# Human Arrangements

*An Introduction to Sociology*

ALLAN G. JOHNSON

Under the General Editorship of
ROBERT K. MERTON
*Columbia University*

HBJ

HARCOURT BRACE JOVANOVICH, PUBLISHERS

San Diego    New York    Chicago    Atlanta    Washington, D.C.
London    Sydney    Toronto

# PREFACE

## To Students

Like many others, I spent much of my undergraduate career trying to discover what I wanted to do with my life. Although I changed majors several times, I always knew that whatever field I entered would have to appeal to several important sides of me. It would have to be challenging and interesting; it would have to stimulate and increase my ability to understand how things work, to see the ways in which things that appear unconnected are in fact connected and affect one another. Perhaps most important, it would have to involve people: it would have to touch my desire to understand not only my own life, but the lives of others and their relations to one another. As a sociologist, I have been able to do all of these things. As a perspective, sociology has enabled me not simply to make a living, but to live with far more awareness and understanding than I would have had without it.

I hope you will experience this textbook on at least two levels. As a writer, I hope you will enjoy what you read, that the care with which I have tried to shape ideas and experience comes across clearly and draws you in as an active reader; and I hope that the examples and analyses of social life will give you reason to stop and reflect on your own life and the circumstances in which you live it.

As a teacher, I hope you will *use* this book as well as read and enjoy it, that you will learn from it and thereby acquire some of the ability to use sociology that has made it such a satisfying part of my life and the lives of other sociologists. This textbook is intended to be worked with, studied, pondered, and, at times, struggled with. It will challenge you to look at the world from what will probably be a very new perspective; to turn the world upside down at times if for no other reason than to get a clearer understanding of what right side up is all about.

Several features of the book were designed to make it more useful to you. Each chapter begins with a detailed table of contents and ends with a summary of major points, a list of key terms, and recommended readings. I suggest you begin each chapter by studying the table of contents and the summary in order to gain an overall sense of what the chapter is about and how it is put together. Each of the key terms is followed by a page number indicating where the term was first introduced and discussed. Together, the table of contents, summary, and list of terms provide an outline for organizing study and review.

You may find several sections at the end of the book useful. The glossary is very extensive and, like the lists of key terms, refers you to the page where each term was first introduced and discussed. The reference list also contains page references to where each book or article is mentioned. This is especially useful if you are trying to locate something written by a frequently cited author. If a term paper is part of the requirements for your course, be sure to read Appendix A.

## To Instructors

At the first meeting of an undergraduate sociology course, I once asked students to take a few moments to write a short paragraph describing sociology as a discipline. For the most part, these students had completed nothing more than an introductory course, and I wanted to get some idea of what I had to work with. None could produce a short, workable definition of the field. I suspect that too many students leave introductory sociology courses with a great many facts and terms but an unnecessarily fuzzy understanding of what it means to observe and explain the social world in a sociological way. What these students lack is a clear sense that no matter what we look at—from informal interactions among strangers to relationships between large organizations, from the structure of a family to the structure of a world economy—a clear framework exists for defining what makes a problem sociological.

In writing *Human Arrangements*, I had two principal goals: to present sociology so that it makes sense on several different levels, and to do so in a way that is both interesting and challenging on the one hand and accessible to students with a wide range of abilities on the other.

The book is based on a definition of sociology that focuses on three conceptual areas: culture, social structure, and population/ecology. Within this conceptual framework there are, of course, many theoretical frameworks—from major perspectives such as conflict, functional, and symbolic interaction to specific theories such as political process theory in the study of social movements, exchange theory in the study of social interaction, or labeling theory in the study of deviance. Students, then, know from the outset that in order to understand any phenomenon sociologically they must begin by paying attention to its cultural, structural, and population/ecological aspects.

I have organized the book to reinforce this approach to making sense of sociology. The book is divided into six parts, the first of which introduces the field in terms of the major concepts that define the kinds of questions we ask as well as in terms of the research methods we use to look for answers. Part II describes in detail the three major concepts that I have used to define the discipline, providing a clear framework that forms the basis for everything that follows.

The remaining parts then apply the sociological perspective in a systematic way to increasingly larger levels of analysis. Part III, for example, moves from relatively small-scale and simple processes to the more complex and large-scale; Parts IV and V focus on social inequality and social institutions; and Part VI ends with detailed discussions of collective behavior and social change. Thus, the book moves from basic conceptual and theoretical views of the sociological perspective to increasingly large-scale and complex areas in which to apply it clearly and systematically.

Most instructors will probably want to begin with Part I; but I have tried to write chapters to maximize your flexibility. Chapter 2 ("Research Methods"), for example, can be assigned at any time, since it relies on no previously introduced sociological concepts; and most of the remaining chapters can be assigned in any order that fits the needs of your class.

It is in the internal organization of chapters that the priority of making sense of sociology is, I hope, most apparent. I have organized chapters around the central concepts of culture, structure, and population/ecology as well as important theoretical approaches to specific areas so that students can develop a sense of sociology as a coherent framework of concepts and theories that can be applied to any aspect of social life.

*Human Arrangements* incorporates a number of features designed to make it both more rewarding and easier to use for teachers and students. "Puzzles" are boxed inserts that pose questions intended to stimulate the reader's curiosity and encourage active participation, while "Voices" boxes provide glimpses of social life as it is lived. Throughout the book, figures and tables abound, both to illustrate and to amplify important points. Each chapter ends with a summary, recommended readings, and key terms with page references.

The glossary is exceptionally complete and includes page references to the major discussions of each entry. The reference list is not only unusually thorough, varied, and up-to-date, but also serves as an author index. This gives students not just a string of page numbers after each author's name, but specific page references for each book or article.

A number of ancillaries are available to assist instructors and students. A *Study Guide* written by the author is available to students. Jeffrey Rosenfeld of Nassau Community College has written a *Test Book* which is available both in print and on floppy disk. Arnold Silverman, also of Nassau Community College, has written an *Instructor's Manual*. In addition, we are making available a powerful computer software package developed by James A. Davis of Harvard University and John G. Kemeny of Dartmouth College. Based on a new version of BASIC (True-BASIC), it will allow users of IBM personal computers to perform a variety of statistical analyses on pooled data from the National Opinion Research Center's General Social Surveys. It is an easy-to-use (completely menu-driven), powerful resource for instructors and students alike.

Throughout the writing of *Human Arrangements* I have worked from a conviction that in teaching introductory sociology, instructors should not have to choose between being understood by their students on the one hand and exposing students to the richness of sociology on the other. I have tried to write a book that does the essential work of giving students sociological literacy as well as a sense of sociological ideas and analysis—for this is the heart of sociology. This is, then, more than anything, a book about how to observe and think about the world. To do that, of course, students need to know something about how to label what they observe; but our field is far more than a set of descriptive terms. In short, my goal has been to give instructors and their students the best of both worlds—a clear textbook that is relatively easy to teach and learn from and an engaging, challenging, lively, and interesting exploration of the field.

## Special Acknowledgments

I doubt very much that I would have written *Human Arrangements* had it not been for Peter Dougherty, the acquisitions editor at Harcourt Brace Jovanovich who first suggested it. His vision of what this book could be, his fine critical judgment, his unwavering support, and his continuing friendship make him the kind of editor few authors ever have the privilege of working with.

As HBJ's advisory editor in sociology, Robert K. Merton has given this project not only a wealth of knowledge and critical insight, but a deep commitment to making this book the best of its kind. His extraordinary attention to detail, his generosity with both praise and criticism, and his appreciation, respect, and support for the struggles of a writer's life have done much to make this one of the most satisfying intellectual and personal experiences of my life.

Many members of the HBJ staff have made important contributions to this project. Marcus Boggs, although assuming the responsibilities of acquisitions editor two full years after the project's beginning, quickly revealed a depth of understanding and support far greater than I had dared to expect. He has shown an unusual appreciation for the essential nature of both this book and sociology. It was he who suggested the "Puzzles" and "Voices" boxes, and he is the author of the opening puzzle box in Chapter 1. Unlike most acquisitions editors, he has also played a role in many aspects of the production of the book.

Natalie Bowen brought her dry wit and keen editor's eye to bear on the first dozen chapters and taught me a great deal about writing and editing in the process. As manuscript editor, Michael Werthman did a superb job not only of editing the remaining chapters but of coordinating the extraordinarily complex range of tasks involved in producing a finished book. As production editor, Kate Duffy was responsible for guiding the manuscript into print, and making sure every word was properly rendered; she did her job exceedingly well. Lesley Lenox, the production coordinator, expertly supervised the many phases of typesetting and printing involved in this large, full-color book.

There are more than 300 photographs in *Human Arrangements*. Each was selected from many possible choices, and each shows a kind of attention to detail not often found in textbooks. All of this is primarily the result of Candace Young's work, for it was her responsibility to transform an enormous list of ideas into actual pictures. Her persistence, enthusiasm, and detective's knack for tracking down the most elusive sources has resulted in an unusually effective illustration program.

Michael Yazzolino is responsible for the physical appearance of *Human Arrangements*, from the basic design of the cover, page layouts, and the striking figures and tables to the choice of color. He has had the difficult job of creating a package for someone else's words, and, as you can see, my words were in good hands.

I also want to express my appreciation to others, members of the HBJ staff and outside consultants, whose skills went into this book. They include Alice Harmon, Cheryl Mergenthaler, Susan Pendleton, David Estrada, Jill Casty, Greg Lloyd, James Chadwick, and Catherine Fauver.

As I write these words I am aware of how difficult it is to accurately describe the contributions of each member of HBJ's extraordinary production staff, for through these many months of long-distance telephone calls and overnight mail deliveries the enthusiasm of their teamwork has shown through again and again. If the production of this book reflects a unity of purpose and a sense of shared enthusiasm, it is due in good part to the very special way in which these people have worked together.

Many of my colleagues have helped by sharing their critical insights as reviewers (their names appear in the separate Acknowledgments list). I appreciate their many suggestions and their sensitivity to the particular difficulties involved in writing an introduction to a field as broad and deep as sociology. I want to thank especially Jeffrey Rosenfeld for his many valuable suggestions, the sensitivity of his criticism, and his enduring interest in this project. I also want to express my appreciation to James A. Davis for his many timely efforts on my behalf and to Hubert J. O'Gorman for his invaluable support during my formative years as a sociologist.

Finally, there are those who have contributed to *Human Arrangements* without perhaps even knowing it. Every book flows from the life of its author, and as my life is connected to many others, so this book is connected to many people. Writing is solitary work, all the more difficult when it takes years to produce a finished product. Throughout this long and difficult process I have been touched by people whose support for my life has supported this work in countless ways: Valdemar, Geraldine, Alice, and Annalee Johnson; Stuart Alpert, Naomi Bressette, George Zepko, Charles Levenstein, Leonard Wallace Robinson, Carol Caputo, Grace Bochain, Brent Harold, Susan Weegar, Ellen Allen, Jan Bidwell, Geoffrey Sandler, Ken Sleight, and Joanne Norton; and above all Nora Jamieson, editor and critic, partner in life, and deepest friend, who has been with me every step of the way. Wherever heart and mind are found working together as one in these pages, there also will be found the mark of these people on my life.

ALLAN G. JOHNSON

# ACKNOWLEDGMENTS

**John W. Bardo,** Southwest Texas State University; **Julie Brown,** University of North Carolina, Greensboro; **Diane M. Bush,** Colorado State University; **Craig Calhoun,** University of North Carolina, Chapel Hill; **Albin J. Cofone,** Suffolk Community College; **Nick Costa,** Greater Hartford Community College; **Clark A. Davis,** California State University, Chico; **Carolyn Ellis,** University of Southern Florida; **Charles F. Emmons,** Gettysburg College; **Robert Freymeyer,** Presbyterian College; **T. Neal Garland,** University of Akron; **Avrama Gingold,** Intermarket Research, Inc. and The Academic Factor; **Vaughn Grisham,** University of Mississippi; **B. G. Gunter,** University of Southern Florida; **Patricia Gwartney-Gibbs,** University of Oregon; **Kelley Hancock,** Portland State University; **Allen C. Haney,** University of Houston; **Charles Henderson,** Memphis State University; **Donald W. Hinrichs,** Gettysburg College; **Walter Hirsch,** Purdue University; **Eric O. Hoiberg,** Iowa State University; **Joan Huber,** Ohio State University; **Sidney J. Kaplan,** University of Toledo; **Will C. Kennedy,** San Diego State University; **Sally B. Kilgore,** Emory University; **Thomas Koenig,** Northeastern University; **Joel Lapin,** Cantonsville Community College; **Charles Levenstein,** University of Connecticut, Hartford; **Gary Madsen,** Utah State University; **John Markoff,** University of Pittsburgh; **Stephen L. Markson,** University of Hartford; **Anselyn Marshall,** San Antonio College; **Joseph A. McFalls,** Temple University; **Robert McLaren,** Portland Community College; **Scott G. McNall,** University of Kansas; **Bernard N. Meltzer,** Central Michigan University; **Eleanor M. Miller,** University of Wisconsin, Milwaukee; **Harvey Molotch,** University of California, Santa Barbara; **Pamela Oliver,** University of Wisconsin, Madison; **Anne K. Peters,** California State University, Dominguez Hills; **Donald R. Ploch,** University of Tennessee, Knoxville; **Jeffrey P. Rosenfeld,** Nassau Community College; **Martin Scheffer,** Boise State University; **Eugen Schoenfeld,** Georgia State University; **Arnold R. Silverman,** Nassau Community College; **Randall Stokes,** University of Massachusetts; **Joseph B. Tamney,** Ball State University; **Edgar Webster,** Oklahoma State University; **Ronald T. Wohlstein,** Eastern Illinois University; **Charlotte Wolf,** Memphis State University; **Thomas J. Yacovone,** Los Angeles Valley College

# CONTENTS

# 2 Research Methods

# PART II

# The Sociological Framework

# 3 Culture

# 4 Social Structure

# 5 Population and Ecology

# PART III

# Social Organization

# 6 Socialization

# 7 Social Interaction

# 8 Groups and Formal Organizations

*Puzzles: What Kept the Wehrmacht Going?*     207

# 9 Life in Communities

# 10 Deviance and Conformity

# PART IV

# Social Stratification

# 11 Social Stratification: Who Gets What, and Why

# 12 Race and Ethnicity

# 13 Gender

# PART V

# Social Institutions

# 15 Marriage and the Family

# 16 Educational Institutions

# 17  Economic Arrangements

# 18 Political Institutions

# 19 Religious Institutions

# PART VI

# Social Change

## 20 Collective Behavior and Social Movements

# ABOUT THE AUTHOR

Since receiving his Ph.D. from the University of Michigan in 1972, Allan Johnson has taught at Wesleyan University, Harvard University, Dartmouth College, Hartford College for Women, and the University of Connecticut, Hartford. His professional interests include social stratification, the sociology of gender, research methods and statistics, and demography.

# Human Arrangements

*An Introduction to Sociology*

# PART I

# What Sociology Is All About

We are surrounded by all kinds of arrangements. Wherever you happen to be sitting right now, look around and you will find that everything can be looked at in terms of its relation to other things. The room you are sitting in differs from other rooms, not only by what is in it, but by how things are arranged (try moving about with your eyes closed and you will see what I mean). This book is at its simplest a collection of electrons, atoms, and molecules that are arranged in such a way as to produce paper, ink, and color. The most important arrangement in this book, however, consists of words arranged into sentences, and the most important thing about them is that you understand them and they are thus the link in the arrangement between you the reader and me the author.

Sociologists, physicists, biologists, psychologists, economists, historians, literary scholars—all are interested in arrangements, whether it be the meter and rhyme in a poem, the structure of an atom, or what goes on among human beings. This book is about sociology, the study of the arrangements through which people know, share, and affect one another's lives.

Sociologists focus on three basic types of arrangements: the arrangement of words and ideas (culture) that we use to make sense of one another and our surroundings; the arrangement of social relationships (social structure) such as those that link authors and readers, parents and children, lovers, enemies, rich and poor, powerful and weak, or spectators and performers at a spontaneous break dance exhibition on a New York sidewalk; and the arrangement of people in physical space (ecology), from how the placement of furniture can affect who emerges as a group's leader to the differences between life in large, populous cities and life in small, rural villages. Whenever one of these basic concepts is emphasized in examining a topic in this book, the passage in question is introduced by the colored symbol shown here, with the concept identified as culture (yellow), social structure (red), or ecology (blue).

Part I introduces you to sociology both as a perspective from which we look at the world and ask questions about it and as a set of scientific methods with which we try to answer those questions and see the world more clearly.

# CHAPTER 1

# A First Look at Sociology

I didn't make this world. It was give to me this way!

Lorraine Hansberry's powerful play *A Raisin in the Sun* is the story of a black American family struggling to escape the urban ghetto. The father, after a lifetime of manual labor, manages to leave his wife a small life insurance policy with which to finally realize her dream, a house of their own.

Their prospective white neighbors, however, want no part of them and send a representative to offer them a cash bribe not to move into their new home. The son, Walter Lee, bitter and cynical after years of trying to find a place for himself in a world dominated by whites, decides to accept the bribe and defends himself against his family's outrage with the words quoted above.

The feelings of anger and helplessness that his words reflect echo the beliefs and feelings of many people. Each of us—rich and poor alike—was born into a world not of our own making, beyond our control, that limits us as profoundly as the pull of gravity. Walter Lee's anger is for the world of

relationships among people, his position as a black man in that world, and the racial prejudice of which he and his family are victims.

> I open and close car doors all day long. I drive a man around in his limousine and I say, "Yes, sir; no sir; very good, sir. . . ." Mama, that ain't no kind of job . . . that ain't nothing at all. . . . Sometimes it's like I can see the future stretched out in front of me—just as plain as day. . . . Just waiting for me—a big, looming blank space—full of *nothing*.

Walter Lee is not completely correct in his assertions, however, for as both a biological and a social being, he participates in some small way in the ongoing development of his physical and social environments. As Hansberry's character discovers, while the social world limits our alternatives, we can still make choices and create new alternatives. When the neighbors' representative returns, Walter Lee faces him: "We have decided to move into our house because my father—my father—he earned it. . . . We don't want your money."

Walter Lee (played by Ossie Davis) expresses his anger and frustration to Mama (played by Claudia McNeill).

## PUZZLES: THE SEARCH FOR ANSWERS

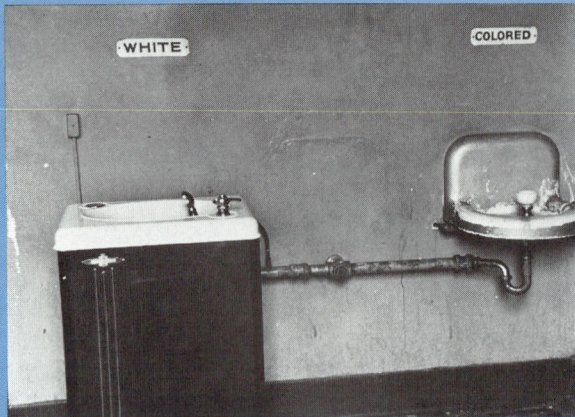

How has the condition of black people changed during the 20-odd years since Lorraine Hansberry published *A Raisin in the Sun* and the Civil Rights Act was signed into law by President Lyndon Johnson?

While reading this book you will encounter a number of questions, puzzles, and riddles much like this one. The answers to them, I think, will not at first be obvious to you. Some may surprise you. You have just read a synopsis of a play depicting a black family's affirmation of pride in itself, in its past, in its future. It is a moving story, filled with human feeling, a story that turns on social conflict and ends in personal triumph. There are many similar stories about the black experience in the United States—the brutality they as a people have endured, their struggle to overcome the conditions imposed on them and to live with dignity. As you think about a question or puzzle such as the one above and try to find the answer to it, you draw upon your store of personal experience, of things heard and seen, which informs you and leads you to a kind of understanding. You have the makings of a common sense.

Sociology, however, challenges our ordinary and limited personal experience by questioning our ready answers even when those answers express our most humane feelings. It upsets our common sense and proposes something better. Consider, for example, the answer to our question about the progress of blacks in the United States.

In the 20 years since passage of the Civil Rights Act, in the 30 years since the Supreme Court ordered desegregation of public schools, in the almost 40 years since Jackie Robinson became the first black to play major league baseball, there has been little significant improvement in the relative position of black people as a whole in American society. The apparent gains— such as increased numbers of middle-class blacks, the election of black officials, and higher salaries paid to black professional athletes— have had little effect on the lives of the vast majority of ordinary blacks. They remain less well paid for their labor, less well housed, less well fed, and less well educated than their fellow citizens. Indeed, many blacks feel farther than ever from full participation in American society despite the years of struggle for recognition and despite the hopes that flared when the Civil Rights Act was signed into law. Some explanations for this distressing and perhaps surprising answer to our question will be proposed later in this book, in Chapter 12.

As you read further, you will find other questions and puzzles similar to this one. It is in them that sociology begins and continues as a way of looking at the world in search of answers. Each question flows from a general wonder about why societies are as they are. Each is a matter of genuine concern that sociologists want to understand, and I put them to you as examples of what it means to observe and think about the world from a sociological perspective rather than rely only on the common sense that arises from personal experience.

This book is an invitation to you to acquire the skills that will enable you to dig deeper in search of understanding about the social world we inhabit. If you acquire those skills, then I will have succeeded in what I set out to do.

## A Sociological View of Familiar Worlds

Each of us lives out our individual life in relation to social and physical environments, and **sociology** *is the systematic study of social and physical environments and their effects on our experience and behavior as individuals.* Sociology is about us—the "us" that preceded you and me and the "us" of which we are now a part.

Sociology helps us see the human arrangements of shared ideas and relationships that connect our otherwise separate individual lives, just as astronomy helps us see constellations where before we saw only a sea of individual stars. The stars were there all the time, but to see Orion's Belt or the Big Dipper, we have to look for patterns; and to see the constellations of social relationships that characterize human life, we have to pay attention to the patterns that exist among vast seas of individuals.

This chapter has two goals: (1) through a series of examples, to introduce some of the major concepts that organize sociological thinking; (2) to sketch the history of sociological thought—to show that this way of looking at the world is, itself, one way in which humans adapt to the world by trying to make a particular kind of sense of it.

Just as we have to learn to see the patterns among thousands of individual stars that make up constellations, so too do we have to learn to see the relationships among individual people that make up the patterns of social life.

### Social Expectations: How Do We Know Who People Really Are?

Perhaps it was just this morning that you entered your first class of the new term, most likely a large room with rows of chairs all facing in one direction. The chairs may even have been bolted to the floor, forcing you to face the front of the room. As students talked among themselves, a person—perhaps it was a woman—entered the room, walked to the front, and stood behind the lectern. Everyone in the room stopped talking soon after she arrived—except for her.

When she wanted to talk, she just talked; when others wanted to talk, they raised a hand and waited for her permission. Students asked questions; she made statements. She did not write down what you said, but you wrote down what she said (or, if you did not, wondered if you should have). This scene repeats itself so often in college classrooms that it may never have occurred to you how remarkable it is.

What is remarkable is that no one ever asks those people behind lecterns if they are who we think they are. Without any personal knowledge of the professor in the scene just described, students pay attention to her and enter into working relationships in which she has power over them and can give or withhold rewards they value highly. Students do "know" something about her, however, knowledge they substitute for details of her personal identity.

They know that according to the catalogue the course was supposed to meet in that room at that time, that everyone involved was expected to read the catalogue and be guided by it. They went to the room at the designated time and found other people there (and perhaps breathed a sigh of relief). Just to be sure, however, many asked, "Is this Soc. 101?" They were told "yes" and believed what they heard.

The woman entered the room and took the position at the front. Anyone in the room could have stood there, but only she did. This is important, for if anyone had challenged her for that spot, your "knowledge" of who she was would have been shaken. No one challenged her, however, because someone was *expected* to occupy that position, someone who looked as though she was supposed to be there.

You expected her to be older than you, to dress in a certain way (no hard hat or bathing suit), to speak English, and behave appropriately (no dancing on the desks or attempts to sell cheap watches). So long as people's appearance and behavior fit our expectations, we treat them accordingly even though their "real" selves may not be what they appear to be (Goffman, 1959). The acceptance of a teacher's authority in a classroom does not depend only on the personalities of individuals but also on beliefs and expectations that students and teachers share about one another as students and teachers, not as unique individuals.

One point of this is that we repeatedly enter into relationships with people without any direct personal knowledge of who they are. We take our clothes off in front of people we believe to be physicians and may even allow them to perform surgery on us. We allow dentists to drill our teeth and airline pilots and bus drivers to take our lives in their hands. Even when we drive a car or walk across an intersection, we depend on the belief that automobile drivers will behave in predictable ways. Rarely, if ever, do we ask doctors and dentists for their credentials or demand assurance that a pilot really knows how to fly a plane.

What we know of other people (and what they know of us) consists primarily of beliefs and expectations about their positions in social relationships (professor, doctor, bus driver) and about ourselves in relation to them (student, patient, passenger). The power of those beliefs and expectations comes in part from the fact that we share them with one another and in part from our general lack of awareness of them as objective characteristics of our social environment. Rarely are we conscious of the complex social relationships that tie us to one another, and, as a result, we often try to understand who we and others really are solely by focusing on strictly personal characteristics such as personality.

The power of social beliefs and expectations is illustrated in Hans Christian Andersen's fairy tale, "The Emperor's New Clothes," in which an emperor is duped by a thieving tailor into buying a nonexistent set of expensive clothes. Everyone in the empire, anxious to fit in, "sees" and admires the naked emperor's "clothes"—everyone, that is, except a small child who does not share the adults' beliefs and expectations and, therefore, does not see what they plainly "see."

## Social Relationships: Mothers

People's positions in social relationships affect not only how they perceive one another, but how they behave. For example, while most of us experience our mothers as unique individuals, from a sociological perspective "mother" is also a social position that profoundly affects how those unique individuals behave.

We enter this world knowing not a single soul. Our knowledge of others is largely sensory, consisting of smells and tastes, touch and sound. We soon learn something very useful, however: the magic of words through which things and people can be named. "Mother" is, when we first learn it, a particular woman's proper name. The word "mother" tells us who that woman is, and so we tend to think that this is who she is to everyone.

Enter confusion: other people do not call mother "mother." We are like the small boy in a television commercial in which other children see his father, a boxing champion, and say, "That's the champ!" The boy only smiles and says, "Naw, that's my *dad*."

Still more confusing is the fact that many women are called "mother"; and our mother herself has a mother, so is both "mother" and "daughter" at the same time. What is hard for small children to understand is that the word "mother" is not like "tree" or "rock," for "mother" describes a *position* in a particular *social relationship* with another person. It need not be the woman who bore the child; it can be any woman who occupies the social position "mother" in relation to someone who occupies the social position "son" or "daughter."

Most of us do not have shared ideas about any particular mother, but we do share ideas about mothers in general, about who they are and what they are like, about their behavior, what is most important in their lives, and how they are supposed to feel in relation to their children. To the extent that a mother shares these ideas, they influence her expectations of others as well as what she herself thinks, feels, and does. To understand a woman's behavior as a mother, we cannot pay attention only to her mental life, the ebb and flow of her emotions. "Mother" represents more than biological fact: it represents a complex set of ideas that she and others use to decide who she is, what her children and she may expect of one another, how she should choose between conflicting alternatives. While she may act and feel contrary to those ideas, she does not have the power to remove them from her social environment.

The point here is that, in a social sense, "who we are" depends on the positions we occupy in relation to other people and the shared ideas attached to us as a result. To ignore the social component of our selves is like trying to explain why apples fall from trees by examining only the characteristics of individual apples without taking into account their relationship to the earth's gravitational pull. It is this attention to the relationship between individuals and their environments that is at the core of sociological inquiry.

## Perspectives: How Did J. J. Riordan Come to Die?

In trying to understand human experience and behavior, sociologists pay attention not only to relationships between individuals, but also to the larger *social environments* in which those relationships exist. More than anything else, it is this focus that distinguishes sociology as a point of view, as the case of James J. Riordan makes clear.

According to the *New York Times*, Riordan, 47, left his spacious apartment on New York City's West Side early on a drizzly Friday morning in October. He went to confession, then to work, but he did not stay very long. Shortly before noon he returned home. At 5:30 that afternoon, his sister and brother-in-law found him seated in an over-stuffed red plush chair in his bedroom at the rear of the house. His jacket and vest hung neatly on a wooden valet; his right hand dangled over the arm of the chair, and directly beneath it, on the floor, was a revolver from which one shot had been fired. He had a bullet wound in his right temple and was dead. How do we figure out how he came to die?

"Figuring things out" is not simple, because there are many ways to do it. We look at things from different points of view, or *perspectives*. Therefore, we can ask different questions about the same thing and arrive at different kinds of explanations. Perspectives direct and focus our attention, influence what we look at and what we make of what we see. For example, it is fairly simple to explain Riordan's death from the perspectives of physics and biology, the points of view coroners use to determine causes of death. These perspectives raise questions about hands holding guns and fingers pulling triggers, about exploding gun powder, the mass and velocity of bullets fired, and bullets' effect on a brain and the life of its owner.

A physical explanation also demands that we determine who pulled the trigger. The gun Riordan was shot with came from a desk drawer in his office; his fingerprints were the only ones found on it; it lay on the floor right where it would have fallen had he shot himself. In the absence of other evidence, we conclude that he committed suicide. From these points of view, then, we know *how* J. J. Riordan came to die.

While these disciplines explain who killed him and how, other points of view produce new questions. Riordan was a human being who had a mind, experienced emotion, sensed the world outside him and responded to it. The psychological perspective raises questions about human choice and the emotional and mental processes that influence what is chosen. The explanations of biology and physics cannot solve the psychological puzzle: *why* did J. J. Riordan come to die?

Riordan's friends told the *Times* that he had been emotionally exhausted for several weeks prior to his suicide; his doctors feared that he would collapse both physically and emotionally. All agreed he was severely depressed. These are classic danger signals of a possible suicide: prolonged exhaustion, feelings of hopelessness and despair, an inability to cope (Lester, 1983). But such an explanation is not a full solution to the psychological puzzle, for other questions remain unanswered: Why, for example, do such emotional states lead some to kill themselves but do not have this effect on others?

Even a complete biological, physical, and psychological explanation of the suicide falls short, for it looks at Riordan's behavior only in terms of his individual processes and characteristics. What is missing is attention to the fact that he made his choice within a social environment. To understand his death from a sociological point of view, we must understand that environment and his position in it.

J. J. Riordan was feeling depressed because he had recently lost a great deal of money. He shot himself on November 10, 1929, just twelve days after the initial crash of the New York Stock Market, which spun the United States and the world into a decade of severe economic depression. It was his speculation in that market that led to his downfall. But why was his downfall so important to him that he would take his own life?

Riordan's social environment was one in which people valued money and its accumulation and accorded both prestige and power to those who had lots of it. He was the president of a large bank, which gave him access to a lot of money to speculate with; it also gave him a great deal of responsibility for the well-being of others. He was a white man in an environment that gave power to white men and expected them to use it successfully. In this environment, Riordan's ability to accumulate things and exercise power was a major source of standing and security.

The sociological perspective suggests that Riordan was hit particularly hard by the stock market crash because of his social positions in relation to that event: a middle-aged, white, male banker

---

## Voices: A Young Poet Chooses Death

This poem was written by a fifteen-year-old and handed to his English teacher. The teacher did nothing and the boy later committed suicide:

> To Santa Claus and
> Little Sisters
>
> Once . . . he wrote a poem.
> And called it "chops,"
> Because that was the name of
> his dog, and that's what it was
> all about.
> And the teacher gave him an "A"
> And a gold star.
> And his mother hung it on the
> kitchen door, and read it to
> all his aunts . . .
> Once . . . he wrote another
> poem.
> And he called it "Question Marked
> Innocence."
> Because that was the name of
> His grief and that's what it
> was all about.
> And the professor gave him
> an "A"
> And a strange and steady look.
> And his mother never hung it
> on the kitchen door, because
> he never let her see it . . .
> Once, at 3 A.M. . . . he tried
> another poem . . .
> And he called it absolutely
> nothing, because that's what it
> was all about.
> And he gave himself an "A"
> And a slash on each damp wrist,
> And hung it on the bathroom
> door because he couldn't reach
> the kitchen.

Source: Giffin and Felsenthal, *A Cry for Help*, 1983.

who not only lost material wealth (as did many others) but suffered from intense guilt and a humiliating loss of social prestige, as well.

If Riordan's social positions influenced him to destroy himself, then we should find similar effects on other people who occupied similar social positions. These effects appear as *patterns* of behavior that differ from one social position to another, and we can see the effects of the social environment by locating Riordan in patterns of behavior. To do this, we look at the suicide *rate* for people like Riordan to see if they were more strongly affected by the crash than people occupying different social positions.

If we look at the suicide rate for white males in the United States, we find that for white men between the ages of 15 and 34, the rate changed very little between 1929 and 1932 when the stock market reached its lowest ebb. For older white men between the ages of 45 and 64, however, who had the greatest investment in the economy, the suicide rate jumped by almost 50 percent. For white women, on the other hand, a great many of whom shared the economic gains and losses of American men, there was no such pattern of response corresponding to the stock market crash. (For comparison, the suicide rate for black males rose only among those 55 to 64 years old.) (National Office of Vital Statistics, 1956)

While suicide rates tell us only about groups and nothing about the individual, J. J. Riordan, they do tell us about the behavior of people who occupied social positions similar to his and, as such, they give us clues about the pressures exerted on such people and the resulting patterns of response to them. (It is important to note, however, that, while we will not go into it further here, the sociological work is not done until we can also explain why so many people in Riordan's position did *not* choose to commit suicide.)

Clearly, Riordan was not just an isolated organism that thought, felt, and lived; although wealthy and powerful, he was part of something much larger than he was, something he neither created nor controlled. He participated in a system of social relationships and shared ideas, through which he constructed his world and made his choices. Had he lived in any of numerous other social environments, his circumstances would have been quite different. There have been and still are

J. J. Riordan responded to the stock market crash by killing himself. Others responded quite differently. To understand such patterned differences in the ways in which people respond to their social environments is a major focus of sociological thought and research.

human groups in which the ideas of private property, money, banks, and speculation do not even exist, in which individual prestige does not depend on owning more than others, and whose material existence is so marginal that there is nothing to accumulate in the first place. Indeed, had Riordan belonged to certain Northwest native American tribes, he would have *gained* social standing by giving away his wealth periodically just to show that he had so much he did not need it (Benedict, 1934; Harris, 1974).

## Potlatch: Having Wealth to Burn

The most bizarre instance of status seeking was discovered among the American Indians who formerly inhabited the coastal regions of Southern Alaska, British Columbia, and Washington. Here the status seekers practiced what seems like a maniacal form of conspicuous consumption and conspicuous waste known as *potlatch*. The object of potlatch was to give away or destroy more wealth than one's rival. If the potlatch giver was a powerful chief, he might attempt to shame his rivals and gain everlasting admiration from his followers by destroying food, clothing, and money. Sometimes he might even seek prestige by burning down his own house.

Source: Harris, *Cows, Pigs, Wars & Witches,* 1974.

*When we pay attention to patterns of behavior among people according to their positions in social relationships, we gain insights that other perspectives cannot provide.* As valuable as it is, for example, to identify psychological conditions conducive to suicide, such understandings are incomplete without an appreciation of the social circumstances affecting the emotional and mental processes through which people make choices. James Riordan's solitary act of suicide tells us things about that particular man; but it also mirrors his social environment.

The crash of the stock market and the Great Depression that followed did not just "happen." They represented the breakdown of an economic system, a way in which humans organized the production and distribution of goods and services. They resulted from a history of events, themselves shaped by the ongoing collective process of social life in the United States.

The nature of that social life did not just happen, either. The ability to accumulate wealth, for example, represents centuries of social development through which it became possible to produce more than people needed for immediate consumption. The development of money and banks, as well as the ideas of private property, credit and the future (about which people might speculate) represents ways in which humans respond to their environment, meeting their needs by organizing social relationships.

Thus, Riordan's solitary act is connected to a collective process unfolding through history, and it is by locating him in that process that we come to a fuller understanding of his individual circumstances, experience, and behavior. Each of the preceding examples shows in its own way that who we are and what we do is affected by our positions both in social relationships and in large social environments. This is never more apparent than when we meet someone for the first time.

### PUZZLES: A SELF-SURVEY

Who do you think you are?

Before reading any further, write down ten words or phrases that, for you, answer the question, "Who am I?" Then, as you read the following section, look again at your answers and think about what this says about "who you are."

## Social Identities: Who Do You Think You Are?

Suppose that you live by yourself in an apartment; to make ends meet, you decide to advertise for a roommate. In response to your ad, someone writes to you: "Most people think I'm intelligent and have a good sense of humor. I'm neat, keep regular hours, don't play music too loudly, pay my bills on time. I enjoy most sports, a good book, lively conversation and meeting new people."

Would this be enough information for you? Would you like to know if this person is male or female, homosexual or heterosexual, 16 years old or 55 years old with two grandchildren? Would it matter to you if this person is a child of the president of the United States, is unemployed, or works as a police officer, a journalist, an assembly-line worker, a farm worker, a computer programmer, a taxi driver, or a restaurant cook? Would you like to know if this person is black, Hispanic, white, or Asian, is fabulously wealthy or desperately poor, went to a posh prep school in Boston or a run-down high school on the south side of Chicago, grew up on a farm or in the Bronx or on an Indian reservation? Does it matter if your roommate is Catholic, Protestant, Jewish, or Muslim, or grew up in a tribe of cannibals on New Guinea (but has since given up the habit of eating people)?

Most likely, most or all of these things would interest you to some degree, despite the fact that none of them tells us about the unique individual you are thinking of living with. They do tell us about people's positions in social environments, and this, in turn, gives us clues about their beliefs, values, and expectations in relation to others. These characteristics help us locate people in relation to sets of shared ideas and social relationships, and it is such characteristics that we use in shaping our initial "knowledge" of others.

People's behavior and expectations in relation to us depend on their ideas of us, and most people never know our private selves. They know our *social* selves—our positions in social environments—and know us through the ideas attached to those "selves." Similarly, our social selves are an important source of ideas about who *we* think we are.

## What Sociology Is All About

The preceding examples stress the importance of our positions in social relationships and environments; but most people find it hard to grasp the idea that social relationships exist independently of the particular individuals who participate in them (Durkheim, 1895). The relationship between children and parents, for example, is defined by shared ideas about children and parents, their behavior, goals, feelings, rights, and responsibilities in relation to one another. Those ideas, and the relationships they define, exist apart from you and your parents.

Without individuals acting in those relationships, however, they would not exist, and there is the crux of it: all of us—students, teachers, mothers, fathers, sons, daughters, bankers, and roommates—participate in something we did not create, and yet through our involvement we give those relationships life; we stamp them with our own individual interpretations and thereby participate in changing or maintaining them as parts of our social environment.

The examples in this chapter center on vital aspects of social life that are at the core of sociology. We use shared ideas to make sense of the

Cultural beliefs are what we use to construct our basic ideas about reality, especially aspects that we cannot directly observe, such as what happens to us after we die. Bosch's vision of hell is a graphic example of cultural attempts to come to grips with the unknown.

## Table 1-1

Culture consists of both material and nonmaterial products. As the examples in this table show, science involves both types of cultural products.

| NONMATERIAL PRODUCTS | MATERIAL PRODUCTS |
|---|---|
| **Symbol Systems and Technical Language** | Test tubes |
| | Syringes |
| 1, 2, 3, 4, etc. | Scalpels |
| +, −, and other symbols. | Laboratories |
| Statistics. | Isotopes |
| Byte. | Artificial hearts |
| Electron. | Microscopes |
| | Prisms |
| **Beliefs** | Atomic clocks |
| | Computers |
| Everything has a cause. | Incubators |
| Evolutionary theory. | Petrie dishes |
| | Telescopes |
| **Values** | Lasers |
| | Cyclotrons |
| Scientists should share their discoveries | Floppy disks |
| with other scientists. | Genetic mutations |
| Scientists should do science and not worry | Scientific books and journals |
| about what is done with their discoveries. | Questionnaires |
| *Before* they conduct research, scientists should | Nuclear reactors |
| consider what will be done with their discoveries. | Fusion reactors |
| | Chemical waste |
| **Attitudes** | |
| | |
| Contempt for astrology as a silly waste of time. | |
| Respect for science as a noble pursuit. | |
| | |
| **Norms** | |
| | |
| Scientists who fake research results will be ostracized | |
| from the scientific community. | |

world, one another, and ourselves; we spend our lives in webs of social relationships with other people, relationships that affect not only how we behave, but who we think we are; and social life is itself affected by physical conditions, including the ways in which societies produce goods. These key aspects of social life correspond to three major concepts that define sociology as a perspective: culture, social structure, and ecology. The next three sections briefly introduce each of them.

## *Culture*

Two basic kinds of cultural products arise from the collective activity and experience of human beings. The first is **nonmaterial culture,** which includes language, art, music, and four major types of shared ideas: beliefs, norms, values, and attitudes. The second is **material culture,** objects that humans make and which become part of our physical environment.

**Beliefs** are statements about what is real and are thus the most fundamental of all cultural ideas. Some examples of such statements are: "The world is round, not flat, and it revolves around the sun." "It is possible to win a nuclear war." "All people are created equal." "People succeed because they work hard." "All parents love their children."

**Norms** are rules about people's behavior according to their positions in social relationships. Some examples: Students are supposed to do what teachers tell them to. Teachers are not supposed to abuse students, sell high grades, or take their clothes off during class. We may not physically attack one another, steal other people's things, or shout people down because we dislike what they say. Parents may not abuse their children.

In addition to beliefs and norms, we share **values,** which are ideas about what is important and unimportant, good and bad, desirable and undesirable. Some examples are: Honesty and fairness are important (we do not want teachers to grade arbitrarily or tell students there are two papers in the course when in fact there are four). People should do whatever their government tells them to. People should always question authority. Wealth, power, and prestige are desirable.

As a fourth component of nonmaterial culture, **attitudes** are evaluations that often predispose us to feel and behave positively or negatively toward people, objects, or situations (Allport, 1935; Fishbein, 1966; Hill, 1981). Many people, for example, have a negative attitude toward people on welfare, based on the value that they should be working and the belief that they could if they wanted to.

While ideas constitute the major part of cultural products, humans have also developed *material* products: objects that both extend our abilities and limit our choices. Automobiles, telephones, forks, plows, pianos, highways, and cities are all examples of material culture. They affect how we eat, communicate, and travel, for example; they affect how we plan our communities and conduct our relationships with one another.

## Social Structure

Beliefs, values, norms, and attitudes are organized into social relationships among people who occupy different social positions (such as mother and child). On the *micro*—or small-scale—level of social life, **social structure** is the arrangement of people in relation to one another and the patterns of expectation attached to each position in social relationships.

When you and I, for example, identify ourselves as children in relation to our mothers and fathers, we define an important part of the social structure of interaction in our families. Parents and children share certain expectations of one another, expectations that are socially prescribed. Each social structure, then, is an arrangement of people in

relation to one another that gives participants a predictable pattern of expectations about who will participate and what will happen.

In addition to social relationships among individuals, the concept of **social structure** has two additional meanings on the *macro*—or large-scale—level. First, groups and organizations interact with one another just as individuals do, and their relationships are guided by patterns of shared expectations. Universities, for example, have structured relationships with government agencies through which universities receive financial support.

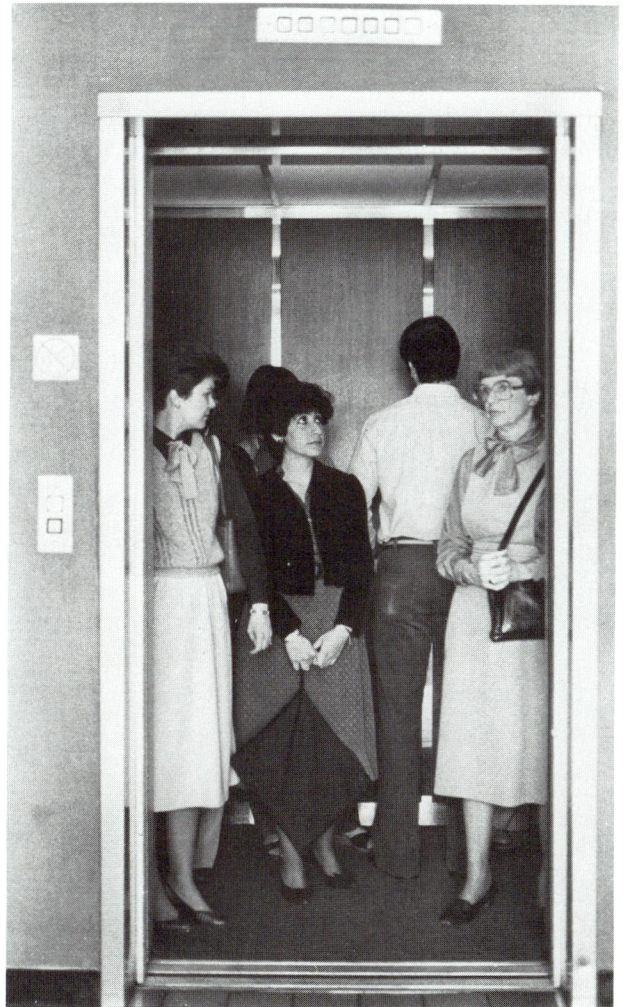

As the ethnomethodologists find, many norms that guide social life are so subtle that we are unaware of them until someone violates them. Face the rear wall of an elevator. The reactions of those around you will reveal a norm you may not have been aware of.

Second, the concept of social structure also refers to the ways in which people are *distributed* among various social positions as well as how major rewards of social life—in particular, wealth, power, and prestige—are distributed among members of a group or society. The medical profession in the United States, for example, is structured in such a way that women rarely occupy the prestigious social position "surgeon" and, as a result, are denied the high incomes that accompany that medical specialty.

Thus, the concept of social structure describes how we are arranged in relation to one another, both in personal interactions and in society as a whole. It describes the patterns of expectation that guide relationships among individuals as well as between groups. As a concept, it is extremely useful, because it draws our attention to the predictable, organized patterns that characterize social life.

Together, the concepts of culture and social structure describe social environments. When we describe something as "social," we are connecting it to one or both of these aspects of a social environment.

As important as social environments are, we cannot overlook the fact that they exist in *physical* environments that include both the physical world and the biological facts of life on this planet. This brings us to the third major concept in the sociological perspective—ecology.

## Ecology

The concept of social structure draws our attention to patterns of social relationships, and culture focuses on shared ideas underlying those relationships, giving them meaning, value, and predictable form. Whereas culture and social structure describe the social environment, the concept of ecology focuses on human beings as physical orga-

nisms who live in relation to physical environments.

In sociology, a **population** is any collection of people who share a physical environment. A population can be as small as a single person living on a desert island or as large as the population of the world, which numbered in excess of 4.8 billion people in 1985. **A society** is a particular kind of population: it is the largest population whose members share a cultural identity and way of life and interact in patterned ways.

**Ecology** focuses on the characteristics of physical environments and the relation of populations to them. The characteristics of physical environments include the availability of resources such as fertile land, water, minerals, and fuel: access to transportation routes such as rivers; and isolation by impassable mountains, deserts, or other barriers. The relation of populations to physical environments includes such characteristics of populations as how large they are, how rapidly they grow or shrink, and how they are distributed in physical space; this relation also includes **technology,** a population's ability to make use of natural resources. Plows, electric generators, printing presses, crop irrigation systems, and computers all represent ways in which human beings make use of the physical environment's resources. Ecology is an important part of the sociology perspective because the physical conditions of human life have important effects on the development of social environments.

If a population grows so large that there is not enough food for everyone, for example, there are only three possibilities: people may migrate to other places; the population may shrink through a decline in the birth rate or a rise in the death rate; or it may be possible to support a larger population through changes in culture (such as inventions) or in social structure (more efficient ways of organizing labor).

This third possibility—changing culture or social structure—illustrates the connection between social and physical environments. The development of large industrial societies, for example, depends on more than culture and social structure, for it also results from rapid population growth, the concentration of vast numbers of workers in large cities, and the successful application of technology to problems of production. In turn, the ability to produce more than people need to survive allows some to accumulate wealth and power at the expense of others.

From this perspective, the social structures that gave J. J. Riordan the power to speculate with other people's money were made possible by an industrialized society with a large, urban population and vast natural resources. Thus, while the concepts of culture and social structure define the social environment, the concept of ecology focuses attention on humanity as a species of life, whose numbers shrink and swell, distribute themselves in the natural environment, and develop relationships with their physical environments. This perspective makes us aware of the connection between the development of social environments, the physical limitations of the natural world, and the reproduction and distribution of human beings within it.

### The Personal and the Social

A crucial element of sociological thinking is the distinction between individuals and their environments. A behavior or experience may be common to many individuals, for example, and yet not be social; or be extremely rare and yet profoundly social.

Every human being, for example, inevitably experiences death, but death remains a personal activity; by itself, the universality of this experience does not make it social. How people respond to us when they know we are dying, however, as well as how we respond to them and to our own condition are *social*, because they are profoundly affected by cultural ideas about death; also, our age at death and the cause of our death are strongly affected by our positions in social relationships (Chapter 5).

I sit alone in my office writing a book about the social world—a rare activity in any society, but nonetheless a highly social one. To explain this activity only in terms of my individual motivation and ability ignores the social and material world within which I act. This book is socially possible because humans invented paper, ink, and printing presses, and developed language and the idea that writing books is socially valuable, allowing me to go about it while at the same time getting a share of what other people produce—food, shelter, clothing. I am also writing this book because humans developed a particular way of thinking about our lives together (sociology) just as they developed ways of thinking about physical life (biology), matter and energy (physics), mental and emotional processes (psychology), the unknown (religion), and truth and beauty (art).

If I belonged to any of a number of other human groups around the world, I would not be writing this book, because in those environments there would be no paper, presses, or audience of college students trying to understand the social world in a systematic way. So, what I do at this moment cannot be explained solely by my individual motives and thoughts; I must also understand my position in the social environment within which I act as a human being, a context I did not create, which consists of objects and particular patterns of thought and social relationships.

Sociology provides us with both a window on the world and a mirror of our participation in it. To use it, however, is difficult, for we actively participate in the very thing we are trying to understand; the intellectual tools, themselves, are part of culture. In addition, the sociological perspective often challenges us to raise uncomfortable questions about the connection between ourselves and social problems.

We could look at J. J. Riordan's suicide, for example, as a personal solution to a personal problem. When, however, we see that people like him (middle-aged, white American men) were far more likely to kill themselves than were Americans not of that age, race, and gender, we can no longer regard his situation and response as purely personal. The patterns reflected in suicide rates for people in different social positions indicate that something is going on in the variety of social environments in which people find themselves, something that makes some people more likely than others to kill themselves (Durkheim, 1895). Like all human behavior, suicide is both a personal act *and* a reflection of social environments (Mills, 1959).

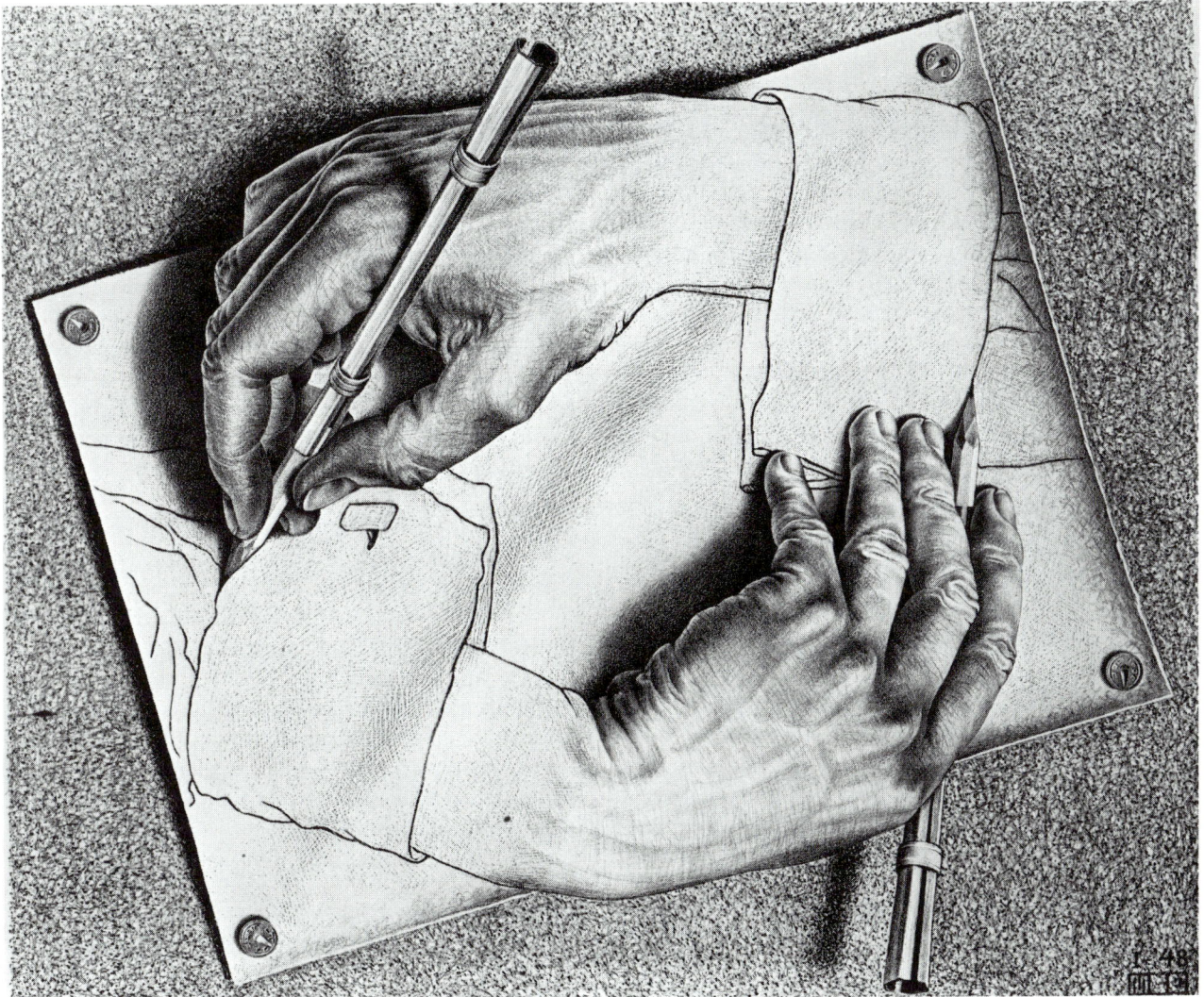

*Drawing Hands*, M. C. Escher, National Gallery of Art, Washington, Rosenwald Collection.

As we begin to understand the social causes of individual troubles, we must acknowledge that as participants in social life we are connected in some way to them. Racism, sexism, and ageism are not problems for only those individuals—such as Walter Lee—who happen to have a particular skin color, sex, or age. We are understandably reluctant to connect ourselves with other people's troubles, and we resist giving up comfortable beliefs in order to see the world in a new way. As Berger (1963) wrote, a social environment

> provides us with warm, reasonably comfortable caves, in which we can huddle with our fellows, beating on the drums that drown out the howling hyenas of the surrounding darkness. "Ecstasy" is the act of stepping outside the caves, alone, to face the night. (p. 150)

To "step outside" is to engage in a particular kind of consciousness, what Mills called "the sociological imagination."

## "Stepping Outside": A Short Social History of Sociology

The concepts of culture, social structure, and ecology are, themselves, cultural ideas, part of our collective scheme for making sense of the world. To understand the origins of sociology, we have to appreciate the social environments that prompted people to make sense of their surroundings in new ways. This section shows that sociology emerged in particular social conditions and that sociologists approach the complex influence of culture, social structure, and ecology on human life from a variety of complementary perspectives.

## Sociology's Beginnings: Comte and Spencer

Prior to the nineteenth century, understandings of the world were based heavily on the concept of "natural order." The rule of kings, for example, was justified as the enactment of God's will. When, in 1543, Copernicus published his idea that the earth revolved around the sun (and not the other way around), he challenged a powerful religious framework that supported many beliefs, including one that the earth was at the center of the universe. A century later, the Italian astronomer Galileo was forced to recant his defense of Copernicus' theory under threats of torture and imprisonment.

Scientists such as Copernicus, Kepler, Galileo, and Newton helped bring about a radical shift in approaches to observing and explaining the physical world. They believed that reason and experience, not religious faith, were the keys to understanding, and it was only a matter of time before their scientific methods were applied to social worlds as well.

During the eighteenth century there was a growing concern for the right of individuals to freedom from oppression by secular or religious authorities, and there was a growing belief that the world was controllable and, above all, perfectible: One need only understand how the social world operates in order to lead humanity on a steady path to enlightenment and progress.

Europeans in the late eighteenth and early nineteenth centuries had good reason to try to make sense of their societies, which were full of chaos, misery, and discontent. The French monarchy was deposed in the revolution of 1789; Napoleon Bonaparte then tried to conquer Europe; and in the wake of his defeat, France was plunged into 50 years of economic and political chaos.

As the Industrial Revolution began to spread throughout Europe, the population concentrated in swelling cities, and poverty and misery were widespread. In spite of enormous leaps in production, most workers remained poor—and many could find no work at all. In 1828, for example, more than half of the artisans in one region of France depended on welfare agencies in order to survive (de Sauvigny, 1966).

In the midst of this scene was the French philosopher Auguste Comte (1798–1857), who was enraged by the "anarchy which day by day envel-ops society." To Comte, the way to bring order out of chaos depended on the idea that societies develop in predictable stages, that in order to understand social conditions, it is necessary to discover the laws that guide the progress of that development. It was Comte who first used the term "sociology" to refer to the systematic, scientific study of social life, and he was one of the first to insist on scientific understandings of social environments.

By the second half of the nineteenth century, England—unlike the rest of Europe—enjoyed relative prosperity. This was the era of Queen Victoria, and England's economic dominance of the Western world created a sense of confidence and complacency. England, of course, had its masses of poor, but farmers and skilled workers enjoyed a rapidly rising standard of living, and to them and the members of the middle and upper classes, the Industrial Revolution was well on its way toward providing a bright future (Clark, 1962).

For the English, the need was not to explain misery and chaos, but to explain and justify prosperity and maintain their belief in the superiority of their way of life. In this kind of social environment, it is not surprising that the philosopher Herbert Spencer (1820–1903) developed the theory that the success of some and failure of others was a "natural" and inevitable occurrence. Social relationships (such as those between rich and poor) evolve "naturally," he argued, according to the principle of the "survival of the fittest." Spencer's ideas led many to believe that Charles Darwin's theories about physical evolution also applied to societies (Jones, 1980). According to the theory of **social Darwinism,** the most capable people will and should gain more in the struggle for survival than the less capable. Spencer's ideas were a staunch defense of individualism: leave things alone, he believed, and, with time, everything would work out for the best. "Things," however, did not work out for the best, and by the late 1870s, English farmers were devastated by foreign competition, England entered a period of economic crisis, and Spencer's theory lost its appeal to Europeans.

## Marx and the Conflict Perspective

While Spencer's views supported the status quo, those of Karl Marx (1818–1883) sharply opposed it. After the defeat of Napoleon, Germans anticipated

Karl Marx

a new era of political freedom, but soon found themselves in a police state that was worse than life under Napoleon. Political meetings were prohibited, universities were tightly controlled, and there was no parliament, trial by jury, or right of free speech. Marx, a German, thus lived in a society in which people's expectations of liberty were thwarted by the power of a relative few to oppress and exploit the masses of people.

Because his ideas made him unpopular at home, Marx did most of his work while living in exile in England, where he saw the misery of workers struggling in a rapidly industrializing country in which the means of production were increasingly concentrated in the hands of comparatively few people. To Marx, the world he found himself in was not a harmonious, natural integration of social relationships serving everyone's best interests. Unlike Comte and Spencer, Marx viewed the world from a **conflict perspective** based on the be-

lief that social environments develop through conflict over control of land, factories, and other means of production and that social relationships and people's experiences in them reflect this continuing conflict between different groups.

Capitalist societies, he argued, are divided into two primary *classes:* those who own the means of production and those who do not (and, hence, must sell their time and energy to whoever will buy it for whatever they choose to pay for it). Cultural beliefs, values, and norms arise not from some "natural" order of things, but from the different positions people occupy in relation to the means of producing what people need in order to survive. Thus, owners tend to believe that inequality is for everyone's benefit, because such a belief supports their privileged position, not (as Spencer maintained) because it accurately describes the natural order of things (Marx and Engels, 1846, 1848).

## Durkheim and the Functional View

While Marx concentrated on how cultural ideas and social structures contribute to conflict and the breakdown of societies, the French sociologist Emile Durkheim (1858–1917) focused on how they help hold them together, and at the heart of his thinking was the concept of society as *more than the sum of its members.*

A human body, for example, is more than a collection of cells, for what makes it human is the *arrangement* of individual cells in *relation* to one another. In a similar way, a group or society is more than a collection of individuals: it is a particular arrangement of individuals in relation to one another and to cultural beliefs, values, norms, and attitudes; and *these arrangements exist independently of the particular individuals who participate in them.*

We cannot explain the existence of money or the power of religion simply by understanding the biology and psychology of individuals, for money and religion endure beyond individual lifetimes and have coercive power over and above the will of any individual (Durkheim, 1895).

Social structures and culture are not the property of any one of us. None of us has the power, for example, to decide the fate of "music" as an idea, as a form we give to sound. While we can enjoy it, play it, compose it, or use it for our own individual purposes, music itself is a cultural creation whose future rests with society as a whole.

If the existence of cultural ideas and social structures cannot be explained solely on the basis of the characteristics of individuals, how do we understand them? Durkheim's response was his **functional perspective,** which focuses on society as a system of interrelated parts. An aspect of culture or social structure is functional for a goal if it contributes to the achievement of it; if it interferes with the achievement of a goal, it is dysfunctional for that goal (Merton, 1968).

The part we intend an idea to play in a group or society is its **manifest function** (Merton, 1968). When Americans are accused of crimes, for example, they are protected by a variety of norms whose manifest function is to support important values: protecting the rights of individuals and preventing the government from abusing and oppressing citizens. Accused criminals are entitled to legal representation, for example, and a trial by jury. In addition, norms restrict the ways in which police can gather evidence, and they allow convicted defendants the right to appeal to higher courts.

In contrast are **latent functions and dysfunctions,** those that we do *not* intend, that are unintended consequences or "side effects" (Merton, 1968). A latent function of the above norms is that they foster a heavy demand for lawyers. If the legal rights to representation and appeal were removed, many lawyers would find themselves out of work. There are also latent dysfunctions: the legal processing of accused criminals is so complex, lengthy, and costly, for example, that criminals often escape through legal "loopholes," as when murderers go free because the arresting officers fail to inform them of their legal rights. Overburdened prosecutors often plea-bargain, charging criminals with less-serious crimes in exchange for confessions of guilt that save the state the expense of a trial. While these norms are functional for protecting individuals and limiting the power of the government, they have latent dysfunctions that interfere with the effective prosecution of those who commit crimes. Most criminals know that even if they are caught, they are unlikely to be prosecuted and punished for their behavior.

It is important to remember that functional ideas are not necessarily "good," nor are dysfunctional ones necessarily "bad." A norm, for example, is functional if it contributes to the achieve-

Emile Durkheim

ment of goals in a society, but the goals it supports may be highly undesirable, as in the case of racism. In similar ways, norms may support valued social goals and yet be dysfunctional for others. The legal norms that protect the rights of accused criminals allow some criminals to escape punishment. In our society, however, this is accepted as the price we must pay in the interests of a goal we consider to be more important—ensuring that the innocent are not punished.

Durkheim was particularly interested in discovering latent functions and dysfunctions. While most early criminologists, for example, explained crime in terms of criminal personalities, Durkheim tried to identify latent functions of criminal behavior. While crime certainly has negative effects on individuals and society, from a functional point of view there are positive effects as well. In response to a serious crime, for example, community members band together in a collective outrage that

## PUZZLES:

## UNEXPECTED CONSEQUENCES

What is *good* about crime?

You can probably think of lots of bad consequences of crime, divorce, nuclear weapons, economic depressions, natural disasters, and wars; but can you think of *positive* consequences of such things? As you will see throughout *Human Arrangements*, sociologists have long been interested in social consequences of events and behavior that tend to jar our expectations by having quite unexpected effects.

strengthens the social ties among them. (They might gather together and march through the streets while shouting their anger and their demands for justice.) In addition, it is impossible for any group to completely control the behavior of its members without stifling individual initiative; thus, the violation of norms is an inevitable part of the functioning of any group that survives through the creative contributions of its members.

Durkheim did not suggest that criminals commit crimes in order to benefit society; but he did suggest that crime, like other social behavior, has latent functions and dysfunctions and that, in spite of its negative effects, from a functional point of view crime is "normal"—that is, inevitable—in any society.

By comparison, a conflict perspective focuses on crime as a reflection of inequality and conflict over scarce resources. When a company overcharges its customers and gains millions of dollars in illegal profits, the people responsible are rarely prosecuted as criminals. But someone who steals a videotape recorder or who fraudulently obtains welfare money is far more likely to be prosecuted. These kinds of inconsistencies reflect unequal distributions of power in a society, and conflict theorists pay special attention to how such inequalities develop and how they are maintained or changed (Chapter 11).

Marx and Durkheim thus focused on two very different aspects of social environments. To Marx, the most important aspects of social life were the conflicts between different classes, through which social relationships develop and change. Durkheim, on the other hand, focused on how cultural products and social structures contribute to or interfere with the attainment of socially valued goals.

### Weber and Social Action

Max Weber (1864–1920) was a German contemporary of Durkheim and, like both Marx and Durkheim, was concerned with the social implications of rapid changes taking place in Europe. Weber (1922a) believed the state would exert mounting control over individuals and saw societies becoming increasingly bureaucratic and coldly rational.

Unlike Durkheim and Marx, however, Weber was interested in **social action**, the behavior of individuals in response to social environments. How do the motives of individuals, for example, reflect cultural ideas? Why are workers in bureaucracies

Max Weber

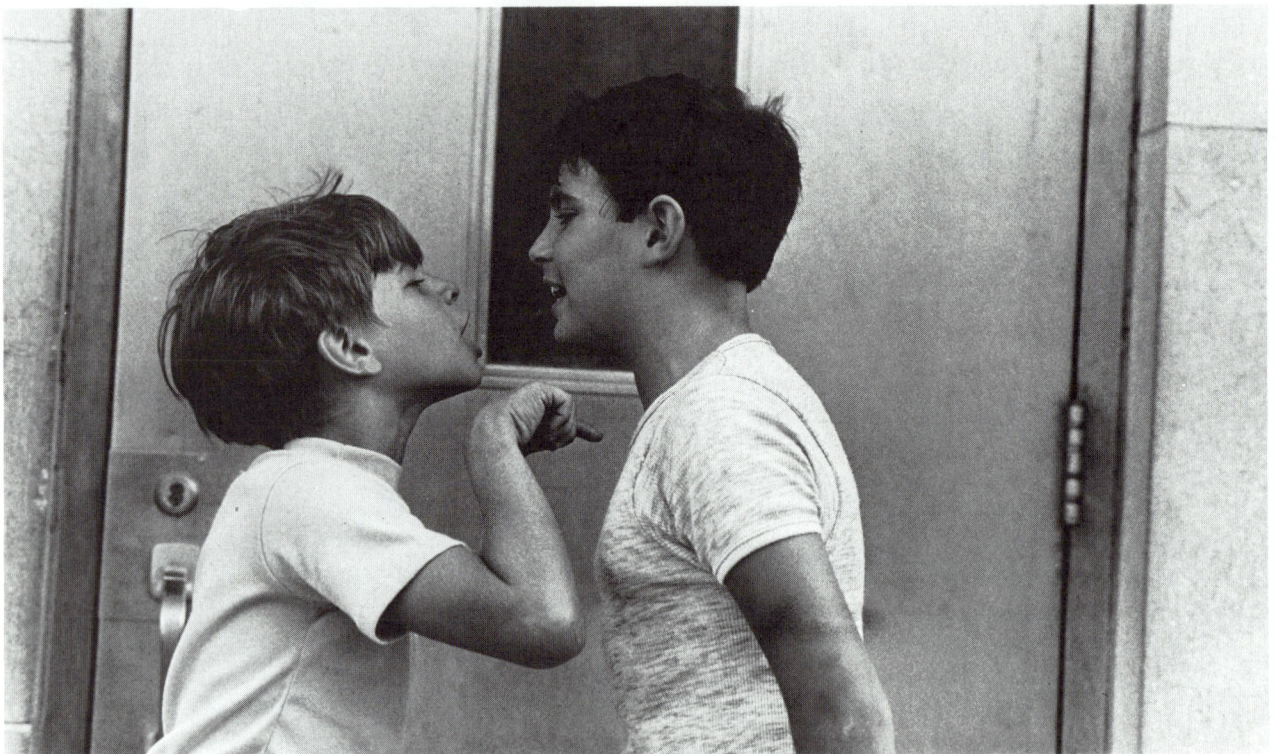

As these pictures show, it is through social interaction that we affect and are connected to each other.

so impersonal and committed to obeying "the rules"? From Weber's perspective, behavior cannot be understood unless we pay attention to the *meaning* individuals attach to their experience and behavior, and culture is the primary source of meaning.

Capitalists, for example, accumulate wealth and invest it in factories, land, and equipment. To Weber (1904), such behavior and the rise of capitalism as a way of life were facilitated by cultural beliefs and values. Weber noted that the religious beliefs of Calvinism provided a cultural environment that supported the accumulation of wealth that is central to capitalism. Calvinists believed that those who would go to heaven were chosen at birth and that worldly success indicated who had been chosen. They also believed, however, that luxurious living was evil. Thus, Weber argued, the cultural beliefs and values in Calvinist doctrine supported capitalist behavior and the development of capitalism as a way of structuring productive work.

## Simmel and Social Interaction

While Spencer, Marx, Durkheim, and Weber focused primarily on the large-scale organization of social life, the German sociologist Georg Simmel (1858–1919) worked on a much smaller scale. To Simmel, social life is a complex pattern of interaction among individuals. To understand social life, therefore, it is necessary to pay attention to **social interaction,** which is *the process through which people act in relation to one another.*

He noted, for example, that people living in large cities treat one another impersonally, rarely making contact with others outside their immediate circles of friends and relatives. This, he argued, is a necessary consequence of urban life, for in cities there are so many people, so many stimuli, that we cannot possibly pay serious attention to everyone. Thus, the social structure of urban environments leads people to "shut down," to narrow their attention.

His observations about urban life reflect an interest in the importance of numbers in social relationships. When there are only two people, for example, each person is necessary for the relationship to exist, and because either can destroy the relationship by leaving it, it is difficult for one to control the other. When we add a third person, however, two can outvote the third, and this, on a

small scale, is the central tension in social life between individual freedom and coercion by social groups (Simmel, 1950).

## American Sociology

It was primarily through the ideas of Darwin and Spencer that sociological thinking took root in the United States late in the nineteenth century. America was then experiencing an orgy of economic speculation; wealthy businessmen built vast fortunes at the expense of exploited workers; the growth of cities was out of control, and millions of immigrants were crowded into dismal living conditions.

There were many demands for social reform, and some of these came from the first American sociologists. Ironically, Darwin's ideas of unity and harmony in the evolution of biological life were used both by social reformers and defenders of the status quo. William Graham Sumner (1840–1910) was a rigid social Darwinist who believed that a society "needs first of all to be free from meddlers—that is, to be left alone" (Sumner, 1883).

Although Lester Ward (1841–1913) was also impressed with Darwin's ideas, he set out to free American sociology from the biological bent of social Darwinism. He adopted the Darwinian concept of evolution; but, like Comte, Marx, Durkheim, and Weber, he believed that human and nonhuman evolution were different: because humans are capable of purposeful action, unlike most animal species, we can change our social and physical environments and thereby affect our own development (Hofstader, 1955). To Ward, unlike Sumner, informed "meddling" in social relationships is what sociology is all about (Coser, 1977).

Sociology became firmly established as a discipline in America with the supportive environment of rapidly expanding universities during the early 1900s. Charles Horton Cooley (1864–1929) and George Herbert Mead (1863–1931) laid the groundwork for what was to become **social psychology,** which is the study of the effects of social environments on the psychological functioning and behavior of individuals. Cooley believed that the individual "self" arises from interaction with other people, especially in small, intimate groups such as the family (Cooley, 1902). Mead believed that thinking and social life were closely related: we think about and respond to the world by attaching cultural meanings to it and to what other peo-

It is not hard to see from this picture the dynamic richness of urban environments in the early 1900s, which fascinated many of the first American sociologists—especially those from the Chicago School.

ple do (Mead, 1934). Both Mead and Cooley were thus deeply interested in the relationship between the "self" and society.

Other sociologists such as Robert Park (1864–1944), Ernest Burgess (1886–1966), W. I. Thomas (1863–1947), and Florian Znaniecki (1882–1938) (all at the University of Chicago) combined a commitment to social reform with an intense curiosity about urban life. They were particularly interested in ecological studies that focused on social problems created by rapid industrialization, urbanization, and massive immigration. Chicago abounded with an extraordinary variety of people's adaptations to the dizzying pace of urban life, and these members of the "Chicago School" used cities as a natural laboratory for the study of everything from urban gangs, slums, dance halls, and racism to life among the wealthy (Coser, 1977).

It was not until the late 1930s that American sociologists paid major attention to questions that had intrigued European sociologists. How do culture and social structure contribute to conflict and cohesion? Why do individuals participate in social life in particular ways? For 25 years, sociologists such as Talcott Parsons attacked these kinds of questions by further developing Durkheim's functional perspective.

**The Conflict/Functional Battle** At the heart of Parsons' functional theory was the concept of society as an integrated system of social structures (such as family, economy, law) supported by cultural norms and values. Each part depends on others and contributes to the whole, allowing it to maintain stability by adjusting to a changing physical environment and internal stresses and strains. Within social systems, individuals choose among culturally defined alternatives and are motivated by norms and values to make choices that ultimately contribute to the survival of the system (Parsons, 1937, 1951).

As America strained under the civil rights movement and the Vietnam War in the 1960s, Marx's focus on social conflict became increasingly popular, and Parsons' critics charged that his functional theory gave a false picture of society as a harmonious, stable collection of social relationships and cultural ideas (Dahrendorf, 1958; Gouldner, 1970; Mills, 1959). Societies, they argued, are not cohesive, unified wholes in which everyone works toward the same goals. All societies experience continuing conflict and change, not stability and equilibrium; and each part of society contributes to that conflict and change. The basis of social order is not consensus, but the coercive use of power (Dahrendorf, 1973).

It makes little sense to contend that either the functional or conflict points of view is sufficient, for social systems are neither stable, smoothly functioning machines nor simply arenas in which people act out endless conflict and struggle. Social life is characterized by cohesion *and* conflict, consensus *and* coercion, as well as uncertainty, ambiguity, ambivalence, and contradiction (Merton, 1976b). Individually, the two perspectives provide us with incomplete, yet complementary views of reality.

**On a Smaller Scale: Symbolic Interaction and Life as Theater** While the advocates of the functional and conflict perspectives battled, other American sociologists followed Simmel's lead and focused on social life on a smaller scale. Within the confines of social structure and culture, we carry on our lives by interacting with one another through the use of symbols. We interpret each other's behavior and continually adjust our behavior in response to others. Mead used the image of a game whose rules we, as players, continually create, maintain, and change (Mead, 1934).

This is the perspective of **symbolic interaction,** and by focusing on how people use symbols, it tends to ignore social structure and culture. A party, for example, is a social situation that is influenced by cultural beliefs, values, norms, and attitudes and by patterns of expectations among the guests. It is impossible, however, to predict people's behavior simply by knowing the cultural and structural characteristics of their situation, for individuals continually interpret one another's behavior and adjust the way they present themselves to other people. Thus, within the large-scale limitations of culture and social structure, individuals use symbols in a variety of ways to interact with one another (Stryker, 1981).

**Ethnomethodology** is a long word that describes one of the simplest aspects of social interaction (Garfinkel, 1967). Ethnomethodologists study the unspoken rules and meanings through which we interpret one another's behavior and form our expectations of one another. When you step into an elevator, for example, you might not be aware of the shared expectation that in elevators people face front; but you would gain that awareness if you stood facing the rear for a few moments and noticed the reactions of other people. Social interaction is full of such subtle and often unconscious understandings and expectations, and ethnomethodologists are interested in uncovering the hidden underside of social life.

Erving Goffman (1959, 1981) went a step further by using a **dramaturgical perspective** that compares social life to the theater. As Shakespeare wrote in *As You Like It,*

All the world's a stage
And all the men and women merely players;
They have their exits and their entrances;
And one man in his time plays many parts.

As actors and actresses, we project images of ourselves to our audiences and construct images of others from their "performances." To Goffman, we are always acting, trying to create favorable impressions from one "stage" to the next. We may be confident and aggressive at work, but meek when a police officer writes out a traffic ticket; wild and crazy at a party, but serious and calm in church. None of this is "faking" to Goffman; there is no "real self" deceiving the world. From Goffman's point of view, this is just the way it is. *We are who we present ourselves to be.* The "masks" do not hide us, they are part of us.

## A Summary of Sociological Perspectives: The New Bedford Case

In March 1983, a woman entered a bar in New Bedford, Massachusetts, for the purpose of buying a pack of cigarettes. According to her later testimony (and that of the bartender), during the two hours that followed she was sexually assaulted repeatedly on top of a pool table by four men, while two other men cheered and the remaining male patrons looked on. No one tried to help her in spite of her pleas. A year later, four men were convicted of sexual assault and the two cheering onlookers were acquitted. None of those who refused to help her were prosecuted (*Newsweek*, March 28, 1983; March 12, April 2, and 9, 1984).

> *Functional:* How well did the men know each other, and how did their behavior affect the strength of their ties with each other?

> *Conflict:* What is the connection between sexual violence and the fact that women as a whole occupy social positions in society that are much lower in wealth, power, and prestige?

> *Social Action:* How was the behavior of the men in the bar affected by beliefs and attitudes toward women, men, sexuality, and violence? What meaning did the participants attach to their own and one another's behavior and how did this affect what happened?

> *Symbolic Interaction:* How did the words and gestures used by the participants contribute to what happened? Why, for example, were the woman's protests and cries for help ignored? Why did no one intervene?

The symbolic interaction perspective draws our attention to fascinating details of human behavior, but like all perspectives on social life, it is incomplete. All exchanges take place in environments, and to interpret one another's behavior we must take into account the cultural, structural, and ecological characteristics of each situation. Goffman's point of view is important, however, because it focuses on the fact that social environments do not determine absolutely our experience or behavior. Cultures and social structures exert their pressures on us, but we continually exercise our ability to manipulate, circumvent, and resist those forces.

Sociologists approach culture, social structure, and ecology from several perspectives and pay attention to social life on different scales, from the large-scale organization of economies and the ecology of cities to the small-scale interactions among individuals. These differences are complementary, not contradictory, and allow sociologists to appreciate fully the complexity of social life. Consider, for example, a society's division of labor: the degree to which tasks are divided among specialists. The functional approach identifies the positive and negative effects of increasingly complex divisions of labor on productivity and efficiency, while the conflict approach reveals the inequalities of power, wealth, and prestige that result from assigning people to different tasks. Weber's focus on social action helps explain why people behave differently in large, complex bureaucracies than they do in small, simply structured organizations; and the symbolic interaction perspective reveals how, for example, people manage their interactions in such settings—deferring to superiors, developing special vocabularies to increase solidarity with co-workers, and presenting different "selves" to different people.

Together, the functional, conflict, social action, and symbolic interaction perspectives dominate current sociological thinking and research on the importance of culture, social structure, and ecology in human life. They constitute a rich set of conceptual tools that approach social life from many directions and thus reveal its inherent complexity. Sociological concepts and theoretical perspectives determine the kinds of questions that sociologists ask about social life; but it is the scientific method that determines how we go about looking for answers. That method is the subject of Chapter 2.

## Summary

1. Sociology is the systematic study of social environments and their effects on the experience and behavior of individuals. Social environments consist of material and nonmaterial cultural products and social structures that exist independently of the individuals who participate in them. To describe something as social is to say that it is related to the collective experience of human beings as they interact with one another. However unique we are as individuals, who we are and what we think, feel, do, and experience are social insofar as they arise from shared ideas and our positions in relation to other people.

2. What we know about one another consists largely of beliefs and expectations we hold about the social positions that we and other people occupy. As individuals we respond to environments in many ways; but sociology focuses on patterns of response that are more likely in some social environments or social positions than in others. Thus, all personal choices in some way reflect the limitations of social environments.

3. Culture consists of nonmaterial and material products. Nonmaterial culture includes language, art, music, and four types of shared ideas: beliefs, norms, values, and attitudes.

4. Social structure is the arrangement of people in relation to one another and the patterns of expectation attached to positions in social relationships. Social structure also refers to patterns of expectation between groups, the distribution of people among social positions, and the distribution of rewards such as wealth, power, and prestige.

5. Individuals and social environments are affected by the characteristics of physical environments, the number of people and their physical distribution in relation to one another and physical surroundings. A population is a collection of people who share a given territory, and a society is a population that identifies with a common culture. Ecology focuses on the relationships between populations and physical environments, including the ability to use technology.

6. Sociologists differ in their views of how societies operate, and they pay attention to social life on different scales—from the organization of society to the most intimate interactions among individuals. Early sociologists tried to makes sense of the chaotic social conditions of late eighteenth-century Europe. Comte believed that societies develop in predictable stages and that humans can use science to affect that development. Spencer also believed in the evolution of societies, but opposed any tampering by human beings.

7. Marx developed the conflict perspective, based on the view that societies develop through continuing conflict over scarce rewards. To Marx, the most important characteristic of a society is how it produces goods, and the most important social characteristic of individuals is their social class, or position in relation to the means of production.

8. Durkheim developed the functional perspective, which focuses on how cultural ideas and social structures contribute to (are functional for) or interfere with (are dysfunctional for) attaining socially valued goals. A manifest function is intended, while a latent function is unintended.

9. Weber focused on social action—the ways in which people's behavior reflects their social environments—while Simmel concentrated on social interaction, the complex process through which individuals act in relation to one another.

10. In the United States, Cooley and Mead focused on the relationship between the self and society while Thomas, Park, and Burgess developed the ecological perspective by studying cities and their neighborhoods. From the 1930s into the 1960s Parsons developed the functional perspective by focusing on how societies maintain themselves, and in the 1960s his work was attacked by conflict theorists who believed his approach falsely portrayed society as based on harmony and consensus. In fact, the conflict and functional perspectives are complementary, for society is characterized both by conflict and cohesion, consensus and coercion.

11. American sociologists such as Goffman built on the work of Mead and Cooley to develop the symbolic interaction perspective, which focuses on how individuals use symbols to present themselves to others just as actors present themselves to audiences.

## Key Terms

## Recommended Readings

BERGER, P. (1963). *Invitation to sociology*. New York: Doubleday (available in paperback). An elegant, personal, and sometimes passionate introduction to the sociological perspective and the dilemmas posed by living as an individual in the social world.

COSER, L. A. (1977). *Masters of sociological thought: Ideas in historical and social context*. New York: Harcourt Brace Jovanovich. A readable, interesting text that takes a detailed look at the historical development of sociology, with an emphasis on the ideas, lives, and times of the sociologists who made it happen, from Comte through the major figures of the 1960s and 1970s.

GOFFMAN, E. (1959). *The presentation of self in everyday life*. Garden City, NY: Doubleday/Anchor. A fascinating classic that introduces the analysis of social interaction from Goffman's dramaturgical point of view.

MILLS, C. W. (1959). *The sociological imagination*. New York: Oxford University Press. This brief paperback is one of the most passionate views of sociology, both as a point of view and as a profession. Pay particular attention to Chapter 1 ("The Promise"), which ranks as the classic statement about the relationship between the "personal" and the "social" and to Chapter 8 ("The Uses of History"), in which Mills argues that an understanding of history is a vital part of the sociological analysis of current social conditions.

# CHAPTER 2

# Research Methods

Chapter 1 introduced major concepts that lie at the heart of most sociological questions. This chapter takes a detailed look at how sociologists use scientific research methods to answer such questions.

We begin by looking at the scientific method itself and its importance in sociology; then we follow the research process from deciding what you want to know to designing research, interpreting results, and wrestling with some of the difficulties of studying human beings and their social world.

## Asking Sociological Questions

Among full-time, year-round workers, why did men earn two-thirds more money in 1982 than women? In the simplest sense, we can answer this or any question by merely sitting back and thinking about it; but, how can we know whether or not such private explanations are correct? If you ask enough people, you will get a variety of answers to the above question, ranging from the effects of genes and hormones to cultural prejudice. How do we decide where the truth lies?

As we will see in this chapter, one response to this problem is the **scientific method,** which establishes objective standards for gathering and interpreting evidence. Unlike personal explanations, scientific results rest on *observable, unambiguous facts that lead everyone to the same conclusion.* Scientists try to rise above subjective beliefs, values, and attitudes by using research methods that confine them to questions about observable facts. Did God intend that men should be more powerful than women? Science can do nothing with this kind of question, because there are no observable facts that provide an answer.

Other questions, however, can be answered scientifically because relevant facts can be observed: Are women discriminated against in the workplace? Are women as capable as men? Do men have advantages in the labor market? How would economic equality between men and women affect other aspects of social life?

Durkheim's study of suicide (1897) was one of the first sociological attempts to answer a question through the use of the scientific method. If suicide is a purely individual act unaffected by social environments, then the *rate* of suicide (the relative number of people who kill themselves each year) should be the same for every group regardless of culture and social structure. Yet when Durkheim

examined death records, he found that Protestants were more likely to kill themselves than were Catholics and that Jews had the lowest suicide rates of all. Single people were more likely to commit suicide than married people and soldiers had higher rates than civilians. Durkheim reasoned that such differences reflect forces that have nothing to do with individual personalities and troubles, forces that affect individual choices according to people's positions in social relationships.

Durkheim considered purely cultural factors—such as attitudes toward suicide—that might explain differences in suicide rates, but logic and evidence led him to quickly discard that explanation. There is no reason, for example, to believe that married people disapprove of suicide more than single people do, and while Catholicism views suicide more seriously than does Judaism (regarding it as a mortal sin), Catholics have higher rates of suicide than Jews.

Durkheim turned to social structure for an explanation, to the ways in which people are connected to one another through social relationships. In particular, he was interested in the degree of *social cohesion* found among people in different social positions. Protestants stress independence and individualism, while Catholics and Jews stress active involvement with other members of their religious communities. In a similar way, married people are likely to have stronger social ties than single people. This is reflected in Durkheim's *theory* to explain observable patterns of suicide that distinguished one social position from another: When social bonds are weak, people are more likely to kill themselves.

Durkheim also noticed, however, that suicide rates tend to be relatively high in groups with very high levels of cohesion. Professional soldiers are more likely than draftees to take risks in battle that lead to their own deaths; and widows in India once committed suicide at the funerals of their husbands because it was expected of them. In both cases, people were more likely to commit suicide because they valued the group and its culture more than their individual lives. Consequently, Durkheim's theory of suicide predicted that suicide rates will be relatively high when social cohesion is either very low or very high.

This first attempt to apply scientific methods to sociological questions was understandably flawed. Durkheim used official records that were often distorted to conceal suicides, and while his theory fit the facts, other explanations might fit them as well. Nevertheless, his attempt to discover possible explanations by systematically observing the world was an important demonstration of a scientific approach to sociological questions. Durkheim tried to find connections between people's behavior and the observable characteristics of their social environments, and in doing so he established a model of sociological research that continues to be one of his most important contributions to sociology.

Sociological research centers on three basic tasks. First, in order to identify the origins and consequences of social structures, cultural ideas, and ecological arrangements, we must be able to *describe* them. What cultural beliefs, values, attitudes, and norms prevail in a particular society? How are families, schools, governments, and economies structured? How are rewards such as power, wealth, and prestige distributed according to people's positions in social relationships?

Second, how do we *explain* what we describe—such as variations in people's behavior? What are the social causes of suicide, for example, or divorce? How is social inequality maintained, and what are the consequences for those involved? How do we explain why societies differ in their cultures and social structures and why social environments change?

Third, how can we use explanations to make *predictions* about the future? Will the American culture's emphasis on individuality and mobility weaken the bonds between individuals and their families and communities, and will this cause a rise in suicide rates? How many children will be born in the next five years? Will there be enough jobs for them when they become adults?

The remaining chapters in this book are filled with the results of sociological research. To prepare you for them, this chapter focuses on the research process that produces such results. Any research project involves four basic phases:

1. Deciding what you want to know.
2. Deciding how you are going to find out.
3. Gathering information.
4. Interpreting your results.

Understanding how research is done will enable you not only to ask critical questions about scientific results, it will also help you do your own research when you write term papers (see Appendix A). In addition, many of the research skills described below are used in a variety of occupations.

## What Do You Want to Know?

If you have ever gotten bogged down trying to write a term paper, it was probably because you did not have a clear idea of just what it was you wanted to know. For undergraduates and research scientists alike, deciding what we want to know is not only the first but often the most difficult part of any research project.

Are we interested in learning about such behavior as lying or telling the truth, stealing, marrying and divorcing, having children or remaining childless, voting or not voting, cheating on college exams or telling on someone who does? Do we want to know about people's beliefs, values, and attitudes and how these ideas are reflected in their behavior? Or are we interested in a society's distributions of wealth, power, and prestige, its vulnerability to social conflict or violent revolution, its ability to function effectively? In short, what aspects of individuals, groups, or societies do we want to understand?

Our interest in trying to understand the income gap between men and women might well lead us to study women's liberation. Before we can begin, we have to answer two questions: What do we mean by "women's liberation" and what, in particular, do we want to know about it? "Women's liberation" can have many meanings. It can mean "removing inequalities of rewards such as wealth, power, and prestige," "changing the structure of family life so that women are no longer solely responsible for child care," or "changing cultural ideas that define women as inferior." It can also refer to the women's movement—how it began and how different segments of it try to achieve different goals.

Suppose we focus on "removing inequalities." Because that problem has many different aspects, we have to narrow it down and ask questions that can be answered by observing measurable phenomena. To show how the research process works, let us ask the following question: Do most Americans favor equality for women?

Favoring or opposing women's equality are values, and before we can do a study, we have to decide how we are going to go out into the world and *measure* them.

## Variables

Because favoring women's equality is a characteristic that varies from one person to another, it is called a **variable.** Variables can be events (such as accidents), behaviors, or any measurable characteristic of individuals, groups, or societies. Thus, group size, body weight, unemployment rates, believing in God, personal income, criminal behavior, and educational attainment are all variables. Having been born and eventually dying, on the other hand, are *constants. When* we are born and how and at what age we die, however, are variables.

Just as we must use a thermometer to measure heat, we now need some way to observe and sort people according to their level of support for women's equality. How might we do this? One simple

---

## How to Read a Table

Most research results begin as a set of observations of the characteristics of anything from individual people to entire societies. Researchers face the problem of organizing and summarizing masses of information in order to answer questions. As a reader, your problem is to understand what researchers present to you. We start with information, such as people's answers to the question, "Are you in favor of the Equal Rights Amendment?" A total of 877 adults answered "yes" in a 1977 national study.

Any arrangement of numbers in columns and rows (such as Table 2-1) is called a *table,* and there are several things we can learn from this one. It shows how supporters of the ERA answered some other questions about men and women. Here is how to go about reading it:

1. Start by reading the title, for it tells you what the table is about. Then look at the column and row headings so you are sure of the meaning of each number. Are the numbers percentages, for example, or are they frequencies, means, or medians? The first column contains a list of the questions the respondents were asked, and the second and third columns give the percentages who answered "Agree" and "Disagree." The last column includes the total (100%) showing that everyone has been included and the number of people—877—who answered each question (this is sometimes represented by the letter "*N*").

A good way to make sure you know what the numbers represent is to pick one and use it in a sentence. For example, 49 is the first number in the "Agree" column: Forty-nine percent of the people who support the ERA agree with the statement that "It is more important for a wife to help her husband's career than to have one of her own."

2. Next, look to see if there are any footnotes. These often provide important information, including when the information was gathered and by whom as well as the meaning of particular words used in the table (for example, the word "adult" might be defined in terms of age).

3. Now you are ready to learn something from the table. This is a relatively simple table because it gives only the percentage breakdown for each variable without comparing the responses of different kinds of people (such as men and women or people of different ages); and yet it has some quite interesting findings. In spite of the fact that all those represented in the table expressed support for the ERA, substantial percentages nonetheless take quite different positions on more specific questions about men's and women's roles. As the text points out, this table raises questions about the meaning of support for the ERA, since many of those who say they support equal rights for women in terms of the ERA seem to oppose equality in more specific areas of social life.

possibility is to ask people if they favor the Equal Rights Amendment, which states: "Equality of rights under the law shall not be denied or abridged by the United States or by any State on account of sex."

We could then interpret "yes" answers as favoring equality and "noes" as opposition. This kind of procedure is a **measurement instrument,** because it clearly classifies people according to some characteristic.

## Measurement, Meaning, and Validity

A measurement instrument is **valid** if it measures what we intend it to measure and not something else. In 1977 a national sample was asked, "Do you strongly favor, somewhat favor, somewhat oppose, or strongly oppose the Equal Rights Amendment?" The result: 57 percent expressed support for it (Davis, 1984). Does this mean that a majority of American adults support women's equality? Is ver-

bal support for the ERA a valid measure of support for women's equality?

Support for the ERA reflects a general value about women's rights, while equality for women involves a variety of specific goals that have direct and immediate implications for people's lives. Thus, it is quite possible for people to support the ERA generally and yet actually oppose equality for women in terms of specific issues. (Before reading on, you might want to take a look at the box, "How to Read a Table," on p. 35.)

For example, Table 2-1 summarizes responses to a series of specific questions about men and women, *among respondents who expressed support for the ERA in 1977.* Among ERA supporters, almost half nonetheless believe that a wife's career is less important than her husband's; 30 percent disagree with the idea that a wife has the right to decide whether or not to bear children; and 57 percent believe that women should stay home and not

**Table 2-1**

Values about Men and Women among Adults Who Support the ERA, 1977

| VALUE STATEMENT | PERCENTAGE WHO AGREE | PERCENTAGE WHO DISAGREE | TOTAL (N) |
|---|---|---|---|
| 1. "It is more important for a wife to help her husband's career than to have one herself." | 49 | 51 | 100(877) |
| 2. "If the husband in a family wants children, but the wife decides that she does not want any children, it is all right for the wife to refuse to have children." | 70 | 30 | 100(877) |
| 3. "It is much better for everyone involved if the man is the achiever outside the home and the woman takes care of the home and family." | 57 | 43 | 100(877) |
| 4. "If there is a limited number of jobs, it is all right for a married woman to hold a job in business or industry even if her husband is able to support her." | 43 | 57 | 100(877) |

Source: J. Davis, 1984.

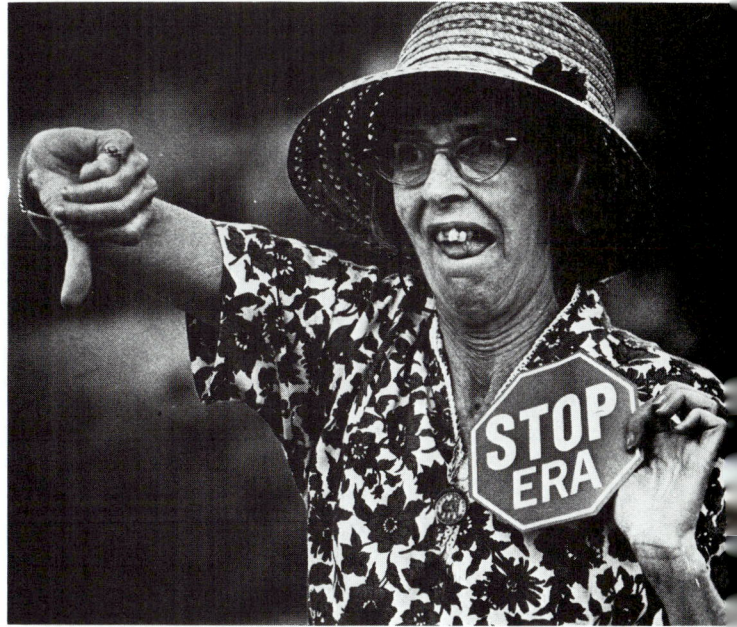

hold jobs (and not get the economic independence that results) if jobs are scarce and their husbands can support them.

While verbal support for the ERA may be a valid measure of support for the *ERA*, the evidence clearly suggests that it is an invalid measure of support for specific aspects of social life that must be changed in order to bring about equality for women. In a similar way, people may support specific aspects of women's liberation and yet oppose the ERA as a means for achieving those goals.

Consequently, "support for women's equality" is too complex to be measured with any one instrument, however tempting and efficient that approach may be. When we hear a statement such as "A majority of American adults favor equality for women," we have to ask a critical question: What does "favoring women's equality" *mean*? In other words, did the researcher use a valid instrument to measure this concept?

**Reliability** Measurement instruments must not only be valid; they must be **reliable:** they must produce the same results no matter who uses them. In addition, if the characteristic they measure remains constant, then the results must remain constant as well.

One way to measure the incidence of crime, for example, is simply to count up the number of crimes reported to police each year. The problem with this is that most crimes are never reported to police (Chapter 10). Thus, the actual incidence of crime might go down from one year to the next, but the *measure* of crime might show an increase if people become more willing to report crimes to police.

Thus, official crime statistics are *unreliable* because they may indicate change even when the behavior in question does not. Their lack of reliability also makes them invalid because they in fact reflect two different things at once: the incidence of crime *and* the willingness of people to report it. Whether the official rates go up or down or remain the same, we cannot be sure about what is actually happening.

**Measurement Problems** The task of measurement poses particularly difficult problems for social scientists (Schuman and Presser, 1981). Much of what we try to measure is difficult to observe directly.

We cannot measure attitudes in the same way that we can measure the weight of an object. We must rely on what people tell us or what they reveal to us through their actions, and even the latter requires some interpretation.

This problem occurs in all sciences. Astronomers rely on what little they can observe in order to construct theories about what they cannot observe—such as the origin of the universe. Atomic physicists developed nuclear reactors long before they could actually see atoms with electron microscopes, and even now the image they see is not the atom itself, but its shadow.

While in some ways the need for interpretation may be viewed as a liability in social research, Max Weber (1949) pointed out that when we study human beings subjective interpretations of behavior are essential. A falling object does not have motives and desires that affect its rate of fall. People are far more complicated than objects, and we cannot understand the effects of social environments on human behavior simply by observing people as if they were objects. Thus, research in the social sciences requires a delicate balance of objectivity and subjectivity: we must be able to put ourselves in another's place while at the same time standing apart and trying to observe with scientific objectivity.

There are additional problems, as well. While the characteristics of objects tend to remain the same over time, people's thoughts, feelings, and behavior are far less stable. Because social research relies heavily on how people present themselves, information about them can easily be distorted. People sometimes lie about themselves in order to make a good impression, or answer questions they do not understand rather than appear to be ignorant. There is evidence that highly educated people in particular tend to give what they believe are "socially acceptable responses" when they report their values, beliefs, attitudes, and behavior (Crowne and Marlowe, 1964).

Sociological research is also difficult because the act of gathering information about people is itself a social process. When people know they are being observed, their behavior is affected by the social situation and the characteristics of the observer. Most of the interviewers who asked the question about support for the ERA were women, and it is reasonable to assume that people are less

willing to express opposition to the ERA to a woman than they are to a man.

Other studies find that whites are less likely to admit racial prejudice in the presence of blacks, even when they are filling out anonymous questionnaires (Summers and Hammonds, 1966), and blacks are more likely to say "whites can be trusted" if the interviewer is white (Schuman and Converse, 1971). Thus, social scientists cannot completely separate themselves from the people they study and take measurements in carefully controlled surroundings.

## How to Find Out: Designing Research

Once we decide what we want to know and how we are going to measure it, we next have to decide how we are actually going to go into the world and *use* our measurement instruments.

Sociologists use a variety of research methods, because all methods have shortcomings. Some, such as in-depth interviews, allow us to examine human interaction "up close" in intimate detail, but restrict us to small numbers of people who may represent no one but themselves. Other methods, such as surveys, allow us to study large representative samples of a population, but limit us to more superficial kinds of information. While all methods have their advantages and disadvantages, combined they produce the varieties of information that can result in understandings that are both detailed and broadly representative.

## Populations

In scientific research, a **population** is any precisely defined set of people, groups, or societies (notice that this definition differs slightly from that used in the study of population and ecology in Chapters 1 and 5). Once we decide what we want to know, we have to define the population, which may be as small as a single group of two people or as large as the entire human race. "Currently married people in Ohio," "Japanese corporations," "cities with a million or more people in 1984," and "countries that use the death penalty" can all be defined as populations.

If we want to find the percentage of Americans who support women's equality, we have to decide *whose* support or opposition we want to measure. We have to define "Americans"—that is, we must precisely define our population. Do we want to include children, or only adults? Or do we want a still narrower focus—American corporations, military units, or professionals such as lawyers and physicians?

Suppose that we decide to include all American adults. However, "American adults" is still not a precisely defined enough population for scientific research, because it does not clearly indicate who is included. What age groups, for example, are considered "adult," and will we include Americans who currently live outside the United States? Will we include people living in Alaska and Hawaii? Will we include people who live in the United States but are not citizens—such as illegal aliens and college exchange students? One solution to the problem is to define our hypothetical population as "American citizens over 18 years old living in the continental United States at the time of the study."

**Censuses versus Samples**  With small populations, it is possible to conduct a **census** by gathering information about all of its members. With large populations, however, the expense and time involved make it difficult if not impossible to observe each member. The U.S. Census Bureau does this every ten years at a cost of tens of millions of dollars (see Mitroff, Mason, and Barabba, 1983) and as you will see throughout this book, it provides a rich source of information about life in the United States.

If we want to know if members of a small labor union support women's equality, we could ask all of them; but if we want to pose this question to our population of all adult American citizens (more than 170 million people), we face an enormous task out of all proportion to what we stand to gain from it. (You only need stop a moment and try to imagine the number of different studies we might want to do on the American population and then realize

*"How would you like me to answer that question? As a member of my ethnic group, educational class, income group, or religious category?"*

Drawing by D. Fradon; © 1969, The New Yorker Magazine, Inc.

that each would cost tens of millions of dollars.) In such cases, practical necessity forces researchers to select a subgroup—called a **sample**—and use it to represent the population.

The necessary use of samples raises important questions about all scientific research: Are some samples better than others? How do we tell? Can a sample accurately represent a large population? How, for example, can the Gallup Poll use 1,500 people to accurately describe the beliefs, values, and attitudes of tens of millions?

**Good Samples and Bad Samples** *Any* set of people, groups, organizations, or societies selected from a population constitutes a sample, and there is virtually no way to be certain that a sample accurately represents the population it came from. How, then, can we use samples with confidence?

The answer to this question lies in the way samples are selected. Suppose there are 10,000 students in your college and you want to find out how strongly they support women's equality. You stand at the library door during the evening and question students as they enter. After you question 200 students, you stop. Do their answers accurately represent the entire student body?

While your sample *may* represent the student population, you have no reason to be confident of this, because you failed to consider all the students who never use the library at night (or who never step foot in it at all); and their views may differ sharply from those of students who routinely spend their evenings in the library. Thus, this haphazard sample is likely to be *biased* because you did not actually select the sample; rather, students selected themselves.

What if you used a different procedure, putting each of the 10,000 students' names into a big bowl and then picking 200 names? You would have good reason to feel greater confidence in this sample *because every member of the population had an equal chance to be included.* Samples selected

The 1940 draft lottery that chose men who eventually served in the American armed services in World War II is a famous life-and-death example of random sampling. President Franklin D. Roosevelt (left) looks on as Secretary of War Henry L. Stimson (blindfolded) selects the numbers of those who would be conscripted.

in this way are called **random samples.** Many sampling methods use the principle of randomness (Kalton, 1984). To save time, you might select at random one of the first 50 names on the list of 10,000 students and use that as a starting point to select every 50th name on the list (a **systematic sample**). Or if you wanted to gather information on all American college students, you might first select a sample of colleges and then randomly select students in each one (a **multistage sample**).

What all of these procedures have in common is the fact that each member of the population and each *combination* of members has an equal chance of being selected, and this is the most crucial characteristic that distinguishes good samples from bad ones.

You might be saying to yourself at this point, "I still don't see how they can use a sample to describe a population with millions of people. So what if it's random?" The answer to this question involves some mathematical reasoning that we will not go into here; but if you are curious, take a look at Appendix B.

## Surveys

A **survey** consists of observations of a sample of members of a population. In most surveys, information is gathered either in **interviews,** in which respondents interact with someone who asks questions, or in **questionnaires,** which respondents fill out in private. In the simplest sense, we use surveys to find out "what's going on out there" by asking respondents to tell us (Schuman and Presser, 1981).

Surveys are useful because they allow researchers to gather large amounts of information from samples that represent populations of interest. Surveys can be used to describe prevailing cultural values, beliefs, and attitudes as in Table 2-1. They also allow us to describe broad aspects of social structure—the number of people who are unemployed, the extent and distribution of poverty, or how income, prestige, power, jobs, and education are distributed in a population.

When surveys focus on specific problems, they often go beyond mere description and shed light on the social processes through which social structure and culture affect individuals' lives. Work in skilled blue-collar trades, for example, requires a period of apprenticeship. While in 1970 there were 280,000 men apprenticed in 350 skilled trades and crafts, there were only 12,000 women. Is discrimination involved?

In a survey of employers in a Wisconsin town, researchers discovered that most employers said they would not admit women to training programs because they would have to work under harsh physical conditions (Hammel, 1974). The researchers also found, however, that women *were* hired to do unskilled work in the same harsh conditions endured by higher-paid, male workers. Thus, survey results, combined with other observations, produced evidence of discrimination in the hiring process.

Another survey sheds light on the process of discrimination in medicine, the highest-paid profession in America. A sample of male physicians was asked to rank different medical specialties in terms of prestige, and their replies placed surgery at the top and pediatrics and psychiatry at the bottom (Quadagno, 1976). Women physicians are overwhelmingly concentrated in pediatrics and psychiatry, specialties with the lowest levels of pay and prestige (Epstein, 1970). How does this happen? When Quadagno asked a sample of female physicians to explain their choice of specialty, two reasons were always given: male surgeons treated them with hostility, and they received far more encouragement from superiors to pursue "feminine" specialties such as pediatrics and psychiatry.

> Their awareness of negative attitudes toward them in certain areas combined with positive reinforcement in others led them to avoid situations where conflict might occur. Rather than confront possible rejection, women selected specialties in which they felt comfortable and welcome. (p. 450)

**Case Studies** While most surveys attempt to represent entire populations, sociologists often begin by studying samples that may or may not represent the population they are interested in. These are called **case studies,** and they allow researchers to explore and clarify research problems and perfect measurement instruments before mounting an expensive survey. W. F. Whyte (1981) was interested in the intimate details of daily life in an urban slum; Helen and Robert Lynd (1929) spent years studying social relationships in a small American city; and Erving Goffman (1961a) observed life in a mental institution for many months.

In each of these studies, detailed descriptions of social life required enormous amounts of time and would have been impossible to obtain if researchers had forced themselves to focus on large samples of slum neighborhoods, small cities, or asylums. Instead, they used case studies to focus on a single instance that was carefully chosen to make it as representative as possible. In effect, they based their conclusions on samples that contained only one "case."

While a study of a single mental hospital cannot be used to describe mental hospitals in general, it can provide insights that can then be tested with more representative samples. In addition, case studies often provide a depth of understanding that is impossible in large surveys. As case studies accumulate, they may provide a bulk of evidence that supports conclusions about entire populations. If Goffman's observations of a single mental hospital are added to other studies, the regular patterns that emerge can tell us much about how people behave in those environments. Thus, while a single case study rarely describes a population, the accumulated findings of many case studies often can.

**Limitations of Survey Research**  In spite of their advantages, surveys have limitations. First, they rely on what people report, either on questionnaires or to interviewers, and individuals may either misperceive the question or, for a variety of reasons, give inaccurate reports. If, for example, we ask someone, "Why did you say you are opposed to the ERA?" the answer we receive may have little to do with actual causes. Some surveys directly observe behavior; but most rely on what people *say* about their behavior. The problem is not that verbal behavior is less "real" than other behavior, for we are quite capable of deceiving others through our actions (Merton, 1940). Rather, surveys limit us to a relatively narrow range of behavior (what people say), which may or may not correspond to their actions.

Second, surveys are limited in time. A survey is like a still photograph, whereas social life is a continuing process through which culture and social structure affect experience and behavior. While surveys measure the results of social processes (gender differences in occupation and income, for example), they are not very effective for discovering how those results come about.

One solution to this problem is a **longitudinal survey,** in which a sample of people is interviewed at regular intervals. This allows researchers to "track" people over time and record changes in their social positions, behavior, beliefs, values, and attitudes. The problem with longitudinal surveys is that keeping track of several thousand people over a period of many years is a difficult and expensive task.

A more practical approach is to use a series of surveys that gather information from *different* samples selected from the *same* population. To find out if support for women's equality changes as people age, for example, we could interview a national sample of 20-year-olds in 1980 and then interview a sample of 30-year-olds in 1990. In both cases, the samples represent the same population: people who were born in 1960.

Because single surveys are "still photographs," however, their results cannot be used to test conclusively ideas about cause and effect, and this is their most serious limitation. For example, a scientist cannot answer the question "Does heat make balloons expand?" simply by gathering a sample of balloons and measuring their temperatures and their volumes. Why not? Because other factors—such as the initial size of the balloons—may account for some of the observed differences.

The only way to answer this question is to take a group of balloons of the same size, heat them to different temperatures, and then record differences in volume. In other words, every factor other than heat must be controlled by holding it constant, and then the suspected *cause* (heat) must be manipulated to see how it (and it alone) produces an *effect* (increased volume). This is the experimental method, and it requires time and controlled conditions, both of which are beyond the capability of single surveys.

## Experiments

An interest in finding out why men earn two-thirds more money than women might lead us to explore the ways in which women are discriminated against. Do people tend to assume, for example, that women are less capable than men and evaluate men more favorably than women even when their performances are of equal quality? Assuming they are even aware of it, people would be reluctant to admit such a bias in survey interviews, and even if they did admit it, we could not use a survey to see if women are actually discriminated against simply because they are women.

To see if gender, by itself, affects people's evaluations of ability and performance, we have to *hold constant all other factors that might affect evaluations*—that is, we must design an **experiment.** In experiments, separate groups of people are exposed to conditions or experiences that are exactly alike in all ways but one. If people's behavior differs from one group to another, then those differences must be due to the different conditions they were exposed to, since the groups are alike in all other respects.

Goldberg (1968) used the experimental method when he randomly selected a sample of 140 female undergraduates, assembled them in a college lecture hall, and asked them to evaluate articles written for scholarly journals. "We are interested in the ability of college students to make critical evaluations of professional literature," he told them. After reading the articles, students filled out questionnaires in which they evaluated them for such things as writing style, the author's professional competence and probable standing in the field, profoundness, and persuasiveness.

Unknown to the students, Goldberg had randomly assigned each of them to one of two groups. Everyone read the same articles, but in one group, the authors had male first names (such as "John T. McKay"), while in the other the authors had female first names (such as "Joan T. McKay"). Goldberg found that the women consistently gave higher ratings to articles they thought were written by men.

Because the students were randomly assigned to their groups, they were, as groups, similar in all important respects. They read and evaluated the same articles in the same social situation; thus, any pattern of differences in their evaluations can be due to only one factor—their perception of the author's gender. Experiments allow researchers to control all factors that might account for different responses and to manipulate the one factor they are interested in. In this way, they are able to demonstrate cause-and-effect relationships between variables.

**Limitations of Experiments** Like all scientific methods, experiments have limitations. When people know they are participating in an experiment, for example, their behavior may be affected

in ways that distort the results. Experimental subjects who know that their behavior is observed, know that what they do (or do not do) is important. Thus, the experimental setting itself may exert an uncontrolled influence on subjects' behavior.

One early study of factory workers suggested that people's behavior in experiments is affected simply because they get more attention than they are accustomed to. Mayo and his colleagues studied workers at the Hawthorne plant of the Western Electric Company to discover how working conditions affect productivity (Roethlisberger and Dickson, 1939). They varied such factors as the amount of lighting and the frequency and duration of coffee breaks and found, to their surprise, that no matter what they did, productivity increased.

They eventually concluded that merely by participating in the experiment, workers received more attention than they were used to, and their increased feelings of being "special" resulted in higher productivity (just as students in "experimental" courses often display unusually high levels of motivation). Such distortions that are caused by experimental situations came to be known as the "Hawthorne effect" and pose considerable problems for experimenters.

Had the researchers been aware of this effect, they might have used a **control group** of workers who were told they were experimental subjects but were *not* exposed to different working conditions. Mayo might then have found that their productivity increased just as the other workers' had.

It is important to note that while the Hawthorne effect made researchers more aware of experimental conditions as sources of error, subsequent studies consistently failed to duplicate Mayo's findings in a variety of settings (Parsons, 1982). This illustrates an important principle in all scientific research: we run a considerable risk of error if we accept the findings of a single study as conclusive proof of any proposition. Science thus depends on **replication**—repeating studies in different settings to see if the initial findings hold up.

**The "Real World" as Laboratory** The experimental method is also limited by the artificial nature of laboratory research settings. The students in Goldberg's study, for example, knew that their evaluations would not affect the authors whose works they read ("It's just an experiment") and it is impossible to estimate how such settings affect subjects' behavior and judgments. If these same students were personnel managers whose decisions affected people's lives, would they still discriminate against women? Laboratory experiments cannot answer such questions, and for this reason experimenters often conduct **field experiments** outside the laboratory.

Fidell (1970) sent fake applications for faculty positions to 238 university psychology departments. The résumés that accompanied the applications were the same in each case, but half of the applicants were identified as males ("Patricks") and the other half as females ("Patricias"). The heads of departments were asked to give a "current appraisal of the applicant's chances of getting a full-time position." The results showed that Patricks were judged to be suitable for more appointments and at higher levels than were Patricias, even though their experience and qualifications were identical; and only Patricks considered to be qualified for full professorships.

Field experiments allow us to control and manipulate key variables in "real world" settings; to do this, however, we must focus on a narrow problem involving only a few variables. This illustrates an important trade-off among different research methods: those that allow a large scope (surveys) make it difficult to test ideas under carefully controlled conditions; on the other hand, those that permit such controls (experiments) require researchers to restrict themselves to simple problems, when in fact behavior is caused by many related factors. When the findings produced by different methods are combined, however, it is possible to piece together richer, more complex explanations.

## Participant Observation

While surveys ask people to describe their social situations, behavior, and experience, and experiments allow researchers to observe behavior in controlled laboratory conditions, **participant observation** allows us to directly observe behavior outside of laboratories (Robert Emerson, 1981). Many sociologists use this technique to gain insights into social behavior. W. F. Whyte (1981), for example, lived for several years in a lower-class neighborhood of Boston and observed urban gangs by participating in their activities. The trust that developed between researcher and subjects allowed Whyte to observe the daily lives of these gang members in ways that would otherwise be impossible.

Goffman (1961a) observed life in a mental hospital and identified ways in which depersonalization and humiliation aggravate mental problems. Festinger, Riecken, and Schachter (1956) joined a religious cult whose members believed the world would soon be destroyed and that only they would be saved by aliens from outer space. The researchers were able to observe firsthand when cult members reacted to the failure of their prophecy.

Kanter (1977a, 1977b) observed employees in a large corporation. Among her many findings, three stand out. First, most women in the corporation were employed as secretaries, and one of their most important responsibilities was attending to such personal needs of their male superiors as listening to personal problems, picking up laundry, and arranging social appointments. Promotions, however, depend on task performance, not attention to personal needs. Thus, many women in corporations are confined to tasks whose successful performance effectively bars them from advancement.

Second, while women numerically dominate secretarial jobs, among managers and executives they are numerical *tokens*—there are but a few women in a vast crowd of men. This, Kanter observed, affects women's behavior in a number of ways. They tend to feel highly visible and often try to "hide" by blending in—wearing man-tailored suits, for example. Their heightened visibility also makes them self-conscious, and they tend to overachieve because they know that everything they do is closely watched and evaluated as an indicator of "what women can do."

Third, Kanter also found that women often perform activities that have little to do with job performance. They may play "mother" (comforting men) or "seductress," treated as a sex object by men who seek to monopolize their attention. They may also play the "pet" who is cute and admiring and presents herself as a self-effacing, unthreatening "girl." Kanter found that women are often unaware of such behavior, and her ability to observe life in corporations allowed her to see the unwitting responses of men and women to their social environment.

**Limitations of Participant Observation**  Participant observation allows researchers to explore aspects of behavior that individuals are often unaware of, to witness and describe daily life as it occurs. While this method has clear advantages over surveys, it also has its limitations. Because participant observers participate in the social situations they study, there is always the danger that their presence will affect other people's behavior and that the observers may identify so closely with their subjects that their own objectivity is impaired. They may develop both positive and negative feelings toward their subjects that lead them to unconsciously select and interpret observations in biased ways.

In the 1920s, anthropologist Margaret Mead lived for several years on the island of Samoa, and her classic book *Coming of Age in Samoa* (1928/1953) described Samoans as a graceful and gentle people among whom adolescence was a trouble-free time of life. Mead's book was particularly important because it was written at a time when Americans were very concerned about the "adolescent crises" that prevailed in American society; her discovery of a society in which such crises did not occur strongly supported the view that culture is more important than biology in determining human behavior.

In 1983 another anthropologist, Derek Freeman, attacked Mead's study. He argued that Mead went to Samoa looking for evidence of the importance of culture, and her observations and interpretations were determined by what she wanted to see. A storm of controversy followed and while Mead's research did have its methodological flaws, it appears that her interpretation of Samoan society in the 1920s was nonetheless basically accurate.

As Marcus (1983) wrote in his comments on this controversy, the outcome is not the most important lesson we can draw from it. More important is the fact that two observers can arrive at "radically different interpretations from fieldwork in the same culture" (Marcus, p. 22). Like all case studies, the results of participant observation must be interpreted in comparison with the findings of other observers. This is an important principle in all scientific research, from physics to biology.

One of the most serious drawbacks of participant observation is that it requires enormous amounts of time—sometimes as long as several

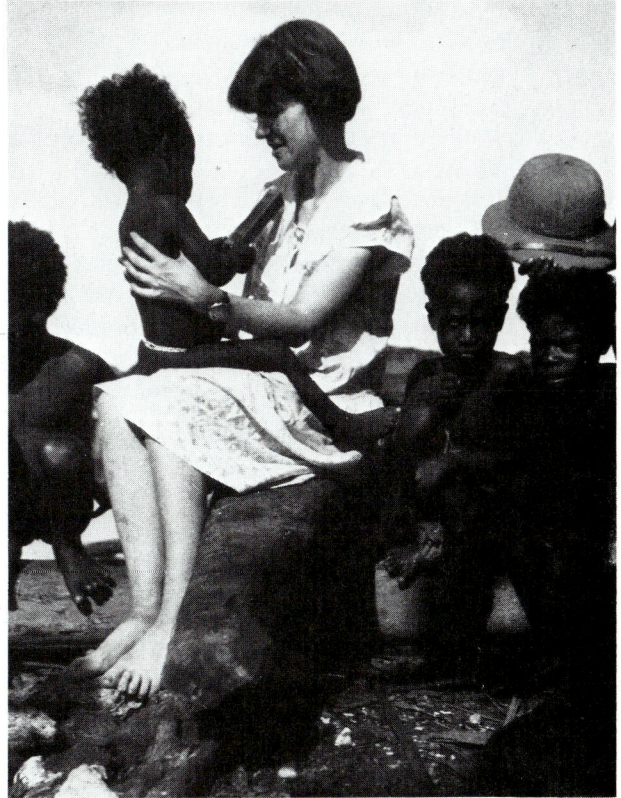

Like many research methods, the strength of participant observation—used to such great effect by Margaret Mead—is also its weakness: by getting close to the subjects of research, observers run the risk of losing their sense of objectivity and, therefore, their ability to see their subjects clearly.

years. An alternative method that gathers extensive information in a shorter period of time is the in-depth interview.

**In-depth Interviews**  Like surveys, **in-depth interviews** gather information by asking respondents questions and recording their answers. Unlike most surveys, in-depth interviews can last for many hours during which the respondent and the interviewer can develop a rapport that enables them to explore issues whose subtlety and personal nature are beyond the scope of most surveys. Researchers are able to explore the reasons that underlie people's behavior and to record many intimate details of their daily lives.

Rubin (1976) studied life in working-class marriages by interviewing each husband and wife in 50 couples. Some of the interviews lasted as long as ten hours and required repeated visits. After spending many hours listening to her respondents, Rubin came to know them and was able to paint a detailed portrait of married life in 50 working-class families, from the struggle to earn a living to sexual relationships.

For hours, wives and husbands talked about their marriages, their early hopes and dreams, how their families and their relationships grew and changed over the years, their disappointments when the reality of married life in the working class collided with their dreams, and how they adapted within the limitations and numerous financial crises of working-class life. The result is a series of richly textured portraits that reveal, among many other things, how husbands and wives often experience their relationship with each other in strikingly different ways.

In-depth studies like Rubin's are limited in several ways. We cannot know if the 50 families in her sample represent anyone other than themselves; and the closeness of her relationship with her respondents carries the danger that her results are distorted because respondents tell her what they think she wants to hear. In spite of these limitations, in-depth interviews and participant observation often yield a wealth of detail about social relationships and human experience, and they remind us that sociological research concerns the lives of real human beings who are trying to come to terms not only with themselves, but the cultural, structural, and ecological conditions of their lives.

## Using What Is Already There: Secondary Analysis

Surveys, case studies, experiments, participant observation, and in-depth interview studies are methods used by researchers to gather fresh evidence that sheds light on sociological problems; but a great deal of information already exists in historical documents, government statistics, and published studies. When researchers apply information gathered by someone else to their own questions, they are using **secondary analysis** (Hyman, 1972). When Durkheim studied suicide, for example, he found a new use for information that already existed—death certificates. Using information that has already been gathered is what secondary analysis is all about.

One of the richest sources of sociological information is the U.S. Census, conducted every ten years by the Census Bureau, which at that time gathers detailed information about every citizen. Additional information is gathered several times a year through the Current Population Survey. Other government agencies gather a wealth of information on births, deaths, marriages, and divorces as part of the vital statistics system.

In addition, organizations such as corporations, military units, universities, public school systems, hospitals, and police departments regularly gather information about their activities. When we add to this the thousands of social science research projects conducted over the last century, we have a rich store of information that can be applied to a variety of research questions never anticipated by those who originally gathered the information.

Sometimes revealing information can be found in the most unlikely places. If you look in the Yellow Pages of your telephone directory under the heading "Physicians," for example, you will find that doctors are listed by their specialties. First names will give you a clue to the gender of each doctor, and by counting patiently you will soon see how women doctors are distributed among different specialties—relatively few in surgery, but many in pediatrics, for example.

Because data gathering is expensive and time-consuming, sociologists are increasingly using secondary analysis. In her study of a large corporation, Kanter (1977a) examined forms used to evaluate the performance of employees. The forms existed for the purpose of making personnel decisions within the corporation, but Kanter found a new use for them as she looked to see which aspects of men's and women's performances led to high overall ratings.

Kanter found that secretaries were evaluated according to two main characteristics: "initiative and enthusiasm" and "ability to anticipate and take care of their bosses' personal needs." Thus, secretaries were rewarded on the basis of personal relationships with superiors, while men were rewarded more on the basis of professional skills and performance.

**Content Analysis** The methods discussed thus far focus primarily on what people do and what they say. **Content analysis,** however, is an additional method that examines not *what* people communicate, but *how* they communicate it, and this often reveals additional messages that are conveyed when people write or talk (Riley and Stoll, 1968). Content analysis is widely used to investigate how the mass media transmit cultural beliefs, values, and attitudes that reinforce the subordinate position of women in society. How is it done?

Suppose you want to find out if school textbooks portray males and females in different ways. You could do this by assembling a collection of textbooks and perhaps counting the number of characters used in stories or examples and determining what percentage of them are male. Content analyses of school texts find that most characters—whether they are human, animal, or fantasy—are male, and almost all important people are presented as male. Working women are rarely portrayed, and when they are, their jobs tend to be low in prestige and pay—secretaries, nurses, and elementary school teachers (St. Peter, 1979; Women on Words and Images, 1975a).

Content analyses of television shows reveal similar biases. Whether the shows are aimed at children or adults, the vast majority of leading characters are male, and successful working women are rarely portrayed (Sternglanz and Serbin, 1974; Weitz, 1977). In commercials, women are often portrayed as bewildered consumers whose most important concern is clean laundry, and in virtually all commercials, the "voice of authority" is male (Women on Words and Images, 1975b).

Thus, while books, television shows, commercials, and movies serve a variety of intended purposes for their creators (education, entertainment, selling products), their contents reveal important aspects of the culture in which they are created, and such messages affect our ideas of who we are and should be as men and women.

**Historical Research** Historical documents are an additional valuable source of information for secondary analysis, for they shed light on the ways in which societies develop and change. What light does history shed on the current standing of women in society?

Historical research methods, by definition, focus on what has already occurred. We cannot, therefore, scientifically observe or experimentally manipulate history. We can learn a great deal, however, from historical records that reflect the social environments in which people once lived. Perhaps the most important lessons to be learned from historical research are that societies are always changing, and that the social environments we live in today developed over long periods of time. This may be the only world we have ever known, but it is not the only world that has ever been known or that ever will be.

Baxandall, Gordon, and Reverby (1976) wanted to understand how capitalism and the Industrial Revolution affected working-class women in America between the early seventeenth century and 1975. How did they do it? Their biggest problem was that most working-class women had neither the time nor the ability to leave written records of their experiences, and even when they did, they often did not consider their lives to be important enough to write about.

By systematically scouring libraries and archives for documents, the researchers found union records, diaries, short stories, poems, songs, letters, advertisements, social-worker reports, factory rules and regulations, petitions, newspaper and magazine articles, government reports, and statistical studies.

They found that in colonial America families met most of their needs through their own labor. While men and women performed different tasks in general, women still played a full role in economic production—weaving fabric, making products such as soap and candles, and trading in the marketplace. It was not uncommon for women to be blacksmiths, tailors, printers, and shopkeepers; and widows often assumed full managerial control of family businesses.

The Industrial Revolution and the rise of capitalism, however, physically separated the family from economic activity, and people no longer worked in the same place they lived. Life in America was divided into the private sphere of unpaid housework and the public sphere of paid employment. Because most work done at home was unpaid, it gradually lost its cultural value, and the self-esteem of women suffered as a result.

Although many women worked outside the home, they were restricted to low-paying service and factory jobs, and census takers routinely ignored wives' earnings when they recorded family income. Because paid work was socially defined as a "secondary" role for women, they were expected

In historical research, many different sources are used to reveal aspects of life in times far removed from our own. Pictures such as this can tell us much about "women's work" at the height of the Industrial Revolution in the United States. Would you want to work in this setting?

to be temporary workers who could be paid little and laid off easily when it suited their employers' interests. Women played an important part in the labor movement's long struggle for better working conditions, and many rebelled against the domination of their husbands.

The most serious limitation of historical studies is that we cannot use them to demonstrate cause-and-effect relationships between variables. We cannot manipulate history in order to see what would have happened in America without an Industrial Revolution and without capitalism.

A partial solution to this problem is to use **cross-cultural studies,** which compare different societies. By comparing Samoa with the United States, Mead (1928/1953) showed that "adolescent crisis" is not an inevitable part of growing up. Studies of the American Hopi Indians show that families are headed by women, not men, and "women's work"—such as making pottery and baskets—is valued just as highly as men's (Leavitt, 1971). Such studies are important because they provide clues to the mystery of why societies develop in so many different ways.

Although we may believe that men are "naturally" stronger than women, cross-cultural research shows that in some cultures women are far more adept at hard physical labor than men.

The preceding sections show how the complexity of social life requires sociologists to draw upon a wide range of research designs as they gather data. What happens, however, after the data are gathered? How are thousands of bits of information used to answer the questions we ask?

## Interpretation:
## Using Information to Answer Questions

Of all research tasks, the interpretation of data is the most fascinating, for it is here that sociologists exercise the skills of a detective in order to discover the clues and patterns that ultimately solve puzzles such as the income gap between men and women. At this stage, statistics are particularly useful.

### Some Useful Statistics

Variables that have a small number of categories (such as the "Agree" and "Disagree" in Table 2-1) are easily summarized with percentages, allowing us to compare different groups. Variables such as income, however, present a more difficult problem, for there are thousands of different numbers that represent people's earnings.

In 1982 the Census Bureau interviewed 60,000 full-time workers—33,000 men and 27,000 women—and recorded annual incomes for full-time, year-round workers (U.S. Census Bureau, 1983b). How can we use this massive set of facts to describe and compare the incomes of women and men? The most efficient solution would allow us to describe each category with a single number.

We could simplify the information by sorting people into a small set of income categories (Table 2-2). We could then compare women and men by seeing which categories they are most likely to be in. Women are more clustered in the lower income brackets than are men. For women, the *most frequent* income category (the **mode**) is between $10,000 and $14,999, while the mode for men is somewhere above $25,000. Although these descriptions show that men are better off than women, they are crude, for they do not allow us to gauge how *much* better off men are.

**Table 2-2**

Annual Income of Year-Round, Full-Time Workers by Gender (United States, 1982)

| INCOME | WOMEN (%) | MEN (%) |
|---|---|---|
| Less than $3,000 | 2 | 2 |
| $3,000 to $4,999 | 2 | 1 |
| $5,000 to $6,999 | 6 | 2 |
| $7,000 to $9,999 | 17 | 6 |
| $10,000 to $14,999 | 33 (Mode) | 16 |
| $15,000 to $24,999 | 32 | 34 |
| $25,000 and over | 8 | 39 (Mode) |
| TOTAL | 100 | 100 |
| (N) | (27,000) | (33,000) |

Source: U.S. Census Bureau, 1983b.

A second approach to this problem is to add up all the money earned by men in 1982 and divide the total by the number of men, giving us the average earnings *per man.* This statistic is what most people think of as an "average" and is called the **mean.** When we calculate means, we find that men earned an average of $24,800—or two-thirds more than the average of $15,100 earned by full-time women workers in 1982.

As a description of groups, however, the mean has its disadvantages, for a few people who make a great deal of money "pump up" the mean and inflate the group's income. For example, suppose we have five people with the following incomes:

| | |
|---|---|
| Vincent | $9,000 |
| Joe | $10,000 |
| Teresa | $10,500 |
| Barbara | $11,000 |
| John | $1,000,000 |
| TOTAL | $1,040,500 |

If we want to summarize the incomes of the people in this group with a single number, would the mean give an accurate picture? Four of the five people have incomes between $9,000 and $11,000, and yet the mean income for the group is $208,100 (or $1,040,500/5). Certainly the mean is not a good indicator of the income of the people in this group. Clearly, whenever a few members of a group have extreme characteristics, the mean is not an effective way to describe the group. The mean does accurately tell us that men *as a group* earned two-thirds more than women did in 1982, but it may give a distorted picture of how *most* men compared with *most* women.

This brings us to a third important statistic— the **median**—which is simply the middle number in any group of numbers that is ranked from high to low or from low to high. In the group above, Teresa's income, $10,500, is the median. In 1982 the median income for full-time women workers was $13,700, while the median for men was $21,700 (U.S. Census Bureau, 1983b). This indicates, for example, that half of all women made more than $13,700 and half made less. Because the median is unaffected by extremely large or small incomes, it is a better summary description of groups.

All these measures describe groups imperfectly, but they are useful because they allow us to

summarize thousands of observations of individuals and use them to compare different groups. We can use means, for example, to see that while in 1955 full-time working women made 64¢ for every dollar earned by men, in 1982 women had actually fallen behind still further and earned only 61¢ for every dollar earned by men (U.S. Census Bureau, 1983b).

Note that such statements do not tell us anything about individual men and women. While there are certainly some women who earn more money than most men and some men who earn less than most women, the focus of sociological research is not on individuals per se. Rather, it is on the characteristics of social environments in which individuals live.

## Causal Relationships between Variables

If men and women were equally likely to fall in each income bracket, we would say that the variables "gender" and "income" are *independent* of each other. As we saw in the previous section, however, if you are a woman, you tend to have a

**Table 2-3**

Occupation by Gender (United States, 1981)

| OCCUPATION[1] | WOMEN (%) | MEN (%) |
|---|---|---|
| Upper white-collar ($18,000 or more) | 25 | 34 |
| Upper blue-collar ($18,000 or more) | 3 | 17 |
| Lower white-collar (Less than $18,000) | 45 | 8 |
| Lower blue-collar (Less than $18,000) | 14 | 32 |
| Farm and service (Less than $10,000) | 13 | 9 |
| TOTAL | 100 | 100 |

Source: U.S. Department of Labor, 1982.

[1]Ranked by average income for full-time wage and salary workers. Excludes self-employed.

lower income than if you are a man, and in this sense, the variable "income" *depends on* the variable "gender."

There is, in other words, a relationship between gender and income. In this relationship, gender is an **independent variable,** because we consider it to affect income. Because income depends to some degree on a person's gender, it is a **dependent variable.** Note that for one variable to affect another, it must occur before the dependent variable. In other words, it would be silly to suggest that income determines whether a person is male or female.

How do we explain the relationship between gender and income? That is the function of a **hypothesis,** a statement that predicts a relationship between variables. The first step is to think of other variables—such as educational attainment and occupation—that we know affect people's income, and these generate several possible hypotheses.

Our first hypothesis is that women work at poorer-paying jobs. In the first column in Table

2-3, for example, we find that only 28 percent of working women are in white-collar or blue-collar jobs that pay more than $18,000 a year. Fifty-nine percent are in white-collar jobs (such as secretaries) or blue-collar jobs (such as assembly-line workers) that pay less than $18,000 a year, and an additional 13 percent are in farm, service, and private household jobs that pay less than $10,000 a year. By comparison, the second column of Table 2-3 shows that 51 percent of all male workers are in white-collar and upper blue-collar occupations that pay more than $18,000 a year. The data support the first hypothesis.

Although part of the relationship between gender and income is due to the concentration of women in poorly paid jobs, we have to consider a second hypothesis: Women are paid less than men even when they work at the same job. To test this hypothesis, we compare the average incomes of men and women who have similar jobs, trying to see if men still earn more money. By looking at men and women who have the same kind of job, we are, in a sense, holding occupation "constant";

**Table 2-4**

Median Income of Wage and Salary Workers by Occupation and Gender (United States, 1981)

| OCCUPATION | MEDIAN INCOME | | FOR EACH DOLLAR MEN EARN, WOMEN EARN: |
| --- | --- | --- | --- |
| | WOMEN | MEN | |
| ALL OCCUPATIONS | $11,600 | $18,000 | 65¢ |
| Professional and technical | $16,400 | $22,800 | 72¢ |
| Accountants | $16,000 | $22,500 | 73¢ |
| Computer specialists | $18,500 | $25,400 | 73¢ |
| Health workers | $14,200 | $16,800 | 84¢ |
| College teachers | $20,200 | $25,200 | 80¢ |
| Non-college teachers | $16,200 | $20,000 | 81¢ |
| Engineers | $19,300 | $28,400 | 68¢ |
| Life and physical scientists | $18,900 | $26,600 | 71¢ |
| Managers and administrators | $14,700 | $24,200 | 61¢ |
| Sales workers | $ 9,900 | $19,000 | 52¢ |
| Clerical workers | $11,400 | $17,000 | 67¢ |
| Blue-collar workers | $12,400 | $18,700 | 66¢ |
| Service workers | $ 8,800 | $12,400 | 71¢ |
| Farm workers | $ 7,600 | $ 9,400 | 81¢ |

Source: U.S. Department of Labor, 1982.

and when we do this, we are using occupation as a **control variable.**

The result is in Table 2-4, which shows the median incomes of men and women according to their occupations. As we saw before, women in general earn 65¢ for every dollar earned by men. For some occupations, however, the gap is smaller: female health workers, for example, earn 84¢ for each dollar earned by men. Thus, *some* of the difference in earnings is due to different occupations; but notice that in almost *no* occupation do women earn as much as men, and in most jobs, women earn far less (see also Treiman and Hartmann, 1981). (Notice how each new explanation generates more questions: for example, why is the gender gap in income smaller among computer specialists than among sales workers?)

By testing our first two hypotheses we found that women have poorer-paying jobs and are paid less for doing the same work. Why, however, are they concentrated at the low end of the job market and paid less for the same work? These questions

lead to our third hypothesis, which focuses on education: Women hold poorer-paying jobs and are paid less for the same work because they have lower average levels of education.

To test the third hypothesis, we control for the variable "education," *by comparing the jobs of men and women who are alike on that characteristic.* Do men and women with similar education hold similar jobs? Table 2-5 provides an answer (this is a multicolumn table, so go through it slowly, one column at a time). The first two columns show the occupations of men and women who have at least a college degree, and while these women are as likely as men to have higher-level white-collar jobs, they are more likely than men to be in lower white-collar positions (20 percent versus 13 percent).

When we look at the occupations of less-educated workers, stronger gender differences emerge. Among workers with nine to fifteen years of schooling (the second pair of columns), men are more likely to have upper white-collar or blue-col-

**Table 2-5**

Occupation by Education and Gender (United States, 1981)

| | College Grads | | 9 to 15 Years | | 0 to 8 Years | |
|---|---|---|---|---|---|---|
| OCCUPATION | Women (%) | Men (%) | Women (%) | Men (%) | Women (%) | Men (%) |
| Upper white-collar | 73 | 74 | 15 | 19 | 4 | 6 |
| Upper blue-collar | 1 | 5 | 2 | 24 | 2 | 23 |
| Lower white-collar | 20 | 13 | 49 | 12 | 24 | 6 |
| Lower blue-collar | 1 | 4 | 14 | 33 | 37 | 43 |
| Service | 4 | 3 | 19 | 9 | 31 | 12 |
| Farm | * | 1 | 1 | 3 | 2 | 10 |
| TOTAL | 100 | 100 | 100 | 100 | 100 | 100 |

YEARS OF SCHOOLING COMPLETED

Source: U.S. Department of Labor, 1983.

*Less than 0.5%.

lar jobs, and women are heavily concentrated in lower white-collar and service occupations. Among the least-educated workers (the last two columns), only 6 percent of women have upper white-collar or upper blue-collar jobs compared with 29 percent of comparably educated men. (Pause for a few minutes and verify these statements by examining the table carefully.)

Table 2-5 clearly suggests that education benefits men more than women in the job market (see also Spenner, Otto, and Call, 1982); but how does education affect income? Do women and men with the same education have the same income? As Table 2-6 shows, controlling for education does not explain the relationship between gender and income, for at each level of education, the median income for men is much higher than that for women. In fact, women with graduate education have almost the same average income as men who never went beyond high school ($21,500 versus $21,300), and women college graduates make less on the average than men who never finished high school ($17,400 versus $17,500) and make just

$1,000 more on the average than men who never went beyond the eighth grade ($17,400 versus $16,400).

This brief analysis reveals some pieces of the puzzle of the relationship between income and gender. Women earn less than men because they hold poorer-paying jobs regardless of educational qualifications, and even when they have similar jobs, they are paid less for the same work. While a complete explanation involves other variables (such as job experience), these findings strongly suggest that women are discriminated against on the basis of their gender, both in getting jobs and being rewarded for their work.

Why, however, are women discriminated against in the workplace? A partial answer lies in cultural values about men and women. In Table 2-1 we saw that even among those who support the ERA, many view women's employment as less important than men's. Thus, the sociological explanation of gender differences in income is both cultural and structural: regardless of education, women have lower average incomes than men be-

**Table 2-6**

Median Income by Years of Education and Gender
for Year-Round, Full-Time Workers
(United States, 1982)

| YEARS OF SCHOOL COMPLETED | MEDIAN INCOME | | FOR EACH DOLLAR MEN EARN, WOMEN EARN: |
| --- | --- | --- | --- |
| | WOMEN | MEN | |
| **Elementary:** | | | |
| 0 to 7 Years | $ 8,400 | $12,400 | 68¢ |
| 8 Years | $10,100 | $16,400 | 62¢ |
| **High School:** | | | |
| 1 to 3 Years | $10,700 | $17,500 | 61¢ |
| 4 Years | $13,200 | $21,300 | 62¢ |
| **College:** | | | |
| 1 to 3 Years | $15,600 | $23,600 | 66¢ |
| 4 Years | $17,400 | $28,000 | 62¢ |
| 5 Years or More | $21,500 | $32,300 | 66¢ |

Source: U.S. Census Bureau, 1983b.

cause of low positions in paid employment, discrimination both in access to good jobs and rewards for their work, and because of cultural values that value employment more for men than for women.

This analysis describes a series of patterns—occupation, gender, education, and income—and examines the *relationships* among them. In this way, we can see how, for example, social characteristics such as being male or female are related to others, such as occupation, education, and income, that have important effects on people's lives. This kind of analysis lies at the heart of sociological research, for it illuminates the complex relationship between the characteristics of social environments and the experience and behavior of individuals.

**Spurious Relationships between Variables** It should be emphasized that the existence of a statistical relationship between two variables does not necessarily mean that one variable causes changes in the other. For example, suppose we gather information on fires and keep track of two variables: (1) the number of firefighters at each fire and (2) the amount of damage caused by each fire. We find this relationship between these variables: the more firefighters at the scene, the more damage. Is the secret to lowering fire losses, then, to reduce the number of firefighters?

Most of us would hesitate to accept such a conclusion. Why? We have to ask a basic question: Why should this relationship exist? In this case, of course, the answer is that both variables are caused by a *third* variable, the seriousness of the fire. Big fires bring more firefighters to the scene *and* cause more damage. If we ignore this third variable, it *appears* that firefighters cause more fire damage when in fact they do not. In scientific terms, the statistical relationship between the number of firefighters present and the extent of fire damage is **spurious,** *for it has nothing to do with cause and effect.*

Since a greater number of firefighters are called in to fight more-damaging fires than to fight less-damaging fires, should firefighters stay away? The obvious silliness of such a conclusion points to an important aspect of statistical relationships: two variables can be related without having any causal effect on each other.

**Table 2-7**

Blood Pressure by Marital Status
(United States, 1959–1962)

| MARITAL STATUS | BLOOD PRESSURE | | |
| --- | --- | --- | --- |
| | High | Normal | Total |
| Single | 10% | 90% | 100% |
| Married | 15% | 85% | 100% |
| Widowed or divorced | 40% | 60% | 100% |

Source: Derived by the author from unpublished data provided by the National Center for Health Statistics.

Whenever we find a relationship between variables, we have to ask ourselves if it might be spurious. Otherwise, we might waste a great deal of time trying to figure out how firefighters cause damage or urging firefighters to stay away from fires. In this example, logic leads us to conclude that the relationship is spurious, but in many cases, relationships may appear to be causal when they are actually spurious, as in the following example.

In the 1960s the U.S. Department of Health, Education, and Welfare conducted a survey of more than 7,000 adults in which each of them received a detailed physical examination. It was found that 40 percent of those widowed and divorced had high blood pressure compared with only 15 percent of married people and 10 percent of single people (Table 2-7).

It is tempting to accept such findings at face value, because it "makes sense" that widowhood and divorce are high-stress social positions and that, in many ways, marriage is more difficult than single life. Scientists, however, are committed to testing common-sense explanations, and so we must consider the possibility that this finding is spurious. Is there a causal relationship between marital status and blood pressure?

To answer this question, we have to rephrase it: Is there a factor that both causes high blood pressure *and* distinguishes widowed and divorced people from others? An obvious candidate is age,

for as people grow older their blood pressure usually increases and they are more likely to be widowed or divorced.

Thus, we test the possibility that widowed and divorced people have higher blood pressure not because of their marital status, but because they are generally older than single and married people. To do this, we control for the variable "age" by asking, "Does marital status make a difference among people of the same age?" When we do this, we find that widowed and divorced people are no more likely to have high blood pressure than single and married people *of the same age*. Thus, by controlling for age, we find that the original relationship between marital status and blood pressure is spurious.

Spuriousness occurs whenever two variables are related to a variable that is causally related to one or both of them. In the firefighter example, both variables were caused by a third variable (seriousness of the fire). In the blood-pressure example, both marital status and blood pressure are related to age, which *does* have a causal effect on the dependent variable, blood pressure.

The possibility of spuriousness is often overlooked when the relationships appear to be reasonable. Scientists are just as human as everyone else, relying on cultural beliefs to decide what "makes sense" and what does not. What sets scientists apart, however, is their continuing skepticism, their reluctance to accept "reasonable" findings at face value, and their use of previous research findings to decide what makes sense. The only way to find out if what appears to be true is in fact true is to gather and analyze objective evidence.

**Correlation** Percentages, medians, means, and modes enable us to describe groups efficiently in terms of single variables, but we also need to describe relationships between variables in a useful way.

A *perfect statistical* **correlation** is one in which two variables overlap completely. In parts *a* and *b* of Figure 2-1, if we know someone's education, we also know his or her income. In *a*, the correlation is *positive*, because the higher education is, the higher income is. In *b*, the correlation is *negative* because the higher education is, the *lower* income is. In *c*, the variables are *independent* of each other, because the chances of having high or low

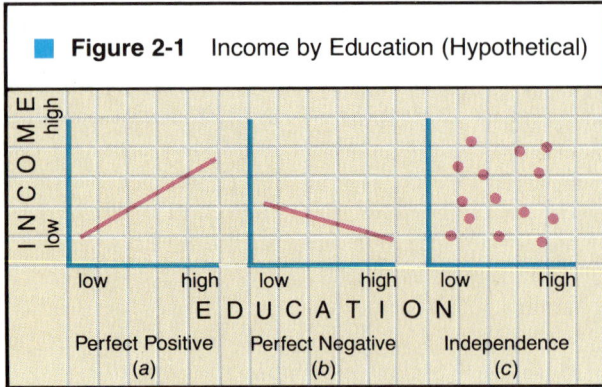

**Figure 2-1** Income by Education (Hypothetical)

income are the same regardless of education: education does not make a difference.

Most relationships between variables are neither perfect nor independent; rather, they are somewhere in between. In Table 2-7, for example, marital status makes some difference in the likelihood of having high blood pressure, but knowing people's marital status does not allow us to know their blood pressure with complete certainty. While widowed and divorced people are more likely than others to have high blood pressure, 60 percent of them have normal blood pressure.

Thus, we need a way to measure the *strength* of relationships between variables. It is not enough to say, "marital status makes a difference." We want to be able to express how much of a difference it makes.

To do this, we use a **measure of association,** which is a number from $-1.0$ to $+1.0$. The association has a value of zero when the variables are independent, a value of $-1.0$ when the relationship is perfect and negative, and a value of $+1.0$ when it is perfect and positive. Note that the "$+$" or "$-$" sign of a relationship describes the pattern of association between two variables, telling us what *kind* of effect the independent variable has on the dependent. The number measures the strength of the relationship, telling us how *much* of an effect it has. Thus, while "$+.60$" and "$-.60$" describe different patterns, they are of equal strength.

## Some Difficulties in Sociological Research

The study of people and the ideas and social relationships that form their social environments poses a number of scientific and ethical problems for sociological researchers.

### Complexity and Objectivity

The forces that influence human behavior and cause changes in social environments are enormously complex. The position of women in American society, for example, cannot be described or explained by a few variables; rather, it flows from many aspects of culture and social structure that are related to each other in complex ways.

In addition, as sociologists study social environments they cannot be immune from the effects of those environments on their own activity as scientists. Survey researchers may ask loaded questions ("You aren't a racist, are you?"); the biases of participant observers may influence what they notice as well as how they interpret their observations; and experimental conditions may themselves produce their own effects.

In comparison with most other scientific disciplines, then, the demands of objectivity are particularly difficult for sociologists to meet. It is for this reason that sociologists so carefully scrutinize their own measures and methods in order to be aware of any possible sources of distorting bias.

As Max Weber argued, however, the complete objectivity of the physical scientist is not only difficult for social researchers to achieve, it is also ultimately undesirable. Unlike rocks, beams of light, and barnyard animals, humans behave according to complex perceptions and interpretations, and all of these are profoundly influenced by orientations to other people and social environments. To understand how the Grand Canyon was formed, we do not have to imagine what it would be like to *be* the Grand Canyon; but we cannot understand people in the same way.

The study of human beings and their social environments thus requires a certain amount of empathy, of seeing the world through other people's eyes in order to understand the choices they make within the limitations of social environments. Unlike physical scientists, sociologists must maintain a delicate balance of objectivity and subjectivity, at best a difficult and demanding task.

It is important to note that no scientist, regardless of discipline, is above the influence of private expectations, values, beliefs, and attitudes. A physicist's choice, for example, to help create nuclear weapons is not a scientific one; nor is a biologist's decision to attempt to prove that nonwhites or women are biologically inferior to whites or

---

## Voices: Sociology as a Humanistic Discipline

Sociology will be especially well advised not to fixate itself in an attitude of humorless scientism that is blind and deaf to the buffoonery of the social spectacle. If sociology does that, it may find that it has acquired a foolproof methodology, only to lose the world of phenomena that it originally set out to explore—a fate as sad as that of the magician who has finally found the formula that will release the mighty *jinn* from the bottle, but cannot recollect what it was that he wanted to ask of the *jinn* in the first place. However, while eschewing scientism, the sociologist will be able to discover human values that are endemic to scientific procedures in both the social and the natural sciences. Such values are humility before the immense richness of the world one is investigating, an effacement of self in the search for understanding, honesty and precision in method, respect for findings honestly arrived at, patience and a willingness to be proven wrong and to revise one's theories, and, last but not least, the community of other individuals sharing these values.

The scientific procedures used by the sociologist imply some specific values that are peculiar to this discipline. One such value is the careful attention to matters that other scholars might consider pedestrian and unworthy of the dignity of being objects of scientific investigation—something one might almost call a democratic focus of interest in the sociological approach. Everything that human beings are or do, no matter how commonplace, can become significant for sociological research. Another

such peculiar value is inherent in the sociologist's necessity to listen to others without volunteering his own views. The art of listening, quietly and with full attention, is something that any sociologist must acquire if he is to engage in empirical studies. While one should not exaggerate the importance of what is often nothing more than a research technique, there is a human significance at least potentially present in such conduct, especially in our nervous and garrulous age in which almost nobody finds the time to listen with concentration. Finally, there is a peculiar human value in the sociologist's responsibility for evaluating his findings, as far as he is psychologically able, without regard to his own prejudices, likes or dislikes, hopes or fears. This responsibility, of course, the sociologist shares with other scientists. But it is especially difficult to exercise in a discipline that touches so closely on the human passions. It is evident that this goal is not always achieved, but in the very effort lies a moral significance not to be taken lightly. This becomes particularly appealing when one compares the sociologist's concern for listening to the world, without immediately shouting back his own formulations of what is good and what is bad, with the procedures of normative disciplines, such as theology or jurisprudence, where one meets with the constant compulsion to squeeze reality into the narrow frame of one's value judgments. Sociology appears by comparison as standing in an apostolic succession from the Cartesian quest for "clear and distinct perception."

Source: Berger, *Invitation to Sociology: A Humanistic Perspective*, 1963.

---

men. The mere selection of research problems is, itself, profoundly influenced by a scientist's beliefs, values, and attitudes.

In addition, even in the most carefully controlled research conditions a scientist's personal expectations may influence the results (Rosenthal, 1967). In one experiment, for example, lab assistants were given the task of training mice to run

through a maze. Although the mice were all the same, the assistants were told that half of them were particularly bright and the other half were from a "slow" learning strain. "Fast" mice learned more quickly than "slow" mice, not because the two groups of mice differed in their abilities, but because the assistants who handled them treated them differently, reflecting their expectations by giving some mice more attention and encouragement than others (Rosenthal, 1982).

We should also remember that individual scientists are not the only ones whose values influence scientific research. Research is expensive, and corporations, government agencies, and foundations have a great deal of power to decide which research projects to support (Kerbo, 1983).

*Ethics, Research, and People's Lives*

Another difficulty in sociological research involves ethical questions (Reynolds, 1979, 1982). While the experimental manipulation of objects and laboratory mice is culturally acceptable, scientists must take far greater care when people are the subject of research. For example, values and norms prohibit researchers from experimentally exploring the effects of child abuse on emotional development by systematically abusing a sample of children and comparing them with a control group of unabused children. In many cases, however, the ethical issues are less clear-cut.

Humphreys (1970), for example, wanted to learn more about men who have homosexual encounters with strangers in public rest rooms. To gather information, he served as a "lookout," and as an observer he was able to gather detailed data about these unusual social interactions. To gather further information, he kept a record of subjects' automobile license plates, which he used to locate the subjects a year later. He then presented himself as a survey researcher gathering general information having nothing to do with homosexual acts, and he found, among other things, that most of these men were married.

In spite of the fact that his study dispelled many myths about homosexual men, Humphreys was criticized on ethical grounds because he lied about his identity and, although he safeguarded subjects' identities, he risked exposing them and their illegal acts. He later agreed that he had improperly invaded the privacy of his subjects and unnecessarily endangered them (Humphreys, 1975). For all scientists, but for social scientists in particular, his methods raise a troubling question: Do the research ends justify the research means?

Ethical questions involve not only research methods, but the possible *uses* of research findings. An important value in scientific work is that knowledge is an important end in itself. Thus, if it were possible to demonstrate, for example, that women's biological makeup generally results in slightly lower mathematical abilities, many scientists would feel obliged by professional values to do so. Many other scientists, however, do not view the ethical implications of their work so narrowly. How would such findings be used outside the scientific community? Would they undermine or support cultural beliefs that women are unsuited for scientific work? How would they affect the lives of those women who have superior mathematical abilities?

Scientists are bound by professional norms that require careful interpretation of findings ("the differences are small and apply only to men and women in general"); but parents, teachers, potential employers, and government policymakers are not. Thus, there is an ever-present danger that scientific findings will be used sloppily or indiscriminately to reinforce damaging cultural stereotypes and the social inequalities they support. Because scientists cannot control the way people will use their findings, they continually confront a moral dilemma: Should they seek knowledge that could be used for destructive purposes?

In the 1960s the U.S. Army provided funds for the study of the social conditions likely to cause or prevent revolutions in Latin American countries. From a scientific point of view, Project Camelot (as it was known) was simply one more set of questions to be answered, but from the Latin American perspective, it involved information that would enable the American government to interfere in the domestic affairs of their countries (Horowitz, 1965).

When news of Project Camelot reached Chile, a public furor erupted, the program was canceled, and the social scientists involved confronted ethical issues they had previously ignored. To a scientist, one bit of knowledge is no better or worse than any other, subject only to rigid standards for determining truth. Outside the scientific community, however, knowledge often represents power that can be used destructively as well as constructively.

In spite of the difficulties inherent in sociological research, the field is firmly committed to scientific approaches to sociological questions. By limiting themselves to objective aspects of reality that can be observed and measured, sociologists necessarily limit the kinds of questions they can investigate. For this reason, few sociologists would suggest that scientific research alone is sufficient to solve the many puzzles of social life; but by systematically observing social environments and their effects on experience and behavior, sociologists obtain the information needed to test a wide range of ideas that contribute to our overall understanding of the human condition.

Edward Teller, one of the driving forces behind the development of the hydrogen bomb, once said, "The responsibility of the scientist is to make science . . . knowing that it could be used for good as for evil purposes." The great potential for disaster prompts many scientists to take a broader view of their responsibility.

## Summary

1. The scientific method involves careful and exacting procedures for gathering and interpreting objective evidence that helps sociologists accomplish the three major tasks of research: description, explanation, and prediction.

2. Research begins with the problem of deciding what it is that we want to know, which variables are involved, and how best to measure them in a valid and reliable way. Measurement is particularly difficult in sociology because much of what is measured is invisible, changes over time, and depends on how people present themselves.

3. The complexity of social life requires sociologists to use many different methods for gathering and interpreting information, and each method has its own strengths and weaknesses. Research design begins with the definition of the population to be studied and the decision to study all its members (a census), a representative sample, or carefully selected cases.

4. Interview and questionnaire surveys allow researchers to gather large amounts of information, but are limited by time and their dependence on the accuracy of people's reports about themselves. In-depth interviews yield greater detail, but must compromise by focusing on a smaller number of people who are less likely to represent a population scientifically.

5. Laboratory and field experiments allow researchers to discover cause-and-effect relationships by carefully controlling the conditions in which variables are measured. Participant observation allows researchers to observe directly the behavior of their subjects, but the involvement of researchers makes it more difficult to maintain an objective perspective.

6. Content analysis and historical research are major types of secondary analysis in which previously gathered information is applied to new research problems. Documents and other records as well as cross-cultural comparisons of different societies help researchers discover how social environments change.

7. Regardless of the research design, sociologists often use statistics both to summarize and condense huge amounts of detailed information and to discover and explain relationships between variables.

8. Sociologists confront a variety of difficulties in their research. They must pay special attention not only to the biases that threaten any scientist's objectivity, but also to the risks their research may pose for the human beings they study. Ethical issues are enormously important in sociology, both in relation to the process of gathering information and to the ways in which that information is eventually used.

## Key Terms

## Recommended Readings

BABBIE, E. R. (1982). *The practice of social research* (3rd ed.). Belmont, CA: Wadsworth. A comprehensive and readable introduction to the research methods sociologists use.

COLE, S. (1976). *The sociological method* (2nd ed.). Chicago: Rand McNally (paperback). A clearly written, lively introduction to the logic of sociological research and the many uses of statistical techniques. Full of interesting examples.

GLAZER, M. (1972). *The research adventure*. New York: Random House. A series of accounts of sociological research projects, the practical problems they encountered, and how the researchers solved them.

JOHNSON, A. G. (1977). *Social statistics without tears*. New York: McGraw-Hill. A brief introduction to statistics written specifically for sociology students who have minimal preparation in mathematics.

KATZER, J., COOK, K., and CROUCH, W. (1978). *Evaluating information: A guide for users of social science research*. Reading, MA: Addison-Wesley (paperback). A book for consumers of research reports. It is lively and clearly written and focuses on basic problems that confront anyone trying to make sense of scientific research and trying to decide which findings to accept and which to reject.

REYNOLDS, P. D. (1982). *Ethics and social science research*. Englewood Cliffs, NJ: Prentice-Hall. A recent examination of the ethical problems encountered by social researchers and some of the ways of dealing with them.

ROSSI, A. C. (1982). *Feminists in politics: A panel analysis of the first national women's conference*. New York: Academic Press. A fascinating account of the process of designing and carrying out a large survey.

WHYTE, W. F. (1981). *Street corner society* (3rd ed.). Chicago: University of Chicago Press. In what has become a sociological classic, pay particular attention to the Appendix, "On the Evolution of Street Corner Society." It is a rare and profound look into the problems and promises of participant observation research.

# PART II

# The Sociological Framework

Because the concepts of culture, social structure, and population and ecology are at the heart of the sociological perspective, if we want to understand why people behave as they do, we must look at the social and physical contexts in which they experience and interpret themselves and others. These contexts, in turn, include the cultural ideas that people share, the relationships that bind them together, and physical factors such as population and the arrangement of people in relation to one another.

In the following three chapters we take a detailed look at these three major areas that define sociology as a perspective. In Chapter 3 we outline different kinds of cultural products and see some of the ways in which they affect our lives. Chapter 4 describes the ways in which our participation in social relationships affects not only what we do but who we think we are; and Chapter 5 shows how the forces of population and ecology affect the cultural and structural characteristics of social environments.

# CHAPTER 3
# Culture

As we saw in Chapter 1, **culture** consists of two kinds of products—the objects that people create and incorporate into their environments and the nonmaterial ideas that members of a society share as a framework for interpreting the world. In this chapter we take a detailed look at language and the ideas that make up most of nonmaterial culture. We close with a brief look at material culture and its connection with cultural ideas.

Because the essence of culture consists of ideas, its existence depends on the human ability to use symbols in order to attach meaning to experience and perceptions and thereby think about the world (Geertz, 1973). Therefore, it is with symbols—the heart of all culture—that we begin this chapter.

## Symbols, Language, and Meaning

Take a moment to look at Figure 3-1. What is it? On a piece of paper make a list of all the answers you can think of. Do not read any further until you have at least four items on your list.

What is Figure 3-1 a picture of? "A bunch of dots?" "Two lines of dots, one shorter than the other, joined at a right angle two-thirds of the way up the longer line?" "*X*- and *y*-axes used to plot data?" "Two roads intersecting?" "A 'cross'?" While the first two answers are a mere physical description of Figure 3-1, the remaining three answers go beyond what the lines look like to say what they *are*. That is, they transform the lines into *symbols* by attaching *meaning* to them; and it is meaning that is at the heart of nonmaterial culture.

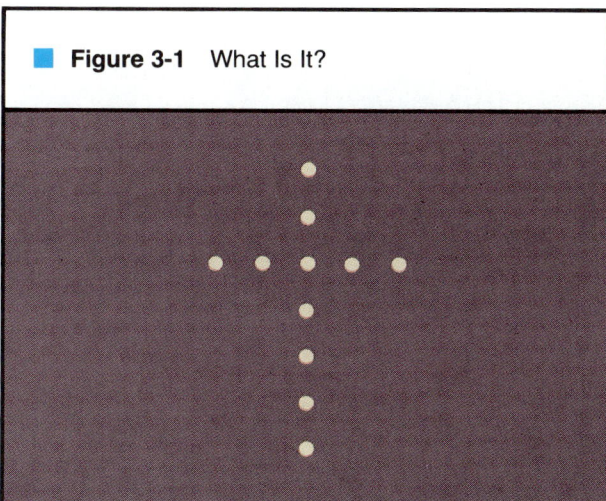

■ **Figure 3-1** What Is It?

A **symbol** is anything that represents more than itself. In many cultures a "cross"—whether made of two sticks or lines on a piece of paper—is more than what our eyes see: people pay great attention to it, carry it around their necks, and hang it in their homes. Members of the Ku Klux Klan gather around large ones and watch them burn in the night. In many places, however, and during many periods of history, millions of people would see nothing more than a pair of sticks held together or two lines joined at right angles.

The four kinds of symbols include, first, symbolic *objects*—flags represent nations and money represents labor and goods; second, symbolic *characteristics* of objects—in our culture purple "stands for" royalty, black for mourning, yellow for cowardice, white for purity. *Gestures* are the third type of symbol. **Gestures** are actions that have symbolic meaning: smiles and winks, the raised right hand in oath taking, an eyebrow raised skeptically, a shrug of the shoulders, a frustrated snap of the fingers—all of these actions have meaning in a particular cultural context (Malandro and Barker, 1983; Patterson, 1983). The fourth type of symbol is the vast range of *spoken and written words* that make up *language*, which is so important that it deserves a separate discussion. Language is the most important set of symbols in any culture, for it embodies the symbolic building blocks used to construct cultural ideas.

In a culture, then, objects, the characteristics of objects, actions, and words are more than our senses perceive them to be; they are what a culture signifies them to be. They *are* what they *mean*. Suppose, for example, you walk down a city street on a summer day and come upon an auction taking place in the front yard of an old house. You spy an empty seat in the shade and, being hot and tired, you sit down to watch. On the auction block is a large ornate desk, and the bidding is very high. "Two thousand dollars," the auctioneer barks. "Do I hear twenty-one hundred? Going once. Going twice . . ." Suddenly, your nose itches and you scratch it with your index finger. Just as suddenly, the auctioneer points a finger at you and shouts, "Twenty-one hundred! Going once! Going twice! Sold!" You have just bought yourself a $2,100 desk.

Strictly speaking, you only scratched your nose, and your reason for doing so was to relieve an itch. You had no intention of bidding for a desk. How do you get out of it? "I didn't *mean* anything

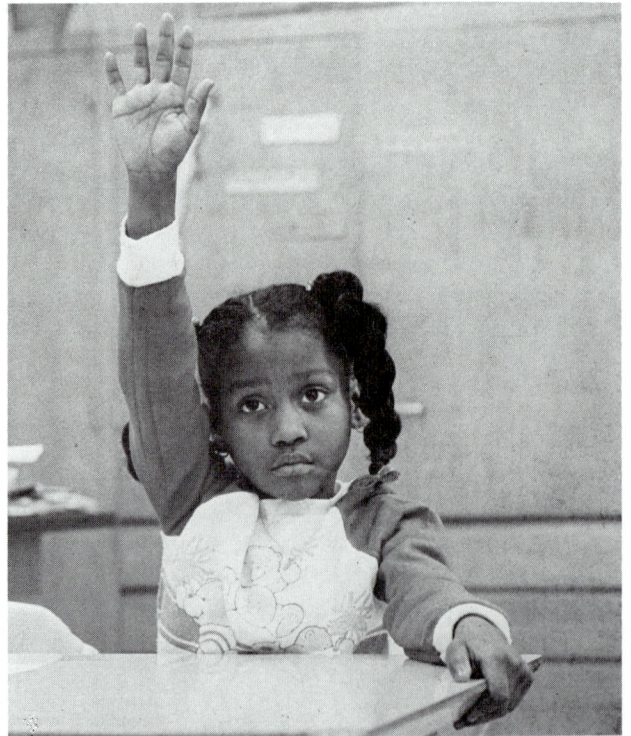

Gestures are physical actions that have meaning, and as in spoken language, the meaning of a gesture often depends on the social context. In this series of pictures, for example, notice how the gesture of a raised hand has a very different meaning in each case.

by it," you say. "I just scratched my nose." Had you been sitting across from the same auctioneer on a subway and scratched your nose in just the same way, the outcome would have been entirely different.

You got into trouble because in the social situation of an auction it is agreed that a nose scratch is more than a physical act; it is a gesture, a symbolic act that represents more than itself: "A nose scratch at an auction is a positive response to the auctioneer's call for bids." Thus, there is no necessary connection between the cultural meaning of a nose scratch (or any other action) and an individual's reason for performing it (Sahlins, 1976).

Symbol systems tell their users how to mark and categorize perceptions depending on the circumstances; hence, the auctioneer categorizes a nose scratch as a bid at certain points in the auction (but not at others) and never does so outside of auctions (and auctioneers may scratch their noses whenever they like). Depending on the situation, the simple act of touching your nose can have many meanings: when con artists are about to "sting" a victim, a finger on the side of the nose means "all is ready"; or a thumb drawn across the nose can signify contempt. Thus, a single action can be transformed into many different meaningful gestures, depending on the cultural context.

This example illustrates a vital aspect of symbols: *we respond to them just as we respond to what they represent.* While the word "fire" represents something that can hurt us, the word itself cannot; yet the word "fire" can make us run just as readily as the sight or heat of fire itself. Without the word, we can experience fire only with our senses, by seeing its color, hearing its crackle, feeling its heat. With the word, on the other hand, fire exists as an *idea* even when there is no fire: it exists in our minds, and when we share the symbol with other people, it exists among us. We can think about it, teach each other about it and its uses. We can attach the idea of "fire" to things that have no concrete relation to it, as "the fiery anger in her eyes." Symbols, themselves, then, are *real* to us; and as W. I. Thomas (1931) pointed out, what we define as real has real consequences.

Symbols are created, which means we have the ability to create symbols to which we orient ourselves and respond just as we do to physical objects and forces. There is nothing inherent in any symbol that gives it power over us; its power lies in what it signifies to those who share its meaning. For example, if children learn the meaning of "danger" by touching a hot stove and hearing the word from an adult, the word "danger" can be used to keep them away from all kinds of things that may not be inherently dangerous at all. Similarly, the symbol "immoral" can be attached to virtually any behavior. This process explains why the meaning of a behavior is often more important to us than its objective characteristics or consequences.

Thus, culture provides a framework of ideas that we use to interpret what we perceive, and people's appearance and behavior are fully understandable only if we pay attention to their cultural context. If we feed our guests roast chicken and after the meal tell them they just consumed the flesh of a dog, their reaction depends only in part on what they actually ate or think they ate. To predict their response, we must know the system of meaning they use to interpret what they did—some Southeast Asians might thank us for the delicacy, while most Europeans would look disgusted (and perhaps make a dash for the bathroom).

## Language

As we noted earlier, of the four types of symbols, the most important is language, for it allows us to organize symbols into ideas about ourselves and our culture, the world we live in. There would be no culture without **language,** the collection of symbols (words) and rules for their use through which we mark and interpret perceptions and communicate with one another. Without culture, humans would be hard-pressed to survive. We are not born knowing what kinds of berries to eat and which are poisonous, or how to catch and eat a wild animal, but we do have the ability to use symbols. Because "edible" and "inedible," for example, are important distinctions for us, we have symbols for them; we can categorize objects and, most important, we can teach those categories to one another.

Every language has two elements: a collection of words and what they symbolize and a set of rules—syntax and grammar—that governs the arrangement of words to express thoughts. Some words—such as "telephone"—have fixed meanings, while many depend on their relation to other words. The phrase "he threw up," for example, means one thing followed by "his lunch," but quite

Drawing by Stevenson; © 1976, The New Yorker Magazine, Inc.

another in the poem, "A Visit From St. Nicholas," in which the father "ran to the window and threw up the sash."

The symbols and their meanings contained in a language represent the distinctions that its users tend to make as they perceive and mark their world. To the Eskimo, a detailed understanding of different kinds of snow is vital for survival. Thus, Eskimo languages typically include as many as 20 different words for "snow"—snow that is good for making igloo blocks, hard and crusty snow, dry snow drifted by the wind, and so on—while English has only one (Hoebel, 1966). The Dugum Dani tribe of New Guinea has more than 60 words that describe their staple crop, the sweet potato (Heider, 1970); and Argentine cowboys ("gauchos") have over 200 separate words that describe the color of horses (Curtis, 1968). English, on the other hand, has an enormous number of words used in making precise scientific measurements—minutes, seconds, milliseconds, meters, centimeters, millimeters, and so on.

The second element of language—syntax and grammar—tells us how to arrange words in order to express ourselves, for different arrangements of the same words convey very different meanings, as in "The whale swallowed Jonah" or "Jonah swallowed the whale," or convey nothing at all, as in "Whale Jonah the swallowed."

The Marx Brothers were famous for manipulating language as a source of humor. In the film *The Coconuts* (1929), Groucho owns a hotel, and his bellboys want to be paid. "Oh," Groucho says, "you want your *money?*" "Yes," they reply. "So, you want *my* money," Groucho says, as he changes the meaning by changing the pronoun. "Is that fair? Do I want *your* money? No, my friends, no. Money will never make you happy. And happy will never make you money."

Meaning also depends on the cultural context. The subtlety of such variations is painfully obvious to those who learn a language as adults and thereby often know only literal meanings. A foreign dinner guest who hears "Oh, you *must* try some of this stew," for example, may interpret the statement as an order, not as friendly encouragement. The social relationship between the speaker and the hearer can also be important in determining meanings: "I love you" spoken by a child to a parent has a different meaning than when spoken between two unrelated adults (or, for that matter, when spoken by a parent to a child).

The complexity of language reflects the complexity of human culture as a system for representing and interpreting the world. As Farb (1975) pointed out, even the simplest statements are impressively complex.

> Children who unravel a simple statement like "The chair broke" must do more than decode a grammatical utterance. They must first master the subtle category of things that *break*, like *chairs* and also *machines* and *windowpanes*. Then they must distinguish the category of things that *break* from things that *tear*, like *paper* and *bedsheets*, or things that *smash*, like *vases* and *cars*. They must next interpret the influence on the chair of the verb *broke* out of all the possibilities that verb implies, such as that the breaking of a chair is conceptually different from breaking the bank at Monte Carlo or from waves breaking on a beach. To achieve all this, children unconsciously unravel the sentence into parts that can be analyzed, and then put the elements together again in a meaningful fashion. (pp. 262–263)

Thus, meaning depends on the symbols used, their arrangement in relation to each other, and the social situation in which they are used.

The language of words is not the only type of language found in human cultures. Mathematics is a language used to represent the quantitative aspects of reality: it is a set of symbols (such as "2," "3," "+," "×," "=") with specific rules that define

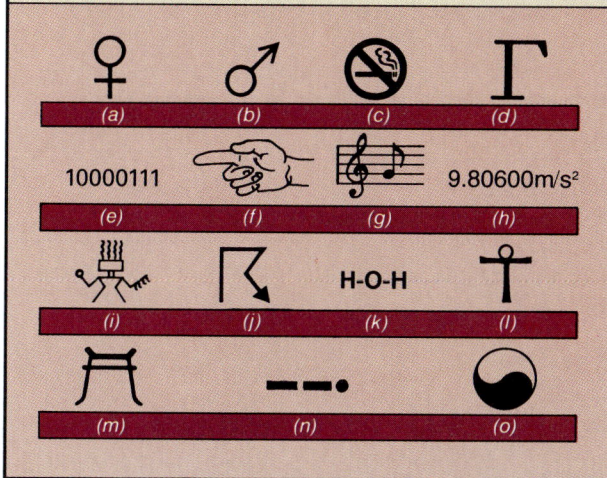

**Figure 3-2** Recognizing Different Types of Languages and Symbols

There are many different symbols and languages found in human cultures. Examples of some of them are shown here. Which ones do you recognize? (Turn the page to learn what each one is.)

(a)    (b)    (c)    (d)

10000111    (f)    (g)    9.80600m/s$^2$

(e)    (f)    (g)    (h)

(i)    (j)    H-O-H    (l)

(m)    (n)    (o)

## The Uses of Language

As a major part of culture, language is more than a system of communication, for it plays important additional parts in the conduct of social life. Sharing a common language fulfills four basic social functions (Farb, 1975). First, our language allows us to assume that those who share it with us (our **speech community**) know what we mean when we talk or write. It is precisely our expectation that strangers will understand us when we speak that makes a language social; a "personal" language is thus not a language at all, for its meanings are not shared. Because there is practically no one who speaks Latin in an existing social environment, it is described as a "dead" language.

Second, the common language of a speech community allows its members to distinguish themselves from outsiders, helping to maintain group boundaries and solidarity. In Shaw's play *Pygmalion* (and later on Broadway as the musical *My Fair Lady*), Eliza Doolittle's cockney accent immediately identifies her social class to Professor Higgins. When American blacks leave urban ghettos to attend college, they often find on their return that subtle changes in their use of language alienate them from friends who now see them as outsiders to their speech community.

Children in school create special languages (such as pig Latin) or use sometimes little-known languages such as American Sign Language as a part of forming exclusive play groups. Prison inmates have their own vocabularies to distinguish them from guards and outsiders (Sykes, 1958). Virtually all occupations use special vocabularies to distinguish themselves from others. Each generation of college students has its own set of slang terms for students who study a lot or who party a lot, for hard courses and easy ones—terms that have different meanings (or none at all) for those outside the college speech community. Ethnic and racial groups have derogatory terms that label the members of other groups; there are more than a thousand such terms in English alone (Allen, 1983).

their relationships to each other ("2 + 3 = 5" or "2 × 3 = 6"). Musical notation is also a language, symbols on paper representing sounds.

Language develops from the interactions of group life, and those who share a culture use its language to represent reality (Berger and Luckman, 1967). The fact that the words "wizard," "bachelor," and "Indian brave" have more positive connotations than "witch," "spinster," and "Indian squaw" reflects long-standing patterns of discrimination against women in life as it is lived. To grow up with these categories of meaning, however, affects the way people think about women and men, and thus, as patterns of living foster certain views of reality, those views in turn help to sustain and reproduce those same patterns of social life.

The limitations of language are clearest when we look at their ambiguities and internal contradictions. Many slang expressions, for example, do not mean what they literally say: "it blew my mind," "a heavy idea," "I'll catch you later," "he spilled his guts," "she picked his brain," and "he shot his mouth off" all illustrate the flexibility with which language can be used to describe reality.

If immigrants do not learn their new society's language, they must restrict themselves to small pockets that contain their speech community. When the children of immigrants learn the new language while their parents cling to the old, the

## Figure 3-2 (Answers)  Identifying the Examples of Different Types of Languages and Symbols

a. Female, Venus, Friday
b. Male, Mars, Tuesday
c. International symbol for No Smoking
d. Letter "g" in Russian alphabet
e. Letter "g" in EBCDIC (Extended Binary Coded Decimal Exchange Code)
f. Letter "g" in American Manual Alphabet sign language
g. Musical notation for eighth note G on G clef (treble clef)
h. In physics, the value of acceleration due to gravity (at 45° latitude and sea level) denoted by the symbol g
i. Symbol for Animiki, the North American Indian god of storm and thunder
j. Meteorological symbol for thunderstorm
k. In organic chemistry, the structural formula for water
l. Ankh, ancient Egyptian symbol of enduring life
m. Torii, emblem of Shinto
n. Letter "g" in Morse Code
o. Yin-yang symbol, used by Taoists to indicate the universal law of existence: the harmonious balance of opposites

## Table 3-1

Reviving Traditional U.S. Navy Terminology

In November 1984, as part of his campaign to increase the pride and professionalism of Navy personnel, Navy Sec. John F. Lehman, Jr., ordered adherence to traditional language (examples appear below, right). He contended that use of this historic vernacular helps Navy men and women appreciate that they are part of a unique institution with its own heritage and military style.

| OLD NAME | NEW NAME |
|---|---|
| Enlisted Dining Facility | Mess Decks or Galleys |
| Dining Room (for officers) | Mess or Ward Room |
| Stairs | Ladder |
| Hall or corridor | Passageway |
| Floor | Deck |
| Wall | Bulwark |
| Ceiling | Overhead |
| Upstairs | Topside |
| Downstairs | Below |
| Replacement when your watch duty is done | Relief |
| The state of suffering late relief | Gapped |
| Double shift | Double (or dual) hatted |
| Shift change | Turnover |
| Advance pay | Deadhorse |
| Putting things away downstairs | Strike it below |
| Ice cream, soda or soda fountain items | Geedunk (slang) |
| Argumentative person | Sea lawyer |
| Older man who teaches a recruit | Sea daddy |
| To be forgotten or go over the side | Go by the board |
| Trash can | GI can |
| Portable radio for distress signals | Gibson girl |

Source: Navy Public Affairs Office and the Naval Institute Press's Naval Terms Dictionary.

result is often distance between family members who participate in different speech communities and, in many respects, different cultures.

When Africans were brought to America as slaves, they were forbidden to speak their native languages and were given new names, all of which undermined their sense of group solidarity. Wars have been fought over which language would dominate in a culture. The struggle between French and English Canadians in Quebec is reflected in the French Canadians' insistence that French have the same importance as English, that bank tellers, for example, be able to speak French (Giniger, 1981).

The third social function of language is that it often serves as a substitute for physical contact: we "keep in touch" by telephone, letter, and small

## Voices: A Family's Language

In a way it didn't matter very much that my parents could not speak English with ease. . . . My mother and father made themselves understood at the county hospital clinic, and at government offices. And yet, in another way, it mattered very much—it was unsettling to hear my parents struggle with English. Hearing them, I'd grow nervous, my clutching trust in their protection and power weakened. . . .

But then there was Spanish, *Espanol:* my family's language. *Espanol:* the language that seemed to me a private language. I'd hear strangers on the radio and in the Mexican church across town speaking Spanish, but I couldn't really believe that Spanish was a public language, like English. Spanish speakers, rather, seemed related to me, for I sensed that we shared—through our language—the experience of feeling apart from *los gringos.* . . .

A family member would say something to me and I would feel myself specially recognized. My parents would say something to me and I would feel embraced by the sounds of their words. Those sounds said: *I am speaking with ease in Spanish. I am addressing you in words I never use with los gringos, I recognize you as someone special, close, like no one outside. You belong with us. In the family.* . . .

Outside the house was public society; inside the house was private. . . . Nervously, I'd arrive at the grocery store to hear the sounds of the *gringo*—foreign to me—reminding me that in this world so big I was a foreigner. But then I'd return. Walking back toward our house, climbing the steps from the sidewalk, when the front door was open in summer, I'd hear voices beyond the screen door talking in Spanish. For a second or two, I'd stay, linger there, listening. . . . All the while her sounds would assure me, *You are home now; come closer; inside. With us.*

Source: Rodriguez, *Hunger of Memory: The Education of Richard Rodriguez, An Autobiography,* 1981.

Disagreements over which language will dominate a culture have been the basis for social conflict that sometimes includes violence. For example, Belgian state police had to use water cannons to disperse members of the Flemish "Language Action Committee" demonstrating in 1975 against alleged disrespect for bilingual administration of a suburb of Brussels.

talk that often appears to be meaningless. When we meet someone and ask, "How are you?", for example, we rarely expect more than a short, uninformative (if not false) reply such as "fine" or "OK," and we may, in fact, become irked if the question is taken seriously.

Many people look upon such exchanges as therefore phony or inessential, but they actually allow us to briefly "touch" one another. It is as if we say, "I see you; do you see me?" and thereby make contact, reaffirming our existence in the eyes of other people (the importance of which is painfully evident when other people ignore us). We also use language as a symbolic substitute for physical violence and yell at each other just as some birds angrily spread their tail feathers or elk toss their antlers.

Fourth, some utterances, referred to as **performative language,** constitute meaningful actions simply by being spoken (Robinson, 1972). To say "I promise" *is* to make a promise, just as "I do" seals a marriage (but only when said by both parties). When a friend looks you in the eyes and says "I love you" for the first time, it is often more than an expression of feeling. It is an invitation to enter into a particular relationship with important expectations; that it is an offer is painfully clear if you fail to reciprocate with "I love you, too." If you do reciprocate, you, too, may have done more than express feelings. The general terms of your new relationship are established simply by uttering such phrases, and they can be undone only with other performative utterances such as, "I don't love you any more."

Perhaps the most marvelous aspect of language, aside from its sheer complexity and seemingly endless variations, is that we are able to participate in it with little or no conscious effort. It is so familiar to us, so close to our everyday lives, that we are likely to think of it as an inherent part of each individual human being.

Language, however, does not arise from the isolated psychological experience of individuals, even though each of us possesses the biological and psychological characteristics that make language possible. The creation of a single word is complete only when two or more people share its meaning. While a single mind can create a sound, until it is shared it is only a noise, not a word. The development of separate languages—English, French, Swahili, Chinese, Hebrew, Arabic, or the thousands of others—does not rest on differences in physiology or psychology, but on the endless variations produced by social interactions extending across many generations.

As a collection of symbols and rules, language is the basis of all beliefs, values, norms, and attitudes. The following sections describe in detail each of these components of culture.

## Cultural Ideas

### Beliefs: The Real and the Unreal

**Beliefs** are symbolic statements about what is real, such as "The earth is round," "There is a God," "There are 100 centimeters in a meter," and "The way to get ahead in the world is to obey the rules and work hard." All of these are beliefs because they try to describe some aspect of reality.

Not all statements about what is real are *cultural* beliefs, however. An individual cannot create or change cultural beliefs by waking up one morning and saying, "The earth is a cube." A belief is cultural only if the ultimate authority for its validity lies outside of individuals—in our shared as-

---

**PUZZLES:**

## WHAT IS A PERSON?

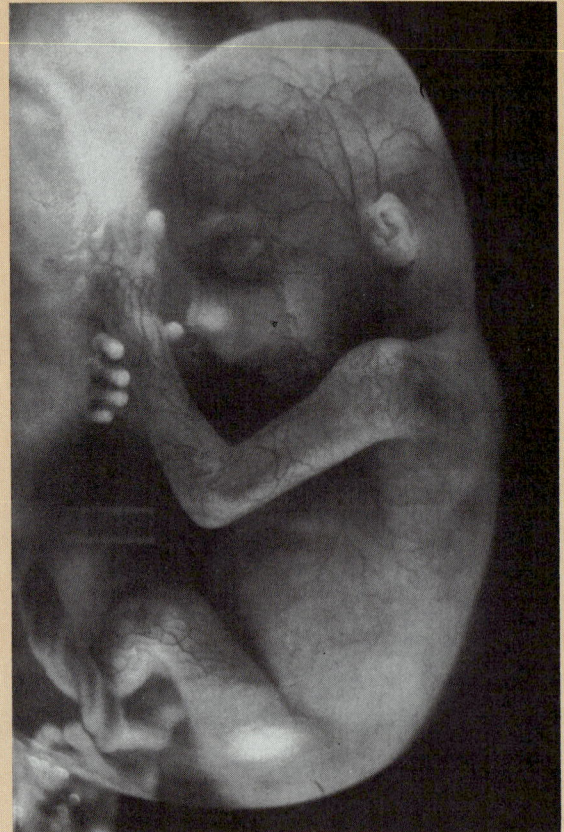

Is this a person? Why or why not? Are you aware of people who would answer these questions differently? What is the basis of the difference? How does this question differ from "Is the earth round?"

On both sides of the abortion controversy, sincere people argue about not when life literally begins, but at what point a fetus becomes a person in a social sense, subject to the protections of its community. As you can see in the section on beliefs, such arguments persist because they have less to do with objective scientific fact than with the beliefs that make up a basic part of culture.

sumption that others share in the particular belief. When the astronomer Copernicus observed the heavens and concluded that the earth was not the center of the universe, his sole authority rested in his own observations, and his belief—at least initially—was strictly a personal one. Copernicus and, later, Galileo were persecuted not because their beliefs were objectively incorrect, but because they contradicted those of the surrounding culture and struck at the heart of an entire system of religious beliefs about the relationship between God and humanity.

Beliefs thus furnish us with the "obvious" facts of our existence: it is "obvious" to anyone reading this book that the earth is round. But it was equally obvious to some living in fifteenth-century Europe that the earth was flat and anyone sailing far enough from land would surely fall off the edge. No thing, then, in itself, is either obvious or obscure. What we call "obvious" is that which we do not question, and whether or not we question it is often more a matter of culture than objective reality. Just as beliefs provide us with categories for sorting perceptions and experiences, so they limit our awareness to those things that have a place in our cultural framework.

## PUZZLES:

## BELIEFS VERSUS REALITY

Who do you think is most likely to say that they can imagine a situation in which they would approve of a man punching an adult male stranger: someone with less than a high school diploma, a high school graduate, or someone who went beyond high school?

In 1980, 78 percent of those with more than a high school diploma said yes to this question, compared with only 52 percent of those in the bottom educational category. If this surprises you, you are not alone, for many Americans share the cultural belief that the more educated you are the less likely you are to approve of violence.

**Cultural Relativism, Subcultures, and Ethnocentrism** Some aspects of culture—such as dancing, games, and language—are found in every known society and are thus referred to as **cultural universals** (see Table 3-2). In general, however, cultural ideas vary enormously among the societies of the world: What is regarded as truth in one culture may be unrecognized or regarded as nonsense in others. Thus, ideas that exist in one culture may

**Table 3-2**

Some Aspects of Culture Found in All Known Societies

| | |
|---|---|
| sports | hygiene |
| bodily adornment | incest taboos |
| calendar | inheritance rules |
| cleanliness training | joking |
| cooking | language |
| cosmology | law |
| courtship | magic |
| dance | superstition |
| decorative art | medicine |
| divination | mourning |
| interpretation of dreams | numerals |
| education | personal names |
| beliefs about death | population policy |
| ethics | property rights |
| etiquette | puberty customs |
| faith healing | religious ritual |
| feasting | sexual restrictions |
| fire making | soul concepts |
| folklore | surgery |
| games | toolmaking |
| gift giving | weaning |
| hair styles | weather control |
| hospitality | trade |

Source: Murdock, 1943.

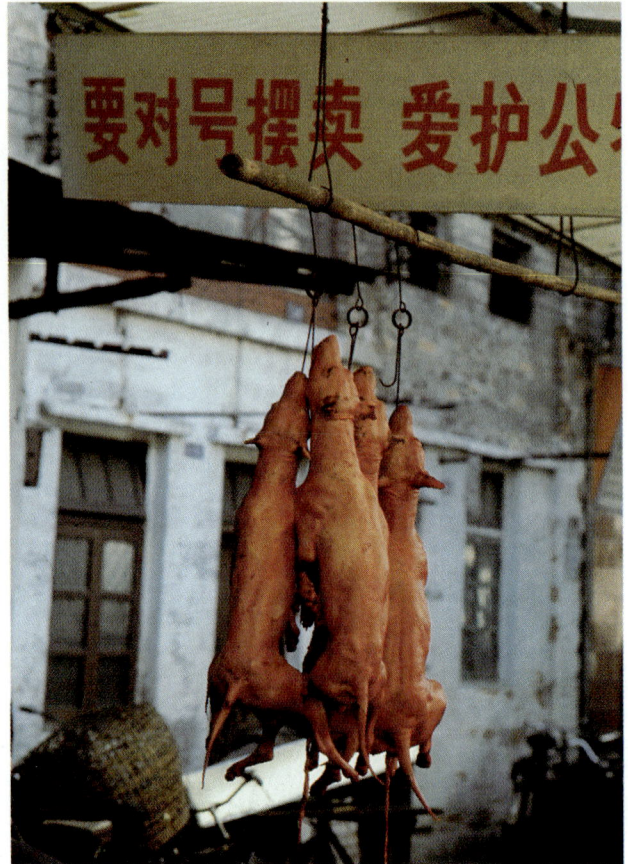

要对号摆卖 爱护公

In some cultures, dogs are cherished as pets who, when they die, are accorded the kind of treatment usually reserved for humans. In others, such as China, dogs are valued in quite a different way. How do these pictures make you feel, and how do you explain your feelings?

not exist in others or, if they do, they may be considered less important. This phenomenon is called **cultural relativism.** The belief that the deliberate killing of a child is murder, for example, does not exist in all cultures, for in some—such as Brazil's Tenetehara tribe—the killing of infants is a culturally legitimate practice.

Ideas also vary within cultures. A **subculture** is a distinctive set of cultural ideas that sets a group of people apart from the culture of its surrounding community or society. While American culture, for example, generally defines marijuana as a dangerous substance, many Americans knowingly share the belief that it is harmless, and such beliefs support and encourage its use among those who share in that subculture.

Because cultural ideas define reality for us, we often judge the ideas of other cultures as incorrect, if not inferior—an attitude called **ethnocentrism** (Sumner, 1906). Most societies have, at one time or another, regarded outsiders as "barbarians" whose cultures were "uncivilized" or "inferior" simply because they were different. "How could they think that way?", we may ask. The essence of ethnocentrism is that we rarely realize that people in other cultures might ask the same question of us.

In our own culture, for example, many of us believe that romantic love is essential for marriage, and if ours is the only culture we have ever known, we might believe that this reflects human nature rather than the beliefs and values of our own culture. If we study history, we find that in Western cultures the idea of romantic love is quite recent, dating back only to the fourteenth century, and in our own time there are many cultures, such as China's, in which the importance of romantic love in marriage is considerably less than in our own.

Western cultures also contain the belief that science is a valid way to understand the world. To a Zen Buddhist, however, all things form a whole to be accepted as it is, not understood by figuring out how things "work." From this cultural point of view, the attempts of Western scientists to explain the world by identifying relationships among its parts is a silly distraction, a futile effort to understand and control a world that is inherently neither understandable nor controllable.

## Values: Shoulds and Shouldn'ts

Whereas beliefs define what is real, cultural **values** define goals by ranking forms of behavior and social arrangements in terms of their relative desirability. "Honesty is better than dishonesty," "Competition is better than cooperation," and "Women and men should have equal rights" are all statements about what *should* be rather than about what *is*.

We are born preferring some states of being over others. Infants, for example, prefer warmth to extreme cold or heat, satiation to hunger or thirst, comfort to pain, and contact to isolation. There are no ideas involved in such preferences, for infants have no knowledge of the symbols we use to construct ideas.

Values, on the other hand, are abstract ideas about goals developed through the use of symbols. Many readers of this book, for example, attend college, even if it involves considerable hardship, because they share the value that education, as an end in itself, is inherently desirable  It is "good" to be educated, and more education is better than less. Many also share the value that being able to use our brains well is more desirable than being able to use our hands well, and that high-prestige, high-paying jobs are more desirable than lower-prestige, lower-paying ones. The cultural desirability of education is thus reflected in individual choices, but as an idea it exists independently of individuals, just as do cultural beliefs.

Also, like beliefs, values are quite different from personal tastes and preferences. If you say, "I like mayonnaise," no one can say "you shouldn't like it," for it expresses a preference whose sole authority is you as an individual. A value judgment, on the other hand, rests on sources of authority outside the individual. "You should not eat mayonnaise because the cholesterol in it is bad for your health" is a judgment that rests on the value we place on good health and long life (and the belief that cholesterol contributes to heart disease).

If you reply, "I don't care if I get heart disease," the response will likely be one of shock (except in a subculture that values eating whatever you like more than health), and the shocked person will know that others share that negative judgment. As a value, health is not more important than self-indulgence because you say it is; its relative "goodness" is part of a culture that ranks some ends higher than others.

Because we share them with others in our culture, such ideas influence our choices. They not only predispose us to strive in competition, to be honest and loyal, but they may also be used to manipulate our decisions. The advertising industry, for example, regularly uses established values to sell merchandise. The interior of a car may be described as "sexy"; spark plugs may be displayed next to a picture of a beautiful woman. In both cases, the values placed on attracting, possessing, or having power over a woman are paired with the idea of buying something that has no inherent connection to them. If we accept the pairing, we are more likely to buy the product, not because we value it but because we value the goals the advertisement associates with it (Slater, 1970).

DODGE 600 ES TURBO

Thus, while we may pursue what we want, values powerfully influence what it is we want in the first place. We may *think* that we "freely choose" to compete with others rather than cooperate, but we are largely unaware that in a different culture we would place different values on such behavior and make very different choices. The Zuni Indians of the American Southwest, for example, value cooperation more than competition:

Personal authority is perhaps the most vigorously disparaged trait in Zuni. A man who thirsts for power or knowledge, who wishes to be as they scornfully phrase it, "a leader of his people," receives nothing but censure and will very likely be persecuted for sorcery. . . . The ideal man in Zuni is a person of dignity and affability who has never tried to lead, and who has never called forth comment from his neighbors. . . . Even in contests of skill like their foot races, if a man wins habitually he is debarred from running. They are interested in a game that a number can play with even chances, and an outstanding runner spoils the game: they will have none of him. (Benedict, 1934, p. 95)

**When Values Conflict** We often hold values that, in a particular situation, produce genuine conflict between alternatives. Suppose, for example, you see a friend cheating on an exam. On the one hand, you value truth and honesty, for these are among the most fundamental values in a university. On the other hand, you value loyalty to friends. No matter what you choose to do—to tell on your friend or not—you will violate a value.

Values collide and produce conflict because they make up a loose "grammar" of thought about the importance of different alternatives, and because we occupy many social positions, each with its own set of values. The values of "respect for the law" and "loyalty to one's friends" are *general* guidelines that do not tell us what to do in specific situations.

By presenting them with a series of dilemmas, Kohlberg (1963) studied how children choose among conflicting values. In one, a man's wife is desperately ill and can be saved only with a new drug invented by a local pharmacist. The pharmacist demands an exorbitant price, far beyond the man's ability to pay. The husband later breaks into the pharmacy and steals the drug. Was he wrong? The answer depends on which value we consider to be more important.

To Kohlberg, we learn moral rules in the same way we learn grammatical rules that allow us to construct and interpret sentences we have never

**PUZZLES:**

## IS HONESTY ALWAYS THE BEST POLICY?

How do you know when to lie and when to tell the truth? Have you ever been in a situation in which you were expected to lie and would be punished if you told the truth?

As you will see in the section on norms, both lying and telling the truth are forms of social behavior and whether or not we are expected to do one or the other depends very much on the social situation.

seen or heard before. We learn only general rules—such as "It's wrong to steal" and "Always put family first"—which we then try to apply to specific situations. Just as no one ever "taught" you the meaning of the preceding sentence, no one specifically teaches us what to do if someone in our family needs a medicine that we cannot afford to buy. To solve moral dilemmas, then, we rely on a general set of rules; and when we participate in a system of values, we continually interpret and choose in search of what Roger Brown (1965) called "some reasonable consistency among judgment, feeling, and action" (p. 414).

## Norms: Dos and Don'ts

Values provide us with loose guidelines for deciding how to behave; norms are specific rules designed to control behavior. A **norm** is a rule that defines punishments or rewards for various forms of behavior according to people's positions in social relationships. While all actions have objective consequences, norms specify *social* consequences for the person performing the action.

If I kill a man, for example, he dies; if I smack my lips at the dinner table, a noise results. The death and the noise are the objective consequences. If I kill a man identified as "the enemy" in a war, however, his death is not the only consequence, for I might be rewarded with a medal. If I kill a man because I do not like the color of his eyes or disagree with his politics, on the other hand, I will be punished. If I smack my lips over dinner in the United States, people may show disapproval by frowning, but if I smack them in India, people are more likely to smile at me. If I am caught stealing a traveler's suitcase in the United States, I might be sent to jail; in the Sudan in 1984, however, the penalty for one unfortunate thief was to have his right hand cut off in a public ceremony.

In each of these cases, the link between the act itself and the consequences for me, the actor, is artificial; it is not inherent in the act itself. The statements "If you kill an enemy, you will get a medal" and "If you kill a man because you don't like him you will be punished" are norms that link specific acts to specific responses that we can expect from other people who share our culture. The responses are called *sanctions*, and they may take the form of rewards (such as medals) or punish-

ments (such as imprisonment). When we are punished for violating a norm (or rewarded for conforming to one), it is not because of what we did, it is because of the *rule;* if the rule changes, the same behavior no longer brings with it the same sanctions (Durkheim, 1924).

The basic types of norms are *folkways, mores* (pronounced "morayz"), and *laws,* each of which we will consider in turn.

**Folkways** In a classic work, William Graham Sumner (1906) defined a society's **folkways** as the set of manners and customary acts that characterize everyday life in a society. As a set of norms, folkways regulate behavior whose consequences are relatively trivial and in which the resulting sanctions tend to be correspondingly mild.

We are not supposed to stare at people or stand too close when talking with them. We are expected to face front in elevators, replace caps on toothpaste tubes, return library books on time, and not refer to our parents by their first name.

Folkways are a particularly fluid form of norm, subject to rapid change, inconsistent application, and enormous variation among the world's cultures. It was not very long ago, for example, that men were expected to open doors for women, but now expectations have changed considerably, and the simple act of passing through a doorway can be an occasion for substantial negotiation and uncertainty (Walum, 1974).

The application of folkways, as with all norms, depends on the situation. Although staring at a stranger on a bus violates an American folkway, we are expected to stare at performers in a theater. To be seen by others is vital to us (imagine if no one ever looked at you), but folkways regulate this simple act.

Folkways also vary enormously from one culture to another. In Latin cultures, for example, people are expected to stand very close to each other when talking, so close that North Americans and Europeans feel very uncomfortable (Hall, 1969). Compared with the British upper class, Americans are far more likely to assume familiarity by calling people by their first name. The Japanese remove their shoes whenever they enter a house and Icelanders consider it impolite to leave a party before three or four o'clock in the morning.

## Voices: Minding Your Manners—and Others'

### Reading at Table

DEAR MISS MANNERS:

Would you please comment on the proper etiquette for reading at the dinner table? In particular, is it considered proper to prop a letter against the salt shaker or to lean the newspaper against a carton of cottage cheese, in order to free the hands for eating?

GENTLE READER:

Miss Manners was about to duck this question, on the grounds that it is never proper to read at the dinner table if anyone else is present and that what you do when you eat alone is between you and your God, and not a matter of etiquette. Then she came to the cottage cheese container. No decent person would put a food package—including ketchup bottles, milk cartons, or cereal boxes—on the table, even at home alone with the shades drawn. . . .

### Extended Nonfamily

DEAR MISS MANNERS:

How do you like this one: my daughter is twenty-six, and lives with a divorced man exactly my age and his twenty-two-year-old daughter who has an adorable eight-month-old baby girl. At this stage in my life, I can't think of anything I want more than a grandchild—I baby-sit this "semi-step-great-granddaughter" (or whatever she is besides being simply darling), but this isn't exactly what I've had in mind. And talk about making introductions when my daughter and I are out to lunch or shopping with the baby—whew! It's one of the few times I'm almost rendered speechless. Any suggestions?

GENTLE READER:

Whew! is right. If you attempt to explain this relationship to people you meet while out lunching or shopping, the baby will probably grow up and move away before you finish talking. Miss Manners suggests you curtail the introduction to merely, "And this is Baby Snooks," or whatever. People will naturally assume that you have kidnapped this child for complex psychological reasons or hope of financial gain, or that she has selected you for her nursery Adopt-a-Grandparent work project. But so what? She will grow up learning that you can't explain everything to everyone, which is a valuable lesson in life. . . .

### "Get Well"

DEAR MISS MANNERS:

Is it considered proper to send a "get well soon" card to a Christian Scientist?

GENTLE READER:

Certainly. A Christian Scientist may disagree with you about treatment but, as Miss Manners understands it, has no objection whatever to the prospect of getting well. . . .

### Improper Remarks

DEAR MISS MANNERS:

I have failed at the art of conversation and most desperately need your help! While my husband and I were sitting at dinner the other night with another married couple, the other man turned to me and, apropos of nothing in the conversation, declared that he was now "safe." Naïve as always, I asked, "What do you mean by 'safe'?" "A vasectomy," he proudly announced.

Nearly speechless, I frantically searched for the proper response, but a splutter and a giggle were all I came up with. Any suggestions?

GENTLE READER:

Ah, isn't it wonderful what passes for conversation these days? You can hardly sit down at dinner anymore without being told what everyone does with the parts of the body that cannot be seen above the table. Miss Manners is going to take to shocking perfect strangers by looking them deep in the eyes and saying, "Beastly weather we've been having lately, don't you think?"

But she cannot improve on your response, which was perfectly proper—unless it would be by accompanying your splutter and giggle with the appropriate gesture of staring the man straight in the napkin.

Source: Martin, J., *Miss Manners' Guide to Excruciatingly Correct Behavior*, 1982.

A society's folkways describe the "fine texture" of everyday life, the thousands of manners and customs that its members take for granted as "the way we do things." Only when we encounter the folkways of different cultures do we become aware of our folkways as peculiar to our own culture rather than as the "natural" way of going about everyday life.

**Mores and Morality** Whereas folkways regulate the trivial aspects of social interaction, a society's mores focus on more serious expectations about behavior. **Mores** are norms that reflect deeply held cultural ideals about how people should behave (Sumner, 1906). While folkways distinguish between relatively unimportant categories—polite and impolite, clean and neat, sophisticated and vulgar—mores make more important distinctions, such as those between "good" and "bad," "virtuous" and "sinful," "laudable" and "repugnant." Thus, a society's mores define standards of behavior that are more serious than those defined by folkways, and punishment for their violation tends to be both more certain and more severe.

There is a story about two children, the first of whom has two apples, one large and the other small. The first offers to share them. When the second child takes the large apple, the first protests, "Hey, why'd you take the big one?"

"Which one would you have taken?" asks the second child.

"The small one."

"Then you got what you wanted, didn't you?"

The first child is outraged because the second ignored an important moral principle: When one person offers something to another, the recipient is expected to reciprocate—to return the favor—by not taking full advantage of the choice. There is actually an exchange going on in this interaction—an apple in exchange for restraint and moderation—and the second child's failure to reciprocate violates important cultural ideas about "fairness" and "reciprocity" (Gouldner, 1960; see also Fisher, Nadler, and DePaulo, 1983).

Mores focus on what most of us think of as morality, and several characteristics distinguish moral acts from immoral ones. First, moral acts never have the actor's self-interest as their only goal. This is what distinguishes Robin Hood's acts of stealing from similar acts by someone who steals for personal gain. This does not imply that an act is immoral if done purely for personal reasons: to run into a burning house to save people's lives is a moral act, but to stay outside out of concern for our own lives usually will be excused. A moral act thus differs from other acts in that it is performed in the interests of other people.

The second characteristic of moral acts is that they have a quality of command. We do them because we are supposed to, out of a sense of duty and obligation, not simply to another individual, but to the values embodied in the act (the value of honesty or of a human life). We refrain from some acts simply because they are forbidden in our culture. If a cashier in a store gives us too much change and we knowingly take it, we do not simply hurt the cashier or the company; we violate one of the terms of our participation in social life. If we return the money, we affirm our place in society and feel the pleasure of belonging.

Third, moral acts have an element of desirability. They are "good," just as immoral acts are "bad," and we feel genuine pleasure simply from doing "the right thing" (and pain from doing "the wrong thing"), whether or not we tell other people and bask in the glow of their approval.

Finally, ideas about morality are sacred. Because they reflect the deepest collective feelings about who we are and should be, we attach strong feelings to them. While specific laws may allow

---

**PUZZLES:**

## MAKING MORAL DECISIONS

Before reading on, imagine that you are a pediatrician and one of your newborn infant patients suffers from a serious condition that will most likely leave it both paralyzed and severely brain damaged. The parents insist that you take no extreme measures to keep the baby alive. One of your colleagues vehemently disagrees, arguing that it is your duty as a doctor to do everything you can to keep every patient alive. What would you do? How would you go about making your decision?

As you read on, think about moral decisions and how we make them.

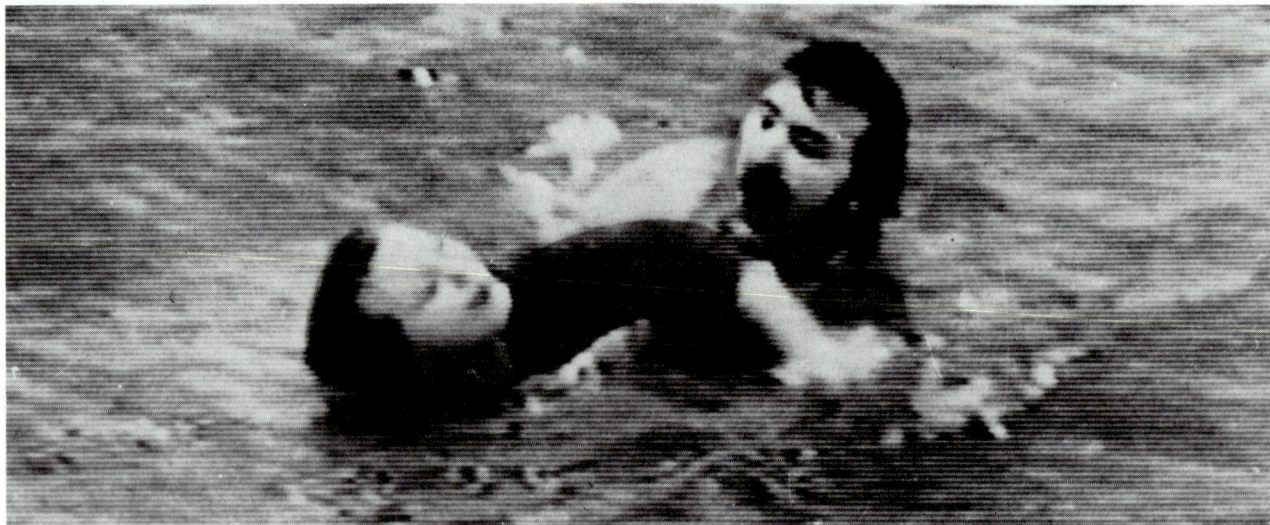

Moral acts typically are performed for the benefit of another. Lennie Skutnik, shown saving Priscilla Tirado, was one of those who braved the icy waters of the Potomac River in Washington, DC, to assist crash victims when an airliner went down in January 1982. At least one such rescuer lost his life in the process.

some people to do things forbidden to others, the idea that "no one is above the law" is a moral one that applies to us all, even, as Richard Nixon discovered, someone who is the president of the United States.

As with folkways, the application of mores often depends on the situation. While dishonesty, for example, violates general cultural mores, there are situations in which it is permitted or expected. As Bok (1979) pointed out, mores permit us to lie in order to save a life or mislead an enemy during wartime. Scientists often deceive and lie to subjects about the aims of their research, parents lie to their children about everything from the existence of Santa Claus to the details of sexual behavior, and physicians often lie by understating the true condition of terminally ill patients.

There is also considerable cross-cultural variation in the definition of moral behavior. Cannibal tribes in Oceania do not consider it immoral to eat human flesh, and the Nayar of India do not define adultery as immoral. Eating pork violates the mores of Orthodox Jews, but in other cultures the consumption of pork is part of an annual celebration of great importance (Harris, 1974). In addition, while the mores of all known cultures prohibit murder, there is considerable variation in its definition. In Western cultures, for example, killing for personal revenge is defined and punished as murder, but in some other cultures killing to

avenge the murder of a family member is expected.

Mores thus extend beyond the rightness or wrongness of certain acts to the most profound ideas of what life in a particular society is supposed to be about, and moral ideas have been used throughout history to justify everything from self-sacrifice and charity to unimaginable cruelty. The murder of over 6 million Jews during the Holocaust was seen by the Nazis as "the final solution" to the "Jewish problem" that, they believed, stood between them and the realization of the "supremacy of the Aryan race." To many Nazis, the execution of millions of men, women, and children was part of a crusade for racial "purity," full of moral self-righteousness; while, to those who did not share their vision, the Holocaust was a crime of unimaginable immorality and horror.

**Laws**  All norms involve sanctions, and sociologists make an important distinction between those that are informal and those that are formal. **Informal sanctions** are not clearly defined and anyone has the right to impose them. If we belch loudly in the company of others, anyone has the right to impose a variety of sanctions ranging from the slightest frown to an angry outburst.

**Formal sanctions,** on the other hand, are clearly defined and people in specialized social positions have the power and responsibility to impose them. If I steal your radio, it is not up to you to enforce the sanctions attached to the norm prohibiting theft. The sanctions as well as the procedures for deciding if and how to apply them are clearly specified; and specific people are authorized to apprehend me, determine my guilt or innocence, and impose punishment. Norms with formal sanctions are called *laws*.

**Criminal law** links specific acts with punishments (expulsion from school for cheating; imprisonment for stealing; fines for reckless driving). To violate such a law is not simply an act against an individual, for it represents an act against society itself. Thus, when someone commits murder, we may feel outrage regardless of our relationship to the victim, and it is the state that prosecutes the case, not the victim's friends and family.

The purpose of **civil law** is to regulate social relationships and, when possible, to undo the negative effects of a particular act. Civil law, for example, regulates relationships among producers, buyers and sellers (commercial law); the functioning of courts and their officers (procedural law); the relationship between citizens and their government (constitutional law); and the relationships among family members (family law), determining, for example, which parent gets custody of children in case of divorce. In addition, if you slip on a roller skate on my front porch and break your leg, the state will not prosecute me under criminal law; but you might sue me in order to pay for your hospital bills and compensate you for the effects of my negligence.

One of the most basic cultural ideas in civil law is that of the *contract*, which is an agreement between two parties to exchange one thing for another: I will give you $5,000 if you will paint my house. The idea of a contract clearly illustrates the fact that norms exist apart from individuals, for the power behind the agreement extends beyond the people who are directly involved. If I refuse to pay you when you fulfill your part of the bargain, society itself supports your claim—*not* out of concern for you as an individual, but to preserve the culturally valued idea of a contract. Thus, society is an "interested party" in all contracts made between individuals (Durkheim, 1893/1933).

Formal and informal sanctions are used to enforce both folkways and mores. While mores usually involve formal sanctions (as in the case of mur-

der), in some cases (such as lying to a friend) the sanctions are informal. Spitting on a sidewalk violates an American folkway, but the sanctions are formal (it is against the law); but if we spit on the floor at a party, the sanctions are informal (the host cannot have us arrested). We should note, however, that while specific laws may or may not have a moral content (overparking is not immoral, but murder is); the *idea* of "the law" is a profoundly moral one.

## Attitudes: Evaluation and Feeling

We have seen that cultural beliefs, values, and norms affect human experience and behavior by defining reality, setting goals, and specifying punishments and rewards for particular behaviors. Another component of culture—attitudes—influences our lives by focusing on emotional feelings. As defined in Chapter 1, **attitudes** are positive or negative evaluations of objects, people, or situations that often predispose us to feel and behave toward them in positive or negative ways (Allport, 1935; Hill, 1981). All attitudes are based on beliefs about people, objects, and situations, and people may share an attitude without sharing a particular belief, just as they may share a belief without sharing a related attitude. The attitude of racial hatred, for example, is often justified by a variety of beliefs. Some people, for example, might justify such attitudes with a belief in the genetic inferiority of a hated group; others, on the other hand, might feel just as strongly but justify their attitude with a different set of beliefs—such as "they're cruel and they murdered my relatives."

As humans, we have the ability to experience and display a wide variety of emotions, but to understand their ebb and flow, we must go beyond the psychology of individual motives to the cultures that produce consistent patterns of belief, feeling, and behavior. The shared love of a country—patriotism—is an attitude that organizes and regulates beliefs ("our country is the best there is") and emotions (pride, excitement, love) and makes us more likely to behave aggressively toward anyone who threatens our positive national image.

In many respects, popular American sports such as hockey and football show many of the characteristics of organized warfare, complete with violent injuries and passionate hatred of the "enemy." From a cultural point of view, hockey players (and their fans) are not violent because of an inherently

In times of war, hostile attitudes toward those designated as the "enemy" play a crucial part in the willingness of people to kill people and risk being killed themselves.

aggressive "human nature"; rather, they are aggressive because they play hockey and share in its subcultural attitudes.

Guilt, pride, and shame are social attitudes directed toward ourselves rather than others, and they exist only in a cultural context (Gordon, 1981). Without culture, there is no occasion for such emotions, for they rest on beliefs and values used to interpret and judge behavior. Fear, for example, exists as a primary emotion in many animal species, but only in a cultural context do we find the concept of "cowardice" and the personal shame that goes with it.

Cultural ideas thus influence what we believe, value, feel, and do. Just as gravity pulls our bodies toward the center of the earth, cultural ideas "pull" us toward centers of meaning, value, and expectation. We resist—even defy—gravity in many ways; in the simplest act of standing up an individual resists gravity's pull. We also resist, and sometimes defy, the constraining force of culture—we play with language, violate norms, or refuse to conform to cultural attitudes.

Consequently, culture does not completely determine who we are, what we feel and think, or what we do. Nor do individuals act in a vacuum, free of the limitations imposed by social environments. The character of our lives and our relationships with one another are, rather, the result of an *interaction* between individuals and their environments.

## Material Culture: Things from Ideas and Ideas from Things

The creation of material objects lies at the core of human existence, and the development of material culture takes place only through a web of social relationships. We produce objects not only to satisfy our needs for them, but also because "free, conscious activity" and "productive life" are important aspects of what makes us human (Marx, in Schaff, 1970, p. 125).

Thus, through the course of history, people have developed an astonishing variety of objects that affect our lives. The invention of the plow and wheel, for example, around 6,000 years ago, revolutionized the ability of humans to travel, produce food, and conduct trade. The development of printing, first by the Chinese in the fifth century A.D. and then with Gutenberg's invention of movable type in the fifteenth century, stimulated a rapid spread of literacy and new ideas.

The Industrial Revolution began in the middle of the eighteenth century with the invention of machines such as textile looms and the use of new sources of power, such as steam. The application of the steam engine to transportation in the mid-1800s vastly expanded the markets for goods and hence stimulated their production. The last hundred years have seen the rapid development of mass production, the automobile, light and durable plastics, and revolutions in communications and computer technology.

Such objects are cultural both in their origins and in the role they play in social life. Most inventions arise from the human ability to think in symbolic terms, to share the resulting knowledge, and to build on previous inventions in the creation of others. They also reflect cultural values and beliefs. The rapid development of industrial technology, for example, reflects not only possessions as a value, but, in capitalist societies, the value of profit, which is increased by mechanization and more-efficient production.

The development of material culture is often a collective response to the pressures of population and ecology. Growing populations, for example, require new methods for satisfying subsistence needs. Those methods, in turn, often create the need for further innovation. When coal was first used as a source of power in the United States, for example, it was easy to obtain: in Pennsylvania, it lay on the surface of the earth. As Americans consumed it in greater and greater quantities, however, it became necessary to go underground to find it, and this required more sophisticated machines to drill and haul the coal.

Material culture is social both in its origins and in its influence on human thought, behavior, and experience. The automobile did more than allow increased mobility; it also contributed to the growth of sprawling cities and "rush hours" with all their tensions. It became a place for young people to be alone, beyond the watchful eyes of parents; and, for many, it provided an instrument for aggression, self-expression, and boastful displays of wealth and individuality.

The relationship between material and nonmaterial culture is both complex and reciprocal. The explosive growth in electronics and computer technology, for example, raises new threats to rights of privacy. Since 1983 there has been growing alarm over the relative ease with which the operators of home computers can gain access to records stored in computers in hospitals, universities, banks, military research laboratories, and other institutions. When such behavior was first discovered in 1983, there were no legal norms that defined it as a crime, because the spread of computer technology had been so rapid that such crimes had not come up as a serious possibility. As new laws are passed in order to protect a host of values that are linked with the security of computers—including the right to privacy—new technology must be invented to secure computers against unauthorized access.

As material culture, computers do more than compute. They also affect social relationships. The students in this picture are not interacting with a teacher or other students but with a machine. The long-term effects of pervasive use of such technology on the social development of children remain to be seen.

An even more important aspect of material culture is that objects, once created, become independent parts of their creators' culture. Computers do only what human programmers and operators tell them to do, and yet we often blame computers for everything from errors on telephone bills to the junk mail we would rather not receive. We often hear people talk about computers as if they somehow have the power to control our lives, as if they have power beyond what their human creators and operators choose to do with them. As machines and other products of material culture assume greater and greater importance in our lives, we may "begin to feel ourselves as things that are parts of the surrounding world of things" (Schaff, 1970, p. 106).

The concepts of material and nonmaterial culture are tools that make up a major part of the sociological perspective. Social environments, however, are more than a vast collection of ideas and objects swirling about us like a thick soup, for beliefs, values, attitudes, and norms are organized into social relationships that produce patterns of expectation and behavior. These patterns represent the second major sociological concept, social structure, which is the subject of Chapter 4.

## Summary

1. Although culture consists of both material and nonmaterial products, the essence of culture is nonmaterial and is made up of abstract beliefs, values, attitudes, and norms. These, in turn, are expressed through symbols: objects, characteristics of objects, gestures, or words that represent more than themselves. Language is a collection of symbols (words) and rules for their use (syntax and grammar), and those who share a language make up a speech community.

2. Language serves several social functions. It allows people to express experience, to store records of it, and to assume that others know what they mean when they write or talk; it allows members of a speech community to distinguish between themselves and outsiders; and it often substitutes for physical contact. In addition, performative language is a meaningful action that alters people's positions in social relationships.

3. Cultural relativism refers to the fact that the importance of a particular cultural product varies from one social environment to another; and ethnocentrism describes the tendency of people to regard other cultures or subcultures as inferior to their own. The concepts of cultural relativism and ethnocentrism can also apply within a society in relation to subcultures, which are distinctive sets of cultural ideas that set a group apart from the culture of a surrounding community or society.

4. Beliefs are statements about reality, and a belief is cultural only if the authority for its validity lies outside of individuals in the shared assumption that other people support it. Values rank forms of behavior and social arrangements in terms of relative desirability. Values often conflict because they are loose guidelines for choosing among alternatives and because we all occupy many different positions in social relationships, each governed by its own set of values.

5. Norms are rules that prescribe sanctions—punishments or rewards—for various kinds of behavior according to people's positions in social relationships. Sanctions may be either informal—loosely defined with no specific people authorized to impose them—or formal—clearly defined with specific people empowered to deliver them.

6. There are three kinds of norms. Folkways are norms (such as table manners) that regulate relatively trivial behaviors in everyday social interactions. Mores, on the other hand, reflect deeply held ideas about how people should behave. Norms with formal sanctions are called laws. Criminal law links specific acts with punishments, while civil law is designed to regulate social relationships (such as marriage and divorce), to deal with contracts, and, when possible, to undo the effects of a particular act (as when someone sues someone else to pay to repair damaged property).

7. Attitudes are predispositions to feel positive or negative emotions toward people and to behave toward them in positive or negative ways. Attitudes also include the feelings people have toward themselves, such as guilt, pride, or shame.

8. Material culture consists of objects people make as they interact with each other and the physical world. The relationship between material and nonmaterial cultural products is complex and reciprocal. Ideas often lead to the creation of objects, but objects (such as computers) can become so important a part of the environment that they affect the beliefs, values, norms, and attitudes that regulate social interaction.

## Key Terms

cultural relativism   74
cultural universals   73
culture   65

   attitude   81
   belief   72
   gesture   65
   language   67

      performative language   71
      speech community   69

## Recommended Readings

BENEDICT, R. (1960). *Patterns of culture*. New York: New American Library (paperback). A classic analysis of cultural relativism with a special emphasis on native American tribes. (Original work published 1934)

FARB, P. (1975). *Word play: What happens when people talk*. New York: Bantam. A serious and yet thoroughly entertaining analysis of the characteristics and uses of language, from the origins of language to the outrageously funny assaults on the English language perpetrated by the Marx Brothers.

GEERTZ, C. (1973). *The interpretation of cultures*. New York: Basic Books (paperback). Not an easy book for undergraduate readers, but it is an important book about the nature of culture and the importance of symbols.

HALL, E. T. (1959). *The silent language*. Greenwich, CT: Fawcett (paperback). An entertaining and insightful look at how cultural differences in language contribute to both variety and misunderstanding among the world's cultures. See also his more recent book, *Beyond culture* (1978). New York: Doubleday.

SLATER, P. (1976). *The pursuit of loneliness* (rev. ed.). Boston: Beacon Press (paperback). A passionate and articulate analysis in which a sociologist shows how major American values promote social isolation and loneliness.

ZBOROWSKI, M. (1953). Cultural components in responses to pain. *Journal of Social Issues, 8*, 16–31. A fascinating exploration into ethnic differences in the ways people experience and respond to pain in a hospital setting.

# CHAPTER 4
# Social Structure

Social structure is the second major concept that defines the sociological perspective. It describes the ways in which values, beliefs, attitudes, and norms are organized in patterns, producing the countless different relationships we participate in during our lives, the limits they impose on our choices, and the conflicts that inevitably result; and it describes the place of each relationship in a complex web of patterns that give predictable form to social life.

This chapter looks closely at the concept of social structure and the many different characteristics of social relationships that affect how people behave in relation to one another.

## The Concept of Social Structure

One night an insurance agent named George feels ill and goes to the emergency room of his local hospital. A doctor named Mary takes his case, and they talk in a small room. They have never met before, yet they share these expectations: he will call her "doctor," not "Mary"; he will answer her questions—even when they are highly personal—as accurately as he can; he will follow her advice; and he will pay for her services. They also share the expectations that she knows what she is doing, that she will confine herself to questions that are relevant to his illness, and that she will keep his answers in strict confidence. While both are capable of a vast array of acts, they limit themselves to a very narrow range: they do not go to sleep or read aloud from the Bible; she does not undress (although he might), and he does not try to sell her an insurance policy.

George and Mary would behave differently relaxing at home with their respective families, eating dinner together in a restaurant, or meeting in the office of his insurance agency. Moreover, if the physician were Harry and the patient were Susan, the expectations would be the same. In a different culture, however—such as one in which witch doctors heal the sick—the patterns would be very different. Among the Mojave Indians in the American Southwest, for example, the "medicine man" was known more for his power to kill than his power to heal, and the Mojave believed that those who were killed by the medicine man's sorcery were under his power in the afterlife. Thus, the Mojave medicine man often had more to gain by the death of patients than by their survival (Benedict, 1934).

The behavior of physicians and patients is thus limited by a set of shared expectations about what is and is not supposed to take place; and these expectations form a pattern that we recognize, a pattern that is different from that of family life or restaurants, and it imposes limits on both participants regardless of who they are as individuals.

### The Three Aspects of Social Structure

The concept of social structure rests on the idea that "a whole is more than the sum of its parts." A human face, for example, is not simply a collection of parts—of two eyes, a nose and mouth, cheeks, lips, chin and forehead. What makes it recognizable as a human face is the *arrangement* of those parts in relation to one another. Similarly, the behavior of physicians and patients cannot be understood solely in terms of their individual characteristics. It is their arrangement in relation to each

Social relationships are a delicate balance of shared expectations.

other, and their individual orientations to that arrangement that produce the unique interactions of doctor and patient (Merton, 1968). Thus, the first aspect of social structure *is the influence of the arrangement of individuals on the individuals themselves.*

The second aspect describes *patterned expectations among groups.* The delivery of medical services, for example, is not simply organized around interactions between individual doctors and patients. Large complex groups such as hospitals, insurance companies, and government agencies also have socially regulated relationships with one another: insurance companies interact with hospitals in setting fees and paying claims; governments make rules that regulate both insurance companies and hospitals and grant physicians the right to practice medicine. If you want to get mental health therapy from a psychiatric social worker, for example, you may have to pay the entire bill yourself, because most health insurance companies will not cover psychotherapy administered by anyone other than a psychiatrist or a clinical psychologist. This, in turn, gives psychiatrists and clinical psychologists a great deal of power by limiting competition in their field by making it difficult for "outsiders" to get patients.

The third aspect of social structure is *the distribution of people among various social positions* (there are many more patients than physicians) *as well as the distribution of various kinds of rewards, the most sociologically important of which are wealth, power, and prestige* (most of the wealth in America is held by a small fraction of the population). The fact that there are relatively few skilled brain surgeons, for example, means that brain surgeons are always in demand; as a result, they can charge very high fees for their work.

Thus, in each of its three aspects, the concept of **social structure** refers to the arrangement of people and groups in relation to one another, and these arrangements exist independently of the people who participate in them. Individuals do not have the power to decide arbitrarily what those expectations will be. An American doctor, for example, does not have the right to suddenly decide to start behaving like a Mojave medicine man.

Expectations that define social relationships are also reciprocal, and vary from one social relationship to another. Both physician and patient, for example, orient their actions in relation to their expectations of the other. A person cannot perform as a physician without a patient, nor can one be a patient without a physician. If George confides a deep dark secret about his health to Mary while he is her patient in the hospital, she may not tell the world about it; but if he meets her in a bar and tells the same secret, she is not bound by the physician-patient relationship to keep it confidential. In addition, while George is legally bound to pay for Mary's advice in the hospital, anything she tells him in a bar is free of charge.

## Social Statuses and Status Sets

At the heart of the concept of social structure, as we just saw, are the social positions that people occupy in social relationships. These positions are called **social statuses** (not to be confused with the common use of "status" to refer to prestige), and they are the building blocks of social structures (Linton, 1936). To say "He is a doctor's patient" describes one of George's social statuses. The definition of a baseball team, for example, centers on a set of statuses—outfielder, pitcher, catcher, shortstop, and so on—that makes up its structure.

The Marx brothers make us laugh because they are so adept at outrageously violating our expectations about how people are supposed to behave as the occupants of social statuses such as physician and patient.

A social status exists only in relation to other social statuses: the status "college student" has no meaning except in relation to other social positions such as "college teacher" or "college administrator." Social statuses thus locate us in social "space" by defining our positions in relation to others.

Not all characteristics are social statuses, because a characteristic is a social status only if it locates us in relation to others and creates sets of shared expectations. Being left- or right-handed, for example, is not a position in a social relationship, for it does not carry with it patterned expectations. Being blind, deaf, or mentally handicapped, however, can represent a social status if the condition affects people's expectations.

Some statuses—the most enduring ones—are **ascribed** (or assigned) to us at birth. These include age, race, ethnicity, and gender. Others are **achieved** (or acquired), such as educational attainment and occupation. Unlike achieved statuses, it is very difficult if not impossible to change an ascribed status. (It is true that some people undergo sex-change surgery, and we all change our age status—but only in one direction.) We can, however, control with greater success how others *perceive* our ascribed statuses. People often alter various aspects of their appearance—with hair styles, clothing, cosmetics, and even plastic surgery—to affect others' perception of their age.

The third type of status is **temporary,** and this can be either *situational* or *transitional*. A **situational status** is a social position that we occupy only so long as we are in a particular social situation. When we walk into a store, we enter the status of "customer," and when we walk out, we leave that status and enter others such as "pedestrian" or "bus passenger." Some states of being are also temporary statuses: when a person believes another to be asleep or sick, for example, their expectations of each other are different from those they might have when both are awake or well (Parsons, 1951).

A **transitional status** is one that is socially structured to be occupied for a limited time as part of a progression toward other statuses (Coser, 1966). "High school junior," for example, is a status that represents a transition from "sophomore" to "senior," just as the status "engaged to be married" is a transition from "single person" to "spouse."

All social statuses, therefore, are positions in social relationships in a particular society, and exist independently of the individuals who occupy them. Even though no one in a given year might occupy the status of "presidential candidate," for example, the social position still exists. This distinction is crucial, for it draws our attention to the limitations of a particular position over and above the personal characteristics of whoever occupies it. A psychologist, for example, might be interested in President *Reagan;* but a sociologist would be interested in *President* Reagan.

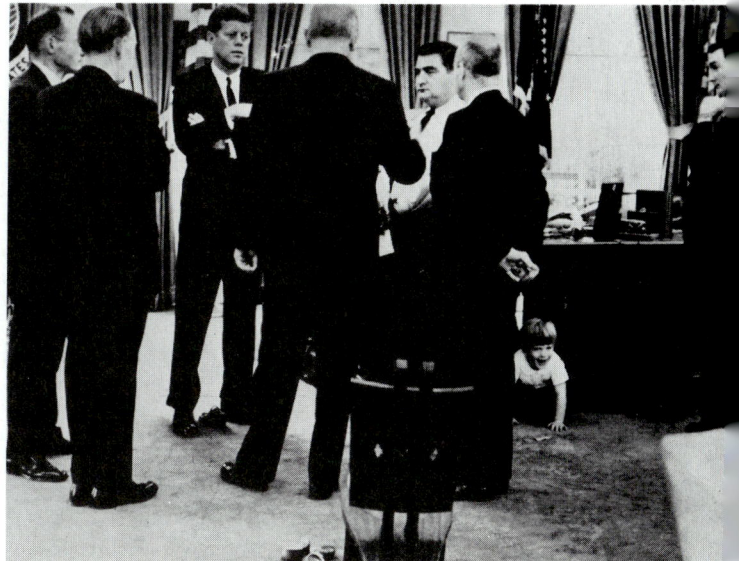

All of us occupy many different statuses that make up our status sets, as this picture of John Kennedy as both president and father illustrates.

## PUZZLES:

## WHAT IS YOUR RACIAL STATUS?

If you got a copy of your birth certificate and found that it described your race as something other than you consider it to be, would it bother you? Why? How would you feel about showing the certificate to other people? Are there some people you would not want to see it? Why? (See also the opening pages of Chapter 12.)

We all occupy a wide variety of social statuses. We occupy some for our entire lives (such as race), whereas most of us never occupy the status of "defendant in a criminal case." The most socially important status we occupy is called a **master status** because it affects almost every aspect of our lives. In racially segregated South Africa, for example, race is a master status. In countries such as the United States, occupation is usually treated as a master status.

If each of us made a list of all the statuses we occupy, the result would be our **status set** (Merton, 1968). Figure 4-1 shows a small portion of the status set for Mary, the doctor in our opening example.

### Roles and Role Sets

Social structure refers to more than any pair or set of statuses, for it represents patterned expectations of those who occupy those statuses. Attached to each social status is a **role,** which is a set of beliefs, values, attitudes, and norms that define expectations shared by status occupants in their relationships with the occupants of other social statuses (Linton, 1936; see also Heiss, 1981). In the example that began this chapter Mary and George are playing the roles of doctor and patient in relation to

each other. Each has expectations—such as Mary will help George get well and George will pay Mary for her services—that affect how they feel, think, and behave.

Roles are collections of ideas about the thoughts, feelings, values, and behavior of status occupants, and **role performance** is behavior that results from our orientation to those ideas. Thus, infants who cry because they are hungry are not performing a role, because they are not orienting themselves to a set of cultural expectations attached to the statuses of infant and parent. When doctors and patients interact, on the other hand, they are limited by a set of cultural ideas attached to the two statuses involved—such as the value placed on health and the belief that doctors know more about medicine than the patients.

Notice, however, that when doctors interact with one another, the expectations change, even though they still occupy the status of "doctor." They are more likely to treat one another as equals, less likely to tell one another what to do. Why does the role change?

The answer is that the content of a particular role depends on the other statuses involved in the relationship. When Mary performs the role of doctor in relation to George in the role of patient,

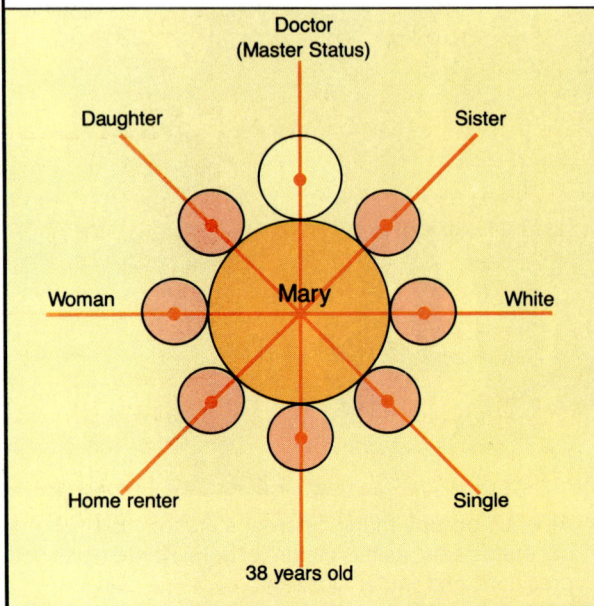

**Figure 4-1** Mary's Partial Status Set

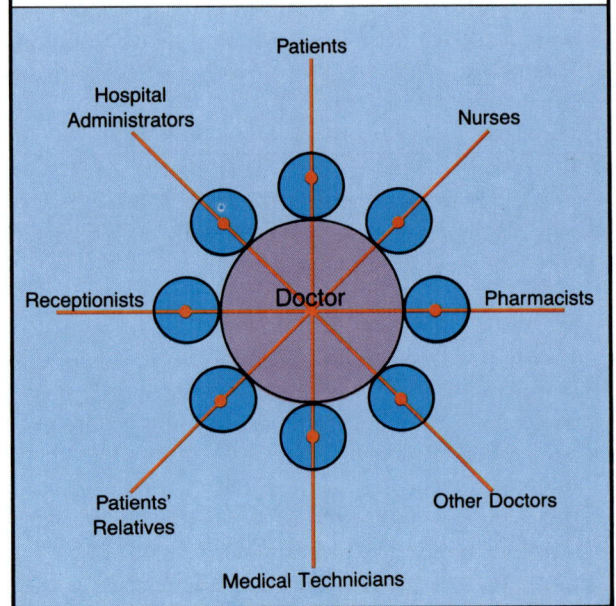

**Figure 4-2** Partial Role Set for Status of Doctor

George is Mary's **role partner** (just as Mary is George's role partner). Thus, a status occupant may have relationships with a variety of different role partners, and each relationship carries with it different expectations.

Doctors have role relationships with patients, patients' relatives, nurses, hospital administrators, receptionists, and other doctors. In other words, "doctor," by virtue of being a doctor, has a *set* of roles (called a **role set**) with the occupants of other statuses (Merton, 1968). Figure 4-2 shows the role set for Mary's master status "doctor."

## Defining Situations (and Ourselves)

Our status and role sets strongly influence who other people think we are and who *we* think we are. If a stranger asks us to describe ourselves, we are unlikely to talk about our personalities, because personalities do not locate us in social space, in relation to patterns of expectation.

Most people want to know our age, gender, occupation, marital status, educational attainment, income, sexual orientation, race, and ethnic background, because such characteristics help locate us in relation to patterns of cultural values, beliefs, norms, and attitudes. If people believe we are married or fabulously wealthy, they treat us very differently than they do if they believe we are single or desperately poor. If a poor young man wanted to marry a wealthy older woman, for example, many people would immediately suspect that he was after her money, even if they had no personal knowledge of the two individuals involved.

When we identify our statuses and those of the people we interact with, we are **defining the situation,** and until we do this, we feel uncomfortable precisely because we do not know "where we are" socially. It is for this reason that people exert so much pressure on us to reveal our social statuses, and take it very seriously when we misrepresent ourselves. If we become romantically involved with someone whom we later discover is married, we are more than disappointed: we feel deceived, embarrassed, and angry because we oriented our behavior and feelings to a social structure (two unmarried people) that did not in fact exist.

The structure of social life—which we take for granted most of the time—is very complex. We all occupy many different statuses (making up our status set), and for each status, we play a variety of

"*Son, I'd like to speak to you in my capacity as a father.*"
Drawing by Richter; © 1983, The New Yorker Magazine, Inc.

roles (a role set). Fathers play one role in relation to their sons, another in relation to their daughters, a third in relation to the children's mother, a fourth in relation to school teachers, and a host of others—with police officers if the children get into trouble, with aunts, uncles, and grandparents, or with parents of the children's playmates.

In addition, we often act under the influence of several statuses or roles at one time. Male patients may feel uncomfortable with female physicians, whereas many females prefer female physicians. Or, in a racist environment, a white patient might refuse the services of a nonwhite physician. To see the inherent complexity of our status and role sets helps us appreciate the inevitability of conflict, ambivalence, and ambiguity as we try to satisfy often conflicting expectations.

## Status Strain and Role Strain

Because we occupy many different statuses, each with its own roles and expectations, we frequently experience **status strain**—the difficulty in satisfying the role requirements of different statuses (Merton, 1968).

In 1982, for example, 59 percent of American working women were married, and 35 percent lived with children under the age of 18 (U.S. Census Bureau, 1983c). As a college professor, a woman is expected to devote her days to her work, while as a mother she is expected to care for her children—to stay home with them when they are sick and respond to emergencies at school. As a wife, she is expected to keep house for her husband and be supportive of him in his career. The three statuses—professor, mother, and wife—carry with them roles whose expectations can often clash and produce status strain within the status set.

Not all status strain is so clear-cut, for we are often unaware of statuses that produce conflict. People's expectations of police officers, for example, differ according to the officer's gender. When police officers are on duty, "police officer" is their **manifest status** because that is the status that explicitly defines their role set. Like everyone else, however, police officers occupy many other statuses—such as male, female, father, mother, husband, wife—that make up their status sets. When these statuses are socially defined as irrelevant in a particular social situation, they are called **latent statuses.** They are important because although they are formally defined as irrelevant, they often form a "background" to performance in a manifest status.

As a latent status, gender often strongly influences people's expectations. Women police officers may be barred from hazardous duty (hence denied a major avenue toward promotion). Or their male colleagues may expect them to be sexually responsive; if they refuse, they often suffer isolation and their colleagues' hostility and lack of cooperation on the job. In some occupations, a latent status is considered to be important enough to be incorporated into the manifest status, creating such statuses as "policewoman," "chairwoman," and "congresswoman."

Strain also occurs within a role set, for when we occupy a status, we must orient ourselves to a variety of role partners. The professor's students expect her to pay attention to them, to give them her time and energy; at the same time, other professors expect her to conduct research, serve on committees, and write books and articles. This kind of conflict, occurring within the role set attached to a single status, is called **role strain.**

**Responses to Strain**   There are many ways of lowering status and role strain (Merton, 1968). We are often more committed to one role than to another, for example, and act accordingly. In the case of the role strain just mentioned, the professor may choose to comply with the expectations that carry the more severe punishment if violated (losing a job is more serious than arousing the animosity of students).

We can also minimize strain by choosing statuses whose roles do not conflict with one another, as students do when they enroll in easy courses to balance their demanding ones. What can we do, however, when we cannot avoid occupying statuses whose roles conflict?

One tactic is to make our behavior in one of the conflicting roles less visible so that we can violate its expectations in greater safety. National politicians, for example, who must satisfy several conflicting constituencies, may express different opinions before different audiences, hoping that one will not hear about the message delivered to the other. For this to work, the actors must *insulate* their behavior from certain audiences; thus, extensive coverage of political campaigns by the mass media makes it difficult for politicians to resolve role conflicts in this way.

Another approach is to **segregate** statuses and roles so that specific individuals are not role partners in more than one of our roles (Goffman, 1961b). Surgeons do not perform operations on members of their own families—in other words, those who are role partners in family relationships are never role partners in surgical relationships. In this way, surgeons avoid the strain of making life-and-death decisions about the people closest to them.

The most drastic response to status and role strain is to abandon a status or role relationship altogether. Quitting a job, divorcing a spouse, dropping a course, and leaving school are frequent responses to conflicting role demands.

There are other sources of strain in role behavior in addition to status and role conflict. To perform a role, we must know what the expectations are and have the ability and motivation to meet them. Few experiences are as anxiety-producing as entering a status and not knowing what is expected of us. First-time parents, for example, are rarely prepared for the demands of child care and often spend a great deal of time and energy worrying about whether or not they are doing what they should ("Should I pick him up when he cries?"). For decades sellers of encyclopedias exploited parental anxieties by claiming that having this or that encyclopedia in the home was crucial for a child's education. (In the 1980s the pitch is the same but the product is different: now it is a home computer that is supposed to make all the difference in getting into a good college.)

Even when we meet the requirements for role performance, we may find the performance itself to be unbearably disagreeable. In combat zones, army doctors are exposed to seemingly endless streams of mutilated bodies day after day, and often use humor or other irrelevant talk in order to distract themselves from what they are doing (as beautifully portrayed in the television show *M\*A\*S\*H*). This is an example of **role distance**— the disassociation from a role—which is often the only way people can endure the strain inherent in the performance of certain roles (Goffman, 1961b).

Throughout our daily lives, we move from one role relationship to another, trying to achieve some sense of harmony and continuity among the roles we are expected to play. In a sense, our lives consist of this delicate juggling of expectations and choices, and how we go about it is a major concern of sociological analysis.

## Groups and Nongroups

The simplest social relationship is a pair of people— a **dyad**—who interact as the occupants of two statuses—for example, father and daughter—with their attached roles. As important as individuals are in our daily lives, we also pay an enormous amount of attention to collections of people—such as families, athletic teams, universities, and governments. These are more than collections of individuals, however, for we often think of and relate to them as if they exist apart from their members.

Families and athletic teams are **groups,** which sociologists define as two or more people who interact with one another in patterned ways and are identified as members by themselves and by others (Homans, 1950). A **subgroup** is simply a group that is part of a larger group. Members of a basketball team, for example, share a subculture whose ideas guide interaction among members both on

Groups—such as the Guardian Angels, whose members work to fight crime in many urban areas—sometimes rely on distinctive styles of dress to draw clear boundaries that both maintain their sense of themselves and identify them to others.

and off the court. The most important ideas are the expectations that govern the game itself—who does what in each situation—the values such as those placed on winning, and attitudes such as loyalty and affection toward the team and competitiveness if not hostility toward other teams. The team, in turn, may include subgroups such as first-stringers and second-stringers, veterans and rookies. Thus, we could not fully describe a group simply by listing the names of its members, for all groups are identified by their cultural and structural characteristics.

Not all collections of people are groups. **Social categories** are sets of people with one or more social statuses in common. Examples include adolescents, college students, lawyers, native Americans, and divorced people. As occupants of similar statuses, they often orient themselves to similar cultural ideas; but they usually do not identify themselves as a unit, nor do they interact with one another in regular, patterned ways, as do the members of a group.

An **aggregate** is simply a collection of people who happen to be in the same place at the same time; that is to say, they share the same situational status. A crowd of pedestrians, the audience at a rock concert, passengers on a bus, and the collection of automobile occupants driving on any highway are all examples of aggregates.

The distinction between groups, social categories, and aggregates is often unclear. "Groupness," for example, is a matter of degree, depending on how often and how much members interact with one another, how strong their sense of "we-ness" is, and how strongly a group's norms affect its members' behavior.

Groups are basic units of sociological analysis. We perform most of our roles in them, and they are important sources of both social control and conflict. In addition, the cultural and structural characteristics of many groups affect not only the lives of individuals, but the fate of entire societies. The relationships in a family, for example, affect not only the happiness and welfare of the individual members, but the ability of societies to teach children the values, norms, beliefs, and attitudes that regulate social life.

As we have seen, the concept of social structure thus includes three major aspects: (1) recurring patterns of expectation that apply to partici-

pants in social relationships, (2) patterns of expectation that apply to relationships among groups, and (3) the distribution of people among social statuses. At the heart of social structures are social relationships, which may extend from the simplest pair of interacting statuses to social categories, aggregates, or the largest, most complex group.

## Characteristics of Social Structures

While cultural ideas are the threads of social life, social structure is the fabric, the weaving together of beliefs, values, norms, and attitudes into a vast and fascinating tapestry of social relationships. Whether we are looking at a huge corporation or two people meeting on a street, we can describe social relationships in terms of nine basic structural characteristics that all have one thing in common: they describe the conditions and circumstances under which people interact with one another. We will look at each of these characteristics.

### Boundaries: Insiders and Outsiders

The **boundaries** of a social relationship specify who may occupy statuses within it. All groups, for example, have boundaries, for by merely saying "We are a group," members distinguish themselves from nonmembers.

The boundaries of social relationships differ in their **clarity**—how easily we can tell who occupies which statuses—and their **openness**—how easily people can occupy or leave social statuses. Table 4-1 shows how these two characteristics interact in describing social situations.

**The Clarity of Boundaries** The clarity of structural boundaries refers to how easy it is for people to identify others and their statuses—and thus plays an important part in social life. Military combat units, for example, must be able to tell the difference between "friend" and "foe" at every moment. They therefore maintain the clarity of their boundaries by wearing similar uniforms and using passwords. One of the most serious violations of the "rules of war" is to impersonate enemy soldiers by wearing their uniforms and blurring their group boundaries.

During the Battle of the Bulge in World War II, some German soldiers dressed in American uniforms, carefully copied American speech

**Table 4-1**

The structural boundaries of social situations differ in their degree of openness and clarity and can best be described in terms of the combination of these two characteristics.

|  | OPEN BOUNDARY | CLOSED BOUNDARY |
|---|---|---|
| **CLEAR BOUNDARY** | A sidewalk | The wall separating East and West Berlin<br>Football team during a game |
| **UNCLEAR BOUNDARY** | Mobs during riots | The population of U.S. citizens<br>College student<br>Terrorist group |

patterns, and even memorized facts about American cities and baseball teams (knowing that American soldiers frequently used such information to keep their group boundaries clear). As the clarity of group boundaries broke down, American soldiers did not know whom they could trust, and the result was enormous confusion and fear (Goolrich and Tanner, 1980).

Some groups deliberately draw vague boundaries in order to avoid offending potential members. Political parties, for example, use positions on political issues to define their boundaries. The candidates of these parties may try to be "all things to all people" by never taking a clear position on controversial issues, so that the vagueness of their boundaries can allow people with very different political opinions to vote for them.

Thus, the boundaries of social relationships are not fixed walls that never change; and they often depend on the social situation. In relation to civilians, for example, soldiers define the boundary of their group as "military vs. civilian"; but in relation to one another, they draw different lines, separating officers from enlisted men and women, "short-timers" from career soldiers, or military academy graduates from reserve officers (Kaplan, 1955).

Some groups misrepresent their boundaries in order to appear to conform to values and norms in the surrounding society. Employers who discriminate against women, nonwhites, and the elderly violate norms and values in the surrounding cul-

ture. To protect themselves, they may lie about the boundaries of their group, claiming, for example, that ability is the only requirement for becoming a member.

**The Openness of Boundaries** The clarity of boundaries is related to their degree of *openness*. While almost anyone can enter the status of "pedestrian" at any time, only a relative few can enroll

"Coming out" parties, in which daughters of prominent families are "presented" to high society, have long been used to maintain the exclusiveness of upper-middle- and upper-class membership.

## Voices: Belonging to the Old Boy Network

In 1979 Sir Anthony Blunt was revealed as the "fourth man" in that seemingly endless spy scandal which began at Cambridge University in the thirties when he, Guy Burgess, Donald Maclean and Kim Philby were undergraduates together.

After a long siege by the Press, Blunt consented to be interviewed by *The Times*, though, following protests, the *Guardian* was present too and television was allowed a ten minute postscript. At the *Times* building in Gray's Inn Road the unmasked traitor was given smoked trout, white wine and, considering the circumstances, a surprisingly easy time.

The question of how Blunt had been recruited by British intelligence was naturally one which exercised his interrogators.

"You went to France, came back, then you joined MI5?" he was asked. "How did you join? Did you apply, or was it arranged for you, or how?"

"Well," said Blunt, playing the half volley gently back to the bowler, "like all those . . . that kind of recruitment, it was done simply. Someone who was in MI5 recommended me. I was recommended."

Evidently this was something that those present, and by extension the readers of *The Times* and the *Guardian*, understood implicitly.

"The old boy network?"

"Yes," said Blunt.

And there the matter was allowed to drop. Everyone—Blunt, the interviewers, the world at large, would, it was assumed, know exactly what was being discussed.

The old boy network.

"Oh that! Of course. Enough said, old boy. Next question."

Source: Heald, *Old Boy Networks: Who We Know and How We Use Them*, 1984.

---

in prestigious universities and fewer still in their graduate schools.

Closed boundaries lie at the heart of discrimination based on such characteristics as race, ethnicity, religion, gender, and age. Many whites, for example, exclude nonwhites from neighborhoods and workplaces in the name of supporting group values, beliefs, and attitudes. Racism, therefore, is a matter both of culture *and* social structure. The forced integration of workplaces and schools is an attempt to open previously closed boundaries, in the hope that by altering the structure of race relations, the increased interaction that results will remove negative cultural beliefs and attitudes about people of different races.

Some groups close their boundaries in order to preserve their *idea* of themselves as a group. The "high society" of wealthy families, for example, strictly limits entry into their social circles. An elite position in society is an essential part of their social identity, and if "high society" is easily entered, it is, by definition, no longer an "elite" group.

### Structuring Time

Within the boundaries that regulate our entry into social statuses, a number of structural characteristics profoundly affect our social relationships and interaction. One of them is the way we **structure time.** In his novel *The Magic Mountain* (1924), Thomas Mann wrote:

> Time has no divisions to mark its passage, there is never a thunder-storm or blare of trumpets to announce the beginning of a new month or year. Even when a new century begins, it is only we mortals who ring bells and fire off pistols.

We "don't have time" to do things; we "make" time, "lose" time, "earn" it, "spend" it, and "waste" it as if it were a physical object. We eat not when we are hungry but when it is "time" for it, even though biologically we are more suited to a continuous string of nutritious snacks than to three meals a day. We go to bed at "bedtime" and—especially for children—whether or not we are tired may be irrelevant.

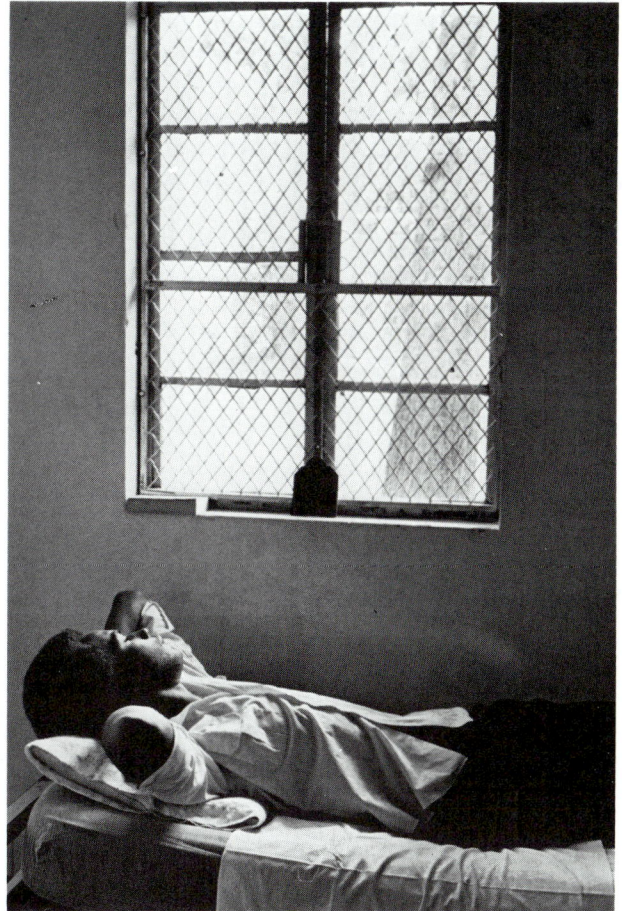

Time is a crucial element in the structuring of social life, whether it is the time that workers sell in return for wages or the time that is "served" by prison inmates.

Most workers return home at the same time, creating "rush hours." School children begin watching clocks in the early afternoon, and around 5:00 adults do, too. College students must learn and write and create works of art in 12 weeks, and at the middle and end of each semester, their behavior often borders on panic. At the stroke of midnight each December 31, millions of people feel as though they can leave the last 12 months behind them and start life anew.

Americans are famous as sticklers for precise schedules; consequently, they are continually feeling "pressed" for time, while Latin Americans are comparatively loose about time, not considering being half an hour late for an appointment to be worthy of comment. Americans routinely orient themselves to the "future," while many Arabs view anyone who tries to see into the future as slightly crazy (Hall, 1959, 1969).

As a cultural idea, time is thus used to structure our relationships with others (Sorokin and Merton, 1937), and it has important effects on social interactions (Lauer, 1981). We tend to make weaker commitments to relationships we expect to last a short time. Thus, we may feel we can afford to be rude to a waitress we will never see again; it is often difficult to arouse the interest of students in the long-term futures of their universities; and military draftees avoid "rocking the boat," because they know they will soon return to civilian life. In prisons, on the other hand, the most dangerous inmates are those with life sentences, for without hope of parole, they feel they have nothing to lose: there is no more time in the outside world to take away from them.

Like most aspects of social environments, the use of time to structure our lives and relationships with others is something we are unaware of until it is disrupted. When students go on long vacations, they often find themselves feeling lost without a schedule to adhere to, and the unemployed, accustomed to years of knowing what they will do in relation to a clock (however much they may have hated it), often feel suspended in time, one day drifting into the next. Our cultural sense of time is thus a vital aspect of the predictable structuring of our daily lives.

### Role Structures: Who's Who

In social relationships, people take on different roles that, together, form a **role structure.** There are many different kinds of roles, but there are two types that are particularly important in most groups—*task* roles and *expressive* roles (Bales, 1950). The first is oriented toward group tasks, ranging from assigning work in an office to being a "critic" who observes and comments on the group but rarely participates in any other way. Expressive roles involve the maintenance of group harmony, soothing frustrated and angry members, breaking tension with humor, or being a "scapegoat" who takes the blame for group failures (Hare, 1962, 1968).

Role structures describe divisions of labor in social relationships. In his study of maximum security prisons, Sykes (1958) identified a number of roles that organize life among prisoners. "Rats," for example, betray other prisoners by giving information to prison officials; "gorillas" use force to take what they want from other prisoners; and "merchants" take advantage of prisoners' misery by selling scarce goods.

Prisoners identified as "wolves" (or "jockers") aggressively seek homosexual contacts; "punks" submit to the aggression of "wolves" without showing any signs of femininity; and "fags" submit and openly assume a passive role that corresponds to cultural ideas of femininity. "Ball busters" openly challenge the authority of guards, and a "real man" is one who serves his time with quiet dignity, neither dominating nor submitting to other prisoners.

Role structures differ not only in content, but in complexity—the number of social statuses recognized in social interactions. When two people play a game of tennis, the social structure of the game is simple not only in the number of people involved, but in the number of statuses as well. Each occupies the status of "player," and one occupies the status of "server" while the other is "receiver."

When four people play doubles, however, we increase not only the number of people, but the number of statuses as well. In addition to those above, we now have the status of "partner," which significantly increases the complexity of the game's structure. The pattern of expectations becomes far more complex as partners orient themselves to each other as well as to their opponents.

While large groups or crowds are usually more complex than smaller ones, this is not always the case. A college lecture course may include hundreds of people, but since all except one of them occupy the same status ("student"), it has a relatively simple structure. A baseball team, on the other hand, has nine different positions. Such a complex structure brings with it a set of rules that define each status' relationships with all the others, and successful players are not simply those with the strongest arms or the sharpest eyes. They are the ones who can quickly and accurately "read" a situation in relation to the structure of the game and their position in it (a good outfielder does not stand there trying to figure out who to throw the ball to).

We can also use the concept of role structure to describe entire societies. Societies that existed some 10,000 years ago fed themselves by hunting small game and gathering food; they therefore tended to be very small. Their division of labor was simple and few people were specialists capable of performing only one particular job (Lenski, 1975).

In the 1980s, by contrast, there are cities with over 10 million inhabitants and the production of goods and services depends on complex social relationships among growers, makers, marketers, and consumers. The division of labor is highly complex and extremely specialized: skills that were shared broadly within smaller, simpler communities (such as how to tan an animal hide) are now possessed by a relative few.

## Voices: Who's Who in Prison Society

The guard who had escorted Fred's group from the clothing room to the cellblock disappeared, and the 8-wing officer took over. "If any of you don't have a mattress on your bunk, let me know," he said. Pointing in various directions, he read off the cell numbers. Fred's was number 1, A deck.

Eight-wing's A deck, the bottom tier on the west side, was "owned" by the bikers, the prison motorcycle club. A tough group of outlaw motorcyclists and hangers-on, the bikers claimed the tier's seventeen four-man cells as their territory. They decided who lived there and who should pay to live there.

Although prison rules prohibited the buying and selling of cell space, the guards felt powerless to enforce them. "There's no way we can prevent it," shrugged Lt. Joseph Colombo, the officer responsible for assigning cells. "That's the problem with multiple cells. You see, the guy who tells me about buying cells is liable to get his head cut off. If I knew about it, I could lock up the other three, but then the guy has to testify against them. If he does, he can't live out there." . . .

Colombo was convinced that inmates preferred to live with their own race, and he tried "to keep 'em happy." He went along with most inmate requests for cell changes except for those that looked coerced or exploitative. Accepting the facts of prison life, Colombo put punks in the same cells as their "jockers," aggressive, macho inmates who played the male role in homosexual relationships. "With these weak kids, one guy will get a hold of them and then the kid's going to be protected. There won't be ten to fifteen guys driving on the kid," he reasoned. When possible, he put the elderly, the lame, the retarded, and the mentally disturbed in one-man cells. When an inmate claimed that his life was in danger, Colombo had guards move the inmate and his possessions to asylum in protective custody.

When Fred meekly introduced himself at the barred door of cell number 1, he did not know that A deck was biker territory. "I guess I'm in here, guys," he said, peering into the dimly lit ten-by-twelve-foot cage.

Inside were two bunk beds, a table, two wooden stools, a sink, a lidless toilet, piles of clothes, an extra mattress flung on the floor, a wall papered with *Penthouse* pinups, a couple of pornographic books, a black-and-white television set, and two of the cell's three occupants. One of them was the cell's owner—Smiley, a stout, bearded biker wearing a plaid lumberman's jacket. Smiley owned the cell because he had lived in it the longest.

"We got a 'bro' coming out of the hole [an isolation cell]," Smiley said, objecting to Fred's assignment to his cell.

Fred hesitantly stepped inside. "I thought they told everybody that we'd be moving in," he apologized.

Grunting, Smiley motioned toward a littered upper bunk and told Fred that he could sleep there for the time being. Fred threw his bedroll on the bunk, ignoring the Harley-Davidson emblems and the pictures of spread-eagled women taped on the wall.

"There ain't nobody going to hassle you tonight. We'll get it straightened out," Smiley said. Fred stood next to the bunk, crossed his arms, and looked around the cell. After a while, Smiley introduced himself and, pointing toward the man sprawled on a lower bunk, he added, "That's Spike." . . .

Two more bikers appeared at the cell door asking Spike and Smiley to join them for dinner. They nodded slyly at Fred, as if to say, "Who's this chump?" Smiley handed Fred a padded jacket to cover up the blue overalls that spelled "fish" and indicated that he could come with them.

Trailing behind Smiley and the three other bikers, Fred plodded off to the south dining hall.

Source: McCoy, *Concrete Mama: Prison Profiles from Walla Walla*, 1981.

## Structures of Affection: Mapping Friendship

While role structures connect people in webs of shared expectations that vary in content and complexity, participants in social relationships also vary in how much they like one another, and this difference affects the way they play their roles. If you watch a group of people discussing a problem, you may notice that some members tend to "stick together," supporting one another's views and whispering quietly to one another. Sociologists have long noted the importance of these structures of affection—subgroups based on friendship—for they can profoundly affect group decisions and performance. How can we identify the existence of such groups within groups?

In 1943 J. L. Moreno developed a method called **sociometry** to identify subgroups. Asking members of test groups how much they liked or disliked each other, he "mapped" their answers in a diagram or **sociogram** that revealed the existence of subgroups based on affection. If we repeat his technique, using six students working together on a group project, what might the sociometric structure look like, and why is it important? The sociograms in Figure 4-3 show two possibilities. In this figure, a single arrow represents one member's affection for another, while an arrow pointing in both directions represents mutual liking between two members.

In (a), all the members like one another, so they will tend to be highly committed to the group and will try to avoid disagreement with one another in order to maintain unity and consensus.

In (b), on the other hand, the group has two subgroups, allowing the possibility of conflicts that could split the group (which member do you think is most likely to smooth relations between the two subgroups?). Opinions will be more varied since members run lower risks of feeling excluded; expressions of frustration and anger are more likely, and decisions may be harder to reach. Thus, sociograms are useful for understanding why groups operate in different ways, for they reveal that members frequently value subgroups more than the group.

In addition to their different structures of roles and affection, social relationships also differ in their distribution of power among the occupants of different statuses.

## Power Structures

**Power** may be defined as the possibility of imposing one's will upon the behavior of others in spite of their resistance (Weber, 1925; Wrong, 1980). Sociology focuses on how such possibilities are distributed among status occupants and how this affects interactions among individuals.

In social relationships, power structures vary both in the degree to which power is evenly distributed among status occupants, and whether or

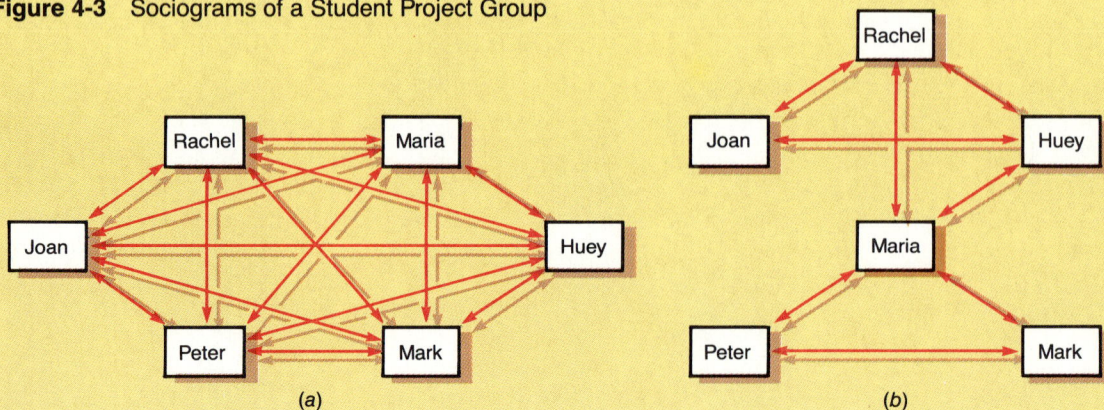

■ **Figure 4-3**  Sociograms of a Student Project Group

Presidents have authority only as long as they occupy the office of president. Richard Nixon resigned the presidency in 1974. While Nixon was flying home to California, Gerald Ford took the oath of office; at that moment Richard Nixon was transformed from the most powerful man in the world to someone with no more authority than any other private citizen.

not power is distributed according to norms. When power is distributed evenly, the power structure is **democratic** (or egalitarian), and as power is increasingly concentrated in the hands of a few people, the structure becomes more **authoritarian.** Most social relationships fall between these two extremes, with some people having more power than others but none having complete control.

Power assigned according to norms is called **authority,** and a group that distributes power in this way has a **leadership structure.** Corporations, military units, and governments all have leadership structures based on authority. It is important to note that power and leadership are not always the same, for leadership represents authority that is supported by group norms and accepted by members. Power, on the other hand, may result

from a person's expertise, persuasiveness, control over valued resources, or physical ability to coerce others. Airplane hijackers, for example, who threaten to blow up an airplane unless their demands are met, have a great deal of power but no authority whatsoever. Thus, while "having power" is sometimes a personal characteristic, "being a leader" is always a social status under group control. For this reason, leadership tends to be more stable over time than personal power, and leadership structures are one of the most enduring characteristics of groups.

Some groups have a **pluralistic structure** in which the right to make decisions is divided among different specialists. Families in which spouses divide task and expressive roles are typical of groups that rely on pluralistic leadership (Bales and Slater, 1955). Groups that exist to accomplish specific goals, however, such as a jury, usually have a single leader who controls group interactions (Bales, 1954).

Many groups have two power structures: a leadership structure defined by norms, and informal structures reflecting the ability of individuals and subgroups to control the group. An army combat platoon's leadership structure, for example, is defined by army regulations; but in combat situations, the greater knowledge and experience of some members may also produce an informal power structure.

A lieutenant is the platoon leader, but his sergeants are often more experienced and command greater loyalty and trust from combat soldiers. Thus, a lieutenant may allow sergeants to overrule his decisions, giving them greater power than the leadership structure calls for. In extreme cases, when lieutenants refuse to share authority with more competent subordinates, enlisted men have murdered their leader rather than suffer from his mistakes in combat situations. Even when lieutenants do share power, of course, they remain responsible for the actions of their men in combat, so the relationship between lieutenants and sergeants is delicate, and requires them to use the informal power structure in order to survive without threatening the leadership structure.

Just as power is socially distributed among status occupants, so are other valued resources such as wealth and **prestige,** the respect individuals ac-cord one another in their relationships (Chapter 11). While power and prestige have similar bases, they are not the same, for people can be respected without having correspondingly high power (Table 4-2). This is true, for example, of England's royal family, spouses of U.S. presidents, and former U.S. presidents.

Nonetheless, power and prestige generally do go together (Markovsky, Smith, and Berger, 1984; Pellegrin, 1953). In Strodtbeck, James, and Hawkins' (1957) study of juries, for example, men and those with more respected occupations not only exercised greater power as jurors, but received higher levels of respect. They were given more opportunities to talk, and their opinions were taken more seriously by others.

The concept of social structure thus describes how roles, affection, power, and prestige are distributed in social relationships, and these structural aspects of social life create **communication structures** that determine how frequently and extensively the occupants of different statuses interact with one another.

## Communication Structures

When four roommates sit down to decide how to arrange furniture, an important characteristic of their interaction is that each person is able to talk with all the others. The pattern resembles a circle in which each person is connected to everyone else. But when they meet with a dean to resolve a dispute among them, the pattern changes: comments are directed mostly to the dean, who acts like the hub of a wheel, holding the four "spokes" together and coordinating their interaction. In armies, the patterns—called a "chain of command"—are dramatically different: generals talk only with high-level officers, and enlisted personnel rarely interact with anyone other than comrades or immediate superiors. Such patterns of communication affect both the performance of groups and the lives of their members (Bavelas, 1950).

In an experiment, Leavitt (1951) gave five-man groups a simple problem to solve: each man had a card with a list of symbols, only some of which were on every card. The task was to find out which symbols were held in common by all members of the group. The men sat around a table, separated from each other by partitions, and communicated by passing written notes through slots in the partitions. By using different arrangements of partitions, Leavitt created four different structures of communication (Figure 4-4).

Leavitt found that the "wheel" structure produced correct answers more quickly than any other, whereas the "circle" was the least efficient. People who occupied central positions (Bill in the "Y" and the "wheel," and Mike in the "chain") tended to emerge as leaders and enjoyed the task the most. He also found that the most efficient groups were the least enjoyed by their members.

Other researchers (Shaw, 1954) repeated Leavitt's experiment using different kinds of tasks and found that with complex problems having more than one solution the resulting group effi-

**Table 4-2**

As these examples show, power and prestige often go together, but not always.

|  | RELATIVELY HIGH PRESTIGE | RELATIVELY LOW PRESTIGE |
|---|---|---|
| **RELATIVELY HIGH POWER** | President of the United States<br>Army general | Blackmailer<br>Airplane hijacker<br>Unpopular dictator |
| **RELATIVELY LOW POWER** | College professor<br>Minister<br>Honorary degree recipient<br>Nobel Prize winner | Someone on welfare<br>Assembly-line worker<br>A child |

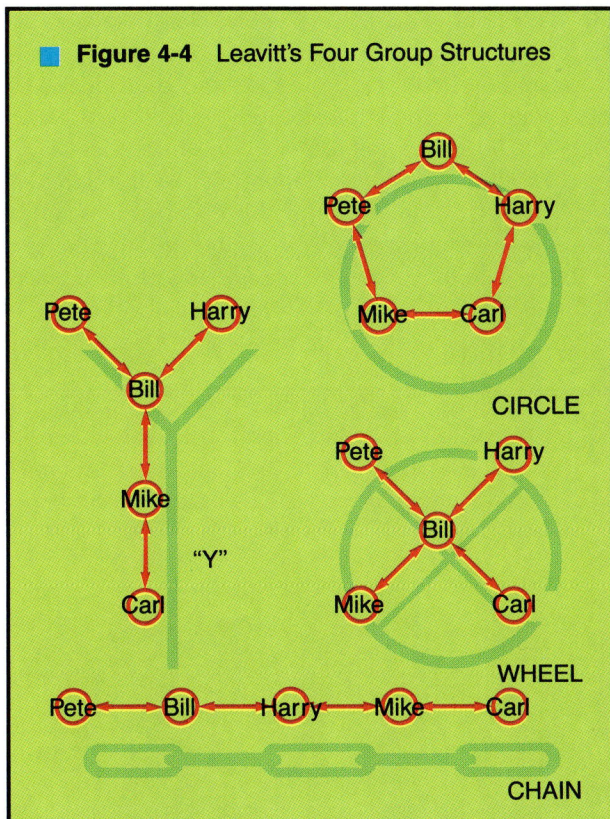

**Figure 4-4** Leavitt's Four Group Structures

ciencies were reversed, with the circle reaching a consensus faster than all the others and the wheel finishing in last place.

Students thus find that lectures (wheels) are boring but efficient ways to pass on large quantities of information, whereas discussion groups (circles) are more enjoyable but often frustratingly inefficient ("We go round and round and never get anywhere"). Complex issues are difficult to discuss in wheel structures, while brainstorming to solve a mathematical problem is fast and efficient. Hence the saying, "A camel is a horse put together by a committee."

Dictatorial, totalitarian governments are structure as "wheels," enabling them to make decisions more efficiently than more democratic "circles" such as the United States Congress, whose decisions are reached only by consensus and whose members are open to the influence of lobbyists. The slow pace of legislation in the United States is due to more than the personalities of legislators: the structure itself is inefficient.

## Primary and Secondary Relationships

**Primary relationships** are the kind we find among friends and within families. Such relationships, in which the welfare of individuals is more important than the achievement of goals, are valued for their own sake. They endure even when circumstances change, and they involve many different aspects of people's lives. Primary ties are based on affection and involve frequent face-to-face interaction (Cooley, 1909). We do not expect to gain from such relationships: we would not say, "She's my friend because she tunes my car and lends me money." It would be more accurate to say, "She tunes my car and lends me money because we're friends."

**Secondary relationships** focus on specific goals that are valued more highly than the welfare of individuals. They involve only the parts of members' lives that are related to achieving those goals, are based on rational considerations of self-interest rather than feelings of affection, and are usually short-lived. Interaction in secondary relationships is limited to specific times and places and is often impersonal. This is the kind of relationship found most often in complex societies such as our own—buyers with sellers, teachers with students, bosses with employees, judges with lawyers, nurses with patients.

The concepts of primary and secondary relations represent what Weber called "ideal types"; "ideal," that is, not in the sense of being desirable, but as purely theoretical. Thus, most relationships contain both primary and secondary characteristics—police officers work together not only to achieve specific, limited goals (such as earning a living and enforcing the law) but, often, because they like one another.

Expectations in both primary and secondary relationships are defined by cultural norms, but sociologists make an important distinction between informal relationships (with norms that are flexible and implicit) and formal relationships (with norms that rigidly and explicitly define expectations).

## Formal and Informal Relationships

**Informal relationships**—such as those among friends—are based on loosely defined, flexible norms that are always open to negotiation. **Formal relationships,** on the other hand, are regulated by clearly stated norms that rigidly prescribe the powers and responsibilities associated with each social status. Such relationships are found in secondary groups—such as those found in most business offices—whose goals require careful control and coordination of people's behavior. Especially when groups are large and members specialize in a variety of tasks, groups cannot depend on members to negotiate the terms of their relationships as they go along (Simmel, 1950).

Suppose 30 people form a group in order to improve conditions in their neighborhood. At first, their group is informal. Without clearly stated expectations, the members frequently interrupt one another and jump from one subject to another with little sense of direction. Sooner or later, someone says, "We've got to get organized," which means "We've got to create a structure that everyone can refer to in order to know what to do next." To do this, they first list their goals and then deal with several important questions.

Who will do what? Who will make decisions? How often will they meet and who will be eligible for membership? Will they have a president and, if so, with what term of office and what authority? How will they collect, spend, and keep track of funds? Does the treasurer need to call a meeting to vote on spending $1.95 for stamps? Or $50 to rent a car?

As these kinds of decisions are made, the group creates a formal structure that is beyond the personal control of any of its members. In its most highly developed form, such a group is a *bureaucracy*.

The bureaucratic organization of universities usually means that activities such as registration involve so many forms and formalities that the paperwork seems more important than the needs of individual human beings.

**Bureaucracy**  In the 1800s, most elementary and secondary schools in the United States had only one teacher who was responsible for everything that happened in the school, from deciding what and how to teach to disciplining students. There were no principals, vice-principals, secretaries, school nurses, or heads of departments.

By comparison, the twentieth-century school is a **bureaucracy,** a complex set of formal, secondary relationships governed by explicitly stated, rigid norms (Weber, 1922a, 1922b). In a bureaucracy, people specialize in narrowly defined tasks, and their roles are rigidly defined by rules and regulations. Teachers, for example, no longer decide what they will teach or, in many schools, *how* they will teach. Jobs once performed by a single teacher arc now divided among a large number of specialists, from the lowest clerk to the most powerful principal.

In a bureaucracy, the occupancy of social statuses is regulated by rigid norms. Students are required by law to attend school and cannot graduate unless they fulfill specific academic requirements. Teachers must be certified by the state in order to work, and the conditions under which they are promoted or fired are clearly spelled out.

Power is distributed in a hierarchical pattern from the principal at the top to the students at the bottom. Written records are kept on every aspect of school life, from the test scores of students to school budgets and teacher performance; and specialists—administrators—do nothing but manage the intricate web of relationships among the various statuses and ensure that everything works as it is supposed to.

One of the most important characteristics of bureaucracies is that decisions are supposed to be based on rational considerations of the best interests of the group, rather than on the personal feelings and welfare of individuals. American schools, for example, commonly promote students to the next higher grade whether or not they have mastered basic skills in reading, writing, and mathematics (National Commission on Excellence in Education, 1983). This is clearly not in the individual student's best interests, but from the school's point of view, it promotes efficiency by ridding the school of students who do not learn easily.

While bureaucracies are relatively efficient producers and distributors of goods and services, their higher efficiency comes at a price (see Chapter 8). People tend to feel lost and invisible, participating in something so complex that they are easily kept from understanding how it works. College students often feel as though they are known more by numbers than by ñames; workers are easily laid off by people they have never met—and then replaced by other workers who are equally unknown as individuals with names and faces. The productive work of the office and the assembly line is split into increasingly specialized tasks performed in efficient, yet impersonal settings. Walk through the offices of any large corporation, and you will see endless rows of desks that, save for a small picture or a flower, are exactly the same.

Bureaucratic norms require people to respond to others as "cases"—not as people with individual needs, desires, and circumstances—and this both solves and creates problems. On the one hand, formal relationships allow us to disclaim personal responsibility for the consequences of our behavior, so long as we strictly adhere to the rules. This, however, requires us to distance ourselves from other people in a way that may make us feel more like machines than human beings.

Consider the example of Marty, who applies for unemployment compensation and is told by the claims processor, Charles, that due to a technicality, he does not qualify for benefits. "If it were up to me," Charles says, "I'd give you the benefits, but the rule is clear. I haven't got a choice in the matter. It's nothing personal; I'm just doing my job."

Marty tries to make eye contact with Charles, to arouse feelings of sympathy and make it a personal matter between the two of them. Charles, however, sticks to the rules, acting not as a feeling individual but as a status occupant who has no personal control over his clearly and rigidly defined role. Marty wants Charles to treat him as an individual with feelings, to relate to him on a personal level that calls upon his human capacity for empathy and compassion. Charles, on the other hand, uses his status and its role requirements as a shield against personal involvement, yet he cannot help feeling some responsibility.

## Institutions: Enduring Social Structures

As we have seen, the characteristics of social structures strongly influence the way individuals expe-

Institutions such as families, schools, courts, and churches differ from other social structures in that they are intended to be enduring blueprints that show us how to accomplish important social goals, from the raising and educating of children to the settling of legal disputes and understanding the unknown.

rience most of their lives—the bonds they feel with their work and with the lives of other people. Although all social structures are patterns of expectation based on underlying beliefs, values, norms, and attitudes, in some cases a social relationship is so important to a group or society that it is preserved as an enduring pattern of expectations—in other words, the relationship becomes an *institution*. An **institution** can be defined as an enduring set of cultural ideas and social relationships organized to accomplish important social goals. Thus, when a social relationship or set of relationships occupies a relatively permanent place in a social environment, it has been "institutionalized."

All societies, for example, rely on the institution of the family to produce, socialize, protect, and care for new members. In many societies, schools are the institutions that provide additional training; economic institutions produce and distribute goods and services; political institutions distribute and apply collective power; and religious institutions help members of society grapple with important questions about morality, life after death, the causes of mysterious happenings, and the meaning of life itself.

It is important to point out that, unlike families or schools, social institutions do not always correspond to groups. Our political institutions, for example, include not only groups such as "the Senate budget committee," but also ways of doing things that have an enduring place in our political system. No one has the right to prevent eligible voters from casting their ballots, and no one has the right to observe voters to see whom they are voting for. These procedures clearly define social relationships in political activities, and are as much a part of "political institutions" as the White House staff, the House of Representatives, the Cabinet, or a town council.

Institutions are designed to accomplish goals that societies define as important and continuing; each existed long before our births and will persist long after we die. While their cultural and structural characteristics change and vary from one society to another, institutions themselves exist as long as the needs they meet persist. The family exists in all known societies, for example, while schools are peculiar to those societies that require (and can af-

ford) specialized, advanced training for their members.

Just as individuals make a variety of choices within the general limitations of social environments, however, individual families vary from the general institutional guidelines laid down by a particular society. As each of us participates in family life, we do so in relation to cultural "models" that indicate how family relationships should be structured and what goals families should pursue. Thus, institutions are social "blueprints" that describe how societies organize themselves to accomplish important goals.

The importance of institutions lies in their relative permanence. Whereas friends can change their expectations of one another and bureaucrats can alter their rigid rules at the stroke of a pen, an institution imposes expectations that are far more difficult to change, for it represents deeply imbedded ideas about how certain social relationships ought to be structured. Thus, bureaucrats might explain a particular rule as "most efficient"; but, if we are asked why American families usually consist of a mother, father, and their children, we would tend to reply, "Because that's what a family *is*."

The preceding sections describe characteristics of social structures that influence everyday interactions among status occupants, from the simple building blocks of status and role to groups and their boundaries; the structures of roles, power, prestige, friendship, and communication; and the types of relationships that tie people together—primary and secondary, formal and informal. Such patterns, however, are themselves embedded in other patterns that describe social environments on a larger scale.

## Structures within Structures

The example that begins this chapter illustrates the fact that most cultures distinguish between "healers" and "patients" and regulate their interactions through social roles. This role relationship, however, exists in a larger structural context that includes *the relative numbers of people who occupy particular social statuses.*

For example, small societies might have only one healer, whose monopoly on a vital social status brings with it great power (you could not afford to

**Table 4-3**

Distribution of the U.S. Population by Age and the
Number of People 20–64 Years Old for Each
Person 65 or Older (1850 to 1981)

| YEAR | LESS THAN 15 | 20–64 | 65 AND OVER | RATIO OF THOSE 20–64 TO THOSE 65 OR OVER |
|---|---|---|---|---|
| 1850 | 42% | 35% | 2% | 17 |
| 1900 | 34% | 50% | 4% | 12 |
| 1940 | 25% | 59% | 7% | 8 |
| 1960 | 31% | 52% | 9% | 6 |
| 1981 | 22% | 58% | 11% | 5 |

Sources: For 1850, 1900, 1940, and 1960: U.S. Census Bureau, 1975a. For 1981: U.S. Census Bureau, 1983c.

be on the wrong side of the tribal healer). In more developed countries, on the other hand, there are thousands of doctors; if you dislike one, you can always find another. Thus, the power associated with the social status "doctor," depends in part on how many doctors are competing with one another. It also depends on the number of available patients relative to the number of doctors: the greater the scarcity of patients, the more eager doctors will be to please. The number of status occupants is an important element of large-scale (or macro) social structures, and profoundly influences the relationships among individuals found in the small-scale (or micro) structures of everyday life.

The distribution of people by age is also important in larger structures (see Table 4-3). In 1850 only 2 percent of Americans were 65 or older, whereas 35 percent were in the more economically productive age-group of 20 to 64. Thus, there were roughly 17 workers to support each elderly citizen in 1850. By 1981, however, the percentage of Americans 65 or older had increased by almost six times to 11 percent, but the percentage of those 20 to 64 years old had increased only to 58 percent. In 1981, then, there were only *five* workers to support each elderly person.

There have been dramatic changes at the lower end of the age scale as well: the percentage

of Americans who were under the age of 15 dropped from 42 percent in 1850 to 25 percent in 1940 and, with the post–World War II baby boom, jumped to 31 percent in 1960. By 1981 it had declined to only 22 percent of the population (Table 4-3).

The effects of such changes have been clear in recent years. The Social Security system is in serious long-term trouble because an ever larger number of people are depending on the labor of an ever smaller number of workers. The elderly, worried over their declining security, have organized politically (into groups such as the Gray Panthers and the American Association for Retired Persons). In addition, the baby boom that followed World War II resulted in the construction of thousands of public schools and an enormous increase in the demand for teachers; and the subsequent decline in the school-age population closed hundreds of these schools (some of which, ironically, are now used as social centers for the elderly) and produced massive unemployment among teachers with all the resulting hardship for individuals and families.

Such long-term structural shifts illustrate the ever changing, fluid nature of social environments. They also illustrate that although social structures are the major source of cohesion in social life, they can produce disruptive change and conflict as well.

## Summary

1. The concept of social structure draws attention to the recurring patterns of relationships through which people live their lives and perform roles as occupants of social statuses. Whether the term is used when considering expectations between lovers, relationships among groups, or the distribution of income, power, and prestige in a society, social structure refers to patterns that are more than a sum of their parts and that exist independently of us as individuals even though we participate in and help perpetuate them.

2. Social statuses and their associated roles are at the heart of any social structure. Our status sets include statuses that are ascribed, achieved, or temporary (situational or transitional), and for each status we occupy, we are expected to perform a variety of roles (the role set) in relation to different role partners. In each case we must define the situation in order to know which role we are expected to perform.

3. Statuses and roles often subject us to strain—role strain when we have difficulty satisfying the demands associated with a role, and status strain when the roles associated with two or more statuses have expectations that conflict with one another. The roles we are expected to perform in a situation are called manifest, whereas those that are defined as socially irrelevant are called latent, and conflict often occurs between manifest and latent statuses. A master status is the most important status in a person's status set.

4. There are a variety of ways to reduce status and role strain. We may insulate our role behavior from those whose expectations we fail to live up to or we may make sure that we do not perform two different roles in relation to the same person. When role performance is unpleasant, we may use role distance to avoid being aware of what we are doing.

5. The simplest unit of sociological analysis is a dyad, a pair of people who interact as the occupants of two statuses. Sociologists, however, also pay attention to larger units: groups, whose members share a common culture, interact with one another, and identify themselves as members; social categories, whose members may have no more in common than a social status (such as race or occupation); and aggregates, which are simply a collection of people who happen to occupy the same temporary status at the same time, such as an audience.

6. The patterns that make up social structures have many characteristics that affect what goes on within them. Group boundaries differ in their clarity and openness. Time structures affect both how long relationships last and how we feel and behave in them.

7. Role structures differ in their content and their complexity. Large groups are usually but not always more complex than small ones, and in complex structures it is particularly important for everyone involved to have a clear idea of what is supposed to happen.

8. Sociometry uses sociograms to map the ties of affection among members of a group. These ties are often the basis for subgroups, which may be sources of conflict within a group.

9. Groups distribute a number of important rewards and resources. The most sociologically important of these are power, prestige, and wealth. Unlike personal power, which is based on individual characteristics, authority is power assigned according to norms, and results in a leadership structure. Authority is evenly distributed in democratic structures; it is shared among several specialists in pluralistic structures; and it is concentrated in the hands of a few people in authoritarian structures.

10. Communication structures determine who interacts with whom and have important effects on the behavior and experience of group members and the effectiveness of groups themselves.

11. There are several kinds of social relationships. Primary relationships, such as friendships, are valued for their own sake, and involve many aspects of our lives. Secondary relationships, such as those between clerks and customers, focus on particular goals and tend to be more impersonal. Informal relationships are regulated by loosely defined norms, while the norms in formal relationships are clearly defined. In their most developed form, formal relationships constitute a bureaucracy.

**12.** Social institutions are enduring sets of cultural ideas and social relationships organized to accomplish important social goals. They include arrangements such as the family as well as those that focus on education, economic activity, politics, and religion.

**13.** Relationships among individuals (found in micro structures) exist within larger social structures called macro structures. A primary element of macro structures is the relative numbers of people who occupy particular social statuses. The distribution of people by age or occupation, for example, is an important aspect of macro social structures.

## Key Terms

aggregate  94
boundary  94
    clarity  94
    openness  94
bureaucracy  105
communication structure  102
definition of the situation  91
dyad  93
formal relationship  103
group  93
    subgroup  93
informal relationship  103
power  100
    authority  101
    leadership structure  101
        authoritarian  101
        democratic  101
        pluralistic  101
prestige  101
primary relationship  103
role  90
    role distance  93
    role partner  91
    role performance  90
    role segregation  92
    role set  91
    role strain  92
    status segregation  92
    status strain  91
role structure  99
secondary relationship  103

social category  94
social institution  108
social status  88
    achieved status  89
    ascribed status  89
    latent status  92
    manifest status  92
    master status  90
    status set  90
    temporary status  89
        situational status  89
        transitional status  89
social structure  88
sociometry  100
    sociogram  100
time structure  96

## Recommended Readings

BIDDLE, B. J., and THOMAS, E. J. (Eds.). (1979). *Role theory: Concepts and research.* New York: Wiley. A rich collection of articles dealing with many aspects of social structure including statuses, roles, and conflict.

BLAU, P. M. (Ed.). (1975). *Approaches to the study of social structure.* New York: Free Press. A demanding but highly informative set of articles on various aspects of social structure, written by leading sociologists.

COSER, L. A. (Ed.). (1975). *The idea of social structure: Papers in honor of Robert K. Merton.* New York: Harcourt Brace Jovanovich. A collection of essays that explore the concept of social structure, from the complexity of roles and the uses of power to the present status of functional theory in sociology.

GOFFMAN, E. (1961). *Encounters.* Indianapolis, IN: Bobbs-Merrill. A pair of essays, the second of which focuses on role distance as a means of resolving role conflict, especially in high-stress situations such as hospital operating rooms.

LAUER, R. H. (1981). *Temporal man: The meaning and uses of social time.* New York: Praeger. A look at an aspect of social structure that we rarely think of as social at all.

MERTON, R. K. (1968). *Social theory and social structure* (revised and enlarged edition). New York: Free Press. Perhaps the classic statement on the importance of social structure as a concept in sociology.

ZURCHER, L. A. (1983). *Social roles: Conformity, conflict, and creativity.* Beverly Hills, CA: Sage Publications. An entertaining look at the creative ways in which we perform roles while trying to maintain some sense of personal autonomy.

# CHAPTER 5

# Population and Ecology

In 1839 Fanny Calderon de la Barca traveled to Mexico City, and as her coach came within view of the Valley of Mexico, she remembered lines from Robert Southey's long romantic tribute to the city:

Thou art beautiful.
Queen of the valley! Thou art beautiful!
Thy walls, like silver, sparkle in the sun.

Later that night, she wrote to a friend:

At length we arrived at the heights on which we look down upon the superb Valley of Mexico, celebrated in all parts of the world, with its framework of magnificent mountains, its snow-capped volcanoes, great lakes, and fertile plains. (Both quotations in Fisher and Fisher, 1966, p. 87)

Robert Southey and Fanny Calderon would hardly recognize Mexico City now. It is rapidly becoming not only the largest but the poorest city in the world. In 1983, 16 million people were living in Mexico City, and by the year 2000 an esti-

To understand how Mexico City, a city celebrated for its beauty, was transformed into a polluted "blueprint for hell," we have to pay attention to the physical and social factors represented by POET.

mated 31 million—more than the number found in many *nations*—will be living there. Half of its adults have no jobs, there is not enough water to drink, and most of its residents live in slums. Rush-hour traffic lasts from 6 A.M. to 10 P.M.; and the air is so polluted with dust, smoke from burning garbage dumps, and automobile exhaust that rarely is there a day when one can see the beautiful mountains that surround the city (on some days visibility is less than two blocks).

Old Mexicans still remember spending afternoons in nearby fields and rivers within view of Popocatepetl, the snow-capped volcano. Many of today's schoolchildren must play in dusty streets or open sewers, and they learn about Popocatepetl from books. (Riding, 1983, p. 12)

What happened to transform the "Queen of the Valley" into a congested, polluted center of poverty that one Mexico City doctor described as a "blueprint for hell"?

To answer this question about Mexico City—and many other cities around the world—we have to understand the ecological perspective, which focuses on how populations adapt to physical environments and how these adaptations affect social life. This chapter describes four concepts that define the ecological perspective and illustrates some of the ways in which ecology helps to explain both how societies change and why so many societies are in a state of crisis in the 1980s.

## POET

The easiest way to remember the concepts that define the ecological perspective is to use the acronym POET, which stands for *population, organization, environment,* and *technology* (Duncan, 1961; Duncan and Schnore, 1959).

In this chapter we will define a **population** as the people who share a geographic territory, and a **society** as a population whose members share a cultural identity and way of life, and who interact in patterned ways. **Demography** is the study of the size, growth, composition, and distribution of human populations: why birth and death rates rise and fall, why populations are distributed over the land in particular ways, and why people migrate (move from one place to another). The inhabitants of Mexico City are a population, and we cannot understand the problems of Mexico City without

As we will see in this and later chapters, the level of technology in a society affects everything from the amount of food that can be produced to the organization of work and the extent of social inequality.

understanding how so many people came to live in one place. A major part of this involves understanding the society of which Mexico City is a part.

**Ecology** is the study of how *populations*—and societies, in particular—adapt to physical *environments:* climate, the shape of the land, and the availability of natural resources. This adaptation is accomplished in two ways. First, populations *organize* themselves in different ways. Hunter-gatherer societies, for example, have relatively simple divisions of labor based on gender and age and do not grow their own food. Industrial societies, on the other hand, have complex divisions of labor and produce goods on a massive scale. Second, societies adapt by using **technology**—the accumulated cultural knowledge of how to use physical environments. The wheel, the horse-drawn plow, computers, automobiles, electricity, telephones,

nuclear energy, and the full range of scientific ideas are all cultural adaptations to physical environments.

This chapter is about the four ecological concepts summed up in POET, which focus on the relationship between the physical conditions of human life and the social environments in which people live. They are useful for understanding the large populations of cities, countries, and the world. They also help us understand the tiny populations of families, school classes, and work groups, all of which profoundly affect our lives.

## Population and Demography

Why have conditions in Mexico City deteriorated so much since Fanny Calderon's visit in 1839? From a population perspective, the problems of Mexico, Mexico City, and much of the world are caused by the size, rate of growth, age characteris-

**Table 5-1**

Crude Birth Rates in Major World Regions, Early 1980s

| REGION | CRUDE BIRTH RATE[1] |
| --- | --- |
| Europe | 14 |
| North America | 15 |
| Soviet Union | 20 |
| Oceania | 21 |
| Asia | 29 |
| Latin America | 31 |
| Africa | 45 |
| World | 28 |

Source: Population Reference Bureau, 1984.

[1]Births per 1,000 people.

tics, and physical distribution of populations. The following sections deal with the central questions of demography: what causes rates of birth, death, and migration to rise and fall?

## Births: Adding People

To survive, every society must reproduce its members, but the *rate* of reproduction in different societies varies enormously. In the early 1980s the birth rate in Mexico (32 births per 1,000 people) was twice that in the United States (Population Reference Bureau, 1984). On a larger scale, birth rates in Africa are roughly three times as high as those in North America and Europe, and rates in Latin America and Asia are about twice as high (Table 5-1). Birth rates also vary within societies. In the United States, for example, people with high education, occupation, and income tend to have fewer children than those who occupy lower positions. Whites generally have fewer children than nonwhites, and birth rates tend to be higher in rural areas than in cities (U.S. Census Bureau, 1979b). From a sociological perspective, such vari-

ations occur because like any other behavior, the decision to have or not to have babies is affected by the ideas and socially structured relationships that make up social environments (Davis and Blake, 1956; Tilly, 1978b).

Birth rates are much higher in Mexico than in the United States for a variety of reasons that include differences in culture and social structure. Mexican women are expected to marry and marry young. If women marry young and quickly remarry after the death of a husband, they are more likely to become pregnant than if they remain single or marry at older ages.

Like most people, Mexican parents prefer male children, in part because the family line is traced through men (see Williamson, 1976). This value encourages higher birth rates, for in order to be sure of having a son, parents whose first children are girls must keep trying (Freedman, Freedman, and Whelpton, 1960). Like people in many less-developed countries, Mexicans also value large families, in part because societies that rely more on manual labor than on sophisticated technology can use children to help produce goods. In industrial societies, on the other hand, children

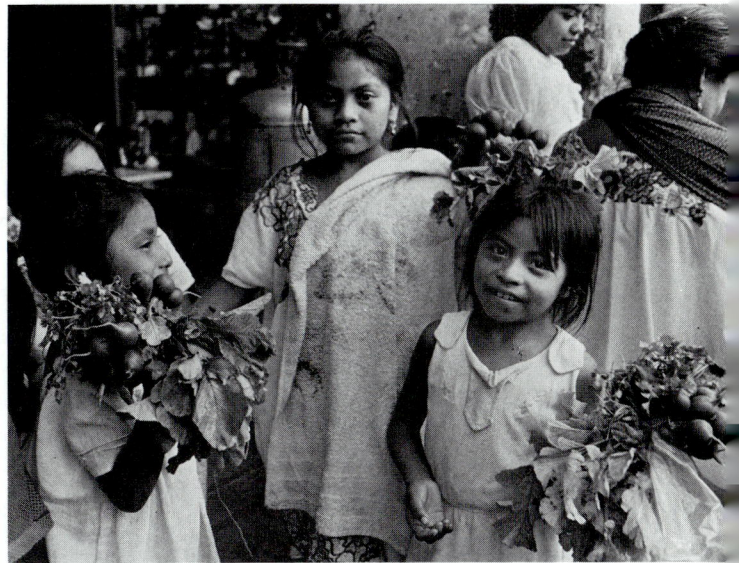

In nonindustrial societies such as Mexico, children have economic value because there are many relatively unskilled jobs they can perform, from shining shoes to selling vegetables in the market.

can perform few productive tasks and are more likely to be seen by parents as economic liabilities. As we will see, it is no surprise that industrialization has brought with it lower birth rates in many countries, including our own.

Mexicans have more children than Americans not only because they want more, but also because their children have a smaller chance of surviving childhood. The **infant mortality rate** is the number of infants under the age of 1 who die each year for every 100,000 births in that year. The infant mortality rate in Mexico is five times that in the United States (Population Reference Bureau, 1984). This means that if Mexican parents want to have four children and expect some of their children to die during childhood, they may compensate by having five or six.

Birth rates are also affected by social policies that encourage or discourage childbearing. During this century, Germany, Japan, France, Brazil, Argentina, Rumania, and the Soviet Union have used rewards ranging from medals to cash payments to encourage parents to have large families.

Norms have also been used to restrict or prohibit the use of contraceptives in many of these countries—as well as among Catholics in many societies (Eldridge, 1968; Schroeder, 1974). Catholic norms forbid the use of contraceptives. As American Catholics have increasingly violated those norms, their birth rates have become very similar to those of non-Catholics (Westoff and Bumpass, 1973).

The governments of China and India have deliberately promoted low birth rates for over a decade. India uses massive advertising campaigns and financial incentives to encourage couples to limit their families to two children—but such programs have had little measurable effect on birth rates. China, on the other hand, has much greater control over its people, and has recently introduced laws that limit each family to one child (O'Callaghan, 1983). Women who become pregnant with their second child are expected to have abortions, and couples who already have more than one child are expected to undergo sterilization.

Given the enormous size of the Chinese population, however—over a billion people—it re-

Many countries, such as China and India, have tried to lower birth rates by actively promoting small families as a cultural ideal.

mains to be seen if the government will be able to enforce its new policy. To this problem must be added the fact that children have economic value in less developed societies, particularly in rural areas where birth rates tend to be relatively high. Children are able to perform farm work from a fairly early age, and it is likely that the Chinese government will have the most difficulty forcing a one-child norm on its rural population.

While pressures to marry and have children are weaker in the United States than they are in countries such as Mexico, they do exist (Blake, 1972). Griffith (1973) asked a national sample of adults 18 to 39 years old to imagine how they would feel and how people would treat them if they never had children. Most believed that family and friends would urge them to have children, and almost half said they would feel out of place among other married people and would be accused of selfishness. Most also believed that having only one child was undesirable, that friends and parents would urge them to have more, and that it would probably be bad for the child. More recent evidence suggests a decline in the judgment that voluntary childlessness is selfish. Huber and Spitze (1983) found that only a quarter of a national sample of adults made such a judgment about a hypothetical couple that chose not to have children.

An important aspect of social structure is the number of people who occupy different statuses, and birth rates are strongly affected by the relative number of women in a population who are of childbearing age. Imagine two populations, A and B, each with 1,000 females (see Table 5-2). In A, 50 percent (500) of the females are of childbearing age, compared with only 10 percent (100) in B. Even if women in both populations have an average of three children apiece, population A will produce five times as many children as will population B (1,500 children in A vs. 300 in B).

During the late 1940s and early 1950s, for example, there was an enormous increase in the American birth rate known as the "baby boom." Accordingly, as these children became adults, the number of young women increased greatly, and although they generally had smaller families than their predecessors, birth rates rose.

## Deaths: Losing People

In addition to the birth rate, population size also depends on how high or low death rates are. The **crude death rate** is the number of deaths in a given year for every 1,000 people in a population. A common way of expressing the rate of death in a population is the concept of **life expectancy,** which is the average number of years people of a given age

---

**Table 5-2**

The Effect of Age Structure on the Birth Rate

|  | CHILDREN BORN IF EACH WOMAN OF CHILDBEARING AGE HAS 3 CHILDREN |
|---|---|
| **POPULATION A: 2,000 PEOPLE** | |
| 1,000 females | |
| 500 of childbearing age | 3 × 500 = 1,500 children |
| 500 too young or too old | 0 × 500 = 0 |
| **POPULATION B: 2,000 PEOPLE** | |
| 1,000 females | |
| 100 of childbearing age | 3 × 100 = 300 children |
| 900 too young or too old | 0 × 900 = 0 |

Both populations have the same number of people and the same number of females, and in both populations each woman of childbearing age has the same number of children; but population A has five times as many children because it has five times as many females of childbearing age.

can expect to live if current death rates remain unchanged throughout their lifetime (Weller and Bouvier, 1981).

Like birth rates, death rates and life expectancy vary enormously among societies (Table 5-3); and once again, cultural, social structural, and material factors help explain why. Causes of death are frequently divided into five categories: infectious, parasitic, and respiratory diseases; circulatory diseases (such as heart disease and strokes); cancer; violent causes (suicide, homicide, and accidents);

and other causes (such as starvation, diabetes, and birth injury). These distinctions are sociologically important, because different causes are related in distinct ways to characteristics of physical and social environments.

Infectious diseases such as tuberculosis, typhoid, smallpox, and diphtheria, for example, are more common among poorly nourished people who live in unsanitary conditions. Prior to the discovery both of vaccines and of the importance of sanitation and nutrition, infectious disease accounted for the major portion of deaths in most societies. Thus, the incidence of infectious disease depends heavily on material living conditions; it accounts for more than 20 percent of all deaths in developing countries such as Colombia but only 6 percent of all deaths in the United States (World Health Organization, 1978).

Cancer and circulatory disease, on the other hand, are the most frequent causes of death in industrial societies, causing almost three-quarters of all deaths in the United States but only a third of those in Colombia (World Health Organization, 1978). In part this difference occurs because wealthy countries have already conquered infectious diseases, and—since people are mortal—they must die from *some*thing. However, the difference is also due to exposure to cancer-causing chemicals produced by industry. Coal miners suffer from black-lung disease, and workers in cotton mills often develop white-lung disease from continually breathing cotton dust into their lungs. Other workers are exposed to dangerous pesticides and cancer-causing substances such as asbestos.

If you look at crude death rates for different countries, you may be surprised to find that the crude death rate is *lower* in relatively poor countries such as Mexico, Chile, and Thailand than it is in the United States. Before concluding that people are healthier in impoverished Mexico than they are in affluent America, you need to understand what it is about crude death rates that makes them "crude."

Specifically, the population of Mexico has a very high proportion of children. If you walk through a Mexican community on a Sunday afternoon, almost *half* (44 percent) of all the people you meet will be under the age of 15. In the United States, on the other hand, only 22 percent of the population is under 15, and the percentage of the

**Table 5-3**

Crude Death Rates and Infant Mortality Rates for Selected Countries, Early 1980s

| COUNTRY | CRUDE DEATH RATE[1] | INFANT MORTALITY RATE[2] |
|---|---|---|
| Mexico | 6 | 55 |
| Japan | 6 | 7 |
| China | 8 | 35 |
| United States | 9 | 11 |
| Brazil | 8 | 76 |
| France | 10 | 9 |
| Soviet Union | 10 | 32 |
| Iran | 12 | 106 |
| United Kingdom | 12 | 11 |
| Czechoslovakia | 12 | 16 |
| West Germany | 12 | 11 |
| India | 14 | 125 |
| Bangladesh | 18 | 148 |
| Afghanistan | 23 | 182 |
| World | 11 | 84 |

Source: Population Reference Bureau, 1984.

[1] Deaths each year per 1,000 people.
[2] Deaths of infants less than one year old for every 1,000 births in a population.

In poor countries death is more likely to be caused by infectious diseases than by chronic diseases such as cancer and heart disease, because living conditions are crowded and unsanitary and people are poorly nourished.

population that is elderly is increasing rapidly (Population Reference Bureau, 1984). How does this affect crude death rates? Children are less likely to die than people at any other age, and a population with a large percentage of children will, as a result, experience relatively few deaths.

Thus, although health conditions are certainly worse in Mexico than they are in the United States, the large percentage of children in Mexico—and the correspondingly low percentage of elderly people—pushes the crude death rate down below that of the United States. Crude death rates do not accurately reflect health conditions in a society, but they are extremely important in determining how rapidly populations grow.

## The Rate of Natural Increase

The rate of population growth is determined primarily by the **rate of natural increase,** which is simply the birth rate minus the death rate. In 1982

the U.S. population increased at a rate of 0.7 percent: the birth rate was 16 births per 1,000 people (1.6 percent) and the death rate was 9 deaths per 1,000 people (0.9 percent). The difference between the two is 0.7 percent (Population Reference Bureau, 1984).

An easy way to see the consequence of a given rate of natural increase is to divide it into 70. The result—100 for the United States—is roughly the number of years it will take for the population to double in size if its current rate of natural increase continues. Rates of natural increase vary widely among the world's societies (Table 5-4).

As Table 5-4 shows, the lowest rate of natural increase in the world today is found in West Germany, where the deaths actually outnumber the births. Britain's rate of natural increase is only 0.1 percent, and at this rate, its population will take 700 years to double. The population of Mexico, on the other hand, is growing at a rate of 2.6 percent

**Table 5-4**

Population Statistics for Selected Countries, Early 1980s

| COUNTRY | CRUDE BIRTH RATE | CRUDE DEATH RATE | RATE OF NATURAL INCREASE | YEARS TO DOUBLE[1] |
|---------|------------------|------------------|--------------------------|--------------------|
| West Germany | 10 | 12 | −0.2% | — |
| United Kingdom | 13 | 12 | 0.1% | 700 |
| Czechoslovakia | 15 | 12 | 0.3% | 233 |
| France | 15 | 10 | 0.5% | 140 |
| United States | 16 | 9 | 0.7% | 100 |
| Japan | 13 | 6 | 0.7% | 100 |
| Soviet Union | 20 | 10 | 1.0% | 70 |
| China | 21 | 8 | 1.3% | 54 |
| India | 34 | 14 | 2.0% | 35 |
| Afghanistan | 48 | 23 | 2.5% | 28 |
| Brazil | 31 | 8 | 2.3% | 30 |
| Mexico | 32 | 6 | 2.6% | 27 |
| Bangladesh | 45 | 18 | 2.7% | 26 |
| Iran | 44 | 12 | 3.2% | 22 |
| World | 28 | 11 | 1.7% | 41 |

Source: Population Reference Bureau, 1984.

[1] The number of years it would take for the population to double in size if its current rate of growth continues.

per year. Its birth rate in 1981 was 32 per 1,000 and its death rate was only 6 per 1,000, which produces a rate of natural increase of 2.6 percent (3.2 percent minus 0.6 percent). At this rate of natural increase, the population of Mexico will double every 27 years.

The rate of population growth in Mexico and most nonindustrial countries is high because birth rates are far higher than death rates. In the United States and Europe, on the other hand, growth rates are low because both birth and death rates are at roughly the same level. The rate of natural increase is already negative in West Germany, and Westoff (1978a) estimates that negative population growth rates are likely to occur in Austria, Great Britain, Luxembourg, Belgium, Sweden, Norway, Denmark, Greece, Italy, and Switzerland by 1990; in the Netherlands and France by 2000; and in the United States by 2020 (see also Westoff, 1983). The government of Rumania became so concerned about the low rate of population growth that in 1984 it announced a campaign to encourage Rumanians to have more children (*New York Times*, March 4, 1984).

Why would fertility decline to levels low enough to cause a negative rate of growth? There are a number of possible answers. The percentage of people who have never married continues to rise; so does the cost of raising children—estimated to be from $60,000 to $120,000 per child when the cost of college education is included (Espenshade, 1980; Hall, 1981). As women become more heavily involved in occupations, the indirect cost of raising children—measured by the income women forgo when they leave work to care for children—also increases (Easterlin, 1978). The dependency of elderly parents on their adult children is lessening as the financial security of the elderly increases (Becker, 1981). In short, "the costs of childbearing are increasing while the rewards are decreasing" (Huber and Spitze, 1983, p. 38).

## The Demographic Transition and the Economics of Childbearing

As we have seen, the sharp differences in growth rates of nonindustrialized and industrialized societies reflect in part changing historical circumstances. One attempt to describe these long-term shifts is the theory of the **demographic transition,** which describes a three-stage pattern of population growth that has occurred in most societies that are now industrialized (see Figure 5-1). In the first

stage of the transition both birth and death rates are high, and the rate of natural increase is therefore low. As far as we know, most early societies had high birth rates balanced by high death rates. When food was plentiful, death rates might drop for a while and populations would increase; and when food was scarce or epidemic diseases struck, death rates would jump and populations would level off or shrink in size.

Although available information is at best sketchy, most demographers agree that the world population was quite stable until around 7000 B.C. when people first started to grow their own food (Weinstein, 1976) (Figure 5-2). Although higher food production probably lowered death rates by improving nutrition, the rate of natural increase was probably very low. Over the next 9,000 years— roughly up to the mid-1600s—growth rates around the world were both low and uneven—going up in some years and down in others. Infectious diseases kept death rates high in most years. During the fourteenth century, for example, the Black Plague killed more than one-third of the entire population of Europe (Thompson, 1942; Tuchman, 1978).

From the seventeenth century on, however, growth rates shot up dramatically in most of the world and especially in Europe. Although the pop-

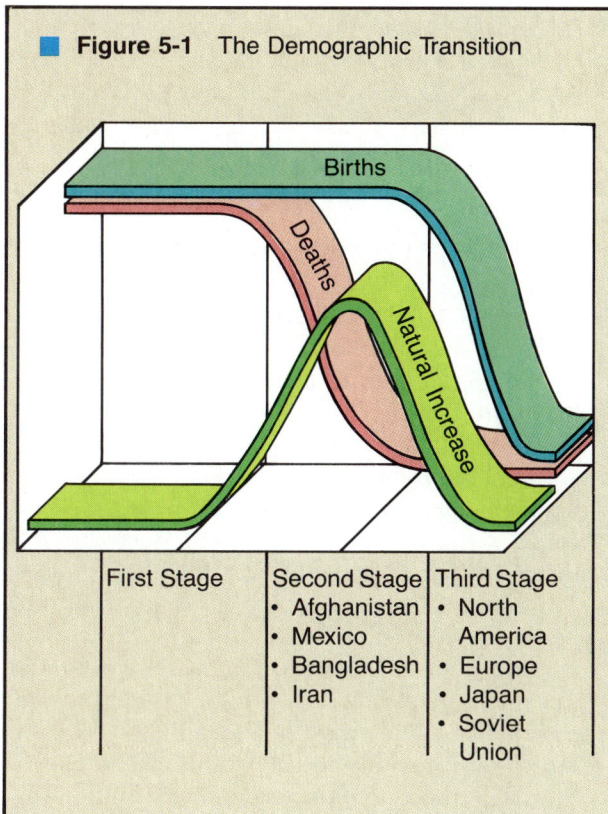

■ **Figure 5-1** The Demographic Transition

| First Stage | Second Stage | Third Stage |
|---|---|---|
| | • Afghanistan | • North America |
| | • Mexico | • Europe |
| | • Bangladesh | • Japan |
| | • Iran | • Soviet Union |

During the Middle Ages, the Black Plague so devastated the population of Europe that people (including artists) became obsessed with death.

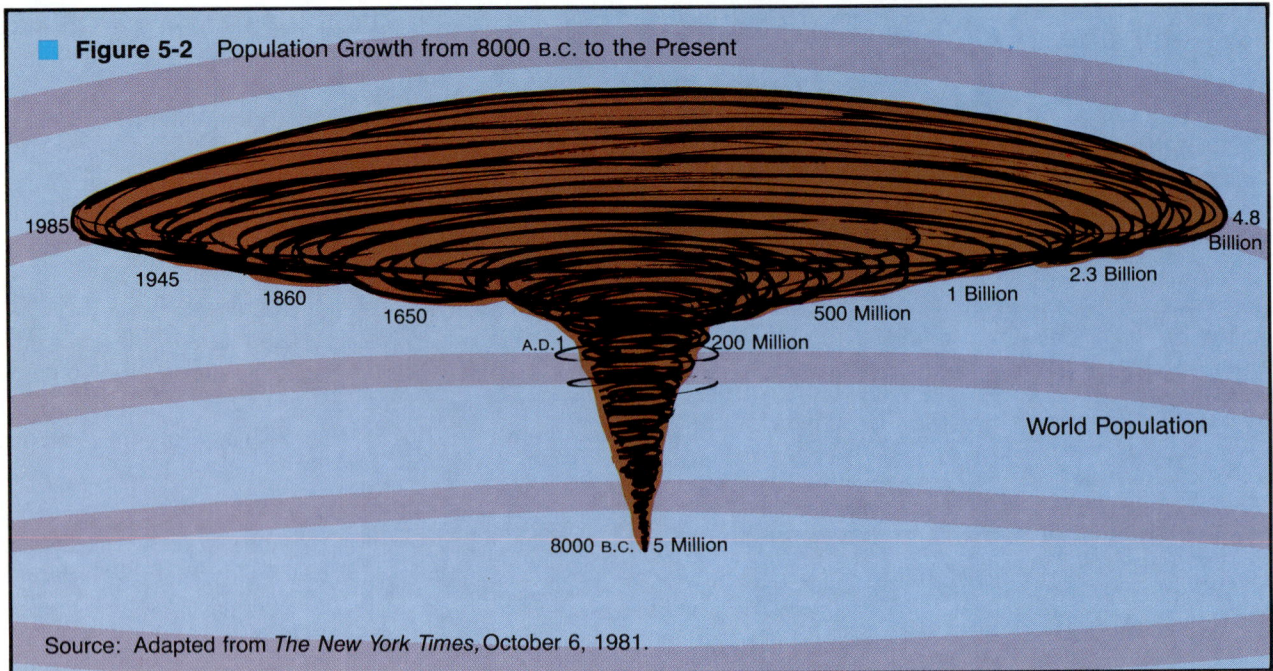

■ **Figure 5-2**   Population Growth from 8000 B.C. to the Present

Source: Adapted from *The New York Times,* October 6, 1981.

ulation of the world took roughly 1,600 years to double (to A.D. 1600), it took only 200 years (from 1600 to 1800) to double again. Improved sanitation and easily administered cures for serious infectious diseases resulted in a redoubling of the world population by 1930, and by 1980—only 50 years later—the population of the world had doubled yet again. In 1984 the population of the world was growing at a rate of 1.7 percent, which may seem like a small figure until it is applied to a base of 4.8 billion people, producing 82 million additional people every year (Population Reference Bureau, 1984). (Question: At this rate, in how many years will the population of the world double to 9.6 billion?)

Declining death rates in the eighteenth century triggered the second stage of the demographic transition, during which birth rates remained high and death rates fell, producing expanding rates of natural increase. As nutrition and sanitation improved in industrializing Europe, death rates continued to fall and the population of Europe doubled between 1800 and 1850. During this period, however, Europe (and, a bit later, the United States) entered the third stage of the demographic transition as birth rates also fell and eventually leveled off close to the level of death rates, producing very low rates of natural increase.

The populations of most nonindustrial and industrializing societies—such as Mexico—continue to grow at rapid rates, for although death rates have fallen sharply through the use of cheap medical technology borrowed from industrial countries, birth rates have remained high. These countries appear, in short, to be taking a long time to get through the second stage of the demographic transition. Why?

You might think that if high birth rates contribute to so much hardship in countries such as Mexico, people would have fewer children. Historical evidence suggests, however, that it is the prosperity brought by industrialization that causes families to control their fertility. Birth rates in Europe and the United States, for example, did not begin to fall until the Industrial Revolution took hold at the beginning of the nineteenth century. Japan experienced a similar decline when it industrialized in the twentieth century (Davis, 1963).

Industrialization not only raises hopes for prosperity, but also converts children from an asset to a liability (United Nations, 1973). Parents who want to exploit expanding opportunities simply have an easier time if they have small families. The desire for upward mobility raises parents' aspirations for their children, and if they have small families, they maximize the resources they can devote to each child's development (Rindfuss, Bumpass, and St. John, 1980).

Thus, at the heart of the ecological problems of Mexico and most other less developed nations are rates of natural increase that add people faster than available jobs and goods can be produced. Natural increase is the most important component of population growth, but migration also plays an important part in the growth of many societies and in the distribution of people within them. The populations of Mexico City and cities in other less developed societies are exploding only in part because fertility is high in their societies.

## Migration: Gains and Losses

**Migration** is the movement of people either within a country or from one country to another. **Immigrants** are people who enter a population, and **emigrants** are those who leave a population (thus someone who moves from Poland to the United States emigrates *from* Poland and immigrates *to* the United States). The causes of migration can be divided into "push" factors—such as poverty or oppression—that drive people away from an area and "pull" factors—such as the promise of higher income or greater freedom—that attract them to a new area.

For many centuries people have used migration to escape poor survival conditions. Hundreds of thousands of Irish immigrated to the United States after the potato famine of 1846. The westward expansion in nineteenth-century America resulted more from crowded living conditions and limited opportunities in East Coast cities than from a curiosity to explore new territories (Morison, 1965). When the farmers of the American Midwest were ruined by years of drought during the Great Depression of the 1930s, hundreds of thousands packed up all they could carry and migrated to

These women, on a ship arriving in the United States around 1910, were among the millions of immigrants who sought a better life by leaving their homelands in the late nineteenth and early twentieth centuries.

what they thought would be better conditions in California (a desperate story powerfully portrayed in John Steinbeck's novel *The Grapes of Wrath*, published in 1939).

Since the 1930s, migration has involved millions of people moving within a short time and under intense pressure. Tens of millions of European civilians were uprooted by World War II and Nazi persecution, and in 1948 thousands of Palestinians fled from the territory that is now Israel (Bouvier, Shryock and Henderson, 1977). Across the world, roughly 50 million people left their

So strong is the determination of many Mexicans and other Latin Americans to escape the poverty of their homelands and take advantage of better opportunities in the United States, that no one knows for sure how many of these illegal immigrants there actually are.

homelands between 1946 and 1955 alone (Cook, 1957), and in the 1970s political and economic upheavals created tens of millions of refugees in Southeast Asia.

In the 1980s many countries, including Mexico and Haiti, still look upon the United States as a place for people who cannot be supported by their economies at home. Illegal immigration of Mexicans into the United States is so massive that no one really knows just how many cross the 1,900-mile border each year (see Massey, 1981a). The figure could be as high as 200,000 (Heer, 1979) and there are an estimated 4 million illegal immigrants in the United States (Robinson, 1980).

Migration is often a major cause of population growth. Between 1840 and 1930, roughly 52 million people emigrated from Europe, mostly to the United States (Davis, 1974). From 1651 to the abolition of slavery in the nineteenth century, between 9 and 11 million Africans were forcibly brought to the United States (Curtin, 1969). These migrations rapidly expanded the populations of receiving countries and substantially redistributed a sizable portion of the world's people. By 1930, for example, one-third of the world's whites lived outside of Europe, and one-fifth of all blacks lived outside of Africa (Davis, 1974).

Migration is the primary cause of the growth of cities around the world. Although birth rates are generally lower in cities than in rural areas, urban populations have increased while rural ones have declined. Only since 1970 has the pattern reversed in a few countries such as the United States as more and more people move away from urban areas (Brown and Wardwell, 1980) (see Chapter 9).

The populations of many cities such as Mexico City, on the other hand, are exploding under the pressures of migration from rural areas. An estimated 1,900 Mexicans migrate from rural areas to the city each *day* in the hope of finding jobs that will improve their standard of living (Fox, 1981). Like many less developed countries, Mexico is trying to industrialize rapidly, and is therefore pouring far more money into industry than into agriculture. Mexico City, then, acts like a magnet that pulls thousands of impoverished, unskilled rural workers who are motivated by the false hope that life in the city will be better. The flood of migrants, however, only makes life in the city worse than ever.

Like a magnet, Mexico City attracts poor migrants from rural areas who find not a better life, but unemployment and continued poverty in overcrowded urban slums.

As in Mexico, migration affects the distribution of people within most populations. Between 1975 and 1980, for example, 45 percent of all Americans moved to a different house, and 33 percent of these moves were across county lines (U.S. Census Bureau, 1983c; Weller and Bouvier, 1981). During the nineteenth century, migration flows in the United States were from east to west and south to north; but since 1970, the northerly flow has reversed as northerners leave home in search of better job opportunities (Biggar, 1979; Long and Hansen, 1975).

Such patterns of migration often have important social consequences. As people move from northern and eastern states to the West and South, for example, the "receiver" areas gain political power in Congress, because representation is based on population. Migration also causes problems for receiver areas, however. The recent massive migration of unemployed workers from northern states to the "Sun Belt" severely strains states such as Arizona, whose job markets, schools, public services, and natural resources (such as water) cannot meet the demands of rapidly expanding populations (Weller and Bouvier, 1981).

"Sender" areas, on the other hand, lose workers, taxpayers, and consumers. Many major U.S. cities—such as New York City—face a financial crisis as those who can afford to move leave behind those who cannot. In the late 1970s New York City almost declared bankruptcy because it could not meet payments on its loans.

Birth, death, natural increase, migration, and population growth are basic processes that define the study of populations by determining a population's *age structure*, *size*, and *distribution*.

## Age Structures

The **age structure** of a population is the distribution of people according to age. Age structures are usually represented by "pyramids," which give a revealing picture of one of a population's most important characteristics.

Figure 5-3, for example, shows age structures for the United States, Mexico, and Sweden. They are all broader at the bottom than at the top, because people die as they grow older. Here, however, the similarities end: the age structure of Mexico is much broader at the bottom than those of Sweden and the United States, and Sweden's is tall and thin. Why do age structures have such different shapes, and why is this important?

In general, age structures reflect the history of births, deaths, and migration in a population; but of these factors, birth rates are by far the most important (Coale, 1964). Mexico has a long history of high birth rates, whereas birth rates in Sweden have remained consistently low. This is why Mexico has such a large proportion of children and Sweden has a large proportion of elderly people. The U.S. age structure, on the other hand, has a bulge that primarily reflects changing birth rates. Prior to World War II, U.S. birth rates had declined steadily for over a century, so that each new generation was smaller than the one that preceded it. Between 1945 and the early 1960s, the United

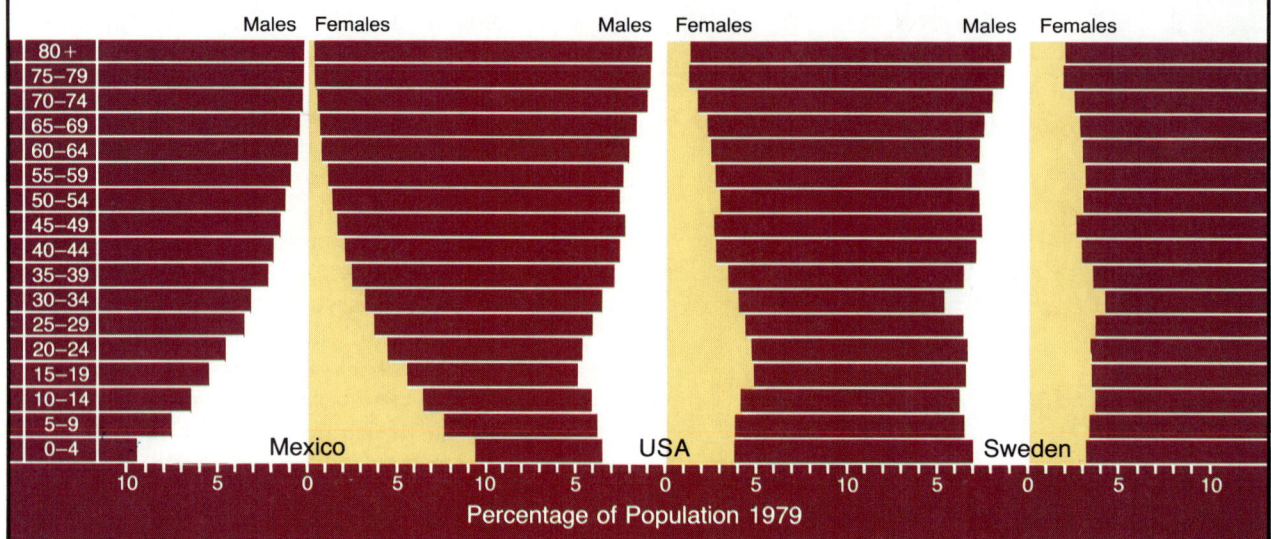

**Figure 5-3** Age Structures

States experienced a "baby boom"; then a drop in birth rates resulted in a "baby bust" in the 1970s. Thus, the "bulge" contains maturing "boom babies" and the relatively narrow base contains the "bust babies" born in the 1970s (Harter, 1977).

Age structures have important effects on both societies and individuals. An "old" population such as Sweden's, for example, must devote a relatively large share of its resources to the elderly, whereas Mexico is burdened with a disproportionately large number of children who produce less than they consume. A large proportion of children in a population poses difficult problems for economic development, particularly in poor societies that are trying to industrialize. Building factories and power plants, for example, is expensive and requires the investment of some of what is produced in a society. Whatever resources are invested in a given year, of course, cannot also be consumed. Just as a family that can barely make ends meet is unable to save any money, so too a poor society has difficulty investing in long-term economic development.

Pakistan, for example, has a hard time setting anything aside because the huge numbers of relatively unproductive children require a great deal just to survive (Easterlin, 1967; Heer, 1966). Thus, rather than investing in higher standards of living, such countries must use much of what they pro-

duce simply to maintain their already poor living conditions; and in order to industrialize, they must go into debt by borrowing money from wealthier countries.

Unlike "old" countries such as Sweden and "young" ones such as Mexico, the United States is in the process of aging and must make a difficult transition between meeting the needs of a young population (building more schools for the "boom babies," for example) and meeting those of an aging one (providing medical care, retirement homes, and social security benefits).

Age structures also affect the frequency of experience and behavior that vary by age. Young people, for example, are more likely to commit certain types of crimes—such as robbery and assault—than are people of any other age. Thus, a young population will tend to have higher crime rates than an old one even if there are no differences in the tendency of individuals to commit crimes (Chilton and Spielberger, 1971).

**Birth Cohorts** Age is an important social status in all societies, but our experiences and opportunities at different ages depend strongly on the period in our society's history in which we reach each age and the relative numbers of people who are younger or older than we are. A **birth cohort** consists of all people who are born at roughly the same time, and the cohort we belong to has important effects on our lives (Ryder, 1965).

If you had been born in the 1930s, for example, your cohort would have been smaller than older ones (born before 1930), because the economic hardship of the Depression discouraged childbearing. As a member of the Depression cohort, you would have enjoyed a relatively rich supply of jobs, housing, and educational opportunities, because *the relatively large cohorts that preceded you created more opportunities than your cohort required.* For this reason, Harter (1977) called the 1930s cohort the "Good Times Cohort":

> By virtue of their smaller number, the thirties cohort, upon encountering each important life cycle event, have experienced relative abundance. . . . In all their important life cycle events, the 1930s cohort has "had it made." . . . Insofar as the number of high school classrooms, glee clubs, athletic teams . . . had not diminished, then the 1950 fifteen-year-old had a greater chance than did the 1940 fifteen-year-old of being in a smaller class, of being a class officer . . . and when the 1930s cohort was 21–30, they required fewer new jobs and housing units than did their predecessors ten years earlier. (pp. 3–4)

As a member of a baby boom cohort, on the other hand, you would encounter enormous competition in the job market for the relatively small number of jobs created by the smaller cohorts that preceded yours. If you were born after the late 1960s (a baby-bust baby) your relatively small cohort will have the greater opportunities enjoyed by those that preceded the baby boom (assuming, of course, that other factors such as the economy do not change for the worse).

## Population Size and Distribution

Along with age structure, population *size* and *distribution* are important both for societies and individuals. In comparison with large, densely settled societies, small, sparsely settled ones require fewer resources, find it easier to move to more supportive environments, tend to have less complex divisions of labor, and tend to be less urban. Tiny societies—such as the Kung Bushmen of Africa—that continually move from one place to another in search of game and wild plants require

relatively little in order to survive and can move to more favorable surroundings with relative ease (Marshall, 1965).

By comparison, the populations of industrial societies all number in the tens and hundreds of millions, most of whom live in cities. Such large populations are a continuing source of diversity and innovation because they allow individuals to specialize in specific tasks, creating complex interdependencies among specialists. Large societies are vulnerable, however, for they demand enormous amounts of natural resources and cannot simply move elsewhere in order to meet their needs.

While large, densely settled populations have greater potential for innovative technology and complex divisions of labor (Bosrup, 1981), their sheer size need not have this result. Many of the poorest countries of the world—such as Bangladesh, China, India, and El Salvador—have among the largest and most densely settled populations. If the United States, for example, were as densely settled as Bangladesh, its population would exceed the current population of the entire world by 36 percent (Population Reference Bureau, 1984).

In part, the poverty of many large, dense populations is due to high birth rates that result in relatively large numbers of children who produce less than they consume. A full explanation, however, involves the characteristics of physical environments and the ways in which human populations organize themselves and use natural resources.

## Physical Environments

The cultures and social structures that develop in a society often reflect the problems of adapting to the characteristics of particular physical environments—from the isolation imposed by a mountain range to the physical splitting of an urban neighborhood by a new highway. For this reason sociologists have paid increasing attention to the relationship between social environments and physical environments, which include nonliving elements such as land, water, and air as well as other species of life.

### Land, Water, and Air

Mountains, deserts, oceans, and seas are barriers to easy movement from one place to another; as a result, they both isolate and protect societies from one another. The vastness and harsh climate of Russia condemned to failure Napoleon's and Hitler's dreams of conquest. The flat, level terrain of Western and Central Europe makes the passage of armies so easy that Europe has been a frequent battleground for centuries. Before the invention of missiles and nuclear weapons, the Atlantic and Pacific oceans virtually ensured that no Asian or European invader could easily attack the United States, just as the stormy English Channel has protected England for almost 1,000 years.

Rivers and seas also allow people to travel and trade over distances that would be difficult if not impossible to cover over land; and landlocked societies without access to major rivers rarely prosper. It is no accident that most of the world's great cities—such as New York, Los Angeles, Chicago, Rio de Janeiro, London, Paris, Rome, Moscow, Bombay, Calcutta, Shanghai, and Tokyo—lie on seacoasts or major rivers.

The physical characteristics of land profoundly affect the way communities develop. The relatively small size of the island of Manhattan, for example, made it inevitable that growth would reach toward the sky in the form of tall skyscrapers. The physical compactness of Manhattan also makes it possible to link all parts of the island with public transportation systems of buses and subways.

Los Angeles lies in what was once a desert, and the long valley extending from the sea to San Bernardino encouraged the development of a sprawling city with relatively low-rising buildings. The geographic vastness of Los Angeles also makes it difficult to use bus and subway transportation efficiently, and so the city developed as a place in which cars are a virtual necessity. The air pollution generated by thousands of cars, in turn, is contained and concentrated by the mountains and hills that line the valley and intensified by the rays of the sun. Thus, the famous smog of Los Angeles has been caused both by geographical factors and by the physical development of the city in response to them.

Life in Mexico City also is affected profoundly by its physical environment. Mexico City is located 7,000 feet above sea level—where the air is relatively thin—in a bowl of mountains that prevents the city's air pollution from blowing away easily. When Cortez came to Mexico City in the sixteenth century, most of the buildings were erected over

In Rio de Janeiro, as in Mexico City and the large urban areas of many developing nations, great wealth and crushing poverty exist side by side.

water on giant "stilts" and platforms. Centuries of urban growth, however, have drained the lake. Now, the dust that is blown up from the dry lake bed by spring and summer winds adds to the air pollution produced by cars and industry.

The mountains surrounding the city also sharply limit its physical growth. In most American cities, middle- and upper-class families have migrated to suburban areas as inner cities have decayed and filled with lower-class residents. The middle and upper classes in Mexico City, however, do not have this option, for there simply are no quiet, green areas left. Thus, poor and wealthy live side by side in Mexico City in ways that are rarely found in American cities.

## Varieties of Life

Within the limitations of the physical environment of land, water, and air, each species of life—including our own—lives in relation to other species of life, and ecology focuses on the place of human beings in such relationships (Hawley, 1968; Park and Burgess, 1921). To survive, each form of life continually exchanges one thing for another. Humans take oxygen from the air and give back carbon dioxide (whereas plants do just the opposite); we take coal and oil from the ground and give back heat and pollution as we burn them; cows transform grass into milk, which we then transform into teeth, bones, muscle, fat, heat (energy), and wastes (which bacteria thrive on).

In addition to eating one another, forms of life often benefit from one another's behavior. Our bodies, for example, are like large "hotels" housing millions of microorganisms whose survival allows us to function: "friendly" bacteria help us eliminate our wastes, and each of our cells contains simple organisms that enable us to transform food into energy (Thomas, 1974). Such mutually beneficial relationships are common in the natural world. As bees gather nectar, they unwittingly pollinate flowers and allow them to reproduce; as worms dig tunnels, they loosen the soil and allow it to absorb air and water more easily, making it more supportive of plants and, in turn, of humans and others who eat the plants.

Just as living things benefit one another, so can they harm one another—and themselves. People, for example, cut down forests in order to build homes, make paper, and keep warm; but, although this benefits us in the short run, it destroys forests that thousands of animals depend on for their survival; in the long run, it also deprives us of vital oxygen that green plants add to the air.

Much of the prosperity enjoyed by the United States results from the richness of its farmland—an ecological condition quite unlike that found during the 1980s in famine-stricken African countries, including Ethiopia, Chad, and Sudan, where despite international relief efforts hungry people such as these have been driven to scavenging grains of cattle feed. The suffering, starvation, and death of tens of thousands have been caused, in part, by deforestation, extensive monoculture (cultivation of a single kind of crop, usually for export rather than to sustain those who grow it), and widespread droughts making agriculture all but impossible and creating new deserts.

One of the most fundamental characteristics of human beings as a species is that we do not simply use the physical environment as we find it: we transform nature by giving it new forms; in this way, we both alter and add to the physical environment. Walk down the streets of any city, and you will have a hard time identifying any part of your surroundings that has *not* been fashioned by human beings. The transformation of nature is so extensive in the United States that we deliberately set aside selected areas—such as national parks—to remind us that there are physical environments untouched by the human urge to turn one thing into something else.

## Organization: Ecosystems and Niches

As we have seen, the life of any species depends on a set of relationships with physical surroundings and other living things. These relationships make up an **ecosystem,** which consists of all forms of life that live in relation to one another and a shared physical environment (the word "ecology" refers to the study of such systems). The limits of a particular ecosystem depend on how we define a "shared physical environment"; thus, a vacant lot in a city, a country field, a small pond, or an entire state, country, or world might all be defined as ecosystems, so long as what goes on in one part of that environment affects life in other parts.

Within ecosystems, species of life survive through relationships with other species and the physical environment, and their positions in such relationships are called **niches.** Thus, while a status refers to an individual's position in a social environment, a niche refers to the position of an entire population in its physical environment. Wheat, for example, draws nutrients and water from the soil and carbon dioxide from the air. As it grows it gives off oxygen, and when it dies it decomposes, providing food for bacteria and fertilizer to be used by

Compared with people in industrial societies, the Australian aborigines occupy a relatively simple ecological niche in which they participate in a set of relationships both with the physical environment and other species of life.

other plants. Much of the carbon dioxide it needs to survive comes from animals (such as ourselves) who extract oxygen from the air and exhale carbon dioxide. Thus, what is "waste" to plant life—oxygen—is vital to animals, and what is "waste" to animals—carbon dioxide—is vital to plants.

Human niches in ecosystems are unique because they are extremely complex and can be altered deliberately. Honey bees can adapt only by changing their biology, but humans adapt by changing cultural ideas and social structures. Human beings do not dominate the earth because they are bigger, faster, or stronger than other creatures. It is through culture and social structure that people organize their activities and vastly extend their otherwise modest biological endowment (Harris, 1979). Whereas most species must adapt through slow biological evolution, humans can quickly adapt to an extraordinary range of environmental conditions.

We have an enormous ability to alter the physical environment itself: we can pollute the waters and clean them, plant trees and cut them down, and build roads and buildings on land that would otherwise sprout vegetation (which would in turn produce oxygen). We can plow the land in such a way that rains wash away the topsoil, ruining it for further cultivation, or we can carefully terrace the land and protect it from erosion.

Most species occupy narrowly defined niches in relation to their natural environment, but the relationship of human societies to ecosystems is far more complex. Tiny fish eat plants and microorganisms, then are eaten by bigger fish, which in turn provide dinner for still larger fish. Humans, however, eat all manner of plants and animals and have the ability to exterminate almost any animal species; we mine the earth and send a vast range of radio waves and chemicals into the air. Whereas most species have biological predispositions to slow their consumption before the food supply becomes too scarce, humans have no such inborn checks.

A major point of all this is that societies have the power to deliberately alter and create ecological conditions within which people and other forms of life must survive. Thus, the populations that make up societies grow, shrink, distribute themselves over physical environments, and survive by organizing their relationships with one another and the natural environment and its many species of life.

## Technology

For humans, a major element of our organization for survival is **technology**—the accumulated cultural knowledge of how to use the natural environment for our own purposes. The number of people who can survive in a physical environment depends on natural resources and the ability to use them, and when a growing population pressures a society's ability to support its people, the range of possible adaptations is limited. The simplest responses are to move the society to a more supportive physical environment or to intensify the use of existing technologies—by increasing kills of wild game, farming more land, or drilling for more oil. These adaptations have limited value, however, for the emigration of an entire society is impractical, and any technology ultimately reaches the limits of its usefulness.

In such circumstances, a society has only four options: to develop new social arrangements and technologies that increase production, to shrink its population through the migration of some of its

---

**PUZZLES:**

## WHY ARE COWS SACRED IN INDIA BUT RAISED FOR SLAUGHTER IN THE U.S.?

A simple answer is that the Hindu religion of India forbids the eating of beef, but this sidesteps the question of why this ever became a part of the Hindu religion. Anthropologist Marvin Harris argues that the holy status enjoyed by cattle in India came about in response to changing ecological and population conditions, that as populations became huge and densely settled and land came under increasingly intense cultivation, the most efficient use of both the cow and the land was to cultivate crops, not raise beef for slaughter. This is one of many examples of the ways in which ecology and population affect human culture in unexpected ways.

members, to control reproduction and death, or to wait for nature to take its toll. Throughout history, societies have relied on the first option—developing new technologies—in order to support larger populations.

## Preindustrial Societies

In the earliest societies—existing between roughly 35,000 and 7000 B.C.—people survived by gathering vegetation and by hunting animals. They lived in small, autonomous communities, and as far as we know they searched for food continually, with everyone kept busy at this task (Murdock, 1967). Their division of labor was simple (there were few if any full-time specialists), and wealth, power, and prestige were distributed fairly equally. Because they did not produce their own food, they had to move whenever they exhausted the supply.

Their technology was primitive, but appropriate to their way of life. They domesticated sheep and dogs, developed basketry and fishing, and invented spears, bows and arrows, lamps, combs, spoons, shovels, fish traps, hooks, and nets (Clark and Piggott, 1965); they had no knowledge of how to fabricate metals, however, and the human body was their only source of energy for work.

**Horticultural Societies** Around 7000 B.C., people in Asia Minor discovered how to cultivate plants, and for the first time in history human beings produced some of their own food. They planted crops with hoes and digging sticks, and after the harvest they burned the stubble (which eventually provided fertilizer) and started again. Although the technology of these horticultural societies was crude and they often exhausted the soil's fertility, these simple innovations were enormously important, for as food supplies grew, so did populations.

Because people could produce more food than they needed for themselves, others could specialize in work that was not necessary for survival, such as pottery and weaving (Childe, 1953, 1964). Plant cultivation provided a more stable food supply, and settlements became more permanent. With a greater variety of goods, people accumulated more possessions and built larger, more substantial dwellings. Although these early communities were still relatively autonomous societies, trade began; this, in turn, made it possible for soci-

eties to support larger populations since they could now acquire goods they did not produce themselves.

Late in the horticultural period, people discovered the beginnings of metallurgy, first with copper in the Middle East and then with bronze—a harder alloy of copper and tin—in Southeast Asia and China. This was a major discovery, for people could now make harder, more durable tools as well as deadlier weapons. The discovery illustrates how one development begets another: without the high temperatures of pottery ovens, it would not have been possible to extract metals from ores and melt, smelt, and mold them into many different shapes. The appearance of metallurgy also illustrates how innovations both solve and create problems. The use of metals to make weapons spawned rulers and conquerors, who required great numbers of workers and artisans to meet their expanding appetite for wealth and power.

Advanced horticultural societies were more permanent, more complex, and larger than their predecessors, averaging just under 300 people. For the first time, they were linked to multicommunity societies with average populations of more than 5,000. Work was more specialized: whereas metal and leather working, boat and house building, pottery making, and weaving were specialties in only 2 percent of the early horticultural societies, they were specialties in almost 30 percent of advanced horticultural societies (Murdock, 1967).

---

### PUZZLES:

### WHICH CAME FIRST, THE KING OR THE PLOW?

If it were not for the invention of the plow, there might never have been kings, queens, emperors, or popes. Why?

The answer is that without the plow societies might never have had the ability to produce a surplus, and as you will see in Chapter 11, without a surplus societies rarely develop social inequalities of wealth and power.

**Agrarian Societies**  What historians refer to as "the dawn of civilization" began around 3000 B.C. Although this period saw the development of the wheel, alphabetic writing, numbers, and the calendar, the most important innovation was the plow (Childe, 1964). The plow helped solve the problems of weeds and the exhaustion of the soil's fertility by digging deeply as it turned over the soil. For the first time, plants could be cultivated in large fields rather than in small gardens, and animal and wind power—useless in a technology dependent on sticks and hoes—were harnessed.

The agrarian age coincided with the development of the first real cities, some with populations exceeding 100,000 (Davis, 1955; Tisdale, 1942). Cities came into being because technology allowed a relatively small portion of a population to produce a society's entire food supply, thus allowing an increasingly large number of people to live in densely settled communities that did not produce their own food.

Permanent settlements were now a way of life, and larger crops produced greater surpluses, which in turn supported still more complex divisions of labor. The agrarian age advanced with the discovery of how to smelt iron and harden it into steel, and by the time of Jesus Christ the new technology had taken firm roots throughout the Middle East, India, and China. In the next 1,000 years, it spread throughout Europe and Southeast Asia and then to the European colonies in the New World. New technology produced new inventions: gun powder, horseshoes and harnesses, screws, wood-turning lathes, magnets, water- and wind-powered mills, the spinning wheel, printing, porcelain, wheelbarrows, and clocks. Later in the agrarian

It was the invention of agriculture and the ability to produce a surplus that made possible the development of ancient cities such as this one in Iraq. With cities, however, came other developments including the emergence of ruling classes.

period, on the eve of the Industrial Revolution, the steam engine and power-driven tools were developed.

## The Industrial Revolution

The Industrial Revolution began in England between 1760 and 1830 with the development of more efficient machinery for making textiles (Mathais, 1983). With a "flying shuttle," one worker could weave as much as two could without one, and the resulting demand for yarn prompted the invention of "spinning jennies," which could spin not one but 120 threads at once. This led to such a large supply of yarn that the weavers could not keep up; so England, lacking a large network of rivers and streams to provide water power, had to find a new source of energy.

The idea of using steam to generate power was not new. Hero of Alexandria—a Greek scientist—invented the steam turbine in the first century A.D. Like Leonardo da Vinci's helicopter, however, it was an idea whose time came only after centuries of social development had produced societies such as England (in which someone like James Watt could invent a workable steam engine to provide power for enormous looms). By the early 1800s England depended more on manufacturing than on agriculture, and was, therefore, the world's first industrial society. Iron and coal production grew rapidly, and machines capable of manufacturing interchangeable, precisely tooled

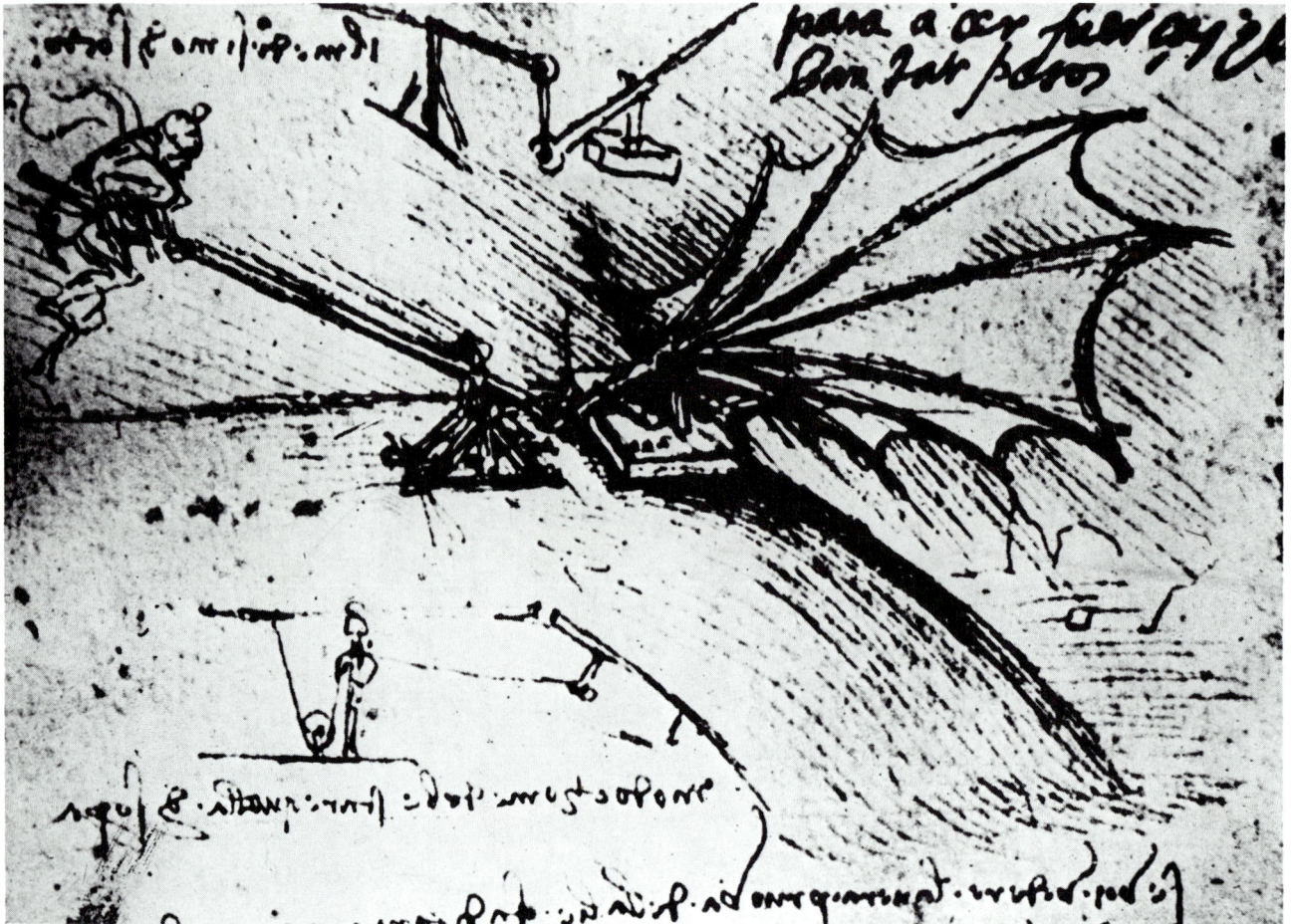

Leonardo da Vinci conceived of helicopters long before a society existed that had the technological resources to bring one into being.

metal parts were developed, paving the way for greater, more efficient production (Woytinsky and Woytinsky, 1953).

It is important to get some sense of the speed of industrial expansion during the early decades of the Industrial Revolution, for it shows how accumulated innovations and key inventions can bring about startling changes. By 1845, for example, the production of textiles in England was 5 times greater than it was in 1760; iron production was 24 times greater; and coal mining was 9 times greater (Deane and Cole, 1962). By contrast, it took horticultural societies the better part of 4,000 years to advance from hoes and digging sticks to the plow.

In the mid-1800s the use of steam power in transportation gave the Industrial Revolution a substantial boost, for by linking distant markets and lowering the cost of moving goods, it stimulated both demand and production. Charles Goodyear discovered how to process rubber so that it could hold up in both extreme cold and heat, and the emerging chemical and petroleum industries added to the momentum of technological change. Farmers traded in their horse-drawn plows for threshers, mowers, reapers, steam plows, and chemical fertilizers; and in 1860 electric power became a reality with the invention of dynamos and transformers. In the twentieth century the pace of technological innovation has increased sharply. Long-distance communications, nuclear power and weaponry, lasers, organ transplant operations, and the widespread use of computer technology in everything from toys to industrial robots are only a few of the major innovations that have appeared.

Most societies continue to rely on technology as a response to the demands of growing populations. In the 1980s, scientists are using discoveries in genetics to create new varieties of food plants that are resistant to disease and produce higher yields (Steinhart, 1981), and the Chinese are attempting to increase their supplies of energy by converting human wastes into flammable methane gas on a massive scale (Wren, 1981).

In comparison with biological evolution, culture allows human societies to alter their relationship with physical environments at lightning speed. The daily expenditure of energy in the large industrial societies is estimated to be 50 *million*

## Voices:
## This Land Belongs to You and Me— An Antipollution Lawyer Speaks Out

This land does not belong to General Motors, Ford, or Chrysler; this land does not belong to Consolidated Edison, Commonwealth Edison, or any other private investor-owned utility company; this land does not belong to Penn-Central, B&O, C&O, Union Pacific, Southern Pacific, or any other railroad; this land does not belong to American Airlines, United Airlines, TWA, or any common carrier; this land does not belong to Minnesota Mining and Manufacturing Company, Minneapolis Honeywell, Xerox, IBM, Eastman Kodak, Polaroid, or any other company marketing technological marvels; this land does not belong to International Paper Company, Scott Paper, Boise Cascade, Weyerhaeuser, Crown Zellerbach, or any other paper products company; this land does not belong to United States Steel, Bethlehem Steel, Inland Steel, Crucible Steel, or any other steel company; this land does not belong to Anaconda, Kennecott, Alcoa, or any other nonferrous metal company; this land does not belong to any soulless corporation!

This land does not belong to the ICC, FPC, FCC, AEC, TVA, FDA, USDA, BLM, Forest Service, Fish and Wildlife Service, or any other federal or state alphabet agency!

This land does not belong to the President of the United States, the Congress of the United States, the governor of any state, or the legislatures of the fifty states. This land belongs to its people. This land belongs to you and this land belongs to me.

Don't just sit there like lambs waiting for the slaughter, or canaries waiting to see if the mine shaft is really safe. Don't just sit around talking about the environmental crisis, or worse yet, just listening to others talk about it.

Don't just sit there and bitch. Sue somebody!

Source: Yannacone, 1970.

times greater than that in the hunter-gatherer societies of only 10,000 years ago (Harris, 1979). (10,000 years may seem like a long time, but it shrinks in the context of some 2 million years of human history.) The human population is estimated to be 880 times greater now than it was at the dawn of horticultural societies around 8000 B.C. The current population of the world constitutes 9 percent of all the people who ever lived (Westing, 1981), and the density of human populations has increased from roughly one person per square mile in 8000 B.C. to more than 65 (Harris, 1979).

While technological innovations often improve the ability to survive, they sometimes have unanticipated consequences that create serious problems. Chemical pesticides have dramatically improved usable crop yields by protecting them against insects; but a negative latent consequence is the chronic introduction of dangerous substances into food supplies—a recent example being the discovery of ethylenedibromide (also known as EDB) in grains and fruits in 1983 and 1984. Growing industries provide jobs and a rising standard of living, but they have also been the source of toxic-waste dumps whose poisons seep into community water supplies. In recent years entire communities have had to deal with the reality of discovering deadly chemicals—such as dioxin—in their wells.

## Too Many People?

Throughout history the size of human populations has been limited by high death rates from infectious disease, but cheap medical technology has sharply lowered death rates without also lowering birth rates. Less-developed countries such as Mexico—whose birth rates remain high—are growing at an unprecedented rate, and their young, rapidly expanding populations severely strain their economies and food supplies (Weller and Bouvier, 1981). Dramatic increases in the size of current populations and projections into the future (Table 5-5)

**Table 5-5**

The Contribution of Regions of the World to Projected World Population Growth

| REGION | PERCENTAGE OF WORLD POPULATION | |
|---|---|---|
| | 1984 (4.76 billion) | 2020 (8.09 billion) |
| Africa | 11.1 | 17.4 |
| Asia | 58.5 | 57.4 |
| North America | 5.5 | 4.1 |
| Latin America | 8.3 | 9.9 |
| Europe | 10.3 | 6.3 |
| USSR | 5.8 | 4.5 |
| Oceania | 0.5 | 0.4 |
| More-developed Countries | 24.5 | 16.7 |
| Less-developed Countries | 75.5 | 83.3 |

Source: Population Reference Bureau, 1984.

have generated widespread concern about the problem of overpopulation.

Many social scientists argue that rapid population growth—particularly in underdeveloped societies—makes economic progress all but impossible and continued widespread poverty, poor health, and starvation inevitable (United Nations, 1973). High-fertility societies tend to have high proportions of young people, and if economies cannot expand fast enough to employ them, they are likely to be a source of social unrest and political instability (Davis, 1976). In addition, larger populations use up natural resources at faster rates and strain the physical environment's ability to absorb growing amounts of waste and pollution.

In 1798 an English clergyman named Thomas Malthus published the first serious discussion of the problem of population size and rates of growth. Malthus used simple reasoning to arrive at a dramatic conclusion: populations grow exponentially (doubling and redoubling as in 2, 4, 8, 16, 32), whereas food supplies grow arithmetically (as in 1, 2, 3, 4) as new land is used for cultivation. Malthus argued that unless birth rates were controlled, the size of a population would inevitably be controlled through higher death rates caused by starvation, disease, or war.

Although it is obvious that there are upper limits on the number of people who can survive on a planet with finite space and resources, determining how many people constitute "too many" is, at best, a complex task. Survival and the material quality of life depend on ecological factors such as the size and distribution of populations, the characteristics of physical environments, and cultural technology. Bosrup (1981) argues that the development of new technology, in turn, has depended historically on the pressures of expanding populations: rather than face starvation, expanding populations *had* to come up with innovative ways to produce food and other necessities.

Survival also depends, however, on social structure—how societies organize productive work and distribute what they produce among their members. Until recently, for example, Mexico had a rapidly expanding economy, but little of the nation's prosperity has been shared with its large population of poor people (Gonzalez Casanova, 1980). From a functional point of view, a population is too large when its social and ecological arrangements are unable to support its members. The functional answer, then, is either to alter those arrangements in order to increase production or to slow—if not reverse—the rate of population growth.

As we saw earlier, many societies with rapidly growing populations have attempted to lower birth rates by actively promoting the use of contraceptives (Symonds and Carder, 1973), but historical evidence suggests that people generally do not lower their fertility in order to improve their standard of living. From this perspective, the connection between population size and poverty is reciprocal: countries are poor because their populations are too large, and their populations are too large because they are poor. All of this suggests that an important answer to the problem of overpopulation is to change social and ecological conditions in ways that will both increase production and raise standards of living—and thereby motivate individuals to have fewer children.

From a conflict perspective, however, those who control societies are unlikely to choose this solution. As we will see in Chapter 11, conflict theorists believe that the widespread poverty found in many rapidly growing societies is due both to overpopulation and to social relationships through which an elite few exploit the mass of people and hoard large shares of wealth (see Mamdani, 1981). Marx (1867) argued that capitalist societies in particular depend on a "surplus" population to provide a supply of "readily exploitable manpower" (pp. 596–597).

This does not mean that the size and rate of growth of populations do not by themselves help perpetuate poverty for much of the population of the world. It does suggest, however, that slowing the growth of populations by controlling births may not by itself do much to improve living conditions. It also suggests that the causes and consequences of and the "cures" for problems of overpopulation depend not only on ecological factors such as technology, but on culture and social structures through which societies organize productive work and distribute the results among their members.

## Summary

1. Each form of life survives through a complex set of relationships with other creatures and with its physical surroundings. Ecology is the study of such relationships, and it focuses on four basic concepts: population, organization, environment, and technology (POET). Demography is the study of the size, growth, composition, and distribution of human populations.

2. The crude birth rate is the number of children born each year for every 100,000 members of a population, and birth rates vary both among and within societies. The number of births depends on both culture and social structure as well as on the proportion of women of childbearing age.

3. The crude death rate is the number of people who die in a given year for every 100,000 people in a population. The infant mortality rate is the number of children under the age of 1 who die each year for every 1,000 births. Death rates differ among societies primarily because of differences in culture (medical knowledge) and material conditions (sanitation and nutrition). They vary within societies because social statuses affect the quality of living conditions and access to medical care and knowledge.

4. The rate of natural increase is the birth rate minus the death rate. The theory of demographic transition is a three-stage pattern of population growth that has occurred in industrialized societies. In the first stage the growth rate is low because the birth and death rates are high. In the second stage the death rate falls while the birth rate remains high, producing a high rate of natural increase. In the third stage the birth rate falls and levels off close to the death rate, producing a low rate of natural increase.

5. Migration is the movement of people from one place to another, either within societies or between them. People who leave an area are called emigrants, and those who enter are called immigrants. Migration is primarily responsible for the growth of cities, often contributes to population growth, and has important social consequences for both receiving and sending areas.

6. The age structure of a population is the relative number of people of each age. Long periods of high birth rates tend to produce a young population, whereas low birth rates produce an old population. Young populations have a relatively high proportion of children who consume more than they produce, whereas old populations must devote a relatively large share of what they produce to the support of the elderly. A birth cohort consists of people born in the same year, and a cohort's experiences and opportunities depend on when in a society's history they reach each age as well as the relative numbers of people who are older and younger.

7. In comparison with small, sparsely settled populations, large, dense ones require more natural resources, find it harder to move to more supportive physical environments, tend to have more complex divisions of labor, and tend to be more urban.

8. The survival of a species depends on its relationships with its physical surroundings and other living things. An ecosystem consists of all forms of life that live in relation to one another and a physical environment. A niche is the position a species occupies in an ecosystem. Human niches are unique because they are very complex and can be altered with relative ease.

9. Technology, which is the accumulated cultural knowledge of how to use the physical environment, is the major way in which humans adapt to physical conditions. Hunter-gatherer societies relied on wild game and vegetation to meet subsistence needs; and in horticultural societies people cultivated small gardens with digging sticks and hoes. In agrarian societies the use of plows allowed people to cultivate large fields and produce a surplus of food. The Industrial Revolution introduced new sources of energy such as steam and electricity, machinery that multiplied the amount of labor one worker could accomplish, and centralized production in factories.

10. Although technology often has beneficial results, it can also have unanticipated latent consequences that create serious problems such as pollution.

**11.** Survival and the quality of human life depend on population size and distribution, the characteristics of natural environments, technology, how societies organize productive work, and how they distribute what is produced among their members. Thomas Malthus was one of the first to pay serious attention to the limited ability of physical environments to support large human populations. Although there is no doubt that the resources of the earth are finite, identifying the causes and consequences of and cures for overpopulation is a complex problem.

## Key Terms

age structure   125
birth cohort   126
crude birth rate   115
crude death rate   117
demographic transition theory   121
demography   113
ecology   114
>   ecosystem   130
>   niche   130
infant mortality rate   116
life expectancy   117
migration   123
>   emigrant   123
>   immigrant   123
population   113
rate of natural increase   119
society   113
technology   114, 131

## Recommended Readings

COALE, A. J. (1964). How a population ages or grows younger. In R. Freedman (Ed.), *Population: The vital revolution*. New York: Doubleday/Anchor (paperback). A readable and classic analysis of how birth and death rates affect the age structure of populations.

EHRLICH, P. R., et al. (1977). *Ecoscience: Population, resources, environment*. San Francisco: Freeman. An excellent introduction to the ecological perspective.

FORD, T. R., and DEJONG, G. F. (Eds.). (1970). *Social demography*. Englewood Cliffs, NJ: Prentice-Hall. Although published some years ago, this collection of articles gives a very useful look at the social aspects of birth, death, migration, and population composition, size, and distribution.

HALL, E. T. (1969). *The hidden dimension*. Garden City, NY: Doubleday/Anchor. A clear, highly readable look at the importance of physical space in social interaction.

HARRIS, M. (1974). *Cows, pigs, wars, and witches*. (1977). *Cannibals and kings*. Both New York: Random House. Harris is now famous for his entertaining and provocative uses of the ecological perspective to identify the origins of a marvelous collection of cultural practices.

JONES, L. Y. (1980). *Great expectations: America and the baby boom generations*. New York: Coward, McCann, and Geoghegan. An interesting look at cohort effects, with an emphasis on the Baby Boom and post–Baby Boom generations.

LENSKI, G. E., and LENSKI, J. (1982). *Human societies* (4th ed.). New York: McGraw-Hill. An excellent description and analysis of the historical development of technology and its effects on human societies.

PAPADEMETRIOU, D. G., and MILLER, M. J. (Eds.). (1984). *The unavoidable issue: U.S. immigration policy in the 1980s*. Philadelphia: Institute for the Study of Human Issues. A thorough, readable, multidisciplinary introduction to the complex issues and debates surrounding immigration to the United States.

SOMMER, R. (1969). *Personal space: The behavioral analysis of design*. Englewood Cliffs, NJ: Prentice-Hall. An important book that explores the effects of architecture and interior design on social interaction.

WEINSTEIN, J. A. (1976). *Demographic transition and social change*. Morristown, NJ: General Learning Press (paperback). A brief and clear description of demographic transition theory with a critical look at its usefulness when applied to nonindustrial and industrializing societies.

WELLER, R. H., and BOUVIER, L. F. (1981). *Population: Demography and policy*. New York: St. Martin's Press. A well-written introduction to the science of demography.

# PART III
# Social Organization

Having read Parts I and II you should now have a solid introduction to the major concepts that define sociology as a perspective. In Part III we begin a task that will occupy us throughout the remainder of the book: to use these concepts to direct our attention to the world in a new way. Along the way, of course, we will introduce you to still more concepts that apply to particular areas of social life.

We begin Part III with Chapter 6, a look at what is perhaps the most important of all social processes, socialization, through which each generation learns the fundamentals of its culture and how to perform the roles that go along with the many social statuses we occupy. Chapter 7 is the first of a series of three chapters that look at social life as it operates on three distinct levels: the level of the individual, the group, and the community. We close Part III with an in-depth examination of deviance and conformity, problems that exist at all levels of social life.

As you work your way through these chapters, keep in mind that the framework we are using rests on three basic concepts: culture, social structure, and ecology.

# CHAPTER **6**

# Socialization

On any given day, an estimated 365,000 babies are born in the world (Population Reference Bureau, 1984). As individuals they vary enormously in the color of their skin, hair, and eyes; in their weight and length; and in the frequency with which they cry or smile. With relatively few exceptions, however, they can all see, hear, smell, touch, taste, eat, cry, move, babble, sleep, play, smile, grimace, smack their lips, and chew their fingers. They can follow a slowly moving light with their eyes, grasp a small object placed in their palm, move toward and suck a nipple, and distinguish light and dark as well as different colors. In addition, they are all completely dependent on other people to take care of them (Fischer and Lazerson, 1984).

With time they will learn to sit, walk, talk, and make choices about what they do, think, and feel in relation to themselves and to the world outside the boundaries of their skin. They will acquire ideas and feelings about who they are, ought to be, and might become. They will, in short, become social actors through **socialization,** the process through which people learn to behave, think, and feel as individuals in relation to social and physical environments (see Bush and Simmons, 1981).

Both what these 365,000 babies learn and how they learn it depend on the characteristics of their social and physical environments, for if we could gather them all together and try to predict something as basic as the language they will speak as adults, we would be wrong much of the time. Even if we knew which infants had Chinese parents, for example, it would still be hard to predict, for those who live in San Francisco's Chinatown will probably never learn to speak Chinese.

If we consider babies who will grow up in a particular society—such as the United States—we can make more accurate predictions. Most will speak English, believe in Christianity or Judaism, aspire to a college education, value scientific thinking, drive cars, and spend more than 15,000 hours in front of television sets by their eighteenth birthday (Leibert et al., 1982). The similarities that reflect their common social environment will be matched by differences, however, for some will be poor and others will be rich; some will raise children but others will not.

Within any given society, then, there is both uniformity and enormous variation in who babies become as adults, and the sociologist's task is to explain how social environments enable people to participate in social life and yet also lead them along divergent paths as they become social actors. Many children play cops and robbers, but only some grow up to be cops, and some to be robbers—and most grow up to be neither.

For individuals, social life is a continuing process of interpreting perceptions and making choices as we think, feel, and act in relation to other people. Babies cannot use symbols to order their world in terms of beliefs and values, nor do they have any sense of themselves and their rights and obligations in relation to others. All of this must be learned by interacting with people who share their environments.

What we learn and how we learn throughout our lives is what socialization is all about; and to see how this happens, we begin by critically examining a long-standing debate about how human beings develop and then go on to explore some theories about how people learn. This leads to a discussion of what it takes to become a social being, and we end the chapter with a detailed look at both the social settings in which socialization occurs and how the socialization process continues throughout the life course.

## PUZZLES: WHICH BABY GREW UP TO BE WHICH ADULT?

Biological maturation turns babies into adults, but it is socialization that determines who and what they will become, how they will perform as social actors participating in social life while developing their own, individual selves. (Turn the page for the answers.)

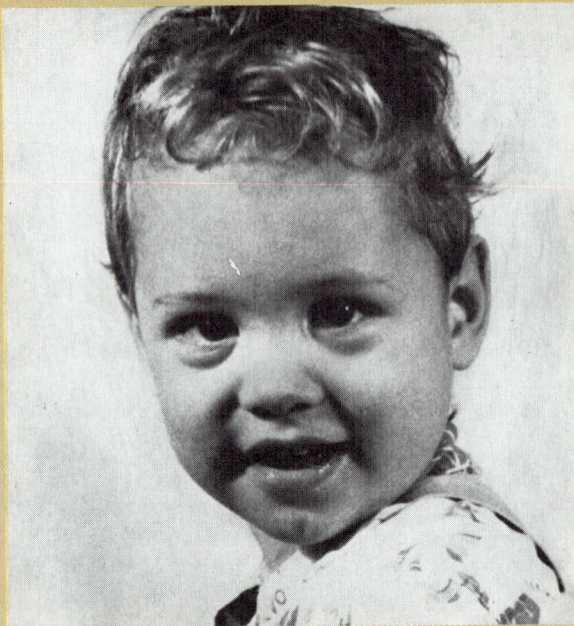

*a*

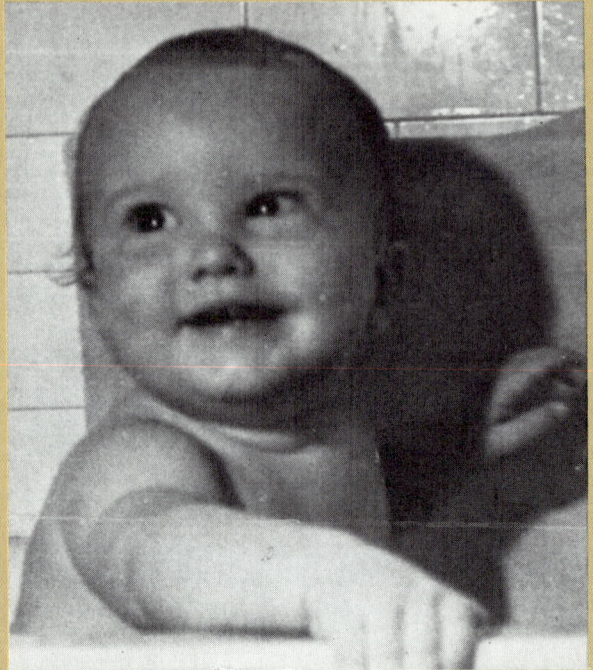

*c*

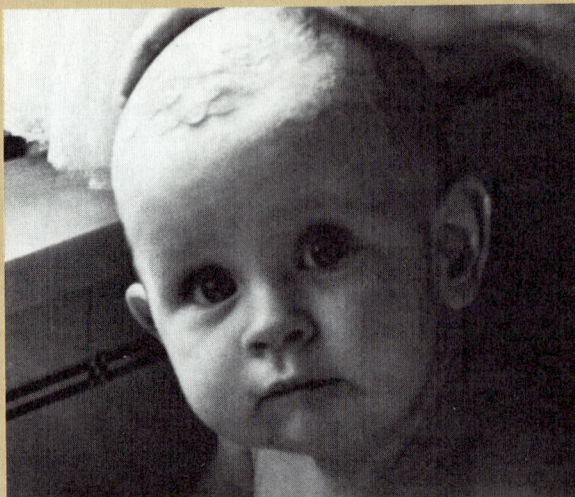

*b*

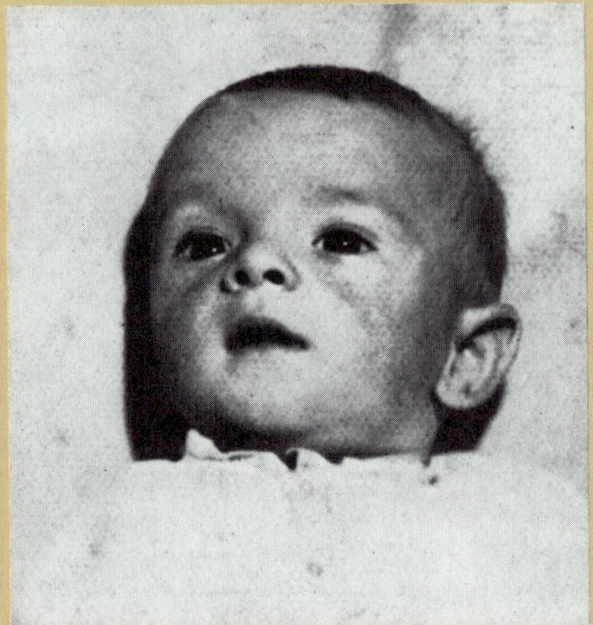

*d*

A

C

B

D

## WHO THE BABIES GREW UP TO BE

Baby *a* is adult C, a business executive; *b* is A, an artist; *c* is D, an engineer; and *d* is B, a jazz musician.

## Genes and the False Debate of "Nature versus Nurture"

The development of a human embryo is guided by 46 chromosomes, which have almost a million parts (genes) whose arrangement provides information—just as the arrangement of dots and dashes of Morse Code, representing letters of the alphabet, provides information. The genetic code determines characteristics such as the color of hair, eyes, and skin as well as a variety of disorders—such as mental retardation—that interfere with learning (Suzuki, Griffiths, and Lewontin, 1981). Genes also seem to affect IQ scores (Munsinger, 1975), certain personality traits (Wilson and Harpring, 1972), and some mental disorders such as schizophrenia (Kessler, 1975).

The most important effect of genes, however, is not on *who* people become, but on *how* they learn and develop. The noted linguist Noam Chomsky (1966), for example, believes that we are born with a "mechanism" that enables us to construct rules from the sentences we hear spoken; and when we begin to talk ourselves, we use these rules to generate grammatically correct sentences of our own. Genes also give us a voracious appetite for new information and experience. From infancy, we absorb knowledge like sponges, and yet—unlike sponges—we do not passively wait for something new to come along. We seem to be innately eager to interact with our environment, to hear, see, smell, taste, and touch as much as we can, and to act in ways that produce movement and change in our surroundings.

When scientists first raised questions about human development, they tended to take one of two extreme positions. Some believed that "nature" controlled every aspect of development—that behavior, feelings, and personality were dictated solely by genetic codes (McDougall, 1908). Others believed just the opposite—that by exposing them to the correct environment, healthy infants could be molded through "nurture" to become virtually any kind of human being (John B. Watson, 1928). During the last 25 years, research in biology, psychology, and sociology has made it clear that both explanations are naive and that the **"nature versus nurture" debate** rests on the false assumption that nature and nurture operate independently of each other (see Reynolds, 1980).

How, for example, do we explain the fact that dogs can see? The "nature" explanation is that they see because they have genes that result in eyes. But if we take a healthy newborn puppy and raise it in total darkness, it will be utterly blind when full grown. The dog's genes ensured that it was born with perfectly good eyes, but now it cannot see.

If eyes are not exposed to light, they deteriorate and become useless. Is sight, then, simply a matter of the right genes? Apparently not. Is it simply a matter of environment? No again, for all the light in the world will not enable an eyeless dog to see. The answer lies neither in genes alone nor in the environment alone, but in the *combination* of the two.

Most scientists no longer consider the issue of nature versus nurture to be a real debate, but its importance extends far beyond academic circles. As we will see in Chapters 12–14, the belief that biological factors cause social differences among races, genders, and people of different ages is often used to justify prejudice and discrimination. If, however, the subordinate social position of some groups—such as blacks, women, and the elderly—is created and reinforced by social environments, then prejudice and discrimination are *not* inevitable.

## The Importance of Human Contact

Like the newborn puppy, we cannot develop unless we are stimulated to use our abilities. Just as the eye needs light in order to thrive, infants require the stimulation of interaction with their surroundings in order to take shape as social beings. How often and in what ways people interact with us are basic characteristics of social relationships, and among infants contact plays an important part in both physical and social development.

Although the skin is actually the largest human organ, it is only since the early 1940s that scientists have begun to understand the importance of touch to human development and growth (Montagu, 1971). Touch, the most fundamental kind of human contact, constitutes our earliest interaction with other human beings. In some cases, touch is the *only* way to communicate (recall the famous story of Helen Keller, who was born deaf and blind). How often infants are touched is part of the social structure of their interactions with others, and social interactions reflect cultural ideas. Thus, social structure and culture are important not only to our physical and mental development, but to survival itself.

As important as physical contact is, it is language that lies at the heart of culture and social life, and without interaction with others we cannot possibly acquire it. Children who are frequently spoken to and played with develop their mental abilities more rapidly than do less stimulated infants (Yarrow, Rubenstein, and Pedersen, 1975). The importance of such contact is illustrated by documented cases of infants raised in isolation (usually because they were illegitimate and their relatives were ashamed of them). In one case, a 6-year-old girl named Isabelle was discovered in an attic in Ohio (Davis, 1940, 1947). From birth her only human contact had been with her deaf and mute mother. When she was found, she could not talk; she could only make a sort of croaking sound. Her performance on intelligence tests was so poor that researchers believed she would never be able to develop normal abilities. After only a week of care and training, however, she began to talk, and within two years her speech was as fully developed as that of any normal 8-year-old.

In another case, a group of children were orphaned after the Nazis killed their parents during World War II. Hidden in attics and basements and moved every night, they had only one another for companions. When they were rescued at the end of the war, they were poorly developed both mentally and physically, and their grasp of language was minimal (Freud and Dann, 1951). As they became attached to their adult teachers, however, their language skills grew rapidly.

Itard (1801/1962) recorded some cases of children who were abandoned by parents and apparently grew up in the wild. The physical development of such "feral" children had usually progressed normally, but their behavior resembled that of a different species altogether: they showed no interest in what went on around them

Although there have been few documented cases of feral children, this portrayal from Truffaut's film *The Wild Child* reflects the human fascination with those who develop outside the boundaries of human society and what they can teach us about ourselves.

and sat in corners and rocked themselves back and forth, not unlike some zoo animals deprived of normal interaction with their kind (Benedict, 1934).

The importance of contact and interaction go beyond normal physical and mental development, however, for through human evolution we have developed the ability to participate in social relationships, and in order to do this we must feel open to contact with other people. Research suggests that the development of trust and responsiveness depends heavily on social interaction during infancy.

There is some evidence that our attraction and responsiveness to other people depend on the amount of nurturing contact we receive as infants. When the children who were hidden from the Nazis during World War II were rescued, they feared and resisted any contact with adults. Only some time later did they learn to trust and form attachments with their teachers, explore their surroundings, and participate in relationships with new people.

Schizophrenics often feel that they have no connection with their own bodies or feelings, and their detachment from themselves is matched by a withdrawal from other people and from reality in general (Weiner, 1958). Clinical studies show that schizophrenics are especially unlikely to have had much (if any) intimate physical contact with others during infancy and childhood (Lowen, 1969), which suggests that awareness of ourselves and others as well as our ability to participate in social life are profoundly influenced by the structure of social contact during childhood.

## Some Theories about Learning

We come into the world with vast potential for exploring and experiencing ourselves and our surroundings, for using language and ideas to negotiate a complex social and physical world. Without sustained interaction with other people, however, we are much like the puppy raised in the dark or the child raised in the attic. It is through contact with other human beings that people learn; but how? This section includes several answers to this question.

### The Behavioral Approach and Albert's Rabbit

The **behavioral approach** to learning focuses on the observable things that people do, rather than on such unobservable things as what we think about what we do. When we eat a piece of food, our mouths produce saliva automatically in a biologically determined reflex action. In the early years of this century the great Russian physiologist Ivan Pavlov noticed dogs salivating at the sight of an empty food dish, and this led him to pose an intriguing question: Can learning affect automatic biological responses? Could he condition dogs to salivate in response to something even as unrelated to food as the sound of a bell ringing?

Pavlov (1927) tested his hypothesis on dogs. When he gave them food they salivated, and when he rang a bell they did not, just as one would expect. He then rang the bell when he gave the dogs food, and after several repetitions he found that they salivated whenever they heard the bell, *even when they were not given food.* He had thus trained the dogs' biological reflex to respond in a new way, a kind of training called *classical conditioning.*

The American physiologists John Watson and R. Rayner (1920) conducted a similar experiment with Albert, an 11-month-old infant who feared loud noises but not rabbits. Whenever Watson presented a rabbit to Albert, he also made a loud noise by banging two steel bars together, and soon Albert cried whenever he saw a rabbit, even in the absence of a frightening noise. Thus, Albert's reflex reaction of fear was conditioned to respond to rabbits. (Watson and Rayner's disregard for the effects of their experiment on Albert raises some serious ethical questions; most scientists would never conduct such an experiment today.)

In the 1930s the psychologist B. F. Skinner (1938) used rats to demonstrate a second form of conditioning. Skinner put a rat in a cage equipped with a lever that, when pressed, released a small pellet of food into the cage. In its normal wanderings about the cage, the rat happened to press the bar and received a bit of food. Soon the rat pressed the bar as fast as it could eat the food. A simple principle emerged from such experiments: we tend to repeat behaviors that are rewarded. A related principle is that we tend to avoid behaviors that are punished.

This second kind of conditioning is called *operant conditioning.* Whereas **classical conditioning** involves automatic reflex actions, **operant conditioning** involves behaviors we can control that are rewarded or punished. When children stop scribbling on walls because that activity brings on a spanking, they are learning through operant conditioning.

The behavioral approach focuses on the effects of conditioning on human behavior and attaches no importance to what people feel or think about what they do (Skinner, 1981). Certainly no one would deny that the effects of reward and punishment are important in our lives. College students may pick courses they do not like (but that promise an easy A) or avoid courses that interest them (in fear of a failing or mediocre grade). We may avoid trying to make new friends because we have been punished with rejection in the past. If we grow up with parents who demand perfection in return for love, we may then struggle to be perfect, believing that only then will people reward us with love.

However, the belief that all behavior is shaped by such conditioning is not supported by the evidence of science or of everyday experience. The complex behavior patterns of 260 million Americans are certainly not due to continuous monitoring of our behavior and the delivery of rewards and punishments. Although punishment is effective with young children, its effectiveness among older children and adults is very limited (Kagan and Havemann, 1980). There is still considerable disagreement about the effectiveness of capital punishment as a deterrent to crime, for example, and punishing older children or adults often results in rebellion, not obedience. If punishment is often ineffective among adults, then reward is the only explanation offered by the behavioral perspective for learning; yet much of our behavior is never rewarded by others.

In addition, behaviorism cannot explain our ability to make choices based on abstract ideas such as moral codes. A bomber pilot who disobeys an order to destroy a village because he believes it contains only innocent civilians can expect to be punished. Unless we assume that the pilot experiences punishment as a reward, it is difficult to explain his decision from a behavioral point of view.

Much of our behavior is learned without ever experiencing external rewards or punishments. Children often copy the behavior of parents and others they admire even when they are told not to. In short, we often use people and groups as **models**—that is, people who exemplify different kinds of behavior that we may or may not choose to imitate.

## Models and Social Learning

The realization that much learning takes place in the absence of rewards and punishments led to the development of the **social learning perspective**, which focuses on the way we select models whose

Much of what children learn comes from copying the behavior of adults.

behavior, attitudes, and beliefs we then imitate (Bandura, 1977). Children often use sexual words years before they have any notion of what the words mean. In the same way, children may imitate parents who contemptuously refer to blacks as "niggers" or to whites as "honkies" long before they understand either the meaning or the consequences of such attitudes (Quinn, 1954).

Most studies conclude that we choose models who are "attractive"; and during early childhood—before we have learned cultural beliefs and values—attractiveness appears to be mostly a matter of power. We imitate those who appear to control events and other people: young girls and boys, for example, both tend to imitate the parent who dominates the family, regardless of that parent's gender (Hetherington, 1967).

Neither the behavioral nor the social learning perspectives includes people's thoughts and feelings in explanations of their behavior; and neither can explain behavior that appears when there is no model present. The pilot in the earlier example, who was ordered to bomb a civilian village, had no "disobedient" model to imitate. He made a difficult moral decision, weighing what others expected of him against his own moral values about duty and the sanctity of life.

If 3-year-old children were confronted with a moral dilemma, however, they would have little idea of what to do, for moral values mean little if anything to them. At that age, moreover, they are incapable of learning how to make such judgments, regardless of the availability of models or the influence of punishments or rewards.

How is it, then, that adults can make such complex judgments and children cannot, regardless of their learning opportunities? One answer comes from the **cognitive development perspective,** which focuses on the growth of our mental abilities to make increasingly complex judgments about ourselves as well as our physical and social environments.

## Learning to Think

A 1-year-old boy sits on the floor next to his mother, who holds out a toy. As he reaches for it, she slowly hides it behind her back, letting him see exactly where she puts it. He wants the toy, but shows no sign that he knows where it is. Even though he saw where she hid it, he acts as though it no longer exists.

A 5-year-old girl sits in front of two sets of ten coins spread out on a table. If asked, "Which group has more coins?" she will reply, "They're the same." If we then stack one group into a column, she will probably say that the stacked group has more coins than the one still spread out on the table. By the age of 8, however, most children will know that the number of coins in each group remains the same no matter how we arrange them.

These kinds of observations led the Swiss psychologist Jean Piaget to believe that children's intellectual development passes through four stages, each bringing with it greater abilities to process information and make judgments. The ages that define each stage are approximate, and children often progress from one stage to another at differing rates (Piaget and Inhelder, 1969).

In the first two years (the sensorimotor stage), infants are able to move around, observe objects, and learn that things exist even when they are out of sight. Although they know some words, they are very limited in their ability to use language. Between the ages of 2 and 7 (the preoperational stage), they can use symbols to label things ("this is a jelly bean"), but they cannot use concepts to express the relation of one thing to another. If I hold up a bag of jelly beans and say to a 4-year-old boy, "There are ten jelly beans in this bag"; then hold up a second bag and say, "This one has just as many beans as the first"; then a third bag, saying "This one has just as many as the second bag," he will not know how many beans are in the third bag, because he cannot yet think in terms of the relationship among the bags.

Between the ages of 8 and 12 (the concrete operational stage), children are increasingly able to group and classify objects as well as see relationships among them. In this stage they know that if A is greater than B, and B is greater than C, then A is greater than C. They can classify objects into different categories, knowing, for example, that a banana can be classified simultaneously as "sweet," "fruit," "food," and "natural."

It is not until about age 12 that children begin to develop the ability to use rules to solve abstract problems (the formal operational stage). If we play the game Twenty Questions, and I say, "I'm thinking of an animal," a child in the concrete operational stage is likely to make an immediate random guess—"A cow!"—whereas an adolescent will approach the problem more efficiently and systematically, asking, for example, "Does it have horns?"

Like the behavioral and social learning perspectives, the cognitive point of view tends to ignore the fact that the decisions and judgments made by people depend on the ideas they acquire about themselves and others. Learning to be a social actor involves more than seeking reward, avoiding punishment, or copying those around us; and it involves more than the ability to think.

The disobedient pilot was not imitating a model or seeking rewards; nor did he make his decision simply because his level of cognitive development enabled him to make a moral decision. He oriented himself to a third source of motivation and guidance: his ideas about himself and his relationships with other people. As a social process, the results of socialization depend on the characteristics of social and physical environments, for these form the contexts in which individuals learn, develop, and behave over the course of their lives.

## Becoming Social Actors

The seventeenth-century philosopher John Locke believed that infants come into the world knowing nothing at all: their minds are a blank slate on which others "write" the sum total of children's knowledge as they mature into adults. To Locke, children were little more than passive receptacles into which knowledge was "poured."

Recent research, however, suggests that infants know more than we might think they do. In one study, 3-month-old infants watched video tapes of a woman reciting nursery rhymes. In the first tape she read the rhyme normally, but in succeeding tapes the voice did not match the movement of her lips. In the distorted versions, infants were more easily distracted and lost interest in the rhymes. Thus, by 3 months of age, infants are already aware of the relationship between the human voice and face. As one of the researchers concluded, the research of the last two decades "shows that the infant, instead of being a blooming mass of confusion . . . is a very complex creature who is capable of thinking, feeling, and processing enormous amounts of information about the world" (Michael Lewis, in Rubin, 1982).

Locke's view that infants' minds are a "blank slate" is correct in a very important sociological sense, however, for they cannot use symbols to represent objects and experience. They do not have to be taught to withdraw their fingers from a hot flame and cry in pain, but they do have to learn the idea of "hot" so that if someone says, "Don't touch that; it's hot!" they can avoid being burned. Thus, although infants are born with some basic drives and reflexes, they are unable to make a connection between abstract ideas and actual experience.

Locke was also correct in the sense that infants have no idea of social relationships and the expectations that govern them. They certainly experience themselves and others—feeling their own hunger and the smell, touch, and taste of their mother's breast—but without words they cannot have an *idea* of themselves or of others. They cannot think about what ought to happen or what they ought to do themselves, about which actions are "right" and which are "wrong," about which goals are worthy and desirable and which are not. They may love to play with their food, but only later will they learn whether or not playing with food is defined as bad manners in their culture. In short, infants are unaware of culture and socially structured relationships. Their awareness grows, however, at an astonishing rate, and an important key to this process is language.

### *Language*

A 1-year-old girl sits on a kitchen floor and watches her father put the groceries away. He reaches into a box of cookies and holds one out to her. Her face lights up and she reaches for it, but he holds it back. "Cookie," he says, and she reaches harder. *"Cookie,"* he says again, and then gives it to her.

Later he gives her another, but only after getting her attention and repeating the word "cookie." Later still, while he sits and reads, a seemingly small event occurs. She crawls to his chair, hauls herself up, tilts her head to get his attention, and says, "cookie!"

This event is in fact tremendous, for it marks the beginning of a revolution in the child's relationship to the social world. The cookie is no longer simply an object: it is represented by a symbol that the little girl can use to affect other people's behavior. No longer does she have to sit and fidget or cry until an adult figures out what it is she wants: now she can *tell* them. The word is a bridge between her desire and its satisfaction, and in the words of the sociologist Charles Horton Cooley (1902), she has "tasted the joy of being a cause, of exerting social power."

Just as she uses symbols to command others, so can others use them to command her, and once the meaning of a word is shared between them, life will never be the same for her again. Consider an-

Language allows us to label both objects and experience, from the danger of a hot stove to the sweetness of falling in love.

other scene: now she is standing next to a flower pot, rocking it back and forth on the table. Suddenly she is startled by a sound from her father: "No," he says. She turns to the sound and sees a stern look on his face. She looks at him for a moment, then rocks the pot one more time, and it falls to the floor and crashes in a messy heap. Suddenly she feels a sharp, painful spank on her behind and hears that sound again—"No!"

The word "no" is no longer simply a sound; it is a sound the infant associates with anger, fear, and pain. If she stops what she is doing, no anger or pain follows; if she continues, the unpleasant experience is repeated. From this she learns that the word is related to both her behavior and the speaker's; *it is a bridge of meaning between them.*

One word begets others, and words are the building blocks of cultural ideas which are organized in role relationships. Just as the little girl learns the names of objects, so too does she learn to name herself and others. This is of enormous social importance, for the act of naming is more than mere pointing: "to tell what a thing is, you place it in terms of something else. . . . To *define* a thing is to mark its boundaries" (Burke, 1945). Language increasingly ties children to a world of meaning and social expectations, boundaries that both require and enable them to participate in social life.

## Cultural Ideas

With language, children acquire beliefs ("There is a God in heaven"; "Santa Claus comes at Christmas"; "What goes up must come down") and use them to interpret the world. Americans allow young children to believe in magic, ghosts, and goblins, but require older children to give up such beliefs. Adults cannot prove that goblins do not exist or that it is impossible to transform a pumpkin into a carriage at the wave of a magic wand; they can only assert these beliefs with words. In order to belong to the adult world around them, children must literally change their beliefs about what is real. If American babies were raised among Korean peasants, they would not surrender such beliefs, for the religion of shamanism rests on the belief that the world is filled with powerful spirits that inhabit trees, rocks, and living things.

Language is also the medium through which children learn values, norms, and attitudes. The value that "it is better to give than to receive" flies in the face of infantile desires to take in as much as they can and hold on tightly to what they have; they literally must learn to give, and they must learn to support such acts as "good."

There is nothing "natural" about eating with silverware (fingers are often more efficient) or defecating and urinating in a toilet, and yet children in Western societies learn that adults expect such behavior. There is also nothing inherent in skin color that would lead children to despise people of different races, nor anything inherent in age that would cause them to despise and fear or to revere the elderly. Like other cultural ideas, attitudes are human creations that are expressed and learned through the use of symbols.

It is important to emphasize that socialization is not a uniform experience in which everyone in a society acquires the same beliefs, values, attitudes, and norms. Although a culture may contain ideas about what everyone should become—honest, for example—it also includes ideas that make distinctions among people who occupy different statuses. When Bem and Bem (1976) asked adults to predict what a newborn boy would be doing as an adult, it was difficult for the respondents to answer the question, because they could imagine many possibilities for him. When asked the same question about a girl, on the other hand, the respondents tended to predict with ease and confidence that she would be a wife and mother and that these would be her most important roles in life.

Variations also occur because in most societies children are exposed only to portions of the surrounding culture. In a small Vermont town, for example, children might never encounter a black or Asian person; they would therefore have little sense of what racism is. The children of professional parents are unlikely to consider coal mining as an occupation, whereas the sons of coal miners may imagine nothing else. Because our social statuses are points of view from which we perceive the surrounding society, they influence our exposure to cultural ideas as well as to the social structures of everyday life.

Thus, it is inaccurate to think of complex societies as having a single, universal culture. Although some cultural ideas apply to everyone—such as laws and a common language—many exist only in subcultures. Russian is the official language of the Soviet Union, but that country includes many different peoples speaking scores of languages that reflect sharp cultural differences. Similarly, walking through Chinatown in San Francisco, a Mexican neighborhood in San Antonio, New York City's Harlem, or the Italian section of Boston makes it clear that although all are located in the United States, they represent subcultures that foster and maintain striking differences in social life within society.

Whatever culture or subculture we are exposed to, however, one aspect of socialization is universal: children learn that their bodies and experiences do not belong solely to themselves, for there is an expanding world of "others" who express active interest in what they feel, think, and do. Children's awareness of other people is perhaps the most fundamental element of socialization, for it underlies the discovery of ourselves and others as participants in webs of social relationships and ideas.

## Socialization and Social Structure

At the heart of socialization is the child's growing awareness that the social world involves more than his or her experiences, desires, and needs. Infants are totally absorbed in themselves and their own needs—they experience themselves and the world through their senses, through hunger and thirst, pain and comfort, cold and warmth, loneliness and contact—but society is more than a population of individuals who act, feel, and think. The core of social life is a complex set of relationships among individual selves, and before children can participate fully they must acquire an awareness of themselves in relation to other selves.

**Id, Ego, and Superego**  To the founder of psychoanalysis, Sigmund Freud, the self consisted of three distinct parts (1923/1960). He believed that all people are born with desires and impulses—to be sexual and aggressive, and to seek pleasure, for example—and these together he called the **id.** After the first few months of life the *ego* begins to develop. According to Freud, the **ego** is the rational part of ourselves that develops as we learn to curb our pursuit of pleasure and instant satisfaction. At about age 6, the *superego*—or conscience—develops in response to feelings of fear of parental power. In Freud's scheme, the **superego** is the source of moral standards and feelings of guilt and shame.

To get a clearer idea of what Freud was trying to describe, consider a teenage boy who steals a cassette tape from a large department store because he wants it and is unwilling to wait until he can earn the money needed to buy it. His id is the source of his desire to have the cassette without having to wait; and his superego is the source of the knowledge that what he is doing is wrong—that the theft violates ideas about what kind of person he should be in the eyes of his parents and adult society. His ego is his "manager," who not only figures out how to steal the cassette and get away with it, but also how to soothe the conflict between his id and superego. One way to do this,

for example, is to say to himself, "It's a big store; they won't miss one cassette." In this way, his ego tries to satisfy the demands of both his id and his superego.

To Freud (1913, 1930), the process of socialization was one of conflict between the desires of infants and the demands of society. But the sociologist George Herbert Mead (1934) focused on a very different aspect of socialization—the process through which we use *symbols* to discover both other people and ourselves and thereby learn to participate in the social world.

**"I," "Me," "Others," and "Mind"** As an illustration of Mead's point of view consider anger, which as an emotion is invisible to others. We may feel enraged, and yet present ourselves to other people as contented and calm. We may even hide the truth of our anger from ourselves. When we make an angry face, shake our fist, and say, "Damn it, I'm mad!" we are using gestures and language to communicate otherwise invisible feelings.

It is through language (both verbal and nonverbal), Mead believed, that we come to know the feelings and thoughts that make up the private lives of other human beings.

Children fear adult anger and may learn to avoid provoking it, but cats and dogs are fully capable of the same kind of learning. It is when children learn to *label* another's feelings, expectations, and actions that they take a crucial step toward full participation in social life. How is this so, and why is it important?

Angry words represent feelings; behind the angry words are selves who think, feel, and act both in relation to themselves and to others. Without symbols, however, infants cannot know that people have points of view; that they think, feel, and make decisions. This is of enormous importance, for "being unaware of other points of view, they are necessarily unaware of their own—as a point of view. It simply is the way things are" (Brown, 1965, p. 220).

When infants are punished for knocking over flower pots, they learn to use the word "angry" to label a person's response. The label marks an important transition because they can apply it to their own feelings as well. Now when someone says, "I'm angry," children know how the speaker feels. Something familiar to them is going on behind the words, in another person.

The transition is completed when children can understand the statement "*If* you do that I *will* be angry." To understand such statements, children must look at their own behavior from another person's point of view. In this way, *they discover themselves through their discovery of others.*

Mead (1934) developed the sociological concept of *mind* to describe this ability to "put ourselves in another's place." **Mind** is the ability to use symbols in order to be aware of other people's feelings, thoughts, and expectations, and we develop mind by using language. Children begin their lives without this awareness, for without symbols they experience the world directly through their senses: things are what they appear to be, not what they mean. Mead identified this "self"—this direct experience of ourselves and others—as "**I.**" "I" is that part of us that feels hunger, satiation, pain, frustration, joy, ecstasy, and desire.

As children acquire language, they learn that they live in a social world in which people share ideas about themselves, the world, and their relationships with one another. In this way, Mead believed, children learn to look upon themselves as others look upon them, to view themselves and

their behavior from other people's points of view. This transition can be seen in small children when they respond to themselves just as their parents respond to them. When children learn "no," for example, they often apply it to themselves: it is not uncommon to hear them say "no" to themselves as they are about to do something they should not, or to scold themselves after the fact ("bad boy"). Who are these "selves" who scold and say "no" to themselves?

To Mead, the voice in children that says, "Knock that thing over and see what happens," is the "I"; but the interior voice that says "no" is enormously important to their social development, because it shows that *they have a point of view on their own behavior*. Language enables us to "talk to ourselves," to conduct internal conversations in which one part of us looks at "I," interpreting its desires, needs, feelings, and behavior in terms of cultural ideas. Mead identified this second voice in such "conversations" as the "**me.**"

Although we are all born with an "I," our "me" arises *only* from social interaction, for the "me" is that part of ourselves that views ourselves and our behavior just as if we were another person. Without language, Mead asserts, the "me" cannot develop, for it is the medium through which we share our different points of view with one another.

Mead uses the example of a game to demonstrate his concepts of "I," "me," and "mind." When several infants play in the same room, they pay very little attention to one another. They may struggle over possession of a toy, but they do not orient themselves to one another's expectations, for without symbols and ideas they can have no expectations. They are "parallel playing"— alongside one another but not *with* one another.

The first step away from parallel play comes when children begin to use language to pay attention to the expectations of particular people, such as a parent or a playmate. When a little girl's "I" is tempted to grab every toy in the room, her "me" may say, "I'd better share them with my brother, because if I don't, mommy will get angry." In this case, the girl is orienting herself to the expectations of what psychiatrist Harry Stack Sullivan called a **significant other**—a particular person who is important to her. She is not yet playing a social role, because she has no awareness that she occupies the social status of "playmate" and that sharing

Unlike older children playing a game, infants in parallel play do not share a set of expectations.

toys is a social expectation of all playmates in her culture.

To learn a game such as baseball, she must orient herself not to the expectations of significant others, but to an abstract set of rules that describe the relationships among the players, telling them who does what in each situation. If she fields a hit while George is playing first base and the bases are empty, she does not base her decision to throw the ball to him on her personal knowledge of what he wants her to do (George, in fact, may be tired and bored and could not care less where she throws it).

She throws it to him because that is what a fielder does in that situation regardless of who is playing each position. The person playing first base may be a total stranger to her, yet she still knows when to throw the ball to first and when not to.

In a game, players orient themselves less to the expectations of significant others than to what they believe are the expectations shared by all players in general. They orient themselves to what Mead (1934) called the **generalized other,** which is our perception of the social environment itself, including the cultural ideas that govern our interactions with others. When we travel in a bus, buy something in a store, or go to the movies, we have no personal knowledge of what other individuals in the crowd expect of us. Instead, we rely on our social knowledge of what people in general expect of one another in those situations; and our perception of these expectations is our generalized other.

When children learn to orient themselves to the generalized other in a game, they take a crucial step toward fully social behavior, for in order to know what to do in each situation, players must put themselves "in the place of" anyone playing each of the other positions. They must, in short, learn to play roles in relation to role partners in social relationships.

**Statuses and Roles**  As we saw in Chapter 4, statuses are positions in social relationships, and roles are the sets of expectations attached to those positions. As children develop an awareness of themselves and others, they learn that their experience and behavior take place in the social context of statuses and roles that affect people's expectations, including their own. The adults who take care of them are mothers or fathers, wives or husbands, employees or bosses. As children begin to understand their positions in a family, they discover that siblings, mothers, and fathers have expectations and obligations that differ from those of casual playmates, aunts, uncles, grandparents, and total strangers. Although their parents, for example, have the legal right to hit them, other adults do not; and even parents do not have the right to physically injure them.

When children are told never to go anywhere with a stranger, they learn to make distinctions among people according to their social relationship with them. They learn that their alternatives depend on the social situation, not merely on their impulses (such as to accept candy offered by a stranger). They are learning the basics of life in social structures, to choose among alternatives according to their positions in social relationships.

As early as the fourth year, American children become aware of racial differences (Ambron, 1978); and they can identify their own gender by age 3. In an experiment involving young children, Thompson (1975) investigated children's understanding of gender. Although 2-year-olds could identify pictures of themselves, they were wrong as often as they were right when asked to label themselves or others as "girl" or "boy," "woman" or "man." By contrast, 3-year-olds not only correctly identified themselves and others in terms of gender, but could see the similarity between themselves and others of their gender. At an early age, then, children are able to use gender as a pair of categories into which they can sort people, including themselves.

How do children tell one gender from another? Thompson and Bentler (1971) showed dolls to a sample of American adults and children between the ages of 4 and 6. The dolls had either male or female genitals, breasts or a muscular torso, and long or short hair. Thus, a doll might have female genitals but no breasts, and a short haircut still typical of American men. The subjects in the experiment were asked to decide how the doll should be dressed for a party, to give the doll a name, and to predict if the doll would be a "mommy" or a "daddy." Only a quarter of the children explained the gender label they used by referring to genitals or the appearance of the doll's upper body; most used hair length as their primary cue. This suggests that younger children use both cultural and biological cues to identify gender.

As children label themselves and others in terms of statuses such as gender, race, ethnicity, social class, age, and family position, they learn to categorize people just as they learn to distinguish rocks from plants and night from day. There is much more involved, however, for cultures attach beliefs, values, attitudes, and normative expectations to each social status and its occupant.

Thus, as children locate themselves in social structures, they learn "who they are" in the eyes of those who share their culture, how they are valued, how people feel about them, and what their rights and obligations are in relation to others. They are, in short, developing ideas about themselves that will become major parts of their *social* selves.

## Self-Concepts and Self-Esteem

Each of us has many abilities, needs, wants, and inclinations. The world outside our skin is a collection of objects that we experience largely through our senses until we learn to use language. With language we construct ideas, and just as we have ideas about objects outside us, so do we have ideas about ourselves. Taken together, these ideas form a **self-concept,** the sum total of our beliefs and feelings about ourselves (Gecas, 1982; Rosenberg, 1979, 1981; Rosenberg and Kaplan, 1982).

Self-concepts are a curious phenomenon. When I describe myself, the object of my attention is "me"—myself. If I say, "I am a good dancer," I describe myself just as I might describe someone else. Thus, we use symbols to "split" ourselves into both subject and object (Mead, 1934), to feel love and hate, respect and contempt, tenderness and rage for our selves, and to hold beliefs about our selves that may or may not be true—that we are God or Wonder Woman, or that we cannot possibly understand calculus. Unlike ideas we have about objects outside ourselves, the self-concept is important to everyone because we bring ourselves and our self-concepts to almost every experience.

Self-concepts are rarely simple or objective, for they include judgments and evaluations of who we are, and corresponding emotions such as pride, contentment, and shame. Self-concepts are also particularly difficult to confirm as true. We may believe that we are intelligent and place a great deal of importance on that image of ourselves, but we are continually vulnerable to evidence to the contrary. Self-concepts are fragile, and given their importance to us, they can produce considerable anxiety as well as a variety of behavior designed to protect our ideas and feelings about who we are.

**The Self in Social Mirrors** Where do self-concepts come from? Imagine Victor meeting Teresa on their first date. In such a situation, Cooley (1927) argued, we have:

**1.** The real Victor, known only to his maker.

**2.** Victor's idea of himself; such as, "I look terrific in this new shirt."

How we think we look has less to do with our reflections in mirrors than with our reflections in the ideas about beauty contained in our culture.

**3.** Victor's idea of Teresa's idea of him, such as "She thinks I look great."

**4.** Victor's idea of what Teresa thinks he thinks of himself, such as "Teresa thinks I think I look terrific."

**5.** Teresa's idea of what Victor thinks of himself, such as "Victor thinks he's something else."

**6.** What Teresa really thinks about how Victor looks, such as "That's the worst shirt I ever saw."

And of course six analogous phrases that apply to Teresa.

In the simplest interaction, we use each other as mirrors, both casting another's reflection and looking for our own. Like the Queen in "Snow White," who chants "Mirror, mirror on the wall, who's the fairest one of all?" we look to others for confirmation of who we think we are. Social relationships are thus "an interweaving and interworking of mental selves" (Cooley, 1902): Victor imagines Teresa's mind, especially what she thinks about him. Unlike a mirror, however, we do not simply reflect each other; we evaluate and judge the selves we encounter, and those judgments are part of the reflection.

We all have ideas about how good looking we are, and they do not come simply from looking in a mirror on the wall. If we think others see us as plain, we think of ourselves as plain (until, perhaps, we meet someone who thinks we are beautiful). Whether or not others consider us beautiful depends in part on our culture, for each culture has its own standards for beauty. Like beauty, many aspects of our selves exist in the eye of the beholder, and each beholder is influenced by culture. Because we depend on other people's perceptions of us in order to see and evaluate ourselves, we tend to perceive ourselves as we believe others perceive and define us (Mead, 1934; Shrauger and Schoeneman, 1979).

When we imagine how others perceive and feel about us, we are constructing what Cooley (1927) called the **looking-glass self.** The looking-glass self is not who we actually are; nor is it how other people actually perceive us. Rather, it is our perception of how other people see and evaluate us.

A few studies show that we tend to see ourselves as others actually see us (Rosenberg, 1979). In one study, 195 adults were divided into ten groups ranging in size from 8 to 48. After some time together, they were asked to rate their own intelligence, likability, physical attractiveness, and self-confidence on a five-point scale. They were also asked to rate each group member and to estimate how others would rate them. In almost every group, people who rated themselves highly tended to be rated highly by others.

There is a stronger relationship, however, between people's self-ratings and their *perception* of how others would rate them (Miyamoto and Dornbusch, 1956), and unlike the studies discussed in Rosenberg above, most studies show relatively little correspondence between people's self-concepts and how they are actually perceived by other people (Gecas, 1982). Our ideas about ourselves strongly reflect how we think others perceive us. In important respects, then, we perceive and experience ourselves indirectly.

In many cases, we form a looking-glass self by using significant others as mirrors; but we also use perceptions of how the generalized other views us according to our statuses. American presidents, for example, are expected to be "presidential"—to be decisive, courageous, and "in charge" of the nation's affairs. Vice-presidents, on the other hand, are generally invisible—little if any real leadership is expected of them and they take a "back seat."

When vice-presidents suddenly become presidents—as Harry Truman and Lyndon Johnson did when Presidents Roosevelt and Kennedy died—they often surprise the public by "rising to the occasion" and displaying leadership abilities that no one thought they had. In many cases, rising to the occasion is a matter of looking at ourselves in a different mirror. When Harry Truman succeeded to the presidency, he was suddenly seen by other people as the president, and so he *became* the president. Thus, self-concepts arise from interactions through which we perceive mirrored reflections of ourselves as seen by others.

**Social Identities** From a sociological point of view, the most important parts of any self-concept are those that reflect our participation in social environments. As we acquire statuses in social relationships and learn the cultural ideas associated with them, we draw upon those ideas to describe ourselves not only to other people, but to ourselves as well. This social component of the self-concept is our **social identity,** a complex set of cultural ideas about us as occupants of social statuses (Rosenberg, 1979; Stryker, 1981).

All cultures contain abstract categories that make distinctions such as "living" and "dead," "animal" and "mineral," "good" and "bad"; and at the moment of birth, children enter a variety of such categories. In Western societies, infants are described in terms of gender, race, age, nationality, and social class. Although such statuses have no meaning to infants, they do influence the beliefs, values, attitudes, and expectations of the adults around them. A male Irish Catholic newborn living in Belfast, Northern Ireland, for example, cannot know that members of society will tend to have differing expectations of him, his sister, and a male Irish Protestant newborn living across town, but as he matures and participates in the life of his society, he is likely to use such external ideas about him as he forms his own ideas about himself.

Children expand their social identities by joining groups formed around shared interests or beliefs. Religious beliefs or interest in sports take on new meaning as children define themselves in terms of group membership. "I play baseball" becomes "I'm a Yankee in the Little League"; "I go to school" becomes "I'm a third-grader"; "I believe in Muhammad" becomes "I am a Muslim."

Social identities are also based on behavior. A child who steals may be labeled a "thief," a girl who is obedient and kind a "good girl," a boy who likes poetry a "sissy," a brilliant student a "genius," and a struggling one a "dummy." Thus, what we do may become an important part of who we think we are, and this, in turn, may influence our behavior and feelings in profound ways. A child who accepts the label of "dummy" may give up in school, whereas a "genius" may live under continuing pressure to live up to extraordinarily high and sometimes impossible expectations.

In forming identities we also draw upon an enormous number of psychological traits such as "generous," "aggressive," or "shy"—just a few examples of the more than 12,000 English words and phrases that describe such characteristics (Gordon, 1976). Although we tend to think of such traits as "personal," they often come from the roles attached to social statuses. "Nurturant" mothers, "serious" bankers, and "scholarly" professors tend to see themselves (and be seen by others) according to the expectations attached to their roles, often regardless of behavior and feelings to the contrary.

Although social statuses, group membership, behavior, and psychological traits refer directly to individual characteristics, culture often extends the boundaries of social identities to include physical objects (Cooley, 1902) as well as other people. When people talk about the objects they own, they often reveal that possessions form an important part of their sense of who they are (Csikszentmihalyi and Rochberg-Halton, 1981). Men often value expensive cars because they believe others will see them as rich and sophisticated. Objects we do not possess can also be important: people often respond to an attack on their nation's flag for example, as if they themselves were the victims.

In a study of 2,000 Baltimore schoolchildren from grades 3 through 12, for example, researchers asked, "If someone said something bad about your mother, would you feel as if they had said something bad about you?" Over 89 percent of the children responded that they would, whereas only 24 percent felt that way about their state governors (Rosenberg, 1979). When children taunt one another by saying, "Your mother has a mustache," it is thus clear to all involved that the attack is on the child, not the mother.

The most stable parts of our identities are those that other people will confirm, and for this reason when we describe ourselves to others, we are likely to focus on our social statuses to define who we are. When Kuhn and McPartland (1954) asked people to answer the question, "Who am I?" with 20 words or phrases, their first answers were most often given in terms of social identities: "Mary Callahan, woman, graduate student, daughter, sister." Only after exhausting social categories did they describe themselves in terms of *personality*—the complex patterns of thought, feeling, and behavior that make each of us unique. Thus, in important ways, we know ourselves as we are known by others, and the vast majority of people know us only through our positions in social relationships with them. If someone points to your sister and asks, "Who is she?" your first response will be, "She is my sister," indicating not what makes her a unique self, but her social structural position in relation to you.

Finally, the last part of our social identity that distinguishes us from all other people as unique individuals is our name and, in complex societies, our numbers: social security, driver's license, credit cards. Although it may seem strange—if not offensive—to suggest that names and numbers are all that socially define us as unique individuals, it is important to remember that other people cannot possibly know the combination of characteristics (many of which are invisible) that presumably make each of our selves unique. I could describe a man's personality in the most minute detail, and yet you could not be certain that you knew him until I told you his name.

We use cultural ideas to construct what we think of as an obvious, natural, commonsense view of ourselves and other people (Garfinkel, 1967). "Obviously" there are two genders, and everyone is either one or the other. Some cultures, however, identify three: male, female, and one in the middle (Kessler and McKenna, 1979). This might seem laughable to one who identifies gender by a person's genitals, yet each year some people are born with a combination of female and male genitals (Money and Ehrhardt, 1972); and in the Olympics, medical examiners use chromosomes, not genitals, to determine the athlete's gender. Each of us, in our daily interactions with others, identifies a person's gender without any knowledge of what his or her genitals look like.

Social identities are powerful because we have little control over many of their aspects. We can hide some statuses from other people (if we lie about our education on a job application, for example), but in many cases we cannot. Race, age, and gender are usually highly visible social statuses, and we are severely limited in how much personal control we can exert over how other people perceive and respond to us as "white," "black," "woman," or "man."

By giving us a sense of who we are (whether we are alone or with other people), social identities are like anchors that hold us in the world by connecting us to other people in social structures. This is never more apparent than when social identities are disturbed, especially when other people do not confirm that we are who we think we are. When people lose their jobs and are unemployed for long periods of time, it is a rude shock to a social identity that includes "self-supporting adult."

When we lose important parts of our social identities—by being expelled from school, fired from a job, or losing a spouse—we often feel a sense of "nonexistence," as if we had been cut loose and were drifting aimlessly through the world, and in a social sense this is true. We still are "who we are" as individuals, but our ties to the social environment have been severely damaged, and until they are replaced or repaired, the feelings of loss, sadness, and disorientation continue.

Social identities, then, are the basis of our participation in social life, our feelings of belonging and being known by others. There is more to self-concepts, however, for social identities indicate not only who we are, but who we *ought* to be as well. (In light of what you have now learned about social identities, look back at Chapter 1, p. 12, and make a new self-survey of who you are.)

**Ideals, Self-Esteem, and Reference Groups**
When children are asked, "What do you want to be when you grow up?" their first answers tend to follow individual interests—to ride red fire engines or dance in the ballet; but they soon learn that there is more involved in such choices than what appeals to them. Americans, for example, have long shared the value that it is better to be a lawyer, doctor, engineer, or business executive than to be a firefighter, coal miner, or carpenter (Hodge, Siegel, and Rossi, 1964), and as children absorb cultural values, they draw upon them to construct their **ideal self.**

In an important sense, culture is "the stuff that dreams are made of," and such dreams become parts of self-concepts: "I am not only a little girl who writes poems and stories; I am a girl who will someday be a great writer." Such images are important not only as descriptions of ourselves that we use as maps to guide our way into adulthood, but also as sources of **self-esteem**—the positive and negative feelings we have about ourselves (Rosenberg, 1979). Feelings such as pride and shame, or confidence and insecurity all reflect different levels of self-esteem (see Helen Lynd, 1958).

As children identify their places in social structures, they learn that cultural values rank some characteristics and social statuses higher than others. In the United States they may learn the fundamentals of racism, sexism, elitism, and ageism: that white is valued above black, yellow, red, and brown; male above female; intellectual labor above manual labor; and young above old (whereas in the Soviet republic of Georgia they would learn to revere the old more highly than the young). We rarely describe anything without at once passing judgment on it: "kind," "intelligent," and "beautiful" are not simply different from "cruel," "stupid," and "ugly"; they are culturally ranked as better.

When self-concepts correspond to culturally valued identities, we tend to feel good about ourselves, and if they do not, our identity and self-esteem suffer, sometimes to the point of being stigmatized by negative labels such as "alcoholic," "mental patient," or "thief" (Goffman, 1963b). Low self-esteem often has substantial conse-

Adolescents often choose as reference individuals people—such as rock musicians—who are considered deviant in the eyes of their parents.

quences: a study of 5,000 high school students found that 80 percent of those with low self-esteem were highly depressed, whereas this was true of only 4 percent of those who reported high self-esteem (Rosenberg, 1965).

Through socialization, we use values to create an ideal self and to make judgments about ourselves. We also compare ourselves to **reference individuals** and **reference groups**—people and groups that we use as models of desirable or undesirable appearance or behavior (Hyman, 1942; Hyman and Singer, 1968; Singer, 1981). We select reference individuals because we want to be like them or because we want to be *un*like them. Children, for example, often say they want to be like their mothers or fathers when they grow up, and evaluate themselves according to their parents' values. As adolescents, however, they often select new reference individuals—from professional athletes and rock musicians to teachers and famous writers—and in many cases this involves a rejection of parental values. In this sense, a punk-rock musician replaces a parent as a positive reference individual, and parents become negative reference individuals ("I sure don't want to be like my parents").

We also compare ourselves with reference groups (Festinger, 1954). Students who are at the top of their high school senior class often find that they are no longer at the top in college, and may as a result feel they are not as capable as they thought they were. Their self-concept may change not because they themselves have changed, but because they are using a new reference group as a point of comparison.

Like reference individuals, reference groups may provide us with models of who we want to be as well as who we do not want to be. And we do not actually have to belong to a reference group in order to use it to evaluate ourselves. For many Americans, for example, the Ku Klux Klan is an example of racism at its worst, and, as a negative reference group, it gives them a point of comparison for favorably evaluating their own racial attitudes.

The fact that we often select reference groups without being members is enormously important for four reasons. First, it explains why our beliefs, values, and attitudes so often differ from those of groups to which we do belong. The children of immigrant families may never learn their native language, because—as they aspire to become members of the surrounding society—they choose a reference group whose language differs from that of their parents.

Second, because we do not need to belong to reference groups, we can have more than one, and this contributes to conflicting self-evaluations. Lesbians may feel good about themselves when they use other lesbians as a reference group, but feel bad about themselves if they use co-workers who disapprove of homosexuality.

Third, the concept of reference groups helps explain why people begin to change their attitudes *in anticipation* of joining a group. This is called **anticipatory socialization** (Merton and Rossi, 1968), and it plays an important part in the learning of roles. When children try to act "grown up," they are using adults as a reference group long before they become adults themselves. Students in graduate schools typically evaluate themselves in terms of the professional group that they hope to join in the future. A great deal of socialization, both among children and adults, is thus anticipatory, because we are acquiring the beliefs, values, and attitudes that are associated with roles we do not yet perform.

Finally, the reference groups we compare ourselves with have an important effect on which parts of our identities we are most aware of and care the most about. Most characteristics have meaning only in comparison with other characteristics: the idea of "female," for example, has no meaning without the idea of "male." To identify ourselves as "female," "black," or "heterosexual," we must have some point of comparison—such as those who are male, white, or homosexual. Without an awareness of people with contrasting characteristics, we have no reason to attach any special significance to our own.

In one study 500 high school students were asked to spend five minutes talking about themselves, saying anything that came to mind. Only 1 percent of the white students mentioned their race, whereas 17 percent of the blacks and 14 percent of the Hispanics mentioned theirs. Why the difference? The study was conducted in a school in which 83 percent of the students were English-speaking whites; only 9 percent were black and 8 percent were Hispanic. As far as racial identity was concerned, dominant whites compared themselves with students of their own race, whereas many of the visible minority of nonwhite students compared themselves with members of the dominant group and were thus more likely to be aware of their racial identity (McGuire et al., 1978).

If we are unhappy with how we compare with reference individuals or groups, we can change our identities by acquiring new statuses that have higher cultural value—getting a better job or going to college—or by concealing those characteristics that lower our self-esteem. We can also choose (or create) new reference groups. When lesbians or blacks separate themselves from society, they are trying to create reference groups in which "lesbian" and "black" are highly valued characteristics.

Another way to narrow the gap between who we think we are and who we want to be is to lower our commitment to various parts of the ideal self. This changes not the content of our self-concept, but its structure, rearranging characteristics in terms of their importance to us. Like James Thurber's character Walter Mitty, we all have fantasies about who we might be, and so long as they are mere fantasies they do not threaten our self-esteem. Most of us spend our lives performing quite ordinary roles, and we protect ourselves when we say, "Sure, I'd like to be rich and famous, but I can live without it."

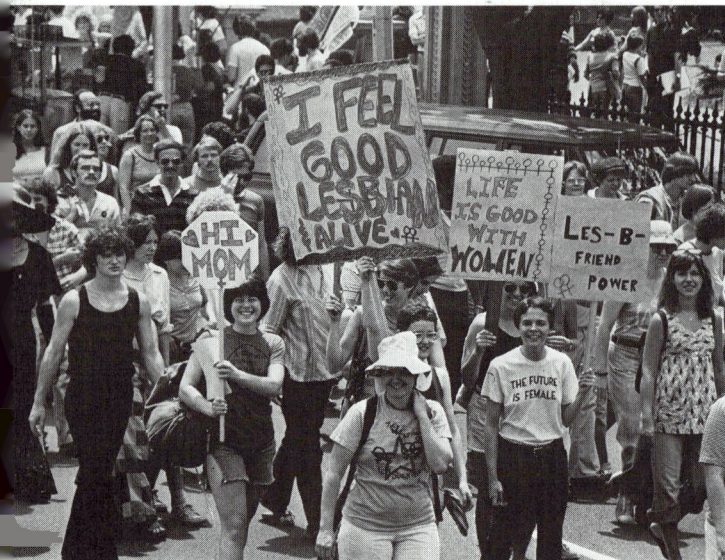

The most radical solution to low self-esteem is not to change from one reference group to another, but to change the reference group itself. This is a major goal of many social movements such as the women's, civil rights, gay rights, and senior citizen movements. When blacks proclaim to a white-dominated society that "black is beautiful" or when feminist artists write song lyrics that celebrate being female, they are supporting their own self-esteem and sending a message to the surrounding society, exerting pressure for change in the prevailing value system. The goal is to create a culture in which people can participate fully and openly and have high self-esteem.

## Socialization and the Life Course

The fact that we adopt many different reference groups during our lives highlights an important fact about socialization. Childhood may be the most intense learning period of our lives, but socialization does not end when we reach adulthood.

The process of socialization takes place over the course of our entire lives, and is affected by major social institutions including the family, schools, the mass media, and the economy (see Part V). We repeatedly discard old roles and learn new ones—a process that is called **resocialization**—and as our reference groups change, so do our perceptions and evaluations of who we are (Bush and Simmons, 1981; Gecas, 1981).

### Rites of Passage

Because people's rights and responsibilities depend not on who they "really" are but on their social identities, control of the statuses people claim as parts of their identities is an important part of all societies. In order to legitimately assume the status of "college graduate" or "married," for example, we must participate in cultural ceremonies that mark our movement from one social status to another. These **rites of passage** mark the transition from one status to another and they represent social control over social identities (Van Gennep, 1909).

The passage from childhood to adulthood is perhaps the most universally important transition in culture, for adulthood brings with it social power. In all societies people are children until they are culturally defined as adults, and this may take place long after they are physically mature.

In some societies the rite of passage from childhood to adulthood is well defined, involving, for example, a ceremony in which the child's genitals are mutilated (Van Gennep, 1909). In others, such as our own, the rites are more ambiguous: in most states young men and women are allowed to marry and have children before they are old enough to vote or purchase liquor. Although the law defines adulthood in terms of age, simply reaching the age of 18 or 21 does not necessarily lead others to define and treat us as adults. As mentioned earlier, the important thing in the social world is not so much who we "really" are, but who other people think we are.

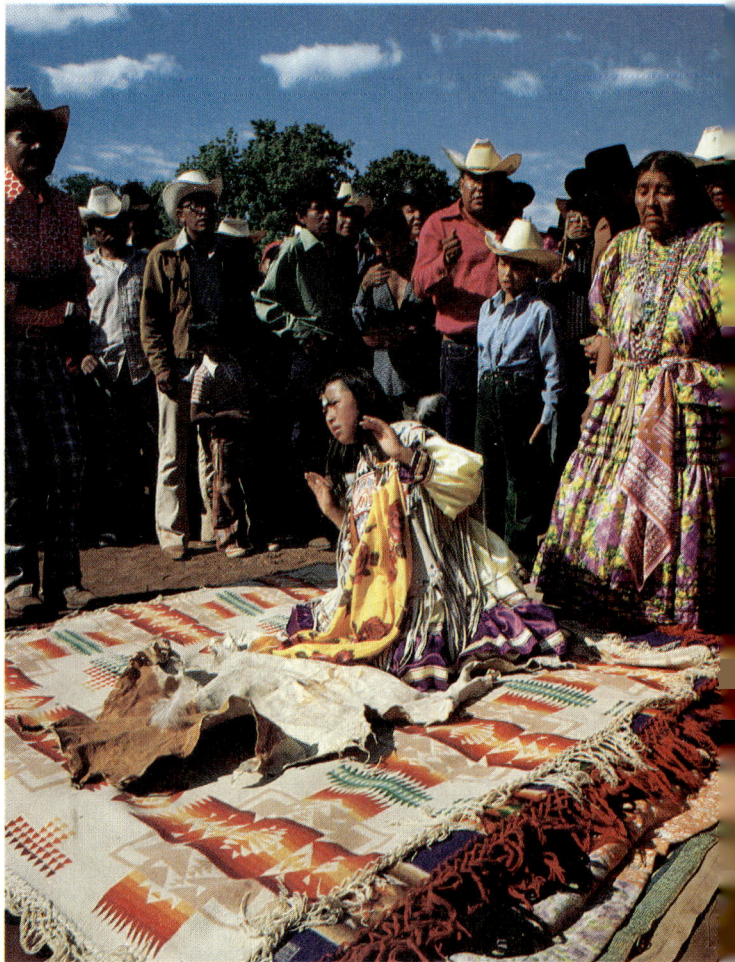

This Apache puberty rite is an example of the ways in which all cultures include rites of passage through which people make the transition from one status to another.

---

PUZZLES:

## ARE YOU A CHILD OR AN ADULT?

How do you know that you are one and not the other? What about other people—do they always agree that you are what you think you are? If not, why?

As you will see in this chapter and again in Chapter 14, age is more than a matter of time. It is one of the most significant and universally recognized of all social statuses. That is why it is so important that we know which age group we are in and why being unsure can generate so much anxiety.

---

The following three sections take a brief look at the importance of social institutions in the socialization process. For more detailed discussions, see Chapters 15 and 16.

### Socialization in Families

One of the primary functions of the family as a social institution is to socialize children. How children are socialized as family members depends both on the reference groups and individuals that parents orient themselves to (such as their own parents, their social class, or their ethnic subculture) and the structure of family relationships.

As they raise their children, lower-class American parents generally value obedience to authority, neatness, cleanliness, and staying out of trouble more than middle-class parents do. Middle-class parents in a variety of societies are more likely to stress creativity, self-discipline, ambition, independence, curiosity, and self-direction (Ellis et al., 1978; Kohn, 1977; Slomczynski et al., 1981). Although lower-class parents evaluate their children's behavior primarily in terms of its positive or negative consequences, middle-class parents pay more attention to their children's intentions (Wright and Wright, 1976).

Class differences in family values produce sharp differences in the methods parents use to socialize their children. Lower-class parents who value obedience, for example, are more likely than middle-class parents to use physical punishment. Middle-class parents rely more on reasoning, guilt, and threatened loss of love to control their children (Maccoby and Martin, 1983; Wright and Wright, 1976).

Class differences in child-rearing values do not occur simply by accident. Lower-class children, for example, can eventually expect to depend on jobs that require them to follow orders rather than make independent judgments, and they are less likely to have advanced educations that lead to higher responsibilities within a given occupation. Middle-class children, on the other hand, are more likely to become professionals, managers, and administrators when they grow up.

Thus, class differences in child-rearing values play an important part in the reproduction of classes. When working-class parents raise their children to be "good workers" who obey authorities, they unwittingly prepare them to participate in social relationships that will give them an unequal share of wealth, power, and prestige in the adult world. In similar ways, when upper-middle- and upper-class parents see to it that their children have the best educations, they, too, play a vital part in the reproduction of class relations (R. Robinson, 1984).

**Birth Order** Of all the structural characteristics that affect socialization in families, one of the most intriguing is **birth order**—a concept that refers to a child's age in relation to the other children in the family. A variety of studies show that birth order affects children's development through their patterned interactions with siblings and parents (see Ernst and Angst, 1983).

Mothers tend to interact more with first-borns than they will with later-borns at the same age, and they also tend to use more complex vocabularies and concepts with them. Mothers tend to expect first-borns to mature more quickly than later-borns; they are more likely to punish, reward, and pressure them to achieve; and they tend to be anxious to help first-borns solve problems, whether or not the help is needed (Lewis and Kreitzberg, 1979; Rothbart, 1971). In comparison, later-borns receive both less attention and less pressure and are more influenced by other children than first-borns are (Dunn and Kendrick, 1982).

Birth order affects patterns of interaction between children and parents, and this, in turn, seems to affect children's development into adults (Vockell, Felker, and Miley, 1973). Hoyt and Raven (1973), for example, found that in comparison with later-borns, first-borns are more likely to seek the company of others during times of stress: during the 15 minutes following an earthquake, first-born women talked with twice as many people as later-borns did. Schachter (1959) found that among experimental subjects who were threatened with a shock, first-borns were twice as likely to choose to wait with others, whereas later-borns more often chose to wait alone. Such birth-order effects have been found in many other studies.

First-borns also tend to trust authorities more than later-borns do (Suedfeld, 1969), and first-born men are more likely to conform to social pressures (Sampson and Hancock, 1967). In addition, Winter (1973) found that first-borns are more likely than later-borns to seek power, probably because they often have power over their younger brothers and sisters during childhood. Prominent leaders—such as U.S. presidents—are unusually likely to be first-born children.

Thus, the earlier we enter a family group, the more attention, stimulation, and pressure we are likely to receive, and the more power we are likely to have in relation to others. As adults, the higher we are in our family's birth order, the more likely we are to strive for power and achievement, to trust those in authority, to experience anxiety and guilt over our personal failings, and to seek the company of others in times of stress. This is a classic example of how people's positions in social structures affect the development of individual characteristics.

## Socialization in Schools

Like the family, the school is an institution whose major manifest function is socialization. What most students learn in school consists primarily of formal studies—math, history, languages, and science—but perhaps the most important contribution of schools to socialization lies in their "hidden curric-

ula": the beliefs, values, attitudes, and norms that are imparted in the process of learning formal subjects.

Students in American schools, for example, learn that they are expected to be punctual, neat, obedient, and polite. What they want to do is no longer important, and activities are rigidly scheduled. They learn that individual competition and success are more valued than working together in groups. For many American middle-class students, the cultural messages in the hidden curriculum are an extension of socialization in their families; but for many others—including blacks, Hispanics, and poor people—the middle-class values of most American schools differ sharply from those they experience at home. In fact, one of the major functions of early public schools in the United States was to weaken the ability of immigrant families to socialize their children according to their ethnic subcultures, so that their children would grow up sharing the dominant white, Anglo-Saxon culture (Lasch, 1977).

Because they help prepare children for adult life, schools play a major role in anticipatory socialization. There is much more involved than mental skills, however, for schools help shape children's social identities, including their visions of which statuses they can occupy as adults. Lower-class students, for example, generally receive less encouragement to go on to college than middle- and upper-class students do; and they—along with blacks—are more likely to be placed in "slow" tracks in school, regardless of their test scores (Shafer et al., 1967).

In comparison with boys, girls receive relatively less encouragement to pursue careers, especially in science and the professions (Schaffer, 1981). As early as nursery school, boys generally receive more attention on academic work and more encouragement to work independently. Girls, on the other hand, are rewarded for showing dependency on the teacher and are more likely to have a teacher offer assistance whether or not they need it (Serbin and O'Leary, 1975).

Most characters in school textbooks are male—especially characters who occupy important statuses—and women are usually portrayed as "helpers": nurses, secretaries, mothers, and elementary school teachers (Women on Words and Images, 1975a; St. Peter, 1979).

Thus, the hidden curriculum of most American schools sends different messages to students of different genders, races, and social classes. In comparison with students who are nonwhite, female, or poor, those who are white, male, and middle- or upper-class generally receive more encouragement to perceive themselves as people who will one day occupy responsible positions that will bring them a disproportionately large share of wealth, power, and prestige. They are more likely to see themselves as people who will go to college and get good jobs, and in anticipation of this, they are more likely to do what they have to do in order to prepare themselves (Smith, 1981).

**Peer Groups**  The concept of **peer group** refers to people who have a similar level of social standing, especially in terms of age. Schools compete with families for influence in the socialization process, but adolescent peer groups compete with both families and schools. In his study of high schools, for example, Coleman (1960, 1961) found that students worried about pleasing their friends as often as they worried about pleasing their parents. Whereas high school teachers generally place their highest values on academic performance, student peer groups do not; rather, they tend to value athletic ability and popularity, and rank academic performance a distant third.

Peer groups are particularly powerful in industrial societies because young people are excluded from most serious adult statuses and their success as adults does not depend on their family ties. In small village societies, on the other hand, the entire village is regarded as a single family, and adult statuses are distributed according to people's positions in the village.

Eisenstadt (1956) believes that adolescents in industrial societies turn to one another because they feel "on their own" and isolated from adult

In industrial societies, the exclusion of young people from important adult statuses greatly elevates the importance—and therefore the power—of peer groups.

society. As they struggle toward adulthood, they are therefore likely to feel that other adolescents are the only ones who really understand what they are going through. The distinctive music, language, and dress of adolescent subcultures exist not in order to set them apart from adults, but as a reflection of the fact that society has already set them apart (Coleman, 1961). Thus, it is not surprising that pressure from peers is a frequent motivation for adolescents to engage in behavior—such as sex and the use of alcohol, cigarettes, and illegal drugs—that violates the restrictions placed on them by adult society.

## The Importance of the Media

The mass media—television, radio, movies, books, newspapers, and magazines—produce a steady stream of images that reflect ideas about how we should look and behave, and the kinds of objects we should own. Punk-rock music celebrates violence and deviant behavior, whereas ballads portray romantic love as the solution for all individual problems.

To sell products in competitive markets, advertisers tell us how we should look, smell, and behave as well as what things we ought to own in order to be attractive to others. Cigarettes are associated with lone, handsome cowboys ("Marlboro Country") and beautiful women who have "come a long way"; cars are described as "sexy" and offered as a way to show how "free-spirited," "independent," or "intelligent" their owners are. Expensive liquor is offered as a sign that those who drink it have succeeded in the world ("Don't you deserve to go first class?").

Like schools, the media often transmit hidden messages by their way of communicating the surface message. Advertisements rarely portray women as the equals of men: women rarely instruct men and voice-overs are always male (Courtney and Whipple, 1983; Goffman, 1976). Advertisements for products designed to make men and women sexually attractive never use men and women of different races in the same situation, which implies that interracial attraction does not exist.

For many of us, the images portrayed in various media are like mirrors in which we look for reflections of ourselves as well as information about other people. "Is *my* breath bad? Is *this* what it's like to be in love? Is this what whites (or Hispanics or Chinese) are *really* like?" The media attempt to portray most aspects of life in our society, from the way police officers perform their jobs to family and work relationships, personal hygiene, and life in different social classes. In *All in the Family*, and, later, *Archie Bunker's Place*, Archie Bunker reinforced the stereotype that working-class people are ignorant racists (which draws attention away from racism among middle- and upper-class people) (Gans, 1980). The general absence of nonwhites in leading roles in television and films reinforces the stereotype that only whites have dramatic lives and are capable of heroic action (Withey and Abeles, 1980). In the same way, the dominant roles generally reserved for male characters in television soap operas reinforce the stereotype that men are more capable than women (Cantor and Pingree, 1983).

The power of the mass media lies primarily in the fact that they portray what is often beyond the experience of many viewers; and thus images of social life can replace direct experience as our source of knowledge about the social environment. Middle- and upper-class people can use television shows like *All in the Family* as a substitute for personal knowledge of life in the working class, just as lower- and middle-class viewers can use *Dallas* to represent the upper class.

When images are oversimplified and distorted, they support stereotypes—oversimplified, distorted views of people in different statuses. But such images also encourage us to experience life at such a distance that we do not feel the consequences of human behavior. Most war movies focus on glory and heroics, not pain and suffering, and the thousands of fictional murders portrayed on television threaten to turn violence into a meaningless event for all but those who are directly involved.

The mass media, of course, also have the power to educate and to challenge stereotypes. Television shows such as *Roots, M*A*S*H, Holocaust,* and *The Day After* may have done much to make people more aware of racism, the human consequences of combat, the realities of persecution, and the horror of nuclear war.

Just how much influence the media have over our perceptions, feelings, and behavior is still unknown (Withey and Abeles, 1980). Whether or not watching violent behavior on television stimulates aggressive behavior in children, for example, is still hotly debated, and there are as yet no consistent findings that point in one direction or the other (Milavsky et al., 1982; National Institute of Mental Health, 1982). Although some critics take the view that the media are a major socializing agent, it has yet to be demonstrated scientifically that they are any more than one piece of an intricate web of social factors.

## It Never Ends: Adult Socialization

"I'm grown up now" is a statement that reflects an important and false belief that socialization is confined primarily to children. Books such as Gail Sheehy's *Passages* (1974) bring our attention to the fact that we acquire new roles, drop old ones, and experience change in existing roles as we age. Thus, socialization continues throughout our lives, and often takes the form of *re*socialization as we adapt to changing circumstances (Gecas, 1981).

**Paper Chases and Professional Training** In the television series based on *The Paper Chase*, John J. Osborn's 1979 book about life at Harvard Law School, Professor Kingsfield gives his first-year law students a crisp and clear statement about professional training: "You come in here with a head full of mush, and if you survive, you'll go out thinking like a lawyer." Notice that he does not say "knowing the law," but "*thinking* like a lawyer." "You will teach *yourselves* the law," he tells them, "but *I* will teach you how to *think*."

Like most people who undergo training for an occupation, many graduate students believe they are in school to acquire specific skills, or to obtain degrees; and although they are certainly correct to some extent, they are often unaware that they are learning more than medicine, law, business management techniques, or sociology: they are also learning to *be* doctors, lawyers, business executives, and sociologists. They are, in short, learning to perform roles that require far more than technical knowledge and skills.

Physicians, for example, are noted for often paying less attention to patients as human beings than as "cases" that offer them opportunities to diagnose and treat "conditions." A common explanation for such behavior is that doctors practice role distance in order to protect themselves from repeated exposures to suffering and death. Becker and Geer (1958), however, offer another explana-

### Voices: Professional Socialization— Learning about Death

People die. I don't like it. I *really* don't like it. I've sat with a lot of people and watched them die. I told the medical students the other day—they thought I was crazy—"Come on, this one's going to die, you've got to watch this." They looked at me like I was *nuts*. I drug 'em in there—*made* 'em. "Watch this person die," I said. "It's going to happen. You've got to think about what's going on in your mind when this person's dying." I know what goes on in my mind. It makes me feel *bad*, it makes me feel weak and impotent, and I think that's good, because there are things that I cannot affect, and I'm not going to die trying to affect them. I'll let them go. But I'll sit here, and I'll take my lumps. (a senior resident)

Source: Harwood, "The Ordeal: Life as a Medical Resident." *New York Times Magazine*, June 3, 1984.

tion based on several years of participant observation in a large medical school.

First-year students, they found, enter medical school full of idealism based on sincerely held values and, in some cases, on a desire to disprove the common belief that doctors are greedy and self-serving. They are eager to help people, to heal the sick, and relieve suffering; but in their first two years, they rarely see—much less actually treat—patients. Instead, they study subjects such as chemistry and anatomy, taught by Ph.D.'s who are not physicians. They soon learn that they cannot possibly learn everything there is to know about medicine, and quickly adjust to medical school as a place in which students learn to please their professors and pay as much attention to passing exams as to learning skills that will enable them to put their ideals into practice.

It is not until their third and fourth years that they actually see patients; but even then, they are constantly quizzed about their technical knowledge:

The student becomes preoccupied with the technical aspects of the cases with which he deals because the faculty requires him to do so. He is questioned about so many technical details that he must spend most of his time learning them. (p. 53)

Thus, there is good reason to believe that physicians who treat patients as "cases" rather than as human beings do so in part because they were socialized to think of patients in this way. As Becker and Geer note, however, many medical students become more concerned with ethical and human factors in medical practice as they near graduation, providing evidence that in even the most intense socialization experiences, individuals often hold on to their values until they are at last in a position to put them into action.

**Starting Out: The Twenties** Between the ages of 20 and 30, a majority of Americans begin their first jobs, marry, and have children. In spite of the fact that most grow up in the presence of their married parents, there are serious limitations on how well anticipatory socialization can prepare anyone for marital roles. Sustained emotional intimacy is one of the most difficult challenges adults face, and Americans in particular place heavy emotional demands on marriage.

In the 1980s young married people must also struggle with rapid change in the roles of women and men. It is no longer taken for granted that wives will stay at home while husbands devote themselves to paid work outside the home. For many couples, the families they grew up in no longer serve as models, and husbands and wives must create their own roles to a considerable degree.

The birth of a couple's first child also brings with it major readjustments. Suddenly a new and demanding member is added to the family, and spouses acquire the new statuses of mother and father. In addition to learning the difficult role of parenting, both must adjust to the loss of the continuous intimacy and free access they had to each other when they were first married.

Those who remain single must also adjust to new roles as they make their way in a society dominated by married couples. In their early twenties, most of their friends are also single, but as they approach 30, many of their friends are married and interact primarily with other married couples. Single people nearing 30 must learn how to satisfy their emotional needs outside of marriage, and find themselves having to consider whether or not they will ever marry at all (Staples, 1981; Stein, 1981).

Whether or not they are married, most people in their twenties are employed, and because occupational roles occupy a large portion of people's time, they are important sources of socialization. Accountants learn to pay attention to small details; lawyers learn to focus more on legally relevant facts and winning arguments than their consequences for people; advertising executives learn to value selling a product more than conveying accurate information about it. Teachers become disciplinarians and guides for their students, and office workers often adapt to bureaucratic settings by becoming rule-minded and rigid themselves (Merton, 1968; Moore, 1969).

Because we frequently change jobs during our lives, occupational resocialization is a common experience. We start our first jobs as the "new kid on the block," and after a period of probation and possible disappointment and confusion, earn our places as work-group members. When we change jobs, however, we must in some ways start all over again and learn a new set of beliefs, values, attitudes, and norms.

**Decision Time: The Thirties** The twenties are generally an exciting and challenging period of trying new roles, and our youth makes us unaware that our life spans are limited. By comparison, the thirties are often a time of serious reflection about our lives (Sheehy, 1974).

Parents must learn to give up control over their children who now approach adolescence. Many couples divorce during their thirties, and must adjust to the disruption of family life and the demands of living alone or raising children by themselves—often in poverty (Gordon, 1981; Rosenthal and Keshet, 1978; Weiss, 1979).

Unmarried people must deal with the difficult question of whether or not to marry at all; and childless women in particular—whether married or not—must cope with the biological fact that their years of potential childbearing are limited. Whether or not to include motherhood as a part of their lives is a difficult and irrevocable decision, because unlike most other statuses, "mother" is limited by biological aging.

The thirties also are a time of intense reflection about occupations. The excitement over a "first job" in the twenties is often replaced by a disturbing question in the thirties: "Is this what I want to do for the rest of my life?" For many people—especially those in the working class—such questions are a luxury, for they have relatively little control over how to earn a living. For middle- and upper-class people, on the other hand, the choice is a real one—between the security of a job they do not like and the risks involved in cutting loose and looking for a better one.

Thus, the thirties appear to be a time for making important decisions about major roles. This period is, for many, like a pivot on which the rest of their lives will turn (Sheehy, 1974).

**Mid-Life Crises: The Forties and Fifties**  At midlife, we begin to adjust to the consequences of all the decisions we have made, and it is often a time of reconciling dreams with reality.

Marriage and parenthood are not the "bliss" that many thought they would be. Children leave home, and even those parents who breathe a sigh of relief must adjust to their shrinking parental roles and a sudden loss of responsibilities. For women who have not had children, their decision is now irrevocable, for childbearing is risky after 40 and by age 55, 96 percent of all women have experienced menopause (U.S. Department of Health, Education, and Welfare, 1961).

By this time, many have also discovered that their dreams of occupational and financial success are not likely to come true, and they must content themselves with what they have (Sheehy, 1974). With fresh generations of workers entering the labor force each year, older workers are less able to take occupational risks, because the chances of successfully competing for new jobs are relatively slim.

Perhaps the most difficult adjustment of midlife involves the realization that we are not immortal, especially in societies in which death before old age is relatively rare. For children and people in their twenties, death often seems so remote that it is no more than an idea; but in midlife, the "end of the tunnel" begins to come into view, and as we adjust to the failure of many dreams to come true, we must also confront the reality of our eventual deaths.

**Learning to Grow Old**  Old age is a time of major readjustments in status and role sets (Riley et al., 1969). Retirement ends occupational roles, which—until old age—occupy most of people's daily lives. Aging can also mean the death of one's spouse and friends. Elderly men who become widowers and who do not remarry have death rates significantly above those for other men of their age (Helsing and Szklo, 1981); but Hyman (1983) found no massive short- or long-term negative effects on elderly women who become widows.

In industrial societies, people are forced to retire by specified ages (65 and 70 in the United States, depending on the job) and people who have worked their entire lives must adjust to the lower prestige of people who no longer earn a living. For many, old age causes sharp declines in income. In 1981, for example, 74 percent of those over the age of 64 had incomes of less than $10,000, compared with only 39 percent of those between the ages of 35 and 44 (U.S. Census Bureau, 1983c).

Because women generally outlive men, a large proportion of older people are widows who live in poverty because Social Security is their only source of income. Elderly women are also more likely to live by themselves: in 1982, 41 percent of elderly women lived alone compared with only 14 percent of elderly men (U.S. Census Bureau, 1983c).

Perhaps of most importance is the fact that the elderly must fully confront the reality of death, because for the first time in their lives many people of their own age are dying (Kübler-Ross, 1969, 1975). Time is literally running out at a rapid pace, and for many elderly people old age is a time of serious reflection about the meaning of their lives.

Stereotyped views of old age often portray it as a negative stage in life in which people are socialized to accept loss of loved ones and important roles and, ultimately, of life itself. It is important to emphasize, therefore, that for many elderly people old age is a very positive experience. The "loss" of roles is also an end to responsibilities—to children, spouses, and employers—and for many, old age is a time in which they have more freedom to run their own lives than ever before.

## Socialization and Freedom

As we have seen, socialization is a lifelong process that brings with it countless changes in the roles we play. It is a process that raises some important issues about the nature of social life, and we close this chapter by examining a few of them.

Infants sometimes wake in the night and cry until someone simply picks them up and holds them for a while. They often have more difficulty falling asleep on a large bed than in a cradle whose size is closer to their own. They seem to need *boundaries*, solid contact with people and things that give them a sense of where, if not who, they are. We are not unlike infants in this way. When we are left without any limits we tend to feel lost, floating in a kind of infinite void, and we reach out for familiar things and people in order to reorient ourselves.

In short, we are social animals who need one another, and yet our relationships with one another are regulated by the ideas we draw from a shared culture. As the studies of isolated children show, we cannot survive as autonomous, lone individuals, and so to satisfy our need for one another we must forgo a good portion of individual freedom.

Socialization is more than a process that prepares individuals for social life, however, for it is

In Nazi Germany, to be a good German was to be a good Nazi.

also a means by which societies are perpetuated. There is more at stake than what we become as individuals, how we adjust to social demands and succeed or fail within their limitations. Also at stake is the kind of society we adjust to and the part we play in changing or perpetuating it. It is ironic that if we are socialized effectively, adjusting perfectly to our social surroundings, we may at the same time perpetuate social injustice and cruelty. For German children who grew up in Nazi Germany during the 1930s, hating Jews and Poles was part of being a "good German," and their adherence to this cultural ideal self ultimately led to World War II, the Holocaust, and the destruction of Nazi Germany.

In similar ways, girls who learn to be "feminine, submissive women," and boys who learn to be "masculine, dominating men," are not merely acquiring roles and identities that allow them to operate in a sexist society. As we will see in Chapter 13, they are also being socialized to participate in the dominance of women by men. Girls who adopt traditional roles learn to accept a subordinate position in society, whereas boys learn to value and hold the power that comes with their gender status. Thus, while we learn to be masculine or feminine in a sexist society, we also learn to participate in and perpetuate sexism.

This raises a crucial point about socialization and the relationship between individuals and societies. All of us are socialized in the sense of becoming social beings. In every society, almost everyone forms a social identity and learns to interact with other people and to perform roles. This does *not* mean, however, that each of us is molded according to a uniform cultural model—that we all become no more than a mirror image of our social environment (Wrong, 1961).

Like individuals, societies constantly change, and how they change depends strongly on the choices individuals make. Without society the individual does not exist; it is also true, however, that without individuals there can be no society or webs of ideas and social relationships that give social life meaning and form. Because we are social beings, our dependence on others makes us vulnerable; and yet we have the power to resist the limitations of social environments, to define and redefine the terms on which we and others will live.

## Summary

1. Socialization involves both what we learn and how we learn as we become social beings; these, in turn, depend heavily on culture and social structure. We learn to orient ourselves to cultural ideas according to our positions in social structures, and through this we acquire an awareness of ourselves and of others and develop self-concepts on which we base self-esteem. Although our ability to be socialized is rooted in biological development, the process itself cannot unfold without social interaction and language—thus, our dependence on both "nature" and "nurture."

2. The behavioral, social learning, and cognitive perspectives are the three principal theories about how people learn. (1) According to the behavioral approach, our behavior results from the application of punishment and reward in classical and operant conditioning. (2) The social learning perspective pays attention to models whose behavior or appearance we choose to imitate. (3) Cognitive development theory focuses on the biological development of the ability to make increasingly complex judgments. Although all three perspectives are useful, they do not take into account the crucial sociological view that behavior takes place within the context of social environments.

3. The process of becoming a social being begins with children's understanding that language is the basis for connecting their experience with the experience of others; through this understanding, children develop mind, the ability to use symbols to put themselves in the place of another person.

4. The "I" consists of our direct experience of ourselves and others, and the "me" is that part of us that looks upon the "I" as an object. Significant others are particular people we orient ourselves to, and the generalized other is our perception of what people in general expect in certain social situations. Through significant others children are able to discover themselves as selves. Our self-concept is the sum total of our beliefs and feelings about ourselves; it is strongly influenced by our looking-glass self, our perception of how other people perceive and evaluate us.

5. As children develop, they enlarge their status and role sets. The cultural ideas people share about the occupants of different social statuses are, in turn, used to form a social identity, an ideal self—what kind of person they think they should be—and self-esteem—the positive and negative ideas they have about themselves. An important part of this process is the use of reference groups and individuals for comparison. This is particularly important for anticipatory socialization, which is learning how to perform a role before we occupy the status that goes along with it.

6. The family, schools, and the mass media are the three major agents of childhood socialization. Past childhood, we continue to adapt and readapt to new social circumstances throughout the life course. Rites of passage mark the transition from one social status to another; and we adjust to change in work and family, modifying relationships as we grow into adulthood and old age. In many ways, we learn to play new roles and to reformulate our ideas and feelings about others and ourselves.

7. As we mature, the socialization process that molds us confers the power of selfhood on us, the ability to make our own choices, which at times may conflict with beliefs, values, attitudes, and norms in the same society that socialized us. We are not simply limited by our social environment; we are part of it, and so long as we participate in social life, we cannot help but punish and reward others and provide them with models. We are born into a world not of our own making, but as we are socialized and participate in social life, we become the makers who help fashion the social environment in which future generations will be born and become social beings.

## Key Terms

behavioral approach   148
   classical conditioning   148
   operant conditioning   148
birth order   166
cognitive development perspective   150
ego   154
generalized other   156
I   155

## Recommended Readings

ARIÈS, P. (1962). *Centuries of childhood: A social history of family life*. New York: Knopf. A fascinating look at how the definition of childhood has changed over the centuries, with a special emphasis on the ways in which this has affected the treatment of children.

BECKER, H. S., et al. (1976). *Boys in white: Student culture in medical school* (rev. ed.). New Brunswick, NJ: Transaction Books. The classic study of the socialization process that turns college graduates into doctors.

BRIM, O. G., JR., and Wheeler, S. (1966). *Socialization after childhood: Two essays*. New York: Wiley. Two classic essays that show that socialization only *begins* in childhood.

BROWN, R. (1965). *Social psychology*. New York: Free Press. In this classic text, chapters on the acquisition of language and morality are both extremely well written and full of ideas and information.

DAVIS, K. (1940). Final note on a case of extreme isolation. *American Journal of Sociology, 45,* 554–565. One of the few existing studies of a documented case of a child raised in isolation, Davis' 1940 article makes for fascinating reading.

FREUD, S. (1961). *Civilization and its discontents*. New York: Norton. Freud's classic theory about the tension between the demands of society and inborn human drives. (Original work published 1930)

GRACEY, H. L. (1972). Learning the student role: Kindergarten as academic boot camp. In D. H. Wrong (Ed.), *Readings in introductory sociology* (2nd ed.) (pp. 243–254). New York: Macmillan. This widely reprinted article shows how early training begins with amusing and sometimes disturbing insights into the world of kindergarten.

KÜBLER-ROSS, E. (1975). *Death, the final stage of growth*. Englewood Cliffs, NJ: Prentice-Hall. Kübler-Ross has been a pioneer in the study of death as a human experience. As the title of this book suggests, Kübler-Ross views death and dying as another stage of life that has its own lessons to be learned.

MONTAGU, A. (1971). *Touching: The human significance of the skin*. New York: Columbia University Press. A fascinating look at the importance of touching in human development with a special emphasis on cross-cultural variation in how people touch each other.

ROSE, P. I. (Ed.). (1979). *Socialization and the life cycle*. New York: St. Martin's Press. A very good collection of readings on the socialization process throughout the life course.

ROSENBERG, M. (1979). *Conceiving the self*. New York: Basic Books. A thorough, thoughtful, and well-written look at key concepts in the sociological study of socialization, based on both a thorough review of existing research and the analysis of new data.

SHEEHY, G. (1974). *Passages: The predictable crises of adult life*. New York: Dutton. A highly readable introduction to the problems of adult socialization.

WRONG, D. H. (1961). The oversocialized concept of man in modern sociology. *The American Sociological Review, 26* (April), 183–193. An important statement of the problems of viewing socialization as a process that is determined either by society or by forces within the individual. Wrong argues effectively for a more balanced view.

# Social Interaction

**Social interaction** is the process through which people act in relation to one another—a complex process through which we organize and interpret our perceptions of people and situations; present ourselves to others; and form impressions of who people are, what they are doing, and why. We weigh expectations and possible consequences in light of cultural ideas. The behavior that results depends in part on the psychological characteristics of individuals; but as the following example and this chapter show, culture, social structure, and ecology influence us in profound ways.

## Action and Interaction

Late one night in March 1964, a woman named Kitty Genovese was murdered outside her New York City apartment in a middle-class neighborhood of Queens. Thirty-nine people watched from the safety of their apartments as she screamed in agony and terror while her attacker stabbed her repeatedly in a struggle that lasted for more than 30 minutes. He left her bleeding, but alive, only to return later and attack her again. During all this time, not one of the witnesses did anything to help her; no one even called the police until the final fatal wound had been inflicted.

The witnesses violated many important norms, values, and attitudes against which we might judge their behavior as outrageously immoral and unfeeling. In the public shock that followed, the question was raised repeatedly: How could people behave that way? For each one who raised that question, there was probably an underlying statement: "*I* would have done *some*thing."

If we think of the witnesses' behavior as simple actions carried out by individuals, our explanations will tend to be psychological: they were perhaps too insensitive, immoral, or frightened to pick up a telephone and call for help. Sociologists, however, are reluctant to settle for that kind of explanation, for it ignores the fact that when we act, we act in *relation* to one another and the cultural, structural, and ecological characteristics of our environments.

Latané and Darley (1970) were among those who tried both to answer the question "How could people behave that way?" and to test the common assumption that most people would have behaved differently (see also Dantin and Carver, 1982; Latané and Nida, 1981). As a participant in their experiment, you would have been invited to take part in a small group discussion about personal problems. You are told that there are six of you, and to help you be more open about yourselves, each of you will sit in your own small room from which you cannot see one another. Each person has two minutes to talk to the others through an intercom system, and during that time, no one else can communicate with other members of the group. After everyone has spoken, each member may speak for an additional two minutes. You will go last.

The first person to talk mentions that he sometimes has violent seizures, especially when he is under strain. After you and other members talk about your lives and problems, the first person speaks again. Suddenly he says:

> I-er-if somebody could help me out it would—it would er-er s-s-sure be—sure be good . . . because er-the-er-er-a cause I-er-I-uh I've got a-a one of the-er-seiz . . . er-er-things coming on and-and-and I could really-er-use some help so uh-er-er-er-er c-could somebody er-er-help er-uh-uh-uh—(choking sounds) . . . I'm gonna die er-er-I'm . . . gonna die er-er-seizure-er (choking sound again; then quiet).

What would you do? Immediately leave the room and look for help? Or sit and wonder if you should do anything? (At the end of the experiment, by the way, you learn that all the voices you heard were recorded.)

Latané and Darley wanted to explain why some subjects respond faster than others and why some fail to respond at all, and they focused not on personality differences but on how the ecological characteristics of the situation affected the subjects' interactions with other members of their group. In particular, they wanted to know how the number of people in a group affects individuals' behavior.

Their results were dramatic. Of those who believed they were in a six-person group, only 30 percent went for help, whereas 62 percent of those who believed they were in a three-person group responded to the plea. Of those who believed they and the victim were the only group members, fully 85 percent went for help. Although individual characteristics may explain why some people in six-person groups went for help and others did not, they cannot explain why those in larger groups were less likely to act than those in smaller groups.

A sociological explanation of why people may not help others combines social and ecological factors. First, the more bystanders there are, the more likely each of us is to assume that someone else will help the victim; we spread our individual responsibility over the entire group, and the larger the group is, the more thinly we can spread responsibility, leaving less for ourselves to assume as individuals (Berkowitz, 1978).

Second, we are always in danger of misinterpreting situations and making fools of ourselves (being an "alarmist," for example), and the larger the number of people present, the more potential witnesses there are to ridicule us. Third, we are often unsure of our individual perceptions and interpretations, and we look to other people for confirmation: if no one else responds, it reinforces the interpretation that action is not called for. This is a classic "Catch-22" (Heller, 1955/1961), for when this happens we wait for someone else to act first: hence, it is relatively common for no one to act, because each potential "someone else" is also waiting for someone else to do something.

Such findings suggest that Kitty Genovese's neighbors were not simply cruel or callous, but that each felt his or her individual responsibility spread out over many others. Ironically, each may have refrained from helping because they could not imagine that *no* one would help the woman. Had they seen someone go to her aid, they might well have called the police; or if each believed he or she was the only witness, they would have been far more likely to respond with assistance.

The sociology of interaction focuses on the way our awareness of ourselves, one another, and social environments influences our behavior. Basic to all social interaction are these two questions: Who are you? and Who am I?

## Visibility: Seeing and Being Seen

Few things are more important to us than to be seen by other people. To be ignored for even a few minutes can make us feel dull, shy, and uninteresting (Geller et al., 1974), and to be shunned, treated as if we do not exist, is one of the worst things that can happen to us.

In the prologue to Ralph Ellison's great novel *The Invisible Man* (1952), a black man accidentally

At the heart of all social interaction is the simple fact of being visible to others. To feel invisible is to feel unknown, a feeling that lies at the core of social isolation and loneliness.

collides with a stranger on a dark street. The stranger insults the black man, and the black man violently attacks him:

> And in my outrage I got out my knife and prepared to slit his throat . . . when it occurred to me that the man had not *seen* me, actually; that he, as far as he knew, was in the midst of a walking nightmare! . . . I ran away into the dark. . . . Poor blind fool, I thought with sincere compassion, mugged by an invisible man!

The black man feels that his low social standing makes him invisible to others, treated with so little regard by white society that he might as well not exist at all. The importance of this for social interaction is clear in his thoughts:

> Irresponsibility is part of my invisibility; any way you face it, it is a denial. But to whom can I be responsible, and why should I be, when you refuse to see me? Responsibility rests on recognition, and recognition is a form of agreement.

Our social statuses affect both whether or not people see us and how they see us; and these, in turn, influence the terms on which we interact with one another, the "agreements" that structure social life.

**Culture, Social Structure, and Perception**  Since we cannot pay attention to everything at once, we necessarily select what we perceive. In order to remember and communicate, we must simplify and organize information. When we describe someone as "intelligent," for example, we select a few observations from many, and simplify, organize, and interpret them in terms of an abstract category. Culture is a framework of ideas that we use in this process, and our social statuses influence which parts of that framework we use and how we use them.

Our perceptions of others depend on two kinds of information. The first consists of *impressions* of personal characteristics such as "kindness" or "cruelty," "beauty" or "ugliness." First impressions are particularly important because they foster expectations that influence our subsequent perceptions, feelings, and behavior.

In one experiment, college students read a short description of a guest instructor just before he arrived (Kelley, 1950). The descriptions gave identical information about his academic back-

ground and experience, but differed in one small detail: half read, "People who know him consider him to be a rather cold person, industrious, critical, practical, and determined," but in the other half, the words "very warm" were substituted for "cold."

The guest led the group discussion for twenty minutes—during which the researcher observed and recorded student participation—and after he left, students anonymously evaluated him. The single piece of information—"very warm" or "cold"—strikingly affected how students interacted with and evaluated him. Among students who were told he was very warm, 56 percent participated in the discussion, whereas only 32 percent of those who were told he was cold took part. When asked to evaluate his performance, students who were told he was cold thought that he seemed more self-centered, formal, unsociable, unpopular, irritable, humorless, and ruthless than did students who were told he was very warm.

Thus, we use first impressions to form expectations around which we organize perceptions and judgments that strongly influence our behavior. From a sociological perspective, however, our expectations depend even more importantly on a second type of information about people: our perceptions of their social identities, their status sets.

**Stereotypes**  Cultures contain thousands of beliefs: that the elderly are less capable than the young, that poor people are lazy (or victims of injustice), or that people from other societies are "barbarians" or value life less than we do. Although it is impossible to avoid using social statuses as a source of information about people, they can lead to a variety of errors, for when we select certain characteristics and make inferences from them, we not only lose the information we choose to ignore, but often add misinformation as well (McCall and Simmons, 1978).

These cultural "sketches" of people in different social statuses are **stereotypes**—rigid, oversimplified beliefs that are applied to all members of a group or social category. We all depend on stereotypes to some degree when we interact with other people. In fact, without them we could not predict other people's behavior in role relationships.

When stereotypes are our only source of information, however, they cause several kinds of misperceptions. First, they oversimplify: we forget that people we regard as heroes are human beings—who sleep, dream, eat, have fears, and make mistakes just like the rest of us. So when they remind us of their human complexity—by making a mistake, for example—our stereotype is shocked by reality.

Second, whereas stereotypes tend to be rigid over time, people rarely are. When we identify people as former mental patients, we tend to interpret their behavior as a reflection of mental instability, and expect them to continue to be "crazy" regardless of evidence to the contrary. Adults often apply stereotyped beliefs to children and are continually challenged to give up their old views as children grow and change.

Third, although some characteristics are more common among those in one social status than another, it is often a mistake to apply group characteristics to individuals. American men, for example, are far more likely than American women to commit violent crimes; but this does not mean that every man you meet is likely to be a criminal.

Fourth, when we define people in terms of a social status, we often mistakenly assume that they represent all occupants of that status. A black college student, for example, may be called upon in class to give "the black point of view" on a particular issue, a request that ignores the enormous variation of beliefs, values, attitudes, and experience among black people. In the same way, a lone man in a women's studies course may find himself called upon to provide the "male" point of view.

Finally, stereotyping may force people to conform to cultural beliefs about them. People often mistakenly assume that deaf people are mentally retarded because they express themselves with difficulty and in unusual ways. If, based on this stereotyped view, we deny deaf children regular schooling, they may in fact grow up with limited intellectual abilities. This is a **self-fulfilling prophecy,** a false belief that comes true because people think and act as if it were, in fact, already true. Our stereotyped beliefs about people lead us to treat them in particular ways; and our treatment, in turn, leads them to fulfill the prophecy contained in the stereotype (Merton, 1968).

Social interaction, then, is based on our perception of other people's personal and social characteristics, from which we identify "who they are."

We do not encounter other people in a vacuum, however, for interaction occurs in social contexts whose characteristics affect both how we perceive others and how we and they define our expectations of one another.

## Defining the Situation

To interact we must **define the situation** by identifying the manifest social statuses of the participants and the roles that define their expectations of one another. If a police officer flags you down for speeding on the highway, the situation is "an apprehension" and the manifest statuses involved are those of "police officer" and "lawbreaker." How people define the situation is enormously important, for as W. I. Thomas once wrote, if we "define situations as real, they are real in their consequences" (Thomas and Thomas, 1928, p. 572).

In his movie *Take the Money and Run*, for example, Woody Allen wants to rob a bank, and he hands a teller a note that reads, "I have a gun. Give me all your cash." The teller, however, is puzzled, because he reads, "I have a gu*b*."

"No, it's '*gun*,'" Allen says.

"Looks like 'gub' to me," the teller says, then asks another teller to help read the note, then another, and finally everyone is in the bank manager's office, arguing over what the note means. Allen never manages to rob the bank, because he is the only one who defines the situation as a robbery.

Woody Allen's predicament reflects an important fact about social interaction: in order for us to interact with one another, we must first define the situation as well as our position in it. Allen wants the teller to define him as a "bank robber" and then to *activate* the corresponding status of "robber's victim" and play the role that goes with it. Without such a shared definition of the situation, Allen is frustrated in his desire to be a bank robber (Watzlawick, 1976).

We continually activate and deactivate social statuses in our daily lives, and as we do, we perform roles through which we express different aspects of our identities. One minute we are riders on a bus, then we are pedestrians, then restaurant customers, employees, or college students in class. When someone gives us a gift, it immediately activates the status of recipient and a role that includes gratitude and some obligation to return the favor (for this reason, there are many people we would just as soon not receive gifts from) (see Fisher, Nadler, and DePaulo, 1983).

The statement "I'm in love with you" is more than an expression of feeling; it is an attempt to define a relationship, and the response "I love you, too" invokes a complex set of cultural ideas. In the same sense, the statement "I don't love you any more" is as much an attempt to redefine a situation as it is an expression of feeling.

When someone approaches us with a definition of a situation—such as "This is a holdup" or "We're lovers"—we must decide whether or not to adopt it, for once we do, we feel bound to perform the role implied by it. Because such definitions carry with them assumptions about shared beliefs, values, norms, and attitudes, they furnish the "obvious facts of existence" that bind us to a particular set of expectations.

Doctors (and others), for example, may lie to terminal patients about the seriousness of their conditions and justify their dishonesty in the name of protecting the patient from a horrible truth the patient cannot alter. From a sociological perspective, however, the deceivers also protect themselves, because once a patient is socially defined as "dying," other people must activate their own status of "attendant to a dying person" (and face all of the sadness and frustration that go with that status) (see Chapter 14).

Our ability to define social relationships gives us considerable creative power. We can be taken care of as though we were children even when we reach adulthood, so long as there is someone willing to play the role of "adult" in relation to us as "child." Or we can be strong and domineering if someone is willing to be weak and submissive in relation to us. In many ways, we seek people who share our definitions of the situation, because they, in effect, allow us to be who we want to be.

The definition of the situation is important not only in the activation of statuses and roles, but also in the way people interpret thoughts, feelings, and behavior. A smile, for example, can indicate many different emotions, including pleasure, embarrassment, affection, friendliness, gratitude, anxiety, sarcasm, and contempt. Only by knowing the social context in which it occurs can we be sure of its meaning.

The definition of the situation also affects which emotions we express (Hochschild, 1979). We often find ourselves in situations in which particular emotions are appropriate—grief at a funeral, silliness at a party—and even if we do not feel those emotions initially, we may work to make them conform with the definition of the situation ("Come on, everybody, laugh it up. This is a *party!*").

Thus, from a sociological perspective, interaction is based on a complex process of perception and interpretation both of people and the situations in which we encounter one another. As we perceive and interpret one another and situations, we activate selected parts of our social selves, and in responding to one another, we interact.

In some ways, interaction is like an elaborate dance in which we move in relation to one another, each creating variations on the "themes" contained in roles. If you observe department store clerks and customers, you will soon discover that although most of the interactions are between complete strangers, the patterns are astonishingly consistent throughout the day.

In this sense, interaction is a vital, functional activity in any society, for it is literally the means through which social life takes place. It is in interaction that social structure and culture become more than ideas, for here they are reflected in what people actually do in relation to one another.

## Social Attribution

When we interact with people, we often use the definition of the situation to solve a recurring problem: explaining other people's behavior. This process of interpretation is called **social attribution** (Heider, 1958; Kelley and Michela, 1980). Suppose a man picks your pocket and gets away with your week's salary, and the police catch him after he has spent your money. How severely would you want him punished? If you learned that he is a professional thief who drives a fancy car, you would feel quite differently than you would if you learned that he is desperately poor, was laid off from his job through no fault of his own, and used the money to buy fuel oil for his family during a bitterly cold winter. He is a thief in both cases, but your response to him depends on how you explain his behavior.

We cannot explain the thief's behavior simply by observing his actions—we must know more. In fact, we need two basic types of additional information (Heider, 1958). First, we need to know the **internal causes** of the thief's behavior: personal motives, abilities, and emotional states. Was the thief desperate or was he just greedy? Or was he mentally ill and unaware of the seriousness of his behavior?

Second, we need to know the **external causes** in order to explain behavior in any social situation. If the thief is unemployed, poor, married, and the father of small children, his family roles require him to earn a living, but his statuses of "poor" and "unemployed" deprive him of socially legitimate ways to do so. Thus, we use people's social statuses and the associated roles to attribute their behavior to a variety of causes.

Several studies, for example, show that people's explanations of behavior vary according to the actor's gender. When asked to explain the success of a "Dr. Mark Greer" or a "Dr. Marcia Greer," subjects tend to attribute the man's success to his abilities and the woman's success to luck, hard work, or a less-demanding job (Feldman-Summers and Kiesler, 1974). They also tend to explain a man's failure as a case of bad luck, while explaining similar failures of women as due to a lack of ability (Deaux, 1972). Thus, we tend to use stereotypes about women and men to explain the behavior of individuals.

We generally use internal causes to explain other people's behavior, but rely on external causes to explain our own (Davis and Stephan, 1980; Monson and Hesley, 1982; Reeder and Spores, 1983). When college students try to explain why their work is late, they are unlikely to offer "laziness," "lack of motivation," or "incompetence" as causes. They are more likely to refer to the demands of other roles ("I have four papers due this week") or circumstances beyond their personal control ("My dog ate my paper").

In other words, we add the demands of latent statuses (student in another course; dog owner) to our definition of the situation in order to explain our failure in a manifest status (notice also, in the "Dr. Greer" example above, how people used the latent statuses "male" and "female" to explain success and failure in the manifest status of "doctor"). Professors, on the other hand, are more likely to attribute the student's performance to internal causes and regard external factors as an excuse for them.

Why should this difference occur? Jones and Nisbett (1971) argued that as actors we "look outward" on the world and are therefore highly aware of the circumstances that affect our own behavior. But, as Tetlock (1981) pointed out, we also want to appear both to others and to ourselves in the best possible light and therefore tend to present ourselves to others as victims of circumstances we cannot control.

As observers of other people, on the other hand, we tend to focus on individual actors, not on their situations. All we see is them and what they do, and we therefore tend to believe that the causes of their behavior rest solely within themselves. Thus, it should not surprise us that when Richard Nixon's employees broke into the Watergate complex in 1973, they protested that their criminal behavior was necessary under the circumstances, whereas the public tended to attribute their actions to "poor character" (West, Gunn, and Chernicky, 1975).

Social interaction is more than a smoothly orchestrated dance between partners who share a rhythm and listen to the same music, for every word, every act directed at someone else crosses a boundary that separates and protects that person from the outside world. To interact is to act *upon* one another. When we hear someone simply say "hello" to us, we may feel ourselves touched by another, as if that single word penetrated some part of ourselves. It thus is important to examine the nature of those boundaries, how we cross them in social interaction, and with what effects.

## Social Boundaries

Some thirty inches from my nose
The frontier of my Person goes. . .
Stranger, unless with bedroom eyes
I beckon you to fraternize,
Beware of rudely crossing it;
I have no gun, but I can spit.
    —W. H. Auden

Physical contact is closely regulated by cultural ideas, social structures, and the ecological uses of physical space. Our skin is a physical boundary that separates us from other people, and we are very careful about whom we allow to touch or cross that boundary. We protect ourselves with clothes that insulate us on crowded buses and shield us from other people's eyes, and only under special circumstances do we allow someone to reach the skin beneath. Strangers may shake our hands, but only those close to us may touch our faces. We allow dentists to work in our mouths and physicians to penetrate our skins, but they may do so only within the strict limits of their roles.

The right to forcibly move us from one place to another is limited to a narrow range of statuses, such as that of police officer (but only when arresting us) or parent (but only when we are still children). In general, people do not have the right to shoot, stab, or hit us; and yet, under culturally defined circumstances—such as "self-defense"—others do have that right.

While our skin separates and protects us from others, the cultural ideas that regulate human contact form an invisible boundary around us, and only those who occupy certain statuses in relation to us have the right to cross it. Thus, our skin is a last line of defense, for the limits of our personal boundaries extend beyond it to include culturally prescribed limits to our selves.

If you are sitting on a park bench, for example, and a stranger sits down right next to you, how do you feel? Chances are you feel less comfortable, as if there were no longer enough room for you, even though in a strict physical sense there is. Hall (1959, 1969) suggests that each culture contains ideas about appropriate physical distances between people for each situation.

In the United States the "zone of intimacy" extends from us to a distance of about 18 inches and is reserved for intimate acquaintances, whereas those who are close friends—but not intimate—must stay at a "personal distance" of 18 inches to 4 feet. Our impersonal interactions—such as those with other workers—take place at a distance that ranges from 4 to 12 feet; and the "public zone" of 12 feet or more is appropriate among strangers.

The use of physical space is an important ecological factor in social interaction. Americans are noted for their opposition to certain physical barriers between people. In spite of Robert Frost's belief that "Good fences make good neighbors," Americans are suspicious of people who erect fences, prefer to live alone, or are uncomfortable

Notice how the way in which the people in this picture have spaced themselves reflects cultural norms about social boundaries.

## Voices: Defending Your Personal Boundaries while Banking

Obviously, hoodlums go where the money is. Therefore, we urge that you consider the following because the places we now discuss are all areas of potential danger.

- When receiving cash from a teller at the bank, count your money at the teller's window. While still at the window, place the money in your side pocket or in your purse. Do not count your money on a table in the bank where someone can watch you counting a significant amount of cash. Never place it in your "sucker pocket" (the rear pocket) or carry it from the bank in an envelope.
- When you leave the teller's window, do your 180-degree turn, which you should now be doing automatically many times every day. See if anyone suspicious is standing by.
- While waiting on line before the teller's window, see who is loitering around and who is standing in front and behind you and at your side.
- Look, look, look! When you go to get cash from a bank money machine, make certain you look the area over before you insert your card. If there is anyone suspicious standing by, don't make the withdrawal.
- At an outside cash machine, do not stand with your back to the street so that someone can come up behind you, grab your money, and then run

off. Stand sideways and continue to look around you, in front and behind, while you are waiting for the money to be released.
- Put the money into your side pocket or your purse while you are standing at the machine. Then do your 180-degree turn before walking away. Do not put money into your sucker pocket or your coat or jacket. Do not walk off carrying money in your hands.
- If you are in an area where you have the choice of walking down a crowded street or a deserted one, walk down the crowded street after you have made your withdrawal. During this period, you then have another opportunity to observe whether you are being followed. If you do not detect a problem before you withdraw your money, you will still have this additional opportunity to observe a possible threat as you walk down a well-trafficked street where help is close at hand.
- Wherever possible, have someone with you if you are cashing a check or withdrawing a considerable amount of money. Take the same precautions with your money as a professional security service would.
- Hoods hang around check-cashing facilities, money machines, and banks. This, after all, is where the money action really is. Don't feel foolish if you seem to be taking unnecessary precautions. Again, rather be safe than sorry.

Source: Sliwa and Schwartz, *Street Smart*, 1982.

in the group living situations of summer camps, army barracks, or college dormitories. During World War II, Americans watched in amazement as German prisoners constructed individual spaces—often no larger than a foxhole—within open barracks, making the space difficult to use efficiently and depriving each man of the precious body heat and company of his fellows during the cold winter months (Hall, 1969).

Americans use automobiles to insulate themselves from interaction with others (although some interaction may result from aggression and competition) and prefer the stresses of rush hour traffic to the forced intimacy of buses and trains. Many Eu-

ropeans (the French, in particular) and Latin-Americans, on the other hand, prefer the feeling of being close to other passengers (Hall, 1969).

Each culture specifies the limits of physical zones. "Personal distance" in Latin cultures, for example, resembles the "zone of intimacy" in the United States, and Americans often feel uncomfortable among Latins who seem to stand "too close" during conversations (whereas Latins often feel that Americans stand too far away). What we experience as natural boundaries are in fact social boundaries whose use depends on how each person defines the situation within a particular cultural context.

In an experiment about the use of physical zones, a researcher sat down six inches from people sitting alone on park benches (Sommer, 1969). He then recorded how long the other person stayed, and compared this with observations of people who were left alone. Almost 50 percent of those whose social boundary was crossed left within five minutes, compared with only 10 percent of those who were left alone.

Norms do more than regulate physical contact, however, for they also specify rights and obligations in role relationships. Although professors may question students about the subject matter of a course, they do not have the right to demand details of a student's sex life, and folkways require others to keep secrets about us to themselves. We may look at strangers, but folkways do not allow staring; even close friends may experience staring as an invasion of privacy, especially when directed at their eyes, which have been aptly described as "the windows of the soul."

Beyond the protection afforded by roles, there are many ways to shield ourselves from other people. As children we tend to reveal ourselves openly and directly in social interactions, but as we are

Norms govern how close people are to each other when they interact, and as these pictures show, distances tend to be greater in the United States than in many other societies.

socialized, we learn subtlety and concealment (Cooley, 1902). Because we rely on gestures to express our feelings and thoughts to others, we can use them as screens that withhold or distort information about ourselves.

Many roles allow us to maintain contact with other people without revealing ourselves. "Hello, how are you?" someone asks, to which we reply, "Fine, how are you?" On one level, such interactions are dishonest, for we rarely want to know how someone really feels when we pass them on the street, and "fine" is often an inaccurate description. Indeed, to describe our feelings in great detail violates the social expectations attached to the role of "acquaintances meeting on the street."

As meaningless as such exchanges appear to be, they play an important part in social life, for without them we feel invisible and uncomfortable ("Why didn't you say 'hello'?"). Although the apparent question is "How are you?" the underlying question is often "How am I?" as we look for our reflection in other people's recognition of us. Without such roles, we would have to choose between extensive, revealing interactions or none at all. No matter how highly placed they are, few people are above the "small talk" that allows them to "keep in touch" with other people safely without revealing more of themselves than they want to.

The importance of small talk illustrates a major tension in social life. We want to be known by others, to break down barriers that isolate us; and yet we are afraid of being known too well by people who may reject or abuse us. The psychotherapist Fritz Perls suggests that our cleverness with words encourages us to interact superficially with one another, to conceal the private feelings and thoughts that give meaning and depth to human relationships (Perls, Hefferline, and Goodman, 1965).

It is ironic that although social boundaries must be crossed if friendship is to occur, the likelihood of forming a friendship is diminished, not enhanced, when those boundaries are unclear or too easily crossed. In one experiment, sailors volunteered to be isolated in pairs for ten days in a small chamber equipped with cots, tables, and toilet and eating facilities, as well as a video camera that recorded their interactions (Altman et al., 1971). In some cases they became friends; but in others they did not get along—sometimes to the point of ending the experiment before the ten days had elapsed.

The researchers noticed that friendship was more likely when the men established clear territorial boundaries at the start of their stay: who would sleep in which bed, what parts of the chamber were reserved for each man, how and when the furniture was to be used. Sailors who failed to establish clear boundaries were far less likely to get along.

Thus, interaction involves a complex balance among individual boundaries; and, as the definition of the situation changes, our social boundaries swell and contract. Among intimate friends we draw our boundaries close to ourselves and allow others to cross them with relative ease, but among strangers our boundaries expand and become increasingly difficult for people to cross.

## Power and Social Interaction

We maintain some control over the extent and strength of our boundaries, but our ability to control contact and interaction with others is often limited by differences in power. There are many different definitions of power, but from a sociological perspective Max Weber's (1922b) is most useful: **power** is the possibility of imposing one's will on the behavior of others in spite of their resistance. Power can take many forms, but most depend on roles. Thus, power often depends more on the definition of the situation than on individual characteristics and will.

Most states define rape as sexual contact gained through the use of force or the threat of force. In rape, the woman's body as well as her right to control it are violated in an interaction dominated by violence and power. As a member of society, she may call upon the legal system to support her right to be protected from assault (Brownmiller, 1975; Medea and Thompson, 1974).

If her attacker happens to be her husband, however, the laws in the majority of states define his behavior as "assault," not rape; and although rape is a serious crime, simple assault is not. In most states, "sexual contact gained through the use of force" simply cannot happen between spouses. Why not?

Criminal laws exist to protect us from other people. Laws that forbid rape, murder, assault, robbery, and harassing telephone calls, or that

## PUZZLES:

# WHEN IS RAPE NOT A CRIME?

When can a man force a woman to have sexual intercourse with him and not be charged with rape even if he confesses?

In most states of the United States, the answer is: when he is her husband and the couple is not legally separated. (A notable "exception that proves the rule" is a 1984 case in Florida in which a husband was tried and convicted of sexually assaulting his wife.) Power is often an important part of social interaction, and as explained in this chapter and in Chapter 13, the statuses of husband and wife have built-in power inequalities that allow husbands to behave toward their wives in ways that are prohibited in relation to other women.

## Voices:
## A Victim of Power Inequalities

One morning in February 1978, Steve Coady came home from night duty and found his wife Carol asleep. He called for some breakfast, so she went down to the kitchen to make his eggs.

"I burned the eggs, because he started screaming at me for how stupid I was because I forgot to put the outside porch light on before I went to bed. . . . When I burned the eggs, he beat me for about half an hour."

She went back to the kitchen and broke some fresh eggs.

"My husband came in the kitchen . . . and said, 'Get upstairs or I'm going to kill you.' He ripped off my pajamas in one pull . . . I never thought he would rape me because rape happens to you from a stranger, not from your husband. . . . It lasted for about five minutes. . . . I took a shower. When I got up, I couldn't stand, because . . . my legs wouldn't hold my weight. . . . Then when I went downstairs, I was sobbing hysterically the whole time."

This incident occurred in Pennsylvania, a state which, like thirty other states, does not allow wives to charge their husbands with sexual crimes. Carol Coady eventually divorced her husband, and in 1984 both houses of the Pennsylvania legislature passed a bill defining rape between spouses as a crime. The governor of Pennsylvania then vetoed the bill on the grounds that "with this bill we would be entering the privacy of the home and the sanctity of an ongoing marriage to allow spousal prosecutions for sexual conduct."

Source: *Hartford Courant*, November 15, 1984, p. F6.

limit a government's power to record our telephone calls, open our mail, or arrest us without good cause, all specify boundaries that people may not cross without risking punishment.

In most states, rape laws grant husbands the right to behave toward their wives in ways that would be criminal in relation to other women. Such laws are based on the English Common Law idea that husbands cannot be held guilty of raping their wives, because upon marriage a wife is assumed to give unconditional consent to her husband's sexual desires, a consent which she "cannot retract" (Hale, 1847). This reflects the historical subjugation of women—in which they have been viewed as property, belonging first to their fathers, then "given" to their husbands in marriage. Thus, in every sexual interaction between spouses, the marriage contract grants a husband the legal right to cross his wife's personal boundaries at will, and although he may choose not to exercise that right, it is always nonetheless available (Weitzman, 1981).

Power in social interaction has two basic sources. In the simplest sense, we all have **personal power,** the ability to coerce others through the strength of our bodies or the persuasiveness of our arguments. Even small children have power in relation to adults: they can refuse to do what they are told, throw embarrassing tantrums in public places, or obey slowly and reluctantly.

Our physical position in relation to others is an ecological aspect of social interactions that also affects personal power. Lying down during an argument is a less powerful position than standing up, just as sitting behind a desk provides more protection, and hence power, than sitting out in the open.

Sociologists, however, focus primarily on the second source of power: the *power of social statuses* and the roles attached to them. Although the husband who sexually assaults his wife uses the personal power of his body, he also draws power from the norms attached to the statuses of husband and wife.

Weber (1925) defined the most important form of social power as **authority.** Authority differs from other forms of power (such as physical strength) in that it is socially supported, and rests on the belief that those who possess it have a right to it, and those who do not have a duty to obey. Thus, it cannot exist without social support. The power that men often enjoy as "the man of the house" is an example of authority, as is the power of people to control who enters their dwellings, of bosses to hire and fire workers, and of parents to control their children.

Our statuses determine who has the authority to invade our boundaries, to act upon us regardless of what we want. The statuses of child, mental patient, and "under arrest" have roles that include little authority, and people in those statuses must rely on personal power to control their interactions with more powerful role partners.

It is important to emphasize that authority is not a form of personal power, for it is attached to particular statuses under socially defined conditions. When military people salute each other, they pay respect to a person's rank, not to the individual who holds it; and when they remove their uniforms, they are no longer saluted.

Sociologically, authority is a particularly important source of power, because it is purely social in its origins. People in positions of authority can exercise power that is vastly beyond their individual resources and abilities, for they act not in their own names, but in the name of an entire group if not society itself. Because society grants some status occupants power they would otherwise never have, authority is particularly subject to abuse (Sennett, 1981).

In a classic experiment (Haney, Banks, and Zimbardo, 1973), male college students volunteered to play the roles of prisoners and guards in a laboratory designed to resemble a prison. The students were paid to participate, and the "guards"

were given complete control over the daily lives of their "prisoners." The experiment began with the handcuffing and arrest of the "prisoners" while they were walking home, and then they were transported to mock prison cells in a university building. The guards stripped and searched them, sprayed them with delousing fluid, took their pictures, and ordered them to remain silent in their cells.

The researchers were testing the common belief that the brutality of guards in real prisons is caused by cruel personalities. Is it possible, they asked, that the situation itself, in which some people have complete power over others, fosters abusive behavior?

As the days passed, the prisoners became increasingly depressed, sometimes crying or showing signs of rage and acute anxiety. Almost half had to be released before a week had passed, and the rest said they would gladly forfeit their pay in exchange for an early release.

The guards, who had almost complete control over their role of maintaining order in the "prison," readily used their authority to abuse the prisoners. They rarely spoke to prisoners except to deliver commands, frequently denied them privileges, and in one case locked a prisoner in the "solitary confinement" of a small closet all night. They concealed much of their abusive behavior from the experimenters, who they believed were "too soft" on the prisoners. Guards appeared to enjoy their work and volunteered to work overtime without pay; and they were very disappointed when the experiment ended prematurely. As one of the experimenters recalled:

> At the end of only six days we had to close down our mock prison because what we saw was frightening. It was no longer apparent to us or most of the subjects where they ended and their roles began. The majority had indeed become "prisoners" or "guards," no longer able to clearly differentiate between role-playing and self. There were dramatic changes in virtually every aspect of their behavior, thinking, and feeling. . . . We were horrified because we saw some boys ("guards") treat other boys as if they were despicable animals, taking pleasure in cruelty, while other boys ("prisoners") became servile, dehumanized robots who thought only of escape, of their own individual survival, and of their mounting hatred of the guards. (Zimbardo, 1971, p. 3)

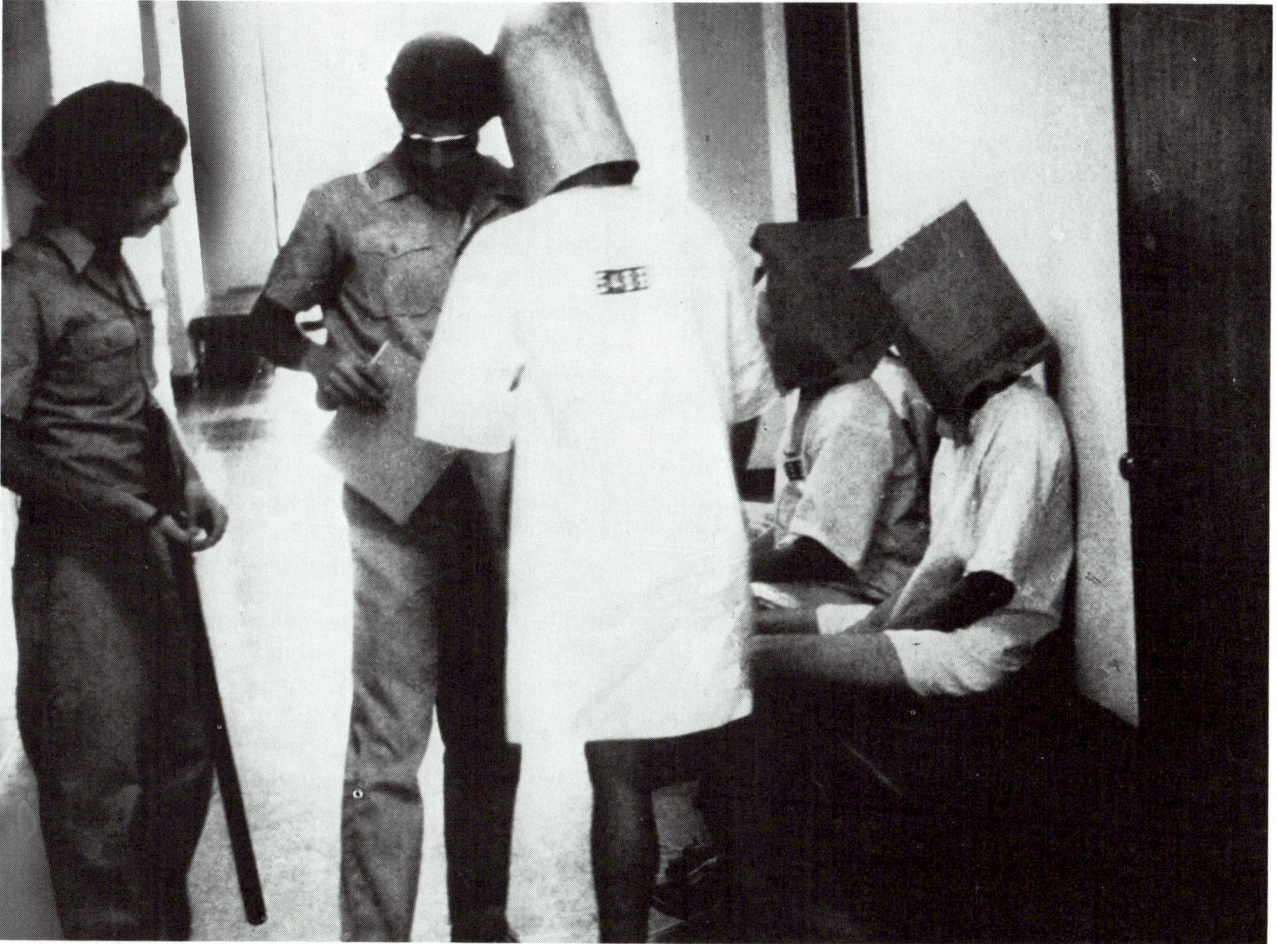

Zimbardo's experiment lends support to Lord Acton's famous statement: "Power tends to corrupt and absolute power corrupts absolutely."

These apparently decent young men gave support to Lord Acton's famous statement that "power tends to corrupt and absolute power corrupts absolutely." Why should power have this effect? Kipnis (1972) suggested that high levels of power lead to abuse for three reasons.

1. Status occupants will use as much power as is available to them. When we have only the power of persuasion, that is what we will use; if our roles allow us to punish and reward others, however, we will rely less on persuasion than on the more powerful means available to us.

2. Power allows people to control other people's behavior. In turn, those who have power may come to believe they are superior to those they control. Power may in fact lead to such a boost in self-esteem that the powerful believe they are exempt from usual standards of moral behavior, and they may feel contempt for those they are able to control.

3. Contempt for others and an exalted self-image cause people to distance themselves from those they control, to shield themselves from an awareness of how their actions affect others. Under such circumstances, abuse is far more likely to occur.

Power, then, tends to corrupt the powerful, but research also shows that powerlessness is equally corrupting. When we believe that nothing we can do will affect what happens to us, we often become victims of "learned helplessness" and its resulting depression (Seligman, 1975). This occurs both in extreme situations, such as prisons, and in everyday life, such as when students receive poor grades after hard work and better grades on papers they write hastily at the last minute. In one experiment, people were subjected to electric shocks and loud noises (over which they had no control), and later, even when the subjects were offered opportunities to learn to control the noises and shocks, they performed poorly. They "gave up" (see Abramson, Seligman, and Teasdale, 1978).

Thus, we all need some sense that we can affect the behavior of other people, and we suffer without it. In one study, students visited elderly people living in homes for the aged. Half of the elderly people had complete control over the timing and length of visits, whereas the other half had no control and were visited at random (Schulz, 1976). At the end of two months, independent evaluators rated the health of the elderly subjects, and the differences were dramatic. Those who controlled this small segment of their lives were judged to be healthier, more active, and more optimistic about life than those who did not. In addition, other studies find that elderly people who *believe* they control their situations live longer than those who do not believe it, even when the actual levels of control are the same (Rodin and Langer, 1977; see also Deci, 1980 and Schulz and Hanusa, 1980).

The importance of power in social interaction is evident in what often seem to be the most insignificant behaviors and situations. When we interact with more powerful role partners, we tend to restrict our movements and sit erect with our legs uncrossed and our hands hanging at our sides or clasped in our laps; whereas more powerful people assume relaxed postures that indicate their relative invulnerability to how we judge them (Mehrabian, 1972).

The more powerful are also more likely to cross the boundaries of the less powerful by touching them, staring at them, initiating conversations, or interrupting during conversations (West, 1982); and observations of men and women show that men are more likely to touch women than women are to touch men (Henley, 1977). This tendency is especially evident in the workplace, where men usually occupy more powerful positions than women (Radecki and Walstedt, 1980).

Power, perception, definitions of the situation, and attribution are basic elements in all social interaction. Like all aspects of social life, however, interaction takes place in physical circumstances that affect what happens.

## Microecology

As we saw in Chapter 5, ecology is primarily the study of the effects of physical environments on societies. The following sections describe **microecology,** which focuses on the ways in which the concepts of population and ecology help explain what goes on in social life on a smaller scale. How, for example, does the size of a group affect relationships among its members? How does the physical design of buildings affect interactions among those who live or work in them? How do individuals use physical distance to regulate the intimacy of their contact with other people?

**Numbers Count** The old saying "Two's company, three's a crowd," is a statement about one of the simplest aspects of human ecology, the number of people involved in a social situation. How many people, for example, does it take to have a party? Two friends sitting around talking and laughing would hardly say, "What a wonderful party!" but 20 certainly might. Why do numbers matter?

Simmel (1908) pointed out that the key to a party is in the number of people present. When two friends share dinner, a single mood dominates; but a party is dotted with small subgroups that display different moods and do different things, from dancing and joking to serious conversation in an isolated corner. We enjoy parties precisely because they allow us to move freely and find a subgroup in which we feel comfortable regardless of our mood. Thus, a party requires enough people to allow subgroups to form.

The smallest group (a **dyad**) has two members, and we can see some of the effects of size by comparing dyads with three-person groups (**triads**). As Simmel (1908) noted, dyads have unique properties, the most important of which is that both members control the relationship's survival, for if either leaves it no longer exists. Thus, so long as each partner is free to leave, a dyad depends on consensus, giving each person considerable control over the other and motivating both to resolve conflicts through compromise. In addition, each member of a dyad is highly visible, and any violation of norms is easily noticed.

With three people, one person can lose control over relationships with the other two as their behavior becomes less visible and they form closer ties, or **coalitions** (Caplow, 1968; Gamson, 1968a; Simmel, 1908). Two roommates (or two siblings) may "gang up" on a third; or when a child is born, one parent may become jealous of the child's bond with the other parent. There is more involved in jealousy than human emotion, for such feelings come about when we perceive a threatening change in our relationships with other people.

As the number of people increases beyond 3, the patterns of interaction tend to change. We have all experienced, for example, the profound effect that class size has on classroom discussions. With 2 people, only 1 conversation is possible; with 3 people, 4 are possible; and with 4 people, 11 are possible (see Table 7-1). As the numbers increase, however, the number of possible combinations of group members rises dramatically. With only 7

people there are 120 possible subgroups involving anywhere from 2 to 7 people at a time. With only 25 people (small by current classroom standards), there are 33,554,406!

In even relatively small groups—say ten—we find that those who are designated as leaders tend to take over more and more of the interaction (group discussions may be little more than conversations between the professor and one or two students). Other group members tend to feel stifled in their ability to express themselves (and guilty about taking up the group's time). Something as simple as "shyness," then, has its roots not only in personality, but in the ecology of groups.

As a characteristic of social interactions, the number of people who are involved is neither a cultural idea nor a set of shared expectations, and yet it clearly affects what goes on in social relationships. It is a *physical* aspect of social situations within which individuals act and experience both themselves and other people.

**Space and Social Interaction** Physical space is another important ingredient in the structuring of social relationships. Space regulates social interaction in many ways. Intimate distances—6 to 18 inches—allow us to see facial details and detect body heat and odors, and make it difficult to be unaware of another's feelings. At moderate distances, we experience people more as objects; that is why we prefer such distances for conducting business or talking with casual acquaintances. Great distances allow us to act without an awareness of others; thus, long-range weapons such as guns and missiles enable us to kill one another with minimal awareness of the harm done to the victim (Hall, 1969; Morris, 1967).

The arrangement of physical environments is often used to reinforce the structure of social relationships (Sommer, 1969). Waiting areas in airports, for example, are usually so large that people have little difficulty avoiding contact with one another. In Britain's House of Commons, members of opposition parties are seated across from one another and at close quarters, which encourages heated debate. By contrast, seating in the U.S. House of Representatives is comparatively spacious, resembling a large college lecture hall, and debate involving several members at once is rare.

Physical space is also used to reinforce status differences in power and is an important tool for

**Table 7-1**

The number of possible combinations of members increases much faster than the size of a group. With two people, only one conversation is possible, but that number quadruples with the addition of a third member and almost triples with addition of a fourth.

| GROUP MEMBERS | POSSIBLE COMBINATIONS OF MEMBERS |
|---|---|
| Anthony Barbara | Anthony-Barbara |
| Anthony Barbara Peter | Anthony-Barbara Anthony-Peter Barbara-Peter Anthony-Barbara-Peter |
| Anthony Barbara Peter Gloria | Anthony-Barbara Anthony-Peter Anthony-Gloria Barbara-Peter Barbara-Gloria Peter-Gloria Anthony-Barbara-Peter Anthony-Barbara-Gloria Anthony-Peter-Gloria Barbara-Peter-Gloria Anthony-Barbara-Peter-Gloria |

social control. Judges in courtrooms and clergy in pulpits sit or stand in physically elevated positions that reinforce their authority. The desks of high-level executives are often placed far from their office doorways, requiring visitors to cross a long expanse while their superiors can sit and examine (or ignore) them. The ability to limit people's access to our physical spaces also reinforces our power in relation to others. In many corporations, for example, the offices of lower-level personnel differ from those of their superiors by not having doors, signifying a lack of power to limit access to their own work space.

People often use space to insulate themselves from others. Privacy and secrecy depend on people not being able to observe other people's behavior. When Americans vote, their behavior is concealed by booths; houses insulate their occupants from observation by others, just as automobiles insulate teenagers from the watchful eyes of their parents. Having "a room of one's own" is an important ecological aspect of family life, for it allows individuals a protected place in which they are safe from observation.

Students who sit in the back rows of large classrooms may do so because it feels "safer" back there where teachers cannot see what they are doing. When students write take-home exams, their role behavior is invisible to their professors,

an ecological problem that is often dealt with through complex norms and values such as honor codes. In the physical environment of in-class exams, however, student role behavior is visible both to the professor and other students, making cheating far less likely to occur. In both situations, the norms and values concerning cheating are the same, but the physical arrangements in which role performances take place are radically different.

One consequence of all this is that we often misperceive reality when we cannot directly observe what is happening. Congressional committees that meet "behind closed doors" force the public to depend on them to accurately report what they do; and isolation from most events requires us to depend on the media for information about what happens in the world. When spatial arrangements limit the visibility of role behavior, it is difficult to make sure others are performing their roles as they should. The president of the United States, for example, is unable to directly observe the actions of most people in the executive branch. This not only makes it impossible to control the everyday workings of government, but also makes the president almost completely dependent on others to act as "eyes and ears," a fact that greatly increases the opportunities for misinformation. Almost every president enters office with plans to bring the government under stricter control, but soon learns the ecological fact that it is almost impossible to control people whose behavior cannot be directly observed.

A second consequence is that we often lack information that is important to us; and when this is the case, we sometimes make it up. In doing this, we may rely on our own beliefs about people: men, for example, may assume that they know what women talk about when there are no men around; whites may assume that they know what family life is like among blacks; citizens may assume that all politicians betray the public behind closed doors; or the Internal Revenue Service may assume that most taxpayers cheat.

Microecology adds an important dimension to the many social factors that affect social interaction, but social interaction is more than the sum of such factors, for they are but pieces of a larger process. What does this process look like? There are several models of social interaction, and we will examine three of them.

# The Dramaturgical Approach: Interaction as Theater

Interaction involves social actors who have ideas about who they are, who present themselves to one another in a variety of ways in order to achieve different effects or simply to act out their ideas of who they are (Tedeschi and Riess, 1981). Officials who act "official" and students who act "studious" are creating and maintaining impressions of themselves in the minds of others, just as actors perform before an audience; and, in this sense, all social interaction is *dramaturgical*—in other words, it includes an element of theater (Goffman, 1959, 1981).

Teachers often present themselves to students as knowledgeable and capable, thoroughly in command of their subject and able to field any and all questions. Students support this image in a variety of ways: by blaming themselves when they do not understand what a teacher says, by assuming they have nothing to teach the teacher, or by refraining from asking challenging questions.

With their colleagues, however, teachers may reveal a very different side of themselves: one that includes feelings of inadequacy, doubts about knowing what they are doing in class, fear of being unable to answer a question, or hostility toward students. Are professors capable, confident, and knowledgeable? Or are they insecure, doubting, and afraid? The most likely answer is that teachers (and everyone else) feel all of these emotions at one time or another, but control how they reveal themselves to others depending on the social situation.

In *The Presentation of Self in Everyday Life* (1959), Erving Goffman described the **dramaturgical approach** to the sociological analysis of interaction as a continuing performance of actors before audiences. As we saw earlier, we approach people with an awareness that their behavior is affected by their impressions of us and their definition of the situations in which interactions occur. We thus have an interest in presenting ourselves to others in ways that produce the results we want (Sagatun and Knudsen, 1982). More important, we have an interest in working together to keep the "play" going, for it is only in this way that we can sustain the definition of the situation in which we perform our roles.

To Goffman, we are actors who interact with other actors who are our audience (Goffman's term for role partners). Our performances take place in physical settings, and are guided by the roles we play—the expected behaviors and feelings that we associate with our social status in each situation. Together, the roles we play make up a **social script.**

When we approach others, we present them with a **front**—our physical appearance, behavior, and definition of the situation—which audiences use to help define the situation for themselves. We thus rely on various cues to define situations, and then orient ourselves to the appropriate script and align our behavior to fit the role we choose to perform.

Like the theater, interaction has a **frontstage** on which roles are performed before an audience, and a **backstage** on which players are freed from the requirements of their role  Just as players are careful not to let the frontstage audience see what they do while backstage, so do social actors **segregate their audiences.**

We can see the sociological usefulness of the dramaturgical approach by seeing how it works in the classroom. Both students and professors are actors who use one another as audiences for their performances in class, a setting arranged to direct attention primarily to the professor's performance.

Before the professor arrives, students sit among themselves and play a variety of frontstage roles appropriate to the "pre-class" situation: "casual acquaintance," "close friend," "stranger," "fellow athlete," and "self-absorbed and not wanting to be bothered." At times, some leave the room to seek a safe backstage area (such as the bathroom) in which they can be alone and free from the demands of being with other students.

During this frontstage performance students often talk about the professor and the course, as if they are sitting backstage and discussing the performance that is about to begin. In this sense, frontstage performances are often at the same time backstage performances in relation to another situation.

The professor's entrance is the first of several cues that redefine the situation. On the first day of class the professor's front is a particularly important set of cues for students, for if professors arrive dressed in dirty jeans and sweatshirts and sit in the back of the room, students lack signals to shift their

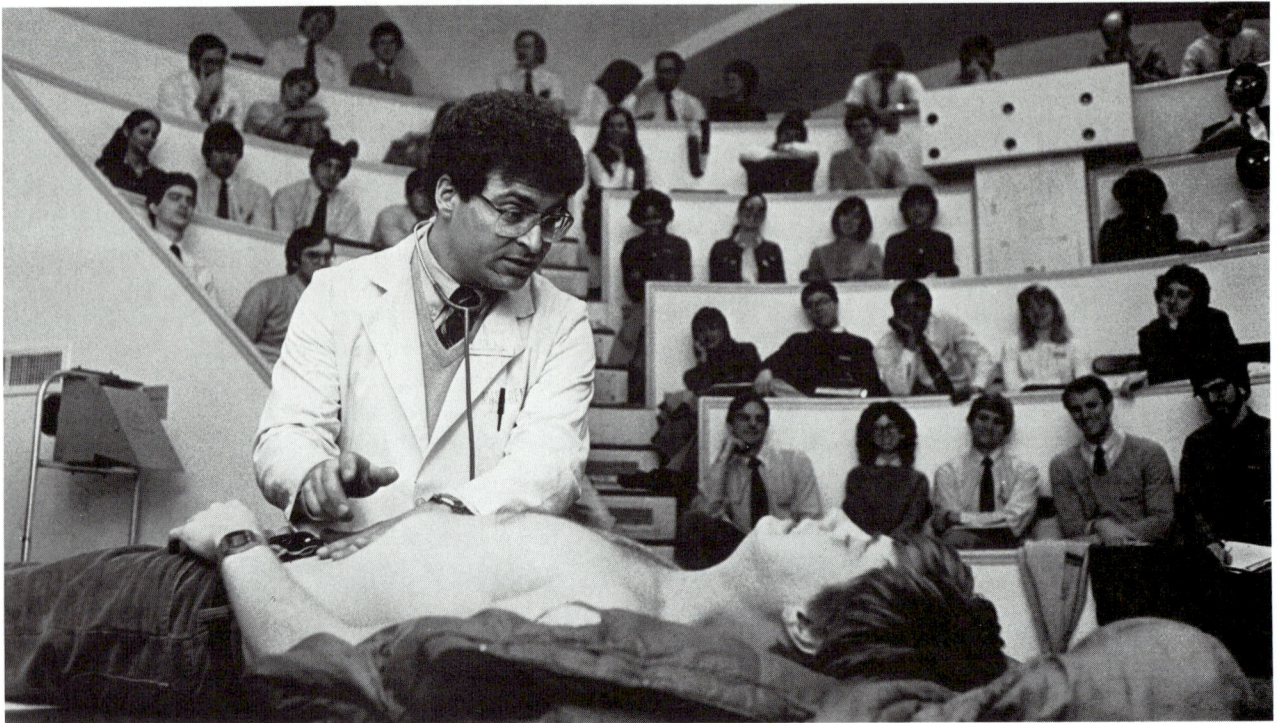

Interaction in the classroom, among students before a class and with the professor once the class begins, shows—according to the dramaturgical approach—that students and professors perform as actors and audiences for one another.

primary orientation from other students to the professor.

Students, of course, present fronts of their own that help professors define the situation for themselves. College professors expect to see a room full of young people dressed for the occasion, and if they found a group of people dressed in gym shorts and sporting tennis rackets, they would think they had walked into the wrong "theater."

When the professor stops shuffling papers and looks at the class, the redefinition of the situation is complete. Students then perform **aligning actions** (part of their front) to signal their acceptance of the new definition: they sit quietly, look at the professor, and perhaps take out pencils and open notebooks. Frontstage is now the performance of students and professor in relation to one another, and the informal interactions among students that once took place frontstage now take place only backstage. Once actors and their audiences agree on the script, the performance begins.

Professors play their role, controlling who talks and when, speaking with confidence, and controlling their use of slang and profanity. Sometimes they deliberately use profanity, both to demonstrate their power to ignore norms and to narrow the gap between professor and students.

Students also play their role, taking notes, looking at the professor, and talking only after raising their hands and being recognized. Students are often reluctant to participate in class discussions because they risk making a bad impression on professors and other students. Yet, their role requires that they "be" there in mind as well as body, and they can indicate their involvement only through behavior.

To protect themselves, many students create an appearance of enough commitment to satisfy their role requirements, but still not exposing themselves to unnecessary risks. They engage in "civil attention"—by nodding their heads or laughing at appropriate moments, taking notes, refraining from talking among themselves—and they participate when there are low-risk opportunities (Karp and Yoels, 1979). Civil attention is important because it allows us to play roles while minimizing the risks associated with them (Goffman, 1961b, 1963a).

Occasionally students go backstage for a moment to talk among themselves, but they must carefully conceal such behavior from their audience, the professor. Not only does such backstage behavior threaten their own performance, but it also threatens the professor's by redefining the situation and making the professor's script inappropriate. As the center of attention, however, professors have no immediately available backstage in which to escape the pressures of performing their role.

Throughout the performance, both students and professors try to manage the impressions that others have of them, and this process lies at the heart of social interaction as theater. In drama, it is not who we really are that matters; rather, it is who we *appear* to be as actors that is central to our performance. Thus, both students and professors try to appear confident and intelligent while concealing ignorance and feelings of insecurity from their respective audiences. They try to maintain the impression that they are seriously committed to the "play" (lest they appear to be cynical or insincere) and avoid behaviors that are "out of character."

Actors defend their performances in a variety of ways. They depend on the loyalty of those who share their status (students do not reveal to the professor that another student did not do the assigned reading); they try to choose their audiences carefully (professors may prefer young students, who are less likely to challenge them); and they use discipline to control their faces, bodies, and voices, keeping them "in character." (Thus, we often prefer to use the telephone or letters to deliver bad news and lies to people, because in such a setting it is easier to control the impression we make on them.)

If they do violate their roles, they often feel acute embarrassment and are quick to align themselves once again to the situation and its script. Goffman (1956–1957) pointed out that embarrassment actually plays an important part in maintaining the integrity of the "play" and the actor's part in it. When people make foolish mistakes, for example, their embarrassed reaction is a way of signaling to everyone that they know what they were supposed to have done and an implication that they will do better from now on. Embarrassment thus expresses a commitment to the script that ties the actors together.

Audiences also feel obliged to help protect an actor's performance. If a professor makes a foolish mistake or stumbles and falls, students will also feel embarrassed and will support the professor's performance by acting as if they are unaware of what happened. Such "tactful inattention" protects both the performer and the audience by maintaining the integrity of the play in which all participate. In this sense, social interaction is unlike the theater, for in social interaction, participants are simultaneously both audience and actors.

When professors give the appropriate cues, students know that the performance is over and all actors may retreat to backstage areas—faculty lounges, student dorms, coffee shops, or campus grounds—in which they are free to relax, drop their classroom fronts, and openly discuss what happened on the frontstage. Because the safety of backstage areas depends on controlling who enters them, both professors and students are careful to stay away from each other's respective backstages. (It is important to note that although college dorms and faculty lounges are backstage relative to the classroom, they are themselves frontstages, each with its own particular script.)

In many interactions the definition of a situation is unclear, and actors negotiate about the scripts they will follow. If a woman and man go out on a first date, for example, their cues are often ambiguous, and they carefully explore ways to arrive at a mutually agreeable definition of the situation. The cues each gives off are invitations—such as an invitation to perform the role of "friend." Having agreed on a definition, one or both may later try to redefine the situation with a **realigning action** (by raising the possibility of sexual activity, for example). Such actions constitute a new invitation (or demand), and both may feel tense while they renegotiate the script.

The negotiation of scripts defines relationships by activating one or more statuses in a person's status set, and the struggle over definitions involves a conflict over which statuses will be de-

Before learning social scripts that enable them to interact with each other in social situations, adolescent girls and boys often act as though they do not know what to do with each other—because they do not.

fined as latent and which will be defined as manifest in a particular situation. In the workplace male employers often try to define a woman employee's manifest statuses as "female" and "sex object," while she struggles to define those statuses as latent, and defines "employee" as her manifest status. Such conflicts may expand beyond the confines of an immediate frontstage to include public legal action to formally define the scripts that are appropriate in such settings.

Goffman's dramaturgical approach is useful because it focuses our attention on the social mechanisms through which we create and maintain impressions of ourselves in the eyes of others, choose and control our audiences, and rely on one another for the successful performance of our roles. The dramaturgical approach reveals how we use others to test and confirm our self-images. Only in the "theater" of social interaction can we perform before others and find out if they see us as we see ourselves. When audiences accept an actor's performance, they are in effect saying, "We believe in you."

Thus, by accepting our presentation of ourselves, they also accept parts of us *as* selves. When audiences reject our performances, on the other hand, we are likely to feel acute embarrassment, if not shame, and we may then defend ourselves by disowning our performances: "I'm not myself today."

## Functions and Conflict: Interaction as Exchange

### Exchange Theory

On one level, the Golden Rule—"Do unto others as you would have them do unto you"—is a norm that commands us to treat others well. We soon learn, however, that it is more than a moral rule; it is also a good strategy for getting what we want from others: If I am kind to others, then they will tend to be kind to me. Because our behavior affects other people just as theirs affects us, social interaction can be described as a process of *exchange*.

Social **exchange theory** rests on four assumptions about human behavior:

**1.** We are motivated primarily to avoid pain and gain pleasure.

**2.** Other people's behavior is a source both of pleasure and pain for us.

**3.** Because human behavior is performed in relation to others, we can use our own behavior to influence what other people do in relation to us.

**4.** We try to maximize pleasure while minimizing our costs: we try to make the "best deal" we can in order to get what we want from others. (Blau, 1964; Richard Emerson, 1981)

While we may believe that we love someone "just because," exchange theory suggests that loving is in part a strategy for gaining love for ourselves. In fact, Homans (1974) suggested that we behave according to an emotional "profit motive," by which we judge relationships according to how much we have to invest in them relative to what we gain from them. Caplow (1982) suggested from his study of families in one community that the giving of Christmas gifts in the United States is often directed toward those whose relationships are both important to us and not secure enough to take for granted.

Gift-giving between spouses, Caplow believed, is particularly important since divorce is relatively easy; and gift-giving from parents to children is important because our norms and values do not oblige children to remain loyal to their parents. By comparison, gift-giving from children to their parents is less important, since the obligations of parents to their children are so strong that children are in a better position to take their relationships with mothers and fathers for granted.

From an exchange perspective, perception, attribution, and definitions of situations are influenced by our efforts to gain pleasure and avoid pain. We perceive others in terms of what they can give to us and what they will demand in return, and we explain their behavior in ways that maximize our own gains ("It's your fault; you owe me"). We also try to define the situation in ways that maximize gains and minimize costs. A man who wants sexual contact with a woman may insist on a definition of "sex in exchange for a fancy dinner," whereas she may define it as "sex in exchange for commitment to a lasting relationship."

The importance of exchange in social interaction is made clear by the fact that virtually all cultures have norms about what constitutes a "fair exchange" (Benedict, 1946; Malinowski, 1922). Norms about fairness and justice are vital to the well-being of any society (Gouldner, 1960), and apply across the entire spectrum of social behavior, from large questions of justice and equality to everyday interactions in which we expect others to do unto us as we have done unto them.

### Competition, Cooperation, and Exploitation: The "Prisoner's Dilemma"

As a process of exchange in which actors try to maximize their gains while minimizing their costs, interaction gives rise to competition and exploitation as well as cooperation. Few studies illustrate the difficult choice between cooperation and exploitation more dramatically than does the "prisoner's dilemma" (Luce and Raiffa, 1957).

Imagine a situation in which two criminals are arrested. The police are certain that these two committed the crime, but without a confession they have insufficient evidence to get a conviction. So the police put each in a separate room and present the following alternatives: "(1) If neither of you confesses, you'll be convicted on a minor, trumped-up charge and spend six months in jail; (2) If you both confess, the district attorney will recommend less than the most severe punishment, say four years; (3) If only one of you confesses, the one who does will go free while the other will receive the stiffest sentence permitted by law, ten years." If you were one of the prisoners, what would you do?

From one point of view, it is best to remain silent, for if neither confesses, both will suffer minimally. The problem with this cooperative strategy is that if you remain silent while your partner confesses, you suffer the maximum penalty while your partner goes free. Hence, there is a dilemma between cooperation and exploitation.

Luce and Raiffa presented volunteers with this dilemma and found that "prisoners" generally do not make cooperative choices: they usually confess, hoping that the other will not, and thus try to gain their own freedom at their partner's expense. Such dilemmas occur frequently in social interaction. When two people consider intimacy, each may feel reluctant to make a commitment, for those who fully commit themselves risk being abandoned or exploited by others. If neither makes a commitment, however, the relationship cannot be truly intimate (Table 7-2).

On a larger scale, the choice between cooperation and exploitation occurs frequently in economic behavior. Economic recessions sometimes confront workers with two alternatives: some lose their jobs so that others may keep theirs at their current rate of pay, or everyone's pay is cut so that no jobs are lost. The first choice is exploitative, for some workers gain only at the expense of others, while the second is cooperative. The prisoner's dilemma experiments suggest that people will exploit in such circumstances, but other evidence suggests that profit is not our only motive. In the 1982 negotiations between auto workers and manufacturers, for example, unions agreed to lower benefits in exchange for greater job security for all their members, a clear instance of cooperative behavior among group members.

Thus, although people rarely cooperate in prisoner's dilemmas in the laboratory, there are many situations whose structure compels us to run the risks inherent in cooperation. In many cases

---

## PUZZLES:

### FACING THE PRISONER'S DILEMMA

Suppose that during an exam you and a friend help each other. Immediately afterward the professor asks your friend to wait in the classroom alone while he talks to you in his office. He tells you that he thinks the two of you cheated. "If neither of you confesses to me now," he tells you, "I'll find a way to give you both a D for the exam. If you both confess, you'll both flunk the course. If one of you confesses and the other doesn't, however, I'll let the one who confesses go unpunished while the one who doesn't will flunk the course and be reported to the dean's office, which could lead to expulsion from school." What would you do? Why?

This is a classic situation in the study of cooperation, exchange, and exploitation in social interaction.

**Table 7-2**

The Prisoner's Dilemma Often Occurs in Social Relationships

Consider two people, Arthur and Valerie, who love each other but are unaware of each other's feelings. They can reveal themselves or not, and each option has its risks.

| VALERIE'S OPTIONS | ARTHUR'S OPTIONS | |
| --- | --- | --- |
| | Reveal Himself | Not Reveal Himself |
| Reveal Herself | They might have a love affair. | Valerie may feel like a fool if Arthur doesn't love her too. |
| Not Reveal Herself | Arthur may feel like a fool if Valerie doesn't love him too. | They may miss out on the love of a lifetime. |

we cannot get what we want without trust and co-operation: For example, when two people want intimacy between them or when nations want to reduce the risk of nuclear war, both parties must make some sort of commitment.

The likelihood of cooperation or exploitation thus depends partly on the structure of interactions. In the prisoner's dilemma experiment, prisoners could not communicate with each other to share intentions, desires, and needs; nor was a long-term relationship involved. Similar structures can also be found outside the laboratory: when people hear rumors of a bank failure, for example, they may rush to withdraw their funds before others do, thus saving themselves at the expense of others. Or, when goods such as food seem to be in short supply, people may buy up more than they can use in a reasonable time, thereby depriving others of having any. Thus, structural aspects of interactions—such as visibility, communication patterns, and the degree of interdependence—affect individual decisions to exploit or cooperate.

Social structures also specify how rewards and costs are distributed in interactions. In a race, for example, there is only one winner, and the prize can be had only at the expense of others. Such "zero-sum" games (Von Neumann and Morgenstern, 1964; Zagare, 1984) exist in many colleges: when grading is done on a curve that limits the number of students who can receive A's (and guar-

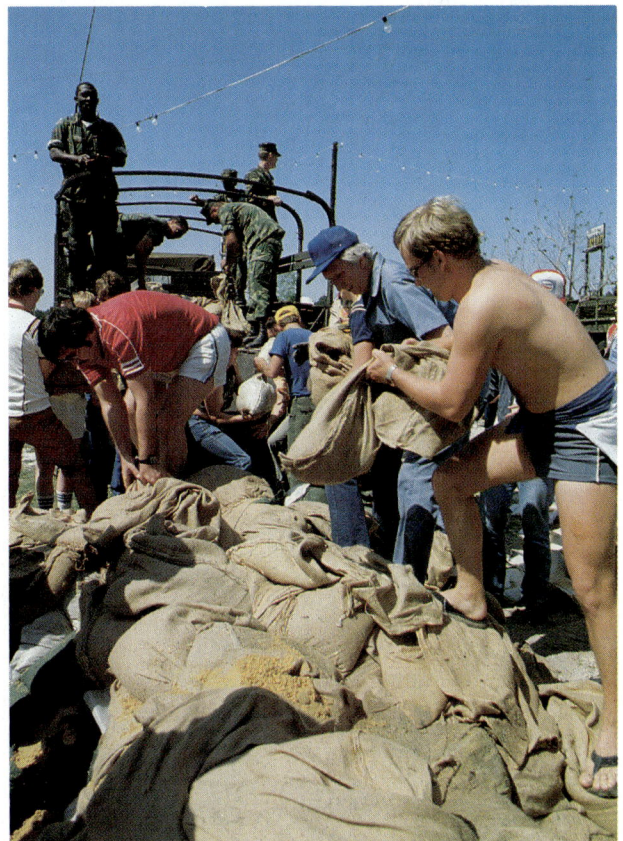

In some social situations, individuals can achieve their goals—including survival—only by cooperating with others.

antees that a certain number at the bottom of the curve will fail), competition and exploitation are likely results, with students not only refusing to help one another, but sometimes going so far as to sabotage one another's work by ruining lab experiments or hoarding library books.

In other situations—such as among combat soldiers in the field or police officers on patrol—the team is no stronger than its weakest member. Each depends on the success of the others in order to survive. When relationships are structured in this way, competition and exploitation threaten the lives of everyone involved. Thus, cooperative, exploitative, and competitive behavior depend on more than individual personalities; they also depend on the structured expectations that individuals orient themselves to as they make decisions.

Whether or not we use profit as our ultimate value, our interactions with others almost always include elements of exchange. Exchange, however, is not the only motivation in social interaction, as we will now see.

## Interaction as a Balancing Act

Why are we attracted to some people, but not to others? Why do we sometimes choose as friends people who do not treat us very well? Why do we feel uncomfortable when two of our friends do not like each other? From an exchange theory perspective, we are attracted to people who give us what we want—such as approval, acceptance, help, or support—and want what we have to give. This does not explain why we sometimes feel attracted to people who think little of us, or why we prefer to have our friends like one another. In all these cases, *balance theory* is a useful theoretical point of view (Heider, 1946).

According to **balance theory,** we organize our perceptions of people (including ourselves) and objects into units, and we strive for some consistency in the positive and negative feelings among them. Consider, for example, a paper you write for a college course. You work hard and feel good about the result. You also respect and like your professor. In terms of balance theory, you, your paper, and your professor are a unit that involves three relationships—each of which can be either positive or negative.

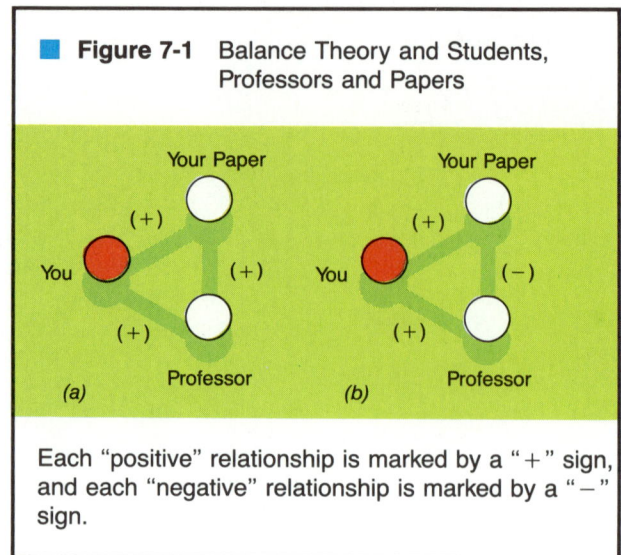

**Figure 7-1**  Balance Theory and Students, Professors and Papers

Each "positive" relationship is marked by a "+" sign, and each "negative" relationship is marked by a "−" sign.

Balance theory can be stated in a generalized form: *if we multiply the "positive" and "negative" relationships together and the result is positive, then the unit is balanced; if it is negative, the unit is unbalanced.* Your professor reads, grades, and returns your paper to you. Look at Figure 7-1 and think about how you would feel in each situation.

In (*a*) the system is balanced and you would feel just fine, but in (*b*) it is not, and to balance the relationships, you must change your feelings toward your paper ("It must not have been good after all") or toward your professor ("What a creep").

If, on the other hand, you did not like your professor to begin with, a low grade will not create an unbalanced situation, whereas a *good* grade will. In the latter situation, you will tend to change your feelings toward the professor ("Not so bad after all") or toward your paper ("If *that* professor liked it, it must not be so hot").

Balance theory also describes what happens to our feelings when we view ourselves or our behavior as objects in a set of relationships. People with low self-esteem are more likely to associate with people who treat them badly than are people with high self-esteem. Balance theory thus explains Groucho Marx's famous statement, "I wouldn't want to join any club that would accept me as a member" (Figure 7-2). If the club likes Groucho (a

**■ Figure 7-2**

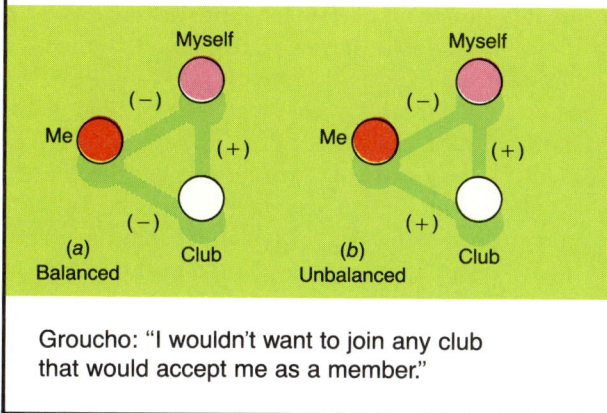

Groucho: "I wouldn't want to join any club that would accept me as a member."

Drawing by Joseph Farris; © 1984, The New Yorker Magazine, Inc.

According to balance theory, it is not surprising that married couples tend to develop similar interests, values, beliefs, and attitudes in order to protect (balance) their relationship with each other.

"+") but Groucho does not like Groucho (a "−"), then Groucho can balance the relationships only by rejecting the club (a "−") or by liking the club *and* himself.

By the same token, if you and I like each other (two "+'s"), but you dislike yourself (a "−"), the relationships will be unbalanced, and I might try to balance them by getting you to like yourself or by changing my feelings toward you. You also might try to balance the relationships by doing things to show me how dislikable you are.

Balance theory suggests that we are attracted to people who share our values, beliefs, and attitudes, for then the relationships are balanced ("I like you, and we both oppose sexism"). Newcomb (1961) invited college students to live rent-free in a house for a semester, asking them during their stay to complete a number of questionnaires about who they liked and disliked. Pairs of students were more likely to become friends if they agreed about themselves, other members of the house, and their values, beliefs, and attitudes. More important, Newcomb predicted friendships with some accuracy using students' values, beliefs, and attitudes measured *before* they ever met.

What, however, of the belief that "opposites attract"? Does this contradict balance theory? Newcomb (1956) suggested that in many cases differences between people reflect an underlying agreement on important values. Dominant and submissive people, for example, may be attracted to each other not simply because they are opposites, but because they both value dominant-submissive relationships.

Balance theory predicts not only that we tend to like people who are similar to us, but also that we tend to agree with people we like. When friends disagree, there are strong pressures to reduce the imbalance by finding a way to agree (Back, 1951; Ofshe, 1970). Married couples often adopt similar beliefs, values, and attitudes in order to balance their relationships (Berger and Kellner, 1964); and if we are strongly attracted to someone, we may change some of our feelings for the sake of balance.

The complexity of social interaction raises a number of problems for us as social actors. We

## PUZZLES:

## ADOPTING NEW ATTITUDES AND ALLEGIANCES

Why is it that young radicals who oppose the "system" so often join the system when they become adults? Why are graduate students who are critical of college faculties often critical of students once they, themselves, become professors? Why do workers become more pro-management after they are made supervisors?

It is tempting to explain such dramatic changes as some kind of sellout; but as we will see below, various theories of social interaction suggest that they are far more complicated than that.

often find ourselves expected to perform according to several different roles at once (resulting in role and status strain), or we may confront several possible definitions of a situation. Role playing also raises disturbing questions about authenticity: Are there real selves behind "exchangers," "balancers," and "theatrical performers"?

## Personal Identity: Authenticity and Consistency

Lieberman (1956) asked 2,354 American rank-and-file factory workers in 1951 a series of questions about unions and management. A year later, he readministered the questionnaires and compared the responses of those who had been promoted to management positions with two other groups of workers: those who had been promoted to union shop stewards and those who remained rank-and-file workers. Lieberman wanted to see how changes in social status affect people's beliefs, values, and attitudes.

He found that after one year, workers who became foremen adopted more pro-management, anti-union ideas, whereas those who became union shop stewards became more pro-union and anti-

management. Before changing statuses, almost none of the workers believed that management "really cared" about them. After a few years in their new statuses, however, 67 percent of the new foremen believed management really cared about workers, whereas none of those who became union shop stewards had this positive view of management. By comparison, workers who experienced no change in status showed little change in their perceptions or feelings about unions and management. When Lieberman returned to the factory in 1954, he found that the foremen who had been demoted to rank-and-file status tended to return to the attitudes they had held prior to their promotions to management. How do we explain such shifts in perceptions and feelings?

A social exchange perspective suggests that workers who become foremen adopt pro-management ideas because it is in their best interests to do so. Balance theory, on the other hand, suggests that when we change statuses, we adopt new reference groups, and our positive feelings toward a new group produce a strain of imbalance if we continue to hold ideas associated with our former status and its reference group. In short, it is difficult to maintain positive feelings toward two reference groups that have a negative view of each other (Figure 7-3).

From a dramaturgical point of view, new foremen adopt roles whose scripts call for pro-manage-

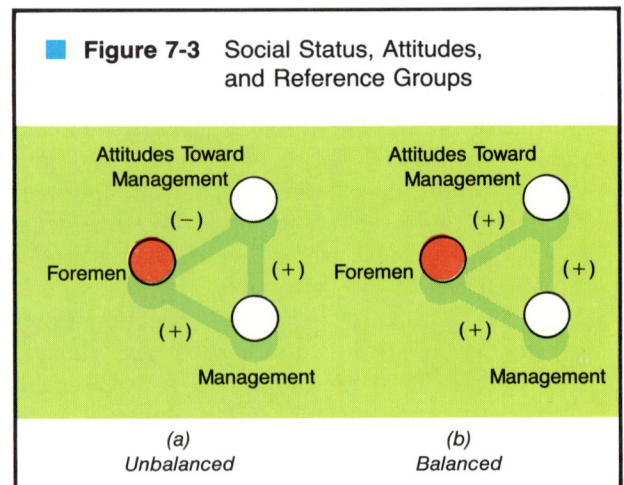

■ **Figure 7-3** Social Status, Attitudes, and Reference Groups

ment ideas and behaviors. Their foreman status becomes part of their social identity, and they can be true to their new self only by feeling, thinking, and acting accordingly. As Goffman (1961b) wrote, "A self virtually awaits the individual entering a position; he need only conform to the pressures on him and he will find a *me* ready-made for him." As we follow a new script, our behavior reinforces new attitudes, values, beliefs, and expectations. In Kenneth Burke's words, "doing is being."

Social life is full of such transformations: the radical political activist is elected to Congress and becomes "one of the boys," and although former friends may use exchange theory to explain the change ("She sold out"), the full explanation is undoubtedly more complicated than this, involving both problems of balance and changing identities (Gecas, 1981). Graduate students are among the severest critics of university faculties, yet when they become professors they often undergo a startling change and become more pro-faculty and anti-student. Although we may act as independent adults while living on our own, in the presence of our parents we may suddenly find ourselves acting like children once again.

Because we play many roles in our lives, we may feel as though we each have many different "selves" that we juggle as we shift from one social situation to another (Alexander and Wiley, 1981; Goffman, 1961b). For many people, the dramaturgical perspective in particular paints a disturbing picture of people adopting one social "mask" after another, continually "playing at" being different people in different social situations. As Robert Park (1950) wrote long before Goffman developed his dramaturgical approach,

> It is probably no historical accident that the word "person," in its first meaning, is a "mask." It is a recognition of the fact that everyone is always and everywhere, more or less consciously, playing a role. . . . It is in these roles that we know each other; it is in these roles that we know ourselves. (p. 249)

Goffman, however, was careful to point out that role playing does not necessarily imply insincerity or falseness. When we play a role, we reveal some aspects of ourselves while concealing others.

Thus, we often put on a "mask" only to the extent that we select which parts of ourselves to reveal, and when we perform a role, we integrate one segment of who we are with selected segments of other people (Goffman, 1961b). In one situation, we display our "intelligent, competent, independent" self, but in another, we display our "insecure, confused, dependent" self. We do not have to decide which is the "real me," for both are merely different parts of extraordinarily complex creatures.

Although we reveal different aspects of ourselves in different social situations, our self-images are relatively stable and enduring, and we strive for some sense of consistency in our presentations of ourselves (Burke and Reitzes, 1981; Mortimer et al., 1981). The desire to maintain a self-image and the self-esteem that goes with it can be as powerful a motivation in social interaction as the desire to gain through exchange, to balance social relationships, or to act according to the expectations inherent in social scripts (Rosenberg, 1979).

We are, of course, perfectly capable of faking performances, of donning masks that represent no segment of ourselves (except, perhaps, our desire for approval and other rewards). When capable, intelligent women act dumb and helpless in the presence of men, for example, or when men who need emotional support act tough and self-sufficient, both misrepresent themselves by pretending to be what they are not. With time, others will expect such false performances (accepting and depending on them as real) and the contradictions between who we are and how we appear to others may cause an identity crisis.

In this sense, we struggle not only for balance in our relationships with others, but for an internal balance between what we do and who we think we are. If Goffman is correct that "we are who we present ourselves to be," then self-images will have powerful effects on how we present ourselves to others. This, then, is a central problem for individuals in social interaction: to satisfy our needs and respond to the demands of social life while maintaining a consistent, stable sense of who we are. Because our identities are heavily anchored in statuses whose roles often conflict, the problem of maintaining an "authentic self" can be formidable.

## Summary

1. Social interaction is the process through which people act on and in relation to one another. It depends on a complex process through which we organize and interpret our perceptions of people and situations.

2. Interaction depends on how we perceive one another, and this often rests on first impressions that rely heavily on stereotypes—rigid, oversimplified beliefs about the members of groups and social categories. When we act as though stereotypes were true, we may help bring about self-fulfilling prophecies.

3. The definition of the situation identifies which statuses and roles are relevant in a given situation. We often use such definitions in social attribution—the explanation of other people's behavior—which focuses on internal causes such as emotional states and external causes such as role requirements.

4. All cultures include expectations about the physical distance between role partners, ranging from the zone of intimacy to personal, impersonal, and public zones. Social boundaries also regulate access to information about ourselves as well as behavior that may not involve physical contact.

5. Power is often an important ingredient in social interaction. Sociologists are less interested in personal power than in authority—power that is socially supported. Authority is purely social in its origins and determines who has the right to do what to whom. Extremes of both power and powerlessness can lead people to do things they would otherwise never consider themselves capable of.

6. Microecology focuses on the ways in which the number of people involved in a social situation and their physical arrangement in relation to one another affect social interaction. One difference between a dyad and a triad, for example, is that in a triad two people can gang up on the third by forming a coalition.

7. The dramaturgical approach to social interaction focuses on individuals as actors who are also audiences for each other as they perform parts of a social script. Like the theater, there is a frontstage and a backstage, and audiences and actors use various techniques to protect performances and ensure the continuation of the "play." Realigning actions introduce new definitions of the situation, and aligning actions signal acceptance of them.

8. Exchange theory looks on social interaction as a process in which we give what others want in exchange for what we want. It assumes that we want to avoid pain and gain pleasure and that these are accomplished primarily in relation to other people. It also assumes that we try to use our behavior in order to maximize our gains while minimizing our costs. This can be accomplished in ways that, depending on the situation, may involve cooperation, competition, or exploitation.

9. Balance theory suggests that we organize our perceptions of people and objects into units, and that we strive for some consistency in the positive and negative feelings among them. Balance theory helps predict not only how we will feel toward others, but also how we may feel toward ourselves in a particular set of relationships.

10. A central problem for us as individuals is to satisfy our needs and respond to social demands while maintaining a consistent, stable sense of who we are.

## Key Terms

## Recommended Readings

BAILEY, F. G. (1983). *The tactical uses of passion: An essay on power, reason, and reality*. Ithaca, NY: Cornell University Press. Evoking feelings of recognition often evoked by reading Erving Goffman's work, a social anthropologist looks at the ways in which we use emotion and reason in "conflict talk."

GOFFMAN, E. (1959). *The presentation of self in everyday life*. New York: Doubleday. Goffman's classic introduction to his dramaturgical perspective. See also *Forms of talk* (1981). Philadelphia: University of Pennsylvania Press. A collection of essays that focus on the importance of how we talk to each other.

HALL, E. T. (1969). *The hidden dimension*. New York: Doubleday. An anthropological look at how the human uses of physical space affect social interaction.

HANEY, C., BANKS, C., and ZIMBARDO, P. (1973). Interpersonal dynamics in a simulated prison. *International Journal of Criminology and Penology, 1*, 69–97. A deeply disturbing report of an experiment that produced astounding and unanticipated results.

# CHAPTER 8

# Groups and Formal Organizations

Families, universities, and government departments are **groups,** which we defined in Chapter 4 as two or more people who interact with one another in patterned ways and think of themselves as members (Homans, 1950). Family members share values, beliefs, and attitudes, and are limited by norms that define their expectations of one another. These ideas, in turn, are organized into social structures—patterns of expectation that guide social interaction.

As you might anticipate by now, this chapter will look at how cultural ideas, structural characteristics, and ecological factors affect groups and what happens to them and their members. The first section briefly examines the sociological importance of groups, and then we move quickly into the importance of group culture with a special emphasis on pressures to conform in groups. Then we look at the complexities of group structures: including boundaries, role and communication structures, distributions of power, prestige, and affection, as well as the primary, secondary, formal, and informal nature of social relationships within groups. From an ecological perspective, the most important characteristics of groups are their size and how they use physical space to regulate social interaction, and this occupies the third major section of the chapter.

We then turn to the problem of what is known as group process, or, what individuals actually do within the cultural, structural, and ecological conditions of group life. This includes how members try to increase their power in the group as well as factors that affect how effectively groups achieve goals and maintain themselves as groups. The chapter closes with a discussion of the tension that always exists between the needs of individuals, freedom, and the demands of group membership.

## The Sociological Importance of Groups

The concept of group is a basic unit of sociological analysis for several reasons. We orient most of our lives to groups, from the intimacy of romantic couples and families to the often overwhelming complexity of large bureaucracies. We experience our most intense desires to "belong" in relation to groups, our greatest fears of rejection, and our deepest conflicts as we perform roles in exchange for the privileges of membership. Some groups are like tiny islands—havens in which we are known and accepted, or prisons from which there is no escape—whereas others are so large and complex that we feel lost and insignificant in them.

Groups meet many human needs, including those for approval and acceptance, protection and safety, and support for our values. We use reference groups to define important parts of who we are and to establish and maintain our self-esteem. We grow up in groups, learn, earn livings, and practice religion in them. It is through them that societies govern and defend themselves, distribute both justice and injustice, heal the sick, distribute rewards and inflict punishments.

Groups are also a source of social conflict and considerable problems for individuals, however. Persecution, discrimination, oppression, and warfare are often based on relationships between groups; and the benefits of membership are not free, for groups require allegiance to their culture and continued interaction with other members.

Groups structure social relationships in many different ways and support a variety of cultural ideas. Their social characteristics affect the way they try to achieve their goals as well as their success in doing so. Social life centers on groups, and by understanding how they work, we can better

---

### PUZZLES:

### WHAT KEPT THE WEHRMACHT GOING?

During World War II, units of the German Army often kept fighting even when things looked hopeless, and long after most American units in similar circumstances would have stopped fighting. Why did the German soldiers hang on so long?

Many observers at the time thought (as you might) that perseverance among the German soldiers came from their dedication to their country and the Nazi cause, but as explained in this chapter, the social organization of military units in an army has more to do with the behavior of individual soldiers than any amount of ideology.

understand our experience and behavior as participants. We can also understand how the characteristics of groups affect the welfare of society itself. The ability of families to raise children, of governments to govern, of criminal justice systems to control crime, of hospitals to provide health care—all are vitally important.

The sociological study of groups centers on several kinds of questions, which this chapter examines in some detail. How, for example, can we describe groups in ways that allow us to see the important cultural, structural, and ecological differences among them? How do they distribute power and assign different roles to their members? How do group structures and cultures affect what goes on in them? How do groups survive over time, manage internal conflicts, and maintain the loyalty and obedience of their members? How are individuals affected by groups? How do groups support or interfere with individual freedom and how is the quality of our lives affected by the kinds of groups we belong to?

# Group Culture

All groups are based on shared cultural ideas. Stein and his colleagues, for example, argue from their research that whites often exclude nonwhites from groups not only because of race, but also because they assume that nonwhites do not share their values and beliefs (Stein et al., 1965).

Researchers asked white high school students to answer questions about their values—such as the desirability of having school spirit, being intelligent, neat, and attractive, or being concerned about other people. They then used these responses to create for each student descriptions of two pairs of fictitious teenagers. One pair of teenagers shared the respondent's values, whereas the second did not. In each pair, one of the teenagers was black, and the other was white.

Respondents were then asked how interested they would be in different kinds of social contact with the teenagers, such as inviting them home to dinner, going to a party together, attending the

same school, belonging to the same social group, living in the same building, or working together on the same committee. Although the willingness for intimate contact was negatively affected by race, a wide range of social contact was not. What did make a difference in these cases was the respondents' perception that they shared values with the teenager.

## Group Norms

The power of group norms is illustrated by a study of workers who built telephone switchboards at the Hawthorne plant of Western Electric (Roethlisberger and Dickson, 1939). In trying to find how to increase productivity, researchers were surprised to discover that workers often violated company norms (trading jobs, for example) and seemed unaffected by company rewards for increased production. They worked quickly in the mornings, but slowly in the afternoons, and never reported fellow workers who failed on the job. Men who worked too hard were labeled "rate busters," whereas those who worked too slowly were "slackers."

By working together, these men formed a subgroup with its own subculture that affected their behavior more strongly than the norms and values of the company in which they worked. That this subculture supported violations of company rules stems in part from the fact that the group members shared a common position in relation to the company and society as a whole. As members of the working class, they shared a long-standing tradition of resistance against the attempts of management to extract as much work from them as possible.

The common circumstances of these workers help explain the formation of their subgroup and the conformity of members to its norms; but in many groups, individuals conform even when they do not want to. What conditions allow groups to exert such power over their members?

## Pressures to Conform

Pressures to conform to group culture have three sources. First, by defining reality, goals, and expectations, group culture specifies requirements for continued membership. Whether we value a group for itself or as a means for achieving personal goals, conformity is the surest way to maintain membership: we conform to keep our jobs, to stay

Pressures to conform apply not only to behavior, but to appearance. There is no compelling reason for these businessmen to dress in the same way—except for the sake of conforming to the norm of their group.

in school, or to keep the love and respect of family members.

Second, we conform to the cultural ideas of reference groups whether or not we are members. Our admiration and affection for the members of a close-knit work group, for example, will lead us to use them as models of who we are or might become; and when such models are part of our social identity, conformity to the ideas that make up group culture is important if we are to maintain a stable sense of who we are. Thus, when we have "heroes and heroines" we often adopt their standards of behavior as our own.

Third, we depend on one another to support our perceptions of reality. If you sit with friends and suddenly smell a faint scent of gas in the air, you are most likely to turn to other people for confirmation: "Do you smell gas?" If they do not support us, we are likely to conclude that our perceptions are faulty; but if they *do* support us, we are far more likely to act on our perceptions as if they were accurate.

The pressures to conform are vividly illustrated by an experiment in which eight-member groups were shown a series of sets of four lines and for each were asked to judge which of three lines was the same length as a fourth "standard" line (Asch, 1952; see also Perrin and Spencer, 1980). Look at Figure 8-1 and imagine that you participated. Each member makes a judgment out loud, and you go last. With the first two sets of lines everyone agrees on which line is the same length as the "standard," but, with the third set of lines, you hear the first member match the standard line with comparison line 1, which is obviously not the same length. As you think about what a colossal mistake that was, you hear the second member make the same error, then the third, the fourth, and all the rest. Now it is your turn. Do you agree with the group's unanimous judgment or insist on your own?

Asch's findings suggest that chances are quite good that you would agree with the majority (all of whom were paid by the experimenter) even

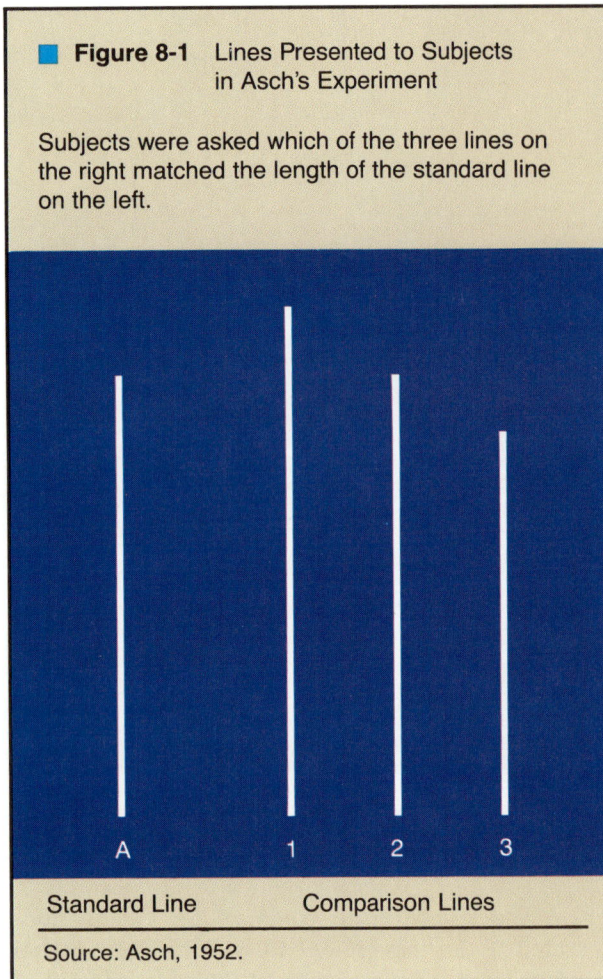

Subjects were asked which of the three lines on the right matched the length of the standard line on the left.

A    1    2    3

Standard Line          Comparison Lines

Source: Asch, 1952.

Then I felt sorry for a person with such poor eyesight."

Other studies found similar effects of group pressure on individuals (Deutsch and Gerard, 1955; Sherif, 1936). Tuddenham and McBride (1959), for example, found that group pressures can convince people that an average person eats six meals a day or that the United States is populated mostly by old people.

Thus, regardless of personal beliefs or perceptions, groups exert strong pressures to conform, especially on people who are attracted to them (Kelley, 1952). Such pressures are particularly important for moral questions that rest less on fact than on values and abstract principles of right and wrong. These studies help us appreciate how extraordinary it is for individuals to defy majority judgments, and how difficult it is to maintain a sense of who we are and what we "know" in group contexts.

## The Social Structure of Groups

As we saw in Chapter 4, social relationships have many structural characteristics that affect what goes on in them. Groups differ in the boundaries that define membership, and in the number and content of the roles their members are expected to perform. They have patterns of affection that may bind some members more closely to one another than to the group as a whole.

Groups differ in the amount of power they have in relation to other groups and the ways in which power and prestige are distributed among their members. Patterns of communication describe which members interact, how often and for what length of time.

Groups such as families and friendship groups are primary, existing for their own sake, enduring through time, and involving members in many aspects of one another's lives. Others—such as many work groups—are secondary, limited to specific goals that, once reached, usually end a member's involvement in the group. Groups may be informal, relying on folkways to control behavior;

though their judgments are clearly contrary to fact. Faced with overwhelming opposition, only 20 percent of Asch's subjects openly disagreed with the group. Those who conformed reported afterward that they both feared ridicule from the group if they disagreed ("Every time I disagreed I was beginning to wonder if I looked funny") and doubted their own perceptions ("Maybe where I'm sitting is making me see the lines wrong").

The fear of ridicule is especially important, as Asch (1952) discovered in a later experiment. In this case, only one of the eight members was employed by Asch and instructed to make errors. As the lone confederate made wrong judgments, the volunteer subjects laughed and openly expressed disbelief and sarcasm. As one subject said later, "I felt the person was attempting a stupid joke. . . .

or they may be formal, with specific rules that rigidly define and control role relationships.

## Boundaries: Members and Nonmembers

All groups have boundaries that distinguish nonmembers from members. Norms define not only who is eligible for membership, but how long the group is expected to exist and individuals are expected to belong.

Membership takes different forms that depend on participation. Members of Congress who rarely talk during sessions, for example, are **peripheral,** for although they are subject to group norms, their interaction with others is minimal. Those who regularly skip legislative sessions are **nominal** members, for although their names are on the list of representatives, the norms that guide congressional interaction do not affect them.

There are also different kinds of nonmembers (Merton, 1968). Some are eligible for membership, whereas others are not; and some want to belong more than others. A large pool of eligible members who openly refuse to join a group can harm it by raising serious questions about its attractiveness. In this sense, groups have relationships not only among their members, but with nonmembers as well.

**Time, Space, and Boundaries** Time is an important factor in defining group boundaries, for whereas some groups exist for short periods of time, others survive across many generations of members. Individual membership also varies in duration from a few hours to a lifetime. Some groups literally use time to define themselves, such as "the college class of 1990."

If you listed the members of your family, you would probably include only living relatives. A family tree, however, spans hundreds of years and includes both living and deceased family members. We expect our membership in a family to endure for our lifetime, and we expect the family itself to endure long after we die. Such expansive time boundaries contribute to a sense of permanence, continuity, and stability, and make the family one of the most important groups in our lives (Back, 1981).

Work groups, on the other hand, are defined primarily by the clock and physical settings (Homans, 1950); and, although the groups may

survive indefinitely, their members generally do not stay very long, which makes it difficult to maintain a strong commitment of members to the group.

During the Vietnam War, American troops were trained in one group, then transferred to others for one-year tours of duty. Because membership was clearly limited in time, soldiers cared less about the goals of their unit or the army than they did about the safety of themselves and their friends (George, 1971; Moskos, 1969). Their attitude toward replacements tended to be, "I've done my time; let the others do theirs."

> The end of the war is marked by the date a man leaves Vietnam, and not by its eventual outcome—whether victory, defeat, or stalemate. Even discussion of broader military strategy and the progress of the war . . . appears irrelevant to the combat soldier: "*My* war is over when I go home." (Moskos, p. 16)

**Clarity and Openness** All groups and organizations need to have clear boundaries in order to tell who is a member and who is not, and all vary in the degree to which their boundaries are open or closed. Intelligence services such as the CIA and the British Secret Service go to great lengths to ensure that their members are not actually enemy spies, and when a spy (often called a "mole") is discovered, it triggers a period during which members cannot be sure of who is a "real" member and who is not.

Whereas some groups try to increase their membership, others restrict it (Simmel, 1950). College fraternities and sororities, for example, deliberately discriminate on the basis of gender. On many campuses, such groups have come under increasing pressure to drop this membership restriction, and in some cases, they have given in to this pressure but insisted on maintaining some semblance of their old boundaries. In one college, for example, a fraternity agreed to admit women, but male members reinforced their gender-based boundary by insisting that female members be referred to as "brothers."

In her study of large corporations, Kanter (1977b) found that since women almost always constitute a tiny minority at middle and upper job levels, men try to "heighten" group boundaries in order to define and exclude women as outsiders.

The men, for example, were more likely to make sexual remarks in front of women than in front of other men. At meetings, they sometimes apologized for an off-color expression they were about to use and then went ahead and used it anyway. This simple act singles women out as outsiders who interfere with what is defined as the normal functioning of the group. Thus, by making the presence of "token" women more visible, men increased their solidarity with one another by heightening their own visibility as the dominant members.

**Voluntary and Involuntary Membership** People often join groups voluntarily because they value the group as an end in itself. Many people are church members, for example, because they enjoy the ritual of the services and the contact with other people who share their faith. Similarly, many people attend college because they enjoy learning, or work because they find it satisfying.

In other cases, individuals join groups as a means to an end. Thus, some people attend church in order to avoid hell and damnation, to make business contacts, or to create a favorable impression in the eyes of their neighbors. Almost a quarter of all employed Americans work only in order to earn money and say they would gladly give it up if they won the lottery (Davis, 1984). In similar ways, students often attend college not to satisfy a desire to learn, but to earn the degrees required for good jobs.

Whereas membership in some groups is voluntary, in others—such as mental hospitals, prisons, and elementary schools—it is involuntary. In such cases, membership is a means to someone *else's* end. Involuntary membership not only ensures a group's survival, but also gives it more control over its members. Involuntary members are deprived of the rights to make many decisions and are vulnerable to abuse and exploitation by those whose ends their membership serves.

The military draft illustrates the importance of involuntary membership for the survival of groups, for many argue that without a draft, the military cannot get the number of members it needs to achieve its goals. While ensuring a sufficiently large membership, however, the draft is dysfunctional for social cohesion, for people who are forced to join have a low commitment to the organization,

which can have disastrous consequences in combat. The draft also raises important questions about individual rights, as it forces young men to kill others and risk their lives in the pursuit of goals they do not choose.

In voluntary groups, members sometimes develop a strong sense of loyalty that may lead them to adopt hostile, superior attitudes toward nonmembers, and these can be an important part of group boundaries.

**In-Groups and Out-Groups** William Graham Sumner (1906) believed that all groups become **in-groups** by developing a strong sense of "we-ness" and hostile attitudes toward **out-groups.** "Loyalty to the group, sacrifice for it, hatred and contempt for outsiders . . . all grow together, products of the same situation" (p. 13). There are many examples of such attitudes: the hostility of college students toward "arch rival" schools, intense hatreds between nations, and the hostility that underlies the use of hundreds of slurs and epithets that different racial and ethnic groups apply to one another (Allen, 1983).

In the late 1970s a religious cult called the People's Temple formed around a single man, the Reverend Jim Jones, and settled in the South American country of Guyana. While the cult gave many downtrodden people a sense of purpose in their lives, it maintained its boundaries by requiring such intense in-group loyalty that members had to cut their ties with all outsiders, fearing out-groups as "the enemy," and labeling criticism from the outside as lies.

When a congressman and several journalists and concerned relatives visited the colony, Jones convinced his followers that the visitors wanted to destroy the cult. Not only were several of the visitors murdered, but over 900 members obeyed Jones' command to commit suicide, accepting his belief that the only alternative was the destruction of their religious colony.

Although there is ample evidence that groups often develop a strong sense of in-group loyalty and a hostile, superior attitude toward nonmembers, such attitudes are by no means inevitable (Merton, 1968). Many groups, for example, are subgroups of larger groups. Members of college athletic teams may have a strong sense of group loyalty, but they are also members of other groups—dorms, fraternities, sororities, and classes—on whom they depend for support.

Boundaries are thus the most fundamental part of any social structure, and within them, groups structure relationships among their members. Role structures divide labor and provide stable patterns of expectation; sociometric structures reflect patterns of affection; power structures rank members by their control over other members' behavior; prestige structures give some members more respect than others; and communication structures describe who interacts with whom.

## Role Structures and Structures of Affection

As groups develop, members take on different roles that form a *role structure.* As we saw in Chapter 4, role structures include two basic types: **task roles,** which focus on achieving goals, and **expressive roles,** which focus on maintaining harmony among members (Bales, 1950). Members of families perform many roles in addition to those of parent, adult, child, and sibling. Parents often divide task and expressive roles between them, and children may play a variety of roles—such as caring for a lonely parent or younger children, or soothing conflicts between parents.

Role structures differ both in content and in complexity. A married couple has two statuses (wife and husband), whereas a group of workers may include hundreds. Large groups are usually more complex than smaller ones, but this is not always true, for a family consisting of two parents, a daughter, and a son has eight statuses (husband, wife, mother, father, son, daughter, brother, and sister), but a college freshman English course has only two: teacher and student (see Table 8-1).

The complexity of groups is reflected not only in the diversity of roles their members play, but also in the emergence of subgroups based on ties of mutual affection. Even in groups with as few as five or six people, members often form such "friendship cliques." If you stand aside at a party, it is possible to identify cliques. Certain people tend to "stick together," whereas others are "loners" or "mixers."

As explained in Chapter 4, patterns of affection in groups define their sociometric structure, and they are important to understand, for they reveal that members frequently value subgroups more than the group as a whole. Office workers may become good friends and may value being with one another at least as much as they value the achievement of company goals. Subgroups often develop their own cultures and share a sense of common destiny. In work situations subgroups may feel

---

**Table 8-1**

As these examples show, groups come in all combinations of size and complexity.

|  | SMALL GROUP | LARGE GROUP |
| --- | --- | --- |
| **SIMPLE STRUCTURE** | Discussion group<br>Dance class<br>Tennis team<br>Jazz trio | Members of a group tour<br>Veterans group<br>Church congregation |
| **COMPLEX STRUCTURE** | Operating room staff<br>Family<br>Basketball team<br>Army squad<br>Movie-making crew (small budget) | Internal Revenue Service<br>Army division<br>U.S. House of Representatives<br>Movie-making crew (blockbuster) |

Even in small groups, as at a party, it is common for cliques to form.

drawn together by shared resentment toward superiors who exploit or pay too little attention to them. They may even sabotage organizational goals in order to protect the interests of their subgroup.

## Power and Leadership

Who controls groups, and why are some groups more powerful than others? In Chapter 7, we defined power as the possibility of imposing one's will on the behavior of others in spite of their resistance. Groups distribute power in distinct ways, and sociologists are interested in the effects of this distribution on both groups and their members. Power differences between groups are also important, for groups are often a source of social conflict.

Members who are able to define a group's culture have considerable control over group life. In Jonestown, for example, Jones had the power to define all nonmembers as "enemies," and his control over group beliefs resulted in mass obedience to his command to commit suicide. Individuals derive power from their ability to control resources: when children play baseball, it is not unusual for the one who supplies the bat and ball to have a disproportionate share of power to decide which rules to play by. Control over patterns of communication is an additional source of power: committee chairpersons, for example, decide who talks during meetings, and can use their power to stifle dissenting points of view. Those who perform roles that are important to a group or organization—and who perform them well—also tend to have a relatively large share of power (Pfeffer, 1981).

In democratic groups, power is distributed evenly among members, but in authoritarian groups, power is concentrated in the hands of a relative few. Most groups are neither purely democratic nor purely authoritarian, but fall somewhere in between.

A group has a leadership structure when power is assigned according to norms, and, therefore, takes the form of authority. It is important to emphasize that power and leadership are not necessarily the same. As Chapter 4 explained, leadership represents authority that is supported by norms and accepted by members. Power, on the other hand, may result from an individual's expertise, persuasiveness, or physical ability to coerce others. If everyone in a group does what you tell them to because they are afraid you will beat them up if they refuse, then you are not exercising either authority or leadership. Only when they accept your *right* to tell them what to do are you using authority. Thus, the social status of "leader" is always under group control.

Leaders perform a variety of roles: coping with external and internal threats, maintaining unity and order, managing anxiety and conflict among members, and motivating them to participate. As Whyte (1981) observed in his study of urban gangs, some groups depend on leaders for their very identity as a group:

> The leader is the focal point for the organization of his group. In his absence, members of the gang are divided into a number of small groups. There is no common activity or general conversation. When the leader appears . . . the small units form into one large group. . . . The leader becomes the focal

point in the discussion. A follower starts to say something, pauses when he notices that the leader is not listening, and begins again when he has the leader's attention. When the leader leaves the group, unity gives way to the divisions that existed before his appearance. (p. 258)

There are three basic types of group leaders, and they have different effects on how groups function (Lippitt and White, 1947). **Authoritarian leaders** dominate group interactions and generally do not participate in group activities. **Democratic leaders** act as guides who give advice and suggest alternatives, but leave decisions to the group. **Laissez-faire** (a French phrase meaning "allow to act") **leaders** rarely participate unless asked to by the group, and withhold positive or negative evaluations of the group and its members.

Many groups do not have leaders, but even in those that do, authority is not necessarily concentrated in a few hands. This is particularly true in large complex groups. The presidents of corporations, for example, are clearly the most powerful leaders in their organizations; and yet their effectiveness depends heavily on hundreds if not thousands of employees organized into small work groups. Leaders depend on their followers to perform their roles and keep them informed of what is happening in the organization, and the ability of

followers to withhold or distort information gives them considerable power in spite of their low position in leadership structures (Weber, 1925).

Different kinds of leaders strongly affect how groups function. A study of adult leaders in children's groups, for example, found that members are more dependent on authoritarian leaders, demand more attention, and take less initiative (Lippitt and White, 1947). They also are more critical of the leader and less friendly and confiding.

Like the moderator in this discussion, democratic leaders play a relatively inactive role and generally do little more than offer guidance to group members.

Authoritarian leaders take an active role in controlling the behavior and appearance of group members. As you can see, they are relatively easy to pick out in a crowd.

Laissez-faire leaders—like the therapist in this group therapy session—actually do very little leading and rarely participate unless asked to by group members. As you can see, it is not at all apparent just who the leader of this group is.

With democratic leaders, members work more independently, are less critical of and more friendly toward the leader, and are more likely to work together as a group. Laissez-faire groups, on the other hand, generate anxiety from members who are far more likely to ask for guidance and suggestions than are those in democratic or authoritarian groups.

Some groups (such as a group of friends) have no leadership structure, whereas others have a **pluralistic** structure, in which decision-making powers in specific areas of group life are assigned to specialists. In colleges and universities, for example, the administration is responsible for financial decisions, admissions, and financial aid, and the faculty controls what goes on in classrooms. Power in the U.S. House and Senate is divided among a number of committees, each of which exerts considerable control over different areas such as defense, budgets, health, and the behavior of group members.

Many groups have two power structures: a leadership structure defined by group norms, and informal structures reflecting the ability of individuals and subgroups to control the group. Although fathers are identified as the leaders of many families, for example, mothers often wield greater power in family decisions, and maintain a balance between formal and informal power structures by leading the father to believe "it was his idea all along."

Some groups have no leaders, while others do. Why?

**When Are Leaders Necessary?** Although people are generally reluctant to surrender individual freedom by giving power to a leader, several social conditions prompt the emergence of leaders (Brehm, 1966). First, members often give power to leaders in order to achieve highly valued goals (Marak, 1964). A group of friends usually lacks specific goals, and, therefore, has no leader; but people adrift in a lifeboat share a deep commitment to survival and are far more likely to appoint one.

Second, the more complex a group's role structure is, the more it needs a leader to coordinate the many different roles its members perform. Thus, a group of students working on a project may not need a leader until they divide tasks in a complex division of labor.

Third, regardless of complexity, large groups are more likely to have leaders than small groups are. Studies of groups of varying sizes reveal that regardless of members' personalities, as group size increases, a few members tend to dominate group interactions (Reynolds, 1971).

Finally, leaders tend to emerge when a crisis threatens group success or survival (Hamblin, 1958). Many nations and organizations have given enormous power to leaders during crises: Robespierre during the French Revolution, Adolph Hitler in Germany, Stalin after the Russian Revolution, Franklin Roosevelt during the Great Depression, and Lech Walesa during the labor crises in Poland in the 1980s. For this reason, times of crisis are particularly dangerous for groups, because leaders are in a position to abuse the power given to them by their members.

**Where Do Leaders Come From?** Crises, group size and complexity, and a commitment to group goals help explain why groups have leaders, but how do group members decide who will lead them? College professors are not hired by the students they teach; nor do office workers appoint managers. In such cases, the selection of leaders depends on norms, and from a sociological point of view, such processes are straightforward and of relatively little interest. A more interesting case is the emergence of leaders in groups that initially lack a leadership structure. How do such groups select their leaders?

During the 1930s and 1940s, researchers identified personality characteristics shared by leaders, including self-confidence, intelligence, dominance, empathy, and an outgoing personality. Their research methods were so varied and ambiguous, however, that later research found many contradictions: traits that were related to leadership in one study were unrelated in others. Although personality certainly makes a difference (shy, retiring people are unlikely to become leaders), the personality approach was abandoned in the 1950s as researchers focused on behavior in groups (Bass, 1960).

One factor that affects the rise of individuals to power and leadership is their *rate of participation in group interactions:* members who talk a lot tend to have more influence than less talkative members. Even shy, retiring people can become leaders if they are encouraged to participate. In one experiment, Hastorf (1965) asked four-member groups to discuss case studies; during the first session, he identified individuals whose participation was next to the lowest. In the second phase, members were separated by panels equipped with green and red lights. Participants were told that experts on group interaction controlled the lights, that "green" encouraged talk, while "red" advised silence.

During this phase, the lights were used to encourage the previously silent members to talk, and their contributions jumped by 50 percent. In the third phase, discussion continued without the lights, yet these members continued to talk the most; and in members' final ratings of one another's contributions, the initially silent member moved from third to second place.

Apparently, under the right circumstances, anyone has the potential to play a leadership role. People who cannot imagine themselves as leaders may find that merely by speaking up, they acquire surprising levels of power. This underscores the fact that leadership is a social status, that leaders are those whom group members *identify* as leaders.

From this perspective, it is easier to see how "unlikely people"—such as Presidents Harry Truman and Lyndon Johnson—who are thrust into leadership positions during crises can yet perform very well. It is also easier to understand how people who are genuinely unfit for leadership nonetheless attain positions of power through frequent, highly visible participation in group activities.

A second factor in leader selection is *latent statuses* that have no recognized role in group activities (Markovsky, Smith, and Berger, 1984; Ridgeway, 1981). F. Strodtbeck et al. (1957) selected people from community jury pools and formed mock juries in order to study how they make decisions. Males and those with high-prestige occupations were the most likely to be elected foremen and to influence jury decisions. Thus, group members use latent statuses as cues to determine which members are likely to make the best leaders and make the most useful contributions. Such early assumptions allow some members to participate more than others and thereby strengthen their leadership positions.

Conformity to norms is a third factor in the selection of leaders, especially in a group's early stages. Hollander (1960) planted confederates in problem-solving groups and supplied them with the correct answers to the problem. The groups established norms, which the confederates violated (by speaking out of turn, for example) at different stages of the meeting.

Although the confederates always offered the correct solution to the problem, when they spoke out of turn at the beginning of the session they were generally ignored; when they obeyed the rules until mid-way in the meeting, the confederates' influence was greater; and when they conformed until the meeting was nearly over, their influence reached a maximum. Thus, members initially identified as nonconformists are unlikely to become leaders regardless of their contributions.

Ridgeway (1981) used a similar experimental design and found that the effect of conformity on influence in groups may not be as simple as Hollander suggests. She found that nonconformity can increase influence by attracting the attention of other members, but that this effect can be tricky since nonconformists may be seen as caring more about themselves than about the group. She found that nonconformity was particularly dangerous for members who occupy latent statuses—such as female—that are relatively low in prestige. Ridgeway concluded that the most important factors in determining influence in groups are other people's perceptions of a member's motivation and competence in performing group tasks and, as we saw above, latent statuses such as gender, age, race, and occupation.

**The Power of Groups** Group power depends on both culture and social structure. Like individual members, groups may exercise authority that rests on cultural norms in the surrounding society. Police departments, the Internal Revenue Service, and employers all hold power over others by virtue of socially defined authority.

Groups also draw power from their structural position in relation to other groups and valued resources. Undergraduate college faculties, for example, control students' access to graduate schools. Thus, students conform to professors' demands not only to maintain their membership in undergraduate classes, but also because professors occupy a key position between undergraduate colleges and graduate schools.

The control of valued resources is also a major source of group power. Employment, professions, governments, and universities, for example, are controlled by people who are white, middle-aged, male, and wealthy, and this gives them power over nonwhites, women, the poor, and the elderly, whom they can exclude from socially legitimate avenues to money, power, and prestige.

Thus, groups draw power from culturally based authority as well as their social structures and positions in the surrounding society. This power is then distributed among group members, whose roles and power affect their position in prestige structures that rank members in terms of the respect they receive from others.

### Distributing Respect: Prestige Structures

Unlike power, the distribution of prestige in groups depends heavily on cultural values. If our culture values possessions such as stereos, cars, and jewelry, we tend to respect those who have them even when they have no power over us. For this reason, people often buy things (such as designer jeans) not simply to use or enjoy them, but to indicate to others that they have achieved an important cultural value and therefore deserve high levels of respect. This is what Thorstein Veblen (1928) called **conspicuous consumption,** owning objects in order to enhance or affirm prestige.

What people buy can be explained only in part by the manifest function of the object (in the case of jeans, to cover our bodies, keep us warm, and improve our physical appearance). Only by paying attention to latent functions such as enhanced prestige can we fully understand trends in what people buy and consume (Merton, 1968).

Prestige is also affected by values attached to specific statuses and their roles. Harris (1977, 1979) argued that in hunter-gatherer and horticultural societies, child-care responsibilities excluded women from the socially valued role of defending communities from outside threats. The male monopoly on warfare resulted in higher levels of prestige for men in general, and helped lay the foundation for male supremacy and sexism.

### Who Talks to Whom: Structures of Communication

As we have seen, groups differ in how they distribute roles, affection, power, and prestige. They also differ in their *communication structures*, which describe how frequently and extensively members of groups and organizations interact with one another—in other words, who talks to whom, how often, and for how long. Figure 8-2, for example, shows several family communication structures. In (*a*), family members interact with one another a great deal, whereas in (*b*), the father interacts heavily with the mother, but little with his children. In (*c*), which represents many families with divorced parents, the father is "absent," interacting minimally with other family members, and in (*d*), the heaviest interaction takes place between the children, as might occur when both parents are employed.

# DOONESBURY                                                    by Garry Trudeau

**Figure 8-2** Family Patterns of Communication

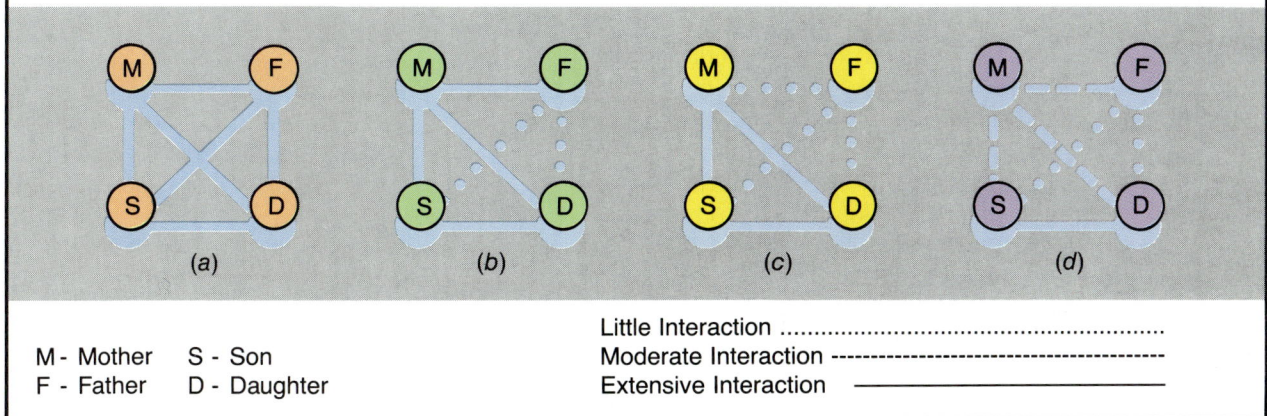

M - Mother     S - Son
F - Father      D - Daughter

Little Interaction ...............................................
Moderate Interaction - - - - - - - - - - - - - - - - - - - - - - - -
Extensive Interaction ─────────────────

Such differences are important in several ways. First, observations of small groups show that frequent interaction strengthens attachments to the group and tends to make them happier. Thus, group cohesion and member satisfaction will tend to decrease as we go from (a) to (c).

Second, members must communicate in order to know about each other and get feedback about their behavior. In (b), the father and children depend largely on the mother for information about each other, while in (c), they are isolated from each other. In comparison with (a), then, the structures in (b) and (c) are likely to result in considerably more misunderstanding and conflict between the father and his children.

Third, because interaction strengthens ties between group members, communication structures affect the formation of subgroups. The tendency to form subgroups will be least in (a), while in (b) three distinct subgroups are likely: mother-father, mother-son-daughter, and son-daughter. In (c), the father is a peripheral or nominal member and may be excluded by the mother-son-daughter subgroup, and in (d) the children may develop a bond that strongly influences family decisions.

## Ties That Bind: Primary and Secondary Groups

In **primary groups** such as families and small groups of close friends, the group is valued for its own sake, and its members' welfare is more important than achieving specific goals. Primary groups endure even when circumstances change, and they involve many aspects of members' lives. Ties in primary groups are based on affection, and interaction among their members is continuous and face-to-face (Cooley, 1909).

**Secondary groups** such as those found in school classrooms and most work settings exist in order to accomplish specific goals that the group values more highly than the welfare of individual members. Secondary ties generally last for a shorter time than primary ones, involve only those parts of members' lives that affect group goals, and are based on rational considerations of self-interest. Interaction is often not face-to-face ("memos" are circulated instead) and is limited to specific times and places.

This distinction is important both to individuals and to groups. Primary groups are at the heart of human social life, for it is within them that we are valued and protected simply because we are members of the group. They give our lives a sense of continuity and stability and provide the only opportunities for affection and being known by others as complex individuals.

Secondary groups cannot give us a sense of stability and continuity, of belonging and worth, for they value group goals more than the welfare of individual members. We can lose our places in them quite easily, and the groups themselves can quickly dissolve. When individuals heavily invest themselves in secondary groups—at work, for example—they often find that their world "falls apart" if they suddenly lose their jobs. Secondary groups, however, offer us greater control over our participation, including the aspects of ourselves we reveal to others (for this reason many people use workplaces as a refuge from the revealing intimacy of family life).

It is generally more difficult for a secondary group to control its members, since their loyalty to the group is usually limited to specific goals and activities. It is, for example, difficult for employers to have much control over what workers do outside of working hours. Secondary groups, on the other hand, are more likely to survive across many generations, because they can replace their members more easily. They can also coordinate large numbers of people in order to accomplish complex goals. It would be impossible, for example, to organize a university or a large army solely around primary relationships.

Primary groups are often regarded as superior to secondary groups because they help meet profound human needs such as those for intimacy and emotional support. They also can be sources of considerable problems for their members, however. We lose a great deal if we "quit" a family (if, in fact, such a thing is possible), and such ties are difficult to replace. By exposing many aspects of our personal lives in them, we make ourselves vulnerable to exploitation, humiliation, and abuse. Many emotional problems that plague us as adults have their roots in our experiences in the family, and studies of family violence identify the family as one of the most dangerous of all groups (Gelles, 1972; Straus, Gelles, and Steinmetz, 1980).

## Formal and Informal Groups

As we saw in Chapter 4, primary groups have an informal structure in which relationships tend to be flexible and group norms are rarely stated explicitly. Although this is true of some secondary groups (such as social clubs), most secondary groups have a formal structure that clearly defines role relationships among groups members (see Table 8-2).

In informal groups, relationships among group members change with varying circumstances, and the terms that guide their interactions are always open to negotiation. An act that is punished in one situation may be overlooked in another: friends may tolerate silly, disruptive behavior one day, but not the next. Thus, **informal groups** are identified by implicit understandings of norms rather than by

**Table 8-2**

Primary groups are always informal, but as these examples show, secondary groups can be either formal or informal.

|  | INFORMAL | FORMAL |
|---|---|---|
| **PRIMARY** | Family<br>Close friends<br>Small commune | None |
| **SECONDARY** | Trial jury<br>Tupperware party<br>College class | Bureaucracy<br>Surgery team<br>Airline crew |

explicit statements, and by flexible relationships among group members.

In groups with specific goals, however, it is difficult to coordinate people's behavior in predictable ways. Especially when groups have many members who specialize in a variety of tasks, they cannot depend on members to negotiate the terms of their relationships as they go along (Simmel, 1950). A response to this problem is the **formal organization,** in which relationships among members are regulated by clearly stated, rigid norms that are oriented to the achievement of specific goals.

## Bureaucracies

As we saw in Chapter 4, the ideal **bureaucracy** is a set of formal secondary relationships that are rationally organized in order to achieve specific goals. People specialize in narrowly defined tasks, and perform roles that are rigidly defined. Power is distributed in a distinct hierarchy, and managers and administrators oversee other people's role behavior to ensure that everything works as it is supposed to. Decisions are supposed to be based on rational considerations of the best interests of the organization, rather than on the personal feelings and welfare of individuals (Weber, 1922a, 1922b).

Bureaucracies are organized around cultural ideas that distinguish them from informal groups. Whereas informal groups place a high value on the welfare of their members, bureaucracies value the organization and its goals most highly, and thus

## Voices: An Encounter with Bureaucracy

My wife and I filed a joint tax return in 1982 and months later received a form from the Internal Revenue Service. According to the form, my social security number didn't match my name; either my name or the number I put on my return was incorrect. They were correct, however, so I called the IRS number listed at the top of the form. "Why did you send me this form?" I asked.

"I don't know," he said.

"Where did the form come from?" I asked.

"Your local IRS service center."

"Can I call them?"

"No," he said. "Try the Social Security Office."

So, I called Social Security.

"Why did I get this form?"

"I don't know," she said. "IRS is the one who sends them out. We get these calls all the time."

"What do I have to do?"

"I'll send you a correction form," she said. "Fill it out, send me something that proves who you are, and everything will be all straightened out. We'll send you a new Social Security card with your correct number on it."

"But there's nothing to correct," I said. "I already *have* a card with my correct number."

"I know; but this is what we have to do."

"That's crazy."

"I know," she said.

"What if I don't do anything about this. What happens then?"

"They'll just send you another form next year and hold up your tax return until the problem is cleared up."

"But there *isn't* a problem," I said.

"I know," she said.

She sent the forms; I filled them out; and now I have a new social security card. Just like my old one.

---

place a premium on technical efficiency, precision, speed, reliability, strict obedience, and the highest possible production at the lowest possible cost.

Bureaucracies also rest on cultural beliefs that the best decisions are made by experts (without regard for feelings) and that efficiency is highest when leaders are authoritarian and members are motivated by the desire to maximize their own rewards, rather than by ties of love and affection. Thus, a bureaucracy is a particularly passionless organization that tries to rely exclusively on rationality, impersonal relationships, inequality, specialization, and loyalty based on calculations of individual self-interest.

Tumin (1964) argued that bureaucracies also rest on beliefs that protect them from external threats. Because the organization (and its survival) is valued more highly than its individual members, bureaucracies share what Tumin called "the myths of infallibility and indispensability." Businesses, Tumin noted, rarely admit violations of the law, no matter how compelling the evidence; and prosecutions of large organizations usually end not in criminal convictions, but in settlements by which the company agrees to "stop doing what it never admitted to doing in the first place" (see Chapter 10). When bureaucracies cannot defend themselves in this way, they usually use individuals (or "the computer") as scapegoats, thus preserving the integrity of the organization itself.

Bureaucracies also use the "myth of indispensability" to fight for survival. When a corporation is in danger of going bankrupt (as Chrysler was in the late 1970s) or when a government agency is about to lose its funding, its leaders often predict that society will suffer immeasurably if their organization does not survive.

Bureaucracies are unique in the norms that structure relationships among their members. The ideal bureaucracy rests solely on norms that clearly specify how roles are assigned, how power and rewards are distributed, and how decisions are made. Such norms specify what members should do in every situation and forbid the use of personal feelings and individual discretion: decisions are made "by the book," not on a case-by-case basis.

Here the distinction between informal groups and bureaucracies is particularly clear, for expectations are not hard and fast in informal groups, and each member has considerable power over the terms of group interactions ("You can't do that." "Who says?"). In a bureaucracy, however, even the most powerful member is limited by clearly stated norms that anyone can refer to ("According to the bylaws, you can't do that").

Bureaucratic norms result in a rigid social structure that links statuses with clearly stated norms specifying areas of competence and responsibility. Individual members are easily replaced, for unlike informal groups, bureaucracies do not depend on particular individuals for their survival.

Whereas a family is a group of specific *individuals*, a bureaucracy is a collection of social *statuses* whose relationships are structured not to benefit individuals, but to achieve goals within a rigid, stable set of mutual expectations among members. Thus, the bureaucratic ideal represents a complete submersion of individuals in a social organization and the resulting irrelevance of individual feelings and needs.

**The Birth of a Bureaucracy** Whyte's (1950) study of restaurants illustrates how bureaucracies emerge as groups grow larger and more complex. Suppose two people decide to open a small restaurant. In its early stages, the structure of the group is informal and may have some of the characteristics of primary relationships. Each member identifies the other as an individual; shares specific tasks such as cooking and serving food, paying bills, and ordering supplies; and handles crises as they arise. Because they interact continually with each other, members can negotiate responsibilities as they go along.

Business booms and they add several employees to cook and serve the food. The owners now face the problem of coordinating the activities of several different people. This requires them to create formal expectations about work hours, dress, and conduct on the job. If their business is highly successful, they might open several restaurants, or perhaps expand into a chain extending across many states. Now they must hire managers to direct each restaurant, accountants to keep the books, and, if they sell stock in their company, a board of directors to oversee the entire operation.

What began as a small informal group grows into a large bureaucracy in which social relation-

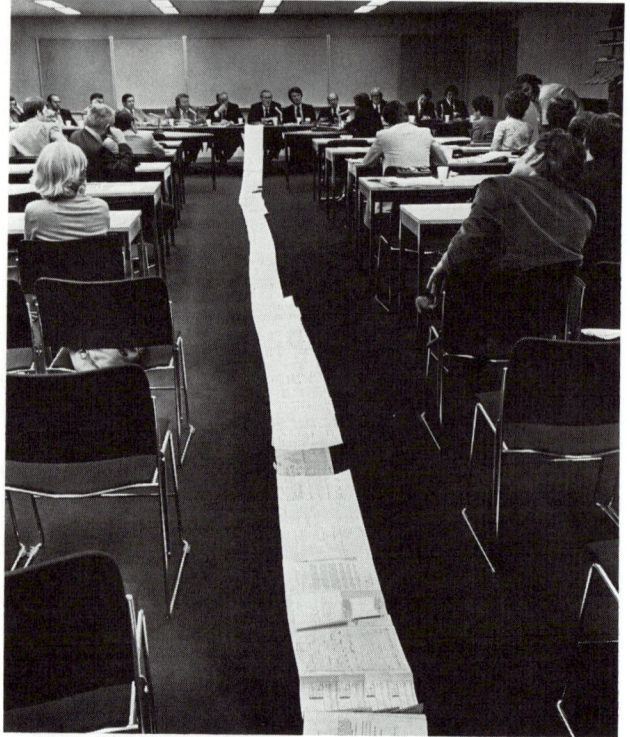

Bureaucracies use written records to control their complex divisions of labor. In this picture the Commission on Federal Paperwork views 45 feet of official forms that are necessary in order to process a request for aid to one dependent child.

ships are formally defined. The company becomes more important than its members, any of whom can be replaced with relative ease. Although the original members had equal levels of power, the more complex, formal organization has a clearly defined hierarchy of power and prestige, with directors at the top and dishwashers at the bottom.

The structural complexity represented by modern bureaucracies is rooted in the development of more complex societies over the last 1,000 years. Murdock's data on primitive societies (1967) show that only 29 percent of villages in advanced horticultural societies were autonomous, free of dominating governments above them, whereas in simple horticultural societies, fully 79 percent were governed solely at the local level. The establishment of central governments spawned increasingly complex societies with formal legal codes, standing armies, and thousands of administrators (Lenski and Lenski, 1982).

**Figure 8-3**    Organizational Chart for the Benguerra Crime "Family"

As you can see, bureaucracy has extended into areas of life where you would not expect to find it. The lines show directions of authority (who is answerable to whom). An underboss sees to it that the orders of the boss are carried out and is like a vice-president who takes over in the absence of the president. The counselor and treasurer are answerable only to the boss and have no authority of their own. There are ten "capos"—leaders of subgroups that control particular areas (such as neighborhoods) or operations (such as numbers, drugs, bookmaking, loansharking, or prostitution)—and below each capo are the lowest-ranking group members who carry out the work of a subgroup (such as collecting bets, enforcing loans, bribing public officials, and murder).

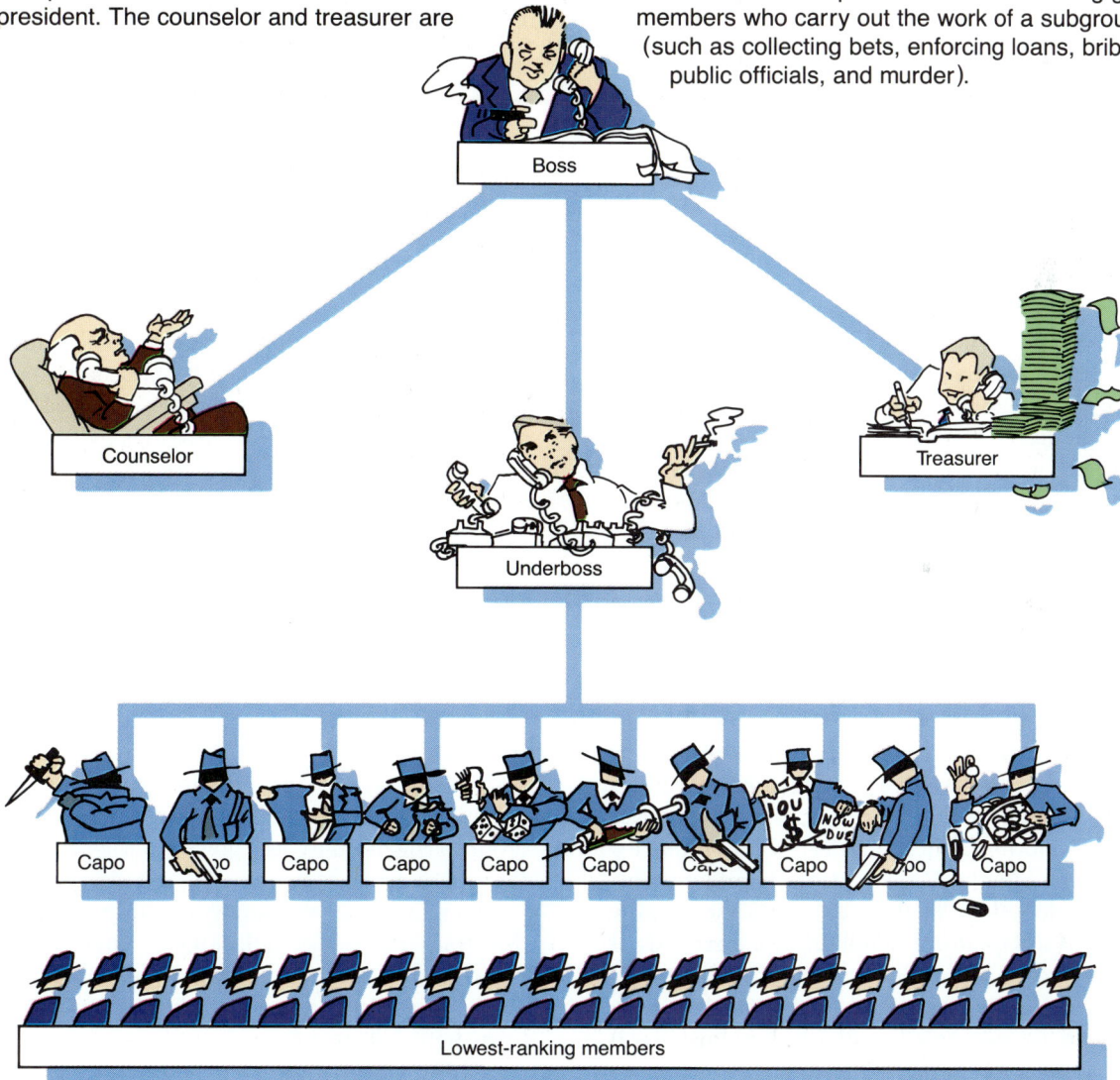

Boss

Counselor

Underboss

Treasurer

Capo | Capo | Capo | Capo | Capo | Capo | Capo | Capo | Capo | Capo

Lowest-ranking members

Source: Anderson, *The Business of Organized Crime,* 1979.

The Industrial Revolution gave the growth of bureaucracy an enormous boost by bringing together large numbers of people who specialized in specific tasks. The increased scale and the complexity of production caused substantial changes in the organization of society itself as governments, schools, hospitals, and other organizations adopted the bureaucratic model (see Figure 8-3) (Zucker, 1983). The bureaucratic ideal has even influenced criminals, for although organized crime once revolved around primary family ties, it now operates much like a large corporation (Chapter 10).

## Population, Ecology, and Groups

As we have just seen, the number of people involved is an important part of the rise of bureaucracy, and the ecological perspective draws attention to both group size and the spatial arrangement of its members. These are the two most important ecological characteristics, and both affect the cultures and social structures of groups.

### Group Size

As we saw in Chapter 4, the smallest group (a dyad) has only two members, but it is difficult to establish the upper limit on possible group size. At some point, however, a group ceases to be a group and becomes a **collectivity,** in which people identify themselves as members but do not interact with one another. The American Civil Liberties Union, for example, began with only a few members who, together, made up a group; but it now has tens of thousands of members and hundreds of chapters across the country. Since many of its members never interact with other members (they join simply by making a donation), the ACLU is no longer a group.

As group size increases beyond three, members tend to specialize in different tasks, and the group may become more formal in order to control a more complex role structure. In addition, members of large groups are less visible than those in smaller ones and can violate group norms with less chance of being detected.

---

### PUZZLES:

## ARE TWO HEADS BETTER THAN ONE? ARE THEY TWICE AS GOOD?

The answer to the first question is "only sometimes" and the answer to the second is "rarely." This chapter explains how and why.

---

Large groups thus allow their members to "hide," which lowers each individual's sense of responsibility to the group. As a result, large groups generally have less cohesion than smaller ones, and individuals tend to feel less valued. Some students prefer small group discussions for this reason—they feel more involved, important, and visible—whereas others avoid such classes for the same reason.

A large group is also more likely to include members who have unusual characteristics. If only 10 percent of a student body are political radicals, a four-member student judiciary board is unlikely to have a radical member. A 100-member Student Senate, on the other hand, can expect to have at least ten radicals (10% of 100) simply on the basis of chance. Thus, larger groups are more likely to be heterogeneous, which increases the chances for internal conflict.

The power of groups in relation to other groups is also affected by size. Although small groups are generally less powerful than large ones, the relationship between size and power depends both on a group's *absolute* size and its *relative* size (Merton, 1968; Simmel, 1950). Three hundred blacks fighting for their civil rights have far less power in a city of a million whites than in a small town with 500 residents.

Group power also depends on the *completeness* of membership—the proportion of eligible members who are actual members (Simmel, 1950). Eighteen million American workers, for example, belong to labor unions; but 66 million workers do *not* belong to unions, even though many of them could if they wanted to (U.S. Census Bureau, 1983c). Thus, while the absolute and relative size of the labor movement gives it considerable power, it is undermined by the visible pool of eligible workers who refuse to join.

## Space and Social Structure

Spatial relationships affect the social structures of groups in a variety of ways. Interaction in families, for example, is frequent simply because members share the same dwelling; and while children are young, frequent interaction supports family unity and allows members to exert considerable control over one another. When children mature and leave home, however, interaction declines, often causing severe shocks to parental power and the family's sense of itself as a group. Members may lose touch with one another, and no longer share important events such as holidays. At best, they may feel they no longer know one another; at worst, they may feel they no longer have a family at all.

The spatial arrangement of people within groups also affects patterns of interaction. When discussion groups are arranged in a circle, for example, people tend to talk with those across from them more than the ones next to them (Steinzor, 1950). At rectangular tables, the people sitting at each end tend to interact more frequently (Strodtbeck and Hook, 1961)—and, as we saw earlier, those who interact the most in groups are the most likely to emerge as leaders.

Seating in public bus, train, and airport terminals is usually in long back-to-back rows, a design that minimizes the chances for interaction. Sommer (1969) observed that patients in a mental hospital rarely interacted with one another in wards whose chairs were arranged much like those in airports. When he rearranged the furniture so that eye contact was difficult to avoid, however, the rate and duration of interaction almost doubled and visitors noticed that the group members seemed more lively and outgoing.

Military organizations often use spatial relationships to build cohesion in small units such as platoons. In the United States, new recruits enter the military with a variety of individual backgrounds and personal characteristics that distinguish them from one another. During training, recruits are housed in open barracks that give them no privacy and force them all to live in ex-

actly the same conditions. No personal articles—such as pictures—can be displayed in the open.

Thus, the physical environment of basic training is designed to submerge the recruits' sense of themselves as unique individuals in order to foster a new, common identity as platoon members. As we will see later, such ties are vitally important for the performance of both groups and individuals. When prisoners of war are isolated from one another, the resulting lack of interaction seriously damages group cohesion and the support that each member receives (Schein, 1957).

Spatial relationships are also used to reinforce distributions of power and prestige in groups. In his study of restaurants, Whyte (1950) observed that cooks often avoid face-to-face interaction with waitresses, because they dislike "taking orders" from workers who are ranked below them in prestige. In most restaurants, cooks and waitresses are separated by physical barriers; and in larger ones, orders are written and then passed to the cooks without any direct contact between cooks and waitresses. Recently some restaurants have taken this a step further by using computers to transmit orders from the dining room to the kitchen.

Corporate leaders typically occupy offices on the highest floors of office buildings, thus using physical space to insulate them from other members while also placing themselves "above" everyone else. In most office settings, workers occupy desks set out in the open where their role behavior is highly visible. As a rule, only managers and administrators have offices of their own, and their power and prestige are reinforced by being shielded from the scrutiny of others.

The preceding descriptions and analyses of how groups vary in their culture, structure, size, and spatial arrangements may give the false impression that groups consist of rigid relationships that lead their members to behave in predictable ways all of the time. What members *do*, as we will see, often changes group structures and cultures.

## What Goes On: Group Process

**Group process** refers to what members actually do in groups; it is a vital aspect of group life, for it causes groups to change as they adapt to new circumstances and respond to the behavior of their members.

After participating in a small group discussion, for example, you would have many impressions of what happened, such as "So-and-so talked a lot," "We got nowhere," "We got the job done," "I felt good," or "I couldn't wait to get out of there." In spite of the fact that such impressions help us make sense of what happens in groups, they are not a scientific description of what is going on. Although you might describe one member's contributions as "stupid," another member might describe that same person as "daring and constructive." In short, you most likely do not use an objective point of view that would yield the same results no matter who did the observing. Your impressions also tend to be highly selective. You may pay little attention to the remarks of people you do not like, for example, or miss large chunks of the meeting while you are thinking about what you are going to do afterwards.

In response to such problems, Bales (1950) and his colleagues developed a method for observing and recording interactions among small group members. Specifically, they developed a set of categories (Table 8-3) to measure who does what in relation to whom, how and when they do it, under what conditions, and with what effects on other members and the group as a whole. To use these

categories, observers must notice everything members say and do and record each act in the appropriate category.

The result is a record of (1) the total number of each type of act; (2) each member's total participation, overall and for each category; and (3) the patterns of interaction—who did what in relation to whom. Such records create a "map" of group interactions. In solving problems, for example, all groups tend to pass through a series of stages that can be accurately charted using Bales' categories (Bales and Strodtbeck, 1951).

Groups begin with pleasantries—such as saying hello and making jokes—that heighten feelings of group solidarity and lower tension. When the group gets down to work, behavior shifts to asking for and giving orientation as members try to see clearly what they are to accomplish. Then orientation declines and opinions and suggestions increase, followed by disagreement and, sometimes, tension and anger.

Tension marks a critical phase, for groups can become bogged down if they cannot release tensions and regain their sense of group solidarity. Acts that increase solidarity ("I think we can work this out if we stop fighting"), release tension (jokes), or orient the group ("I think we've lost sight of the problem") are very important; for, as groups thrash their way toward a solution, they are in danger of tearing themselves apart with anger, disagreement, and frustration. If the group passes through this difficult phase, the interaction shifts to releasing tension and repairing any damage to group solidarity.

## Group Process and Changing Power Structures

Clearly, groups need members who specialize in task roles (offering suggestions, opinions, and orientation) and expressive roles (providing solidarity and releasing tension). Bales' system allows observers to identify how and when group process breaks down, and is a useful tool in explaining why some groups succeed and others fail. It also reveals how individual members change their position in group structures.

Unlike less-powerful members, for example, leaders tend to speak to the group as a whole more

**Table 8-3**

Bales' Group Process Categories

| TYPE OF ACT | EXAMPLE |
|---|---|
| Shows Solidarity | "I think we've done well." |
| Shows Anger | "You stink." |
| Agrees | "I'll vote for that." |
| Disagrees | "That's not how it happened." |
| Shows Tension | Taps a pencil on the table. |
| Releases Tension | "I'll drink to that!" (laughs) |
| Makes a Suggestion | "Let's take a vote." |
| Asks for Suggestion | "Any ideas?" |
| Gives an Opinion | "I don't think it'll work." |
| Asks for Opinion | "Will it work?" |
| Gives Orientation | "We're running out of time." |
| Asks for Orientation | "What was the assignment?" |

than to specific individuals. When a member begins to speak to the group as a whole ("This is what *we* should do" instead of "This is what *I* want to do"), it often indicates an attempt to raise his or her position in the group's power structure.

If individual members support such bids for power by not arguing, the power seeker is free to continue addressing the group as a whole and is likely to compile a high rate of overall participation. As Bales (1968) noted, "For most individuals there is no better indicator of relative power or . . . position in the evaluation of the group than his total participation compared to that of others." Especially in formal groups, such bids for power can create substantial tension by challenging group leadership structures and even altering actual distributions of power and prestige.

## Powerful Combinations: Coalitions

A second avenue to power is to form **coalitions,** subgroups of two or more members who join forces in order to increase their control over a group. Since Simmel's (1950) observations about the tendencies of two people to combine forces against a third member of a triad (see Chapters 1 and 7), two theories have emerged to explain why coalitions occur in groups. Caplow (1956, 1968) suggested that members form coalitions to maximize their control over others and minimize the control others have over them.

Gamson (1961, 1964), on the other hand, argued that power is not the only motivation—that members also try to maximize their rewards. In doing so, they realize that if they form a coalition with other members, their share of any rewards may depend on the size of their contribution. From this perspective, coalitions tend to form when (1) there is a decision to be made and individuals want to maximize their own gains from it; (2) no alternative will maximize every member's gain; (3) no member has the power to make decisions alone; and (4) no member has veto power.

The two theories lead to similar predictions except in the case of a weak member who contemplates joining with a strong member when there are substantial rewards at stake. To see how these theories predict coalition formation in groups, let us apply them to three different situations (see Figure 8-4).

In the first there are three roommates—Sam, Bill, and Mark—who have equal amounts of power. Three coalitions are possible: Sam-Bill, Sam-Mark, and Bill-Mark. Which is most likely to occur? Both theories predict that all three are equally likely: Sam's power, for example, is increased no more by joining with Bill than with Mark; nor does his share of any rewards depend on whom he chooses for a partner.

The second case is a family consisting of Ann and her parents, both of whom have equal amounts of power. Which coalition is the most likely? Ann increases her power regardless of which parent she joins with, and in both coalitions her partner has more power than Ann does. The parents will tend not to form a coalition between them, because they already have more power than Ann. On the other hand, a parent who forms a coalition with Ann gains increased control over the other parent. Thus, the most likely coalition is between Ann and one of her parents.

The third case is a group of nations, one of which is more powerful than any of the others and yet is *less* powerful than all of the others combined. Which coalitions would you predict? In this third situation, Caplow and Gamson make different predictions.

Caplow's theory predicts that weak nations will join with the strong in order to increase their power in relation to other weak countries. The strong country, of course, would welcome such a coalition because it increases its power while still controlling its partners. Gamson's theory, on the other hand, predicts that the most likely coalition combines the weaker nations against the strongest. Why?

Weak countries increase their power by combining with the stronger one, but when it comes time to divide up any rewards, they cannot prevent their more powerful partner from taking the lion's share. By combining only with each other, weak countries can both control a stronger one *and* share equally in the rewards, since their partners are equally powerful.

Vinacke and Arkoff (1957) tested coalition theories by asking subjects to play a modified game of Parcheesi. Players were allowed to multiply their dice rolls by "weights" ranging from 1 to 6, giving some members more power than others. Thus,

**Figure 8-4** Possible Coalitions in Three Situations

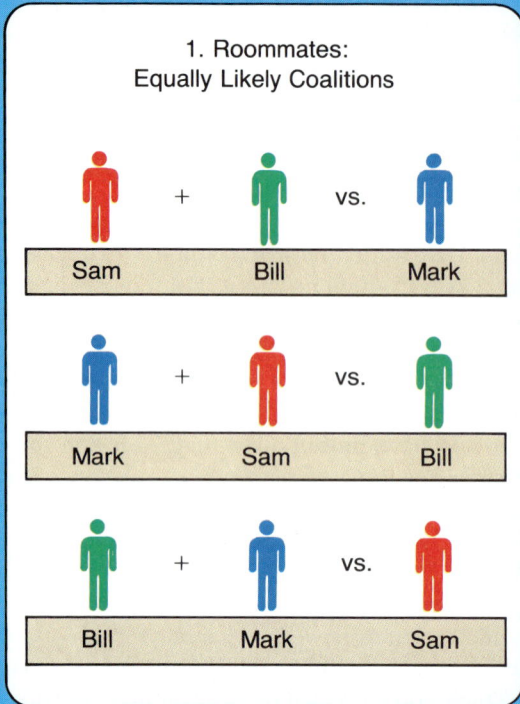

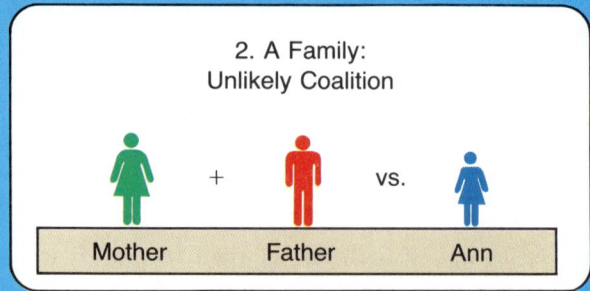

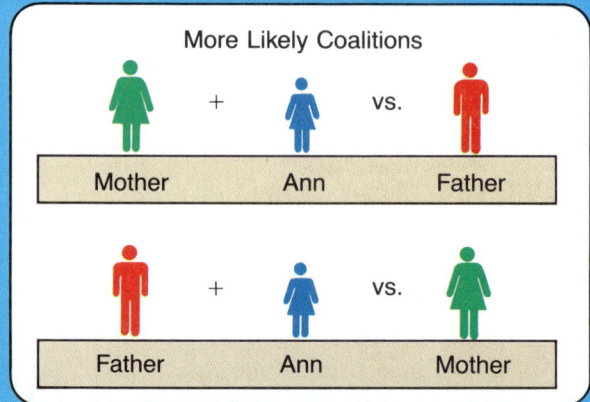

1. Roommates: Equally Likely Coalitions

Sam + Bill vs. Mark

Mark + Sam vs. Bill

Bill + Mark vs. Sam

2. A Family: Unlikely Coalition

Mother + Father vs. Ann

More Likely Coalitions

Mother + Ann vs. Father

Father + Ann vs. Mother

3. Nations: Equally Possible Coalitions

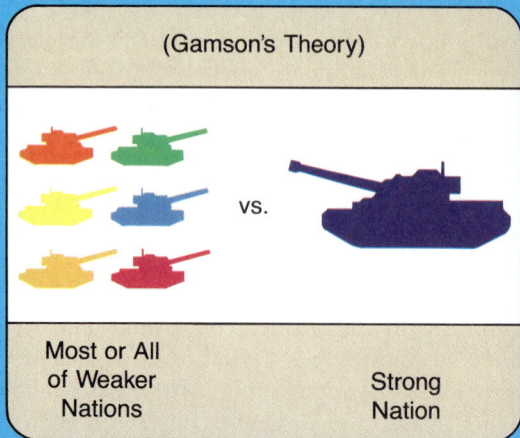

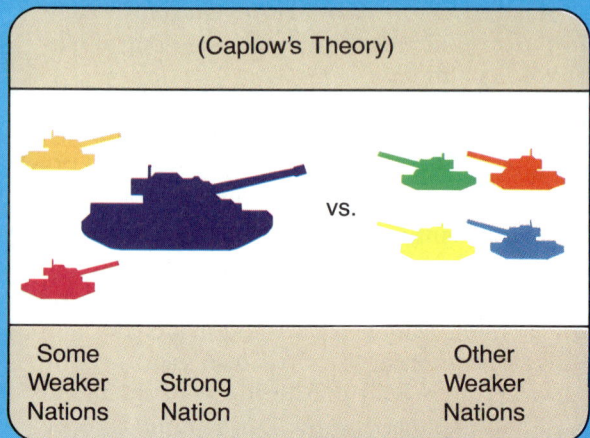

(Gamson's Theory)

Most or All of Weaker Nations vs. Strong Nation

(Caplow's Theory)

Strong Nation vs. Some Weaker Nations Other Weaker Nations

when players rolled a 7, the most powerful were allowed to move their pieces a total of 42 squares (6 × 7), whereas the weakest players could move only 7 squares (1 × 7).

In addition, players were allowed to form coalitions at any time during the game, pooling dice throws and using one set of game pieces. The winner received 100 points, but if the winner was a coalition, its partners shared the points *according to their power at the beginning of the game*. Thus, in a winning coalition consisting of a powerful member (weight 6) and a weak member (weight 1), the powerful partner would receive a share six times larger than that of the weaker partner. The results supported Gamson's predictions in every case and Caplow's in all but one: weak players combined with other weak members both to increase their chances to win *and* to maximize their share of the rewards.

The study of coalitions is important because it helps us understand how members of groups and organizations combine to change distributions of power even when there is no formal leadership structure. Weak members of groups and societies can use coalitions to end domination and exploitation by other groups. As individuals, for example, black members of Congress have no more power than white representatives, but as a coalition, they have considerable power over legislation.

It is through social interaction that groups and organizations achieve their goals. Although the failure of groups to cope with disagreement and tension is an important factor in their performance, group cultures and social structures also influence their effectiveness.

## Getting the Job Done: Explaining Group Effectiveness

Groups confront a variety of tasks. They produce objects, solve problems, win ball games, make judgments, learn skills, and try to satisfy their members. Factory workers produce objects, and universities produce graduates and research. Groups of scientists solve problems involved in sending a rocket to a distant planet, and families figure out how to balance their budgets. Research teams judge the effectiveness of new drugs and juries judge the guilt or innocence of defendants in criminal trials.

Most group work involves one or more of these areas: balancing a family budget, for example, requires both judgment (estimates of future needs and income) and problem solving (how to raise income or cut spending). Regardless of the mix of tasks involved, all groups must cope with the problems of keeping their members satisfied (if not happy) and maintaining the commitment of their members to the group.

The sociological study of group performance grew out of the Industrial Revolution and the concentration of production in larger and more complex groups. Although early research focused on finding ways to increase productivity (and therefore profits), the study of group performance now includes many groups, such as schools, government bureaucracies, the military, and scientific research laboratories. The settings vary, but the sociological question remains the same: How do the cultural and structural characteristics of groups influence their performance?

We should note at the outset that **group effectiveness** is relative, depending on different groups' goals. A group that is effective in solving mathematical problems, for example, may be ineffective with problems that have no single correct answer (such as how to design a house).

The effectiveness of groups depends on their cultural, structural, and ecological characteristics—in particular, on group norms, size, and role, leadership, and communication structures. Before describing the importance of such characteristics, we should first examine a fundamental question: Do groups perform better than individuals?

**Individual versus Group Effectiveness** "Two heads are better than one," the poet John Heywood wrote, and most research comparing the performance of individuals and groups bears the poet out. Individuals usually learn better and faster in the presence of others (Perlmutter and Montmollin, 1952), and groups solve puzzles more quickly than individuals do (Hill, 1982; Laughlin, 1980). When Warnick and Sanders (1980) asked both groups and individuals to recall details of a videotape portraying a crime, the groups produced more accurate and more detailed accounts.

Although two heads are often better than one, are they *twice* as good? Research suggests they are not, because individuals tend to reduce their effort as a group grows in size (Harkins, 1981; Harkins, Latané and Williams, 1980). In one experiment, for example, Moede (1927) asked men to pull as hard as they could on a rope attached to a machine that, unknown to them, measured their pull. By themselves, men pulled twice as hard as they did in groups of eight.

Although groups are generally more effective than individuals, they do have their disadvantages, especially when they are small and members want to maintain group harmony at all costs. When the desire for unity is strong, individuals are less likely to object to poor decisions and suggest alternatives. Groups, in other words, are vulnerable to what Irving Janis (1968, 1982) called **groupthink,** in which the desire for consensus overpowers group members' better judgment.

Hall and Watson (1970) asked groups of management trainees to decide what equipment would be needed in order to live on the moon. "Consensus groups" were instructed to reach a collective solution, whereas "conflict groups" were told to avoid changing views simply for the sake of harmony, to view differences of opinion as healthy and constructive, and to *not* use majority votes to reduce conflict.

Both individuals and their groups submitted solutions, which were compared to solutions prepared by experts. Not only did conflict groups produce better solutions than consensus groups, but 75 percent of the conflict groups produced better solutions than their most capable individual member. By comparison, only 25 percent of the consensus groups performed better than their most capable member.

Groups and individuals differ not only in effectiveness, but in willingness to take risks as well. When stakes are high, groups tend to be more cautious than individuals (Knox and Safford, 1976). When the Soviet Union placed nuclear missiles in Cuba in 1964, for example, most of President Kennedy's advisers initially urged an extreme response: the invasion of Cuba. Kennedy, however, insisted that his advisers reach a group consensus and, as a result, they made a "conservative shift" to a more moderate solution: a naval blockade around Cuba.

In less dangerous cases, groups make riskier decisions than individuals do. In one study, for example, groups were asked to consider the following situation (Stoner, 1961):

> A man with a severe heart ailment must seriously curtail his customary way of life if he does not undergo a delicate medical operation that might cure him completely or might prove fatal. What would you advise? (p. 58)

Members were asked to consider the problem alone first and then as a group, and the results showed that group decisions were consistently more risky than those reached by individuals. Thus, in a group, individuals made a "risky shift."

Such findings raise disturbing questions: Do governments make group decisions that are riskier than those individuals would reach? Is group decision making more conducive to recklessness? Were decisions such as those to drop the atomic bomb on Japan or to seize the American Embassy in Iran caused by risky shifts in groups? Why do such shifts occur?

In some cases, group cultures value risk taking as a sign that the group is "tough" and unafraid, and members increase their prestige by suggesting and supporting risky alternatives. Also, people tend to feel less individual responsibility when they are in groups and may thus feel less responsible for any failure that results from a risky decision. Finally, as Simmel (1950) noted, groups tend to release the inhibitions of their members: we often feel freer to act out wild impulses at a large party, for example, than we do in a small group.

Thus, groups tend to be more effective than individuals in achieving goals, but the results depend on the task and the size of the risks involved. Groups differ not only from individuals, however, but from one another, both in their cultures and their social structures, and such differences strongly influence their effectiveness.

**Effectiveness and Group Culture** Although norms are supposed to help groups achieve their goals, they sometimes have just the opposite effect. Bureaucratic norms, for example, cannot anticipate all possible situations, and yet members are expected to obey the rules no matter what. Soldiers are required by law to obey the orders of their commanders, no matter how foolish those orders may appear to be.

Bureaucratic norms often become ends in themselves, obeyed not because they help accomplish group goals, but because "a rule is a rule." Procedures that work in one situation, however, may be totally inappropriate in another. In such cases, highly disciplined training becomes what Veblen called a "trained incapacity." During the Japanese attack on Pearl Harbor in 1941, some American officers refused to issue weapons to soldiers without "proper written authorization" from the commander, even though they were being shot at by enemy planes. Such red tape clearly interferes with group effectiveness.

No set of rules can govern all possible situations, especially emergencies. In a situation such as this—in the midst of the Japanese attack on Pearl Harbor—the rigid application of bureaucratic rules can have disastrous consequences.

In some cases, the content of norms affects group performance. In bureaucracies, for example, members are supposed to ignore individuals' feelings as they make decisions, to deal with each person as a "case," not as an individual. This often causes the arrogance, abruptness, coldness, and harshness that so many of us associate with "bureaucrats," and creates hostile attitudes between bureaucracies and those they serve.

**Effectiveness and Group Size** Larger groups tend to perform better than smaller ones when problems require a large number of skills or have a single solution (Watson, 1928). Small groups, on the other hand, tend to be more stable (James, 1951), and their members can communicate more easily than in large groups. Thus, small groups perform better when tasks require a limited range of skills and more creative solutions (such as when auto makers decide how to design a new car).

Small groups also appear to be more successful at satisfying their members, but such appearances can be deceiving. Slater (1958) gave problems to 24 groups ranging in size from two to seven members and afterward asked members if they thought their group was too small or too large. The proportion of "too small" responses decreased steadily with increased size, whereas the proportion of "too large" responses increased (Table 8-4). Only in groups of five members did no one feel the group was either too large or too small. In addition, members of large groups were consistently more likely to report a variety of complaints about the group and its

**Table 8-4**

Percentage of Occasions on Which Subjects Felt Group Was Too Small or Too Large to Carry Out Assigned Task, by Size of Group

| SIZE | PERCENT TOO SMALL | PERCENT TOO LARGE |
|------|------------------|-------------------|
| 2 | 34 | 0 |
| 3 | 17 | 0 |
| 4 | 11 | 0 |
| 5 | 0 | 0 |
| 6 | 0 | 14 |
| 7 | 0 | 13 |

Source: Slater, 1958.

**Table 8-5**

Issues on Which Large-Group Members Agreed More Often Than Small-Group Members[1]

1. The time available to solve the problem was insufficient.
2. This group doesn't make the best use of its time.
3. This group needs somebody to keep it on track.
4. Some people in this group talk too much.
5. Some people in this group are crowded out of the discussion.
6. Some people in this group should participate more.
7. There are considerable differences of ability and competence between members of this group.
8. There is too much competition among members in this group.
9. This group is not accomplishing as much as it could.

Source: Slater, 1958.

[1]Small groups have 2, 3, or 4 members, large groups 5, 6, or 7.

members (Table 8-5), whereas those in the smallest groups expressed no complaints at all. Why should size have this effect?

One might argue that in small groups members feel more important than in larger groups and freer to speak their minds. Yet, when Bales and Borgatta (1955) examined Slater's data, they found that in smaller groups members rarely showed tension or anger, whereas in larger groups anger and disagreement were frequently expressed.

Bales and Borgatta explained these findings by suggesting that as groups increase in size, some problems are diminished while new problems emerge. The smallest groups depend on agreement and harmony for their survival (Simmel, 1950), and although they may lack the resources they need to accomplish a task, members are likely to conceal disagreement and anger and therefore give a rosy picture of group life.

Large groups, on the other hand, have more resources and do not need the agreement of all their members in order to survive or reach a decision. Thus, members feel freer to disagree and show anger because such expressions pose a less serious threat to the group and their standing in it. This suggests that whereas our *physical* freedom (to talk, for example) is greater in smaller groups, our *psychological* freedom (to express opinions, for

example) is greater in larger groups (Mullen, 1983).

This contradicts the common belief that small groups are the only places where individuals can truly be themselves. Large groups limit members' participation, but small ones limit expression of feelings and outrageous impulses (Simmel, 1950). Whereas large groups tend to make people feel insignificant and lost, small groups tend to inhibit their members by making them feel highly visible.

**Effectiveness, Roles, and Leadership** As we saw earlier, the more complex a group is, the better it accomplishes complicated tasks that require a wide range of skills. Complex groups, however, also find it more difficult to coordinate and control their members' behavior.

Group complexity creates problems when it *becomes an end in itself*. The essence of a bureaucracy is the management of some members by others; and in order to demonstrate their importance, bureaucrats often create work that requires assistants, which results in more paperwork as assistants

*"It's been moved and seconded that some of us will keep our mustaches, some of us will shave them off; some of us will wear gray flannel, some of us will wear brown flannel; some of us will wear rep ties, others foulards; some of us will wear horn-rimmed glasses, some steel-rimmed; et cetera."*

Drawing by Opie; © 1983, The New Yorker Magazine, Inc.

must report to their bosses. More assistants are then added, and the organization continues to grow and use increasing portions of its resources simply to manage its mushrooming staff (Parkinson, 1957).

Additional problems arise from the ways in which groups decide who plays which roles. Bureaucracies, for example, try to secure the loyal, devoted service of their members by offering them job security and clear lines of promotion so long as they obey the rules. This causes three main problems for such groups.

First, members may use their security to do no more than what the norms require of them. College professors, for example, are often criticized for working less after achieving the security of ten-

ure. Second, because advancement in bureaucracies requires obedience to norms, people may become timid and overly conservative, afraid to show initiative for fear of risking their promotion to higher positions (Merton, 1968).

Third, members of bureaucracies tend to be promoted to higher positions on the basis of performance in *lower* positions. Inevitably, members reach positions that are beyond their abilities and there they stay, unable to perform well enough to reach the next rung on the ladder.

Peter and Hull (1969) called this phenomenon the Peter Principle: "In a hierarchy each employee tends to rise to his level of *in*competence; every post tends to be occupied by an employee incompetent to execute its duties." Peter and Hull suggested that the only reason top positions are sometimes occupied by competent people is that "there are not enough ranks for them to have reached their level of incompetence: in other words, *in that hierarchy* there is no task beyond their abilities." Thus, although complex role structures increase group effectiveness in many ways, they also produce unanticipated negative consequences that affect their individual members and interfere with group performance.

Social situations affect not only the emergence and selection of leaders in groups, but their effectiveness as well. Task leaders, for example (those most concerned with seeing to it that the group achieves its goals), are most effective in extreme situations—when groups verge on falling apart during disasters or when they are cohesive and strong.

Expressive leaders, on the other hand (who specialize in the feelings that underlie group relationships), are more effective than task leaders in more moderate circumstances, when members have less need of a task leader and are in a stronger position to question a leader's authority (Fiedler et al., 1976). Thus, a leader who improves group performance in one situation may damage it in another.

**Effectiveness and Communication** We saw in Chapter 4 that communication patterns affect both success at different tasks and member satisfaction. When members can interact freely with one another (a "circle"), groups have more difficulty solving puzzles with single solutions than they do with tasks having many workable solutions (Shaw, 1954). In addition, although groups that limit interactions by channeling communication through a single member (a "wheel") are efficient problem solvers, their members are less satisfied.

From this point of view, it is easier to see why large numbers of people with free and open communication structures (such as street mobs) are inefficient at solving problems. It is also easier to see why bureaucracies—in which interaction is limited and tightly regulated—have so much trouble satisfying their members and performing efficiently. Their structures of communication often leave members feeling insignificant and powerless to affect decisions. They also make it difficult for one part of the organization to know what other parts are doing, for each piece of information must

It is easy to understand why large groups such as street mobs are inefficient at—even incapable of— solving problems.

pass through many hands before reaching its ultimate destination.

Thus, the ability of groups and organizations to achieve their goals depends heavily on their cultural and structural characteristics. No group, however, can perform well if it cannot maintain its members' commitment to the group. All groups must continually cope with the problem of social cohesion.

## Staying Together, Falling Apart: Cohesion and Conflict in Groups

What makes groups stay together? When membership is involuntary as in junior high schools, **social cohesion** is maintained by the power of authority; but in voluntary groups, the attraction of members to a group is more difficult to maintain. In the simplest sense, a group cannot exist unless individuals are motivated to interact with one another, and a group survives only if the forces keeping it together are stronger than those that would tear it apart.

In many groups, members are joined by shared cultural ideas. Family members value family life itself, for example, and members of rural communities or urban neighborhoods may feel bound together by shared values about what constitutes "a good life," norms that regulate relationships among neighbors, attitudes toward "outsiders," and religious beliefs. Group cohesion that is based on common experience and culture is called **Gemeinschaft** ("community") (Tönnies, 1887) or **mechanical solidarity** (Durkheim, 1893). Because of the closeness of social relationships in Gemeinschaft groups, they are almost always primary.

The primary ties of Gemeinschaft relations are often the source of social cohesion in the subgroups that make up much larger organizations. In the last days of World War II, for example, the German army maintained its combat effectiveness even though it was badly outnumbered and undersupplied, and had to rely on damaged and inferior equipment. Some military analysts believed that the German army continued to function as a cohesive unit because its soldiers strongly believed in their cause; but in their postwar study, Shils and Janowitz (1948) found that German soldiers were generally indifferent to Nazi ideology.

What held them together? Shils and Janowitz concluded that it was the loyalty that each soldier felt toward the members of his small combat squad or platoon (see also Van Creveld, 1982). The German soldier, they wrote,

The kind of cohesion found in neighborhoods such as Little Italy in New York City at the turn of the century is based primarily on the sharing of a common culture and similar life experiences.

was likely to go on fighting, provided he had the necessary weapons, so long as the group possessed leadership with which he could identify himself, and so long as he gave affection to and received affection from the other members of his squad or platoon. . . . As long as he felt himself to be a member of his primary group and therefore bound by the expectations and demands of its other members, his soldierly achievement was likely to be good. (p. 284)

Studies of American soldiers during World War II also showed that primary ties were vital sources of group cohesion in small combat units (Stouffer et al., 1949). A study of American soldiers in Vietnam, on the other hand, suggests that although primary group ties were important, they arose in part from the fact that soldiers could not survive on their own.

The fact is that if the individual soldier is realistically to improve his survival chances, he must *necessarily* develop and take part in primary relationships. Under the grim conditions of ground warfare, an individual's survival is directly dependent upon the support . . . he can expect from his fellows. He gets such support to the degree that he reciprocates to the others in his unit. In other words, primary

Small combat units are usually held together more by primary relations than by the structural cohesion binding the larger units of which they are also a part.

relations are at their core mutually pragmatic efforts to minimize personal risk. (Moskos, 1969, p. 18)

The primary ties in Gemeinschaft groups are based on common experience and shared cultural beliefs, values, attitudes, and norms; but the example of American soldiers in Vietnam introduces a second major source of social cohesion: the degree to which members depend on one another in order to achieve their goals. The concepts of **Gesellschaft** (Tönnies, 1887) and **organic solidarity** (Durkheim, 1893) describe groups that stay together because their structures make it difficult to achieve important goals unless their members cooperate with and depend on one another in spite of cultural differences. Thus, whereas *culture* is the major source of cohesion in Gemeinschaft, cohesion within the secondary relations of Gesellschaft is largely a matter of *social structure*.

The most recognizable example of Gesellschaft is the bureaucracy. While small combat units are often held together by primary relations, the larger organizations of which they are a part—the battalions, divisions, and armies—cannot function unless each of the units that make them up does its specialized job. A small unit that specializes in delivering food, ammunition, and other supplies, or one that specializes in communications can stay together as a unit based on the primary ties among its members. An army, however, stays together only insofar as its various units function effectively as parts of the whole.

Social structure affects group cohesion by defining not only relationships within groups, but among them as well. As Thomas Jefferson and Winston Churchill noted, groups that conflict during peacetime suddenly pull together during wartime in the face of a common enemy, burying their differences and sacrificing individual interests for the common good. When the external threat is removed, old differences resurface, unity breaks down, and group conflicts resume (Coser, 1956).

During World War II, German leaders believed that continuous bombing of Britain's cities would beat its population into submission; but the bombings had the opposite effect, for they aroused a sense of solidarity and defiance in the British people. Later in the war, Allied commanders failed

to learn from the German mistake, and researchers discovered after the war that saturation bombing of German cities only increased German resistance and prolonged the war (Janis, 1951).

Thus, when group cohesion is low, leaders may increase solidarity by convincing members that other groups threaten their survival (Markides and Cohen, 1982). During its recent revolution, for example, Iran was torn by power struggles and disagreements about how the country should be run, and its leaders frequently unified their followers by directing attention to "foreign devils"—such as the United States—who, the leaders claimed, wanted to destroy them.

Within the boundaries of all groups, members interact as they struggle toward their goals and try to maintain a sense of cohesion. These are the basic elements of life in groups, but what are the implications of group life for their individual members? How do the characteristics of human groups affect the quality of our lives?

## Individuals, Freedom, and Life in Groups

The cultural and structural characteristics of groups have profound effects on societies and their members. Groups are capable both of supporting and protecting their members and of corrupting and harming them. Through groups, human beings have accomplished stunning and wonderful things, but groups are also the source of humanity's most astonishing cruelty and destruction. How do cultural and structural characteristics of groups and organizations affect their individual members?

### Culture, Groups, and Individuals

Perhaps one of the most significant cultural changes during the last 2,000 years has been the enormous increase in the social value of individuals and their freedom in relation to groups. Durkheim (1893) went so far as to suggest that in the simplest societies with their uncomplicated divisions of labor, the idea of an "individual" simply did not exist. The group, he argued, was everything, and it never occurred to people to stand apart from it as unique individuals.

From Durkheim's point of view, "individuality" cannot exist without supporting cultural beliefs (that such a thing is possible), values (the individual is important), and norms (individuals have rights in relation to the group); and these cultural ideas are relatively new in human history. In this sense, if sociology had existed as a discipline thousands of years ago, it would not even have recognized the effects of groups on individuals as a problem.

The social value of individuals has reached its highest point in complex industrial societies such as the United States. As societies increasingly recognize the worth of individuals, their members are less vulnerable to being "buried" in the group, to having no right to stand apart and celebrate their uniqueness. This, however, creates the danger of being *isolated* from groups, of feeling alienated and lonely.

In complex industrial societies, for example, we spend increasingly large portions of our lives in groups and organizations that value efficiency, precision, speed, control, production, and obedience more than they value the happiness and satisfaction of their individual members. In addition, Slater (1971) argued that an extreme emphasis on individuals and their uniqueness creates a cultural environment that frustrates basic human needs to trust and cooperate with others, to deal directly with interpersonal problems, and to share responsibility for the conduct of our individual lives.

In short, Slater argued that modern cultures not only raise the social value of individuals to new heights, but also create unprecedented levels of isolation and loneliness. "Who am I?" Is perhaps the most common and profoundly disturbing question individuals face in modern cultures, because simple group membership is no longer a complete basis for our existence. Whereas ties between individuals and groups may have been too strong in the simplest societies, in complex societies they are in danger of being too weak (Durkheim, 1897).

Such cultural changes, however, do not simply "happen" by accident; they are often responses to changing social structures that define human relationships. Weber (1946) and Durkheim (1893) were two early sociologists who saw in the Industrial Revolution a threat to human welfare. What changes in the structure of group life did they see and why were they so concerned?

## Social Structure, Groups, and Individuals

In Gemeinschaft societies, members are held together by their common culture, and groups tend to be small, informal, and primary. Work, family, and religion form a unified whole. Those who share in the culture and obey its norms have a secure place in the social world.

The Industrial Revolution, however, gave an enormous boost to a long-term change in which social relationships became increasingly rational, secondary, and formal in Gesellschaft societies based less on shared culture than on rational calculations of individual self-interest (Weber, 1922a). This change resulted from the rise of large bureaucracies of specialists connected to one another in complicated role structures.

In complex industrial societies people are known as individuals, and as individuals, they are known primarily by the social statuses they occupy. Children no longer grow up confident of their place in society, knowing exactly what is expected of them, what roles they will play as adults. To survive in modern societies, each of us must achieve a place for ourselves somewhere in the complex division of labor.

In industrialized societies, work is a specialized activity separate from other aspects of social life. People not only play a wide variety of roles, but differ sharply from one another in power and their share of what is produced. They are bound to one another by rational ties of formal secondary relationships, and nowhere are the consequences of these social structures clearer than in modern bureaucracies with their formal rules, rigidly defined relationships, and inattention to individual feelings and needs.

Argyris (1957) suggested that bureaucracies interfere with the needs of healthy individuals. Maturity includes the ability to act and make judgments independently, to think abstractly and in terms of long-term consequences of behavior. Bureaucracies, however, encourage dependency and timidity, short-term thinking, and ignorance of long-term consequences of behavior.

Thus, Argyris concluded, "Formal organizations are willing to pay high wages and provide adequate seniority if mature adults will, for eight hours a day, behave in a less mature manner." As a result, members often feel frustrated and helpless because they have little control over their environment, goals, or behavior, and the lack of control creates anxiety and uncertainty. Karl Marx described the resulting feelings of being lost and insignificant as *alienation*—a feeling of helplessness and detachment in relation to work and its results (see Chapter 17).

Unlike primary groups, bureaucracies do not derive their security from the welfare of their individual members. We may be fired when it is no longer in an employer's "best interests" to keep us, regardless of our abilities. Middle-aged American executives often lose jobs because they are *too* experienced and *too* capable and therefore command higher salaries than younger employees.

Some members defend themselves by leaving the organization (a risky choice), or by achieving more powerful positions within the organization. Others, however, who can neither advance nor afford to leave, retreat into apathy and daydreams, or create informal groups that support their feelings of alienation.

Thus, the rational basis of bureaucracy leads many to participate in order to achieve personal—not organizational—goals, the most important of which is earning a living (Moore, 1962). We can work in a bureaucracy without valuing its goals or liking our jobs or other workers. This often minimizes feelings of loyalty to large organizations and encourages members to exploit every opportunity

While bureaucracies are able to manage complex divisions of labor with considerable efficiency, the price is often exacted in human terms—in the isolation and alienation of people whose lives are touched by them.

for personal gain—whether on the large scale of criminal embezzlement or the small scale of stealing office supplies and equipment, padding expense accounts, or using company cars for personal trips—a clear example of social factors that foster criminal behavior (Gracey, 1972a).

As bureaucratic organizations spread, we find ourselves with fewer and fewer groups in which we are known and valued as individuals. We spend increasing portions of our lives in secondary groups that involve limited parts of ourselves, and our lives are segmented—divided into separate spheres of family, work, friendships, and religion that have little if any connection to one another. In such social environments, it is difficult to maintain a sense of "wholeness" about our lives; rather, we tend to feel torn in many directions at once as we divide our time, energy, and loyalty between family, friends, and the formal demands of work (Moore, 1962).

The structures of complex societies create feelings of insignificance and rootlessness in their members, yet how do they differ from Durkheim's vision of simple societies in which individuals are indistinguishable from their groups? Is it not true that individuals have little significance in both simple Gemeinschaft societies and the bureaucracies of modern Gesellschaft societies?

Although individuals tend to be "lost" in both types of societies, there is an enormously important difference between the two. In the simple societies Durkheim referred to, individuals had no need to stand apart from their groups, because groups and their members depended on each other for their survival. There was thus a close connection between the welfare of groups and the welfare of their members.

A large bureaucracy, on the other hand, uses people as a means for achieving goals that they neither determine nor control, and may not even share. The essence of a bureaucracy is that it exists independently of its members and therefore has no strong vested interest in their welfare. In a bureaucratic society, individuals cannot afford to place their welfare in the hands of organizations that can and often do quickly dispense with them.

It is no accident of history that as social structures become increasingly bureaucratic, concern for the rights and welfare of individuals emerges and grows stronger. Whereas primary groups value their members most highly, bureaucracies value their rules, leadership structures, and goals more than the fate of any individual, and thus are likely to exploit individuals whenever possible. As groups become more exploitative, members must establish new sources of protection and security, and aside from the family, the lone individual is the last line of defense.

The increased size, complexity, and formality of groups and organizations also affect the welfare of entire societies, for although bureaucracies support efficiency, control, and complex divisions of labor, they also oppose the strong emotional ties that are the basis of human morality, compassion, and empathy. Members of bureaucracies are supposed to simply do their jobs and leave the establishment of group goals to their leaders. Thus, bureaucracies have what Sabini and Silver (1982) called "a genius for organizing evil."

Nazi Germany, for example, was a model of bureaucratic efficiency, and prided itself on the strict formal organization of its society. When Adolph Eichmann managed the railway systems that transported millions of people to their deaths in concentration camps, he behaved as a model bureaucrat, carrying out his instructions quickly, efficiently, and without question. In the final chaotic months of World War II, when Germany was defending itself on three fronts, Eichmann's proudest achievement was his astonishing ability to keep the trains running on time.

Marx believed that bureaucratic structures turn individuals into cogs in vast machines and that as people are increasingly alienated from their work and its results, they also feel increasingly alienated from one another. In bureaucratic societies, in which organizations and their rules assume primary importance, it is not surprising that individuals are often motivated by rational self-interest ("What's in it for *me*?") and insensitive to the fate of others.

For better or for worse, groups will always be a major part of human life, and it is for this reason that decisions about their social structures and guiding cultural ideas are so important. We cannot survive alone, and the characteristics of groups set the terms on which we live our lives in relation to other human beings.

The same bureaucratic structures that enable subways and railroads to perform the complex and demanding tasks of transporting large numbers of people and shipping food, clothing, and countless other necessary goods from one place to another were also used by the Nazis to efficiently ship millions of victims to their deaths in concentration camps. They represent, as Sabini and Silver (1982) wrote, "a genius for organizing evil."

## Summary

1. A group is two or more people who interact with one another in patterned ways and identify themselves and one another as members. The group is an important sociological concept because individuals perform their most important roles in groups; groups both meet many human needs and are an important source of social conflict; and the performance of groups strongly affects the achievement of important social goals such as socialization.

2. All groups rest on a shared culture to which members are expected to conform. In most cases, it is very difficult for individuals to defy the majority opinion in a group to which they belong.

3. Group structures differ in many ways, defining their existence in terms of time and space, and drawing boundaries that differ in their clarity and openness. Membership in some groups is voluntary, whereas in others it is compulsory. Group members may think of themselves as members of superior in-groups and express hostile attitudes toward out-groups.

4. The division of labor in groups is reflected in their role structures, and the distributions of affection, power, respect, and communication are revealed in sociometric, power, leadership, prestige, and communication structures.

5. Primary groups such as the family are valued for their own sake, endure through time, and involve many aspects of members' lives. Secondary groups such as many work groups are valued for limited goals, are relatively short-lived, and involve limited aspects of members' lives. Secondary groups range from informal organizations (in which norms are often vaguely stated and loosely applied) to formal organizations (in which norms are clearly stated and rigidly applied).

6. Democratic, authoritarian, and laissez-faire leaders emerge under a variety of conditions as groups struggle to stay together and achieve goals. Some groups have no leadership structure, whereas others have more than one.

7. As we saw in Chapter 4, a bureaucracy is a set of formal relationships that are rationally organized in order to achieve goals. People perform specialized tasks according to rigid norms. Power is distributed hierarchically and managers have the job of ensuring that the organization performs effectively. The growth of bureaucracy as a form of social organization is one of the most significant transformations of the past two centuries and was given an enormous boost by the Industrial Revolution.

8. Groups can be as small as a two-person dyad or as large as an army of tens of thousands. Absolute and relative size are important factors in the power of groups and in the complexity of their structures.

9. Spatial relationships among members affect the frequency and duration of interaction, which in turn affects the level of social cohesion. Spatial relationships also serve to reinforce distributions of power.

10. Group process refers to what members actually do, regardless of the expectations attached to roles. Bales' techniques for recording group process are useful in identifying critical stages in the life of a group.

11. Members may try to form coalitions to increase their power or the rewards they receive. Coalition theorists try to predict the conditions under which coalitions will occur and which individuals are most likely to be involved.

12. Many factors affect group effectiveness, depending on the goals involved. Factors include group size, the formality norms, the complexity of role and communication structures, and the presence of leaders.

13. Group cohesion has two main sources: the degree to which members share a common base of culture and experience (Gemeinschaft) and the degree to which members depend on one another in order to accomplish goals (Gesellschaft). Cohesion based on Gemeinschaft is called mechanical solidarity and is most often found in primary groups such as the family and preindustrial communities such as the hunter-gatherers. Cohesion based on Gesellschaft is called organic solidarity and is most often found in bureaucratic organizations and complex industrial societies.

14. The characteristics of groups profoundly affect the experience and behavior of their members, their levels of self-esteem, their feelings of belonging and security, their ability to determine and pursue their own goals, and their power to control others and protect themselves.

## Key Terms

## Recommended Readings

JANIS, I. (1973). *Victims of groupthink.* Boston: Houghton Mifflin. A look at the sometimes disastrous effects of groupthink on decision making, focusing on U.S. foreign policy.

KANTER, R. M. (1977). *Men and women of the corporation.* New York: Basic Books. An important study of how male dominance is maintained in large formal organizations.

KANTER, R., and STEIN, B. A. (Eds.). (1979). *Life in organizations.* New York: Basic Books. A collection of essays about work experiences in formal organizations.

OLMSTEAD, M. S., and HARE, A. P. (1978). *The small group* (2nd ed.). New York: Random House. A well-written summary of important research on small groups.

SLATER, P. E. (1971). *The pursuit of loneliness.* Boston: Beacon Press. Slater's compelling analysis of a central tension in group life between independence, freedom, and a sense of belonging and commitment is one of those books that many people read more than once.

WEBER, M. *From Max Weber: Essays in sociology.* (1946). Edited and translated by H. H. Gerth and C. Wright Mills. New York: Oxford University Press. One of the best and most accessible sources of Weber's ideas on bureaucracy.

WHYTE, W. F. (1981). *Street corner society* (3rd ed.). Chicago: University of Chicago Press. Whyte's classic participation observation study of groups in an Italian slum in Boston.

# CHAPTER 9

# Life in Communities

What does the word "community" make you think of? Friends, family, home town, neighborhood, politics, school, church, work, "a place where I belong," busy streets, quiet country lanes, burglar alarms, doors locked only at night? Whatever the association, "community" refers to one of the most important aspects of our lives—where we live; and where we live profoundly affects *how* we live, for it is in communities that we are born, attend school, make and lose friends, find jobs or suffer unemployment, grow old, and die. Communities may be sources of deep feelings of attachment that make us feel rooted in the world; they may be like prisons from which we see little chance of escape; or they may be no more to us than places we see as stopovers on the way to someplace else.

A **community** is a collection of people who share a physical environment and meet their needs through daily interaction with other members (Schnore, 1973). (Groups, by contrast, often are not defined in relation to a physical territory.) From a sociological perspective, communities differ in cultural ideas, which define the terms of social life; in social structures, which include com-

## Voices: Big City, Small Neighborhoods

The oft-quoted thumbnail sketch of New York is, of course: "It's a wonderful place, but I'd hate to live there." I have an idea that people from villages and small towns, people accustomed to the convenience and the friendliness of neighborhood over-the-fence living, are unaware that life in New York follows the neighborhood pattern. The city is literally a composite of tens of thousands of tiny neighborhood units. There are, of course, the big districts and big units: Chelsea and Murray Hill and Gramercy (which are residential units), Harlem (a racial unit), Greenwich Village (a unit dedicated to the arts and other matters), and there is Radio City (a commercial development), Peter Cooper Village (a housing unit), the Medical Center (a sickness unit) and many other sections each of which has some distinguishing characteristic. But the curious thing about New York is that each large geographical unit is composed of countless small neighborhoods. Each neighborhood is virtually self-sufficient. Usually it is no more than two or three blocks long and a couple of blocks wide. Each area is a city within a city within a city. Thus, no matter where you live in New York, you will find within a block or two a grocery store, a barbershop, a newsstand and shoeshine shack, an ice-coal-and-wood cellar (where you write your order on a pad outside as you walk by), a dry cleaner, a laundry, a delicatessen (beer and sandwiches delivered at any hour to your door), a flower shop, an undertaker's parlor, a movie house, a radio-repair shop, a stationer, a haberdasher, a tailor, a drugstore, a garage, a tearoom, a saloon, a hardware store, a liquor store, a shoe-repair shop. Every block or two, in most residential sections of New York, is a little main street. A man starts for work in the morning and before he has gone two hundred yards he has completed half a dozen missions: bought a paper, left a pair of shoes to be soled, picked up a pack of cigarettes, ordered a bottle of whiskey to be dispatched in the opposite direction against his home-coming, written a message to the unseen forces of the wood cellar, and notified the dry cleaner that a pair of trousers awaits call. Homeward-bound eight hours later, he buys a bunch of pussy willows, a Mazda bulb, a drink, a shine—all between the corner where he steps off the bus and his apartment. So complete is each neighborhood, and so strong the sense of neighborhood, that many a New Yorker spends a lifetime within the confines of an area smaller than a country village. Let him walk two blocks from his corner and he is in a strange land and will feel uneasy till he gets back.

Storekeepers are particularly conscious of neighborhood boundary lines. A woman friend of mine moved recently from one apartment to another, a distance of three blocks. When she turned up, the day after the move, at the same grocer's that she had patronized for years, the proprietor was in ecstasy—almost in tears—at seeing her. "I was afraid," he said, "now that you've moved away I wouldn't be seeing you anymore." To him, *away* was three blocks, or about 750 feet.

Source: E. B. White, "Here Is New York."

munity boundaries, patterns of communication, and distributions of power, prestige, statuses, and roles; and in ecological arrangements, which describe the size, density, and composition of community populations and the way they use natural resources.

We begin by describing basic types of communities, and then use sociological analysis to examine how their cultural, structural, and ecological characteristics both affect the lives of the people who live in them and cause communities to change.

## Some Basic Types of Communities

There are many ways to describe cultural, structural, and ecological differences among communities, but perhaps the two most important distinctions sociologists make are *rural* or *urban* and *traditional* or *modern*.

## The Rural-Urban Continuum

**Rural communities** consist of small, homogeneous, sparsely settled populations, whereas **urban communities** are large, heterogeneous, and densely settled (Wirth, 1938).

How large and densely settled must a population be in order to be considered "urban"? Any limit will be somewhat arbitrary, but most sociologists use the 1982 U.S. Census Bureau definition of 2,500 or more people. Although this figure has the practical advantage of being clear and precise, the concepts of urban and rural are most useful if we think of them as describing two extremes of a continuum.

At one end are tiny, isolated villages such as those that characterized early American settlements. The larger and more densely settled a population is, the more urban it is. An **urbanized area,** for example, is a city and the densely settled territory around it (its **suburbs**) that together contain 50,000 or more people.

On a larger scale, a **metropolitan area** is either a city with 50,000 or more inhabitants or an urbanized area that is socially and economically linked with surrounding counties that bring its total population to 100,000 or more (U.S. Census Bureau, 1983c). The specific definitions of urbanized and metropolitan areas are less important, however, than the basic concept behind them: they are large, densely settled population centers whose economic and social activities are closely linked with those of surrounding communities.

New York City, for example, contains almost 8 million people, and activities in the city are closely tied to the populations of surrounding counties in New York, New Jersey, and Connecticut. Many residents of these neighboring counties work and shop in New York City, making the city and its

Hasidic Jews, like the Amish, maintain their traditional beliefs, customs, and manner of dress, even while living within modern communities such as New York.

adjacent counties an integrated unit containing more than 9 million people (U.S. Census Bureau, 1983c).

Urban communities are divided into **neighborhoods**—collections of people who live close to one another—which often serve as communities for their residents (Gans, 1982; Greer, 1968; Hallman, 1984). Neighborhoods are where people carry out most of the small details of everyday life: they are where children play and "hang out," and where adults shop for groceries and have shoes repaired and clothing cleaned. Neighborhoods are communities in which people are most aware of and affected by other people's behavior and where, therefore, conformity to norms is most highly valued.

## Traditional and Modern Communities

Communities differ in the degree to which they are *traditional* or *modern* (Inkeles and Smith, 1974). The American Amish live in **traditional communities** that are culturally isolated from the rest of society (Kephart, 1982). Their religious beliefs preclude the use of scientific technology, and they reject most aspects of the modern society that surrounds them—including electricity, indoor toilets, jewelry, machinery, political involvement, watches, life insurance, loans, and social security. Their style and color of dress—mostly simple and black—is the same in the 1980s as it was 250 years ago.

In comparison with traditional communities, **modern communities** tend to have more-complex divisions of labor, more-sophisticated technology, more highly developed mass media, and higher levels of education and literacy. Residents of modern communities are more likely to accept new ideas, and social relationships tend to be more secondary and formal than primary and informal.

Urban communities are not necessarily modern, nor are rural communities necessarily traditional. Many cities in less-developed countries—particularly in Africa and Asia—are traditional communities, while many rural communities in Europe and North America are, in relative terms, quite modern.

The concepts of urban, rural, traditional, and modern describe communities only in very general terms. In the rest of this chapter, we will focus on

the detailed cultural, social structural, and ecological characteristics of communities, which affect the lives of those who live in them.

## Communities and Culture

Community cultures vary both in content (the specific beliefs, values, norms, and attitudes that guide life within a community) and in homogeneity (the degree to which residents subscribe to the same set of cultural ideas).

## Beliefs, Values, and Attitudes

Like groups, communities are characterized by sets of beliefs, values, and attitudes, which in some cases lie at the core of a community's existence: the early Puritan settlements in the United States came into being because their members wanted to sustain their religious beliefs in a social environment free of persecution. Throughout history, groups such as communes have been based on decisions to live according to cultural ideas considered deviant in the surrounding society (Kanter, 1972; Zablocki, 1980). The Twin Oaks commune in Louisa, Virginia, for example, was inspired by the community described in B. F. Skinner's novel *Walden Two*. At Twin Oaks, cooperation is valued more than competition for individual advantage, and decisions based on consensus are valued more than leadership by a few. With the exception of private belongings, which members must keep in their rooms, all property is held in common and all that is earned or produced is contributed to the group (Cordes, 1984; Kanter, 1972).

Sociology's roots lie in the Industrial Revolution, which brought with it an enormous increase in urban populations; thus it is no accident that a major focus in sociological analysis has been on cultural differences between rural and urban communities. As politicians need to remember, most rural communities rest on traditional values, and their members tend to be less open to change and less tolerant of strange life-styles than their urban counterparts. In the United States, rural dwellers are more likely to be religious fundamentalists and

As communities, communes are often organized around specific cultural ideas such as religious beliefs, values, attitudes, and norms.

political conservatives: major opposition to the Equal Rights Amendment, for example, has come mostly from sparsely settled rural states.

In comparison with urban dwellers, people in rural communities generally place less value on literacy, formal education, the arts and mass media, the use of sophisticated technology, and individual advancement through competition (Inkeles and Smith, 1974; Larson, 1968). They tend both to share a common set of cultural ideas and to place higher values on large families, traditional roles for men and women, conformity, cooperation, and loyalty to the community.

City populations, on the other hand, represent a great diversity of beliefs, values, and attitudes (diversity was, in fact, a major part of Wirth's 1938 definition of cities as communities). Cities contain a vast array of people in different occupations, social classes, and racial and ethnic groups. Cities are more likely to have substantial numbers of artists and musicians, judges and college professors, political radicals, the very wealthy and the very poor, as well as criminals and their victims. The mix of people from different cultural backgrounds is also far greater in cities: there are, for example, more Poles in Chicago than in Warsaw.

One result is a generally higher level of tolerance for nonconformity in urban areas (Wirth, 1938). Stephan and McMullin (1982) found that people who live in the largest cities report far more tolerance for homosexuality, pornography, and extramarital and premarital sex than do people living in smaller cities and towns. They found even greater differences in attitudes toward sexual nonconformity when they compared people in terms of the size of the communities they lived in as adolescents (see also Wilson, 1985).

Why should such cultural differences occur between small, sparsely settled communities and large, densely populated ones? Early sociologists such as Simmel (1908) and Wirth (1938) attributed urban-rural differences to the physical characteristics of the communities themselves—the number of people who occupy a given area. Large populations are bound to be more heterogeneous than small ones, and conformity will be valued more highly in small communities where people cannot escape awareness of one another's behavior. When we are surrounded by large numbers of people, we protect our privacy, Simmel believed, by adopting attitudes of aloofness and superficiality in social interactions.

Simmel's approach is purely ecological, because it suggests that physical differences between urban and rural communities (such as population size and density) cause their inhabitants to adopt different beliefs, values, and attitudes. The ecological approach, however, ignores the effects of culture on the formation of communities. In other words, as more recent urban sociologists argue, it is culture that created the city—not the other way around (Castells, 1977; Gans, 1962; Jaret, 1983).

Since the beginnings of the Industrial Revolution in the eighteenth century, the most important characteristic of urban places has not been their mere size and density; rather, it is their *industrial and commercial activity* that has profoundly affected both community culture and social structure. Industrial and commercial communities require large pools of workers who occupy a vast array of statuses in a complex occupational structure; to advance, individuals must compete with one another for jobs and be ready and willing to move to different neighborhoods or communities in search of better opportunities. These two facts help explain why industrial communities attract large numbers of people with a variety of cultural backgrounds.

People also choose to live in cities because cities foster the development of a variety of subcultures, communities-within-communities in which shared interests draw people together. People with unusual interests or beliefs—such as homosexuals, vegetarians, lovers of Baroque music, communists—often feel isolated in small towns, but city populations are so large that such people can find a supportive subculture with relative ease (Fischer, 1975, 1982, 1984).

The cultural differences between urban and rural communities are not caused simply by the population characteristics that define communities as urban or rural, and nowhere has this misinterpretation been more evident than in early sociological studies of "suburbia."

## The Myth of Suburban Culture

Suburbs first appeared in the United States at the turn of this century and were inhabited by people who could afford country homes from which they commuted by train and streetcar to work in cities.

In the 1920s, suburbs grew rapidly with the mass production of cars and paved roads, and after World War II they were built on a massive scale for returning veterans and their families (Long, 1981).

Suburbia received considerable attention from sociologists because it appeared to represent a new kind of community with a distinctive culture that emphasized family life, home ownership, security and safety, active community involvement, and close, friendly relations among residents—all the things that made for "the good life." It was also seen as a social environment in which conformity and "keeping up with the Joneses" were valued more than anything else; in which young people were restless and rootless, and their parents were imprisoned on a treadmill of trying to keep up—if not get ahead. Wives were captives of their new homes, and husbands could not escape the deadening daily commute to the city. With the help of movies (such as *Rebel Without a Cause*) and literature (such as John Cheever's short stories), suburbia was identified in American culture as a unique form of community life.

In the last 20 years, however, sociologists have challenged the idea that suburban culture exists at all. Rather, they argue that the cultures found in suburban communities depend on the social statuses of their residents: their social class, occupation, age, marital status, and race. Berger's 1960 study of a working-class suburb in California, for example, reveals a social life that contradicts the suburban ideal: a social life with little participation in local affairs, limited social involvement with neighbors, and an almost exclusive concentration on the family, its home, and its television.

Numerous other studies report a wide variety of cultures in different suburban communities (see Bell, 1969; Gans, 1962, 1982). Knowing that a woman lives in a suburb or city tells us far less about her than do social statuses such as occupation, ethnicity, race, income, education, age, and marital status.

Outside the United States the variety of suburban life-styles is even more apparent. In suburbs of Rome, for example, residents focus almost completely on their families and have little to do with neighbors or community decisions (Ferrarotti, 1970). In the suburbs surrounding Kampala, Uganda, on the other hand, close ties with neighbors and active participation in community life are

The explosive growth of suburbs—especially following World War II—gave rise to the erroneous belief that suburbs represent a unique set of cultural beliefs, values, attitudes, and norms. The key to the culture of suburban communities lies in the social statuses of their residents, not in the fact that they are suburbs.

highly valued (Gutkind, 1966). Thus, for the most part there is little about the physical characteristics of suburbs that dictates a particular kind of culture.

## Norms and Community Life

Like all norms, those that regulate life in communities differ in their formality, the strictness with which they are applied, and their content.

The small populations and relatively simple division of labor in traditional communities such as the Amish allow them to control their members with informal sanctions that are strictly applied. Individual behavior and appearance are highly visible in such communities: any member of an Amish community who violated prohibitions on smoking cigarettes, for example, or who dressed inappropriately would be quickly noticed. Because most residents know one another and interact on a regular basis, there is little need for formal mechanisms—such as police departments, courts, and correctional systems—for enforcement of norms. The community itself, acting as a whole, enforces its norms.

In cities it is impossible to regulate people's behavior through such informal mechanisms, because populations are large and culturally heterogeneous. It is relatively easy for people to conceal their behavior in such communities. In cities, therefore, norms tend to be formal rather than informal, enforced through a complex division of labor designed to discover, prosecute, and punish those who violate laws. Urban neighborhoods, however, are often small communities themselves and can often enforce norms with the same informal mechanisms used by traditional communities (Jacobs, 1961).

Because cities offer residents a variety of neighborhood environments and a relatively high degree of anonymity, norms cannot be strictly applied, especially if they apply to personal lifestyles—sexual preferences and clothing, for example. Thus, urban communities tend to be far more tolerant of individual differences than rural communities (Fischer, 1982, 1984).

Urban and rural communities differ not only in the formality of norms and how strictly they are enforced, but in their content as well, and this fact, too, results from the cultural and structural complexity of industrial and commercial communities. In his classic book *The Division of Labor in Society* (1933), Durkheim identified differences in the *con-*

*tent* of norms that hold communities together by regulating the behavior of their members (see also Lukes and Scull, 1983). He described two types of social solidarity that correspond to the content of community norms: mechanical and organic solidarity.

As we saw in Chapter 8, the concept of **mechanical solidarity** refers to social cohesion that is based on a relatively simple division of labor and the sharing of a common culture—conditions found most often in small, traditional communities. In communities that are held together in this way, most norms take the form of criminal laws that prohibit specific behaviors because they are considered "wrong."

**Organic solidarity,** on the other hand, is based not on how alike people are, but on how different they are. City residents, for example, are connected to one another not so much by a shared culture as by their dependency on one another. Each resident performs a specialized task—food store manager, doctor, police officer, trash collector, department store clerk, electrician—in a complex division of labor. Because each person specializes in only a narrow portion of the activities required to meet people's needs, city dwellers depend on people with whom they often have very little in common.

In communities that depend on organic solidarity—most of which are urban—only a relatively small proportion of the norms focus on forbidden behaviors. Instead, most norms that govern community life are civil laws that regulate relationships involving groups and individuals who may never be more than strangers to one another. Commercial law regulates relationships among producers, buyers, and sellers; procedural law regulates interactions among police, defendants, and courts; constitutional law limits the power of government in relation to citizens; contract law settles disputes over agreements made between individuals or groups; and tort law provides compensation for those who suffer loss or injury at the hands of others. In all of these cases, norms regulate social relationships rather than prohibit specific behaviors because they are culturally defined as wrong.

To Durkheim, such differences in norms reflect profound differences in how communities stay together. The Industrial Revolution brought with it communities of such complexity and diversity that a vast body of civil law was needed to regulate a complex web of social relationships involving enormous numbers of people.

The concepts of organic and mechanical solidarity represent theoretical ideal types, and social cohesion in communities is rarely based purely on one or the other. Mexican villages and small African tribes are examples of communities held together primarily by mechanical solidarity, but many small, rural communities combine the two. Farming communities in most industrial societies, for example, have close relationships with urban and international markets.

To sum up, we have seen that it is impossible to fully understand cultural differences between communities without paying attention to the way social relationships among individuals and groups are structured: how boundaries are drawn and maintained, how roles, power, and prestige are distributed, and how interaction is patterned in predictable ways.

## The Social Structures of Community Life

On the level of role relationships, social structures are patterns of expectation that influence the feelings and behavior of individuals who occupy social statuses. At the community level, however, social structure also refers to relationships among groups as well as to the mix of social statuses found in community populations.

The following sections describe basic structural characteristics of communities: boundaries that separate members from nonmembers; the uses of time; the social composition of community populations; the distribution of power and prestige among individuals and groups; and the kinds of social relationships through which residents know and interact with one another.

### Community Boundaries and Xenophobia

Like groups, communities have boundaries that are defined by cultural beliefs, values, attitudes, and norms. In addition to such social distinctions, however, community boundaries have a physical dimension, for a shared physical space is part of the definition of a community. In both their social and physical aspects, community boundaries vary in clarity and openness.

Physical boundaries may be actual barriers—such as the walls that protected ancient cities—or they may be somewhat arbitrary geographic boundaries that are politically determined (the "city limits"). Political boundaries are important because they define the area within which local officials have jurisdiction and, thereby limit their use of authority. One of the most important aspects of communities, however, is that they provide us with a sense of belonging. Newcomers may be able to cross physical boundaries, but it does not necessarily follow that they will be accepted as members of the community; it is here that the clarity and openness of a community's social boundaries are important.

In small communities, the clarity of boundaries depends on the simple fact that all of the residents know one another. In some cases—such as seasonal resort communities and university towns—the massive influx of outsiders blurs community boundaries and leads permanent residents to adopt new mechanisms for maintaining their sense of community, including hostile attitudes toward the "invaders." Each summer in Nantucket, a small island community lying just off the Massachusetts coast, the tourists outnumber the permanent residents. Some residents spend most of their time at home in order to avoid feeling that they have lost their community to strangers; others may display bumper stickers that read "Native."

Particularly in urban neighborhoods, people often draw symbolic boundaries that define the area with which they identify (Suttles, 1972). Such boundaries often do not correspond to physical or political boundaries and may include a variety of ethnicities, races, and social classes. Harlem and Greenwich Village in New York, the Back Bay and Beacon Hill sections of Boston, and the Nob Hill and Haight-Ashbury sections of San Francisco are all examples of widely known neighborhoods whose residents often think of them as their "real" home.

Community boundaries are sometimes drawn in ways that select residents on the basis of social statuses such as race, ethnicity, and religion; the exclusion of blacks, Jews, and various ethnic groups is a longstanding practice in American communities. Until recently, for example, the only

Most community boundaries lack the clarity of this medieval walled French city.

true national urban policy in the United States centered on the value of "culturally homogeneous neighborhoods"—a thinly disguised way of saying that nonwhite and poor families should be excluded from white, middle-class neighborhoods. During the housing construction boom that followed World War II, the National Association of Real Estate Boards' code of ethics discouraged realtors from selling housing to members of "incompatible"—that is, black—groups. This deliberate policy of segregated housing was supported by the Federal Housing Administration, whose official guidelines for realtors and banks (which provided mortgages) forbade integration (Berry and Kasarda, 1977, pp. 369–370).

In many cases, attempts to maintain closed community boundaries are based on **xenophobia**—the fear of strangers. The United States is a nation of immigrants (with the exception of American Indians), but this has not prevented generations of Americans from claiming their communities as their own and telling succeeding waves of immigrants to "go back where you came from."

The Protestant English who inhabited the early colonies attempted to exclude Jews and Catholics, and in the seventeenth century, Mary Dyer was hanged in the Massachusetts Bay Colony for preaching Quaker religious doctrine. The Pennsylvania Quakers, on the other hand, opposed the influx of German Protestants in the 1750s, and Benjamin Franklin (1751) was among those who believed that America should be reserved for Anglo-Saxon whites.

Throughout the nineteenth century, cities such as New York, Boston, and Philadelphia experienced widespread fear over the massive influx of

Catholic immigrants, most of whom were Irish and German. The late 1800s was a period of bewildering social change in the rapidly industrializing Northeastern states, and residents found a convenient explanation for crime and corruption in the expanding population of "foreigners." Numerous groups—such as the Oriental Exclusion League, the Native American Party, and the Immigration Restriction League—tried to limit immigration into the United States (Curran, 1974). In California the excluded became the excluders as Irish workers formed the Workingmen's Party in 1877 and urged exclusion of Chinese immigrants who competed with them for jobs. In 1915 the Ku Klux Klan expanded its list of enemies to include Jews and Catholics (Curran, 1974).

Xenophobia and efforts to prevent outsiders from crossing community boundaries have not ended in the United States; all that has changed are the social statuses used as a basis for defining community membership. Now Mexican-Americans, Puerto Ricans, and Asian refugees are per-

THE GREAT FEAR OF THE PERIOD
THAT UNCLE SAM MAY BE SWALLOWED BY FOREIGNERS.

THE PROBLEM SOLVED.

ceived by many as a threat to jobs held by "natives," a burden on public welfare systems, and a source of crime. Whites continue to resist the movement of blacks into their neighborhoods and, if unsuccessful, are likely to move because they now consider their neighborhoods to be "less desirable" (Farley et al., 1978).

To some degree, it is probably inevitable that communities will accept some newcomers more readily than others, for a boundary that anyone can cross is no longer a boundary. When large-city communities become "wide open," residents often lose their sense of community and then create smaller communities within the city (Gans, 1982). The ethnic neighborhoods of large cities around the world attest to the continuing human desire to maintain physical spaces within which life goes on according to predictable cultural and structural arrangements.

The continuing problem with closed community boundaries is that some communities and neighborhoods offer better schools, housing, health care, and jobs than others do. In this sense, boundaries not only maintain a community's cultural homogeneity, but also serve to perpetuate inequalities of wealth, power, and prestige.

### The Importance of Time

Time is an important aspect of community social structure because communities and their neighborhoods differ in age, and the people who make up community populations stay for varying lengths of time.

In the simplest sense, the age of communities and neighborhoods is important because physical objects deteriorate over time. As communities age, so do their buildings, roads, sewer and water systems. It takes a considerable amount of time to transform a neighborhood of large, stately homes into an urban slum that is falling apart.

Because communities differ so widely in age, it is often difficult to compare them. The first American suburbs, for example, were primarily "bedroom" communities in which people lived but did not work. Early suburbs, therefore, were strikingly different from cities. In more recent years, however, businesses—including factories—have begun to move from central cities to the suburbs. As a result, the suburbs of today may in time resemble cities with all their problems of overcrowding, pollution, and physical decay.

Time is also important because the longer we live in a community, the more likely we are to make the status of "resident" a part of our social identity ("I'm a Chicagoan"), and this motivates us to conform to community norms and values. We are also more likely to care about a community if we believe our membership will last a long time, because we cannot comfort ourselves by thinking, "I'll be out of here soon." If we are "short-timers," we have less stake in community conditions, because however bad they may be, we expect their effect on us to be temporary.

In highly mobile societies—in which job changes usually involve a change of residence—it is difficult for communities to foster strong feelings of loyalty and involvement among highly mobile residents. The populations of college towns, vacation resorts, and communities near military bases are heavily populated with temporary residents whose home towns are far away. In such cases the problems of community loyalty and unity are particularly acute.

### Who Lives Here?
### The Social Composition of Communities

People's status sets tell us a great deal about their probable beliefs, values, attitudes, and expectations. Similarly, the mix of statuses in a community tells us a great deal about its social life. Retirement communities face different problems from those that small suburbs with relatively large numbers of young children face; and wealthy suburbs offer a social environment very different from that of a working-class suburb or an inner-city neighborhood in which most residents live in poverty.

Thus, many of the differences between communities are caused by the relative numbers of different social statuses found in their populations. In comparison with suburban populations, for example, central-city residents in the United States are more likely to be nonwhite, elderly, female, single, unemployed, and poor. Nonmetropolitan communities (almost all of which are rural) have a racial composition similar to that of suburbs, but tend to be poorer than central cities (Table 9-1).

Central cities and suburbs, however, are equally likely to include financially well-off families. In other words, central cities have a wider *mix* of family incomes, with relatively high proportions of both the very poor and the well-to-do. Bloomfield, Michigan (the home of many auto company

**Table 9-1**

Type of Community by Various Characteristics
(United States, 1981)

| | TYPE OF COMMUNITY | | |
| --- | --- | --- | --- |
| | Metropolitan Areas | | |
| CHARACTERISTIC | Central Cities | Suburbs | Nonmetropolitan Areas |
| Race | | | |
| % White | 68 | 90 | 88 |
| % Black | 22 | 6 | 9 |
| % Hispanic | 11 | 5 | 3 |
| Median Family Income | | | |
| Whites | $21,300 | $25,100 | $18,800 |
| Blacks | $12,900 | $16,200 | $10,300 |
| Spanish Origin | $13,400 | $17,000 | $13,900 |
| % Below Poverty Level | 14 | 6 | 12 |
| % Above $50,000 | 6 | 7 | 3 |
| % Nonfamily | 28 | | 23 |
| % Couples | 57 | | 65 |

Source: U.S. Census Bureau, 1982.

executives) is homogeneously prosperous, whereas Manhattan contains both the wealthy residents of Park Avenue apartments and the poorest ghetto inhabitants.

Central cities tend to be poor and nonwhite because for centuries they have been a receiving area for impoverished migrants seeking industrial jobs (Goldstein and Mayer, 1965). The heaviest concentrations of blacks in the United States, for example, are in industrial cities such as Atlanta, Detroit, Newark, and Gary, Indiana.

Until the 1970s, blue-collar workers were heavily represented in urban labor forces, but as many manufacturers have moved to suburbs in the last ten years, the mix of occupations in cities has become more concentrated in white-collar jobs: professionals, administrators, clerks, and secretaries. Blue-collar jobs, however, have long been the major source of employment for poor migrants; and because they cannot afford to follow manufacturing jobs to the suburbs, many of them are trapped in central cities. This helps explain why unemployment rates in central cities are twice as high as those in suburban communities (Berry and Kasarda, 1977).

White-collar workers are increasingly likely to live in suburbs and work in central cities. Those who *work* in cities, then, tend to be in white-collar occupations, but those who *live* in cities are more likely to have blue-collar job skills. Unlike rural and suburban communities, then, the urban population during the day differs substantially from the nighttime population (Melbin, 1978).

In cities, women tend to outnumber men, whereas rural communities have more men than women. The reason is the relative scarcity of opportunities for women in rural areas compared with the relative abundance of jobs in cities and suburbs (Hunt, 1965). Cities are also more likely to include single people and childless couples because people tend to prefer the physical and social conditions in suburbs for raising children (Frey, 1983).

Such differences are not found in all societies or in all American cities. In many developing countries, poverty is more severe in rural areas than in cities, and men are more likely to migrate to cities than women are. Mexico City's poorest neighborhoods are on the city's fringe, not at its center, primarily because the city lies in a "bowl" of moun-

In urban areas such as Los Angeles, the flow of traffic each evening is predominantly outward, away from the center of the city.

tains and the most desirable land is in the middle of the city. There are, in other words, few "green suburbs" to which the wealthy can flee. One of the wealthiest sections of Boston is Beacon Hill, located in the middle of the city. Although wealthy families left Beacon Hill for the nearby Back Bay neighborhood at the turn of the twentieth century, the poor people who moved in were eventually displaced by affluent Bostonians whose sentimental attachment to Beacon Hill prompted them to buy and restore its stately homes (Abrahamson, 1980; Firey, 1945).

In spite of such exceptions, the social composition of American central cities differs sharply from suburban and rural areas, and such differences are important because the mix of social statuses found in communities profoundly affects the beliefs, values, attitudes, and expectations of their inhabitants. In other words, the values people place on personal advancement, music and the arts, material possessions, conformity, and family life are determined more by their social class than

whether their community is urban, suburban, or rural.

Communities with young populations reflect different values than do those with larger proportions of the middle-aged and elderly. In the United States, for example, Ann Arbor, Michigan, and Berkeley, California, are sites of major universities, and have been the birthplaces of radical social movements. Ann Arbor was the first American community to pass a local ordinance classifying the possession of marijuana as a minor offense, with no punishment except a $5 fine.

## The Scale of Community Life: Groups and Formal Organizations

In addition to the mix of statuses, communities also differ substantially in the degree to which social life is organized around various groups. Life in small, rural villages is often organized on a small scale in the sense that relationships among individuals are more important than those among groups. In the cities of industrial societies, however, groups are more important in community life and tend to hold a relatively large share of wealth and power. In a few small New England towns, decisions are still made at town meetings in which all residents have an opportunity to present their views and cast their votes. In larger, more complex communities, power is primarily concentrated in groups and formal organizations such as labor unions, government agencies, businesses, political parties, neighborhood associations, and civic groups.

The large scale of city life makes it difficult for individuals to participate directly in community decisions. At best, city residents are heard only through groups that represent them; and those who do not belong to influential groups are virtually powerless.

## Distributing Power

In social interaction the concept of power centers on the ability to control people's behavior; but at the community level, power takes on an added dimension. Here the focus is on the ability to make decisions that affect community members' lives, regardless of the effect on their behavior (Polsby, 1968).

Sociologists focus on several questions about the distribution and use of power within communities: What are the sources of power within communities? How are decisions made? What are the social relationships among those who have power?

**Sources of Power in Communities**  Within communities the occupancy of important social statuses and control of valued resources such as land, wealth, and jobs are two main sources of power (Spinrad, 1965).

Some statuses are recognized by residents as legitimate authorities whose roles require them to make decisions about the community. Mayors, city managers, and councils pass laws and ordinances and decide how to spend tax revenues; police officers decide when to enforce particular laws; school boards decide which books students will read and how many teachers to hire.

Such statuses also include that of "voter"; and, when organized, voters can exert considerable power in decision making. In many small towns, for example, voters have the power to approve (or reject) local budgets and to override the decisions of elected officials. In cities, neighbors often form associations that, because they represent relatively large numbers of voters, vastly multiply the power of individual residents.

A more subtle source of power lies in the functional importance of a particular status. Trash collectors, for example, are not recognized as powerful by most community members, but if they go on strike their power is revealed as residents watch garbage pile up on the sidewalks. This source of power is particularly important in communities that rely on complex divisions of labor through which everyone depends on everyone else to perform their specialized roles.

Social statuses also give power to their occupants by allowing easy access to local officials. Business leaders and local politicians, for example, often belong to the same clubs, and in locker rooms and private dining rooms both business and political leaders have far greater access to one another than do other citizens.

In addition to social statuses, power also comes to individuals and groups who control valued resources. Landowners, for example, can tear down low-rent tenements in order to build office buildings or luxury condominiums. Valued resources also include the ability of affluent residents to affect local government decisions by giving or withholding contributions to political campaigns. Bankers decide how to invest the money that residents put into savings, and their decisions can have important effects on community life. Recently, for example, communities have become aware of the practice of "redlining," in which bankers decide that some neighborhoods are poor investment risks and refuse to give home improvement loans in those neighborhoods. In some cases, residents have expressed outrage at the fact that their money is being used to improve other neighborhoods at the expense of their own.

Control over jobs often gives businesses considerable power within a community. Companies may threaten to move and take hundreds if not thousands of jobs with them unless they receive special treatment (such as tax breaks or exemption from antipollution laws) from local governments. Such decisions affect not only workers and their families, but the financial health of the entire community: businesses are major sources of tax revenues, both directly through the taxes they pay and indirectly through the taxable income of their employees; and small local businesses cannot survive if residents have little money to spend (Bluestone and Harrison, 1982; Raines, Berson, and Gracie, 1982). This is especially true in communities whose economies are dominated by a single company that shuts down (Buss and Redburn, 1983).

These, then, are basic sources of power in communities; but a major focus of sociological research has been to understand how these different kinds of power fit together to produce power structures. How is power distributed, and who influences which kinds of decisions?

**Structures of Power: Who Rules?** Since sociologists began to study community power structures some 50 years ago, two major views have emerged. The first theory argues that power in communities is concentrated in the hands of a **power elite** whose members dominate decision making in all important areas of community life. A second and more recent view is that of **pluralist theory,** which holds that power in communities is distributed *pluralistically*, that a wide variety of groups and individuals influence decisions in different areas of community life.

The power-elite view first appeared in Robert and Helen Lynd's monumental "Middletown" studies (1929, 1937), in which they tried to identify a community's most influential individuals. They did this by living in the community for many months, interviewing residents, examining newspaper articles and official records, and acquainting themselves with the community's historical background. From this emerged their conclusion that local decisions were dominated by an elite group of upper-class residents who dominated community life in their own interests.

Floyd Hunter (1953, 1980) studied Atlanta, Georgia, and reached similar conclusions with a more efficient research methodology—the "reputational" method. Hunter located people he believed to be knowledgeable about various aspects of community life and asked them to compile a list of influential people. A panel of judges then used these lists to compile a final list of people whose names were mentioned most often, and these people were then interviewed and asked such questions as: "Which ten people on this list would you choose to make a decision about the community?" and "Who is the biggest man in town?"

The problem with these studies and their findings is that they focus not on who actually *makes* decisions in such areas as school expenditures, zoning, housing policy, or attracting new businesses, but on who people *believe* make decisions or have the greatest potential to make decisions. More recent studies try to remedy this problem by focusing on events rather than individuals: Who makes actual decisions, and what does this reveal about a community's power structure?

Dahl (1961) studied decisions made in New Haven, Connecticut, and Banfield (1965) conducted similar research in Chicago. Both studies (as well as many others) suggest that decisions in urban communities are influenced by a broad range of groups and individuals; that is, power is pluralistic, distributed widely rather than being concentrated among the members of a single elite. Although specific decisions—such as how to zone a particular area or whether to build a new school—are usually controlled by small segments of a community, elite groups are not unified into a single, integrated whole that dominates community life, and they often have competing interests (Weissberg, 1981). Insurance companies, police departments, and groups of citizens, for example, may favor raising the legal drinking age in a community, but liquor companies and bar owners may oppose it.

Dahl found that few business leaders influenced community decisions, and then only in the area of urban redevelopment. None participated in decisions affecting education, and only a few were involved in political parties. The mayor and school officials made most decisions about education, and political party regulars were most influential in nominating candidates. Banfield found, in fact, that business leaders tended to ignore community decisions unless their interests were directly threatened: "Big businessmen are criticized less for interfering in public affairs than for 'failing to assume their civic responsibilities'" (p. 287).

In general, the larger and more diverse a community's population is, the more pluralistic its power structure. No single group can hold absolute power in cities such as Dallas, Chicago, or Los Angeles, for the structure of city life depends on too many different groups, any one of which has the power to cause conflict simply by refusing to perform its role. As societies become more urban, therefore, communities are increasingly vulnerable to disruption as different groups struggle to improve their conditions by increasing their power.

Whichever view of community power structures we adopt, the fact remains that in most communities power is unequally distributed among individuals and groups. Immigrants and the poor generally have little if any influence over community decisions, and in cities, residents are governed by representatives who clearly have more power than those they represent. The distribution of power in communities is thus an enduring source of conflict in community life and an important area of sociological analysis.

## Relationships: Gemeinschaft and Gesellschaft

To sociologists such as Simmel, Weber, and Tönnies, industrialization and urbanization caused a disturbing shift in social relationships. Small, intimate communities gave way to large cities and the complex divisions of labor characteristic of mass production and bureaucracy. Weber (1922a) was disturbed by the increasing importance of rationality in social relationships, the rise of the "specialist," and impersonal bureaucratic ideals as social models for groups. To Simmel, city populations were so large and diverse that individuals protected themselves from overstimulation by becoming distant and aloof from other people.

Tönnies used a pair of concepts— *Gemeinschaft* and *Gesellschaft*—to describe this shift in social relationships. **Gemeinschaft** refers to a "'community of feeling' . . . that results from likeness and from shared life-experience" (Miner, 1968). Gemeinschaft relationships are what Cooley later referred to as "primary" (such as those between family members), and in their purest form such relationships are often organized primarily around kinship networks—who is related to whom by blood or marriage.

A **Gesellschaft** relationship, on the other hand, is held together less by a common culture than by rational considerations of self-interest and role structures that make people depend on one another in order to achieve important goals. The divisions of labor found in highly bureaucratic societies such as China and the United States, for example, create interdependencies among people

who share different cultural ideas. The city dweller who manufactures farm equipment and the farmer who uses it live sharply different lives, but each depends on the other in order to survive.

Whereas Gemeinschaft rests on shared values and interpersonal liking, the secondary relations of Gesellschaft do not. Thus, lawyers in small towns might refuse to defend an innocent man for fear of alienating a community certain the defendant is guilty, and city lawyers may represent clients they personally dislike and believe to be guilty.

The concepts of Gemeinschaft and Gesellschaft are **ideal types;** that is to say, there is no such thing as a community with social relationships that are purely one or the other. The concepts are useful, however, for comparing the general character of relationships in different communities or in the same community over time. Since the colonial period, for example, social relationships in the United States have dramatically shifted from Gemeinschaft toward Gesellschaft.

In colonial America, people who grew food and exchanged it for products such as candles knew personally those they were dealing with. In the 1980s, however, the social structures through which goods are produced and exchanged are vastly more complex and impersonal. The lettuce eaten by someone in Kansas City was probably grown in California, picked by migrant farm workers from Mexico, sold to a wholesaler and then to a retailer, transported by truckers, and ultimately sold to an individual in a supermarket for money earned, perhaps, by working in a candle factory. Thus, our relationship with lettuce growers is now based less on a shared culture than on a complex set of social structures through which we exchange goods and services and thereby satisfy our needs and desires.

The first urban sociologists were as pessimistic about cities as they were optimistic and romantic about life in Gemeinschaft communities. To Wirth (1938), rural communities were cozy and intimate: people knew one another well, actively participated in community life, and could turn to others for comfort and support in times of trouble.

Cities, on the other hand, were seen as cold and impersonal places in which people disappeared in anonymous and superficial relationships and rarely participated in community affairs, because they were "just passing through." As Tönnies (1887) wrote, in Gesellschaft communities,

Everybody is by himself and isolated, and there exists a condition of tension against all others . . . intrusions are regarded as hostile acts . . . nobody wants to grant and produce anything for another individual . . . (p. 65)

Sociological research, however, suggests that neither the Chicago School's pessimism about urban life nor its romanticism about what anthropologist Robert Redfield (1947) called the "folk society" represents reality. When Kasarda and Janowitz (1974) interviewed residents of urban and rural communities in Britain, they found little difference in the satisfaction people reported about their social lives. In fact, urban residents tended to report more friendships than their rural counterparts. In two American studies, Fischer (1982, 1984) found that urban dwellers reported no more isolation than rural residents, no less involvement with their families, and, in some cases, higher levels of social support. Fischer found no evidence that would justify the conclusion that urban and rural dwellers differ in the amount or the quality of their social relationships.

People who live in cities are no more likely than others to report feeling always rushed in their daily lives. Nor are they more likely to report dissatisfaction with community conditions such as schools and police protection. Indeed, they are *less* likely to report dissatisfaction with health care, transportation, and annoyances such as street noise or poor street lighting or repair (U.S. Census Bureau, 1980b).

How do people maintain their ties with others in enormous cities? One explanation is that when confronted with astounding numbers of people and a dizzying array of cultural ideas, people tend to form their own communities within cities. Whereas Simmel believed that urban dwellers orient themselves to the entirety of a city and its population, Gans (1982) argued that the neighborhood is their primary focus. The size and diversity of city populations foster and sustain the strong ethnic subcultures found in many urban neighborhoods, and it is within them that individuals and groups meet their needs for a sense of belonging and involvement (Fischer, 1975, 1982, 1984).

Even those who appear to be isolated—such as elderly people living alone—often form "telephone communities" through which they maintain contact with one another. Whereas Simmel and Wirth believed that the size of cities caused isolation and weak social ties, Fischer's analysis suggests just the opposite: although city dwellers may avoid interaction with *most* people they encounter, they have such a wide range of possible subcultures to choose from that their ties to other people are often stronger than they might be in small communities.

Although cities certainly have their share of serious problems—including higher crime rates and higher percentages of poor people—they are free from the stifling pressures to conform found in small communities where "everyone knows your business." Life in Gesellschaft communities can be as overstimulating as Simmel suggests, but it is no less true that the homogeneity and closeness of a Gemeinschaft community can be very boring.

For over 1,000 years, people have migrated from rural communities to the attractive diversity of cities. Although the population of American inner cities is now decreasing, people are moving not to the more Gemeinschaft conditions in rural communities, but to nearby suburbs that still afford full access to cities, which offer both "the wonders and the terrors of human life" (Aronson, 1971, p. 300).

## Community Ecology

Whereas the concepts of culture and social structure draw our attention to the social environments that distinguish one community from another, ecology focuses on characteristics of populations and their physical environments. Communities differ in the size and density of their populations as well as in how rapidly they grow or shrink. In addition, they find themselves in a variety of physical settings to which they adapt by organizing activity and using technology.

### Community Populations

The size and density of a community's population are sociologically important in several ways. In comparison with small, sparsely settled communities, those that are large and densely settled can support a more complex division of labor—a greater variety of people performing specialized tasks. They tend to be culturally more heterogeneous, including people with a greater diversity of cultural backgrounds. Because they cannot grow their own food, they are more dependent on technology—both in agriculture (so that farmers can grow enough to feed themselves as well as the urban population) and in industry (to provide employment for city residents).

By current standards, the earliest cities hardly qualified as cities at all, for their populations rarely exceeded 20,000. In comparison, New York City had 7 million inhabitants in 1980 and Mexico City had over 11 million. Such large populations allow a division of labor whose complexity dwarfs that of previous cities. Tax records for fourteenth-century Paris, for example, list 157 occupations (Russell, 1972), but the number of different jobs found in New York City is in the thousands.

In comparison with small rural communities, large cities are more vulnerable to social disruption for three reasons: their division of labor is complex, they are highly dependent on energy such as electricity, and they are far less self-sufficient. An electrical blackout in a city brings economic activity to a virtual halt, and if transportation from rural areas is disrupted by a strike, no food can reach city dwellers.

Although much has been written about the supposed negative effects of crowded living conditions on human health and behavior, the evidence is far from conclusive (Baldassare, 1983; Simmel, 1950; Winsborough, 1965; Wirth, 1938). Simmel and Wirth, for example, argued that crowded living conditions in cities cause social relationships to be superficial and transitory; and others argue that crowding causes deviant behavior, mental illness, and poor physical health.

Most arguments linking high population density to deviant behavior and poor health are based on animal studies (such as Calhoun, 1962) and have yet to be demonstrated conclusively in human populations (Hawley, 1981). International comparisons also raise serious questions about the effects of population density on human behavior. The overall density of Japan's 1983 population, for example, was almost 13 times greater than America's, and individual housing units were twice as crowded. Yet, in comparison with Japan, infant mortality rates in the United States were 57 percent higher, homicide rates were 9 times higher, and suicide rates were only slightly lower (U.S. Census Bureau, 1982, 1983c).

It cannot be denied, however, that social life in communities is affected by the size and density

The effects of crowding on human behavior and experience depend on the cultural context. What is experienced as overcrowding in one society may be just right in another.

of their populations, for these basic aspects of community ecology affect both the diversity of cultures found among residents and the ways in which communities organize human activity in relation to physical environments.

## Niches and Ecosystems

Each community participates in an ecosystem—a physical environment that includes both natural resources and other species of life—and survives through its relationships with it. The ways in which a population participates in an ecosystem comprise its ecological niche, and communities differ both in the kinds of ecosystems they inhabit and how they interact within them.

Communities that survive by hunting game and gathering wild food can support only small, sparsely settled populations with minimal divisions of labor. The earliest cities were made possible by

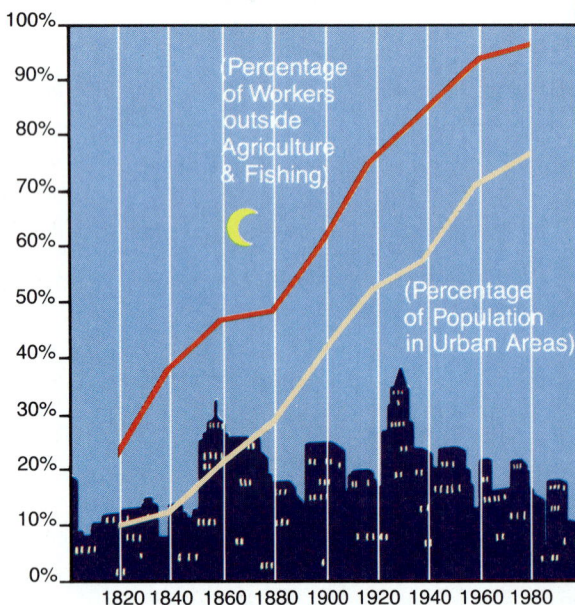

**Figure 9-1** Percentage of U.S. Population Living in Urban Areas and Percentage of Workers outside Agriculture and Fishing, 1820–1980

Sources: U.S. Census Bureau 1975, Tables D 167–181, A 57–72; U.S. Census Bureau 1981, Tables 10, 390.

revolutionary advances in cultural technology—such as the plow—that enabled people to produce more food than they needed for their own survival; this surplus, in turn, supported cities, whose residents did not grow their own food.

The greatest leap in world urbanization resulted from the Industrial Revolution, which rested on innovative technology and changing cultural values. When machines were introduced on farms, the increased efficiency that resulted created a labor surplus in rural communities. At the same time new machinery, sources of energy, and ways of organizing factories allowed the owners of factories to pursue the goals of vastly increased production and profits.

These changes profoundly affected urban communities. Masses of people who could no longer find work in rural communities—both here and in Europe—migrated to urban areas in search of factory jobs (the enormous influx of Irish immigrants to American cities in the middle of the nineteenth century, for example, was caused in large part by the Irish Potato Famine of 1846). Figure 9-1 shows how profound this change was in the United States during the last two centuries. Between 1820 and 1980 the percentage of people employed in nonagricultural occupations increased from a low of 21 percent to a current high of 98 percent. At the same time the percentage of people living in urban areas increased from around 10 percent to 76 percent.

Work became increasingly specialized as production was divided into narrower and narrower tasks, and this fostered diversity by attracting migrants with a vast range of backgrounds. The welfare of individuals depended increasingly on their ability to compete with others for social statuses in complex divisions of labor.

Thus, the phenomenal growth of cities during the last two centuries did not just "happen" and then create cultural differences between rural and urban communities. Rather, the size and density of city populations were caused by changes both in culture and in social structure: in technology, the values of profit and mass production, and the increasingly complex divisions of labor that resulted.

The Industrial Revolution transformed community life by creating enormous cities whose survival depended on increasingly complex technology, vast amounts of energy, and expanding markets in which to sell manufactured products.

This change in the ecological niche of communities profoundly altered societies and relations among them. The colonial expansion of urbanizing European nations during the eighteenth and nineteenth centuries was the direct result of industrial needs for raw materials and markets in which to sell finished goods. In the late twentieth century, the phenomenal growth of industrial cities across the world created an enormous demand for energy that dominates international politics. Industrial nations such as the United States, Japan, the Soviet Union, and most of Europe depend heavily on the stability of oil-producing countries in the Middle East, because without a steady supply of oil, the urban centers that dominate these countries cannot survive.

Thus, the ecological shift from communities based primarily on agriculture to industrial cities dependent on technology, huge supplies of energy, and vast markets brought with it increased interdependency among communities and nations and, therefore, increased vulnerability to economic disruption and heightened international tensions. A downward slide in the international demand for oil in 1982, for example, brought the economy of Mexico to the edge of bankruptcy, and a major war in the Middle East could seriously damage the economies of countries located thousands of miles away.

The shift to industrial communities also increases the danger of damaging the physical environment, for large, densely settled populations produce enormous amounts of waste. Until quite recently, death rates in cities were far higher than in rural areas, largely because human wastes were simply thrown into the streets or into rivers and streams that were also used as water supplies. As recently as the nineteenth century, for example, the Thames River in London was an open sewer, and London streets were littered with tons of horse manure. In the 1980s Mexico City is in serious danger of depleting its supplies of drinkable water, New York City produces more waste than it can dispose of without seriously threatening the natural environment, and raw sewage from Tijuana, Mexico, is polluting the beaches of San Diego. The population of Houston, Texas, has grown so rapidly that its water supply is decreasing, and because most of its water is in the ground beneath the city, the city is steadily sinking as the water is consumed (Reinhold, 1982).

## Land Use: Where People Do What They Do

Within any community, people and their activities are distributed spatially; the larger a community is, the more complex these arrangements are. With the boom in urban growth during the last century, ecologists and urban sociologists have tried to discover patterns that describe how the uses of space give communities their physical shape (Figure 9-2).

Early in this century Park, Burgess, and McKenzie (1925) theorized that cities develop in *concentric zones* or "rings" of activity around a core devoted to business and entertainment. As commercial activity "spills" into the next ring, its residents flee outward, leaving behind a mixture of commercial activity and relatively impoverished residential neighborhoods, including ethnic neighborhoods such as "Chinatown" and "Little Italy." The next ring consists mostly of the homes of blue-collar workers, and as we move farther from the core, neighborhoods rise in social class, with the upper-middle and upper classes living in the outermost rings (Guest, 1976).

The **concentric-zone** view of city growth assumes that business activities are concentrated in a single core, and that rings develop as people compete for land away from industrial activity and poor neighborhoods. Although this model fit Chicago early in this century, city development is generally more irregular than a smooth set of concentric rings. Paris, for example, has no single business district (Caplow, 1952).

Hoyt (1939) introduced a variation on the concentric zone model by taking into account the effects of transportation on patterns of land use. Like the zone model, Hoyt's **sector model** suggests that cities develop outward from a central core. Instead of a ring pattern, however, cities grow along transportation lines that go out from the center like pieces of a pie. According to Hoyt, upper-class neighborhoods are not necessarily clustered in an outer ring, but can be found at varying distances from the center of the city along transportation lines.

Harris and Ullman (1945) suggested the **multiple-nuclei theory,** which de-emphasizes central business districts and suggests that cities have centers for different kinds of activities—such as finan-

■ **Figure 9-2**  Models of Urban Growth

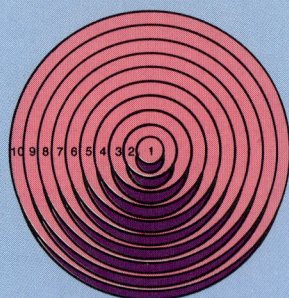

|  |  |  |
|---|---|---|
| Concentric-Zone Theory | Multiple-Nuclei Theory | Sector Theory |

1. Central business district
2. Wholesale light manufacturing
3. Low-class residential
4. Middle-class residential
5. High-class residential
6. Heavy manufacturing
7. Outlying business district
8. Residential suburb
9. Industrial suburb
10. Commuters' zone

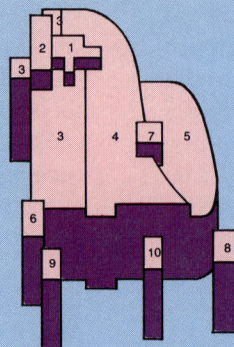

Source: Adapted from Chauncy D. Harris and Edward L. Ullman, "The Nature of Cities," *Annals of the American Academy of Political and Social Science*, 242 (November 1945).

cial, theater, restaurant, clothing, and industrial districts.

What do we make of these theories, none of which accounts for the variety of community spatial arrangements? Perhaps their greatest usefulness lies in the one thing they have in common: they acknowledge that the intensity of land use for different purposes varies from one part of a community to another, which affects not only what people do in communities, but how communities change.

## How Communities Change

The process of community change involves a combination of cultural, structural, and ecological factors. Although large cities have existed for many centuries, the rapid urbanization of the world was created by the Industrial Revolution, which represented both a shift in cultural values and technology and a profound change in social structure toward increasingly complex divisions of labor.

These cultural and structural changes, however, produced cities only in combination with ecological factors such as massive immigration of

workers. The poverty of American cities results not simply from social inequality in the distribution of wealth, but also from the migration of businesses and middle- and upper-class families away from central cities. Thus, community change is a complicated process, and it is for this reason that finding solutions to community problems continues to be a particularly difficult task.

## World Patterns of Change

Across the world there are some clear patterns of change in the cultures, social structures, and ecological arrangements of communities. There is, for example, a general trend toward modernism—evidenced by the acceptance of change, the increased use of scientific technology, and the spread of mass media such as newspapers and television (Inkeles and Smith, 1974).

The most dramatic trends, however, are ecological and structural, for the world's population is increasingly concentrated in urban areas. Only about 3 percent of the world's population lived in urban communities in 1800, but by the year 2000,

**Table 9-2**

Degree of World Urbanization, 1800–2000

| YEAR | PERCENTAGE LIVING IN CITIES OF 5,000 OR MORE | PERCENTAGE LIVING IN CITIES OF 100,000 OR MORE |
|------|------|------|
| 1800 | 3 | 3 |
| 1900 | 14 | 5 |
| 1950 | 28 | 16 |
| 1975 | 41 | 26 |
| 2000 | 55 | 40 |

Source: Population Reference Bureau, 1975.

cities will contain an estimated 55 percent of all people in the world (Table 9-2). As industrialization attracts migrants, cities mushroom in size and their populations come to include an astounding diversity of races, ethnic groups, occupations, and social classes.

Increasingly complex divisions of labor cause social relationships to shift in character from Gemeinschaft to Gesellschaft. The organization of community life around family ties and local economies gives way to mass markets and rational, contractual relationships (Miner, 1968). As the scale of communities grows larger, power is increasingly concentrated in large, formal organizations such as governments and corporations, and as this happens, individuals are further and further removed from the decision-making process.

The rise of the city as the dominant form of community life also affects rural communities (Larson, 1968). The increased use of agricultural technology makes farm communities both less autonomous and less isolated. Rural villages, for example, are increasingly oriented to distant urban markets on which they depend for cash income as well as for bank loans to finance investments in machinery, seed, pesticides, and irrigation.

The growing orientation to distant markets—rather than to local subsistence needs—encourages farmers to specialize in only a few crops, many of which (such as coffee) cannot be used as food. This specialization, in turn, makes them still more dependent on urban markets, for they can no

longer survive simply by consuming what they produce themselves. Rural farm populations such as those in Mexico—who spend their lives growing food—thus often find themselves in the ironic position of starving when the prices offered for their cash crops decline in urban markets.

## Trends in the United States

Although the world trends described above also apply to the United States, since 1970 American urban areas have experienced significant structural and ecological changes that are not typical of the world as a whole. Between 1970 and 1980, for example, the combined population of central cities remained unchanged while the suburban population grew by almost 16 million, a rate of increase almost double the national average (U.S. Census Bureau, 1982, 1983c). While the *size* of central-city populations remained generally unchanged, however, their social *composition* changed dramatically (Frey, 1983).

The number of blacks living in central cities, for example, grew by almost 2 million, whereas the number of whites declined by over 6 million. Because those who left central cities generally had higher incomes than those who stayed behind and those who moved into them, the percentage of people below the poverty level increased in central cities from 13 percent to 16 percent, but the incidence of poverty in suburban communities remained unchanged at 7 percent. In the central cities of large metropolitan areas, median family income actually dropped by almost $800 while family incomes in the suburbs of these cities increased by $700 (U.S. Census Bureau, 1980b, 1983c).

What caused these shifts in the composition of central-city populations? To some extent, the flight of middle- and upper-class whites from central cities is due to racism. The answer is not this simple, however, for affluent blacks have also been leaving central cities at an accelerated rate (Long and De Are, 1981).

An additional piece of the explanation lies in the relocation of many businesses to suburban communities—a movement due in part to the attraction of less-congested environments, but also to the fact that as central cities become poorer, governments must increase tax rates in order to maintain levels of essential services such as sanita-

The relocation of businesses from cities to suburbs contributes to the vicious circle through which American cities are becoming increasingly poor and debt-ridden.

tion, fire and police protection, and welfare programs.

It is here that cities find themselves in the midst of a vicious circle, for as businesses and their middle- and upper-middle-class employees move to the suburbs, living conditions in cities (including tax levels) become worse, precipitating still more flight (Bradbury et al., 1982). In this way many cities find themselves in a downward spiral toward greater poverty and—as in New York City in the late 1970s—on the edge of virtual financial collapse.

Community change in the United States has not been confined to urban areas, for in the last half-century the use of sophisticated agricultural technology has caused the decline of small family farms, which have been replaced by huge corporations. Between 1930 and 1983 the number of farms dropped from 6.5 million to 2.4 million, and the average size of farms almost tripled. This, coupled with the migration to cities, has dramatically lowered the populations of rural communities: between 1930 and 1983 the number of Americans living on farms dropped from 30 million to just under 5.6 million (U.S. Census Bureau, 1983c).

Migration from rural areas, however, has been selective: those who leave tend to be young adults. Thus, rural communities generally have relatively high percentages of children and the elderly—people who produce less than they consume—which helps explain why the highest percentages of people below the poverty level are found in rural communities (U.S. Census Bureau, 1983c).

## Community Change in Developing Nations

Many early urban sociologists and human ecologists shared the belief that the process of urbanization took the same form in all societies (Wirth, 1938). The experience of the past 20 years, however, suggests that urbanization in developing countries is quite different from the urban growth in Europe and the United States that accompanied the Industrial Revolution (Hawley, 1981). Whether or not these different lines of development will ultimately converge and produce cities much like those of industrial societies is still an open question, for too little time has passed to arrive at any firm conclusions.

Urbanization in developing countries is unique in four ways. First, urbanization in Europe and the United States took place in response to the needs of rapidly expanding industry. By comparison, the world's most rapid urbanization now takes place in poor, nonindustrial countries.

Second, the Industrial Revolution prompted a decline in birth and death rates in Europe and the United States. Together, rapidly expanding industry and lowered birth rates allowed these countries to keep industrial production ahead of population growth. In developing countries, however, birth rates remain high while death rates have fallen sharply through the use of cheap medical technology. Thus, in the rapidly urbanizing countries of Latin America, the Middle East, North Africa, and Asia, populations increase faster than production, and urban economies cannot absorb enormous numbers of migrants from rural areas.

A third unique aspect of urbanization in developing countries is the spatial distribution of residents (Peattie and Aldrete-Haas, 1981). In most American cities the social class of residents increases with distance from the center of the city (although many city centers attract a small elite of wealthy residents, such as those who live in the expensive apartments and condominiums around Central Park in New York City). Urban growth in most developing countries, however, reverses this pattern, with poor immigrants settling at the outskirts of cities (Berry and Kasarda, 1977).

Fourth, changes in culture and social structure predicted by early sociologists have not occurred in many developing countries. Tönnies, for example, believed that the shift from Gemeinschaft to Gesellschaft relationships was inevitable—that all cities would be dominated by formal, secondary relationships in which the individuals' primary loyalties are to themselves, rational thought is most highly valued, and people are rewarded strictly according to their performance.

Kolb (1954) and Hauser (1959) argued, however, that early predictions were based on an American model of city life that does not apply in the cultural context of many nonindustrial societies. The cultures of developing societies, for example, are more likely to value spiritual life, tradition, extended family ties, rigid roles, and religion—none of which match the "rational" model of Western bureaucracy. Although urbanization in Europe and the United States was synonymous with industrialization in a modern cultural context, this is often not the case in today's developing countries.

The most important consequence of this difference lies in the social relationships among urban dwellers in developing countries. In Africa, urban and rural culture are similar because migrants to the cities bring their village culture with them. Many writers describe the "gusto," "camaraderie," and "casual ease with which social relations are established" in many African cities, and attribute this to the fact that "the African who comes to town rarely arrives as a complete stranger" (Epstein, 1967, p. 206). This pattern is repeated throughout the world in "squatter" settlements outside cities in countries such as India, Turkey, Mexico, Egypt, and Kenya, where traditions are grounded in family and tribal ties that do not give way to the kinds of rational, secondary relationships found in the cities of industrial nations.

Despite the variety of their forms and patterns of growth, however, the world's cities have one thing in common: as communities, they find it increasingly difficult to feed, house, and employ their residents, and still preserve their physical environments.

## Communities in Trouble: Possibilities for Change

The most serious problems facing urban communities are overcrowding, poverty and unemployment, and deteriorating physical and natural environments. It is important to remember that all but the first of these are not unique to cities. Some of the worst poverty is to be found in rural communities, as are some of the most dangerous environmental conditions, such as land erosion and droughts. Revolutions in developing countries such as El Salvador often focus on the problems of rural communities where most of the land is owned by single families and farmed by poor peasants who may face starvation while their crops are exported abroad for sale in cash markets (Weller and Guggenheim, 1982).

Most of the world's population, however, will soon live in urban areas; and for this reason, poverty, overcrowding, and deteriorating physical conditions are most visible and serious in cities. What are some possible solutions? In the simplest sense, the answers are obvious: redistribute populations in order to alleviate overcrowding, provide jobs for community residents, rebuild cities. *How* to accomplish these goals, however, is another matter, and it is here that we find three major approaches to solving community problems: government planning, private enterprise, and social movements among community residents.

The most notable examples of government planning are found in Britain, the Soviet Union, Israel, and China. In the early years of this century, the British government decided to build a series of "New Towns" near urban centers such as London. They were designed as self-contained communities—not suburbs—in which people would both live and work; by 1971 their combined population had reached almost half a million. The planners seem to have achieved most of their goals: most residents work in their local areas, and physical conditions are better than those in crowded cities (Berry and Kasarda, 1977).

After the Russian Revolution in 1917, the Soviet government began long-term planning to organize cities according to the number of workers needed for local industries and to ensure socialist ideals of equality and eradication of social class differences. The result in many Soviet cities (and in those of some eastern European communist countries that used the Soviet Union as a model) has

been massive construction of cheap, uniformly designed apartment houses forming neighborhoods whose residents represent a broad mix of occupations. Although physical conditions in the Soviet Union are harsh by Western standards, Soviet urban planners appear to have achieved some of their goals (Berry and Kasarda, 1977).

In Israel the construction of planned communities, or *kibbutzim*, continues to be a major part of Israeli nation building. In a kibbutz, property ownership and decision-making power are shared among all residents, and the community as a whole provides care for children and the elderly (Bettelheim, 1969; Spiro, 1956). There is some dissatisfaction among kibbutz members—primarily among younger people who strain under the intense pressures to conform to community norms and values—but in general, community planning in Israel has resulted in high production, emotional support for residents, and a high degree of community cohesion and loyalty.

China has tried to stem the flood of migrants from rural areas in order to combat enormous overcrowding in its major cities. Migration is tightly

Community planning in England, the Soviet Union, and Israel is representative of the handful of such attempts that have had some success. In most societies, community change involves little or no centralized planning.

controlled by the government, and it is illegal to change residence without permission. China has also made major investments in the development of rural areas in an attempt to make rural life more attractive.

In developing countries such as Egypt, urban planning focuses on increasing urban employment through industrialization and luring migrants back to rural communities. In such countries, however, planning has been generally unsuccessful. Their populations grow so rapidly that industrial development cannot meet the demand for jobs; and rural poverty is so extreme that migrants are reluctant to leave the cities that, however unpleasant by Western standards, provide better conditions than rural areas do.

Although many countries have adopted national planning strategies for community change and development, the approach in the United States has been quite different. Americans have steadfastly resisted government participation in community planning, preferring to leave the fate of communities in private hands; the piecemeal planning that has taken place has often ignored the needs of residents and the social arrangements that brought cities to their current crises in the first place.

The current problems of American cities, for example, result in part from uncoordinated decisions of business owners and families over the past 200 years. City populations grew rapidly in the nineteenth century because immigrants were attracted to factory jobs. Because cities have been like lightning rods—attracting the poor who seek a better life—they have for two centuries been the home of large populations of poor people crowded into substandard housing.

In many urban neighborhoods, low-income families have been forced to leave even sub-standard housing through a process called **gentrification,** in which individuals or real-estate developers buy up old, deteriorating housing largely inhabited by poor people who pay low rents. They then remodel the buildings and rerent or sell them at rates far beyond the means of their original tenants (Laska et al., 1982). Although gentrification restores old neighborhoods, increases property values (and therefore city tax revenues), and makes large profits for developers, it also displaces low- and middle-income residents who often find themselves with no choice but to move to less desirable neighborhoods (Besser, 1979).

For millions of Americans who have no place to move, the result is homelessness (U.S. Department of Housing and Urban Development, 1981). Flophouses once provided more than 2 million single-occupancy rooms for many of the poorest people in the United States; but between 1970 and 1980 almost half of these were either destroyed or converted to higher-priced dwellings. New York City lost 87 percent of its single-occupancy rooms during this same period, and Denver, Seattle, and Rochester lost more than 50 percent (*Newsweek,* January 2, 1984).

The scattered efforts to improve life among poor populations in cities have generally failed because many planners have worked from the assumption that the social aspects of community life

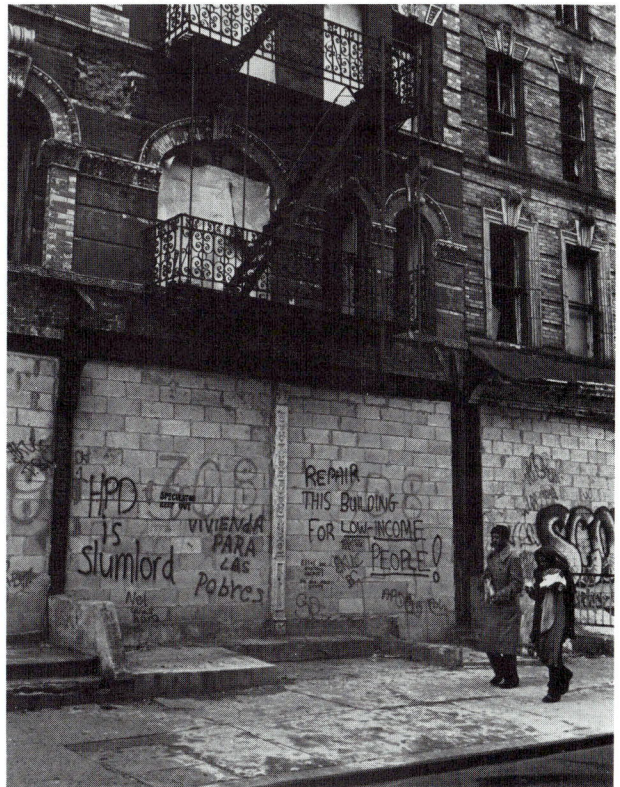

While gentrification is profitable for developers and offers attractive urban housing for those who can afford it, for others it results in homelessness as the stock of inexpensive housing is depleted.

## Voices: Two Sides of Gentrification

A group of Hartford residents fighting a trend toward office conversions in their neighborhood, protested Monday against a request for tenants to move from two more buildings.

"I've been here in this country for 37 years and I've never seen a damned thing like this," said Marcelino Guzman. He and 15 others live at 61 Russ St., a 109-year-old apartment building with splintered wooden trim and grimy brick walls in Hartford's Frog Hollow neighborhood.

"It isn't fair, but look around. It's happening all over," Guzman said, pointing to former apartments across the street and up toward the new Superior Court complex being built on Lafayette Street.

He and the other protesters instead urged support for a proposed moratorium against conversions from homes to offices.

Led by the Hungerford Street Block Club, the residents said they have counted at least 29 apartment buildings in the area that have been converted to offices for lawyers and professionals who do business at nearby courts and state offices.

They fear their neighborhood is becoming an office park. They say tenants, many of them poor, are being forced to look for housing in a city where decent apartments for low- and moderate-income families are scarce.

David Dubay was among the protesters. He lives two blocks from Guzman, at 154-156 Hungerford St., a building where tenants last week were served with a 30-day notice to move.

"I've lived there for 18 years and put about $3,000 to $4,000 into my apartment," Dubay said. "I think it's unfair. The landlord should have given us more notice. Thirty days ain't nothing."

As Dubay spoke, about eight members of the Hungerford Street group and its parent group, Hartford Areas Rally Together, marched in a circle, carrying placards protesting office conversions.

"I know this neighborhood is only so-so," he said. "I could move to a better neighborhood. But where am I going to find a place to rent for the $200 I pay now?"

Neighborhood leaders are supporting a City Council proposal to impose a six-month freeze that would suspend building permits for converting residential property to commercial and business uses. . . .

"I think that kind of (real estate) speculation is something we don't have to put up with," said Councilman Allan B. Taylor, an ardent supporter of the moratorium. "I think a majority of the council feels that way."

M. Donald Cardwell, a Hartford attorney and owner of Guzman's building, disagreed. Cardwell said he sold the building to another attorney who wants to renovate it. The tenants have until February to move out, he said.

"I have been in this area for 15 years, and I have no equivocation of saying that the lawyers were responsible for the neighborhood's renaissance," Cardwell said. "There's been an awful lot of heat on this. Protest is easy; constructive decisions are difficult."

Source: Rodriguez, *Hartford Courant*, December 4, 1984, p. B.11.

depend primarily on ecology—the size and density of populations and the quality of buildings. In doing so, they have largely ignored cultural and structural factors that affect life in communities—such as the inequalities produced by race and social class (Gans, 1982; Keller, 1975).

In the last few decades, conditions in older American cities have grown worse as businesses leave (to lower their tax burdens and thereby increase their profits) and take with them thousands of jobs. As cities become poorer, taxes increase, and to save money, landlords let their buildings deteriorate. This, in turn, makes cities increasingly unattractive places to live in, and middle-class families move to the suburbs (Gans, 1968).

The development of American communities has thus depended primarily on what businesses and middle- and upper-class families consider to be in their own best interests, *not* on the overall needs of communities. What substitutes for a national urban policy

> is a complex set of uncoordinated, often contradictory . . . random public policies and programs provided in the wake of strong economic forces which set the agenda for urban growth. Thus, if in the past urbanization has been governed by any conscious public objectives at all, these have been, on the one hand, to encourage growth, apparently for its own sake; and on the other hand, to provide public works and public-welfare programs to support piecemeal, spontaneous development impelled primarily by private initiative. (Berry and Kasarda, 1977, p. 371)

The populations of American cities are increasingly poor, elderly, and nonwhite; and yet these groups have little power over the economic and political decisions that profoundly affect community development. So long as American culture values the right of organizations such as banks and corporations to act only in their self-interest—without regard for the fate of communities—how can conditions in American cities improve?

One answer lies in the ability of community residents to organize and exert pressure on the decisions of business and government (Hallman, 1984; Van Til, 1980). Neighborhood groups have successfully opposed the building of highways that threatened to split neighborhoods down the middle; tenants have successfully opposed the demolition of apartment houses or their conversion into luxury condominiums they cannot afford to buy. When companies that provide most of a community's jobs move out, residents sometimes pool their resources and become owners as well as workers, saving both themselves and their community.

Examples of residents organizing to fight for their communities are increasingly common in the United States, but perhaps even more so in less-developed countries. In their extreme form, local efforts such as these are part of social movements that are sometimes revolutionary in scope. El Salvador and Mexico are vivid examples of citizen-initiated revolutions based in large part on the desire to improve economic and social conditions in communities.

The populations of American cities now include growing numbers of people who are not only poor, but homeless.

## Summary

1. A community is a population that shares a territory and meets basic physical and social needs through daily interaction among residents. Rural communities are small, homogeneous, and sparsely settled; urban communities—or cities—are large, heterogeneous, and densely settled. Suburbs are densely settled communities around a city.

2. In comparison with modern communities, traditional communities tend to resist change, have relatively simple divisions of labor, use unsophisticated technology, have less highly developed mass media, and rely more on informal relationships than on secondary, formal relationships.

3. Community cultures differ in content and the homogeneity of community residents. There are no distinct urban, suburban, and rural cultures.

4. Community norms vary in their formality and strictness of application. They also differ in their content, and this difference corresponds to different sources of social cohesion. Mechanical solidarity refers to communities held together primarily by criminal laws; organic solidarity refers to communities held together by civil laws that regulate relationships in complex divisions of labor.

5. Communities differ in the clarity and openness of their physical and social boundaries. Closed boundaries are often based on xenophobia, the fear of strangers and outsiders, which occurs in most known societies.

6. Community structures also differ in age and how long residents stay; in social composition and the importance of groups and formal organizations; in distributions of power; and in the social relationships through which residents know and interact with one another.

7. Power in communities depends on the occupancy of social statuses and control of valued resources. Power-elite theory argues that an elite group dominates decision making; pluralist theory maintains that power is spread out among various interest groups.

8. Gemeinschaft communities are held together by primary relationships based on likeness and shared life experiences; Gesellschaft communities are held together by secondary relationships based on rationality and interdependencies in a complex division of labor.

9. Communities differ in population size and density, and this affects the complexity of the division of labor. The Industrial Revolution caused a major change in the human niche by using technology and concentrating both production and people in relatively small areas (cities).

10. According to concentric-zone theory, cities develop in rings around a core of business activity. Outer rings are higher in social class than inner rings. The sector model states that cities grow in pie-shaped segments going out of a central business core. The multiple-nuclei theory maintains that cities have many different cores of activity. According to all three theories, the intensity of land use for different purposes varies from one part of a community to another, and residential neighborhoods tend to be segregated according to important social statuses.

11. Communities change through a complex process involving social and ecological factors. The world population is becoming increasingly urban and modern. In the United States, suburbs are growing faster than central cities, and city populations are becoming poorer and blacker, while suburbs are becoming wealthier and whiter. Urbanization is not the same in developing countries that lag behind in industrial growth.

12. The major approaches to solving community problems are government planning, private enterprise, and social movements among residents, and these can both solve and create problems.

## Key Terms

## Recommended Readings

ABRAHAMSON, M. (1980). *Urban sociology* (2nd ed.). Englewood Cliffs, NJ: Prentice-Hall. A useful text that summarizes major aspects of the sociological study of cities.

BOGGS, V., HANDEL, G., and FAVA, S. F. (Eds.). (1984). *The apple sliced: Sociological studies of New York City.* New York: Praeger. Drawing on the classical approach of the Chicago School, these 19 articles provide a richly entertaining and informative look at life in New York City.

BUSS, D. M., and REDBURN, F. S. (1983). *Shutdown at Youngstown: Public policy for mass unemployment.* Albany, NY: State University of New York Press. An examination of what happens when a "one-factory town" loses its factory.

FISCHER, C. S. (1984). *The urban experience* (2nd ed.). San Diego: Harcourt Brace Jovanovich. A critical appraisal of urban research with a particular emphasis on subcultures.

GANS, H. (1982). *The urban villagers* (2nd ed.). New York: Free Press. The second edition of an important study of tight-knit ethnic communities that struggle to maintain themselves in the midst of modern urban decay.

JACOBS, J. (1961). *The death and life of great American cities.* New York: Random House. Although more than 25 years old, Jacobs' observations about the problems of urban planning, urban renewal, and life in American cities are still of great value and make for interesting reading.

ROBERTS, B. (1979). *Cities of peasants.* Beverly Hills, CA: Sage. A look at the unique problems of cities in newly industrializing countries, with an emphasis on Latin America.

# CHAPTER 10

# Deviance and Conformity

**Deviance** is any behavior or appearance that violates a norm, and **conformity** is behavior or appearance that is consistent with norms (Merton, 1968; Schur, 1971). We all violate norms—by overparking, telling "little white lies," failing to surrender a bus seat to an elderly passenger, or keeping a library book past its due date—but most of the time we do not risk serious punishment even, as in the case of traffic violations, when we have broken a law.

Other deviant acts, however, have more serious consequences if they are detected. When people lie compulsively, commit murder or armed robbery, or cheat on college exams, they are in danger of being severely punished. Convicted criminals are confined in prisons, and students who cheat may be expelled from school. Thus, deviance and conformity are related to group boundaries; and, although everyone violates norms, we need to distinguish between the *kind*

and the *intensity* of social sanctions applied in response to deviance, sanctions that depend on cultural interpretations of behavior.

This chapter focuses on three kinds of sociological questions about norms, deviance, and conformity. First, how do groups use norms to draw their boundaries, and what are the resulting varieties of deviance? Second, how do culture, social structure, and ecology affect deviant behavior? (What kinds of people, for example, are the most likely to violate norms, and why? Why are some violators punished, but others are not? Why is deviance more common in some societies than others?) Third, how do conformity and deviance affect societies and their members? What are their positive and negative consequences? (Why, for example, does Durkheim assert that a society without criminals would have to invent them?)

In short, what are deviance and conformity all about, and why are they important?

## Norms and "The Norm"

In any society, people behave in many different ways. Some behaviors are unusual—never eating meat, for example—but their rarity in itself does not make individuals socially unacceptable. Most people in the United States eat meat, and such common behaviors are referred to as **"the norm"**; but the mere fact that individuals behave in ways that are statistically rare does not necessarily mean they are committing deviant acts. Performing heart transplant operations, for example, is an extraordinarily rare behavior in any society.

What, however, of an American who eats people? Cannibalism is not simply unusual in the United States; it also violates norms that define the moral acceptability of different behaviors. In our culture there are thousands of different "acceptable" foods, but individuals who cross the cultural boundary and eat people are classified as *abnormal* and, to put it mildly, risk their standing as members of society.

Thus, norms are not merely ideas used to control individuals; they also establish social boundaries of acceptable and unacceptable behavior. This is clear in social responses to what is defined as immoral behavior: "You are not one of us, and must either become one of us or leave." People who are identified as criminals or insane, for example, are either "rehabilitated" so they can once again fit

## Voices: The Morality of Cannibalism

One evening just before the sun had set, and when the twenty-seven survivors were preparing to take shelter from the cold in the fuselage of the plane, Liliana turned to Javier and told him that when they returned she would like to have another baby. She felt that if she was alive it was because God wanted her to do so.

Javier was delighted. He loved his children and had always wanted to have more, yet when he looked at his wife he could see through the tears in his eyes the poignancy of her suggestion. After more than ten days without food the reserves had been drawn from her body. The bones protruded from her cheeks and her eyes were sunk into their sockets; only her smile was the same as before. He said to her, "Liliana, we must face up to it. None of this will happen if we don't survive."

She nodded. "I know."

"God wants us to survive."

"Yes. He wants us to survive."

"And there's only one way."

"Yes. There's only one way."

Slowly, because of their weakness, Javier and Liliana returned to the group of boys as they lined up to climb into the Fairchild.

"I've changed my mind," Liliana said to Marcelo. "I will eat the meat."

Marcelo went to the roof of the plane and brought down a small portion of human flesh which had been drying in the sun. Liliana took a piece and forced it down into her stomach. . . .

The meat was strictly rationed, . . . The basic ration which was given out at midday was a small handful, perhaps half a pound, but it was agreed that those who worked could have more, because they used up energy through their exertions, and that the expeditionaries could have

almost as much as they liked. One corpse was always finished before another was started. . . .

"You cannot condemn what they did," said Monsignor Andrés Rubio, Auxiliary Bishop of Montevideo, "when it was the only possibility of survival. . . . Eating someone who has died in order to survive is incorporating their substance, and it is quite possible to compare this with a graft. Flesh survives when assimilated by someone in extreme need, just as it does when an eye or heart of a dead man is grafted onto a living man. . . . What would we have done in a similar situation? . . . What would you say to someone if he revealed in confession a secret like that? Only one thing: not to be tormented by it . . . not to blame himself for something he would not blame in someone else and which no one blames in him."

Carlos Partelli, the Archbishop of Montevideo, confirmed his opinion. "Morally I see no objection, since it was a question of survival. It is always necessary to eat whatever is at hand, in spite of the repugnance it may evoke."

And finally the theologian of *L'Osservatóre Romano*, Gino Concetti, wrote that he who has received from the community has also the duty to give to the community or its individual members when they are in extreme need of help to survive. Such an imperative extends especially to the body, which is otherwise consigned to dissolution, to uselessness. "Considering these facts," Father Concetti went on, "we justify on an ethical basis the fact that the survivors of the crash of the Uruguayan airplane fed themselves with the only food available to avoid a sure death. It is legitimate to resort to lifeless human bodies in order to survive."

Source: Read, *Alive*, 1974.

within culturally defined limits of normality, or are excluded from society, through isolation in prisons and mental hospitals or—in more extreme cases—through death or exile.

Suicide clearly illustrates the connection between deviant behavior and social boundaries. By

definition, suicide is an act in which the offender and the victim are one and the same (although other people certainly are affected). Even the most isolated individual, however, is legally forbidden to commit suicide. In England suicide was once viewed as so grave an act that the penalty for attempted suicide was death. How can we explain so extreme a response?

An obvious answer is that antisuicide laws support values about the importance of human life, but it is not this simple. Perhaps the clearest social boundary is the one that separates life from death. Life is difficult, and it is not uncommon for people to contemplate leaving society by ending their lives. In its simplest sense, the will to live is a basic prerequisite for the existence not only of individuals, but of groups and societies.

A society that allows suicide undermines its most fundamental hold on its members: "If you don't think life is worth living, why should anyone else?" Each time we prevent a suicide, we both save the potential victim's life and reaffirm the belief that even the most unhappy life is worth preserving. Thus, even the most solitary act often has profoundly social consequences.

What of societies in which suicide is sometimes permitted or expected? In eighteenth-century India, Hindu widows were expected to commit suicide by allowing themselves to be burned alive on the husband's funeral pyre (Stein, 1978); and in feudal Japan, suicide was expected of those who had dishonored their families or their emperor (Douglas, 1968). The key to these exceptions is that such suicides are not seen as rejection of life itself or of society; rather they affirm important values. When Japanese pilots committed suicide during World War II by crashing their planes into American ships, they strengthened social boundaries by reaffirming the value that the emperor was more important than any citizen.

Although deviant behavior is by definition forbidden by norms, it is nonetheless common in many cases. In 1984, 73 percent of American adults supported laws prohibiting marijuana use

All cultures have norms that regulate the circumstances under which people may take their own lives and the meaning attached to such behavior. This Buddhist monk committed ritual suicide in Saigon in 1963 in order to protest the policies of the South Vietnamese government.

(J. Davis, 1984); yet an estimated 50 percent of all Americans aged 26 to 34 had smoked marijuana at least once (*Newsweek*, 1982, p. 40). Alcoholism is also considered deviant in the United States; yet in 1984, 72 percent of American adults were alcohol users and almost a third of these reported that they sometimes drink more than they think they should (J. Davis, 1984).

The line between acceptable and deviant behavior varies both among cultures and within them. Although ancient Greeks considered homosexuality a higher form of love than heterosexuality (Licht, 1932), most societies have persecuted homosexuals in one way or another (an extreme case being the murder of thousands in Nazi concentration camps). In colonial America, adulterous women were severely ostracized by society (a situation described vividly in Nathaniel Hawthorne's novel *The Scarlet Letter*). Although 69 percent of American adults profess the belief that adultery is always wrong (J. Davis, 1984), adulterers today are far less likely to be shunned and are no longer punished under the law.

Prior to 1914 there were no legal controls on the use of addicting drugs such as opium and heroin in the United States. Cocaine, in fact, was an early ingredient in Coca Cola, and heroin and morphine were publicly advertised as over-the-counter drugs (just as aspirin is today). In 1914 the federal government passed the Harrison Act, prohibiting the sale and use of opiates (Clausen, 1976). In 1937 marijuana was added to the list, as were LSD and other psychedelic drugs in the 1960s.

Boundaries that define deviant behavior, then, are cultural creations, which means that deviance itself is a cultural creation (Durkheim, 1895). Merely by passing a law defining drug use as a crime, the United States created hundreds of thousands of criminals. Laws now under consideration by Congress define abortion as murder and—if passed—would instantly transform thousands of women into criminals, including those who use certain forms of contraception such as intrauterine devices. Under such laws, women who miscarry because of accidents or poor nutrition could be charged with manslaughter or negligent homicide. Thus, statements such as "marijuana use is deviant" describe not the individual user, but the *cultures* that define certain behaviors as deviant.

## Social Control and Social Conflict

From his study of Puritan society in colonial America, Erikson (1966) concluded that the social basis of deviance was primarily cultural, that laws reflect a moral consensus among society's members:

> The deviant individual violates rules of conduct which the rest of the community holds in high respect; and when these people come together to express their outrage over the offense and bear witness against the offender, they develop a tighter bond of solidarity than existed before. (p. 4)

Erikson focused on deviance as functional for society. Deviant acts violate a "**collective conscience**" (Durkheim, 1924), and the outraged reaction of citizens increases social cohesion by reinforcing each member's sense of commitment and attachment to the community and its standards. (In a related sense, as kings and their court jesters have long known, comedians do more than entertain. Their routines, which often make a shambles of "proper behavior," both highlight group boundaries and reassure members of the audience that they are safely inside those boundaries.)

The conflict perspective focuses on the uneven distribution of the power to define behaviors as deviant in a society, and the ways in which laws serve the interests of some groups more than others. Norms that define deviance can serve the function of maintaining inequality as a structural characteristic of societies. Both the functional and conflict perspectives, then, challenge the idea that norms reflect *only* a moral consensus in society, and lead us to focus on social distributions of *power* in which some groups use norms in order to dominate others (Turk, 1969, 1976).

In eighteenth- and nineteenth-century America, blacks were not allowed to learn to read, nor were others allowed to teach them. They were not allowed to sue in courts of law or testify against whites. They could not vote or sit on juries, and the law specified harsher penalties for blacks than for whites convicted of the same crime (Burns, 1973).

We can explain such laws as reflecting a moral consensus among society's members only if we ignore the glaring omission of blacks and abolitionist whites from that consensus. From a conflict perspective, acts are defined as criminal when it serves the interests of those who dominate society. Members of dominant groups are allowed to violate laws, whereas those in subordinate groups are punished (Chambliss, 1973). As Quinney (1972) wrote,

> The established authority is thus able to use the law in the attempt to maintain control over the people. Furthermore, those in power are able to justify their actions through law. And most critically, they can pursue *their own* criminal activities without being defined as criminal. The police are seldom charged and convicted of crimes when they murder, violate constitutional rights, assault, and so on. The government itself, when engaging in an illegal policy, is not prosecuted as criminal. All of this is understandable . . . *since those in power, those who control the legal system, are not likely to prosecute themselves and define their official policies as criminal.* (p. 29, italics mine)

Dominant groups use the law to maintain their power by controlling which acts are defined as serious crimes. When people call for "law and order," they usually refer not to tax evasion, corporate fraud, or violations of civil rights by police and government agencies; rather, they refer to acts such as burglary and theft, which are committed more frequently among middle- and lower-class people. A man who steals a television set worth several hundred dollars is likely to be prosecuted as a criminal. When a corporation robs customers by deceptively advertising its products, or causes death and injury by ignoring worker safety regulations or dumping hazardous wastes, however, the individuals involved are rarely prosecuted or imprisoned (Clinard and Yeager, 1980; Mitford, 1973).

Dominant groups also create laws that favor their members. Housing codes favor landlords over tenants, and credit laws favor lenders over individual borrowers. Laws that require people to retire at age 70 increase the economic power of younger people at the expense of the elderly. Tax laws favor the rich over the middle and lower classes.

Dominant groups benefit in several ways from their control over cultural definitions of deviance. First, they do not *need* to resort to burglary or larceny in order to steal, so that laws prohibiting such acts do not threaten them. Laws often are changed only when they threaten members of dominant

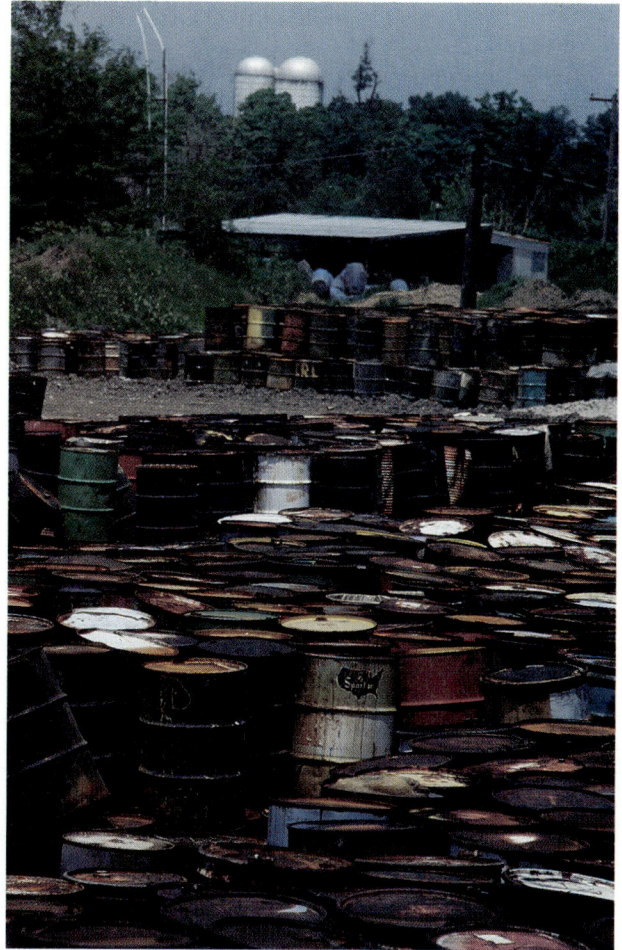

The illegal and improper disposal of toxic waste endangers the health of entire communities; but business owners found guilty of illegal dumping are rarely defined and punished as criminals.

groups. As long as drug use was confined to the poor, there were no strong public pressures to legalize it. When it began to spread to children of upper-middle- and upper-class families in the 1960s, however, there was sudden public pressure to remove criminal penalties.

Second, dominant groups perpetuate inequality by using laws to limit poor people's options, forcing them to choose between the risks of criminal prosecution and the likelihood that they will never escape their social class by socially legitimate means. After blacks were granted the right to vote following the Civil War, many Southern states enacted "literacy laws" and "poll taxes" that denied the vote to anyone who could not read from the Constitution or who was too poor to pay a tax. These laws diluted blacks' newly won political freedom and power, thereby protecting the privileged position of whites (Burns, 1973).

Third, by limiting cultural definitions of deviance, members of dominant groups draw public attention away from their own criminal methods, thus protecting themselves and their elite positions (Chambliss, 1973).

To sum up, although norms often reflect a moral consensus in society, they are also used to exploit others and maintain positions of dominance. Whenever we discuss deviant behavior, we have to keep in mind that *deviance is a cultural category*, and that people differ in their power to control such categories in their own interests.

## Varieties of Deviance

Sociologists make three basic distinctions concerning deviance. First, although all deviant behavior violates norms, individual violators may or may not accept the values enforced by these norms (a murderer may or may not value human life). Second, although deviance is often defined in terms of behavior, it also includes **stigmas**—personal characteristics (such as personality or the appearance of our body) and social statuses (such as religion) that threaten an individual's standing in groups and society (Goffman, 1963b). Thus, we need to distinguish behavior from personal characteristics as bases for cultural definitions of deviance. Third, the social response to deviance may be informal or formal. Informal sanctions are most common when folkways are violated, and formal sanctions are used when laws are violated.

### Values, Norms, and Deviance

As rules of behavior, norms specify socially acceptable means for achieving valued goals. Although all deviant acts violate norms, social responses to deviant behavior depend on how people perceive the connection between specific norm violations and the violator's support of cultural values. To illus-

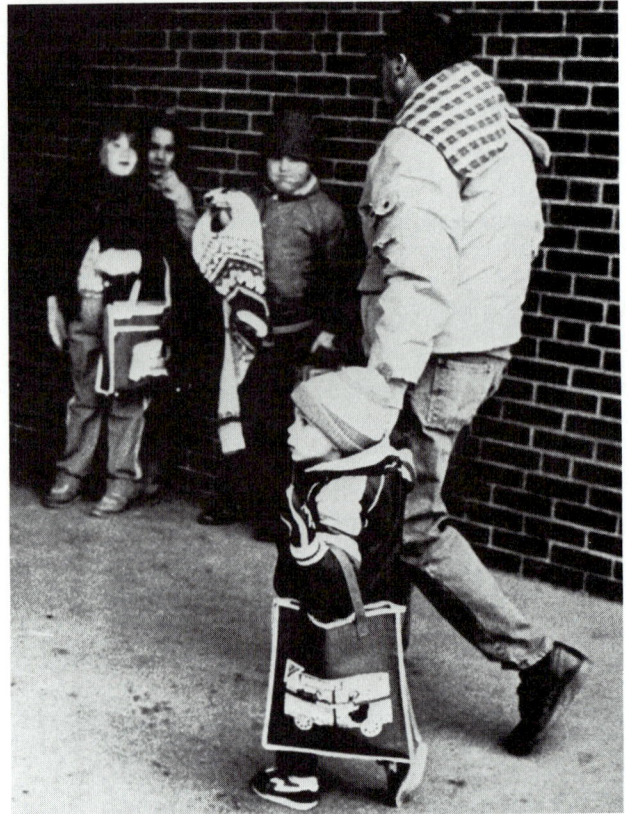

This little boy carried the stigma of having herpes, a disease that frightened his schoolmates and their parents, who demanded that he be kept out of school and away from other children. Even after he returned, under a court order, he had to be taught by a substitute teacher because his regular teachers and the members of his old class rejected him.

trate, let us consider the deviant behavior of three college students. The first deeply believes that grades and exams destroy the learning process by turning students into "machines" who care about nothing but grades. She believes this so strongly that she steals the exam and the answer sheet beforehand, distributes copies to students, and publicly announces her action as a "protest against grades and examinations."

The second student, in desperation, steals the exam and answer sheet and secretly uses them to prepare for the test. The third student is so frustrated with college work that he abandons all attempts to get good grades. He spends most of his time under the influence of drugs, rarely studies, and fails to appear for the exam at all.

The first student is a **rebel** (Merton, 1968)—someone who openly violates a norm in order to challenge and change both the norm and the values it supports. Her actions are also **nonconformist,** for she committed them openly and without consideration for personal gain (Merton, 1976a). When faced with punishment, she may defend herself by appealing to other values shared by her community—the importance of learning and of inquiring minds—values that, in her view, are more important than the specific norm she violated.

The second student's actions are **innovations,** for although he accepts the value of good grades, he rejects culturally legitimate means for achieving them (Merton, 1968). His behavior is also **aberrant** (Merton, 1976a), because he stole the exam answers secretly and for personal gain. He is concerned not with challenging university norms, but with escaping their sanctions. If caught, he will defend himself not by appealing to higher values served by his behavior, but to circumstances that explain his actions ("I was desperate; I was overloaded with courses this term").

The third student's behavior represents **retreatism** (Merton, 1968), a stance that rejects both norms and values without any interest in changing them. Like the rebel, he refuses to accept the university's norms and its values; but the retreatist offers nothing as a replacement. He has simply "dropped out" by refusing to participate. The retreatist's behavior is also aberrant, for it represents not an active concern with university culture, but a self-serving, apathetic rejection of the community itself.

Innovative behavior may be either aberrant (as in the case of the second student) or nonconformist. A student might share the cultural values of good grades and success and yet believe that exams are the wrong *means* for measuring accomplishment. Openly stealing the exam answers would then be an innovative, nonconforming act designed to protest norms while supporting cultural values.

These distinctions (shown in the box on this page) are important because social responses to deviant behavior depend on the type of deviance the act represents. Nonconforming rebels and innovators act in the name of important values and without consideration of personal gain, so other members of the community are more likely to support them. In addition, nonconformity often leads to positive social change. When blacks refused to sit in the back of buses or be turned away from "Whites Only" restaurants in the 1960s, they did so in order to change cultural ideas and the structures of human relationships. There can be little doubt that without such "civil disobedience," the black civil rights movement would never have achieved as much as it has.

## Types of Deviant Behavior

**NONCONFORMING BEHAVIOR** Done openly in the name of positive social change, not for personal gain; appeals to "higher values."

**Rebellion** Openly rejects *both* norms and the values they support, and offers alternatives.

*Example:* Revolutionary.

**Innovation** Openly rejects norms and offers alternatives; supports values that rejected norms enforce.

*Example:* Publicly burning a military draft card while calling for a volunteer army to meet defense needs.

**ABERRANT BEHAVIOR** Done secretly for personal gain; concerned more with avoiding punishment than with positive change.

**Retreatism** Rejects *both* norms and the values they support, but does not offer alternatives. Uses illegitimate means to achieve culturally illegitimate goals. "Dropping out."

*Example:* Skid row drug addict.

**Innovation** Rejects norms, but accepts the values they support. Uses illegitimate means to achieve culturally legitimate goals.

*Example:* Robbing banks.

Source: Adapted from Merton, 1968, 1976a.

Aberrant behavior, on the other hand, provokes harsher punishment because the act is committed for personal gain, not for the improvement of society. Unlike nonconformists, people who commit aberrant acts such as theft cannot say to society, "I did this for your own good." Thus, the behavior of nonconformists reflects a concern for values that connects them with the society that considers punishing them, whereas aberrant and retreatist behavior identifies individuals as "outsiders."

The severity of punishment for aberrant behavior depends on the values involved. A starving woman who steals in order to feed herself violates a norm while conforming to important values about the preservation of human life. If she steals in order to feed starving children, she conforms to even more powerful values—helping others and caring for children. A man who steals simply because he wants to possess a luxury he cannot afford, however, acts only in his self-interest and conforms to a less-valued goal—accumulating possessions—and is therefore more likely to be punished harshly.

The social response to deviant acts as well as their ultimate effects on society depend heavily on the actors' orientations to values and norms as revealed by *how* they present themselves and their behavior to others. For this reason, people who describe themselves as "political terrorists" have something to gain by defending their behavior with appeals to "higher values" rather than personal gain (Rappoport and Alexander, 1982). In this way, they seek to define killing as something

Terrorists try to defend their behavior by portraying it as nonconformist rather than aberrant, as motivated by important cultural values rather than self-interest.

other than murder, and abduction as something other than criminal kidnapping, hoping to thereby escape severe punishment (Schafer, 1974).

## Stigma:
## When Who We Are Is against the Rules

**Stigmas,** Goffman (1963b) wrote, are characteristics that render people "not quite human" in the eyes of others, who reduce them in their minds "from a whole and usual person to a tainted, discounted one." Bernard Pomerance's recent play (and, later, movie) *The Elephant Man* tells the true story of an Englishman who was horribly disfigured by a disease. Like many disfigured people, he was regarded as a freak and accepted only by a sympathetic physician and a rare few who were willing to seek out the witty, charming, and intelligent human being who lived within the deformed body. The 1985 movie *Mask* tells a similar story.

Stigmas are also attached to personality characteristics such as dishonesty or mental instability. Former convicts and mental patients, for example, may be treated as outcasts even when they "go straight" (or "go sane"). The mentally retarded are often subjected to humiliation even by those responsible for taking care of them (Dudley, 1983). Even the relatives of stigmatized people may suffer from people's assumptions about their characters:

> Dear Ann Landers,
>
> I'm a girl 12 years old who is left out of all social activities because my father is an ex-convict. I try to be nice and friendly to everyone, but it's no use. The girls at school have told me that their mothers don't want them to associate with me because it will be bad for their reputations. . . .
>
> Is there anything I can do? I am very lonesome because it's no fun to be alone all the time. My mother tries to take me places with her but I want to be with people my own age. Please give me some advice—An OUTCAST. (Berkeley *Daily Gazette,* April 12, 1961)

Stigmatized people are treated as deviants not for what they do, but because of who they *are* or are thought to be. It is, for individuals, perhaps the most damaging form of deviance, for while we can control our behavior, it is all but impossible to change our bodies or our pasts, no matter how much we may want to do so. Cultural stigmas have the power to condemn individuals to lives of shame and isolation over which they have little if any personal control.

## Formal and Informal Sanctions

In most cases, telling lies violates folkways that have **informal sanctions** such as expressions of anger. If we lie habitually, however, people may refuse to trust or associate with us, and as informal as such sanctions are, they can be powerful reasons to tell the truth.

Informal sanctions, however, are not strong enough to compel people to tell the truth in court. People often have powerful personal reasons for lying in court, and such behavior (perjury) can have serious consequences. In many cases, therefore, norms take the form of *laws* with **formal sanctions** and specialists such as police officers, judges, juries, and prison officials to enforce them. In general, *crime* is deviant behavior that violates the law, and the social nature and causes of criminal behavior are a major focus of sociological research.

# Crime, Criminals, and Victims

Although **crime** technically includes all acts that violate laws, it is important to note at the outset that many violations of law are not socially defined as crimes, and some crimes are not defined as deviant. Few people consider speeding on the highway a criminal act, for example; and although restaurant waiters who fail to report all their tip income to the Internal Revenue Service are committing a crime, most people—including restaurant owners—do not treat such people as deviants.

"There is no society that is not confronted with the problem of criminality," wrote Durkheim (1895), and the United States is a prime example. In 1981 a murder was reported to police every 23 minutes, a sexual assault every 6 minutes, an assault every 49 seconds, and a theft every 4 seconds (Table 10-1). In comparison with other modern

### Table 10-1

Reported Incidence of Crimes
(United States, 1960 and 1981)

| TYPE OF CRIME | HOW FREQUENTLY EACH TYPE WAS REPORTED | |
| --- | --- | --- |
| | 1960 | 1981 |
| All violent crimes | 2 minutes | 24 seconds |
| Murder | 60 minutes | 23 minutes |
| Sexual assault | 30 minutes | 6 minutes |
| Assault | 3 minutes | 49 seconds |
| Theft | 10 seconds | 4 seconds |

Source: U.S. Census Bureau, 1980b, 1982.

### Table 10-2

Homicide Rates for Selected Countries, 1980
(Rates per 100,000 People)

| COUNTRY | HOMICIDE RATE |
| --- | --- |
| United States | 9.1 |
| Australia | 1.9 |
| Israel | 1.8 |
| Denmark | 1.4 |
| Great Britain | 1.2 |
| Austria | 1.2 |
| Sweden | 1.2 |
| Norway | 1.1 |
| Japan | 1.0 |
| Switzerland | 1.0 |
| Netherlands | 0.8 |
| Greece | 0.7 |
| West Germany | 0.7 |

Source: U.S. Census Bureau, 1983c.

industrial societies, the United States is the undisputed "murder capital of the world" (Table 10-2).

The **crime rate** (the number of crimes per year per 1,000 people) increased sharply during the last two decades. Between 1960 and 1981 the U.S. population grew by 28 percent, whereas the rate of reported crime grew by more than 300 percent—in spite of doubled public spending for law enforcement (U.S. Census Bureau, 1980b, 1982). In 1973 about 16 percent of adults had had the experience of being shot at or threatened with a gun, but by 1984 the figure had risen to 20 percent (J. Davis, 1984).

We must remember that these statistics include only crimes that are reported to the police, and as people become more or less willing to report crimes, the trends in *official* crime rates may not accurately reflect trends in *actual* rates. In the 1970s the U.S. Department of Justice began a series of large national surveys to measure the incidence of crime by interviewing individuals (see Gottfredson and Hindelang, 1981). By comparing the results with police statistics, the researchers found that crime often goes unreported to the police (U.S. Department of Justice, 1980a). The victimization studies found, for example, that the incidence of violent crimes in 1980 was almost six times higher than that recorded by police (U.S. Census Bureau, 1982).

Like most human behavior, criminal acts are influenced by the characteristics of social environments. Criminals are more likely to occupy some social statuses than others, as are their victims. Criminal behavior occurs in social environments in which criminals have social relationships with one another. In addition, criminals, their victims, and those charged with law enforcement have social relationships with one another that affect not only themselves, but the capacity of society to prevent crime as well.

## Who Are the Criminals?

From a sociological point of view, our behavior is strongly influenced by our social statuses and the ways in which societies organize social relationships. This suggests that criminal behavior is at least partly due to social structure, that criminals as a group differ from noncriminals in their likelihood of occupying important social statuses such as gender, age, race, and social class.

**Gender**  More than 10 million people were arrested in 1981, and 84 percent of them were male (U.S. Census Bureau, 1983c). The gender difference in known criminal behavior occurs in virtually all societies, all communities within them, and among all age groups; and it has existed as long as statistics on crime have been gathered. Prostitution is the only crime committed primarily (although not exclusively) by females (Cohen and Short, 1976).

In recent years the gender difference in criminal deviance has narrowed slightly in the United States, particularly among nonwhites and for relatively minor crimes. Smith and Visher (1980) suggested it may be due in part to a growing similarity in the social positions—such as occupation and education—occupied by males and females. As males and females increasingly come to occupy similar positions, their behavior—including deviance—should become more similar as well. Gora's 1982 study of arrest rate trends, however, found no support for the common belief that increases in female criminal activity have been caused by the women's movement and a redefinition of women's roles.

**Age**  Some crimes are defined literally by the age of the criminal. *Juvenile delinquency*, for example, refers specifically to illegal acts committed by people under 18 years of age. Prior to the nineteenth century, "child criminals" were either shielded from the law or treated as adult criminals, but during the last 100 years Western societies have created a separate legal category for youthful offenders, with its own set of procedures for handling them (Sutton, 1983).

Age is also important because the likelihood of criminal behavior varies strikingly and consistently by age (Hirschi and Gottfredson, 1983). More than a third of all people arrested for theft in 1982 were under the age of 18, as were 44 percent of those arrested for arson (U.S. Census Bureau, 1983c). Adults are more likely to be arrested for violent crimes such as assault and homicide and for crimes that require expertise (counterfeiting and forgery), money (drug smuggling and gambling), or special opportunities (embezzling bank funds) (Cohen and Short, 1976).

The high rate of arrests for teenage arsonists underscores the problem of estimates of crime

**PUZZLES:**

## WHO CONSTITUTES THE CRIMINAL CLASS?

Who is most likely to break the law—someone from the lower class, the middle class, or the upper class?

If you answered, "the lower class," you might be right; and you might also be wrong. Popular stereotypes portray members of the lower class as particularly prone to criminal behavior, but, as this chapter shows, a long history of scientific research challenges this view amid a continuing debate among sociologists.

based on arrests. Arrest information does not measure the *frequency* of crime, for it misses all unreported crimes as well as those reported crimes for which police are either unwilling or unable to make arrests. That teenagers are particularly likely to be arrested for arson may indicate not a greater likelihood of committing arson, but a lack of adult skills needed to get away with it.

**Race and Social Class**  The inadequacy of official statistics is particularly apparent when we try to estimate racial and social class differences in criminal behavior. Nonwhites made up 14 percent of the U.S. population in 1982, but they accounted for 30 percent of all arrests (U.S. Census Bureau, 1983c). The criminologists Wolfgang, Figlio, and Sellin (1972) kept track of almost 10,000 boys throughout adolescence and found that lower-class boys were twice as likely to be arrested as middle- and upper-class boys.

Do the findings in the preceding paragraph indicate that nonwhites and the poor are more likely to commit crimes or that they are simply more likely to be singled out by police? Many studies that rely on private interviews suggest that official crime records are biased against nonwhites and people from the lower class. Hindelang (1978) reviewed studies based on reports from victims and concluded that whites and nonwhites have very similar overall rates of criminal behavior; and another review of 35 studies of crime and social class concluded that social class has no effect on the likelihood of committing criminal acts (Tittle, Villemez, and Smith, 1978). Although nonwhites living in inner cities are more likely to commit theft and violent crimes, the overall criminal tendencies of youths at all socioeconomic levels are strikingly similar (Elliott and Ageton, 1980; R. Johnson, 1980).

The criminal acts of middle- and upper-class adults are more likely to go unrecorded because they tend to be **white-collar crimes,** crimes that people are able to commit because of the social statuses—usually occupations—that they occupy (Mars, 1983; Reiss and Biderman, 1980; Sutherland, 1949, 1983). Now that computers are used so heavily in a variety of businesses, for example, employees have new opportunities to steal from companies. One computer operator with access to company payroll records modified the computer program so that each employee's paycheck was rounded down to the nearest ten cents, with each small reduction transferred to the thief's own paycheck. With 3,500 employees this amounted to an additional $300 a week for the computer operator, whose real salary was only $120 (*New York Times*, January 29, 1984).

Much white-collar crime—such as the theft of office supplies by employees—costs businesses millions of dollars each year and yet is rarely defined or punished as criminal behavior.

White-collar crimes may be committed by individuals, as in the previous example, or by groups (corporate crimes such as price-fixing). Factories that violate worker safety laws may cause the severe injury or death of employees. Companies that fix prices, violate patent and copyright laws, engage in fraud, or evade taxes cause three times more economic loss than do thieves and vandals (President's Commission on Law Enforcement, 1967). Although such acts violate laws, they often go undetected; and, even when they are discovered, they are rarely considered true "crimes."

If, for example, an executive criminally mismanages company funds, higher officials may fear that stockholders will lose confidence in their investment if they find out. Thus, they may deal with the executive's crime privately, requesting a quiet resignation in return for protection from the police. This is precisely what Richard Nixon and his aides did during the Watergate scandal: they tried to cover up illegal acts for fear that exposure would destroy Nixon's presidency (which it eventually did).

Even when companies are found guilty of criminal acts, the white-collar criminals involved are often not prosecuted; rather, the company itself suffers punishment (usually a fine) and individual criminal behavior goes unrecorded. Douglas and Waksler (1982) suggested that social ambivalence toward white-collar criminals reflects a deep underlying value conflict. On the one hand, we value honesty; but on the other hand, we also value "making the best deal" and "looking out for Number 1." W. C. Fields was not speaking only for himself when he said, "Never give a sucker an even break."

Because official statistics overlook most white-collar crime, some researchers suggest that middle- and upper-class people may actually be *more* prone to criminal activity than people from lower classes (Reckless, 1973). Tittle and Villemez (1977) interviewed a large sample of adults and found no evidence of greater criminality in lower classes (Table 10-3). In fact, petty theft, gambling, and tax evasion were more commonly reported by upper- and upper-middle-class respondents.

There is, of course, reason to be suspicious of any study that relies on people to report their own criminal behavior. What is important to note here, however, is that these data do not support the common belief that lower-class people are more

**Table 10-3**

Percentage of White Males Admitting Criminal
Behavior during Last Five Years, by Social Class
(United States, 1977)

| | SOCIAL CLASS | | | | |
|---|---|---|---|---|---|
| CRIME | Upper | Upper-middle | Middle | Lower-middle | Lower |
| $5 theft | 19 | 36 | 29 | 31 | 25 |
| $50 theft | 4 | 8 | 10 | 12 | 7 |
| Gambling | 38 | 54 | 50 | 48 | 36 |
| Tax cheating | 16 | 22 | 19 | 13 | 7 |
| Assault | 14 | 17 | 17 | 12 | 13 |
| Marijuana use | 16 | 25 | 19 | 13 | 24 |

Source: Tittle and Villemez, 1977.

**Table 10-4**

Violent Crimes and Property Crimes by Size of
Place, United States, 1970 and 1982
(Rates per year per 100,000 population)

| SIZE OF PLACE | VIOLENT CRIMES | | | PROPERTY CRIMES | | |
|---|---|---|---|---|---|---|
| | 1970 | 1982 | % CHANGE | 1970 | 1982 | % CHANGE |
| Large metropolitan | 458 | 662 | +44 | 4389 | 5660 | +29 |
| Smaller cities | 182 | 332 | +82 | 2727 | 4651 | +71 |
| Rural | 121 | 171 | +41 | 1233 | 1893 | +54 |

Source: U.S. Census Bureau, 1983c.

prone to criminal behavior than everyone else. The debate continues (see, for example, Braithwaite, 1981) and, so long as problems of measurement are as difficult to solve as they appear to be, it may be some time before the longstanding issue of social class and deviance can be resolved.

**Urban, Rural, and In-between**  The likelihood that people will commit crimes depends not only on social statuses such as gender, age, race, and social class, but also on their ecological (or spatial) relation to one another. People who live in large cities, for example, are more likely to commit crimes than those who live in small cities or rural areas (Table 10-4). In some cities the rate of violent crime is extraordinarily high: The overall reported rate of violent crime in 1982 was 691 in large metropolitan areas, but the rate was over 2,000 in Baltimore, New York, and Washington, DC (U.S. Census Bureau, 1983c).

Historically, large cities have experienced more criminal behavior than smaller communities, but as Table 10-4 shows, small cities and rural communities are rapidly catching up. Between 1970 and 1982, for example, violent crime rose by 44 percent in the largest cities, but by 82 percent in small cities. Small cities and rural areas both had higher rates of increase for property crimes.

As we found earlier with age and social class, the effect that the size of a community has on crime rates depends on the type of crime. Reported rates of violent crime, for example, are 99 percent higher in large cities than in smaller ones, but the difference in property crime rates is only 22 percent. The answer to the question "Who are the criminals?" depends, then, on which crimes are involved. Among adults, reported violent crimes and thefts involving the use of force are more common in urban areas and among their impoverished residents, whereas white-collar crimes are more common in the middle and upper classes. Among adolescents, juvenile delinquency is no more common among nonwhites and the poor than among whites and the more affluent, although poor nonwhites are more likely to be arrested and prosecuted.

The fact that crime is a social interaction involving both criminals and their victims brings us to a second question: What social characteristics distinguish victims from nonvictims?

## Who Are the Victims?

Just as social statuses influence the likelihood of committing criminal acts, they also affect the likelihood of being victimized, and this also depends on the type of crime involved. Table 10-5, for example, shows that for all major crime categories, men are more likely than women to be victimized. In the case of sexual violence, however, almost all victims are women (U.S. Census Bureau, 1983c).

We can also see in Table 10-5 that nonwhites are more likely than whites to be victimized by murder, robbery, and assault. The murder of black men is astoundingly frequent, occurring at a rate almost seven times greater than among white men.

The data in Table 10-6 show that victims of all major types of crime are heavily concentrated in the younger age groups. In the case of sexual violence, most victims are young women between the ages of 16 and 24 (U.S. Department of Justice, 1983).

The effect of social class on criminal victimization also depends on the type of crime. Lower-income people are more likely to be victims of violence (U.S. Department of Justice, 1983) and burglary (see Table 10-7). Higher-income people,

**Table 10-5**

Who Are the Victims? Violence and Theft by Victim's Gender and Race, United States, 1980 (Rates per year per 100,000 Population)

| VICTIM'S RACE AND GENDER | TYPE OF CRIME | | |
| --- | --- | --- | --- |
| | Murder | Robbery | Assault |
| White males | 10 | 800 | 1300 |
| White females | 3 | 400 | 500 |
| Nonwhite males | 65 | 2000 | 1800 |
| Nonwhite females | 14 | 900 | 700 |

Source: U.S. Census Bureau, 1982.

**Table 10-6**

Who Are the Victims? Violence and Theft by Victim's Age, United States, 1981 (Rates per year per 1,000 Population)

| VICTIM'S AGE | TYPE OF CRIME | |
| --- | --- | --- |
| | All Violent Crimes | Theft |
| 12–15 | 59 | 128 |
| 16–19 | 68 | 132 |
| 20–24 | 68 | 133 |
| 25–34 | 44 | 101 |
| 35–49 | 23 | 78 |
| 50–64 | 13 | 51 |
| 65+ | 8 | 22 |

Source: U.S. Department of Justice, 1983.

**Table 10-7**

Victims of Theft, by Income, United States, 1981
(Rates per year per 1,000 Households)

| HOUSEHOLD INCOME | TYPE OF CRIME | |
|---|---|---|
| | Burglary[1] | Larceny[2] |
| Less than $3,000 | 132 | 118 |
| $3,000 to $7,499 | 99 | 120 |
| $7,500 to $9,999 | 89 | 121 |
| $10,000 to $14,999 | 87 | 123 |
| $15,000 to $24,999 | 80 | 129 |
| $25,000 or More | 83 | 123 |

Source: U.S. Department of Justice, 1983.

[1]Burglary is unlawful entry in order to commit a crime.
[2]Larceny is stealing without illegal entry into a dwelling, force, violence, or fraud (e.g., shoplifting, pocket-picking, and auto theft).

## Structures of Crime

The simplest element of crime's social structure is the number of people involved, ranging from lone individuals to large groups. Crimes may be committed by a small adolescent street gang, a crime syndicate that includes hundreds of members, or a major corporation. In the same way, victims may be either groups or individuals. Social relationships among criminals also vary in their complexity, from the simplicity of a pair of bank robbers to the bureaucratic complexity of organized crime. We need, then, to take a closer look at two kinds of social relationships—those among criminals and those between criminals and their victims—in order to describe crime as social behavior.

**Relationships among Criminals**  Although violent crimes tend to have simple structures involving single offenders, crimes such as theft, prostitution, and drug smuggling involve more complex relationships among criminals (Miller, 1978). Thieves, for example, rely on "fences" to buy what they steal, and fences, in turn, rely on people who are willing to buy stolen property (which is itself a crime). A fence may sell a truckload of stolen stereos to legitimate dealers who then sell them to an unsuspecting public. Thus, a simple act of theft often involves a variety of people playing different roles.

Just as industrialization made business, government, and education more bureaucratic, it also changed the organization of crime. **Syndicated crime** is highly bureaucratic, with rigid authority structures controlling complex divisions of labor among criminals (Abadinsky, 1983; Block and Chambliss, 1981; Cressey, 1969). The smuggling and distribution of illegal drugs such as heroin and cocaine, for example, require large amounts of cash and precise coordination among overseas buyers, smugglers, and distributors, from the wholesaler to the lowliest pusher.

Syndicated crime may be organized in a variety of ways, from a rigid military model of bureaucratic efficiency complete with salaried employees, to a tight-knit "family business." In some cases, syndicates operate as franchises (like fast-food chains), providing capital and expertise to local operators who then share their profits with the "parent company" (Anderson, 1979; Ianni, 1972).

on the other hand, are slightly more likely to suffer larceny (theft that does not involve breaking and entering or the use of force).

The most important thing these findings tell us about crime is that as far as *non-white-collar* crime is concerned, the social statuses most likely to produce criminals are also those most likely to produce victims. For many types of crime, people who are young, nonwhite, poor, or city dwellers are more likely to be involved in crime either as offenders or as victims than are those who are older, white, with higher income, or living in smaller communities. Thus, both criminals and their victims tend to occupy some social statuses more than others and to occupy similar social statuses.

As we will see later in this chapter, the social characteristics of criminals and victims provide a basis for sociological explanations of criminal behavior. Before considering the causes of deviance, however, we must first examine criminal activity as a structured set of social relationships among criminals and between criminals and their victims.

Thus, the social structures of crime and those of legitimate business are often quite similar.

**Criminals and Victims** Crime involves social interaction in which criminals victimize groups or individuals (Table 10-8). Most violent crimes involve individuals who know each other: a majority of murders, sexual and other assaults involve family members or acquaintances (U.S. Department of Justice, 1980a). White-collar crimes (such as evading taxes or dumping hazardous chemicals in water supplies), however, tend to victimize groups, as do crimes that systematically victimize people on the basis of social characteristics such as race, ethnicity, age, or gender (illegal job discrimination or sexual harassment, for example).

In some cases, the distinction between individual and group victims is unclear, for if a black man is lynched by the Ku Klux Klan as an example to blacks in general, the effects ripple beyond the immediate victim to all who share his racial status. Brownmiller (1975) made a similar point about sexual assault: the fact that some women are assaulted encourages all women to fear men.

**Victimless Crime** Although most crimes involve an individual or group as victim, in **victimless crimes** there either is no victim or the criminal and the victim are one and the same. Most states define prostitution, some types of gambling, homosexual acts, and the use of certain drugs as illegal, but who are the victims? If one argues that drug addiction victimizes the abuser, this means society punishes those who victimize themselves.

Schur (1965) and others argue that norms defining victimless crime exist not to protect individuals from victimization, but to use laws to prohibit behavior that is culturally defined as immoral. Because victimless crimes involve voluntary interactions, laws that prohibit them are difficult to enforce, for legal authorities are the only complainants.

The connection between victimless crime and morality helps explain why the response to such crimes is so severe even though individuals are not victimized. A society's mores reflect deeply held ideas about right and wrong and are an important part of the boundaries that define membership. In the case of prostitution, for example, society itself is defined as the victim, and the punishment does more to maintain clear social boundaries than to protect individuals.

By definition crimes violate laws, and unlike other norms, laws are enforced by specialists who are responsible for arresting, prosecuting, and punishing criminals.

## Table 10-8

Individuals and Groups as Criminals and Victims

| CRIMINAL | VICTIM | |
| --- | --- | --- |
| | Individual | Group |
| Individual | Assault<br>Mugging<br>Auto theft<br>Sexual assault | Treason<br>Tax evasion<br>Bank robbery<br>Embezzlement |
| Group | Gang burglarizes a home<br>Mob collects "protection money" from merchant<br>Ku Klux Klan lynches a black man | Job discrimination<br>Mob bribes government officials<br>Nazi group bombs Jewish synagogue |

The use of illegal drugs such as cocaine is a crime whose primary victim is society itself.

## Structures of Justice and Injustice

Police, courts, and prisons constitute a **criminal justice system,** which carries out three basic social processes: identifying and arresting criminals, determining guilt and innocence, and deciding how to treat those who are convicted. How do culture and social structure affect who is arrested, prosecuted, and convicted? How effectively does the criminal justice system control crime?

**Arrest**  Arrest is a social process through which individuals enter the criminal justice system, and like all interactions, it is affected by culture and social structure. Police face the impossible task of enforcing thousands of laws, and therefore have considerable discretion in deciding when to arrest someone. Police responses to criminal behavior depend on cultural definitions of situations and the social statuses of those involved.

American culture defines wife beating as a "family matter," not a crime, so police are reluctant to arrest men who abuse their wives, and usually persuade the victim not to press criminal charges (Flynn, 1977). Enforcement agencies tend to ignore white-collar crime because our culture defines it as a less serious offense. In 1978 the U.S. Justice Department allocated only 5 percent of its budget to fighting white-collar crime, although such crimes result in annual losses of billions of dollars (Conyers, 1979; United Press International, 1978).

Participant observation studies of police reveal considerable racial prejudice, but also suggest that the high rate of black arrests is not due simply to race. Rather, police are more likely to arrest those who are disrespectful or—as members of the lower class—objects of stereotypes that include shiftlessness, irresponsibility, and criminal tendencies (Piliavin and Briar, 1964). Donald Black (1971) suggested that racial prejudice among police officers leads blacks to assume they will be treated unfairly, and therefore approach police with defiance and hostility. Whatever the effect on their behavior toward police, blacks are far more likely than whites to perceive the police and courts as being unfair (Hagan and Abonnetti, 1982).

Although the evidence on racial discrimination is mixed, it is clear that poor people are frequently singled out for arrest. Chambliss (1973) studied the Saints and the Roughnecks—two gangs in the same town—and found that Saints committed more criminal acts than Roughnecks, caused more property damage, and often endangered other people's lives with their stunts and practical jokes. The Saints, however, were never arrested during Chambliss' two-year study, whereas the Roughnecks regularly found themselves in trouble with the law. Why? The Saints belonged to middle-class families, drove new cars, spoke politely to teachers, police, and others in positions of authority, and had parents whom the police knew might cause trouble if their children were arrested. Most residents looked upon the Saints as no more than a group of "good boys" who were having a good time. The Roughnecks, on the other hand, were from the lower class and were assumed by residents to be "bad characters."

University students often escape prosecution for minor crimes on the grounds that it would ruin their career chances (in some cases, as future lawyers). Middle- and upper-class parents have resources to shield their children (and themselves) from arrest—resources that are unavailable to poor people. They are more aware of their legal rights, and their relatively high prestige gives them credibility when they guarantee their children's future good behavior (Mitford, 1973).

Thus, police officers' perceptions influence their decisions to arrest individuals, and such perceptions are affected by cultural beliefs attached to social statuses. Most evidence shows that the social statuses of defendants continue to influence the criminal justice system after arrests are made.

**Prosecution**  From the moment of arrest, legal procedures discriminate against the poor (Forer, 1984). Middle- and upper-class defendants can afford to hire their own lawyers rather than depend on overworked public defenders. Poor people are also more likely to stay in jail while awaiting trial, for the bail system allows the wealthy to buy their freedom (even though under the law the rich and the poor are equally presumed to be innocent until proven guilty) (Foote, 1965; National Conference on Bail and Criminal Justice, 1964).

Trial verdicts may depend more on stereotypes about defendants and victims than on factual evidence. Under the law, for example, the only issues in a rape trial are the fact of sexual contact and whether or not the victim consented at the moment the act took place. Americans, however, often blame the victim and treat her as if she were the actual defendant (Holmstrom and Burgess, 1983; Medea and Thompson, 1974).

Judges are obliged to decide cases on strict legal grounds, but juries are allowed to take extra-legal factors into account, including stereotypes about women. Even when victims have been brutally beaten, their attackers may go free if the woman appears to be of "poor character" (typically, unmarried and sexually active). Juries often believe that such women "ask for it" and "deserve what they get." In so doing, they ignore the fact that a crime took place.

Defendants have the right to choose to be tried by a jury or by a judge alone, and Kalven and Zeisel's classic study, *The American Jury* (1966), shows why accused rapists prefer jury trials. Kalven and Zeisel examined 106 jury trials for aggravated rape (with physical evidence of brutality) and "simple" rape (when the victim was threatened with a weapon, for example, but not visibly beaten), and compared jury verdicts with those favored by the judge. In aggravated rape cases in which judges favored conviction on the basis of the evidence, juries acquitted defendants 14 percent of the time; but in "simple" rape cases in which judges favored conviction, *juries found defendants "not guilty" 95 percent of the time.*

In cases of "simple" rape, therefore, juries often ignore legal evidence, and judge the victim rather than the defendant. Judges favored conviction 52 percent of the time, whereas juries found defendants guilty in only 7 percent of such cases. By choosing a jury trial in which stereotypes about women can overshadow the facts of the crime, defendants are seven times more likely to go free.

**Punishment** Once convicted, a defendant's statuses significantly affect the sentencing process. White-collar criminals usually receive lower sentences than other criminals (Seymour, 1973). In the aftermath of the Watergate scandal, Vice President Spiro Agnew pleaded "no contest" to a charge of tax evasion (for which he was only fined) in exchange for immunity on more serious charges of bribery and extortion (from the proceeds of which he illegally paid no taxes).

In comparison with whites, black juvenile delinquents are more likely to be prosecuted and to be committed to juvenile homes at younger ages, for less-serious crimes, and with less-damaging criminal records (Axelrad, 1952; Wilson, 1968). Nonwhite adults typically receive stiffer sentences than whites who commit the same crime (Derrick Bell, 1973), especially if the victim is white (LaFree, 1980). Black men are far more likely than whites to receive death sentences, especially when convicted of raping white women. Sociological documentation of such unequal treatment in fact formed the basis for the Supreme Court's 1968 decision to ban the death penalty (Wolfgang and Reidel, 1973).

Judges have great power to decide the severity of punishment, and an ingenious experiment illustrates the effects of a defendant's race on how judges use that power. Jackson (1974) gave descriptions of a typical case to 36 judges and asked them to decide on an appropriate sentence:

> "Joe Cut," 27, pleads guilty to battery. He slashed his wife on the arms with a switchblade. His record showed convictions for disturbing the peace, drunkenness, and hit-and-run driving. He told a probation officer that he acted in self-defense after his wife attacked him with a broom handle. The prosecutor recommended not more than five days in jail or a $100 fine.

Unknown to the judges, Jackson varied one detail in the descriptions: to half of the judges, the defendants were described as white; to the other half, they were described as black. White defendants received sentences ranging from three to ten days, compared with five to thirty days for blacks.

Criminologists have long maintained that the severity of punishment depends on the defendant's race and social class (Chambliss, 1969; Thornberry, 1973); but more recent evidence suggests that this kind of discrimination may have declined substantially in the last decade (Chiricos and Waldo, 1975; Hagan and Bumiller, 1983; Willick, Gehlker, and Watts, 1975).

Sentences *do* depend on the culturally defined severity of the crime, however, and here there is a clear bias in favor of white-collar criminals. Newfield (1974), for example, cited a 1973 case in which a nursing home director swindled 2 million dollars from stockholders. Although the law allowed a maximum prison sentence of five years, the defendant was sentenced to one year and was eligible for parole after only four months. The next day the same judge sentenced a Puerto Rican youth to five years in prison for stealing a car valued at no more than $100.

Sentencing is only a part of the criminal justice process. There is little convincing evidence that criminal behavior is more likely among nonwhites and poor people than among whites and the middle and upper classes, and yet the American prison population is overwhelmingly black and poor. Taken as a whole, the social processes of arrest, prosecution, and sentencing clearly discriminate against people in these categories.

**Does the System Work?** Criminal justice systems are organized around a variety of values that define their goals (Cohen and Short, 1976). The most important of these are prevention, deterrence, and the infliction of punishment. How effectively does our criminal justice system achieve its goals, and how is its effectiveness related to its social characteristics?

Criminal justice systems combat crime by increasing the size of police forces and, therefore, the ability to observe criminal acts; by imprisoning and thereby isolating criminals from potential victims; by imposing harsh penalties; and by attempting to alter the personalities of people who commit crimes. The evidence is clear that none of these methods has been very effective.

Between 1960 and 1977, per capita expenditures for police protection in the United States more than doubled (after adjusting for inflation); but in the same period, the rate of reported violent crime tripled and the rate of property crime almost tripled (U.S. Census Bureau, 1980b). Thus, a doubled investment in crime prevention did not cut crime rates in half; instead, all types of crime far outran police efforts to prevent it. (It is of course possible that crime rates would have increased even more if police expenditures had not increased.)

Most people who commit crimes are never caught, much less imprisoned. In 1980 the Justice Department's victim survey conservatively estimated a total of 45 million criminal acts (which do not include the vast majority of white-collar crimes). Of these, only 30 percent were reported to police and only 6 percent resulted in an arrest (U.S. Census Bureau, 1982). Thus, more than 90

percent of criminal offenses never result in an arrest, much less in prosecution, conviction, and punishment (Table 10-9).

Since the vast majority of criminals are never caught and convicted, the threat of punishment is too low to effectively discourage criminal behavior. In 1984, 81 percent of American adults believed that courts do not treat criminals harshly enough (J. Davis, 1984), but dozens of studies show that long prison sentences are no more effective than short ones in preventing crime (Babst et al., 1976).

What does make a difference is the *certainty* of punishment (Chapman, 1976; Silverman, 1976; Tullock, 1974). In the United States over 90 percent of kidnappers are caught, convicted, and severely punished, and as a result, kidnapping is quite rare (*New York Times Magazine*, 1976). When public perception of the certainty of punishment for drunken driving increases, the incidence of drunken driving tends to decline (see Ross, 1984). In Norway if automobile drivers are discovered with the slightest odor of alcohol on their breath, they face certain jail sentences. Drunken driving is, therefore, rare in Norway: when cou-

---

**Table 10-9**

Arrest and Prosecution for Personal Crimes of Violence and Theft, United States, 1980[1]

**TOTAL CRIMES[1]** 45,000,000

| Of All Crimes, Those Resulting in: | Number | Percentage |
|---|---|---|
| Reports to Police | 13,290,000 | 30 |
| Arrests | 2,844,000 | 6 |
| Prosecutions | 1,250,800 | 3 |
| Convictions | 913,000 | 2 |
| Imprisonment | 419,980 | 1 |

Sources: Federal Bureau of Investigation, 1976; U.S. Census Bureau, 1976, 1980b.

[1] Ignores most white-collar crime.

ples go to parties, for example, if one drinks, the partner does not.

Finally, efforts to rehabilitate criminals by altering their personalities through therapy or by providing them with occupational skills have had, at best, mixed results (Lipton, Martinson, and Wilks, 1975; Martinson, 1974). A sociological point of view suggests several reasons for this failure.

Prison is what Goffman (1961a) called a **total institution**—in which inmates' lives are almost completely controlled by others. They are isolated from society, deprived of meaningful work and heterosexual contact, and can make few decisions for themselves. On entering prison, inmates experience **degradation ceremonies** (Garfinkel, 1956),

in which they are stripped, searched, and labeled as inferior human beings. The physical and social organization of prisons is designed primarily to prevent escape, a goal that has little effect on crime rates since, as we have seen, few criminals are ever imprisoned. With prison inmates learning to adapt to and function in a social environment whose culture and structure bear little resemblance to the outside world (Sykes, 1958), it should come as no surprise that 74 percent of inmates are arrested for new crimes within four years of their release (Federal Bureau of Investigation, 1976).

A second reason for the failure of the American criminal justice system lies in its assumptions about the *causes* of deviant behavior. In particular,

In prisons and other total institutions, degradation ceremonies are an important part of the socialization process.

it rests on three questionable assumptions: (1) people conform primarily because they fear punishment; (2) people commit crimes because they do not fear punishment enough; and, most important, (3) the causes of deviance rest in individuals.

Fear of punishment has relatively little effect on behavior; and the choices people make (including the choice to commit a deviant act) are profoundly affected by cultural ideas and the structures of social relationships. The criminal justice system, however, responds to deviance *as though criminal behavior had little to do with the pressures and limitations imposed by social environments.*

All of this points strongly to the importance of sociological explanations of deviant behavior. How do cultural ideas and the structures of human relationships increase the chances that people will commit crimes?

## What Causes Deviance?

Researchers have tried for many years to identify biological and psychological causes of deviant behavior. Lombroso (1911), for example, examined criminals and concluded that crime results from "animalistic body types"; but Goring (1913) later discovered that the physical appearance of criminals differs little from that of noncriminals. Sheldon (1949) found that delinquents tend to have sturdy, muscular bodies, and suggested that this fact increased the likelihood of aggressive behavior. The problem with such findings is that they ignore the ways in which people's social responses to physical appearances affect behavior (Glueck and Glueck, 1972). Muscular boys, for example, are more likely to be chosen as members of gangs that regularly engage in fighting, but this is a far cry from concluding that muscularity in itself causes deviant behavior.

More recently, Danish researchers discovered that male prisoners are unusually likely to have a genetic disorder. Whereas normal men have an X and a Y chromosome, some males have an additional Y chromosome. The finding that male prisoners are more likely than other men to have this disorder—the extra Y chromosome—suggested that criminality might have a genetic basis. They also found, however, that the extra chromosome is not related to aggressive behavior; rather, it appears to be related to lower intelligence. The XYY

syndrome thus seems to affect the likelihood of being caught by police more than the likelihood of committing a crime (Witkin et al., 1976).

Personality characteristics certainly play a part in deviant behavior, but psychologists have been unable to identify personality types that are consistently related to deviant behavior (Schuessler and Cressey, 1950). Glueck and Glueck (1950) found that delinquents were only slightly more likely than nondelinquents to suffer from emotional disturbances, and mental illness appears to be no more common among prison inmates than among ordinary citizens (Coleman, 1959; Hakeem, 1958).

Social environments affect how we perceive the world, what we think and feel about it, what we want for ourselves, and how we think we can get what we want. Our positions in them affect what other people expect of us and what we expect of them. Sociologically, then, choices between conformity and deviance depend a great deal on the social environments people find themselves in. This does not mean that sociological explanations of deviance relieve individuals of personal responsibility; rather, they help identify social factors that encourage people to make deviant choices. To the extent that society itself fosters deviance, all the individual therapy in the world will only treat the symptoms of deviance, not its causes.

Deviant behavior is an enormously complex puzzle, and researchers in all disciplines are far from identifying all its pieces, and even farther from putting them together. The following sections identify some of the pieces revealed by sociological analysis and research.

## Deviance and Culture

In the simplest sense, culture contributes to deviance merely by defining some behaviors as deviant. Social boundaries guarantee that some people will be excluded on the basis of their behavior, for a boundary that includes everyone and excludes no one is, by definition, not a boundary at all. Without boundaries, members can have no solid sense of an "us" in relation to a "them." Thus, as Durkheim (1895) asserted, deviance is an inevitable consequence of social life, for societies use categories of deviant behavior to draw their boundaries and maintain social cohesion (Erikson, 1966).

The United States, for example, could reduce the annual number of arrests by more than 2 million if the law no longer defined public drunkenness, drug use, liquor sales to minors, prostitution, gambling, and vagrancy as crimes (U.S. Census Bureau, 1983c). When drugs such as heroin and cocaine are outlawed, their price skyrockets because they can be obtained only at great risk. This forces addicts to find great sums of money, and for most of them crime is the only way to do it. Many suggest that the criminal justice system would in fact be far more effective if certain behaviors, especially victimless crimes, were no longer defined as crimes (Schur, 1965).

Since some deviance is inevitable in all societies, however, we are confronted with the problem of explaining why some people deviate from norms and others do not. Two sociological theories help explain the role of culture in promoting deviant behavior.

**Deviance and Anomie** According to the first of these theories, we tend to conform to norms only insofar as we identify ourselves as members of society and feel an attachment to its values. Norms regulate social relationships, and if we feel cut off and isolated from groups, the norms of these groups will have little influence over our behavior. In a related sense, if we live in a society in which there is wide disagreement and confusion about which behaviors are acceptable, we lack clear guidelines for our behavior and are more likely to create new ones.

Durkheim (1897) believed that human desires have no natural limits, and that if it were not for the pressure of norms and values, societies would be unable to control violence and other destructive behavior. When norms break down and people no longer feel a solid connection between themselves and society, the result is what Durkheim called **anomie.** During electrical blackouts in large cities, for example, people often feel that "anything goes," and commit acts they would never consider in less chaotic conditions.

Even in relatively stable societies, the weak ties to values and norms that characterize anomie are often common. In 1976, for example, 26 percent of American adults agreed that "To make money, there are no right and wrong ways anymore, only easy ways and hard ways," and 40 percent agreed that they "sometimes can't help wondering whether anything is worthwhile anymore" (J. Davis, 1980).

As Durkheim (1897) noted in his study of suicide, anomie is a dangerous social condition, for it "deceives us into believing that we depend on ourselves only." In the same 1976 survey cited above, 59 percent of American adults expressed the belief that "Most people don't really care what happens to the next fellow," and 75 percent agreed that "These days a person doesn't really know whom he can count on" (J. Davis, 1982).

As Hirschi (1969) found in his comparisons of delinquents and nondelinquents, feelings of isolation are associated with deviant behavior. Typical delinquents are weakly attached to friends and family, and lack the close relationships, values, and beliefs that motivate most people to obey the law. Wiatrowski, Griswold, and Roberts (1981) supported Hirschi's findings and emphasize the particularly strong effects of adolescents' attachments to parents and school as inhibitors of delinquent behavior.

The characteristics of individuals are thus often less important than the cultural *bonds* that tie individuals together. In her study of elderly Americans, Blau (1973) found that when older people lose important roles either through retirement or the death of a spouse, they often protect themselves from the pain of the present by retreating into daydreams and nostalgia. This defense leads them to lose interest in social activities, isolating them from human contact and support.

In some cases, groups feel so weak a connection to society that they deviate by retreating, creating their own communities with deviant subcultures that define their goals and means for achieving them. In 1875, for example, a religious group called the Hutterites rejected the capitalist, competitive way of life, and forbade marriage between their members and outsiders. Early in the same century, another religious group—called the Oneida Community—rejected American ideas of marriage, the family, and private property. Sexual relations were unrestricted, and children were raised not by parents, but by the entire community of adults. In more recent years, there have been numerous attempts in the United States to form "communes" that represent a rejection of values and norms that dominate our culture (Kephart, 1976; Zablocki, 1980).

Thus, culture creates deviance by defining deviant behavior itself, and when values and norms are not strong enough to maintain substantial conformity, new ones emerge that may be defined as deviant by those who dominate society.

**Deviance as Conformity** A second cultural perspective on deviance raises the paradoxical idea that deviance often represents conformity. Even when there is general agreement about which behaviors are deviant and how serious each is, the larger and more complex a group or society is, the more likely subgroups are to form, and their subcultures may include norms, values, attitudes, and beliefs that conflict with those of the surrounding society (Newman, 1976; Newman and Trilling, 1975).

American culture, for example, defines drug use, vandalism, theft, and teenage drinking and sex as deviant behaviors; but adolescents form friendship groups that serve as powerful reference groups that may support such behavior. Not yet recognized as adults with important roles to play, adolescents must find other ways to feel rooted in society, and when they turn to peer groups to satisfy their desire to "belong," they encounter strong pressures to conform to adolescent subcultures.

In defiance of an adult society that refuses to grant them full membership, adolescent subcultures often include norms that require *noncon*formity to norms and values in the surrounding culture (Coleman, 1961; Douvan and Adelson, 1966). Adolescents who refuse sex, drugs, and alcohol often find themselves treated as deviants by their peers, excluded from group activities and ridiculed.

Thus, although many adolescent behaviors are deviant in the eyes of society, they represent conformity to the norms of important reference groups. Society defines car theft as criminal devi-

ance, but a street gang's subculture may define it as conformity—that is, as obeying a norm. Reporting crime to the police conforms to legal norms, but criminal subcultures define it as seriously deviant ("ratting," "snitching," and "finking"). For this reason, gang members who act as police informants occupy an insecure position between two cultures and may find themselves in a no-man's-land in which neither group is willing to support or protect them.

The pressures to conform in small groups are often rooted in larger subcultures. Miller (1958), for example, spent three years observing lower-class gangs of adolescent boys, and concluded that the high value they place on toughness (being brave, daring, and physically strong), autonomy ("No one tells me what to do"), smartness (ability to "con" others), excitement (risk and danger), and fate (luck), reflected not the deviant subculture of the gang itself, but elements of lower-class culture as a whole.

Miller did not suggest that lower-class subculture values criminal behavior; rather he suggested that values prevalent in that subculture increase the likelihood of behaviors defined as deviant by middle- and upper-class authorities. We should also note that the lower class has no monopoly on values such as "toughness" and "machismo." In comparison with men in Northern European countries, for example, American men in general place a high value on such characteristics (Block, 1973). Many American presidents have been strongly motivated by the desire to maintain a "tough" and "manly" image (Halberstam, 1972).

From this perspective, deviant behaviors are often *learned* through socialization. Toughness and defiance are learned through the same process as politeness and respect for the law. Prostitutes learn their craft just as plumbers, lawyers, and accountants learn theirs (Heyl, 1977). Why, however, are some people socialized into deviance, but others are not?

According to Sutherland's theory of **differential association,** complex societies offer many beliefs, values, and attitudes, including both respect and disrespect for the law (Matsueda, 1982; Sutherland and Cressey, 1978). Which ideas we adopt depends on the intensity of our exposure to competing alternatives. If we grow up associating pri-

The value placed on masculine toughness is not restricted to the lower class.

marily with professional thieves who define burglary as acceptable behavior, we are more likely to accept it as a legitimate activity. In the same way, if our parents regard income tax evasion as acceptable, we are likely to evade taxes ourselves, *unless we experience more intense exposure to alternative values and beliefs.*

Thus, complex societies contribute to deviance by fostering the formation of subcultures whose values, beliefs, norms, and attitudes may conflict with the surrounding culture. Complex cultures also contain a variety of conflicting values, beliefs, and attitudes; and differences in exposure to competing alternatives during socialization produce a variety of definitions of acceptable behavior.

Although cultural explanations reveal that deviant behaviors are often learned and transmitted from one generation to the next, they do not explain where such patterns come from in the first place. Why would anyone choose crime as an occupation? Why do some groups require their members to conform to norms and values that society defines as deviant? A sociological response to such questions depends on a second major concept in the sociological perspective—social structure.

## Deviance and Social Structure

If we focus on how social statuses and roles limit people's choices, three theories help explain deviant behavior from a structural perspective. First, people may violate norms from a sense of *duty*— because they believe that the legitimate demands of their roles require them to do so. Second, societies often create deviant roles by *labeling* people as deviants and expecting them to violate norms. Third, people often find themselves in social situations in which they can achieve legitimate goals only by violating norms—in other words, situations in which legitimate means will not work. The following section discusses each of these theories in turn.

**Deviance as Duty**  According to the Uniform Code of Military Justice, American soldiers are required to obey the orders of their superiors; during wartime, the penalty for disobedience is death. This raises a serious dilemma: What happens when a commanding officer orders troops to commit illegal acts?

In Vietnam a platoon of American soldiers, demoralized by ambushes and booby traps and frustrated by their inability to strike back at an enemy they could not find, wandered into the village of My Lai (Hersch, 1970). Most of the residents were women, children, and old men, and there was no reason to believe they threatened the Americans in any way. Yet, within minutes, the GI's had killed several Vietnamese, and shortly thereafter both the platoon leader (Lieutenant Calley) and the company commander ordered the soldiers to kill everyone in the village.

By the end of the day, between 450 and 500 civilians had been murdered in spite of their cries and pleas for mercy. They were stabbed, thrown down wells, pushed into ditches and shot, or forced into dwellings and then blown up with grenades.

> One further incident stood out in many GIs' minds: seconds after the shooting stopped, a bloodied but unhurt two-year-old boy miraculously crawled out of the ditch, crying. He began running toward the hamlet. Someone hollered, "There's a kid." There was a long pause. Then Calley ran back, grabbed the child, threw him back in the ditch and shot him. (Hersch, 1970, p. 74)

How could people commit such acts? Although their state of mind—frustration and depression— helps explain their behavior, one thing is clear: had their leaders not ordered them to fire, or had they

---

**PUZZLES:**

## AT WHAT POINT WOULD YOU STOP OBEYING LEGITIMATE ORDERS?

If the president of the United States ordered you to push a button that would execute a stranger for no good reason that you could see, would you do it?

If your answer is "no," pay particular attention to the following discussion of the Milgram experiment, for it suggests that you may not know yourself as well as you think you do.

---

ordered them *not* to fire, the massacre never would have happened.

From a sociological point of view, the soldiers did their duty by obeying orders. As Hersch noted, those who did not like what was happening "kept their thoughts to themselves," for disobeying direct orders during wartime is a serious crime. It seems incredible to most people that anyone would obey such orders, and yet, as Milgram discovered in his classic experiments, most people tend to violate norms when an authority they define as legitimate tells them to.

Milgram (1965) conducted an experiment in which people volunteered to assist in a "learning experiment" at a prestigious university. Each subject, who was paid $4.00 an hour (plus 50¢ carfare) to participate, was told by a man dressed in an official-looking white lab coat that researchers were interested in the effects of punishment on learning.

The subjects stood in a small room equipped with a large electronic panel with a series of 30 buttons, each of which, they were told, delivered increasingly severe shocks to a man strapped to a chair in the next room. The lowest shock level (15 volts) was labeled "SLIGHT SHOCK," the third highest (420 volts) was labeled "DANGER: SEVERE SHOCK," and the last two switches (435 and 450 volts) had the ominous label "XXX." Subjects were told to read a list of words to the "learner" in the next room, and to punish him with shocks when he failed to recite the list correctly.

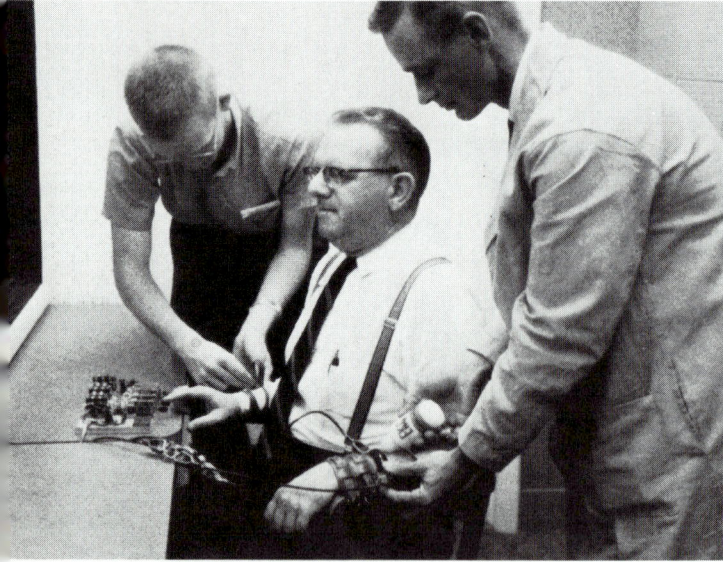
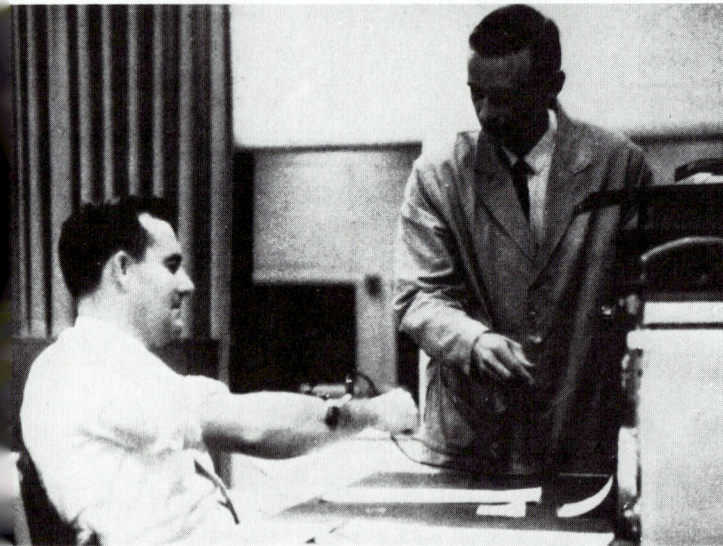

In these pictures from the Milgram experiment, the "learner" is "wired" for electric shocks and the "teacher" is instructed in the use of the control panel.

(In fact, the "learner" worked for Milgram and there were no actual shocks.) A window allowed each "teacher" to see the "learner."

The learner consistently failed, and with each failure, the experimenter told the teacher to increase the shock by 15 volts. At 75 volts, the learner grunted, and by 150 volts, he banged on the walls after each shock and begged to be released. When subjects protested to the experi-

menter, they were told, "The experiment requires you to continue" or "You have no other choice; you must go on." The learner said he had a weak heart, and after a level of 330 volts was reached, he no longer responded at all. How do you think these ordinary citizens behaved? Did they refuse to endanger a person's life in the name of scientific research?

Milgram expected few subjects to deliver what they believed to be dangerous shocks, and a sample of 40 psychiatrists predicted that most subjects would stop at the 150-volt level and that only a rare neurotic individual would deliver the maximum shock (Milgram, 1974). In fact, however, almost *two-thirds* of the subjects were fully obedient and went all the way to the most dangerous shock level. In doing so, they showed a great deal of anxiety—verbally attacking the experimenter, twitching or laughing nervously—but, nonetheless, most did as they were told.

Some argue that Milgram's experiment was unethical, that he did not have the right to manipulate people's beliefs and coerce them into committing what they believed were harmful acts (Baumrind, 1964; Mixon, 1972). In fact, only 2 percent of the subjects expressed regret that they had participated; the rest said they were glad.

Milgram's experiment dramatically illustrates the ability of authorities to force people to violate norms. Thus, when presidents order illegal wiretaps or the assassination of foreign leaders, or when business executives order subordinates to fire an employee without good reason, they are likely to be obeyed by people who define obedience to legitimate authority as part of their role obligations.

In the simplest sense, then, social structure often encourages deviance by giving some people authority over others, thereby giving them the power to demand deviant behavior as a requirement for successful role performance. Deviant behavior is also encouraged, however, when societies label deviance as a social status whose role includes the violation of norms.

**The Power of Labels** When people steal, they are usually punished if discovered; but the social response to deviance often goes beyond mere punishment. In some cases, both the actor *and* the behavior are labeled as deviant: the person who steals is labeled a "thief," or the student who cheats on an exam is labeled a "cheater." In this sense, behaviors such as theft, cheating, or drug use are transformed into social statuses that may become part of people's social identities (Becker, 1964, 1973). According to the **social labeling perspective,** societies often reinforce their boundaries by labeling *people* as deviants as well as their behavior.

Deviant acts that are performed before any labels are applied (such as trying illegal drugs while out with your friends) are called **primary deviance.** People—including those who perform the act—do not consider primary deviance to be deviant, either because they are unaware of the behavior or because they think it is trivial. If you were caught and arrested, however, and referred to and treated as a "junkie" and a criminal, you might find that the deviant label itself fosters further deviant acts—called **secondary deviance** (Lemert, 1951). If people who shun drug use also shun you once the label of junkie is applied, for example, then you are more likely to seek the company of others who are also labeled as junkies; and at this point you might be on your way to a career of deviant behavior and repeated encounters with the police. Secondary deviance, then, may have nothing to do with the original cause of the primary deviance—such as giving in to peer pressure to use drugs. Secondary deviance represents a way of responding to or defending against the labeling and punishment that occur when primary deviance is discovered.

As the case of the Saints and the Roughnecks showed, high school students are often labeled as "troublemakers" or "good students." When a student is labeled a troublemaker, it alters other people's expectations and interpretations of behavior: if teachers catch a "troublemaker" outside of class without a hall pass, they are likely to assume the student is doing something wrong. Finding a "good student" under the same circumstances, however, teachers are more likely to assume the student is there for a good reason, "to joke with him a minute and let him go" (Balch and Kelly, 1974).

Although students who get into trouble may not initially define themselves as deviant people, cultural labels are sticky, and make it difficult for people to resist seeing themselves as others see them. As Hawthorne wrote in *The Scarlet Letter,*

## Voices:
## Labeling, Deviance, and Denial

My name is Kathleen. I have Jellinek's disease. . . .

Jellinek's disease is responsible for:
- 50 percent of all auto fatalities.
- 80 percent of all home violence.
- 30 percent of all suicides.
- 60 percent of all child abuse.
- 65 percent of all drownings.

It is estimated that when a woman contracts the disease, her husband leaves her in 9 out of 10 cases; when a man contracts it, his wife leaves in 1 out of 10 cases. . . .

Jellinek's disease is another name for alcoholism, the most neglected health problem in the United States today. Neglect springs from denial, the hallmark of alcoholism. In other words: if I say that I am not an alcoholic, then I am not an alcoholic and I do not need help. Consequently, it is a fact that only 5 to 10 percent of alcoholics recover. (Not that we can ever drink again, but we can learn to live happily without it.) . . .

One of the major causes for the denial, shame and neglect is the name by which we call it: *alcoholism.* It is replete with negative social and moral implications: skid row; bag ladies; a crazed, drunken father murdering his seven children; a priest stumbling on the altar; red roses for a very blue lady; William Holden cracking his head and dying alone. . . .

As long as we cling to the name alcoholism we relegate the disease to the dark chambers of sin and shame and preclude its righteous acceptance as an illness. The name, likewise, resonates as an ism, an abstract, theoretical entity that deflects from the reality of a disease that can be treated and healed.

Sticks and stones will break my bones and names, indeed, do hurt me.

My name is Kathleen. I have Jellinek's disease.

Source: FitzGerald, *Newsweek,* October 17, 1983.

his novel about a colonial woman labeled an "adulteress" by her community,

> No man, for any considerable period, can wear one face to himself, and another to the multitude, without finally getting bewildered as to which may be the true.

In some cases, a deviant status becomes a **master status**—a status viewed by others as the most important part of a person's status set. Others use cultural stereotypes attached to the deviant master status to form their expectations, interpret the deviant's behavior, and decide how to respond. When former convicts apply for jobs, for example, they often find that their status as "ex-cons" overshadows all others in the eyes of potential employers (Schwartz and Skolnick, 1962).

Thus, former statuses may become the most important part of a person's current status set, a fact that can lead to secondary deviance whether or not stigmatized people actually accept the label as part of their social identities. If the "thief" or "drug addict" label excludes them from jobs, for example, they may then have to steal in order to survive. Whether or not individuals accept the deviant label, secondary deviance is an example of a self-fulfilling prophecy: people are treated in ways that increase the chances that they will violate norms, so they do.

In a dramatic illustration of the power of cultural labels, Rosenhan (1973) planted volunteer "patients" in 12 different mental hospitals. Each reported a single, simple symptom—hearing a voice that said "empty," "hollow," and "thud." All were admitted with diagnoses of schizophrenia, and all *stopped reporting symptoms immediately after being admitted as patients*. They openly made written observations of ward activity, and when asked how they felt, replied that they felt fine and no longer heard voices.

"Despite their public show of 'sanity,' the pseudopatients were never detected" by the hospital staff (although they were detected by many patients). They were hospitalized for an average of 19 days (some as long as 52 days) and all were discharged with diagnoses of "schizophrenia in remission." Once the "mentally ill" label was applied, the staff used it to interpret patients' behavior. Note taking was described as "behavior indicative of psychological disturbance." When a "patient" paced up and down a hospital corridor, a nurse asked, "Are you nervous?" "No. Bored," he replied. When a psychiatrist saw a group of patients sitting outside the lunchroom half an hour before mealtime, he remarked to other staff members that this was a compulsive behavior typical of schizophrenics, ignoring the fact that meals are one of

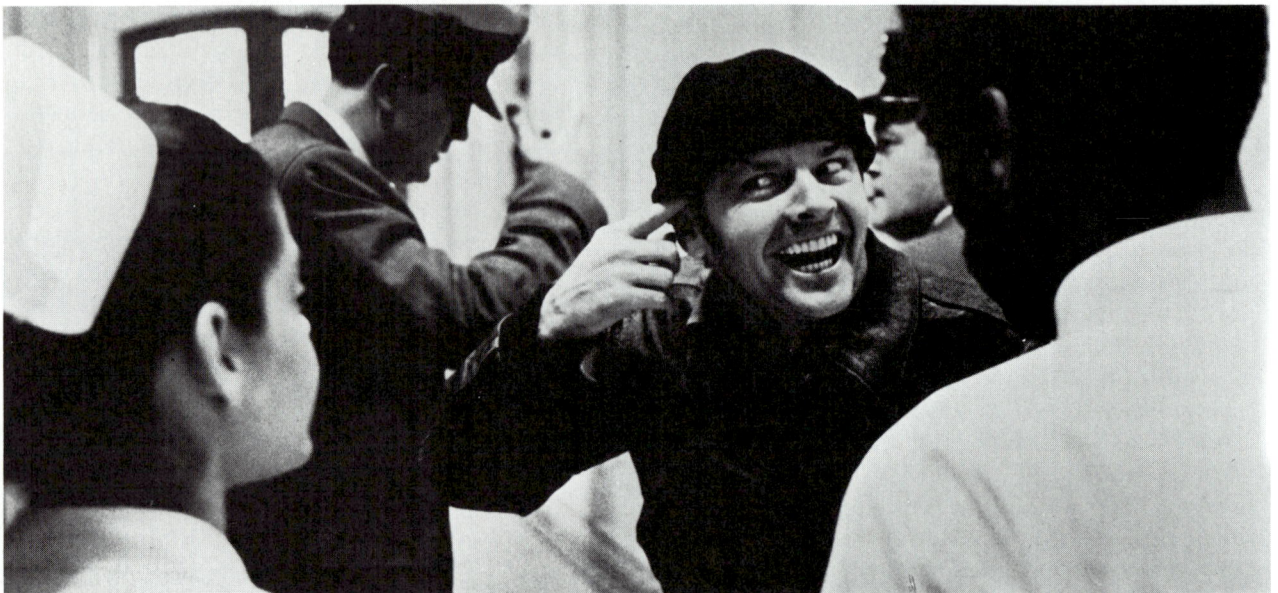

Jack Nicholson, in the movie version of *One Flew Over the Cuckoo's Nest*, portrayed an inmate of a mental institution who heroically resisted the labeling and the consequent dehumanization imposed upon him and the other patients by the staff.

the few events that interrupt the boredom of hospital life.

Rosenhan's study clearly shows the power of labels such as "crazy," "insane," and "schizophrenic":

> Once the impression has been formed that the patient is schizophrenic, the expectation is that he will continue to be schizophrenic. When a sufficient amount of time has passed, during which the patient has done nothing bizarre, he is considered to be in remission and available for discharge. But the label endures beyond discharge. . . . Such labels, conferred by mental health professionals, are as influential on the patient as they are on his relatives and friends, and it should not surprise anyone that the diagnosis acts on all of them as a self-fulfilling prophecy. Eventually, the patient himself accepts the diagnosis, with all of its surplus meanings and expectations, and behaves accordingly. (pp. 253–254)

Some authors use the labeling perspective to argue that "mental illness" is as much a social role that is forced upon certain people as it is an actual illness (Scheff, 1975, 1984). Others note, however, that although such labels have devastating effects on people, they cannot account for the years of serious emotional disturbance that precede most mental-hospital admissions. As Clausen (1976) wrote:

> It is probably true that in the past we launched many acutely disturbed persons on careers of chronic mental illness by keeping them in mental hospitals until every spark of motivation and zest for life had been snuffed out. But mental illness existed long before psychiatry and mental hospitals, and it simply will not do to blame psychosis on labeling. (p. 127)

**When It Pays to Break the Rules** Although labeling often limits people's access to legitimate ways of achieving their goals, such limitations also exist on a broader level. A major characteristic of social structures is the distribution of opportunities to attain wealth, power, and prestige. Roles include values that define goals, but they also include norms that define the appropriate *means* for achieving those goals. From a structural perspective, the likelihood of deviance depends on people's access to legitimate means for achieving their goals, the *adequacy* of legitimate means, and their access to illegitimate means. In other words, people are more likely to commit deviant acts if they cannot achieve their goals in legitimate ways and if they are in a position to achieve them in illegitimate ways.

Earlier in this chapter, we saw how social responses to deviant behavior depend in part on the relationship between deviant acts and cultural values. "Innovators," for example, support cultural values, but reject norms when they use deviant methods to achieve them. This approach helps explain the *causes* of deviance as well as social responses to it.

Merton (1938) expanded Durkheim's concept of anomie to pose a fundamental question about structural causes of deviance: What happens when people share important values but, because of their social statuses, are cut off from socially legitimate ways of achieving them? Many poor people, for example, share the American value of financial success and yet find themselves hopelessly cut off from high-paying jobs. They tend to have few marketable skills, are chronically unemployed, and have poor schooling opportunities. How then are they to share in the "American dream" of prosperity and financial security?

Merton argued that people often conform to norms when they do not *need* to break laws in order to get what they want, and people may violate norms when their positions in social structures leave them no alternative but to change their values and abandon their goals. People who are limited in this way are more likely to find new means to achieve their goals; and these means are often defined as deviant by elites who *do* have access to legitimate means. Cultures that emphasize that everyone can and should succeed ("*Any* citizen can become president of the United States") exert strong pressures on disadvantaged people to commit crimes.

> Given the American stigmatization of manual labor, *which has been found to hold rather uniformly in all social classes,* and the absence of realistic opportunities for advancement beyond this level, the result is a marked tendency toward deviant behavior. (Merton, 1968, p. 199)

In his study of crime rates in large metropolitan areas of the United States, Jacobs (1981) found that levels of property crime—burglary and larceny—tended to be higher in areas in which income inequality was the greatest. Property crime rates were *not* related, however, to the absolute levels of poverty—only to the size of the gap between the rich, the poor, and those in the middle.

Merton's theory is important because it focuses on how a significant aspect of social structures—the **opportunity structure**—distributes legitimate opportunities among the occupants of different social statuses and predicts that deviance is more common when legitimate means for achieving important values are unequally distributed.

Conflict theory also explains deviance as a response to political and economic conditions. Industrial societies—capitalist societies in particular—depend on consumers to buy the products produced by the system, most of them luxuries not necessary for survival. Capitalism also depends on workers who are willing to spend their lives at dull, tedious, unrewarding jobs; and in order to motivate them, capitalists depend on large pools of impoverished people who stand ready to take the jobs of dissatisfied workers ("If you don't like this job, there are plenty of people who will take your place") (Bottomore and Rubel, 1965; Marx, 1867; Marx and Engels, 1846).

08-22-79    12:43:25

In the Abscam case, politicians were offered bribes by FBI agents who then arrested those who accepted. These cases prompted the charge that the FBI was acting improperly by entrapping otherwise innocent people in the name of enforcing the law.

Thus, industrial societies create "both the desire to consume *and*—for a large mass of people—an inability to earn the money necessary to purchase items they have been taught to want" (Chambliss, 1978, p. 192). Many crimes are committed because the opportunity structure limits people's opportunities *without* limiting their goals. Crime is not caused simply by "deviant subcultures" that create and support "criminal personalities" and disrespect for the law. It also depends on values (such as owning luxuries) and the structural distribution of opportunities for achieving them. The conflict perspective also implies that the criminal justice system is not simply the protector of a "moral consensus," for it is also used by privileged classes to control the deviant behavior created by a social environment they control.

It is important to point out here that Merton relies on a functional approach to deviant behavior, identifying how the "normal" operation of societies often creates deviant behavior. That some conflict theorists explain deviance from the same perspective underscores the fact that the functional and conflict points of view are not inherently contradictory, because societies often produce social conflict as part of their normal functioning. Although some sociologists argue that these perspectives are incompatible with each other, they are, in fact, often complementary.

Societies distribute not only legitimate opportunities but illegitimate ones as well (Cloward and Ohlin, 1960). Government officials, for example, occupy social statuses that allow them to do favors for others in exchange for bribes; computer programmers who work for banks are in an ideal position to embezzle funds by altering bank records; police officers who use their discretion in making arrests or responding to calls for help can demand various kinds of "payoffs" ranging from bribes from criminals to free services from local merchants who want to ensure adequate protection. Regardless of individual motives and personalities, social structures themselves create opportunities and temptations that increase the likelihood of certain types of deviant behavior.

Social structure also contributes to deviance when culturally defined ways of achieving goals are *available*, but *inadequate*. The most important cultural goals of police officers, for example, are to prevent crime and apprehend criminals; and, on every level, they are rewarded only when they produce results. A police officer's role also includes norms that define legitimate *means* for controlling crime. American police officers are not allowed to torture prisoners in order to get confessions, to wiretap telephones without a court order, to arrest people without informing them of their rights, or to search people's homes without due cause.

The best efforts of police to control crime, however, have been largely unsuccessful. If you were a police officer, what would you do in the face of repeated failures to achieve the goals that define your job? Many officers believe that their roles limit them so severely that it is impossible for them to control crime. Thus, public pressures on police officers provide strong incentives for them to *break laws in the name of enforcing the law* (Reiss, 1971; Jerome Skolnick, 1975). (As recent news stories make clear, police officers in many societies are not as restrained as they are in the United States. Torture, for example, is widely used by authorities in many countries, including Chile, Argentina, Uruguay, Iran, and the Philippines [*Newsweek*, February 14, 1983].)

Maximizing business profits is a value supported by most Americans; and in pursuit of this goal businessmen may resort to crime by bribing public officials, misrepresenting income to tax collectors, falsely advertising products, or disposing of hazardous wastes in economical but dangerous ways. Many corporations contend that if they obeyed all antipollution laws, they could not survive and many jobs would be lost.

Faced with bankruptcy, some business owners hire arsonists to burn their buildings so that they can collect insurance payments (*Business Week*, May 21, 1979). Similarly, government agencies (the CIA, for example) have been known to illegally wiretap telephones or break into homes or offices in search of information—all in the name of "national security."

Another response to the inadequacy of legitimate means is **ritualism**—which results when people, convinced they cannot achieve their goals, "go through the motions" by conforming to norms without fully supporting the values those norms support (Merton, 1938, 1968). Office workers who see no hope for promotion may simply show up each day and do no more than their roles require of them. College students who believe their grades will be mediocre no matter how hard they work may also "give up" by lowering their aspirations

and working only hard enough to guarantee passing grades. Although ritualism is often not viewed as true deviance (since norms are obeyed), it clearly poses a problem for societies by undermining cultural values and productive activity.

Sociologists thus approach the complex problem of explaining deviant behavior within societies by relating the behavior of individuals to the cultural and structural characteristics of social environments. This perspective helps us understand why some people conform to norms and others deviate from them, but additional questions remain: Why do *rates* of deviant behavior change over time and why is deviance more likely in some societies than in others? Such questions require us to think of culture and social structure in larger terms: How do the characteristics of populations and their ecological relationship to physical environments affect rates of deviant behavior in societies?

## Population, Ecology, and Deviance

As mentioned earlier, young people are particularly likely to commit crimes, and crime rates tend to be higher in large cities. In addition, sociological explanations of deviance suggest that (1) large societies support a variety of subcultures (including those supporting deviance); (2) heterogeneous societies whose members differ widely from one another will be less cohesive and, therefore, more prone to anomie and deviance; and (3) inequality of opportunity encourages crime. Rates of crime thus vary according to population characteristics such as age, urbanization, complexity, diversity, and equality.

Between 1960 and 1982, crime rates in the United States tripled. During this same period, the population became younger (as the percentage of people 14 to 24 years old increased by a third) and 5 percent more urban (U.S. Census Bureau, 1983c). Thus, some of the increase in crime rates may be the result of increasing proportions of the U.S. population concentrated in the high crime statuses of "youth" and "urban resident" (Blumstein and Nagin, 1974; Ferdinand, 1970).

Population characteristics also help explain variations in crime rates among social categories. Because birth rates are higher among blacks than among whites, for example, the black population has a higher percentage of young people (U.S. Census Bureau, 1983c). Blacks are also more likely to be poor and to live in crowded cities. Thus, the distribution of blacks by age, residence, and income contributes to higher rates of deviance. (Remember, however, that these statements do *not* include white-collar crime, most of which is committed by adults and rarely included in official crime statistics.)

Differences in age structures and urbanization also suggest a partial explanation for cross-cultural differences in crime rates. Crime rates in European countries, for example, are generally lower than in the United States. Only one-fifth of the people of Europe live in large cities, compared with more than a third of all Americans (Goldstein and Sly, 1977; U.S. Census Bureau, 1978b). Decades of low birth rates have also made European populations considerably older than the population of the United States.

Durkheim's theory of anomie suggests that deviance is more likely when social cohesion is low, and this implies that large, complex societies with a variety of subcultures will have higher rates of deviance. It also suggests that highly *mobile* societies, in which people frequently move to new communities, will be more vulnerable to deviance because people will have weaker ties to communities and their norms.

International comparisons provide some support for Durkheim's position. The United States, for example, has one of the most heterogeneous and mobile populations in the world, as well as one of the highest known crime rates. More than one-third of the American population changes residence every three years, producing an average of 13 moves in each person's lifetime. In comparison with countries such as Iceland, Sweden, Japan, and Ireland, the American population is far more heterogeneous and mobile (Long and Boertlein, 1976).

Iceland provides a particularly interesting comparison, for its population is homogeneous and stationary (the vast majority of its 230,000 inhabitants are native born and share a common heritage). There is only one jail in the entire country, and it is rarely used (Markham, 1982).

Iceland's low crime rates are not due simply to a small, homogeneous population, however, for Iceland's opportunity structure is far more egalitarian than that of the United States. The Icelandic standard of living is considerably higher than the American, and prosperity is distributed far more evenly among Icelandic citizens. Literacy is universal in Iceland and unemployment is virtually nonexistent. These cultural and social structural differences offer a tentative explanation for Iceland's low rate of crime in comparison with the United States.

It is important to emphasize the *tentative* nature of such explanations: evidence from so few comparisons is not conclusive, and the effects of population and ecology are complex. Japan's population, for example, is more urban than America's, but its crime rates are lower, not higher. Why? One explanation is that the Japanese population is more homogeneous, resulting in stronger bonds between the Japanese, their culture, and its norms. No single factor operates alone to encourage or discourage deviant behavior: the high rate of crime in the United States is produced, in part, by a *combination* of population and ecological factors.

## Social Consequences of Deviance

Most of this chapter has focused on descriptions and explanations of deviant behavior (for a summary, see the box on p. 309). We come now to a final sociological question: What are the consequences of deviance, both for individuals and for societies?

Much deviant behavior exacts enormous costs from individuals, groups, and societies. In the United States in 1982, 21,000 people were murdered and 6 million assaulted—including 78,000 sexual assaults (U.S. Census Bureau, 1983c). In 1984, 41 percent of all Americans reported that they were afraid to walk alone at night within a mile of their homes (J. Davis, 1984).

Crime not only causes suffering and fear, it results in enormous economic losses. Seventeen million people are robbed each year; automobile thefts in New York City alone amount to annual losses exceeding $400 million (Basler, 1982); and, nationally, the profits of syndicated crime amount to tens of billions of dollars a year. Conservative estimates put annual losses from white-collar crimes such as embezzlement and tax evasion at more than $250 million a *day*, and this excludes

# Causes of Deviance:
# A Summary

## Cultural Explanations

*Anomie (**Durkheim**)*
Confusion, disagreement, ambiguity
Weak social ties of individuals or groups
to society

*Deviance as Conformity*
Socialization in subcultures (Miller)
Differential association in complex cultures (Sutherland)

## Social Structural Explanations

*Deviance and role behavior*
When legitimate roles require deviant
behavior
Social creation of "deviant roles"—
labeling (Becker)
"Primary" and "secondary" deviance

*Deviance and culturally defined means for
achieving goals*
Unequal access to legitimate means
(Merton)
Unequal access to illegitimate means
(Cloward and Ohlin)
Inadequacy of legitimate means

## Population and Ecological Explanations

*Age of population*
*Urbanization*
*Diversity of population*
*Size, complexity, and formation of subcultures*
*Mobility and cohesion*
*Equality of distribution of opportunity*

the damage that white-collar crime does to public confidence in those who occupy positions of authority in organizations and institutions (Conyers, 1979; Meier and Short, 1982). Even "victimless" crimes such as alcoholism cause losses of more than $25 billion a year (HEW, 1974).

The costs of deviance are not quite this simple, however, for the line between "victim" and "offender" is often unclear. Criminal behavior results in the disproportionate labeling and punishing of thousands of lower-class, nonwhite people; and thousands of people labeled as "mentally ill" are forcibly committed to mental institutions. Homosexuals are regularly discriminated against in housing and jobs—37 percent of American adults believe homosexuals should be denied teaching jobs in colleges and universities. Almost half would also bar communists and atheists from college faculties (J. Davis, 1984). Thus, deviants themselves are often the victims not only of structural inequalities of wealth, power, and opportunity, but of cultural stereotypes and stigmas as well.

Many people benefit from deviance. The jobs of tens of thousands of people depend on the existence of crime, for without it there would be no need for police officers, criminal lawyers, judges, prison guards, probation officers, locksmiths, and the thousands of people who record and report criminal activity. Thus, although it is in the interests of some of these people to diminish crime (if only to justify keeping their jobs), it is not in their interests to eradicate it completely (Chambliss, 1978).

Furthermore, behaviors that some regard as problems are regarded by others as *solutions* to problems (Merton, 1976a). Homosexuality, adultery, divorce, drug use, alcoholism, prostitution, and tax evasion are culturally defined as deviant behaviors that constitute social problems. Yet, divorce is a common solution to the problem of unsatisfying and destructive marriages, homosexuality allows millions of people to express themselves sexually, and families and businesses often rely on tax evasion in order to survive.

Conformity is important because it gives social life a sense of predictability, continuity, and stability. As important as these manifest functions of conformity are, however, there are also latent dysfunctions that no group or society can afford to ignore. Too high a level of conformity, for example, tends to stifle creativity and constructive criticism. Conformity can also be disastrous when the values and norms involved are destructive as in the case of racism. Deviance also has unanticipated consequences, some of which are functional for important goals. Nonconformity, for example, stimulates social change by challenging the status quo. The well-being of society and its members, then, depends on a delicate balance between deviance and conformity.

## Summary

1. Deviance is any appearance or behavior that violates a norm; conformity is obedience to norms. What most members of a group or society actually do is the norm, but the rarity of certain behaviors does not make them deviant. Because deviance is a cultural creation, the classification of behaviors as deviant varies historically between and within cultures.

2. The functional perspective views deviant acts as violations of a moral consensus, and outraged responses of citizens as beneficial for social cohesion. The conflict perspective argues that deviance reflects social inequality, and that the law protects the interests of the powerful rather than a moral consensus.

3. Nonconformists openly violate norms in order to bring about positive change. Nonconformists may be either rebels who challenge both norms and values, or innovators who accept values but reject the norms that define legitimate means for achieving them. Aberrance is the secret violation of norms for personal gain. It may be either retreatist, in which a person withdraws from social life by rejecting values and norms without offering alternatives, or innovative, in which a person secretly uses illegitimate means to attain valued goals.

4. A stigma is a personal characteristic (such as a physical deformity) that others treat as deviant.

5. Some violations of law (such as overparking) are not defined as crimes or as deviance; many forms of deviance (lying to a friend) are not defined as crimes; and an act defined as criminal by law may be regarded as normal by one or more subcultures.

6. Males are more likely than females to commit crimes. Young people are more likely to commit many traditional crimes such as burglary, but older people are more likely to commit job-related, white-collar crimes. Nonwhites and the poor are more likely than whites and the nonpoor to be arrested; but most evidence shows that class and race differences in crime influence the kinds of crime committed, not the amount. Crime is more common in urban areas than in suburban or rural areas, but the difference is greater for violent crimes than for those against property, and it has been shrinking in recent years.

7. Men are more likely than women to be victimized by crime, except in the case of sexual assault. Nonwhites are more likely to be victimized than whites, and young people are more vulnerable than older people.

8. Relationships among criminals vary from simple to complex. Both criminals and victims may be either individuals or groups, and most victims of violence know their assailant. Some crimes—such as prostitution—are victimless; they represent an offense against society itself.

9. Social class and race affect the likelihood of being arrested, prosecuted, and convicted of a crime, as well as the length of sentence. At all stages, the criminal justice system discriminates against blacks and lower-class people.

10. The American criminal justice system responds to crime with punishment, rehabilitation, and isolation of criminals from society. Most evidence indicates that these do not control crime.

11. Culture contributes to deviance in several ways, the most basic of which is the designation of some acts as deviant. When norms are unclear or disputed, or when individuals are weakly attached to their society, anomie results, and under such conditions deviance is more likely to occur. Deviance may also be conformity to subcultural values and norms that support behavior regarded as deviant in the surrounding society. In complex cultures, individuals are exposed to competing standards, and differential association—differing degrees of exposure to cultural ideas—helps explain why some individuals adopt cultural ideas that are defined as deviant in society at large.

12. Social structure also contributes to deviance. Deviance is sometimes required in the performance of legitimate roles (such as when military commanders order soldiers to shoot civilians).

13. Primary deviance refers to behavior that people do not treat as deviant—either because they are unaware of it or because they regard it as trivial. Secondary deviance occurs when people are labeled and treated as deviant, and "deviant" becomes an important part of their identity. Such

labeling encourages secondary deviance, which conforms to people's expectations of those labeled deviant.

**14.** Structure also contributes to deviance by un- equally distributing legitimate opportunities for achieving culturally valued goals; by creating ille- gitimate opportunities for some status occupants; and by providing inadequate means for achieving culturally valued goals.

**15.** In general, deviance is more likely in popula- tions that are large, diverse, young, urban, and marked by social inequality.

**16.** Deviance results in considerable negative consequences for individuals, groups, and socie- ties, including physical injury, fear, and economic loss. Widespread deviance weakens group bounda- ries and lowers social cohesion. Deviance also damages groups and individuals identified as devi- ant. Despite the costs of deviance, however, some groups benefit from it by holding jobs designed to record and control deviant behavior.

## Key Terms

anomie   298
"collective conscience"   280
conformity   277
crime   285

> crime rate   286
> syndicated crime   291
> victimless crime   292
> white-collar crime   288

criminal justice system   293

> degradation ceremony   296
> total institution   296

deviance   277

> aberrance   283
> innovation   283
> nonconformity   283
> rebellion   283
> retreatism   283

ritualism   307
stigma   282,   285

differential association   299
formal sanction   285
informal sanction   285
"the norm"   277
opportunity structure   306
social labeling perspective   303

> master status   304
> primary deviance   303
> secondary deviance   303

## Recommended Readings

BECKER, H. S. (1963). *Outsiders.* New York: Free Press. An important, well-written statement of the labeling per- spective on deviance.

GOFFMAN, E. (1963). *Stigma: Notes on the management of a spoiled identity.* Englewood Cliffs, NJ: Prentice-Hall.

KADISH, S. H. (1983). *Encyclopedia of crime and justice* (3 Vols.). New York: Free Press. An extraordinarily com- prehensive, interdisciplinary summary of what is known about criminal behavior and social responses to it.

KALVEN, H., JR., and ZEISEL, H. (1966). *The American jury.* Boston: Little Brown. A fascinating study of what happens in juries and how they arrive at their decisions.

REASONS, C. E., and RICH, R. M. (Eds.). (1978). *The soci- ology of law: A conflict perspective.* Toronto: Butter- worths. A provocative set of articles that examine the ways in which the law and definitions of deviance help maintain social inequality and oppression.

SCHUR, E. (1965). *Crimes without victims—Deviant behav- ior and public policy.* Englewood Cliffs, NJ: Prentice- Hall. One of the clearest statements of the problem of "victimless" crime.

SILBERMAN, C. E. (1980). *Criminal violence, criminal jus- tice.* New York: Vintage. A powerful, insightful analysis of the causes and consequences of criminal behavior in the United States.

SYKES, G. (1978). *Criminology.* New York: Harcourt Brace Jovanovich. An excellent introduction to criminology by one of the foremost sociologists in the field.

# PART IV
# Social Stratification

Few areas of social life provoke as much strong feeling and conflict as social inequality. The gulf that separates rich and poor, the damage to individuals, families, communities, and societies caused by racial, ethnic, and sexual prejudice and discrimination—all touch some of our most deeply held values about justice and fairness. The problem is far from simple, however, for in many societies, including the United States, the issue of how valued rewards such as wealth, power, and prestige are distributed also touches deeply held values about individualism, hard work, self-reliance, and the importance of merit. In short, while there is widespread support for justice and fairness in our society, there is also strong support for cultural and structural arrangements that produce inequality, in spite of the damage it inflicts on millions of people's lives.

We begin with Chapter 11, a detailed examination of the general problem of social stratification—the process through which wealth, power, and prestige are distributed. We will look at the nature and extent of inequality both within societies and between them and consider some major theories that try to explain why inequality exists at all. We will also look at the social processes through which some people gain a greater share of wealth, power, and prestige than others. In the remaining three chapters of Part IV we look at prejudice, discrimination, and social inequality based on the ascribed statuses of race, ethnicity, gender, and age.

# CHAPTER 11

# Social Stratification: Who Gets What, and Why

All societies produce a variety of rewards that are valued in their culture. Some are physical possessions such as land, automobiles, or buildings; money represents the power to buy possessions and services. Others, such as the respect we receive from people, are nonmaterial, but are very important to us, nonetheless.

The central question in Chapter 11 is this: How do societies distribute valued rewards among their members? In other words, who gets what, and why? In this chapter we look at how sociologists use the functional and conflict perspectives to describe and explain inequality in societies, and we apply both of them to the United States and other societies. We also look at the causes and consequences of inequality *among* societies.

## Stratification, Inequality, and Social Class

"Justice," "fairness," "respect," "equality," "discrimination," "exploitation," and "oppression"—these are words that evoke strong feelings because they refer to fundamental aspects of social life among human beings: how we are treated by other people and how we treat them; also, how we share in the wealth, power, and prestige that are distributed among the members of society. The concept of **social stratification** refers to the social structures through which wealth, power, and prestige are distributed unequally among the occupants of different social statuses. The definition of stratification has three aspects that you should understand before going on in this chapter.

First, stratification is a social *process*, even though the word calls up images of layers of rock that just sit there. Societies continually sort people into different social statuses and distribute wealth, power, and prestige among them.

Second, a society is stratified only if wealth, power, and prestige are distributed unequally according to people's social statuses—such as age, gender, education, occupation, and ethnicity. If we took all the income produced in the United States during each year and distributed it through an enormous lottery that gave more money to some than others, the distribution of income would be unequal but *not* stratified. The difference is that in a stratified society rewards are distributed *systematically* according to social status, not randomly.

Third, *what* is distributed in a society varies according to cultural values. In a poor village society, food and clothing may be the major rewards, while in wealthier, more complex societies, political power, leisure time, health care, and luxuries are also distributed.

Social stratification has long been a major area of sociological analysis because few aspects of social environments affect the quality of people's lives as profoundly as the distribution of wealth, power, and prestige. Our positions in stratified societies make the difference between respect and contempt, full stomachs and starvation, keeping warm and freezing during harsh winters, working and being unemployed, living long and dying young, living in hope and in despair, controlling our own lives and being controlled by others.

One of the most important concepts used in the study of stratification is *social class*, an idea that was developed most notably by Karl Marx and Max Weber. Their perspectives on class differ in important ways, however, and lead to different views of social stratification.

### Marx: Class, Production, and Social Relationships

To Marx, the most basic human activity is the production of necessities such as food, clothing, and shelter, and he focused on two key questions about the production process: How do societies produce goods and services and how does the relationship between people and the ways in which goods are produced affect their lives?

Because Marx (1867) was primarily interested in how societies produce goods, he defined **social class** as an aggregate of people who occupy similar positions in relation to the production process. Although he identified several social classes, the most important are the **capitalists (the bourgeoisie),** who own the means of production (capital) such as factories, and the **workers (the proletariat),** who survive by selling their *labor power* to capitalists.

The distinction between labor and labor power is important in Marx's theories. **Labor** refers to the production of products and services that can either be *used* (shoes to wear, food to eat) or *exchanged* for something else (one farmer trades his surplus wheat for another's surplus milk, or farmers sell crops or milk in the marketplace).

The hired hands who work in the fields sell their labor power in exchange for wages. Their employers, on the other hand, own the means of production and control what is produced; when they sell their produce on the market, they are selling their labor.

Farm workers, however, who spend their days picking lettuce that grows in someone else's fields are not selling their labor. It is not as if they pick the lettuce and "sell" it to the farmers, who then sell it on the market. The workers do not own the lettuce, the fields, or the machinery. What, then, *do* they sell? They sell their *time* in exchange for *wages*. What they do with that time and what becomes of the products (e.g., lettuce) are not under their control. Thus, workers sell their **labor power**—so many dollars for each day's work—and not their labor.

In any society, Marx argued, the mode of production and the kinds of technologies that are used determine social relationships, and to understand human behavior and experience, we must pay attention to people's positions in those relationships. Those who control the means of production also control jobs, while workers must sell their labor power for whatever wages they can get—or not work at all. When the means of production are privately owned, the capitalist class is in a position to exploit workers and accumulate wealth and power.

The complexity of modern societies makes it difficult to categorize everyone as either owners or workers. The vast range of professionals, such as physicians and lawyers, cannot easily be categorized as capitalists or workers; nor can the thousands of upper-level managers and administrators in government and business (Gagliani, 1981).

For this reason, it makes more sense to define classes according to *control* over production, which may or may not take the form of ownership. Wright et al. (1982) use this perspective to divide the American labor force into six class categories based on the amount of control workers have over the means of production, other workers, and their own work (Figure 11-1). Using data from a national survey, Wright and his colleagues estimated that roughly 45 percent of all workers are in Marx's working class, 2 percent are capitalists (the bourgeoisie), and 7 percent are "small" capitalists, or what Marx called the "petit bourgeoisie." The remainder are in the "gray areas" of social class: 30 percent are managers or supervisors, 6 percent are small employers, and 10 percent are semiautonomous wage earners such as college professors.

This approach still has some ambiguity, for ownership and control of the means of production are matters of degree (one person might own one share of IBM stock, while another owns a million shares). To Marx, however, this is not a problem, for he did not try to create categories into which everyone could be unambiguously sorted. Rather, he focused on the *process* through which societies produce goods and services and urged us to pay attention to the variety of roles people play in it.

## Weber: Class, Prestige, and Power

Whereas Marx focused on how modes of production cause inequality, Weber (1946) paid more attention to the levels of wealth, power, and prestige people actually have than to how they come to have it. From Weber's perspective, stratification has three major dimensions—wealth, power, and prestige—and to identify social classes, we must first decide which one we are referring to.

Weber used **"class"** to describe people in terms of material "life chances"—their wealth and

**Figure 11-1**  The American Class Structure from a Marxist Perspective

Percentage of All Workers

2%  6%  7%  30%  10%  45%

### Social Class

*Bourgeoisie* (capitalists): Own means of production; ten or more employees (the owners of a factory; the controlling stock holders of a major corporation)—2%.

*Small employers:* Own means of production; two to nine employees (an electrical contractor with three employees)—6%.

*Petite bourgeoisie* (small capitalists): Own means of production; no more than one employee (people who knit sweaters at home and sell them through stores)—7%.

*Managers and supervisors:* Do not own means of production; moderate to high levels of autonomy and authority (office supervisor; personnel manager; military officer)—30%.

*Semiautonomous wage earners:* Do not own means of production; low to moderate levels of autonomy and authority (journalist; teacher)—10%.

*Proletariat* (workers): Do not own means of production; little autonomy; no authority (assembly-line worker; secretary; telephone operator)—45%.

Source: Adapted from Wright et al., 1982.

property. He referred to power as **"party,"** and to prestige—the amount of respect we receive from others—as **"status."** Unlike Marx's approach to stratification, Weber's leads us to rank people from "upper" to "lower" in terms of these three different dimensions.

People who rank high on one dimension usually rank high on the other two. For example, it takes a great deal of money to be elected to powerful, prestigious political offices in the United States, and the winners tend to be those who spend the most money in their campaigns (U.S. Census Bureau, 1983c).

The tendency of wealth, power, and prestige to go together leads many sociologists to classify people according to **socioeconomic status,** a concept that combines wealth, occupational prestige, and educational attainment into an average rank, usually expressed in terms of "upper class," "middle class" and "lower class" (see Powers, 1982). There are countless exceptions, however, that make it difficult to assign people an overall rank that means anything. Successful criminals may rank high on wealth and power, but low on prestige; college professors and religious leaders rank high on prestige, but relatively low on wealth and power; a United States senator ranks high on both power and prestige, but is not necessarily wealthy. Which of these has the highest overall rank in the stratification system and which has the lowest?

Many sociologists (such as Parsons, 1964) believe that prestige is valued more highly than wealth and power. Even if we confine ourselves to this single aspect of stratification, however, ranking individuals is difficult because each of us occupies a variety of social statuses whose levels of prestige may be *inconsistent* with each other (a phenomenon called **status inconsistency**). Physicians, for example, rank higher on prestige than do factory workers, and heterosexuals rank higher than homosexuals. Who, then, will be treated with greater respect in a heterosexual society—homosexual physicians or heterosexual factory workers?

We tend to emphasize our highest prestige statuses, while minimizing those of lower prestige. Some women executives try to play down the fact that they are female, perhaps by wearing "mannish" clothes. A male colleague, on the other hand, may try to emphasize a woman executive's gender in an effort to increase his prestige relative to her (Kanter, 1977a).

One way of identifying who is in which social class is simply to *ask* people which class they think they belong to. In 1984, for example, 4 percent of American adults placed themselves in the lower class, 46 percent in the working class, 45 percent in the middle class, and 3 percent in the upper class (Davis, 1984). This is a useful measure insofar

as self-perceptions of class position affect people's expectations and behavior, but it is misleading insofar as *actual* positions in a stratification system are more important than *perceived* positions. For example, only 5 percent of Americans placed themselves in the lower class in 1982, while 15 percent had incomes below the poverty level (Davis, 1982; U.S. Census Bureau, 1983c). It is doubtful that *thinking* we are not poor is enough to undo the effects of poverty.

In spite of these complications, most sociologists use Weber's framework when they refer to social class—from the upper class, whose members generally rank high in prestige, wealth, and power, to the lower class, whose members rank at the bottom in all three areas. In addition, sociologists commonly make a class distinction based on occupation. The term **blue-collar workers** refers to people—such as factory workers, carpenters, and plumbers—whose jobs involve manual labor. **White-collar workers**—such as professionals, business executives, and secretaries—have jobs that are more mental than manual. Blue-collar occupations are also divided according to the skills involved. Carpenters, for example, depend on their mental abilities far more than do assembly-line workers. In fact, highly skilled blue-collar workers rely on mental abilities more than do many white-collar workers such as file clerks.

Neither Marx's nor Weber's approach allows us to unambiguously assign everyone to clearly defined categories, but we do not need to do this in order to understand how societies distribute resources and rewards. Marx draws attention to how the means by which goods and services are produced affect social relationships; Weber focuses on the *results* of the distribution process in a stratified society: sets of people with similar levels of wealth, power, or prestige. Thus, Marx and Weber concentrate on different aspects of a complex social process. The difference between their approaches is important because each leads us to pay attention to fundamentally different aspects of stratification and its effects on people's lives.

### Comparing Marx and Weber: The Case of Carol, Susan, and George

Carol is a self-employed plumber in a small city. She owns her own tools, employs an apprentice, and, after paying all her expenses, earns $12,000 a year. She rents a modest apartment, drives an old Ford pickup truck, rarely takes vacations, and usually dresses in jeans and sneakers. She never attended college, is divorced, and her daughter attends a community college.

Susan works on an assembly line in a Detroit automobile plant. She earns $16,000 a year, drives a three-year-old car, takes a week off every year, rents a large new apartment, and generally wears jeans and work boots to work. She earned a college degree by taking night courses at a community college. She is married and has three teenage children.

George is a design engineer at Susan's plant. He earns $50,000 a year (plus a bonus in good years), supervises ten employees, owns his own home, drives a new car, takes a three-week vacation each summer, and wears tailored suits. He has a graduate degree in engineering, and his only child attends an Ivy League college.

How would we compare these three people in terms of their relative standing in the American stratification system? From Weber's perspective, George ranks highest because he has more wealth, a graduate degree, a more powerful and prestigious job, enjoys long vacations, and can point with pride to his child's Ivy League education. Susan comes in a distant second and Carol a close third, because although Susan has a higher income and a college degree, most Americans rank Carol's occupation slightly higher in prestige (Hodge, Siegel, and Rossi, 1964).

Marx would look at these people very differently, however, for while Carol sells her labor and owns some capital—her plumbing equipment—George and Susan neither own nor control any means of production and must sell their labor power to whoever will pay them for it. From Marx's perspective, Carol is a small capitalist (a "petit bourgeois") and George and Susan are workers; and there may be reasons to prefer Carol's class position to George's and Susan's.

Susan and George have little control over their jobs and, therefore, little control over the rewards they receive by performing them. In the early 1980s, for example, the U.S. automobile industry experienced a deep slump in sales, and unemployment in Detroit was the highest in the nation. While George's position as an engineer is better protected than Susan's, if a company closes an en-

tire plant, virtually everyone except top managers is likely to be laid off.

Carol's position has an important advantage, for, as she might put it, "People always say, 'you can never find a plumber when you need one,'—and that's me. I can always get work, because people are forever stopping up toilets and sinks (you wouldn't believe the things they try to put down drains)."

Thus, Marx and Weber lead us to pay attention to fundamentally different aspects of people's positions in stratification systems. Weber focuses on how much wealth, power, and prestige people have, while Marx concentrates on how means of production foster social relationships through which wealth, power, and prestige are distributed. Because our positions in social relationships determine our rights and obligations, Marx's perspective focuses on an important fact that Weber's does not: whatever our class position may be now, our security depends on our control over the social relationships that keep us there.

## Explaining Inequality

Sociologists use two major perspectives to explain social stratification. A functional view tries to identify ways in which inequality contributes to or interferes with the achievement of culturally valued goals. A conflict perspective focuses on inequality as the result of power inequalities that enable some members of society to exploit others and take a disproportionately large share of rewards and resources for their own use.

There are many ways in which these two perspectives generate different explanations of inequality, but they are most useful if we think of them as revealing different aspects of a complex puzzle. If we adopt either of them as "the one true perspective," we inevitably produce an oversimplified and, therefore, distorted explanation.

### The Functional View:
### Social Structure and Cultural Values

To explain the existence of a cultural idea or social relationship, the functional perspective pays attention to how it contributes to or interferes with the achievement of culturally valued goals. Kingsley Davis and Wilbert Moore's functional theory of stratification focuses on two contributions of inequality: first, differences in the level of rewards are necessary to motivate individuals to perform important roles; second, a complex division of labor requires unequal distributions of power, because some must be in a position to coordinate the activities of everyone else.

Davis and Moore pointed out that each culture values some activities more than others, in part because not all activities contribute equally to the well-being of society. They then argued that the most important tasks require abilities that relatively few people possess, and that to prepare themselves, these individuals must undergo rigorous training that requires considerable personal sacrifice.

Given these requirements, societies inevitably confront the major problem of motivating individuals to play important, demanding roles. How, for example, do we motivate young people to endure the long years of study required to become physicians? How do we motivate people to run businesses, command armies, or govern societies?

Davis and Moore's answer is quite straightforward: in order to ensure that the most important roles are adequately performed, we must offer relatively high levels of prestige and wealth to those who are able and willing to perform them. If important jobs requiring extensive training are not performed, society suffers. Conversely, jobs which rank lower on cultural scales of values—washing dishes, driving trucks, or assembling cars—will carry lower levels of prestige and wealth, because it is relatively easy to find people who can and will adequately perform them and there is, therefore, no need to offer special rewards in order to make sure such jobs are performed.

If the Davis-Moore theory is correct, we should find that the most highly trained people receive the highest levels of reward. This is generally true for formal education (Table 2-6, p. 53): for both men and women, more years of schooling mean higher average incomes.

Studies of occupational prestige in the United States and in other societies are also consistent with the Davis-Moore argument. Hodge, Siegel, and Rossi (1964), for example, analyzed national survey data in which adults rated 91 occupations from "excellent" to "poor" in terms of how much respondents "look up to them." The most important finding is that the relative prestige of these occupations has remained essentially unchanged since the first study was done in 1925. The stability of occupational prestige rankings may be interpreted as a reflection of stable cultural evaluations of jobs and their importance to society.

In an international study, Hodge, Treiman, and Rossi (1966) compared prestige ratings of occupations in 31 countries that varied considerably in culture and level of industrialization. In general, there was strong agreement across societies about which occupations are most prestigious, which, the authors suggest, supports the idea that some occupations are more important than others regardless of the society:

> Specialized institutions to carry out political, religious, and economic functions, and to provide for the health, education, and welfare of the population, exist in one form or another in all national societies. Considering the importance of these functions to the maintenance of complex social systems, it is not surprising that occupations at the top of these institutional structures should be highly regarded. (p. 310)

The functional explanation also emphasizes that complex divisions of labor require extensive coordination of people's activities, and this means that some individuals must have authority to make decisions about what people do and how resources are distributed and used. To Parsons (1964, 1971), equality of power is simply impossible in any society with a complex division of labor.

While Davis and Moore's theory identifies some important functions of inequality, it has been criticized on six major grounds (Tumin, 1953). First, motivation to perform roles competently is a problem for *all* jobs—if garbage collectors fail to perform, life rapidly becomes intolerable for everyone. That our culture values the performance of engineers or business managers more than that of garbage collectors has less to do with maintaining society than with maintaining the privileged position of managers and engineers.

Second, Tumin challenged the belief that those who occupy highly rewarded positions have made sacrifices for which they must be compensated with a lifetime of privilege. The costs of professional education, for example, are often borne by families and government, not the individual trainees themselves. Even when they bear a considerable portion of the cost, they quickly earn it back with higher-than-average incomes and then go on to 20 or 30 years of relatively high prestige

and income. In addition, while trainees are in professional schools, they enjoy a higher level of prestige than many who work in low-level jobs and have greater opportunities for leisure.

Third, Tumin questioned the belief that wealth and prestige are necessary to motivate people to perform important roles. Davis and Moore minimized the importance of the satisfactions that come with important roles: the challenges, creative opportunities, high levels of control over work conditions, and the chance to make an important contribution to one's community and society.

Fourth, the Davis-Moore theory cannot explain why some people in some social categories—such as women and blacks—receive less wealth, power, and prestige regardless of their training. Table 2-6, for example, shows that the average income of women with graduate training is only $200 higher than that of men who never went beyond high school, and women college graduates average $100 less than men who never finished high school. Nor can their explanation account for wide

Although many people who work in advertising agencies earn more money and have higher prestige than people who collect garbage, it is not at all clear that their contribution to society is also greater.

variations in income among people who work at the same jobs and have the same levels of education, skill, and experience (Thurow, 1975).

Fifth, Tumin criticized Davis and Moore for not making full use of the functional perspective, which focuses on *dys*functions as well as functions. Social stratification is dysfunctional for many culturally valued goals. For example, the talent of those at the "bottom of the heap" is less likely to be discovered, encouraged, and developed; and, as a result, society is denied the full range of its population's abilities. Inequality encourages hostility, suspicion, and distrust between those at the top and those at the bottom; and those who must go through life with little prestige and little hope of a better life are less likely to be loyal to a society that deprives them. Thus, in focusing on functional aspects of stratification, Davis and Moore paid too little attention to its dysfunctional consequences.

Finally, while Davis and Moore argued that people receive high incomes because their jobs are perceived as being more important, some sociologists argue just the opposite—that we tend to perceive those who make a lot of money as being more important than the rest of us *because* of their high incomes and not because their jobs make a more important contribution to society (Jenkins, 1981a).

If the best interests of society do not explain the existence of stratification, why is systematic inequality so pervasive? Marx and other conflict theorists propose an answer.

## The Conflict Perspective: To Each According to the Ability to Take

If societies cannot produce an abundance of food, clothing, and shelter to satisfy everyone's needs fully, it is inevitable that some will be in a position to take more than their share; and, as they accumulate wealth and power, they will use their dominant position to create and sustain a social environment that perpetuates their privileged position (Marx and Engels, 1846). Thus, Marx explained stratification as the result of conflict over scarce resources and of the ability of those who dominate society to maintain their privileged position by exploiting those below them.

Lenski (1966) supported Marx's view by tracing the development of societies and showing that stratification exists only in those that produce a surplus. (He does not say that there is no inequality in societies that barely survive; only that inequality is not determined by social statuses.) Hunter-gatherer societies such as the Kung Bushmen of Africa do not produce their own food, and they move from place to place in order to find it. This way of life discourages the production of surpluses and the accumulation of private property:

> It is not advantageous to multiply and accumulate in this society. Any man can make what he needs when he wants to. Most of the materials he uses are abundant and free for anyone to take. Furthermore, in their nomadic lives, without beasts of burden, the fact that the people themselves must carry everything puts a sharp limit on the quantity of objects they want to possess. (Marshall, 1965, pp. 257–258)

As technology created greater surpluses, settlements became more permanent, elite groups accumulated both wealth and power, and eventually the existence of privileged and disadvantaged classes became an enduring characteristic of societies.

Conflict theorists argue that stratification is functional only for the dominant class, not for society as a whole (Gans, 1973). The existence of poverty, for example, ensures that "dirty work" will get done: cleaning streets, collecting garbage, digging ditches, picking lettuce, scrubbing floors, and emptying bedpans in hospitals. Such jobs would go undone if no one was driven by the threat of poverty to perform them. Poverty also creates jobs for welfare and social workers, pawnbrokers, and government bureaucrats who administer antipoverty programs.

In addition, the lower class usually bears a disproportionately large share of the costs of social change: they are the first to lose their jobs when factories are automated in order to lower costs; when homes are torn down to make way for highways, it is the poor, not the wealthy who lose. Even unemployment works to the advantage of those who own or control the means of production. When there are many people without jobs, competition among them leads them to accept lower wages, for if they refuse to work for low pay, there is always someone else desperate to take their place. Low wages, in turn, mean higher profits for the owners.

John Steinbeck vividly portrayed this in his novel, *The Grapes of Wrath*, in which Oklahoma farmers who were wiped out by the Great Depression go to California in search of jobs in fruit orchards. Each day, the owners spread rumors that large numbers of jobs are available; an enormous crowd gathers at the gate, and the owners announce a pitifully low rate of pay. The people looking for work can see that only a few of them will get jobs, that they are all hungry and homeless, and that even a low wage is better than no wage at all.

This scene is not unique to the Great Depression. In 1983, for example, 10,000 people stood in freezing rain for four hours in Cleveland, Ohio, to apply for 1,000 public-service jobs that paid $4.50 an hour, were to last only 12 weeks, and involved cleaning up public parks and vacant lots. Some of the applicants were unemployed auto and steel workers with 25 years of experience in the steel industry (*New York Times*, March 22, 1983).

If inequality results from the ability of some to accumulate power and wealth, why does the lower

The desperation of the Oklahoma farmers who fled west from the devastation of the Great Depression gave them little choice but to accept whatever wages they could get for their labor power—however low and exploitative those wages were.

class stand for it? The first response is, "They often don't." Throughout the last thousand years, people have been drawn to the idea of equality. During the Middle Ages, European peasants often joined bands of robbers and revolted against landowners. The story of Robin Hood, who "stole from the rich to give to the poor," has found a place in the folk histories of many societies (Hobsbawm, 1971). Peasant revolts were common in England, France, and other European countries (Froissart, 1961; Genicut, 1966).

Why, then, does stratification persist? Part of the answer lies in the ability of powerful classes to use force to take what they want and keep what they have—by controlling police, armies, and governments. Moreover, stratification is an enduring characteristic of most societies, few of which resemble a police state. The rest of the answer lies deeper, in the *acceptance* of inequality by members of *all* social classes.

## Culture, Ideology, and Inequality

In the *Manifesto of the Communist Party*, Marx and Engels (1848) argued that members of dominant classes use their privileged positions to influence the cultural ideas that affect individuals' perceptions of reality, aspirations, feelings, and expectations. Upper-class people tend to be among the best-educated members of society and occupy positions of authority—in government, university boards of trustees, and legal systems. They provide financial support for political candidates and universities. They are thus in a position to foster beliefs, values, attitudes, and norms that keep those in lower classes "in their place."

**Norms**  Norms are an important tool through which the upper class perpetuates its privilege. Norms that protect private property, for example, favor the wealthy more than the poor, and most inheritance laws allow families to accumulate wealth over many generations. By extreme contrast, in some American Indian tribes, no one is allowed to own land. An individual may lease land for a lifetime, but when he or she dies, the land becomes community property once again, to be leased to someone else (Matthiessen, 1984).

In the United States, income tax laws *appear* to tax the wealthy at higher rates than the poor. Those in the top income brackets, for example, are

taxed at a rate of 50 percent, while those in the lowest bracket pay no tax at all. This is based on several principles: the wealthy are more able to pay and therefore should pay more; they have more to gain from a healthy society and therefore should contribute more; and they receive a disproportionately large share of income, and therefore the burden of supporting society should fall more heavily on them.

In practice, however, income tax laws always allowed many wealthy Americans to avoid paying taxes on much of their income (Devine, 1983). When the wealthy profit from the sale of property, stocks, and bonds, for example, the law requires them to pay tax on only half of their long-term profits. In addition, tax deductions that appear to apply to everyone usually benefit the wealthy far more than others.

We are allowed, for example, to deduct and therefore not pay taxes on income we use to pay interest on loans. A wealthy family, paying $1,000 a year in interest charges, avoids paying $500 in tax (50 percent times $1,000). A middle-income family, on the other hand—taxed at a rate of 20 percent and paying $1,000 a year in mortgage interest—avoids paying only $200 in tax (20 percent times $1,000). Thus, tax laws allow the wealthy family to keep $500 that would otherwise be paid in taxes, while allowing the middle-income family to keep only $200.

Such deductions sometimes enable millionaires to pay no tax at all, and few wealthy individuals pay the full rate. In 1977 the top income tax rate was 70 percent, but the wealthiest 5 percent of American taxpayers paid only 25 percent of their income in federal taxes (U.S. Census Bureau, 1980b). Because upper-class people have considerable influence over the passage of laws, they are often able to bring about laws that serve their best interests (such as lowering the 70 percent rate to 50 percent in 1982).

The effects of this are clear in Table 11-1, which shows the effect of income taxes on the distribution of income in the United States in 1982. In terms of before-tax income, for example, the poorest 20 percent of the population received only 4 percent of all income, while the richest 20 percent received 45 percent. The second column shows the distribution of after-tax income, and you can see that it differs very little from the distribution of

**Table 11-1**

Distribution of Before-Tax and After-Tax Household Income (United States, 1982)

| INCOME GROUP | SHARE OF BEFORE-TAX INCOME (Percentage) | SHARE OF AFTER-TAX INCOME (Percentage) |
|---|---|---|
| Lowest Fifth | 4.0 | 4.7 |
| 2nd Fifth | 9.9 | 11.2 |
| 3rd Fifth | 16.5 | 17.5 |
| 4th Fifth | 24.6 | 24.8 |
| Top Fifth | 45.0 | 41.8 |
| | 100.0 | 100.0 |

Source: U.S. Census Bureau, 1984a.

before-tax income. Income taxes have a very small effect on the distribution of income in the United States (see also Pechman, 1984).

**Culture and the Uses of Ideology**  When Marx (1843) described organized religion as "the opiate of the masses," he was not attacking religion itself; rather, he was pointing to the ways in which religion functions as a distraction for workers. The more attention they pay to heaven, hell, and the "hereafter," he argued, the less attention they pay to social relations on earth through which they are exploited.

Thus, religious beliefs often cloud awareness of classes and their relationships with each other, especially in societies whose workers are poorly educated. Religion focuses attention on individuals, and this, too, draws attention away from social factors that affect living conditions, experience, and behavior. Marx called this lack of awareness of the true extent and causes of social inequality **false consciousness,** an important concept that shows how social conditions persist because some participants misperceive important aspects of reality.

Religion is not the only potential source of false consciousness. Americans, for example, com-

monly believe that the United States is a "land of equal opportunity," and most value the right of individuals to own property. In 1984, 66 percent of American adults reported the belief that hard work is the most important factor in "getting ahead" (Davis, 1984), and most Americans believe that success and failure are due primarily to individual, not social, causes (Kluegel and Smith, 1982). A major part of the "American Dream" is to "make it big" and share in the affluence of the upper class.

Such aspects of culture support stratification by legitimating the social arrangements that produce it and by explaining individual success or failure in purely individual terms. The value of private property, for example, underlies the upper class's ability to accumulate wealth and power; and, for the classes below them, it rarely amounts to more than a sometimes-realized dream of a single-family home.

There are three ways in which the belief in the importance of hard work is highly functional for maintaining the privilege of dominant classes: It keeps the lower classes hard at work; it keeps them in a state of false consciousness; and it does not threaten members of the upper class, most of whom depend heavily on inheritance (rather than their own labor) for their wealth (Projector and Weiss, 1966). Instead, it legitimizes their privilege (if they are wealthy, they must have worked hard). When lower-class people fail to get ahead, they tend to blame themselves rather than a stratification system that severely limits their opportunities no matter how hard they work. After all, the United States was founded on the idea that "All men are created equal" (a constitutional ideal that still excludes women). By blaming themselves, members of lower classes tend to ignore the fact that while higher-class people may work no harder than they, they still receive far more wealth, power, and prestige.

When cultural ideas are used to justify either change or maintenance of the status quo, they constitute an **ideology.** In the late eighteenth and early nineteenth centuries, for example, Spencer's interpretation of Darwin's theory of evolution led to social Darwinism, the belief that those who survive and prosper do so because they are more "fit." In his book, *What Social Classes Owe to Each Other,* the American sociologist William Graham Sumner argued that members of the upper class deserve their privilege because the mere fact of *having* it proves its members are more "fit." Sumner's view illustrates the "circular arguments" that are typical of ideologies intended to justify rather than explain social conditions: Only the most fit prosper; the wealthy, by definition, prosper; therefore, they must be the "fittest."

In general, those members of society who benefit most from ideologies that support existing conditions are their strongest advocates. In their 1970 study of adults in Muskegan, Michigan, for example, Rytina, Form, and Pease found that 76 percent believe that in America "there is plenty of opportunity, and anyone who works hard can go as far as he wants." When people were asked more specific questions about the opportunities of the rich and poor, however, as well as questions about the causes of poverty and affluence, the answers of people in different social classes differed sharply from one another (Table 11-2).

The higher people's incomes are, the more likely they are to believe that rich and poor have an equal chance to go to college and make a given amount of money, that personal attributes account for both wealth and poverty, that the poor do not work as hard as the rich and do not want to get ahead. Such findings support Marx's view that cultural beliefs often support the privileged position of the dominant class.

The preceding sections briefly introduce the major perspectives sociologists use to describe and explain social stratification, and those that follow apply these perspectives to the United States and less-developed societies as well. How would Marx and Weber describe social stratification in the United States?

## Social Stratification in the United States

The United States was founded, in part, as a reaction against the aristocracies of Europe with their rigid divisions between nobility and commoners, and we like to think of our society as classless. We may locate ourselves in the "lower class," "middle class," or "upper class," but we tend to believe that in America people who work hard can go as far as they want. Is America a classless society?

### From Marx's Perspective

To Marx, there are two basic social classes in industrial societies, those who own or control the means of production and those who do not. A classless

**Table 11-2**

Perceptions and Explanations of Inequality, by Respondent's Income (Muskegan, Michigan, 1970)

| | PERCENTAGE WHO AGREE | | |
| --- | --- | --- | --- |
| **PERCEPTIONS** | **Lower Class** | **Middle Class** | **Upper Class** |
| All young people of high ability have a fairly equal chance of going to college. | 45 | 67 | 96 |
| Young people whose parents are poor are just as likely to be in college as anyone else. | 29 | 35 | 43 |
| If they both work hard, a rich man's son and a poor man's son have equal chances of making a given amount of money. | 34 | 42 | 57 |
| Poor people generally don't work as hard as rich people. | 10 | 24 | 39 |
| Poor people basically don't care much about getting ahead. | 12 | 23 | 46 |
| Personal attributes account for wealth. | 28 | 34 | 72 |

Source: Computed from Rytina, Form, and Pease, 1970, Tables 1, 3, & 4.

Prior to the Industrial Revolution in the United States, most people were self-employed as farmers and owned their own means of production.

society is one in which the means of production are collectively owned and controlled by everyone, and in which no one has the power to deny someone the right to earn a living. No society has achieved Marx's ideal; but we can use his perspective to describe the American class structure by answering two questions: (1) How likely are Americans to work for themselves rather than for someone else? and (2) How concentrated is the ownership of the means of production?

In the early 1800s around 80 percent of working Americans were self-employed, mostly as farmers. By the 1870s, when the Industrial Revolution was in full swing, roughly 33 percent worked for themselves; and by 1982 the figure was only 9 percent (Mills, 1951; U.S. Census Bureau, 1983c). Thus, while America began as a country in which most people owned and controlled the means through which they produced goods, the vast majority of contemporary workers are employees of someone else.

While this suggests the existence of capitalist and worker classes in the United States, before reaching such a conclusion we have to remember that ownership and control of the means of production is not as simple now as it was in the 1800s when most businesses were family-owned. Most businesses are now owned by stockholders, and anyone who has money to spare can own a "piece of the action" by purchasing stocks and bonds.

This brings us to the second question: How *concentrated* is ownership of business in the United States? In 1976 the wealthiest 5 percent of the population owned 52 percent of all bonds and 82 percent of all corporate stock; the wealthiest *one* percent owned 30 percent of all bonds and 46 percent of all stocks; and in 1981, 82 percent of all Americans owned *no* stocks or bonds at all (U.S. Census Bureau, 1983c).

The above, when added to the findings shown in Figure 11-1, shows that from Marx's perspective, America is divided into classes defined by their relationship to the means of production. The dominant class consists of a small minority who are either self-employed professionals, own the means of production, or occupy top management positions. Most of us, then, belong to the working class; for whether we are professors, engineers, fire fighters, or clerks, we cannot work unless those who control jobs are willing to buy our labor power.

The importance of Marx's concept of class was painfully evident to millions of American workers in 1982, when almost 20 percent of those who wanted to work were either out of work and still looking for jobs or had given up the effort. Many of the newly unemployed had occupied well-paid positions, lived in mortgaged houses, and had children in college; they were shocked to suddenly find themselves without a way to earn a living. By drawing our attention to the importance of owning and controlling the means of production, Marx reveals that whatever our level of rewards may be today, in a class society, what workers earn today may be gone tomorrow no matter how hard they work or how competent they may be.

It is thus no accident that in the 1980s, American labor unions are shifting their focus from the rewards of work—such as pay, benefits, and vacation time—to control over working conditions. Auto unions now demand membership on corpo-

For the vast majority of American workers, who neither control nor own any means of production, unemployment is a continuing threat whose occurrence is largely beyond their control.

rate boards of directors, so that workers can have some control over the organizations on which they depend for a living. While pay was the issue of the 1960s and 1970s, job security is the issue of the 1980s, and this inevitably involves a struggle over control of the means of production (*New York Times*, June 3, 1982; Raskin, 1982).

## Through Weber's Eyes: Dimensions of Inequality

While Marx described stratification in terms of ownership of the means of production, Weber divided societies according to the distribution of wealth, power, and prestige. How evenly are wealth, power, and prestige distributed in America? Who gets what?

**Wealth and Income**   It is important at the outset to distinguish between wealth and income. **Wealth** refers to valued possessions, including cash, property, stocks and bonds, buildings, jewels, and cars. **Income** refers to money that we receive each year. Thus, wealth is what we *have*, while income is what we take in each year. The distinction is important because wealth is often a source of income: interest on investments, rent payments from tenants, or profits from a business or the sale of property that has increased in market value.

A small minority of Americans owns most of the wealth in the United States. In 1976, for example, the richest 5 percent of the population held 39 percent of all the wealth, including 27 percent of all cash, 32 percent of all real estate, and 74 percent of all stocks and bonds (U.S. Census Bureau, 1983c).

Like wealth, the distribution of income is also unequal. In 1982 the wealthiest 5 percent of the population received 16 percent of all money income—more than three times what they would have received if everyone got equal shares; and, the wealthiest 20 percent received 43 percent of all money income. Meanwhile, the lower 60 percent of the population received only 33 percent of all income; the poorest 20 percent received 4.7 percent—less than a quarter of what they would have received if income were distributed equally; and the income of one out of every seven Americans fell below the poverty level (U.S. Census Bureau, 1983c).

## DOES EDUCATION INCREASE MOBILITY?

In the last twenty years, the educational attainment and level of training in the American population has grown dramatically. As a result, has the distribution of income in the United States become less unequal, more unequal, or stayed just about the same?

The answer is that the distribution of income has become *more* unequal in the last ten years. This chapter explains why.

It is important to note that income figures based on tax returns understate the true extent of inequality in the United States, for much of the income of wealthy families and individuals is never reported to the Internal Revenue Service. Top executives, for example, enjoy large expense accounts that pay for travel and entertainment, and are often given the opportunity to buy stocks at a cost far below their actual value. The most lucrative tax-free investments are typically beyond the reach of all but the wealthy (often requiring investments of $100,000 or more); and when people profit through the sale of property, bonds, or stocks, only half of their profit is taxable.

**Living Long and Well** The consequences of unequal distributions of income and wealth go beyond how much we own or the things we are able to buy, for the material conditions in which we live profoundly affect our physical and mental health.

In comparison with those with income of $15,000 or more, poor people are almost twice as likely to be hospitalized, and when they are disabled by disease or injury, the average period is three times as long. They are three times more likely to have heart disease, anemia, and arthritis, and almost four times more likely to suffer from diabetes. They are only half as likely to assess their own health as "excellent," and eight times more likely to assess it as "poor"; and they are only half as likely to see a dentist each year (U.S. Census Bureau, 1980b, 1983c).

## Voices: When Coke Is the Only Thing

Unlike the affluent, to whom soft drinks are snacks or even no-calorie refreshment, the desperately poor may have to rely on such beverages for clean drinking water and carbohydrates otherwise unavailable to them at the very bottom of our stratification system.

You spend a lot of your time worrying about water. That's the truth. You just don't begin a day without deciding who's going to get the water, and when, and how good it'll be when it comes back. That's why I use Coke for my children, right from the start I do. It's the best thing you can get to take away their thirst, and give them the sugar they need. They drink it all over the country; it's made for the rest of the people. If they use it, we can. We have to, though. We can't turn to much of anything else. There's the milk you have in your body to start out with, and that goes real fast—I hear say because we can't get enough for ourselves. My grandma, she used to say that nothing comes free, even a mother's milk; and that you plain run dry if you can't keep yourself fed up good. The one thing you can do is keep plenty of water inside, and that's what Cokes do, and as I say they give you your sugar. And when the babies get on their own they drink those Cokes and you can see them perk up, perk right up. They'll be lying around, tired-like, and waiting on me to figure out what I can find for them, and then I'll get the bottle opener and they know what's coming. My grandma, she said we'd all be dried up and dead and gone from starvation if God didn't send us Cokes.

Source: Coles, *Still Hungry in America*, 1969.

**Power** How is power divided according to social statuses in the United States? C. Wright Mills (1956) argued that power in the United States is concentrated in the hands of an elite, that business, political, and military leaders share common backgrounds, values, and attitudes, and cooperate with each other in order to maintain their dominant positions. He noted, for example, that individuals often move among high positions in business, government, and the military. Business leaders are often appointed to top positions in government agencies designed to regulate business; or, those in charge of government agencies that regulate business may later work for corporations, using their special knowledge to help businesses avoid government regulations.

Alexander Haig was an army general until the 1970s, when he became a close aide to President Nixon. He then served as president of United Technologies, a large corporation that specializes in making jet engines for the military. In 1980 he became Ronald Reagan's secretary of state, and after resigning that position, returned to United Technologies. From Mills' point of view, Haig is an example of elite individuals who move from one powerful position to another—whether economic, political, or military—and because these people know each other well and share values and experiences, they are in a position to exercise considerable control over important decisions.

Domhoff (1967, 1971) compiled a list of the American upper class—those at the highest levels of wealth and education—and found that while its members may belong to different political parties, they are closely related through intermarriage, attendance at the same schools, and club memberships. Most important, they strongly value free enterprise and the rights to accumulate private property and make profits, and they are far more likely to occupy powerful positions in business and government than are those in the social classes below them. Useem (1983) conducted in-depth interviews with 72 British and 57 American leaders of large corporations, and his findings were very similar to Domhoff's (see also Domhoff, 1983).

Riesman (1961), on the other hand, argued that Mills overstated the power of elites in the United States. To Riesman, power is *pluralistic*, concentrated in a wide variety of interest groups: labor unions, professional organizations such as the American Medical Association, consumer action groups, political parties, the National Association for the Advancement of Colored People (NAACP), the Civil Liberties Union, the Urban League, the Congress of Racial Equality (CORE), and the National Organization for Women.

Both views are correct to a degree. The upper class clearly has more control over economic and political decisions than do people in any other class; and yet, the power of the upper class is by no means absolute. While no group controls American society, it is also true that individual citizens have good reason to feel powerless unless they are represented by an interest group.

**Prestige: Distributing Respect** There are few things more important to us than how other people perceive and evaluate us as human beings. There are few things worse than being treated as "inferior," and few things are as satisfying as being treated with respect, as though we and what we do are valuable and worthwhile in the eyes of others.

While wealth, power, and prestige have similar bases, they are not the same, for people can be respected without having very much power. This is true, for example, of England's royal family and the spouses of American presidents.

Unlike power and wealth, however, the distribution of **prestige** depends heavily on cultural values. Parsons (1964) argued that the respect we receive from others depends on how our culture values *possessions, qualities* (such as "natural talent" or ascribed statuses such as race, gender, and the social class of our parents), and *performance* (including achieved statuses such as education, marital status, and occupation).

If our culture values possessions, such as cars, stereos, and jewelry, we tend to respect those who have them even when they have no power over us. For this reason, people often buy things (such as "designer jeans") not simply to use or enjoy them, but to indicate to others that they have achieved an important cultural value and therefore deserve high levels of respect. This is what Thorstein Veblen (1928) called conspicuous consumption, owning objects in order to enhance or affirm prestige. What people buy can be explained only in part by the manifest function of the object, (in the case of jeans, to cover our bodies, keep us warm, and improve our physical appearance). Only by paying attention to latent functions such as enhanced prestige can we fully understand trends in what people buy and consume (Merton, 1957, 1968).

Conspicuous consumption, however, has not always brought with it higher levels of prestige, and Harris (1974) argued that historical shifts in the *basis* for distributing prestige have helped perpetuate stratification in industrial societies. In the

**Table 11-3**

Occupational Prestige Rankings (United States, 1963)

| OCCUPATION | PERCENTAGE RATING OCCUPATION'S PRESTIGE AS | | OCCUPATION | PERCENTAGE RATING OCCUPATION'S PRESTIGE AS | |
|---|---|---|---|---|---|
| | "Excellent" | "Good" | | "Excellent" | "Good" |
| U.S. Supreme Court justice | 77 | 18 | Police Officer | 16 | 38 |
| Physician | 71 | 25 | Newspaper reporter | 7 | 45 |
| Scientist | 68 | 27 | Tenant farmer | 11 | 37 |
| State governor | 64 | 30 | Carpenter | 7 | 36 |
| College professor | 59 | 35 | Manager of small store | 3 | 40 |
| Representative in Congress | 58 | 33 | Local labor union official | 8 | 36 |
| Lawyer | 53 | 38 | Mail carrier | 7 | 29 |
| Dentist | 47 | 47 | Railroad conductor | 6 | 33 |
| Member of board of directors of a large corporation | 42 | 51 | Plumber | 6 | 29 |
| Mayor of a large city | 46 | 44 | Factory machine operator | 6 | 24 |
| Civil engineer | 40 | 52 | Garage mechanic | 4 | 22 |
| Airline pilot | 41 | 48 | Truck driver | 3 | 18 |
| Banker | 39 | 51 | Clerk in a store | 1 | 14 |
| Large business accountant | 27 | 55 | Gas station attendant | 2 | 11 |
| Public school teacher | 31 | 46 | Dockworker | 2 | 9 |
| Owner of small factory | 28 | 49 | Night guard | 3 | 10 |
| Building contractor | 22 | 56 | Coal miner | 3 | 13 |
| Symphony orchestra musician | 25 | 45 | Restaurant waiter | 2 | 8 |
| Electrician | 18 | 45 | Taxi driver | 2 | 8 |
| Trained machinist | 15 | 50 | Farm hand | 3 | 12 |
| Farm owner and operator | 16 | 45 | Janitor | 1 | 9 |
| City welfare worker | 17 | 44 | Garbage collector | 2 | 5 |
| | | | Shoe shiner | * | 3 |

Source: Hodge, Siegel, and Rossi, 1964.

---

*less than 0.5 percent

early stages of capitalism, for example, prestige went to those who were frugal and wealthy. When the privileged position of the rich became more secure, they engaged in conspicuous consumption—building enormous estates (such as the mansions in Newport, Rhode Island) and spending their wealth openly and freely as a symbolic expression of their power and privilege.

As production increased and capitalists needed people to buy their goods, conspicuous consumption became associated with prestige among the middle and lower classes, as well. Most recently, as the gap between rich and poor has become a source of social conflict, the "old rich" protect their high prestige by regarding conspicuous consumption as "vulgar." This shift both lowers their visibility and changes the "rules of the game," once again putting the highest levels of prestige out of reach of everyone but themselves.

Prestige is also distributed according to ascribed statuses such as race, gender, ethnicity, and our parents' social class—characteristics that we are born with and powerless to change. When black men are referred to as "boys," or when adult women are referred to as "girls," their ascribed statuses are being used to lower their value in other people's eyes. Children who can say, "My father is a U.S. senator," are likely to receive levels of respect that have nothing to do with their individual characteristics or accomplishments.

Prestige is also affected by cultural values attached to achieved statuses and their roles. Since 1947, several studies have attempted to measure the amount of prestige attached to different occupations (Hodge, Treiman, and Rossi, 1966; North and Hatt, 1947; Treiman, 1977). In such studies, respondents are asked to rate the prestige of occupations as "excellent," "good," "average," "somewhat below average," or "poor" (see Table 11-3), and researchers used the ratings to give each occupation an average rank.

The most prestigious occupations are those that either require extensive formal education or involve high levels of responsibility and power—professionals and technical workers, business owners and managers, and administrators. At the bottom are jobs that depend mainly on manual work, require relatively little training, and involve little or no power.

In 1980 only 27 percent of working Americans held jobs whose prestige was rated "good" or "excellent"—professionals and technical workers, managers, and administrators. Thus, like wealth, income, and power, the distribution of prestige in the United States is highly unequal; and, as Studs Terkel (1974) found when he interviewed people in many different occupations, the high prestige of those at the top is paid for by those at the bottom. As a washroom attendant in a large Chicago hotel put it:

> I'm not particularly proud of what I'm doing. . . . I don't go around saying I'm a washroom attendant. . . . Outside of my immediate family, very few people know what I do. . . . This man shining shoes, he's had several offers . . . where he could make more money. But he wouldn't take 'em because the jobs were too open. He didn't want to be *seen* shining shoes. . . . No, I'm not proud of this work. (p. 108)

Whether we view stratification from Weber's point of view or Marx's, the United States is, like every complex society, clearly divided into social classes. The degree of inequality is only one aspect of stratification systems, however, for societies also differ in how *rigidly* they are stratified. In other words, societies differ in how easily individuals can change their social class or their standing within a class. Such changes, of course, can be positive or negative, for people can move down as well as up. Together, the movement of individuals within and between classes is called **social mobility**.

---

**PUZZLES:**

## WHAT ARE THE MOST IMPORTANT FACTORS THAT DETERMINE WHO GETS AHEAD?

If your answer includes "education" and "hard work," you agree with most Americans. But as this chapter explains, if your answer includes "luck," "race," "sex," and "who your parents are," you might be closer to the truth.

The following sections look at social mobility in terms of Weber's and Marx's concepts of social class. As you might guess, the resulting picture of social mobility in the United States depends on which concept we use.

## Social Mobility: Going Up and Going Down

Mobility occurs when individuals start from one position and end up in another that is either higher or lower than the original. There are two ways of defining "starting positions," however, and each corresponds to a different type of mobility. First, we can think of *lifetime* mobility—a woman begins as a researcher in a publishing company and retires as a senior editor; or, she becomes an editor at age 36, loses her job when the company goes bankrupt, and ends her work life as a waitress. Second, we can compare people's social class position with that of their parents in order to detect *intergenerational* mobility.

In a **closed stratification system,** social classes are called **castes.** Caste membership is based on ascribed statuses such as ethnicity and race, and because it is assigned at birth according to the parents' caste, it cannot be changed. While individuals can improve their position within a caste, it is impossible for them to change their caste. Before the abolition of slavery in the United States, caste was an important aspect of race relations, and in some respects it still is (Frederickson, 1981). Housing continues to be strongly segregated by race, and most whites disapprove of racial intermarriage.

As one of India's "untouchables," the lowest among the caste of laborers, the woman holding a broom she uses to clean toilets was assigned her status (and even her occupational specialization) at birth. The teacher is a member of a higher caste, but her status, too, was ascribed, based on her parents' caste. This traditional closed stratification system has been undergoing changes since India achieved its independence.

In an **open stratification system,** individuals may freely compete for wealth, power, and prestige regardless of their ascribed statuses. In the United States, as in most of the world's societies—whether capitalist or socialist—the stratification system is open to a degree and allows some mobility from positions of lower power, wealth, or prestige to higher ones. Most Americans believe that whatever our class position is today, with hard work, education, and a little luck, there are few limits on what we can achieve. Sociological research suggests that our perceptions are accurate in the sense that Americans often do improve their positions; but it also shows that how *far* we can move is, for most of us, very limited.

The next three sections try to answer three basic questions about social mobility. First, what characteristics of societies determine how much mobility there is in their populations? Second, which social characteristics allow some individuals to be more mobile than others? Third, does mobility lead to greater equality in society as a whole?

## *How Much Mobility?*

The extent of upward mobility in any society depends on two basic aspects of its social structure. People cannot move up to better positions if there are none available; and in order to occupy higher positions, we must have the characteristics and abilities required for entry into those statuses.

Feudal societies were divided into two classes—the land-owning nobility and the peasants—and mobility was severely limited. There were very few positions available, and since only the eldest son could inherit his father's estate, the younger sons had few options other than an ecclesiastical career. The daughters of nobility had three choices: to marry a nobleman, spend their life in their father's house, or enter a convent. The caste system made it impossible for peasants to move upward, since the only higher status in the system was the ascribed status of "noble."

Industrialization and complex divisions of labor account for the relatively high rates of mobility found in the United States and other modern societies (Blau and Duncan, 1967; Lipset and Bendix, 1959). Industrialization caused a vast expansion of educational opportunities: of people 18 to 24 years old, the percentage in college increased from 1 percent in 1870 to 25 percent in 1982, and since 1918 the number of people in vocational training programs has increased from under 100,000 to more than 16 million (U.S. Census Bureau, 1980b, 1983c).

By creating thousands of different jobs as well as opportunities to acquire necessary skills, industrialization created mobility by dividing the distance between the highest and lowest class into a series of very small steps. Whereas in feudal societies the "ladder" of success had only two rungs—with the top rung hopelessly beyond the reach of those on the bottom—the "ladder" in industrial societies has thousands of "rungs." While the poor still have almost no chance of reaching the top rung (the upper class), they can experience some progress and may eventually make it to the middle class.

Kahl (1961) found that between 1920 and 1950, 67 percent of sons were in higher-ranked occupations than their fathers. Blau and Duncan (1967) compared the educations and occupations of fathers and sons and found that 37 percent of men with white-collar jobs had fathers who worked in blue-collar jobs. Both of these studies, however, find that the *degree* of movement from one generation to the next is quite small. The vast majority of those who occupy high statuses in government and business come from upper-class families, and a study of professionals in the 1960s found that 40

In feudal societies, the nobility was at the top and the peasants were at the bottom, and there were few social positions in between.

percent had fathers who were professionals as well (Jackson and Crockett, 1964; Lipset and Bendix, 1959).

In the 1980s the job market is expanding in industries that require technical training—such as computer programming—and service occupations such as veterinarians, legal assistants, tax preparers, and employment interviewers (*Newsweek*, Oc-

tober 18, 1982). There are not enough children of upper- and middle-class parents to fill these jobs—fertility is lower in the middle and upper classes than in the lower class. Thus, structural changes in the economy and relatively low birth rates in the middle and upper classes have created opportunities for the children of lower-class parents to move into the middle class.

Technological advances that create thousands of jobs for those with technical training can spell disaster for millions of manual workers. The automobile industry, for example, will increasingly replace workers with robots on assembly lines, and while this creates jobs for engineers and technicians, it causes severe downward mobility for many skilled and unskilled blue-collar workers.

Some can go back to school to train themselves for new opportunities; but this is a long-term solution that ignores short-term effects of downward mobility. Bills—including medical bills and those for college tuition and home mortgages—must be paid now, not later. In many cases, the shock of downward mobility is so severe that families never recover. Thus, as the structure of the job market—the kinds of jobs available—changes, it causes both upward and downward mobility.

## Who Goes Up and Who Goes Down?

Sociologists identify several social statuses that affect who moves up and who moves down in the stratification system, the most important of which are education, social class of parents, race, gender, occupation, and age.

Americans generally agree that education is the most important factor in upward mobility. In 1976 almost half of all parents hoped their young children would eventually receive a college or graduate degree; and in 1978, 35 percent of adults believed that a college education is "very important." The perceived importance of higher education is strongest among those with the most to gain: 45 percent of those with incomes below $7,000 consider college "very important," compared with only 32 percent of those with annual incomes above $15,000 (U.S. Census Bureau, 1980b).

The introduction of robots on assembly lines has led to the replacement—and unemployment—of thousands of workers.

## Voices: The Shock of Downward Mobility

*Now what will happen to me?* The wording suggests an uncharacteristic passivity, even despair. But the lesson of the past several years is that taking charge doesn't always yield results. Fred O'Connor, a 40-year-old lathe operator from Rockford, trekked across the Midwest in search of new employment after his layoff six months ago. From Logansport, Ind., to Marysville, Ohio, the response has been the same: no vacancy. "I've been practically spit on when I've tried to apply for a job," he says. "They don't want to hire you; they don't even want to see you coming." At Rockwell International's Rockford printing-press plant, O'Connor had been earning more than $12 an hour, but he's becoming reconciled to the idea of a new line of work for less money. "In a few years I imagine I'll be in some job paying $4 to $5 an hour," he says. "*If* I can get it."

Meanwhile, life must go on. "I used to have all the money in the world but no time," says Don Brooks, a furloughed electrician at the National Steel Pellet Co. mine outside Hibbing. "Now I've got all the time in the world but no money." He also has an eight-month-old son with serious medical problems: the child was born with no connection from his esophagus to

his stomach and required surgery. Next came a virus that hospitalized him for four weeks. In all, the baby's health-care bills have mounted past $30,000, and the family budget is showing the strain. "My mortgage payment and health insurance take up three unemployment checks a month," says Brooks. "That leaves one week's check for utilities and food—not to mention car insurance and all the rest." He smiles ruefully. "I used to make more than $12 an hour," he adds. "Our contract says I've gotten a raise since I got laid off. Now I'm making more than $13 an hour."

Brooks remembers happier days when all the workers enjoyed the middle-class life. "Most people around here spent their money on toys," he says. "Boats, cars, four-wheel drives—the idea was to go anywhere you wanted to go. It was as if nothing could stop you." Overtime was so plentiful a worker could afford to take days off on a whim—"It was all gravy . . . You'd get up in the morning and you'd say, 'It's Wednesday—that's a good reason not to go to work today.' So you call the mine to say you weren't coming in, and then you'd head uptown. The question used to be, 'What do we want to do?' Now it's 'What *can* we do?'"

Source: *Newsweek*, March 21, 1983.

---

Research generally supports our faith in education. Blau and Duncan (1967) determined that education has a greater effect on mobility than parents' education or occupation. Although education generally increases mobility, its effects are not guaranteed. In 1982, 27 percent of college-educated workers had lower incomes than the average worker with only a high school diploma; and 26 percent of workers with high school diplomas had *higher* incomes than the average college-educated worker (U.S. Census Bureau, 1983c). As Thurow (1975), Jencks et al. (1972), and Bane and Jencks (1972) concluded, training and skill cannot explain why some people have more income than others. Bane and Jencks went so far as to suggest that "luck" is the single most important factor.

If we compare the incomes of brothers who have similar IQ scores and similar educations, for example, they differ by an average of $5,300. If we choose pairs of men at *random*, however, the average difference between their incomes is only slightly higher—$6,200. As explained by Bane and Jencks:

> These estimates mean that people who start off equal end up almost as unequal as everyone else. Inequality is not mostly inherited: It is re-created anew in each generation. . . . Adult success must depend on a lot of things besides family background, schooling, and the cognitive skills measured by standardized tests. (p. 39)

The positive effects of education also depend on ascribed statuses such as race and gender. In

Table 2-6, for example, we saw that while education increases women's incomes, they still lag far behind men with far less formal education.

Although education has long been viewed as a great "equalizer" in American society, this belief depends on the belief that everyone has an equal chance to go to college; but, of course, this is far from true. In 1982, 52 percent of children with family incomes of $25,000 or more attended college; but in families making less than $10,000, only 25 percent were enrolled (U.S. Census Bureau, 1983c). Thus, while education promotes mobility regardless of parents' class, and lower-class parents are the most likely to value higher education, *access* to education strongly depends on parents' resources.

Even when children begin schooling with equal IQ and grow up to have equal education, class background strongly affects adult income. Bowles and Nelson (1974), for example, found that among white males 35 to 44 years old with nonfarm family backgrounds, children from families in the top tenth of the population were three times as likely to wind up in the top fifth of the population as children from families in the poorest tenth of the population (Table 11-4).

## Table 11-4

The Effect of Class Background on the Chance of Winding Up in the Top Fifth of the Income Distribution as Adults, for Those with Equal Childhood IQ and Educational Attainment

| INCOME OF FAMILY OF ORIGIN (10th) | CHANCE OF BEING IN THE TOP 5th OF INCOME AS AN ADULT (Percentage) |
|---|---|
| Bottom 10th | 10 |
| 2nd 10th | 14 |
| 3rd 10th | 16 |
| 4th 10th | 17 |
| 5th 10th | 19 |
| 6th 10th | 20 |
| 7th 10th | 22 |
| 8th 10th | 24 |
| 9th 10th | 27 |
| Top 10th | 32 |

Source: Bowles and Nelson, 1974.

The ability to move upward also depends on our initial occupations. Newly created jobs in the United States increasingly require advanced training and intellectual rather than manual skills. Technological advances, then, degrade the value of certain kinds of skilled and unskilled labor, and these workers are the most likely to be downwardly mobile as they are replaced by machines and find themselves unable to find new jobs in an increasingly sophisticated and educated work force (Braverman, 1976).

Studies of mobility in the United States, then, give us a mixed picture. People often enjoy higher incomes and more prestigious occupations than their parents, but in general the differences are small. Achieved statuses such as education are important, but they offer no guarantee of success and their effects are often limited by ascribed statuses such as race, gender, and the social class of parents. The number and variety of jobs available is a structural characteristic of society itself and is beyond the control of workers. As that structure changes, it inevitably produces opportunities for some and hardship for others.

We come now to our third question about social mobility: What effect does it have on stratification? Does mobility lead to a less-stratified society? Or, does it actually help maintain inequality?

## Is Mobility an Illusion?

While upward mobility appears to be a common occurrence that justifies the common belief that the United States is a "land of opportunity," in several respects our faith in the equalizing effects of mobility is not justified. First, in spite of the findings of mobility studies, Americans increasingly believe that their financial conditions are growing worse, not better. Second, so long as the stratification system remains intact, mobility has little effect on the relative standing of social classes and the ability of their members to control their society and their own lives.

Between 1960 and 1981, for example, the percentage of Americans living in poverty dropped from 22 percent to 14 percent, and, after taking inflation into account, the median income of husband-wife families increased by 39 percent. In addition, luxuries such as cars, washers, dryers, and stereos became increasingly common: between 1970 and 1982 the worth of all such goods in American households increased by 70 percent over and above the effects of inflation (U.S. Census Bureau, 1983c).

During much of this period, however, American adults continued to believe that their financial positions were growing worse. Between 1972 and 1984 the percentage of adults who reported that their financial condition had grown worse in recent years held steady at around 20 percent, and the percentage who agreed that "the lot of the average man is getting worse, not better" never dropped below 50 percent. In addition, people's perceptions of which class they belong to shifted downward between 1964 and 1984: in 1964, 61 percent of adults placed themselves in the middle class, and 35 percent in the working class (Hodge and Treiman, 1968). By 1984 only 45 percent placed themselves in the middle class and the working class swelled to 46 percent (Davis, 1984). How can things be getting better and worse at the same time?

Part of the answer is that while incomes rose between 1960 and 1981, the relative position of the middle class grew worse. The richest 40 percent of American families actually enjoyed a slight increase in their share of national income, while of the rest, the share of all but the poorest fell, even though actual incomes rose (U.S. Census Bureau, 1983c).

Under these conditions, people tend to feel **relative deprivation** (Williams, 1975). Whether or not we feel deprived depends only in part on *absolute* levels of income and wealth; it also depends on how much other people in our community and society have. If everyone lives at the same standard of living, no one is likely to feel deprived; but, if some live at a moderate level while others are wealthy, even a moderately good standard of living no longer feels adequate in comparison with others.

A second part of the answer lies in the *source* of increased family income. Between 1960 and 1980, the percentage of husband-wife families that depended on the earnings of both spouses rose from 43 percent to 65 percent. Thus, although family income rose by 39 percent, this was caused in part by a 51 percent increase in the percentage of families depending on the earnings of both spouses. Making a living also became more difficult for single, widowed, and divorced people: between 1965 and 1980, the percentage of people working at two or more jobs increased by 42 percent among single people and by 26 percent among those widowed or divorced (U.S. Census Bureau, 1981).

What of our increased stock of luxury goods? Does this represent upward mobility? It does, but only if we ignore the fact that between 1970 and 1982, the amount of consumer debt more than *tripled* (U.S. Census Bureau, 1983c). This means that a substantial portion of these new possessions is owned not by individuals and families, but by banks and loan companies that allow people to buy on credit. Thus, Americans increased their stock of luxuries in large part by going into debt. In fact, if spread evenly over the population, unpaid consumer debt in 1982 amounted to about $1,500 for every man, woman, and child.

While it appears on the surface that Americans are better off than ever before, most are working harder just to keep up, while those in the upper class maintain their privileged position with relative ease. This brings us to a deeper level, on which social mobility is an illusion: in spite of all the moving around within social classes, the class structure itself remains intact, and except for those in the poorest class, movement of people to a higher one is not common. Why is this true, and how is the illusion of mobility perpetuated?

Stone (1974) examined the steel industry in the early part of this century and argued that employers created mobility within the working class in order to encourage them to work harder and to control their dissatisfaction with working conditions and pay. Before the Industrial Revolution, goods were produced by skilled workers who were familiar with all aspects of production. From roughly the 1870s on, however, the factory assembly line, by splitting the production process into a series of small steps, few of which require great skill, led to a decline of skilled workers. Thus, as the range of skills in the steel industry narrowed, workers could be replaced with relative ease, and most found themselves stuck in "dead-end" jobs (Gordon, Edwards, and Reich, 1982).

Employers responded by creating "job ladders." Put simply, they took a narrow range of jobs and made fine distinctions among them, attaching slightly higher levels of pay to each. Thus, while the jobs were as "dead-end" as before, the job ladder gave workers the *feeling* of moving upward. Job ladders also encouraged workers to compete with each other for promotion, rather than unite against their employers.

*"If debt is a measure of consumer confidence, we have become very confident indeed."*

Drawing by Lorenz; ©1983, The New Yorker Magazine, Inc.

The illusion of mobility is also supported by the greater value placed on white-collar jobs than on blue-collar jobs. Blau and Duncan (1967), for example, interpreted the white-collar jobs of the children of blue-collar workers as a sign of upward mobility; but "white-collar," includes many low-level occupations: clerks, security guards, telephone operators, mail carriers, welfare workers, and day-care workers; and many blue-collar jobs require more mental ability than do many white-collar jobs. Is a typist's work any less "manual" or any more "mental" than a skilled tool and die maker's?

Stone argued that the distinction between mental and physical labor is both unnecessary and artificial, and "only serves to maintain the power of employers over their workers" (p. 28). It does this by fostering the illusion that becoming a white-collar worker—no matter how lowly the position may actually be—is a step upward in the stratification system.

Many Americans improve their levels of income, wealth, and prestige, both during their own lifetimes and in comparison with their parents; but the gap between those who own or control the means of production and those who do not is virtually unaffected by such individual progress. For the vast majority of Americans, upward mobility is strictly limited by the stratification system. Most of us spend our work lives inching up a short ladder with many rungs, and even when we reach the top of it, we are not very high and do not have much of a view.

## Marx:
## Mobility as an Uninteresting Problem

The tendency of Americans to focus on social mobility and competition for wealth, power, and prestige *within* a stratified society leads us to ignore the stratification system itself. From Marx's perspective, so long as the upper class controls the means of production and the working class must sell its labor power for whatever wage employers are willing to pay, mobility from one income or occupational level to the next is largely a case of those at the lower levels fighting to keep from being on the bottom. After all, if every American made it to the middle class, the middle class would no longer be "middle"—it would be the lower class in comparison with everyone else.

To Marx, the key to understanding how wealth, power, and prestige are distributed in societies lies in how goods are produced and whether or not the means of production are privately owned. The self-employed, for example, who by definition control their own means of production, are twice as likely to be in the top income brackets as are those who work for someone else (U.S. Census Bureau, 1981).

To Marx, social mobility from Weber's point of view is largely irrelevant and only contributes to false consciousness. More important, Marx's concept of social class focuses on the considerable *downward* mobility that most sociological studies of social mobility ignore. As we saw earlier, the percentage of people who are self-employed dropped from around 80 percent in the early 1800s to less than 10 percent in 1980. In addition, the *control* of the means of production remains concentrated in a relatively small portion of the population. Between 1900 and 1980, the percentage of employed people who were managers, administrators, or officials only increased from 6 percent to 10 percent (U.S. Census Bureau, 1980b, 1983c).

If we define "upward mobility" as movement from less control over the means of production to more control, then Americans have been *downwardly* mobile for almost two centuries, and only a small percentage of Americans have risen to social statuses that afford any major degree of control

over the means of production that form the basis for the distribution of wealth, power, and prestige.

What of societies other than our own? How does stratification differ among societies, and why are some societies wealthier than others?

## International Stratification

**International social stratification** has two aspects. First, countries differ in the degree of inequality and the amount of social mobility they allow. Second, there is enormous inequality between countries. International stratification is particularly important, for the amount of wealth that is available for distribution *within* a society often depends on relationships between societies.

### Varieties of Inequality within Societies

Although wealth, power, and prestige are unequally distributed in the United States, in many societies inequality is far more severe. In the United States, for example, the distribution of wealth is in the shape of a "diamond," with a relatively small percentage who are poor or wealthy and a large middle class. In most less-developed countries, however, the distribution looks like a pyramid, with a small elite at the top, a relatively small middle, and a broad base of poor people at the bottom.

In general, wealth is distributed more equally in industrial countries than in poor countries that are just beginning to industrialize (Kerbo, 1983; Weede, 1980). In 1970, for example, the richest 5 percent of Brazil's population received 50 percent of all income, compared with 20 percent in the United States. In 1969, the richest fifth of Mexico City's population received 63 percent of all income, while the bottom fifth lived on a meager 1 percent (Barnet and Muller, 1974; U.S. Census Bureau, 1980b).

The early stages of industrialization generally create more, rather than less inequality. Per capita income in Mexico almost doubled between 1960 and 1972, but Mexico's prosperity was not shared with its poor people. Mexico is typical of industrializing countries: when the economy grows, the rich get richer and the poor get poorer. Increased production is used not to better the living and working conditions of the entire population but to satisfy the elite's desire for luxuries (Herman,

In countries such as Mexico, which are just starting to industrialize, inequality generally becomes more, not less, severe; and the extremes of wealth and poverty become more apparent than ever.

1975). As a former president of Brazil put it, "Brazil is doing well but the people are not" (in Barnet and Muller, p. 149).

Increased production in less-developed countries is also used to protect the privileged position of the upper class. Countries such as Argentina, Chile, Indonesia, the Dominican Republic, and South Korea invest heavily in military and police units whose primary function is to control the local population and prevent revolutions that would threaten the privileged upper class.

In socialist countries such as the Soviet Union and China, wealth, power, and prestige are unequally distributed, just as they are throughout most of the world. Party leaders are wealthier, live in better housing, and have access to a variety of luxury goods beyond the reach of most people. While the means of production are not owned by the elite, they are tightly controlled by a relative few (Connor, 1979; Hollander, 1982).

Thus, while the vast family fortunes of the American Rockefellers and Hunts have no parallel in socialist countries, socialist and capitalist societies are similar in an important way. In socialist societies surpluses are appropriated by the state and the party elite decides how they will be used. In capitalist societies surpluses are appropriated by capitalists who can then use them for their benefit. In neither type of society, therefore, do the workers have the power to control and dispose of what they produce.

**Social Mobility** Nineteenth-century India was divided into four castes: priests and scholars at the top, then nobles and warriors, merchants and skilled workers, and common laborers. Below all of these were the outcasts, or "untouchables," with whom physical contact was avoided at all costs by members of castes. In 1949 the Indian caste system was officially abolished; and its importance has declined in urban areas, where it is difficult to maintain caste identity in crowded living conditions; but caste remains an important force in traditional rural areas (Berreman, 1973).

South Africa is one of the few remaining caste societies. Blacks and whites constitute two castes, and it is impossible to move from one to the other. Although whites make up only 17 percent of the population, they dominate all aspects of social life through a rigid policy of racial segregation called

## Voices: Social Immobility

Mataji and Pitaji had a servant called Fikan. A servant was expected of a respectable Jat family, and Mataji thought herself very respectable. Fikan was a low caste Hindu boy of twenty who had lived in the house for the past five years. He slept apart from the family, moved about noiselessly and didn't speak unless he had to: I was scarcely aware of his presence.

Four hundred miles away in Uttar Pradesh, Fikan had a wife and child. He sent them most of his monthly income of £9; once a year he went home on leave. His wife, meanwhile, made a rudimentary living by breaking up stone for road repairs. I had often passed groups of such labourers squatting by the roadside hammering rocks into smaller and smaller pieces. They hammered all day and every day, on frosty winter mornings, in torrential rain and exposed to the noonday heat, and they lived in temporary makeshift huts by the roadside, huts made of sacking and bitumen drums.

Fikan's lot was better than his wife's and, according to Jungli, better than most other servants kept by Jat families. Other people didn't buy their servants such nice clothes as Mataji did, nor give them the same food the family ate. Other people only gave them pickles with their chapattis, or watered buttermilk with salt and green chillies. And other people worked their servants hard all day in the fields. Fikan's duties were light—four animals to graze in the daytime and water evening and morning, the night fodder to bring in from the fields and push through the chopping machine, and sundry errands to run. In the afternoon lulls he would squat with his cronies (Hindu boys who worked in other Jat houses), pound cannabis with a pestle and mortar and drink it, watered down, with salt. It was his chief pleasure in life.

Source: Lloyd, *An Indian Attachment*, 1984.

South Africa is one of the few remaining caste societies in which race affects virtually all aspects of social life.

**apartheid.** Interracial marriage and sexual relations are forbidden by law. Blacks are not allowed to vote in national elections, are forced to live in impoverished areas, and are allowed to enter "white" areas only to work for whites. All skilled and the better unskilled jobs are reserved for whites, blacks are forbidden by law from striking, and the average black worker's income is only one-seventh that of the average white (Frederickson, 1981; Lever, 1981).

In comparison with caste societies, stratification systems in most of the world are relatively open, allowing varying degrees of mobility from lower to higher positions and using a variety of criteria to determine who is most likely to move. Does the United States offer more or less opportunity for mobility than other industrial societies?

If we measure mobility in terms of moving from blue-collar to white-collar jobs, the rates in West Germany, Sweden, Japan, France, and Britain are similar to those in the United States (Lipset and Bendix, 1959). If we define mobility more narrowly—focusing on movement from the working class to professional or highly technical occupations—the U.S. seems to offer better opportunities than most countries. In the 1960s roughly 10 percent of the American working class advanced to professional and technical jobs, compared with 2 percent in West Germany, 7 percent in Japan, and 4 percent in France (Blau and Duncan, 1967; Fox and Miller, 1965). Note, however, how small the percentages are, even in the United States.

Inequality is a pervasive feature of the world's societies, and although they differ in the extent of inequality, virtually all known societies are dominated by elite, privileged groups. Perhaps the most striking levels of inequality in the world, however, are found *between* societies, not within them.

## Inequality between Societies

In 1980, *per capita income* (what each person would receive if income were distributed evenly) in industrialized societies ranged from highs of $16,200 in Switzerland and $10,400 in the United States to a low of $8,900 in Japan. In socialist countries (excluding China), per capita income ranged from a high of $4,900 in the Soviet Union to a low of $3,000 in Yugoslavia. In the remaining countries, per capita income was startlingly low: $500 in China and Egypt, $700 in Uganda, $200 in Zaire, $200 in India, and $100 in Bangladesh, (U.S. Census Bureau, 1983c).

These differences are even more striking if we remember that per capita income is the amount of money each person would receive *if* income were distributed equally *within* countries. Thus, while under conditions of equality each person in India would receive $200 a year, the vast majority of Indians must actually live on far less. Even if income were distributed equally within countries, the people of the wealthiest countries would receive more income each *week* than most of the world's inhabitants would receive each *year*.

The effects of world stratification extend to every aspect of living conditions. Almost half of the people in Africa and Asia can neither read nor write. The United States contains only 5 percent of the world's people, and yet we use 28 percent of all the energy consumed each year. China, on the other hand, contains roughly 23 percent of all the people in the world, and yet its annual share of energy is only 7 percent. In the world's industrial societies, less than 2 percent of all infants die during their first year of life; but in many nonindustrial societies, between 15 and 25 percent of all infants die. The average person in Japan can expect to live

76 years, but in Nigeria life expectancy is only 41 years (U.S. Census Bureau, 1983c). In industrial societies, death by starvation is rare; but in Ethiopia, hundreds of thousands died of starvation when prolonged drought and crop failure wiped out the country's food supply in 1984 and 1985.

Part of the explanation of international inequality is ecological. The United States, for example, is rich in natural resources, and industrialization both here and in Europe took place when populations were relatively small. In most of today's poor countries, on the other hand, populations already outstrip food supplies and are growing faster than the ability to provide jobs and basic necessities.

The answer, however, is not this simple, for the poverty of most of the world's people is linked with the prosperity of the rest. The Industrial Revolution in Europe, for example, depended on **colonialism,** an arrangement through which a "parent" country controls and dominates another. England's colonies provided raw materials for its industry, and England then sold the finished goods to colonies. Because England controlled its colonies, it would not allow them to trade with any country other than England or develop industries of their own. Colonialism consequently guaranteed colonial powers a continuing source of raw materials and a "captive" market in which to sell their manufactured products (Emerson, 1968; Fieldhouse, 1968).

This arrangement was functional for the economic growth of colonial powers; but for the colonies themselves it was an exploitative relationship that left them poorer. Although the colonialism of the seventeenth, eighteenth, and nineteenth centuries no longer exists today, the relationships between rich and poor countries still contain elements of it.

For example, many of the industries in less-developed countries are owned and operated by American or European corporations such as Ford and Sears. Many people believe that poor countries should be grateful to wealthy foreigners who build businesses and provide jobs, but this belief ignores some important facts (Barnet and Muller, 1974).

When an American corporation builds a factory in Brazil, it often uses little of its own money.

Instead, it borrows from Brazilian banks that prefer to risk their money on established U.S. corporations. Between 1960 and 1970, about 78 percent of all U.S. manufacturing operations in Latin America were financed with Latin American money. Thus, many new industries in less-developed countries do not represent a flow of resources (capital) from the wealthy countries to the poor.

Although less-developed countries provide most of the financing for new industry, they receive a small share of the profits. Between 1965 and 1968, for example, 52 percent of all profits from U.S.-owned businesses in Latin America went back to the United States. In some industries—such as mining—American parent companies returned as much as 79 percent of all profits to the United States.

The results of such relationships resemble those of colonialism. Poor countries are less likely to develop industries owned and controlled by local inhabitants. They become highly dependent on the dominant country. Most important, they stay relatively poor, partly because profits are not reinvested in their own economies. Thus, in many respects international stratification is functional for the economies of wealthy nations whose power enables them to dominate and exploit other countries (Evans, 1981; Evans and Timberlake, 1980). (See Chapter 17.)

Why do the people in less-developed countries tolerate such exploitation? In many cases, the exploitation of poor nations by rich ones is supported by the poor countries' wealthy elites, who grow richer while the vast majority of the population stays poor. They often maintain stability (and, therefore, their privileged position) by employing large numbers of soldiers and police, often financed with generous contributions from the United States and other wealthy nations (Herman, 1975).

**Mobility among Nations** For the world, estimated per capita income increased by 13 percent between 1970 and 1980, over and above the increase caused by inflation. While all but a handful of small countries shared in this progress, some took a much larger share than others. Between 1970 and 1980, per capita income increased by 17 percent in the wealthiest 15 countries (from $7,100 to $8,300)

and by only 2 percent in the remainder (from $632 to $645) (U.S. Census Bureau, 1983c).

In the poorest 15 countries, per capita income rose to a new high of about $360; but in the wealthiest countries, the *increase* in per capita income ($1,200) was more than three times larger than *total* per capita income in the world's poorest countries. These figures are even more disturbing when we remember that the 15 poorest countries contain 48 percent of the world's population and income is distributed very unequally within them. This means that most of the world's inhabitants receive a very small share of what is *already* a very small share of all that is produced in the world (U.S. Census Bureau, 1983c).

While virtually all countries improved their incomes during the 1970s period, the gap between the wealthiest and the poorest remained unchanged. In both 1970 and 1980, the wealthiest fifth of the world's population received around 75 percent of all income (U.S. Census Bureau, 1983c). In many Third World countries, per capita income has actually been falling since 1980, and in parts of Africa "there is now the real possibility that it will be lower by the end of the 1980s than it was in 1960" (World Bank, 1983, p. 2).

There is little question that stratification among societies is similar to stratification within them. Like upper-class elites, wealthy countries maintain the gap between themselves and those who have less. Although individual countries make progress, the international "pecking order" remains largely intact, just as the relative positions of social classes remain unchanged. It is a dismal picture and raises important questions: What are the prospects for change? Is such extreme inequality inevitable? Under what social and ecological conditions is equality most likely to come about, both within societies and between them?

## Prospects for Change

Aristotle once defined justice as "a virtue of the soul distributing that which each person deserves," and this is a major problem in all societies that produce a surplus. How can wealth, power, and prestige be distributed in ways that satisfy both the functional requirements of a society and cultural beliefs and values about justice and fairness? Debate over stratification centers on two basic kinds of change: equality of *opportunity* in the form of increased mobility *within* a stratified society and equality of *outcomes*—an end to stratification itself.

## Mobility and Equal Opportunity

In the early 1830s Alexis de Tocqueville visited America and recorded his impressions of the new country. In *Democracy in America* he wrote:

> I know of no country . . . where the love of money has taken stronger hold on the affections of men and where a profounder contempt is expressed for the theory of the permanent equality of property.

Tocqueville's observation remains largely true today. In their study of adults in Boston and Kansas City, Coleman and Rainwater (1978) found that most people did not favor an end to social stratification. In explaining their positions, people mentioned beliefs that America is a land of opportunity, that inequality is an important source of motivation for hard work, and that the possibility of mobility gives people a feeling that their lives are going somewhere. In fact, one of the major suggestions for change was to increase mobility by making higher education available to all and ending discrimination based on ascribed statuses such as race, ethnicity, and gender.

Coleman and Rainwater's study also revealed several important misperceptions of the U.S. stratification system. First, people commonly reported the belief that the gap between the upper class and those below is closing, although evidence presented earlier in this chapter shows that it is widening. Second, they used a definition of social class that narrowly defines a class society as one organized around rigid castes.

Third, they reported a great deal of faith in education as a route to upward mobility. Recent evidence suggests, however, that while higher education aids upward mobility more than any other factor, it is no guarantee of success, and its impact is growing weaker as college degrees become more common (Freeman, 1976; Jencks et al., 1979; Thurow, 1975). If a relative few have college degrees, its value is high, but when college education is a common characteristic of job applicants, it

represents less of an advantage. It is much like the inflation of money: when everyone has little money, each dollar is worth a great deal; but if money is plentiful, each dollar is worth less.

Fourth, and perhaps most important, Coleman and Rainwater's respondents generally thought of social stratification in individualistic terms. The responses of many are summarized by one answer: "We're still a competitive society; *people are still trying to get ahead of the next person*, and if that ever changes, it won't be America anymore" (p. 294).

This kind of response suggests that Americans accept social stratification because they believe that mobility will allow them to escape being at the bottom of the distribution system. In effect, they are saying, "Inequality is acceptable so long as I can feel that I'm doing better than someone else."

This ignores the fact that the *structure* of stratified societies severely limits mobility. Few people ever achieve elite statuses, and so long as an elite controls most of wealth and income, a stratification system can become open only to a very limited degree, regardless of whether the society is capitalist or socialist. However freely Americans may move from the lower to the middle class, 80 percent will still be competing with one another for the relatively small portion of wealth and income that remains after the wealthiest 20 percent takes its "share."

Herman (1975) argued that a significant shift toward equality will occur only when the lower 80 percent of the people focus their attention not on competition among themselves, but on the share of wealth and income left to them by the top 20 percent.

> Change, if it comes, will likely arise out of a continued series of shocks and a failure of the system to "deliver," not only to the bottom 20 percent, but to the lower 80 percent. Only substantial material blows are apparently capable of breaking through false consciousness. (p. 117)

## Equality and Classlessness

To Weber, a classless society is one in which everyone receives an equal share of wealth, power, and prestige. Marx went further by defining a classless society as one in which the distinction between owners and workers is removed and no one has the power to control opportunities to earn an equal share of what a society produces. Weber's view tells us little about how to achieve a classless society, because it pays little attention to the ways in which classes are created and perpetuated. Marx, on the other hand, was primarily interested in change, and by focusing on modes of production and social relationships, he suggested how it might come about.

Davis and Moore (1945) held that inequality is functional in existing societies, but they were less certain about its inevitability (Davis, 1953). Marx believed that inequality will persist until societies are able to produce an abundance of goods without depending heavily on physical labor. Consequently, he saw capitalism as a necessary step in a long historical process toward the utopian goal of equality, because capitalism dramatically increases production. Marx believed that *all* forms of inequality will disappear in advanced societies—for which he reserved the term "communist"—and capitalism will no longer be necessary. Indeed, Marx (in Marx and Engels, 1846) contended that the division of labor itself will disappear in communist societies:

> In a communist society, where nobody has one exclusive sphere of activity, but each can become accomplished in any branch he wishes, society . . . makes it possible for me to do one thing today and another tomorrow, to hunt in the morning, fish in the afternoon, rear cattle in the evening, and criticize after dinner. (p. 22)

This vision is clearly utopian, and even Marx's colleague, Engels, believed that the most advanced societies will depend on complex divisions of labor that require some people to occupy positions of authority. Between 1955 and 1965, for example, the Chinese army stopped dividing its soldiers by rank. The Chinese returned to the use of ranks in 1984, in part to avoid the kind of battlefield confusion that occurred during the short border war with Vietnam in 1979.

Many functional theorists also regard inequalities of prestige as inevitable, for high prestige is, by definition, always in short supply: There is no

such thing as "high prestige" except in relation to those who have lower prestige. What is unclear, however, is whether or not inequalities of prestige require that some members of society receive levels of respect so low that it damages their self-esteem.

The United States appears to have achieved the ability to produce the material abundance that Marx believed is necessary for equality. If all income for 1980 were distributed evenly among families, each would receive $24,000. In fact, however, 47 percent of all families had incomes more than $4,000 below this amount, and almost a third had incomes more than $10,000 below. In order for family income to be equally distributed (20 percent going to each fifth of the population), 26 percent of all income would have to be redistributed from the top 40 percent of the population to the lower 60 percent (U.S. Census Bureau, 1982).

Thus, while the United States clearly produces enough to provide an abundance of material goods for all its people, the actual distribution is far from this goal. Efforts to redistribute income in the United States—by taxing the rich at higher rates and supplementing poor people's incomes with welfare payments, food stamps, and free medical care, for example—have only slightly increased the share of income going to the poorest class, but at the same time have lowered the share received by the middle class (Beeghley, 1983; U.S. Census Bureau, 1983c). Thus, efforts to redistribute income have not weakened the dominant position of the upper class (Devine, 1983; Page, 1983).

In addition, by defining the problem of inequality primarily in terms of poverty, the American approach ignores the fact that even if poverty were eradicated entirely, the enormous gulf separating the wealthiest 20 percent from everyone else would remain. In many ways, a single-minded concentration on poverty as *the* problem in stratification systems maintains inequality by distracting both lower- and middle-class people from the fact that they have far more in common with each other than either has with the upper class.

Why does stratification persist, even though we produce a huge economic surplus? Marx argued that change will not occur until the working class becomes aware of the true nature and causes of its condition. Even then, it is doubtful that the upper class will give up its privileged position without a sustained struggle.

**Class Consciousness and Social Change**  Marx believed that even in societies that produce an abundance of goods, classes will disappear only when members of the working class achieve **class consciousness**—in other words, when they become aware of the true extent of inequality as well as its social causes. Without such consciousness, social classes are little more than social aggregates—collections of people who have a social status in common. With class consciousness, however, people can use common interests as a basis for organizing social movements.

Why have middle- and lower-class Americans not achieved class consciousness and demanded change in the stratification system? As we saw earlier in this chapter, Americans strongly believe in a cultural ideology that supports stratification; but, there is more involved than simple ideology. Americans *have* improved their lives within the existing class system, and each small step upward reinforces the belief that it is possible to reach the top. This belief, in turn, supports competition as a way of life, and when people are competing with each other, they are unlikely to come together and recognize their common interests.

An additional piece of the answer lies in the concept of **alienation**—a psychological condition in which people feel disconnected from other people or their own behavior (Marx, 1884). When we work for someone else rather than for ourselves, we lose control over the conditions under which we live and work. In extreme cases—such as China and the Soviet Union—workers do not choose what they will do, but merely do what they are told to do. The resulting lack of autonomy and self-control causes us to be something less than fully human, for as we lose control over work, we feel separated from it—alienated—and because work is such an important part of our lives, alienation from it produces feelings of alienation from each other. The alienation produced by a class society, then, makes it less likely that members of the working class will critically examine the true nature of their condition.

C. Wright Mills (1951) suggested that an important part of alienation is fear. Because those who control the means of production control our ability to make a living, we tend to live in a constant state of anxiety over our future. If we fear what employers may decide to do with us, we are less likely to threaten them and more likely to turn our anxieties on those who have less power over us—in other words, on other workers. In socialist countries fear is directed at the state, which, like employers in capitalist societies, controls people's ability to earn a living.

This explains why to many white male American workers the "enemy" is not the upper class, but blacks, Hispanics, and women who compete with them for jobs; and to many blacks, Hispanics, and women the "enemy" is the white male worker who stands in the way of their upward mobility by trying to maintain a monopoly over skilled jobs. As a result, members of different racial, gender, and ethnic categories fail to see what they have in common—membership in the working class. Instead, they tend to explain their circumstances in terms of *each other*, rather than as the inevitable consequence of the stratification system itself.

While inequality within societies is likely to cause severe strains in the coming years, inequality between nations is an increasingly serious source of international tension and conflict. Countries that once supplied industrial nations with raw materials—such as rare metals and oil—are becoming more militant and demanding an end to relationships through which wealthy nations prosper at the expense of poorer ones. Less-developed countries, realizing that industrial nations depend on them for raw materials, are using this awareness to exact higher prices for their goods.

While it may seem unlikely that Aristotle's notion of justice will ever come to pass in industrial societies, one thing is certain: change toward a more equitable and just system for distributing wealth, power, and prestige requires a full understanding of the social structures and supporting cultural ideas that produce and sustain social stratification. In short, the lot of individuals will improve little until we appreciate that each of us participates in socially structured relationships that profoundly affect our lives.

## Summary

1. Social stratification refers to the social structures through which the products of social life—including wealth, power, and prestige—are distributed unequally among members of society. Stratification is a process in which social statuses determine one's position in the system.

2. One of the most important concepts in the study of stratification is social class. To Marx, class position depends on a person's relationship to the means of production. Capitalists own or control the means of production, while workers sell their labor power to capitalists.

3. To Weber, class position depends on the *outcomes* of stratification; in other words, on how much power, prestige, or wealth a person has.

4. Davis and Moore's functional theory of stratification argues that inequality exists because some tasks are more important than others and it is necessary to offer higher rewards in order to motivate individuals to acquire the training to perform them. Complex divisions of labor also require that some people have authority over others.

5. Conflict theorists such as Marx argue that inequality benefits only those who are in dominant positions and that it results from a scarcity of valued goods. Conflict theorists also argue that culture often serves the interests of the privileged elite and constitutes an ideology that supports the status quo. False consciousness exists when members of a group misperceive the true nature and causes of the inequalities in their lives.

6. From the perspectives of both Marx and Weber, almost all societies are stratified. In the United States, for example, the control of the means of production is concentrated in the hands of a small minority and the distributions of wealth, power, and prestige are far from equal.

7. Social mobility is the movement of people within or between social classes. In closed systems class position is based on ascribed statuses (or castes) and no movement between them is allowed. There is a moderate amount of mobility in the United States and other industrial societies, but most upward moves are quite small.

8. The most important factors in mobility are education, social class of parents, race, gender, occupation, and age. Mobility has little effect on the relative positions of social classes. Family mobility often requires that both spouses work and that the family go into considerable debt. Job ladders often foster the illusion of mobility by dividing a short distance into many small steps.

9. Societies differ in the degree of inequality and there is great inequality between societies. Inequality is more severe in poor and newly industrializing societies than in industrial countries. While socialist countries do not base inequality on ownership of the means of production, they still have considerable inequality.

10. The gap between rich and poor nations is stable, in part because wealthy nations are in a position to exploit poorer ones.

11. Debate about change in stratification focuses on two issues: an end to the inequality and social classes of stratification and equality of opportunity within a stratified society.

12. Marx's communist utopia, in which social classes would disappear, is unlikely to ever come to pass. Both conflict and functional theorists believe that inequality of authority will always be necessary, and functional theorists also believe that inequality of prestige is inevitable.

13. Efforts to redistribute income in the United States have slightly improved conditions among the poor but have had no effect on the position of the upper class.

## Key Terms

alienation   349
blue-collar worker   318
class consciousness   349
closed stratification system   333

    apartheid   344
    caste   333

false consciousness   325
ideology   325
income   328
international stratification   341

    colonialism   345

labor   315
labor power   316
open stratification system   334

## Recommended Readings

BEEGHLEY, L. (1983). *Living poor in America*. New York: Praeger. An important book that challenges many common beliefs about welfare and the causes of poverty.

BENDIX, R., and LIPSET, S. M. (Eds.). (1966). *Class, status, and power* (2nd ed.). New York: Free Press. A comprehensive collection of articles about social stratification.

BOWLES, S., and GINTIS, H. (1976). *Schooling in capitalist America: Educational reform and the contradictions of economic life*. New York: Basic Books. An important book about the ways in which schooling reproduces social classes and inequality in the United States.

KERBO, H. R. (1983). *Social stratification and inequality*. New York: McGraw-Hill. A clear, interesting, and thorough introductory text.

LENSKI, G. (1966). *Power and privilege*. New York: McGraw-Hill. A fascinating look at the relationship between historical changes in the mode of production and the emergence of social inequality. The early chapters are particularly useful as overviews of the general problem of social stratification.

MARX, K. (1964). *Selected writings in sociology and social philosophy*. Edited by T. Bottomore and M. Rubel. Baltimore, MD: Penguin. A highly accessible introduction to Marx's major ideas on social stratification.

SENNETT, R., and COBB, J. (1972). *The hidden injuries of class*. New York: Vintage. A thought-provoking look at the ways in which social class differences affect how people feel about themselves and one another.

# CHAPTER 12

# Race and Ethnicity

Chapter 11 described basic aspects of all social stratification systems through which culturally valued rewards such as wealth, power, and prestige are distributed within and among societies. Whereas Chapter 11 focused primarily on the importance of achieved social statuses such as education and occupation, in this and the next two chapters we take a detailed look at the importance of ascribed social statuses such as race and ethnicity, gender, and age in the distribution of wealth, power, and prestige.

We begin with some basic concepts—race, ethnicity, minority group, and social oppression—and then examine cultural, social structural, and ecological aspects of social inequality based on race and ethnicity. Then we use conflict and functional perspectives to explain why societies have for centuries used ascribed statuses as bases for social inequality, and, finally, we explore what it will take to end social oppression.

## Race and Ethnicity

Imagine that you apply for a copy of your birth certificate one day, and when you receive it, you discover that it lists your "race" as something other than what you and everyone else always considered it to be. You are black, and the certificate says you are white; or you are white, and it says you are black. How would you feel?

This is exactly what happened in 1977 to Susie Guillory Phipps—a New Orleans resident who had always been white, both to herself and to everyone who encountered her. She had twice married white men, and her family album was filled with pictures of blue-eyed, white ancestors. The state of Louisiana, however, defined her as "colored."

When she protested to state authorities, they carefully traced her ancestry back 222 years and found that although her great-great-great-great grandfather was white, her great-great-great-great grandmother was black. Under Louisiana law, anyone whose ancestry was at least 3 percent black was considered black. Thus, even with an ancestry 97 percent white, the state defined her as black (Jaynes, 1982).

Susie Phipps spent $20,000 to force Louisiana to change her birth certificate, and in 1983 Louisiana repealed the law. Why did she go to such expense? Beyond the obvious shock to her personal identity, there are larger issues: Why does the state have a formula for officially deciding what each person's race is? Why would a tiny percentage of black ancestry cause her to be considered black, while an overwhelmingly white ancestry would not mean she is white?

The key lies in the word "mean" in the previous sentence, for as we have seen, what things objectively *are* is often less significant to human beings than what things *mean* in cultural frameworks of beliefs, values, and attitudes. As a biological concept, **race** refers to people who share a genetic heritage that results in distinct physical features, such as the color of skin, eyes, and hair, or the shape of the nose or eyes.

The biological concept, however, is useful only if members of different races remain separate from each other and do not combine their genes in reproduction. Most scientists agree that the genes that determine biological race have become so mixed across the world that the vast majority of people have a mixed racial heritage. Thus, from a biological point of view, the concept of race has lost most of its usefulness (Dobzhansky, 1973; Richardson and Spears, 1972).

Most cultures, however, define **race** as an ascribed social status to which they attach values, attitudes, and norms that produce important consequences for the occupants of different racial statuses. A biologist would have to say that Susie Phipps is certainly more white than black, but her dilemma has little to do with biology and everything to do with her society's culture. Once she is defined as black, she is perceived, evaluated, and treated as black.

The cultural meaning of race, then, is far more important than biological distinctions. Although Adolph Hitler's claim that there exists a distinct Aryan "race" of tall, blond, blue-eyed people is scientifically incorrect, his error (as well as the fact that he was a short, dark-haired man) did not prevent him and his followers from identifying Jews, Gypsies, Poles, and others as members of inferior "races." Nor did it prevent them from exterminating millions of people who fell into the wrong "racial" group.

Whereas the sociological concept of **race** refers to statuses based on a shared biological heritage, **ethnicity** refers to a shared cultural heritage. An **ethnic group** is a collection of people who identify

with a common culture. They share a common heritage of food and styles of dress, music and literature, and look back upon a history that reflects the collective experience of "their people." Thus, Jews, Italians, Egyptians, white Anglo-Saxon Protestants (WASPs), Irish, Ugandans, and Mexicans all constitute distinct ethnic groups whose members identify with a particular cultural and historical heritage.

American society contains an extraordinary variety of ethnic backgrounds. In 1980, 10 percent of all those 5 to 17 years old spoke a language other than English at home, and 14 percent spoke English only with difficulty. Fifty-four percent of adults trace their origins to single ethnicities—the largest of which are German, English, Italian, Spanish, Polish, and Irish—and 46 percent report multiple ethnic origins (U.S. Census Bureau, 1982).

Race and ethnicity are often a major basis for feelings of pride and solidarity among people, but they also have been used for centuries as a basis for distributing wealth, power, and prestige; and race and ethnicity have often been the basis for systematic violence, exploitation, and oppression.

## Minorities and Social Oppression

All of us trace our origins to ethnic groups that constitute relatively small percentages of the American population. For example, the largest set of people who cite only one ethnic origin are German, but they make up only 10 percent of the population. In terms of *numbers*, we all belong to ethnic minorities.

Sociologists, however, are less concerned with relative numbers than with the social consequences of ethnic and racial differences. From this point of view, a **minority** is a group of people

> who, because of their physical or cultural characteristics, are singled out from the others in the society in which they live for differential and unequal treatment. (Wirth, 1945, p. 351)

**PUZZLES:**

# WHEN IS 80 PERCENT OF A POPULATION NOT A MAJORITY?

When they are blacks living in South Africa. It is also true that women do not rule any known societies even though they are a numerical majority in virtually all of them.

Thus, a minority is defined not by relative numbers of people with certain physical or cultural characteristics, but by how they are treated as a result of such characteristics. In South Africa, for example, blacks are a minority because they are singled out for unequal treatment in spite of the fact that they make up the vast *majority* of the pop-

ulation. Regardless of their relative numbers, South African blacks would not be a minority in a society that treated whites and blacks in the same way. What all minorities have in common is that their members are the objects of socially supported mistreatment, injustice, and exploitation that are the essence of **social oppression.**

It is important to understand that individuals may be abused or exploited without it being an example of oppression, for the concept of oppression describes relationships in which minorities, as groups, are defined as inferior by dominant groups. Individual members of minorities are mistreated simply because they are members, regardless of their behavior or personal characteristics. When a man is beaten and robbed because his attacker wants his money, he is not being oppressed; but, if he is beaten and robbed because his attacker hates Jews and identifies him as a Jew, then he is a victim of oppression.

In South Africa, blacks are treated as a social minority even though they are an overwhelming numerical majority.

Moreover, a group may be defined as a minority even though some members are not oppressed; and a group may be socially dominant even though some of its members do not personally oppress minority people. Oppression is a social phenomenon that is based on the relative standing of different groups. Because some are culturally defined as superior to others, their members are in a social position that allows them to benefit from the exploitation and mistreatment of those defined as inferior.

Whether or not individuals behave as victims or victimizers, the oppressive relationships between groups nonetheless exist. Thus, I, as a white man, may not personally oppress blacks; but my behavior does not wipe away the fact that blacks as a group occupy an oppressed position in the United States, and I, as a white man, may benefit from their oppression whether I want to or not.

The word "may" in the previous sentence is significant, because members of dominant groups do not share equally in the benefits of oppression. For example, as explained later in this chapter, racism can discourage lower-class whites from joining with blacks to change the social class system.

What are the social bases of oppression? What forms does it take and what are the consequences both for societies and their members? As with other social phenomena, the sociological perspective focuses on three basic aspects of oppression—cultural, structural, and ecological—and the following sections look at each of these in detail.

## Culture, Race, and Ethnicity

As a set of shared ideas, culture plays an important part in the mistreatment of minorities, for how people perceive and evaluate others, as well as how they feel and behave toward them, is strongly affected by beliefs that describe them, values that rank them, attitudes that direct positive and negative feelings toward them, and norms that restrict people as participants in social relationships. Thus, underlying oppressive behavior are cultural ideas that affect relationships between minority and dominant groups.

### Prejudice: Racism and Ethnicism

**Prejudice** is a positive or negative attitude based on stereotyped beliefs about the members of a group (Allport, 1958; see also Seeman, 1981). Like all attitudes, prejudice includes beliefs that describe different kinds of people as well as values that rank their relative worth. Prejudice based on race is **racism;** and prejudice based on ethnicity is **ethnicism.**

Prejudice may be either positive or negative: the belief that Hindus are superior to Muslims is just as prejudiced in favor of Hindus as it is against Muslims. Whether positive or negative, however, all prejudice has four key characteristics that make it an important part of social oppression (Memmi, 1964).

First, prejudice is based on real or imagined differences between groups. Prejudice against blacks includes the belief that they are lazy, stupid, happy-go-lucky, dirty, musical, and oversexed—descriptions that have also been applied to European Gypsies and poor people in southern Italy (Pettigrew, 1968). American movies often portray Mexicans as lazy men slumbering under sombreros or unshaven bandits waving pistols as they grin broadly through broken teeth. Family life among nonwhites is rarely portrayed, and nonwhites rarely have lead roles in television shows. When they do, they are usually cast in comic, servile roles (Unger, 1983; Withey and Abeles, 1980).

Say the words "organized crime" and many people immediately think of Italians; and our humor is full of "dumb Polack" jokes. Many people think of all Jews as ambitious, sly, and dishonest, and of white Anglo-Saxon Protestants (WASPs) as snobs who only attend Ivy League schools.

People often form beliefs about personal characteristics of people in ethnic groups even when they have no personal experience of them (Karlins, Coffman, and Walters, 1969; Katz and Braly, 1933). In one study, college students even had beliefs about ethnic groups that do not exist—"Wallonians" and "Pirenians"—and their beliefs were usually negative (Hartley, 1946).

Second, prejudice attaches values to differences in ways that benefit dominant groups at the expense of minorities. To many Irish Protestants—who dominate Northern Ireland—"Protestant" is good and "Catholic" is bad. The drive to feel superior then leads people in the dominant group to *maximize* the perceived difference between themselves and minorities, for "the smaller he makes his victim, the bigger he becomes" (Memmi, 1964,

"Amos 'n Andy," a radio program on which white actors portrayed blacks whose behavior and attitudes were largely modeled on unflattering stereotypes, was enormously popular with white audiences in the 1930s and 1940s.

p. 189). Many Irish Catholics, of course, respond with prejudices of their own against all Protestants.

Third, prejudice is generalized to all members of a target group—in other words, each individual's self is summarized by stereotypes (Lieberson, 1982). Stereotypes often have a "grain of truth"— the average black score on school achievement tests is lower than the white average; there are Mexicans who take a "siesta" every afternoon; the Italian word "Mafia" does describe *some* criminal organizations; and WASPs are more likely than others to occupy top positions in most large corporations.

Stereotypes, however, ignore enormous differences between individuals who share social characteristics: many blacks are more intelligent than most whites; most Mexicans work hard in order to make a living; most Italians are not criminals; and the vast majority of white Anglo-Saxons are neither executives nor professionals and do not attend Ivy League colleges.

Fourth, in order to ensure their superior position, members of dominant groups support the belief that the inferior position of those in a minority is absolute and inevitable because it results merely from membership in the group. This is often extended both back in time and into the future: "Jews have always been greedy and blacks have always been inferior; therefore, they always *will* be." In the case of racism, biology is often used to explain the disadvantaged position of minorities, and biological racism is enormously powerful because, once accepted, it defines differences as absolute and, therefore, unchangeable. As Memmi (1964) put it:

> biological racism . . . penetrates the flesh, the blood and the genes of the victim. It is transformed into fate, destiny, heredity. From then on, the victim's very *being* is contaminated, and likewise *every manifestation of that being:* behavior, body, and soul. (p. 190)

For centuries, scientists and others have tried to prove that members of minorities are biologically inferior. Jensen (1969), for example, has asserted that most of the difference between the average IQ score of blacks and that of whites is due to genetic differences. The crux of his position is that racial differences in IQ persist even among people who have similar social class backgrounds. From this he argued that since racial differences persist even when social environments are similar, then genetics must be the cause. He concluded that blacks as a group will always be intellectually inferior to whites, regardless of educational efforts.

There are several problems with Jensen's argument (Tumin, 1973). First, IQ tests measure a set of mental skills that are developed in and reflect a particular cultural context—that is, the world of the American white middle class. Many black children do relatively poorly on IQ tests, not because they are less intelligent, but because the examples and language used in test questions reflect white middle-class culture and experience (see Chapter 16). Thus, the tests used to measure IQ are to some degree *culturally biased* in favor of whites, especially those in the middle and upper classes.

Second, a genetic explanation of racial differences rests on the assumption that blacks and whites represent pure racial types, and this assumption is false. Hunt and Walker (1974), for example, estimated that 70 percent of all American blacks have some white ancestors and that 20 percent of all whites have some black ancestors.

The most serious criticism of Jensen, however, is that he misinterpreted his own evidence (Lewontin, 1970). Specifically, Jensen assumed that when he compared the IQs of blacks and whites who came from the same social classes, he was comparing people whose social environments were the same. As we have seen in earlier chapters, however, the measurement of social class is, at best, quite crude. For example, to conclude that people whose parents had similar educations and occupations are alike on all the known and unknown social factors that affect the development of intelligence is simply unjustified. In other words, we do not *know* how social environments affect intelligence, and controlling for social class does not eliminate all social causes of racial IQ differences.

Racism and ethnicism therefore rest on negative stereotypes about all members of minorities and positive stereotypes about all members of dominant groups. They are more than simple sets of ideas about racial and ethnic groups, however, for they play a vital part in justifying and perpetuating the interests of people in dominant groups. Racism and ethnicism, in other words, are used as *ideologies.*

## Ideology and Oppression

Racism and ethnicism support oppression by denying the existence of oppression itself. This is accomplished primarily by blaming the negative consequences of oppression on its victims.

Many Americans, for example, believe that America is a land of opportunity in which individual ability and motivation largely determine success and failure. Such a belief can be used to "mask" the oppression of minorities, however: "America is a land of equal opportunity; if you have failed, you must be at fault." Not surprisingly, whites are far more likely than blacks to believe that blacks have equal opportunity, for such a belief effectively blames blacks for their disadvantaged position in society (L. Harris, 1977).

Blaming victims often takes a more direct form. In 1977, for example, 25 percent of white adults believed that blacks have worse jobs, income, and housing than whites because blacks have "less in-born ability to learn"; and 66 percent answered that blacks "don't have the motivation or will power to pull themselves out of poverty" (Davis, 1980). In 1981, 41 percent of whites believed that laziness was the major cause of black unemployment (Clymer, 1981).

Within the framework of prejudiced ideologies, members of minorities are not perceived as varied and complex individuals who have many of the same feelings, goals, and needs as other people. This view makes it easier to perceive minority individuals as faceless objects, and once people are perceived as objects, they may be treated in ways that members of dominant groups would never accept for themselves.

Consequently, during the Vietnam War, Asians were labeled "gooks" and were stereotyped as people to whom "life is cheap." This made it easier to kill large numbers of Vietnamese civilians since, after all, the American military was not taking away something of much importance to *them*. Members of minorities, of course, often have ideologies of their own that justify violence toward members of dominant groups. During the 1960s some black militants labeled all police officers "pigs," and some used this stereotyped label to justify killing them.

### The Destruction of Culture

How is a society's culture affected by the coming together of people from a variety of ethnic backgrounds? Mexico is a good example of **amalgamation,** which occurs when diverse cultures within a society merge into a single new culture. Modern Mexican culture is a mixture of native Indian culture and that of Spanish conquerors. This is what Zangwill (1909/1933) meant when he mistakenly described America as a "melting pot."

**Assimilation,** on the other hand, occurs when people from different ethnic backgrounds conform to the dominant culture; and **pluralism** occurs when people of different ethnicity live side-by-side and maintain their cultural diversity.

Assimilation best describes cultures in most heterogeneous societies, including the United States. In spite of our immigrants' varied backgrounds, the most important elements of our culture are Anglo-Saxon. English is our language, our legal system is based on English Common Law, and basic cultural ideas about liberty and the rights of individuals are based on the English Magna Carta. In fact, the American Revolution was initially an attempt to secure for colonists the same rights enjoyed by English living in Britain.

Assimilation often requires ethnic minorities to abandon their distinct cultures as the price of escaping minority status and participating fully in the life of a society. The first American public schools were designed to enforce "Anglo-conformity" among immigrants (Cole and Cole, 1954), and immigrant children still find that their native lan-

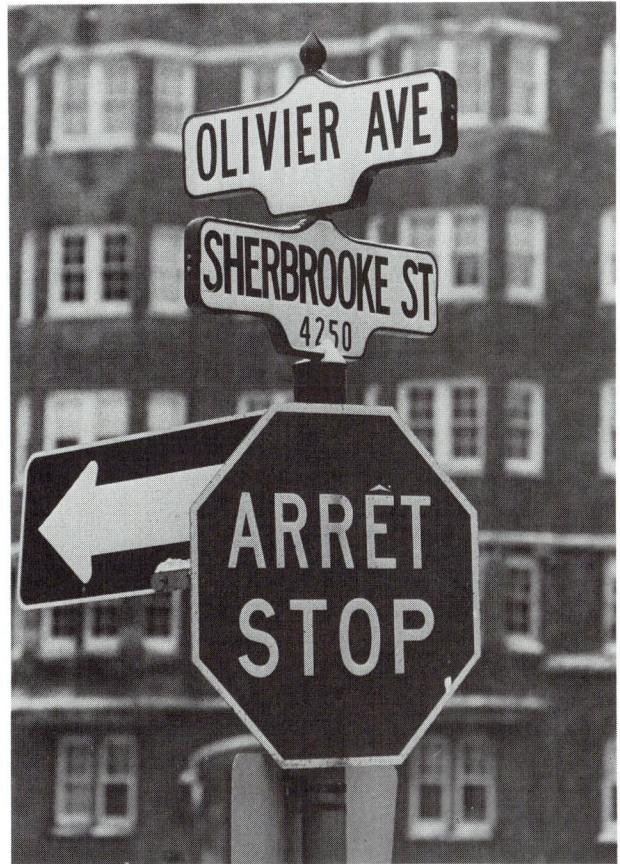

Until recently, in the Canadian province of Quebec, the coexistence of two languages—English and French—paralleled the class division between the dominant English-speaking population and the minority French-speaking population. Those who could not speak English were excluded from the best occupational opportunities. Recent laws, however, require all signs to be in French only and business may no longer be conducted in English only.

guage and customs are unacceptable in white schools that regard non-Anglo-Saxon cultures as inferior. The children of American immigrants typically do not learn the language of their parents, and it is not uncommon for children to have difficulty understanding their own grandparents. As a result, entire cultural traditions may eventually be lost (see Conklin and Lourie, 1983; Stevens, 1985).

Thus, by devaluing ethnic and racial differences, racism and ethnicism tend to destroy cultural diversity (Blauner, 1972). When blacks were brought to America as slaves, their African cultures were systematically destroyed by their white owners. They were forced to take new names, and family members were separated from one another. They were not allowed to govern themselves, to administer justice, or practice their religions. Blacks found themselves in the midst of a white culture that excluded them in every way except as slaves (Frederickson, 1981).

American Indians also experienced systematic efforts by whites to destroy their culture. For centuries, they had been free peoples who effectively governed themselves and administered justice. Since their conquest by whites, however, they have been forced to adopt a uniform type of government modeled after Anglo-Saxon institutions: constitutionally elected tribal officers, tribal courts, and legislatures (Josephy, 1973). Most power, however, is vested in a federal agency—the Bureau of Indian Affairs—not in the tribes (Barsh and Henderson, 1980).

Although the normal expectation in American society is that a private individual may do anything unless it is specifically prohibited by the government, it might be said that the normal expectation on the reservation is that the Indians may not do anything unless it is specifically permitted by the government. (Cohen and Mause, 1968, p. 1820)

With autonomy and self-government went a host of Indian beliefs and values. Some Indian tribes valued cooperation more than competition, group success more than personal ambition, the careful management of nature more than its conquest and exploitation. Human beings were seen as an integral part of the natural world, not separate from it, and had neither the need nor the right to dominate it.

Such values were unacceptable in the Judeo-Christian tradition of whites, a tradition that included centuries of individualism, political domination, economic development, and exploitation of the natural environment. Indians and their culture stood in the way of white "progress," and so the dominant whites forced the Indians to choose between adopting white culture and being exterminated (Josephy, 1973).

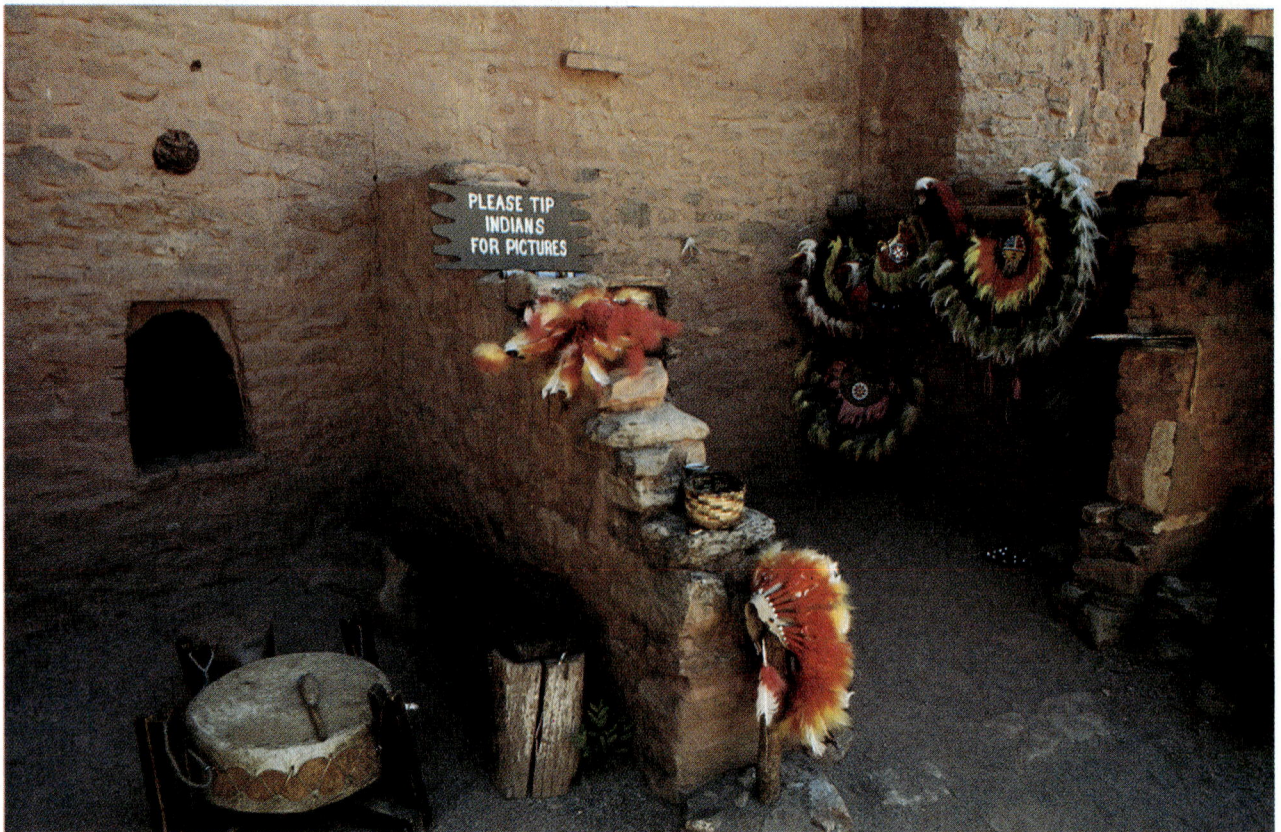

## Voices: Our Cup Is Broken

A chief of the Digger Indians, as the Californians call them, talked to me a great deal about the ways of his people in the old days. He was a Christian and a leader among his people in the planting of peaches and apricots on irrigated land, but when he talked of the shamans who had transformed themselves into bears before his eyes in the bear dance, his hands trembled and his voice broke with excitement. It was an incomparable thing, the power his people had had in the old days. He liked best to talk of the desert foods they had eaten. He brought each uprooted plant lovingly and with an unfailing sense of its importance. In those days his people had eaten 'the health of the desert,' he said, and knew nothing of the insides of tin cans and the things for sale at butcher shops. It was such innovations that had degraded them in these latter days.

One day, without transition, Ramon broke in upon his descriptions of grinding mesquite and preparing acorn soup. 'In the beginning,' he said, 'God gave to every people a cup, a cup of clay, and from this cup they drank their life.' I do not know whether the figure occurred in some traditional ritual of his people that I never found, or whether it was his own imagery. It is hard to imagine that he had heard it from the whites he had known at Banning; they were not given to discussing the ethos of different peoples. At any rate, in the mind of this humble Indian the figure of speech was clear and full of meaning. 'They all dipped in the water,' he continued, 'but their cups were different. Our cup is broken now. It has passed away.' . . .

These things that had given significance to the life of his people, the domestic rituals of eating, the obligations of the economic system, the succession of ceremonials in the villages, possession in the bear dance, their standards of right and wrong—these were gone, and with them the shape and meaning of their life. The old man was still vigorous and a leader in relationships with the whites. He did not mean that there was any question of the extinction of his people. But he had in mind the loss of something that had value equal to that of life itself, the whole fabric of his people's standards and beliefs. There were other cups of living left, and they held perhaps the same water, but the loss was irreparable. It was no matter of tinkering with an addition here, lopping off something there. The modelling had been fundamental, it was somehow all of a piece. It had been their own.

Source: Benedict, *Patterns of Culture*, 1934.

---

The destruction of cultural diversity often takes more subtle forms. Many Americans (and the U.S. Census Bureau), for example, use a single term, "Hispanic," to refer to people with enormously varied backgrounds—such as Mexicans, Puerto Ricans, Cubans, Brazilians, Colombians, Chileans, Argentinians, Salvadorans, and Nicaraguans. In each of these countries, people certainly distinguish themselves from other Latin American peoples; but in the United States, Hispanic is used by the white majority to conveniently label nonwhites who are not black. We also tend to refer to Africans as if they are culturally homogeneous, when in fact there are hundreds of different languages and cultures on the African continent.

Racist and ethnicist ideologies thus support socially structured relationships in which minorities are oppressed, particularly through the destruction of their cultures. What do the social structures that result from racism and ethnicism look like?

## Social Structure, Race, and Ethnicity

On the microlevel of role relationships, oppression occurs as exploitation, abuse, and injustice in social interactions between members of different ethnicities and races. On the macrolevel of social structure, race and ethnicity are statuses that powerfully affect the distribution of wealth, power, and prestige. Thus, racism and ethnicism are sets of cultural ideas whose effects on the lives of individuals are felt through social structures.

It is important to note, however, that people have been oppressed in many societies without suffering the social stigmas of extreme racial and ethnic prejudice. Both Spain and Portugal, for example, practiced slavery long before the discovery of the New World; and while their slaves certainly suffered, they were not dehumanized to the extent that American blacks were by the English colonists, who regarded nonwhites as inferior beings (Conrad, 1983; Tannenbaum, 1947). As a result, there is less racism in former colonies such as Mexico and Brazil than there is in the United States, whose legacy of racism continues to stigmatize black people.

## Patterns of Interaction: Discrimination

Whereas prejudice is an attitude, **discrimination** refers to unequal *treatment* of people based on stereotyped beliefs about them. Expectations and feelings during interactions depend on how people define social situations, and this, in turn, depends on how they perceive the statuses of other people. Race and ethnicity are far more than physical or cultural characteristics; they are symbols that stand for sets of beliefs, values, and attitudes directed toward those who display them.

When we see people dressed in police uniforms, we immediately act and feel as though we have significant information about them. In the same way, when we identify people's race or ethnicity, we draw upon cultural beliefs, values, and attitudes that identify how we should behave, what we should expect of them, and how we feel toward them.

In 1970 college students conducted an experiment in which pairs of black, Mexican, and white students tried to rent apartments in Los Angeles. All 12 students dressed similarly, spoke English equally well, and had equal educations. They applied for a total of 25 apartments, and in virtually every case the white couples were the most likely to be accepted. Black and Mexican couples were more often told there were no apartments available, or were quoted higher rents. Only 5 of the 25 apartment managers did not discriminate in any way (Johnson et al., 1971).

Thus, prejudice differs from discrimination in the same way that our beliefs about people differ from what we *do* in relation to such people. In this sense, our behavior and attitudes may often contradict each other (Merton, 1948). For example, some members of dominant groups are not prejudiced and do not discriminate against minorities, while other unprejudiced people may nonetheless discriminate against minorities when it is expedient or profitable to do so ("Some of my best friends are Jews, but if I let you into the club the other members will raise hell").

Prejudice does not necessarily result in discriminatory behavior. American culture strongly values equality for all, and both prejudice and discrimination are against the "American creed." Prejudiced people are under pressure to conceal their prejudice, and for this reason some people are what Merton (1948) called "timid bigots."

In the 1930s, a Chinese couple stopped at 250 restaurants and hotels as they traveled across the United States and were refused service only once. Later, they sent letters to all the establishments and asked if they served "members of the Chinese race." About half replied, and of these, 90 percent said they did not (Lapiere, 1934). A later study in a northeastern suburb, had similar results: both white and black couples were treated well in restaurants, but attempts to make telephone reservations for black groups were strongly resisted (Kutner et al., 1952).

Regardless of our attitudes, whether or not we *act* on them depends strongly on the social situation. It is far easier for people to discriminate over a telephone or through the mail than it is when they are face-to-face with the person who will be hurt by discriminatory behavior. It is also easier to discriminate in secondary relationships ("It's nothing personal"), because people can then claim that they are simply following rules formulated and enforced by others. In this way, they are able to conceal their own motives, which may or may not rest on prejudiced attitudes.

Social interaction is an important arena in which the attitudes of racism and ethnicism are played out to the benefit of dominant groups and at the expense of minorities. It is here, on the smallest level, that cultural ideas about race and ethnicity become visible in social relationships. On a larger structural level, however, race and ethnicity profoundly affect the material conditions of people's lives, for it is here that these statuses play an important part in social stratification.

## Wealth, Income, and "Life Chances"

Race appears to exert a powerful effect on the distribution of income and wealth in the United States. The 1981 average income of white households was $20,200, but it was only $15,300 for Hispanics and $11,300 for blacks. Black households constituted 11 percent of the population and yet received only 7 percent of all income, 64 percent of what they would receive if income were distributed equally. Only 1.7 percent of black households had incomes of $50,000 or more, compared with 3.1 percent of Hispanics and 7.8 percent of whites. Blacks were three times more likely than whites to have incomes below the poverty level and 30 percent more likely than Hispanics (U.S. Census Bureau, 1982).

Why do whites make so much more money than nonwhites? Education appears to explain some of the difference, for whites are 22 percent more likely than blacks to have high school diplomas and more than twice as likely to have college degrees. There are three problems with education as an explanation, however.

First, average education is slightly higher among blacks than among Hispanics, but average income is lower. Second, when we compare families whose adults have similar educational levels, the racial difference remains: in families with a college-educated householder, average income in 1980 was $32,900 for whites, $26,000 for Hispanics, and $24,800 for blacks. Third, unemployment is more likely among nonwhites regardless of education: blacks and Hispanics with four or more years of college are two-thirds more likely to be unemployed than are similarly educated whites (U.S. Census Bureau, 1982).

What about occupation? Do whites have higher incomes because they have better jobs? Here the evidence is more convincing: whites have

Blacks in the United States are three times more likely than whites to live in poverty, a gap that has remained virtually unchanged in spite of a vigorous civil rights movement and numerous antipoverty programs.

**Table 12-1**

Representation of Nonwhites in Various Occupations (United States, 1982)

### OCCUPATIONS IN WHICH NONWHITES ARE UNDERREPRESENTED, BY DEGREE

| Severe[1] | Substantial[2] | Slight[3] | Overrepresented |
|---|---|---|---|
| Engineer | Accountant | Chemist | Social worker |
| Lawyer | Computer specialist | Nurse | Military, enlisted grade |
| Judge | Scientist | Elementary teacher | Vocational counselor |
| Librarian | Personnel worker | Electronic technician | File clerk |
| Dentist | Military officer | Clerical supervisor | Key punch operator |
| Social scientist | Pharmacist | Mail carrier | Recreation worker |
| College teacher | Physician | Computer operator | Mail clerk |
| Research worker | Health technician | Shipping clerk | Stenographer |
| Journalist | Bank teller | Stock clerk | Telephone operator |
| Writer | High school teacher | Storekeeper | Crane operator |
| Artist | Drafter | Painter | Typist |
| Entertainer | Science technician | Punch and stamp press operator | Brickmason |
| Editor | Billing clerk | | Stonemason |
| Business manager | Health administrator | Welder | Factory assembler |
| Sales worker | Public administrator | Truck driver | Seamstress |
| Bookkeeper | Restaurant or bar manager | Stock handler | Laundry worker |
| Secretary | Counter clerk | Food service worker | Machine operator |
| Carpenter | Cashier | Barber | Meat or produce packer |
| Electrician | Police officer | | Textile factory worker |
| Sheet metal worker | Investigator | | Chauffeur |
| Tool and die maker | Insurance adjustor | | Bus driver |
| Radio and TV repair | Receptionist | | Fork lift driver |
| Type compositor | Plumber | | Taxi driver |
| Typesetter | Machinist | | Freight handler |
| Mine worker | Auto mechanic | | Construction laborer |
| Farmer or farm manager | Butcher | | Cook |
| Waiter | Blue-collar supervisor | | Practical nurse |
| | Aircraft mechanic | | Gardener |
| | Baker | | Cleaning worker |
| | Hairdresser | | Guard |
| | Telephone installer | | Hospital orderly |
| | Electric line worker | | House servant |
| | Printing press operator | | Outside labor force |
| | | | Unemployed |

Source: U.S. Census Bureau, 1983c.

[1] Percentage less than half the percentage of nonwhites in the labor force.
[2] Percentage between half and three-fourths of nonwhite percentage in the labor force.
[3] Percentage just under nonwhite percentage in the labor force.

a 60 percent greater chance of holding upper-level white-collar jobs, a 25 percent greater chance for lower-level white-collar jobs, and a 40 percent greater chance for upper-level blue-collar jobs. Nonwhites, on the other hand, are 55 percent more likely than whites to have low-paying, unskilled jobs (Table 12-1). Take a moment to study Table 12-1. Check the jobs you would like to have, and then see which columns they are in.

Racial differences in income are affected not only by the kinds of jobs people have but also by whether or not they have jobs at all. In 1980 the unemployment rate among black males was 24 percent—more than three times as high as the rates for whites and Hispanics. Thus, it is generally true that unemployment levels whites experience as a recession—6 or 7 percent—represent relative prosperity for nonwhites. If whites experienced the unemployment risks that are usual for blacks, they would consider themselves in the midst of a deep depression (Fein, 1966).

Whites are not only more likely than nonwhites to have *a* job, but are also more likely to be working at two or more jobs. What is most interesting, however, is that the reasons for working at more than one job vary by race. Blacks are more likely than whites to have extra jobs in order to pay regular bills, pay off debts, or save for future needs. Whites, on the other hand, are more likely to work at extra jobs in order to gain new work experiences or to make "special" purchases (U.S. Census Bureau, 1982). Even though whites are more likely to have two or more jobs, they are less likely to have them because they *must*.

While blacks generally have poorer jobs and less education than whites, these differences do not fully explain why the income of black families is so much lower. Nor do education and occupation fully explain the income gap between blacks and other nonwhites and their greater likelihood of being unemployed. What, then, is left?

What is left is racial discrimination—the cost of being black in America. As Duncan (1969) demonstrated with his sophisticated analysis of data describing American men 25 to 64 years old,

> At least one-third of the income gap arises because black and white men in the same line of work, with the same amount of schooling, with equal ability, from families of the same size and same socio-economic level, simply do not draw the same wages and salaries. (p. 108)

Poorer jobs and lower income exact additional costs for blacks. In comparison with whites, black infants are almost twice as likely to die during their first year; black children are only two-thirds as likely to be immunized against polio; and among those who survive to adulthood, blacks live an average of four fewer additional years than do whites (U.S. Census Bureau, 1982). Average black workers are in occupations that are between 37 and 52 percent more likely to produce serious illness or accidents (J. Robinson, 1984).

Although discrimination certainly plays a major part in perpetuating the minority standing of blacks, William J. Wilson (1978) and Hout (1984) believe that race, itself, is slowly losing its importance. Until recently, blacks were discriminated against universally simply because they were black; but, during the last few decades, some blacks have entered the middle and upper-middle classes. While the historical legacy of racism still affects *all* blacks, Wilson believes that the disadvantaged position of most blacks is now caused more by social *class* than by race.

> In the economic realm . . . the black experience has moved historically from economic racial oppression experienced by virtually all blacks to economic subordination for the black underclass. And as we begin the last quarter of the twentieth century, a deepening economic schism seems to be developing in the black community, with the black poor falling further and further behind middle- and upper-income blacks. (William J. Wilson, 1978, p. 152)

Wilson, therefore, is arguing that the majority of blacks are poor not because of *current* racial discrimination, but because a history of systematic racism and discrimination has concentrated them in the lower class, thereby confining them to unemployment and jobs that offer little hope of advancing into the middle class.

Blacks are the largest racial minority in the United States, but American Indians are in the worst position. Most of the roughly 1 million American Indians are confined to impoverished reservations. Unemployment averages roughly 45 percent, and average family income is under $2,000 (Burnette, 1971; Rose, 1981; Thurow, 1975).

Clearly, race is an ascribed status that profoundly affects class membership. Nonwhites are heavily overrepresented in the lower class and virtually absent from the upper class. Ethnicity also affects class membership, although to a lesser degree than race. White Anglo-Saxon Protestants and Jews have higher average incomes, better jobs, and more education than do members of most other ethnic groups (see Farley and Neidert, 1984).

Ethnicity played its strongest role in social stratification during the nineteenth and early twentieth centuries. Successive waves of immigrants—Germans, Irish, Poles, Scandinavians, and Jews—were confined to the worst jobs and living conditions in urban ghettos. Mexicans were perceived as "aborigines" who were inferior to white Anglo-Saxons (Pratt, 1935). Each new wave of immigrants, however, brought a fresh supply of poor people to occupy the bottom rung of the stratification ladder, and those who had come before were able to move upward, although only with considerable effort (Hutchinson, 1965).

Those whose culture was most similar to that of the dominant Anglo-Saxons—Germans and Scandinavians—were able to move upward with greater ease than those who were culturally more different: Catholic Irish, Poles, and other East Europeans. Ethnicity has thus become a relatively minor determinant of social class among whites.

Nonwhite ethnics, on the other hand, continue to lag behind whites in average income. Among college graduates, average income among American Indians, Chinese, and Filipinos amounted to only two-thirds of the average income for all college graduates; and Hispanic and Japanese earnings amounted to roughly 85 percent of the national college-graduate average (Jencks, 1983a; see also Farley and Neidert, 1984).

The legacy of racial prejudice and oppression persists largely because race is more visible than ethnicity, but also because nonwhites have a unique history in America. Whites, most of whom believed nonwhites were inferior, killed Indians in vast numbers as they seized their land. Blacks were property to be bought and sold and used in any way their owners saw fit. As oppressed as minorities such as the Irish once were in the United States, they were never slaves, were never systematically slaughtered, were never forced to abandon their cultural heritage, and were never treated like animals placed outside the boundaries of the human race.

Prejudice against most European minorities was largely sporadic—there were many places in the United States where the Irish were not treated as a minority—but prejudice against blacks and Indians was universal and has lasted for generations.

> Discrimination only poses a serious barrier to economic success if it is almost universal, or if its existence transforms the victims' behavior in self-defeating ways. Discrimination against European minorities was common but never anything like universal. The descendants of European immigrants have almost all had the option of shedding their ethnic identity and "passing" as just plain "Americans." Physical differences, combined with extreme social sensitivity to the significance of these differences, made this much more difficult for most blacks and somewhat more difficult for Asians, American Indians, and even Latin Americans. (Jencks, 1983a, p. 34)

As an ethnic group, Jews are an exception to these generalizations. For centuries, Jews were not allowed to own land, were regarded by Christians as the embodiment of evil, and were periodically murdered in large numbers, culminating in the World War II Holocaust during which an estimated 6 million Jews were murdered. A few, however, were allowed to flourish in financial pursuits such as banking and tax collecting, for when banking first came into being, it was regarded as immoral, and tax collectors were far from popular. Thus, some Jews were allowed to be "middlemen" between the upper and lower classes. This allowed the upper class to profit from Jewish activities while avoiding the resentment of people in the lower class.

Through this, however, many Jews developed important skills and maintained the integrity of their culture; and when banking and business became more culturally respectable, many Jews flourished. Because they made the best of what was left to them, Jews have, for centuries, been both despised and envied. Their somewhat unique position is duplicated by some racial and ethnic minorities in other societies: Chinese merchants in Indonesia and Malaysia, for example, and Muslim merchants in eastern and southern Africa (Pettigrew, 1968).

It is important to remember, however, that while American Jews have relatively high *average* education and income, most Jews are in the middle and working classes, and many are poor. The popular image of Jews as bankers and wealthy doctors

In Nazi Germany, Jews were required by law to wear yellow stars of David in public; they were regularly stopped on the street by police and interrogated, detained, or arrested; and their businesses were boycotted and vandalized. All of this, of course, was preliminary to the Holocaust and the concentration camps in which millions of Jews were murdered.

is nothing more than a stereotype. Jews are rarely found on the boards of large corporations, including those of commercial banks (Domhoff and Zweigenhaft, 1983).

## Power

In caste societies such as South Africa and, until recently, India, power is sharply divided according to race. The Indian constitution specifies which castes are eligible for benefits such as college scholarships, welfare, and government jobs. South African blacks are denied the vote in national elections and representation in the national parliament. They cannot travel freely, conduct strikes against employers, or choose where they will eat, work, live, or educate their children. Every aspect of life in South Africa is segregated by race—including public transportation, restaurants, beaches, residential neighborhoods, and schools—and marriage and sexual relationships between blacks and whites are forbidden by law (Price and Rosberg, 1980). In 1985 Desmund Tutu—1984 winner of the Nobel Peace Prize—became the first black bishop of the Anglican Church in Johannes-

burg; but he had to obtain special permission to enter the white neighborhood where the ceremony appointing him to his office took place.

Until quite recently, the situation of American blacks was as bad as or worse than that of today's South African blacks (Elkins, 1963; Frederickson, 1981). Slavery flourished for 200 years before the Civil War, and even "free Negroes" were denied the rights to vote, testify in court, own land, or make contracts. In spite of federal efforts after the Civil War, the late 1800s and early 1900s were a period in which blacks had little power to participate in their society or to live in safety. In southern states, "Jim Crow" laws restricted blacks in every conceivable aspect of their lives. Literacy tests and poll taxes prevented many from using newly won voting rights, and they were "kept in their place" by the terror of lynchings and church burnings.

In the last 20 years blacks have greatly increased their collective power in the United States, largely by using the federal courts to fight discrimination, registering as voters, running successfully for public office, and conducting disruptive mass demonstrations. After the passage of the

1965 Voting Rights Act, the registration of black voters in the South more than doubled, and the percentages of whites and blacks registered are now nearly equal. Between 1970 and 1984 the number of political offices held by blacks increased from 1,472 to more than 5,600. Blacks have become mayors of large cities: Chicago, Philadelphia, Los Angeles, Atlanta, Washington, D.C., Detroit, Cleveland, and Newark. In 1966 Edward Brooke became the first black senator in this century, and between 1962 and 1981 the number of black representatives quadrupled (U.S. Census Bureau, 1982).

While such gains are important, power in the United States is still disproportionately concentrated in the hands of whites. In 1980 blacks were 12 percent of the U.S. population but held only 1 percent of all public offices (Joint Center for Political Studies, 1975). There is no longer a black in the U.S. Senate, and blacks make up only 4.6 percent of the House of Representatives (*Congressional Quarterly,* November 10, 1984).

Nowhere is inequality of power between whites and blacks more evident than in the criminal justice system. Because blacks are more likely than whites to be poor, they are more often unable to use bail in order to stay out of jail during their trials; and numerous studies show that accused

In spite of the fact that blacks, such as Tom Bradley in Los Angeles, have become mayors of some of our largest cities, blacks still hold a disproportionately small share of political power in the United States.

criminals are more likely to be convicted if they are imprisoned during their trials (Wice, 1973). Once convicted, blacks receive harsher sentences than whites—more than 10 times greater for murder or kidnapping, and twice as great for rape, robbery, or the sale or possession of illegal drugs (U.S. Census Bureau, 1975c).

## Prestige and Self-Esteem

When we find ourselves in an achieved status—such as education, occupation, or income—that commands little respect from others, we may suffer; but we may have the chance to increase our standing in other people's eyes by achieving a higher-level status. With ascribed statuses such as race and ethnicity, however, there is, by definition, no possibility of raising our social standing by changing statuses, unless we are willing to misrepresent ourselves to other people.

Both racism and ethnicism attach strong cultural values to people of different race and ethnicity, attributing superior qualities to members of dominant groups and inferior qualities to those subordinate to them. Just as the relative ranking of occupations has remained quite constant in the United States, so, too, has the ranking of different ethnicities and races (Bogardus, 1928, 1959). Generations of American whites have defined nonwhites as undesirable and inferior: light skin is better than black, yellow, brown, or red skin; wavy and straight hair is better than "wooly" hair. Generations of white Anglo-Saxon Protestants have defined those who do not speak English or who are non-Protestant as inferior and undesirable. The world, they believed, was reserved for those of "superior" ethnicity and race—in other words, for them and those like them (Hofstadter, 1955).

Inevitably, the low cultural value placed on minority groups is attached to their individual members, and each must confront a fundamental problem: How do I perceive and value *myself* in a culture that thinks so little of me? If my life is bad, does that mean *I* am bad?

As we grow up in a society, we acquire social identities that define who we are in relation to other people, and an important part of our identities is self-esteem—how we evaluate who we are. We are social creatures and cannot define and evaluate ourselves without taking into account how we think others see and evaluate us—what Cooley (1927) called our looking-glass self.

Farley and his co-researchers tested two additional explanations of racial segregation in the Detroit metropolitan area. First, they tested the hypothesis that blacks overestimate the cost of housing in white neighborhoods or differ from whites in their evaluation of the relative attractiveness of different neighborhoods. Second, they used a new measure of white attitudes toward integration, for they suspected that the "black on your block" question was too general because it failed to confront white respondents with specific residential possibilities.

Their findings show clearly that whites and blacks accurately perceive the cost of housing in different areas and share views of which areas are the most attractive to live in. In addition, while blacks report a strong preference for integrated neighborhoods, whites generally believe that blacks want to "stick to their own kind." In other words, whites seriously underestimate blacks' preference for integration.

Apparently, this misperception reinforces the reluctance of whites to share neighborhoods with blacks, for Farley's most important finding is that whites do not want to live in integrated neighborhoods. Rather than ask whites if they would mind living near a black family of similar economic status, Farley presented them with diagrams that showed different neighborhood mixes of black and white families. The diagrams showed 15 houses colored white or black with the center house labeled "your house." Hypothetical neighborhoods ranged from all white to just over half black (8 out of 15 houses).

Whereas in most surveys a majority of whites say they would not mind living near blacks, Farley's results tell a very different story (Table 12-2). As the hypothetical neighborhoods become increasingly black, the reported discomfort of whites, their desire to move out, and their reluctance to move in all rise sharply.

If Detroit is typical of American cities, Farley's results offer little hope that racial segregation in housing will ease in the near future. While better-educated whites tend to be more tolerant of integration, the differences between the least and most educated are small. Higher-*income* whites, however, are *less* tolerant of racial integration than are lower-income whites, while higher-income blacks are *more* likely to accept integrated neighborhoods

**Table 12-2**

White Responses to Racial Integration Possibilities (Detroit, 1976)

| PROPORTION OF WHITE RESPONDENTS WHO WOULD: | HYPOTHETICAL NEIGHBORHOODS: PERCENTAGE OF FAMILIES THAT ARE BLACK | | | |
|---|---|---|---|---|
| | 14 | 20 | 33 | 53 |
| Feel uncomfortable in the neighborhood | 24 | 42 | 57 | 72 |
| Try to move out of the neighborhood | 7 | 24 | 41 | 64 |
| Would not move into such a neighborhood | 27 | 50 | 73 | 84 |

Source: Farley et al., 1978, Figure 7.

than are lower-income blacks (Farley et al., 1978). Racially segregated housing, complete with its negative effects on black people, is likely to remain an enduring aspect of American communities for some time to come.

**Segregated Schools and Living with Contradictions** There are two basic causes of school segregation. *De jure* segregation is required by law; this type of segregation prevailed in southern states until the 1954 Supreme Court decision outlawed separate schools for blacks and whites (Ravitch, 1983). *De facto* segregation, on the other hand, is caused by residential segregation: most children live in segregated neighborhoods and, since they attend neighborhood schools, their schools are segregated, as well.

As of 1976, 52 percent of all public school students would have had to change schools in order to make the racial composition of schools match the racial composition of the American population (Wurdock and Farley, 1979). School segregation both denies white and black children the opportunity to know one another and negatively affects the educational careers of black children. Blacks who attend segregated schools are less likely to finish high school, attend college, and secure white-collar jobs than are blacks who attend integrated schools (Crain, 1975).

Racial segregation also affects whites, for those who attend integrated schools are least likely to prefer all-white classes and all-white friends (Coleman et al., 1966). White adults who attended integrated schools are also more willing to live in integrated neighborhoods, have their children attend integrated schools, and have black friends (U.S. Commission on Civil Rights, 1967).

Residential and school segregation illustrate a basic contradiction in American culture, for while most whites say they do not object to living in inte-

White opposition to busing students to achieve racial integration of Boston schools was so great that police had to protect school buses from demonstrators.

grated neighborhoods, most reverse their position when they are presented with specific integration possibilities. A similar reversal occurs with school segregation. In 1984, 90 percent of American adults believed white and black students should attend the same schools; and yet, 78 percent opposed the busing of black and white students from one school district to another and 45 percent supported the right of whites to deliberately exclude blacks from their neighborhoods by refusing to sell their houses to them (Davis, 1984).

These contradictions illustrate that individuals may support general cultural values and yet violate them when they believe their interests are threatened. Many Americans are what Merton (1948) called "Fair-Weather Liberals," who support the "American Creed" until it threatens them personally. As Americans, we value equality and fairness, but we also live with a centuries-old legacy of racism and value the right of individuals to control basic aspects of their lives, including who will live near them and where their children will attend school. These are contradictions that will not be resolved easily or quickly, for the values involved are all deeply held.

## Population and Minorities

In the simplest sense, superior numbers make it easier for people in one group to oppress those in another. In the late 1800s and early 1900s, for example, many prominent Americans worried that relatively high rates of fertility and population growth among nonwhite peoples of the world (including those in the U.S.) would soon make it difficult for whites to maintain their dominant position (Hofstadter, 1955).

In some cases, those who dominate a society try to control the size and growth of minority populations. The most extreme form of population control is **genocide,** the deliberate attempt to exterminate an entire racial or ethnic group. The most brutal was the Nazi Holocaust during World War II (Davidowicz, 1975), but history is full of examples. The early Hebrews tried unsuccessfully to exterminate the Canaanites; entire tribes of American Indians were all but exterminated during the nineteenth century; between 1917 and 1919, Turks massacred over a million Armenians (Dadrian, 1971); and massacres have plagued many newly independent African states (Kuper, 1977). In a single attack in 1983, 600 Moslems were slain by Hindus in the rural area of Assam, India (Hazarika, 1983).

A less-extreme form of population control is **expulsion**—forcing everyone of a particular race or ethnicity to leave a community or society. In 1830, for example, the Indian Removal Act forced thousands of American Indians of many different tribes in the Southeast to move west of the Mississippi, primarily to allow whites to seize their tribal lands. During their long forced marches—often covering thousands of miles—some tribes lost as many as 40 percent of their people to disease and starvation (Morison, 1965).

In 1972 Uganda's black leader, Idi Amin, ordered nearly 50,000 Asians—many of whom were second- and third-generation Ugandans—to leave the country; and in the process, they were forced to leave everything behind, including their savings (Kramer, 1974; Weintraub, 1975). Between 1961 and 1965 the government of the Assam state in India deported 136,000 Moslems to what is now Bangladesh (*New York Times*, February 23, 1983, p. 10).

In 1983, thousands of foreign workers and their families were forced to leave Nigeria.

After the Japanese attacked Pearl Harbor in 1941, thousands of American citizens of Japanese descent were forcibly confined to "relocation camps" for the duration of the war. They were loyal Americans, many of whose sons fought in Europe as members of an all-Japanese unit that earned more battle decorations than any other in the American Army. Nonetheless, Japanese-Americans were removed from their homes and effectively imprisoned simply because of their ancestry, while Americans of German and Italian descent—culturally and racially more similar to the dominant Anglo-Saxons—retained their rights as American citizens. It was not until 1983 that the U.S. courts awarded financial compensation to the Japanese-Americans who were interned (Irons, 1983).

Oppression is often a response to environmental conditions and the technology of production. Physical space is used to segregate minorities; and, in oppression's most extreme forms, minority populations, themselves, are either forcibly removed from their communities or killed.

We come now to the major problem in understanding social oppression and prejudice—explaining their existence. Why do they exist at all?

## Explaining Social Oppression

Sociologists use both the conflict and functional perspectives to explain the mistreatment of minorities. A conflict perspective focuses on competition for scarce resources and the resulting ability of

During World War II, entire Japanese-American families were "relocated" to remote internment camps, such as Manzanar (shown above) in the California desert.

some people to exploit others. A functional view tries to identify how oppression contributes to or interferes with the achievement of culturally valued goals.

## The Conflict Perspective

There is historical evidence that prejudice and discrimination are most likely to occur when there is intense competition over scarce resources and rewards (Noel, 1968; Vander Zanden, 1972). In Hawaii and on the U.S. West Coast, for example, there was little open prejudice against Japanese until whites and Japanese competed for the same jobs; and the economic success of Chinese in Southeast Asia and Indians in Uganda preceded sharp rises in prejudice against them.

In the United States, lower-class whites are more likely to report racist attitudes to interviewers than are middle- or upper-class whites, and this is consistent with a competition explanation of discrimination against minorities. Until recently, for example, many white-dominated labor unions resisted increases in black membership, in part because unemployment was already a problem for the white members (Gould, 1968). Large unions— such as the AFL-CIO—however, are among the most integrated of all organizations in the United States.

The openness of large labor unions to minority members suggests that prejudice is not simply a result of competition, for we need to remember that competition among the lower and middle

Although lower-class whites are the most likely to belong to racist groups such as the Ku Klux Klan, this does not mean that those in the middle and upper classes hold less-racist attitudes. Because middle- and upper-class whites are less threatened by the progress of minorities, they have less reason to express openly any racist attitudes they may hold.

classes is caused in large part by the fact that the upper class takes a disproportionately large share of wealth and income. Thus, the scarcity of rewards in the lower class is, itself, a product of a class system.

To Marx, the most important aspect of any society is the division of people into two classes, those who own the means of production (capitalists), and those who do not (workers). From this perspective, racism and ethnicism are two forms of prejudice that benefit the capitalist class (Reich, 1981). The existence of minorities provides a continuing source of cheap labor, for "inferior" people cannot demand high wages. In fact, the growth of American industry during the nineteenth century was made possible by successive waves of immi-grants—Irish, Germans, Scandinavians, East Europeans, and Asians—each of which, in turn, was the object of prejudice and discrimination that increased the profits of business owners.

Prejudice against minorities also creates divisions within the working class by setting workers of different ethnicity and race against one another. This perpetuates inequality by contributing to false consciousness and interfering with social solidarity within the working class: rather than blame the upper class or the class system itself, lower-class groups blame each other. As Lipset and Bendix (1959) put it:

A real social and economic cleavage is created by widespread discrimination against minority groups, and this diminishes the chances for the development of solidarity along class lines. . . . This continued splintering of the working class is a major element in the preservation and the stability of the class structure. (pp. 105–106)

During the first three decades of this century, few blacks belonged to unions, and white employers actively recruited blacks as strikebreakers—workers who take the place of union workers who are on strike (William J. Wilson, 1978). This intensified racism among working-class whites and, until they responded by actively recruiting blacks as union members, divided the working class along racial lines.

Thus, to Marx, prejudice and exploitation are all but inevitable in class societies—whether the targets are defined by race, ethnicity, gender, or age. Oppression contributes to upper-class privilege and helps maintain the class system. It also encourages members of the lower class to vent their anger and frustration on relatively safe—and undeserving—targets; in other words, to use minorities as **scapegoats.**

**Scapegoats** In the ancient Roman Empire, Christians were "thrown to the lions" whenever disaster struck. When Christians became a majority, Jews replaced them as scapegoats, and when plagues ravaged Europe during the fourteenth century, Jews were blamed and hundreds of their communities were exterminated (Graebner and Britt, 1942). The ruling class often used Jews as tax collectors, making them convenient targets for the dissatisfaction of those whose taxes supported the wealthy (Pettigrew, 1968). During the Great Depression of the 1930s, Hitler used Jews and Communists as scapegoats on which Germans could blame all their political and economic troubles (Davidowicz, 1975).

In nineteenth-century America, Irish immigrants were blamed for crime, poverty, political corruption, and deplorable urban living conditions. When they became established, prejudice was turned against other ethnic and racial groups—Germans, Polish Catholics, Chinese, and Japanese. During the Depression, anti-Semitism grew

Although thousands of illegal aliens from Mexico and other Latin American countries are arrested and deported every week, more of them continue to enter the United States, find work, and elude capture by the Immigration and Naturalization Service.

sharply in America (Strong, 1941), and after World War II, returning veterans who felt they had received bad breaks in the army were more likely than others to report anti-Semitic attitudes (Bettelheim and Janowitz, 1950).

Campbell (1947) found that people who report themselves as being dissatisfied with economic and political conditions in the United States are almost three times more likely than satisfied people to express dislike for Jews, avoid them, or show active hostility toward them. Whites who are dissatisfied with community services and local government are more likely than others to express hostile attitudes toward blacks (Campbell, 1971).

Hispanics, blacks, and Asian refugees are now the most convenient scapegoats on which to blame urban decay, the "welfare mess," unemployment, disorder in schools, and "crime in the streets." There is considerable hostility toward Vietnamese refugees who fish along the Gulf Coast in Texas, Louisiana, and Florida. Illegal immigrants from Mexico are often blamed for high unemployment rates, even though they perform jobs that most Americans will not.

Social oppression is thus connected to both competition for scarce rewards and the exploitation of classes, and from this perspective it is easier to understand why racial and ethnic prejudice is more commonly expressed by lower-class people (Adorno et al., 1950; Selznick and Steinberg, 1969). The upper class can *afford* to appear liberal and unprejudiced because minority gains pose no threat to their position (Kerbo, 1983). Members of the lower class, however, are more vulnerable to unemployment and a loss of prestige and income; and, because they depend on the upper class for their jobs, they are more likely to vent their anger and frustration on people who are less powerful than they.

From a conflict perspective the existence of minorities is functional only for members of dominant groups, particularly those in the upper class. Does this mean that oppression never contributes to the achievement of culturally valued goals?

**Voices:**

## The Pressure Is Greatest at the Bottom

(In August, 1984, riots between whites and Hispanics broke out in the city of Lawrence, Massachusetts. The violence was confined to Oxford Street, "a 400 yard long slum of rotting tenements and trash-filled vacant lots ending at a dreary red-brick public housing project.")

Who's to blame for the riots? "It's the (Puerto) Ricans! They are taking over the town. The Ricans are always saying, 'Kill the whites.' But they say it in that Rican language so you won't understand them. See them two walking by now? Talking that Rican junk! They could be saying, 'We'll burn his house down tonight.' Hey! That IS what they're saying. I can tell just by looking at them." (Sal, a young white man).

Source: *Hartford Courant*, August 12, 1984.

"Many non-Hispanics are always calling the young Hispanic girls 'spics' and 'whores.'" (17-year-old Hispanic girl).

"When we ride our bicycles, they always say they are stolen" (15-year-old Hispanic boy).

"If we work, they say we are stealing jobs from them. If we don't work, they say we are welfare bums." (Hispanic employee of local antipoverty agency).

"People here are frustrated and angry and they don't understand. They need a focus for their anger, so they fight each other. But they are really angry because they can't get jobs, because the schooling they got wasn't any good, because federal programs were cut back, because they have to live in a place like this. Would you want to live here?" (An Hispanic social worker).

"Look around you. Look at this place. Why not fight? People here don't have anything better to do." (a young black man who lives in the neighborhood).

## Functions and Dysfunctions of Prejudice and Discrimination

The oppression of minorities is often a part of the basic fabric of social life in a society. On the simplest level, racial and ethnic stereotypes help maintain social boundaries. In homogeneous societies, negative stereotypes about outsiders (and positive ones about insiders) allow insiders to draw clear boundaries between themselves and the rest of the world, boundaries that often reinforce superior self-images.

In eighteenth- and nineteenth-century America, ethnic and racial stereotypes about immigrants contributed to social solidarity among Anglo-Saxons by heightening awareness of racial and ethnic differences and by devaluing all non-Anglo-Saxons. Racism was functional for the economy of southern states prior to the mechanization of agriculture; many whites of that period believed they were doing blacks a *favor* by enslaving them, for this was a way of introducing Christianity to the "African heathen" (Pettigrew, 1976).

In spite of their negative effects on minorities, prejudice and discrimination still play a part in the achievement of some goals in American society. Oppression ensures that "dirty work" will be done: cleaning streets and collecting trash, emptying hospital bedpans, maintaining and cleaning buildings (including college classrooms and dormitories), washing dishes in restaurants, digging ditches, and performing the countless tasks required in low-paid, unskilled factory jobs. The oppression of migrant farmworkers—most of whom are nonwhite, illegal aliens—keeps the price of fruits and vegetables relatively low.

The functional perspective also identifies *dys*functions of oppression, in addition to the obvious negative consequences of prejudice and injustice. It keeps substantial portions of the population in poor health and contributes to hostility, suspicion, and fear. It denies millions of people the opportunity to develop fully and use their abilities; and this not only deprives society of the full range of talents found in its population, but also contributes to crime, growing welfare and unemployment rolls, and the decay of communities.

Ethnic and racial groups themselves are not the problem. The problem is the mistreatment of minorities that has become an enduring structural, cultural, and ecological aspect of social environments. The elimination of prejudice and discrimination involves more than changes in attitudes, for the oppression of minorities is deeply embedded in socially structured relationships and ecological arrangements.

# Social Change: Ending Prejudice and Oppression

The oppression of minorities has three major sociological aspects: prejudice (culture), discrimination and inequality (social structure), and population control and segregation (ecology). What are the prospects for change in each of these areas?

## Cultural Change: Reducing Prejudice

There are two basic ways to reduce prejudice: by attacking the legitimacy of prejudice itself and by reducing perceived differences that form the basis for prejudice.

Racial and ethnic prejudice runs deep in American culture; and yet, at the same time, we value equality, fairness, equal opportunity, and freedom from oppression. Our culture pulls us in opposite directions; and as Myrdal (1945) wrote in his classic analysis, *An American Dilemma*, the resulting strain makes social change inevitable.

One of the major accomplishments of the civil rights movement of the 1960s was that it forced many Americans to confront serious cultural contradictions. As Myrdal predicted, Martin Luther King, Jr., and other civil rights activists used one part of American culture—beliefs and values about equality—to attack another, racial prejudice. This is a particularly effective method of bringing about social change, for it forces people to confront uncomfortable contradictions between what they envision as their *ideal* culture and the cultural ideas they actually live by.

As prejudice is exposed and negatively valued in a culture, however, people often respond merely by withholding the expression of prejudice while keeping their attitudes, beliefs, and values intact. Thus, surveys that show a steady decline in outward expressions of racial and ethnic prejudice in the United States do not prove that prejudice itself is declining. This is an important distinction, because if prejudice remains strong while its outward expression declines under increased social pressure, it can quickly reemerge under less-restrained conditions.

A second approach to reducing prejudice is to change people's perceptions of members of different racial or ethnic groups, and this often involves the destruction of stereotypes as bases for our knowledge about each other.

**Changing Perceptions of Minority Groups** When prejudice focuses on differences between groups, one solution is for members of a minority to assimi-

---

**Voices:**

**The Corrosiveness of Stereotypes**

In 1970, elementary school teacher Jane Elliott devised an experiment for her all-white class in Riceville, Iowa. She divided her class into two groups—those with brown eyes and those with blue.

"I told them that brown-eyed people are better than blue-eyed people—they are smarter and cleaner. And within 15 minutes after the exercise started, the brown-eyed children became viciously cruel, condescending, elitist.

"The blue-eyed students became unclean, belligerent, angry, frustrated, defeated. They couldn't read, they dropped their pencils. They did all the things that are supposed to be limited to minority groups.

(The next day the roles were reversed and the brown-eyed children were defined as a minority. The results were similar, although the blue-eyed children were slightly kinder.)

"The blue-eyed kids said afterwards, 'I didn't want to make my friends feel the way I felt when I was on the bottom.'"

On the third day, Elliott explained there is no real difference between blue and brown eyes.

"After they hear that, they get back together, they hug, they cry, you get the feeling what society could be like if it was non-judgmental."

Source: Associated Press, in the *Hartford Courant*, August 14, 1984, p. 2.

---

late—to change their culture so they no longer differ from those who dominate society. When Hispanics or Asians adopt English as their primary language, or when Jews change their names, they may become more acceptable in the eyes of dominant whites and less visible as members of a minority (my great grandfather, for example, emigrated from Norway to the United States and changed his name from Mokestaad to Johnson in order to fit in as a new American). Many immigrants to the United States reduce prejudice by replacing ethnic customs, styles of dress, and modes of speech with those favored by dominant ethnic groups.

The problem with this solution is that it requires minorities to surrender unique cultural identities, and this can be yet another form of social oppression. In addition, while assimilation is often effective for reducing ethnic prejudice, it is largely ineffective for reducing racism, for the physical characteristics of race can neither be changed nor concealed (except after generations of interbreeding that blends the characteristics of different groups). Black Americans are oppressed, in part, simply because of their race. How, then, can minorities both keep their unique cultural identities and free themselves from negative stereotypes and prejudice attached to them?

**Stereotypes** are beliefs that we use as substitutes for direct experience and knowledge of individuals. They lead us to overestimate differences between groups, to underestimate the amount of variation within them, and to apply general descriptions of entire groups or social categories to all individuals within them. Thus, they distort reality in many different ways.

It is easiest to maintain stereotypes if we avoid evidence that contradicts them, and one way to avoid contradictory evidence is to avoid interacting with people of different races or ethnicities; then there is no opportunity to compare stereotypes with the actual people those stereotypes describe. In addition, so long as we are isolated from one another, we can make up our own private explanations for people's behavior without ever taking their point of view into account (Newcomb, 1947).

This suggests that we can reduce prejudice if we change the structure of social relationships by increasing interaction among members of different groups. Contact with people of other races or ethnicities makes us more likely to see them as unique individuals, not copies stamped out by a single stereotype. Contact also allows us to discover that we often have more in common with members of other racial or ethnic groups than we do with many members of our own.

Many studies support the idea that increased interaction reduces prejudice. Deutsch and Collins (1951), for example, compared two housing projects. In one, residents were randomly assigned to dwellings; in the other, blacks and whites were segregated from one another. Blacks and whites in integrated housing were more likely to interact informally and to report interracial friendships. Other studies show that integrated housing reduces the tendency to stereotype members of minorities (Kramer, 1950; Wilner et al., 1955); and the desegregation of elementary schools increases both interaction among children of different races and desire for friendships with one another (Koslin et al., 1969).

A simple increase in the rate of interaction is not a guaranteed cure for prejudice, however. Blacks and whites interacted with each other for several hundred years in the American South without decreasing the levels of racism. Increased interaction is most likely to reduce prejudice when people: (1) occupy the same social status (such as co-workers); (2) share common goals (as in problem-solving groups); (3) can achieve their goals only by working together (as in athletic teams and military units); and (4) have the support of authorities (Allport, 1954). After President Truman ordered an end to discrimination and segregation on American merchant ships, for example, racial prejudice among white seamen decreased with each integrated voyage.

The reduction of prejudice through increased interaction illustrates how cultural, structural, and ecological factors affect one another. New ecological arrangements (physical integration of schools, workplaces, or neighborhoods) change a basic aspect of social structure (the frequency of interaction among people of different races or ethnicities) that, in turn, often reduces prejudice (a cultural attitude). Other structural changes—such as putting people of different races or ethnicities in similar statuses in which they must depend on one another for the achievement of common goals—also affect how we value, feel and think about, and behave toward other people.

Clearly, the reduction of racist ideas in a group, community, or society, depends heavily on related social structures or ecological arrangements. The 1954 Supreme Court decision to integrate public schools attacked cultural racism by creating ecological arrangements and patterns of interaction in which stereotypes are more difficult to maintain.

## Structural Change: Reducing Inequality

Expressions of racial and ethnic prejudice seem to be declining in the United States, and many American whites infer from this that blacks are no longer oppressed. In 1977, for example, roughly 60 percent of white adults reported the belief that blacks receive equal treatment when applying for housing and white-collar jobs, or when dealing with police; and 68 percent reported the belief that blacks are treated equally when they apply for skilled-labor jobs (Harris, 1977).

Blacks, on the other hand, reported very different perceptions of their position (Table 12-3). Less than a quarter said they receive equal treatment in the economy, housing, and by police. In

**Table 12-3**

Perceptions of Discrimination against Blacks, by Respondent's Race (United States, 1977)

| ARE BLACKS DISCRIMINATED AGAINST IN: | PERCENTAGE SAYING, "NO DISCRIMINATION" | |
|---|---|---|
| | WHITES | BLACKS |
| Getting white-collar jobs? | 59 | 18 |
| Getting skilled labor jobs? | 68 | 23 |
| Getting decent housing? | 61 | 23 |
| The way they're treated by police? | 60 | 23 |
| The way they're treated if arrested? | 61 | 23 |

Source: Louis Harris, 1977, p. 3.

more recent studies, blacks were far more likely than whites to perceive the police and courts as unfair (Hagan and Abonnetti, 1982). In short, most whites seem to believe that race is no longer an important factor in social stratification, while most blacks believe just the opposite.

There is little question that certain segments of the black population have made considerable gains over the last 20 years, especially those who are young, married, and well-educated; but, in general, the relative standing of American blacks has improved very little (Farley, 1980). During the 1970s, the earnings gap between white and black *workers* decreased slightly, but the gap between white and black *families* did not change at all. How could this happen? The answer is that for both blacks and whites single-parent families headed by women became increasingly common during the 1970s, and such families have lower average incomes than two-parent families. Because this trend was stronger among blacks than among whites, black gains in the labor market were offset by changes in family structure (Farley, 1980).

In spite of black gains in occupational status, an enormous racial gap remains, and Kluegel and Smith (1982) estimated from a national study of white adults that almost three-quarters of whites overestimate recent economic progress by blacks and the level of their opportunities. In 1980 white workers had a 67 percent greater chance than blacks to have upper-level white-collar jobs and a 39 percent greater chance to have skilled blue-collar jobs (U.S. Census Bureau, 1981). In fact, the percentage of blacks with upper-level white-collar jobs was lower than the comparable percentage for whites in *1950* (Farley, 1980).

For many black workers, the old rule still applies: last hired, first fired.

While employed blacks have made some progress, even they are vulnerable, for when unemployment increases, blacks are among the first to be laid off (Freeman, 1975). In each year since 1947, unemployment rates have been twice as great among nonwhites as among whites. Compared with whites in 1982, unemployment rates were twice as high among blacks and 60 percent higher among Hispanics (U.S. Census Bureau, 1980b, 1983c).

It is important to point out that the progress made by skilled and educated blacks came about only with the assistance of the federal government and a decade of mass protests and riots in cities such as Los Angeles, Detroit, and Washington, DC. Freeman (1975) showed that there has been a close relationship between black progress and antidiscrimination activities of federal government agencies such as the Equal Employment Opportunity Commission. The likelihood that companies would hire blacks was directly related to the amount of pressure applied by the federal government, as were changes in discriminatory hiring, firing, and promotion practices.

The most controversial attempt to eliminate economic inequality is **affirmative action,** the practice of giving minorities preferential treatment when they apply for jobs or college. Opponents argue that it is little more than "reverse discrimination"—progress for minorities at the expense of others. American culture, they argue, values individual ability as the main consideration in distributing resources and rewards, and affirmative action violates this important value.

Supporters of affirmative action point out that individual ability has relatively little to do with the distribution of wealth, power, and prestige in the United States (see Chapter 11). In addition, the ability argument ignores the cumulative effect of centuries of oppression, because it assumes that blacks and whites are now in equally strong positions to compete. It is not enough to say, "From now on, everyone has an equal chance," when history has left minorities with relatively low levels of education, training, and job experience.

While affirmative action programs have helped blacks who are highly skilled, well-educated, or who have long, steady work histories, in some ways it has hurt blacks by reinforcing racial preju-dice. The mere existence of a double-standard reinforces the belief that blacks are inferior to whites. As Jencks (1983b) points out, when colleges recruit blacks whose average preparation for college is weaker than the average white's, it reinforces whites' perceptions that "blacks just aren't very bright":

> The logic is precisely the same as the logic that convinces students and faculty that athletes, who are also admitted even if they are academically unpromising, aren't very bright. The difference is that encouraging the nation's future professional and managerial elite to think athletes are nitwits does no serious social harm, whereas encouraging the belief that blacks are nitwits does incalculable harm. (Jencks, 1983b, p. 14)

Thus, racial oppression is strongly linked with social class systems, with both upper- and middle-class whites benefiting from the exploitation of nonwhites. Many nonwhites consequently suffer from the double disadvantages of lower class status and nonwhite racial status.

Many white Americans have relatively little to lose by giving up racist ideas; but unequal distributions of wealth, income, and power will be with us for a long time to come, for they have been deeply embedded in the American economic, social, and political fabric for centuries. As Farley (1980) wrote:

> We are a long way from the segregated society of 1950, but we are still far from the dream of Martin Luther King. If the next generation of blacks is not to remain a generation behind whites, society has a long road ahead. (p. 16)

**Violence and Social Change** Just as those who dominate societies often use violence to oppress minorities, so, too, do minorities sometimes resort to violence as the only way to end prejudice and discrimination.

Gandhi and his followers freed India from Britain's colonial rule largely without the use of violence, and Martin Luther King, Jr., used Gandhi as a model. There can be little doubt, however, that Americans did not pay serious attention to civil rights until blacks asserted their willingness to engage in violence. The riots in Detroit, Los Angeles, and other American cities during the 1960s prompted the appointment of a national commis-

Although it is undeniable that blacks have made some progress since the beginning of the civil rights movement, it is unlikely that much change would have occurred had blacks not called attention to their plight with violence such as the Newark riots in the summer of 1967.

sion whose conclusions focused on the frustrations of blacks in a racist society.

More recently, many South African blacks have concluded that peaceful, legal action will not bring about an end to their oppressed minority status. Denied any effective voice in government and forbidden to protest by breaking even the most minor laws, many blacks believe that their government will only allow opposition that it knows will be ineffective; this leads them to the conclusion that "the only language the government understands is force" (Slambrouck, 1983, p. 13).

Gamson (1974, 1975) studied 53 social movements in American history and found that the more "unruly" social movements were, the more likely they were to gain concessions from those in power. As Gamson concluded, it appears that "the meek don't make it."

## Ecological Change

One of the most important ecological aspects of social oppression is physical segregation. Paradoxically, both more and less segregation have been proposed as responses to the oppression of minorities in the United States and elsewhere.

For years many French Canadians in the province of Quebec have urged a separation of Quebec from the rest of Canada and the establishment of an independent state in which "French Canadian" is no longer treated as a minority status (Hughes, 1963). Israel is the only country in the world in which "Jew" is not a minority status. During the 1920s Marcus Garvey proposed seizing European colonies in Africa and transforming them into a free United Black Africa populated by American blacks and sympathetic Africans. More recently, the Republic of New Africa movement in the United

States pursued the goal of taking over several southern states for an independent black nation (Weisbord, 1975).

All of these efforts to preserve cultural diversity and escape exploitation and mistreatment involve **separatism,** which calls for greater segregation, not less, and rests on the belief that separation is the only way people can control the social and ecological conditions in which they live. In most cases, they have not been successful, primarily because those who control necessary resources benefit from the oppression of minorities.

In contrast to separatists are those who advocate greater integration, and their efforts have focused on two major areas—housing and schools.

**Desegregation and Resegregation** In 1954 the Supreme Court established the doctrine that separate schools for whites and blacks are "inherently unequal," and it ordered an end to segregated schools. As we saw earlier, however, segregation persists in American schools.

When measuring change in the distribution of blacks and whites, it is important to distinguish between racial **integration** and racial *isolation.* Within school districts, schools are integrated if whites and blacks are evenly distributed among schools. In other words, if the population is 10 percent black and 90 percent white, full integration exists only if every school has that racial composition.

Racial **isolation,** on the other hand, refers to comparisons *between* school districts. Suppose one district's population is entirely white and another's is entirely black; *within* each district, schools are integrated, because the racial composition of the schools matches the racial composition of the communities they serve. Black and white students, however, are isolated from each other, because they live in different school districts.

Although segregation has decreased, it remains high in many large cities such as Chicago, Cleveland, and Newark. In fact, segregation in these and other cities actually increased between 1967 and 1976 (Wurdock 1979; Wurdock and Farley, 1979). This occurred primarily because *residential* segregation *within* school districts increased: whites moved from integrated neighborhoods to all-white neighborhoods in the same school district. Thus, de facto *re*-segregation is slowly undoing much of the desegregation achieved between 1954 and 1967.

Racial isolation fell between 1967 and 1976, but as whites leave central cities in increasing numbers, the separation of white and black students is likely to increase once again. Only two of the nation's 20 largest cities—Phoenix and San Jose—have school districts in which whites outnumber nonwhites; and whites make up only 4 percent of enrolled students in Washington DC, 18 percent in Detroit, and 25 percent in Chicago (Wurdock and Farley, 1979). Thus, increased interaction between blacks and whites made possible by desegregation is likely to be undone by increased racial isolation caused by changing racial compositions of America's communities.

Coleman, Kelly, and Moore (1975) argued that desegregation in many communities has actually caused increased racial isolation, because white parents leave rather than send their children to integrated schools. Farley, Richards, and Wurdock (1980), showed, however, that the migration of whites away from cities has been going on continuously for the last decade, and when such communities desegregate their schools, white migration increases only for the following year and then settles back to its former rate. In other words, school desegregation has a relatively small and temporary effect on the "flight" of white families from communities.

Migration is only one factor in racially segregated schools, however, for in the last decade the number of private schools in the United States has grown rapidly while the number of public schools has decreased (U.S. Census Bureau, 1983c). Many of these schools exclude blacks—some of them on supposedly religious grounds—and this introduces a major new way for whites to separate their children from blacks.

If the goal of integration is to reduce prejudice and discrimination by improving educational opportunities for blacks and by increasing contact between students of different races, the United States clearly has a long way to go. In fact, there is reason to believe that we are retreating from the goal of a society in which people from different ethnic and racial backgrounds can share the same neighborhoods and schools.

## Summary

**1.** Biological races are collections of people whose distinct physical characteristics are passed on through reproduction. Social race is a status defined in physical terms. An ethnic group is a collection of people with a common cultural heritage.

**2.** A minority is a group of people who are singled out for unequal treatment. Social oppression is the systematic, socially supported abuse or exploitation of one group by another.

**3.** Prejudice is a positive or negative attitude directed toward members of a group. Prejudice is based on real or imagined differences between groups, attaches values to group differences, is generalized to all members of a target group, and usually includes the belief that group differences are absolute and inevitable.

**4.** Prejudice functions as an ideology by denying the existence of oppression and by blaming minorities for the effects of oppression.

**5.** Cultural differences within societies are dealt with in several ways. Amalgamation occurs when several cultures mix to become a new culture; assimilation occurs when ethnic groups conform to the culture of a single group; and pluralism occurs when diverse ethnic groups maintain their differences within a society.

**6.** Discrimination is unequal treatment of people because they belong to certain groups. Whether or not our treatment of each other is consistent with our attitudes depends on the situation.

**7.** Race strongly affects the distribution of wealth, occupation, education, income, prestige, employment, power, health, and living conditions. Ethnicity has weaker effects because it is less visible and has weaker prejudices attached to it.

**8.** Upward mobility among blacks has been slow and has barely affected the distribution of wealth, income, power, and prestige. Blacks are handicapped not only by poorer education and occupation, but by the stigma of race itself. Prejudice often creates self-fulfilling prophecies.

**9.** Ecology often affects the creation and perpetuation of minorities. Discrimination and prejudice often are encouraged by the mode of production in a society.

**10.** Segregation often reinforces the disadvantaged position of minorities. Residential segregation is common in the United States and results mostly from the refusal of whites to live near blacks. *De jure* segregation is required by law; *de facto* segregation is a latent consequence of other social or ecological arrangements. Most American children attend segregated schools because they live in segregated neighborhoods.

**11.** Genocide is the systematic killing of members of a group. Expulsion is a form of oppression in which minorities are forced to leave their community or society.

**12.** Conflict theorists believe that prejudice and discrimination arise out of competition for scarce resources in which some groups are able to exploit others. Prejudice serves the interests of dominant groups and contributes to false consciousness among subordinate groups that often use minorities as scapegoats.

**13.** The functional perspective identifies both functions and dysfunctions of prejudice and discrimination. In spite of their negative consequences both for minorities and societies, prejudice and discrimination do contribute to the achievement of some social goals.

**14.** Prejudice may be reduced by attacking its social legitimacy or by reducing perceived differences between minorities and dominant groups. Increased interaction often lowers prejudice when people occupy the same social statuses and share common goals that can be achieved only through cooperation. Affirmative action programs—preferential treatment given to minorities—have generally had little effect on the disadvantaged position of minorities in the U.S.

**15.** Separatism is a belief in increased segregation as a way of preserving minority culture and ending discrimination.

**16.** Racial integration of schools exists when the racial composition of schools matches the composition of their communities. Racial isolation refers to comparisons between school districts and communities and the degree of contact between people of different races. American schools have become more racially integrated and less isolated since

1954, but in many large cities the trend toward less isolation is reversing as whites move out of integrated neighborhoods.

## Key Terms

affirmative action 385
amalgamation 359
assimilation 359
discrimination 362
ethnicity 353
   ethnic group 353
expulsion 375
genocide 374
integration (racial or ethnic) 387
isolation (racial or ethnic) 387
minority 354
pluralism 359
prejudice 356
   ethnicism 356
   racism 356
race 353
scapegoat 379
segregation (racial or ethnic) 372
   *de facto* 373
   *de jure* 373
separatism 387
social oppression 355
stereotype 382

## Recommended Readings

ALLPORT, G. (1958). *The nature of prejudice.* Cambridge, MA: Addison-Wesley. A classic exploration of the nature of prejudice, including a look at the ways in which minorities often respond.

CONKLIN, N. F., and LOURIE, M. A. (1983). *A host of tongues: Language communities in the United States.* New York: Free Press. A study of linguistic assimilation through which the diverse cultural origins of the American people are dominated by a single language.

DUNBAR, L. W. (Ed.). (1984). *Minority report: What has happened to blacks, Hispanics, American Indians, and other American minorities in the eighties.* New York: Pantheon. Seven civil rights activists argue that while many cultural aspects of racial and ethnic inequality have changed, economic discrimination continues and will continue without government intervention.

FERNANDEZ, J. P. (1981). *Racism and sexism in corporate life.* Lexington, MA: D. C. Heath. A study of attitudes among managers toward existing company-sponsored affirmative action programs. One major finding is that the more highly placed executives are, the more racist and sexist their personal attitudes tend to be.

SIMPSON, G. E., and YINGER, J. M. (1985). *Racial and cultural minorities: An analysis of prejudice and discrimination* (5th ed.). New York: Plenum. The latest edition of an important source book on discrimination and prejudice, which pays attention to both theory and research.

WILSON, W. J. (1978). *The declining significance of race.* Chicago: University of Chicago Press. A provocative book that argues that class, not race, is the most important impediment to progress for American blacks.

To begin, consider the following riddle:

> A man and his son go for a walk. The boy falls and injures himself seriously. The father rushes his son to a hospital, and while the father waits, his son is taken into a treatment room. A doctor enters the room, looks at the boy and exclaims, "My God! It's my son!"
>
> Who is the doctor?

People come up with a variety of complex solutions for this riddle (such as the doctor is the boy's real father and the other man is his stepfather), but it also has a very simple answer: the doctor is the boy's mother. When most of us hear the riddle for the first time, the "obvious" answer is not obvious at all; Russians, however, would probably figure it out quickly since most physicians in the Soviet Union are women.

The riddle reveals a fragment of a much larger phenomenon found in most societies: people make social distinctions among other people based upon their biological sex, and this profoundly affects their perceptions, evaluations, feelings, and behavior. Most important, however, is the fact that in most societies sex plays a part in social stratification, the unequal distribution of wealth, power, and prestige. In many cases, it is also the basis for prejudice and discrimination; that is, the treatment of females as members of a social minority.

Unlike most other minorities, females are a numerical majority in virtually all known societies, which makes their minority standing all the more compelling (Hacker, 1951). How have culture, social structure, and ecological arrangements been used to transform a numerical majority into a social minority?

We begin by looking at the difference between sex as a biological characteristic and gender as a social status. From there we go into a detailed analysis of cultural, structural, and ecological aspects of social inequality based on gender and the socialization process through which we learn to take our place as males and females and play the roles associated with them. The rest of the chapter uses the ecological, functional, and conflict perspectives to explain why gender is used as a basis for inequality, and closely examines the myths and realities of change in contemporary American society.

## Biology, Culture, and Social Structure

Biologically, sex is a crucial and relatively simple characteristic, for it takes two types of people—male and female—to create new people. All fetuses initially look the same, but after the first few months, changes occur: males develop testicles and penises and females develop vaginas, clitorises, ovaries, wombs, and fallopian tubes. These differences occur because males have an "X" and "Y" pair of chromosomes and females have two "X" chromosomes.

Males and females also differ in body chemistry, for while both have the same hormones in their blood, they differ in how much of each they have. Females generally have more estrogen and males more testosterone, and this difference plays an important part in the physical development of girls and boys into women and men (determining among other things the size of their bodies, amounts of body hair, potential for muscle development, and the size of breasts and hips).

Sociologically, however, there is more to being male or female than chemistry, physiology, and the parts we play in reproduction, for these *physical* differences have been culturally transformed into two **genders,** which are distinguished by profoundly different social characteristics. Cultural beliefs define the basic nature of males and females in different ways; values generally rank males higher than females; norms generally support male privilege; and females are the object of both positive and negative attitudes—from the adoration of the Virgin Mary to the contempt for women expressed in pornography.

Most societies also assign males and females to sharply different statuses and, on this basis, distribute wealth, power, and prestige unequally. Women are almost always the ones who care for children, whereas most men spend their time producing goods. Even among people who work outside the home, there are sharp differences in what men and women do: all but a few women follow instructions given by men; men are far more likely to make decisions and supervise other people. Women are also more likely than men to live in poverty, and to have no paid work at all.

People differ by gender not only in what they do, but in how they do it, for in most societies, male and female patterns of response to other people differ in many ways. Men, for example, tend to display more aggressiveness and self-confidence, whereas women display more tenderness, vulnerability, and emotion in social interactions.

Thus, biological differences between males and females correspond to a variety of cultural and structural distinctions: different sets of beliefs, values, norms, and attitudes; complex divisions of labor and rewards; and different styles of interacting with other people. Because all societies make important social distinctions between females and males, it is tempting to conclude that such distinctions are biologically determined and are, therefore, "inevitable" and "natural."

Edward O. Wilson (1975) recently revived this point of view in his study of the genetic basis of social behavior among humans and other species. Females, he asserted, are nurturant toward children because the species needs such behavior in order to successfully reproduce itself. There is, he contended, a nurturant gene that causes such behavior, and biological differences between males and females explain many important differences we observe in what men and women do and how they do it.

This conclusion, however, fails to pay enough attention to the crucial fact that cultures distinguish between males and females in very different ways, and the distinctions made within cultures often change over time. As Wilson (1977) later acknowledged, "The evidence is strong that almost but probably not quite all differences among cultures are based on learning and socialization rather than on genes" (p. 133).

Biological determinism also ignores the fact that aside from the roles males and females play in reproduction, there is little scientific evidence that other differences are biologically caused; and those differences that are biological are relatively few in number (Maccoby and Jacklin, 1974). Males are more vulnerable than females to hemophilia and color blindness. They tend to have better visual-spatial and mathematical abilities but poorer verbal abilities, and they tend to be more active physically (Petersen, 1980).

Females display more sensitivity to sound, odor, and touch, are more dexterous in the use of their fingers, and are more likely to sing in tune. Males are generally more sensitive to light and are more adept at manipulating objects in space and

"seeing" spatial relations in their minds—as in reading a map or getting through a maze. Female infants pay more attention to facial expressions than to moving objects, whereas the pattern in infant males is just the opposite (Durden-Smith and DeSimone, 1983; Gove and Carpenter, 1982; Parsons, 1980). In each of these cases, however, the differences are between *averages* for males and females, and there is considerable overlap: many girls, for example, have better spatial ability than many boys do.

There is little evidence that hormones cause gender differences in behavior (Maccoby and Jack-

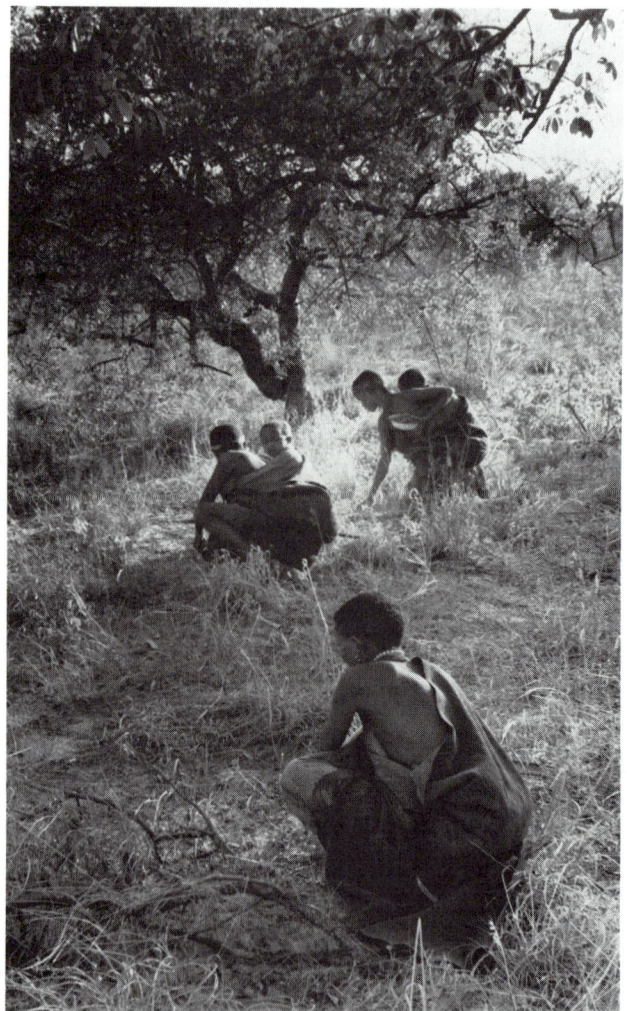

In many hunter-gatherer societies, women played an important role in production—especially of food—and equal standing with men was the rule, not the exception.

lin, 1974). In one study, for example, Kreuz and Rose (1972) found no consistent difference in testosterone levels when they compared male prison inmates on the basis of fighting behavior. Other studies of testosterone levels and hostility and aggressiveness in men also find no consistent relationship (Doering et al., 1974).

The lack of scientific support for biological determinism does not mean there is no connection between "male" and "female" as biological and as social characteristics, however (Rossi, 1984). The confinement of women to child care, for example, is no mere accident of history. The important point is that biological differences do not *determine* social differences, although they are often used as the basis for them.

This chapter focuses on two major sociological questions about gender: How do societies use biological characteristics to distinguish among their members, and under what social circumstances do these distinctions lead to the definition of women as a minority? From a sociological perspective, the position of women as a minority depends on the cultural, structural, and ecological aspects of our environments, and each of these factors is connected to the other two in often complex ways.

# Gender, Culture, and the Ideology of Sexism

Male and female are ascribed statuses that identify positions in social relationships. Attached to these statuses are *gender roles*—sets of expectations about how males and females should appear and behave. As you read the following sections, it is very important to keep in mind that although females are treated as a minority in most societies today, this has not always been the case. In most hunter-gatherer and some horticultural societies, the division of labor was based on gender, but women were not treated as inferior people (Etienne and Leacock, 1980).

In social interaction, we first define the situation; that is, we decide who other people are in relation to us. Culture is the source of such definitions, providing us with the categories through which we "know" and evaluate people, decide whether we like them, and know what to expect of them as well as what they will expect of us. The building blocks of cultural ideas are found in language, which—to varying degrees—makes important distinctions between females and males.

## Language and Gender

Language is more than a tool for communication, for people also use it to label people, things, and experiences; and their use of a particular language focuses their attention on some aspects of reality more than others. For example, we are less likely to focus on women's adult strengths if we think of them as "girls" rather than "women."

Language reinforces the minority status of females in four basic ways (Richardson, 1981). First, in many languages, females do not exist independently of males. In English, "man" and masculine pronouns such as "he" are commonly used to refer to both males and females (as in "Peace on earth and good will toward men"). When American women marry, they usually replace their own last name with their husband's, surrendering a unique part of their social identity. In general, men are referred to as "Mr."—a title that reveals nothing about their marital status—while women are known either as "Miss" or "Mrs."—in other words, according to their legal relationship with men. In French, the word "femme" means both "woman" and "wife," but "husband" and "man" are distinct words—"mari" and "homme." Thus, a French man can be referred to independently of his relationships with women, whereas a French woman's identity as "woman" is synonymous with a relationship with a man.

**PUZZLES:**

### WHAT WORD MEANS "HATRED OF MALES"?

There is no such word. This chapter explains why this is so, even though we have the word misogyny, which means "hatred of females."

Some argue that "it's only semantics" and "everyone knows that 'man' and 'he' refer to both males and females"; but both common experience and research suggest otherwise. When the word "man" is used, it is more likely to evoke male images than female ones, so the idea that women can be "congressmen" often puzzles children. Scheider and Hacker (1973) asked college students to submit photographs for a new textbook. Half the students were given chapter titles such as "Urban Life" and "Political Behavior," and the other half received titles such as "Urban Man" and "Political Man." The second group produced far more pictures of men than of women, reflecting the subtle but powerful influence of cultural imagery.

Second, we tend to associate masculine and feminine pronouns with specific social statuses. We refer to telephone operators and elementary school teachers as "she," but use "he" to refer to college professors, engineers, and physicians. When men or women hold jobs dominated by the other gender, we draw attention to the exception by using titles such as "male nurse" and "policewoman" (Lakoff, 1975; Weitz, 1977). In both cases, the language reflects cultural beliefs about who occupies each status, rather than the objective fact that both men and women are found in them.

We also use masculine and feminine pronouns to label nonhuman objects in ways that reflect the subordinate social position of females. Things that men build and control (or try to)—such as airplanes, ships, and nature—are "she's," while forces that are too powerful for men to control—the Devil and God—are "he's" (see Griffin, 1978).

Third, we use language in ways that portray women as weak, incompetent, and undesirable, and men as strong, competent, and socially valued. Women are commonly called "girls," but men are rarely called "boys" unless they occupy inferior statuses such as "busboy," "shoeshine boy," or, in some cases, "black." Unmarried older men are called "bachelors," a far more flattering label than comparable words for women—"old maid" and "spinster."

Most sexual slang that is applied to women describes their desirability to men (for example, "fox," "chick," "broad," and "nice piece"), whereas slang that applies to men refers to power over women (such as "stud"). Many people are familiar with the word for "excessive sexual desire in a fe-

---

## PUZZLES:

## IS YOUR LANGUAGE SEXIST?

Read the following sentences, filling in the masculine or feminine pronoun (his/her, he/she) you think is most appropriate. Do not take a lot of time thinking about your choice. The point is to discover if you have internalized the sexist tendencies of our language, not to identify you as a sexist.

Professor Blandon of Oxford won the Nobel Prize for _____ discoveries in biochemistry.

_____ sang softly to the baby cradled in _____ arms.

The memo from the boss said _____ would award bonuses next Friday.

As the senator accepted the presidential nomination, _____ eyes filled with tears of joy.

My secretary has increased _____ average typing speed to 80 words per minute.

The smartest student in the class often waited until the last minute to finish writing _____ term papers.

If you can honestly say that both male and female pronouns seem equally right for most or even all these sentences, you may have learned to go beyond the gender orientation of language and to concentrate on what people, as individuals, can do and be.

---

male" (nymphomania), but few have ever heard the word for comparable males (satyriasis). In addition, although English includes words for the hatred of females (**misogyny**) and the hatred of all people (**misanthropy**), there is no word for the hatred of males.

Japanese contains two vocabularies and grammars—one of which expresses ideas more directly and assertively than the other—and females are expected to use the less-assertive form (Farb, 1973). American speech produces parallel examples: women, for example, are more likely than men to use words such as "lovely," "cute," and "precious," and less likely to use strong profanity or make direct, powerful statements (Lakoff, 1975). Not only do males and females tend to use different vocabularies, but in some cases people assign different meanings to words depending on the speaker's gender. Many people, for example, support the belief that when a woman says "no," she really means "yes."

Women and men also tend to use different tones of voice. If we think of speech as music, males use fewer tones and are more likely than females to end a sentence on a relatively low tone, indicating firmness and finality (Brend, 1975).

Language reinforces the minority status of women in a fourth way: there is a clear historical trend through which words used to describe women acquire negative meanings. "Madam" and "mistress" went from respectful forms of address to "keeper of a whorehouse" and "lover kept by a man." "Hussy" once meant "housewife"; "tart" and "biddy" were affectionate names; "whore" once meant "lover of either sex"; "nymph" meant "beautiful young woman"; and "broad" meant "young woman," with no negative connotations. Words that describe men, however, have not been degraded in this way. In fact, favorite insults directed toward men are often derived from words that describe women—as in "sissy" (from "sister"), "pussy," and "son of a bitch" (which attacks men by insulting their mothers).

Language does not cause women to occupy inferior positions in societies, but it plays an important part because we use it to think about ourselves and other people. The fact that there is no English word for "the hatred of males" does not mean that no one hates males; it does mean, however, that systematic, socially supported negative attitudes toward males are unlikely to be a part of a society whose culture includes no such word. In the same way, the existence of the word "misogyny" does not mean that everyone will hate females, but it reflects a cultural idea that lends legitimacy to prejudice and discrimination against females.

## Beliefs: Masculine and Feminine

At the heart of cultures are beliefs that people use to define reality, and when applied to social categories, they are stereotypes: men are smarter than

### Voices: Who Has the Right Stuff?

Sally Ride, first American woman crew member on a space flight.

A young man might go into military flight training believing that he was entering some sort of technical school in which he was simply going to acquire a certain set of skills. Instead, he found himself all at once enclosed in a fraternity. And in this fraternity, even though it was military, men were not rated by their outward rank as ensigns, lieutenants, commanders, or whatever. No, herein the world was divided into those who had it and those who did not. This quality, this *it*, was never named, however, nor was it talked about in any way. . . . As to just what this ineffable quality was . . . well, it obviously involved bravery. . . . The idea was to prove . . . that you were one of the elected . . . ones who had *the right stuff* and could move higher and higher and even . . . that you might be able to join that special few at the very top.*

The stereotype depicting men as the only ones with "the right stuff" to be test pilots and even astronauts is breaking down as women demonstrate their ability to perform efficiently and professionally as members of space craft crews. What remains of the stereotype is the notion that such highly demanding work requires special skills, competence, and qualities of mind and spirit of which only a few extraordinary men—and women—are capable.

*Source: Wolfe, *The Right Stuff*, 1979.

women; women cannot take pressure like men can; men are less emotional than women and are only interested in sex; women make better parents and housekeepers than men; aggressive men are "go-getters" and aggressive women are "pushy"; women's talk is all chatter and women only think about clothes; women want to be raped; menstruation makes women unreliable; there is something wrong with women who enjoy sex; there is something wrong with men or women who do *not* enjoy sex.

These are only a few examples of the beliefs that have been used to distinguish between males and females. Together, they portray a vision of the "true nature" of females and males, and in our culture these "natures" are summarized by the concepts of "masculine" and "feminine."

Regardless of gender, race, age, or social class, American adults generally agree that **masculinity** describes people who are aggressive, rational, strong, independent, competitive, self-confident, dominant, active, tough, emotionally insensitive, and reluctant to show their feelings. **Femininity,** however, describes people who are intuitive, emotionally excitable, weak, vulnerable, dependent, insecure, submissive, noncompetitive (except with other women), passive, tender, sensitive, and quick to show their emotions (Broverman et al., 1972).

Like all stereotypes, the concepts of masculinity and femininity describe people in oversimplified terms that bear little relation to what individual men and women are really like (Lott, 1981). No one is aggressive or passive all the time; we all have both moments of intelligence and moments of stupidity. Gender stereotypes also ignore the enormous variation *among* women and *among* men: there are many men, for example, who come closer to the feminine ideal than many women do. Perhaps most important, stereotypes about gender are strongly linked to cultural values.

## Values: Vive la Différence?

To many people, beliefs that distinguish females and males do no more than just that: the two genders differ from each other, and what is the harm in that? The harm lies in the fact that most cultures also generally value the ascribed status of male higher than the status of female, and different criteria are used to evaluate men and women.

Several studies reveal a preference for male children among parents in most societies (Coombs, 1977; Williamson, 1976). In parts of rural India, infanticide—the killing of infants—is relatively common and is more likely to be inflicted on female children (Korbin, 1983). Not only is maleness a preferred characteristic, but traits associated with masculinity are valued more highly than those associated with femininity. Broverman et al. (1970), for example, asked male and female mental health professionals to use lists of personality traits to describe the "mature, healthy, competent" male, female, and human being. Although they described the ideal male and ideal human being in similar terms, they described the ideal female in sharply different terms. Thus, American females who fulfill cultural ideals about them are valued less than men who conform to cultural ideals about them.

The higher value placed on maleness leads to different perceptions and evaluations of men's and women's behavior. In a study of 600 male and female undergraduates (Lao et al., 1975), students watched videotapes of men and women playing roles that differed in assertiveness. Role players were matched for age, physical attractiveness, and intelligence; but, in every case, male role players were judged to be more intelligent and likable than their female counterparts. Highly assertive men were evaluated as more intelligent than less-assertive men; but the results for women were in the opposite direction: higher assertiveness resulted in *lower* evaluations of intelligence.

It is significant that cultures commonly value maleness and masculinity more highly than femaleness and femininity; but we also tend to evaluate men and women according to different criteria. An important basis for evaluating women in the United States, for example, is their physical attractiveness to men, and women often go to great lengths to force their bodies to conform to male values about how they should look. As Chernin (1981) describes in her powerful analysis of values about female slenderness, dieting and being thin are a national obsession among American women, all in the name of being attractive to men.

Slenderness is far from a natural or universal criterion for beauty in women. In Western Samoa most women gain weight with each pregnancy and are, by American standards, "fat" by the time they reach middle age. Rather than suffering shame, they are widely admired and are usually the ones who perform "humorous, almost lascivious" dances on public occasions (MacKenzie, 1980). In addition, the women portrayed in classic paintings by European artists such as Rubens and Renoir reflect standards of female beauty that are quite different from our own.

To make their legs appear attractive, many American women wear shoes whose high heels make it difficult to walk or run and cause back pain. In 1984, 95,000 women submitted themselves to surgery in order to increase the size of their breasts (American Society of Plastic and Reconstructive Surgeons, 1985). Between the ninth and eleventh centuries, the Chinese practiced footbinding, the gross distortion of women's feet that made it both painful and difficult—sometimes impossible—for them to walk (Dworkin, 1974; Levy, 1966). Tiny feet were culturally valued as delicate, beautiful, and feminine, and feet of normal size were considered ugly.

Footbinding was accomplished by bending all toes except the big one under a girl's foot and into the soles of her feet. A long cloth wrapped around the toes and the heel drew them as close together as possible. The result—in addition to excruciating pain, chronic bleeding, and infection—was a woman who could barely do more than shuffle. "Perfect 3-inch form and utter uselessness were the distinguishing marks of the aristocratic foot" (Dworkin, p. 106). Although footbinding is a far cry from chronic dieting and wearing high-heeled shoes, it is hard to escape the parallel, for in each case, women's bodies are subjected to distortion and pain in order to conform to cultural values.

The major criteria for evaluating men, however, are power, wealth, and prestige, not physical attractiveness. As the psychologist Theodor Reik wrote, "Women, in general, want to be loved for what they are, and men for what they accomplish. The first for their looks and charm, the latter for their actions" (in Morgan, 1970, p. 38). The values applied to women do not increase their power, except through relationships with men who find them attractive. Such power, however, is very insecure, for it depends on men's evaluations of women. Thus, the cultural values that apply to women encourage them to depend on men, and provide them with no independent basis of social power; values that apply to men have just the opposite effect.

## Attitudes

Several authors argue that beneath beliefs and values that define females as inferior are negative attitudes. Pornography usually portrays women as objects that exist to please men, and women are often the victims of verbal abuse and physical violence (Carter, 1978; Lederer, 1980).

Chernin's (1981) analysis of values about female beauty shows their relationship with negative attitudes toward females. American women, she observes, are often dissatisfied with their bodies and regard them as enemies that refuse to conform to cultural ideals of slenderness. The desire to live in a different body reflects

> a bitter contempt for the feminine nature of my own body. The sense of fullness and swelling, of curves and softness, the awareness of plentitude and abundance, which filled me with disgust and alarm, were actually the qualities of a woman's body. (p. 18)

The dislike that many American women feel for their bodies reflects negative cultural attitudes toward the natural physical characteristics of female bodies (Chernin, p. 22), just as the Chinese belief that normal female feet were crude and unattractive reflected attitudes of that culture.

Negative attitudes toward females are common throughout the histories of many societies. Ancient Greeks believed women were evil, and misogyny was a recurring theme in literature that portrayed women as the cause of all human problems (Pomeroy, 1975). The Greek philosopher and mathematician Pythagoras wrote, for example, "There is a good principle which created order, light, and man, and an evil principle which created chaos, darkness, and woman" (in Morgan, 1970, p. 34). In the 15 centuries after the death of Christ, women and sexuality were increasingly associated with evil in many cultures, and negative attitudes toward women peaked in Europe during the Middle Ages when hundreds of thousands are persecuted as witches (Ben-Yehuda, 1980; Dworkin, 1974).

Why have such attitudes been directed at females? Kipnis (1972) and colleagues (Kipnis et al., 1976) provide a partial answer: when people have power over others, they tend to see them as being

In classical mythology, Pandora was credited with opening a box that loosed on the world all the evils that trouble humanity, claiming men, as this etching shows, as the first victims.

of less value than themselves because they appear to be weak. As the value of women is decreased in the eyes of men, men's self-evaluations are inflated, and, ultimately, the result is contempt for "inferior" women.

## Norms

Laws have been used to limit the rights and power of females in many societies. Until quite recently, American women could not vote, own property, dispose of their earnings, or enter into contracts. A majority of states still do not include a husband's use of force to have sex with his wife in their legal definition of rape (an omission that clearly supports inequality of power within marriages). In 1982 the Equal Rights Amendment to the Constitution was defeated, and women do not yet enjoy equal standing and protection under the law. The debate over abortion still rages, and many women believe that without the right to choose abortion, they do not have complete control over their own bodies and, therefore, over their lives. This is particularly true of highly educated professional women, who have been at the forefront of the movement supporting abortion rights (Luker, 1984).

The effects of the folkways and mores on the everyday lives of men and women are no less important than the effect of law. Women are expected to marry and, once married, to have and raise children, leaving the job of breadwinning to men. In 1977, 65 percent of American adults agreed that, "It is much better for everyone involved if the man is the achiever outside the home and the woman takes care of home and family," and only 36 percent approved of married women working if their husbands could support them and job opportunities were limited (Davis, 1982). Even when women do work outside the home, they are expected to put family obligations before their jobs (Pleck, 1977).

In their interactions with men, women are expected to conceal their intelligence and physical strength. When a man is sexually aroused, many women feel an obligation to do something to satisfy his desire. Many men feel they should open doors for women, defend them if another man offends them, and pay the check when they go out with them.

On a superficial level, these parts of the folkways appear to be no more than harmless courtesies that make life more pleasant for everyone. On a deeper level, however, they reinforce the minority status of women: women are expected to pretend they are inferior even when they are not; to subjugate their own feelings to men's sexual desires; and to pretend that they are incapable of providing for, taking care of, and defending themselves in the adult world.

Because we use culture to make sense of the world, we are often unaware that it is a human creation until we look at cultures other than our own. In her classic study of New Guinea tribes, Margaret Mead (1935) found startling departures from Western ideas about gender. Among the Arapesh, both men and women conformed to our ideas about femininity: both took care of children, aggressive behavior was discouraged for both genders, and gentleness and warmth were highly valued.

Among Mundugamoors, however, the opposite prevailed: both men and women were aggressive and violent, and men and women attacked each other with equal ferocity. The third tribe—the Tchambuli—distinguished between men and women, but the behavior of women corresponded to our ideas of masculinity, whereas the men conformed to our ideas of femininity.

In a study of college students in various Western societies—Norway, Sweden, Denmark, Finland, and the United States—Block (1973) found that American men place more importance on "manliness" than do men from the other countries, and American women describe the ideal woman in more masculine terms than other women do. American students also place more importance on competitive achievement and less emphasis on the control of aggressive behavior in males.

Culture is a framework that we use to make sense of ourselves and others. Ideas that apply to males and females, however, go beyond the task of "making sense" of the world, for they also help justify and perpetuate social structures in which females are treated as a minority. Most cultures are **sexist** because they support prejudice against females; and because sexism is used to justify inequality, it is an *ideology*. The inequality supported by sexist ideology is found in social structures—the complex webs of social relationships through which we affect one another's lives. What do these structures look like, and how do they affect the lives of males and females?

## Gender and Social Structure

Although culture consists mostly of ideas, their influence can be seen in social structures. On the microlevel of everyday interactions, social structure refers to statuses we occupy and roles we play in relation to role partners. It is through such relationships that we affect other people and are affected by them. On the macrolevel, social structure refers to the distribution of individuals among social statuses—such as the relative numbers of women and men in different occupations—as well as distributions of wealth, income, power, and prestige.

The social structures of most of today's societies clearly place women in the position of a minority; but, as we saw earlier, gender-based inequality is by no means a universal characteristic of all known societies. In most hunter-gatherer and in some horticultural societies, women and men have shared equally in wealth, power, and prestige, in spite of their different positions in divisions of labor (Etienne and Leacock, 1980; Sanday, 1981).

### Gender Roles, Status Sets, and Social Identity

Male and female are ascribed statuses, and **gender roles** are cultural ideas that define expectations for males and females as they interact with other people. When we interact with people of different genders, we use beliefs to identify and describe them as male or female, values to determine their rank in relation to us, attitudes to direct positive and negative feelings and behavior toward them, and norms to form expectations of them and ourselves in relation to them.

Of course, we do not have to think, evaluate, feel, and behave according to gender roles, but we have strong reasons to do so. Roles have coercive power over us both because reward and punishment depend on our performance and because we use roles to orient ourselves to other people. In short, if we deviate from our gender role, we take risks: we may be punished or refused rewards, or, at the very least, we may lose our sense that we know who we are and who other people are in relation to us.

What do gender roles look like? In our culture, they correspond to definitions of masculinity and femininity (Chafetz, 1978). Thus, females who conform to their gender role define physical beauty as "slenderness"; value the ability to be attractive to and supportive of men more than they value independence; admire and look up to men; and behave in a variety of ways that perpetuate their subordinate position (letting men interrupt them, asking men to do things for them that they could easily do themselves, or allowing men to dominate them sexually).

Men who conform to their gender role believe they are more intelligent than women; value wealth, power, and prestige more than intimate relationships; feel hostility toward women (often expressed as humor); and behave in ways that reinforce their dominance (controlling conversations, "defending" women without asking them if they want to be defended, or being sexually aggressive regardless of women's feelings).

As important as gender roles are, however, they are only the "tip of the iceberg," because gender is a status that profoundly affects which other statuses are included in our status sets. Men dominate society not simply because they are masculine, but because they have greater access to powerful achieved statuses. They control legislatures, governments, courts, labor unions, corporations, religious organizations, schools, universities, and important professions such as law and medicine.

Women's inferior position thus rests on more than the demands of femininity, for women are confined to relatively powerless statuses. As wives or mothers, they have little power outside the home, and those who do not work for pay must depend on men for their security. Even within families, they enjoy few legal protections from abuse by their husbands. In the workplace, they are confined to the lowest-paying, least-powerful occupations.

Gender roles have an enormous impact on our status sets and, with them, on our identities. In our culture a successful woman is not simply femi-

nine: she is also a supportive wife and devoted mother who values her children's happiness and her husband's occupational success more than her own. She is content with poorly paid or part-time jobs. In the same way, a successful man is not simply masculine. He has a beautiful wife and bright children to whom he can point with pride, a highly paid, prestigious job, his own home, a new car, and other luxuries.

Thus, gender roles are not single, unified roles. There are several that make up much of men's and women's social identities (Janeway, 1971). Each of us is far more than female or male, but the sum total of who we are in the social world is vitally affected by our gender.

**Role and Status Conflict: Binds and Double-Binds** We occupy many different statuses, and each includes a role set—the roles we perform in relation to different role partners. Both the variety of statuses we occupy and the complexity of their role sets often produce conflicting expectations that cause status and role strain.

Working mothers, for example, experience status strain because men and other women expect them to both stay home to care for a sick child and go to work to keep their jobs and earn a living (see Barnett and Baruch, 1983). Added to this is the widespread belief that children's development suffers if women work (Davis, 1982)—a belief that consistently finds no support in scientific research (Hayes and Kamerman, 1983). Men experience role strain because other men (and many women) expect them to be strong and domineering, and yet many women expect them to behave with tenderness and treat them as equals.

Although both men and women experience conflict because of gender, a society that treats women as a minority generally produces more strain for them than for men. Unless women are wealthy enough to hire someone else to care for their children, for example, they have a difficult time combining marriage, motherhood, and full-time work. Men are in less of a bind, for our culture makes relatively few demands on husbands and fathers, and this enables men to both have families and commit themselves to demanding and rewarding careers. Men are thus able to separate their different roles from one another in time and space. One result of this is that early marriage dis-

*"Can I call you back? Jim and I are struggling with our roles."*

©Drawing by Koren; © 1983, The New Yorker Magazine, Inc.

rupts the educational progress of women but not that of men (Alexander and Reilly, 1981).

Women who marry and bear children, however, cannot separate family and nonfamily role obligations so easily (Janeway, 1971). The result is considerable strain for many women who want to work or who must work (either because their husbands cannot earn enough to support their families or because they are divorced and are the sole source of support for themselves and their children).

The conflicts and dilemmas that confront males and females in social relationships are most apparent in the interactions of everyday life.

**Patterns of Interaction** In interactions we use symbols—from words to facial expressions and the angle at which we hold our bodies—to make sense of ourselves and others, to know what people think and expect of us and how they feel about us. We are generally unconscious of how we use cultural meanings in daily interactions, just as we do not pause to think of the meaning of the word "rain" before or after we use it. Nonetheless, we rely on them to make our way through interactions with people of different genders.

We saw earlier that American men and women tend to use different vocabularies and speak with different tones of voice, and that such differences contribute to the often inferior social position of women. Observations of interactions between men and women reveal inequality of power in other ways as well, most notably in the control men tend to exercise over conversations with women (see Kollock, Blumstein, and Schwartz, 1985).

Women generally say less than men and more often abandon topics they introduce in favor of what men want to talk about (Fishman, 1975). In mixed-gender couples, men are usually the ones who interrupt; but, when men and women talk with people of their own gender, interruptions are more evenly distributed among the participants (Zimmerman and West, 1975). When women interact with men, they often appear to be "a class of speakers . . . whose rights to speak are casually infringed upon by males" (p. 117). As a female student wrote in her journal, "he assumes that *whatever* I'm doing is interruptible; that I will be ready to do what he wants to do when he wants to do it" (in Richardson, 1977, p. 29).

Women who want to both work and have a family inevitably face status strain that men for the most part are able to avoid.

Men and women differ not only in control over conversations, but in the content of what they say. It is generally true, for example, that people of higher status are not required to reveal as much of themselves as are people of lower status (Goffman, 1967), and this appears to be true for women and men. Masculine men are expected to hide emotion and weaknesses, while feminine women are expected to be open and vulnerable (Henley, 1973).

Language, of course, is only one of the tools we use in social interaction, and in many cases our bodies send nonverbal messages that are more important than what we say in words. Women, for example, tend to smile more frequently than men (often a sign of a desire to please, if not of submission), regardless of how they are feeling (Deaux, 1976). Females tend to remember people's faces more accurately than males, a difference that has been detected in children as young as 4 years old; females also are more willing to make eye contact with others and to hold it for longer durations (see Haviland and Malatesta, 1981). A substantial body of research shows that women are more sensitive than men to people's nonverbal expressions of how they are feeling (see Hall, 1978), and that women tend to be more emotionally expressive than men (see Friedman, Riggio, and Segall, 1980).

Men are more likely to touch women than to be touched by them (Henley, 1973, 1977; Mayo and Henley, 1981); and, as Goffman (1967) reminds us, if we are more powerful than others, we feel greater freedom to touch them when we want to (teachers touch students more than students touch teachers). In public we are more likely to see a man's arm around a woman's shoulders than the other way around, and even when holding hands, men tend to hold the back of their hand facing forward, as if leading a child.

Men and women also tend to touch in distinctly different ways. When a man "cuddles" a woman in his arms, for example, his physical position is a controlling one, for her arms are confined by his. Men, however, rarely allow themselves to be cuddled, especially in public, because this threatens to reduce them to a childlike status (Henley, 1973).

Women encounter a variety of difficulties in their interactions at work. Both men and women, for example, generally prefer to have male supervisors and resent women who are placed above them (Greene, 1976; Kanter, 1976). When competent women have jobs that match their abilities, male co-workers tend to dislike them and exclude them from informal activities such as meeting for lunch or coffee—all of which are important in being accepted as members of work groups (Hagen and Kahn, 1975).

Women may find their work abilities and performances devalued because of their gender. Nurses, for example, often find their notes on patients "not being read, or being read derisively" and their observations and suggestions regarding patients "ignored until either a male nurse or another doctor comes up with the same thing" (Gilbert, 1970, p. 70).

In large corporations, highly placed women are often the only women in their workplace. Such "tokens" are pressured to conform to stereotypes that have nothing to do with their jobs. Executive women may be expected to "mother" male executives—by preparing coffee or providing emotional support. They are often looked upon as sexual objects that men compete for, or as "office pets" who play the role of a "younger sister" who adds humor and does not threaten men (Kanter, 1977b). As one business woman described her experience,

> I was introduced to an audience of fellow consultants as "our cute, little bright girl consultant." When I said I was far from a little girl, being in my mid-forties, and that gender had nothing to do with this kind of work, I was labeled again, "difficult." (Willett, 1971, p. 520)

Among all the pressures and conflicting expectations American women face in their interactions with men, one of the most serious is sexual harassment—repeated and unwanted sexual comments, looks, propositions, and physical contact. Whether at work or on the street, women often experience a violation of their social boundaries:

> "Hey honey, where you going? Can I go too? Where's your bra, honey? Don't they get cold that way? I'll keep 'em warm. . . . What a nice piece. . . . You got real nice legs. . . . Got anything between 'em? What's the matter with you? You stuck up or something?" (in Medea and Thompson, 1974, p. 47)

Most women can tell stories of similar experiences, including "those mysterious hands that suddenly appear from under attaché cases, coats, or

Power inequality encourages men to assume they have the right to violate women's social boundaries; and this lies at the heart of sexual harassment, especially in the workplace, where power takes the form of authority.

**Voices: Sexual Harassment**

"I said no. I simply was not going out with him after work and, no, I simply was not going to have an affair with him, because I thought I could rely on my job skills. . . . I was fired with 25 minutes notice on a Friday." (From House of Representatives hearings on sexual harassment in the federal government)

"There are sexual feelings here, we can't totally dismiss that. But mostly it's a question of power. Either a man isn't powerful and uses harassment to make himself feel like he is, or he is in a powerful position and just expects that women are part of the benefits." (Peggy Crull, research director of the Working Women's Institute)

Source: *Christian Science Monitor,* February 9, 1984.

simply out of nowhere"—what Medea and Thompson call "little rapes." One study estimates that 75 percent of working women have experienced sexual harassment at work (Kolson, 1979). That men so often assume that women actually enjoy such experiences reflects a culturally supported lack of regard for women's right to choose the circumstances under which they will interact with other people.

Members of minorities are commonly the victims of such violations of social boundaries, and victimization often extends to physical violence. Using data from the National Victimization Studies, for example, Johnson (1980) estimates that as many as one-third of American females will experience an attempted or completed criminal sexual assault in their lifetime. Virtually all rape is committed by males against females and damages the victim's life in serious and often irreparable ways (Brownmiller, 1975; Holmstrom and Burgess, 1983; Medea and Thompson, 1974).

Gender roles affect interactions among women and among men, as well as between them. Except for handshaking and contact during sports, men rarely touch each other, for to do so may threaten the power of the man who is touched (Deaux,

1976). Women, on the other hand, have less power to lose through touching, and are considerably more likely than men to touch people of their own gender (Rands and Levinger, 1979). In one experiment, male and female experimenters stood very close to men and women on a street and found that men moved away from men but not from women. Women, on the other hand, were more tolerant of such "invasions" of space, regardless of the "invader's" gender (Dobbs, 1972).

Gender roles affect not only inequalities of power in social interactions, but also the kinds of relationships people are likely to have. Friendships among women tend to be more intense than among men (Rubin, 1973), tend to last longer (Wheeler and Nezlek, 1977), and involve more emotional support (Weiss and Lowenthal, 1975). The evidence suggests that men pay a price for their dominance—fewer enduring, self-revealing, personal ties that provide emotional support.

## Divisions of Labor: Ecology and Social Structure

Divisions of labor in all known societies use gender as a basis for sorting people into adult statuses (Nielson, 1978), but only a few statuses—mother and father, for example—are directly tied to sex as a biological characteristic. Historically, however, the statuses of mother and father have been of enormous importance in creating and perpetuating gender inequality in many societies (Huber, 1976).

In early societies that survived through hunting and gathering, the dependence of children on their mothers confined women to tasks that allowed them to remain in one place for long periods. Men were thus in the best position to be hunters, to leave their villages for many days at a time in search of wild game. Some anthropologists argue that hunting provided the most important source of food for these societies, and biological roles thus allowed men to monopolize the most culturally valued social roles (Friedl, 1975).

Harris (1977) argued that different reproductive roles also created gender inequality in early societies by allowing men to dominate warfare and weapons:

Warfare required the organization of communities around a resident core of fathers, brothers, and their sons. This led to the control over resources by paternal-fraternal interest groups and the exchange of sisters and daughters between such groups . . . to the allotment of women as a reward for male aggressiveness. . . . The assignment of drudge work to women and their ritual subordination and devaluation follows automatically from the need to reward males at the expense of females. (p. 86)

Thus, early ecological arrangements enabled men to monopolize the most important tasks and laid the groundwork for cultural values that rank males higher than females.

Others maintain that the gender division of labor did not result in inequality in hunter-gatherer societies or in most horticultural societies. In all societies, people are considered to be adults only if they perform socially productive labor (Huber and Spitze, 1983). In the earliest societies, all labor contributed to communities as a whole, and the family barely existed as a distinct social unit. The "domestic" work of women was no less socially productive than the hunting and warfare conducted by males, and although women were less powerful than men, they were treated as full adults.

Among the Hopi Indians, families are headed by women, not men; Hopi women do not depend on marriage for their security; and privilege based on gender does not exist. Although men are primarily responsible for hunting, herding, and farming, these tasks are not more highly valued than women's work—such as making pottery, baskets, and clothing. It is revealing to note that Hopi society differs sharply from our own in another crucial way: child care is the responsibility of the entire community, not of women alone (Leavitt, 1971).

Engels (1891), Sacks (1974), Goody (1976), and others argue that it was when agricultural technology enabled societies to produce surpluses that the position of women dropped dramatically. The ability to produce surpluses created two distinct types of production: production of goods that were consumed and of goods that were used for trade. It was here that the concept of "private property" emerged, and while men monopolized the production of surplus goods that were used for exchange, women were confined to producing goods for immediate consumption.

The distinction is crucial because surplus goods can be accumulated as wealth and used as a basis for exchange and social power. The family emerged as a social unit separate from the community as a whole; production was for the family, not the community; and because women's domestic work no longer contributed to the community, women lost adult standing and were viewed as little more than the wives and daughters of men (Etienne and Leacock, 1980).

As divisions of labor became more complex, gender distinctions went far beyond childbearing, child care, hunting, and warfare to include a wide range of occupations. In colonial America, families produced most of what they consumed, and although men and women usually did different things, women performed important productive roles—weaving cloth, making products such as soap and candles, and trading in the marketplace. Some women worked as blacksmiths, tailors, printers, and shopkeepers, and when husbands died, wives often assumed full control of family businesses (Baxandall et al., 1976; Demos, 1970).

In colonial times, family life and production of goods were usually carried on in the same place, but this ecological arrangement changed with the Industrial Revolution in the late eighteenth century (Cherlin, 1983; Tilly and Scott, 1978). Home and work became increasingly separate activities with the introduction of factories, and home became a "private sphere," separated and isolated from the "public sphere" of paid work. Thus, ecological changes made it increasingly difficult for women to both occupy the statuses of wife and mother and perform more highly valued and powerful roles outside the family. This, in turn, affected the division of labor within families.

**Divisions of Labor in Families** In most American families, husbands are considered to be the "heads" of their households and dominate decision making. However, women who work outside the home, and who have more education than their husbands, tend to have more power within their families than women who do not (Gillespie, 1971; Hood, 1983).

In American families, it is still the case that women do most of the housework (Miller and Garrison, 1982), and a recent study of high school seniors reveals little interest in changing this division of labor (Herzog, Bachman, and Johnston, 1983). In families with two working parents, husbands generally do only a small fraction of the domestic work their wives do, and most of their contribution consists of shopping or doing dishes (Huber and Spitze, 1983). Fathers, as a whole, spend an average of only 12 minutes a day alone with their children (Tavris and Wade, 1984), and this time is

## Voices: Fathers Have it Great

"The responsibility of feeding the babies and changing the diapers is mine and that's grossly unfair. Garry is a very involved father, but even with as much of a contribution as he makes, he is less likely to take responsibility for items like . . . When was the last time the diapers were changed? . . . or, Do they need lunch? (Fathers) get the rewards of being daddy and from time to time they change diapers and play with and get to know their children. They get a second income from the wife who is working so the family coffers are enriched. They don't feel the guilt and they are relieved of the stress of being the sole breadwinner in their family. They have it great."

Source: Newswoman Jane Pauley writing about her marriage to *Doonesbury* cartoonist Garry Trudeau. *Hartford Courant*, October 17, 1984.

more likely to be spent in play than in caretaking (Berk and Berk, 1979).

Women are not only expected to devote themselves to family life, but must live with a disturbing cultural contradiction: they are expected to value family roles more than any others, yet those roles are ranked relatively low by cultural values. We tend to value people who work more than we value those who do not, and family roles are not defined as "productive work." The U.S. Census Bureau does not include homemakers in the labor force, and if you ask a full-time homemaker, "Do you work?" she will most likely say, "No, I'm a housewife."

The relatively low value placed on family roles puts women in an insecure position in which they receive little outside support. Few businesses provide day-care facilities for employees; the demands of child care make it difficult for women to establish themselves in secure, well-paying jobs; and the status of "homemaker" has little financial security (it lasts only as long as the marriage remains intact).

The division of labor within families thus profoundly affects the position of women in society. The domestic responsibilities of women are not only the historical root of gender inequality, but a major aspect of social structure that continues to deny women equality.

**Gender and the "Public" World** Most women in all societies are part of the labor force. In 1982, 62 percent of single American women were in the labor force, as were 52 percent of married women, including 49 percent of those with preschool children and 63 percent of those with children of school age. Among divorced women, 75 percent were in the labor force, including 67 percent of those with young children and fully 84 percent of those with school-age children (U.S. Census Bureau, 1983c).

In general, women find themselves in jobs that involve taking care of the needs of others and working under the authority of men.

The persisting American ideal—"woman's place is in the home"—clearly does not describe our society and is, in fact, a curious idea, both in comparison with other societies and in the context of history. Yet, while most women work, they are still less likely than men to be in the labor force. In 1982, 77 percent of all males over the age of 15 were in the labor force, compared with 53 percent of all females over 15. Women are also more likely than men to work at part-time jobs: in 1982 only 5 percent of men over the age of 19 worked part-time, compared with 20 percent of women over 19 (U.S. Census Bureau, 1983c).

Even among those who work full-time, however, women find themselves in jobs at the lowest levels of wealth, power, and prestige (Rytina, 1981). There is also increasing evidence that when men and women perform different jobs that require comparable skills, the women are consistently paid less simply because the job is defined as a woman's job (Bureau of National Affairs, 1984; Treiman and Hartmann, 1981; Women's Research and Education Institute, 1984).

The contents of Table 13-1 are important enough to study carefully. Each column shows occupations according to how well women are represented in them, *relative to their representation in the entire labor force.* In 1980, for example, women made up 43 percent of the labor force. Thus, if women had an equal share of all jobs, they would comprise 43 percent of every occupation, but they make up only 4 percent of engineers, 26 percent of computer specialists, and 36 percent of accountants (top of first three columns). Whereas 47 percent of all librarians and personnel workers (top of last two columns) were women.

The table reveals three patterns that describe the position of women in the labor force. First, they are overrepresented in jobs that involve taking care of other people's needs (such as nurses, clerks, secretaries, elementary school teachers, and child-care workers), few of which include authority over other adults, and all of which carry low pay and prestige. Second, women are severely or substantially underrepresented in the best white-collar jobs (engineer, lawyer, physician) as well as blue-collar jobs that are highly skilled or represented by unions (such as plumbers and electricians, machinists, truck drivers, and police officers). In 1979 only 14 percent of employed women belonged to unions, compared with 28 percent of

**Table 13-1**

Representation of Women in Selected Occupations, United States, 1982

| UNDERREPRESENTED | | | OVERREPRESENTED | |
| --- | --- | --- | --- | --- |
| Severely[1] | Substantially[2] | Slightly[3] | Moderately[4] | Heavily[5] |
| Engineer | Computer Specialist | Accountant | Personnel Worker | Librarian |
| Dentist | Lawyer | Social Scientist | High School Teacher | Nurse |
| Senator or Representative | Judge | College Teacher | Vocational Counselor | Therapist |
| Carpenter | Scientist | Writer | Editor | Health Technician |
| Plumber | Chemist | Artist | Buyer | Social Worker |
| Electrician | Physician | Entertainer | Health Administrator | Elementary/Kindergarten Teacher |
| Firefighter | Pharmacist | Bank Officer | Building Manager | Bank Teller |
| Construction Worker | Science Technician | School Administrator | Real Estate Agent | Office Manager |
| Metalcraft Worker | Public Official | Restaurant Manager | Insurance Adjustor | Computer Operator |
| Machinist | Sales Manager | Typesetter | Assembly-Line Worker | Clerk |
| Auto Mechanic | Insurance Agent | Postal Clerk | Bus Driver | Cashier |
| Police Officer | Stockbroker | Cleaning Worker | Commercial Cook | Bookkeeper |
| Telephone Installer | Sales Representative | Baker | | Secretary |
| Heavy Equipment Operator | Mail Carrier | | | Telephone Operator |
| Meat Cutter and Butcher | Storekeeper | | | Clerk Supervisor |
| Mine Operative | Machine Operator | | | Stenographer |
| Welder | Farm Supervisor | | | Typist |
| Taxi and Truck Driver | Security Guard | | | Receptionist |
| | Salesworker (except clerks) | | | Textile Worker |
| | Blue-Collar Supervisor | | | Laundry Worker |
| | Religious Worker | | | Dressmaker |
| | Precision Machine Operator | | | Waiter |
| | Farmer or Farm Manager | | | Child-Care Worker |
| | | | | Household Servant |

Source: U.S. Census Bureau, 1983c.

[1] Equal to less than ¼ of women's share of the labor force.
[2] Equal to between ¼ and ¾ of women's share of the labor force.
[3] Equal to between ¾ and all of women's share of the labor force.
[4] Less than ⅓ more than women's share of the labor force.
[5] More than ⅓ more than women's share of the labor force.

working men (U.S. Census Bureau, 1983c). Third, in virtually all jobs in which women are heavily overrepresented, they are supervised by men.

Women not only occupy inferior positions *among* occupations, but within them as well (Brown, Moon, and Zoloth, 1980). In medicine, women are rarely surgeons or gynecologist/obstetricians (the highest-paid specialties) and are more likely than men to be psychiatrists or pediatricians, both of which are at the bottom of the medical hierarchy. In college and university faculties, women are far less likely than men to have tenure or full professorships, and women in the military rarely reach the rank of general. Among lawyers, women are more likely than men to work in government agencies, whereas men more often work in higher-paying private law firms (Epstein, 1983). Women who manage to make it into large private firms are overrepresented among associates but severely underrepresented among partners (Table 13-2). Over the course of their lives, women as a whole tend to be somewhat downwardly mobile, whereas men tend to move upward in the occupational hierarchy (Marini, 1980; Sewell et al., 1980). Spenner, Otto, and Call (1982) found that the greater opportunities for men mean that over the course of their working lives, the educational "payoff" in terms of occupation prestige, complexity, and skill is nearly three times as great for them as it is for women.

Divisions of labor that place women in inferior positions are found throughout the world. In socialist countries such as the Soviet Union and China, women are far less likely than men to occupy positions of high income, prestige, or power. The Chinese family, for example, is still heavily dominated by men (Johnson, 1983; Stacey, 1983); and although roughly three-quarters of all Soviet physicians are female, they have less prestige than American physicians, and earn only two-thirds the income of skilled Soviet workers (Lapidus, 1978).

## Wealth and Income

In 1976 men were twice as likely as women to be among America's top wealthholders under 50 years of age. Among older top wealthholders, women fared better, but this is largely because women outlive men and therefore outnumber them at the older ages (U.S. Census Bureau, 1983c).

**Table 13-2**

Representation of Women Lawyers among Associates and Partners in Selected Large U.S. Law Firms

| LAW FIRM (City) | PERCENTAGE OF ASSOCIATES WHO ARE WOMEN | PERCENTAGE OF PARTNERS WHO ARE WOMEN |
|---|---|---|
| Sidley & Austin (Chicago) | 31 | 6.2 |
| Shearman & Sterling (New York) | 34 | 1.7 |
| Morgan, Lewis, & Bockius (Philadelphia) | 28 | 1.4 |
| Gibson, Dunn, & Crutcher (Los Angeles) | 35 | 3.7 |
| Skadden, Arps, Slate, Meagher & Flom (New York) | 29 | 3.1 |
| Vinson & Elkins (Houston) | 28 | 3.4 |
| Jones, Day, Reavis, & Pogue (Cleveland) | 30 | 3.7 |
| Finley, Kumble, Wagner, Heine, Underberg, Manley & Casey (New York) | 22 | 2.4 |
| Squire, Sanders, & Dempsey (Cleveland) | 31 | 4.0 |
| Fulbright & Jaworski (Houston) | 26 | 2.0 |

Source: *National Law Review*, May 21, 1984.

Among full-time workers in 1981, women earned only 60¢ for every dollar earned by men; and families headed by unmarried women were more than twice as likely to live in poverty than were those headed by unmarried men (U.S. Cen-

**Figure 13-1**  Incomparable Pay Levels for Jobs Judged to Be of Comparable Worth

Below is a comparison of predominantly male and female occupations judged to be of comparable worth, based on a study of monthly salaries for Government jobs in designated locations.

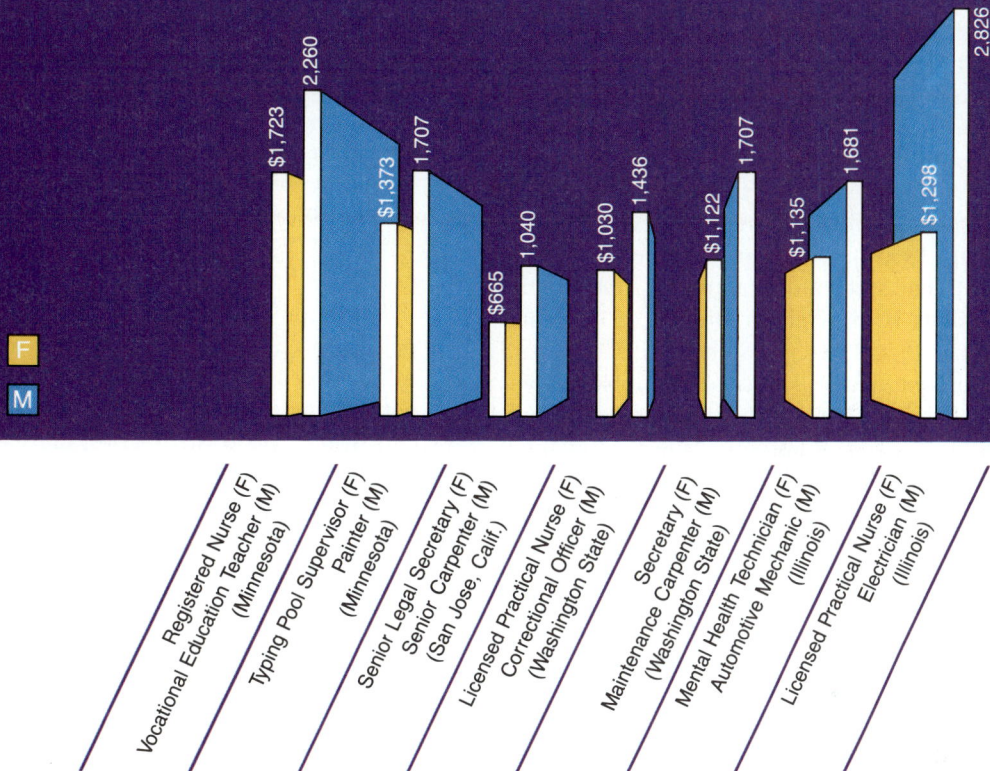

F
M

$1,723 — Registered Nurse (F) (Minnesota)
2,260 — Vocational Education Teacher (M) (Minnesota)
$1,373 — Typing Pool Supervisor (F) (Minnesota)
1,707 — Painter (M) (Minnesota)
$665 — Senior Legal Secretary (F) (San Jose, Calif.)
1,040 — Senior Carpenter (M) (San Jose, Calif.)
$1,030 — Licensed Practical Nurse (F) (Washington State)
1,436 — Correctional Officer (M) (Washington State)
$1,122 — Secretary (F) (Washington State)
1,707 — Maintenance Carpenter (M) (Washington State)
$1,135 — Mental Health Technician (F) (Illinois)
1,681 — Automotive Mechanic (M) (Illinois)
$1,298 — Licensed Practical Nurse (F) (Illinois)
2,826 — Electrician (M) (Illinois)

Sources: Council on the Economic Status of Women, State of Minnesota; Hay Associates; Norman D. Willis & Associates.

sus Bureau, 1983c; U.S. Department of Labor, 1981). As we saw in Chapter 2, women earn less than men in part because they are concentrated in relatively poorly paid jobs regardless of their educational qualifications, and even when they work at the same jobs or jobs requiring comparable skills, they tend to be paid less (Treiman and Hartmann, 1981).

Income inequality between men and women exists regardless of race, but it is more severe among whites than among nonwhites. This is largely because nonwhites are crowded into a narrow range of low incomes, and so the potential for large gender differences in income *among* nonwhites is relatively small. Black women, for example, constituted 55 percent of the black population

in 1980 and received 43 percent of all income received by blacks—three-quarters of what they would receive under conditions of equality *among* blacks. White women, on the other hand, made up 52 percent of the white population, and yet received only 30 percent of all income received by whites—just over half of what they would receive under conditions of equality.

*Power, Patriarchy, and Matriarchy*

Power is the ability to impose one's will on the behavior of others in spite of their resistance; and a **patriarchy** is a society in which power resides in the eldest male in a family, who passes it on through his eldest son. In a **matriarchy,** women are the formal and official heads of their families, but the actual power resides in their brothers, and children inherit through their maternal uncle. There are no matriarchies in the world today, and there is some debate over whether or not there has ever been a society in which women actually ruled (Bamberger, 1974).

In industrial countries, men control business and banking, government, religious organizations, the mass media (including most magazines written for women), schools and universities, legal and correctional systems, prestigious professions (such as law, medicine, and science), the military, and most of the nation's wealth (Epstein and Coser, 1981). In the early 1980s, for example, women held only 12 percent of all state and local public offices in the United States (U.S. Census Bureau, 1983c) and made up less than 2 percent of the U.S. Senate and only 5 percent of the House of Representatives (*Congressional Quarterly*, November 10, 1984).

Goldberg (1973), however, argued that women have great power, because their feminine qualities and child-rearing role make them "the directors of societies' emotional resources" (p. 140). That men control virtually every other aspect of social life, he argued, merely compensates them for their otherwise fragile place in the life of our species.

Most of women's power is over children, however (and most who have spent time raising children will agree that it is often difficult to tell just who is raising whom). Such power is both short-lived and ironic in its consequences: in patriarchies, women both prepare sons to dominate other women and raise daughters who are culturally defined as inferior to their brothers. Insofar as they raise their children to conform to cultural definitions of masculinity and femininity, they are, like the Chinese mothers who bound their daughters' feet, perpetuating a society in which females are treated as a minority (Rich, 1976).

Goldberg is correct, however, in asserting that women *do* have some power in relation to men; but as Hacker (1951), Janeway (1971), and others point out, it is the peculiar kind of power wielded by people who are dominated by others. Few would argue that small children are powerful in our society, and yet they often control their parents with astonishing effectiveness (by embarrassing their parents with tantrums in public, for example). Like children, women are often

stereotyped as "manipulative," *but their social status gives them few other sources of power.*

> As part of her traditional role, it is only in intimate situations that she can use power and feel its rewards. The more she is precluded from acting for herself in man's world and limited to managing emotions . . . the likelier it becomes that her need for autonomy, her search for identity . . . and the unused energies she possesses will come to expression in private because they can't be put to work in public. The negative role of bitches is almost built into a woman's role and it surfaces at the heart of the duality of marriage *if this is to be the only place where she has a chance to exercise power* [italics mine]. (Janeway, 1971, p. 205)

Women also derive power from their unique position as a minority, for while virtually all other minorities are segregated from those who dominate them, intimate relationships between men and women lie at the heart of the most universal of all social institutions, the family. Thus, although women are a minority, most women also live in relationships in which they depend on men and men depend on them.

Women, Virginia Woolf (1929) noted, serve as "looking-glasses possessing the magic and delicious power of reflecting the figure of man at twice its natural size" (p. 35). She then described how men depend on women to play this role in order for men to feel powerful:

> Without that power, the earth would still be swamp and jungle. The glories of all our wars would be unknown. . . . mirrors are essential to all violent and heroic action. That is why Napoleon and Mussolini both insist so emphatically upon the inferiority of women, *for if they were not inferior, they would cease to enlarge. That serves to explain the necessity that women so often are to men. And it serves to explain how restless they are under her criticism;* how impossible it is for her to say to them that this book is bad, this picture is feeble, or whatever it may be. . . . For if she begins to tell the truth, the figure in the looking-glass shrinks; his fitness for life is diminished. How is he to go on giving judgement, civilizing natives, making laws, writing books . . . unless he can see himself at breakfast and at dinner at least twice the size he really is? (italics mine) (pp. 35–36)

As Janeway (1971) put it, "Here is the paradox: women are weak because they can be strong only through giving. They are strong because what they give is needed" (p. 57). Such power, however, is fragile, for if one woman does not give a man what he wants, he can (and often does) seek out other women who will. Although women also have this option, their exclusion from public sources of power and income makes it more difficult for them to prosper on their own.

Social structures thus distribute power unequally between women and men in complex ways. Men dominate all existing societies, but unique relationships between men and women create interdependencies that provide women with sources of power unavailable to most other minorities.

## Prestige

In most societies, males generally have more prestige than women do, both because they are male and because the roles they perform are culturally valued more highly. When men conform to cultural expectations by committing themselves more heavily to work roles than to family roles, they increase their prestige. Women who fulfill cultural expectations by adopting feminine behavior, marrying, having children, devoting themselves to being wives and mothers, and working only at low-level jobs, however, automatically place themselves in low-prestige positions.

The generally low prestige of women is powerfully reflected in everyday experience. A woman's "no" is commonly interpreted by men as a "yes," thus depriving her of the right to be taken seriously. Women office workers are often treated as servants who are incapable of making independent decisions, who are expected to perform personal services such as picking up a male boss's laundry or selecting presents for his wife (Ann, 1970). Many domestic tasks that women are regularly expected to perform involve chores—such as washing floors, changing soiled diapers, and cleaning bathrooms—that, as occupations, rank at the bottom of the prestige scale (Oakley, 1974). Women's work, therefore, is work that men avoid because it detracts from their prestige (Polatnick, 1973).

The preceding sections have tried to give a detailed look at cultural ideas and social structures that perpetuate gender inequality. Male and female are far more than physical traits that we ac-

quire before birth—they are positions in social structures within which we conduct our lives in relation to other people. Just as we must learn to play the roles associated with statuses such as "teacher" or "lawyer," so, too, must we learn to play the gender roles of "male" and "female" as our culture defines them.

# Socialization: Learning to Be Male and Female

Sociology focuses on two types of socialization. Most learning centers on roles we are currently trying to play, as when children learn to play a game or adults learn to perform in a new job. Anticipatory socialization, however, involves preparation for roles we hope to perform when we are older. Gender roles involve both types of socialization, for as we learn to be feminine or masculine, we also prepare ourselves for adult statuses that are defined as appropriate for men and women. In the socialization process, we locate ourselves in relation to our families, and then in a continually widening scope of relations in the larger social world.

The beliefs, values, attitudes, and norms attached to gender are transmitted to new generations in many ways; but the most important agents of socialization are the family, schools, the media, and training for occupations.

## Gender Roles and the Family

Most studies show few gender differences in the behavior of infants, but many show that parents tend to treat infant girls and boys differently and to have different expectations of them. Parents generally give boys and girls different toys to play with, and they would tend to stop a wrestling match involving girls even though they would ignore the same kind of behavior between two boys. They also tend to give sons less help than they give to daughters. When parents are asked if they treat sons and daughters differently, however, they generally report no awareness of the differences observed by researchers (Fischer and Lazerson, 1984).

The expectations adults have of male and female children also tend to lead them to perceive the behavior of children differently. In one study, parents watched videotapes of infants at play, and

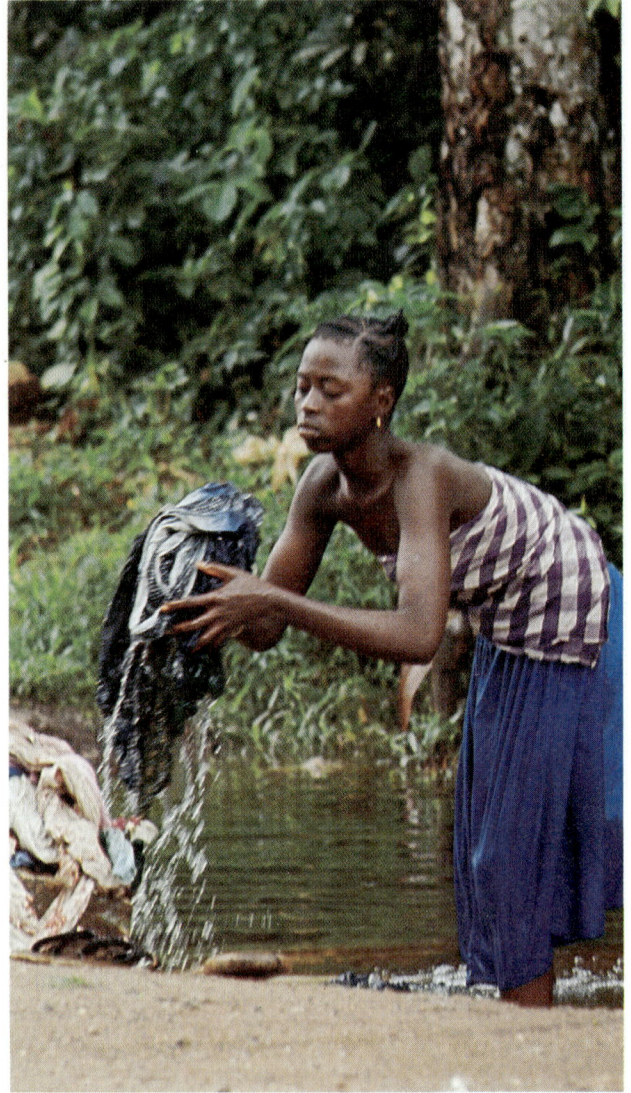

In almost all societies, it is women who tend to people's personal needs, including the washing of dirty laundry.

when they were told the infant was a boy, men tended to describe "his" behavior in terms of independence, aggressiveness, activity level, and alertness. When the infant was identified as a girl, on the other hand, men described "her" behavior in terms of passivity, delicacy, and dependency. Although women also made such distinctions, men paid more attention to gender-appropriate behavior than women did (Meyer and Sobieszek, 1972).

Both social learning and developmental theory have been proposed as explanations of gender-role socialization in childhood. Social learning theorists argue that children learn gender roles through a combination of conditioning—reward and punishment—and imitation of adults of their own gender. Most studies, however, show that conditioning and imitation explain only part of the socialization process. Both boys and girls, for example, imitate adults who display warmth, dominance, and power, regardless of the adult's gender (Bandura et al., 1963b); and most studies find no consistent evidence that young children imitate adults of one gender more than the other (Maccoby and Jacklin, 1974).

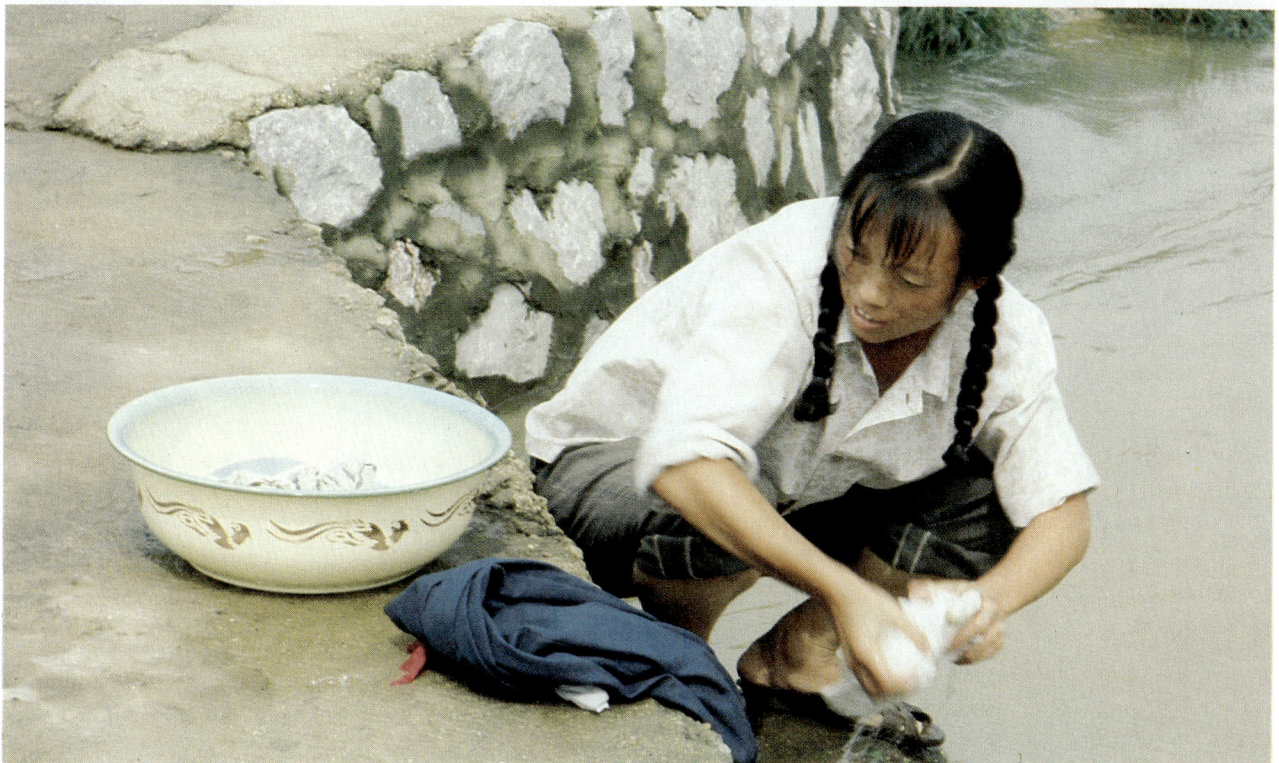

Developmental theorists focus on the way children think about gender. In the first stage of development, children discover that there are two sexes and learn to identify both themselves and others as male or female. At first they use physical characteristics such as hair length to distinguish males and females, but by age seven their idea of gender is more stable and they begin to identify which behaviors are appropriate for each. Most studies, however, reveal few gender differences in actual behavior among young children (Maccoby and Jacklin, 1974).

In the second stage, children develop a sense of value about their gender and begin to imitate people of their own gender as they strive for acceptance as males or females; and in the third stage, children develop deep emotional bonds with their same-sex parent, bonds that generally assure gender-role socialization.

Developmental theory is more comprehensive than social learning theory, but does not explain how children select behaviors from the many that are defined as appropriate for their gender. In ad-

dition, both perspectives ignore the fact that the particular set of abilities children develop depends in part on the activities they are encouraged or allowed to perform. In most families, for example, there is a tendency for sons and daughters to be assigned domestic tasks that conform to traditional views of gender roles—such as cooking and cleaning for girls and lawn mowing for boys (White and Brinkerhoff, 1981). Thus, relative lack of self-confidence among women reflects more than conformity to roles or imitation of models. It also rests on the fact that girls tend to be excluded from activities such as sports, through which children develop self-confidence.

Children observe more than masculine and feminine behavior in adults, for adults also offer them a preview of the statuses they can expect to occupy as adults. Most research on occupational mobility, for example, uses only the father's occupation to predict mobility among sons and daughters. More recent research, however, shows that whether or not a mother works, as well as the kind of job she holds, affects career plans and mobility

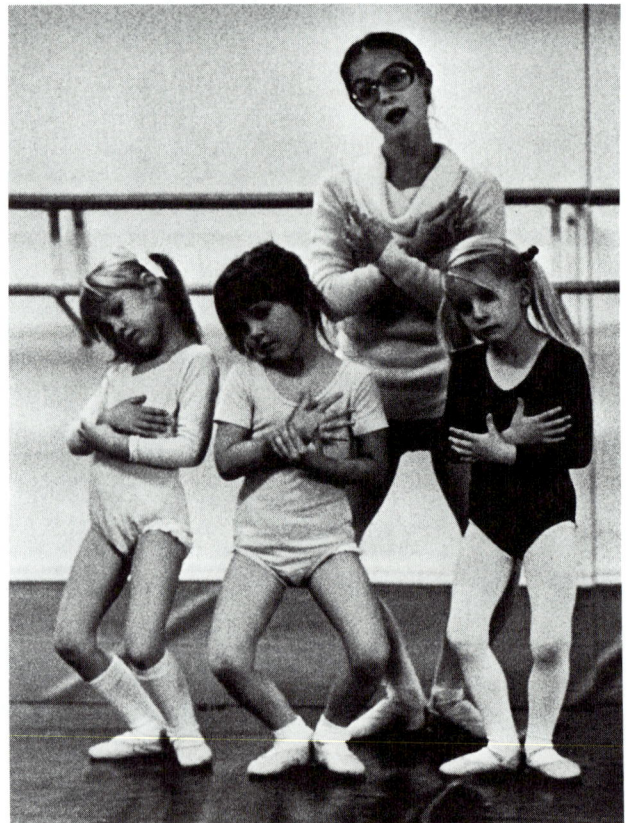

among both daughters and sons (Hoffman, 1977). Not only do working mothers provide role models of mothers who work outside the home, but fathers in such families often provide role models of men who both work outside the home and share domestic tasks as well.

## Schools and Gender Roles

Children begin school with a clear idea of their own gender, but know relatively little about adult gender roles. In schools, children learn about gender roles both from what they learn and the social structure of the school itself, which serves as a mirror of the adult world.

School textbooks, for example, reinforce gender roles. Most characters—whether they are human, animals, or fantasy—are male, as are almost all important people. Men are shown in a wider variety of jobs than women; in rare instances where working mothers are portrayed, they are in support roles as nurses, secretaries, and elementary school teachers. Girls are portrayed as passive—jumping rope and playing with dolls, or performing traditionally female chores such as cooking—while boys are portrayed as active—climbing mountains or saving girls who are in danger (St. Peter, 1979; Women on Words and Images, 1975a).

The social structure of schools also reinforces gender roles in a variety of ways. In elementary grades, when school work has little prestige in the outside world, most teachers are female. Their role is similar to a mother's, and much of the day is spent in play, nurturing, and discipline. Most principals, on the other hand, are male. In high school and college, work is more demanding and more prestigious, and most teachers are male. Thus, the structure of schools reinforces cultural expectations that women take care of others and men are authorities with serious roles in the world outside the home (Mickish, 1971).

There is some evidence that teachers treat girls and boys differently as early as nursery school. One study found that nursery school teachers gave twice as much instruction to boys as they gave to girls. Boys were given more attention on academic subjects and were encouraged to work independently. Girls were rewarded for showing dependency and staying close to their teachers; and teachers were more likely to intervene in a girl's work and complete it for her (Serbin and O'Leary, 1975).

In higher grades, girls are often discouraged from participating in serious athletic competition and advanced courses in mathematics and science, whereas boys are encouraged to study science and mathematics but are discouraged from developing their skills in less-marketable areas such as language, home economics, or literature (Schaffer, 1981). Thus, as children strive for stable identities as males or females, schools play an important role—by presenting cultural images of men and women, by mirroring adult gender roles, and by selectively encouraging boys and girls to engage in activities that develop different skills.

## Gender Roles and the Media

Television, radio, films, literature, and journalism provide us with streams of images in words, pictures, and sound. Such images do more than represent the world as it is; they also reflect beliefs, values, and attitudes about how the world ought to be. On television shows, for example, most leading characters are male (McArthur, 1982; Women on Words and Images, 1975b). In his analysis of the uses of gender in advertising, Goffman (1976) identified several ways in which men and women are presented that contribute to gender inequality (see also Courtney and Whipple, 1983, for a recent review of research findings). In most ads, clear patterns appear repeatedly:

1. Women are taller than men only when they are their social inferiors.

2. Women's hands are rarely portrayed as holding anything firmly—only touching it lightly.

3. Women never instruct men; even among children, the boy is the one who instructs the girl.

4. Men are rarely portrayed lying down; it is usually a woman or child who assumes this vulnerable pose.

5. The eyes of men focus only on important people; the eyes of women focus on men.

6. Women are often portrayed as "dreamlike" and physically close to a man, as if they did not need to be aware of their surroundings so long as there was a man present to look out for them.

7. Women are more likely than men to be shown in a state of shock or surprise.

Particularly in commercial advertising, images of women and men do more than sell products. As Gornick (1979) wrote, they also

> serve the social purpose of convincing us that this is how men and women are, or want to be, or should be, not only in relation to themselves, but in relation to each other. . . . That orientation accomplishes the task a society has of maintaining . . . order, an undisturbed on-goingness, *regardless of the actual experience of the participants* [italics mine]. (p. vii)

The media often appear to be an independent force in society, but it is important to remember that the images they present are designed to fit the expectations of their audience (when did you last

Most married women who survive to old age will experience widowhood at some time in their lives.

see an ad for laundry detergent in which a man was trying to remove a stubborn stain?). As such, the media often function as mirrors in which we look for familiar reflections, both of ourselves and the social world we live in.

## Gender and Adult Socialization

Learning to be male or female involves more than the prescriptions of masculinity and femininity, for the place of men and women in society depends on their entire status sets. For this reason, socialization extends throughout our lives as we learn to perform roles associated with adult statuses considered appropriate for our gender.

It is often not until after women marry that they learn how their new status limits their rights in relation to husbands, and for many women, childbearing confronts them with the fact that they no longer control their own bodies. As Rich (1976, p. 28) wrote, "The new life of my third child was a kind of turning point for me. I had learned that my body was not under my control; I had not intended to bear a third child."

At work, men learn that women are there to serve them, and that their success in the world is measured by the size of their paycheck and their ability to compete successfully with other men (Gould, 1973; Silverstein, 1972). Women learn that they are expected to occupy subordinate, inferior positions (Epstein, 1970). Even in the professions, they are excluded from informal social interactions through which vital professional knowledge is passed. They are less likely to be made assistants to those in powerful positions, and are thus more likely to find their upward mobility blocked (Speizer, 1981).

When their children reach adulthood, most mothers must adjust to the fact that their major activity in life is now a low-level job that offers few rewards (Moss, 1970). Although men escape this adjustment, they face their own crisis when retirement forces them to surrender their most important social status and live at a diminished standard of living (Bock, 1972). Among the elderly, women must learn to live as widows (Lopata, 1979): among people 65 years old and older who lived alone in 1982, for example, there were more than four times as many women as there were men (U.S. Census Bureau, 1983c). This is due in part to the fact that women generally live longer than men do (which may reflect a negative cost associated with conforming to the male gender role). It is also due, however, to the tendency of men to marry women who are younger than they. Thus, elderly women have relatively few potential husbands who are their age or older.

Socialization is a lifelong process through which we learn to participate in a society that treats men as a privileged class and women as a minority. All of this, however, begs the most important question of all: Why are women a minority in the first place?

## Explaining Inequality

Both the functional and conflict perspectives have been applied to stratification based on gender, and each contributes important pieces of the puzzle.

### The Functional View: Are Gender Roles Necessary?

The functional perspective focuses on the ways in which cultural ideas and social structures contribute to or interfere with the achievement of culturally defined goals in groups, communities, and societies. This point of view raises a basic question: For which goals are gender inequality and the division of labor between men and women functional, and for which are they dysfunctional?

Ecological conditions in early societies encouraged divisions of labor in which women took primary responsibility for child care and men monopolized hunting and warfare—tasks that required long periods away from home. In these societies, gender divisions of labor were clearly functional for the physical survival of populations; but even here, women were rarely treated as a minority.

Ecological conditions in modern countries, however, are a far cry from those of hunter-gatherer societies. Bottled formulas free women from having to remain close to children in order to breastfeed them when they are hungry; contraceptives allow women to limit childbearing to relatively small periods of their lives; women live much longer now and have many years to live after their children have grown; and people no longer range far from home for weeks at a time in search of food (Rossi, 1984). For what goals, then, are inequality and a gender division of labor functional in this kind of society?

Parsons and Bales (1953) argued that because people live and work in different places in the United States, the most efficient division of labor is one in which parents split employment and domestic tasks. If we accept the belief that all women are better suited for child care than all men are, then the gender division of labor is functional for the goals of caring for and socializing new human beings and making sure that economic, political, and other public roles are performed properly.

Americans certainly *believe* that "child care" and "mother" are two terms that mean the same thing. Most interpret the verb "to mother" as meaning "to care for," but attach an entirely different meaning to the verb "to father" (to impregnate a woman). Although the association between women and child care is strong in our culture, there is considerable evidence that it is based more in myth than in fact. As Albert (1971, p. 29) put it, "Having babies is one thing, raising them another."

In his famous experiments, Harlow (1958; see also Harlow and Harlow, 1969) raised monkeys with a variety of nonliving "mother substitutes" (such as wire cages shaped like adults) and found that providing food is not the most important part of "mothering"; rather, warmth, cuddling, and physical comfort make the most difference in the healthy development of infant monkeys. "The American male," he concluded, "is physically endowed with all the really essential equipment to compete with the American female on equal terms in . . . the rearing of infants" (Harlow, 1958, p. 685).

People, of course, are not monkeys, but Harlow's evidence challenges the notion that only women can give infants what they need. To this we must add the fact that some women dislike children and show little inclination to take care of them, and many men care for children very well. A recent experiment in Washington, DC (Herzig and Mali, 1980), found that ten-year-old boys welcomed the opportunity to take care of babies and eagerly learned how to take care of them (their first response on entering the nursery was characterized by the title of Herzig and Mali's book—*Oh, Boy! Babies!*). In their exhaustive review of the research literature, Maccoby and Jacklin (1974) concluded that whether or not people are "positively nurturant or indifferent" toward children "depends in large measure on how much contact they have with children and how much responsibility they have for child care" (p. 372).

Even if we believe that females are better suited than males for child care, a functional analysis shows that discrimination against women either is unrelated to the achievement of culturally valued goals or actually interferes with it. A large number of women, for example, never marry or have children. In 1981, of all adult American women over the age of 44 (that is, beyond childbearing age), almost 6 million—or 15 percent—had either never married or were childless (computed from U.S. Census Bureau, 1982); and an estimated 29 percent of white women born after 1950 may not have children (Bloom, 1982). Even those women who do marry and have children have, on the average, around two children, and children begin to spend their days in school by the age of six.

Davis and Moore (1945) argued that social inequality is functional for ensuring that the most qualified people perform the most important roles, but evidence strongly suggests that discrimination against women does not serve this end. As Table 13-3 shows, for example, women college graduates have lower average incomes than men who never finished high school, and women with graduate training have average incomes only $200 above those of men who never went beyond high school. Thus, discrimination against women in the United States appears to have little to do with ensuring that the most capable or highly trained people perform the most important roles (Treiman and Roos, 1983).

A functional analysis also leads us to identify the ways in which the exclusion of women from important nonfamily statuses is *dys*functional for important social goals, for it excludes more than half of our population from contributing their talents and abilities to important roles in business, government, education, and a host of other vital institutions. There is also evidence that gender roles are dysfunctional for women's mental health

**Table 13-3**

Median Income by Years of Education and Gender
for Year-Round, Full-Time Workers
(United States, 1982)

| YEARS OF SCHOOL COMPLETED | MEDIAN INCOME WOMEN | MEN | FOR EACH DOLLAR MEN EARN, WOMEN EARN: |
|---|---|---|---|
| **Elementary:** | | | |
| 0 to 7 Years | $ 8,400 | $12,400 | 68¢ |
| 8 Years | $10,100 | $16,400 | 62¢ |
| **High School:** | | | |
| 1 to 3 Years | $10,700 | $17,500 | 61¢ |
| 4 Years | $13,200 | $21,300 | 62¢ |
| **College:** | | | |
| 1 to 3 Years | $15,600 | $23,600 | 66¢ |
| 4 Years | $17,400 | $28,000 | 62¢ |
| 5 Years or More | $21,500 | $32,300 | 66¢ |

Source: U.S. Census Bureau, 1983b.

(see Franks and Rothblum, 1983). For every category of mental illness, married women have higher rates than single women, whereas married men have lower rates than single men (Gove and Tudor, 1973). Weiss (1981) found that female graduate students who were divorced or separated were more productive and self-confident than those who were married, but that the effect was in just the opposite direction among men.

Bernard (1972) argued that the role of "housewife" is so boring and frustrating, and brings so few social rewards or supports, that it contributes to disillusionment and depression among American women; and depression is the most prevalent mental illness among middle-aged American women (Bart, 1971). Kessler and McRae (1981), however, reported that in the last decade the great influx of women into the labor force has narrowed the gender difference in symptoms of psychological distress.

The pressures men experience appear to be dysfunctional for *their* health, as well. Their heavy investment in work makes them particularly prone to depression when they lose their jobs or retire (Schaffer, 1981), and weak family ties often leave them without emotional support during personal crises. The strains of male gender roles may be reflected in suicide rates, for men are almost three times more likely than women to kill themselves, and among older men—who face retirement and the end of their work lives—suicide rates are six times higher than for women of the same age (U.S. Census Bureau, 1983c). The masculine ideal of "toughness" may also be dysfunctional for men's health, for men are four times more likely than women to be murdered (U.S. Census Bureau, 1983c). Men are also more likely than women to be treated for psychotic disorders involving drug and alcohol abuse and violence toward others (Dohrenwend and Dohrenwend, 1976).

A functional analysis makes it clear that a division of labor based on the demands of child care, and the inequalities between men and women that result, are not necessary for achieving culturally valued goals. Many women never become wives or mothers, and those who do become mothers spend a small portion of their lives with small children; and men, with proper socialization, can perform most child-care tasks. The gender-based division of labor and its resulting inequalities also appear to

be dysfunctional for both society and the health of men and women. How, then, do we explain the persistent and pervasive position of women as a minority? One approach to this question is to rephrase it from a conflict perspective: Whose interests does gender inequality serve?

## The Conflict Perspective: Perpetuating Patriarchy

The conflict perspective focuses on the ways in which cultural ideas and social structures are functional for some groups or social categories in the struggle over the distribution of wealth, power, and prestige, and dysfunctional for others. From this perspective the gender division of labor benefits males at the expense of females. Child care is the key to women's inferior position in patriarchal societies: so long as women are held responsible for child rearing and men are not, women will be unable to securely establish themselves outside the family, and it is such work that primarily determines shares of wealth, power, and prestige. Why do women accept child-care responsibility and why do men avoid it?

Polatnick (1973) and others argue that women accept child-rearing responsibilities because existing societies are dominated by men and offer women few socially supported alternatives. Most men, on the other hand, avoid child-rearing responsibilities because cultural beliefs, values, attitudes, and norms do not require them to take care of children, and because taking care of children does nothing to improve or maintain their dominant position in society.

Although women have long been treated as a minority, Marxian analysis argues that industrialization—and capitalism in particular—sharply lowered the social standing of women. Engels (1891) argued that when the family became the "private sphere" in industrializing nations, women were denied full and equal participation in production, and their resulting dependency on men rendered them little more than domestic slaves.

Capitalists have been quick to exploit women, using them as cheap labor during periods of expansion and quickly dispensing with them when they are no longer needed (Smith, 1981). Women contribute domestic labor each year that, by market standards, amounts to billions of dollars; and yet, they do so in return for only a share of their husbands' earnings over which they have only partial control. Domestic labor, however, includes socializing future workers, and thus the domestic exploitation of women also serves the interests of capitalism (Sacks, 1974).

Gender statuses—like those of ethnicity and race—are also part of a larger system of classes that share unequally in the control over the means of production and the distribution of wealth, power, and prestige. Thus, the treatment of women as a minority does not result simply from a "war between men and women," but is also tied to larger structures that maintain general inequality as a characteristic of societies. It is here that the functional and conflict perspectives come together.

Unlike other minorities, the subordinate position of women results from more than their relationship to the means of production, for in a patriarchy, *that* relationship is directly tied to women's roles in reproduction and child care (Mitchell, 1966). Thus, *within* each social class, women have unequal standing, just as do the members of other minorities. From this perspective it is easier to understand why lower-class men are more likely to oppose equality for women, for gender divides the working class in the same way that race and ethnicity do. Working-class men are already at the bottom of the stratification system and are likely to experience women's equality as a threat to their already deprived conditions (explaining, in part, why some labor unions exclude women). Black women in particular find themselves doubly discriminated against because they occupy two minority statuses—black and female—that they are powerless to change.

Just as the most highly placed black is, in some ways, culturally defined as inferior to lower-class whites, so, too, is the most wealthy woman culturally defined as inferior in some ways to lower-class men. The parts of our language that degrade women, and the beliefs, values, and attitudes that describe masculinity and femininity, apply to males and females of all social classes.

Both the functional and conflict perspectives make it clear that gender inequality is deeply rooted in cultural, structural, and ecological characteristics of societies. How, then, do we move from a patriarchal society to one in which females and males have equal standing?

## Gender Roles and Social Change

To understand how gender roles and inequality might change, we need to appreciate how we got to where we are now, and this involves ecological, cultural, and structural aspects of social life.

Most families in frontier America lived in isolated farm communities. Families were large, and women were valued primarily as domestic laborers. Children were valued as economic assets, for the cost of raising them was relatively low and they began to share the load of farm work at an early age (Riley and Waring, 1976).

Urbanization and the Industrial Revolution caused major shifts in the social positions of men and women (Harris, 1979). Children became less valuable as producers—and, therefore, more costly to raise—and the only way that women could participate in paid labor was to limit childcare responsibilities by limiting their fertility. From 1800 on, the average number of children born by each woman in the United States and Europe steadily declined.

As nineteenth-century women became increasingly aware that wealth, power, and prestige were distributed according to social statuses outside the family, dissatisfaction over their confinement to family roles formed the basis for the early stages of the women's movement, which sought, among other goals, the right to vote, own property, and enter into contracts, as well as equal access to higher education and the professions. The first Equal Rights Amendment was proposed in the 1920s, but received little support.

Women made slow progress in education and employment until World War II created a massive demand for industrial workers. At the war's end, however, women workers were displaced by returning veterans, and as the postwar economy boomed, women retreated to traditional domestic labor in the newly emerging suburbs (J. Freeman, 1975), and the long downward trend in fertility reversed itself in the "Baby Boom" that followed.

After 1950 women's participation in the labor force increased dramatically, in part because as the American economy expanded, so, too, did the demand for low-level service workers such as secretaries, bookkeepers, and waitresses. In the 1960s the Baby Boom ended and the costs of raising children increased as more and more young people

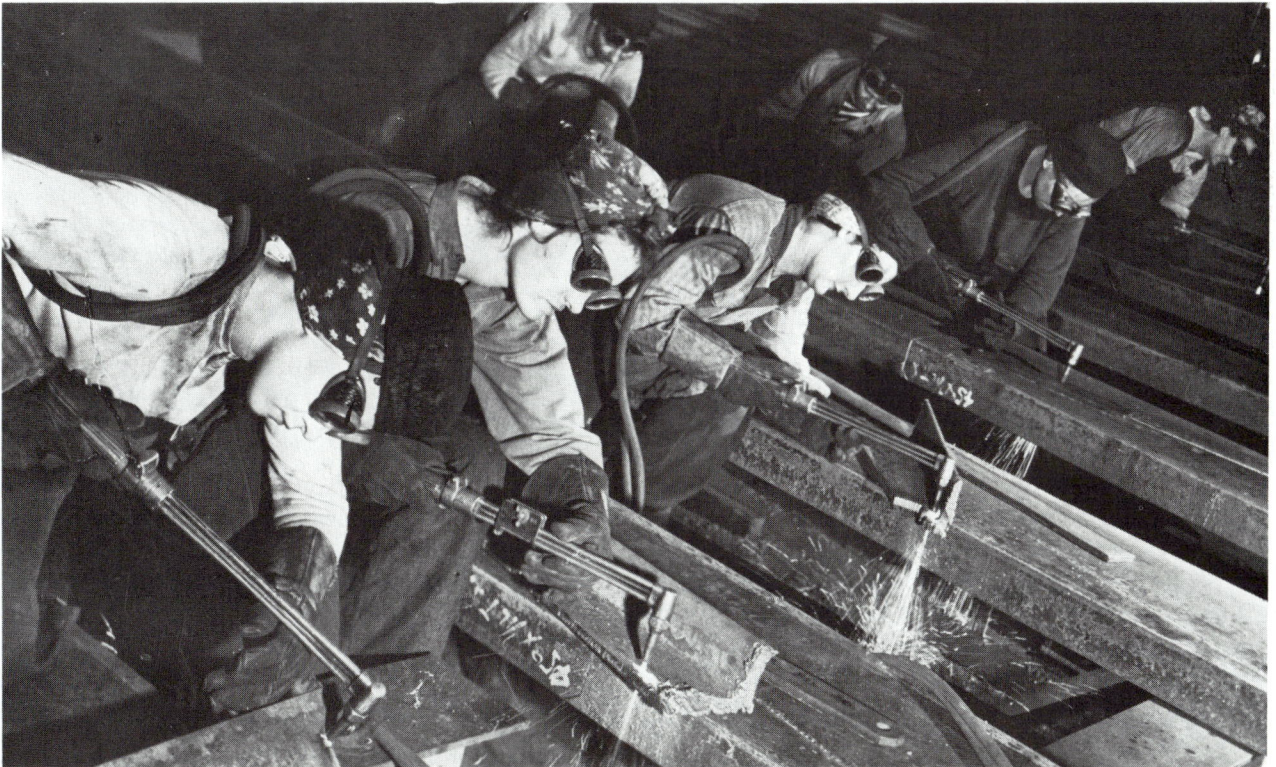

Women's labor has been exploited for well over a century in the United States, from providing cheap labor in nineteenth-century factories to performing vital industrial jobs during World War I and World War II, only to be replaced by returning veterans at war's end.

attended college. As women devoted less time to child care, they once again looked outside the family for roles that would both redefine their social identity and increase their share of wealth, power, and prestige. In 1963 Betty Friedan published *The Feminine Mystique* in which she urged women to reevaluate their traditional roles and demand the opportunity to fully develop their abilities; and in 1966 Friedan and others formed NOW—the National Organization for Women—and the politically organized women's movement was rejuvenated.

Pressures for social change, therefore, did not occur simply because people began to change their ideas about men and women. Rather, changes in economic production coupled with a decline in the birth rate provided new opportunities for women. As they took advantage of them by dramatically increasing their participation in the labor force, their social position as a minority became increasingly obvious as they were systematically excluded from all but the most low-level occupations.

Thus, changes in population and the economy created ideal social conditions for a new and pervasive "consciousness-raising" among American women, and many began a concentrated attack both on the inferiority of their social statuses *and* on the cultural ideas that underlie them.

### New Ideologies and Cultural Change

A major focus of the women's movement is sexism, particularly the beliefs, values, and attitudes associated with masculinity and femininity. Just as cultural ideas about gender have been used as an ideology supporting patriarchy, the women's movement is based on **feminism**—an ideology that directly opposes sexism by supporting gender equality and portraying women and men as equals (Firestone, 1970; Rossi, 1969).

The cultural ideas of masculinity and femininity often portray females as inferior and require men and women to limit their behavior to a narrow portion of their full potential. Thus, the women's movement focuses on masculinity and femininity by publicly challenging the definition of females as inferior people and by promoting **androgyny,** a concept that combines masculinity and femininity (de Beauvoir, 1952; Unger, 1979).

Androgynous people are neither masculine nor feminine. Rather, they choose their behaviors without regard to gender. Androgynous men would not avoid child care simply because they feared others might consider them "feminine" (although they might choose not to father children because of personal preferences). In the same way, androgynous women base their decisions about bearing and caring for children on their personal preferences, not to protect an image as "feminine" women.

Lott (1981) criticized the concept of androgyny on the grounds that it depends on and therefore supports the practice of thinking of people in terms of the masculine and feminine stereotypes. Masculinity and femininity, she argues, are artificial concepts that arbitrarily divide the wide range of human traits into two sets that are then associated with each gender. To talk of somehow combining these two sets of traits still treats them as if they are real.

> To label some behaviors as feminine and some as masculine, as androgyny researchers do, and then to put the two artificial pieces back together again to conform with the reality of human functioning and capability (and to suggest that the "whole" is preferable to the parts because it provides for greater flexibility and range) is to reinforce the verbal habits which undermine the possibility of degenderizing behavior. (Lott, 1981, p. 178)

A very different approach would be to end *all* references to gender when discussing behavior and personality, a position that argues against the use of androgyny as much as it does against the concepts of masculinity and femininity.

The women's movement also focuses on norms that perpetuate their oppression. Working primarily through legislatures and courts, women have struck down discriminatory laws (such as those excluding women from military service academies) and have lobbied successfully for new laws that equalize opportunity (such as those forbidding employers from discriminating against women in pay, hiring, firing, and promotion).

The more subtle norms found in the American folkways are also the target of the women's movement. Women's insistence that they pay their own bills on social occasions, that they be referred to as "Ms." rather than "Miss" or "Mrs.," that men stop rushing to open doors for them, that women be respected when they say "no" in sexual situations, or that they no longer be expected to clean up after men at home—all reflect a growing awareness that an end to patriarchy depends on more than what happens in courts, and legislatures, and in the boardrooms of large corporations. It also depends on what happens in the interactions of everyday life—on the street, in offices, college classrooms, and bedrooms.

We often feel surrounded by rapid social change, and there are many who believe that most aspects of sexism have been eliminated in our society. However, although awareness of sexism has certainly increased during the last two decades, there is little evidence that women have been accepted as equals. The Equal Rights Amendment was defeated in 1982; and clear majorities of Americans believe that children suffer when their mothers work, that things work better if women stay at home, and that a husband's career is more important than a wife's (Davis, 1982).

Perhaps most serious is the enduring appeal of the masculine ideal. As Roszak and Roszak (1969, p. viii) wrote, "the world belongs to what . . . masculinity has become"—we value rationality more highly than intuition, control of emotions more highly than their open and free expression, toughness more than vulnerability, the conquest of nature more than respect for it, independence more than dependence, being perceived as right more than admitting we are wrong. For many Americans, then, the liberation of women merely allows them to participate in a male-dominated society according to the values and attitudes embodied in the concept of masculinity. In this sense, the liberation of women implies the *negation* of women and the cultural ideas associated with them.

On a deeper level, some segments of the women's movement seek to change our culture from one based on masculinity to one based on the full range of human behaviors. This is a radical goal, for it would affect not only the relative standing of men and women, but our basic cultural assumptions about how people in general ought to think, feel, and behave.

## Voices:
## They Work Hard for Their Money

In arduous, low-status jobs like coal mining, a sense of honor develops "which says that they are special to be able to do this work. Lily-white office workers can't do it, women can't do it, nobody can do it but them because they're strong, they're tough, they're special. And then these women come, and lo and behold, they *can* do it. So the men have to admit that they're not so tough after all." (Jacqueline Boles, sociologist who has conducted surveys on sexual harassment)

(Voices of female coal miners):

"I'm in love with my job. To get me out of the mines, the 'godfather' would have to make me an offer I couldn't refuse."

"Every man has to prove himself, but it's different with a woman. A woman has to prove herself a lot more."

"Trying to get accepted by the guys is just as hard as the work. You feel like an alien, like something from outer space. The men look at you as if to say, 'What's she doing down here?' Some guys still don't think women belong here, that it's no place for a woman."

"It was tough at first. The jokes and the propositions were the hardest. And you had to work twice as hard to get half the credit. The men don't harass much anymore. It's gotten better. But I'm still proving myself. A coal mine isn't a place for a woman. But it's not a place for anybody—period."

Sources: *Christian Science Monitor*, February 9, 1984; *New York Times*, October 11, 1982.

## Social Change and Social Structure

A second major focus of the women's movement is on the confinement of women to social statuses that offer relatively low levels of wealth, power, and prestige. This includes access to higher education and occupations previously monopolized by men; but on a deeper level it extends to the family, for a division of labor that leaves child care to women lies at the heart of their minority status.

It is true that American women "have come a long way" since the earliest women's movement.

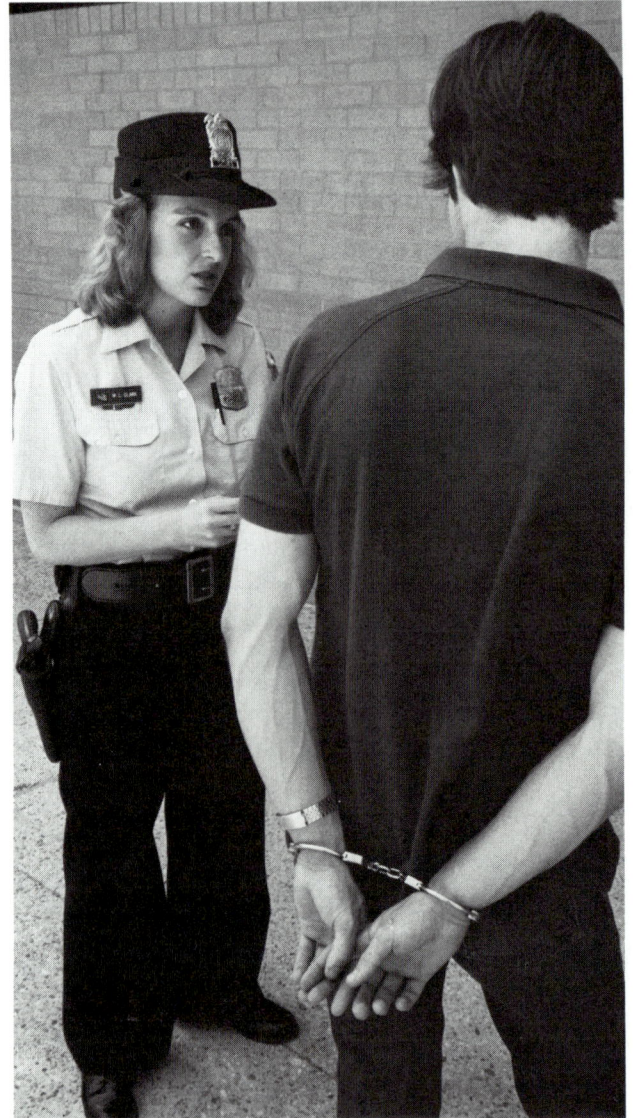

Women now perform many jobs once reserved exclusively for men, but their numbers are still relatively small. More important perhaps is the fact that the movement of men into female-dominated jobs—child care in particular—is even more rare.

They are more likely now to be in the labor force than at any time since the Industrial Revolution, and they occupy many positions previously reserved for men. They work in coal mines and in police and fire departments; they drive trucks, work on construction crews, manage businesses, and teach in universities. In art, music, and literature, there has been a virtual explosion in new works created by women. In 1981 the first woman was appointed to the Supreme Court, and women are found in increasing numbers among lawyers, judges, and physicians. In 1983 the first American woman astronaut was included in the crew of a space shuttle. In 1984 the top-ranked graduate of the United States Naval Academy was a woman, and Geraldine Ferraro became the first woman

nominated by a major political party as a candidate for vice-president of the United States.

Within families, there is evidence that some men are making greater commitments to child care, most notably in seeking custody of their children during divorce proceedings (Schaffer, 1981). During the last few years, there has been a dramatic increase in research examining the importance of fathers for child development (Cath, Gurwitt, and Ross, 1982) and the ways in which married couples can adjust to the demands of work and family. There is also evidence that wives who seek careers are increasingly likely to have the support of their husbands (Huber and Spitze, 1981; Wallston et al., 1978).

Although such gains sound impressive—especially when highly publicized—the vast majority of middle- and lower-class women are still heavily concentrated in low-level, poorly paid occupations. Relative to men, American working women were less well-off financially in 1981 than they were in 1950, in spite of the fact that women now outnumber men among college students (U.S. Census Bureau, 1983c). Men still rarely involve themselves in the care of infants (Entwistle and Doering, 1981; Lamb and Goldberg, 1982), and the high divorce rate means that the overall child-care burden still falls overwhelmingly on women (Rossi, 1984).

## Why Is Change So Difficult and Slow?

It will be difficult for women to free themselves of their minority standing because their position in the public world is strongly tied to their roles in the family; they are a minority in all classes, including within other minorities; and gender is one of the most important bases for the identities of both men and women.

**Social Structure**  Even if women were not discriminated against in the public world, so long as men avoid the responsibilities of child care they will have a distinct advantage in the marketplace. Coverman (1983), for example, found that among married, white, employed men and women, the more time people spend on domestic tasks, the lower their income tends to be, especially if they are working-class men or middle- to upper-class

women. It is for this reason that many feminists look upon the right to choose abortion as critical for women's liberation, for without that right they cannot control their commitment to child care (Luker, 1984). Even in socialist countries that proclaim equality for women as one of their major goals, gender equality does not include bringing large numbers of men into child care (Huber and Spitze, 1983).

Thus, industrial societies are structured in ways that make it convenient to hold women responsible for child care—"If women are allowed to have careers, who will take care of children?" It is vital to remember, however, that such a question is relevant only in societies that isolate the family from other social institutions by separating production from reproduction; and if the family is isolated, women are isolated with it (Sacks, 1974).

Most societies are controlled by men, and it serves men's interests if society is structured so that it is difficult for women to gain equal standing. It is true that the liberation of American women would destabilize society to some degree, requiring massive change in social institutions such as the family, government, and the economy. The other side of this, however, is that in order to perpetuate

## PUZZLES:

### WHY ARE THE HUSBANDS OF SOME WORKING WIVES SO TROUBLED?

White husbands whose wives work often report more symptoms of psychological distress (such as difficulty sleeping and nervousness) than those whose wives do not work. Why?

If your answer is that husbands whose wives work have harder lives because they have to do more housework, you are wrong. As this chapter explains, working wives still do most of the housework and husbands tend to feel threatened by a wife's earning power.

patriarchy, domestic labor must continue to be defined as nonwork; and, therefore, females must continue to be a treated as a minority.

Faced with the choice between child care and careers, American women are increasingly choosing to remain single, at least during their twenties. Between 1970 and 1981 the number of unmarried couples in the United States tripled, and the number of young adults living alone more than doubled. Between 1960 and 1982 the percentage of women who had never married rose from 28 to 53 percent among women from 20 to 24 years old, and from 10 to 23 percent among women from 25 to 29 years old (U.S. Census Bureau, 1983c).

Changing the division of labor within families may be the last and most difficult goal of the women's movement, for as long as wealth, power, and prestige are distributed according to performance in the public world rather than in the family, and as long as child care is a poorly rewarded occupation, most men will resist substantial commitments to domestic labor (Coverman, 1983; Polatnick, 1973).

There is also recent evidence that married men have a difficult time coping with their wives' full-time employment. In a national study of white married couples, Kessler and McRae (1982) found that although employment lowered the incidence of depression, poor self-esteem, and psychological distress symptoms (such as insomnia and trembling hands) among wives, it increased such problems among their husbands. Nothing in the data indicated that the increased problems of married men resulted from demands such as a greater contribution to domestic work. The problem, concluded the authors, seemed to be largely a matter of men having a difficult time accepting new definitions of the roles of husbands and wives.

**Women as a Unique Minority** The fact that the formation of families requires women to join with members of the social category that dominates them means that they are at the bottom of whatever other minority they belong to. This means that men will dominate social movements that promote an end to inequality based on social class, race, and ethnicity. Historically, women have made enormous contributions to movements for

social justice (including the movement to abolish slavery in the early nineteenth century and the labor union movement in the late nineteenth and early twentieth centuries); but their own cause has been, for the most part, ignored (Kessler-Harris, 1982; Stimpson, 1971).

This is due, in part, to the fact that women's liberation threatens the social standing of all men regardless of their minority status. During the 1960s the United States experienced violent social movements protesting injustice against blacks and the poor; and yet women were often treated as a minority *within* these movements. In extreme cases, some leaders looked upon women as no more than envelope stuffers, bed partners, and domestic workers (Morgan, 1970).

**Identity and the Power of Social Mythology** Janeway (1971) observed that many cultural ideas about men and women are myths—beliefs that are rooted more in emotion than in factual evidence. Such mythology is "illogical—or, at least, pre-logical" and rarely describes real men or women accurately; but *this has nothing to do with their importance to us*, for "from this very fact, it gains a certain strength: logic may disprove it, but it will not kill it" (p. 27).

Myths are important because regardless of their accuracy, they are beliefs that give us a feeling that the world makes sense and will always make sense. We also value them because as social beings, we locate ourselves within them and depend on them for a stable sense of who we are. From this point of view, it is easier to understand why many women resist their own liberation, for they can free themselves only by shattering myths that define important parts of their social identities. It is often easier to hang on to social arrangements that are familiar and yet oppressive than it is to give them up in favor of new ones that are both alien and only potentially better.

As Langer (1962, p. 147) wrote, "We live in a web of ideas, a fabric of our own making." However necessary it may be to tear the web that holds us tightly in a world of meaning and social relationships, once we do, we experience the chaos of not knowing who we are, until we create a new social environment in which to live.

## Summary

1. Women are a minority in most societies in spite of the fact that they are a numerical majority. Sex refers to the physical characteristics that distinguish males and females; gender refers to social distinctions between them.

2. There is little scientific evidence that biological factors cause more than a very few gender differences in behavior or ability.

3. As part of culture, language reinforces gender inequality by always connecting the status of women with men, by associating male and female pronouns with social statuses, by portraying men and women in different terms, and by degrading the words used to describe women.

4. Masculinity and femininity are sets of beliefs about men and women and comprise most of gender.

5. Cultural values both rank maleness above femaleness and evaluate men and women according to different criteria.

6. Historically, cultural attitudes have long reflected hostility toward females.

7. Both laws and folkways are used to reinforce the subordinate position of females.

8. Gender roles define expectations for people according to sex. Gender roles cause considerable status and role strain for both men and women and result in many different patterns of interaction that reflect the subordinate status of females.

9. In most societies, adult standing depends on contributions to productive labor, and as production has become increasingly separated from the home, the standing of women has steadily declined.

10. In families, women still perform the majority of domestic work. Outside the home, women are concentrated in the poorest-paying, least-prestigious jobs with the lowest chance of advancement.

11. The concept of patriarchy refers to dominance by men, and the concept of matriarchy refers to formal dominance by women. There is some debate over whether there has ever been a matriarchal society.

12. Gender role socialization takes place primarily through the family, schools, and the media. It depends both on portrayals of what males and females are supposed to be like and on the different ways we are treated depending on our gender. Socialization continues throughout adulthood as we occupy marital, parental, and occupational statuses.

13. Functional analysis shows that gender inequality is not functional for important goals in an industrial society and that it is dysfunctional for many goals, such as the health of men and women.

14. Conflict analysis shows that women are a minority in all social classes and that the gender division of labor serves the interests of men as a group and rests primarily on the ability of men to avoid domestic work.

15. Pressures for change have grown in recent decades as women have entered the labor force in greater numbers and birth rates have declined.

16. The passage of the Equal Rights Amendment and the elimination of sexism are major cultural goals of the women's movement. Major structural goals include access to better occupational statuses and a fuller sharing of domestic responsibilities with men.

17. Change in gender inequality is slow because women are a unique minority, because many ideas about gender are deeply rooted in cultural mythology, and because gender inequality is rooted in the structure of important institutions such as the family and the economy.

## Key Terms

androgyny   422
femininity   396
feminism   422
gender   391
gender role   399
masculinity   396
matriarchy   409
misanthropy   394
misogyny   394
patriarchy   409
sexism   399

# Recommended Readings

BERK, S. F. (1985). *The gender factory: The apportionment of work in American households*. New York: Plenum. A recent study of the gender division of labor in families and the ways in which this affects both family life and gender stratification.

COOK, A. G., LORWIN, V. R., and DANIELS, A. K. (1984). *Women and trade unions in eleven industrial countries*. Philadelphia: Temple University Press. A collection of articles that compare the status of women in unions and segmented labor markets in Denmark, West Germany, Finland, France, Great Britain, Ireland, Italy, Japan, Norway, the United States, and Sweden.

EPSTEIN, C. F. (1983). *Women in law*. New York: Anchor Press/Doubleday. An insightful study of what women encounter as they try to enter, survive, and succeed in the male-dominated legal profession.

ETIENNE, M., and LEACOCK, E. (Eds.). (1980). *Women and colonization: Anthropological perspectives*. New York: Praeger. A collection of articles on non-Western societies that focus on the sources of gender inequality.

HAYES, C. D., and KAMERMAN, S. B. (1983). *Children of working parents: Experiences and outcomes*. Washington, DC: National Academy Press. A thorough examination of the ways in which the participation of both parents in the labor force affects the education and everyday experience of children. A major finding is the absence of any direct negative effect of mothers' working on child development.

PETRAS, J. W. (1975). *Sex:Male/Gender:Masculine*. Port Washington, NY: Alfred. A stimulating collection of articles about men.

*SIGNS: Journal of Women in Culture and Society*. Chicago: University of Chicago Press. Probably the most important scholarly journal devoted to the study of women and gender roles.

TAVRIS, C., and WADE, C. (1984). *The longest war* (2nd ed.). San Diego: Harcourt Brace Jovanovich. A well-written, comprehensive text on gender and society.

# Age Stratification

How old are you? Are you a child, adolescent, adult, middle-aged, or old? If your answer is, "adult," how would you feel if people thought of you as an adolescent or a child? Or, if your answer is "adolescent," how would you feel if people thought of you as an "adult?"

As your feelings about these questions probably tell you, the importance of age goes far beyond the number of years that have passed since birth. Biologically, age is simply a matter of time, and aging is a physical process through which people develop from infants to adults and gradually deteriorate as they move toward the inevitability of death.

Age and aging are sociologically important because all cultures divide the human life span into **age groups** and apply different beliefs, values, attitudes, and norms to each. Age is a social status that affects your relationships with people who are younger, older, or your own age; and aging is a social process of transition from one status to another.

We begin by comparing biological and sociological approaches to age and aging; then we see how age inequality is reflected in cultural ideas, social structures, and ecological arrangements. We then draw upon the functional, conflict, and ecological perspectives to help explain the existence of age stratification; and we close by showing how cultural ideas, social structures, population dynamics, and ecological arrangements both promote and interfere with the achievement of equality among people of different ages.

## Some Different Views of Age and Aging

As a status, age is unique in three ways. First, age is always a temporary, transitional status. While we may spend our lives as females or our adulthood as lawyers, we continually move from one age status toward another. Second, unlike other statuses (except, perhaps, for gender), age provides a cultural "map" of our entire lives. All cultures include ideas that describe the **life course**—the "normal" set of passages from one age to another (Eisenstadt, 1956; Hogan, 1980; Sheehy, 1974). Our "map" tells us where we are expected to be and what we are expected to be doing: in school as children, at work in our early twenties, married and raising families by our thirties, and at our peak

Drawing by Chas. Addams; © 1983, The New Yorker Magazine, Inc.

of wealth, prestige, and power by our fifties. When we are defined as elderly, we are expected to stop working, lose interest in sex, and become less active, less intelligent, and more rigid and conservative in our beliefs, values, and attitudes.

As individuals, of course, we can deviate from cultural expectations tied to stages in the life course; but like all deviants, we then risk being treated as outsiders and losing our sense of who and where we are in cultural frameworks that we use to make sense of ourselves and the social world. Thus, age is more than a set of statuses whose roles influence our thoughts, feelings, and behavior in a given time and place, for it also defines our futures. It describes where we are going as much as where we are and where we have been.

Third, more than any other social characteristic, age affects which statuses we achieve. It determines when we go to school, how we are treated when we break the law, and when we can get a driver's license, free ourselves from parental authority, vote, sign an apartment lease, be drafted into the military, marry and have children, work, or run for public office. Not only does age profoundly affect which statuses we may occupy, but it is often viewed by others as a *master status*—one that is treated as more important than any other status we occupy.

Of all the social statuses that affect our lives, few are as obvious as age. "Everyone knows," for example, the differences between children, adults, and the elderly; but as we will see, age affects our lives in many different ways of which we are often unaware. We will also see that what people take to be "obvious" facts about age and aging in one culture are quite different in others, have changed considerably over the last several centuries, and often have little to do with the biology of aging.

## Age Stratification and Minorities

The structure of every known society includes age stratification in which some age groups are more wealthy, powerful, and privileged than others. The unique aspects of age as a status, however, make age minorities equally unique, for people of different ages do not stand apart from the rest of society in the same way that other minorities do.

Blacks do not spend part of their lives as whites and men do not spend part of their lives as women, and no one can control the aging process; this means that *we all belong to subordinate and dominant age groups at one time or another in our lives*. The most powerful American adult was once a powerless child and has the potential to one day be defined as "old" and suffer a loss of prestige, power, and wealth. Thus, subordinate age groups are only "quasi-minorities" (Birren, 1968), for while we cannot change such statuses as race, gender, and ethnicity, age is unique because we cannot *stop* it from changing so long as we live.

The uniqueness of age as a status also produces ironic twists and turns in social relationships as each generation moves through the life course.

Age is always a temporary, transitional status placing all of us, at one time or another, in both dominant and subordinate age groups.

Middle-aged adults who treat the elderly as a minority perpetuate inequalities that will eventually work against their own interests. Similarly, the children we raise will someday be middle-aged adults whose position allows them to treat *us* as a minority.

How do sociologists describe and explain the part that age plays in social life and its importance in social stratification systems? The answer should, by now, be a familiar one: the social position of different age groups depends on cultural ideas about age and aging, on social structures that define role relationships and distribute wealth, power, and prestige, and on ecological conditions under which populations grow and people use the physical environment to produce goods.

## Culture, Age, Aging, and Ageism

All cultures abound with ideas that distinguish one age group from another, and these profoundly affect our experience and behavior in socially structured relationships. In addition, cultural ideas about age often take the form of **ageism**—prejudice based on age—and ageism, in turn, is related to unequal distributions of wealth, power, and prestige.

### Beliefs: "Funny, You Don't Look Old"

The most basic cultural beliefs about age define it as a social status, not just a numerical label. In some African societies, for example, individuals do not know their exact age, for the number of years they have lived is not a culturally significant fact (United Nations, 1956). In China, the age of infants who have lived for 1.5 years is "two"—which means they are in their second year of life. In the United States, however, age is defined as the number of years we have *already* lived, and those same infants are only one year old.

Cultures also differ in the number of age groups that define social positions in the life course. The Nupe of Nigeria have 3—children, young people, and the old—while the Nandi of Kenya have 28 (Eisenstadt, 1956). American cul-ture recognizes 6 age groups as distinct social statuses: infancy, childhood, adolescence, young adulthood, middle age, and old age.

Cultural beliefs not only define age groups, but also describe people who belong to them. Many Americans, for example, think of elderly people as asexual, and this often causes younger people to ignore gender distinctions among them, in spite of the fact that gender is one of the most important parts of our social identities. As Burnside (1975) wrote:

> I once asked a class to draw two pictures, one of an old man and one of an old woman. One student said, "What's the difference?" (p. 31)

Cultural beliefs also portray the elderly as mentally and physically slow, inactive, and unproductive. A majority of adults under the age of 65 believe that those over 65 spend most of their time staring out windows or watching television; but most people over the age of 65 disagree (National Council on Aging, 1975). Television frequently portrays the elderly as "doddering old fools who cause problems for their relatives or as wise old ancients who are always ready with a pithy saying or a piece of warm gingerbread" (Jones, 1977, pp. 89–93).

Most of these beliefs, however, are stereotypes that do not accurately describe the majority of elderly people. Sexuality is an important part of people's lives well into old age (Pfeiffer et al., 1972). Many artists and scholars are most productive after the age of 50; workers' accuracy, steadiness, and reliability decline only slightly with age (Riley and Foner, 1968; Riley et al., 1970); and with moderately good health, "individuals can expect high levels of mental competence beyond the age of 80" (Birren, 1968, p. 19).

None of this means that biological age does not affect abilities (Kart and Manard, 1976). Infants are far less capable physically and mentally than older children and adults. Among the elderly, aging has many negative effects: slower physical reactions, poorer hearing and eyesight, and less physical strength and agility. In 1980, 39 percent of people 65 and older had chronic medical conditions that limited major activities, compared with only 19 percent of those 45 to 64 years old and 4 percent of those under 45 (U.S. Census Bureau, 1982).

Cultural beliefs about the incompetence of the elderly are based more on stereotypes than on reality.

Like most cultural stereotypes, beliefs about age often have some basis in fact; but they are often exaggerated, and even when they accurately describe differences between age groups, they oversimplify and distort reality by ignoring substantial variation within them. For example, people over 65 years old are *generally* weaker physically than those under 65, but there are many elderly people who are considerably stronger than many who are much younger than they.

It is also important to remember that, as with all stereotypes, the facts that seem to confirm beliefs about age often derive from the stereotypes themselves. In other words, stereotypes about age promote self-fulfilling prophecies. Elderly people, for example, may suppress and deny sexual needs and desires because they share the cultural belief that they do not even *have* them. The negative effects of self-fulfilling prophecies can extend to virtually all the roles we perform:

> For all age strata, barriers in the social structure can destroy the motivation to perform in accustomed roles. And once motivation is lost, a vicious circle sets in: Skills and capacities deteriorate through disuse, and the disuse fosters actual physical and mental incompetence. As incompetence becomes apparent, social stereotyping . . . follows, and this stereotyping in turn further undermines motivation to perform. (Riley and Waring, 1976, p. 373)

Thus, cultural beliefs about age often have little to do with biologically determined differences, and this fact is clearest when we look at different cultures, as well as historical change within cultures. Beliefs about children, for example, have changed dramatically over the last several hundred years. Most Americans think of children as distinct kinds of people: innocent, helpless, and unable to participate in adult activities. Ariès' (1962) careful study of diaries, clothes, tapestries, and paintings from the last 10 centuries, however, reveals that until the twelfth century, children were portrayed as no more than short adults. In one miniature painting, for example,

> the subject is the scene in the Gospels in which Jesus asks that little children be allowed to come to Him. . . . Yet the miniaturist has grouped around Jesus what are obviously eight men, without any of the characteristics of childhood; they have simply been depicted on a smaller scale. (p. 33)

As recently as the eighteenth century, children and adults wore identical clothes and children were often treated like "small adults." It was not until the Industrial Revolution that cultural beliefs began to describe childhood as a special and unique stage in the life course (see also Pollock, 1984).

Like all cultural ideas, beliefs about age and aging are important ingredients in our construction of reality and cannot help but affect our perceptions of other people and ourselves.

## Values:
## "Why Jack Benny Died So Young"

One of the longest-standing jokes in show business was the late Jack Benny's insistence that he was only 39 years old, even though he was well into his seventies when he died. The joke became funnier the older he got, but beneath its humor lay an unpleasant reality: to be defined as old in American culture is something most of us want to avoid, because it diminishes our value in other people's eyes.

Children and adolescents understandably want others to perceive them as older than their years, and they often overstate their ages, especially when they approach ages that substantially increase their legal rights (16 and 21). Middle-aged people, on the other hand, often *under*state their ages in an effort to put off the inevitable cultural devaluation that comes with retirement and the status, "old." Elderly people often protect themselves from cultural devaluation by believing that they are not really old (Riley et al., 1970): those over 65 years old, for example, tend to believe that

"old age" starts at an older age than younger people do (Riley and Foner, 1968).

Age understatement is common among women, perhaps because age devalues them more than it does men. American adults are 1.5 times more likely to attach the label "old" to a woman under the age of 60 than to a man (Riley and Foner, 1968). This may reflect the fact that men and women are evaluated according to different cultural values—women according to their physical attractiveness to men and men according to wealth, power, and prestige (Chernin, 1981). As a consequence, men in their fifties are generally at their peak of wealth and power, while women are losing the ability to conform to cultural definitions of feminine beauty that influence how other people evaluate them.

In the United States, the cultural value of individuals usually increases as they move from childhood, through adolescence, into adulthood, but then declines in old age. In many other societies, however—such as among the Andaman Islanders, the Soviet Georgians, and the Chinese—the values attached to age groups are highest among the elderly (Davis-Friedmann, 1983; Radcliffe-Brown, 1948; Weg, 1975).

## Attitudes: "Never Trust Anyone over 30"

American culture abounds with positive and negative attitudes toward age groups. Insults such as "old bag," "old biddy," and "old as the hills" reflect negative attitudes toward the elderly, just as com-

In many cultures—especially those in less-industrialized societies such as China—the elderly are venerated rather than pushed aside by institutions such as forced retirement.

pliments such as "venerable," "dignified," "stately," "statesmanlike," and "wise old woman" and "wise old man" reflect positive ones.

Negative attitudes toward the elderly are particularly important because, although each of us can grow beyond the devalued statuses of child and adolescent, death is our only escape from old age. Not only is old age devalued in our culture, it also signals the approaching end of our lives, and beneath the contempt often expressed toward the elderly is a cultural attitude of genuine fear. As Mary Gordon (1978) wrote in her novel, *Final Payments*,

> "The old are the invisible minority," she said. "They have no power; they're worse than blacks or women."
>
> "But they do have the power to menace us with our own inevitable futures. White people aren't afraid of becoming black or men of becoming women. Many people act as they do to old people because they're afraid of being like them." (p. 137)

One rare example of negative attitudes toward middle-aged Americans appeared in the 1960s with the phrase, "Never trust anyone over 30"; but this hostile attitude was limited to a subculture of young people who were actively involved in social movements such as the anti-Vietnam War and civil rights movements. Ironically—and inevitably—the leaders of those movements are now over 30 years old and certainly do not define themselves as untrustworthy.

This illustrates one of the unique aspects of age as a social status. Young radicals can afford to rebel against adult society, because, as members of an excluded age minority, they have relatively little to lose. As they approach middle age, however, opportunities for wealth, power, and prestige increase and the price of expressing contempt toward adult society rises with each passing year.

## Norms: Acting Your Age

All societies use norms to assign rights and responsibilities to people in different age groups. In the United States, laws distinguish between children and adults and adults and the elderly. Laws confine children to schools and generally exclude them from most jobs until they are 16 years old. They control the age at which young people can drive cars, leave home, sign leases and other contracts, join the military, and marry. The law sometimes allows adults to have elderly parents declared legally incompetent, deprived of control over their money and assets, and committed to institutions against their will. In employment, by forcing them to retire by a given age—now around 65 to 70—norms deprive older workers of control over their work lives and ability to earn a living.

Although many laws enhance the power of middle-aged adults at the expense of children and the elderly, some help protect those groups from exploitation and abuse. Parents can lose custody of their children if they abuse or neglect them. Children and elderly people who commit crimes are not treated as harshly as young and middle-aged adults; boys under the age of 18 are protected from the military draft; and the Age Discrimination Act of 1967 prohibits employers from discriminating against employees 45 to 64 years old on the basis of their age.

The American folkways that regulate everyday interactions also distinguish between age groups in ways that reinforce differences in power. Children are expected to respect their elders and to "be seen and not heard." Adults may call children by their first names, but children generally use more formal titles such as "Mr." and "Mrs." when they speak to adults. Elderly people are not supposed to show interest in sex ("You dirty old man!") or interfere in the lives of their adult children.

Thus, cultures include formal and informal norms that define appropriate behavior for people in each stage of the life course. "Act your age," applies to everyone—from children to the most elderly person—and reflects the importance of norms in relationships both between and within age groups. In a stratified society, such relationships are also important because they result in socially structured inequality among age groups.

## Age, Social Structure, and Inequality

As we have seen, on the microlevel of role relationships, social structure refers to the statuses we occupy, the roles we perform, and the resulting patterns of interaction among role partners. On the macrolevel, social structure refers to the distribution of people among social statuses—such as the relative numbers of children, middle-aged adults, and elderly people who are full-time workers. It also describes the distribution of wealth, power, and prestige among status occupants.

At both levels of social structure, few statuses are as important as age, and because of this, the ability to clearly define membership in age groups is particularly important.

### Rites of Passage and Age Group Boundaries

Like all statuses, age groups have boundaries that determine who occupies each age status, and the most important characteristic of such boundaries is their clarity. I once asked some first-year college students, for example, if they considered themselves to be adults or adolescents, and the most surprising result was that many of them were unsure. What does this tell us about our society and why is it important?

Many societies practice **rites of passage**—rituals that mark the transition from one social status to another—that allow members to know their exact social standing in terms of age (Van Gennep, 1909). In such cultures, members of different age groups have clearly prescribed rights and obligations and often dress in distinctive ways. Among the Masai of Africa, "learning warriors" help protect the community, carry messages, repair fences, and water the stock. They may not marry or eat meat in public, and wear clothes and hair styles that clearly identify their age group (Gulliver, 1968).

By comparison, rites of passage between age groups in the United States are rare and provide few clear guidelines that unambiguously distinguish one age group from another. Adolescence, for example, generally begins at puberty; but, when does it end? How many of us can identify the day on which we become adults? What events unambiguously tell us when a girl becomes a woman, a boy becomes a man, or a middle-aged adult becomes old? Americans do not agree, for example, on the age that defines "elderly": 38 percent of adults under the age of 45 define men 50 to 59 as "old," but another 30 percent do not consider men to be old until they reach age 70 (Riley and Foner, 1968).

This lack of clarity about age groups has a number of consequences, the most important of which is the awkwardness and anxiety that afflict individuals who find themselves in the "gray area" between one age group and another. Adolescents are given few clear signs by adult society that they have passed into adulthood (except, perhaps, for the ceremony of "bar mitzvah" for Jewish boys) and yet "man," "woman," and "adult" are enormously important statuses. Nor are there cultural ceremonies that mark the entry of people into old age and give broad recognition and support for a major change of status. As Pauline Bart (1970) wrote of aging women, "There is no Bar Mitzvah for menopause."

The absence of rites of passage raises a number of questions that are worth thinking about. For example, is there a connection between the lack of clarity about manhood and the fact that older adolescence is the most violent and aggressive period

Rites of passage that clearly mark the vital transition from childhood to adulthood are far more common in preindustrial societies than in industrial societies such as the United States.

in the lives of American males? Does this reflect the continuing effort of young males to prove their manhood in the absence of clear rites of passage? Do high rates of sexual behavior and pregnancy among adolescent girls reflect a desire to be regarded and treated as adults, even though such behavior violates cultural norms? Is the "identity crisis" that seems to be so common among American adolescents an inevitable consequence of age, or is it caused by cultural ambiguity about the passage from adolescence to adulthood?

Margaret Mead's (1928/1953) study of life in Samoa during the 1930s suggests that the answer to these questions is "yes." Samoan adolescents, she observed, were fully integrated into adult life: they participated in production, observed sexual behavior among adults, and freely experimented

with sexuality. They were not confined to a vaguely defined gray area between childhood and adulthood, and they exhibited little of the awkwardness and anxiety so commonly associated with American adolescents.

By telling us who we are in relation to other people, social identities are like anchors that hold us firmly in our social environment. We may know how many years we have lived, but it is our social age that really matters. The clarity of the boundaries that distinguish one age group from another is thus enormously important, for without it we may find ourselves feeling lost, as if we do not know where we are in social space. This, in turn, makes it difficult for us to clearly define social situations, including our expectations of ourselves and other people.

> ## Voices: Age and Social Identity
>
> The first week I began working as a rabbi, someone called the temple to say that his mother had died. I went to see the man, who didn't know I had never conducted a funeral. I was twenty-seven years old. He opened the door and I said, "Hi. I'm your new rabbi." His response was, "You're too young. My mother was ninety-five. You are much too young." And, of course, he was right.
>
> —Rabbi Douglas E. Krantz
>
> Source: Quoted in Secunda, *By Youth Possessed*, 1984.

Drawing by Richter; © 1985, The New Yorker Magazine, Inc.

## Age, Role Sets, and Social Interaction

Like all social statuses, age affects our choice of role partners—whom we are most likely to interact with; and the role sets attached to age affect our perceptions, evaluations, feelings, and expectations of ourselves and our role partners. This, in turn, produces patterns of interaction that vary according to the ages of those involved.

**Cohorts, Peer Groups, and Subcultures** One of the most important concepts in the sociological study of age is the **cohort,** which is defined as an aggregate of people who experience the same events during the same time interval (Ryder, 1965). Strictly speaking, a birth cohort is an aggregate of people born in the same year, but sociologists often use a wider range of time—usually 5 years—to define birth cohorts. Thus, we could define those born between 1930 and 1935 and those born between 1960 and 1965 as two different birth cohorts.

The birth cohort is an important concept because it defines peer groups on the basis of age and because it draws our attention to the fact that different groups of people experience the stages of the life course during different historical periods. Each cohort, for example, tends to identify with its own unique history. Members of my cohort became adults during the turbulent 1960s, and many of us identify with the trauma of Vietnam, the civil rights movement, and the protest music created by people such as Bob Dylan. In similar ways, today's

elderly are drawn together by the shared previous experience of the Great Depression and World War II, as well as by current anxieties over the financial insecurity of old age in America.

Such shared experiences tend to create subcultures that isolate cohorts from each other; but many aspects of social environments—such as primary family ties—encourage interaction among members of different cohorts. Almost 75 percent of Americans over age 65 have living children, for example, and 25 percent live with them. The percentage of adults who think it is a good idea for elderly parents to live with their children increased from 31 percent in 1973 to 50 percent in 1984; and those who thought it was a bad idea dropped from 58 percent to 36 (Davis, 1984).

Parents and adult children interact quite frequently in the United States. In 1983, 30 percent of adults with living parents reported spending social evenings with them at least once a week, and 45 percent did so at least several times a month (Davis, 1983). In addition, most people—regardless of age—say they *prefer* to spend their time with people of different ages rather than with peers (National Council on Aging, 1975).

It seems our society both encourages and discourages interaction between age groups. On the one hand, we benefit by interacting with people who are younger and older than we are, for it gives us a continuing sense of where we are in the life course by reminding us of where we have been and where we are going. On the other hand, the unique experience of each cohort as it moves along the life course encourages its members to limit themselves to their peers, and the more isolated people are from other age groups, the less aware they are of the effects of ageism, age discrimination, and age inequality on their interactions with other people.

**Age and Patterns of Interaction** Like every status, each age group has a role set. Young adults orient themselves to different sets of expectations when they interact with children, adolescents, peers, middle-aged adults, and the elderly. We readily call a boy by his first name, but would probably wait for permission to call a 70-year-old woman by hers.

In all societies, role sets change as people move from one age group to another. In the United States, children have few responsibilities or rights in role relationships, and their roles consist more of what they should *not* do than what they should do: do not work, do not be sexual, do not talk back, do not run your own life. They are surrounded by an adult world whose statuses are forbidden to them, and aside from attending school and doing what they are told, they live with relatively few important expectations from their society.

Rights and responsibilities change and increase in adolescence and adulthood, especially in relation to people in younger age groups. As adolescents, for example, we feel obliged to help a lost child or an ailing elderly person in ways that rarely occurred to us as children. The older we become, the more responsible we tend to feel for other people and the groups, organizations, and communities we belong to.

In the United States, however, old age reverses the upward trend of rights and responsibilities. The social position of the elderly reverts in many ways to the position of children, which consists more of what they should not do than what they should: do not work, do not show a lot of interest in sex, do not "get in the way," and "take it easy."

Like members of other minorities, both children and the elderly are often treated by young and middle-aged adults as if they were socially invisible, and this both reflects and perpetuates their subordinate position in society. Adults, for example, frequently discuss children's problems with other adults even when the children are present and often refer to them in the third person, as if they were not there. The elderly also find themselves treated in this way, often because younger people assume they are senile and either unable to hear what is said or to understand what they hear.

There is a deeper reason for treating the elderly as if they were invisible, however. Especially in industrial societies, the death of young people is a rare event, so most of our awareness of death is associated with the elderly, who remind us that death is inevitable. In the United States, for example, people over the age of 85 constitute only 1 percent of the population but account for 17 percent of all deaths each year (Brody, 1983).

> Although the old have always died, the dying have not always been old. It is only in very recent decades that death has become primarily the province of the elderly, rather than an event scattered erratically across the life span. . . . Because of the close association between old age and death in modern industrial societies, the individual and social issues relating to death are in many ways individual and social issues of aging. . . . One of the significant reasons that the old are avoided and isolated is their proximity to death. (Kalish, 1976, p. 494)

The fear of death profoundly affects interactions with the elderly when they are identified as terminally ill. Dying is a social event as well as a biological one, and it involves relationships among people who occupy different statuses and perform different roles (Kalish, 1981; Sudnow, 1967).

Most elderly people die in hospitals or nursing homes, and they are often treated in ways that protect other people's feelings more than their own. Terminally ill patients are often treated as though they were already dead: autopsies are arranged, relatives are asked to approve donation of vital organs after death, and patients may find themselves isolated and shut away in back hallways.

Doctors and nurses as well as family members may pretend that terminally ill patients are not dying (Benoliel, 1973; Glaser, 1966), and they may justify this as a way to avoid upsetting the patient. A number of studies show, however, that most patients would rather know the truth (Glaser and Strauss, 1965). How, then, do we explain such deliberate deception?

One answer is that people deceive dying patients in order to control the definition of the situation, which, in turn, determines the roles they must play. By lying about patients' true conditions, doctors, nurses, and family members promote a definition of the situation that prevents dying patients from expressing the grief, rage, and need for emotional support that often accompany awareness of impending death (Kübler-Ross, 1969, 1975).

Such pretenses enable people to avoid performing painful roles. Doctors and nurses can avoid the frustration of being unable to keep an elderly person alive, and family members can postpone their grief and avoid feelings of helplessness and rage. While this protects the feelings of doctors, nurses, and family members, however, it denies dying patients both the emotional support of other people and the opportunity to prepare themselves emotionally for death.

Concern for the needs of dying patients has recently prompted the development of alternative social institutions for them. Unlike most hospitals and nursing homes, a **hospice** is designed specifically for the terminally ill; it supports patterns of interaction that differ sharply from those found in most hospitals and nursing homes. Hospices are designed to be as homelike as possible and allow frequent contact between patients and other people. Awareness of death is openly shared, and this calls upon family, friends, and health professionals to perform roles in which they confront their own feelings and support patients during their final transition to death (Munley, 1983).

This example illustrates an important dilemma in social interactions involving dying patients. The hospice movement is based on the value judgment that it is preferable for dying patients to be fully aware of what is happening to them. The deliberate avoidance of such awareness, on the other hand, is based on the judgment that awareness of dying unnecessarily adds fear and anxiety to what is already probably the most difficult experience in the life course. It is a difficult value judgment to make, for those who make it are not themselves approaching death and yet have a great deal of power and responsibility to define the social situations in which people die.

Apparently the American medical profession has moved rapidly toward greater openness with dying patients during the last two decades. A 1961 study of physicians found that only 10 percent favored telling terminal cancer patients the truth about their conditions; but a similar study in 1979 found that the percentage who favored candor with terminal patients had risen to 90 percent (reported in John Riley, 1983).

## Status Sets and Divisions of Labor

All societies use age as a basis for assigning roles, and the resulting divisions of labor profoundly affect the distribution of wealth, power, and prestige among different age groups. Work and family roles, for example, depend strongly on cultural ideas about age—both in terms of when we are eligible to start performing them and when we are expected to stop (Neugarten et al., 1965).

Throughout history, age stratification has resulted from two factors: the confinement of children and the elderly to low-level occupations and, most recently, the exclusion of children and the elderly from productive work itself. Prior to the nineteenth century, production centered on the family, and children were trained for work from an early age. Children were a source of cheap labor in agrarian societies, and by the time they reached adolescence they were full-grown workers (Ariès, 1962; Coulton, 1926).

The Industrial Revolution separated production from the family, and during the eighteenth and nineteenth centuries lower-class children as young as 4 or 5 often worked 14-hour days in dark, filthy, and dangerous mills, mines, and factories. These conditions are powerfully described in Charles Dickens' novels—*Oliver Twist* and *Hard Times*—as well as Engels' 1845 study, *Conditions of the Working Class in England in 1844* (see also Smelser, 1959). As the Industrial Revolution advanced in the late nineteenth and early twentieth centuries, however, and machines steadily replaced human labor, new laws prohibited the employment of children and increasingly confined them to schools.

Although these laws reflected humanitarian concern for lower-class children, they also reflected the fact that the employment of children was becoming less profitable for employers. In the process, they transformed children and adolescents from productive workers into full-time students. Between 1850 and 1982 the percentage of children 5 to 17 years old enrolled in school

climbed steadily from 47 to 89 percent (U.S. Census Bureau, 1975a, 1983c). During the same period, the percentage of those 10 to 15 years old who were employed dropped from 18 percent (25 among boys) to virtually zero. Even though a substantial percentage of older adolescents are in today's labor force, they are more than twice as likely as older workers to be unemployed (Riley and Waring, 1976; U.S. Census Bureau, 1975a).

The elderly have experienced a similar historical transition. Between 1890 and 1981, the percentage of American men over the age of 65 who were in the labor force dropped from 68 to 18 (U.S. Census Bureau, 1975a, 1983c). Mandatory retirement laws created "room at the top" for upwardly mobile younger workers, which increased business profits by allowing employers to replace experi-

enced, higher-paid older workers with younger less-experienced workers who were willing to accept much lower wages (Haber, 1983). In 1967 the Age Discrimination Act protected workers between the ages of 40 and 65, and in 1978 the act was amended to forbid forced retirement before age 70 (Graebner, 1980).

It is important to note that the exclusion of children and the elderly from productive work does not occur in many societies, especially those that are not yet industrialized. The elderly in Soviet Georgia, for example, as well as those in many other less-developed societies, continue to work as long as they are able, in part because they own their own land (Nash, 1965; Weg, 1975). In industrial societies, however, both the youngest and the oldest age groups have, over the course of the last

As long as it was profitable, industrialists readily exploited child labor, even when this exposed children to dangerous working conditions such as those found in mills and coal mines.

200 years, been virtually excluded from the productive work through which wealth, power, and prestige are distributed.

## Wealth and Income

The elderly constitute the poorest age groups in the United States, and incomes are generally highest among people 35 to 54 years old (Table 14-1). In 1982, 12.2 percent of Americans 22 to 64 years old lived below the poverty level, but the figure was 14.6 percent for those over 65. Individuals had an average income of $10,100, but for those 65 and over, the average was only $7,500. Of all the money earned in 1980, 10.5 percent went to the elderly, although they made up 14 percent of the adult population (U.S. Census Bureau, 1982, 1983c). Thus, their share of the national income was 75 percent of what they would have received if income were distributed equally among age groups.

Among the elderly who belong to other minority groups, income inequality is even more severe (Table 14-1). Elderly women and blacks have far lower incomes than do men and whites. Only 13 percent of elderly whites lived in poverty in 1981, compared with 39 percent of blacks and 26 percent of Hispanics. If we count those whose incomes are below or *near* the poverty level, the figures jump

## Voices: The Pitfalls of Age Discrimination

Eugene B. Goodman, an executive with a multi-national corporation, Heublein, Inc., sued his employers when he was denied a promised promotion to vice-president. His career had been paralyzed, he claimed in his largely successful age-discrimination suit, by the firm's "youth policy" on promotions. Goodman eloquently explained why such wasteful policies work against the interest of the young, the old, and the companies themselves:

At the time of Heublein's centennial, the chairman was 58, the president, 52. I was 53. I did not think that 48 was so young, nor did I think that 58 was so old. At 53 I did not feel unvigorous. In my vision of America, there was a place for the experience of older persons and a place for the aspirations of the younger. In my previous experience in other American corporations, mentors were older and younger executives learned from them. In the International Division, I reported to younger men.

It was now clear to me that the older officers at the top had decided to emphasize age as a determining factor in career progress. They had arrived where they wanted to be, and had changed the traditional rules. I had been prevented from arriving where I wanted to go, not because of lack of experience or effective performance, but because of the arbitrary perception that youth was better. In my opinion, it was a perverse and irrational value judgment. The presidium had imposed senescence by decree.

Youth-oriented employment and promotion practices have serious pitfalls. For instance, they ignore the value of experience and set youth and age in an unnatural relationship. However, on Wall Street, the stock analysts presumably are impressed with reports of a management of young tigers, rather than old lions. Heublein, Inc. sponsored that image. In such a looking glass, there would ultimately be no place for me.

This did not jaundice me, however, against the younger International executives. My quar-rel was not with the beneficiaries of the program but with the top management who had capriciously arranged for them to go to the head of the line. My perception that there was no logic, and that there would be no profit for the corporation, in such a policy was eventually confirmed. By the time my case was over in 1982, none of the International protégés was employed by Heublein. Instead of growing a new crop of loyal managers, Heublein's harvest had been a lawsuit.

In other times, I also had been a younger executive and considered it appropriate to learn from older, more experienced superiors. In other major corporations, I had also known younger men who deserved their early advancement. I had been among them.

They did not win their promotions because there was a youth-oriented personnel policy in effect but because the corporate management was acknowledging achievement, rewarding for results obtained, or encouraging entrepreneurial skills. Merit, not age, was the criterion for promotion: the younger, meritorious executive was not arbitrarily held back because of his age, nor was the older executive arbitrarily denied advancement by reason of age.

American business needs a cadre of younger executives to learn to handle increasing responsibilities. It ensures the continuity of experienced management. America does not need the corporation whose employment practices discriminate against the older, seasoned executive in order artificially to create opportunities for younger executives who may not be meritorious. In such a situation, the younger executive who is promoted beyond his ability or his experience may become a victim, psychologically and professionally. He is often intimidated by his own realization that he knows less about most business situations and the solutions of business problems than his subordinate but can scarcely admit this, especially to himself. Because of the awkward reporting relationship, he omits the formality of learning from an older, more experienced executive in a proper mentor-protégé relationship. "Brain-picking" replaces the learning process.

The disregard of experience, or its discard, is the ultimate, profligate waste in a society that is just beginning to cope with the realization that our planetary resources are finite. Aside from merit, whether for special skills or achievements, the only legitimate basis for preferring youth to experience in the corporate milieu is the potential for innovation and creativity. But these have never been the exclusive attributes of the young. They appear in the individual, younger or older, not in the generation.

Source: Goodman, *All the Justice I Could Afford*, 1983.

---

to 23 percent for whites, but to 54 percent for blacks and 41 percent for Hispanics (U.S. Census Bureau, 1982).

Households headed by elderly women were 71 percent more likely to live in poverty in 1980 than were those headed by elderly men. Elderly men's share of national income equalled their share of the population (5.8 percent); but, whereas women over the age of 65 made up 8.4 percent of the population, they received only 4.7 percent of all income (U.S. Census Bureau, 1982).

The poor position of elderly women in the United States clearly illustrates how cultural, social structural, and ecological factors combine to produce minorities. Cultural values rank elderly women relatively low, but this alone does not explain their high rates of poverty. Their position as women excludes them from good jobs for most of their adult lives, which, in turn, makes them highly dependent on their husbands. In addition, women live considerably longer than men, which means that widowhood is far more common among women than among men. In 1981, 51 percent of women over the age of 64 were widows, while only 13 percent of men over 64 were widowers.

Widows are also more common than widowers because elderly widowers are more likely than widows to remarry. Cultural values encourage

---

**Table 14-1**

Average (Median) Money Income by Age, Gender, and Race
(United States, 1982)

| AGE GROUP | TOTAL POPULATION | GENDER | | RACE | |
|---|---|---|---|---|---|
| | | MEN | WOMEN | WHITES | BLACKS |
| 15–19 | $1,700 | $1,800 | $1,700 | $1,800 | $1,700 |
| 20–24 | $6,600 | $7,700 | $5,500 | $7,000 | $4,000 |
| 25–34 | $12,100 | $16,400 | $8,000 | $12,400 | $10,100 |
| 35–44 | $14,200 | $21,600 | $7,900 | $14,900 | $10,500 |
| 45–54 | $13,200 | $21,500 | $7,500 | $14,000 | $10,100 |
| 55–64 | $10,800 | $17,800 | $5,900 | $11,400 | $6,900 |
| 65–69 | $7,700 | $11,400 | $5,500 | $8,200 | $4,600 |
| 70+ | $6,200 | $8,100 | $5,300 | $6,500 | $3,800 |

Source: U.S. Census Bureau, 1984b.

The elderly—and elderly women in particular—constitute one of the poorest age groups in the United States.

men to marry younger women, while elderly women are expected to look for husbands among men who are *older* than they. Thus, widowed elderly men have a larger pool of prospective mates than do elderly women. Among people 65 years or older in 1982, for example, there were only 23 unmarried men for every 100 unmarried women (U.S. Census Bureau, 1983c).

Unlike income, the distribution of wealth favors the elderly—especially women—because the longer we live, the more wealth we can accumulate. In 1976, 55 percent of the nation's wealthiest individuals were more than 49 years old, even though this age group made up only 24 percent of the population. Among the wealthy, at least, age generally favors women, because they tend to outlive their husbands and become wealthy through inheritance. The majority of wealthy women are over the age of 50; the majority of wealthy men are less than 50 years of age (U.S. Census Bureau, 1983c).

Much has been made in recent years of the economic progress made by the elderly, especially through increased Social Security benefits (Pear, 1982). In general, the "poverty gap" between the elderly and the rest of the population has closed substantially since the 1950s, and the elderly are only slightly more likely to be poor than the population as a whole.

The incidence of poverty, however, is only one way of comparing the incomes of people in different social categories and ignores the fact that age generally acts as an income "leveler" because most people are downwardly mobile after the age of 65. This is especially true for women and those who spend their adult lives in the middle class (Tissue, 1979).

Table 14-2 shows how the relationship between education and income differs according to age and gender, and it clearly shows the negative effects of aging on mobility, particularly among women (there are a lot of numbers in this table, so take your time as you study them). Columns I and II, for example, show incomes for men and women 45 to 54 years-old with different educational levels. As you can see, higher education brings higher income, and the income difference between the highest and lowest education groups is $26,800 for men and $16,200 for women.

The picture is much the same among those 55 to 64 years old (columns III and IV); but look at what happens after age 65 (columns V and VI). The income difference between the most- and least-educated men drops by one third (from $25,800 to $16,700) and as does the corresponding difference for women (from $14,900 to $10,400). Thus, while America's elderly are only slightly worse off than everyone else, most of them are considerably worse off than they were as younger adults, especially if they are women.

## Power, Prestige, and Self-Esteem

A **gerontocracy** is a society ruled by an elderly elite, and this describes the governments of most societies. The most powerful members of the U.S. Congress, for example, are those who have been there the longest and whose seniority puts them in control of important committees. Presidents of the

**Table 14-2**

Average (Median) Money Income by Age, Education, and Gender
(United States, 1982)

| EDUCATION | 45–54 YEARS OLD (I) Men | (II) Women | 55–64 YEARS OLD (III) Men | (IV) Women | 65 AND OLDER (V) Men | (VI) Women |
|---|---|---|---|---|---|---|
| Elementary 0–8 | $10,100 | $4,100 | $8,500 | $3,600 | $5,900 | $3,900 |
| 8 | $12,900 | $5,100 | $11,700 | $4,000 | $7,500 | $4,700 |
| High school 1–3 | $15,700 | $5,300 | $14,300 | $4,300 | $8,500 | $5,000 |
| 4 | $21,100 | $7,700 | $19,100 | $6,700 | $11,100 | $6,300 |
| College 1–3 | $25,000 | $9,400 | $22,300 | $8,200 | $13,900 | $7,700 |
| 4 | $33,200 | $11,700 | $32,400 | $12,000 | $17,400 | $10,200 |
| 5 or More | $36,900 | $20,300 | $34,300 | $18,500 | $22,600 | $14,300 |
| **Highest-Lowest Income Gap**[1] | $26,800 | $16,200 | $25,800 | $14,900 | $16,700 | $10,400 |

Source: U.S. Census Bureau, 1984c.

[1]Equals highest income minus lowest for each age-sex group.

United States, top leaders in business, the military, universities, and organized religion all tend to be elderly. Ronald Reagan, for example, was 74 when he was reelected president in 1984. This pattern repeats itself in a variety of societies—from China, the Soviet Union, and Japan to the Andaman Islanders. In 1985, 73-year-old Konstantin Chernenko died while serving as president of the Soviet Union and was replaced by 54-year-old Mikhail Gorbachev, who, in comparison with most of his predecessors, was regarded by many as a "youth." Both of China's top leaders were 81 years old in 1985, and the Prime Minister of Japan was 67.

Although many top leaders are elderly—usually because they were chosen over younger candidates with less experience—such high leadership positions are relatively rare, and in most societies the elderly as a whole are neither powerful nor prestigious. The United States is ruled primarily by elderly leaders, but most Americans experience a sharp decline in power and prestige when they enter old age, primarily because they are excluded from important work and family statuses. The majority of elderly people live on fixed retirement incomes; they can no longer take good health for granted; most no longer work, in a society that values workers more than nonworkers; and they are expected to depend on others to take care of them, to "enjoy" depending on other people for a change (Barton, Baltes, and Orzech, 1980).

All of these social factors add up to a general loss of control by the elderly over important parts of their private lives and their environments, and this explains in part why they often appear to be depressed (Gergen, 1980). Elderly residents of nursing homes, for example, often have little power over the most fundamental aspects of their daily lives—when they will eat or sleep, or when they can see visitors—and this loss of control often damages their health and lowers their level of activity and enthusiasm for life (Schulz, 1976).

The cultural devaluation of the elderly in the United States might lead us to conclude that ours is a "youth-oriented" society, but the high value that many adults place on delaying the loss of their *own* youth does not mean that our culture values young *people*. As a characteristic, a youthful appearance may enhance the power and prestige of older adults, but it diminishes the power and prestige of the young.

American children have little if any power, either over other people or their own lives. They cannot vote, work, decide where or with whom they will live, or marry. Throughout history, fathers in many societies have had the power to kill children who displeased them. Even in modern societies such as our own, children are highly vulnerable to physical abuse by parents, and police and other authorities are reluctant to intervene unless they have overwhelming proof of abuse (Allan, 1978).

As we have noted, it would be difficult to argue convincingly that children are an oppressed minority in the same sense that nonwhites and women are, for children eventually become adults, and the powerlessness of children results in part from biological limitations. Many 13-year-old boys and girls are biologically capable of having children, but they certainly are unable to care for them or earn a living in industrial societies.

American culture, however, extends childhood to include older adolescents and even those in their early twenties; and while adolescents are also not an oppressed minority, their levels of power and prestige are greatly out of line with their abilities. Denied power and prestige in the adult world, many adolescents compensate by expressing power among their peers—especially through the use of violence—and often direct their frustration toward adults by rebelling against parental and legal authority.

The low social standing of adolescents may explain in part their unusually high levels of deviant behavior. In 1980 those 15 to 17 years-old made up only 6 percent of the U.S. population, but accounted for 11 percent of all arrests for rape, 23 percent of arrests for robbery and larceny, 34 percent of arrests for car theft, 19 percent of arrests for arson, and 26 percent of arrests for vandalism. Overall, they accounted for 15 percent of all arrests for serious crimes—a share 2.5 times larger than their share of the population (U.S. Census Bureau, 1981).

The dependency of children on adults makes them highly vulnerable to physical and mental abuse.

Exclusion from valued statuses contributes to lowered levels of power, prestige, and self-esteem among both children and the elderly, who are more likely than those in other age groups to feel useless, trivial, and socially invisible. Children who grew up during the Great Depression of the 1930s often made important contributions to the survival of their families and had good reason to feel that they were needed and valued (Elder, 1974). The primary role of many of today's children is that of consumer, and they often have good reason to feel superfluous, as if their dependent emotional attachment to their families is their only meaningful connection to adult society.

In other ways, however, historical changes have increased the relative power of adolescents. When the family was the center of production, adolescents had few alternatives to working under the authority of their parents, their fathers in particular. As the Industrial Revolution shifted productive work away from the family, the availability of paid employment outside the family provided adolescents with a way to escape the power of their parents.

## Explaining Age Stratification

Age stratification can be both functional and dysfunctional for the achievement of various culturally valued goals, and this often depends on the characteristics of populations and ecological arrangements through which goods are produced in a society. Age stratification also reflects the ability of some age groups to dominate others in the competition for wealth, power, and prestige. Thus, the functional, ecological, and conflict perspectives help answer a question that can be stated far more simply than it can be answered: Why does age stratification exist at all?

### Functions and Dysfunctions of Age Stratification

Perhaps the most important functional requirements of any society are to perpetuate itself and to ensure that adult roles are adequately performed. Age stratification is functional for these goals in most societies (Eisenstadt, 1956).

Young children, for example, are physically, emotionally, and mentally incapable of performing adult roles in industrial societies that rely on skilled labor and sophisticated technologies. Continuity from one generation to the next requires that children be socialized so that they will be able to perform adult roles when they grow up. This requires training, and adults can train their children only if they have power over them.

Successful performance of any role requires motivation as well as ability, and all societies use inequality between adults and children to encourage children to strive for adult standing. Because adults are wealthier, more prestigious, and more powerful than children, children are motivated to learn what they have to in order to escape the limitations and disadvantages of childhood.

Consequently, age stratification is functional for some important goals; but as we have seen before, social arrangements may be functional for some goals and dysfunctional for others. Forced retirement, for example, is functional for creating opportunities for younger workers, but is dysfunctional for keeping the most experienced workers in the labor force. This creates a growing class of older people who must be supported by younger adults who are already feeling the strain of trying to provide for their own growing families. As explained later in this chapter, this increases social conflict between different age groups.

Forced retirement is dysfunctional in other ways. When people lose important work roles, their incomes often fall and they lose a sense of control over their lives. A large body of scientific evidence shows that people who no longer feel in control of their own lives are more vulnerable to psychological depression and chronic illness (Brim, 1974). This, in turn, produces an enormous demand for medical care and institutions for the elderly.

The exclusion of adolescents from the labor force is functional for lessening competition for jobs; but it also creates a large number of people who produce far less than they consume, feel disconnected from their society, and often express their resulting frustration in deviant, if not destructive, ways.

Ultimately, the distribution of wealth, power, and prestige depends on divisions of labor through which societies accomplish important tasks. Divisions of labor, in turn, are closely related to ecological arrangements: population size, growth, and age structures, and how societies use technology and the physical environment to produce goods.

### Population, Ecology, and Age Stratification

The ecological perspective reveals two key aspects of age stratification. First, it focuses on the relationship between population *age structures* and *role structures* through which societies produce goods and services. Second, it draws attention to the fact that each cohort experiences childhood, adolescence, young adulthood, middle-age, and old age at different times in a society's history and, therefore, in different social circumstances. Such differences, in turn, often affect levels of social inequality.

**Age Structures, Role Structures, and Age Inequality**  As we saw in Chapter 5, the **age structure** of a society is the relative number of people who are of each age. The population of Mexico, for example, has a high proportion of children, whereas Sweden has a high proportion of elderly people. In both cases, a relatively large proportion of the population (children plus the elderly) depends on a relatively small adult population to produce goods that everyone consumes.

Populations in Europe and North America have been growing older for over a hundred years. Between 1870 and 1981 the percentage of the U.S. population under the age of 15 fell from 39 percent to 22, while the percentage over the age of 64 quadrupled from 3 percent to 12 (U.S. Census Bureau, 1975a, 1983c).

The **role structure** of a society has three different aspects: the *number of different roles*, the *number of openings* that exist for each role, and the *requirements for role performance*. Role structures depend heavily on the level of technology in a society and how labor is organized in relation to it. Hunter-gatherer societies use simple technologies and have relatively simple role structures; but industrial societies use sophisticated technologies and divide labor into thousands of different jobs, some of which employ far more people than do others. In 1982, for example, there were 3,847,000 secretaries in the United States, but only 168,000 pharmacists, 100 U.S. senators, and one president of the United States (U.S. Census Bureau, 1983c).

On the one hand, all societies have role structures that determine the kind and number of roles that are available for people to perform, and age is an important characteristic used to assign people to those roles. On the other hand, populations have age structures that determine the relative numbers of people available to perform roles that are culturally defined as appropriate for each age group.

If we consider age and role structures simultaneously, we can see that *age structures and role structures always have the potential to be out of balance with each other* (Riley, 1976). Productive work in agrarian societies, for example, requires relatively little sophisticated training, and children

and the elderly can perform many productive roles. In agrarian economies—where machines do none of the work—the more workers there are, the higher production will be. Thus, in agrarian societies, age structures are rarely out of balance with the opportunities provided by role structures.

Industrial societies, however, have less use for unskilled workers and rely heavily on machines to replace human labor; and this provides few work opportunities for children. The relative scarcity of jobs also creates pressures to exclude the elderly in order to make room for young adult and middle-aged workers. The more numerous children and the elderly are in industrial societies, the more likely they are to be excluded from the labor force.

This means, however, that "young" and "old" age structures—those with large percentages of children or the elderly—create more strains in industrial societies than in agrarian ones, because the role structure provides relatively few positions for large portions of the population. Thus, *the relationship between age and role structures* determines their effect on age inequality: the more out of balance with each other they are, the greater age inequality will tend to be.

**Age Cohorts and the Importance of Generations**  At any one time, a population includes people from a series of cohorts, each of which may pass through important stages of the life course under widely differing social circumstances that produce what are called **cohort effects** (Riley and Foner, 1972; Ryder, 1965).

People's ability to compete successfully in industrial societies, for example, depends on two key cohort effects. First, historical trends in birth and death rates produce cohorts of different sizes. Between 1800 and the late 1940s, birth rates fell steadily in the United States and Europe, and this meant that each new cohort was smaller than the next older cohort. In addition, the Industrial Revolution rapidly expanded the demand for workers. Together, these ecological, population, and structural changes meant that an economy that had enough jobs for one generation of workers could easily absorb the smaller generations that followed.

From the late 1940s through 1960, however, the post–World War II "Baby Boom" temporarily reversed the fertility decline, and adults who are

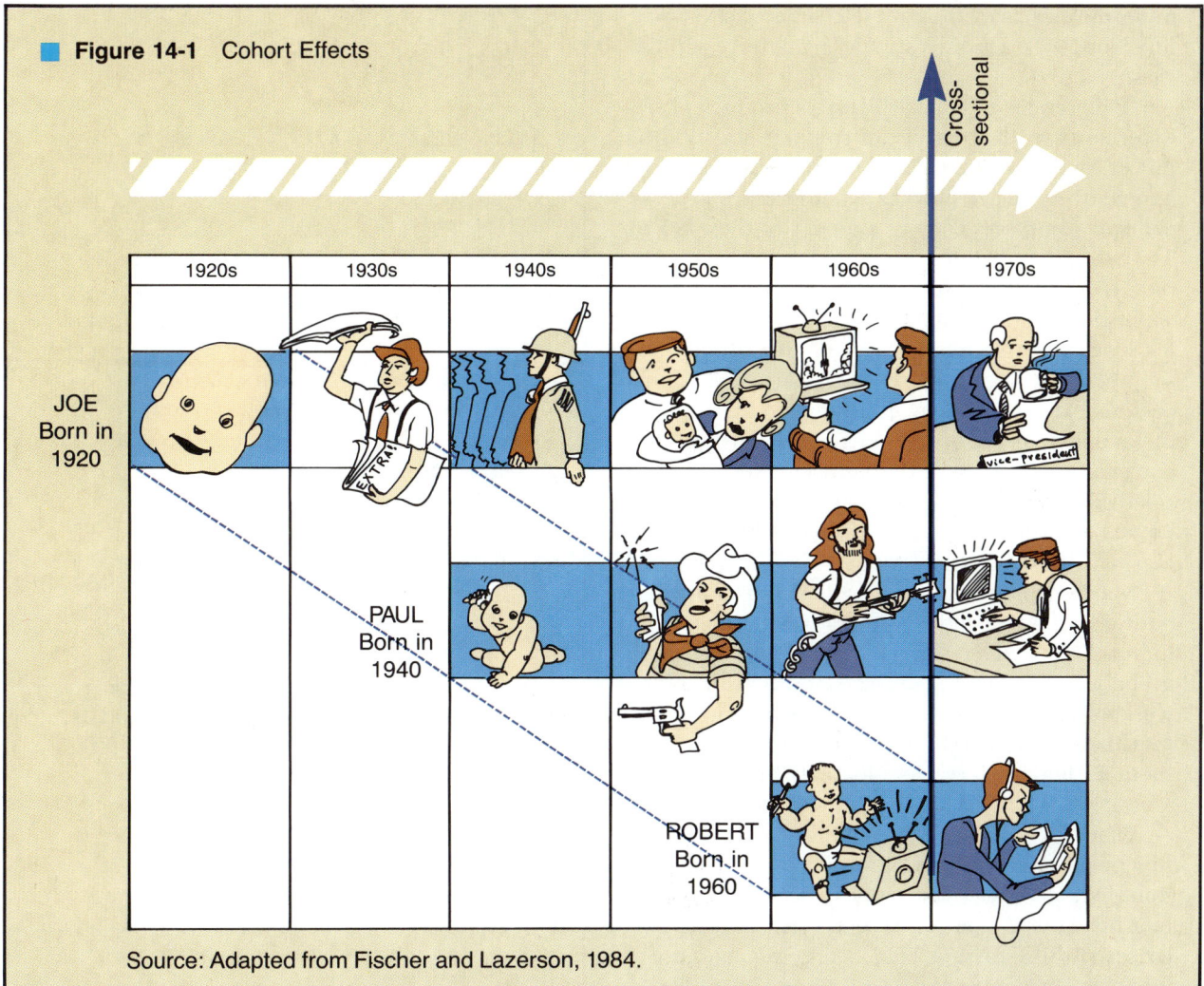

**Figure 14-1**  Cohort Effects

1920s  1930s  1940s  1950s  1960s  1970s

JOE Born in 1920

PAUL Born in 1940

ROBERT Born in 1960

Source: Adapted from Fischer and Lazerson, 1984.

now in their thirties are far more numerous than were older generations. The result is a role structure whose opportunities are out of balance with the age structure of the population: the number of jobs being vacated by the relatively small generations of people who are now in their fifties and sixties is insufficient for the larger "Baby Boom" generation. It is, in part, for this reason that there is so much pressure on older workers to retire in order to make room for upward mobility among younger workers.

A second key cohort effect arises from the fact that each cohort experiences stages in the life course under different social conditions, and this produces differences in characteristics, such as educational attainment, that strongly affect our

share of wealth, power, and prestige. The cohorts born between 1915 and 1920, for example, are among today's elderly. They experienced childhood in the "Roaring Twenties," adolescence during the Great Depression when educational opportunities were very limited, young adulthood during and after World War II when the job market exploded with new opportunities, and middle age during the turbulent 1960s.

The 1945–1950 cohort, on the other hand, experienced childhood during the relatively prosperous 1950s, adolescence during the 1960s that saw an explosion of educational opportunities, and young adulthood during the economic recessions of the 1970s. In the 1980s, this cohort approaches middle age in an economy that has severely limited opportunities, and they must compete for upper-level jobs with a rapidly expanding elderly population.

Differences in cohort histories produce sharp differences in their ability to compete for wealth, power, and prestige. In 1980, only 8.5 percent of people over the age of 65 had four or more years of college, compared with 21 percent of those 35 to 44 years old and 26 percent of those 30 to 34 years old (U.S. Census Bureau, 1981). As new, more sophisticated technology redefines requirements for successful role performance in the job market, members of older cohorts inevitably find themselves at a competitive disadvantage. Computer technology, for example, is one of the most rapidly expanding segments of the labor market, and the relatively poor education of older workers poorly equips them to compete in this sector of the labor market.

As each new cohort benefits from expanded educational opportunities, it enlarges its advantage in relation to older cohorts, but eventually *loses* ground in relation to *younger* cohorts. While older workers are less likely than younger workers to *lose* their jobs, if they do, it is much harder for them to find new ones (Riley and Foner, 1968).

The preceding sections indicate some of the functional and ecological aspects of age stratification. While these perspectives contribute important pieces of the puzzle of age stratification, other pieces are still missing. Many consequences of age inequality are *not* in the best interests of society or of age minorities, and yet still exist—a fact that brings us to the conflict perspective.

## Age and Social Conflict

From a conflict perspective, inequality is caused by competition over wealth, power, and prestige, through which members of some social categories are able to dominate and exploit others. Thus, the conflict perspective identifies relationships between age stratification and the conditions that create and maintain social classes.

For example, beliefs that portray adolescents as incapable of performing adult roles and that define the elderly as senile arose in part from class conflict. Nineteenth-century laws that prohibited child labor were strongly supported by labor unions that wanted to protect their members' jobs by

---

## PUZZLES:

## AGE, EDUCATION, AND UNEMPLOYMENT

Who do you think would be more likely to have been unemployed for at least one month during any recent 10-year period—someone with at least a high school diploma or someone who had never graduated from high school?

As the table below shows, the more highly educated person is more likely to have been unemployed. Why?

Unemployment Experience by Educational Attainment
(United States, 1978)

| EDUCATION | PERCENTAGE UNEMPLOYED FOR AT LEAST 1 MONTH DURING PAST 10 YEARS |
|---|---|
| Less than high school graduate | 24 |
| High school graduate or more | 32 |

Source: Data from the 1978 National Opinion Research Center's General Social Survey.

The answer is that over the past several decades each generation of young people has been better educated than the one before it, and this upward trend in education means that the most highly educated people in the population tend also to be the *youngest*. Since people are generally more likely to experience unemployment when they are just starting out in the work world, then those who are the best educated will also tend to experience unemployment the most. What is going on here has nothing to do with education per se and everything to do with cohorts. For more on this, see Chapters 5 and 21.

reducing the amount of competition. Mandatory retirement for older workers began to increase in popularity during the 1930s—the years of the Great Depression—when jobs were scarce and labor unions were becoming increasingly powerful (Atchley, 1982).

The minority standing of the elderly in the United States is also related to class conflict, because the scarcity over which different age groups compete is produced by the concentration of wealth and income in the upper class. Forced retirement, for example, benefits the capitalist class by lowering costs and therefore increasing business profits. Employers can replace experienced— and more expensive—older workers with younger workers who, although they are generally better-educated, are willing to work for lower wages because they are inexperienced.

As the age structure of the population becomes older, the pressures toward conflict among age groups increase. When Social Security was enacted in 1935, it was designed as a self-supporting fund that would provide *supplementary* benefits for all elderly people who contributed to the fund during their working years. Workers and employers would contribute over the years, and when workers retired they would then draw from the fund. By design, then, each cohort contributed to a "safety net" that would protect those who survived to old age from living in poverty.

In practice, however, the system has worked quite differently. In 1956, disabled workers under age 65 became eligible for benefits; in 1961, workers retiring before age 65 also became eligible; and in 1965, hospital insurance under the Medicare plan was added to the list of benefits. Because the elderly population was still relatively small in the early 1970s, the fund had a huge surplus, and Congress decided to adjust social security payments according to the level of inflation.

In the 1970s, however, the cost of living—as measured by inflation—was rising *faster* than the income of workers. Between 1970 and 1981 average real family income actually *dropped* by almost one percent, but social security benefits increased by 40 percent. At the same time, the age structure of the population was becoming older at a rapid rate. Together, these two factors meant that for the first time money was flowing *out* of the fund faster than it was coming *in*, and by 1983 the social security system was losing money at the rate of $20,000 each *minute*.

As benefits rose rapidly, retired workers were drawing far more from the social security fund than they and their employers had contributed. The average person who retired in 1980, for example, had, together with his or her employer, contributed $24,000 to the system; but those retirees could expect to draw $125,000 in benefits over the rest of their lives.

The result is a growing burden on the young and middle-aged working population, whose contribution to social security is now used immediately to pay *current* benefits to those who are already retired. In 1945 there were 42 workers to provide benefits for each retired person. The elderly population is now much larger relative to the working population that pays social security taxes, and there are only 3 workers to support each retired person (*Newsweek*, January 24, 1983).

This situation is ripe for social conflict between the elderly and younger workers who must pay taxes to support them, particularly workers in the lower and middle classes. Social security taxes are only applied to the first $32,400 of earnings, which means that people with a taxable income of $1,000,000 a year pay no more in social security taxes than those earning $32,400.

It is important to point out that conflict over the social security crisis is *within* the lower and middle classes. Eighty percent of those over the age of 65 have incomes below $10,000 and depend on social security for more than half their annual income (*Newsweek*, January 24, 1983; U.S. Census Bureau, 1982). As we saw in Chapter 11, the lower and middle classes are hardly in a position to support the elderly, but the burden, nonetheless, falls largely on them.

Consequently, the social security crisis is not simply a matter of changing age structures and rising retirement benefits, for it also reflects the larger economic structure of our society. The large population of retired people is produced in part by an economic system that cannot provide jobs for everyone who wants to work, and from this perspective, retirement programs benefit upper-class capitalists as well as (if not more than) middle- and lower-class workers. Without such programs, workers would either insist on remaining in the labor force well into old age or would demand

The emergence of groups such as the Gray Panthers signaled a major growth in the organized political influence of the elderly in the United States.

wages high enough to adequately provide for them in retirement (Smith, 1981). In this way, retirement programs operate as "a kind of insurance for capitalists and corporations" (O'Connor, 1973, p. 138).

The position of the elderly, like that of other minorities, rests on both functional requirements of societies and conflict over wealth, power, and prestige. Unlike the situation of other minorities, however, the position of the elderly is closely tied to changing age and role structures of populations and to biological aspects of age and aging. The uniqueness of age as a social status produces both unique barriers to social change and unique pressures for change.

## Age Stratification and Social Change

Ageism and age stratification are deeply rooted in culture, social structures, population dynamics, and ecological arrangements. What are the social pressures toward equal distributions of wealth, power, and prestige among age groups? Is equality possible at all?

### Avenues to Change

Pressures toward equality between age groups come from organized social movements, the unique characteristics of age as a social status, changing age structures of populations, and the changing characteristics of age cohorts.

As a whole, the elderly have greatly increased their political power in the last decade. They are not only more numerous than ever before but are more likely to vote in elections than any other age group (U.S. Census Bureau, 1983c). The American Association of Retired Persons has 14 million members, and the Gray Panther organization has over 60,000 who actively challenge cultural stereotypes while promoting equal rights for the elderly. Says Maggie Kuhn, the 78-year-old founder of the Gray Panthers:

> We have used street theater, we have marched, we have demonstrated, we have picketed. . . . But more than that, we have brought together a group of people who have first-class minds and who read a lot, who have the ability to think and who have a creative social analysis. (*Hartford Advocate*, July 28, 1982, p. 6)

Kuhn emphasizes that the Gray Panthers is an intergenerational organization that attracts people of all ages. In part, the attractiveness of the Gray Panthers rests on the uniqueness of age as a social status, for everyone faces the inevitable time when they will be culturally defined as "old." Whites can ignore the oppression of blacks; men can ignore the oppression of women; and adults can ignore the disadvantaged position of children. Few can totally ignore the fate of the elderly, however, without also ignoring the inevitability of old age itself.

Perhaps the most important pressure for change, however, results from long-term shifts in the age structure of populations and the inevitable flow of generations through the life course.

**Population, Ecology, and the Graying of America**
For almost two hundred years, birth rates have declined steadily in Europe and North America, and this has caused major shifts in population age structures. By the year 2025, an estimated 20 percent of our population will be over the age of 64, compared with 11 percent in 1980 and only 4 percent in 1890 (U.S. Census Bureau, 1975a, 1982).

The resulting "graying" of America will inevitably increase the political power of the elderly and pressure decision makers to devote larger portions of national resources to elderly people's needs, such as health care and retirement income and housing. Opposition to mandatory retirement laws will grow along with the size of the elderly population, and this will put pressure on a job market that excludes the elderly in order to provide jobs for young and middle-aged adults.

Such changes are particularly important in southern parts of the United States—the "Sun Belt"—whose populations have swelled with elderly migrants attracted by warm climates and relatively low costs of living. People over the age of 65 made up 11.6 percent of the U.S. population in 1982, but 17.4 percent of Florida's (U.S. Census Bureau, 1983c). Many communities in Florida and other Sun Belt states are being designed and built specifically to meet the needs of older residents, and the elderly increasingly dominate both local and state politics.

Increased power among the elderly also results from the different social characteristics of cohorts. In 1980, 43 percent of Americans over the age of 65 had never gone beyond elementary school; only 8 percent had college degrees; and 20 percent were foreign-born and thus relatively unfamiliar with U.S. laws and the political process. By comparison, less than 10 percent of the elderly in 2010 will have never gone beyond elementary school; roughly 20 percent will have college degrees; and almost all will be native-born (U.S. Census Bureau, 1981). This, combined with an increasing consciousness of the importance of age as a social status will probably result in considerable increases in the social power of the elderly.

Increased tension between different age groups appears to be an inevitable consequence of changing age structures and the increased political

power of each succeeding generation of elderly people. How might these tensions be resolved? Is equality of wealth, power, and prestige a possible answer?

## Is Equality Possible?

Age stratification results primarily from the use of age to determine which statuses people may occupy and, therefore, which roles they may perform in the division of labor. Equality among age groups implies that age would no longer limit people's access to statuses, especially jobs. This kind of arrangement, however, would inevitably result in renewed age stratification, because societies still have to allocate roles among their members, and the most likely criteria are strongly related to age (Riley and Waring, 1976).

Suppose, for example, that work roles were allocated on the basis of skill and ability. Adolescents would be at a distinct disadvantage, and the middle-aged and elderly would have to compete with healthy and vigorous younger cohorts fresh out of college where they have learned the latest technological skills (Young, 1961). If work experience were the most important factor, both young and middle-aged workers would lose their competitive edge over the elderly. If jobs went to those who needed them most—such as those with families to support—the middle-aged would benefit, because they are the most likely to have families whose children are approaching college age (Oppenheimer, 1974).

This analysis suggests that age stratification among adolescents, adults, and the elderly is unavoidable, but it rests on an assumption that may not be. All of these hypothetical consequences of age equality would occur only in a society that cannot provide jobs for everyone, thus making it necessary to exclude some people from the labor market in order to employ everyone else. Competition between groups tends to breed prejudice, and prejudice is the cultural bulwark of discrimination (Noel, 1968; Vander Zanden, 1972).

To Marx, such conditions are main features of capitalist, industrial societies in which the means of production are privately owned, and competi-

Drawing by Ziegler; © 1984, The New Yorker Magazine, Inc.

tion among workers for scarce jobs keeps wages low and profits high. Marx argued that these conditions would disappear in an advanced, technologically sophisticated communist society, and, with them, all forms of social inequality. Thus, from Marx's perspective, age inequality is directly related to the same social conditions that produce and perpetuate social classes.

Marx's view, of course, is utopian, and we cannot know if the ideal society he envisions is possible. His perspective is powerful, however, because it underscores the fact that social change is severely limited by the basic ways in which societies organize production and distribute wealth, power, and prestige. It is impossible to eliminate age stratification in industrial societies—including both capitalist and socialist countries—without changing fundamental economic and political structures that perpetuate social inequality. To see why this is true, consider the recommendations of two panels of scientists who studied the disadvantaged positions of the young and the elderly in the United States (Coleman et al., 1974; Riley, 1974).

In industrial societies, education is confined primarily to children and adolescents who, in turn, spend most of their time in school. Similarly, young and middle-aged adults are confined to work, and the elderly are largely excluded from productive work. In spite of the fact that they focused on dramatically different age groups, the panels made similar recommendations: education, work, and leisure should not be rigidly distributed among age groups; rather, they should be distributed evenly throughout the life course.

Under this arrangement, adolescents would split their time between school and on-the-job training. Young and middle-aged adults would work less in order to make room for continuing education and increased leisure. The elderly would continue to work—although perhaps at reduced levels—while enjoying increased amounts of leisure and continuing their educations. In essence, these proposals rest on the idea that the total amount of time devoted to education, work, and leisure would remain the same in the population as a whole. What would change would be the distribution of these activities over the life course.

There is some evidence that this kind of shift has already begun in the United States. Adults are increasingly likely to change careers at least once during young adulthood and middle age, and such changes often require them to return to school for additional training. Between 1960 and 1982 the percentage of adults over the age of 29 who were enrolled in school almost tripled (U.S. Census Bureau, 1983c).

Unless total production and income increase, however, redistribution of education, work, and leisure across age groups will reduce inequality of income only if people in higher-income age groups are willing to lower their incomes. Raising the average income of elderly people to the 1980 national average of $10,100 would cost more than $64 billion, or $500 for every adult under the age of 65.

Where would this money come from? From the 53 percent of young and middle-aged adults who *already* earn less than the national average? Or from the upper-middle and upper classes that not only control a disproportionate share of the nation's wealth and income but also heavily influence those who make our laws? Will the upper class weaken its own position in order to bring about equality for the elderly, especially given that old age does not threaten *them* with financial insecurity? Certainly this kind of change is unlikely to occur.

Minorities—whether they are based on gender, race, ethnicity, or age—are ultimately created by social conditions that produce and perpetuate social stratification itself. In capitalist societies, an end to age stratification would require the redistribution of the enormous wealth, power, and prestige now concentrated in the upper class. In socialist societies, the state and those who control it would have to surrender their power over the economy and the distribution of what is produced. So long as control over the means of production is unequally distributed, there will be scarcities and competition; and so long as people must compete for scarce rewards, privileged groups will use their advantage in the fight to maintain their position in the stratification system (Lenski, 1966).

Thus, in order for some groups to be privileged, minorities must pay the cost. In both capitalist and socialist societies, the most important question is not, Will minorities continue to exist? but, Who will the minorities be?

## Summary

1. All societies divide the life span into age groups, each of which is a social status with its own role set.

2. Like other statuses, such as gender and race, age affects the distribution of wealth, power, and prestige. Age is unique, however, because it is always temporary, provides a map of the life course, and affects the content of status sets more than any other status. Because we all belong to both subordinate and dominant groups at one time or another, subordinate age groups are only quasi-minorities.

3. Relationships between age groups are supported by a variety of beliefs, values, attitudes, and norms; and in many societies, the prejudice of ageism perpetuates age stratification and creates self-fulfilling prophecies.

4. Like other statuses, age groups have boundaries that determine who occupies which age status; and in some societies rites of passage clearly indicate when someone moves from one age group to another.

5. In social interaction, age affects our choice of role partners, and the role sets attached to age groups affect our perceptions, evaluations, feelings, and expectations. In many relationships age acts as a latent status that affects how we play other roles.

6. The birth cohort is an important concept because it defines peer groups on the basis of age and because it draws attention to the fact that different groups of people experience the stages of the life course during different historical periods.

7. The division of labor in all societies uses age as a basis for assigning tasks, and this, in turn, creates and supports social inequality. In the United States, children and the elderly generally occupy lower positions than young and middle-aged adults, and while most elderly people are not poor, they are worse off than they were as younger adults, especially if they are women.

8. Age stratification is functional for the socialization and motivation of children to perform adult roles, and is also closely connected to ecological arrangements and the dynamics of population growth and changing age distributions. Important work and family roles are assigned according to age, and when the role structure in a society is out of balance with the population age structure, opportunities increase for some age groups at the expense of others.

9. Age stratification is also dysfunctional for important goals. It creates large numbers of dependent people who consume more than they produce. Exclusion from productive work damages the health of the elderly and fosters feelings of alienation and frustration among the young.

10. While age stratification is functional for many goals, it is also perpetuated by conflict among social classes for wealth, power, and prestige. The exclusion of children and the elderly from employment lessens competition for jobs made scarce by a class society. It also contributes to false consciousness among young and middle-aged adult workers by focusing attention on competition between age groups rather than on the upper class whose privileged position creates the scarcities over which people in the lower and middle classes compete.

11. While social movements for equality among age groups have benefited the elderly, the strongest pressures for change center on changing population age structures and characteristics of new generations. Each new cohort of elderly people is more numerous, educated, and politically aware than the last, and these changes inevitably increase their political power in relation to other age groups.

## Key Terms

age group    431
ageism    433
age structure    450
cohort    439
    cohort effect    450
gerontocracy    446
hospice    441
life course    431
rite of passage    437
role structure    450

# Recommended Readings

ARIÈS, P. (1962). *Centuries of childhood.* New York: Vintage. A fascinating look at the emergence of childhood as an age group and historical changes in its definition.

ATCHLEY, R. C. (1980). *The social forces in later life* (3rd ed.). Belmont, CA: Wadsworth. An effective and well-written introduction to the study of aging as a social process.

MCPHERSON, B. D. (1983). *Aging as a social process: An introduction to individual and population aging.* Toronto: Butterworths. An excellent introduction to aging as a social process, including the ways in which that process is affected by historical, gender, racial, social class, and cross-cultural factors.

POLLOCK, L. A. (1984). *Forgotten children: Parent-child relations from 1500 to 1900.* Cambridge: Cambridge University Press. A recent book that directly challenges several of Ariès' (1962) most popular conclusions.

RILEY, M. W. (1976). "Age and Aging." In R. K. Merton and R. Nisbet (Eds.), *Contemporary social problems* (4th ed.). New York: Harcourt Brace Jovanovich. A brief, useful sociological overview of the problems of aging and age as a basis for social inequality by one of the foremost sociologists involved in the study of age and aging.

RILEY, M. W., HESS, B. B., and BOND, K. (Eds.). (1983). *Aging in society: Selected reviews of recent research.* Hillsdale, NJ: Lawrence Erlbaum Associates. An excellent collection of papers originally written for the 1981 White House Conference on Aging, and touching on topics such as aging and economics, the family, work, retirement, mortality, stress, learning and memory, health and mortality, nutrition, and geographic mobility.

STEARNS, P. N. (Ed.). (1982). *Old age in preindustrial society.* New York: Holmes and Meier. A revealing study of the day-to-day lives of the elderly in preindustrial societies, which challenges many of the romanticized beliefs about age and aging in previous societies.

# PART V

# Social Institutions

In Parts I and II we laid out a basic conceptual framework of sociological analysis—the organization of human life through cultural, structural, and ecological arrangements. In Part III we applied this to basic aspects of social life: the socialization process, interaction, groups, formal organizations, communities, and the ways in which groups and societies try to control the behavior of their members. In Part IV we focused on the ways culture, social structure, and ecology produce and perpetuate inequality based on characteristics such as social class, race, ethnicity, gender, and age.

Part V focuses on social *institutions*, the most important arrangements in any society. As we saw in Chapter 4, institutions are enduring sets of cultural ideas and social relationships organized to accomplish important social goals. All societies rely on some variation of the *family* to produce, socialize, protect, and care for new members. In many societies, *schools* provide additional education and skills; *economic institutions* produce and distribute goods and services; *political institutions* distribute and apply collective power; and *religious institutions* help members of society grapple with enduring questions about the meaning of life itself.

# CHAPTER 15

# Marriage and the Family

Look through a Sunday newspaper and you will find announcements of engagements, weddings, births, and divorces. Read the obituary columns and you will find the names of people who "survive" those who die. Walk down a residential street and you will see houses and apartments, each containing its own assortment of people living together. Sit back and think about your childhood, and more than anything else you will probably think of your family—a group of people that may include no more than you and one parent or scores of people from parents, stepparents, sisters, and brothers, to grandparents and distant cousins, aunts, and uncles, some of whom are no longer alive.

On the surface, such aspects of marriages and families seem to involve no more than people's personal decisions about their lives, and we may think that each relationship is unique for each group of people who define themselves as a married couple or a family. From a sociological perspective, however, marriages and families exist in social and physical environments that profoundly affect how they are formed, how they fall apart,

"We are gathered here to join together this man and this woman in matrimony—a very serious step, with far-reaching and unpredictable consequences."

Drawing by Booth; © 1985, The New Yorker Magazine, Inc.

and what goes on among their members; just as what goes on in families also affects the nature of those environments.

Like all other groups, families are affected by cultural ideas; all families have social structures; and in spite of individual variations from one family to another, families tend to conform to predictable cultural, structural, and ecological patterns within societies. These patterns, and their importance to both society and individuals, are what this chapter is all about.

We begin by looking at cultural ideas and social structures that characterize the family in different societies and how these are affected by ecology and population. We then use the functional and conflict perspectives to better understand the place of families in societies. The closing sections include a systematic sociological analysis of family disorganization—divorce and violence in particular—and the causes of change in the family as a social institution.

## Marriage and the Family as Institutions

The definition of marriage is relatively simple, regardless of the society. **Marriage** is a socially supported union between individuals in what is intended to be a stable, enduring relationship that involves sexual interaction as one of its key elements. As such, the institution of marriage forms the basis for the institution of the family.

If asked to define a "family," you would probably describe it as a group consisting of parents and their children. In an Israeli kibbutz, however, the entire community serves as a family, and all women take collective responsibility for child care (Rabin, 1965); among India's Nayar, fathers have no role relationship with their children (Gough, 1952); and Indonesia's Dani have no word for "family" at all (Heider, 1972). Although these examples reveal cultural differences in the definition of the family, all three have one thing in common. In each case the family is a social institution—an enduring set of cultural ideas and social relationships that contribute to the achievement of social goals.

In virtually all societies the **family** performs six basic social functions, and these define the family as an institution. First, it regulates sexual behavior by specifying who may have sexual contact with whom. In all societies **incest taboos** prohibit sexual contact between people who are culturally defined

Although all societies have family institutions that perform key social functions, there is enormous variation in the cultural and structural forms these institutions take.

as close relatives. Second, the family is responsible for *reproduction;* and the norms, values, and beliefs that regulate family life often affect the number of children born.

Third, families nurture and protect children and provide emotional support for adults. Fourth, the family is the main socializing institution charged with teaching new members of society what they need to know in order to participate in their social environment.

Fifth, the family plays a part in the production and consumption of goods. In many societies the family is a center of economic production, and its members produce most of what they consume. In others, such as our own, families produce little of what they consume.

Finally, families are a source of ascribed social statuses—such as race, ethnicity, and social class—that profoundly affect people's life chances. Caste membership in India and South Africa, for example, depends solely on the characteristics of families into which people are born.

Thus, even among the Dani—who have no word for the family—the institution nonetheless exists in social relationships that play important parts in the perpetuation of the cultural ideas and social structures that make up the Dani social environment. Since the essence of the family lies in *why* it is organized rather than *how*, we should not be surprised by the astounding variety found among different societies, for the same goals can be achieved in a variety of ways.

## Your Family, My Family, and The Family

If we compared your family and mine, we would find many differences—in values, beliefs, and attitudes that family members share; in norms that define rights and responsibilities in role relationships; and in the number of children, patterns of interaction and affection, and divisions of labor and power. Just as no two individuals are exactly alike, individual families also have some unique characteristics.

As an *institution*, however, the family is more than a collection of families, just as a group is more than the sum of its members. An institution is a social "blueprint" that defines how family relationships ought to be structured and what goals families and their members should pursue in order to make sure that important social goals are achieved.

Each of us participates in family life in relation to cultural models that produce patterns of family relationships, and these patterns are at the heart of the family as an institution. In the United States fathers generally have more power than mothers;

### Do you know your way around your own family tree?

How well do you know your family, its members, and the relationships among them? Fill in as many spaces as possible on this blank family tree.

(Such a tree could, of course, be extended to earlier generations from memory or family records.)

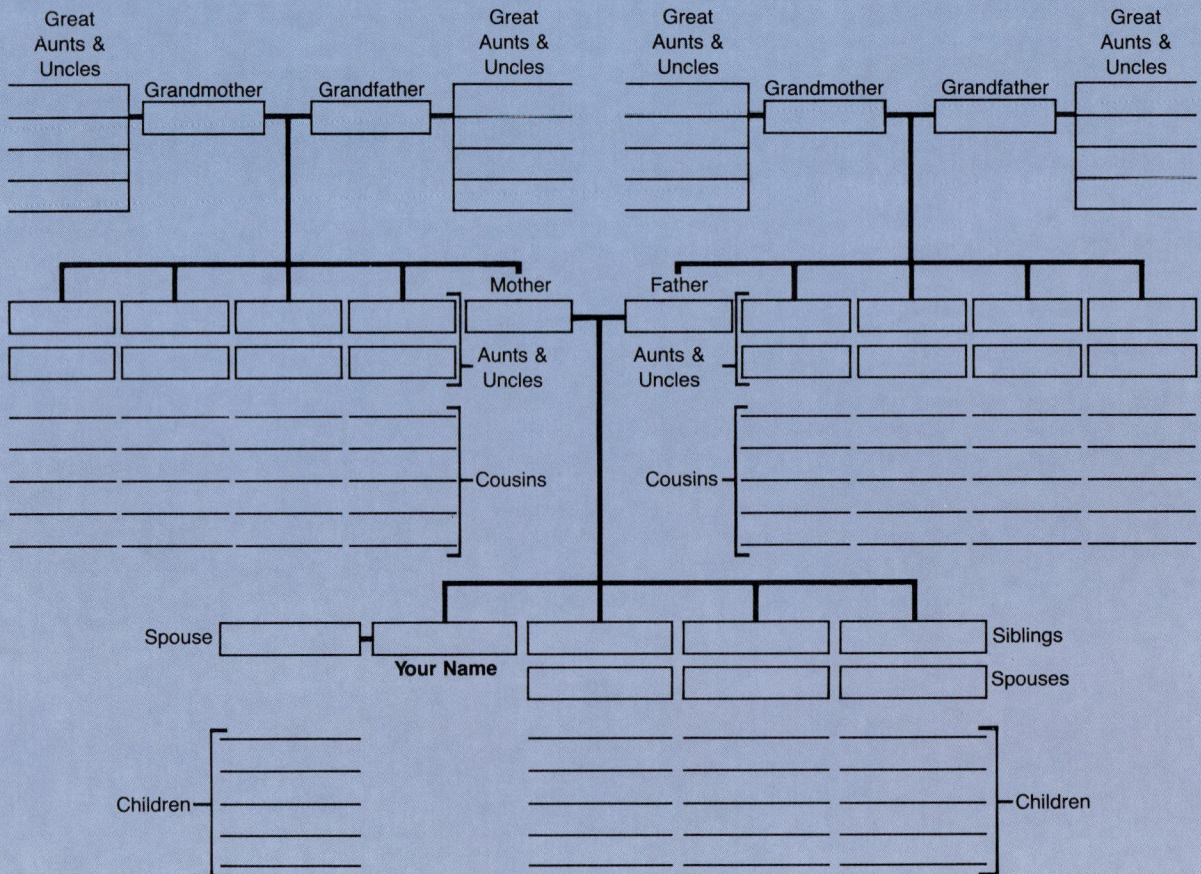

children have few legal rights until they reach 18 years of age; and most families have three or fewer children and do not have aunts, uncles, and grandparents living in the same dwelling.

Although some societies have a single model for the family, others—such as ours—include several, each of which reflects a different subculture. In some ways all American families are alike, but ethnic and racial subcultures often produce unique patterns of family relationships. Thus, it is misleading to refer to the institution of "the American family" as if it has only one meaning.

This chapter focuses on six of the many aspects of marriage and the family that interest sociologists: How do cultural ideas define marital and family relationships and regulate behavior within them? How are these relationships structured? How do ecological arrangements in a society affect family life? What are the relationships between families and the rest of society? How do we explain the problems that threaten the well-being of indi-

vidual marriages and families? How and why do the institutional characteristics of marriage and the family change?

## Cultural Variations

Marriages and families are affected by a variety of beliefs, values, attitudes, and norms. Beliefs define who is related to whom; values motivate us to form families and guide our choices within them; attitudes affect our feelings toward family members and outsiders; and norms define family roles and govern how family relationships are established, maintained, and broken.

### Beliefs and the Concept of Kinship

At the heart of all family institutions is the concept of **kinship**, which refers to social relationships

Kinship provides what is perhaps our most important social connection, one that can extend backward in time across many generations. In this picture more than 200 descendants of a Cape Cod pioneer celebrate their heritage as one of America's oldest families.

based on common ancestry, adoption, or marriage. In all societies children and their mothers are culturally defined as relatives (or *kin*); but beyond this core there are great differences among the world's cultures.

American culture, for example, includes special terms for hundreds of different relatives: spouses, parents, children, aunts, uncles, nieces, nephews, in-laws, grandparents, and a host of distant relatives. To these we can add fictive kin, such as godparents and "honorary aunts and uncles," who are not formal members of a family but nonetheless play important roles when family ties weaken. The number of possible kin relationships is enormous, and for this reason virtually all societies simplify kinship by considering only some to be "true" relatives.

Trobriand Islanders are unaware of the biological connection between fathers and their children, and although fathers have affectionate relationships with their children, they are regarded as outsiders (Malinowski, 1929). Southern India's Nayar do acknowledge the biological role of fathers; but, as in several other societies, the mother's eldest brother is responsible for her children (Gough, 1974).

Kinship, therefore, depends more on cultural definitions than on biology, and if "fate makes our relatives," then part of that fate is the culture we happen to be born into (Sahlins, 1976). For societies kinship provides continuity from one generation to the next by establishing ties between the generations who carry a society's culture and those who must learn to live by it. For individuals kinship is important because it links each of us to the past, present, and future.

Unlike all other social relationships, those among kin often have the power to transcend death itself. In most horticultural societies, for example, people worship their ancestors, believing that if they do not appease them, their spirits might return to harm them (Shiels, 1975). Even in societies such as our own that do not worship ancestors, we often refer to deceased relatives as living parts of our social identities.

Kinship is generally defined in one of three ways. In societies characterized by **matrilineal descent,** ancestry is traced through mothers and their blood relatives. Children, for example, are not defined as relatives of their father's family.

Matrilineal descent is relatively rare, and is found most often in horticultural societies, in which women produce most of the food (Aberle, 1961; Murdock, 1967).

The situation is reversed in societies with **patrilineal descent,** in which children are related only to their father's blood relatives. In most of the world's societies, descent is either matrilineal or patrilineal (Murdock, 1949); there are only a few with **bilateral descent,** tracing ancestry through both the mother's and father's families. Murdock (1949) found that of the 86 societies on which information on descent is available, fully 71 percent are patrilineal, compared with 27 percent that are matrilineal, and only 2 percent that are bilateral.

While kinship defines basic family ties, other beliefs affect relationships within families. Until rather recently, Americans believed that when men and women marry, they become "one," and the "one" is the husband. This belief profoundly affects family relationships by undermining a wife's standing as a separate individual with her own rights in relation to her husband and the rest of society. It is still evident in the tendency of most American married women to adopt their husband's last name as their own. In contrast, the Swedish Parliament ruled in 1982 that husbands and wives are free to choose their own last names, and that if they choose no last name for a newborn child, after three months it automatically takes its *mother's* name (*Ms.* magazine, 1982).

Many Americans believe that marriage is better for women than it is for men, a belief reflected in jokes about women "trapping" men into marriage and about husbands continually trying to escape the limitations of married life. Most research, however, shows that just the opposite is true: single women report greater happiness and less psychological stress than married women of the same age, while married men report fewer symptoms of psychological distress than single men.

## Values

Cultural values rank behavior and experience in terms of social desirability, and strongly affect both the formation and dissolution of marriages and families and social interactions within them.

There are many reasons for marrying, and Americans generally consider romantic love to be the most important. Rural Greeks, however, still arrange marriages as economic exchanges between the bride's family and the groom's, and spouses rarely know each other before they marry (Friedl, 1962). Similar arrangements are found among North America's Blackfeet Indians and the Swazi of southeast Africa (Kuper, 1963; Wissler, 1911). In northern Australia, the marriages of Tiwi girls are arranged before they are even born, and they grow up as members of their future husband's family (Hart and Pilling, 1960).

Many Americans flinch at the idea of basing marriage on economic and political values; but these values offer distinct advantages. Romantic love thrives on rushes of excitement that come with exploring the mysteries of another person (as well as the mystery of why they find *us* so exciting). Married life, however, makes heavy, practical demands on husbands and wives, from earning enough money to live on and deciding how to spend it to cleaning houses, caring for children, and managing relationships with in-laws. Romance consumes enormous amounts of energy, and at the end of a hard day's work, most people do not have enough left over to stay up all night and wait to share a breathtaking sunrise.

Americans also value virginity in brides and sexual fidelity in marriage, particularly on the part of women. In 1984, for example, 87 percent of American adults considered extramarital affairs to be wrong, and in spite of rapidly changing values, 36 percent held similar values about premarital sex (Davis, 1984).

Strong values supporting virginity at marriage are relatively rare among the world's societies—Murdock (1949) estimated that premarital sex is prohibited in less than 5 percent of them. Virginity has no value among Samoans or Trobriand Islanders, and the Mentawei of Indonesia go so far as to require women to give birth before marriage in order to prove they are fertile (Malinowski, 1929; Mead, 1953; Murdock, 1949). Women in Scandinavian countries increasingly choose to have children without marrying the father (Westoff, 1978b), and Blake (1982) believes that similar trends are occurring in the United States as social disapproval of premarital sexual behavior declines and social acceptance of children born out of wedlock increases.

Values about adultery also differ among societies. Eskimos and Australian aborigines consider it to be good manners to share wives with visitors

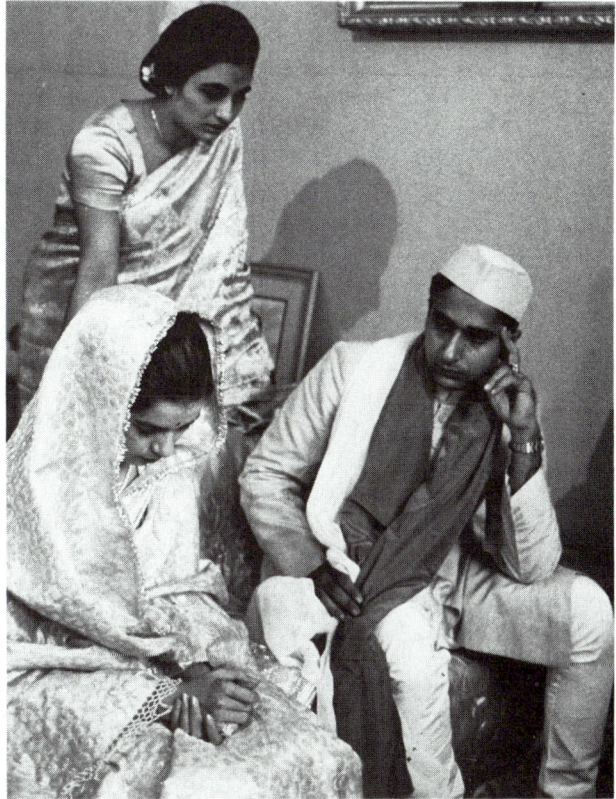

The idea of people choosing their own spouses makes little sense to traditional Indian Hindus whose marriages are arranged for them by their elders.

(Montagu, 1971), and a Nayar wife is free to have sex with any man, so long as he belongs to her husband's caste (Gough, 1974).

Although many societies place a lower value on virginity and fidelity than we do, others value them much more highly. In Muslim societies, for example, a family's honor depends on the virginity of its daughters (Pastner, 1974), and although Trobriand Islanders do not value virginity, they strongly value fidelity between spouses. Virginity was a required condition for marriage among ancient Hebrews, and a bride who failed to show certain signs of virginity on her wedding night (such as telltale spots of blood) was killed and her family was shamed (Brownmiller, 1975). More recently, when thousands of single women in Bangladesh were raped by invading Pakistani soldiers, they lost all prospects of marrying, even though they had no control over the loss of their virginity.

It is important to note that in no society are virginity at marriage and marital fidelity valued more highly in men than in women, and this clearly reflects the subordinate position of women, especially in societies that regard them as actual property of their fathers or husbands.

Other values also play a part in family relationships. Americans, for example, tend to value the self-advancement of individuals more than loyalty to kin, and value marital ties more highly than those to the families in which they grow up. In contrast with children of traditional Japanese families, adult offspring in the United States are expected to make their own decisions about their lives, even when they conflict with their parents' desires, and the independence of husbands, wives, and their children from the influence of parents-in-law is closely guarded.

Values also affect how many children parents have. The cultural value of small families, for example, tends to increase with the level of industrialization. In the United States lower-class families generally have more children than those in the middle and upper classes, but this difference is due more to ineffective birth control than to differences in values. Income makes little difference in the number of children people say they would like to have, only in the number they actually do have (Ryder and Westoff, 1971).

## Attitudes

American attitudes toward marriage and the family are a curious blend of opposites. Regardless of social class, Americans attach intense emotional needs to families and look upon the idea of the family with a great deal of reverence. We worry about whether or not the family is being destroyed by a rapidly changing industrial society; over 90 percent of Americans marry at some time in their lives and although roughly half will experience a divorce, around 65 percent of those who divorce remarry within five years (Grady, 1980; Thornton and Rodgers, 1983; U.S. Census Bureau, 1982). We celebrate Mother's Day and Father's Day and regard holidays such as Thanksgiving, Christmas, and Hanukkah as important family events.

Such positive attitudes, however, exist side by side with negative ones. Hostile jokes about mothers-in-law, "hen-pecked husbands," and "Jewish mothers" are a staple ingredient of American humor, and comedians typically include hostile remarks about spouses in their routines. "I had a rotten childhood" is a phrase familiar to most of us, even if we do not use it to describe ourselves.

We often avoid revealing our negative attitudes toward families—even to ourselves—in part because cultural ideas influence our perceptions of reality and our interactions with others. The ideal of the happy family is so strong that we tend to bury feelings of disappointment, frustration, and bitterness that inevitably arise in intense primary relationships. Perhaps this is why hostile jokes about marriage and families are so popular, for they express negative feelings that we, ourselves, would rather not see or let others see in our own lives.

Cultural ambivalence is, of course, not uncommon in complex societies. The importance of marriage and the family—both as institutions and as basic aspects of people's lives—causes us to make heavy emotional investments in them. Both individuals' needs and the perpetuation and stability of societies require their continued existence in one form or another. We cannot live without them, and we often find it difficult to live with them. From this point of view, the existence of ambivalent cultural attitudes about marriage and the family should not surprise us.

## Norms

Cultural norms affect almost every aspect of social relationships in marriages and families, and generally fall into one of two categories: norms that regulate the formation and dissolution of marriages, and norms that regulate role behavior among kin.

**Marriage Rules** All cultures include **marriage rules** that put limits on whom people may marry, when, and under what conditions. They also have incest rules that prohibit marriage between people who are defined as close relatives, and with the exception of a few ancient societies in Hawaii, Egypt, and Mexico, all societies include parents and their children, as well as brothers and sisters, in that category. Even in Hawaii and Egypt incest was regarded as a privilege reserved for royal families (see Rubin and Byerly, 1983).

United States law prohibits marriages involving parents and their children, siblings, grandparents and grandchildren, aunts and nephews, and uncles and nieces; and 30 states prohibit marriages between first cousins. Shoshone Indians, however, do not distinguish between siblings and cousins, and therefore prohibit marriages that involve even the most distant cousins.

That incest taboos are universal suggests a biological basis for them, but cross-cultural differences in the definition of incest and illogical definitions within cultures show that incest rules are more a matter of culture than biology. In some societies people commit incest if they marry a child of their mother's sister or father's brother; but they are often *expected* to marry a child of their mother's *brother* or father's *sister*. Biologically, the son of a mother's sister is no closer a relative than the son of a mother's brother, but the incest rule clearly defines marriage to the first as revolting and marriage to the second as socially desirable.

Incest taboos are not the only norms that regulate who marries whom. Norms of **endogamy** require people to marry those belonging to their own group. South Africa forbids marriage between people of different races—as did most of the United States until recently—and Nazi Germany forbade marriage between Jews and gentiles. Orthodox Jews may not marry gentiles, and a Balinese woman may not marry a man from a caste lower than her own (Mead, 1968). Norms of **exogamy,** however, require marriage to someone who is culturally defined as an *outsider.*

American norms are generally endogamous in relation to race and religion. In 1977 only 24 percent of American adults said they would feel comfortable if a close relative married someone of a different race, and in 1984 almost a quarter favored laws prohibiting interracial marriage (Davis, 1984). Our marriage rules are exogamous, however, in relation to gender, for the law does not yet provide for marriage between people of the same gender. In contrast, East Africa's Nuer allow childless women to marry younger women and claim their children as heirs (Lévi-Strauss, 1956).

Norms also specify how many people can be married to each other at one time. In his survey of 238 societies, Murdock (1949) found that 18 percent insist on **monogamy**—marriage to only one spouse at a time—while the remainder permit some form of multiple marriage, or **polygamy.** Men are allowed to have more than one wife (**polygyny**) in 80 percent of all societies, including

A Bakhtiari man stands with his three wives and many children.

the Swazi of Africa, the Tiwi of Australia, and, until 1896, American Mormons. Murdock found that women may marry more than one husband (**polyandry**) in only three societies: the Toda of India, the South Pacific Marquesian Islanders, and the Sherpa of Nepal.

Most of these 238 societies are small, preindustrial, and contain a small fraction of the population of the world. Thus, although most societies permit some form of multiple marriage, most people in the world live in societies that expect monogamy.

Once couples marry, norms also affect where they can live. In **matrilocal societies**—such as the American Hopi Indians—married couples are expected to live in or near the wife's mother's household, whereas in **patrilocal societies**—such as Greek villages and Africa's Swazi—they are expected to live in or near the husband's father's household. In **bilocal societies**—such as the Blackfeet Indians—couples may choose between the husband's and the wife's families (but they are not free to choose neither). In contrast, couples may live wherever they want in most industrial societies, which are usually **neolocal,** with couples start-

married couples in the United States involved people of different races (U.S. Census Bureau, 1983c). We also tend to marry people who are similar to us in educational attainment, social class, and religious background. In the late 1970s, 93 percent of Protestants, 89 percent of Jews, and 81 percent of Catholics married people of their own religious faith (Smelser, 1981).

The relative frequency of intermarriage across ethnic, class, and religious boundaries is strongly affected, however, by how homogeneous the population of a community is. Intermarriage is far more common in large heterogeneous cities, for example, then in relatively homogeneous rural communities (Blau, Blum, and Schwartz, 1982).

Although marriage patterns—like those of age, race, and religion—are largely due to cultural values, norms, and attitudes, they are also affected by socially structured relationships that limit our interactions to people who have important statuses in common with us. We live in neighborhoods that tend to be homogeneous with respect to social class, race, and ethnicity; college students are more likely to meet and fall in love with each other than with high school graduates who are already in the labor force.

Just as norms regulate the conditions of marriage, so, too, do they regulate their dissolution. Until quite recently, most U.S. states permitted divorce only under a limited set of circumstances—such as adultery and desertion—and the Catholic Church does not recognize divorce as legitimate although the practice of annulment is often used to accomplish the same end. Only in recent years have states adopted no-fault divorce laws under which spouses can divorce each other by nothing more than mutual consent.

**Norms and Family Relationships** In addition to regulating the formation and dissolution of marriages, norms define role relationships within marriages and families. Incest taboos prohibit sexual relations between close relatives. While most norms about sex set limits on it, marital norms define sexual access to spouses as a right, and refusal to have sex is grounds for divorce in most U.S. states.

Although all societies define sex as a basic part of marriage, norms regulate sexual behavior in sharply different ways. In India and most Muslim

ing new households. Murdock's (1949) survey of 238 societies shows that 73 percent are patrilocal, 18 percent are matrilocal, and 9 percent allow a free choice of residence.

These patterns describe residence rules in most but not all societies. Among western Africa's Ashanti, for example, husbands and wives do not live together at all—each lives with his or her own mother's relatives. Children may eat meals at their father's house and then return to their mother's house for the night (Fortes et al., 1947). In India, once a Nayar husband has spent three nights with his wife, he leaves her, and the wife lives as a member of her mother's household (Gough, 1974).

Together, values and norms affect who marries whom in other ways as well. In most societies, for example, spouses tend to have similar social statuses. Americans generally marry people of similar ages (Leslie, 1982) and rarely marry people of different races. In 1982 just over 1.4 percent of all

countries, for example, husbands may not sexually approach wives who are menstruating or who have recently given birth. In America many states still have laws that specifically prohibit certain sexual behaviors—such as oral and anal sex—even between spouses.

Family norms differ sharply from those found in other groups in their informality and the way in which they are applied. In comparison with other groups, family norms are often applied in different ways to each member depending on his or her personal characteristics and needs. Because families are intimate primary groups, members are more likely to be treated as unique individuals, each with his or her own special needs, abilities, and limitations.

Much of the world outside the family, however, operates under formal norms that apply to everyone who occupies a particular social status. Relationships in school, for example, are secondary, and when children first attend school they are often jarred by the fact that they no longer receive the individual attention and special considerations that they enjoy as family members.

Norms define role relationships, both within marriages and families and between them and the surrounding social environment. Major aspects of these relationships include the distribution of labor, wealth, power, and prestige among family members, and the patterns of interaction that are the social fabric of everyday life in families.

# Varieties of Social Structure

On the microlevel the concept of social structure refers to the statuses we occupy, the roles we perform in relation to other people, and the patterns of interaction that result. On the macrolevel it refers to the numbers of people who occupy different social statuses and the distribution of wealth, power, and prestige that result. In addition, macrostructures also describe relationships among groups, organizations, communities, and societies.

Sociologists study the institutions of marriage and the family on both of these levels of analysis, for what goes on within families is profoundly af-

fected by the relationships between family groups and other institutions. It is no less true, however, that change within societies is affected by what goes on in its families. The following sections describe some basic family structures and then look at variations in their major characteristics: role structures, patterns of interaction, and distributions of wealth and power.

## Basic Elements of Family Structures

Boundaries are basic attributes of all groups since they define who is included as a member. Although kinship includes people who are related to us whether they live with us or not, the concept of a family is generally restricted to people who live together. From this point of view, the composition of families usually takes one of four forms.

A **nuclear** family consists of parents and their natural or adopted children, and this structure describes most families in industrial societies. **Extended** families include additional relatives such as grandparents, aunts, uncles, or cousins.

The remaining two family structures are variations on the nuclear family. **Single-parent** families are nuclear families in which one parent is absent. In **compound** families children are directly related to only one of the two parents. When a divorced parent with custody of children remarries, for example, the resulting family—parent, children, and stepparent—constitutes a compound family.

Even when they are relatively small, compound families can have particularly complicated structures. Both wife and husband may bring to their new family children from prior marriages and then have children together. Thus, compound families have the potential to include a variety of complicated relationships in which children have closer family ties to one parent than the other and, in the most complicated cases, other children have equally strong family ties to both parents.

Although these four structures describe families in most societies, there are other variations as well. In the Israeli kibbutz child care is the responsibility of adult females as a group; and yet, nuclear family ties exist within the larger structure and parents spend time with their children at the end of each day. Among Indonesia's Dani the family as an isolated social group barely exists at all; the community as a whole is the major focus of social life. Spouses, parents, and children spend rela-

■ **Figure 15-1** Some Types of Families

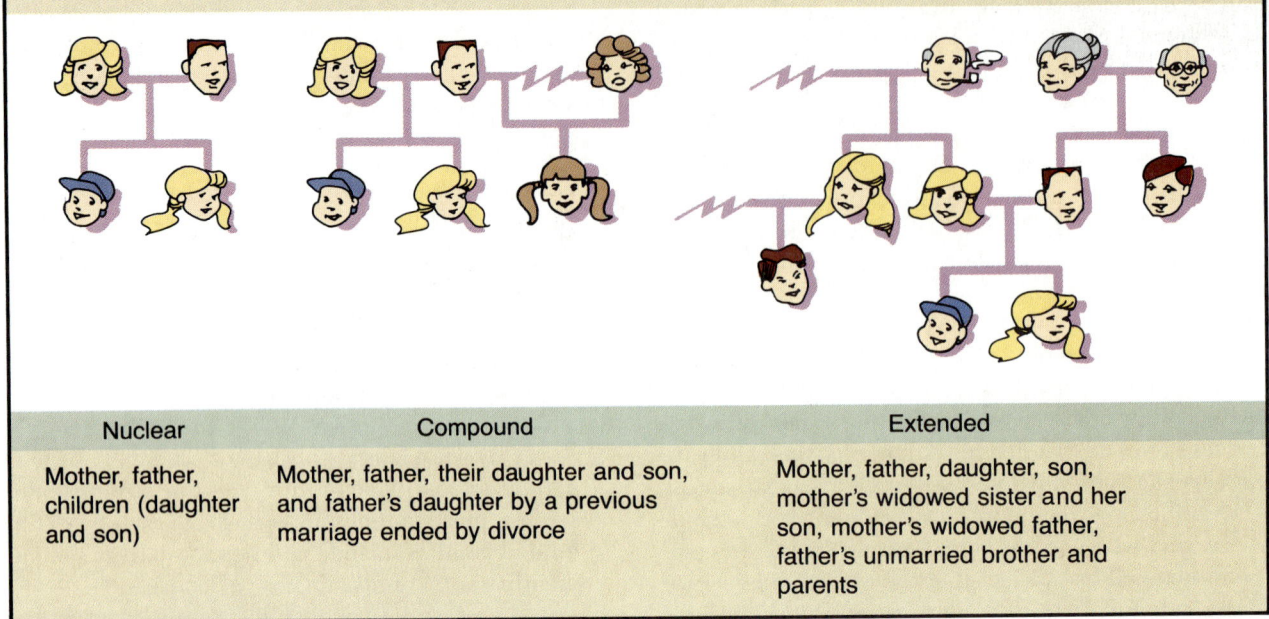

| Nuclear | Compound | Extended |
|---|---|---|
| Mother, father, children (daughter and son) | Mother, father, their daughter and son, and father's daughter by a previous marriage ended by divorce | Mother, father, daughter, son, mother's widowed sister and her son, mother's widowed father, father's unmarried brother and parents |

tively little time with one another, and children move away to live with other relatives by the time they arc ten years old (Heider, 1972).

## Divisions of Labor and Role Structures

The basic statuses in any family are those of husband, wife, mother, father, child, brother, and sister; and the social roles attached to them profoundly affect the behavior and experience of family members. Family role structures vary in complexity from a single parent and child to families that include spouses, children and stepchildren, grandparents, aunts, uncles, and cousins.

Biological reproduction, socialization, consumption, and the regulation of sexual behavior are the most important functions of families in all societies; and in nonindustrial societies the production of goods and services is still a major family function. It is around such functions that family divisions of labor are organized.

In virtually all societies responsibility for child care falls primarily, if not exclusively, on women; but women are also economically active, playing a part in production. The American "ideal" division

of labor—in which women are confined to housework and child care and men are solely responsible for breadwinning—has not been achieved in any society, including our own.

Fifty-one percent of all married American women were in the labor force in 1981. Among those with preschool children, 48 percent were in the labor force, and the participation rate rose to 62 percent among women with school-age children. Divorced mothers had the highest participation rates—fully 84 percent of those with school-age children were in the labor force in 1982 (U.S. Census Bureau, 1983c).

In all societies, then, women contribute heavily to important family functions—reproduction, socialization, and production—while in almost all societies fathers focus most of their attention on production. This is true even in the Israeli kibbutz, for while child-rearing tasks are not the responsibility of each individual mother, child care and other domestic work are still defined as "women's work" (Lesser-Blumberg, 1983). Within this basic structure, however, there is much variation between and within societies.

While the structure of work in Senegal allows women to take their children with them, American mothers usually must choose between work and child care, often having to resort to hiring other women to take care of their children.

Women in industrial societies are not only less likely to be economically active than are women in agricultural, horticultural, or hunter-gatherer societies, but the higher their family's class position, the more likely it is that outsiders will be hired to perform major housekeeping and child-rearing roles.

Child rearing, however, is a complex role, and families often assign different aspects of child rearing to mothers and fathers. In working-class families, mothers have primary responsibility for meeting children's emotional needs, while fathers generally play the role of punisher ("Just you wait until your father gets home") (LeMasters, 1975). Regardless of social class, fathers rarely participate in child care before their children are 18 months old (Entwistle and Doering, 1981); and while fathers are more likely to play with children than care for them, the pattern is the opposite for mothers (Lamb and Goldberg, 1982).

Divisions of labor are different in middle-class families, for both parents are expected to support their children emotionally. These variations reflect different child-rearing values, for middle-class families tend to stress children's emotional development, while working-class families are more concerned with obedience to authority.

Children, of course, are also included in family role structures. In nonindustrial societies, they play full economic roles from an early age, whereas in industrial societies, they are usually confined to schools and nonproductive household chores. Children in lower- and working-class families are far more likely than their middle- and upper-class counterparts to work in order to help support their families.

## Patterns of Interaction

Patterns of interaction consist of who interacts with whom, when, how often and how long, as well as the content of interactions. Like all groups, individual married couples and families develop their own patterns, but because each is part of a social institution, interactions in families often have similar structures.

Unique as each married couple is, for example, interactions between spouses within a society often have similar patterns. In our society nighttime is identified as the "appropriate" time for sex, in part because the structure of work in industrial society requires absence from the home during the day. This pattern may give rise to rigid expectations ("It's night; we're in bed; therefore we should make love") that can convert a natural pleasure into a burdensome social obligation.

In monogamous societies the frequency and intensity of interactions between spouses often profoundly affect their perceptions, values, and attitudes. As Berger and Kellner (1964) suggested, when marriage involves intense and relatively exclusive relationships between wives and husbands, spouses tend to adopt similar beliefs, values, and attitudes, even when they initially disagree. They may enter their marriage disagreeing about everything from politics to the likability of friends; but the longer they live together, the more similar their beliefs, values, and attitudes become.

This occurs for two reasons. First, we all depend on other people to confirm our perceptions of reality and support our values and attitudes, and we tend to depend the most on the people with whom we interact the most. In the United States in particular, when people marry they tend to focus their attention more on each other than on friends they had before marrying. Friends often perceive a husband and wife as a couple—not as two distinct individuals—and no longer feel free to spend time with one without including the other. It is difficult, for example, to invite a married woman to a dinner party without including her husband. Thus, cultural ideas about married couples help produce exclusive and intense interactions between husbands and wives.

Second, the stability of intense and exclusive marital relationships depends in large part on the *perception* of a strong common bond between husbands and wives. Constant disagreement produces a strain in relationships, and this encourages the creation of a "common ground" on which spouses can live together in relative peace.

Marital interactions are also affected by major structural characteristics of families. In matrilocal societies—where married couples join the wife's mother's household—the husband occupies the status of "outsider." This undermines his position in the family, contributes to his being left out of important interactions, and makes him vulnerable to coalitions formed against him by family "insiders." All these observations, of course, apply equally to wives in patrilocal societies.

Patterns of interaction in families are even more complex than those between spouses. In American nuclear families, where child care is the responsibility of the wife alone, children tend to interact far more with mothers than with fathers. In many cases mothers are children's only source of adult contact and, as a result, mothers frequently feel "overloaded" and children become heavily dependent on a single adult. This problem is especially acute in single-parent families—which made up almost 12 percent of all families in 1982—and affects both single mothers and single fathers (U.S. Census Bureau, 1983c).

Such patterns of interaction help explain why children often feel jealous of newborn babies with whom they must compete for the parent's attention. If the family structure includes more than one adult who is available to children, they are less likely to feel that the attention paid to newborns necessarily causes a loss of attention for them. In extended families the availability of several adults means that children have more than one adult to choose from, and no one adult must bear the entire burden alone. This is also true of societies—such as the Dani of Indonesia and the Israeli kibbutz—in which entire communities share the responsibility of child care.

The structure of compound families can create very complex patterns of interaction (Cherlin and Furstenberg, 1983; Matilda Riley, 1983). Because children have a closer tie with a natural parent, they may form coalitions with that parent against the stepparent and defy a stepparent's authority ("You aren't my *real* mother"). Stepparents may feel "left out" of family jokes, secrets, and memories that were created before they joined the family, and often feel in competition with the natural parent who no longer lives with the children.

A large body of research (summarized in Hess, 1970) shows that family interactions vary considerably among social classes. In general, the higher a family's social class position, the more likely parents are to talk with their children, reason with them, use complex language in talking to them, express warmth and affection, and avoid physical punishment. These social class differences in family interactions have been found in a variety of societies, and among both blacks and whites in the United States (Hess and Shipman, 1965; Kamii and Radin, 1967).

## Power, Matriarchy, and Patriarchy

Who rules the family? In a **patriarchy** husbands are culturally defined as the heads of major institutions, including the family; in a **matriarchy** women are the official heads of their families, but actual power resides in the wife's eldest brother; and in **egalitarian marriages** power is shared equally between husbands and wives. In spite of variations among individual families, almost all existing societies are patriarchies. Even in matrilineal societies—such as the Trobriand Islanders—which trace kinship through the mother's family, family power structures are patriarchal. There is, in fact, some debate over whether or not there has ever been a society in which women held most of the power (Bamberger, 1974).

Although patriarchy describes family institutions in most societies, the distribution of power varies considerably both among societies and among individual families. This depends on a variety of cultural and social structural factors. The cultural valuing of egalitarian marriage, for example, tends to be stronger in the middle and upper classes than in the working and lower classes. This may be due in part to the fact the husbands in higher classes have more power outside the home than lower-class husbands do, and therefore have less need to use the family as a social situation in which they can feel powerful. Although middle- and upper-class families tend to be more egalitarian, they are still patriarchal, and husbands generally control most important decisions, such as what kind of car to buy or where the family will live.

In all societies individuals' authority depends in part on their contribution to production, and the productive roles of husbands and wives strongly affect their authority in marriages. In the United States wives who work tend to have more power than wives who do not; and the higher a wife's education or income is, the more power she tends to have in family decision making (Gillespie, 1971; Hood, 1983).

Residence rules also affect authority relations in families. In a matrilocal society a husband's authority is undermined by the fact that his wife's kin can "gang up" on him. In patrilocal societies, however, the patriarchal dominance of men is increased enormously by the wife's isolation from her family, and her greatest source of power is to simply leave the marriage and return to her parents' house. From this point of view, matrilocal residence supports egalitarian marriage by giving the wife more authority in a patriarchal society. Societies that allow married couples to freely choose where they will live also support equality by separating husbands and wives from their families.

Keep in mind that the concepts of matriarchy, patriarchy, and egalitarianism refer to cultural models of the family and prevailing patterns of authority, and although some women in patriarchal societies may be in charge of families, this does not mean that matriarchy prevails. If we describe single-parent families headed by divorced women as "matriarchal," for example, we distort the basic meaning of matriarchy, for these women dominate by default, not because society defines women as the legitimate heads of families. Single-parent families headed by women deviate from the American cultural ideal.

This distinction is important because single-parent families are increasingly common in the United States, particularly among blacks. Without this distinction, we might conclude that black families are more matriarchal than white families simply because they are more likely to be headed by women. Among intact families, however, patriarchy prevails among both blacks and whites.

The preceding sections describe basic structural characteristics of families and how they affect relationships and interaction within families. As groups, however, families occupy positions in relation to their surrounding societies, and one of the most important of these is their position in systems of social stratification.

## Family Wealth and Power in Stratified Societies

In hunter-gatherer and horticultural societies community life is organized around kinship ties, and the family is the most powerful institution. Even in agrarian societies political authority rests largely in family units. Industrial societies, however, are too large and complex to be dominated by even the largest kin group, and authority lies in institutions outside the family—in schools, governments, courts, corporations, churches, and the professions. Legal norms prohibit preferential treatment for relatives in occupations and the legal system.

Families, in short, are not powerful groups in industrial societies.

This does not mean that all families have equal amounts of power. Inequality of wealth and income among families is common, and wealth is a source of power. Engels (1891) went so far as to argue that the existence of family units in communities and societies is a basic cause of social stratification itself. It is only when families can accumulate wealth and have an interest in passing it on to their heirs that intense competition within societies comes into being.

The chapters in Part IV describe a variety of social statuses—such as race, ethnicity, gender, age, education, and occupation—that affect the distribution of income in stratified societies, and these characteristics affect inequality among families as much as they affect inequality among individuals. The structure of families, however, in addition to the social statuses of their individual members, also affects the distribution of income.

In the United States, for example, family income is greatest in intact families (especially if both parents work) and single-parent families headed by men. The families with the lowest income are those headed by unmarried women, a pattern that holds regardless of race (take a moment to study Table 15-1 carefully).

Clearly, families headed by unmarried women—whether they are divorced, single, or widowed—are in a poor economic position, especially if they are nonwhite. In comparison with intact families, families headed by white females are over four times as likely to live in poverty and over seven times as likely to depend on food stamps. These differences are less severe among blacks, primarily because black families are crowded into a much narrower income range (U.S. Census Bureau, 1983c).

## The Social Ecology of Family Life

Ecology focuses on the physical aspects of social life: the processes of birth, death, and migration through which populations grow and distribute themselves, and the ways in which societies use

**Table 15-1**

Median Family Income, by Race and Family
Structure (United States, 1980)

| FAMILY STRUCTURE | All Families | FAMILY INCOME Whites | Blacks | Hispanics |
|---|---|---|---|---|
| Intact married couple | $23,100 | $23,500 | $18,700 | $17,400 |
| Wife works | $27,000 | * | * | * |
| Wife does not work | $19,800 | * | * | * |
| Male head—wife absent | $17,500 | $19,800 | $13,600 | $13,900 |
| Female head—husband absent | $10,400 | $12,300 | $ 7,700 | $ 7,200 |

Source: U.S. Census Bureau, 1982.

*= Not available.

physical environments to produce goods and satisfy material needs. The ecological perspective is basic to any study of marriage and family institutions since reproduction, production, and consumption are among their most important social functions.

## Reproduction: Marriage, Family, and Society

All societies use marriage and the family to regulate sexual behavior, and this, in turn, affects the rate at which children are born and populations grow. Most societies both limit sexual intercourse to those who are married and expect married couples to have children. Thus, cultural and structural aspects of marriage and the family affect birth rates and population growth in several important ways.

The more common marriage is and the younger the age at marriage, the higher birth rates tend to be. As of the 1970s, for example, an estimated 44 percent of all African females 15 to 19 years old were married, and in countries of Western Africa the estimate is 70 percent. By comparison, only 11 percent of American females 15 to 19 years old were married in 1980, and in European countries the percentages were typically less than 10 percent (Population Reference Bureau, 1980).

Birth rates also depend on the degree to which married couples limit childbearing. Contraception is used by 64 percent of married women in the United States, and this results in longer periods between births and fewer births over the life cycle. Between 1955 and 1975 the percentage of women who had a child within two years of their first marriage dropped from 68 to 48 percent, and birth rates among married women 20 to 24 years old dropped by 50 percent. The result has been a steady decline in the average size of American families. Between 1967 and 1982 the percentage of women 30 to 34 years old who expect to have two or fewer children increased from 31 to 68 percent, and the percentage who expect to bear four or more children dropped from 55 percent to 12 (U.S. Census Bureau, 1983c).

While Americans are delaying marriage and childbearing in increasing numbers, men and women are more likely than before to live together without marrying and to have children without marrying. Between 1960 and 1983 the number of unmarried couples increased from just over 100,000 to almost 2 million (Glick and Norton, 1979; U.S. Census Bureau, 1983a). In the same period birth rates increased by 29 percent among all unmarried women and by 76 percent among unmarried teenagers, the latter increase being due largely to increased sexual activity among young people coupled with a failure to use effective contraception (U.S. Census Bureau, 1981; Zelnick and Kantner, 1976 and 1978). Thus, as the institutions of marriage and the family lose control over sexual behavior and reproduction, birth rates are pressured upward.

Values and norms about family life also affect birth rates, and as they change, birth rates change with them (see Mason, 1982). Hindus in India's West Bengal, for example, prohibit sexual intercourse between husbands and wives for almost 100 days out of every year, and in some societies intercourse is forbidden for two or three years after childbirth (Nag, 1962, 1967). Before 1975, birth rates among American Catholics were higher than among non-Catholics primarily because Catholicism forbids the use of contraceptives and encourages childbearing. Since 1975, however, Catholics have increasingly ignored their Church's ban on contraceptive use, and their birth rates are virtually equal to those of other major religious groups (Westoff and Jones, 1979).

Finally, the size of families is strongly related to the nonfamily statuses that wives and mothers occupy. In both nonindustrial and industrial societies women who work in paid employment outside the home tend to have fewer children than women who do not, especially if their work is highly paid (Weller, 1977; Weller and Bouvier, 1981). In addition, the more highly educated women are, the fewer children they tend to have. Education lowers fertility not only by increasing the chances that women will work outside the home, but also by delaying the entry of women into marriage and increasing the chances that they will never marry (Abu-Lughod, 1965; U.S. Census Bureau, 1983c).

Thus, the institutions of marriage and the family affect birth rates and population growth; but changing birth rates, death rates, and age structures also have important effects on individual families and the institution of the family.

## Birth Rates, Death Rates, and the Structure of Family Life

As birth and death rates fall and families grow smaller and people live longer, the structure of the family tends to change. In colonial America the average married woman bore an estimated eight children during a lifetime that, by current standards, was relatively short (Grabill, Kiser, and Whelpton, 1959). Thus, each woman could expect to have very few years during which she was not either pregnant or responsible for young children.

By comparison, average lifetime fertility among today's married women is just over two children apiece, and life expectancy is far higher than it was in colonial times. This means that married women spend a relatively small portion of their lives bearing and caring for children. By the time most married women reach their early thirties, their children are in school, and these mothers have an average of 43 more years of life ahead of them (U.S. Census Bureau, 1983c).

These population changes encourage women to perform nonfamilial roles, especially in professional and other career occupations that require years of training and involve steady advancement over the life course. This, in turn, breaks the monopoly that husbands have had over the breadwinner role ever since the Industrial Revolution separated the family—and mothers—from production. As women increase their share of family breadwinning, they tend to increase their prestige and power in marriages and in families.

Falling birth rates have had the additional effect of decreasing the number of relatives people have. As children, today's elderly had an average of 5 siblings, 20 uncles and aunts, and perhaps as many as 40 cousins. Children born in the last decade, however, have on the average less than half that number of relatives with whom they can form close ties (Bane, 1976). As the number of kinship ties falls, so does the importance of extended kinship networks in everyday life.

Thus, population processes and family structures affect one another in a variety of ways. The ecological perspective also pays attention to how technology and modes of production affect the institutions through which societies accomplish important goals.

## Technology, Production, and Families

From an ecological perspective, social institutions change in response to changes in physical environments and the ways societies use them to produce goods. As a basic social institution, the family is no exception; it has changed dramatically over the last several centuries in response to industrialization.

Because their populations are small and their division of labor is relatively simple, hunter-gatherer societies organize social life almost exclusively around kinship ties (Coon, 1971; Service, 1966). Economic production, education, religious observances, law, and government are all administered by and depend on membership in kinship groups. The extended family is the source of individual rights, responsibilities, and social identities, and marriage is based more on economic and political exchange than on the preference of individual men and women.

By comparison, the greater size and complexity of agricultural societies means that each society includes a variety of kinship groups, none of which can dominate all aspects of social life. Even here, however, family membership is closely related to wealth and political power, for some families have virtual monopolies on political offices that they pass from one generation to the next.

The Industrial Revolution rapidly accelerated a process that began centuries before: kinship ties were losing their importance as families lost control over societies. This ecological change profoundly affected families in important ways and continues to affect families in societies that are beginning to industrialize today.

As production shifts to factories and relies on more sophisticated technologies, child labor loses its value and large families become a liability rather than an asset. Birth rates began a steady decline in Europe in the early 1800s and somewhat later in the United States—well over a century before the invention of effective medical contraceptives. Thompson and Whelpton (1933) estimated that the U.S. birth rate was 55 births per 1,000 people at the end of the eighteenth century, but by 1900 it had fallen to 30 per 1,000 (Weller and Bouvier, 1981).

While hunter-gatherer and horticultural societies revolve around the primary ties of kinship, industrial societies are dominated by secondary relationships and formal bureaucracies; and many of the functions once performed by the family are transferred to other social institutions. Responsibility for educating children shifts to schools; wealth and power in the public world depend more on individual performance and characteristics than on family ties. While discrimination in favor of relatives in politics and employment is expected in preindustrial societies, it is commonly outlawed (although not unknown) in industrial societies. Kinship groups no longer control the passage or enforcement of laws or the administration of justice.

As vital social functions are transferred from the family to other institutions, the importance of economics and politics in the formation of marriages declines. This is one reason why romantic love is far more important in industrial than in preindustrial societies (Goode, 1959). As a basis for marriage, romantic love allows individuals to separate from the families they grew up in. Young people no longer have to wait patiently to inherit the positions held by their elders, and can escape their parents' authority at a relatively early age (Cherlin, 1981). Romantic love also promises to provide the emotional support once provided by tightly bonded extended families, and encourages individuals to marry in societies in which marriage is no longer required to preserve the economic and political dominance of kinship groups.

The extended family's loss of control over marriage increases the power of women. In agrarian societies, for example, women were property to be exchanged by families for economic and political gain. In industrial societies, however, women are freer to choose their own husbands and have more bargaining power in the "marriage market." This, of course, is only one aspect of social power, and industrialization has certainly not led to equal standing for women (see Chapter 13).

Industrialization also creates social conditions in which the importance of nuclear families increases at the expense of extended families (Goode, 1963). Industrial societies need workers who can move from one place to another with relative ease as new industries are built, and the loose ties of nuclear families to relatives increases their geographic mobility. Industries also need people who are willing to be *socially* mobile—who will, for example, break away from the lower-class occupations of their parents and strive for middle-class jobs.

Finally, industrialization and the rise of the nuclear family affect the division of labor within

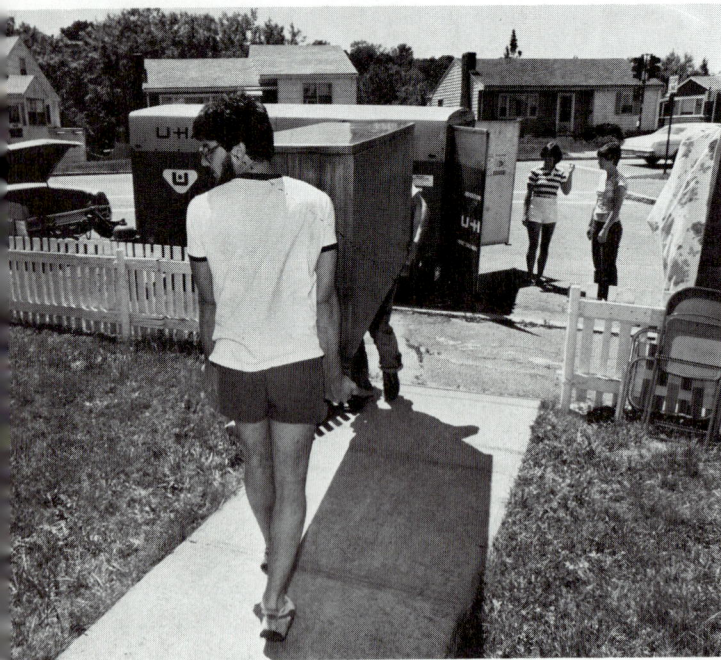

The importance of geographic mobility for social mobility promotes the nuclear family structure's relatively weak ties to extended kin.

families. Among Alaskan Eskimos and the Gusii of Kenya, for example, women work in or near their homes and strap their infants to their backs while they work (Montagu, 1971; Whiting, 1963). In industrial societies, however, production and the home are separate, and it is difficult for both parents to work outside the home (Cherlin, 1983). As a result, child care and productive work are more specialized in industrial than in preindustrial societies: child care is the exclusive province of women, and men are the primary breadwinners.

Over a period of many centuries, then, the family has been dramatically transformed from an extended kinship network that dominated social life to a relatively small primary group whose most important functions are to meet the emotional needs of its members, care for young children, and regulate sexual behavior. The geographically fixed extended families of hunter-gatherer and horticultural societies—whose culture and socially structured relationships varied little from one generation to the next—have been replaced in industrial societies by families that are both geographically and socially mobile.

This analysis reveals an additional consequence of ecological change that profoundly complicates family life. The powerful extended family of preindustrial societies has been largely replaced by a variety of social institutions such as schools and government, and the nuclear family in industrial societies exists through a complex set of relationships with these institutions. What goes on in families is affected by what goes on in economic, educational, and government institutions, for families are not isolated groups insulated from the outside world. They are a vital part of the social environment, charged with the responsibility for reproducing that environment in new generations. As such, they both affect and are affected by surrounding social institutions.

## Marriage, Family, and Society

As institutions, marriage and the family are defined by the functions they perform in relation to social goals. This does not mean, however, that the social characteristics of families are always functional. Nor does it mean that conflict does not exist, both within families and between them and society as a whole.

### Functions and Dysfunctions

While marriage and the family are defined in terms of major functions discussed earlier in this chapter, particular cultural and structural aspects of family life—such as incest taboos and marriage rules—are often functional for both families and societies (Mead, 1968).

Incest taboos draw clear group boundaries that distinguish close kin from everyone else and promote family stability by preventing hostility and jealousy among family members. They help keep family structures unambiguous and clear, and this minimizes status strain. If a mother and son had a daughter, for example, the son would be the newborn's father and her brother. By forcing people to look outside the family for sexual partners, incest taboos also encourage social ties between families and the growth and solidarity of larger kinship networks and communities.

Incest taboos are related to rules of exogamy that require people to marry outside their group, and exogamy performs an important function for communities. Among hunter-gatherers, for example, marriage between people of different communities helps establish cooperative political and economic ties (Service, 1962).

Endogamous marriage can also be functional because by restricting marriage to group members outside the immediate family, it keeps group boundaries clear and helps maintain group solidarity. Thus, endogamy among Orthodox Jews helps ensure the perpetuation of their religious and cultural traditions and strengthens the in-group loyalties that support them against anti-Semitism. Ironically, Nazi Germany also imposed endogamous marriage to isolate Jews from the rest of German society.

The dysfunctions of the cultural and structural characteristics of families illustrate again that all social arrangements have costs as well as benefits. The nuclear family, for example, is by definition isolated from extended kinship networks, and this means that its members depend on relatively few people for emotional and material support. If a spouse dies in an extended family, other adults are available to assume important roles in production and child care; but in nuclear families the absence of a spouse through death or divorce can cause a major crisis that threatens the survival of the family unit itself.

Extreme interdependency among nuclear family members may create severe emotional strain. We spend most of our lives in secondary relationships and often rely on the family as our main source of emotional support. This makes nuclear families particularly vulnerable to emotional overload, and the intensity of family relationships may breed hostility and bitterness as well as love (A. Skolnick, 1975).

The structure of the nuclear family—unlike that of the extended family—excludes the elderly from meaningful roles, and this is dysfunctional for the well-being of the elderly and for society as well. Thousands of widowed, elderly parents spend their last years alone or in institutions, and even those who live with their children's nuclear families often find that they have no meaningful part to play in family life. In Japan, however, the extended family is more common, and this not only provides meaningful family roles for many elderly people, but—since live-in relatives provide alternative child-care arrangements—also supports

women working outside the home (Morgan and Hirosima, 1983).

Thus, although the nuclear family is functional for many goals in industrial societies, it brings with it social costs. Its structure contributes to family vulnerability, instability, and strain, and leaves elderly people in a "roleless" position. Like all social structures, its form produces both positive and negative consequences.

## The Conflict Perspective on Marriage and the Family

While the functional view focuses on positive and negative consequences of cultural ideas and social structures, the conflict perspective focuses on social institutions as arenas in which struggles for wealth, power, and prestige take place. From this perspective, conflict takes place both within marriages and families and between them and society, and is related to the social characteristics of institutions in different societies and historical periods.

In lower- and middle-class families relationships among family members are strongly affected by the family's position in relation to economic institutions. In industrial societies—whether capitalist or communist—workers have little control over work conditions that often have negative effects on family life. Many industries, for example, operate 24 hours a day. Although this increases industrial efficiency and profits, it creates severe strains on the families of both blue- and white-collar workers (Lipset, Trow, and Coleman, 1956; Rowbotham, 1973). Working spouses often must be away from their families during the night, and repeated changes in work shift assignments subject individuals to a variety of negative effects—such as insomnia and chronic fatigue.

Work conditions also affect families in the middle and upper-middle classes. Managers are under intense pressure to care more about their jobs than their families, and because their jobs often take them away from home, they must choose between family life and the rewards of their occupations (Pleck, 1977). Given the emotional needs that nuclear families are expected to satisfy, it is easy to see how industrial economies create strains within families by calling upon workers to neglect their families in some ways in the name of supporting their families.

A more important effect of economic institutions on marriages and families lies in the structure of the economy itself. In industrial societies families do not produce the goods they consume and must sell their labor power for money they can exchange for goods and services. In both capitalist and socialist societies, however, families do not receive a substantial portion of what is produced by their members' labor power—a large percentage is kept as profit in capitalist societies or is appropriated by the state in socialist societies. The resulting strain on families is inevitable, for whatever amount workers may be paid to make a product, they must pay far more than that to buy it.

One result of this is that most families in industrial societies have a hard time making ends meet and must increasingly depend on the earnings of both spouses. In 1890, for example, only 14 percent of all women in the labor force were married. In 1982, however, 59 percent of women in the labor force were married, and almost 54 percent of these were also mothers (U.S. Census Bureau, 1975a, 1983c).

Most goods and services produced in industrial societies—food, clothing, appliances, housing, and medical care—are consumed by families, and this means that the way in which goods and services are produced and distributed affects life in families, whose members must participate in the economy in order to survive. The stresses and strains that workers experience are inevitably reflected in the families that depend on their occupational success (Rubin, 1976). In a study of urban husbands and wives, Blood and Wolfe (1960) found that disagreements about money made up 42 percent of marital disputes, while sex, in-laws, religion, politics, and family roles together accounted for only 22 percent.

It thus should not surprise us to find that marital instability goes right along with financial instability. Goode (1976) estimated that marriages involving service workers and laborers are twice as likely to be unstable as are those involving professional and technical workers; and such differences are found in many industrial societies (Goode, 1962).

It is ironic that the family's most important function as an institution is to reproduce the very society that often has profoundly negative effects on families (Landes, 1977–1978). Families are not simply isolated groups that are affected by social conditions. Whether they live in Manhattan or Moscow, parents who raise children to obey authorities and be "good workers" reproduce not only people, but the social relationships that create and sustain social inequality. In turn, they also help reproduce and perpetuate the stressful conditions under which their children will, themselves, marry and raise families. In this way, the victims of social inequality are expected by their society to perpetuate the social conditions that victimize them and their children.

## Family Disorganization

A group is organized if all its statuses are occupied by people who adequately perform their roles. Thus, a nuclear family is organized if it includes a mother and father and children, all of whom perform their roles. **Family disorganization** occurs either when an important status is unoccupied or when one or more family members fail to perform their roles adequately. Family disorganization is of interest to sociologists both because it affects a family's ability to perform important social functions and because it affects the lives of family members.

Structural incompleteness of families takes a variety of forms, the most common of which is separation of spouses through divorce. It also occurs, however, when women have children without marrying at all or when one spouse dies. Inadequate role performance also takes many forms—from mental or physical breakdowns or a breadwinner's unemployment to an "empty shell" family

---

**PUZZLES:**

### WHY DO FAMILIES PLAY SO ROUGH?

If you wanted to avoid being physically assaulted, what common group would you avoid?

The answer is the family. This chapter explains why.

in which members go through the motions of performing task roles while totally ignoring the emotional roles that make up the core of primary relationships (Goode, 1976).

Divorce was outlawed in Catholic Europe during the Middle Ages and in Puritan New England, and most family disorganization was caused by the death of a spouse (Stephens, 1963). In mid-eighteenth-century Sweden, roughly half of all marriages ended because one spouse died, as did approximately 60 percent of all marriages in France and 70 percent of all marriages in India (Lenski and Lenski, 1982).

As death rates fell over the past century, divorce became the major form of family disorganization. Between 1860 and 1982 the divorce rate in the United States increased from 1.2 per 1,000 married couples to 22.8 per 1,000—a nineteenfold increase (Thornton and Freedman, 1983; U.S. Census Bureau, 1975a). In 1984, 31 percent of Americans who had ever been married had also experienced a divorce or legal separation (Davis, 1984), and an estimated 50 percent of recent marriages will end in divorce if current rates continue (Weed, 1982). None of this means that marriage has lost its appeal among Americans, however, for as we mentioned earlier, around 65 percent of those who divorce remarry within five years.

## Understanding Divorce

Sociological research has much to say about the causes of rising divorce rates. Once again, the explanation rests on three key sociological concepts: culture, social structure, and ecology.

**Divorce and Culture**  Just as cultural beliefs, values, norms, and attitudes affect the organization of marriages and families, so, too, do they affect their disorganization. As one would expect, divorce rates tend to be highest in societies whose norms restrict it the least and whose values and attitudes place little social stigma on divorced people.

Socially legitimate grounds for divorce vary enormously among cultures (Stephens, 1963).

Stinginess and laziness are legitimate grounds among the Hopi Indians, and the Iban of Borneo may divorce a spouse if they see a bad omen or have an ominous dream. In patrilocal societies the husband's parents can initiate divorce by simply sending his wife home if they do not like her. Di-

---

**Voices:**
### Divorce—A Solution and a Problem

When we children were at home during these years between 1969 and the mid-1970s, my parents would have dinner together at the long table in front of the downstairs fireplace as they always had, but they could rarely get through the meal without a fight. She would leave the table in tears, or he would get up in a cold, self-righteous rage. His drinking had begun to have remarkable physical effects. His speech slurred and his step was unsteady. Often after he left the table we would hear him stamp and stumble up the stairs and then there would be a series of crashes and thuds as he tried to get down the narrow hall and up the two steps into the bedroom. Both of my parents began to talk a lot about other people in their lives—people who understood them. They both confided at length and in explicit detail to me, or anyone else who would sit still long enough to listen. Not only did I wish they wouldn't; I began to wish they would get divorced. A tension seemed to be building up between them that was almost intolerable—certainly more intolerable than the wreck of their marriage, the shattering of our family, and the sale of what we jokingly referred to as "the ancestral homestead." The house was at the center of things. My father had turned over the soil, taken down dead trees, cleared the brush, and paid off the mortgage. My mother had planned and nurtured the flower gardens, furnished the rooms, fed the dogs, established her life and work there. Neither of them would leave. It came to seem a matter of angry stubbornness rather than of any kind of virtue.

Source: Cheever, *Home Before Dark*, 1984.

vorce rates in nineteenth-century Japan were very high for this reason (Goode, 1976).

In some societies—such as the Navaho Indians—divorce involves no elaborate public ceremonies (Stephens, 1963). In pre-Civil War New England, however, married couples could not divorce without a special act of the state legislature (Goode, 1976). Divorce rates in the United States have risen as the legal grounds for divorce have expanded and become less specific. In the nineteenth century the only grounds for divorce were desertion, adultery, and physical abuse, but since then "abuse" has been expanded to include mental cruelty, and the new grounds of incompatibility include virtually any behavior that one spouse dislikes in the other (Bane, 1976). Almost half of all the states in the United States now have "no-fault" laws that allow couples to divorce without proving that either spouse was guilty of behavior that "deserves divorce" as a punishment.

Divorce has also been made easier by changing values about marriage, the family, and individual happiness. In societies that base marriage and the family primarily on economics and alliances between different kinship groups, the fact that spouses are unhappy with each other is relatively unimportant. In industrial America, however, marriage is valued primarily as a relationship that satisfies the emotional needs of individuals, and when those needs are not met divorce is culturally defined as a legitimate solution.

As values and norms about divorce have changed in the United States, so, too, have attitudes. It was not that long ago, for example, that no divorced person could hope to run for the office of president and win; but that changed with the election of Ronald Reagan. Until the 1960s most Americans looked on divorce as a shameful admission of failure, and divorced women were assumed to be "loose," "wild," and sexually promiscuous. These stigmas have lost most of their importance.

**Divorce and Social Structure** The structural causes of rising divorce rates take three forms: the changing relationship of married couples to kinship networks, the changing internal structure of nuclear families, and increased visibility of divorced people in the population.

First, the more people a marriage involves, the higher the pressures are against divorce. Among the Subanum in the Philippines, for example, marriage involves economic exchange between two families, including a "bride-price" paid by the groom's family to the bride's. If couples divorce and the wife is found to be at fault, her family must repay up to twice the bride-price to the husband's family and turn over the children and most of the couple's property to them. Among the Navaho marriage joins two kinship networks and divorce thus threatens to disrupt important social ties (Stephens, 1963). In such cases extended families often oppose divorce because they stand to lose a great deal. In industrial societies, however, extended families lose relatively little when couples divorce and so offer less opposition.

The isolation of nuclear families from extended kin also makes divorce more likely by increasing the emotional and financial insecurity of married couples. In prerevolutionary China, the relationship between spouses was less important than the contribution of each to the extended family, and spouses depended on a large set of family relationships to satisfy their individual needs (Goode, 1976). Married couples in industrial societies, however, are both more independent and more isolated: spouses must depend on each other to satisfy important needs, and in times of emotional or financial stress they can count on relatively little social and material support from kinship networks.

Paradoxically, the increased importance of the nuclear family has contributed to higher divorce rates in some societies and lower divorce rates in others. In Japan, for example, divorce rates have fallen as parents-in-law have lost the power to send their daughters-in-law home. In the United States, where in-laws never had the power to initiate divorce, the isolation of nuclear families has had just the opposite effect on divorce rates.

A second structural cause of rising divorce rates lies in the changing structure of the nuclear family itself and its relationship with the economy. In extended families production is shared among many adults, and divorce has little effect on either spouse's ability to survive. Each can simply return to the extended family from which they came. Divorce in nuclear families, however, threatens the financial security of both spouses (but particularly of wives, who generally have little income of their own). Thus, divorce rates normally drop during economic depressions, because most couples cannot afford to separate (Jacobson, 1959).

Divorce rates increase as wives participate more heavily in the labor force and become more financially independent of their husbands (Kephart, 1981). Part of this is due to the increased strains that occur when both husbands and wives pursue careers. When both spouses are heavily committed to demanding jobs, conflicts inevitably occur around the performance of domestic work, and although many couples succeed in creating marriages that are more egalitarian, it is, at best, a difficult and challenging process (Wallston et al., 1978).

Husbands who earn less than their wives often feel threatened. If one spouse wants to accept a job offer in a distant city, the other must confront the choice of whether or not to move at the expense of an existing job. In some cases, husbands and wives decide to live in different places—maintaining a "commuter marriage"—in order to keep their relationship intact while pursuing their occupational goals (Gerstel, 1976; Ngai, 1974). How the stability of such marriages compares with that of other marriages is yet to be seen.

Family finances and economic relationships between husbands and wives help explain historical changes in social class differences in divorce rates. In the nineteenth century, when divorce was expensive and difficult to obtain, it was more common in the upper class than in the middle and lower classes (Bane, 1976). Since that time, however, legal costs of divorce have dropped sharply and are within the reach of a much larger number of lower- and middle-class couples, and divorce is now more common among lower-class couples than among those in the upper class.

As divorce has become more accessible to all classes, other legal changes encourage upper-middle and upper-class couples to stay together. In particular, community property laws force divorcing couples to split their property evenly, and wealthy couples often own valuable assets such as

stock and real estate. This means that both spouses—but husbands in particular—have a great deal to lose in a divorce and may stay with an otherwise unattractive marriage (Goode, 1976).

The third structural change that helps explain rising divorce rates is the sheer increase in the number—and therefore the visibility—of divorced people. When divorce was rare, people who contemplated it correctly believed that such a decision would place them in a small, deviant minority. Their only reference group consisted of married couples, and they got little support for the decision to end a marriage.

As more and more people occupy the status of "divorced person," however, divorced people are increasingly visible to married people who contemplate divorce, and this provides unhappy spouses with a new reference group on which they can model their behavior and from which they can draw emotional support and social approval.

**Divorce, Population, and Ecology** Changes in population and ecology have contributed to rising divorce rates by making divorce easier and by making lifelong marriage harder.

When nuclear families produce most of the goods and services they need, each spouse needs the other to perform important productive work. Prior to the late 1800s most American families lived on farms, and it took at least two adults working together to produce enough to support them. A man who divorced his wife lost far more than a companion, for he also lost a producer of a variety of essential goods such as food, cloth, clothing, and pottery.

By shifting production out of the home, industrialization creates economies in which people work for money that they use to buy what other people produce. This means, in turn, that wives and husbands can survive by their own labor, and this weakens the economic dependency of spouses on each other. As their dependency on each other lessens, so does the material cost of divorce.

In industrialized societies, in which long lives are becoming the rule rather than the exception, "'Til death do us part" is an increasingly difficult commitment to honor.

Population trends also affect divorce rates by making lifelong marriage more difficult. In the eighteenth century, adult death rates were relatively high—especially among women of child-bearing age—and people rarely spent their entire lives with a single spouse. Thus, high death rates contributed to relatively low divorce rates by ending marriages before the need for divorce ever arose. Death rates have fallen sharply over the last century, however, and this means that people who married in their early twenties could look forward to roughly 50 years of married life (U.S. Census Bureau, 1983c). This inevitably increases the chance that divorce will occur, because it is simply much harder to spend 50 years with one person than it is to live together for 10 or 20 years.

Population changes, therefore, have made "'Til death do us part" an increasingly difficult ideal to achieve.

## Family Violence

One of the most important functions of families is to provide a safe haven for its members. The Constitution of the United States protects us in our homes from unlawful intrusions. Families, we believe, should be groups that take care of us, and for this reason family violence is particularly disturbing—and difficult to control.

Straus, Gelles, and Steinmetz (1980) conservatively estimated that 8 million Americans are assaulted by family members each year. Sixteen percent of all married couples hit each other, and in a third of these cases, violence includes severe kicking, punching, or biting. One study found that 8 percent of college freshmen reported having been physically injured by their parents during the preceding year (Mulligan, 1977). In the United States between 20 and 40 percent of all murder victims are killed by members of their own family (Curtis, 1974); and more police officers are killed trying to stop domestic violence than in any other situation (Parnas, 1967).

These data paint a picture of American family life that is a far cry from our cultural ideal of harmony and love. From a sociological perspective, however, the level of violence in American families comes as no great surprise. Why?

**Ecology and Family Violence**  Interpersonal violence depends on people being physically close, and the nuclear family brings a small group of people into close and frequent interaction. Physical proximity is just as necessary for hitting another person as it is for hugging.

The chance of violence is also increased by the isolation of the nuclear family, since outsiders cannot see what goes on inside the home. The less publicly visible our behavior is, the more likely we are to commit deviant acts.

**Violence and Social Structure**  Ironically, the very fact that the nuclear family functions as a "haven in a hostile world" increases the chances for violence. Most families, for example, have difficulty satisfying all their members' needs. The extreme emotional and material dependency of nuclear family members on one another inevitably creates some tension, anger, and bitterness because many family decisions—such as how to spend money—cannot satisfy everyone (Gelles, 1972).

Defining the family as a haven also supports violence because the family becomes the only place in which we feel free to "let off steam." You pay a much higher price if you punch your boss than you do if you punch your spouse, because your boss has far fewer reasons to tolerate such behavior. As Coser (1956) put it, the nuclear family

is a "safety-valve institution," and this makes it conducive to violence.

Because the family and its home are valued as private places beyond the reach of government, public officials are reluctant to intervene in what is culturally defined as a "family affair" (Berk and Loseke, 1981; U.S. Department of Justice, 1980). This insulates family members from standards of behavior that prevail in the outside world and makes violence more likely to occur (Sherman and Berk, 1984).

Structural distributions of power in patriarchal families also contribute to violence by placing both women and children in highly vulnerable positions (Dobash and Dobash, 1979; Klein, 1982). Children are generally powerless to leave abusive families, and wives often find themselves in the same position because they cannot support their children and themselves with their own earnings.

**Culture and Family Violence**  Although American culture includes values, norms, and attitudes that disapprove of family violence, it also contains ideas that support it. Most parents, for example, regard the physical punishment of children as both legitimate and necessary and rarely define it as violence (Gelles, 1972).

Our norms often allow behavior within families that would not be tolerated among nonfamily members. Parents may slap children who refuse to eat their vegetables and the police will not intervene; but they risk punishment for criminal assault if they slap restaurant customers who do not eat their vegetables. The social sanctions are quite different in these two situations, even though in both cases the violent behavior might be defended as "for the victim's own good."

In a majority of states in the United States, a husband may force his wife to have sex with him by threatening violence if she refuses; but the same behavior toward any other woman is legally punishable as rape. How do we live with such contradictory norms? One way is to use cultural beliefs to define many physically violent acts as "nonviolent." In general, we do not define an injurious act as violent if the act is permitted or required by a social role. A national study of American men, for example, found that most do not define the killing of a criminal by police as violence (Blumenthal et al., 1972), and most parents do not define spanking a child as a violent act, because they regard it as a necessary part of their role (Gelles, 1972).

From this perspective, family violence is often neither defined nor treated by outsiders as such because family roles condone violence within limits that are always subject to interpretation. Field and Field (1973) found that police officers in Washington, DC, will not arrest a husband who beats up his wife unless she requires a specific number of stitches; and Calvert (1974) found that under California law physical assaults within families have to cause more damage than those taking place outside families in order to be defined as criminal by the authorities.

Culture, social structure, and ecology help explain many aspects of family disorganization. As disorganization becomes more visible in American families, however, we must confront issues about the future of the family that have disturbed many Americans for a number of years: Is the family as an institution in danger? Can it be destroyed?

## Families and Social Change

Like all groups, families change in response to changes in their social and physical environments; but unlike most other groups, change is an inevitable part of family life. Membership in families spans the entire life course, and as individuals inevitably move from one age status to another, their families must also change their values, norms, and socially structured relationships (Boss, 1980).

In families with young children socialization, protection of the young, and children's obedience to their parents are highly valued, and family norms support those values. Interaction among family members is frequent because they live in the same household, and power is unequally divided between parents and children and between husbands and wives.

When children reach adulthood, however, family culture and structure change dramatically. Children are expected to make their own deci-

sions, and parents lose much of their authority along with their socializing roles. Interaction among family members drops sharply as children move away from home; and as parents enter old age, inequality between them lessens, particularly when the husband is no longer the primary breadwinner. In many societies family changes over the life course are not as dramatic as they are in the United States. In patrilocal and matrilocal societies newlyweds live with their in-laws, and adult children have far less autonomy than they do in the United States.

Our concern in the following sections, however, is less with internal changes over the life course than with changes in the family as an institution. What kinds of changes are taking place in the cultural ideas and social structures that define and regulate marriage, divorce, and relationships among family members? What is the future of the family as an institution in the United States?

### Cultural Change and the Family

Some of the most profound cultural changes during the last few decades focus on marriage and divorce. One of the most important social functions of marriage is the regulation of sexual behavior, and Americans increasingly support values that promote sexual unions between unmarried people. Between 1960 and 1983, for example, the percentage of adults who believed that premarital sex is always or almost always wrong dropped from 80 to 36 percent (Davis, 1977, 1983).

Americans are also increasingly tolerant of interracial marriage. Between 1972 and 1984 the percentage of adults who favor laws prohibiting interracial marriage dropped from 38 to 25 percent. Disapproval of homosexual unions, however, has remained virtually unchanged over the last ten years. In 1984, 75 percent of American adults believed that sexual relationships between adults of the same sex are always or almost always wrong (Davis, 1984).

Values and norms about relationships within marriages and families are also changing. Marriage, for example, has always been a contract relationship—the moment we say, "I do," we enter into a culturally defined set of rights, obligations, and expectations that are not explicitly stated in marriage ceremonies. Increasingly, however, cou-

When parents reach old age, they and their children (like this 98-year-old man and his daughter) sometimes experience a sharp role reversal as children take care of their parents.

ples are basing marriage on written contracts that clearly specify the spouses' expectations of each other—sometimes including details about who does which domestic tasks (Weitzman, 1981).

Both the surge of women into the labor force and the efforts of the women's movement have contributed to a shift toward egalitarian values in some middle- and upper-class marriages in the United States. As wives become financially independent and husbands lose their monopoly over the breadwinning role, the tendency toward greater equality is inevitable, and husbands have less and less choice about whether or not they will share in the less-prestigious household tasks.

Values about adultery have remained virtually unchanged since 1973; and in 1984, 87 percent of all adults disapproved of it. Perhaps in reaction to the fact that divorce has become increasingly easy to obtain both legally and financially and no longer carries the stigma it did 10 or 20 years ago, a slim majority of Americans believe that it should become *harder* to obtain (Davis, 1984).

Changing values also affect the composition of families. Although the value of large families has declined sharply in the United States, other values have changed in ways that may increase the size of households. Between 1973 and 1984, for example, the percentage of adults who believe that it is a good idea for elderly people to share a home with their grown children increased from 31 to 50 percent (Davis, 1984).

What do all these statistics tell us about the American family? As a set, they seem to describe changes that go in more than one direction. We are more tolerant of premarital sex, but oppose adultery; divorce is easier to obtain, but a majority of Americans would make it harder. In an important sense, such patterns of change in our most important social institutions are just what we should expect.

In a rapidly changing society, marriage and the family inevitably reflect those changes since they are the focal point of most people's lives. Nevertheless, because marriage and the family are so important to us as individuals, we tend to resist change in the interests of stability and continuity. When it comes to changing major institutions, in other words, we tend to be cautious. A liberal attitude toward change in some areas is often balanced

by conservative attitudes toward change in others.

As ideas about marriage and the family change, what corresponding changes occur in social structures? What changes have there been in the composition of families and their role structures?

## Shifting Structures

The composition of families is the most observable change in American family structure. In general, adults are less likely to live in nuclear families and families are becoming smaller, less likely to be headed by a married couple, and more likely to include nonrelatives as members of the household.

Between 1960 and 1982 the percentage of Americans living in families dropped from 93 to 88 percent. During the same period the number of people living alone more than doubled to 19 million, and more than quadrupled to 7 million among those under 45 years old. In the last ten years, the number of households whose members are unrelated to one another—including unmarried couples—more than doubled to 22 million, while the number of families rose by only 35 percent (U.S. Census Bureau, 1983c).

These numbers suggest that Americans are experimenting with alternatives to nuclear family living arrangements. For many unmarried couples living together is a new form of courtship that eventually leads to formal marriage—a pattern that exists in a number of societies, including Poland and Sweden. It is possible, however, that a growing minority of Americans are reluctant to take on the burdens and restrictions of marriage and parenting, and although more than 90 percent of young Americans say they intend to marry eventually, that figure may come down in the future (Thornton and Freedman, 1982).

What about the structure of American families themselves? How are they changing? (Before you read on, take a moment to study Table 15-2 carefully.)

Between 1960 and 1982 average family size dropped by 11 percent among whites and 16 percent among nonwhites. Although the nuclear family headed by a married couple is still the most common family structure in the United States, it is losing ground to other forms. Between 1960 and 1982, for example, the percentage of families

**Table 15-2**

The Changing Composition of American Families, by Race, 1960 to 1982

| FAMILY STRUCTURE | ALL FAMILIES | | WHITES | | BLACKS | |
|---|---|---|---|---|---|---|
| | 1960 | 1982 | 1960 | 1982 | 1960 | 1982 |
| Average Family Size | 3.7 | 3.3 | 3.6 | 3.2 | 4.4 | 3.7 |
| **Percentage of Families with:** | | | | | | |
| Married Couple | 87 | 82 | 89 | 85 | 74 | 54 |
| Female Head | 10 | 15 | 9 | 12 | 22 | 41 |
| Other | 3 | 3 | 2 | 3 | 4 | 5 |
| **Percentage of All Children Who Live with:** | | | | | | |
| Both Parents | 89 | 75 | 92 | 82 | 69 | 43 |
| Mother Only | 8 | 18 | 6 | 14 | 21 | 43 |
| Other | 3 | 6 | 2 | 4 | 10 | 14 |
| **Percentage of All Children Who Live with:** | | | | | | |
| Single Mothers[1] | 0.8 | 2.8 | 0.2 | 1.0 | 4.4 | 12.8 |

Source: U.S. Census Bureau, 1983c.

[1]Single means never married, children are those under 18 years old, and figures are for 1970 and 1981, rather than for 1960 and 1982.

headed by a divorced, separated, or single mother increased by 33 percent among whites and 86 percent among nonwhites.

As a result, a growing percentage of children are living in single-parent families. Between 1960 and 1982 the percentage of all children living with both parents dropped from 89 to 75 percent, and in 1982 less than half of all nonwhite children were living with both parents. Since 1970, single-parent families headed by women who have never married have also become more common. The percentage of all children living in such families was more than three times greater in 1982 than in 1970, and among whites the percentage was five times greater.

The nuclear family is also changing by becoming more extended in some ways and less extended in others. A **subfamily** is a family that lives in the household of another family, and subfamilies can be either related or unrelated to the host family. Between 1960 and 1980 the number of related subfamilies in the United States dropped by 26 percent, indicating a decline in extended family networks. By 1982, however, the number of related subfamilies had climbed by 63 percent to its highest level since 1950. At the same time the number of unrelated subfamilies increased by 80 percent. In addition, the percentage of families sharing a household with unrelated individuals jumped from 14 to 26 percent (U.S. Census Bureau, 1983c).

The surge of women into the labor force has increased the involvement of fathers in child care to some degree; but the most rapidly increasing family type is the single-parent family headed by a woman who is highly likely to live in poverty.

America has never been a society in which most households included extended families (Thornton and Freedman, 1983), and although the importance of kinship seems to be declining, families also seem to be expanding their households by including nonrelatives. This trend is paralleled by the increased number of nonfamily households in which unrelated adults live together and share expenses and housework. Americans, in short, seem to be trying out a number of alternative ways of meeting their needs for companionship and both financial and emotional security. The fact that we are less likely to live with extended kin does not mean that we have become a nation of "loners" and isolated nuclear families.

## Families Come and Families Go, but The Family Is Here to Stay

In spite of rising divorce rates and a growing minority of young people who postpone marriage or forgo it altogether, there is little doubt that the family as an institution will always be a part of society. Americans end marriages in record numbers, but they also remarry in record numbers. Although many grow disillusioned with particular marriages, or delay marrying, there is little evidence that marriage itself is losing its appeal.

Both historical and cross-cultural variations in marriages and families highlight the fact that social institutions are defined by the functions they perform, not by particular cultural and structural arrangements. From this perspective, institutions may radically change their structures or the cultural ideas that guide them; but they "die" only if other institutions take over their functions or the functions themselves lose their importance as social goals.

Many social functions of the family have been taken over in part by other institutions such as schools, but there is no society in which the family does not exist in some form. Even the Soviet Union—which tried to replace the family with schools and day-care centers in the years following the Russian Revolution—returned to the family as the primary group in which children are cared for and socialized.

Thus, the family as we know it is changing and will most certainly continue to change; but primary groups in which people are born and grow up, and which meet their needs for emotional support and a sense of continuity in their lives are, as Bane (1976) put it, "here to stay."

---

## Voices: The Family and Future Shock

The flood of novelty about to crash down upon us will spread from universities and research centers to factories and offices, from the marketplace and mass media into our social relationships, from the community into the home. Penetrating deep into our private lives, it will place absolutely unprecedented strains on the family itself.

The family has been called the "giant shock absorber" of society—the place to which the bruised and battered individual returns after doing battle with the world, the one stable point in an increasingly flux-filled environment. As the super-industrial [postindustrial] revolution unfolds, this "shock absorber" will come in for some shocks of its own. . . .

Seldom discussed, there is a hidden rhythm in human affairs that until now has served as one of the key stabilizing forces in society: the family cycle.

We begin as children; we mature; we leave the parental nest; we give birth to children who, in turn, grow up, leave and begin the process all over again. This cycle has been operating so long, so automatically, and with such implacable regularity, that [it has been] taken for granted. It is part of the human landscape. Long before they reach puberty, children learn the part they are expected to play in keeping this great cycle turning. This predictable succession of family events has provided [everyone], of whatever tribe or society, with a sense of continuity, a place in the temporal scheme of things. The family cycle has been one of the sanity-preserving constants in human existence. . . .

If industrialism, with its faster pace of life, has accelerated the family cycle, super-industrialism now threatens to smash it altogether. With the fantasies that the birth scientists are hammering into reality, with the colorful familial experimentation that innovative minorities will perform, with the likely development of such institutions as professional parenthood, with the increasing movement toward temporary and serial marriage, we shall not merely run the cycle more rapidly; we shall introduce irregularity, suspense, unpredictability—in a word, novelty—into what was once as regular and certain as the seasons.

When a "mother" can compress the process of birth into a brief visit to an embryo emporium, when by transferring embryos from womb to womb we can destroy even the ancient certainty that childbearing took nine months, children will grow up into a world in which the family cycle, once so smooth and sure, will be jerkily arhythmic. Another crucial stabilizer will have been removed from the wreckage of the old order, another pillar of sanity broken. . . .

In our family forms, as in our economics, science, technology and social relationships, we shall be forced to deal with the new. . . .

As we hurtle into tomorrow, millions of ordinary men and women will face emotion-packed options so unfamiliar, so untested, that past experience will offer little clue to wisdom. In their family ties, as in all other aspects of their lives, they will be compelled to cope not merely with transience, but with the added problem of novelty as well.

Source: Toffler, *Future Shock*, 1970.

## Summary

1. An institution is a social "blueprint" for groups. Thus, the family as an institution is not the same as your family or mine.

2. Marriage is a socially supported union between individuals in what is intended to be a stable, enduring relationship that involves sexual interaction. It is the basis for the family, an institution defined by social functions. These are regulation of sexual behavior, reproduction, nurturance and protection of children, socialization, production and consumption, and the passing on of ascribed statuses such as race.

3. Marriage and the family rest on many beliefs, the most important of which is kinship, which defines who is related to whom. Matrilineal societies trace descent through the mother's blood relatives, whereas patrilineal societies trace descent through the father's. In bilateral societies descent is traced through the relatives of both parents.

4. Among the most important values and attitudes in marriage and the family are those focusing on the basis for marriage (such as love or economic exchange), sexual experience before and during marriage, and the relative importance of family ties and those with outsiders.

5. Marriage rules limit whom people may marry, when, and under what conditions. Incest rules prohibit marriage between kin; rules of endogamy require marriage outside the group; and rules of exogamy require marriage within it. Marriage rules define the acceptability of multiple spouses (polygamy), whether it be multiple wives (polygyny) or husbands (polyandry). In matrilocal societies married couples must live with the wife's family, whereas in patrilocal societies they live with the husband's. In bilocal societies couples must choose between the two.

6. Families have a variety of structures, from the nuclear family consisting of parents and children, to extended families that include additional relatives, single-parent families, and compound families that include children from other marriages.

7. In all societies women are the primary caretakers of children, but they also participate in economic production. In general, the more industrial a society is, the less likely women are to be economically active.

8. Patterns of interaction in families depend heavily on the structure of family institutions. The intensity of monogamy, for example, encourages couples to reach agreement on important perceptions and issues.

9. Most societies are patriarchies, in which the official head of the family is the husband, but a very few may have been matriarchies, in which the official head is the wife. Power is shared equally between spouses in egalitarian marriages.

10. The characteristics of families strongly affect birth rates. The younger the age at which people marry, for example, the higher birth rates tend to be. Changes in birth rates, in turn, affect family structure. Compared with colonial women, women in the 1980s bear far fewer children and are more likely to work outside the home.

11. The way in which goods are produced in a society profoundly affects both the power of family groups and the ways in which families are organized. In industrial societies, for example, many of the functions once performed by the family have been transferred to other institutions.

12. The functional perspective identifies both functions and dysfunctions associated with different aspects of family organization. A conflict perspective shows how the interests of individual families and economic and political institutions clash.

13. Family disorganization occurs when statuses are not occupied or roles are not performed adequately. Divorce, death, and violence—which are themselves caused by cultural, structural, and ecological factors—are major causes of family disorganization.

14. As an institution, the American family has undergone a variety of cultural and structural changes, particularly as families adjust to change in the economy and the roles of men and women.

## Key Terms

bilateral descent   468
egalitarian marriage   477
family   463

    extended   473
    nuclear   473

## Recommended Readings

BANE, M. J. (1976). *Here to stay*. New York: Basic Books. An insightful look into the ways in which the American family is changing.

GOODE, W. J. (1976). Family disorganization. In R. K. Merton and R. Nisbet (Eds.), *Contemporary social problems*. New York: Harcourt Brace Jovanovich. A useful sociological overview of the various forms of family disorganization.

HOOD, J. C. (1983). *Becoming a two-job family*. New York: Praeger. An in-depth study of 16 married couples in which both spouses work. Hood sheds light on a number of important issues, including the effects of a wife's work status and earnings on her power in the family and the ways in which spouses negotiate domestic responsibilities. See also LEIN, L. (1984). *Families without villains: American families in an era of change*. Lexington, MA: D. C. Heath.

*Journal of Marriage and the Family*. Minneapolis, MN: National Council on Family Relations. The leading scholarly journal that focuses on marriage and the family.

KORBIN, J. E. (Ed.). (1983). *Child abuse and neglect: Cross-cultural perspectives*. Berkeley: University of California Press. A collection of papers that includes a disturbing study that finds that behaviors such as child abuse are more common in "developed" societies than in what many people think of as "primitive" societies.

SPIRO, M., and SPIRO, A. G. (1975). *Children of the kibbutz: A study in child training and personality*. Cambridge, MA: Harvard University Press. An analysis of the effects of a radically different approach to family life on the development of children.

STAINES, G. L., and PLECK, J. H. (1983). *The impact of work schedules on the family*. Ann Arbor: University of Michigan Press. A clearly written, interesting study that shows how work schedules for both men and women affect the feelings and behavior of family members.

STRAUSS, M., and GELLES, R. J. (1980). *Behind closed doors: Violence in the American family*. New York: Doubleday/Anchor. An analysis of the extent and causes of one of the most disturbing forms of family disorganization by two leading authorities.

# CHAPTER 16

# Educational Institutions

Students often describe everything outside of schools as the "real world." "School," they say, "isn't part of the real world. It's just a place I have to go if I want to get a decent job or have my parents approve of me. *Real* life doesn't begin until after graduation." They could not be more mistaken. Few social institutions mirror the social environment as faithfully as schools do, and that so many students are unaware of this fact gives schools enormous power and influence in their lives.

What are schools and how do their cultural, structural, and ecological characteristics define them as social institutions? How are they related to other social institutions, such as families, religions, economies, and governments? For what goals are they functional and dysfunctional, and what part do they play in the distribution of wealth, power, and prestige in stratified societies? How do they affect their societies and the lives of the people who pass through them? These are the kinds of questions that this chapter will try to answer.

We begin with the history of schools as educational institutions and then take a detailed look at the cultural, structural, and ecological characteristics of schools, which affect not only how they function, but the experience and behavior of the people who participate in them. From there we examine the complex relationships between schools and other social institutions, such as the family and economy, and we assess the importance of schools in maintaining stratification systems. We close with a critical look at some recent proposals for changing schools.

## School as a Social Institution

All societies socialize their members to perform adult roles. In nonindustrial societies, children learn adult roles through the informal interactions of their everyday lives. In hunter-gatherer and horticultural societies, children learn informally from the adults who happen to be around them. They learn the same way in agricultural societies, but because skills are more specialized and the division of labor is more complex, some children are apprenticed to adults—such as carpenters and blacksmiths—and also learn through on-the-job training.

Training in industrial societies, however, is too complex to be left to informal relationships, and

Although many students think school is something separate from the "real world," the fact is that few social institutions reflect the social environment as faithfully as schools do.

families do not have the resources to prepare their children for adult work roles. As a result, children spend large portions of their childhood in **schools**—formal organizations whose primary purpose is to educate people. From this perspective, **education** is a special form of socialization, which involves the systematic, formal transmission of skills, knowledge, beliefs, values, attitudes, and norms.

### A Short Social History of Schools

Schools have existed for centuries, but until the late nineteenth century they were restricted largely to the children of elite families. The ancient Chinese used schools to train government officials, just as medieval Europeans used them to train priests. In Victorian England, elite private schools trained the future high-level government officials and business leaders (Wilkinson, 1964), and this is still largely true today. In 1977, for example, 86 percent of all senior officials in the Foreign Office (the British counterpart of the U.S. State Department) were graduates of just two elite colleges—Oxford and Cambridge (Sampson, 1983).

Education not only prepared the elite for prestigious and powerful occupations; it set them apart symbolically from the classes below them. The ability to read and write, for example, or to speak Latin and Greek, was a cultural indicator of "high breeding" and superiority. Schooling was thus a major way for members of the upper class to prepare their children to be defined and treated as members of the upper class.

As the Industrial Revolution took hold in the nineteenth century, the upper class monopoly over formal schooling began to loosen. Social life became more bureaucratic and rational, and the

At the height of the Industrial Revolution in the United States, public schools served to assimilate immigrants into the dominant Anglo culture and to socialize an obedient work force.

demand for training in specialized skills—from typing and filing documents to operating telegraphs, engineering, and managing complex business organizations—grew rapidly (Trow, 1961). Examinations and grades were used to certify competence. Education as a symbol of "cultured," elite status, in short, was gradually replaced by education as a means for producing a large number of workers with a wide range of skills (Weber, 1946).

In addition to a skilled work force, industrialists wanted "good" workers whose values and attitudes served the interests of employers and helped increase production. Horace Mann—one of the strongest early supporters of public education—won the support of manufacturers by promising that educated workers would be "docile and quick to apply themselves to work," disciplined, punctual, and loyal (Mann, 1842).

By the 1850s every state in America supported public education. Between 1870 and 1900 the number of high schools grew from 160 to more than 6,000, and the percentage of young adults with high school diplomas more than tripled. By 1982, 86 percent of those 25 to 29 years old were high school graduates, and illiteracy had dropped from 11 percent of the population in 1900 to less than 1 percent (U.S. Census Bureau, 1975a, 1983c).

The growth of colleges and graduate schools was slower than that of public high schools, in large part because most families could not afford to send their children to college and higher education was widely perceived as a luxury until well into the twentieth century. In fact, around 1900, popular books giving advice on "success" generally told their readers that college was a waste of time for all but the wealthy, who did not have to worry about making a living (Huber, 1971).

Although the dramatic rise of schooling resulted largely from the Industrial Revolution, other factors played a part as well. Nations used schools to create and maintain patriotism and national solidarity ("I pledge allegiance to the flag . . . "). In the late 1800s and early 1900s the United States was flooded with immigrants, and schools were used to assimilate the newcomers into Anglo culture.

Over the last century education has also been perceived as the major source of upward mobility, an escape route leading out of poverty into the middle class. By the late 1970s—in sharp contrast to the early 1900s—79 percent of American parents said they would like their children to go beyond high school, and 36 percent of all adults rated college education as "very important." Most significant, the perceived importance of college is highest among people who are at the *bottom* of the stratification system—nonwhites and those with relatively low incomes and educations—not among those at the top (U.S. Census Bureau, 1975a).

Whether or not such perceptions of education are accurate, one thing is certain: institutionalized learning profoundly affects not only societies, but the lives of millions of people. Given this, we need to understand how schools work—how cultural ideas, social structures, and ecological arrangements affect what goes on in them—as well as how schools affect and are affected by the social environment in which they exist. The next three sections analyze the cultural, structural, and ecological characteristics of schools. Then, we take a broader perspective and examine the relationships between educational and other institutions and the effects of education on social inequality.

## Cultural Variations

Like other institutions, schools rest on sets of cultural ideas that define reality, establish goals, and regulate the behavior of people who occupy social statuses within them. To understand what people do in schools, we first have to understand how people think about schools and about what goes on in them.

### Beliefs

The most fundamental belief that underlies schooling is that in order to learn what we need to know as adults, someone must both decide what it is that we need to know and then teach it to us. From the earliest grades, most students and teachers share the belief that teachers know what is true and students do not. Thus, it is not surprising that college students seldom challenge their teachers—even when they believe their teachers are wrong—for

to do so challenges a major belief that underlies schooling itself.

A second important belief is that knowledge is the key to individual happiness and the solution to social problems. Jefferson argued that a healthy democracy depends on a well-educated public capable of making critical, independent decisions about social issues and the actions of government officials. Almost half of American adults believe that blacks and other minorities are relatively poor because they "don't have the chance for the education it takes to rise out of poverty" (Davis, 1982), a belief that, as we will see later in this chapter, is largely untrue.

A third belief underlying schooling in America is that tests and grades accurately measure student's mental abilities and how much they have learned. Most research shows, however, that this belief is at best only partly true (Kirschenbaum et al., 1971). Standardized tests—such as IQ tests and college SATs—have recently come under heavy criticism for being biased in favor of white middle- and upper-class students. Tests depend on language and on examples that reflect cultural background and life experiences as much as—if not more than—mental ability.

Consider the following questions:

1. A "handkerchief head" is:
   (A) A bad dude, (B) A porter, (C) An Uncle Tom, (D) A preacher

2. Which word is most out of place here?
   (A) Bagel, (B) Lox, (C) Gefilte

Blacks have an edge with the first question ("C"—An Uncle Tom; do you know what that is?), and Jews have the advantage on the second ("A"—the other two are seafoods). The second question is designed to measure the ability to categorize objects on the basis of similar characteristics; but clearly the correct answer depends on more than this. If you have never heard of gefilte fish and lox (seafood dishes popular among Jews), you might answer incorrectly regardless of your ability to distinguish between objects. You first have to know what the words mean, and that depends on your cultural background.

The validity of standardized tests is only part of the problem, however, for a large body of research suggests that teachers are very subjective when they grade papers and tests (Kirschenbaum et al.,

## PUZZLES:

## ACADEMIC PERFORMANCE AS A SELF-FULFILLING PROPHECY

Do teachers' beliefs about how well their students will do affect how well their students do?

The answer is yes, and what teachers expect from their students often depends on their students' social class, race, and gender. This phenomenon is discussed here and in Chapters 12 and 13.

1971). For example, when teachers from a variety of disciplines are asked to grade student papers, they vary enormously in the range of grades they assign to the same work. One teacher's "A" is often another's "C."

This finding will surprise relatively few students and even fewer teachers, and this is, in itself, an important point. All of us suspect at some level that grades are meaningless, and yet most of us continue to act as if they were not. Since the entire system hinges on the belief that grades are at least roughly valid, those who refuse to go along cannot succeed within it. Students who do not care about grades risk flunking out; and teachers who do not take grading seriously seldom escape the criticism of their peers.

### Values

As a socializing institution, the school reflects important values, the most important of which is the value placed on socialization itself. Most American students learn quickly that their teachers regard such middle-class values as obedience, punctuality, politeness, neatness, individual competition, and "playing by the rules" more highly than independent thought, rebelliousness, creativity, and group work. Whereas primary groups such as families value their members because they are members, secondary groups such as schools value students for their performance at standardized tasks; and for most students, schooling is their first experience of being ranked and graded in relation to other people.

Values also change. Standardized tests, grading, ranking, and individual competition were relatively unimportant in American schools until the middle of this century, because the primary purpose of early schools was to socialize young people, not to identify those most likely to succeed in the marketplace. The progressive education movement, which began late in the nineteenth century, favored learning through experience rather than through reading and rote learning, greater attention to the needs of each child than to the requirements of rigid curricula and the needs of society, cooperation rather than competition, schoolroom democracy rather than the unquestioned authority of teachers and administrators, and preparation for the everyday tasks of life rather than the development of intellectual ability (Ravitch, 1983).

From the 1920s through the late 1940s the progressive value system dominated much of American public schooling; but from 1949 to 1953 opponents of the progressive model mounted a concerted attack, in part based on the belief that the prevailing educational value system was a communist conspiracy aimed at undermining the youth of America by substituting training in basic intellectual skills with "life-adjustment" courses such as how to behave on a date and "how-to" courses on decorating the interior of a home. The supporters of progressive education were unable to deny that the study of mathematics, literature, history, science, and foreign language had been severely curtailed in public education, and the following decade saw public education turn "back-to-basics" (Ravitch, 1983).

In the late 1960s two important values about education clashed head-on once again: Should schools exist for social purposes (to socialize the young) or should they exist to serve individuals (to provide them with resources controlled and used by them for their own benefit as they see it)? In the midst of antiwar and civil rights struggles that questioned the legitimacy of authority itself, many students demanded social and personal relevance in school courses and greater control over their own education.

Like the earlier progressives, reformers in the 1960s advocated personal growth and autonomy for students, and many schools abolished grades and required courses. As requirements were loosened, students increasingly replaced courses in language, mathematics, and science with a range of "electives"—from driver education to home economics (National Commission on Excellence in Education, 1983; Ravitch, 1983).

As unemployment has soared in the early 1980s and parents have become increasingly anxious about the job prospects of their children, support has grown for a "back-to-basics" movement that advocates a rigid curriculum and a heavy emphasis on language, mathematics, computers, and science.

**Value Conflict and Role Strain** Values also conflict within schools and often produce considerable role strain for both students and teachers. College students, for example, are encouraged to value learning for its own sake, to think for themselves, critically examine ideas, and take challenging courses that force them to grow. They are also encouraged, however, to achieve high grades, and they know that their grades will heavily affect their future once they leave school.

These two values often conflict with each other: students must choose between challenging courses that offer slim prospects of an "A" and easy ones whose chief benefit may be a high grade. If they read unassigned books, they risk not having enough time to prepare for exams. If they challenge what their professors say in class, they may risk appearing to be foolish or disrespectful, and may fear (with some justification) that this will negatively affect their grades. Consequently, they often find themselves in what appears to be a "no-win" situation: "If I don't speak up in class, the professor may think I'm dumb; if I *do* speak up, the professor will *know* I'm dumb."

Teachers also face value conflicts in performing their roles. In helping students to learn, they often feel the need to be close to students, to know and care about them as individuals, to gain their trust so that they will openly reveal their doubts and weaknesses. As evaluators, however, who report student performance to schools and, eventually, to the outside world, they are expected to treat their students according to fixed standards, to ignore their unique characteristics, and to make decisions that may hurt the same students who trust and confide in them.

Schools are complex institutions that serve the interests of many constituencies and attempt to achieve a wide range of culturally valued goals. This makes value conflict inevitable, both within schools and between them and the outside world.

## Norms

Values define goals; but norms define legitimate *means* for achieving those goals. Most American schools are bureaucracies—complex, formal organizations in which role relationships are rigidly defined by clearly stated norms. Although people below the age of 16 are required by law to attend school, older adolescents and adults must satisfy specific requirements in order to attend. Teachers must be properly certified, and hiring, firing, and promotion are regulated by rules of seniority and specific procedures. Administrators oversee the performance of both students and teachers. Written records of student performance are maintained, and access to them is restricted by law (only recently have students begun being allowed to see their own files).

Of all school norms, the ones with the most immediate impact on students are those that determine how rewards and punishments are actually distributed. "What do I have to do to get an 'A'?" is the number one topic of conversation among many college students at the beginning of a term. "How many papers and exams? How long should the papers be? What percentage of the final grade is determined by each exam and paper? How much does classroom participation count? Does she want footnotes? Does he *really* want us to talk in class? Is she a hard grader? Does he expect us to actually read *all* of the reading list? Does she give extensions? Can I take my personal problems to him?"

Such questions are even more important when grading is done on a curve that limits the number of high grades that can be assigned and requires a certain number of low grades. This is a classic example of a **zero-sum game**, one in which the success of one player requires the failure of another (Morgenstern, 1968; von Neumann and Morgenstern, 1964). Forced to operate under these kinds of norms, it is not surprising that students often spend a great deal of time doing detective work in order to figure out the norms that actually determine success and failure.

Listen carefully to what students ask professors in the early weeks of a term and you will notice that many questions are attempts to force the professor to reveal the "rules of the game," which often vary considerably from one course to another. Students must often wait for several weeks for the professor to reveal the entire set of norms, and they are sometimes shocked to learn that they misperceived important norms or that norms have been suddenly changed. It is thus understandable that some students study the course as much as they do its subject.

The importance of grades and the norms that determine them are at the heart of a fundamental dilemma in American education. On the one hand, students learn more if they study because they are interested in the subject itself—in other words, if their primary rewards are the **intrinsic rewards** they give to themselves: personal satisfaction, excitement, and growth. On the other hand, from their earliest grades, students learn that everything they do is connected to **extrinsic rewards**—a grade or expression of approval given to them by someone else—and several research studies suggest that interest in activities declines when outside rewards are introduced.

In one experiment, preschool children were offered an art project, and the experimenters identified those children who showed the greatest interest (Lepper, Greene, and Nisbett, 1973). These children were then divided into three groups. In the first, children were told beforehand that they would receive a "good player" certificate if they took part. The second group unexpectedly received a certificate afterward; and the third group received no external reward.

Two weeks later, the same children were again offered an art project—but with no promise of reward—and the children who were rewarded the first time spent the *least* amount of time working on the project. Even though all of these children had shown great interest in art work, external rewards apparently tended to replace internal rewards, for when external rewards were no longer offered, the children's motivation decreased. This effect has also been found among older children and adults (Deci, 1975).

## Attitudes:
### "No More Teachers' Dirty Looks"

Value conflicts, compulsory schooling, and the ambiguity of classroom norms inevitably result in both positive and negative attitudes between teachers and students. Perhaps the most common student attitude about school work is that they do not like it—especially those who are relatively unsuccessful in obtaining the reward of high grades.

For many students—especially those whose social class or race severely limits their life chances—school is not a positive experience that will "pay off" someday with a good job. It is, instead, a place they have to be, a forced alternative to being on the street. For many students, school is like a prison, and the crime is being younger than 16 years old (Carnegie Council on Policy Studies in Higher Education, 1979).

Negative attitudes between students and teachers and among members of each group are common; and they rest on beliefs and values that affect perceptions. Teachers often assume that students value grades more than learning (which is not surprising given the normative structure of schools) and believe that students will cheat if they can get away with it. This not only supports negative attitudes toward students, but also toward teachers that students openly like. Teachers commonly believe that since students value grades above everything else, popular teachers must be easy graders (and, therefore, bad teachers).

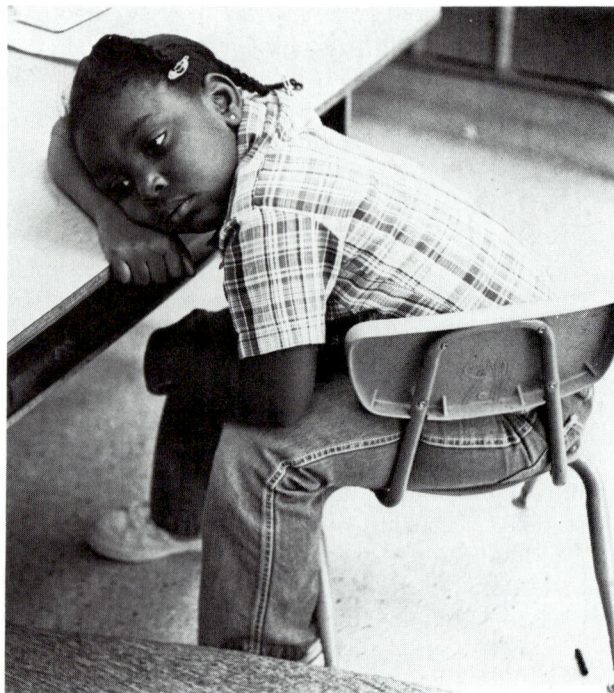

Values and norms also encourage students to become highly dependent on teachers, to wait anxiously for teachers to tell them exactly what to do, instead of using their own judgment. This, in turn, often makes teachers feel angry, resentful, and "overloaded" by demands from the long lines of students waiting anxiously outside their offices. Although many students may not be aware of it, they are not the only ones who breathe a sigh of relief at the end of a term.

Students, on the other hand, often resent the power that teachers wield over their future, the arbitrary ways in which grades are sometimes assigned, and teachers' reluctance to pay attention to students as individuals. They also tend to resent other students who are successful at the academic "game," especially those who "butter up" the teacher. This is due in part to the fact that schools are organized in such a way that students and teachers are adversaries who strive for different and often conflicting goals. Students who try to "get in good" with the teacher are seen by many students as "going over to the other side" for their own personal gain. In contrast, successful athletes may be perceived as adding to the glory of the entire student body (Coleman, 1960).

## The Importance of Subcultures

The preceding sections show that although schools are regulated by an institutional culture, what goes on in them depends on subcultures that affect the experience and behavior of students and teachers. Student behavior is affected as much by the beliefs, values, attitudes, and expectations of other students as it is by the formal and informal expectations of teachers and school administrators.

For example, in his study of high schools in the early 1960s, sociologist James Coleman (1960, 1961) found that while teachers value academic achievement more than anything else, students do not. Among males, athletes were the most likely to belong to the leading crowd, followed by popular students, and, a distant third, by high academic achievers. Among girls, being considered good looking and popular were valued far more highly than academic success, and the best students tended to have the fewest friends.

College students belong to one or more of four distinct **student subcultures** (Clark and Trow, 1966). The **vocational** subculture, because it de-

fines college as a route to good jobs, values hard work for its "pay off" after graduation. The **academic** subculture also encourages hard work, but in the name of a different value—learning for its own sake—which is the classic "liberal arts" goal. The **collegiate** subculture values social activities—parties, football games, and drinking—while the **nonconformist** subculture values rebellion against authority and open deviation from the other three subcultures (and, of course, conformity to its own).

Teachers are also influenced by their peer subculture (Caplow and McGee, 1958). Professors are often expected by their peers to value research and publishing more than any other goal, including teaching; and their peers are the ones who control their professional future. College students are often puzzled and frustrated by their teachers' apparent reluctance to spend time with them, to help

them learn difficult materials. Few students realize that the cultural values, norms, and systems of reward that define student-teacher relationships compete with those that define relationships among teachers.

School culture is thus both complex and riddled with competing values, attitudes, and norms. Far more is going on in a school than simply the transmission of knowledge and skills. Merely by participating in the cultural environment of schools, students learn other lessons that make up what Jackson (1968) called the "hidden curriculum."

## Cultural Lessons in the Hidden Curriculum

In many ways, the cultural ideas that regulate the social relationships through which students learn formal subjects are subjects in themselves—the **hidden curriculum.** Academic performance, for example, is measured by objective tests whose questions usually have only one correct answer. In addition to learning specific facts, such learning contains a hidden lesson: all questions have a single correct answer, and that is what the teacher is looking for (Holt, 1964). Students are thus taught to *know* answers, not to search for them, and to value questions that have a single correct answer more than those that do not.

When students enter college, they are often disturbed when professors ask questions that do not have a single correct answer ("Why do people commit crimes? How can nuclear war be prevented? What is the poet trying to say in this poem?"). All of us have experienced the uneasy silence that sometimes comes over a class when this kind of question is asked, the fear that the professor will call on us, the frantic searching of our memories for the "right" answer contained somewhere in the readings, and the nagging question, "Will this be on the exam?"

The hidden curriculum contains many such lessons (Gracey, 1972b; Holt, 1972). Even in kindergarten, children learn to value punctuality and being "good." They learn to value themselves according to their performance and their ability to compete with other students, and to value an "expert's" judgments more than their own. Whether or not they personally want to do something is no longer important.

Minority students often learn to devalue their own subculture and replace it with the language, beliefs, values, attitudes, and norms of white, middle-class America. For example, at home Puerto Rican children learn that it is impolite to look directly into an adult's eyes; but their middle-class, white teachers often interpret—and punish—such behavior as "shifty" and untrustworthy. Until the late 1960s, the Spanish language was forbidden by

In American schools students quickly learn the importance of competition through which some students gain at the expense of the failure of others.

law in Texas schools, and Mexican-American children were often punished—sometimes by having to kneel and beg forgiveness—for saying a Spanish word (Silberman, 1971).

School norms emphasize order, obedience, and uniformity; and a student's reward is usually gained at the expense of others (Henry, 1963). In elementary classrooms, when one student cannot answer a question, the others often hold their hands high in the air, straining for the teacher's attention ("He doesn't know the answer. This is my chance.") (Henry, 1963). Students are also encouraged to adopt attitudes of cheerful, willing acceptance of authority—to do what they are told to do until they are told to stop, without complaining or questioning.

As we will see later in this chapter, the importance of hidden cultural lessons extends far beyond the confines of schools, for they play a major part in the perpetuation of social inequality and social classes.

## Varieties of Social Structure

Like all organizations, schools are held together by social relationships in which the occupants of social statuses perform roles in relation to role partners. To understand schools from a sociological perspective, we need to take a detailed look at the structural characteristics of these relationships.

## Boundaries

Organizational boundaries vary in their clarity and in how open they are. Of these two characteristics, the degree of openness of school boundaries is far more important, for schools control the distribution of knowledge and skills as well as the credentials that are often used as job requirements. Prior to the mid-nineteenth century, virtually all schools were privately owned and reserved for the children—especially sons—of wealthy families. As recently as 1982, fewer than a third of all American high school graduates went on to college (U.S.

In most industrial societies, schools act as a sorting mechanism that determines, among other things, who is allowed to go on to the next higher level of schooling.

Census Bureau, 1983c). In most other societies, higher education is even more restricted. In Britain, Japan, Switzerland, and France, for example, competition for college entrance is fierce, and only an elite few are able to go beyond secondary school (Eurich, 1981).

Public education made elementary and secondary education available to most Americans, but "white" schools regularly excluded blacks until the 1954 Supreme Court decision outlawed separate schools for whites and blacks (Ravitch, 1983). Until quite recently, women were largely excluded from professional education in law, medicine, business, engineering, and science.

Boundaries become more closed with each additional level beyond high school, owing primarily to competition for limited places and the high cost of college and professional education. This, in turn, affects the racial and class composition of college enrollments.

As Table 16-1 shows, white male high school graduates are considerably more likely than comparable blacks to go to college, and enrollment increases steadily with each rise in family income (although the effect of income is less pronounced among blacks than among whites). The negative effects of race and family income on college enrollment among blacks and the lower-class are compounded by the fact that nonwhites and lower-income families attach *more* importance to college education than whites and higher-income families do (U.S. Census Bureau, 1975a).

The exclusiveness of higher education has been lessened by the enormous growth of two-year junior colleges—especially the relatively inexpensive community colleges. Between 1960 and 1981, the number of junior colleges more than doubled; enrollments increased by ten times; and the number of part-time college students grew at a rate 55 percent higher than the number of full-time students (U.S. Census Bureau, 1983c).

Junior college students differ sharply from those in four-year colleges. They are more likely to be black, twice as likely to be married, are generally older, and most are employed. Thus, the rapid growth of alternatives to four-year colleges has opened up higher education for social categories that were generally excluded in the past, and almost half of all junior college graduates eventually transfer to four-year schools (AACJC, 1977).

**Table 16-1**

College Enrollment among Those 18 to 24 Years Old, by Sex and Race and by Family Income (United States, 1981)

| RACE AND SEX[1] | PERCENTAGE ENROLLED |
|---|---|
| White males | 35 |
| White females | 31 |
| Black males | 28 |
| Black females | 28 |
| **RACE AND FAMILY INCOME[2]** | |
| **Whites** | |
| Under $10,000 | 32 |
| $10,000–$14,999 | 37 |
| $15,000–$19,999 | 37 |
| $20,000–$24,999 | 42 |
| $25,000 and over | 53 |
| **Blacks** | |
| Under $10,000 | 24 |
| $10,000–$14,999 | 31 |
| $15,000–$19,999 | 38 |
| $20,000–$24,999 | 42 |
| $25,000 and over | 44 |

Source: U.S. Census Bureau, 1982.

[1]For sex and race, figures are percentages of high school graduates who are enrolled in college.
[2]Figures are percentages of all those 18 to 24 years old.

## Patterns of Interaction

Like other organizations, schools produce patterns of interaction as students, teachers, and administrators attach meaning to behavior, define situations, and perform roles. In most classrooms the teacher is the focus of all interaction. Students speak only when asked and are generally forbidden to communicate with each other. This pattern is reinforced by physical arrangements in classrooms: students sit in fixed chairs facing the front of the room while teachers are free either to face the entire class or walk about and monitor students' behavior.

Some schools have "open" classrooms in which students are allowed to move about the room and interact with one another more freely (Silberman, 1971). Open classrooms were introduced to encourage student autonomy, initiative, and creativity, but they also tend to undermine the teacher's control both over students' behavior and over the content of what they learn. Thus, some critics of open classrooms suggest that autonomy and creativity are gained at the expense of basic skills such as reading, writing, and mathematics.

The physical and social arrangement of open classrooms encourages independence, autonomy, and creativity at the expense of discipline and control.

Any pattern of interaction depends on how the participants use symbols to define the situation, including the meaning of behavior, values, attitudes, and normative expectations. Karp and Yoels (1979) used this perspective to explore a simple question about college classrooms: Why do so many students remain silent? They observed ten classes in a private northeastern university for an entire term and then asked students and teachers to complete questionnaires designed to measure perceptions of themselves and each other in classroom interaction.

While most students and teachers said that large class size inhibits student participation, the number of students who actually participated was roughly the same, regardless of class size. Karp and Yoels concluded that early in each term students identify a few students who will take primary responsibility for class discussions.

This is similar to Latané and Darley's (1970) findings about bystanders who do not help people in distress (see Chapter 7). Responsibility becomes diffused in groups of strangers so that most can remain passive. In classrooms, however, responsibility is consolidated in a few individuals, with the same effect. Professors support this by rarely calling on specific students to contribute. Professors are twice as likely as students to believe that the fear of looking foolish to other students is an important reason for student silence, and they often protect students from embarrassment by not calling on them.

Although consolidation of responsibility protects students in some ways, it threatens them in others, because students who participate too much may raise the professor's expectations. Thus, interaction in college classrooms is a fine balance in which participants and nonparticipants must carefully control how they present themselves to the professor and other students.

Consolidation of responsibility in classrooms also encourages students to come to class unprepared, for they know that a few students will carry the load of interacting with the professor. It is not surprising, therefore, that students rate lack of preparation, ignorance of the subject, and a feeling that their ideas are not well formulated as the most important reasons for their silence; and this finding reveals the importance of students' and teachers' definitions of the social situation itself.

To many students, teachers are like banks that hold knowledge, and students make withdrawals, not deposits (Freire, 1972). Their classroom role, then, is to absorb truth from the teacher, not to participate in a dialogue whose purpose is to determine what is true and what is not. Students frequently express reluctance to question the validity of what they read, much less to openly challenge what a professor says in class.

In performing their role, professors contribute to these perceptions by coming to class fully prepared—they have had many hours to carefully work out what they are going to say—and from this perspective, it is easy to see why students often feel intimidated. It is here, however, that students and professors rely on sharply different definitions of the situation, which often contribute to serious misunderstandings.

From their precollege experience, most students believe that giving the correct answer is the most important part of their role, and if they are unsure, the best strategy is to remain silent. To many professors, however, uncertainty is at the heart of intellectual work, "truth" is always open to question, and the most important thing that students can learn is how to think critically and analytically.

The result is often a vicious circle. Students feel "put down" when professors challenge their ideas, for given their definition of the situation, an attack on their ideas is an attack on their role performance and, therefore, on their selves; and this makes them still more reluctant to speak out. Professors feel frustrated by students' silence, and may wonder if their students *have* any ideas. The harder a professor pushes, the more students feel vulnerable and under attack; and the more defensive students become, the harder professors feel they have to push.

To protect themselves in what they perceive as a threatening situation, students often use what Goffman (1963a) called "civil attention." They maintain the *appearance* that they are involved in the classroom—by taking notes, nodding their heads, or laughing at appropriate moments—without becoming so involved that they risk exposing themselves to an "attack" from the professor. Many students become skilled at knowing when to look at the professor and when not to—if the professor is looking around the room as if searching for someone to call on, many students immediately look away, preferably to write some notes.

Perceptions and expectations thus play an important part in classroom interaction, and an intriguing experiment shows how teachers' expectations of students affect how well students perform. Rosenthal and Jacobson (1968) administered a test to elementary school students at the start of a school year and told teachers that the results would accurately predict which students would be "spurters"—that is, had high potential to achieve. In fact, however, the test was not intended to be valid, and students were randomly assigned to the "spurter" group. At the end of the year, students whose teachers *perceived* them as "spurters" increased their IQ scores by an average of 12 points, while the other students' scores increased by only 8 points. Among first and second graders, IQ gains by "spurters" were over twice as large as they were for other students. More recent studies find similar effects of teacher expectations, although the effects are considerably more complex than originally believed (see Cooper and Good, 1983).

This illustrates an important sociological insight: self-fulfilling prophecies are the rule, not the exception, in social life, because our expectations of other people affect how we behave toward them, and *their* behavior as well as their perceptions of themselves are affected by ours (Merton, 1957, 1968). All of us have experienced the rush of energy, excitement, and pride that comes when teachers tell us they think we are smart, or the crushing disappointment when they tell us that we are not; and when we feel intelligent, we are more likely to act intelligently.

**PUZZLES:**

## IS EDUCATION THE GREAT EQUALIZER?

If every American had equal education, training, and intellectual ability, would the result be substantially less inequality of wealth, power, and prestige?

Probably not. This chapter and Chapter 11 explain why.

As we will see later in this chapter, self-fulfilling prophecies are particularly important when entire social categories, such as nonwhites and the poor, are perceived by teachers as poor prospects for education. When that happens, the assignment of students to the "spurter" category is not random and reflects racial, ethnic, and class prejudice.

### Complexity and Role Structures: The School as Bureaucracy

Since the start of this century, the size and complexity of American schools have increased enormously, and the structure of schools has been dramatically transformed from a relatively simple role relationship between students and teachers to a large bureaucracy involving administrators, clerical workers, and public officials.

In 1916 there were 200,000 schools in the United States that had only one teacher; but by 1980 the number of one-teacher schools stood at roughly 900. During this same period the average size of schools increased by over seven times. Most important, while the number of public school students doubled and the number of teachers more than tripled, the number of principals and administrators increased more than sevenfold (U.S. Census Bureau, 1975a, 1982).

The historical transformation of American schools closely paralleled a trend toward bureaucracy that was occurring throughout society. Business leaders dominated school boards and evaluated schools with the same criteria of efficiency and productivity they applied to their businesses: How many math problems do students solve per hour? How high are student grades? How many students are graduated each year, and how much does it cost per student? As Callahan (1962) put it:

> They saw schools not as centers of learning, but as enterprises which were functionally efficient if the students went through without failing and received their diplomas on schedule and if the operations were handled economically. (p. 247)

The signs of bureaucracy are found everywhere in schools. Public school teachers must be certified by state agencies. Formal records are kept not only on student behavior and performance but on teachers. Relationships between teachers, students, and administrators are clearly defined by school norms, as are those between administrators and outside authorities such as school boards, boards of trustees, and, in public institutions, state legislatures. Look at any college's "Student Handbook," and you will quickly see how many areas of student life are explicitly regulated by institutional norms.

College students are assigned identification numbers, and in many classes enrollments are so high that teachers do not know which student names go with which faces. Students are judged by their performance on tests that ignore individual needs and abilities, for attention to individuals is almost impossible under such circumstances. In many courses, students never meet their professors face-to-face, and when they need help, they turn to specialists—graduate students who run study sessions. Students thus have good reason to often feel lost in the crowd, because in today's bureaucratic schools, they often are.

In bureaucracies attention is on the organization as a whole rather than on individuals. The negative effect of this on educational goals is clear in the practice of **social promotion,** through which students who have not mastered the skills of the current grade are nevertheless sent to the next higher grade. Part of this is undoubtedly due to the desire of many teachers to spare students the humiliation of repeating a grade. We also have to remember, however, that one function of schools is to produce graduates, and if large numbers of students are not promoted, the schools' efficiency and productivity appear to decline.

How does this affect educational goals? In 1977, 40 percent of high school juniors in Florida failed a functional literacy test that included such questions as:

**1.** Joe gave a clerk a dollar for two dime candy bars and a nickel for a package of gum. If the tax was one penny, what change should he get back?

**2.** You want to call Mr. Jones on the telephone. You look in the telephone book for his number. You would find it between which names?

    A. Jackson and Jacobs
    B. James and Johnson
    C. Johnson and Judson
    D. Judson and Justus

In 1977 a 19-year-old sued a New York State school district for "educational malpractice," because although he was a high school graduate, he could not read above the fourth grade level (Hentoff, 1977). In 1979 the Carnegie Foundation's nationwide study found that 20 percent of American high school graduates lacked basic skills in language and mathematics. In addition, the national average score on college entrance examinations has been declining steadily for over a decade, and in 1983 the National Commission on Excellence in Education concluded that a "tide of mediocrity" has seriously damaged education in America.

The negative effects of social promotion are most glaring among minority students. In 1975, one out of every five 17-year-old students in inner-city schools could not read a newspaper or the directions on a can of food (NAEP, 1977). While many may feel tempted to blame the students involved, such explanations ignore the fact that they were promoted in spite of the fact that they had not mastered basic skills.

It would be a gross oversimplification to suggest that bureaucratic structure is responsible for the decline of learning in American schools. It is apparent, however, that the educational needs of many students have been ignored by an institution that serves many different interests—including those of providing jobs for teachers and administrators—and that like all bureaucracies, schools may neglect individuals within them while perpetuating the organization itself (see Baldridge and Deal, 1983).

## Distributions of Power

As institutions, schools are tied to the surrounding society. This means that power is distributed both within schools and between them and other institutions. Whether or not they are structured as bureaucracies, most schools rely on highly unequal distributions of power, with students placed at the bottom. Distributions of power vary substantially, however, from one level of schooling to another.

In public elementary and secondary schools, administrators have power over teachers, teaching methods, and curriculum, and students have little power in relation to anyone but their peers. To some degree, however, the power of administrators over teachers is balanced by the fact that most public school teachers belong to labor unions that can use strikes to achieve their goals.

In colleges and universities, the distribution of power is more complex. In many colleges, the administration controls the flow of money, which, in turn, allows it to affect the resources available to academic departments. Unlike public school teachers, college faculties generally control what goes on in classrooms—the kinds of courses that are taught and standards for grading—and play the most important role in deciding who will be hired, fired, or promoted.

In other ways, however, professors have less power than public school teachers. While most public school teachers belong to organized unions, professors often depend solely on the support of their own departments, which may consist of only a few members. Because faculty power generally lies in each department rather than the faculty as a whole, the administration is often able to overcome opposition to unpopular decisions because the faculty does not speak or act as an organized group.

The power of college faculties is also weakened by conflicting values and internal divisions of power. Senior, tenured members have a great deal of power over the careers of junior members, for promotions and tenure depend primarily on their recommendations. Heads of academic departments are almost always tenured professors, and the interests of senior members often conflict with those of junior members. Tenured professors do not have to worry about job security and may value the long-term survival of their departments more than anything else. Junior members, however, often have young families and must worry about their individual futures. When a college administration suggests saving money by cutting the size of the faculty, junior members are the ones most likely to lose their jobs. Tenured members, on the other hand, are less affected since the department

The fact that public school teachers are organized into unions often gives them more institutional power than higher-prestige college professors.

can still survive, and it is through departments that they exercise much of their power.

## The Social Ecology of Schools

Schools exist primarily to socialize young people, and this means that the demand for schooling depends directly on the number of young people in a society's population. In addition, the existence of schools depends on a society's material resources, for schools are expensive to build and maintain, and if children are in school, they are not available for productive work.

### Population and the Business of Schooling

In societies that use schools for education, when birth rates increase, so does the demand for schooling. Before reading on, take a moment to study Table 16-2, which shows how enrollment at the elementary, high school, and college levels has changed over the last 50 years.

Enrollment in elementary school was stable until the effects of the post–World War II Baby

**Table 16-2**

School Enrollment (1,000s) by Level of Schooling (United States, 1930–1981)

| YEAR | LEVEL OF SCHOOLING | | |
| | ELEMENTARY | HIGH SCHOOL | COLLEGE |
|---|---|---|---|
| 1981 | 28,440 | 14,771 | 12,097 |
| 1970 | 34,190 | 14,418 | 7,136 |
| 1960 | 30,119 | 9,600 | 3,126 |
| 1950 | 21,033 | 6,453 | 2,281 |
| 1940 | 20,466 | 7,130 | 1,494 |
| 1930 | 22,954 | 4,811 | 1,101 |

Source: U.S. Census Bureau, 1975a, 1982.

Boom were felt in the 1950s and enrollment jumped by almost 50 percent. In the next decade it rose by only 14 percent, because the Baby Boom was winding down; and in the last decade, enrollment has actually declined as birth rates have fallen.

High school enrollment jumped by almost 50 percent in the 1950s and by another 50 percent in the 1960s; but it barely grew at all in the 1970s, and began to fall in the 1980s. Notice that enrollment began to fall earlier in elementary schools than in high schools. This occurs because high school students are older, and it takes longer for falling birth rates to affect the number of teenagers in a population.

College enrollment rose sharply in the late 1940s because government benefits under the GI Bill allowed many returning World War II veterans to afford a college education. As the economy boomed and a college degree became an important factor in the job market, enrollment continued to climb in the 1950s and 1960s, and as the Baby Boom generations reached college age, enrollment rose sharply through the 1970s.

In spite of the importance attached to a college degree, falling birth rates may cause college enrollment to decline in the next 20 years. This is not inevitable, however, because there is already some evidence that although the number of people 18 to 23 years old is declining, the age structure of the college population is shifting upward. A large percentage of students in junior and community colleges, for example, are more than 21 years old (AACJC, 1977). Large numbers of married women are returning to school in order to improve their chances in the job market. Thus, while the age group traditionally served by colleges—those 18 to 22 years old—is shrinking, other age groups may make up the difference.

Why are these trends important? One answer is that education is the biggest business in America. Over 5 million people earned a living by working in schools in 1979, and many more—from book publishers to construction workers—benefit from an expanding school population. The rapid increase in the student population over the last 30 years caused a dramatic increase in the number of teachers, and as the school population shrinks, thousands can no longer find work (U.S. Census Bureau, 1983c).

College faculties more than doubled in size between 1960 and 1975, and tenure was relatively easy to achieve. After 1975, however, college faculties barely grew at all, but the percentage having tenure did—to 61 percent in 1982 (U.S. Census Bureau, 1983c). So long as the number of college professors remains stable, the percentage with tenure will remain high, and the prospects for those who have yet to achieve tenure are grim regardless of their individual qualifications. In short, there is "no room at the top," and many college professors have been forced to change careers or wander from one part-time job to another (*Newsweek*, 1983a; *New York Times*, 1982; Robertson, 1982).

## Segregation and Learning

When public schools were first introduced on a large scale at the end of the nineteenth century, blacks were largely excluded, either by law or because they had to work (Beale, 1975). In the early 1900s public education was available to most American blacks, but the distribution of funds clearly favored whites. In one Southern county, for example, expenditures per child in white schools were 33 times greater than in schools attended by blacks (Nasaw, 1979).

In 1954 the Supreme Court's landmark decision ruled that separate schools for blacks were inherently unequal, and the Court ordered an end to segregation "with all deliberate speed" (Ravitch, 1983). More than 30 years later, blacks and whites still attend schools that are predominantly of one race. As of 1976 full racial integration would have required the reassignment of 52 percent of all students (Wurdock and Farley, 1979).

In Chapter 12 we discussed the causes of racial segregation; but here we are concerned with its effects on students. It has long been noted that average scores on standardized tests are lower among blacks than among whites. Does segregation help explain this difference? Do blacks achieve higher scores in integrated schools?

At the request of the U.S. Civil Rights Commission, James Coleman and his colleagues conducted a survey of 570,000 students and 60,000 teachers in 4,000 public schools (Coleman et al., 1966). They expected to find lower quality in predominantly black schools than in predominantly white schools: older buildings, fewer library and science facilities, less-qualified teachers, larger classes, fewer textbooks, and poorer funding. They were surprised, however, to find little difference between them. Average test scores for blacks were 15 points lower than for whites, and 84 percent of black students scored below the median score for whites; but Coleman's analysis showed that his study's measures of school quality explained very little of the difference in black and white academic achievement.

The factor that had the greatest impact on scores was social class. Regardless of race, students from middle-class families score higher than lower-class students. Most important, when students attend schools whose students come from families of a lower class than their own, their test scores suffer. When they attend schools whose students come primarily from higher social classes than their own, their scores tend to increase. For example, lower-class blacks who attend black schools whose students are mostly middle-class do better than lower-class blacks who go to school with other lower-class blacks. Coleman concluded that blacks generally score lower than whites because they are more likely to come from the lower class *and* attend school with other lower-class children.

Coleman's findings laid the groundwork for racial integration, and a number of later studies showed that, under the right circumstances, inte-

Although integration affects people's racial attitudes, it has a relatively small effect on student performance over and above the effects of social class.

gration increases the average score of black students by 2 to 3 points, thus narrowing the gap slightly (Jencks, 1972). Notice, however, that most of the racial difference remains. It is apparent from these studies that changing the racial mix of student populations has only a limited effect on racial differences in educational achievement. As we will see later in this chapter, this has important implications for ending racial inequality in American society as a whole.

## Technology, Production, and Schools

More than 98 percent of Americans 5 to 17 years old were enrolled in school in 1982, and less than 1 percent of Americans over the age of 15 were illiterate. In many countries, however, illiteracy is common and only a small fraction of young people attend school. More than half of the populations of Africa and South Asia are illiterate, and in Ethiopia, Afghanistan, and Saudi Arabia, among other countries, over 80 percent are illiterate (U.S. Census Bureau, 1983c).

A major reason for such wide variations in education and literacy is that formal schooling is expensive. It not only takes an enormous investment in buildings, teachers, and equipment, but also requires that young people spend their time away from productive labor. Most societies simply cannot afford to formally educate their young on the scale found in the United States.

If all the money spent on education in 1983 were equally distributed among all Americans, it would amount to $900 for every woman, man, and child. For many countries, however, this level of spending would exhaust the entire national income: more than half of all the people in the world live in countries whose total per capita income is less than $400, a figure just over the U.S. per capita expenditure on higher education alone (U.S. Census Bureau, 1983c).

Take a moment to study Figure 16-1, which shows the relationship between per capita income and secondary school enrollment for a number of countries, each of which is represented by a dot. Note that most countries are clustered in the lower left-hand corner, with very low per capita income and secondary school enrollment. Most important is the fact that these countries contain almost three-quarters of the world's population, while the "educational elite" countries contain only 17 per-

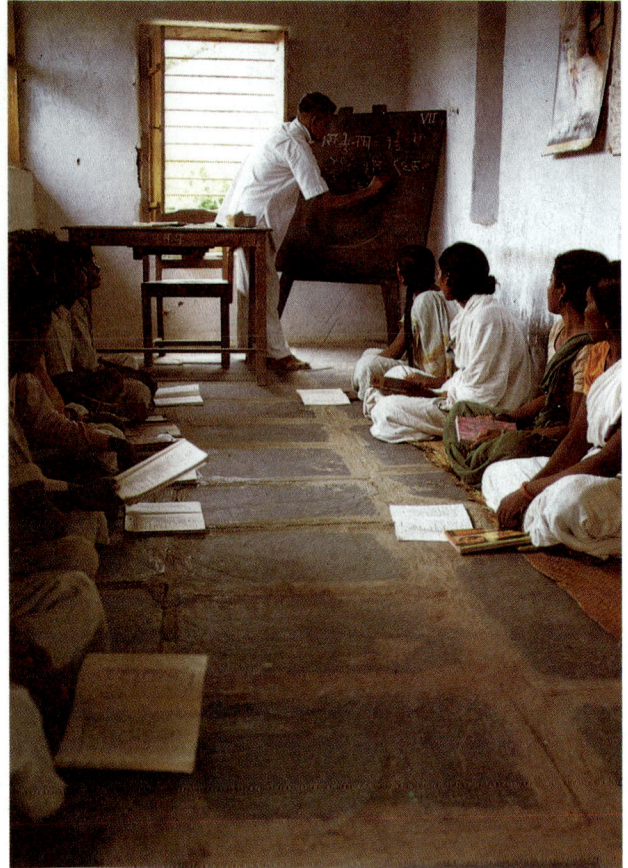

The great expense of schooling results in the exclusion of much of the world's population from all but the most elementary formal training.

cent. Thus, the distribution of formal education among societies is just as unequal as the distribution of wealth and income.

While literacy and elementary education are nearly universal in industrial societies, secondary education is not. In the United States and Japan, over 72 percent of all those 15 to 19 years old are full-time students; but in France and West Germany, the figure is only 51 percent, and in Great Britain, only 44 percent (U.S. Census Bureau, 1980b).

The staggering expense of institutionalized learning raises serious questions about education and economic development in underdeveloped countries. Although universal literacy is relatively easy to achieve, it may be that the American model of education with its heavy emphasis on advanced training beyond the elementary school level will

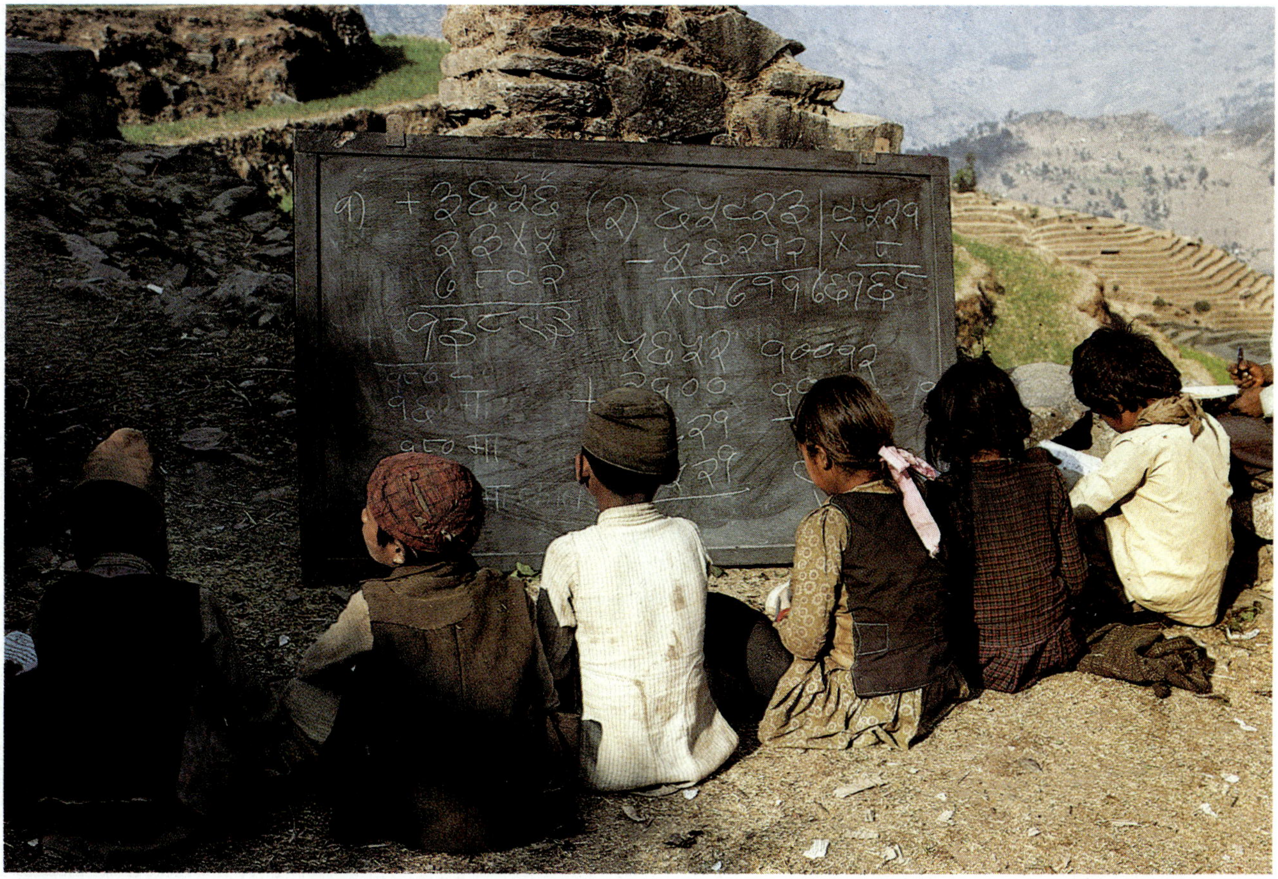

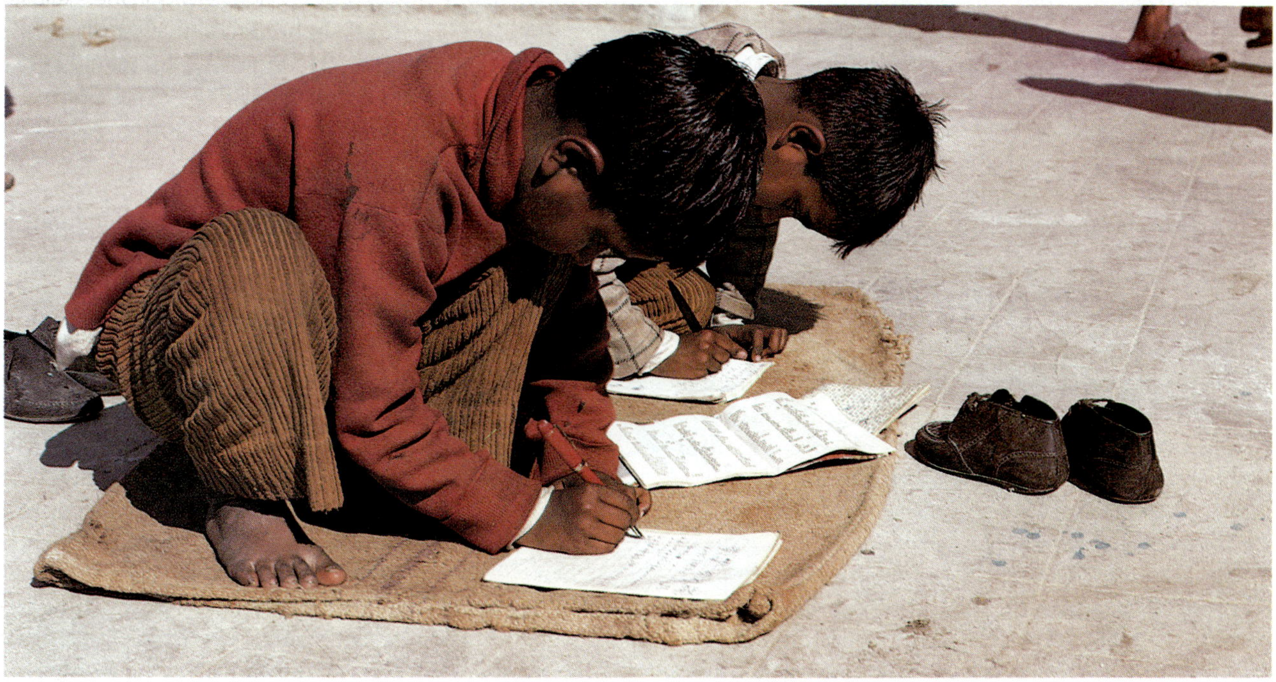

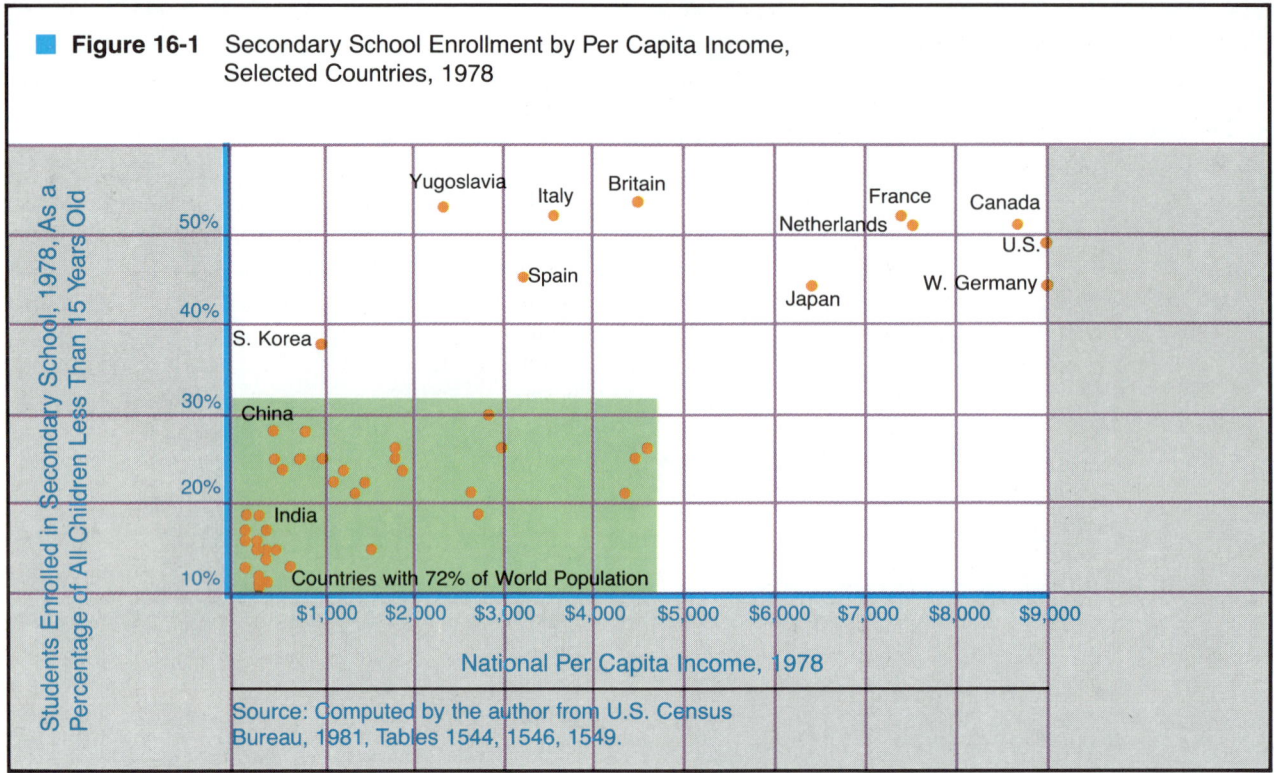

**Figure 16-1** Secondary School Enrollment by Per Capita Income, Selected Countries, 1978

Students Enrolled in Secondary School, 1978, As a Percentage of All Children Less Than 15 Years Old

National Per Capita Income, 1978

Source: Computed by the author from U.S. Census Bureau, 1981, Tables 1544, 1546, 1549.

be beyond the means of most of the world's population for a long time to come.

## Schools and Other Institutions

As an institution, the school does not exist in a vacuum. Its very existence, as well as its cultural and structural form, is connected to other social institutions: economies, the family, and government. To understand what goes on in schools, we must pay attention to the relationships between schools and such institutions.

### Schools and Families

Latent consequences of compulsory schooling affect families in a variety of ways. By acting as "baby-sitters," schools make it easier for both parents to work outside the home. In their role as socializers, schools relieve parents of much of the burden of preparing their children for adult work roles. In many schools, the food provided is cheaper and better than what is available at home, and schools thus contribute to children's nutrition.

While such transfers of family functions to schools make life easier for parents in many ways, they also create problems. As responsibility for

socialization shifts to schools, so does power over children. Before education became compulsory, families had greater control over socialization and could pass on subcultures to their children. Many advocates of public schooling, however, saw the family's influence as dysfunctional for social progress and wanted to use schools to break the family's hold on children, to replace "old-fashioned" ideas of many ethnic immigrants with the "modern" ideas of dominant groups (Lasch, 1977).

In many ways, parents feel threatened by schools, not because schools have so much power, but because they separate children from the family and give parents little control over what their children do all day long. In his study of high schools, Coleman (1961) found, for example, that students valued pleasing their friends almost as much as pleasing their parents. As we saw earlier, schools have played a major role in the creation of adolescent peer groups and subcultures, and it is in response to peer pressures that young people often have their first exposure to alcohol, drugs, cigarettes, and sex.

Thus, as responsibility for children has shifted away from families, so has power and control over their socialization. Families must compete both with the formal and hidden curricula of schools and with the strong influence of student peer groups.

## The Social Economics of Schooling

School and economy are related in several important ways. So long as young people are in school, for example, they cannot compete with adults for jobs. In 1982 there were 110 million people in the U.S. labor force, of whom over 10 million were unemployed. Almost 27 million people were enrolled in high schools and colleges (U.S. Census Bureau, 1983c). If all those students suddenly entered the labor force, the number of unemployed could almost quadruple. Because schools serve the latent function of delaying the entry of young people into the labor market, they help minimize competition for jobs.

By evaluating and sorting students according to ability, schools also help determine which jobs students will qualify for as adults. As early as 1908, many educators shared the view of the president of Harvard who believed that schools "ought to sort the pupils and sort them by their evident or probable destinies" (in Nasaw, 1979, p. 138). Many American and European schools assign students to "tracks." In Swiss schools, children are assigned to one of three tracks after four years of primary education. The lowest achievers finish primary school and then learn a manual trade; the middle group goes on to high school and trains for jobs in business and management. Only the highest achieving track leads to college and graduate education and work in the professions, universities, and leadership in business and government.

Because schools do not produce a product that they sell in the market, they are not self-supporting; public schools must depend on tax revenues, local school boards, and state and federal governments for funding. When the economy is in a slump, schools are often among the first institutions to feel the effects as teachers are laid off and programs are cut.

The dependence of schools on outside support makes them vulnerable, for if they displease their supporters, they may lose the funds they need to operate. During the 1960s the University of California had a running battle with Governor Ronald Reagan, who disapproved of student demonstrations against the war and student demands for greater control over the university. One of his major weapons in that struggle was his influence over the state budget on which the university depended.

Finally, schools are connected to the economy because they are *part* of it. Most public school teachers belong to unions whose interests may conflict with educational goals. For example, the National Commission on Excellence in Education (1983) recommended merit pay for teachers and regular evaluation of teacher performance. The American Federation of Teachers, however, opposed merit pay because it would weaken the union's bargaining position; it also opposed teacher evaluation because it would undermine job security (*Newsweek*, 1983b).

Even college professors have unionized on some campuses in order to protect job security and pay levels—even though professors traditionally look upon unions as being inappropriate for middle-class professionals. The unionization of professors shows clearly that in spite of the fact that many people like to think of colleges as "Ivory Towers" that stand aside from the mundane affairs of society, colleges and universities are organizations in which people earn a living, and the economic interests of different groups often conflict.

## Politics: Schools and Nationalism

> If an unfriendly foreign power had attempted to impose on America the mediocre educational performance that exists today, we might well have viewed it as an act of war. . . . We have in effect been committing an act of unthinking, unilateral educational disarmament. (National Commission on Excellence in Education, 1983)

This startling conclusion about the current state of American education reflects a strong belief in a connection between student achievement in schools and the attainment of national goals. The Commission clearly defines education as a national armament that helps protect the United States from other nations.

The use of schools to promote national goals is not a new practice. The first public schools appeared in Germany at a time when Germans were trying to build a sense of national solidarity and patriotism, and in the 1930s the Nazis used children's literature to foster the image of Germans as a master race that would rule the world

There is a strong connection between schooling and nationalism in most developed societies, whether in the recitation of a pledge of allegiance or in the rewriting of history.

(Kamenetsky, 1984). Students in American schools pledge allegiance to the flag every day and sing the national anthem at sporting events. Courses in American history tend to neglect the more unattractive aspects of our past—including racism, imperialism, and atrocities committed during wars—while emphasizing our accomplishments, praising the benefits of capitalism, and highlighting the shortcomings of socialism and communism.

Japanese textbooks were recently criticized for ignoring atrocities committed by Japanese troops during World War II; and German textbooks pay little attention to the Nazis and the Holocaust. Lessons in Russian schools glorify socialism and communism, condemn capitalism, and, depending on the political climate, either attack or glorify various leaders of the past. The tendency of the Russian leadership to rewrite history is so pervasive that it has found its way into Russian jokes, one of which defines a Russian historian as "someone who can predict the past." Until as recently as the 1960s, the study of sociology was not allowed in China or the Soviet Union; and current sociological work in the Soviet Union rarely raises issues and problems that challenge basic characteristics of its society (*Footnotes*, 1980).

After World War II the United States and the Soviet Union engaged in a "Cold War" in which both sides struggled for economic and military superiority. In 1957 the Soviet Union launched the world's first space satellite—Sputnik I—and the United States reacted in fear to this startling technological advance. President Eisenhower argued that scientific education lay at the heart of America's ability to defend itself and called for nationwide testing of high school students, incentives to pursue scientific careers, increased laboratory facilities, and better training for math and science teachers (Ravitch, 1983; Spring, 1976).

Within a year of the launch of Sputnik I, Congress passed the National Defense Education Act, which provided substantial federal funding for counseling programs designed to sort out the most gifted students, training programs for science teachers, graduate fellowships, and undergraduate student loans. American schools were clearly being regarded as an instrument of national political policy.

On many levels, then, schools perform a variety of functions—from socializing the young to advancing political goals. Because schools distribute skills and credentials, they have often been criticized as supporters of social inequality. Conflict theorists in particular focus on the ways in which cultural, structural, and ecological aspects of schools perpetuate inequality based on race, gender, and social class.

## Schools and Social Conflict: Class and Classrooms

In the 1960s the civil rights movement targeted education as a major way of removing racial inequality (Bane and Jencks, 1972). A basic assumption was that lower-class children could not escape poverty without the basic cognitive skills—such as the ability to read, write, and do arithmetic—required in the job market.

As explained in the following sections, the assumptions underlying this strategy are false, both because cognitive skills do not explain why some people are rich and others are poor, and because there is little evidence that schools can substantially reduce class or racial differences in basic skills. Social characteristics of schools, however, do help perpetuate social inequality in other ways, for

> the real achievement of schools consists in their ability to train children to accept the prevailing class structure and their fate as workers within the industrial system. . . . What is learned in school . . . is rarely related to specific skills. . . . Rather students learn . . . to accommodate to the first requirement of industrial labor: respect for authority, the self-discipline needed to internalize the values of the labor process, and the place of the worker within the prevailing occupational hierarchies. (Aronowitz, 1973, p. 74)

## Inequality and the Hidden Curriculum

There is a New England town in which most of the residents are connected in some way to a local private, elite college. The public schools are relatively new and well staffed, and a large percentage of the students are the children of college professors and administrators. The neighboring town is inhabited primarily by working-class people, some of whom are maintenance workers at the college (Smith, 1981).

In both towns high school students study the same subjects, but the hidden curriculum is very different. The working-class students cannot leave classrooms without a "hall pass"; their behavior is watched closely by teachers and principals; they have little choice over the courses they will take; and the subject of college education is rarely brought up. In the college town, on the other hand, students are not required to have hall passes; they are allowed to make many decisions for themselves, including selection from a wide variety of elective courses; and their teachers often express the assumption that most if not all of them will go on to college.

If they learn their "lessons," students in these two towns will graduate with quite different ideas about themselves and their place in society. Working-class students will learn that they are not to be trusted, that important decisions about their lives

The students in these two classes—one in a public school and the other in a private school—are receiving very different messages about who they are in the world and what is expected of them.

will rest in the hands of others. The middle- and upper-class students in the college town, however, will learn that they can be trusted to control their own lives and, most important, that they will become adults who will make decisions about *other* people's lives. The working-class students are being prepared to be workers under the authority of managers and professionals, while the middle- and upper-class students are learning to *be* managers and professionals.

Such differences between schools intensify class differences among adults by transmitting different expectations to students. When Leacock (1969) repeated the Rosenthal and Jacobson (1968) experiment in which teachers' expectations and behavior were affected by false reports of student potential, she found that the results were themselves affected by the school's social class. Teachers in schools whose students came primarily from the middle class treated students better if they were identified as bright and promising; but in lower-class schools, just the opposite occurred: "promising" students were treated as "wise guys."

This raises a serious question about the study (Coleman et al., 1966), discussed earlier. Coleman and colleagues found that many objective measures of school quality did not explain the racial gap in academic achievement. Although these researchers did measure "teacher qualifications," they did *not* measure the many beliefs, values, attitudes, and expectations that affect teachers' perceptions and behavior in relation to students. This suggests that the relatively poor performance of students in lower-class schools—many of whom are black—may be in part a self-fulfilling prophecy: they achieve less because their teachers *expect* them to, regardless of the "quality" of schools and their teachers.

**Tracking and Inequality   Tracking** is used to divide students according to tests designed to measure academic ability. The manifest function of tracking is to allow "slow" students to get attention that would otherwise be given to "bright" students, and to allow "bright" students to move at their own speed, rather than having to wait for the "slow" students to catch up.

Nonwhite and lower-class students are more likely than others to be assigned to "slow" tracks, regardless of their test scores (Edelman et al., 1985; Shafer et al., 1967). Given what we know about the effects of expectations on student achievement, it is tempting to conclude that tracking helps explain why black and lower-class students have lower average levels of achievement. It is not this simple, however.

In 1968 the National Education Association reviewed hundreds of studies on the effects of tracking and concluded that regardless of the track students are in, tracking is no more likely to hurt student performance than it is to improve it. In a study of British primary schools (Acland, 1972), students whose initial ability levels were similar had similar levels of achievement even though they were assigned to different tracks. Heyns (1971) found similar results in a study of predominantly white American high schools.

Does this mean that tracking plays no part in the perpetuation of inequality? There is little evidence that tracking affects levels of cognitive ability to any significant degree, but tracking may have a more important effect that has nothing to do with achievement. By affecting students' expectations, beliefs, values, and attitudes, tracking may reinforce their acceptance of their position in society, whether it be high or low. In this sense, tracking may contribute to false consciousness and, therefore, to the perpetuation of social classes.

**Grades, Ideology, and False Consciousness**
Grades are functional for a number of goals in schools. They reinforce the power of teachers, motivate many students to work, and are fairly accurate predictors of how well students will perform at higher levels of schooling.

The use of grades is dysfunctional for other goals, however. Grades and standardized tests are poor predictors of adult performance outside the school environment (McClelland, 1973); they create tensions and anxieties that interfere with creativity and discourage close relationships between students and teachers; and they encourage students to manipulate teachers, to compete rather than cooperate with each other, and to avoid taking initiative (Hoyt, 1965; Kirschenbaum et al., 1971; Sawyer, 1970).

The finding that grades are inaccurate predictors of adult performance is important, because schools are often viewed as sorters of talent for the adult job market. If grades are poor predictors of which students will make the best lawyers, business managers, scientists, or teachers, then why are they still used to "sort" students? Part of the answer comes from the conflict perspective.

As we saw in Chapter 11, the perpetuation of social classes depends in part on people's acceptance of their class position. Part of the basis for this acceptance is the belief that the system through which rewards are distributed is fair, that everyone has an equal opportunity to achieve desirable jobs and relatively high standards of living. If individuals support the belief that the system is basically

## Voices: Tracks that Lead Nowhere

In most schools and school systems, in this and a number of other countries, poor children are in a great many ways discriminated against, humiliated, and often brutally treated. Wherever schools allow what they call "corporal punishment," by which they mean the practice of allowing teachers, on whatever pretext they may choose, to assault and beat children, it is poor children who get beaten the most and the worst. Indeed, even for the severest offenses, upper-class children are rarely beaten at all. In all schools and school systems that divide children by so-called ability—tracking as it's called here, streaming as it's called in Great Britain—the poor children are almost all and always in the lower tracks. Studies have often shown an almost perfect correlation between family income and school tracking—rich kids at the top, poor at the bottom. Furthermore, the poor kids are put into the lowest track almost from the moment they enter school. Once in, they have little chance of getting out. Teachers of low tracks have often told me that even when a student was doing very good work the school would not allow them to give him a high grade, on the grounds that if he were capable of doing that good work, he wouldn't be in the low track. That he had been in the low track almost from the first day he entered school was dismissed as irrelevant.

An even more horrifying example of the way this discrimination works in a *kindergarten* class can be found in the article "Student Social Class and Teacher Expectations: The Self-Fulfilling Prophecy in Ghetto Education" by Ray Rist, in the August, 1970 issue of the Harvard Educational Review. The kindergarten teacher described, after only eight days of school, and entirely on the basis of appearance, dress, manners, in short middleclassness, divided her class into three tracks by seating them at three separate tables, which remained fixed for the rest of the year. One of these tables got most of her teaching, attention, and support; the other two were increasingly ignored except when the teacher told them to do something or commented unfavorably on what they did. Worse yet, the children at the favored table were allowed and encouraged to make fun of the children at the other two tables, and to boss them around.

Some of this has changed a little, for a number of reasons—bad publicity, poor people's militancy, the growing crisis of schools in cities and out—but it is not likely to change very much. Once reason is simple and hard to escape. The schools, particularly the schools where poor kids go, are filled with people who don't like poor kids. Almost everyone I know who has had wide experience with inner city schools has found this to be true.

Source: Holt, *Freedom and Beyond*, 1972.

fair, then they have no one but themselves to blame if they are in the lower class, and no one but themselves to credit if they live a life of privilege (Jencks and Riesman, 1968).

Students generally enter college with unrealistic job aspirations, for there simply are not enough good jobs to go around (Guzzardi, 1976). Grades thus serve the function of dulling the aspirations of many students, but particularly those from the working and lower classes, for they are most likely to have below-average grades (Clark, 1960). Many students with low grades are advised to drop out of school altogether; but many others are encouraged to remain in school but to accept lower aspirations.

This helps ensure that society's less-desirable jobs will be performed; but, most important, it helps maintain the ideology of equal opportunity and, with it, the unequal distribution of wealth, power, and prestige.

Trimberger (1971) and others consequently claim that grading contributes to false consciousness among lower-class students by supporting the false belief that their class position as adults results more from their individual abilities and performance than from the limitations imposed by a class society. Grading, however, also contributes to false consciousness among middle- and upper-class students, for it supports the equally false belief that their success is due entirely to their individual talent and effort.

You might be tempted to conclude from this analysis that if schools devised a grading system that did accurately predict adult performance, then actual ability would be the only basis for assigning people to adult roles, and the resulting distribution of rewards would be fairer. The problem with this solution, however, lies with the fact that the distribution of wealth, power, and prestige has relatively little to do with ability, however accurately it may be measured.

## Opportunity and Outcome

From their earliest years, public schools were looked to as sources of economic prosperity, social equality, and upward mobility. A major part of the American dream is that individual ability and effort

In spite of our deep faith in higher education, equality of educational opportunity would probably have a relatively small impact on the social and economic factors, outside of schools, that produce a stratified society.

are the only limits on achievement, and equal opportunity for education is the key to equality of outcomes (Binder, 1974).

We saw earlier in this chapter that lower-class and minority members do not have equal access to higher education; but as many sociologists point out, even if there *were* equal educational opportunity, this would not eliminate social classes, because inequality is created by economic arrangements, not educational ones (Bane and Jencks, 1972).

The educational attainment of the American labor force, for example, rose sharply over the last two decades (see Table 16-3). Between 1960 and 1981 the percentage of adults with high school diplomas increased by almost 70 percent, and among blacks the percentage almost tripled. Among both blacks and whites, the percentage of adults with four or more years of college more than doubled. As we saw in Chapter 11, however, inequality between social classes *increased*, which suggests that while education is certainly not irrelevant to economic success, other factors play an equal, if not more important, part.

**Table 16-3**

Educational Attainment, by Race and Sex, (United States, 1960–1981)

| RACE AND SEX | HIGH SCHOOL GRADUATE | | COLLEGE GRADUATE OR MORE | |
|---|---|---|---|---|
| | 1960 | 1981 | 1960 | 1981 |
| White males | 22% | 34% | 10% | 22% |
| White females | 29% | 42% | 6% | 14% |
| Black males | 11% | 31% | 3% | 8% |
| Black females | 14% | 32% | 3% | 8% |
| Hispanic males | * | 24% | * | 10% |
| Hispanic females | * | 28% | * | 6% |

Source: U.S. Census Bureau, 1982.

*Not Available.

If, for example, we compare the incomes of brothers who have similar IQ scores and similar education, they differ by an average of $5,300 (Bane and Jencks, 1972). If we choose pairs of men at random, however, and compare their incomes, the average difference is only slightly higher— $6,200. As Bane and Jencks concluded:

> These estimates mean that people who start off equal end up almost as unequal as everyone else. Inequality is not mostly inherited: It is re-created anew in each generation. . . . adult success must depend on a lot of things besides family background, schooling, and the cognitive skills measured by standardized tests. (p. 39)

Like all major structural characteristics of societies, inequality is not the result of any one aspect of social life. No institution has the power to remove the inequalities of race, gender, or social class. That schools have been looked to so often as a remedy for inequality is due less to the actual power of schools than to the importance Americans attach to the cultural ideas of equal opportunity and reward based solely on ability and effort.

## Schools and Social Change

If you wanted to change a major aspect of society, where would you begin? When I pose this question to college students, more often than not they reply, "You have to start with kids." It is an obvious solution: it is easier to teach children new ideas than to change old ideas that are already deeply embedded in adults.

For this simple reason, schools have often been a battleground in struggles for social change. Racial integration increases interaction between children of different races before they firmly adopt the fundamentals of racism. A major focus of the women's movement has been on the images of males and females in school textbooks. Sex education is offered as a way to increase young people's understanding of their sexuality and decrease the likelihood of teenage pregnancy.

Opponents of change focus on schools as sources of social opportunity and stability. Religious fundamentalists oppose the teaching of the theory of evolution, and 14 percent of American adults are against sex education. Just under half would prevent atheists, communists, or advocates of military rule in the United States from teaching

in colleges or universities, and 40 percent would also exclude homosexuals (Davis, 1984).

Values also conflict in less-specific areas. For many, schools exist in order to teach students to think for themselves, to solve problems, and to ask critical questions about prevailing beliefs, values, attitudes, and norms—Thomas Jefferson's prescription for a healthy democracy. To others, however, the idea that any question can have more than one correct answer is unacceptable because it threatens the stability of a predictable, orderly view of the world.

From their home in Texas, Mel and Norma Gabler organized a national campaign to censor textbooks that do not adhere to their rigid set of views. From their perspective, students should not read sympathetic stories about Robin Hood, because he stole. Students should not be allowed to discuss questions of morality, because the very act of posing such questions implies that moral decisions have no single correct answer (*Time*, 1979).

Schools embody a fundamental value conflict in social life: The freedom of people to think for themselves is highly valued in our culture and is the major source of innovation and creativity; and yet, at the same time, free inquiry inevitably leads to critical questions about cultural ideas and social relationships. The Brazilian educator, Paulo Freire (1972) was expelled from his country because he taught peasants to read. The dominant groups— especially the landowners who exploited the peasants—felt threatened because literacy increased the peasants' ability to understand their oppressed position in Brazilian society.

Higher education, in particular, contributes to social change in ways that have nothing to do with what students learn. For example, many college students are free of work and family responsibilities, and this gives them time and energy to participate in social movements. The civil rights and anti-Vietnam War movements of the 1960s drew heavily on the support of students, and in the 1970s university students in France succeeded in leading what became a paralyzing national strike.

Education has also fostered the growth of intellectuals as a category—people who are separated from production and are therefore free to analyze and criticize the cultural, structural, and ecological characteristics of a society (Flacks,

1970). The roots of sociology itself extend back to the turbulent 1800s in which scholars such as Durkheim, Weber, and particularly Marx, were motivated as much by a desire for positive social change as they were by intellectual curiosity. Most of the first American sociologists saw themselves primarily as social reformers, not detached intellectuals. Many of today's sociologists believe that it is their responsibility to use their research and analytic skills to bring about positive changes in the social conditions that so profoundly affect people's lives.

Writers, artists, scholars, and professionals such as Lenin, Leon Trotsky, Fidel Castro, and Che Guevara have played major roles in revolutions. For this reason, intellectuals are often viewed with considerable suspicion, if not hostility. When the Nazis seized power in Germany in the 1930s, university professors and other intellectuals were among their first targets as they tried to stifle criticism and dissent.

As institutions, schools thus contribute both to social change and conflict *and* to continuity and stability; but schools, themselves, have also been the objects of movements for social change.

Among the many alternatives to traditional education that have appeared in recent years are schools such as the one formed by this group in southern Kentucky. In that school the children have a program of learning emphasizing the group's belief in the importance of "getting back to the land."

## Changing Schools

As we have seen, schools may be understood both in terms of how they operate and in terms of their relationships with the rest of society. In order to understand changes in educational institutions, therefore, we have to pay attention to both of these levels of analysis.

Because the functions of schools are so highly valued in societies that use them, criticism of schools and efforts to change them are almost as old as schools themselves. The practice of grading students, for example, has a long and checkered history in American education. Over the last hundred years, schools have adopted grading, dropped it, re-adopted it, and modified it with innovations such as "pass-fail" (Kirschenbaum et al., 1971). In the 1980s there is a renewed call for higher standards and stricter grading of student performance (National Commission on Excellence in Education, 1983).

Such changes reflect competition between competing beliefs and values. Opponents argue that grading inhibits creativity and independent thought, that it encourages students to care more about grades than learning. Supporters stress different values—the importance of motivating students to learn what they need to know whether they like it or not, and sorting out students of different ability levels.

Underlying such positions are beliefs about the nature of childhood and values about how much power children should have, and such differences have produced some radical alternatives to traditional schooling. At a British school called Summerhill, teachers exercise virtually no authority over their students, who run the school through democratic meetings and decide what they will learn and when they will learn it. The school's founder, A. S. Neill, maintained that the most important thing for young people to learn is how to live with others and make decisions for themselves. Subjects such as history and science can be learned later, when children decide they need them (Neill, 1961).

Illich (1971) went so far as to advocate abolishing schools altogether and replacing them with "learning centers" in which people who want to learn get together with those who have something to teach. He objected to formal schooling not only because of his belief that it stifles the motivation to explore the world and learn about it, but also because its hidden curriculum promotes control, obedience, and conformity more than enlightenment and independent thought.

Illich and Neill were both embraced and ridiculed by experts in many fields, including education (see Gartner, Greer, and Riessman, 1973; Hart, 1970). Supporters generally applauded the values, beliefs, and attitudes reflected in Illich's and Neill's proposals, while detractors questioned their practicality, and argued that student autonomy will seriously undermine the goals of socialization and social control.

Beyond a few private experiments, it is unlikely that elementary and secondary schools will stray far from their current bureaucratic form in which power is sharply divided between adults and children. In 1983 the National Commission on Excellence in Education strongly recommended that school days and years be lengthened, that student freedom to decide which subjects to study be severely limited, and that requirements for graduation be raised and strictly enforced.

There is evidence, however, that in higher education students are controlling their own education to an increasing degree. For the most part, this results from the fact that an increasing proportion of students are adults who are returning to school after spending several years in the labor force. It also results from the fact that many colleges are experiencing financial difficulties and skrinking enrollments, and they see the adult market as a new source of income.

In 1982, 13 percent of American adults participated in some kind of education program, and only a quarter of these were enrolled in traditional schools—elementary or secondary schools or four-year colleges (U.S. Census Bureau, 1983c). In a California study, three out of four adults said they wanted to continue their education, and almost a third of these preferred informal arrangements with teachers rather than formal enrollment in an institution (Peterson, 1976). Thus, for many adults, schools increasingly serve as providers of services in a market in which schools depend on students to buy education.

This raises once again the economic reality that schools must have money in order to operate; and some of the most heated debates about American schools focus on the issue of who will pay for them and how, and how this will affect the quality of education.

## Money and the Quality of Education

Many reformers would improve schools by forcing them to improve—by raising graduation standards, for example, and by requiring teachers to pass competency tests at regular intervals. Others, however, suggest that the best way to improve schools is to set them in economic competition with each other. If parents can send children to the school of their choice, then schools will have to compete in order to survive.

One suggestion is to take a community's school budget and distribute it among parents in the form of "credits" or "vouchers" (La Noue, 1972). Parents could then redeem their vouchers in any way they wished, either by enrolling their children in a public school, or by seeking out private education. The best schools, of course, would get the most "business," and this would encourage inferior schools to improve their performance.

A second proposal would allow parents who send their children to private schools to pay less federal tax (Hegedus, 1976; Thomas and Levin, 1983). By subsidizing private schools, supporters argue, this plan would increase healthy competition between public and private schools and give parents greater freedom of choice and control over their children's educations.

Critics—including the NAACP, the Civil Liberties Union, and professional educators—argue that both plans would make the distribution of education even more unequal than it is today. As additional family income, vouchers would enable middle-class parents to send their children to private schools, but would not be enough to give lower-class parents the same option. Tuition tax credits discriminate against lower-class families, who cannot afford private schools and already receive a relatively small share of educational resources. Critics fear that both proposals would further divide schooling into two separate and unequal systems: one well-financed, middle-class, and predominantly white, and the other poorly financed, lower-class, and predominantly nonwhite.

The characteristics of educational institutions seem forever tied to social conditions in society itself. Schools have been, are, and will continue to be important parts of the "real world."

## Summary

1. Education is a form of socialization that involves systematic, formal transmission of skills, knowledge, and other aspects of culture. In many societies this takes place primarily in schools—formal organizations whose primary purpose is education.

2. Education was once restricted to the upper classes, but with the Industrial Revolution public schooling gradually included increasingly large segments of the population.

3. Like all institutions, schools are organized around cultural ideas such as a belief in the accuracy of grades, values of punctuality and competition, and norms such as those embodied in honor codes. Within this environment, there are subcultures such as those among students. While the manifest function of schools is to teach subjects such as math, they also teach a hidden curriculum that consists of values such as obedience to authority and the relative desirability of different social classes or of different ethnic backgrounds.

4. In general, the higher the level of schooling, the more likely school boundaries are to exclude students from disadvantaged backgrounds.

5. Like all social behavior, patterns of interaction in schools are affected by definitions of the situation and people's perceptions of each other. Teachers and students often feel frustrated with each other, for example, when students define their role as giving correct answers and teachers expect students to think independently.

6. Schools, like many other institutions, have become bureaucratic. Some argue that this interferes with educational goals by creating competing interests such as those of teachers and administrators.

7. Distributions of power differ sharply among schools, according to the level of schooling. For example, students generally gain power as they advance to college, and power structures are more complex in college than in elementary school.

8. Population affects schools primarily through changes in the birth rate, increasing or decreasing the number of potential students. This profoundly affects both communities and professionals who make a living from the business of schooling.

9. Ecological factors, such as the use of space, also affect schools. Racial segregation, for example, and different models of classroom interaction, such as open classrooms, affect how much students learn and what they learn. The mode of production in a society is also important, because schooling is expensive. Industrial societies are in a far better position to school their children than are underdeveloped countries.

10. Schools are related to other institutions in many ways. They have taken over many functions once reserved for families; compulsory schooling keeps young people out of the job market; and schools are often used to promote national political goals such as allegiance to the state.

11. Schools play an important part in social conflict. The hidden curriculum, tracking, and grades, for example, support social class differences by sorting students according to class and preparing them to accept their class position. While schooling has long been perceived as a solution for social inequality, most research shows that the causes of inequality are to be found primarily outside of schools.

12. Because they socialize the young, schools have been viewed as vehicles for social change. This has made them an ongoing scene of conflict as various interest groups vie to determine school policy and curriculum.

## Key Terms

education 499
extrinsic reward 504
hidden curriculum 506
intrinsic reward 504
school 499
social promotion 512
student subcultures 505
    academic 505
    collegiate 505
    nonconformist 505
    vocational 505
tracking 522
zero-sum game 503

# Recommended Readings

BOOCOCK, S. (1980). *Sociology of education: An introduction* (2nd ed.). Boston: Houghton-Mifflin. An excellent introduction to the field. See also Parelius, A. P., and Parelius, R. J. (1978). *The sociology of education.* Englewood Cliffs, NJ: Prentice-Hall.

BOWLES, S., and GINTIS, H. (1976). *Schooling in capitalist America: Educational reform and the contradictions of economic life.* New York: Basic Books. An important analysis of the ways in which schools and formal education help to reproduce social classes in America.

ILLICH, I. (1971). *Deschooling society.* New York: Harper and Row. A revolutionary plan to do away with schools as we know them. For an equally provocative collection of critical articles written in response to Illich's ideas, see A. Gartner, C. Greer, and F. Riessman (Eds.). (1973). *After deschooling, what?* New York: Harper and Row.

JENCKS, C., et al. (1972). *Inequality.* An energetic challenge to the belief that education is the key to social mobility and reduction of social inequality.

RAVITCH, D. (1983). *The troubled crusade: American education 1945–1980.* New York: Basic Books. A thoughtful, well-written analysis of 35 years of attempts at educational reform in the United States.

ROHLEN, T. P. (1983). *Japan's high schools.* Berkeley: University of California Press. A highly recommended study that tries to explain how Japan's high schools produce levels of achievement unheard of in the United States. See also Cummings, W. K. (1980). *Education and equality in Japan.* Princeton, NJ: Princeton University Press.

# CHAPTER 17

# Economic Arrangements

Stop for a moment and look at the characteristics of this book as an object: the print, pictures, cover, binding, use of color, and strings of words that communicate ideas. Now think about two questions: What did it take to bring this book into being, and how did it wind up in your hands?

In the simplest sense, this book has physical origins: lumber and paper mills, photographic equipment, typewriters, word processors, artists' pens and brushes, typesetting machines, printing presses and ink, glue and binding machines. In order to get to you, it had to be packed, shipped to a store, and then given to you in exchange for money. This book is also the result of energy—from electricity produced by giant turbines to gasoline refined from crude oil. Together, these constitute what Marx called the **means of production.** They are the physical means through which goods and services are produced in a society.

All this, however, is not the whole story of where this book came from, for the means of production were used by people who worked in relation to one another and to the means of production. The author, editors, administrators and managers, sociologists, clerks, secretaries, artists, designers, photographers, typesetters, bookbinders, market researchers, salespeople, bookstore owners—all these and many more (including janitors in the publisher's office building) participated in a set of social **relations of production** through which this book and thousands like it are produced and distributed. Together, the means of production and the relations of production constitute the **mode of production.**

**Economic institutions** are enduring sets of cultural ideas and objects and social relationships through which goods and services are produced and distributed in societies. Cultural characteristics of economic institutions include values that define the goals of productive activity (do we publish a book to help educate young people, to make a profit, or both?). Structural characteristics of economic institutions refer to how people work both in relation with one another and to the means of production: who owns and controls the means of production, who decides what will be produced and how, who controls what is done with the results, and the kinds of roles people play in the production process.

Like this free-lance writer, those who control a means of production can decide what they will produce and how and what will be done with the results.

I, for example, work under contract with my publisher. I agree to produce a manuscript by a certain date, in return for which I am paid a share of the returns from selling the book. I work in my apartment and use a word processor that I own. No one checks to see if I am at work this morning. So long as I get the job done on time, *I* decide how and when I work.

Most of the others who helped produce this book, however (like most people in our society), work for employers who buy their time for wages and decide what they will do with that time. These employees do not help decide which books will be published; they do not get a percentage of the proceeds from selling what their labor power helps to produce; they do not decide how and when they will work; and, most important, they do not own any means of producing goods or services other than themselves.

The characteristics of economic institutions determine both how societies produce goods and services and how individuals participate in the production process; and one way to see how economic institutions affect societies and their people is to look at how those institutions have changed over the course of human history. Imagine that we can condense 35,000 years into a single life span, so that each of us can experience the changes that have occurred. Where do we begin, where do we end up, and how do we get from there to here?

## The Roots of Capitalism

We begin with tiny societies whose members survive by hunting wild game and gathering plants. There are neighboring societies some distance

In hunter-gatherer societies such as the Bushmen of southern Africa, virtually everyone contributes to production in a communal economy in which control over production is collective.

away; but we rarely encounter them except on long hunting expeditions, and generally have little to do with them. Virtually everyone except the smallest child produces something; we share what we produce with everyone else; and kinship is the most important tie that binds us together into a single society (Murdock, 1967). Our division of labor is simple and based entirely on age and gender. Although each of us contributes to production in different ways, in general no one's contribution is valued so highly that it gives him or her a great advantage of prestige or power.

We consume everything that we produce, which means that the value of everything from meat to clothing is based solely on its **use value.** Control of the means of production is *collective,* and our economy is *communal,* much like that of the Melanesian tribes that Malinowski (1922) studied in the 1920s. We help one another as friends and family members—not for personal gain, but because we feel a social obligation to cooperate with and help one another.

Thousands of years pass (until roughly 7000 B.C.), and we discover how to grow some of our own food. We invent simple tools, and as our technology grows—especially with the invention of the plow—we are able to produce more than we need in order to survive. Our population grows because we can feed more people with better diets; but, most important, our ability to produce a surplus affects both the internal structure of our society and its relation to others.

Everyone no longer must produce food. Some can make clay pots, mats to sleep on, or fancy clothes to wear during celebrations. Whereas we once produced things only for their use value, we can now use some of what we produce to *exchange* for goods that we do not make ourselves. We can trade some of our pots, mats, and fancy clothes for things produced in other societies: arrows, plows, or medicinal herbs. Even food—if we produce a surplus—takes on **exchange value** in addition to use value.

When goods have exchange value, they are **commodities.** For the first time, we trade with each other—commodity for commodity—and our economy is changing into a **market economy** in which the exchange value of goods determines what can be bartered for what. I make fancy clothes but I do not grow food; you grow food but

As the number of different goods and services expands, we discover that bartering is a very inefficient way of getting what we need and want from each other. Once you have all the clothes you want, or if you think the clothes I make are ugly, how do I get food from you? How, in short, can I get something that you produce when you do not want what I produce? The answer that developed around 2000 B.C. was money, and it profoundly affected the social relationships through which goods and services were produced and distributed.

Instead of trading commodities for commodities, we now use money. I trade my clothes for money and then trade my money for food. Exchanges now take the form of commodity-money-commodity, rather than the simpler form of commodity-commodity.

## Feudalism: A Shift in Power

As the centuries pass (we are up to the early Middle Ages), populations grow more rapidly, divisions of labor become more complex, trade expands rapidly, and money is increasingly important as a medium of exchange. All of this supports an elite of nobles, kings, and queens, who maintain their positions by accumulating wealth in the form of money and land. The most significant aspect of this society, however, lies in the social relationships between producers and the elite.

Nobles use their power to protect people from other nobles; and many of these people are *serfs*, who give some of what they produce to the nobles in exchange for protection (Bloch, 1961). Although serfs are bound to the land and live generally miserable lives, both they and free workers control the means of production. They use land or tools and decide how much to produce. Unlike slaves, then, serfs control their own labor.

Serfs, however, are not allowed to dispose of what they produce as they choose. Even independent producers are regulated by craft guilds whose norms specify where and when they work, and what and how much they produce. Clearly, this new system—called **feudalism**—marks the beginning of a historical transformation that ultimately will affect almost every aspect of social life: *the control over the production process is shifting out of the hands of those who actually produce goods and services.*

The introduction of markets in which commodities are traded accompanied an important shift from use values to exchange values.

do not make fancy clothes; so we trade one for the other. This means, of course, that we have to deal continually with the problem of deciding what amount of clothing is "worth" what amount of food, and the basic mechanism in bartering is the balance between how much labor it takes to make clothing and food and how much each of us wants or needs what the other produces.

Although many aspects of our society—such as family life—do not operate like a market, a market economy significantly changes the culture and structure of our society. Getting a fair (if not the "best") deal in market exchanges replaces sharing as our most important economic value, and the means of production are no longer collectively owned. Each producer owns and controls some means of production—whether it be tools, land, or labor. Thus, we use our labor and what it produces to get what we need and want through market exchanges.

## Buying, Selling, and the Rise of the Merchant Class

Around the eleventh century, towns develop outside the walls of feudal estates, and after considerable struggle their inhabitants free themselves from the dominance of the nobility (Dobb, 1947). Producers are now free to produce what they want, make the best trades they can, and accumulate a surplus.

At about this time some powerful residents of towns make a discovery that will dramatically affect the development of societies: since economic exchange primarily involves money, why not use money to buy commodities and then sell them for still more money? These innovators—**merchants**—withdraw from the production process and make a radical transition from a commodity-money-commodity exchange to one that is money-commodity-money.

The new exchange is revolutionary because it represents a profound change in values that govern economic behavior. Previously, the purpose of exchange was to get something that we did not produce ourselves; and we were content to wind up with something whose value was comparable to what we gave up. Merchants, however, want to end up with more money than they start with. They are in the business of making a profit by taking a share of what is produced through the labor of other people.

The appearance of merchants introduces a new social relationship—between producers and merchants; and the idea of profit is based on the terms of that relationship. In our earliest society goods had use value only; later they acquired exchange

The merchant class introduced a revolutionary type of exchange—money-commodity-money—that laid the groundwork for the emergence of capitalism centuries later.

value determined by the value of the labor it took to produce them. Now, however, merchants want to sell goods at a higher price than they pay for them. One way to do this is to try to sell the goods for more than their value; but this makes it difficult to compete with other merchants.

A second alternative is to pay workers less than the value of their labor and keep what is left over. "What is left over" is called **surplus value,** and it is created by money-commodity-money exchange (Marx, 1867; see also Braverman, 1976). For the system to operate, workers must receive enough of the value of what they produce to maintain a standard of living that allows them to work (to buy enough food, shelter, clothing, and medical care to remain productive) and raise children who will become new workers. Thus, the "surplus" value consists of what is left over after taking out what is needed to maintain and reproduce workers.

Merchants increase profits by maximizing the difference between the value of goods and what it costs to produce that value—that is, by maximizing surplus value. Those who produce goods, however, can refuse to sell them to merchants if the offered price is too low, and consumers can refuse to buy if the price is too high. How, then, can merchants maximize their profits?

One answer is to increase control both over those who produce goods and over the markets in which goods are sold—in other words, to change the structure of economic institutions. Before we see how this is accomplished, we have to understand the cultural and structural characteristics of *capitalism*—the economic arrangement toward which these changes are bringing us.

## Capitalism as an Economic Arrangement

As Adam Smith outlined in his enormously influential book, *The Wealth of Nations*, the most important values that underlie capitalism are those of private property, profit, rational self-interest, and free competition. The idea of private property does not refer to personal items such as clothing and books, but to **capital,** which is wealth—from hand tools to factories—that can be used to produce new wealth. **Capitalism** is an economic arrangement in which private individuals and groups have the authority to use and dispose of the means of production as they see fit. Capitalism values most highly the capitalist's own self-interest—not loyalty to

community, society, or kinship ties. Capitalists compete with other capitalists, and the one who produces commodities at the cheapest cost and sells them at the highest price will be the most successful.

The cultural seeds of capitalism are sown in the sixteenth century when John Calvin founds the Calvinist religious sect. In his classic book, *The Protestant Ethic and the Spirit of Capitalism*, Max Weber argued that Calvinist religious doctrine and practices created conditions that contributed to the rise of capitalism as an economic arrangement. Calvinists believe that work is a "calling" done in the service of God, and that living in luxury is a sin. They also believe that whether people will go to heaven or to hell is decided at the moment of birth. Understandably, this creates a lot of anxiety since those who are to go to heaven do not know it and those who are condemned to hell can do nothing about it. In the face of this, it makes sense that people look for some sign of their eventual fate, something that indicates that they are among the select few who will go to heaven.

Given their beliefs about work and the importance of setting aside rather than consuming their wealth, it also makes sense that they interpret financial success as just such a sign. In the seventeenth century, Calvinism takes strong root in England and Scotland, and the accumulation of wealth becomes not only respectable, but almost a moral imperative. Members of the aristocracy, of course, were wealthy long before the seventeenth century, but Calvinism encourages them to accumulate their wealth rather than use it to live luxuriously. Since capital—such as a factory—is relatively expensive, a religious doctrine that encourages the accumulation of wealth was, Weber argued, an important cultural ingredient in the emergence of capitalism.

The rise of capitalism and the form it eventually acquires depends on far more than cultural values and beliefs about work and wealth. In the 300 years following Calvin's death, both technological revolutions and structural change will profoundly affect the social relations of production and produce capitalism as we know it today. This brings us back to the fundamental problem of both merchants and capitalists: how to control the costs of buying or producing goods in order to maximize surplus value.

## The Transformation of Labor

As goods increasingly are valued for exchange, landowners begin to use land in ways that radically alter social relationships. In feudal societies the ownership of land was the basis of power for the aristocracy: peasants grew food on land owned by the nobility and gave a share of what they produced to the lord in exchange for protection. Beginning in the sixteenth century, however, the demand for wool grows so large that landowners realize that they can do far better if they become capitalists and use their wealth to buy and use land to support sheep rather than to grow crops. Over a period of some 200 years, a great deal of agricultural land in England is "enclosed" and used entirely for sheepraising, and thousands of peasants become landless (Lazonick, 1974).

During the same period the cultural value placed on the right to own private property and do as one pleases with it reaches new heights (Dobb, 1947). The centuries-old relationship between serfs and the nobility begins to fall apart, producing thousands of landless peasants who, lacking a viable alternative, sell their labor power to capitalists. It is here that capitalists try to solve their problem of competing with one another by minimizing the cost of producing goods.

Landless peasants no longer control their own **labor** and are forced to sell their **labor power** to capitalists for whatever price capitalists are willing to pay. Thus, labor power is transformed into a commodity: capitalists purchase it, put it to work on land or in factories, and then sell what is produced. Unlike previous economic arrangements, this system allows people who sell their labor power to receive in return only a portion of the value of what they produce. For example, when I sell chairs that I have made, I receive in return their full value, a value that is determined by the labor that went into them. If I sell my labor *power* to someone else, however, I receive less, because capitalists keep some of the value of what I produce—the surplus value—for themselves.

Capitalists increase their profits in four basic ways. First, they try to control the cost of production, which is facilitated by a growing class of landless peasants who have no choice but to work for someone since they no longer own or control any means of production. Capitalists are therefore in a position to exploit the landless peasants by paying them just enough to maintain and reproduce themselves (Dowd, 1974). Costs of production can also be minimized by introducing new ways of using labor power—assembly lines, for instance—or by replacing people with machines. In both cases, costs are reduced by increasing efficiency of production, which has become one of capitalism's most important values.

Second, capitalists can try to increase sales—through advertising, for example. Once they maximize the surplus value of each object they produce, they can then increase overall profits by selling as many of them as possible.

Third, capitalists can introduce new products and, possibly, new markets. Home video games and personal computers, for example, were unheard-of just ten years ago, but have since opened up vast new markets for existing manufacturers and have spawned a large number of new companies. To sell such products, however, capitalists must convince potential buyers to purchase them; and, as we will see later, advertising plays an important role in this by "manufacturing desire."

Fourth, they can increase profits by maximizing the price at which they sell finished goods, and one way to do this is to have a *monopoly*—in other words, to be the sole provider of a particular product. If everyone likes to drink tea, and I am the only one who imports tea from India and China, then you will either pay the price I ask or go without tea. This is, in fact, how some early English capitalists became rich—the king sold them monopolies over the tea trade (Hill, 1961).

Few sixteenth- and seventeenth-century English capitalists are able to buy monopolies from the king, and this means that the best way to increase profits is to exploit workers, and the control of labor power becomes one of the most important goals of capitalists. To compete with one another, capitalists must continually expand by making more and more profit and by acquiring still greater productive power. To expand, however, they must increase the surplus value of what their workers produce, and this means that they must give workers a shrinking share of what they make. Thus, whereas expansion is the basic economic process through which capitalism develops, exploitation is the basic social process (Dowd, 1974).

We are now up to the nineteenth century, and the Industrial Revolution is in full swing. Before

Since expansion lies at the heart of capitalism as an economic system, the Industrial Revolution and the rise of capitalism to the dominant position it occupies today went hand in hand.

looking at modern capitalist societies as well as some alternative economic arrangements, go through Table 17-1 carefully, for it summarizes the major changes we have just described.

Notice how values and the social structures through which goods are produced and exchanged have changed. The value of goods has shifted from use to exchange to the surplus value that constitutes profit. Social obligation, cooperation, and the importance of meeting social needs are giving way to rational self-interest, control over labor power, the ideal of free competition, and efficiency in the name of greater profits and capitalist expansion. Although the types of exchange are similar in feudal and capitalist societies, *what* was exchanged changed dramatically when labor power became a commodity to be bought and sold in markets.

All of these changes were accompanied by rapid population growth, increasingly complex divisions of labor, and a shift in social organization from Gemeinschaft to Gesellschaft and from primary work groups to bureaucracies. Bureaucracy reinforces the separation of workers from the means of production, for they rest on such narrowly defined tasks and limited areas of responsibility that control over production is impossible for most who work in them; and in modern industrial societies, if people want to work, they must sooner or later find a place in bureaucratic organizations.

Before we examine twentieth-century capitalist societies in some detail, it is very important to raise some warning flags. The Industrial Revolution and the rise of capitalism were closely intertwined with each other. Like all social arrangements, capitalism has both desirable and undesirable consequences, but it is difficult to know whether some of these are due to capitalism or simply to industrialization. Some of the negative

**Table 17-1**

Summary of Economic Transformations: From Communalism to Capitalism

| CHARACTERISTIC | COMMUNAL ECONOMIES | FEUDAL ECONOMIES | CAPITALIST ECONOMIES |
|---|---|---|---|
| Dominant Economic Values | Obligation to kin<br>Use value of goods<br>Cooperation<br>Tradition<br>Community control<br>Social needs | Obligation to nobility and kin<br>Exchange value of goods<br>Regulated competition<br>Tradition<br>Control over labor<br>Maintaining nobility | Rational self-interest<br>Surplus value (profit)<br>Free competition (capitalists)<br>Innovation<br>Control over labor power<br>Efficiency |
| Types of Exchange | Sharing | Commodity-commodity (early)<br>Commodity-money-commodity (early)<br>Money-commodity-money (later) | Money-commodity-money (capitalists)<br>Commodity-money-commodity (workers) |
| What Is Exchanged? | Labor | Labor, goods, and money | Labor *power*, goods, and money |
| Who Owns the Means of Production? | Collective | Individual producers | Capitalists |
| Who Controls How Goods Are Disposed Of? | Collective | Individual producers<br>Nobles | Capitalists |
| Division of Labor | Simple ——————————→ Complex | | |
| Technology | Simple ——————————→ Sophisticated | | |
| Social Organization | Gemeinschaft<br>Primary group ————→ Gesellschaft<br>Bureaucracy | | |

aspects of capitalist societies—such as the alienation of workers—may occur in any industrial society whether it is capitalist or not.

As you read about capitalist societies you may also be tempted to conclude that their problems are not shared by noncapitalist societies such as the Soviet Union and China; but this is far from the truth. As ideal types capitalism and socialism differ sharply from each other. In practice, however, countries that are called "capitalist" and those that are called "socialist" have many of the same problems; and although socialist societies claim to have corrected many of the negative aspects of capitalism, in many areas of social life conditions are far worse than they are under capitalism. Both kinds of societies, in short, have a long way to go before achieving their ideal economic arrangements.

Finally, the fact that socialist and capitalist countries share many common problems does not mean that the differences between them are merely theoretical. For example, workers in both types of societies have very little control over the economy; but the state has most of the power in socialist countries, whereas private individuals, groups, and organizations have most of the power in capitalist societies. The difference is a profound one, even though many of the consequences for workers are similar.

## Advanced Capitalism: Relations of Production

With the exception of the Soviet Union, the capitalist model guides the leading industrial societies of the world—Japan, the United States, West Germany, Great Britain, and France. What does capitalism look like in the twentieth century? How do

## PUZZLES:

### WHAT MARX DID NOT FORESEE

Karl Marx predicted revolutions in advanced industrial societies such as England and the United States, revolutions in which the working class would overthrow capitalism and install socialism. Obviously Marx's prediction has not yet come true. Why not?

The answer has to do with many social changes that Marx did not foresee, including the increasing power of the modern state and divisions within the working class, matters examined later in this chapter.

capitalists pursue the goals of greater profit, efficiency, and control over both labor power and markets? What does the division of labor look like, and how does if affect the perpetuation of capitalism and the positions of different social classes?

### Distributions of Power

The ability of capitalists to compete with one another depends on two main factors: control over labor power through which goods are produced and the control over markets in which they are sold. In order to protect their own positions, workers resist the attempts of capitalists to extract sur-

## PUZZLES:

### WHY DO WORKERS FEEL POWERLESS?

In spite of the fact that labor unions are supposed to benefit workers, almost 80 percent of American workers do not belong to one. Why not?

While part of the answer certainly has to do with the bad reputations of many unions, most of the answer has to do with the structure of the American economy and job market and the relatively powerless position of most American workers within it, as this chapter explains.

plus value from their labor power, and this, in turn, creates continuing social conflict.

**Controlling Labor** When wage labor was first introduced in the sixteenth century, landless peasants in England openly protested the exploited position they were being forced into, and the most radical among them believed that to be forced to work for wages was to lose their birthright as free Englishmen (Hill, 1967; Macpherson, 1973). It was a losing battle, however, for they eventually realized that they had few viable alternatives to selling their labor power as a commodity. Unlike feudal serfs, workers in capitalist societies are not obliged to work for anyone, but they are obliged to sell their labor power to *some*one; and this basic structural fact about capitalist societies explains most of the power difference between capitalists and workers.

Although workers in the United States no longer protest the selling of labor power itself, they do make an issue of the terms on which it is sold. In the nineteenth and twentieth centuries, workers began to organize unions because they knew that employers were powerful primarily because they could replace dissatisfied workers with others who also had no choice but to sell their labor power wherever they could find a buyer for it. If all workers refused to work under certain conditions, however, they would then have far greater power.

Capitalists retaliated with the aid of government, and labor strikes—particularly in the late 1800s—involved unprecedented violence. In 1894 workers in factories that manufactured Pullman railway cars went on strike because their wages were cut so drastically that they could not afford to live in company-owned "villages." They were then joined by the American Railway Union, whose members refused to handle Pullman cars. The company owners refused to negotiate and hired nonunion strikebreakers, many of whom were poor, unemployed blacks. When union members interfered with trains, violence escalated and President Cleveland sent in federal troops to both operate and protect the trains. A federal court order forbade interference with the railways, and the president of the striking union—Eugene Debs—was imprisoned for defying that order. Within a few months, both the strike and the Pullman workers' union were broken (Morison, 1965).

During the late nineteenth and early twentieth centuries, the U.S. government openly acted against the rising tide of labor organizing. In 1912, for example, mill workers in Lawrence, Massachusetts, struck in protest over wage cuts, and the intervention of state militia troops resulted in both the end of the strike and the death of one of the strikers.

Since the beginning of the twentieth century, relations between capitalists and workers have lost most of their violent character; but control of labor power continues to be a major means for increasing profits. How is it done? The most obvious source of control still lies in the structure of capitalist society, for so long as workers do not control the means of production, they do not control their own jobs. In his influential book, *White Collar*, C. Wright Mills wrote of the "new middle class," whose insecure position in the labor market contributes to increasing feelings of anxiety and powerlessness.

A second source of control lies in the fact that the vast majority of American workers—almost 80 percent—do not belong to unions (U.S. Census Bureau, 1983c). Why is union membership so low? Part of the answer is that most workers in industrial societies (nearly two-thirds in the United States) hold jobs that require relatively unsophisticated skills—clerks, assembly-line workers, farm laborers, and restaurant workers, for example (U.S. Census Bureau, 1983c). Because there are always workers willing to take their places, most

workers have a great deal to lose by making trouble, and employers generally define attempts to form unions as just that.

Union membership is also low because those who are most likely to hold relatively unsophisticated jobs—nonwhites, married women, college students, teenagers, and the elderly—tend to have little social power (Smith, 1981). Their position in both society and the labor market gives them little ability or incentive to take the risks and make the investment of time and energy that it takes to form unions and improve working conditions and pay levels.

A third source of control lies in the segmented, bureaucratic nature of work in industrial societies. This not only makes it easier for employers to replace discontented workers, but puts most day-to-day power over production in the hands of bureaucratic managers and administrators who specialize in controlling labor power. The proliferation of "management seminars" and courses in "labor management" and "labor relations" attests to the growing sophistication of capitalist methods for controlling workers.

One of the most important sources of control is the continuing drive for greater efficiency. In 1911 Frederick Winslow Taylor published *Principles of Scientific Management*, in which he espoused the use of scientific principles to determine the most efficient way to use workers. In time-and-motion studies, for example, he tried to identify the single most efficient way for workers to accomplish narrowly defined physical tasks—such as screwing two pieces of wood together. The design and control of the human work process, he believed, should be no less rigorous and scientific than the design of machines.

In the 1920s industrial sociologists focused on how to maximize the productivity of workers (and, therefore, the surplus value that could be extracted from them). The famous Hawthorne studies, for example (discussed in Chapters 2 and 8), were attempts to identify working conditions—such as the amount of lighting and the frequency of rest periods—that would maximize the productivity of each worker. Studying productivity from another angle, Mayo and his colleagues discovered that small primary work-groups establish norms about a "fair day's work" that often exert more control over worker productivity than do employers.

The replacement of human workers with machines has accelerated in recent years, and perhaps no better symbol of this trend lies in the fact that this machine—which puts automobile engine parts on an assembly line—even has a name: "Sweet William."

One of the most effective ways to both increase efficiency and weaken the control of workers over productivity is to replace them with machines—a process known as **automation.** In the eighteenth century, British textile manufacturers developed power looms with which a single worker could replace hundreds; and as industrialization has expanded over the last two centuries, increasingly sophisticated technology has rendered ever greater numbers of skills—and, in some cases, workers themselves—obsolete. Automakers in Japan and the United States now use robots to perform many assembly-line tasks that once provided jobs for thousands of workers. In order to cut costs and maintain profits, the American printing industry has introduced so much high technology that skills among printers have declined and the printing craft has lost its once envied position as the epitome of skilled craftwork (Wallace and Kalleberg, 1982).

The capitalist valuing of efficiency increases productivity enormously, but workers often bear the costs. Productivity—as measured by the average value of goods produced by each worker in a day—is lower in Japan than it is in the United States. The reason for this lies not with the characteristics of workers, the use of technology, or the organization of work; rather, it lies with the structural relationship between employers and workers.

In capitalist Japan workers generally are not laid off when sales decline; thus, during economic "slumps," production is cut back while the number of workers remains the same, and productivity per worker falls. In the United States, however, efficiency is often increased by laying workers off when sales decline; and this keeps the statistical measure of worker productivity at a higher level. Thus, increased efficiency often benefits capitalists more than workers. Understandably, some labor unions have opposed automation and have been accused by many as being opposed to progress and efficiency. This is one of the major contradictions of capitalism, for greater efficiency often worsens the relative position of workers (Smith, 1981).

Under pressure from unions, some employers have experimented with giving workers more power, but the profitability of controlling labor power is so great that such experiments often fail. In the early 1970s the General Foods pet food plant in Topeka, Kansas, changed the structure of work by allowing workers to work in teams that shared many of the day-to-day decisions normally controlled by management (Walton, 1972). Productivity increased along with the satisfaction of workers, but after five years management decided that the workers had too much power and—in the name of higher profits and greater productivity—ended the new arrangement (Zwerdling, 1980).

In industries whose labor unions are most powerful, workers have gained some increases in power. At Chrysler, for example, the auto workers union now has a representative on the board of directors. It is important to note, however, that this kind of structural shift in the distribution of power is achieved only under intense pressure, for it works against one of capitalism's primary values: the maximization of surplus value by controlling labor power.

**Controlling Markets: Monopoly and Oligopoly**
Adam Smith believed that capitalist economies, in their ideal form, are controlled not by individuals, groups, or organizations (including governments), but by the "invisible hand" of economic forces that underlie market activities. Detroit automakers lost ground to foreign competition in the 1970s because they continued to manufacture large, expensive, gas-guzzling cars long after Americans developed a preference for small, inexpensive, efficient cars. From Smith's point of view, they suffered losses because they did not match consumer demand with a supply of desired goods at a price people were willing to pay.

Smith believed that in order to make a profit and compete successfully with one another, capitalists must give consumers what they want at prices they are willing to pay. Competition forces them to introduce both new products at attractive prices and more efficient ways of producing them, and in the end everyone benefits. Thus, in the

ideal capitalist society, the market is controlled by competition among producers and by the balance of supply and demand—the market forces that make up the "invisible hand."

In practice, capitalist economies do not come close to Adam Smith's ideal. Increased profits depend on control over both production and markets. Not only is free and open competition among capitalists anxiety-producing, but it also poses a constant threat to the ability of businesses to survive. Understandably, then, capitalists prefer an economy in which they are protected from competition (while at the same time perpetuating the belief that the market is free), and this has led to increasing control over production and marketing in the hands of a relatively few organizations—a condition known as **oligopoly** (Chamberlin, 1962).

Many Americans believe that small businesses are the "bedrock" of our economy, but the truth is that businesses owned and operated by a few individuals have only a tiny share of production and income. In 1980 such businesses received only 11 percent of all business income, and corporations received the rest. Most important is the fact that a small minority of corporations controls the majority of economic activity in America. In 1982 there were more than 250,000 corporations in the United States; but the largest 100 of these owned 48 percent of all business assets, and the largest 200 owned 61 percent. The 500 largest U.S. corporations had sales in excess of almost 1.7 *trillion* dollars, *an amount that exceeds the gross national product (GNP) of every other country in the world, with the exception of the Soviet Union* (U.S. Census Bureau, 1983c).

Oligopoly describes markets for many important products and services. More than 1,800 different makes of automobiles have been manufactured in the United States. Table 17-2 lists some of them. In 1985 there were only 4 major U.S. automakers. A handful of companies control the entire American supply of oil and natural gas, a situation that is also true for cigarettes, beer, breakfast cereals, coffee, aluminum, and personal computers (Standard and Poor, 1978, 1979). Just 10 corporations control NBC, ABC, and CBS (both television and radio); 34 affiliated television stations; 201 cable television franchises; 59 magazines including *Newsweek* and *Time;* 20 record companies; 41 book publishers; and 58 newspapers including the *Wall Street Jour-*

## Table 17-2

Some of the Makes of Automobiles Once Manufactured in the United States

| PRODUCTION DATES | NAMES | PRODUCTION DATES | NAMES |
|---|---|---|---|
| 1914–1922 | Allen | 1909–1958 | Hudson |
| 1916–1926 | Anderson | 1888–1941 | Hupmobile |
| 1901–1926 | Apperson | 1905–1912 | Johnson |
| 1904–1913 | Atlas | 1908–1928 | Lexington |
| 1900–1936 | Auburn | 1904–1925 | Maxwell |
| 1899–1911 | Autocar | 1910–1925 | Mercer |
| 1915–1922 | Bell | 1918–1958 | Nash |
| 1915–1937 | Brewster | 1907–1932 | Oakland |
| 1871–1873 | Cahart Steamer | 1906–1930 | Overland |
| 1909–1927 | Case | 1899–1958 | Packard |
| 1908–1923 | Chalmers | 1900–1932 | Peerless |
| 1913–1922 | Commonwealth | 1901–1938 | Pierce-Arrow |
| 1929–1937 | Cord | 1904–1936 | Reo |
| 1910–1936 | Cunningham | 1896–1925 | Stanley |
| 1950–1955 | Cunningham | 1912–1930 | Stearns Knight |
| 1915–1924 | Dixie Flyer | 1906–1966 | Studebaker |
| 1921–1934 | Dusenberg | 1913–1935 | Stutz |
| 1915–1933 | Dupont | 1908–1928 | Velie |
| 1910–1932 | Essex | 1908–1923 | Washington |
| 1902–1934 | Franklin | 1908–1925 | Westcott |
| 1946 | Frazer | 1914–1932 | Willys-Knight |
| 1919–1931 | Gardner | 1896–1924 | Winton |

Source: Ash, *Automobile Almanac*, 1967.

nal, the *Washington Post*, the *Los Angeles Times*, and the *New York Times* (Parenti, in press).

The importance of oligopoly lies in the ability of an organization to control prices while maintaining the appearance of a competitive marketplace. For example, Americans spend more than $200 billion on food each year, but less than 40 cents out of every dollar goes to farmers. Most of what we spend on food goes to "middlemen"—food processors—and only 50 companies control 90 percent of the food market (Hightower, 1980). Beatrice Foods, for example, owns more than a hundred different companies that produce, among other things, ice cream, yogurt, bread, milk, pickles, bottled water, cheese, Chinese food, cat food, whiskey, orange juice, hot dogs, taco sauce, peanut butter, nuts, ketchup, sausage, tomato sauce, cocoa mix, turkeys, popcorn, smoked meats, cooking oil, pudding, refried beams, "sloppy Joe" mix, and soup mix.

Judging from commercials on Saturday morning television, you might think that there is intense competition among the enormous number of different breakfast cereals—Wheaties, Fruit Loops, Total, and so on; but most of these brands are made by a handful of companies that, to a degree, compete only against themselves. Thus, the extensiveness of oligopoly results in considerably less competition than there appears to be (Hightower, 1980).

Judging from the last decade, the trend toward oligopoly is upward. In 1970 the 100 largest corporations had gross sales that equalled 29 percent of the entire U.S. GNP, and the sales of the 500 largest corporations amounted to 47 percent of the GNP. By 1982 sales had increased to 37 percent of the total GNP for the 100 largest corporations and to 54 percent of the GNP for the top 500 (U.S. Census Bureau, 1983c).

When production of goods or services is controlled by a single corporation, that corporation is said to have a **monopoly.** For example, most people buy utilities such as natural gas and electricity from companies that control the entire market in a given geographical area, and until recently, telephone service in the United States was controlled entirely by the American Telegraph and Telephone Company.

A **conglomerate** is a collection of companies in different industries that are owned by a single corporation. Conglomerates form and expand when one company uses its profits to buy others, or when two or more companies merge to form a single organization. The International Telephone and Telegraph company, for example, owns more than 150 different corporations that provide products and services that have nothing to do with telephones—including Wonder Bread and Hostess Twinkies.

Conglomerates have enormous power in the marketplace because they have great financial resources and the decisions of a single board of directors affect many different markets. Suppose, for example, that the "Big C" conglomerate owns 50 different companies, most of which make a profit each year. One of Big C's companies makes portable typewriters, and its competitors are relatively small, independent firms. Big C's board of directors decides to "take over" the portable typewriter market by cutting prices so much that the competition cannot stay in business and still compete. How might this happen?

Even though its typewriter company will lose a lot of money during the "takeover" phase, the profits from the *other* companies in the conglomerate will keep the conglomerate going by making up the difference. In short, the vast and diversified resources of conglomerates allow them to compete in the marketplace in ways that are beyond the resources of independent companies. As conglomerates increase their control over markets and drive smaller, independent firms out of business, oligopoly tends toward monopoly.

**The Manufacture of Desire** All economies shape people's needs to fit what is produced to some degree; but the capitalist imperatives of expansion and profit through competition raise the importance of controlling what consumers think they want and need. In order to expand, capitalists must increase people's perceived needs and then try to meet them, but only if it is profitable to do so.

The manufacture of desire is an important part of capitalist economies and is often accomplished by introducing "new" products. In many cases, the products are not new at all: new dishwashing detergents, for example, often differ from old ones only in their packaging and smell. Production goes on as usual, but advertising campaigns foster the illusion of new, innovative products (Baran and Sweezy, 1966).

Desire is also manufactured by introducing products that substitute new ways of doing things for old ways that were quite sufficient. People have always managed to entertain themselves—with singing, parties, games, dancing, storytelling; but now "entertainment" generally involves products or services that are sold in markets—television,

*"Lester, shouldn't we be upgrading something?"*

Drawing by Saxon; © 1984, The New Yorker Magazine, Inc.

records, radios, cassettes, and movie theaters. Home computers are now advertised heavily, and suddenly we are told that the "old" ways of balancing checkbooks, filing recipes or making Christmas card address lists are not good enough, and that without computer literacy children will not succeed in college.

In many cases the production process creates real needs that create new sources of profit. As Best and Connolly (1976) wrote:

> When industrial production pollutes the air, urban dwellers come to equate the need for air with a vacation, air conditioning, or a more expensive home in the suburbs. . . . When food packaging, processing, and distribution create tasteless food fortified with potentially dangerous preservatives, consumers identify the need for nutrition with expensive organic foods and natural vitamins. (pp. 57–59)

The effort to manufacture the desire to consume products that generate profits for capitalists often leads to contradictions. In a single issue of a national magazine, for example, full-page advertisements for cigarettes pictured people smoking after they had obviously engaged in healthy exercise—a handsome man sitting in a locker room and a beautiful young dancer sitting next to a dance studio mirror (*Newsweek*, July 11, 1983).

**Who's in Charge?** That the economies of most advanced capitalist societies are dominated by large business organizations raises the important question of who, in turn, dominates these powerful corporations? In the early stages of industrial capitalism there were no corporations, and businesses were owned and operated by no more than a few individuals who often belonged to the same family. Family control of business organizations continued well into the twentieth century and formed the basis for the fortunes of families such as the Rockefellers, Vanderbilts, Kennedys, and Hunts.

As the twentieth century unfolded, however, ownership of large businesses appeared to slip from the control of families and individuals as stock ownership became increasingly common. As business became more and more bureaucratic, large numbers of managers and administrators took over control of day-to-day decision making. These two developments led some to believe that ownership and control of the means of production were no longer in the same hands, and that economic

power was, therefore, becoming less concentrated than it once had been (Berle and Means, 1968).

This view is sharply countered by a number of social scientists. Burch (1972) gathered data on the largest U.S. corporations and divided them into two groups. Corporations that were controlled by single families or groups of families who both owned a controlling interest and placed some of its members in key management positions (such as chairman of the board or a top executive) were classified as "owner-dominated." If controlling interest was owned by a family or group of families who did *not* also have family members in key management positions, then the corporation was classified as "management-dominated."

Burch concluded that "owner-dominance" characterized almost 60 percent of the top 300 industrial corporations, 72 percent of the top 50 merchandising corporations, and just over half of all corporations that deal in banking and transportation. In addition, the wealthiest 5 percent of Americans own more than 80 percent of all corporate stock, whereas 82 percent own no stock at all (U.S. Census Bureau, 1983c). Thus, although bureaucracy and its managers play increasingly important roles in the production process, economic institutions in capitalist societies remain primarily under the control of a small elite group.

Herman (1981) studied the 200 largest U.S. corporations and disagreed with Burch by concluding that there is no small elite that controls American economic institutions. He agreed with Burch in an important sense, however, when he noted that many high-level managers own substantial amounts of stock in their companies; and even those who do not own very much stock are constrained by the same goals and interests as those who do. In short, Herman concluded that managers and owners have essentially the same interests (see also James and Soref, 1981).

**The Role of Government** To Adam Smith, government never interferes with the economy in the ideal capitalist society: "laissez faire" (or, "leave it alone") was his motto. Early in this century, however, federal government officials came to believe that unrestrained capitalist expansion threatened to severely damage and deplete natural resources, and that individual corporations were amassing so much power that monopoly and oligopoly threatened both free competition and the welfare of consumers. Railroads, for example, typically charged "what the market would bear," and their monopoly over the hauling of freight allowed them to charge exorbitant prices.

The American government played an expanding role in the regulation of business activities, primarily in order to ensure a stable social environment in which capitalists could pursue their interests (Weinstein, 1969). Antitrust laws were passed that forbade monopolies; and in 1983 the government won a long legal battle to end the American Telephone and Telegraph's monopoly over telephone service. During the Depression of the 1930s, Franklin Roosevelt's administration set a precedent for government action that persists to this day. Unemployment compensation, farm subsidies, the minimum wage, social security, regula-

tion of the banking industry and the stock exchange, and vast government spending in the marketplace—all signaled the growing role of government in the economy (Heilbroner, 1977).

The list of areas in which the federal government plays a regulatory role includes work-safety regulations; control of natural resources; antipollution laws; fair trade practices (such as rules that govern our rights and obligations when we sign a lease or credit agreement); regulation of nuclear power plants; product safety (such as new drugs, standards for food, and the safety features of cars); and labor-management relations (such as laws that forbid employers from firing employees who promote unions).

The Federal Reserve Board controls the nation's money supply and determines, among other things, how much money is available for business

investment and personal loans. When the government charges tariffs on goods imported from abroad, it helps protect U.S. industries from competition. The government subsidizes the production of various agricultural products—such as tobacco—by guaranteeing a certain level of prices. The price of vital commodities such as oil, gasoline, and natural gas is regulated by the federal government.

The state seems to have a great deal of power, but how and in whose interests particular administrations use that power, and how effectively they control what goes on in the marketplace, are other matters. The trend toward oligopoly in the United States strongly suggests that the federal government's ability (or willingness) to limit the power of corporations is quite limited.

## Occupational Structures and Segmented Labor Markets

As we have seen, labor power is a commodity that is bought and sold in capitalist societies—just as food, steel, and electricity are bought and sold. Although complexity is the most obvious characteristic of **labor markets** in industrial societies (the Labor Department lists over 35,000 different occupations), of more interest to sociologists is the fact that modern labor markets are divided into separate and distinct parts: they are *segmented,* and this profoundly affects the opportunities available to different workers (Gordon, Edwards, and Reich, 1982).

The American labor market is divided into two basic segments (study the characteristics of different jobs in Table 17-3 and see which labor market you would prefer to be in). The **primary** labor market includes jobs that encourage stable work habits, involve skills that are often learned on the job, are relatively high-paying, and have job ladders. The primary segment is, itself, divided into two smaller segments. **Subordinate** primary jobs involve routine tasks that encourage workers to be dependable and obedient to authority. **Independent** primary jobs, on the other hand, involve more creativity, autonomy, and power. Roughly 70 percent of all American workers were in the primary labor market in 1982, but only around 16 percent of all workers had "independent" jobs (com-

piled from U.S. Census Bureau, 1983c, Table 692).

The **secondary** market does not require stable work habits, is relatively low-paying, has few chances for advancement, and, as a result, has a high rate of turnover (people leave jobs after relatively short periods of time). Almost a third of all American workers (30 percent) were in this segment of the labor market in 1982.

**Table 17-3**

Segmented Labor Markets

| LABOR MARKET SEGMENT | CHARACTERISTICS |
|---|---|
| **Primary** | Encourages stable work habits. Skills often acquired on the job. Relatively high-paying. Job ladders. Strong unions. |
| Subordinate primary | Routine jobs that encourage dependability, discipline, obedience to authority. EXAMPLES: Police officer, skilled blue-collar worker, bank teller, office supervisor, computer programmer, public school teacher, military officer. |
| Independent primary | Creative jobs that require problem solving, initiative, and decision making. EXAMPLES: Scientist, executive, college professor, public official, school principal, lawyer, newspaper editor, police chief. |
| **Secondary** | Does not require stable work habits. Relatively low-paying. High turnover. Few job ladders ("dead end jobs"). Weak unions or none at all. EXAMPLES: Laborer, clerk, day-care worker, factory assembly-line worker, restaurant worker, taxi or bus driver. |

The occupational structure of labor markets in capitalist societies reflects the importance attached to controlling labor power, for only a small minority of all workers have jobs that bring them some measure of power, autonomy, and creativity. In their theory of **labor market segmentation,** Reich, Gordon, and Edwards (1973) argued that the goal of controlling labor power actually caused the development of distinct labor markets. During the late nineteenth century industrialization had the effect of homogenizing labor—factory work fragmented the production process and no longer required highly skilled workers who were familiar with all phases of production. This, combined with having to sell their labor power for wages, gave workers a common bond around which they began to organize unions and oppose the power of capitalists.

Reich, Gordon, and Edwards believed that twentieth-century capitalists responded to the threat of organized labor in part by creating different jobs—in other words, by making the division of labor more complex than it needed to be for efficiency. The steel industry, for example, created job ladders that made trivial distinctions between job levels and assigned slightly higher pay levels to each (Stone, 1974). This both fostered an illusion of upward mobility and weakened the bond of common experience that held the labor movement together. Unlike workers in the nineteenth century, in other words, twentieth-century workers had less in common with one another because some were better off. Thus, the "division of labor" literally "divided" the labor movement.

The structure of the economy also changed in ways that reinforced a segmented labor market. In the nineteenth century the economy was competitive, with large numbers of small businesses competing against one another. In the twentieth century, however, some areas of business—such as the steel, auto, and chemical industries—were slowly dominated by monopolies and oligopolies, largely because there was a steady demand for their products. Others—such as restaurants, stores, construction companies, and auto dealers—remained competitive because the demand for their goods fluctuated and they had to compete in order to stay in business.

As a result, a **dual economy** emerged—part monopolistic and part competitive—and the posi-

tion of workers in the two economies strongly affects their position in the labor market. Primary and secondary jobs exist in both sectors of the economy; but primary workers are far more likely to be found in the monopoly sector, whereas almost all secondary workers are in the competitive sector.

Unions are weak in the competitive sector (in which most people work) because most of the workers are in the secondary labor market and can be replaced with relative ease. Low rates of pay and job insecurity are, in fact, major ways in which competitive businesses remain competitive and control their workers: when demand for goods or services falls, employers simply "lay them off." For example, in late 1983 the Greyhound bus company insisted that workers agree to a cut in pay so that

the company could remain competitive. Workers went out on strike, and the company threatened to replace them with new workers. After almost nine weeks the workers finally accepted the pay cut and returned to work.

Monopolistic business, however, depends on a stable demand for products and employs a larger number of highly skilled workers who cannot be replaced easily. If employees leave because they dislike working conditions, monopoly businesses stand to lose far more than competitive businesses; and, for this reason, workers have more leverage in monopoly industries, and unions are more common and more powerful.

When people think of "labor," many think of highly publicized unions such as the Teamsters or the United Auto Workers, who often use their power to exact relatively high wages from their employers. It is important to remember, however, that the vast majority of American workers—roughly 80 percent—do not belong to unions, and only a portion of the 20 percent who are members belong to powerful unions. When the United Auto Workers gains major concessions from employers, it results in relatively few benefits for the vast majority of American workers. For most working Americans, low pay and job insecurity are permanent features of their positions in a segmented occupational structure.

**Professions and Professionalization**  Some occupations—both within and outside the primary labor market—are **professions**, and these have unique cultural and structural characteristics (Greenwood, 1962). Professional jobs are based on systematic, formal knowledge about a particular field, such as law, medicine, or engineering. Compared with other occupations, professionals as a group are relatively autonomous and can determine the conditions under which they work.

Professionals, however, are generally bound by codes of conduct and standards that are determined by professional organizations. Physicians and lawyers, for example, are answerable primarily to other physicians and lawyers who decide what constitutes malpractice. In similar ways, scientists establish norms for competent research and ethical conduct, and reporters and editors establish standards for accuracy and objectivity in reporting the news.

The boundaries of professional statuses are usually tightly controlled. Scientists and college professors must have advanced degrees in order to practice their profession; doctors, lawyers, registered nurses, and engineers must pass rigorous licensing examinations and be certified by state boards; public school teachers must be certified by the state in order to teach; and only lawyers with special training are allowed to argue cases before the Supreme Court.

Because professions provide valued services, are relatively free of outside interference, require extended training, control the size of their membership, and enjoy relatively high levels of prestige, they generally have high levels of income. The average income of American physicians in 1981, for example, was over $70,000; and the average starting salary for graduates with Ph.D.'s in engineering, chemistry, mathematics, and physics was more than $30,000. By comparison, the average wage of all full-time workers amounted to $15,000 (U.S. Census Bureau, 1983c).

Roughly 12 percent of working Americans are professionals, and most of these work for someone else—in other words, they are part of the labor market. Engineers, accountants, librarians, religious workers, scientists, nurses, reporters, and teachers sell their labor power as members of what Marx considered to be the working class. Most of them, of course, are much better off than other workers, and many have authority over secondary- and subordinate primary-sector workers (such as secretaries). Nonetheless, as members of the working class, these professionals must live with the uncertainties of a job market they do not control.

An even smaller minority—just over 2 percent—of working Americans are professionals who work outside the labor market—such as physicians, dentists, and lawyers in private practice. It is among these professionals that autonomy, financial well-being, and job security reach their maximum level in a capitalist economy.

Some occupations are "semi-professions" that have only some of the characteristics of professions (Etzioni, 1969). A growing number of business executives have graduate degrees, and they often like to refer to business as a profession with its own code of ethics. In addition, professions that exist primarily as part of the labor market—such as public school teaching—have less autonomy and control over their members than do those that are largely outside the labor market.

The attractiveness of professional standing encourages people in many occupations to try to *professionalize* their occupation (Caplow, 1964). The first step in **professionalization** is to form some kind of professional group or organization whose boundaries restrict membership and create a sense of occupational identity for its members. Often, a new name for the occupation (such as "educator" for "teacher") is a part of establishing boundaries, for it helps to break the cultural association of an occupation with its previous nonprofessional standing.

The second step is to create a code of ethics to indicate to the outside world that the group intends to regulate its own members. It is an early assertion of one of the most important characteristics of a profession—autonomy from outside control. The third and final step is to gain formal public recognition—usually from political authorities—that establishes the autonomy of the organization and, in some cases, creates legal criteria for membership (such as state licensing).

Once an occupation is professionalized, its members may gain a substantial increase in collective power. Until recently, for example, the American Medical Association prevented chiropractors from gaining professional recognition from state authorities—an effort that included frequent public reference to chiropractors as "quacks" and the exclusion of chiropractic services from insurance policy benefits. Since people are less likely to use uninsured medical services, the AMA effectively limited competition. The American Psychological Association (as well as the AMA) also limits competition by opposing the professionalization of psychotherapists who are not psychiatrists (with M.D.'s), or clinical psychologists (with Ph.D.'s). Only recently have some states included the services of psychiatric social workers in health insurance benefits.

**Postindustrial Society and Changing Occupational Structures** In preindustrial societies, most people earn a living by working directly with raw materials—by growing or gathering food. As Daniel Bell (1973) wrote, such economies are primarily a "game against nature" (p. 126). In industrial societies, however, most economic activity involves

manufactured goods. Since the early 1950s the United States has entered a third stage in which most economic activity involves neither raw materials nor manufacturing, but *service* occupations such as sales clerk, telephone operator, travel agent, secretary, banker, real-estate agent, office manager, public official, teacher, police officer, and soldier.

Bell believed that this signaled the beginning of **postindustrial society**—in which the production of goods is overshadowed by the provision of services, and relations between people and machines are gradually replaced by relationships between people and other people. In this kind of society, he argued, social interaction becomes the most important aspect of work; disputes between workers and employers are handled through negotiation rather than through angry confrontation; and most people work for relatively small organizations rather than large corporations.

Braverman (1974) and others, however, have pointed out that although the content of occupational structures is changing from factory work to office work, the relations of production—between workers and employers and between workers and their work—have not changed at all. The central values of capitalist societies—expansion, profit, and the exploitation and control of labor power—are as strong as ever. The most rapidly expanding occupations—sales and service—are in the secondary, competitive labor market, where unions are weak or nonexistent and where wages are relatively low and profits relatively high.

## Life in the Labor Force

How do different economic arrangements affect the lives of workers? Do relations of production in a postindustrial society differ substantially from those in an industrial society? Are the divisions between the social classes narrower? Do people enjoy coming to work to a greater degree? Do they feel any higher level of control over what they do all day long?

Sophisticated technology—computers, word processors, and sophisticated telecommunications equipment—is used increasingly in office workplaces, but it is unclear whether this improves the lives of workers as much as it increases profits. Textile workers once stood for hours tending machines that turned thread into cloth; but secretaries and clerks now sit for hours in front of computer terminals and word processors. They "process" information—taking it from one place and putting it in another—without affecting it in any way (see Zuboff, 1982).

One study of clerical workers in two New England companies, for example, found that computer operators were instructed to enter information just as they received it even when they spotted obvious errors. "They were not expected to be able to decide if the information was correct." The work of customer representatives (who work primarily over the phone) was closely monitored by computers that allotted them a specific number of minutes to handle each customer; and if workers paid extra attention to a difficult case, they were often penalized for falling short of their work quota for the day (*Hartford Courant*, January 5, 1983).

The use of high technology in a postindustrial society certainly has the potential to make work more interesting; but the drive for greater efficiency and profit has created enormous numbers of "dumb," rigidly controlled jobs that involve "intelligent" technology. Just as early machines degraded the skilled labor force by taking over complex productive tasks, so too does computer technology further this process by taking over increasing numbers of productive mental tasks (Braverman, 1974).

Clearly, computer technology and automation are functional for productivity and profits, but how do they and other characteristics of capitalist societies affect the lives of workers?

**Going through the Motions: Alienation in the Workplace** To Marx (1845), **alienation** is the feeling that the world we live in is, itself, alien to us. In the workplace alienation represents a lack of connection between people and what they produce and between themselves and other people. It is the feeling that they do not know why they are doing what they are doing, and yet must go on doing it anyway.

Imagine for a moment that you are a bootmaker in seventeenth-century Paris. You own a little shop, and on a typical day a man comes in and tells you he wants a pair of boots. If he is insulting and orders you around, you might tell him to go to another shop and leave you alone. If not, you discuss different styles and kinds of leather, measure

his feet, fix a price, and tell him when they will be ready.

Your life is far from ideal. You are relatively poor, and there are months when it seems that no one needs boots. You do, however, decide when you will work, whose boots you will or will not make, how you will make them, and for what price you will sell them. Most important, you produce and sell boots by interacting both with materials that you transform into finished boots and with other people—from the purchase of leather to the final sale.

Now imagine that you work in a twentieth-century boot factory. You do not make boots; you cut out soles on a stamping machine—thousands of them every day—and you are paid a wage for each hour of work. While you work, you stand alone and tend the machine, feeding the leather in and taking the soles out. You do not control which kinds of boots are made in the factory, the leathers that are used, the style, the quality, the price for which they are sold, or to whom they are sold. Your wages are determined by your employer. You punch the time clock at 8:00 A.M., work until noon with a ten-minute break at 10:00, and then punch out at 4:00 and go home. The next day, you return to the factory and cut out thousands of soles again; and this is what you do year after year.

Stop for a moment and imagine yourself in each of these situations. Which would you prefer and why?

In comparison with the seventeenth-century worker, the twentieth-century factory worker lacks control over the process of work and the results. The process of making boots is now fragmented into many separate tasks, and what workers do has little connection to their thoughts or feelings about what they do. The shopowner could sit back occasionally and think about what he was about to do with the leather, and the unity of thought and action is what produced the boots. In the factory, however, the boots are disconnected from what the workers think or feel about them.

When we have no control over our work or what is done with the result, we lose our sense that work has meaning and value; and work is one of the most important of all human activities. If what we do lacks meaning and value, and if our social identities are bound up in what we do, then we are in danger of feeling that *we* are meaningless.

Alienation is one of the most important concepts in the sociological analysis of work in industrial societies (see, for example, Seeman, 1959). In his classic study of alienation in four American industries—car, textile, chemical, and printing—Blauner (1964) tried to identify structural characteristics of work that affected what he believed were four key aspects of alienation: powerlessness, meaninglessness, isolation from social interaction, and a lack of personal attachment and commitment to work.

Alienation was highest among auto workers, most of whom performed dull, repetitive jobs on assembly lines that isolated them from other workers and gave them no control over the work process. Alienation was lowest among printers who performed a craft with deep historical roots and controlled many aspects of production, including the pace at which they worked. Printers were able to interact with one another on the job, and rather than perform a tiny portion of a work process, they did the "whole job" and had the satisfaction of seeing the final product, much as our seventeenth-century bootmaker was able to do (see Lipset, Trow, and Coleman, 1956, for an in-depth, classic study of the work life of printers).

Chemical workers were only slightly more alienated than printers. Although they had relatively little control over production, they worked in teams of skilled workers who closely monitored production and made many on-the-job decisions. In comparison with auto workers, chemical workers enjoyed far more social interaction with one another and their decision-making powers gave them a stronger basis for feeling an attachment to their work.

Alienation thus seems to be closely tied to powerlessness, meaninglessness, social isolation, and fragmentation of work tasks (see also Kalleberg and Griffin, 1980; Kohn and Schooler, 1983; and Mottaz, 1981). In 1984 American workers were asked which aspects of occupations were most important to them; whereas half ranked "a feeling of accomplishment and importance" at the top, only 19 percent placed "high income" in that position (Davis, 1984).

How widespread is alienation among American workers? One clue may be found in a 1973 study by the U.S. Department of Health, Education, and Welfare in which workers were asked if they would choose their present occupation again. Forty-three percent of all white-collar workers said "yes," compared with only 25 percent of blue-collar workers (Table 17-4). You can see in Table 17-4 that as the level of skill, prestige, and control over work increases, so does satisfaction with work.

The structure of occupational life in industrial societies thus makes it difficult for people to care about and feel attached to their work. What, however, of those who want to work, but are unemployed? What are the social causes of unemployment, and how does it affect people's lives?

**Causes and Consequences of Unemployment**
Wanting a job but not having one is often a personal problem that individuals must deal with on their own. Unemployment has obvious financial consequences for families and individuals; when workers are the only earners in their families, the loss of a job is like firing the entire family. One study of workers who lost their jobs when a plant closed found a sharp increase in symptoms of poor physical and mental health. Reported levels of anx-

**Table 17-4**

Answers to "Would you choose the same job again?" for Different Occupations (United States, 1973)

| WHITE-COLLAR OCCUPATIONS | PERCENTAGE WHO WOULD CHOOSE THE SAME OCCUPATION AGAIN |
|---|---|
| All white-collar workers | 43 |
| University professors | 93 |
| Mathematicians | 91 |
| Physicists | 89 |
| Biologists | 88 |
| Chemists | 86 |
| Lawyers | 83 |
| Journalists | 82 |
| **BLUE-COLLAR OCCUPATIONS** | |
| All blue-collar workers | 25 |
| Skilled printers | 52 |
| Paper workers | 42 |
| Skilled auto workers | 41 |
| Skilled steel workers | 41 |
| Textile workers | 32 |
| Unskilled steel workers | 22 |
| Unskilled auto workers | 17 |

Source: U.S. Department of Health, Education, and Welfare, *Work in America*, 1973.

the weekend in line, sleeping on the sidewalk to assure acceptance of their applications as carpenters' apprentices. Some of the out-of-work families who left the industrial mid-west for the supposedly greener pastures of Texas are being forced to live in their cars. In Austin, 2,817 applicants lined up for 187 jobs.

The above is not a description of the Great Depression of the 1930s; it was written in 1982 (*New York Times*, November 3, p. C1). Between 1980 and 1982 the number of unemployed people increased by 37 percent, as did the average number of weeks that people were out of work; and in many countries—including France, Great Britain, and most of Latin America—the picture is far bleaker than it is in the United States (U.S. Census Bureau, 1982). In addition to these grim statistics, Gordon (1977) estimated that as much as a third of the American labor force may be "underemployed"—which means that although they are employed, their jobs are either part-time or so poorly paid that they cannot earn enough to live on.

Most of us look upon unemployment as a fact of life. We are so accustomed to the monthly unemployment statistics that it is hard to imagine a society in which everyone who wants to work has a job. The fact that we tend to accept it as an inevitable part of economic life strongly suggests that its causes lie in the nature of the social environment that we also tend to take for granted.

As Smith (1981) pointed out, once labor power becomes a commodity, then the demand for labor (and the opportunity for work) is no longer controlled by the willingness of individuals to work and the demand for the goods they produce. New factors come into play, such as the desire of capitalists to expand, to increase their profits, or to compete more successfully with one another. Most important is the fact that the historical transformation of labor into a commodity has created an ongoing conflict between employers and workers.

One of the most important types of unemployment is called **structural unemployment**—so called because it is caused by changes in the structure of occupations. The mechanization of agriculture throws unskilled farm laborers out of work, just as the automation of factories and offices

iety, tension, pessimism, depression, and insomnia increased, as did the incidence of high blood pressure and ulcers (Institute for Social Research, 1980; see also Buss and Redburn, 1983).

From a sociological perspective, unemployment is also a social problem with cultural, structural, and demographic causes. When unemployment rates are high, the personal desperation and despair of individuals is multiplied by thousands:

> In Detroit last month, several thousand desperate people, ranging from a 19-year-old unmarried mother to a 55-year-old unemployed automobile worker, lined up for a handful of job openings as unskilled laborers. In New York, 60 people spent

## Voices: What It Feels Like to Be a Surplus Person

He is 52, father of two, and the unemployment checks are running out. He did not miss a day unless sick in 15 years on the last job. When he lost it, he sent out 235 résumés seeking another chance to do what he's good at: technical-engineering writing. On our psychological tests, his self-esteem is now low, his alienation index very high.

But he maintains a strict schedule on his job hunts, and stays in writing trim by unpaid work, such as a novel about an executive who suddenly finds himself moved out of the mainstream and into the backwater of surplus people. When we asked precisely where the pain is, he told us without whining:

I thought my conscientiousness and diligence would pay off. Hard work, you know, the old go go go. Nothing could be more erroneous. The ones that were brown-nosing the boss, that went to his house and painted it, that mowed his lawn, that washed his cars, that took him to the ball game, drove him to the A & P, bought groceries for him, maybe babysat for his children, washed out his swimming pool, took care of his winter cabin—painted it, refurnished it—with their own materials, mind you. They're still doing it. With half the education I had, half the perseverance, half the talent, they are still here.

The hardest part for me to swallow is my pride and have some blue-collar worker say, right to your face, "With all your education now, Bob, how far did it get you?" Do you believe I have friends that work overtime now, running a lathe, working on machines?

You have no friends when you're unemployed. They think it's a disease that is contagious and might jump on them. I've found open resentments like, "I'm glad it happened to you and not me, brother." Without my writing I would be out. I would be with the rest of the boys in a tavern drinking and drowning my troubles. If a man is gainfully employed, and then you take away his employment, he's like a tool and just what happens to an idle tool. It's like being in a prison. If a man is going to contribute to society, he has to be gainfully employed.

Source: Braginsky, D., and Braginsky, B., "Surplus People: Their Lost Faith in Self and System," *Psychology Today*, August 1975.

creates unemployment by replacing workers with machines (Rasmussen, 1982). Automated bank tellers replace human tellers; word processors enable secretaries to do work that once required several people; robots on auto assembly lines not only take over dull "dumb" jobs, but leave many assembly-line workers with no jobs at all. Since the cost of labor power is the largest single production expense in many industries, automation increases profits by lowering costs; but it does so at the expense of workers.

In some cases structural unemployment has demographic causes, for as populations grow and age structures change, so does the size of the labor force in relation to the number of available jobs. In the 1950s, for example, the labor force grew slowly because the low birth rates of the 1930s resulted in a relatively small number of young adults. The Baby Boom of the late 1940s and 1950s, however, created a huge influx of young people looking for jobs in the 1970s and 1980s. Combined with a surge of women into the labor force (see Chapter 13), the labor force expanded more rapidly than the job market.

As age structures change, so does the demand for certain goods and services. The large numbers

In Chester, Pennsylvania, in 1983, when it was announced that 30 jobs would be available, more than 1,000 people lined up to apply for them.

of children produced by the Baby Boom, for example, fostered a sharp rise in the demand for teachers; in the 1980s, however, the size of the school-age population is considerably smaller, and thousands of teachers must choose between unemployment and training for new occupations.

Sweezy (1942) also argued that the antagonistic relations between workers and employers in capitalist societies create recurring crises that inevitably raise unemployment levels. A basic tension in capitalist societies is between the desire of capitalists to expand by giving workers the smallest possible share of what they produce and the desire of workers to increase their share. When profits are high (a "boom"), workers are in a better position to demand a bigger share—in other words, an increase in wages. If their wages go up, then business profits go down, and economic growth slows (a "slump" or, in the worst cases, a "bust"). If employers are able to keep wages from rising, then workers do not have enough money to buy all of the goods being produced in a "boom" period, and this in turn causes business profits to fall and, with them, the expansion of the economy.

When the economy goes into a slump, wages fall (as they did during the Great Depression and as they have during the last decade) and workers are in a weak bargaining position. This sets the

d services are
iow goods and
, 1982; Lane,
ire dominated
d oligopolies,
y state-owned

economically
ieties because
est interests of
socialist socie-
ct between the
o control their
e in China and
ted States and
untries are try-
large, complex
urces of author-
iciency. Goods
d for them has
t supply go un-
large new opti-
cow and lacked
nd lenses, wait-
veral months to

quality that the
. Effort and re-
o to the Soviet
h Galbraith told

and socialism differ dramatically from each other, many socialist and capitalist societies have certain problems in common—problems that stem from industrialization and the complexity of their societies.

## The Social Structure of Socialist Economies

The distribution of power is the most important structural difference between socialist and capitalist societies. Under **socialism** the party and its government officials decide what wages are paid for

I was taken out to sp         y at . . . the state planning committee. Bureaucratic inflexibility was one of the topics. When it was over, the deputy head of the planning committee . . . walked out to make sure my car was there.

It was *pouring* rain. As we waited for the car, a sprinkler came on down the street, sprinkling the road. The deputy head of the planning apparatus of the whole Soviet Union said, "There you see, professor, what we've been talking about. He's fulfilling his plan!"
(*Christian Science Monitor,* November 1, 1983, p. 1)

Inefficiency is the least of the problems of most industrial socialist countries, for most are also authoritarian states in which governments rule by force and are not elected by the people (see Chapter 18). In practice, the socialist ideal of a workers'

As the Solidarity union in Poland showed in the early 1980s, socialist societies also have their share of conflict between those who control the means of production and those who do not.

state has not yet come into being and brought an end to social conflict (Hollander, 1982). For the last several years workers in Poland have repeatedly defied government authorities with national strikes. They have insisted on the right to organize unions and to have greater control over production and wages.

Labor power is less likely to be sold as a commodity in socialist countries than it is in capitalist societies, however. Unemployment is rare in the Soviet Union, and groups of workers sometimes work under contract with the government. In farming, the contract specifies a level of payment for a certain level of production, and if bad weather produces a poor harvest, the workers are paid anyway. The workers do not own the land, however,

nor do they own machinery or raw materials (Lane, 1982; Silk, 1983).

Countries like Great Britain and France practice a modified form of socialism called *democratic socialism*. Under **democratic socialism** the government owns and controls only the most important means of production that supply necessary goods and services. Airlines (such as British Airways), railways, and major television stations (such as the British Broadcasting Corporation or "BBC") are all publicly owned; and in some countries banks, mines, and telephone systems are also publicly owned and operated. Even in the United States, the government owns and controls a railroad (Amtrak) and a power-generating system (the Tennessee Valley Authority).

Although it may appear that government ownership of some means of production in societies such as the United States indicates a movement toward socialism, it is important to remember that socialism is not simply a matter of government ownership. The fact that the federal government owns Amtrak does not mean that it is representing the interests of the working class.

In its most extreme form, the ideology underlying socialism represents **communism.** A *communist* society is a utopia in which the means of production are owned and controlled neither privately nor publicly, but collectively. In fact, in a communist society there would be no state. There are no communist societies in the world today, although many people in capitalist societies mistakenly label socialist countries such as Poland, the Soviet Union, and China as "communist." Since there are no existing examples of a communist society, it is difficult to know just how or if it could operate in an industrial world.

It is important to remember that capitalism, socialism, and communism are all ideal types. No capitalist society conforms to Adam Smith's vision of free competition and the universal benefits created by the "invisible hand"; governments in socialist societies do not act solely in the best interests of workers; and communist societies do not exist at all. It is also important to remember that there is a great deal of variation among capitalist and socialist societies. With the exception of a limited number of small free markets, for example, private enterprise is not allowed in the Soviet Union; but it is allowed on a limited scale in some other socialist societies such as Hungary and China. In Poland 75 percent of all farming is private; and in Yugoslavia the government subsidizes numerous private businesses. Agriculture is no longer owned and controlled by the state in Yugoslavia and there are more than 200,000 private shops (*Christian Science Monitor,* December 5, 1983).

**Table 17-5**

Cross-National Comparison of Government Ownership of Basic Industry

Percentage of government ownership in

| INDUSTRY | Australia | Austria | Belgium | Canada | England | France | W. Germany | Italy | Japan | Mexico | Netherlands | Spain | Sweden | Switzerland | United States |
|---|---|---|---|---|---|---|---|---|---|---|---|---|---|---|---|
| Telecommunications | 100* | 100 | 100 | 25 | 100 | 100 | 100 | 100 | 100 | 100 | 100 | 50 | 100 | 100 | 0 |
| Electricity | 100 | 100 | 25 | 100 | 100 | 100 | 75 | 75 | 0 | 100 | 75 | 0 | 50 | 100 | 25 |
| Gas | 100 | 100 | 25 | 0 | 100 | 100 | 50 | 100 | 0 | 100 | 75 | 75 | 100 | 100 | 0 |
| Oil production | 0 | 100 | NA | 0 | 25 | NA | 25 | NA | NA | 100 | NA | NA | NA | NA | 0 |
| Coal | 0 | 100 | 0 | 0 | 100 | 100 | 50 | NA | 0 | 100 | NA | 50 | NA | NA | 0 |
| Railways | 100 | 100 | 100 | 75 | 100 | 100 | 100 | 100 | 75 | 100 | 100 | 100 | 100 | 100 | 25 |
| Airlines | 75 | 100 | 100 | 75 | 75 | 75 | 100 | 100 | 25 | 50 | 75 | 100 | 50 | 25 | 0 |
| Auto Industry | 0 | 100 | 0 | 0 | 50 | 50 | 25 | 25 | 0 | 25 | 50 | 0 | 0 | 0 | 0 |
| Steel | 0 | 100 | 50 | 0 | 75 | 75 | 0 | 75 | 0 | 75 | 25 | 50 | 75 | 0 | 0 |
| Shipbuilding | NA | NA | 0 | 0 | 100 | 0 | 25 | 75 | 0 | 100 | 0 | 75 | 75 | NA | 0 |

Source: Adapted by Kerbo from *The Economist,* December 30, 1978.

*The approximate percentage of the industry government controls in each nation. NA = not applicable or negligible production.

## The World Economy

Before the Industrial Revolution capitalism existed primarily through long-distance trade. Seventeenth-century merchants might buy grain and then hold onto it until conditions—such as food shortages—in distant places created a sharp rise in the demand for grain and the willingness to pay high prices for it. Braudel (1983) argued that it was here that the biggest profits were to be made, and capitalism took on an international scope long before the Industrial Revolution.

While capitalism has become a dominant economic arrangement within many societies over the past 500 years, it has also come to dominate economic relationships among societies. There is a *world economy* (Bergesen, 1980; Wallerstein, 1976, 1979, 1980) with a division of labor (Froebel, Heinrichs, and Kreye, 1980). Many American cars contain parts manufactured in West Germany, Japan, and Brazil, as well as the United States; a few countries—the United States, the Soviet Union, and France—supply most of the world's sophisticated weapons; a few nations, including South Africa, control much of the world's supply of metals such as nickel and chromium that are in increasing demand; Middle Eastern countries such as Saudi Arabia depend primarily on the export of oil for their entire national income; and the bulk of the national income of Mexico comes from the sale of minerals and oil, tourism, and the earnings of many thousands of Mexican immigrants working in the United States.

In a **world economy** no nation is self-sufficient, and this means that each must sell its goods in world markets in order to purchase everything they need. The United States, for example, buys most of Nicaragua's sugar and beef production as well as almost all of its lobster and shrimp catch. If the United States suddenly stops buying Nicaraguan goods (as it did in 1985 as part of its opposition to Nicaragua's socialist government), Nicaragua's economy would suffer enormously. Many countries are in similarly vulnerable posi-

tions because they depend on a relatively few goods that they sell in markets they cannot control. Several South American countries—Colombia and Brazil, for example—depend heavily on a few cash crops such as coffee for much of their national income.

Many other countries—including the United States—are vulnerable because of international competition. European and Japanese steel manufacturers, for example, have for years offered their products at prices below those charged by American manufacturers, and as a result the share of the steel market going to American steelmakers has steadily declined. In 1983 the American government imposed heavy import duties on certain kinds of steel in order to protect domestic manufacturers from foreign competition. In similar ways, American car manufacturers have tried to limit the number of Japanese cars imported into the United States; and the Japanese have tried to limit the importation of American beef and other products into Japan.

Although all nations are vulnerable to some degree in the world economy, the worldwide distribution of wealth and power is extremely unequal. **World-system theory** divides nations into three groups (Wallerstein, 1976, 1980). The most powerful are the *core* societies such as the United States, France, Japan, West Germany, and Great

### PUZZLES:

### WHO PROFITS FROM A WORLD ECONOMY?

As foreign corporations invest more money in underdeveloped economies (to build factories, for example), does the relative position of the lower and working classes get better, worse, or does it stay the same?

The gap between social classes tends to get wider—which is to say, the position of the working class in relation to the upper class grows worse, not better. Why? World-system theory provides one answer.

Britain. **Core societies** control most means of production such as factories and scientific technology, are relatively autonomous and stable, and have great economic and military power. They have complex divisions of labor and do not specialize in producing only a few goods or services—which is to say they are diversified. Their economies are geared to manufacturing goods, not to providing raw materials.

At the other extreme of wealth and power are the *peripheral* societies, which include underdeveloped countries such as Uganda and Nicaragua. **Peripheral societies** own little or no means of production, are relatively dependent on other nations, tend to be politically unstable, and are weak militarily. They have relatively few highly skilled workers and are more likely to specialize in the production of a few raw materials.

The third group of nations lies in-between the core and peripheral societies. These **semiperipheral societies**—such as Taiwan—are generally moving toward a diversified industrial economy and provide cheap skilled labor for core nation industries. Many electronic devices produced for U.S. firms, for example, are assembled in Taiwan or South Korea.

The position a society occupies in the world system profoundly affects its ability to develop economically and, therefore, the living conditions of its population. Most core countries, for example, developed during the early stages of the Industrial Revolution. Because industrialization was new to the world, there was a great deal of room for expansion, and countries who are now the world's great industrial powers developed in a world environment that imposed few serious limitations on them. Today's semiperipheral and peripheral societies, however, face a much more limiting set of circumstances: they must try to industrialize in a world *already* dominated by core societies such as the United States. Core societies have little to gain by the addition of new sources of competition in world markets for manufactured goods, and their monopoly over technology and their enormous economic power allow them to limit the industrialization of most of the semiperipheral and peripheral countries.

Economic arrangements on a world scale produce problems not only for nations, but for the world as a whole. Because economies of individual countries are so tightly connected to a world economy, the fate of all nations is affected by the success or failure of a few. In the late 1970s American and European bankers made huge loans to developing nations such as Brazil, Mexico, and Argentina (Brazil alone had a debt of over $90 *billion* in 1983). A worldwide recession and a decline in international trade in the early 1980s meant sharply lower incomes for these countries; and as interest rates in the United States skyrocketed, the debtor nations were hard-pressed to meet their loan payments.

What would happen if they defaulted on—refused to repay—their loans? The grimmest possibility would be that the banks who extended the loans in the first place would lose so much money that they and their investors would face ruin. If the largest American and European banks are ruined, then the entire world economy would be threatened. Thus, in the mid-1980s the world's affluent societies were waiting anxiously to see if a handful of relatively poor countries would be able to solve their financial problems.

## Power and Multinational Corporations

A small number of elite nations control most of the world's wealth, receive most of its income, and consume most of what is produced each year. As some sociologists and economists point out, however, the distribution of power in the world economy is shifting away from national governments to *multinational* corporations whose operations extend across national boundaries (see Evans, 1981).

IBM, for example, is based in the United States, but more than half of its earnings comes from its foreign operations; and almost half of the Ford Motor Company's work force is in foreign countries. U.S. and Western European firms own all of Brazil's automobile and tire plants and over half of its electrical equipment, and Brazil is not an unusual case among less-developed countries: more than a *third* of all production in the entire capitalist world is controlled by the 650 largest industrial firms (Smith, 1981).

Whereas the economies of all industrial societies are controlled by government to some degree, the world economy is independent of the control of any one government or set of governments. There is no world government to control the world economy, and multinationals are relatively free to shift operations to countries that offer the most profitable conditions. If labor costs rise in one country, a multinational can move to another where wages are lower (the next time you buy clothing with an American label, look carefully to see in what country it was actually made). Multinationals can also plan their operations so that they earn the highest profits in countries with the lowest income taxes.

Although multinationals play a vital part in the economic life of most societies, they often feel little loyalty to their host countries and are subject to relatively few legal restrictions. To keep multinationals from moving to other countries (and taking jobs and tax revenues with them) national governments must bargain and make concessions that vastly increase the power of multinational corporations. This is—on a larger scale—the same problem faced by communities when national businesses threaten to move a branch office or plant to another part of the country (see Chapter 9).

Fatemi et al. (1982) and other social scientists believe that multinational corporations rival the power of most nation states. More radical writers such as Amin (1975) believe that the rising power of multinational corporations will inevitably bring about a socialist revolution as governments and citizens assert control over corporations and the means of production. These writers were responding to the phenomenal growth rates of multinationals during the 1960s, and in more recent years multinational growth rates have fallen to more moderate levels (Goodman, 1980). Nevertheless, multinational corporations retain enormous amounts of economic power (Evans, 1981).

## The Social Consequences of Economic Arrangements

Like any set of social arrangements, the cultural ideas and social structures that make up economic institutions produce consequences that either contribute to or interfere with the achievement of culturally valued goals. In addition, economic arrangements play a particularly important part in social stratification, for it is through them that wealth—and to a considerable extent, power and prestige as well—is produced and distributed.

### Functions and Dysfunctions

Capitalism has produced and continues to produce a phenomenal volume of goods and services. Marx, in fact, believed that solving the problem of producing enough to satisfy the needs and wants of everyone would be the most important social function of capitalism. Competition among capitalists has also produced a staggering array of inventions and innovations—from the airplane, television, and computer to the permanent press shirt, artificial sweeteners, and Coca Cola. There is simply no comparison between the average standard of living in today's industrial, capitalist nations and any other type of society that has ever existed.

Capitalism is also dysfunctional for a variety of goals, the most notable of which is the narrowing of social class differences. As an economic system, capitalism also creates recurring patterns of "boom" and "bust" and requires periods of high unemployment that are disastrous for members of the labor force (Institute for Social Research, 1980; Smith, 1981). We have also seen that industrialization in general and capitalism in particular contribute to alienation among workers by fragmenting the work process and denying them meaningful work over which they exercise control.

Capitalism is also dysfunctional in ways that affect every segment of society. Because profit and expansion are the primary goals of capitalism, social needs may be adequately met only if it is profitable to do so. Drug companies, for example, resist investing in research to find cures for diseases that are relatively rare—even though they may also be highly fatal. The reason is simple: there is little profit in discovering a medicine for which the market is small. Cigarettes, on the other hand, are produced by the billions each year simply because they sell.

The high value placed on profit affects not only which needs are met, but how they are met. Hard, juiceless tomatoes were developed not to improve nutrition, but because they can be shipped with less damage; and less loss during transit means higher profits. Chemical preservatives in foods are used to prolong the shelf life of products—and, therefore, the chances that they will be sold—but they may threaten the health of those who eat them. Sugar-coated cereals promote tooth decay and substitute for more healthy nutrients (such as

One of the most glaring dysfunctions of most existing socialist societies is gross inefficiency resulting in shoddy goods and chronic shortages of both luxuries and many necessities. Waiting for hours in long lines for most consumer items is a way of life in the Soviet Union.

protein), and yet there are now so many different kinds of such cereals that most supermarkets cannot stock them all.

Although competition among capitalists is functional for increasing organizational efficiency and introducing new and innovative products, it also creates a great deal of waste. Building cars that last only four or five years (a practice once known as "planned obsolescence" in Detroit) increases profits by increasing sales; but it also wastes enormous amounts of raw materials, energy, and labor power.

Competition also generates wasteful duplication: instead of one or two companies producing a product, we have several that all produce essentially the same thing and compete with one another primarily through clever (and expensive) advertising. Go to a supermarket and look at the number of different brands of laundry detergent—any one of which will clean your clothes. Then stop and ask yourself, "What social needs could be met with the billions of dollars spent each year on advertising?"

Like capitalism, socialism produces both functional and dysfunctional consequences. In the Soviet Union, for example, everyone is guaranteed a job and the extreme differences between rich and poor found in the United States are relatively rare. One dysfunctional consequence of full employment, however, is that workers know they will keep their jobs no matter how badly they perform. Shoddy goods and low productivity are widespread problems in the Soviet Union and many socialist countries in eastern Europe and are often blamed by Soviet economists on the structure of socialism itself. As one Moscow economist said, "The Americans are lucky because they do not have the problem of full employment to deal with" (*New York Times*, June 12, 1983). On a larger scale, business and industry in socialist countries have relatively few incentives to improve productivity and efficiency, because they cannot fail in the way that capitalist enterprises can. Since they are owned and operated by the government, they cannot go bankrupt unless the government goes bankrupt.

The fate of both workers and managers rests with a central government that rules the country through enormously complex bureaucracies with characteristically rigid rules and procedures. It is simply safer for workers and managers to follow the rules and do as they are told than it is for them to try new techniques, experiment with new technologies, or restructure relations among workers in promising new ways.

As we would expect, the cultural and structural differences between capitalism and socialism produce different consequences. Competition under capitalism produces both positive and negative consequences, just as the general absence of competition does in socialist countries. In many important respects, the two kinds of society are quite similar: both face the problems of industrialization—such as pollution and bureaucracy—and both alienate workers who control neither the physical means nor the social relations through which goods are produced (Welsh, 1981).

Capitalism and socialism, however, are not simply two different and unrelated economic systems that sprang up all by themselves. Capitalism developed over a period of many centuries, and socialism emerged as a response to capitalism. To many socialist thinkers, socialism is both a response to capitalism and an inevitable consequence of it (Amin, 1975).

## Conflict, Change, and the Contradictions of Capitalism

Marx (1884) and others have pointed out that capitalism embodies a series of contradictions that, they believe, will ultimately lead to social change through which the means of production will be taken out of private control and placed under the collective control of the workers.

The most fundamental contradiction is one we have seen repeatedly in this and earlier chapters: the division of society into social classes based on control of the means of production produces inevitable tension and antagonism between social classes. The capitalist system itself pits workers and owners against each other: capitalists compete successfully by extracting as much surplus value from workers as they can; workers improve their position only by keeping as much of what they produce as they can. Thus, capitalism creates class conflict, and the only real question is, who will come out ahead?

The capitalist imperatives to expand production and increase profits create a second contradiction: the more productive the work force becomes, the less able the working class is to purchase all the goods that are produced. This, in turn, creates recurring crises for capitalist societies—recessions and depressions.

In this sense, capitalism creates its own crises that are more than inevitable ups and downs in business cycles. They are more than mere technical problems to be solved by fine-tuning the economic system—by increasing the number of public service jobs, changing the level of interest rates or taxes, increasing unemployment benefits, encouraging new business investment, or changing the level of government spending. Beneath the recurring crises in capitalist societies are social relationships between capitalists and workers—relationships whose effects reverberate throughout the entire society (Castells, 1980). As we will see in the next chapter, many government programs are designed to temporarily correct for economic "ups and downs" while keeping the basic economic arrangement of society intact.

Socialist societies also struggle with contradictions. Socialist governments ideally govern in the interests of the workers and have as their major goal a communist state in which there is no government. To control a nation, however, the government gathers to itself enormous power that its officials are, of course, reluctant to share or surrender, even to the workers for whom the government supposedly exists. Thus the irony is that in practice, socialism, which is supposed to be the path to freedom from exploitation, tends to have just the opposite effect in many areas of social life (Stojanovic, 1981).

Socialist societies, of course, have not been in existence nearly as long as capitalist societies have, and it remains to be seen how they will change. Thus far, however, no socialist society has come close to a workers' state in which people are free of political oppression and are able to control the means of production. The most critical contradiction for socialist societies may eventually lie in its failure to deliver the material basics of human life—good food, shelter, clothing, and other necessities—to a majority of their populations.

## Summary

1. Economic institutions are enduring sets of cultural ideas and objects and social relationships through which goods and services are produced and distributed. They include the means of production and the relations of production.

2. The development of capitalism depended on long historical transformations through which goods took on exchange value as well as use value and ownership of the means of production shifted from communities to individual producers, and then to employers.

3. Feudal nobles protected serfs in exchange for a share of what the serfs produced. This arrangement began to break down as independent merchants bought and sold what was produced by others, often paying producers less than the cost of production and keeping the difference between that and the selling price—surplus value—for themselves as profit.

4. The key to capitalism is the private ownership of the means of production. Calvinist religious beliefs supported the emergence of capitalism by making a virtue of hard work and the accumulation of wealth.

5. The development of capitalism also depended on the transformation of labor through which feudal ties between land, nobles, and serfs broke down and landless peasants were available as sources of cheap labor power to the rising urban capitalist class. In this way, labor power became a commodity that was bought and sold in the marketplace.

6. Capitalists try to maximize profits by controlling labor power and markets. Monopoly describes a market dominated by a single organization, whereas oligopoly is a market dominated by a few. A conglomerate is a centrally owned and controlled collection of organizations that produce goods and services in a wide variety of different markets. Most powerful business organizations are controlled by a small elite that generally includes high-level executives.

7. Industrial society labor markets tend to be segmented, divided into jobs that have different requirements and prospects. The primary market is divided into subordinate and independent sectors, and the secondary market includes low-level jobs that carry with them little power, income, or chance for advancement. Professionals are relatively autonomous and well paid and determine the conditions under which they work. For this reason, people in many occupations try to professionalize their work.

8. The economy is also divided into two parts, one noncompetitive and the other competitive. In general, workers in the noncompetitive economy earn higher wages and are more likely to belong to unions.

9. The United States is one country moving into a postindustrial era in which people are increasingly likely to provide services rather than produce goods. Although this changes the job market, it has little effect on the relative standing of employers and workers.

10. Alienation is the feeling that we lack a connection with the work we do, and it is closely tied to work that is experienced as powerless, meaningless, socially isolating, and fragmented.

11. Unemployment has many social causes, the most important being structural. Changing job markets, shifting age structures, and ongoing tension between workers and employers are continuing causes of unemployment.

12. Socialism differs from capitalism in that the means of production are owned by the state, not by private individuals or groups. Existing socialist societies tend to be far less efficient than capitalist ones and are often governed by authoritarian states. Under democratic socialism, only major industries are owned by the state. Communism is a utopia in which all means of production are communally owned and there is no state.

13. Regardless of its economic institutions, each society has a place in a world economy in which nations are divided into the core, the periphery, and the semiperiphery. In this system multinational corporations wield enormous power, in many cases rivaling that of nations.

14. Both capitalism and socialism have a number of functions and dysfunctions. Capitalism, for example, generates enormous wealth but also classes of the very poor. Socialist societies, however, have eliminated gross class differences, but are generally inefficient and politically repressive.

# Key Terms

# Recommended Readings

BRAVERMAN, H. (1974). *Labor and monopoly capital: The degradation of work in the twentieth century.* New York: Monthly Review Press. An important analysis of the transformation and control of labor power in capitalist societies.

HARRISON, M. (1982). *A woman in residence: A doctor's personal and professional battles against an insensitive medical system.* New York: Penguin Books. The essence of a profession is that the power of regulation lies largely with its own members. In this book a daily journal provides an inside look at the need for reform of the medical profession and what it will take to bring it about.

MARX, K. (1964). *Selected writings in sociology and social philosophy.* Edited by T. Bottomore and M. Rubel. Baltimore, MD: Penguin Books. A highly accessible introduction to Marx's major ideas on social stratification and alienated work.

NELKIN, D., and BROWN, M. S. (1984). *Workers at risk: Voices from the workplace.* Chicago: University of Chicago Press. The authors forcefully counter the belief that workers are free to choose among jobs according to how much danger they are willing to expose themselves to in the workplace.

SMELSER, N. J. (1975). *The sociology of economic life* (2nd ed.). Englewood Cliffs, NJ: Prentice-Hall. A useful guide to the sociological approach to the analysis of economic behavior and institutions.

SMITH, J. (1981). *Social issues and the social order: The contradictions of capitalism.* Cambridge, MA: Winthrop. An interesting, well-written book that tries to understand the ways in which economic arrangements such as capitalism contribute to social problems.

TERKEL, S. (1974). *Working.* New York: Pantheon. Studs Terkel is a journalist with a marvelous talent for getting people to talk about themselves. This collection of interviews in which people talk about "what they do all day long" is fascinating and thought-provoking.

# CHAPTER 18

# Political Institutions

In 1983 the government of Rumania, a socialist country in southeastern Europe, banned the private ownership of typewriters by former convicts or anyone who posed "a danger to public order or state security" (*New York Times,* April 24, 1983). People could not buy a typewriter without official permission from the government, and those who already owned one had to register it with the police, including a sample of the typewriter's print (so that anything written on the machine could be identified later). In short, it is easier to own a gun in most of the United States than it is to own a typewriter in Rumania.

**Politics** refers to the social process through which power is distributed among and used by groups, organizations, communities, and societies, and the preceding example illustrates important aspects of the political structures of social life. Clearly, the Rumanian government's decision is an exercise of power that affects all members of its society, and this by itself is enough to make it a political decision.

It is also political because it was designed to make it more difficult for opponents of the government to publish antigovernment leaflets. The government's attempt to control the distribution and use of something as simple as a typewriter is an attempt to keep that government in power and to perpetuate the form of government that rules Rumania.

Previous chapters explored the importance of power in social interaction (Chapter 7), groups and organizations (Chapter 8), and communities (Chapter 9). In this chapter, we are interested primarily in the distribution of power in societies. In particular, we focus on **political institutions**—the relatively permanent cultural ideas and social structures through which power is distributed and exercised in societies. Who has the power to make what kinds of decisions? How evenly distributed is decision-making power? How are decisions actually made and how are they put into effect? How do political institutions affect the people who occupy different social statuses in a society? What are the functions and dysfunctions of different political arrangements, and what is the relationship between political power and social change?

Since the sociological study of politics centers on the concept of power, we begin by taking a closer look at this by-now-familiar concept.

## Political Power and the State

We have defined power as the ability to impose one's will on other people in spite of their resistance. This includes not only direct control over people—such as the conditions under which they can own typewriters or guns—but also the ability to decide how the resources of a society will be used. Thus, deciding how tax money will be spent is as much an exercise of political power as is the ability to force people to pay taxes in the first place.

As we saw in Chapter 7, Weber (1925) defined the most important form of social power as **authority.** Authority differs from other forms of power in that it is socially supported and rests on the beliefs that those who possess it have a right to it and those who do not have a duty to obey. Thus, it cannot exist without social support. From a cultural point of view, parents have authority over their children, but only so long as members of a society recognize and define it as legitimate. When children reach ages that legally define them as adults (usually 18), parents lose much of their authority; and parents who abuse their children may also lose their authority over them if, for example, a court orders the children's removal from their home.

Weber identified three types of authority, the first of which is **legal-rational authority,** that is, power based on culturally defined rules that regulate social interactions. The power of professors to grade and discipline students, of people to control who enters their houses, of bosses to hire and fire workers, and of congressional representatives and senators to enact laws are all examples of legal-rational authority. The norms that define legal-rational authority specify who holds power in relation to whom and under what circumstances. In the United States the police may not enter your home without a proper warrant; but in many countries such as Chile and Argentina, it has not been uncommon for the police literally to kidnap "suspects" who are never heard from again.

Unlike legal-rational authority, **charismatic authority** is power that is based on people's beliefs that a particular individual possesses special abilities or characteristics. Prophets, heroes, demagogues, and mass-murderers—from Jesus Christ to Gandhi, from Napoleon Bonaparte to Adolph

The authority of these Supreme Court justices is primarily legal-rational.

Hitler—all exercise this type of authority over their followers (Willner, 1984). When the more than 900 disciples of the religious cult leader, Jim Jones, obeyed his instructions to commit suicide by swallowing poison (and poisoned their children, as well), they dramatically illustrated the power of this kind of authority (although it should be noted that some members were forced to take the poison). In this case, Jones' power came not from the social status of "religious leader," but from his followers' close identification with him as an individual.

The third form is **traditional authority;** it rests on the belief that the occupants of certain statuses are legitimately powerful because "that's the way it's always been." The authority of kings, queens, and emperors and, on a smaller scale, of elderly Japanese over their adult children—does not depend solely on legal-rational rules; rather, it also flows from a commitment to traditional arrangements that confer power on the occupant of particular statuses.

It is important to emphasize that legal-rational and traditional authority are not forms of personal power, for they are attached to particular social statuses under socially defined conditions. When soldiers salute each other, they pay respect to a person's rank, not to the individual who holds it. When police officers go "off-duty," they lose much of their authority, just as former U.S. presidents no longer control the use of nuclear weapons.

A number of sociologists (see Haskell, 1984) point out that in technologically sophisticated societies *expertise* in a specialized area is becoming an increasingly important source of authority in addition to Weber's three classic types. Experts in fields such as medicine, computer science, economics, business management and accounting, and nuclear weapons technology often exercise considerable authority because they command information necessary for vitally important decisions.

In sharp contrast with authority, **coercive power** lacks social legitimacy. When one country invades another and imposes its will on the inhabitants, its control over that society's resources and the behavior of its members is not socially supported. Rather, it is based on fear and, for this reason, tends to be relatively unstable. In the after-

Gandhi had enormous authority as a leader, virtually all of which was charismatic, based on the extraordinary characteristics attributed to him by his followers.

The authority of Japanese Emperor Hirohito, like that of most monarchs, was primarily traditional. Although Hirohito (shown here at his accession in 1926) is still nominally an emperor, he has lost virtually all of his authority.

math of revolutions (such as that in Nicaragua) and invasions (such as the Soviet Union's invasion of Afghanistan), guerilla warfare often becomes a fact of everyday life, and the new leaders live with continuing awareness that they might be overthrown at any time. In countries such as Japan and the United States, on the other hand, leaders know that while they may lose office with the next election, their opponents do not question their basic right to use the powers of their office.

Weber's three forms of authority are ideal types that rarely exist by themselves. A president's power may combine legal-rational, charismatic, and traditional authority, and the power of parents in relation to their children combines both traditional and legal-rational authority. If one source of power declines, status occupants rely more heavily on others. Former national leaders, for example, have no legal-rational authority over government decision making but may try to use charismatic or traditional authority to influence decisions long after they leave office.

How is authority organized in societies? This question brings us to perhaps the most important concept in the study of political institutions—the *state*.

## The Emergence of the State

Weber (1921) defined the **state** as the institution that "claims the monopoly of the use of force within a given territory" (p. 78). Like other social institutions, the state is defined in part by the social functions assigned to it to perform. It is responsible for establishing and enforcing legal norms; it sets social goals; it acts as an "umpire" in disputes among individuals, groups, and communities; and it establishes and maintains relationships with other societies, including trade agreements and military alliances. One basic function underlies all of these: the state is the institution charged with the responsibility for maintaining order and stability in a society.

States vary both in the process through which they perform these functions and the results of that process—such as which norms are enforced and which goals are pursued—and it is these differences that are the focus for most of this chapter. In this sense, the state is not a static "thing"; rather, it is a set of cultural ideas and dynamic social relationships through which power is exercised by some individuals and groups over others.

The American judicial system, for example—going all the way to the Supreme Court—is, above all, a social mechanism for resolving disputes and using the social power to determine guilt and innocence and inflict punishment. The rules that regulate what happens in courts of law are part of the normative structure of the state and profoundly affect what happens to individuals, groups, communities, and society itself.

The state is not the same thing as the *government,* just as "The American Family" is not the same thing as your family or mine. The **government** of a society is the collection of people who happen to occupy positions of authority within the framework of social relationships that define the state. Thus, there are two answers to questions such as "What is the Soviet Politburo?" As a part of the Soviet government, it is simply a collection of leaders who come and go, different people at different times. As part of the Soviet state, it is a group whose members—*whoever they may be*—have particular powers in relation to the citizens of the Soviet Union and particular relationships with the leaders of other societies.

The American government may change considerably with each presidential election, but the state remains virtually unchanged. For example, the Bill of Rights (the first 10 amendments to the Constitution, reprinted on the next page), is a set of norms that defines relationships between the state and its citizens, and it applies no matter which government is in power. The distinction between the state and the government is perhaps clearest when we remember that although many governments during our history have violated the Bill of Rights by abusing the power of the state, such violations have had a relatively small effect on the basic nature of the state itself.

Historically, the state is a relatively recent social institution. Hunter-gatherer societies had no state; decisions generally rested on community consensus, and the kinship group was the most important focus of power. Horticultural societies often had a few leaders who depended on traditional authority, but it was not until the agricultural era produced surpluses of goods and wealth that social classes and governments emerged.

Kings and emperors were at the center of the first states. Their authority was strictly traditional, and they were involved in continuous power struggles with nobles and with religious and military leaders. It was not until the last few centuries—particularly in Europe and then the United States—that the state began to acquire a monopoly over political power and the many social functions that characterize its modern form. With the emergence of the state came new cultural concepts—"nation" and "patriotism"—that have become basic organizing concepts in relations between societies. As the Industrial Revolution spawned a growing middle class of well-educated citizens who demanded a voice in the exercise of power in their societies, and as divisions of labor made social life increasingly complex, the functions of the state—and its power—expanded enormously.

Some authors believe that the emergence of powerful states was inevitable as societies industrialized and became vastly more complex (Davis, 1949; Service, 1975); but as explained later in this chapter, the development of the state and its enormous power has served some social classes more than others. Since the prime function of the state is to maintain the cultural ideas and social structures that make up a social environment, and since a given social order usually favors some groups and social categories over others, the state inevitably plays an important part in social conflict and the perpetuation of social inequality. This also means, of course, that the cultural and structural characteristics of the state inevitably mirror to some degree the social environment it is designed to protect and perpetuate.

## Culture, Politics, and the State

The power exercised by the state represents the collective ability of a society to "mobilize its resources in the interest of goals" (Parsons, 1969, p. 204). In other words, the state operates to select

# The Bill of Rights of the United States

## AMENDMENT I

Congress shall make no law respecting an establishment of religion, or prohibiting the free exercise thereof; or abridging the freedom of speech, or of the press; or the right of the people peaceably to assemble, and to petition the Government for a redress of grievances.

## AMENDMENT II

A well regulated Militia, being necessary to the security of a free State, the right of the people to keep and bear Arms shall not be infringed.

## AMENDMENT III

No Soldier shall, in time of peace, be quartered in any house, without the consent of the Owner, nor in time of war, but in a manner to be prescribed by law.

## AMENDMENT IV

The right of the people to be secure in their persons, houses, papers, and effects, against unreasonable searches and seizures, shall not be violated, and no Warrants shall issue, but upon probable cause, supported by Oath or affirmation, and particularly describing the place to be searched, and the persons or things to be seized.

## AMENDMENT V

No person shall be held to answer for a capital or otherwise infamous crime, unless on a presentment or indictment of a Grand Jury, except in cases arising in the land or naval forces, or in the Militia, when in actual service in time of War or public danger; nor shall any person be subject for the same offence to be twice put in jeopardy of life or limb; nor shall be compelled in any criminal case to be a witness against himself, nor be deprived of life, liberty, or property, without due process of law; nor shall private property be taken for public use, without just compensation.

## AMENDMENT VI

In all criminal prosecutions, the accused shall enjoy the right to a speedy and public trial, by an impartial jury of the State and district wherein the crime shall have been committed, which district shall have been previously ascertained by law, and to be informed of the nature and cause of the accusation; to be confronted with the witnesses against him; to have compulsory process for obtaining witnesses in his favor, and to have the Assistance of Counsel for his defence.

## AMENDMENT VII

In suits at common law, where the value in controversy shall exceed twenty dollars, the right of trial by jury shall be preserved, and no fact tried by a jury, shall be otherwise reexamined in any Court of the United States, than according to the rules of the common law.

## AMENDMENT VIII

Excessive bail shall not be required, nor excessive fines imposed, nor cruel and unusual punishments inflicted.

## AMENDMENT IX

The enumeration in the Constitution, of certain rights, shall not be construed to deny or disparage others retained by the people.

## AMENDMENT X

The powers not delegated to the United States by the Constitution, nor prohibited by it to the States, are reserved to the States respectively, or to the people.

both the values that influence collective decisions about goals and the norms that define the legitimate means for achieving them. How do the cultural ideas fostered and maintained by the state differ from one society to another, and how are they reflected in the state as an institution?

Does the state, for example, value personal freedom more than social order and conformity, a strong military more than a healthy population free of poverty, equality more than the freedom to pursue individual gain, the rights of accused criminals more than the rights of their victims? The answers to such questions define a basic aspect of any state—the goals it pursues in the name of society—and profoundly affect how particular governments go about the business of using political power.

In the United States and other capitalist societies, the right to own and use the means of production for private gain is an important value in economic life. The state, in turn, is responsible for protecting private property rights and fostering social conditions in which capitalists can maximize profits (see Smith, 1981). From Marx's perspective, economic arrangements form the most important institutions in any society, and the most important function of a capitalist state is to enact and enforce legal norms that support the values of the capitalist class.

Consider, for example, antitrust laws that forbid the formation of monopolies in which a single business organization completely dominates a particular product or service. Whose interests do such laws best serve? Do they protect consumers from the ability of monopolies to dictate any price they want? Apparently not, for a few large companies in an industry can maintain high prices even though no one of them has a monopoly. There are four major American automobile manufacturers, for example, and yet there is little price competition among them. Each waits for one of the others to raise prices at the beginning of the new model year and then one by one the others raise their prices by a comparable amount. The only serious price competition in the automobile market has come from Japan, which has nothing to do with U.S. antitrust laws.

From Marx's perspective, antitrust laws primarily serve those who own and control the means of production. This appears to be a contradiction, for why would the state serve the interests of capi-

talists by restricting them? One answer is that antitrust laws protect capitalists from being driven out of business by other capitalists who monopolize a market. The breakup of the American Telephone and Telegraph Company in 1983 was urged less by consumer groups than by companies that wanted a larger slice of the telecommunications market. The long and unsuccessful antitrust suit against IBM was inspired primarily by IBM's competitors—such as Xerox—not by consumers. In both cases, the tens of millions of dollars spent by the government to sue the companies involved were supplied by taxpayers.

The protection of private property rights is, of course, not the only function of the state in the United States and other capitalist countries. Values such as privacy and the freedoms to vote, express opinions, move from one place to another, and follow religious beliefs are also protected by legal norms. The state takes major responsibility for providing for the poor, for protecting consumers against fraud or the hazards of dangerous products, for supporting mass education, and for protecting the natural environment.

Some of the values supported by the state in socialist countries such as the Soviet Union and Rumania are very different from those emphasized in capitalist countries. Personal freedom is far more restricted, and people live in continuing fear that they will be reported to the authorities for performing some act that might offend government officials. Rock music was recently banned in the Soviet Union because of its supposed "subversive" effects on the stability of Soviet society; and artists, musicians, and writers are regularly persecuted for "undermining" the state.

The announced aim of such societies is to promote equality by refusing to support what is, in capitalist societies, one of the most important personal freedoms—the right to own the means of production. The welfare of the community, socialists argue, is of more value than the freedom of individuals to exploit the community for personal gain. Consequently, full employment is more highly valued than efficient production.

The contrast between capitalist and socialist states might lead one to conclude that personal freedom and equality are inherently incompatible values, that it is impossible for a society to vigorously support both at the same time. It is important to remember, however, that the right to own property is only one of many personal freedoms, and human history is full of examples—including most hunter-gatherer and horticultural societies—of societies in which people owned little private property and inequality was minimal and in which personal freedom in other areas of life was *not* tightly restricted as it is in so many socialist societies today. Whether or not freedom and equality can be achieved simultaneously in industrial societies remains to be seen.

It is also important to remember that most socialist societies were created through violent revolutions or foreign invasions that transformed societies in which private property rights and severe inequality had existed for hundreds of years. To Lenin (1917), the most powerful leader of the Russian Revolution, the state had to assume great powers over individual freedom in order to crush opposition to the revolution and break the control of the ruling class over the means of production.

Regardless of the differences among them, all societies where the state has developed as a powerful social institution have one value in common: the preservation of the state itself. The state is the institution that monopolizes the use of force in a society, and when the perpetuation of the state itself is threatened, the governments of the United States or Britain are no less likely to respond with force than are those of China, Rumania, or the Soviet Union. It is a federal crime, for example, to advocate—even by merely writing a letter or making a speech—the violent overthrow of the U.S. government; but it is perfectly legal for the state to

As these antigovernment demonstrators in Santiago, Chile, experienced in 1984, the state's monopoly on the use of force puts it in an ideal position to perform what might be viewed as one of any institution's most important functions—to perpetuate itself.

use police and soldiers to violently disperse a crowd of demonstrators.

The state, then, is an institution that, at best, walks a fine line between the protection of citizens and their oppression. In the name of safeguarding society, it seeks to increase its powers; but those same powers—the monopoly of violence—can then be used against those same citizens.

## Structures of Power: Basic Types of Political Institutions

Cultural ideas often provide an ideological basis for political institutions that justify their existence and determine the goals for which political power is used. However, it is in the social structures of power—how it is distributed and used—that the greatest differences between societies are found. As we have seen before, power structures have two basic characteristics: the distribution of power, and the amount of power a group, organization, community, or society has.

### Distributions of Power: Democracy, Oligarchy, and Autocracy

The word **democracy** joins the Greek words "cracy" ("rule") and "demo" ("of the people"), and in pure democracies power is shared equally by all members of a society. In ancient Greece, decisions were made at meetings in which every citizen had a vote. Virtually all hunter-gatherer societies operated as democracies, and some New England towns still have town meetings in which residents are free to voice their opinions and ultimately vote on the issues at hand.

It is important to note that democracies always place some restrictions on who is defined as a "citizen" eligible to participate in decision making. Children, for example, cannot vote, just as slaves and women could not in ancient Greece.

Few states take the form of pure democracy, in large part because it is impractical in large complex societies. How, for example, would millions of Americans meet to thrash out national issues? If every decision required a vote by the entire popu-

lation, we would spend most of our time at the polls. One common response to this problem is the **representative democracy,** in which citizens delegate authority to elected representatives—such as those who serve in legislatures. Theoretically, the elected representatives speak for the voters, who are too numerous to speak for themselves.

Representative democracy is the political institution found in countries such as the United States, India, Canada, France, Britain, Norway, Mexico, and Italy. Lipset (1959) studied 48 societies and concluded that democracy depends on several key cultural and structural characteristics. Countries with advanced economies and urban, literate, middle-class populations tend to be more democratic than societies that are underdeveloped and have largely illiterate, rural, peasant populations.

Bollen (1983) studied 100 societies and supported Lipset's view that economic development and democratic institutions tend to go hand in hand; but he also found that democracy depends on the position of a country in the world economy (see Chapter 17). Democracy is most common in wealthy core countries such as the United States and Japan and least common in peripheral countries such as Nigeria.

Cultural characteristics of a society also play a part in supporting democracy. The culturally homogeneous population of Iceland has created and supported the longest-lasting representative democracy in the world. Countries such as Chad and Lebanon, however, have populations that are so diverse and conflicting that a stable democracy is virtually impossible to achieve.

The norms that define the means for achieving social goals are an important ingredient in the creation and perpetuation of democracies. In particular, democracy depends on strong norms that restrict the power of the state in relation to the people—such as the U.S. Constitution and its Bill of Rights.

Values and attitudes are also important, especially those that tolerate and support dissent (see McClosky and Brill, 1983). In the United States, for example, **civil disobedience**—the deliberate and open violation of a norm for the purpose of changing it because it is perceived as being unjust—is culturally defined as legitimate behavior, even though those who engage in it are punished. Our culture reserves a special respect for those who openly defy unjust laws and willingly accept the consequences in the name of improving society. Many observers have noted that Russians, on the other hand, tend to hold just the opposite view and value conformity and obedience to authority far more highly than do Americans (Shipler, 1983).

Two important aspects of social structure also support democracies. Since citizens must be in a position to elect representatives who act in their best interests, it is important for citizens to have access to information that reveals just what their representatives are doing with the authority that is given to them. This produces a continuing tension in democracies between the desire of those in authority to keep their activities secret and the need of the people to have continuing access to information about government decisions and activities.

In some cases, secrets do protect "national security." If the American public had access to the military's plans for national defense, so would its enemies. In other cases, however, secrecy serves the interests of leaders who want to preserve their positions by concealing activities that the public would oppose. Many instances of official misconduct—such as illegally wiretapping telephones—are concealed by government officials on the grounds of "national security," when in fact the only security involved is that of the government officials themselves.

Democracy also depends on diffusion of power among many different individuals, groups, and organizations, for when power is concentrated in the hands of a relative few, democracies are in danger of becoming *oligarchies* and, in the most extreme cases, *autocracies*.

**Oligarchy and Autocracy** Michels (1911) argued that the mere existence of leaders in a society guarantees that democracy cannot last, because the availability of power is corrupting no matter how noble a leader's initial intentions may be. Thus, Michels believed that an "Iron Rule of Oligarchy" dictates that complex societies inevitably become **oligarchies,** in which the power of the state is monopolized by a privileged elite.

Michels based his rule on three arguments, the first of which is that most people, either because of apathy or incompetence, would rather let others make decisions for them. It is, for example,

difficult for most Americans to actively involve themselves in debates over nuclear weapons and the economy without a thorough understanding of the complex issues involved.

Second, Michels argued that in complex societies it is impossible to pay attention to every individual's point of view. Although we may have opinion polls, elections, and referenda on important issues, it is impossible to conduct a "national debate" that includes the active participation of more than 230 million Americans. Thus, important decisions are left in the hands of a relatively small number of leaders.

Third, leaders enjoy the privileges that come with power and, therefore, want to keep their positions of power. This separates them from the people they lead and, in the interests of keeping their power, leaders seek more power, trying to control their rivals or silence their opposition by controlling criticism in the media.

From Michels' point of view, the increasing complexity of societies and their reliance on leaders results in a loss of individual power and freedom and growing opportunities for abuses of power that result in social oppression. As Tannenbaum (1968) pointed out, however, things are not so simple in many of today's societies. Industrial societies are organized around complex bureaucracies that control complex divisions of labor. No small group of people can control national governments in countries such as the United States. Every four years, a new American president vows to control the vast federal bureaucracy and, inevitably, realizes that he and his aides cannot possibly do it. As Etzioni-Halévy (1983) argued, bureaucracy is necessary for managing the affairs of a complex representative democracy such as our own, and yet its size and power coupled with its inherent rigidity constitute a threat to democratic institutions.

Socialist countries such as the Soviet Union and China are, in comparison with North American and most European countries, far more oligarchic and bureaucratic. When Soviet jet fighters shot down a Korean airliner that strayed into Soviet airspace in 1983, one fact that became clear in the aftermath was that the Soviet oligarchy—the Politburo—had great difficulty monitoring and controlling military units far on the other side of the country. As tightly controlled as many aspects

A true autocrat—such as Paraguay's General Alfredo Stroessner—is a relative rarity in the world today.

of social life are in socialist countries, gross inefficiency is one of their hallmarks, and this is due in no small part to the vastness and complexity of the bureaucracies through which a relatively small number of leaders try to govern entire societies.

The most extreme concentration of political power is found in an **autocracy** in which the power of the state is wielded by a single leader. Hitler in Germany, Stalin in Russia, Idi Amin in Uganda, and the Shah of Iran were all autocrats, as were most kings and queens prior to the twentieth century. Autocracy describes only a few national leaders in recent years, including the head of the royal family in Saudi Arabia, Muammar al-Qaddafi in Libya, the Ayatollah Khomeini in Iran, and Augusto Pinochet in Chile.

The scale running from pure democracy to pure autocracy describes the range within which states distribute political power. A second important dimension of the state, however, is the amount of power it wields in relation to members of a society.

## How Much Power?
## Authoritarianism and Totalitarianism

The concept of **authoritarianism** describes the degree to which the state controls the lives of its citizens. Since all states, by definition, monopolize the use of force, they are all authoritarian to some degree; but sociologists generally reserve the term "authoritarian" for states that exercise high levels of control over people's lives.

Most of the population of the world lives in authoritarian states, from China, the Soviet Union, and the countries of Eastern Europe to military dictatorships in Latin American countries such as Chile, Paraguay, and Guatemala. Under authoritarianism, the state has the power to control the mass media, schools, and the economy. It often uses terror—inflicted by military and secret police organizations—to control its citizens. The ability of people to migrate—especially to other countries—often is restricted, and there are few restraints on the government's ability to enact and enforce laws, however unjust they may be (Friedrich and Brzezinski, 1965).

The most extreme form of authoritarianism is **totalitarianism,** under which the state attempts to control not only people's behavior, but virtually all aspects of their private lives. Best described in George Orwell's 1949 classic novel, *Nineteen Eighty-four,* the totalitarian state tries to control what people think and feel as well as what they do, and it accomplishes this goal through complete control over all social institutions, from the family and mass communications to religion. In Orwell's nightmarish vision, a society is ruled by "Big Brother"; television sets are two-way, allowing authorities to monitor what goes on in people's homes; history is methodically rewritten in order to conform to the state's version of the truth; and those who refuse to conform are tortured until they think and behave "correctly."

Of all the forms that characterize the state in different societies, totalitarianism is probably the least stable and is as uncommon as pure democracy (Walzer, in Howe, 1983). In the twentieth century, Nazi Germany and Russia under Stalin came closest to Orwell's vision of totalitarianism, but even these extreme cases were far from monolithic

## Voices: Totalitarian Terror

Total terror, the essence of totalitarian government, exists neither for nor against men. It is supposed to provide the forces of Nature and History with an incomparable instrument to accelerate their movement. This movement, proceeding according to its own law, cannot in the long run be hindered; eventually its force will always prove more powerful than the most powerful forces engendered by the actions and will of men. But it can be slowed down and is slowed down almost inevitably by the freedom of man, which even totalitarian rulers cannot deny, for this freedom—irrelevant and arbitrary as they may deem it—is identical with the fact that men are being born and that therefore each of them *is* a new beginning, begins, in a sense, the world anew. From the totalitarian point of view, the fact that men are born and die can be only regarded as an annoying interference with higher forces. Terror, therefore, as the obedient servant of natural or historical movement has to eliminate from the process not only freedom in any specific sense, but the very source of freedom which is given with the fact of the birth of man and resides in his capacity to make a new beginning. In the iron band of terror, which destroys the plurality of men and makes out of many the One who unfailingly will act as though he himself were part of the course of History or Nature, a device has been found not only to liberate the historical and natural forces, but to accelerate them to a speed they never would reach if left to themselves. Practically speaking, this means that terror executes on the spot the death sentences which Nature is supposed to have pronounced on races or individuals who are "unfit to live," or History on "dying classes," without waiting for the slower and less efficient processes of Nature and History themselves. . . .

In a perfect totalitarian government, where all men have become One Man, where all action aims at the acceleration of the movement of Nature or History, where every single act is the execution of a death sentence which Nature or History has already pronounced, that is, under conditions where terror can be completely relied upon to keep the movement in constant motion, no principle of action separate from its essence would be needed at all. Yet as long as totalitarian rule has not conquered the earth and with the iron band of terror made each single man a part of one mankind, terror in its double function as essence of government and principle, not of action, but of motion cannot be fully realized. Just as lawfulness in constitutional government is insufficient to inspire and guide men's actions, so terror in totalitarian government is not sufficient to inspire and guide human behavior.

Source: Arendt, "Ideology and Terror: A Novel Form of Government," 1953.

states that effectively ruled the private lives of their citizens. In both cases dissent was not uncommon, there was continual infighting, and there were frequent power struggles. History seems to indicate that the totalitarian state is unattainable, for "thus far, 'human nature' has proved too stubborn, devious, recalcitrant, and . . . courageous to submit to total transformation" (Schlesinger, 1983, p. 24).

In general, the likelihood of authoritarianism increases as the surrounding society becomes more unstable. The most authoritarian states in the world today—China, the Soviet Union, and military dictatorships in a number of countries—all came into existence in the aftermath of violent revolutions. In general, the state in all societies—including the United States—becomes more authoritarian during times of crisis such as wars and internal upheaval.

In 1798, shortly after the American Revolution, Congress passed the Sedition Act, which allowed the government to prosecute anyone who wrote or published anything that was "false, scandalous, or malicious" against any branch of the federal government (Beard and Beard, 1944). In short, open criticism of the government was banned by law. In the early 1950s the fear of communism allowed Senator Joseph McCarthy to conduct his infamous Senate hearings to identify communists. Hundreds of people were subpoenaed to testify before his committee, and anyone who had ever belonged to a communist organization, or who had associated with those who had, was labeled a communist (or, at the very least, a communist sympathizer). McCarthy never managed to identify a single communist in the government, but by the time he was stopped, hundreds of innocent people—from government employees to writers, artists, and actors—had lost their jobs and suffered permanent damage to their reputation.

There is no such thing as a state that cannot become more authoritarian under the control of a particular government, and the state's monopoly over the use of force creates a continuing tension between the functional importance of state institutions and the potential for abuse of power by groups and individuals. Nor is "majority rule"—one of the hallmarks of democracy—a guarantee that the power of the state will not be used to oppress citizens. More than a century ago, Alexis de Tocqueville (1835/1954) visited America and warned of the possibility of a "tyranny of the majority," in which the rights of blacks and other minorities would not be protected. In a racist, sexist,

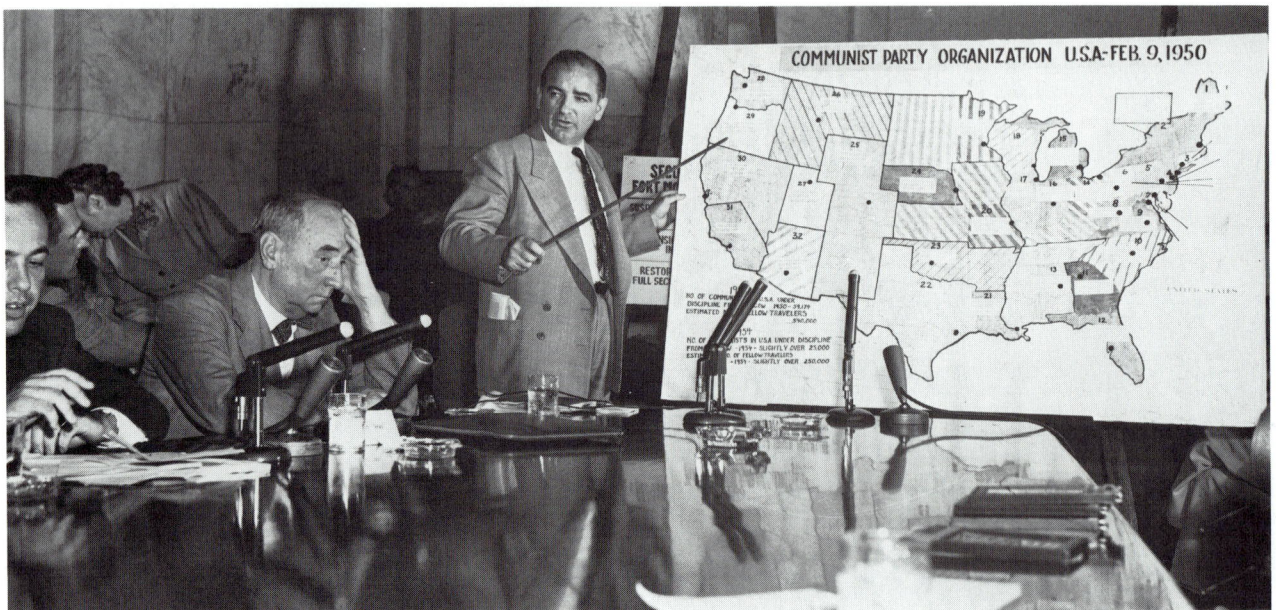

Senator Joseph McCarthy presenting "evidence" of communist subversion in the U.S. government. Not one of his charges was ever supported by evidence.

anti-Semitic society conformity to prevailing norms results in the oppression of nonwhites, women, and Jews for whom the law—which is controlled by the state—is "a sword, not a shield" (Burns, 1973). Without the acceptance of Nazi values, beliefs, attitudes, and norms by millions of Germans, the Nazi state never would have been able to perpetrate the Holocaust in which more than 6 million people were murdered.

It is important to note that while many of the authoritarian states of the world are also socialist countries, there is no necessary connection between economic and political arrangements. Nazi Germany was both capitalist and intensely hostile toward socialism; some of the world's most oppressive military dictatorships are allies of the United States; and in semi-socialist countries such as Sweden and Norway, the state is not authoritarian.

## Who Rules? Power in American Politics

Sociologists have developed several views of the distribution of political power in societies, two of which we encountered in Chapter 9. Mills (1956) and Hunter (1953) argued that power is virtually monopolized by a power elite of leaders in business, government, and the military, who enjoy common backgrounds and move easily from one sphere of power to another (see also Useem, 1983). Below the power elite a variety of interest groups exercise some power, and at the bottom of the power distribution lies the mass of unorganized people who have little power at all to affect national decisions.

The power elite, Mills argued, is bound together by common interests. Military leaders, for example, want to expand the number and sophistication of weapons, and corporations want to build such weapons for huge profits. As a result, decisions about the nuclear arms race are based not only on considerations of national defense, but on the economic interests of corporations as well. The concept of a power elite identifies several consequences of such concentrations of political power, the most important of which are the growth of corporate power and the decline of public participation in decision making (Domhoff and Ballard, 1968).

Riesman (1961) offered a very different view of the distribution of power, arguing that it is plural-

istic—divided among a variety of separate interest groups over which the mass of unorganized citizens has some power. Different interest groups dominate decision making in different areas, and interest groups generally recognize that they have limited power and depend on others in order to accomplish their goals.

Riesman (1961) believed, however, that when pluralism is taken to extremes it interferes with leadership because each interest group exercises "veto" power over the issues that define its goals. Governing bodies such as the Congress have difficulty making decisions because they are besieged by well-organized interest groups at every turn. The result is often legislation that offends a minimal number of people but also fails to establish clear and decisive directions for national programs and policy.

Lieberson (1971) also contended that when interest groups become so numerous and powerful that they dominate political decision making it is difficult for a national consensus to emerge on any given issue. Each group tends to fight for its special interest and for nothing else, and this tends to fragment society and break down social cohesion.

There is little doubt that political power is concentrated in the United States, although certainly not to the degree found in authoritarian societies. Domhoff's 1967 study and Freitag's study in 1975 both support Mill's belief in the existence of a power elite (see also Domhoff, 1983). Freitag found, for example, that almost 90 percent of cabinet officers in the federal government between 1897 and 1973 had also served as high-level officers in corporations.

This does not mean the power elite is a unified group whose members meet in an enormous room to agree on how political decisions are to be made. It does imply that a relatively small number of people have far greater access to political power than do most citizens, and their interests tend to coincide far more than they diverge.

Middle- and lower-class people certainly have some voice in selecting presidents and congressional representatives, but they have virtually no power in choosing cabinet members and the heads of powerful federal agencies such as the departments of State and Defense. Nor does the average citizen have any access to these officials once they are appointed (when was the last time you or your

**Table 18-1**

Voter Participation in Selected Countries

| COUNTRY AND (YEAR) | PERCENTAGE VOTING[1] |
|---|---|
| Switzerland (1975) | 52 |
| United States (1976) | 59 |
| India (1977) | 60 |
| Canada (1974) | 71 |
| Finland (1975) | 74 |
| Ireland (1977) | 76 |
| Israel (1977) | 79 |
| Great Britain (1974) | 79 |
| Norway (1977) | 83 |
| Denmark (1977) | 89 |
| West Germany (1976) | 91 |

Source: U.S. Census Bureau, 1980b.

[1] Percentage of population of voting age that actually voted in national elections.

**Table 18-2**

Selected Political Perceptions and Attitudes, American Adults, 1984

| | |
|---|---|
| "Most public officials are not really interested in the problems of the average man." | 68% agree |
| "I have a great deal of confidence in the Executive Branch of the federal government." | 18% agree |
| "I have a great deal of confidence in the Congress." | 12% agree |

Source: J. Davis, 1984.

parents attended a dinner party whose guests included high-level government officials?).

Members of the power elite certainly differ on various issues and may oppose one another; but when they choose to work toward common goals, they wield enormous political power. If the American political system is pluralistic, it is what Kornhauser (1966) called an "elite pluralism," in which a select few vie with one another over control of the state (see also Knoke, 1981).

The following section gives a broad outline of the distribution of power in American politics, and the sections following take a more detailed look at the different "players" in the political "game": voters, political parties, interest groups, and political coalitions.

**The American Voter** The right to vote is the most direct form of political power available to most Americans. Although we rarely use it to decide

specific issues, we can use it to elect nominated candidates for public office. This, of course, represents a very indirect form of power in an important respect, for once candidates are elected, their need to worry about pleasing their constituents lessens considerably until the next election. In the 1964 presidential election, for example, Lyndon Johnson overwhelmed his opponent, Barry Goldwater, in large part because voters feared that Goldwater would be too quick to involve the United States in war. Within a few years after his election, however, Johnson had led the United States deep into the disastrous war in Vietnam.

Americans are considerably less likely to vote in national elections than are the citizens of other industrial societies (Table 18-1). This may be due in part to the fact that in the United States responsibility for registering as voters rests entirely with the individual, whereas in Canada, Finland, Great Britain, and West Germany registration is either required or actively facilitated by the government by, for example, allowing registration by mail or automatically registering all citizens. Among American registered voters, fully 74 percent voted in the 1980 election, which suggests that if registration were more widespread in the United States, voting might be as well.

There is also evidence, however, that Americans generally pay little attention to political issues. In 1982 only 36 percent of adults reported

## Table 18-3

Selected Political Values, American Adults, 1983–1984

| POLITICAL VALUE | ADULT POPULATION | GOVERNMENT POSITION |
|---|---|---|
| 1. Death penalty | 70% in favor | Opposed |
| 2. Registration of guns with police | 70% in favor | Opposed |
| 3. Wiretapping by law enforcement officers | 84% opposed | In favor |
| 4. Decrease spending to improve and protect the environment | 93% opposed | In favor |
| 5. Spending too little for defense | 82% disagree | Agree |
| 6. Verifiable freeze on nuclear weapons | 64% in favor | Opposed |
| 7. Assist anti-communist guer-rillas in Nicaragua | 56% opposed | In favor |

Sources (percentages): #1–#5: J. Davis, 1984; #6: *Newsweek*, January 31, 1983, p. 17; #7: *Newsweek*, May 9, 1983, p. 21.

## Table 18-4

Who Votes in National Elections? (United States, 1980)

| CHARACTERISTIC | PERCENTAGE VOTING[1] |
|---|---|
| **Gender** | |
| Male | 62 |
| Female | 62 |
| **Race** | |
| White | 63 |
| Black | 52 |
| Hispanic | 45 |
| **Age** | |
| 18–20 | 38 |
| 21–24 | 45 |
| 25–34 | 58 |
| 35–44 | 68 |
| 45–64 | 71 |
| 65 and older | 67 |
| **Education** | |
| 8 years or less | 47 |
| 1–3 high school | 47 |
| High school graduate | 60 |
| 1–3 years college | 70 |
| College graduate or more | 83 |
| **Employment Status** | |
| Employed | 64 |
| Unemployed | 43 |

Sources: U.S. Census Bureau, 1982, 1983c.

[1] Percentage of adult citizen population that actually voted in the 1980 presidential election.

that they "follow what's going on in government and public affairs most of the time," and more than a quarter said they did "only now and then" or "hardly at all" (Davis, 1982).

National surveys suggest that these relatively low levels of political involvement may reflect a lack of faith in government and the belief that government is not responsive to the people. In 1984, for example, more than two-thirds of Americans reported the belief that most public officials have little interest in the average citizen's problems, and less than 20 percent expressed a great deal of confidence in either the Congress or the executive branch (Table 18-2). In addition, the adult population held values that were strikingly at odds with government policy in a number of important areas, from gun control and the federal budget to nuclear weapons and foreign aid (Table 18-3).

Voter nonparticipation is also related to the social statuses people occupy. In general, those who occupy the highest positions are the most likely to vote (Table 18-4). The one exception to this general finding is that women and men are equally likely to vote, even though women as a social category occupy an inferior social position in American society (see Chapter 13).

Is our general lack of political interest and participation some kind of national "personality trait"? While this is a possible explanation, sociologists are more likely to consider how the structure of American political institutions affects the ability and motivation of individuals to participate in them. For more insight into this, we turn to political parties, which represent the first level of political organization above the "unorganized mass of people."

**Political Parties** A **political party** is an organization whose main goal is to acquire power by placing members in positions of authority. In authoritarian countries, such as the socialist countries of Eastern Europe, a single party dominates the state and voters must choose between voting for the official party candidates or not voting at all. In a few countries, such as Mexico, the state is not authoritarian, but the ruling party is so firmly entrenched that opposition parties rarely win elections. Most countries—including the United States—have a handful of political parties, and a few, such as Italy, have a dozen or so.

Since political parties are the main source of candidates for public office, they are an important link between citizens and their government. Through their candidates, parties define positions on important issues, map solutions to pressing problems, and transmit public opinion to the decision-making apparatus that is the state. If voters, then, feel unmotivated to participate in political activities, part of the explanation may lie in the characteristics of political parties through which most of the power of voters is exercised.

The sociological importance of political parties lies in two main areas that sharply distinguish political parties in the United States from those in most other representative democracies. The first concerns the legal norms that control elections, which, in turn, define the relationship between parties and the state. The second focuses on the structural and cultural characteristics of parties themselves, both of which are closely tied to the first.

Unlike elections in most democracies, American political norms dictate a "winner-take-all" system (Duverger, 1959). To win a seat in the U.S. Senate, for example, a candidate must receive more votes than any other candidate. Thus, the

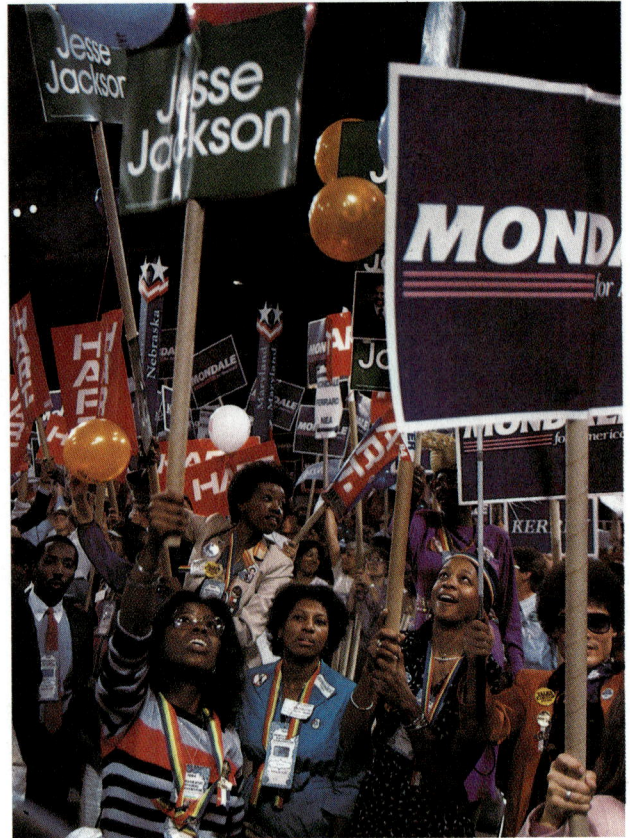

composition of Congress is determined by the outcome in each of 50 state elections. Under this system, even if 49 percent of the voters favor candidates from party "A," it is possible that *none* of those who are elected will be from that party. In this extreme hypothetical case the interests of almost half of the adult population would have no representation in Congress.

In most other representative democracies, the composition of legislatures is proportional, which is to say it is determined by the percentage of the vote received by each party, not whether individual candidates get more votes than do their opponents. If only 10 percent of the voters favor party "A," then 10 percent of the seats in the legislature will be filled by members of that party. Such legislatures reflect the diversity of their populations in a way that is almost impossible under legal norms in the United States.

Thus, the norms that govern elections profoundly affect the composition—the social structure—of governing bodies such as the U.S.

Congress and state legislatures or European parliaments. If Americans want to use their votes to elect candidates, their only hope is to vote for a candidate who can beat all other opponents. If the candidate who seems most likely to win does not represent their views, then from a practical standpoint, their votes have no effect on the ultimate composition of the government.

The effects of the winner-take-all system extend to the cultural and structural characteristics of parties themselves, and American parties differ from those in other representative democracies in several important ways (Lipset, 1959). Suppose, for example, that you belong to the "Freedom Party," whose members favor, among other things, legalization of marijuana, a position shared by only 22 percent of American adults in 1984 (Davis, 1984). How does your party win seats in Congress?

In most democracies, you could hope to gain as many as 22 percent of the legislative seats—in other words, representation in direct proportion to the percentage of your supporters in the population. In the United States, however, you would win no seats unless you ran candidates in congressional districts where most voters favor legalization of marijuana—an extremely unlikely possibility. If you are serious about winning—rather than merely expressing your views—one response to this problem is to do whatever you can to avoid offending potential supporters, and one obvious way to do this is not to take a clear and open stand in favor of legalizing marijuana.

In most representative democracies, when parties take a clear, unambiguous stand on the issues, it does not destroy their chances of gaining some political power; but in the United States, such behavior has disastrous consequences, as Barry Goldwater and George McGovern discovered in the presidential elections of 1964 and 1972. Both took clear positions in their campaigns and both were defeated overwhelmingly by their opponents—Lyndon Johnson in 1964 and Richard

Nixon in 1972. In 1984 many analysts agreed that Ronald Reagan's landslide victory over Walter Mondale was helped considerably by the President's avoidance of controversial issues and his refusal to reveal his plans for a second term. Mondale, for example, openly announced that he would raise taxes in order to lower the federal budget deficit, while Reagan said he would not raise taxes but did not reveal any alternative approach.

To avoid such defeats, American parties try to appeal to the broad center of political opinion in order to attract a majority of voters by offending as few people as possible. As a consequence, **party platforms**—statements of party positions on important issues—tend to be vague and wishy-washy, and members of the same party may hold sharply different views. Southern Democrats, for example, are often more conservative than northern Republicans.

This, in turn, makes it difficult for parties to be tightly organized on a national level. More important, it forces voters to choose between candidates whose political differences are often hard to detect and who do not represent what voters want. (The disaffection of American voters was perhaps best expressed by a candidate who tried to change his name to "None of the Above," figuring that such a name on a ballot would surely attract a large number of voters. The courts denied his request.) As a result, we tend to base our votes more on our perceptions of candidates' personalities than on the political beliefs and values that define their positions on issues. In most other democracies, however, people vote for the party, not for the individual candidate.

The relative importance of parties and individual candidates profoundly affects the characteristics of parties. In France, for example, individuals can gain public office only through the success of their parties. There are no primary elections; party officials decide who will actually occupy the seats won in an election. This gives parties enormous power over officeholders, for representatives who fail to support party positions on important issues may be expelled from the party and, therefore, virtually denied access to public office. Under this system, representatives have no individual base of power and must either reflect the views of those who elected them or leave office.

In the United States, by contrast, the focus is on the individual candidate, not the party, and this means that parties have virtually no control over those they help put in positions of authority. Individuals can defy their parties and maintain their power on the basis of their own resources. Since most Americans do not actively follow politics, they often have no idea of what their representatives are actually doing on their behalf, and when election time rolls around, personality often plays a far more important part than ability or political ideology.

It should thus come as no surprise that Americans are less and less likely to vote in elections and increasingly identify themselves as "independents" rather than as members of a political party. Between 1972 and 1984 the proportion of adults who identified themselves as independents rose from 26 to 36 percent, and in 1984 only 26 percent classified themselves as strong members of a major political party (Davis, 1984).

Political parties, then, are not very powerful in the United States. Given the fact that voters are, for the most part, disorganized and not very committed to actively following political affairs, where else can we look for concentrations of political power? One answer is the interest group.

**Interest Groups**   Whereas the avowed goal of political parties is to place their members in positions of authority, an **interest group** is an organization that attempts to affect political decisions by supporting candidates who are sympathetic to their interests and by influencing those who are already in positions of authority.

Parties generally have broad platforms that cover a wide range of issues, but interest groups usually focus on single issues such as abortion, gun control, product safety, the arms race, prayer in public schools, pollution of the environment, benefit levels for retired people, the Equal Rights Amendment, or legislation that affects a particular business, industry, or category of workers. As you can see, the list could go on and on, and this gives you some sense of how many different interest groups focus their attention on government officials.

Interest groups influence government officials primarily by providing them with expert information on complex issues and by contributing money to election campaigns. When legislators, for example, consider bills that would regulate, encourage, or discourage nuclear power plants, they must take into account a vast array of scientific information that describes, among other things, the risks of nuclear disasters. No legislators in the U.S. Congress in 1983 were scientists (most, in fact, were lawyers), and they therefore depended on outsiders to provide them with the accurate technical information needed to make informed decisions.

This is where interest groups often exert influence by employing **lobbyists**—representatives of interest groups who meet with government officials and provide expert information on issues, information that, of course, tends to support the interest group's goals. Lobbyists for pronuclear power groups, then, might provide studies that indicate that nuclear power is both safe and economical, while lobbyists for antinuclear interest groups might provide information that underscores the dangers and high cost of nuclear power. Since legislators usually lack independent sources of expertise on complex issues, their own positions on the issues often result from the relative persuasiveness of different lobbyists.

Because some interest groups are well organized and can hire full-time lobbyists, they can exert far more influence over government decisions than citizens who have neither the time nor the money to lobby in state or national capitols. This is particularly true of those large corporations whose financial resources are greater than those of any other organization with the exception of the state itself.

The importance of money in politics goes beyond the lobbying efforts of interest groups, for elected officials depend on contributions in order to finance their campaigns for reelection. As the late humorist, Will Rogers, put it in 1931, "Politics has got so expensive that it takes a lot of money even to get beat with," and this simple fact of political life gives interest groups powerful leverage with elected officials who want to stay in office. When politicians take positions on issues that affect interest groups, they cannot ignore the fact that they might offend those whose contributions could make the difference between defeat and reelection in the next election.

Some political writers, such as Drew (1983), argue that the connection between money and politics is unnecessary. The greatest campaign expense is television advertising, and in Great Britain television time is given to candidates free of charge, substantially reducing candidates' dependence on private contributions from interest groups who can take advantage of their influential position. Others urge public campaign financing through which candidates receive equal amounts of money from tax revenues and are forced to rely exclusively on these funds.

Efforts to limit the dependency of political officeholders on financial supporters have generally been unsuccessful in the United States. The Federal Election Campaign Act severely limited the amount that each individual could contribute to a campaign, but interest groups soon found a way

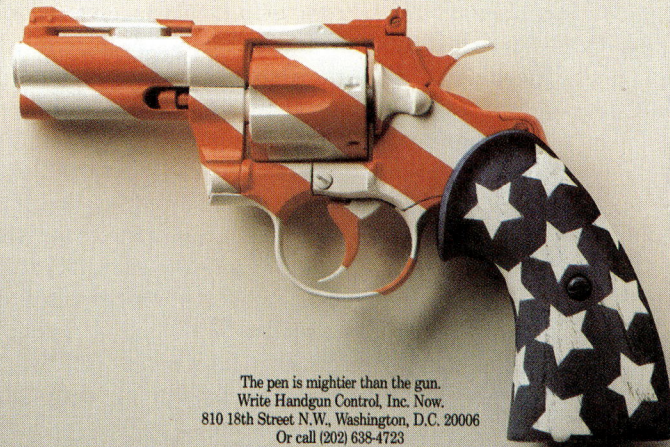

IN 1980, HANDGUNS KILLED 77 PEOPLE IN JAPAN. 8 IN GREAT BRITAIN. 24 IN SWITZERLAND. 8 IN CANADA. 23 IN ISRAEL. 18 IN SWEDEN. 4 IN AUSTRALIA. 11,522 IN THE UNITED STATES.

GOD BLESS AMERICA.

The pen is mightier than the gun.
Write Handgun Control, Inc. Now.
810 18th Street N.W., Washington, D.C. 20006
Or call (202) 638-4723

STOP HANDGUN CRIME BEFORE IT STOPS YOU.

around the law. There is no limit on the amount that groups and organizations can contribute, and interest groups—from corporations to social movements—have formed countless political action committees (called "PACs") through which vast amounts of money from individuals are funneled into political campaigns.

Organized interest groups are a major focus of political power in many countries, including our own; but groups often multiply their power by temporarily combining with other interest groups to form coalitions.

**Political Coalitions**  As we saw in Chapter 8, a **coalition** consists of two or more members—who can be anything from individuals to entire societies—who combine forces so that each will have more power than they would have by themselves. Interest groups often combine in this way in order to accomplish goals that temporarily overlap, and this can produce strange combinations. The American Civil Liberties Union, for example, generally fights against the activities of the Ku Klux Klan; but when the Klan tries to conduct demonstrations in public, the Civil Liberties Union has often defended the right of Klan members to assemble publicly and express their views. As Charles D. Warner (1870) put it almost a century ago, "politics makes strange bedfellows."

Coalitions abound in the political life of any complex society, in part because as the number of competing interest groups grows, the relative power of any group declines in relation to all the rest. In the ongoing debate over abortion, for example, organizations that favor free choice for women include the Planned Parenthood Federation, the American Civil Liberties Union, the National Organization for Women, and a variety of religious and feminist groups. While these groups form a coalition around the issue of abortion, however, they sometimes find themselves on the opposite sides of other issues. Some feminist groups, for example, oppose the free availability of hard-core pornography; the Civil Liberties Union, on the other hand, opposes this position on the grounds that it interferes with constitutionally guaranteed freedoms, including freedom of speech.

Coalitions are also a part of everyday life within governments themselves. In Congress, for example, senators and representatives regularly form temporary coalitions in order to muster enough votes to pass their favorite bills ("I'll vote for your bill if you'll vote for mine"). In some countries—such as Italy and Israel—there are so many political parties that it is rare for any one party to win a majority of the vote in elections; so they are forced to form a coalition government in which several parties share ruling power.

The stability of such governments depends on the ability of diverse groups to maintain a consensus, and if that consensus breaks down, the government falls and new elections are called. This is in sharp contrast to America's winner-take-all system in which one candidate controls the entire administration after being elected president.

While most political coalitions are temporary and focus on specific issues, some appear to be permanent. In the United States, one of the most powerful coalitions is what President Dwight D. Eisenhower (himself a former army general) called the **military-industrial complex**—a coalition consisting of the military and industrialists who make huge profits by manufacturing arms and selling them to the government. Both share the goal of developing expensive new armaments, but for different reasons. The military justifies its budget and its importance as an institution only by justifying the need for more and better weapons. Industry makes profits from the sale of weapons. Thus, both parts of the coalition use their enormous expertise and financial resources to lobby Congress to authorize increased spending for new military hardware.

As we have seen in the preceding sections, the cultural and structural characteristics of political arrangements define them as social institutions through which decisions about life in a society are made and enforced. Political power is also affected by ecological arrangements, for the definition of the state itself includes the physical territory within which governments exercise authority.

## Political Ecology

Geography and population are two of the most important factors that affect the ability of a government to exercise the power of the state in a given territory. The territory of the Soviet Union, for example, is more than twice as large as the United States, four times as large as Europe, and slightly larger than all of Latin America. Obviously, for a central government to control a vast territory is at best an enormously difficult task, and that helps explain why the state in societies such as the Soviet Union, China, and the United States depends so heavily on a huge bureaucracy, military, and police force. It also helps explain why the Soviet (and American) government is so inefficient, for it is very difficult for central planners in Moscow (or Washington) to monitor what is happening 4,000 miles away in Vladivostok (or 3,000 miles away in Los Angeles).

The government of China faces additional obstacles to controlling its population, for not only is China large (roughly the size of the United States) but it has a population of more than 1 billion people—four times larger than the U.S. population and amounting to almost a quarter of all the people in the world (Population Reference Bureau, 1984). It is one thing for the government to institute a policy—such as limiting families to one child each in order to lower population growth rates—and quite another to enforce it.

In any society, regardless of its size, the state cannot effectively control its citizens without their cooperation; but this is particularly true in societies with large populations, territories, or both. If just 20 percent of American tax payers openly refused to file federal income tax returns, the Internal Revenue Service would be faced with tracking down and prosecuting 18 *million* lawbreakers distributed over a land area of almost 4 million square miles.

## The Geography of Political Power

Geography is an important aspect of the distribution of political power. In the simplest sense, geographical boundaries define legal jurisdictions—the territories that are under the authority of the governments of towns, cities, counties, states, and nations. Geography, however, often plays a more complex part in political life.

Consider, for example, the problem of adding the Equal Rights Amendment to the U.S. Constitution. The amendment was passed by both houses of Congress and sent to state legislatures, 38 of which had to ratify the amendment in order for it to become part of the Constitution. In the spring of 1982, 91 percent of all American adults reported that they had heard of and understood the ERA, and of these, 75 percent favored its passage (Davis, 1982); yet when the deadline for passage—June 30—came, the amendment had fallen 3 states short of ratification.

There are many explanations for the ERA's defeat (see McGlen and O'Connor, 1983), but one aspect simply involves the social geography of political power in the United States. Regardless of the relative size of its population, each state has an equal vote in deciding the fate of proposed constitutional amendments. A significant portion of ERA opponents are religious fundamentalists, most of whom live in rural southern and western states with relatively small populations. The combined populations of the states whose legislatures did not ratify the ERA made up only 28 percent of the U.S. population, and yet because each of these sparsely settled states had an equal vote, they were able to block the amendment.

From an ecological point of view, the fate of the ERA depended in part on the fact that most of its supporters were heavily concentrated in a relatively small number of states, each of which could cast only one vote for the amendment (this arrangement was designed by the framers of the Constitution to ensure that large urban states could not completely dominate and exploit small, rural states).

In some cases, the geographical distribution of citizens is deliberately used by some segments of a population to increase their power, a practice that is known as **gerrymandering,** named after Elbridge Gerry, whose party first used the technique in Massachusetts in 1812. Gerrymandering is a way of defining election districts in ways that maximize the political power of a particular group or social category. To see how it works, look first at Figure 18-1, which represents the outlines of a city that is divided into four election districts, each of which sends a representative to the city council (the election districts are drawn with solid lines). In this city, 60 percent of the voters in *each* district belong to Party A and 40 percent belong to Party B. Thus, Party A stands to win all four seats on the council.

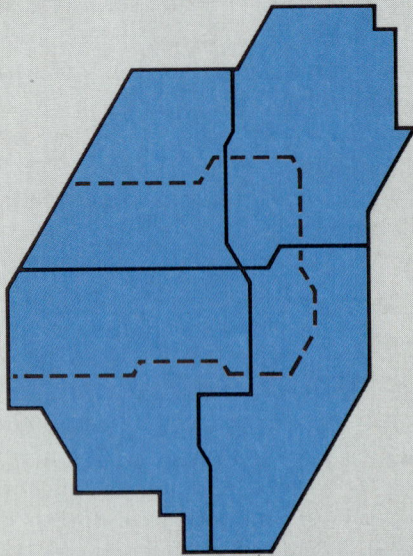

**Figure 18-1**  Election Districts in a Hypothetical Community*

*Solid lines indicate community and election
district boundaries. Dotted line marks area
in which most members of Party "A" live.
In each district, 40 percent of residents belong
to Party "B," and 60 percent belong to Party "A."

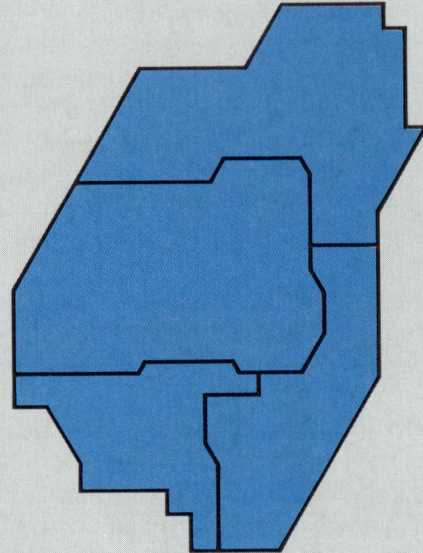

**Figure 18-2**  Election Districts in a Hypothetical
Community, Showing the Effects
of Gerrymandering
(Compare with Figure 18-1)

Notice, however, that Party A's supporters are concentrated in a series of neighborhoods that lie next to each other (the dotted line in Figure 18-1). To see why this is important, suppose that in an unusual year, Party B manages to win a majority on the council and decides to use its power to redraw the election district lines. Figure 18-2 shows one possible outcome, and if you compare it with Figure 18-1, you can see that the new lines concentrate almost all of Party A's supporters in a single district, leaving the remaining three districts dominated by Party B. By simply redrawing election district lines, Party B assures itself three out of four seats on the council and a long term in office.

In nineteenth-century Massachusetts, Governor Gerry used this technique to increase his party's control over state offices, and the resulting election district map created some strange-looking counties. Essex County, in fact, looked very much

like a salamander—hence the word gerrymander. Gerrymandering has been used in many representative democracies, including Belfast, Northern Ireland, where Irish Protestants used the technique to increase their power over Irish Catholics.

## The Uses of Political Power

Like all social institutions, political arrangements have cultural, structural, and ecological characteristics that affect not only how the institutions perform a variety of intended and unintended functions, but, in turn, how they affect social life in societies. For what goals are political institutions functional and dysfunctional, what part do they play in social conflict, and how are they related to social change? These are the kinds of questions that we address now.

### *Functions and Dysfunctions*

Like all social institutions, political arrangements are functional for some goals and dysfunctional for others. Representative democracies, for example, allow a great deal of public debate and criticism of government. Many officials—from presidents, governors, and mayors to congressional representatives and city council members—are elected by the people and can, therefore, be held accountable for their decisions at predictable intervals.

These characteristics of democracies are functional for restraining the power of government and encouraging authorities to weigh their decisions carefully. Public debate and criticism encourage the development of new ways to accomplish socially valued goals, as well as changes in the goals themselves. Compared with authoritarian states, governments in democratic states have much less authority to abuse the rights of citizens, to arrest, detain, and punish people without due cause, to invade privacy or use torture to extract information.

Widespread opportunities for participation in the political process strengthen the social legitimacy of the state and, therefore, help to perpetuate it. We may openly oppose a particular government, but the representative democracy as a state, since it is the source of our ability to protest in the first place, is less likely to be challenged.

These same characteristics of representative democracy are also dysfunctional for other goals, however. Public debate over important issues often requires a great deal of time, and as a result it often takes years for new policies to emerge and take effect. While the accountability of authorities to the public limits their power, it also tends to make officials wary of making decisions that will offend voters, especially voters who are represented by powerful interest groups. In 1984, for example, the federal budget deficit was projected to be in the neighborhood of 200 billion dollars, and although most officials agreed that programs such as Social Security would have to be cut in order to bring the budget under control, neither the president nor Congress was willing to "do what was necessary" and risk alienating elderly voters so close to an election.

The relative openness of democratic societies also encourages a considerable amount of conflict as different interest groups clash with one another both over the goals a government pursues and the means it uses to accomplish them. The turbulent decade of the 1960s is a perfect example of the great instability that can occur when the public takes full advantage of the rights to protest government policies publicly.

Finally, while it is said that most members of democratic societies can influence government decision making, we have seen in earlier chapters that social characteristics such as race, age, and social class profoundly influence the amount of power people actually have. In this sense, the democratic ideal can produce false consciousness that leads citizens to underestimate the concentration of political power.

As you might expect, political institutions in authoritarian states have quite different effects on their societies. Unlike democracies, for example, governments in authoritarian states can make decisions with relative speed and efficiency because they do not have to first consider public opinion. There was no public debate in the Soviet Union, for example, over the invasion of Afghanistan; the violent and nonviolent protests that took place in the United States over the Vietnam war and civil rights never would have been tolerated in the Soviet Union. Nor is there public debate in Russia over the Soviet position at international arms control negotiations. Governments in authoritarian states, then, enjoy much greater freedom to make decisions and act on them as they see fit, which can lead to greater efficiency.

The price that is commonly paid for this kind of efficiency, however, is rigidity, stagnation, and oppression (Stojanovic, 1981). Without criticism and public debate, governments can easily fall into a set of inflexible policies that discourage the introduction of new and better ideas. The Soviet state's control over the economy is a perfect example of inefficiency and backwardness that is so extreme that it is a favorite source of sarcastic humor among Russian citizens themselves.

The primary goal of governments in authoritarian states is to control as many aspects of social life as is possible, and this produces a number of dysfunctions. Beyond the obvious problem of abuses of state power through which people in countries such as Argentina, Chile, and the Soviet Union have simply "disappeared" or been arrested, tortured, and imprisoned without legal representation or due process of law (Stojanovic,

The primary dysfunction of authoritarianism is the oppression of the people by governments and their agents. This picture shows part of the funeral for a priest murdered by Polish secret police. The murderers were eventually brought to trial, but only in response to vigorous public protest.

1981), there are several less-obvious dysfunctions.

The most important, perhaps, is the fact that it is almost impossible for a central authority to manage a complex society efficiently. As we saw in the previous chapter, for example, economies in socialist societies tend to be highly inefficient—producing too much of one product and too little of another.

Another dysfunction is less apparent, but important. Authoritarian societies often appear to be very stable, as if the government is in complete control of the population and can do as it pleases. Authoritarian governments, however, stay in power by taking maximum advantage of the state's monopoly over the use of force, and this means that the stability of the state depends heavily on its coercive power. "The one means," wrote Adolph Hitler (1924, p. 53) "that wins the easiest victory over reason: terror and force."

Leaders in all societies face the problem of discovering just what the people are thinking, but the problem is even more acute in authoritarian states because they forbid open dissent. This necessitates enormous and complex institutions—such as secret police—whose sole function is to find out if people are thinking and doing anything that might threaten the government or the state (Hollander, 1982).

Authoritarian leaders sometimes try to increase their security by identifying themselves with the state—in other words, by removing the distinction between the state and a particular government. "I am the state," declared Napoleon Bonaparte to the French Senate in 1814. This statement, in effect, implied that since Napoleon was the state, the state as a social institution could not be used to limit his power or bring his legitimacy as a ruler into question.

The dangers inherent in Napoleon's assertion make clear why the separation of government from the state is an important principle in representative democracies. The principle—"no one is above the law, not even the president"—was the basis for Richard Nixon's forced resignation in 1974. His removal from office underscored the supremacy of the American state and its legal norms over any particular government.

## The State and Social Conflict

As the social institution responsible for maintaining social order and stability in society, the state inevitably plays a part in social conflict. The state, however, is rarely if ever a neutral "umpire," for by preserving the cultural ideas and social structures that make up a society, it also preserves social arrangements through which some enjoy higher levels of wealth, power, and prestige than others.

This is most apparent in authoritarian states. In socialist authoritarian societies, such as East Germany and the Soviet Union, the power of the state is used to maintain the wealth, power, and prestige of government and military leaders, and the basic conflict in such societies is between the government and the people. In capitalist authoritarian societies, the state also supports the interests of capitalists, whether or not they occupy formal positions in the government. In El Salvador, for example, leaders of labor unions are regularly harassed by the police and military, and many have been kidnapped and murdered by "death squads" who support the government.

State support for categories of people who dominate society is less visible in representative democracies, but it is important and widespread nonetheless. The United States, for example, is a capitalist democracy where government rarely uses the power of the state to hurt the interests of capitalism as an economic system. This means that most government programs support the interests of capitalists and capitalist organizations as a whole.

The French philosopher Jean-Jacques Rousseau (1762/1950) believed that the state came into being as an institution because the right to own private property caused such chaotic competition over ownership that an institution was needed to restore order. Rousseau also believed, however, that the state did more than restore and maintain order: It also became the defender of the wealthy—the largest and most influential class of property owners.

Marx expanded Rousseau's analysis and concluded that democracy is an illusion, that because the masses of people do not control *economic* institutions the belief that we can still control political institutions is false. It is of course true that we can elect anyone we want to public office, but Marx believed that the basic structure of the state supports the interests of capitalism and capitalists, not the vast majority of people who must sell their labor power in order to survive.

In the simplest sense, the state in capitalist democracies supports capitalism by refraining from doing anything that hurts the interests of capitalists as a class. Although many laws have been passed that defend the interests of working people—minimum wage laws, occupational health and safety laws, and laws protecting labor unions, for example—none of these threatens capitalism as an economic system. Nor have they significantly altered the unequal distribution of wealth, power, and prestige between social classes (see Chapter 11).

In a more complex sense, the state actively supports capitalism by creating and maintaining social conditions that enable capitalists to expand their operations and more efficiently profit from the labor power of workers. In the world economy,

for example, the State Department conducts relations with other countries in ways that foster a stable social order in the world, within which capitalists can invest money in other countries and be assured that their investments are safe. This often puts the United States in the position of supporting authoritarian states in other countries—such as South Korea, Chile, and the Philippines—because American corporations have huge investments in those countries.

Within the United States, many government policies and programs that are officially defined as for the benefit of workers also support capitalism (O'Connor, 1973), particularly those that increase the productivity of labor and help to train and educate new workers. Each year the federal government spends billions of dollars on research that benefits industry and to maintain railroads, highways, airports, and other utilities that directly benefit businesses. The military provides huge sources of income and profit to business, and policies of the Treasury Department and the Federal Reserve profoundly affect interest rates and the money supply—both of which are vital to the investment needs of capitalists.

Businesses depend on a steady supply of trained, educated workers. Public education, subsidized housing, federally guaranteed mortgages, school lunch programs, and publically funded daycare centers not only benefit families and children but also capitalists, by helping to prepare each new generation of workers at public expense. Without such programs, individuals would have to shoulder the expense and would, therefore, be far more likely to demand much higher wages from their employers.

A variety of other social programs benefit capitalists in ways that are not readily apparent. Welfare programs and unemployment insurance, for example, obviously benefit workers and families; but they also soften the negative effects of job shortages, and this makes it easier for employers to lay off workers when it is profitable to do so. Social Security lessens the need for workers to set aside money during their working years, and this lessens the pressure for higher wages.

Perhaps the most important way in which all states—whether authoritarian or democratic, capitalist or socialist—maintain economic arrangements and the resulting inequalities is by

Many government programs benefit capitalists as much as—if not more than—workers. Day-care centers, for example, make it possible for lower- and working-class parents to work—most often at the poorly paid jobs available to them. For capitalists, on the other hand, such programs increase the pool of workers willing to work for low wages rather than face not working at all.

legitimating them by identifying with them. We tend, for example, to think of America as both capitalist and democratic, and most of us have a hard time imagining an America that is not both. We tend to believe that democracy *implies* capitalism and that capitalism implies democracy; that socialism implies authoritarianism (and, erroneously, that authoritarianism implies socialism). Because economic institutions affect so many aspects of life in a society, and because the state's prime function is to maintain a particular way of life, when people

affirm their loyalty and affection for their country, they also tend to affirm their support for its economic system. Thus, when children learn the pledge of allegiance to the flag and develop a love for their country, they also are socialized to accept prevailing economic institutions as the "right" way to produce and distribute goods and services.

In this sense, political and economic institutions are so intertwined that we need to think in terms of **political economy**—the sets of social arrangements through which political and economic institutions support and maintain each other (see Froman, 1984). The state and the economy are not separate parts of a society that operate independently of each other (Domhoff, 1983). We may think of them as separate, but as is true of so many social arrangements described in earlier chapters, these two institutions are integral parts of the same whole. Whatever happens in one inevitably affects and is affected by what happens in the other.

The state cannot single-mindedly pursue the interests of one class or interest group, however, without alienating the vast majority of its citizens, thereby threatening to undermine the legitimacy of state authority. As O'Connor (1973) put it, this produces a serious tension:

> The state must try to maintain or create conditions in which profitable capital accumulation is possible. However, the state also must try to maintain or create conditions for social harmony. A capitalist state that openly uses its coercive forces to help one class accumulate capital at the expense of other classes loses its legitimacy and hence undermines the basis of its loyalty and support. But a state that ignores the necessity of assisting the process of capital accumulation risks drying up the source of its power, the economy's surplus production capacity and the taxes drawn from this surplus. (p. 6)

This source of social conflict and tension is even more apparent in authoritarian states such as the Soviet Union. On the one hand, civilian leaders must support the interests of powerful groups such as the military, who demand a huge share of national resources for weapons and other defense spending. On the other hand, however, high levels of defense spending leave a relatively small share for consumer goods—from meat and home appliances to decent housing and transportation. One of the most persistent social problems of Soviet society is the demoralization of its people, who are frustrated in their desire to improve their standard of living; and their frustration often supports a crisis of faith in society itself (Shipler, 1983; Silk, 1983).

In most societies, then, governments use the power of the state to maintain what is often a delicate balance between the demands of powerful interest groups, the needs of the population, and the pressures of maintaining the legitimacy of the state itself. When a government can no longer maintain that balance, political change may be unavoidable.

## Politics and Social Change: Rebellions, Coups, and Revolutions

Political change generally takes one of three basic forms. A **rebellion** challenges the policies of a particular government without trying to change the cultural or structural characteristics of the state. In 1786, for example, poverty was widespread in the American colonies in the aftermath of the Revolutionary War; and poor farmers, unable to pay their debts, were stripped of their possessions—their land, animals, and equipment—by the courts. Led by Daniel Shays, mobs of farmers prevented Massachusetts courts from meeting to prosecute indebted farmers; eventually there was an armed confrontation between Shays' followers and the Massachusetts militia (Morison, 1965). "Shays' Rebellion" was not an attempt to change the form of American political institutions. Its goal was to change the policies of government—in other words, to change the ways in which the government used the power of the state.

In 1982 Polish shipyard workers went on strike, not to call for an end to socialism in Poland,

Shays' Rebellion, 1787.

A coup d'état in progress in Chile.

but rather to demand better living and working conditions for workers (Ash, 1984).

Like rebellion, a **coup d'état** (pronounced "coo day ta"—whose meaning in French is "a blow concerning the state") does not try to change the character of the state; but unlike rebellion, a coup is an illegal attempt to replace one government with another, often with the use of force. In many countries—especially in Latin America and Africa—coups are so frequent that they have become the primary way in which leadership passes from one group to another. Because the military has a virtual monopoly on the instruments of force, it is often the source of coups. In the simplest case, military leaders decide that they can do a better job of governing a country than civilian leaders can. One morning the president wakes up to find that the presidential residence is surrounded by tanks and that key resources—television and radio stations, telephone exchanges, airports, and power plants—are under military control. In other cases, coups occur while the leader is out of the country.

November 6, 1917 (October 24 by Julian calendar). Revolutionaries led by Lenin storm the Russian Winter Palace in Petrograd (now Leningrad) and topple the provisional government.

Of all the forms of political change, **revolution** is by far the most serious, both in its goals and its methods. Unlike rebellions and coups d'état, revolutions seek to install a new government *and* to change the fundamental character of the state and society (Skocpol, 1979). Because revolutions seek to change the most fundamental cultural and structural characteristics of a society and its institutions, they almost always include considerable violence. In 1789 French revolutionaries toppled the autocracy of Louis XVI in what was to be the first stage of a prolonged period of violence and chaos as France searched for new political and economic institutions. In March 1917 the Russian Revolution forced Czar Nicholas II to give up his throne (he and his family were killed) and installed a new provisional government; but in October, a second revolution brought Lenin and his communist followers to power, and Russia became the Soviet Union. In the decades that followed—particularly under

the rule of Stalin—millions of Russians who were suspected of opposing the new state were imprisoned, exiled, or executed.

Revolutions have been common occurrences in the twentieth century. In 1949 the Communist forces of Mao Tse-tung defeated the armies of Chiang Kai-shek and established a socialist state in mainland China. In 1954 Vietnamese revolutionaries under the leadership of Ho Chi Minh defeated a French army and ended French colonial rule in Indochina. North Vietnam became an authoritarian socialist state and South Vietnam became an authoritarian capitalist state. In 1959 revolutionaries under the leadership of Fidel Castro overthrew Batista's authoritarian capitalist state and replaced it with an authoritarian socialist state. In 1973 the socialist government of Salvador Allende was overthrown by a military coup and replaced by an authoritarian capitalist state. In 1979 Marxist revolutionaries overthrew the government of Nicaragua,

PUZZLES:

## WHEN ARE REVOLUTIONS MOST LIKELY TO OCCUR?

Are revolutions more likely when injustice and miserable living conditions persist for long periods of time or when there are rapid improvements in social justice and standards of living?

As surprising as it may seem, revolutions are more likely when conditions are getting better than they are when they remain steadily poor. This apparent paradox is explained here and in Chapter 21.

and Islamic revolutionaries replaced the Shah of Iran with an authoritarian state based on Islamic religious law.

The American Revolution actually began as a rebellion in which colonists demanded the same rights as those enjoyed by British citizens living in Britain. It became a revolution when colonists declared their independence from Great Britain and precipitated a war that resulted in a new country with political institutions that differed sharply from those of the past. Although the new state borrowed heavily from British political institutions, the Constitution, the office of the president, and the two houses of Congress were all major departures from the British form of government.

Why do revolutions occur? Sociologists have identified several cultural and structural characteristics of political institutions and societies that are conducive to revolution (Goldstone, 1982). From a cultural perspective, revolutions are based on a profound shift in beliefs and values and a sharp drop in the acceptance of norms.

Belief in the legitimacy of the state tends to crumble before revolutions occur and this is often due to a chronic inability of the state to solve routine problems of government and meet the needs of the people, coupled with a rising expectation among the people that those needs should be met. The Russian Revolution, for example, occurred in a society in which a huge peasant class had, for centuries, lived in poverty under the oppressive rule of the czars and their nobles. In 1914 Germany declared war on Russia and in the three years that followed, millions of Russians died and shortages of food and other necessities became critical. Russia's continued participation in the war greatly aggravated long-standing social problems (Skocpol, 1979).

Revolution is also more likely to occur when people begin to share the beliefs that inequality and injustice are widespread and that more effective political institutions are possible. Perhaps most important is the shared belief that radical change cannot be achieved peacefully, that the state can be changed only through violence because the government will not respond positively to the needs and desires of the people.

Shifts in cultural beliefs are closely related to changing values, particularly those that affect what people expect for themselves. When expectations are rising—when people think that living conditions, freedoms, and other aspects of social life should improve—they are far more likely to question the legitimacy of a state that offers little hope of making those expectations a reality.

As values change, so too does allegiance to norms that define legitimate means for achieving goals. If the legal norms of the state support values that the people oppose, then the norms begin to lose their power over people's behavior.

Cultural shifts are closely tied to important aspects of social structure. The belief that peaceful change is impossible, for example, is often based on the refusal of government authorities to communicate with the people. In January 1905, 12 years before the 1917 Russian Revolution, a crowd of thousands of Russian workers peacefully marched to the czar's winter palace to protest poverty and hunger. They were met by troops who attacked the crowd, wounding and killing hundreds of unarmed people. The response to "Bloody Sunday" was a series of strikes and protests. Since even these did not bring about change, the eventual response was revolution.

As a population's allegiance to state-supported beliefs, values, and norms erodes, and as lines of communication are blocked (or shown to be nonexistent in the first place) the state loses its authority and the government increasingly relies on coercion in order to stay in power. This, of course, further

The Russian Revolution was caused in part by World War I, which inflicted enormous losses and suffering on the Russian army and eventually turned tens of thousands of soldiers against their officers and, eventually, the czarist state itself.

erodes the population's belief that the state and its government are legitimate, and only increases the chances for a violent revolution.

In the aftermath of revolution, the state is often authoritarian—sometimes more authoritarian than the state it replaced (Goldstone, 1982). This occurs primarily because the new government sets as its first goal the crushing of all opposition. There were even hints of this in the years following the American Revolution. As we saw earlier, for example, the Sedition Act made it a crime to publish any opinions that were harshly critical of the government or its leaders.

It should come as no surprise that true revolutions are as violent or rare as they are, for no social institution regularly serves the function of deliber-

ately turning itself into something else. What Miliband (1969) observed in capitalist societies is true in virtually all societies in which the state exists as a social institution:

> The politics of advanced capitalism have been about different conceptions of how to run the same economic and social system and not about radically different social systems. (p. 72)

In most societies, governments and leaders may come and go and the balance of power between interest groups may shift one way or another; but the cultural and structural form of the state remains largely intact. As with economic arrangements, real change in political institutions is a rarity.

## Summary

1. Political institutions are enduring sets of cultural ideas and social structures through which power is distributed and used in societies.

2. Authority is the most important form of political power; it may be based on legal-rational, charismatic, or traditional grounds, or on expertise in an important field. Coercion, on the other hand, is the use of power not considered legitimate by those who are subject to it.

3. The state is the institution that has a monopoly over the use of force. It is not the same as government, which is a collection of people who happen to occupy the positions of authority that make up the state.

4. As an institution, the state may support a variety of cultural values, such as those promoting equality or individual freedoms.

5. States differ in how power is distributed. In a democracy, power is shared equally by all citizens, whereas in a representative democracy, citizens elect people to exercise authority in their name. Democracy is fostered by a number of social factors, including economic development, cultural homogeneity, norms that restrict the power of the state, tolerance of dissent, and access to information about government activities.

6. Unlike democracy, an oligarchy is ruled by an elite, and an autocracy is ruled by one person. According to Michels' "Iron Rule of Oligarchy," oligarchy is inevitable because of citizen apathy, the complexity of societies, and the desire of leaders to keep their power.

7. States also vary in how authoritarian—or powerful—they are in relation to their citizens. Totalitarianism is an extreme in which the state tries to control virtually all aspects of life in a society.

8. The power structure in the U.S. is neither dominated by a unified power elite nor spread pluralistically among many different interest groups. Rather, it is an elite pluralism in which a relatively small number of interest groups struggle over control of the state.

9. Americans are less likely to vote and be involved in politics than citizens of most democracies. Generally those in the most advantaged social positions are the most likely to vote and be involved in politics.

10. Political parties are organizations whose main goal is to place members in positions of authority, and parties in the U.S. differ sharply from those in European democracies. American elections are based on a winner-take-all system that encourages candidates to take ambiguous positions on important issues and weakens the ability of parties to control their candidates once elected. Unlike parties, interest groups do not try to place members in positions of authority but rather try to influence elected officials, sometimes through representatives called lobbyists.

11. A political coalition is a set of interest groups who temporarily combine in order to increase their power. This often means that groups that oppose each other on one issue work together on another.

12. Geography often plays an important part in political life. The larger a society is, for example, the more difficult it is for the state to control its citizens. Since representatives in most democracies are chosen by geographical areas, the distribution of representatives may be altered to favor one group or another through gerrymandering.

13. Like all social institutions, a given political arrangement will have both functions and dysfunctions. Democracy, for example, is functional for protecting individual freedoms but is dysfunctional for reaching rapid decisions in times of crisis.

14. Its monopoly over the use of force inevitably means that the state will play a role in social conflict. While it sometimes acts as an umpire between conflicting groups, it more often promotes the interests of dominant groups. This is particularly true of those who dominate economic institutions. Through political economy, political and economic institutions support each other and promote the interests of those who dominate them.

15. Political institutions change through rebellion, in which policies are changed without affecting the state, through coups d'état, in which only the government is changed by forcibly replacing old lead-

ers with new, and through revolution, in which the state itself is changed. Revolution is most likely to occur in societies in which the state is no longer able to perform basic governmental tasks, citizens no longer view the state as a legitimate wielder of authority, and beliefs in the existence of injustice and inequality become widespread.

## Key Terms

## Recommended Readings

ELDER, C. D., and COBB, R. W. (1983). *The political use of symbols*. New York: Longman. A valuable introduction to the use of symbols in the political processes through which power is distributed, held, and used.

FROMAN, C. (1984). *The two American political systems: Society, economics, and politics*. Englewood Cliffs, NJ: Prentice-Hall. How does the U.S. political system *really* operate? The author provides one answer in a clear, straightforward look at political economy—the important relationship between political and economic institutions—in the United States.

MILLS, C. W. (1956). *The power elite*. New York: Oxford. A sociological classic in which Mills provides a provocative answer to the question, "Who rules America?"

ORUM, A. M. (1983). *Introduction to political sociology* (2nd ed.). Englewood Cliffs, NJ: Prentice-Hall. A comprehensive text on the many sociological aspects of politics, from socialization to the structures of power.

REJAI, M., and PHILLIPS, K. (1983). *World revolutionary leaders*. New Brunswick, NJ: Rutgers University Press. A short, highly readable book that uses hard data to explore the relationship between leaders and revolutions. Do revolutions create great leaders or do great leaders make revolutions?

SKOCPOL, T. (1979). *States and social revolutions*. New York: Cambridge University Press. An important study of the causes of revolution in China, Russia, and France.

TUFTE, E. R. (1978). *Political control of the economy*. Princeton, NJ: Princeton University Press. An important and highly interesting exploration of the connection between politics and economics.

# CHAPTER 19

# Religious Institutions

Have you ever taken the time to sit down and seriously ask yourself, "What will happen to me after I die?" I vividly remember the first time I thought about that question and the other questions it inevitably raised: What do I mean by "me"; what is there about me that might exist after my body does not; and what might that existence be like? In struggling over the meaning of death, I inevitably had to think about the meaning of life.

As I thought about it that first time, I imagined my life as a slender slice out of time that stretches infinitely in both directions—an infinity of time before my birth and an infinity of time after my death. Suddenly, I felt frightened, as if my life would be replaced by nothingness and meaninglessness. I would simply cease to exist and I had no idea of what that meant. The most frightening thing was to realize that I did not know what would happen.

People have wrestled with the idea of death and the meaning of life for thousands of years. Sociologically, the most important thing about these concepts is that they deal with the known, the unknown, and meaning. Although individuals and groups place great emphasis on the truth of their efforts to understand these concepts, our interest centers on the fact that people in all cultures wrestle with these fundamental themes.

At the core of culture are symbols and ideas that people use to attach meaning to objects, events, and experiences. Just as we can attach meaning to aspects of reality that we can see and touch and smell, so too can we attach meaning to that which we cannot perceive. An important latent consequence of the ability to give meaning to life is that it creates the possibility of meaninglessness. I doubt very much that my dog contemplates the meaning of life after death, just as he never contemplates the meaning of life before death. Meaning and meaninglessness, the known and the unknown are not problems for him; but they are for us.

As social animals, we tend to join together to solve such problems, and these collective solutions lie at the heart of religion and religious institutions. We begin our examination of these subjects by defining some basic concepts and then look at the variety of religious ideas and ways of structuring religious institutions. From there we explore the effects of population and ecology on religious

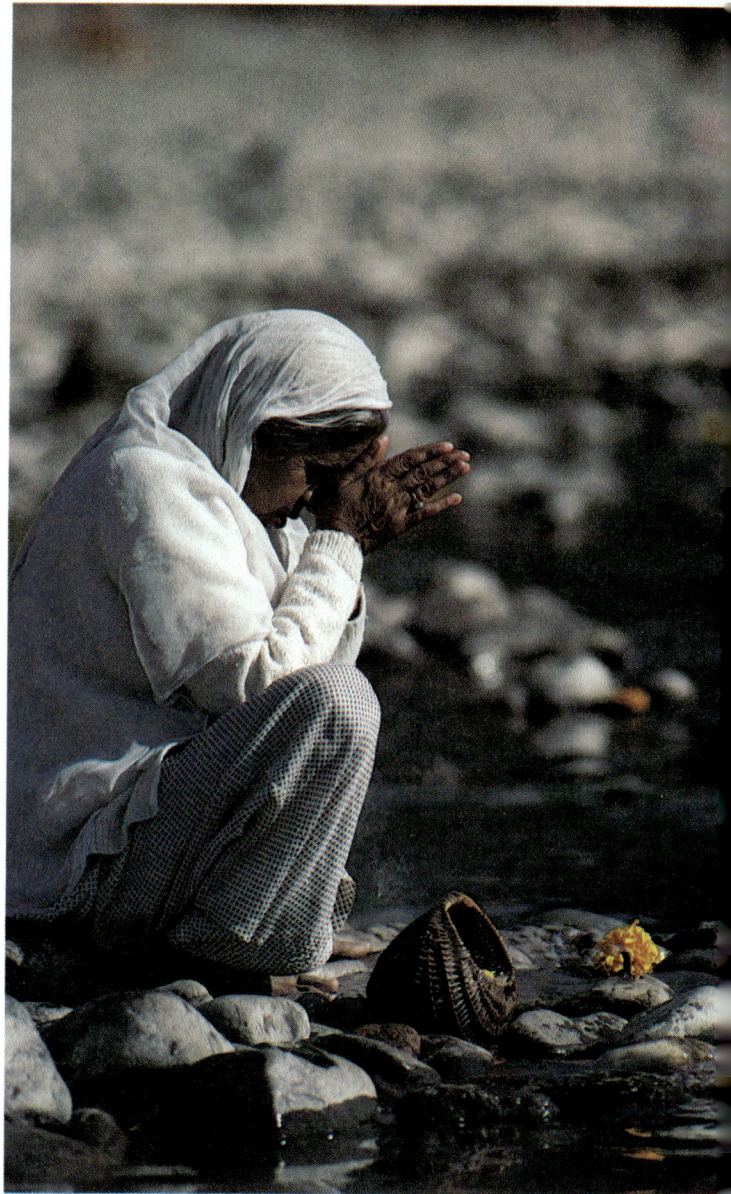

institutions, and we use the functional and conflict perspectives to better understand the relationship between religion, society, and social change.

## What Is Religion?

The substance of **religion** is a set of cultural symbols and ideas that focus on the meaning of human life and the nature of the unknown. The symbols are important because they describe visions of the ultimate nature of both the world and human experience in it, and they establish in people "powerful, pervasive, and long-lasting moods and motivations" that profoundly affect their feelings and behavior (Geertz, 1973, p. 90).

Just as words do not constitute a language unless they are shared by members of a speech community, ideas about human existence and the unknown constitute a religion only when they are shared among members of a community of believers. I may believe that there is a heaven and that no one who flies in an airplane or talks on a telephone can go there after they die; but, from a sociological perspective, my beliefs are not part of a religion unless a group of people shares them.

Of course, religion is not the only source of cultural ideas about the unknown. Scientists spend their lives trying to expand our understanding of the unknown. How, then, do science and religion differ? In the simplest sense, science looks upon the unknown as something that is ultimately knowable through observation, experiment, and verifiable fact.

Religion, however, is not a method for pursuing truth; it is the embodiment of what is already believed to be true. Christian beliefs about the origins of the universe, for example, are regarded as truths to be learned and shared in the community of believers; the only confirmation of such beliefs lies within the community itself: individuals must look to the faith of others in order to confirm their own. To cosmologists, on the other hand, beliefs about the universe are scientific hypotheses waiting to be tested.

There is a more important difference between religion and science, a difference that focuses both on the aspects of the unknown to which people pay attention and on how they pay attention to them. In his classic sociological study of religion, Durkheim (1912/1965) noted that all religions distinguish between the *sacred* and the *profane*. To consider an object, experience, or unknown force as **sacred** is to give it meaning and value that inspire feelings of awe and place it outside of the natural human world. To Christians, the cross, the idea of God, and the life of Jesus Christ are all sacred, just as the city of Jerusalem is sacred both to Jews and Muslims, and the cow is sacred to Hindus.

The concept of the **profane** refers to what we can experience directly as ordinary aspects of the natural world. As a profane experience, death involves the cessation of biological functioning (the stopping of the heart and of electrical activity in

The concept of the sacred can apply to virtually anything, from objects to places to species of life.

the brain) and of a dying person's physical and mental experience. The concept of the sacred focuses on the *meaning* of death, on its place in a cosmic order of things. In sacred terms, we are concerned not with what death consists of or how it happens, but why people die and what it means to die—and, therefore, what it means to live—in an ultimate sense.

Thus, science and religion pay attention to fundamentally different aspects of the unknown. What causes a dying person to suffer is something that scientists can determine; but why suffering seems to be an inherent part of human experience is a question that scientists consider to be unanswerable in scientific terms and therefore irrelevant to scientific inquiry. In most religions, however, the meaning and reason for earthly suffering are major concerns.

The sacred and the profane are not two separate and disconnected cultural realms; on the con-

trary, the sacred is used to give a sense of ultimate understanding and meaning to the profane, and by doing so it profoundly affects it (Geertz, 1973). In a religion that includes the belief that death is always a matter of divine will that is not to be interfered with, believers will refuse medical intervention and will be much more likely to die. Thus, by providing an account of what the world is like in an ultimate sense, religion can powerfully affect what the world in fact becomes.

In some cases, science and religion try to solve similar problems, but in doing so they draw on very different perspectives. In the ongoing debate over the origins of human life, for example, some religions frame explanations in sacred terms, as Christianity does with the belief that a male God created man in "His" own image and then created woman from Adam's rib. As far as we know, the existence of God cannot be proved or disproved with objective evidence and, hence, the Christian explanation of the origin of human life holds little interest for scientists. By definition, science cannot draw upon supernatural explanations, for the province of science is the natural world.

Religion, then, is defined by its concentration on the sacred and supernatural. The sociology of religion is principally concerned with the place of religions and religious institutions in societies.

## Religion and Society

The distinction between the sacred and the profane lies at the heart of religion, but religious institutions are sociologically significant primarily because of their social functions and dysfunctions. From a cultural point of view, religion attaches meaning and value to human life and supports major cultural ideas. All religions offer believers some form of salvation—whether it be the heaven of Christianity, the earthly peace offered by Buddhism and Taoism, Hindu reincarnation into a higher social caste, or the simple curing of an illness (Wilson, 1982).

Most important, religion helps believers explain and accept the suffering that plagues human life, by offering a coherent world view in which suffering makes sense and is, therefore, sufferable.

> The dumb senselessness of intense or inexorable pain, and the enigmatic unaccountability of gross iniquity all raise the uncomfortable suspicion that perhaps the world, and hence man's life in the world, has no genuine order at all—no empirical regularity, no emotional form, no moral coherence. And the religious response to this suspicion is in each case the same: the formulation, by means of symbols, of an image of such a genuine order of the world which will account for, and even celebrate, the perceived ambiguities, puzzles, and paradoxes in human experience. The effort is not to deny the undeniable—that there are unexplained events, that life hurts, or that rain falls upon the just—but to deny that there are inexplicable events, that life is unendurable, and that justice is a mirage. (Geertz, 1973, p. 108)

Religion thus locates a community of believers in relation to spiritual and supernatural forces as well as the whole profane world (the meaning of life, the nature of the universe) and this is an important ingredient in our collective definitions of who we are in the ultimate scheme of things—both as individuals and as groups (Mol, 1976). In most religions, people are not lost bodies floating aimlessly through time and space. Life has meaning and an ultimate purpose, and people are part of something larger than themselves and their societies. Religion, then, can serve to reduce anxiety and uncertainty in its believers by connecting the profane world with the mysteries of life, which are given sacred meaning and value. In the same way, of course, religion can serve to increase anxiety—by, for example, leading people to believe that they will suffer endless torture in another world after they die.

Religion can also perform important structural functions, for it is a major source of social cohesion. The roots of the word "religion" lie in the Latin words "re" and "lig" which together mean to tie or bind again. A community of believers shares basic ideas about both the known and the unknown. They can therefore give one another comfort and support when suffering and misfortune strike their members or share in joy or ecstasy when something happens that suggests that their profane lives are in harmony with the sacred order of things. When people come together for a funeral or other religious ceremony, they reinforce their bonds with one another through their religious institutions. When two people marry, religious ceremonies bind them to their cultural community as well as to each other, for it is their society and its religious institutions that legitimate and assign meaning, value, and normative expectations to their relationship.

The bonds created by a shared faith lie at the heart of religion as a social institution.

Religious institutions also legitimate other social institutions. In medieval Europe, the Church supported the "divine right of kings" to rule: the coronations of kings and queens were, more than anything else, religious ceremonies in which rulers of the profane world identified with the sacred and therefore drew power from those who represented sacred powers (Kendall, 1962). In return, religious institutions often received large amounts of property and other wealth from kings and emperors (Lenski, 1966).

Most modern states no longer depend on the blessing of religious institutions and their leaders to justify their power; but they often identify with religious symbols in order to reinforce their authority (Warner, 1961). American coins bear the words "In God We Trust"; political leaders often refer to God as being "on our side"; the Pledge of Allegiance to the Flag includes the words "one nation, under God"; the song "America the Beautiful" includes the words "God shed his grace on thee"; both houses of Congress begin their sessions with prayer.

Hunter-gatherer and horticultural societies had no state (see Chapter 18); and in his studies of such societies Durkheim (1912/1965) first formulated his theory of the relationship between religion and society. In the aboriginal tribes of Australia, each clan worshiped a **totem**—an animal or plant considered sacred in that society. Each totem represented not a god, but the clan itself, and from this simple observation, Durkheim argued that religion is in fact a way in which people worship their own societies. A totem gives supernatural significance and power to the social bonds that hold people together and through which they survive both as individuals and as societies.

Durkheim was one of the first in a long line of sociologists who accepted the belief that religion and religious institutions are part of culture and are, therefore, of human and not divine origin. Is it therefore necessary to accept this belief in order to study religion from a sociological point of view?

## Can a Sociologist Believe in God?

The first sociologists who studied religion—Comte, Marx, Durkheim, and Weber—were part of a social revolution in which science challenged religion as the dominant cultural framework that people used to interpret and explain the physical world and human experience. These early sociologists were in the thick of an intense conflict between the supporters of religion and of science as points of view. In that social environment, they

**Voices:**
**The Defense Budget and the Bible**

WASHINGTON—President Reagan asserted twice Monday that U.S. arms spending is sanctioned by scripture and said defense budget cuts would weaken the nation in the face of the "unprecedented military buildup of the Soviet Union."

"You might be interested to know that the scriptures are on our side in this," Reagan told a group of business and trade representatives in the White House. "Luke 14:31, in which Jesus in talking to the disciples spoke about a king who might be contemplating going to war against another king with his 10,000 men, but he sits down and counsels how good he's going to do against the other fellow's 20,000 and then says he may have to send a delegation to talk peace terms."

"Well, I don't think we ever want to be in a position of only being half as strong and having to send a delegation to negotiate under those circumstances—peace terms—with the Soviet Union," Reagan continued.

Later in the day he cited the biblical passage again in a speech to the National Religious Broadcasters Conference meeting at the Sheraton Washington hotel.

"I don't think the Lord that blessed this country as no other country has ever been blessed intends for us to someday negotiate because of our weakness," the president said.

Source: *Washington Post*, February 5, 1985.

found themselves trying to explain the existence of religion—why, for example, people hold beliefs even though they may appear to be untrue—and to explain religion *away* (Wilson, 1982).

Modern sociology is not antireligious, but the definition of religion as a humanly created part of culture is generally accepted in the sociological study of religion. This, of course, raises a disturbing question for those who both use sociology as a perspective and who belong to a community of religious believers: Can sociologists be religious? Can a Christian, Muslim, or Jewish sociologist both study religion as a set of cultural ideas and believe in the existence of a Supreme Being?

The answer to all these questions is yes, and the reason is quite straightforward: It is not the goal of sociologists to test the truth or falsity of religious beliefs. "Does God exist?" is not a sociological question; but "Do people believe that God exists?" is. Sociologists want to understand how religious ideas and practices affect the lives of those who belong to a community of believers and influence the societies in which those people live. They want to understand how religious institutions are organized and how they affect other institutions. They want to understand the manifest and latent functions and dysfunctions of religion and the part religion plays in social conflict and social change.

None of these sociological problems requires that we assume that particular religious beliefs are either true or false. Wherever specific religions may have come from, they affect social life in a variety of ways in different societies, and it is the job of sociology to understand those effects. To do so, we must look at religion from the three points of view that define the sociological perspective: culture, social structure, and ecology.

## Culture:
## Linking the Known and the Unknown

The core of any religion is a set of cultural ideas and practices that constitute a framework for interpreting both the known and unknown in relation to the sacred world of the supernatural. While all four components of culture are important parts of religion, beliefs are what distinguish different religions most clearly from one another.

### Religious Belief:
### Some Major Types of Religions

Religious belief systems focus on describing the ultimate nature of reality and the place of human beings in it. Most religions can be categorized as one of only a few major types, each of which corresponds to a different view of the sacred, the profane, and the relationship between the two.

Mass at St. Peter's in Rome

Siva—the Hindu god representing destruction—is part of a triad of gods (Trimurti) that includes Brahma the Creator and Vishnu the Preserver and Renewer.

**Theistic Religion** A theistic religion includes the belief in one or more supreme beings. Christianity, Judaism, and Islam, for example, are **monotheistic** religions because each recognizes the existence of only one Supreme Being. To Christians it is God; to Jews it is Yahweh; and to Muslims it is Allah; but what all have in common is a single Supreme Being who allows allegiance only to himself (note that all also envision the Supreme Being as male).

Hinduism is a **polytheistic** religion; it allows for the existence of five gods. The concept of god is not central in the Hindu religion, for the power of the supernatural is vested in a spiritual concept of "Oneness" through which people are born into social castes (see Chapter 12) and are **reincarnated** in succeeding lives as members of higher or lower castes, depending on how well they satisfy the duties associated with their current caste. The

Hindus of India, Pakistan, and Bangladesh do not believe in a single supreme being that decides their fate but in a vision of life as a succession of lives in which the ultimate goal is a state of unity with supernatural forces.

**Animistic and Totemic Religion** Many religions ignore the idea of a Supreme Being. Some African and American Indian tribes, for example, practice **animistic** religions in which spirits and ghosts are believed to inhabit sacred objects such as trees, rocks, or animals. To the Mbuti of Africa, the forest is the sacred giver of life and death (Turnbull, 1965). The Shinto religion of Japan vests supernatural power—Kami—both in objects such as stones and trees and in ancestors (and, for this reason, Shintoism is also a religion involving **ancestor worship**). As we saw earlier, **totemic** religions believe that certain objects—or **totems**—have supernatu-

Animistic funeral dancers on Mali in western Africa.

Australian aborigines with a religious totem.

ral powers. The totemic approach to unknown forces is similar to the way people think of "good luck charms" (such as rabbits' feet).

**Abstract Ideals** A large portion of the world's population—living mostly in India and East Asia—have religions that focus more on sets of abstract ideals than on supernatural powers vested in gods, objects, or animals. The largest of these religions are Buddhism, Confucianism, and Taoism, and they are concerned with how believers can achieve a better life on earth by living according to a set of ethical principles. Buddha, for example, was a sixth-century B.C. Indian Hindu who believed that people can escape suffering by freeing themselves of all desire, an ideal state that he called Nirvana.

Confucius was a Chinese contemporary of Buddha who believed that salvation depended on behaving according to correct manners and respecting those of higher social rank. Taoism is still more abstract and focuses on harmonious living and personal ethics that conform to concepts of a

universe that is held together by ethical principles. Thus, in both Confucianism and Taoism, supernatural power lies in the universe itself and the harmonious relationships among all the things and creatures in it. The task of believers in these **ethical religions** is to behave in ways that enable them to fit into the scheme of things in a harmonious way.

**Ritual** Religions use a variety of practices—called **rituals**—for maintaining relationships between believers and the supernatural and between believers and one another. Ritual may be as simple as uttering a sacred word or as complex as an elaborate ceremony in which people manipulate sacred objects and perform specialized roles. Religions that include a belief in one or more gods use ritual to reaffirm believers' loyalty to supernatural powers and to satisfy their gods' demands. The ancient Aztecs of Mexico performed gory rituals in which a priest cut the heart from a living person, in the belief that this would appease their gods (Diaz,

1974). Christians, Jews, and Muslims use prayer to maintain their connection with the supernatural. Christianity is one of the few religions that emphasizes the concept of sin and uses ritual to reestablish a state of "grace" that will enable sinners to enter heaven when they die (Wilson, 1982).

The Trobriand Islanders use magic in their efforts to control the powers of the unknown (Malinowski, 1948), and the followers of the Shinto religion worship both nature and their ancestors in order to maintain a relationship with the supernatural power of the Kami. Buddhists, Taoists, and Confucians mediate in order to establish an inner sense of harmony between themselves and the ethical principles they believe tie all the parts of the universe into a single, integrated whole.

These are only major differences between the belief systems of the major religions of the world, to which must be added thousands of specific beliefs about the nature of the universe and the place of humans in it. Most religions, for example, pay little or no attention to life after death.

It is very important to point out that there is enormous variation in religious belief not only between religions, but within them as well. Some Orthodox Jews, for example, differ sharply from other Jews in their strict adherence to the belief that the Jews may not have their own homeland until Yahweh sends a Messiah. This means that these Jews oppose the existence of the state of Israel.

There is also enormous variation in belief among Christians, even on such central beliefs as the existence of God, Jesus as the Son of God, and life after death, and on such central values as the importance of religious belief. Sharp differences exist not only between denominations in the United States (Table 19-1) but also between societies that are predominantly Christian (Table 19-2). In societies whose people are predominantly

**Table 19-1**

Percentage of American Christians Reporting Various Religious Beliefs, 1960s

|  | CONGREGATIONAL | METHODIST | EPISCOPALIAN | PRESBYTERIAN | CATHOLIC |
|---|---|---|---|---|---|
| I know God exists and I have no doubts about it. | 41 | 60 | 63 | 75 | 81 |
| Jesus is the Divine son of God and I have no doubts about it. | 40 | 54 | 59 | 72 | 86 |
| It is completely true that Jesus was born of a virgin. | 21 | 34 | 39 | 57 | 81 |
| Miracles actually happened just as the Bible says they did. | 28 | 37 | 41 | 58 | 74 |
| It is completely true that there is life beyond death. | 36 | 49 | 53 | 69 | 75 |
| It is completely true that the Devil actually exists. | 6 | 13 | 17 | 31 | 66 |

Source: Glock and Stark, 1968.

**Table 19-2**

Percentage of People Reporting Belief in God or
Universal Spirit and in Life after Death
(Selected Countries, 1976)

| COUNTRY | PERCENTAGE WHO REPORT BELIEF IN "GOD" OR A "UNIVERSAL SPIRIT" | PERCENTAGE WHO REPORT BELIEF IN LIFE AFTER DEATH | PERCENTAGE WHO VALUE RELIGIOUS BELIEFS AS "VERY IMPORTANT" |
|---|---|---|---|
| United States | 94 | 69 | 56 |
| Canada | 89 | 54 | 36 |
| Italy | 88 | 46 | 36 |
| Australia | 80 | 48 | 25 |
| Belgium | 78 | 48 | 26 |
| United Kingdom | 76 | 43 | 23 |
| France | 72 | 39 | 22 |
| West Germany | 72 | 33 | 17 |
| Sweden, Norway, Denmark, and Finland | 65 | 35 | 17 |

Source: Gallup Report, September 9, 1976.

white, for example, Christians believe that Jesus was white; but many African Christians believe he was black.

### Religious Values, Norms, and Attitudes

One of the most important goals in any religion is salvation, although each religion defines salvation in its own way (Wilson, 1982). To the Melanesian tribes of Southern Indonesia, salvation is safety on the sea when they go fishing. In Christianity, one aspect of salvation is people going to heaven rather than hell when they die. In Judaism, salvation is the coming of the Messiah, signaling that Jews once again enjoy the favor of Yahweh.

In Hinduism, salvation is reincarnation into a higher social caste in the next life, which, after an appropriate number of lives results in a complete identification with the Divine. In Buddhism, salvation represents the achievement of a mystical state of "Oneness" with the Divine. In Taoism and Confucianism, salvation is oriented to the present life. In Taoism, it takes the form of withdrawing from all

earthly pleasures and ending all desire and, therefore, all feelings of deprivation and suffering; in Confucianism, it represents harmonious living by the principles of a unified universe. In animistic and totemic religion, salvation often takes the form of deliverance from the misfortunes of everyday life such as disease and accidents.

Religious norms define socially approved means for achieving salvation. Orthodox Judaism requires obedience both to the Ten Commandments and to the complex set of laws contained in the Talmud, which includes dietary laws forbidding the eating of pork. Among Hindus, reincarnation into a higher social caste depends on performing the duties associated with their current caste, including obedience to sacred laws such as those forbidding the killing of cows.

In Buddhism, meditation is the chief means for achieving the end of desire, which is believed to lead to the salvation of a nonexistence free from earthly suffering. As in animistic religions, the Shinto of Japan appease the spirits in objects and ancestors by worshipping them and by taking special care not to harm them. Followers of totemic religions appease the forces of the supernatural by carrying totems.

Ethical religions such as Taoism and Confucianism stress respect for others and goodness and love in human relationships as the means for achieving the goal of harmony with the universe. Confucianism in particular stresses respect for the family and for those in higher social classes. Thus, Confucianism demands support for the existing social system as the means for achieving its most important religious value.

To sociologists, the most important religious attitudes focus on relationships among people, not between believers and the sacred and supernatural. Among Hindus, for example, religious beliefs and values underlie a caste system that includes attitudes of respect for those in higher castes and attitudes of contempt for the "untouchables" in the lowest caste. Confucianism stresses attitudes of respect and subservience toward family elders and those in higher social classes. Christianity and Ju-

daism both tend to regard females as inferior to males, and Catholicism in particular—in spite of its adoration for the Virgin Mary—carries a deep tradition of negative attitudes toward women, beginning with the belief that Eve was responsible for Adam's fall from grace in the Garden of Eden (Daly, 1973).

Together, beliefs, values, attitudes, and norms form the cultural core of religion, but a full sociological understanding of the importance of religion in society must also pay attention to how religious ideas are expressed through socially structured relationships.

## Social Structure: The Social Organization of Religion

As social institutions, religions are more than collections of cultural ideas about the sacred and the unknown, for they also include social relationships

**Table 19-3**

Membership in Major Religions of the World, by Region, Early 1980s

| RELIGION | NORTH AMERICA | SOUTH AMERICA | EUROPE | ASIA | AFRICA | OCEANIA | TOTAL |
|---|---|---|---|---|---|---|---|
| Total Christian | 252,459,000 | 196,600,000 | 337,678,000 | 104,099,000 | 147,076,000 | 18,782,000 | 1,056,094,000 |
| Roman Catholic | 138,876,000 | 185,251,000 | 178,033,000 | 57,265,000 | 56,999,000 | 5,215,000 | 621,639,000 |
| Eastern Orthodox | 5,649,000 | 335,000 | 47,069,000 | 2,763,000 | 9,402,000 | 408,000 | 65,626,000 |
| Protestant | 107,935,000 | 10,993,000 | 112,577,000 | 44,071,000 | 80,765,000 | 13,158,000 | 369,499,000 |
| Muslim | 1,581,000 | 406,000 | 20,190,000 | 380,069,000 | 152,944,000 | 87,000 | 555,277,000 |
| Hindu | 309,000 | 637,000 | 443,000 | 459,708,000 | 1,166,000 | 326,000 | 462,589,000 |
| Buddhist | 336,000 | 241,000 | 238,000 | 250,097,000 | 15,000 | 24,000 | 250,951,000 |
| Confucian | 100,000 | 59,000 | 450,000 | 162,500,000 | 3,000 | 18,000 | 163,130,000 |
| Shinto | 50,000 | — | — | 33,000,000 | — | — | 33,050,000 |
| Taoist | 33,000 | 13,000 | 13,000 | 20,500,000 | 1,000 | 3,000 | 20,562,000 |
| Jewish | 7,611,000 | 750,000 | 4,644,000 | 4,009,000 | 232,000 | 74,000 | 17,320,000 |
| Zoroastrian | 3,000 | 3,000 | 14,000 | 224,000 | 1,000 | 1,000 | 245,000 |

Source: *The 1984 Encyclopedia Britannica Book of the Year.*

both within a community of believers and between it and the surrounding society. These relationships affect both how religious ideas are expressed and in many cases how social life in general is carried out in a society.

Religious institutions have boundaries that define both active and potential membership, role structures that divide labor and power, and patterns of interaction through which religious ideas are expressed and perpetuated. In relatively simple societies, religious institutions are not separate from other institutions such as the family and economic and political arrangements; but in complex industrial societies, religious institutions stand apart, and sociologists try to understand the complex ways in which they are related to other social institutions.

These structural differences between religious institutions can be described in terms of several major types: the *ecclesia*, the *church*, the *denomination*, the *sect*, and the *cult*.

## The Ecclesia

The ecclesia is the most powerful of all religious institutions. Islam in Iran and Catholicism in Italy are both examples of an **ecclesia,** in which all or most of the people in the society belong to the community of believers from the moment they are born. Thus, religious affiliation is an ascribed status that is occupied by almost all members of the society regardless of social class.

The role structure of an ecclesia is formal and bureaucratic. It has a highly trained corps of religious leaders and workers, and one leader usually dominates the entire structure. Authority is primarily traditional and legal-rational, although in some cases charismatic leaders, such as Iran's Ayatollah, emerge. In no ecclesia, however, is charismatic authority (authority based on the personal attributes of the leader) the main source of power.

The time structure of an ecclesia is indefinite—Islam's followers, for example, expect it to last forever—and religious practices consist primarily of rigid rituals that include relatively little expression of emotion.

Perhaps the most important structural characteristic of the ecclesia is its relationship with other social institutions. Unlike all other religious institutions, the ecclesia is closely identified and allied with political, economic, and family institutions. In

In Iran, the Ayatollah Khomeini dominates both the state and the Iranian ecclesia of Islam.

ancient Egypt, for example, the Pharaohs were, themselves, regarded as gods and thus the rulers of both the profane and sacred worlds (Woolley, 1963).

The ecclesia is less common today than it once was, but it still exists. In Iran, for example, the Islamic ecclesia is virtually amalgamated with the government. Criminals are tried in religious courts under religious law, and no major governmental decision can be made without the approval of the country's highest religious leader, the Ayatollah Khomeini.

In Italy, the position of the Catholic ecclesia is not so powerful, but the pattern is fairly similar in form nonetheless. The Pope is a powerful figure in Italian life and politics, and while the government often makes decisions that the Pope condemns—such as allowing divorce or abortion—the government cannot afford to ignore completely the views of the Catholic ecclesia.

## The Church

A **church**—such as the Church of England, the Catholic Church outside of Italy, the Methodist, Episcopalian, and Lutheran churches in the United States, and the Greek Orthodox Church—is similar to an ecclesia in several ways. Membership is usually ascribed at birth and includes people from all social classes. There is a formal bureaucracy that includes a highly trained priesthood, authority is based more on tradition and legal-rational rules than on charisma, the institution is expected to last indefinitely, and religious practice is highly ritualized and involves relatively little display of emotion (Troeltsch, 1912).

Two important structural characteristics distinguish churches from ecclesia, however. Membership does not include all members of a society, and the relationship between churches and other social institutions is far looser. Churches such as the Church of England, for example, generally ally themselves with the ruling class and support the status quo; but they do not have the enormous power of an ecclesia to influence political and economic institutions.

In many authoritarian societies, churches oppose the power of the state, in some cases because the state at best only tolerates religious belief and practice. In Poland, for example, the Catholic Church has often been a source of opposition to government policy, although its leaders must be careful not to go too far in their criticisms. In some Latin American countries, such as Chile, El Salvador, and Nicaragua, that are ruled by single political parties, the Catholic Church is virtually the only institution through which political opposition to the government can be expressed.

## The Denomination

**Denominations**—such as Congregational and Unitarian Christians—are the smallest religious institutions that still have a formal role structure with trained religious leaders. Like churches and ecclesiae, denominations generally draw new members from families that already belong to the community of believers, and religious rituals usually involve little expression of emotion.

Unlike churches and ecclesiae, denominations generally draw members from a limited range of social class backgrounds. Congregationalists and Unitarians, for example, are most likely to come from the upper-middle and upper classes, while almost 70 percent of all Baptists are in the working and lower classes (Chalfant, Beckley, and Palmer, 1981).

Denominations also lack the bureaucratic structure and sharp divisions of power that are hallmarks of ecclesiae and churches. The power structure of denominations is much looser and based almost entirely on traditional authority. The relationship between denominations and other social institutions is also far more remote. Rather than allying themselves with governments, for example, denominations are more likely to coexist with them and refrain from actively supporting or opposing political or economic arrangements.

The United States is one of the world's few religiously pluralist societies, in which no single church dominates. As described later in this chapter, this results in a relatively high degree of religious tolerance and freedom, but also tends to lessen the influence of religion on nonreligious ideas and behavior.

## The Sect

**Sects** such as the Seventh-Day Adventists and Jehovah's Witnesses are religious groups that have broken off from churches and denominations, and their structures are radically different (Troeltsch, 1912; Wilson, 1982). Membership is usually through conversion rather than ascribed at birth, and new members are converted through persuasion. The role structure of sects is informal and leaders have little if any formal training. There are minimal divisions of power and leaders are usually chosen by the community. Religious ceremonies encourage spontaneous shows of emotion and have little of the rigid, abstract form found in the ecclesia, church, or denomination.

Sects also differ from other religious institutions in their active opposition to other institutions. Seventh-Day Adventists and Jehovah's Witnesses, for example, oppose standard medical care and public education, and there are occasional legal battles in which parents refuse to permit medical treatment for their children (Findley and Redstone, 1982; Anderson, 1983).

Members of the lower classes are more likely than others to belong to religious sects, perhaps because they have less to gain by supporting existing political and economic institutions that place them at the bottom of the social stratification system. Engels (in Feuer, 1959) draws striking parallels between revolutionary movements and the early history of Christianity as a religious sect:

> Christianity was originally a movement of oppressed people; it first appeared as the religion of slaves and emancipated slaves, or poor people deprived of their rights, of peoples subjugated or dispersed by Rome. (p. 168)

In the 1970s roughly 55 percent of sect members in the United States belonged to the working and lower classes, compared with just over 40 percent of Presbyterians and Jews and just over 30 percent of Episcopalians. Only around 14 percent of those who belong to sects are from the upper class, compared with 30 percent of Presbyterians and Jews and 40 percent of Episcopalians (Chalfant, Beckley, and Palmer, 1981).

The deviant status of many sects often causes tense and hostile relationships both with the parent church and the surrounding society. In the fifth century B.C., the first Buddhists were defined and persecuted as a heretical sect of Hinduism. Early Christians were a sect of Jews who believed that Jesus was the Son of God, and they were persecuted by the Romans. In the seventeenth century, English Quakers were persecuted by Christians, as were Mormons in the eighteenth century; in this century, members of the Baha'i sect are persecuted in countries such as Iran; and in India, members of the Sikh sect of Hinduism have frequent violent confrontations with other Hindus.

## The Cult

**Cults** are the least organized of all religious institutions. The vast majority of their members join through conversion—usually in response to a personal emotional crisis—and their members are largely from the poorest social classes. Religious ceremonies tend to be highly emotional and spontaneous. The role structure of cults is informal, but power is concentrated in a single charismatic leader.

Members of the Sikh sect of Hinduism in India.

Cults depend heavily on highly emotional spontaneity in their religious ceremonies and on charismatic leadership. As the tragedy in Jonestown shows, the strong emotional ties and charismatic leadership found in cults create social conditions in which power is easily abused.

The cult is the only religious institution in which charisma is the main form of authority. For this reason, the time structure of a cult tends to be no longer than the life of its leader, for once he or she is gone (or loses charismatic appeal), the central organizing force in the cult disappears. The importance of charismatic authority in cults also creates conditions in which leaders may easily abuse their power. For example, in 1978 the Reverend Jim Jones led 900 of his followers in a mass suicide (Hall, 1979).

Cults also differ from other religious institutions in their complete rejection of and withdrawal from the rest of society. While sects are critical of other social institutions, cults reject them entirely. This perhaps explains why cults attract so many people from the poorest social classes, people who see little to be gained by trying to participate in the existing institutions of their society.

The followers of Jim Jones, for example, were almost all poor people who saw the Jones cult as their last hope for a decent life, and who willingly left the United States to create their own colony in the small South American country of Guyana. Their mass suicide (in which a few unwilling participants were murdered) was based on the same kind of fear of outsiders that prompted them to move to Guyana: they believed that outsiders were coming to destroy their cult.

Thus, religions not only differ sharply in their ideas; the ways in which institutional arrangements are structured also vary in many important ways that affect social relationships both within a community of believers and between the community and the rest of society (see Table 19-4).

Not all religious institutions can be classified in terms of the major types described in the preceding sections, for the social structures of religious institutions are connected with the cultural ideas contained in religions. Ecclesiae and churches are more common among monotheistic religions such as Christianity, Judaism, and Islam than they are among polytheistic religions such as Hinduism and

**Table 19-4**

Summary of Major Types of Religious Institutions

| STRUCTURAL CHARACTERISTIC | ECCLESIAE | CHURCHES | DENOMINATIONS | SECTS | CULTS |
|---|---|---|---|---|---|
| **Boundaries and Membership** | Ascribed; most people belong | Mostly ascribed; broad membership | Mostly ascribed; limited in social class | Mostly achieved, through persuasion; lower class | Mostly achieved, through emotional crisis; poor people |
| **Time Structure** | Indefinite | Indefinite | Indefinite | Moderately long | Usually temporary |
| **Role Structure** | Formal and bureaucratic with trained clergy | Formal and bureaucratic with trained clergy | Formal but not bureaucratic; trained clergy | Informal with relatively untrained leadership chosen by community | Informal, loosely organized; charismatic leadership |
| **Authority Structure** | Legal-rational and traditional | Legal-rational and traditional | Traditional | Minimal authority structure | Charismatic |
| **Patterns of Interaction** | Highly abstract ritual; relatively little emotion | Highly abstract ritual; relatively little emotion | Abstract ritual; relatively little emotion | Few formal rituals; spontaneous show of emotion | No formal rituals; highly emotional |
| **Relation to Other Institutions** | Closely identified with political and economic institutions | Often allied with ruling class and status quo | Coexist with political and economic institutions | Oppose institutions; nonconformist | Reject institutions; retreatist |

ethical religions such as Taoism and Confucianism. Religions based on belief in a single all-powerful god are more likely to develop complex social structures—including bureaucracies—through which religious leaders represent and administer what is believed to be the will of the Supreme Being. Monotheism also creates a need for institutions that have power to force followers to be religiously faithful, for monotheistic gods are generally viewed as jealous and intolerant of allegiance to any other sacred force (Wilson, 1982).

Ethical religions, on the other hand, do not view sacred power as flowing from a single source such as a god; rather, the sacred consists of all things—of which each believer is a part. This cultural aspect of ethical religions gives them less need for formally structured religious institutions. It is one thing to have a church leadership that "represents God on earth"; but it makes little sense to have church leaders who represent the entire universe.

**Table 19-5**

Membership in Major Religions (United States, 1981)

| RELIGION | NUMBER OF MEMBERS | PERCENTAGE OF U.S. POPULATION |
|---|---|---|
| Protestant | 76,300,000 | 33.3 |
| Roman Catholic | 51,200,000 | 22.4 |
| Other Catholic | 900,000 | 0.3 |
| Eastern Orthodox | 3,900,000 | 1.7 |
| Jewish | 5,900,000 | 2.6 |
| Other | 211,000 | 0.1 |
| Nonmembers | 90,600,000 | 39.6 |

Source: U.S. Census Bureau, 1983c.

## The Social Ecology of Religious Institutions

Like all cultural and structural aspects of social life, religions and religious institutions are affected by how populations grow and distribute themselves and the ways in which societies use physical environments to meet their material needs.

### The Importance of Size

The number of people who belong to a community of believers directly affects the power of religious institutions; but as we saw in Chapter 8, the effect of numbers on group power depends as much on relative size as it does on absolute size (Merton, 1968; Simmel, 1950).

As an ecclesia, for example, the Iranian Islamic religion is powerful both because its membership is large and because it includes almost all of Iran's population. Under such conditions, it is difficult for other religious institutions to survive, much less compete successfully. In a religiously pluralistic society such as the United States, however, no single religion dominates religious life, in part because there are so many different communities of believers. Absolute size alone, then, does not determine social power.

Size helps account for several social characteristics of smaller religious groups such as sects and cults. Small numbers not only lessen the power of such groups but also make it more difficult for them to perpetuate themselves across generations. This problem is particularly acute in the predominately black Father Divine cult in the United States, whose norms forbid marriage and sexual relations among its members, thereby removing what is obviously a very important source of new members (Kephart, 1976).

The instability of cults reinforces members' fears of the surrounding society and their urge to isolate and protect themselves from it; but this is not restricted to sects and cults. The state of Israel is attractive to many Jews, for example, in part because while Jews are a tiny minority around the world, in Israel they constitute an overwhelming numerical majority. Thus, vulnerability to persecution and discrimination is substantially lessened by the ecological arrangement that exists in Israel.

Israel offers Jews their only opportunity to live as members of an overwhelming numerical majority.

## *Technology, Production, and Religion*

Sociologists and anthropologists have long noted distinct patterns of religious ideas and institutions that vary between societies according to the ways in which they use physical environments to produce goods (Table 19-6). The religions of most hunter-gatherer societies, for example, do not include belief in a Supreme Being who created the earth, while this belief is found in the religions of almost all herding societies. Among hunter-gatherers, animism is the most common form of religion (Turnbull, 1961).

Notice in Table 19-6 that as we move toward societies that use more advanced technology, belief in a Supreme Creator who is active in human affairs and supports moral behavior becomes more common—with the interesting exception of herding societies, 80 percent of whose religions do include this belief. Although we do not know just why the belief in an active and caring creator is so

common among herders, it is possible that they draw upon their own experience as herders to envision a Supreme Being that cares for them in the same way that they care for their animals (Lenski and Lenski, 1982).

The mode of production in a society is also related to whether or not its religion includes the worship of ancestors. Ancestor worship is found in only 17 percent of hunter-gatherer societies, but in more than two-thirds of simple and advanced horticultural societies. This difference may be due to the simple fact that unlike hunter-gatherers, peoples who live by tending small gardens tend to live in one place and this keeps them near the graves of their ancestors (Shiels, 1975).

Before the explosive growth of scientific thinking and knowledge in seventeenth- and eighteenth-century Europe, **fatalism**—the belief that humans can do nothing to control events—was a common religious belief, and magic was often

**Table 19-6**

Percentage of Societies Whose Religion Includes Selected Beliefs, by Type of Society

| RELIGIOUS BELIEF | TYPE OF SOCIETY | | | | |
|---|---|---|---|---|---|
| | Hunting and Gathering | Herding | Simple Horticultural | Advanced Horticultural | Agrarian |
| No concept of a Supreme Creator | 61 | 4 | 61 | 21 | 23 |
| Belief in a passive Supreme Creator who is unconcerned with human affairs | 29 | 10 | 35 | 51 | 6 |
| Belief in an active Supreme Creator who does not support human morality | 8 | 6 | 2 | 12 | 5 |
| Belief in an active Supreme Creator who supports human morality | 2 | 80 | 2 | 16 | 66 |
| PERCENTAGE TOTAL | 100 | 100 | 100 | 100 | 100 |
| (Number of Societies) | (85) | (50) | (43) | (131) | (66) |

Source: *Human Societies*, Lenski and Lenski, 1978.

viewed as the only way to escape complete helplessness (Banfield, 1967; Levi, 1947). Scientific thought, however, offered the possibility of control over the physical world, and with the rising influence of science, fatalism and belief in magic declined.

Technology and modes of production are also related to the size, power, and complexity of religious institutions. As is true of political institutions, a full-time, highly trained, and powerful class of religious leaders can only be supported in a society that is able to produce a surplus of goods, and it was not until the agrarian age that ecclesiae and churches came into being.

Religious institutions in industrial societies, however, are far less powerful than they were in agrarian Europe of the Middle Ages. As we saw in Chapter 18, church and state in medieval Europe were the two dominant and competing sources of power, but religious change, scientific thinking, and the Industrial Revolution weakened the economic and political power of religious institutions. The Protestant Reformation inspired by Martin Luther in the sixteenth century challenged the absolute authority of the Catholic Church and undermined its claim to obedience and surplus wealth. In the eighteenth and nineteenth centuries, science weakened the monopoly of religion over cultural explanations of the world; and with the Industrial Revolution the state and the emerging capitalist class claimed an increasingly large share of surplus production. The result was a dramatic decline in the economic and political power of religious institutions.

Here it is especially important to remember that religions and religious institutions are not the same thing. Nowhere in the world, perhaps, has the power of the state caused so dramatic a decline in the power of a church as it did in Russia after the 1917 revolution that began the transformation of feudal Russia into the socialist Soviet Union. In today's Soviet Union, the Russian Orthodox Church has no authority as a social institution; but the religious ideas and practices of Christianity still have considerable power in a large segment of the Russian population (Shipler, 1983).

## Function, Dysfunction, and Social Conflict

All social institutions are defined in part by the functions they perform in a community of believers. As we have seen repeatedly in other chapters, however, this does not mean that institutional cultures and structures cannot also have dysfunctional social consequences, or that they never play a part in social conflict.

### Some Dysfunctions of Religion and Religious Institutions

Religious ideas often have dysfunctional consequences for societies. Because religious communities often view their beliefs and values as absolutely correct, it is only a short step to the ethnocentric view that their religion is superior to all others. The absoluteness with which many religious ideas are held also increases the chance that religion will serve as an ideology.

No war is so fierce as a "holy war" fought in the name of religion, and as the seventeenth-century French philosopher and mathematician Pascal wrote, "Men never do evil so completely and cheerfully as when they do it from religious conviction." As long as the religion of ancient Rome was polytheistic, Christians were favorite objects of persecution; but when Christianity became the official religion of Rome in the fourth century, Jews became the new target and have remained an object of persecution based on the mistaken belief that Jews were responsible for the death of Christ. The crusades of the eleventh, twelfth, and thirteenth centuries pitted Christians against Muslims. The Spanish Inquisition at the turn of the sixteenth century sent thousands of suspected heretics to their death, focusing particularly on Jews and Christians with Moorish backgrounds. In the sixteenth century, French Catholics and Protestants fought for more than 30 years during which massacres and other atrocities were commonplace.

Religion still plays a part in aggression and war. Catholics and Protestants in Northern Ireland have been fighting for most of this century. Muslims and Christians in Lebanon have fought with each other in religious wars that continue into the 1980s. Violence against Jews in France, the Soviet Union, and in the United States and many other western countries still occurs. In India, violence between Muslims and Hindus is common, and in 1984 members of the Sikh religious sect assassinated Prime Minister Indira Gandhi in retaliation for alleged mistreatment at the hands of the Indian government. The 1979 revolution in Iran replaced the oppressive authoritarian state of the Shah with an equally or more oppressive authoritarian state based on Islamic religious law. Arrest, torture, and execution of those who oppose Islamic rule has become common in Iran, and the ensuing war with Iraq has been characterized by Iranian leaders as a "holy war" whose ultimate goal is to bring about the supremacy of Islam as the basis for all political institutions in the Middle East.

Religion, of course, is not the sole cause of such violence; as in the case of Northern Ireland, conflict often has more to do with economic and political issues than with differences of faith. Reli-

During the Spanish Inquisition, thousands of suspected heretics were tortured and killed in the name of religious purity.

gion, however, fuels conflict by giving each side the belief that their cause is "just" in an ultimate and absolute sense.

Social conflict is more likely to involve monotheistic religions such as Islam, Christianity, and Judaism than polytheistic religions such as Hinduism or ethical religions such as Buddhism, Confucianism, and Taoism. By definition, monotheism includes the belief that there is not only a god, but one god only. Thus, any other religion that does not focus on a single god is likely to be seen as a threat to believers in a monotheistic religion.

The divisive effects of religion also occur in less-violent forms. In the United States, for example, religious beliefs and values are often the basis for social conflict. Prayer in public schools and abortion are two issues that deeply divide Americans—a situation that would be less likely to exist if all Americans shared a single religion.

Violence is not the only dysfunction of religion. The Hindu belief that the only route to a higher social caste lies with performing the duties associated with people's present caste may interfere with motivation for upward mobility and improvement of their lives within their own lifetimes; and this effect may extend beyond the lives of individuals to the standard of living in India as a whole.

This is also true of Buddhism, for the Buddhist emphasis on people removing themselves from earthly concerns and putting an end to all feelings of desire tends to remove them from the ongoing conflict through which positive social change often occurs (Wilson, 1982). The Islamic religion carries a strong sense of fatalism in the belief that everything that happens on earth is a matter of Allah's will. This interferes with economic progress that usually involves long-range planning and a belief that the future can be affected by what people do in the present (Hall, 1959).

In the simplest sense, religion can be dysfunctional for certain social goals when it includes beliefs that are empirically false. In Europe of the Middle Ages and into the eighteenth century, the advance of science and technology was slowed by deeply entrenched religious doctrines that offered a very different view of how the world and universe work. Scientists such as Galileo and Copernicus were persecuted by the Catholic Church for their theories about the solar system, and early medical researchers were forbidden from cutting open corpses and had to steal them from graveyards.

In general, sociologists are not very interested in the truth or falsity of particular religious beliefs, because the social power and importance of religion does not lie in the content of religious ideas; rather, it lies in the commitment of a community of believers to a set of ideas that form a sacred framework within which people interpret and explain the world and their experience in it. In general the ideas that make up a religion are far less significant than the fact that people believe in them.

## Religion, Class, and Social Conflict

The relationship between religious institutions and class systems in stratified societies is both long-standing and widespread in human history. The historical rise of religious institutions was spurred by the same ecological and social changes that supported the emergence of social stratification systems and the state. Since religious and political institutions both depend on wealth that they do not themselves produce, it is not surprising that they have often found themselves either supporting each other or competing for a greater share of power. Religious leaders constituted one of the first elites to emerge when societies developed the ability to produce a surplus of goods that allowed the accumulation and concentration of wealth and power.

Religious beliefs and values have supported social inequality in many different cultures. The Hindu caste system, for example, is supported by the religious belief in reincarnation and the importance attached to caste boundaries. Respect for elders and others in positions of authority is an important part of Confucianism that supports inequality of wealth and power. Buddhist values and beliefs support the status quo by denying the importance of anything that occurs in the profane world and striving for a cessation of all desire for wealth, power, and prestige (Wilson, 1982).

For centuries the Catholic Church was one of the most powerful social institutions in Europe, rivaled only by the nobility; and even when the state emerged as the dominant social institution, the church continued to have great wealth and influence. In Mexico, the Catholic Church was so closely allied with the upper class that during the violent revolutions of the nineteenth century the church and the priesthood were direct targets of the anger and frustration of the peasant class. Not only did the church lose most of its wealth, but for several years priests were forbidden to wear religious clothing in public.

Religion does not always serve the interests of dominant social classes and the status quo, however. While the Mexican revolutionaries identified the church as a major enemy, the Mexican people were at the same time deeply religious. Here the distinction between religion and religious institutions is once again important, for it was the church and not religion that Mexicans rejected in the nineteenth century.

In some societies, religious institutions openly oppose the state, especially when it is oppressive and authoritarian. This is true of most religious sects and cults that draw their members largely from the lowest social classes; but it is also true of the Catholic Church in Latin American countries that are ruled by dictatorships. The church in such societies becomes a place for people to meet, to discuss political and social issues that affect their lives, and to make plans for change. In a few Latin American countries, such as El Salvador, the priesthood serves as an active source of criticism of government policy and of awareness of the true conditions of life in the profane world. Most important, religion in these societies—and others such as socialist Poland—is a source of emotional attachment and power whose mere existence threatens the dominance of the state. In 1984, for example, the Polish government ordered the enforcement of a previously passed law banning the display of crucifixes in public schools and universities, a move that prompted violent demonstrations against the government.

**Religion and False Consciousness**  When Karl Marx described religion as the "opium of the people," he was saying that the focus of religion on the sacred and unknown world distracted people's attention from the realities of life in the profane world of wealth, power, prestige, inequality, and social class. As Max Weber (1923) wrote, "It was possible for the working class to accept its lot as long as the promise of eternal happiness could be held out to it" (p. 369).

Marx's use of "opium" as an image is powerful because opium is a depressant drug that dulls sen-

sation, including pain. To Marx, religion often serves to explain and justify the suffering that people experience during their lives. The key, however, is that religion explains earthly conditions not as the result of social relationships but as part of a natural, sacred order.

Religion thus contributes to false consciousness by substituting a sacred explanation of earthly conditions for a social one. The problem, argued Marx, lies not with the conditions created by sacred or supernatural forces, but with those created by societies and institutions, and when people focus attention on the sacred as the source of all things—including poverty, oppression, and suffering—they are less likely to identify the true sources of inequality and the suffering and deprivation that result.

Slaves in the American South were told that their condition was a matter of God's will (Stampp, 1956); and mill owners in North Carolina near the turn of the twentieth century supported local churches primarily in order to distract workers from the social causes of their deprivation (Pope, 1942). Many Christians believe that inequality between men and women is based on the word of God as revealed in the Bible (Daly, 1973), a belief that prompted pioneer feminist Elizabeth Cady Stanton to argue that "The first step in the elevation of women under all systems of religion is to convince them that the great Spirit of the Universe is in no way responsible for any of these absurdities" (in Daly, 1973, p. 13).

Harris (1974) argued that false consciousness lay at the heart of the persecution of witches throughout Europe during the Middle Ages. In those times of severe economic hardship, women accused of being witches served as scapegoats, which encouraged the poor to believe that "they were being victimized by witches and devils instead of princes and popes" (p. 237).

Christianity is of course not the only religion that contributes to false consciousness in this way. The Hindu religion is a perfect example, for people who are born into lower castes cannot hope to return in a higher caste unless they accept their current lot in life and meet their prescribed obligations to the castes above them.

In a deeper sense, all religion contributes to false consciousness by alienating human beings from the simple fact that the social world and its institutions are the products of human activity. When family roles, the roles of men and women, or the roles of kings are shrouded in religious symbolism, we then tend to treat them as inevitable parts of the ultimate reality that religious ideas purport to describe.

> Just as religion mystifies and thus fortifies the illusionary autonomy of the humanly produced world, so it mystifies and fortifies its introjection in individual consciousness. The internalized roles carry with them the mysterious power ascribed to them by their religious legitimations. Socialized identity as a whole can be apprehended by the individual as something sacred, grounded in the "nature of things" as created or willed by the gods. As such, it loses its character as a product of human activity. (Berger, 1967, p. 95)

There is nothing about religion that necessarily means that it supports false consciousness and, therefore, existing social conditions. Jesus Christ was one of many Jews who led the Jewish rebellion against the Roman Empire. The Mexican revolution that overthrew Spanish rule early in the nineteenth century was led by a soldier and a priest named Hidalgo, and radical Catholic priests continue to play revolutionary roles in some Latin American countries.

In the 1960s American priests and ministers played active roles in the civil rights movement, and Martin Luther King, Jr.—one of the most powerful of all black civil rights leaders ever to emerge—was himself a minister. On the other side of the world in 1963, Vietnamese Buddhist monks set themselves afire on public streets and burned themselves to death in dramatic protest against the oppressive authoritarian regime of Ngo Dinh Diem (Karnow, 1983). In the 1980s many American religious leaders are playing an active part in the nuclear freeze movement that opposes the spread of nuclear weapons (Castelli, 1983).

Religion and religious institutions, therefore, have both opposed and inspired social conflict aimed at changing the social conditions in which people live. Religions and religious institutions themselves, however, are also subject to the pressures that lead to change.

## Religion and Social Change

Like all aspects of social environments, religions and religious institutions change, for they do not exist in a vacuum and thus are affected by change in the surrounding society.

### Cultural Change

In general, the ideas that constitute a religion change less easily than the social structures through which a community of believers practices its religion, for these ideas form the most basic visions of what life is about, both in this world and in the unknown.

Nevertheless, they do change. Norms once forbade the participation of women in religious services among Catholics, Jews, and several Protestant denominations; but under the pressure of the women's movement, those norms are slowly breaking down. There is continuing pressure on the Catholic Church to relax norms that forbid abortion, divorce, and the use of contraceptives, as well as those that forbid priests from marrying.

In 1983 the National Council of Churches released a new translation of key passages in the Bible, designed to remove the male-oriented, sexist bias of earlier translations (*Newsweek*, October 24, 1983). The new version, for example, replaces "mankind" with "humankind," refers to God as "my Mother and Father" and to Jesus as the Child of God rather than as the Son of God. For all of the protest and praise the new version has inspired, it is important as an institutional acknowledgment of the impact of religious ideas on the most basic aspects of social life and of the pressures exerted on religion by change in the surrounding society.

Specific changes such as these are not isolated social phenomena, for they are part of a much broader and more powerful trend in industrial societies called *secularization*.

**Secularization**   Secularization refers to a social process through which "beliefs concerning the supernatural and practices associated with them are discredited and the institution of religion loses social influence" (J. Wilson, 1978, p. 397). Secularization involves both cultural and structural change within religions as well as changes in the relationship between religious and other institutions.

A 1976 survey found that only 31 percent of Catholics believed that the Bible was a literal record of actual events (Chalfant, Beckley, and Palmer, 1981), and in the late 1960s as many as 60 percent of the members of some Protestant denominations had doubts about the existence of God (see Table 19-1). In 1984 only 31 percent of American adults had "a great deal of confidence" in the leaders of organized religion (Davis, 1984). For many Americans, religious holidays are no longer occasions of worship but opportunities to escape the demands of work and spend time with their families.

The declining influence of religion is common in industrial societies, and sociologists have identified several likely causes. The most obvious is the steady rise of scientific thinking that began in the seventeenth century and undermined religion as a framework for explaining the natural world (Berger, 1967). For example, physical science challenged the Christian view of the origins of the universe and human life, and in no industrial society is the Biblical version of creation widely used as an explanation (Wilson, 1982). As we saw earlier in this chapter, Weber, Marx, and Durkheim challenged religion by focusing on social rather than divine causes of social conditions. They even went so far as to argue that religion, itself, was a human creation.

The Industrial Revolution added to this an explosion of material goods and, with it, an increased social value placed on material prosperity at the expense of religion's orientation to the sacred and spiritual worlds (J. Wilson, 1978). Industrialization also brought with it the need for increased mobility and migration, and with this the ties between church and community became increasingly difficult to maintain. Perhaps most important, the Industrial Revolution rested on a rationalization both of thought and of human relationships, and this undermined the importance in human life of unknown, sacred forces.

As a cultural system, religion has not simply changed in response to cultural changes in society, however, for as the structures of industrial societies have become more complex, religious institutions have faced and continue to face challenges from other institutions.

## Changing Structures

Secularization affects not only the cultural ideas that constitute religions but also the structures of religious institutions and their relationships with the rest of society. Most American churches and denominations, for example, have experienced a decline in active membership over the past century. Between 1972 and 1984 the number of people who reported attending church at least once a week declined slightly from 35 to 33 percent, while the number who reported attending no more than once or twice a year increased slightly from 29 to 32 percent (Davis, 1984).

The most dramatic structural change in religious institutions has been a drastic decline in power and authority. In preindustrial societies religion is directly involved in virtually all aspects of social life, from the rituals that mark the passage from one stage of the life course to another—birth, adulthood, marriage, and death—to healing the sick, caring for the poor, administering justice, explaining the world, and educating the young.

In industrial societies, however, many of these social functions are performed by other institutions. It is now possible to marry and have children with no involvement with religious institutions; physicians heal the sick, schools educate the young, scientists in universities and business provide socially acceptable explanations of the world, and the state determines what the law will be, administers justice, and provides for the poor.

In comparison with preindustrial societies in which religion and religious institutions are deeply embedded in all aspects of social life, religious institutions in industrial societies are separate and isolated. They must compete with a variety of other institutions that both perform many of the former functions of religion and place demands on the attention of believers (Luckmann, 1967). Religious institutions are no longer the major source of cultural ideas that they once were, a fact that is particularly apparent in the high degree of religious tolerance found in most industrial societies. As Wilson (1982) wrote:

> The very fact that religion becomes an optional matter, the fact that there is freedom of religion, tolerance, and choice, is an indication that religion is apparently of little direct consequence to the functioning of the social order, at least as that order is understood by those who have helped to build it, modify it, and maintain it. (p. 46)

Religious institutions in general have declined in importance in industrial societies, but this has been confined largely to ecclesiae, churches, and denominations. Although cults such as the Unification Church of Sun Myung Moon and the Hare

## Voices: The Fundamentalist Furor

As America nodded at the end of the seventies from its liberated binge of sex, drugs, self-discovery, and disco, a motley cluster of short-haired prophets concluded the Me Decade with a flurry of jeremiads. While historians and sociologists were discovering in American civilization such fin-de-siècle symptoms as the culture of narcissism and the twilight of authority, religious conservatives were finding auguries of Armageddon, and political conservatives were foretelling the fall of liberalism. It was a time of strange coincidences and unlikely conversions.

In the autumn of 1979, when the Reverend Jerry Falwell was launching the hastily soldered conservative coalition known as Moral Majority, rock and roll veterans Bob Dylan, Van Morrison, and Arlo Guthrie released portentous religious albums. Shortly after Catholic charismatics braved the Bronx and gathered in the thousands for a tongue-loosing rally in Yankee Stadium, the exiled Dalai Lama arrived in Manhattan to begin his first tour of America with an appearance at St. Patrick's Cathedral, urging peace and simplicity on the mildly curious crowd that turned out to welcome him. And as the Tibetan holy man was humbly greeting millionaires and assorted Buddhists in a heavy Houston downpour, Pope John Paul II was energetically upstaging him in Massachusetts. Hard-nosed newsmen found themselves melting like communion wafers before the hearty charisma of the peripatetic pontiff, until John Paul's beaming pink-cheeked visage was superseded by the pale omnipresent scowl of the Ayatollah Khomeini.

It seemed that America was being held hostage by an alien zealotry, both at home and abroad. The sleek triumphant smile of the Reverend Falwell began to appear everywhere, like the tacked-up icon of a fundamentalist führer. In the wake of a decade of experiments in moral relativism, the minions of moral absolutism were on the march, using the media to amplify their message and their numbers. In America's heartland, the phantom army of the Moral Majority, whose legions were counted in computerized lists, mounted the attack through the mails and on the airwaves, collating the power of elemental Protestantism. It appeared that a thoroughly modernized machine was being built in order to deliver a very dated message.

. . . In the spring of 1980, a quarter of a million born-again Americans converged on Washington, DC, to pray for the purification of national politics. . . .

Jimmy Carter looked up from his Bible to find that fundamentalism was running amok and he himself had become a false prophet. Carter's election did not usher in an old-fashioned religious revival so much as a new phase in the clash between Christ and culture. It was a clash that not only set millenarian against humanist, pro-lifer against abortionist, and creationist against evolutionist but Christian against Christian, evangelical against evangelical, and preacher against preacher. The fundamentalist war against modern culture was also a war among the churches. Politics was a new front in a long-standing conflict among American Protestants that had culminated with the establishment of fundamentalism during the first part of the twentieth century.

. . . Tutored by conservative political organizers, fundamentalist leaders mastered the grass-roots rallying techniques of the sixties counterculture, including music, marches, and mass gatherings, as well as the sophisticated technology of secular culture. Setting themselves against the Eastern liberal "establishment," whom they felt ruled the nation without the consent of the governed, conservative Christian leaders attempted to smooth over long-standing doctrinal differences and territorial disputes among themselves in order to present a united front—a "Moral Majority," a "disciplined, charging army." They created a new common cause—the family—and identified a new common enemy—secular humanism. As Jerry Falwell described it, fundamentalists had hijacked the jumbo jet of evangelicalism and directed it on a new conservative course.

Source: Flake, *Redemptorama*, 1984.

Krishna movement and the various fundamentalist Christian sects involved in the new evangelicalism still constitute a very small portion of the American population, they have enjoyed large increases in membership over the last decade (Hadden and Swann, 1981; Lofland, 1977). In comparison with larger religious institutions, cults and sects offer their members a mystical and absolute view of the world that may be a backlash against the secularization process that renders the world increasingly rational, bureaucratic, impersonal, unemotional, and profane.

## Civil Religion and Other Alternatives

If involvement in religious institutions is declining, what becomes of the most important social functions of religion—increasing social cohesion and providing a sense of individual and group identity that rests on a set of shared beliefs about the meaning of life and the place of human beings in relation to the unknown?

Durkheim once argued that religious institutions in preindustrial societies allowed people to worship their own societies. The sociologist Robert Bellah (1973) contended that in industrial socie-

ties, the state itself has become a religious institution. Through **civil religion,** he maintained, we now worship society directly rather than indirectly through religious institutions. Civil religion cuts across all lines drawn by churches, denominations, sects, and cults and helps to unite a pluralistic society (Bellah and Hammond, 1980).

The evidence of civil religion is everywhere. God is mentioned at most important public occasions: at the opening of Congress, in courts of law, in the Pledge of Allegiance to the Flag, at presidential inaugurations. The words "In God We Trust" appear on money; the bald eagle and the American flag are sacred symbols of national unity, purpose, and strength; the Fourth of July and Memorial Day are ritual celebrations of a common heritage and the belief that God is somehow on America's side. National monuments such as the Lincoln Memorial in Washington, DC resemble religious shrines.

Perhaps the most striking example of civil religion is the Soviet Union, which, paradoxically, officially opposes religious institutions. From its revolutionary beginnings in 1917, the Soviet state identified religious institutions as a negative force

that did little more than contribute to false consciousness and the dominance of the ruling class. The Soviet state has tried to replace religion with the state itself and with a Marxist theory of the world based entirely on the social relationships through which goods are produced and distributed (Duverger, 1959). Yet in this society that officially opposes the very idea of the "sacred," Russians stand in line for hours to visit the tomb of Lenin in which Soviet Union's first Marxist leader lies in his casket, perfectly preserved for all to view with quiet religious reverence.

In some ways, both the concept and the reality of civil religion represent a contradiction in terms. Religion focuses on sacred and unknown forces that are believed to affect human life, whereas the word "civil" refers to the profane world of people's ordinary lives as members of a society. Marxism is clearly grounded in the material conditions of human existence, not in unknown forces that are beyond the understanding of everyday experience. This is also true of civil religion in America: we may love our country, we may feel awe in the presence of monuments, and we may feel full of emotion when we hear "America the Beautiful"; but it remains to be seen if our attachment to our country can substitute for answers to the ultimate questions that all religions try to answer.

Civil religion cannot explain why we were put on this earth; nor can it tell us what will become of us when we die. It cannot, by definition, provide a meaning of life grounded in beliefs that have a sacred source beyond everyday human experience. While it can, in short, bind us to our society, it cannot secure a place for us in the universe and the endless stretches of time that include our short earthly existence.

Thus, while civil religion performs some of the functions once performed by religious institutions, it is not a true religion. Bellah (1973), in fact, believed that civil religion is little more than a "broken and empty shell" (p. 142) and that our increased reliance on science, technology, and the state to provide ultimate solutions to human dilemmas will cause a crisis of major proportions.

The rise of the state and civil religion and the declining influence of religious institutions do not necessarily mean that people are no longer concerned with understanding the unknown and attaching a cosmic meaning to life. While sociologists can measure how often people attend church, it is very difficult to measure aspects of religious faith and concern scientifically. In 1984, 73 percent of American adults reported a belief in life after death, and although only a minority of adults attend church on a regular basis, just over half oppose the Supreme Court's ban on religious observances in public schools (Davis, 1984). One out of every three adults opposes allowing atheists to give speeches in their communities and half do not think atheists should be allowed to teach in colleges and universities (Davis, 1984).

Again we can see the importance of the distinction between religion and religious institutions. Although attendance at church services in many industrial societies is declining, there is some evidence that people are turning to more private settings for religious behavior. Televised services, for example, have a growing—although still relatively small—audience in the United States (Hadden and Swann, 1981). In 1983 the coach of a professional football team, a U.S. senator, professional athletes, and prominent businessmen all appeared on television to promote a book that, they promised, would give its readers "a personal relationship with God."

Major religious institutions appear to be losing much of their former authority as sources of the ultimate meanings and truths that make up a religion, and, at the same time, religion has become a more private matter. Rather than adopting the organized beliefs of a particular religion, individuals are now more likely to construct their own view of ultimate truth from a variety of available beliefs and values. With the decline of primary religious institutions, other institutions have taken over some of the role of spreading ideas that ultimately become part of people's religious framework. The family, schools, and the media all offer and support an assortment of ultimate truths from which individuals construct what amount to private religious systems (Luckmann, 1967).

Thus, it appears that religion is becoming less visible as people turn away from major institutions as the major setting for expressing religious beliefs and feelings; but a lack of visibility does not mean such feelings and beliefs no longer exist. It does suggest, however, that religion is on the decline as a social force that binds people together and forms a basis for group identity. Whether or not other institutions can perform this important social function remains to be seen.

## Summary

1. Religion consists of symbols and ideas that focus on the meaning of life and the nature of the unknown. The profane is what we can experience directly as ordinary aspects of the natural world, but the sacred is outside the natural world and inspires feelings of awe.

2. Like all institutions, religion is defined in part by the functions it performs. It helps believers cope with pain and suffering, for example, and contributes to social cohesion.

3. It is not the task of sociology to prove the truth or falsity of religious beliefs; rather, sociologists try to understand how religion affects the lives of individuals, groups, and societies.

4. Religions differ primarily in their beliefs. Theistic religion includes the belief in one (monotheism) or more (polytheism) supreme beings. Animists believe that spirits inhabit objects such as trees, and totemists believe objects (totems) have supernatural power. Ancestor worshipers believe the dead can influence life among the living. Religions such as Buddhism and Confucianism focus more on abstract ideas as guides for ethical living than on supernatural forces. Religions employ practices called rituals through which religious beliefs are acted out.

5. Some form of salvation is one of the most important values in any religion, and many religious norms define appropriate means for achieving it. Religions also include a variety of attitudes, from adoration of sacred figures to hatred of nonbelievers.

6. Ecclesiae, churches, denominations, sects, and cults are five basic structural types of religious institutions. They differ from each other in how powerful they are and how universal their membership is in a society; in how bureaucratic they are; in the closeness of their ties to other institutions, especially the state; in the selectivity of their membership, especially in terms of social class, and in the ways in which people become members.

7. As with all institutions, religions are affected by population and ecology. The relative and absolute number of followers, for example, helps account for both the power of ecclesiae and the weakness of cults. Religious ideas are also affected by technology and the mode of production in a society. The more technologically advanced a society is, for example, the more likely are its religions to include belief in a supreme being who takes an active interest in human affairs.

8. Like all institutions, religion is functional for certain goals but dysfunctional for others. Beliefs in the absolute truth of religious ideas, for example, fosters ethnocentrism and conflict with followers of other religions. Hindu beliefs support a rigid caste system and the Islamic religion carries a strong sense of fatalism that interferes with economic progress.

9. Frequently religious institutions are either allied with or actively opposed to the state and dominant social classes. Marx believed that religion often contributes to false consciousness by distracting members of oppressed groups from the true nature and causes of their oppression.

10. A major trend in religious change has been secularization, the process by which religious institutions lose influence to nonreligious institutions such as the state and schools. Compared with religious institutions in preindustrial societies, those in industrial societies have far less authority and influence over people's lives.

11. Some have pointed to the emergence of civil religion as a substitute for the declining influence of religious institutions. In civil religion, society is the focus of worship.

## Key Terms

ancestor worship   607
animism   607
church   613
civil religion   626
cult   614
denomination   613
ecclesia   612
ethical religion   608
fatalism   618
monotheism   607
polytheism   607
profane   602
reincarnation   607
religion   601

## Recommended Readings

BERGER, P. L. (1969). *A rumor of angels: Modern society and the rediscovery of the supernatural.* New York: Doubleday. A thoughtful exploration of the place of religion in modern industrial societies.

FOWLER, J. W. (1981). *Stages of faith.* New York: Harper and Row. A study of religious socialization that focuses on the ways in which people acquire religious faith.

HUNTER, J. D. (1983). *American evangelicalism: Conservative religion and the quandry of modernity.* New Brunswick, NJ: Rutgers University Press. A historical study that shows how the traditional basis of evangelicalism has adapted and survived alongside modernization in most major regions of the world.

ROBBINS, T., and ANTHONY, D. (Eds.). (1980). *In gods we trust: New patterns of religious pluralism in America.* New Brunswick, NJ: Transaction Books. An important set of articles that focus on religious change in the United States, from social conflict to the rise of civil religion and new religious institutions.

WILSON, J. (1978). *Religion in American society: The effective presence.* Englewood Cliffs, NJ: Prentice-Hall. An excellent introduction to the sociology of religion in the United States. See also Wilson, B. (1982). *Religion in sociological perspective.* New York: Oxford.

# PART VI
# Social Change

Most of this book has focused on trying to describe the cultural, structural, and ecological aspects of social life and to explain how they operate as human arrangements that affect our lives. We have covered a considerable distance—from the process through which children learn language and discover themselves and other people to the ways in which political and economic systems work.

Most of the chapters end with a section on change, and this in itself indicates an important sociological problem that extends across all of the areas we study: it is not enough to describe and explain human social arrangements, for the arrangements change, and each change presents us with new problems to solve. It is one thing to see clearly how things are and to describe how they work; but it is quite another to understand how things got to be the way they are, and still another to have some idea of how things will be in the next year or the next decade. And given the rapid pace of change in today's societies, it is more important than ever that we wrestle successfully with these kinds of problems.

These last two chapters look at two areas of sociology that focus on social change. Chapter 20 focuses on collective behavior, an area that includes a variety of behaviors. The most important of these is social movements, which are organized efforts to either bring about or interfere with social change. Why do social movements emerge when they do, and how do we account for the success of some and the failure of others? What causes revolutions to occur? In the final chapter we examine specific theories that try to explain the patterns, speed, and causes of change.

# Collective Behavior and Social Movements

In the spring of 1982, 700,000 people marched peacefully in New York City to protest the nuclear arms race. There was little violence associated with the demonstration, and no clashes with police. In the months just before Christmas in 1983, however, the "Cabbage Patch" brand of dolls became wildly popular in the United States. In Charleston, West Virginia, 5,000 shoppers started a near riot in a department store. "They knocked over tables, fighting with each other—there were people in mid-air," reported the store manager. "It got ugly." Huge crowds waited for hours—often in biting cold winds—for a chance to snatch up the dolls, and the rush often resulted in injuries, including broken bones (Associated Press, 1983).

In that same fall hundreds of thousands of people gathered in cities across Western Europe to protest the deployment of nuclear missiles aimed at the Soviet Union. In England protesters chained themselves to fences surrounding military bases; many people were arrested and police used water cannons to disperse some of the crowds. In late 1984, two members of the Sikh religious sect in India murdered Prime Minister Indira Gandhi, and in the days of enraged rioting that followed, more than 1,000 people were killed, most of them Sikhs.

In November 1983, millions watched *The Day After*, a television movie depicting the fate of an American community in the aftermath of a nuclear

In 1982, more than 700,000 people gathered peacefully in New York City's Central Park in support of a freeze on the production and deployment of nuclear weapons.

## Voices: Murder on the Rajdhani Express

"Had I read about this, I might have dismissed it as far-fetched. But I saw it.

"The Rajdhani Express, India's premier train, a 17½-hour, 1,000 mile run from Bombay to New Delhi, arrived at its second stop, Ratlam, on schedule at 1 A.M. Friday. Passengers were roused by an announcement warning them there was 'trouble' ahead and they could disembark there if they wished. Few did. . . .

"At Mathura a teenage Sikh boy . . . was advised by some passengers to take shelter at Mathura station where he would be safe with some soldiers. He took the advice, but two other Sikhs in the car—identifiable by their beards, turbans, and long hair—declined. One was alone, the other had his wife and a son and daughter with him.

"On the outskirts of New Delhi, the train stopped again at a small station. A voice announced that passengers should lock all doors and keep all windows curtained. We didn't know why. . . . Three minutes later we knew.

"About a hundred people, all young men, began hammering on the doors of the halted train, pounding at the compartment door windows with iron rods and stones. There was a crunching sound, then a cheer. The window had broken. Four youths, unkempt and wielding sticks, came into our car. I was sitting near the door and one glanced at me, pondering over my beard.

"'Come out, all the Sikhs in here!' one shouted.

"'There are none here,' a passenger said softly. Just then, a few of their companions entered the car, some with iron rods, others with long black rubber pipes. The armed brigade marched down the aisle between the seats. 'Here! Here! Come here! We got one of these fellows.'

"As the passengers slowly got to their feet and turned to look there was a sound of scuffling and a series of sickening thuds. Two teenage girls, traveling with their mother, screamed hysterically. The other passengers did not react. They just looked on silently.

"One of the marauding youths was pulling a Sikh man by his long hair. Three other attackers followed, hitting the Sikh with their rods. He held onto the seats, refusing to move. His shirt became spattered with blood. A girl screamed and one of the mob looked at her soothingly and said: 'Don't worry, sister. We will not do anything to you. We are after them. . . . We will not spare them.'

"Finally one of the youths broke the Sikh's hold on a seat. They hauled the beaten, deeply wounded man outside. The crowd collected around him and continued their relentless onslaught. We could only watch from the windows. No one got down onto the platform.

"A few moments later an acrid smell floated into the car through the broken window. The crowds parted, and we saw flames leap up from the body of the Sikh, a man who just 15 minutes before had been riding peacefully from Bombay. Inside the train, none of us spoke.

"The train remained there for three hours. . . . At 1:30 P.M. it departed, carrying many passengers who had been stranded on an earlier train at the same station. They spoke of similar incidents. . . . A fellow passenger said police were standing by, doing nothing . . . while the killers rampaged.

"The Rajdhani Express arrived in New Delhi at 2 P.M. A curious crowd gathered around a body lying in the entrance to a car. I did not know whether it was the Sikh who had been in my car. The body was charred and unrecognizable.

"'This is just the beginning,' muttered an old man, shaking his head.

Source: Associated Press, in the *Hartford Courant*, November 3, 1984, p. 1.

Enraged members of a Hindu mob attack a Sikh in New Delhi after the assassination of Prime Minister Indira Gandhi in 1984.

war. A storm of controversy preceded the movie, and for many it was a deeply moving and frightening experience that they shared with millions of other people.

Where in the sociological framework do we find a place for people pushing and shoving over a doll, battling with police in the streets, calmly marching in huge numbers without violence, killing strangers only because they belong to the same religious group as two murderers, or sharing an important experience with people we never know but can only imagine? A clue lies in the concept of collective behavior, and in this chapter we examine the many kinds of collective behavior and some major attempts to understand them sociologically. We begin with a look at some basic concepts.

## Crowds, Masses, and Collective Behavior

**Collective behavior** refers to how people think, feel, and behave as members of crowds and masses (Lofland, 1981). **A crowd** is a relatively temporary collection of people who happen to be in the same place at the same time in close enough proximity to one another so that they can interact with and be affected by one another. A collection of people on a sidewalk, the audience at a rock concert, passengers on a bus—all are examples of crowds, in which membership is a temporary, situational social status. Standing in a telephone booth, we are not part of a crowd; but when we open the door and step out on the sidewalk, we suddenly are.

Unlike a crowd, a **mass** is a collection of people who pay attention to and react to the same thing without being in one another's presence. For example, the 1963 assassination of President John F. Kennedy set off a wave of shock and sadness that went around the world and was shared by tens of millions of people who were thousands of miles apart. The collective shock and mourning were examples of mass shock and grief, within which people also expressed their feelings as members of crowds such as those that lined the route of the funeral procession. One of the most telling indicators of the mass experience of Kennedy's assassination is that virtually everyone who was old enough to be aware of the event knows exactly what they were doing when they first heard about it.

Since collective behavior refers to what people think, feel, and do as members of crowds or masses, what distinguishes it from other types of behavior is not so much what people do, but the structure of the social situations in which they do it.

There are four basic types of collective behavior (Blumer, 1939) that can occur either in crowds or in masses (see Table 20-1). **Casual** collective behavior—such as people walking on a sidewalk—involves no common purpose or goal around which people interact or focus their attention. **Conventional** behavior, on the other hand, involves a specific purpose such as watching a parade.

**Expressive** collective behavior—as you might suppose—centers on the expression of feelings toward some common object or event. Protest marches, riots, religious revival meetings, funerals, and the annual congregation of tens of thousands of people in New York City's Times Square each New Year's Eve are all examples of expressive collective behavior. Finally, **acting** collective behavior is oriented to specific goals—whether it be to lynch someone, block traffic, prevent workers from crossing a picket line, elect a new government, or topple an old one.

These four general categories include most types of crowd behavior that interest sociologists, but miss several kinds of collective behavior that take place in masses rather than crowds. **Fashion**

**Table 20-1**

Examples of Collective Behavior in Crowds and Masses

| TYPE OF BEHAVIOR | IN A CROWD | IN A MASS |
|---|---|---|
| Casual | Waiting for bus | Watching the Superbowl |
| Conventional | Church service | 4th of July celebrations |
| Expressive | Protest march | Nationwide fear over poisoned Tylenol capsules |
| Acting | Lynch mob Social movement | Voting Social movement |

Sources: Based on Blumer, 1939, and Lofland, 1981.

At the height of the Cabbage Patch doll fad, a New Jersey dentist opened a summer camp for dolls in his home. He received responses from 200 people—some from as far as Germany and England—and had a final enrollment of 53 "campers." About 20 percent of the dolls were sent by adults.

refers to relatively temporary standards of appearance and behavior that are considered to be socially acceptable or desirable. For example, men's hairstyles in this country were generally short in the 1950s, longer in the 1960s and 1970s, and shorter again in the 1980s (although not so short as the "butch" and "crew" cuts of the 1950s).

**Fads**—such as owning a Cabbage Patch doll—have a shorter life span than fashions and rarely become general standards for behavior or appearance; but what they lack in staying power and social acceptability they make up for in the enthusiasm of their followers. In the 1930s trying to swallow goldfish was popular among college students, just as trying to fit as many people as possible into a telephone booth (or a Volkswagen Beetle) was in the 1950s.

Collective behavior has long been an important problem for sociologists because it so often has a profound impact on societies. Crowd behavior is highly visible, and when it is focused on grievances over social conditions, it openly threatens the status quo and stability of social institutions and those who occupy positions of authority in them. People in crowds also have the collective capacity to seriously threaten both life and property, from killing people and burning and looting buildings to unseating governments in violent revolutions. Such violence may provoke equal or greater violence from authorities, resulting in a polarization of society as people take sides. It is also not uncommon, however, for authorities such as the police to violently attack a peaceful but disruptive crowd. This, in turn, often provokes a violent response from the crowd.

Most important, the behavior of people in crowds seems to be highly unpredictable, and the combination of danger and unpredictability provides a compelling reason to understand it. In addition—as we will see later in this chapter and in Chapter 21—social movements are, as the definition implies, a form of collective behavior aimed directly at changing or maintaining the cultural, structural, or ecological conditions of social life.

## Mobs

**A mob** is an emotionally aroused, acting crowd that typically has a leader and focuses on a specific goal; and the achievement of this goal usually involves some form of violence. In the late 1800s and early 1900s, for example, lynch mobs were common in the United States and accounted for the murder of more than 5,000 people, most of them blacks living in the South (Cantril, 1963; Raper, 1933).

Mobs often play an important part in bringing about or preventing social change. In the 1930s mobs of Nazis roamed German cities and established a pattern of intimidation of opponents and persecution of Jews that solidified Adolph Hitler's authority and laid the groundwork for the Holocaust. In the 1970s mobs of Japanese tried to prevent the opening of a new airport near Tokyo. In 1980 a mob of Iranians seized the American em-

bassy in Tehran, made hostages of the embassy employees, and precipitated an international crisis that—among other things—played a major part in ending President Carter's hopes for a second term.

Its potential for violence has always made the mob an object of fear. Authoritarian governments rarely allow crowds to gather in public unless they are tightly controlled, in part to prevent a crowd from turning into a mob. In some cases, however, authorities allow mobs to act when this supports the social order. In the American South early in this century, for example, the mutilation and lynching of blacks served to keep blacks "in their place," and it was often inflicted as punishment for "offenses" such as trying to vote or daring to use facilities reserved for whites (Raper, 1933). The mobs in Nazi Germany served Hitler's purposes in a similar way.

In 1985, rioting soccer fans of rival teams in a Brussels stadium caused a wall to collapse, killing dozens of people.

## Riots

Unlike mob action, a **riot** lacks leadership, organization, and clear goals. Riots often allow people to express frustration and anger that have been contained for years. Riots may involve the destruction or theft of property or attacks on people. In 1984, for example, thousands of people in the Tunisian capital of Tunis rioted for three days after the government doubled the price of bread and other staples. Shops that sold luxury goods were attacked, as were drivers of expensive cars, and some 50 people were killed. The government then restored the lower prices, and within a few hours the streets were filled with people in a festive mood celebrating their victory.

As a form of violent collective behavior, the riot has played an important part in the life of most societies. India is struck periodically by riots over the unavailability of food. In the 1960s French students rioted over unpopular government educational policies and the riots eventually resulted in a national strike that brought down the government.

In 1863 residents of New York City rioted in protest against military draft laws instituted to recruit soldiers for the Civil War. In Chicago in 1919 and in Detroit in 1943 rioting whites attacked blacks in two of America's worst race riots. In the 1930s conflict between striking workers and management resulted in frequent riots. In the 1960s blacks rioted in American ghettos to protest poverty and racial discrimination. In 1968 at the Democratic National Convention in Chicago, hundreds of anti-Vietnam War demonstrators clashed with police in the streets outside the convention hall, and although many observers defined the demonstrators as the rioters, an Illinois Commission later decided that it was the police who had rioted by attacking nonviolent demonstrators indiscriminately and without justification.

Riots often pose a more serious danger to social order than mobs do precisely because they have neither leadership nor clear goals. A mob, for example, can often be stopped by affecting or removing its leader or by meeting its goals without the use of violence. Once a riot has started, however, it is difficult to stop without the use of equal or greater violence, and each use of official violence often has the effect of only deepening the anger and motivation of rioters.

## Panics

As a form of collective behavior, a **panic** is an attempt by people in a crowd or a mass to escape some kind of perceived danger or respond to a situation of acute uncertainty. By definition a panic is an irrational response in that cooperation breaks down completely and this usually results in greater danger, not greater safety. When someone yells "Fire!" in a crowded theater, for example, a panic reaction would be for everyone to try to run to the exits at once. The result would most likely be injury or death for most of the people and escape for a relative few.

Panics can also occur at the level of masses. When people hear that a bank is about to fail, for example, they may panic and rush to withdraw their money, an action that ensures the bank's failure. In 1984 false rumors that the Continental Illinois bank was about to fail began to spread, and large-scale depositors withdrew billions of dollars in a matter of weeks. The bank—the eighth largest in the United States—was not in good financial

Thousands of residents of Bhopal, India, fled in panic when deadly gas from a Union Carbide plant was accidentally released into the air, killing and seriously injuring tens of thousands of people. Panic also struck thousands of depositors who raced to withdraw their funds from Ohio savings and loan institutions after one of the largest S&L's in the state failed in 1985.

shape when the rumors began to circulate, but it was not in immediate danger of failing. By mid-summer, however, more than $20 billion had been withdrawn and neither the federal government nor the bank management was able to restore public confidence in the bank. Finally, the Federal Depositor's Insurance Corporation had to step in and make an arrangement that ensured the bank's survival. Panic withdrawals were prevented in Ohio in 1985 because the governor ordered the temporary closing of the state's savings and loan institutions after one of the largest of them failed.

### Hysteria

Panic in crowds and masses is often preceded by mass **hysteria,** which is defined as a state of rapidly spreading anxiety based on a danger or opportunity that is usually misperceived.

In 1982, for example, Americans became aware of a new disease called Acquired Immune Deficiency Syndrome (or AIDS) that appeared to be confined to a small subgroup of the population—most notably male homosexuals (Fettner and

Check, 1984). AIDS victims lose their ability to combat even the simplest illnesses, and in a majority of cases at that time the disease was fatal.

Anxiety over AIDS spread quickly. Although discrimination against homosexuals was certainly nothing new in the United States, it now took on an added dimension of open fear of any physical contact with homosexuals, a fear based on the mistaken belief that the disease could be transmitted merely by being near or touching an AIDS victim. Suddenly, homosexuals were losing jobs and being denied housing that was formerly open to them. Many health workers and ambulance personnel refused to handle possible AIDS victims; some police officers wore rubber gloves and protective masks while arresting homosexuals.

As telephone hot lines were flooded with thousands of anxious calls from around the country, it became clear that mass hysteria had set in and that a medical emergency was compounded by widespread fear based on false beliefs. For homosexuals, the result was a double-victimization—once by the disease and again by the mass hysteria that fol-

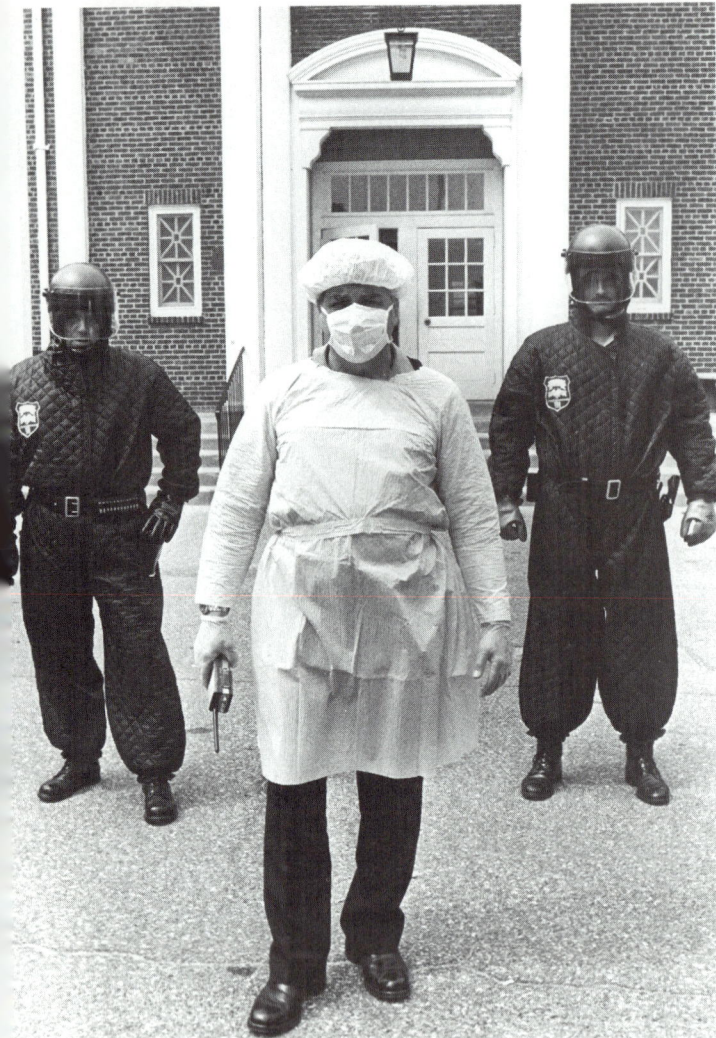

In the hysteria that accompanied the AIDS epidemic, police and other public workers responded with extreme measures to protect themselves from what they erroneously believed to be a highly contagious disease.

lowed. In 1984 Australia went so far as to pass a law making it a felony for homosexuals to donate their blood.

Mob action, riots, panics, and mass hysteria are forms of collective behavior that have attracted much attention from sociologists, and for more than a century they have tried to explain why and how they occur.

## Some Theories of Behavior in Crowds

Perspectives on crowd behavior can be divided into roughly two types. The earliest theories—and some later ones—looked upon behavior in crowds as largely a matter of psychology. Crowds were viewed as having personalities and tendencies that explained the behavior of people in them. In fact, the earliest theories treated crowds as if they were some kind of distinct organism with a mind and life of their own. Later theories have placed much more importance on the social conditions that cause collective behavior and the social processes through which it occurs. In short, over the last century thinking about collective behavior has become much less psychological and much more sociological.

Like sociology itself, theories of crowd behavior first emerged in the nineteenth century, a period of history that was full of rapid social change that often involved violent social upheaval and revolution. While this led social thinkers to pay a lot of attention to social conditions and the characteristics of social environments, it provided particular reasons to focus on crowds and masses, for in many cases—one of the most notable being the French Revolution—they played a direct and important role in bringing about social change.

Those who opposed change tended to see crowds and masses as menacing forces that threatened the very fabric of civilized society, whereas those who favored radical change were more likely to see them as evidence of an aroused lower class whose awareness of social conditions was, to paraphrase Marx, the engine of social change and progress. Clearly, many early theorists of collective behavior were particularly affected by the times they lived in; they used unscientific data and often had a personal ax to grind. Nowhere was this more apparent than in the nevertheless pioneering work of Gustave Le Bon.

### Le Bon and "Mob Psychology"

Writing at the end of the nineteenth century, Gustave Le Bon made one of the earliest serious attempts to analyze collective behavior with a psychology of crowds—**mob psychology.** Like all thinkers, his ideas reflected both the social conditions and the dominant ideas of his time. France had endured a violent revolution a century before and the pace of social change had, if anything, quickened since. The working class struggled for better working conditions and a greater share of political power, and the emerging middle class of capitalists threatened the dominant position of the aristocratic upper class. The old order of feudalism was gone, but capitalist society was too new to provide a sense of order and continuity in social life.

In short, social change was rapid and often accompanied by violence, and Le Bon (1895/1960) feared that his society was going out of control. The social bonds and obligations of feudalism were gone, and Le Bon feared that his society would be ruled by mobs drawn from masses of ignorant and irresponsible members of the lower class. As he put it,

> Today the claims of the masses are becoming more and more sharply defined, and amount to nothing less than a determination to utterly destroy society as it now exists, with a view to making it hark back to . . . before the dawn of civilization. (p. 16)

Le Bon believed that collective violence occurs because people who are prone to violence are drawn together by some event. This is what Turner (1964) called Le Bon's **convergence theory:** crowds consist of like-minded people who assemble in one place. Thus, collective violence depends initially on a collection of individuals who are prone to violent behavior.

Perhaps most important in Le Bon's theory is his reliance on leaders who control crowds through a kind of hypnotism. "A crowd," he wrote, "is a servile flock that is incapable of ever doing without a master" (p. 118). Le Bon believed that leaders exert power by flattery, strong rhetoric, the presentation of only one side of an issue, repetition, and the clever use of symbols. In short, they succeed by appealing to the nonrational, emotional, and unconscious motivations of people in crowds. People can be controlled through such techniques, he believed, because when in crowds they are "leveled"—which is to say, everyone comes to think, feel, and behave in the same way. Le Bon believed that in a crowd people no longer exist as individuals: only the crowd exists.

According to Le Bon, once a crowd forms, several consequences follow. People lose their ability to think rationally, and they lose touch with abstract ideas (especially those about right and wrong). Crowd members are very suggestible in this state and will readily do what they are told. They become shortsighted and misperceive what is going on around them. To Le Bon, then, crowds are suggestible, blind, and fickle.

As a process, crowd behavior in Le Bon's view was quite simple and depended on what he called **contagion.** People copy one another's behavior, and this sets off a chain reaction—much like the effect of throwing a tennis ball onto a floor covered with cocked mousetraps.

Le Bon deserves credit for making an early connection between social conditions and collective behavior and for drawing attention to the importance of unconscious psychological motivations (such as those that play a role in lynch mobs). Most important, he focused serious attention on crowds as a subject of study. His ideas, however, have little credibility among sociologists. There is no compelling evidence that contagion either describes or explains what goes on in crowds, or that social influence in crowds differs substantially from social influence in general. Nor is there any evidence that hypnotism operates in crowds.

Le Bon's most serious shortcomings are his view of the nature of crowds and his reliance on the power of leaders as an explanation of collective behavior. As we will see shortly, many studies find that people in crowds are far more rational than Le Bon thought they were; and there is a division of labor in most crowds that is ignored by Le Bon's view of crowds as a group in which all members are alike. For example, during anti-Vietnam War demonstrations in the 1960s, some demonstrators specialized in acting as "medics" who took care of the injured, while others looked out for police movements and possible avenues of escape.

People do not all think, feel, and act alike in crowds (see McPhail and Wohlstein, 1983). Watch a crowd at a sporting event and you will see a lot of variation in what people do and appear to feel. Some watch the game enthusiastically; some talk with friends and seem to ignore the game; some play games that compete with what is happening on the field—such as passing a person from row to row. Le Bon barely scratched the surface of the complexity of collective behavior in even the most common social situations.

**Blumer and Stampeding Cattle** In the 1930s the American sociologist Herbert Blumer (1939) used many of the same assumptions that underlay Le Bon's work. Unlike Le Bon, however, Blumer focused on interaction among crowd members rather than on what happened between leaders and followers, and this was an important shift in emphasis.

Like Le Bon, Blumer assumed that crowds were homogeneous and that individuals in crowds were irrational. Blumer also relied on a concept he called **circular reaction,** which was like the concept of contagion in viewing crowd behavior as a chain reaction, but differed in an important respect: people in crowds do not simply set each other off; rather, when one person affects a second, the act of witnessing the result acts back on the first person and *amplifies* the affect. So, my excitement stimulates excitement in you, and when I see your heightened excitement I become still more excited, and so on. In this way, Blumer believed, feelings and tendencies in crowds spread and increase rapidly. To describe this process, Blumer used the image of a herd of cattle in which cows progressively become more and more excited until they stampede.

Blumer believed that crowds form around some precipitating incident. Then people "mill around," talking with one another, being stimulated by and amplifying one another's moods. Someone does something, and instead of interpreting the behavior as they would normally do, people react without thinking. As collective excitement builds, it becomes focused on a common object, and in the final stage of crowd excitement, people act impulsively and irrationally toward the object.

Blumer's ideas have many problems in common with those of Le Bon—most notably his reliance on the idea of circular reaction and his assumptions about the homogeneity and irrationality of people in crowds. Also like Le Bon's theory, Blumer's theory of circular reaction describes more than it explains and cannot explain why not everyone in a crowd is aroused or why the mood in a crowd can change quickly.

Both Le Bon's and Blumer's theories have a deeper problem, however. Both viewed crowds as irrational, uncivilized collections of people, and Blumer went so far as to liken them to herds of cattle. This meant, of course, that neither fully appreciated the fact that many crowds contain people who can protest social conditions in no other way. Thus, unlike the views of theorists discussed later in this chapter, those of Le Bon and Blumer de-emphasize the importance of collective behavior as both a reflection of social problems and an important vehicle for positive social change.

## Collective Behavior as Social Interaction

Social interaction is the process through which we interpret one another's behavior, define the situation, and act in relation to one another and to the cultural and structural factors that make up a social environment. From a social interaction perspective, collective behavior poses no theoretical problems that are any more challenging than those posed by any other social behavior. How are collective situations defined? How do people make choices within them? What do the patterns of interaction in crowds look like?

**Emergent Norms** One of the paradoxes of collective behavior is that individuals in crowds behave in a variety of ways, but at the same time often feel a sense of shared purpose with people they have never met. Often there is no prior planning in crowd behavior, and yet clearly discernible patterns of expectation and interaction emerge from crowd situations, and participants feel constrained by a set of informal norms. How does this happen? Where do these norms come from?

Turner and Killian (1972) offered **emergent norm theory** to explain how patterns of interaction and expectation evolve in crowds. In most social situations, we rely on the definition of the situation in order to know "what is going on" and, therefore, what is expected of us and others. When shopping in a store, for example, we are bound by certain legal norms (we have to pay for what we buy) and informal folkways (we have to wait our turn).

In a crowd, however, the definition of the situation may be quite unclear and fluid. Suppose, for example, that we have been waiting for eight hours outside a department store in Buffalo, New York, in order to buy Cabbage Patch dolls as Christmas presents. People are cold, a little irritable, and anxious that there will not be enough dolls to go around or that the announcement of a new shipment was false. What norms apply here as the store-opening time nears? How do you know "what goes" and what does not?

Chances are that you would look around at what other people are doing. Are they staying in line? Are people slowly inching their way toward the door so that they will be in a better position when the manager opens it? In usual circumstances the norms about waiting in line would be clear; but the anxiety and tension in this situation create unusual circumstances in which no one is quite sure if other people will abide by the usual norms. There is, in short, a sense of anomie—or normlessness—in this crowd. In this situation people look at what people are actually doing in order to establish the norms that will apply. This is just the opposite of what usually happens: rather than having the patterns of interaction emerge out of an established set of norms, the norms emerge out of a pattern of interaction.

According to emergent norm theory, people in crowds look for signs of what norms will apply in that situation. This is due, in part, to earlier experiences in groups in which behavior is rewarded or punished depending on whether or not it conforms to group norms. Since people are actively looking for norms to emerge, they are unusually susceptible to suggestion and are likely to accept emerging norms with little criticism. They tend, in short, to approach all collective situations with a certain amount of anxiety and, therefore, a desire to define the situation quickly so that they know what is going on. This, in turn, means that people tend to accept definitions of crowd situations without exercising very much independent critical judgment.

The desire of crowd members to identify quickly a set of norms to guide their behavior means that some visible members can have considerable power to define the situation through the example set by their behavior. In a tense, yet ambiguous crowd situation, the difference between violence and peaceful protest may hinge on whether someone yells "Get them!" or "Everybody stay calm!"

Emergent norm theory is useful because it focuses on the ways in which social interaction in crowds leads to the emergence of norms. Crowds generally contain a diverse collection of people who have diverse motives, feelings, and beliefs about what is going on, and yet somehow through social interaction a common purpose and set of shared expectations often emerge. From this perspective, behavior in crowds—like any social behavior—is governed by norms. It is not a unique kind of behavior whose causes lie outside the boundaries of regular social life.

Emergent norm theory contains traces of a problem found with its predecessors: a tendency to view behavior in crowds as less rational than that in other social situations. More recent theories have directly challenged that longstanding view, arguing that interaction is no less rational or intelligent in a crowd than in any other social situation.

**Decision Theory**  As a view of human nature and behavior, decision theory is about as far as one could get from Le Bon's view of uncivilized mobs. **Decision theory** has been applied to many aspects of human behavior, and essentially rests on the idea that people usually act rationally in order to solve problems. From this perspective, collective behavior represents the efforts of people in crowds to act together in order to solve problems.

Problem solving—whether by an individual on a desert island or by members of a crowd at a football game—is a process that may be thought of as consisting of a series of steps (Luce and Raiffa, 1957; Raiffa, 1970). We gather and interpret information about what is happening and about what might happen; we may list our options and rank them according to the desirability of their probable consequences; and we make choices in order to gain the best possible outcome.

Suppose, for example, that you are eating lunch in a college dining room and suddenly some people start throwing food at each other. It is the last day of the term and there is a lot of laughing as food flies through the air. What do you do? According to decision theory, the behavior of most people will depend on some weighing of the probable consequences: What happens if I join in? What happens if I just sit here? If I try to stop it? If I leave?

If you join in, you might have some fun or release some tension; you might also get covered with food, be punished by college authorities, and offend other students. If you just sit there, you run the risk of having some students think you do not like to have a "good time"—and you will probably end up with food on you anyway. If you try to stop it, even those students who do not participate might think you are being a "wet blanket"; and if

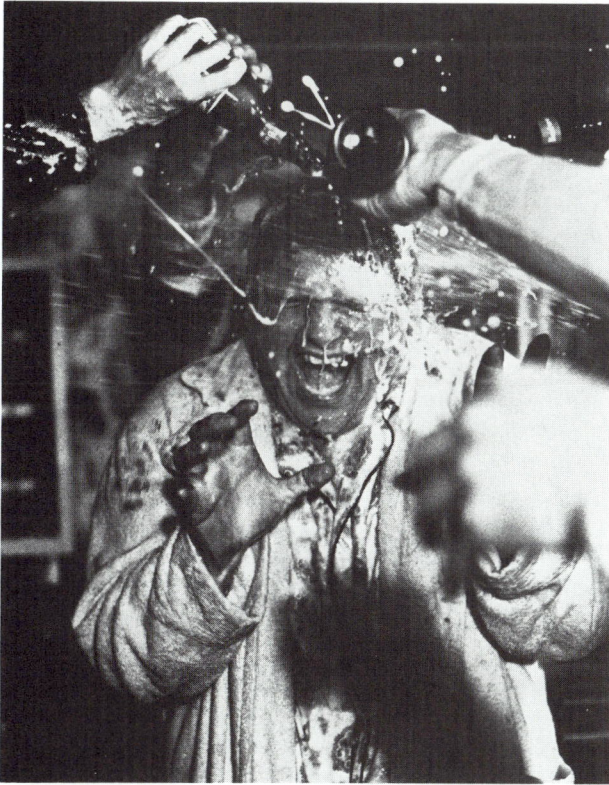

you leave, you leave your lunch behind along with everything else.

Somewhere among those options you will decide which consequences are the most important to you, and this will be the basis of your decision. Notice that in this and many other crowd situations, people are not all behaving in the same way, even though you might later describe the incident as a "food riot" in which everyone was throwing food around. Thus, there is at least circumstantial evidence that people are making decisions about their behavior, rather than blindly copying the behavior of the food throwers.

Notice also that your decision depends heavily on how other people react, both to your behavior and to the behavior of others. This kind of situation—in which the consequences for an individual depend on what other people decide to do—is called a *game*.

**Game Theory** According to **game theory,** each of us tries to achieve what is called a "minimax" solution, one that minimizes our costs and maximizes our rewards (Luce and Raiffa, 1957; Zagare, 1984).

In order to discover such a solution in a crowd situation, each member has to consider what other people in the crowd are likely to do, and this process is at the heart of the game theory approach to collective behavior (Berk, 1974a, 1974b).

In game theory, the decision facing crowd members boils down to two problems: Will others support what I do, and what difference will it make? Of the two, predicting whether or not other people in the crowd will support what we do is the most difficult problem, and the ability to predict depends on a number of structural and ecological characteristics of crowds (Berk, 1974b). For example, the more people there are who appear to act in a particular way and the more visible their behavior is, the more likely we are to perceive support for ourselves if we join in.

From a gaming perspective, collective behavior is a case of collective problem solving in which individuals compromise and cooperate with one another in order to maximize their rewards through the support of one another. "Each crowd member tries to make the most of the situation while constrained by the need for support from others" (Berk, 1974b, p. 73). This approach is most useful in explaining why people participate in crowds that require some measure of cooperation.

It is also useful, however, for understanding crowds that involve competition among members (Berk, 1974b). Suppose, for example, that you hear on the radio that a nuclear power plant is about to "melt down" and cause a nuclear disaster in your city. A rational response would be for everyone to leave the city in a rapid but orderly manner, for if everyone makes a mad dash for the highways and public transportation systems, the confusion and inevitable accidents might make it virtually impossible for all but a few to escape danger.

Suppose, however, that you notice a few people driving wildly toward the highway entrance ramp, screaming out their car windows for everyone else to get out of the way and waving pistols in the air just to make sure everyone gets the point. You might conclude that those few people have panicked unnecessarily and that the best thing for everyone to do is to proceed in a quick and orderly manner and ignore the panicked few.

It is also possible, however, that the mad dashers know something that you do not—that, perhaps, the reactor has already melted down and fatal radiation is only minutes behind you. In that case, it may be impossible for everyone to get out alive, and only those who force their way through will escape unharmed. This is a very different kind of game from a peace demonstration in which individual crowd members cooperate with one another in order to accomplish desired goals, for in this game the rational choice is to maximize the chance of achieving your goal of survival by struggling against everyone else.

The line between cooperation and competition, then, is a thin one, and which side of it you wind up on depends on your perceptions of what is going on; and, as we have seen before, our perceptions of the world are strongly affected by the social environment. The environment provides us with *information*, a key ingredient in collective behavior; and *rumor* is an important social mechanism through which information is communicated.

**Rumor**  A **rumor** is an unverified belief that arises from informal social interaction. Most rumors arise in situations in which people need to have information that is otherwise unavailable to them (Rosnow and Fine, 1976): when daily routines are disrupted (the buses are all running late); when the environment changes drastically (there is an earthquake or a hurricane); when we must make choices but are uncertain of the outcomes (which courses do you sign up for?); when there is sustained tension (the families of prisoners of war must wait for news); or when there is prolonged boredom without knowing the cause (people wait in a theater line that stretches halfway around a city block and does not move).

That rumor spreads informally does not mean that it is a random process in which all people are equally likely to be included. Instead, most rumors are nurtured by established social networks of people who share social positions that make the content of the rumor particularly relevant to them (Milgram, 1977). In Lillian Hellman's powerful play, *The Children's Hour*, a girl in a boarding school mentions to her grandmother that she saw the two women who run the school hugging each other in their room. This simple observation soon becomes embellished into a supposed lesbian relationship, and the rumor spreads quickly among the parents of girls who attend the school—but not in

the community as a whole. In similar ways, rumors about proposed tax changes affecting business will spread more quickly among business executives and corporate secretaries than among poor people living in urban ghettos.

As a social process, rumor has been viewed both as an example of human failing and as an important and normal part of social life. In early studies of rumor, Bartlett (1932) and later Allport and Postman (1947) treated rumors as accounts that are passed in series from one person to another, and they used experiments to explore how this kind of rumor occurs. They asked one person, for example, to describe a picture or repeat a simple statement to the next person in a chain and recorded each transmission at every step until the last person was reached.

In these and many subsequent experiments the findings were the same: as the account is transmitted down the line, it tends to become shorter, more concise, and easier to understand (an effect called *leveling*); limited to a relatively few details (*sharpening*); and more coherent and consistent with the interests and beliefs of the participants (*assimilation*). The general conclusion from these experiments was that distortion is inevitable in rumor because of faulty perception and memory, and the inability to repeat a message verbatim.

In spite of the fact that many replications of the Allport and Postman experiments generated similar results, many researchers have challenged the results because they were obtained in an artificial laboratory setting. Caplow (1947), for example, argued that in many situations—such as combat—the accuracy of information is so important that people are critical about what they accept and what they subsequently pass on to others. The fact that rumor usually travels through established social networks means that unreliable people tend to be discounted and eliminated from the network. The result, he believed, is that rumors may become more—not less—accurate as they go along.

Others, such as Festinger (1948) and Peterson and Gist (1951), have also pointed out that in many situations rumors become longer and more elaborate—not shorter and simpler—as they are spread through a social network. This may be due in part to the fact that since rumors are social beliefs they must be plausible and complete before we believe in them; and this requirement encourages the development of details related to the main piece of information.

Several researchers have argued that rumor is part of a collective effort to define social situations (Shibutani, 1966, 1968; Turner, 1964). So long as something important is unexplained, there is "a distracting sense of incompleteness" and a desire "to understand the new circumstances by completing the incomplete" (Shibutani, 1968, p. 579). The more important it is to us to understand a situation and the more ambiguous the available information is, the more likely it is that rumors will develop as a way for increasing our understanding and defining the situation with greater clarity (Jaeger, Anthony, and Rosnow, 1979). As rumors develop, they tend to become more plausible and complete. Details that do not fit are eliminated, whereas those that are consistent with the rumor are added, thereby making it more convincing.

According to Shibutani, the ways in which rumor develops depend on the social situation. When the situation is relatively unimportant to the participants, information is handled through established social networks. In situations of high excitement, on the other hand, such as when a natural disaster strikes, established networks tend to break down and new lines of communication spring up quickly and spontaneously. Under such conditions, it is harder to verify new information before it is spread further.

When people are bored, rumor can serve quite different social functions: it can be a source of entertainment or a vehicle for expressing social attitudes. Students may spread bad rumors about a disliked teacher because it allows them to express their negative feelings; and by passing it through the social network of students, they strengthen the bonds between them. The ultimate truth or falsity of the rumor is, in this case, irrelevant to its social functions.

Like all social behavior, the process of spreading rumors has a structure that can involve a variety of different social roles (Shibutani, 1966, 1968). Transmitters simply pass on messages ("I heard that today's final exam is going to include the whole book, not just the last four chapters."), while interpreters place them in context, evaluate their truth or falsity, and speculate about details that are left out ("Where'd you hear that? That doesn't make any sense; I was in class when the announcement was made. Then again, worse things have happened in that course."). Skeptics play the important role of challenging new information ("That can't be true."), and agitators urge action based on the rumor ("That's totally outrageous; let's go see the dean.").

This model of the rumor process clearly reflects more recent views of collective behavior, in that it looks upon such behavior as a rational process through which collections of people try to achieve goals, define situations, and take action that they perceive as being in their best interests. From this perspective, collective behavior is to be understood as a normal consequence of the cultural, structural, and ecological conditions in which people live.

Nowhere is this more apparent than in social movements—collective behavior organized for the purpose of preventing or bringing about social change.

## Social Movements

**Social movements** are organized attempts to change or preserve aspects of a social environment. In addition to being organized, they are social in that they attempt to change cultural or structural aspects of society; but they are social in another perhaps more important respect as well. For example, so long as members of minorities do not identify themselves as members of a minority, they have no other explanation for their disadvantages and mistreatment than their own personal characteristics or luck, fate, or other factors beyond their control. Once the existence of prejudice and discrimination are identified for them, however, the social problems of which their personal troubles are a part become apparent to them. It is only when individuals go beyond psychological and biological frameworks and focus on their relationships to their environments that social movements become possible.

Social movements usually focus on reform, revolution, or resistance to change. **Reform movements** try to improve existing arrangements by altering specific cultural, structural, or ecological aspects of them. Various civil rights move-

ments—of blacks, women, or gays, for example—do not seek to dismantle and change the entire society; rather, they demand that members of those social categories have the right to participate fully in political, economic, and other social structures and receive a fair share of wealth, power, and prestige. In similar ways, movements to save the physical environment often focus on specific cultural, structural, or ecological arrangements (such as the choice between solar or nuclear technology to provide energy) rather than society as a whole.

Unlike reform movements, **revolutions** attempt to replace an existing social or ecological arrangement with a different one (Goldstone, 1982; Skocpol, 1979; see also Chapter 18). The French Revolution attempted to replace a monarchy with a more democratic government; and the American Revolution—which began as a reform movement to guarantee colonists the same rights as other British subjects—rapidly turned into a revolution that completely separated the colonies from the British Empire. In early 1917 the Czar of Russia was overthrown and replaced by a government that began to introduce a kind of Western democracy. Later in that same year, the Bolsheviks under the leadership of Lenin carried out yet a second revolution that led to the socialist state that rules the Soviet Union today.

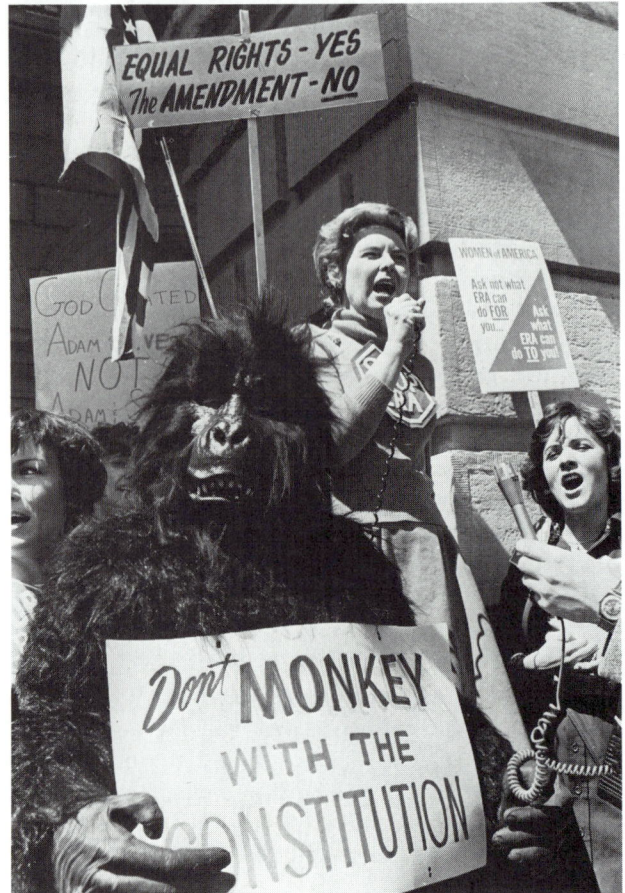

everyone has some access to major institutions. In such a world, it makes sense to view social movements and other forms of collective behavior as aberrations, as the result of the personal troubles of individuals. Why else, after all, would anyone take to the streets and protest when legitimate avenues were available to them to make their grievances known and to effect change?

One answer, of course, is that the distribution of power is not pluralistic. From a conflict point of view, legitimate means for changing a society are controlled by an elite, and the only way for subordinate groups to bring about change is through some kind of organized action. To go against dominant groups, however, requires *resources* as well as motivation, and this brings us to more recent—and more sociological—theories of social movements.

## Resource Mobilization Theory

Inequality, discontent, frustration, anxiety, and social isolation are nothing new to complex societies, and the relative rarity of social movements underscores the fact that such conditions, even when shared by many people, are not in themselves sufficient to bring about collective action (Jenkins and Perrow, 1977; Oberschall, 1973). In response to this inadequacy of classical social movement theories, **resource mobilization theory** argues that people with common interests form social movements only when they have access to resources—such as time, people, leadership skills, money, and organization—that give them some hope of achieving their goals in spite of opposition from the powerful groups that dominate society (Jenkins, 1983).

It takes time, energy, and money to change the world, and most people can spare little of either, especially if they are poor. This simple fact helps explain why so many social movements—even those that act in the interests of poor people—tend to draw heavily on the time and energy of middle- and upper-class, relatively well-educated people. The Cuban Revolution that brought Fidel Castro to power was founded by young professionals and well-educated intellectuals (Draper, 1962). Over two-thirds of the founders of the Chinese Communist Party came from upper-class—not peasant—backgrounds (Lee, 1968). A large percentage of the activists in the civil rights, anti-Viet-nam War, women's, and nuclear freeze movements have been young college students, middle-class, nonworking women, professionals such as physicians and lawyers, and the elderly—all of whom have relatively high levels of free time and autonomy (Snow, Zurcher, and Eckland-Olson, 1980).

The fact that disadvantaged groups—the ones most likely to want social change—are the least likely to command the resources necessary to sustain a social movement has led several theorists to argue that such movements succeed only with support from the outside. In the civil rights movement, blacks had to attract the support of elite outsiders—in this case the federal government,

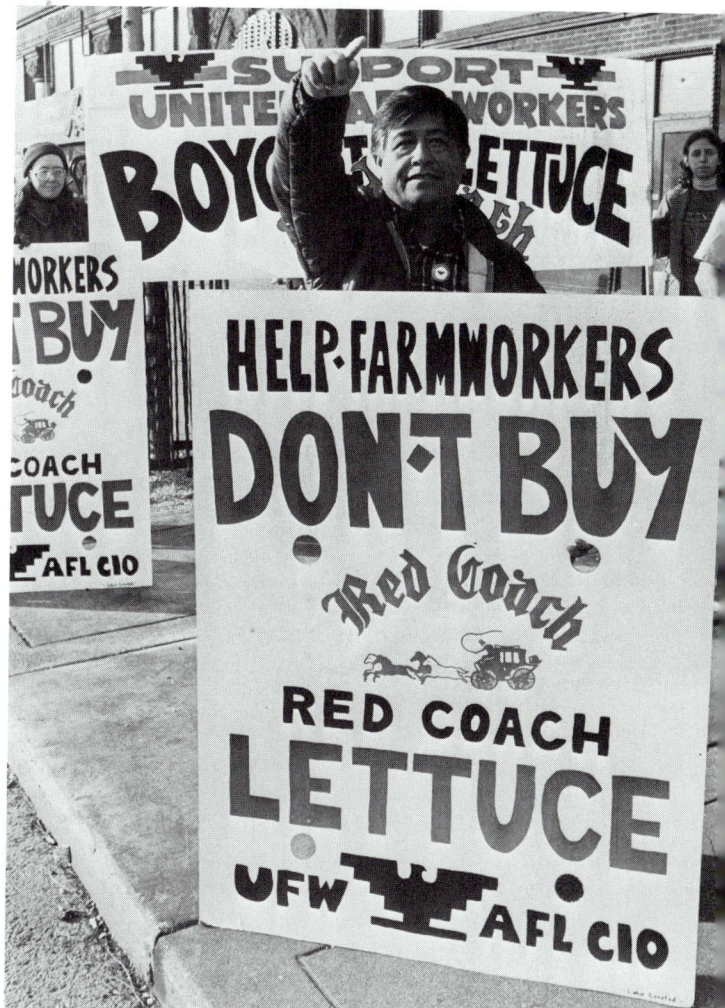

Cesar Chavez's United Farm Workers movement drew significant outside support from sympathetic organizations.

In 1968, strikes by students, later joined by workers and farmers, managed to topple the French government and bring the economy to a virtual halt.

upper-middle- and upper-class Northern whites, and young college students (McCarthy and Zald, 1973; Oberschall, 1973). Similarly, the farm workers movement relied on strong support from liberal churches and powerful labor unions (Jenkins, 1981b, 1983). As Jenkins and Perrow (1977) wrote, "collective action is rarely a viable option because of a lack of resources and the threat of repression. . . . When deprived groups do mobilize, it is due to the interjection of external resources" (p. 251).

As McAdam (1982) pointed out, this view suggests that most groups in a population are powerless and that initiation of social movements lies with those groups that control crucial resources. It is they, and not deprived groups, who are ulti-

mately responsible for social movements and, therefore, for social change.

Resource mobilization theory is a substantial improvement over classical theories in several respects (see McAdam, 1982). First, it explicitly defines social movements as organized social behavior rather than characterizing them as little more than manifestations of shared feelings of tension, anxiety, and discontent. It has, in short, put the "social" back into social movements. Second, by taking social movements out of the realm of the psychological problems of individuals, mobilization theory makes movements more understandable as political actions that are as rationally motivated as any other political behavior including that of those who control social institutions.

Third, mobilization theory includes the influence of groups outside social movements in order to explain the emergence and development of social movements. Classical theories focused primarily if not exclusively on the characteristics of movements and their participants. Finally, resource mobilization theory underscores the importance of organization to the success of social movements. Movements do not depend only on the motivation and intensity of feeling among their participants; rather, like all organizations, they require a steady supply of resources that include everything from money to people with administrative skills.

Although mobilization theory has stimulated a great deal of interest in what was considered by many to be a dying field in sociology, it has several weaknesses. In general, it is more effective at explaining the success or failure of movements initiated by those who already have some power in society, as was the case with environmental and consumer groups (McCarthy and Zald, 1973). It is less successful at explaining movements among minorities who are generally excluded from legitimate means for bringing about change (Piven and Cloward, 1979).

It is important to note that the involvement of elites in social movements by powerless groups can have negative as well as positive effects (Jenkins, 1981b). If a movement becomes dependent on outside support from elite groups, it may take fewer risks for fear of alienating its sponsors. Since members of the elite have an interest in preserving the social arrangements that support their elite status, they may support some social movements in order to ultimately gain control over them and limit their effectiveness.

A more serious problem with resource mobilization theory is that by focusing on the importance of outside support, it underestimates the resources of minorities and their ability to bring about change on their own. For example, McAdam's (1982) analysis of the black civil rights movement during the late 1950s suggests that it was not a sudden infusion of outside support that led to an increase of black civil rights activity; it was just the other way around. Increased militancy led to increased levels of outside support. In their analysis of strikes in France, Shorter and Tilly (1974) emphasized the importance of preexisting orga-

nization among workers and "the availability of a structure which identifies, accumulates, and communicates grievances on the one hand, and facilitates collective action on the other" (p. 284).

An additional problem with mobilization theory is that it has yet to include a clear definition of "resources." Since the concept can include anything from organizational skills to money, it is usually possible to find an increase of some kind of resource that precedes the emergence, rise, or decline of a social movement. It is also possible, therefore, to find many instances in which resources of some kind increased without leading to a social movement. As theorists define resources more narrowly, it will be possible to test the theory more conclusively.

## Political Process Theory

As we have seen, whereas classical movement theory focuses on the intensity of feeling among participants, resource mobilization theory focuses primarily on the importance of support (or the lack of it) from outside the movement. Skocpol (1979), Tilly (1978a), McAdam (1982), and others concentrated on an important additional aspect of the problem: what goes on both inside and outside social movements. At the heart of what is called **political process theory** is the idea that social movements "develop in response to an ongoing process of interaction between movement groups and the larger sociopolitical environment they seek to change" (McAdam, 1982, p. 40).

The emergence of a political protest movement depends on a combination of factors. First, there must be an opportunity to bring about change, which means that the more vulnerable dominant groups and institutions are, the more likely open opposition to them will be. When, for example, the general political situation in a country is unstable, protest movements are more likely to occur, because the forces that might oppose them are weaker and less well organized. In their analysis of strikes in France, Shorter and Tilly (1974) found that strike activity in France was most common during times of intense struggle over who would rule the country.

As Skocpol (1979) argued in her analysis of the French, Chinese, and Russian revolutions, this is

When students demonstrate on American campuses against university investments in corporations doing business in or with the South African government, they are part of a complex international social movement aimed at pressuring American institutions (the U.S. government, universities, and corporations) as a way of bringing about social change in another country.

particularly true in the case of revolutions through which entire social systems may undergo radical change. In each of these cases the state was in crisis, and its inability to perform the basic tasks that defined its role as a social institution prompted opposition from deprived groups such as the peasantry and aggravated old conflicts among dominant groups as well. The 1917 Russian Revolution, for example, took place while the Russian state was in turmoil over repeated defeats in World War I. More recently, the Solidarity labor movement in Poland began amid general social unrest over poor economic conditions (Ash, 1984).

Second, the emergence and success of movements depends on the level of organization that exists among opposing groups. The black civil rights movement, for example, owed much of its success to the existing organizational network of black churches. Widespread church membership among southern blacks provided a source of social movement members, facilitated communication, gave members a sense of belonging that encouraged them to stay with the movement, and generated leaders such as Martin Luther King. Tilly's (1978a) studies of social movements in Europe show a steady change over the past 400 years from temporary disorganized movements to more organized efforts with lasting influence (see also Shorter and Tilly, 1974; Tilly and Tilly, 1981; and Tilly, Tilly, and Tilly, 1975).

Third, even when dominant groups and institutions are vulnerable to pressure and subordinate groups have the potential to organize a social movement, collective action depends on how po-

**Figure 20-2** Political Process and the Emergence of Social Movements

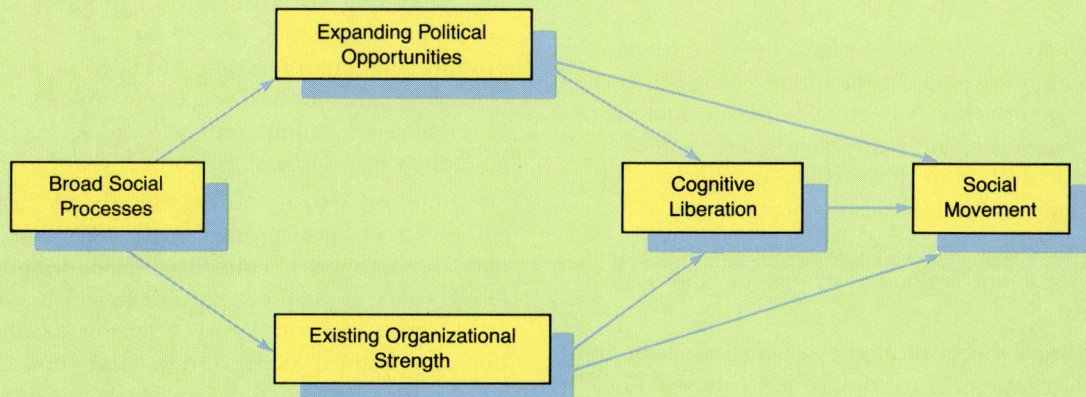

Source: McAdam, *Political Process and the Development of Black Insurgency: 1930–1970,* 1982.

tential participants *think* about their situation. Movements tend to emerge only when people begin to (1) question the legitimacy of dominant authorities, (2) assert what they want as rights, and (3) believe that they are not helpless and that they have the potential to bring about change (Piven and Cloward, 1979).

As McAdam (1982) summarized this part of political process theory, the emergence of social movements depends on expanding political opportunities, the organizational strength of subordinate groups, and "cognitive liberation," or new ways of thinking about their situation and prospects for change (see Figure 20-2). Both the availability of political opportunities and organizational potential are the result of long-term social changes, and "cognitive liberation" results both from the perceived vulnerability of dominant groups and institutions and from the organizational strength of the subordinate group.

Once a movement emerges, its success depends on a variety of factors that involve dynamics within the movement, within its opposition, and in the relationship between the two. Protest movements, for example, may encounter enormous, often violent opposition from governing institu-

tions. This, in turn, may provoke outraged responses that serve to strengthen the movement's organization by increasing membership and outside support. It may also produce a response that is so violent and repressive—as was the case with the Solidarity movement in Poland—that even the most well organized movement cannot sustain itself.

A political process approach offers some promising advantages over its predecessors. Its most important feature may be its inclusiveness, for it tries to cover the entire range between the characteristics of participants and their groups and the society in which they and the forces they oppose exist. It both fills an enormous gap between classical and resource mobilization theory and goes significantly beyond them. Sociological understanding of collective behavior in general and social movements in particular has come a long way from Le Bon's crowd psychology.

As we have seen, social movements often play an important part in changing the cultural, structural, and ecological conditions in which people live, but they are only one of many sources of social change. A fuller discussion of these appears in the next chapter.

## Summary

1. Collective behavior refers to how people think, feel, and behave as members of crowds and masses. In crowds, collective behavior includes casual, conventional, expressive, and collective action. In addition to these kinds of collective behavior, fads and fashion also occur in masses.

2. Some of the most volatile forms of collective behavior are mob actions, riots, panics, and hysteria.

3. Le Bon's theory of mob psychology was one of the earliest attempts to understand collective behavior. His theory places a great deal of importance on leaders, the like-mindedness and irrationality of crowd members, and people copying one another's behavior. Blumer also viewed crowds as essentially irrational, uncivilized collections of people.

4. From a social interaction perspective, collective behavior involves interpretations of behavior and defining the situation. Emergent norm theory, for example, argues that people observe one another's behavior in crowds in order to establish the norms that will apply in that situation. Decision theory and game theory emphasize the rational calculations that people make in deciding how to behave in crowd and mass situations.

5. Rumor is an important ingredient in the social interaction that makes up collective behavior because it is often a major source of information. As in all social situations, people perform different roles in the rumor process, and the patterns through which rumor develops and spreads depend on the social situation.

6. Social movements are organized, collective attempts to change or preserve some aspects of a social environment.

7. Classical theories have in common a reliance on the view that movements develop in order to relieve psychological strain brought about by strain in the social environment. Frustration-aggression theory, for example, argues that relative deprivation leads to frustration, which in turn leads to social movements. Rising expectations as well as rapid improvement followed by sharp declines (the J-curve) have also been suggested as causes of frustration and social action.

8. According to Kornhauser, the existence of mass society in which people feel socially isolated produces feelings of anxiety, and people engage in collective behavior and social movements in order to relieve such feelings and restore a feeling of connection with others.

9. Smelser's structural strain theory is more complex than most preceding theories, but shares with them a view of collective behavior and social movements as based in psychological needs that arise from social conditions. Strain in social conditions, he argues, leads to uncertainty and tension among people who then seize upon generalized beliefs to explain their condition in much the same way that people appeal to magic. Such beliefs are then used to justify collective action around a precipitating incident. The success of collective behavior depends both on the ability of the movement to mobilize participants and on the ability of authorities to exercise social control.

10. Classical theories have been criticized on many grounds, including their reliance on psychological mechanisms to explain collective, social phenomena; their failure to link changes in the level of psychological states such as frustration and relative deprivation with the occurrence of collective behavior; and their failure to acknowledge the importance of social change as a major goal of social movements.

11. Resource mobilization theory focuses on social organization by explaining the emergence and development of social movements in terms of the resources available to the members of discontented groups.

12. Political process theory goes beyond both resource mobilization and classical theory by looking at what goes on both within social movements and in their relationship to a social environment that includes major social institutions. In this model, movements depend on opportunities (such as when the state is weak), existing organizational resources, and a shared perception that collective behavior both is legitimate and has some chance of success.

## Key Terms

## Recommended Readings

FREEMAN, J. (Ed.). (1983). *Social movements of the sixties and seventies.* New York: Longman. A penetrating look at the factors that affected the emergence and progress of 18 social movements of the 1960s and 1970s.

GAMSON, W. A., FIREMAN, B., and RYTINA, S. (1982). *Encounters with unjust authority.* Homewood, IL: Dorsey Press. An intriguing experimental study in which the researchers try to understand what it takes for small groups to rebel against the unjust demands of those in authority.

GENEVIE, L. (Ed.). (1978). *Collective behavior and social movements.* Ithaca, IL: Peacock. A useful collection of articles that survey the broad range of collective behavior.

LIEBMAN, R. C., and WUTHNOW, R. (1983). *The new Christian right.* New York: Aldine. A collection of 12 essays that try to explain why many conservative evangelicals have joined social movements to bring about political change in the United States, and the significance of this political activism for both religion and politics.

NYDEN, P. W. (1984). *Steelworkers rank-and-file: The political economy of a union reform movement.* New York: Praeger. Based on interviews with dozens of union workers in a midwest steel plant, this excellent study shows how rank-and-file union members rebelled against union authorities in an attempt to gain a voice in the affairs of their own union.

WELLER, R. P., and GUGGENHEIM, S. E. (Eds.). (1982). *Power and protest in the countryside: Studies of rural unrest in Asia, Europe, and Latin America.* Durham, NC: Duke University Press Policy Studies. An interesting, well-written collection of articles that explore the origins of protest and rebellion in the rural areas of a variety of societies.

# CHAPTER 21
# Social Change

**Social change** refers to the ways in which the cultural and structural characteristics of social environments change. Questions about change are relatively easy to ask, but they are among the most difficult of those that sociologists try to answer. Why did the women's movement emerge with such strength in the 1960s? Where did capitalism and socialism come from? Will the widespread use of computers make it easier for government to invade the privacy of individuals, and will this threaten democratic institutions?

Much of the relevant information about social change is historical, and it is, therefore, especially difficult to scientifically measure the factors that might account for the change. Added to this is the difficulty with most research problems that sociologists deal with: social change involves simultaneously many factors that affect one another in complex ways. New social ideas and relationships do not come about through "events" that can be precisely located in time or simply explained. We cannot say, for example, that the modern women's movement began on January 4, 1963, in New York City. History is not a simple sequence of events, each of which is neatly caused by previous events. It is, rather, like a river into which flow many streams that mingle and affect both one another and the river itself in countless different ways.

## Culture, Structure, and Social Change

As we have seen in many previous chapters, the functional and conflict perspectives provide two major sociological frameworks for explaining what goes on in societies. These perspectives have also been applied to the problem of social change, and both depend heavily on culture and social structure as sources of change. Before discussing and evaluating their usefulness, we turn first to a look at some of the ways in which culture and structure contribute to change.

### Cultural Sources of Change

As we saw in Chapter 1 and again in Chapter 17, Weber's classic book *The Protestant Ethic and the*

*Spirit of Capitalism* analyzed sociologically the impact of beliefs and values on the structure of economic activity. According to the Calvinist religion, the assignment of people to heaven or hell is determined at birth, and nothing a person can do will alter that fate. Calvinism also placed a high value on frugal living and hard work, and only through success in a "calling" could people lower their anxiety over what their fate would be. Prior to Calvin, the idea of a "calling" in Christianity applied only to religious occupations. Calvin, however, defined all occupations as callings and this injected into everyday work a new religious fervor.

Weber argued that Calvinist beliefs and values contributed to a social environment that fostered the emergence of capitalism, for as an economic system capitalism depends on the accumulation of wealth, which is then available for investment in capital. Weber did not argue that Calvinism alone *caused* capitalism to appear, but he did believe that in this case religious belief played an important part in fostering the development of a new economic system.

There are countless examples of the effect of ideas on social environments. Albert Einstein's theories about the laws that govern the universe were basic to the discovery of atomic fission and the invention of nuclear weapons that have changed the nature of warfare and the structure of political power in the world. The writings of Karl Marx and Friedrich Engels became the cultural basis for revolutions that have radically affected social life in a wide range of societies from the Soviet Union to China to Cuba and Nicaragua. In similar ways the American Declaration of Independence and Constitution embody ideas that have been used as inspirations and blueprints in the transformation of many societies.

As the last two examples show, the effect of culture on social change is particularly evident when ideas take the form of ideology, for an ideology is a set of ideas that serves the function of explaining or justifying particular social arrangements. In his role as leader in the civil rights movement, for example, Martin Luther King, Jr., increased his support among whites by appealing to strongly held values placed on equality, fairness, and justice. He was thus able to enlist the support of whites who otherwise did not share the high value he placed on racial equality in its own right.

Culture also affects social change in more direct ways, especially through norms that explicitly require change. For example, the 1954 Supreme Court decision that outlawed racially segregated schools and the 1983 decision that banned the use of gender by insurance companies in setting rates for life insurance and annuities changed aspects of the social environment, as did federal regulations requiring affirmative action in hiring and federal legislation requiring equal treatment of male and female students in schools that receive federal aid (see Chapters 12 and 13).

## Structural Sources of Change

Just as new ideas often bring about change in social structure, so too does structural change affect culture. One way to break down stereotypes about the members of groups or social categories, for ex-

Our stereotyped beliefs about members of different groups usually do not hold up in the face of direct experience of individuals. Increased interaction is a structural change that can produce profound cultural change.

ample, is to increase social interaction between those who hold stereotypes and those who are the object of them. This is particularly true when the people involved must cooperate with one another in order to achieve shared goals (Allport, 1954).

Laws that forbid racial segregation are aspects of culture that affect the structure of social relationships. Increasing the frequency of interaction between people of different races is a structural change that can, in turn, have the effect of acting back upon culture by weakening stereotyped beliefs. It has long been noted that it is difficult if not impossible to change people's beliefs about and perceptions of others by requiring them to do so; but this example shows how changes in the structure of social relationships—how often people of different races interact with one another—can affect how they perceive and think about other people.

Such effects of social structure on culture are common in social life. Over the last several decades, for example, Americans have become increasingly tolerant and supportive of women working outside the home and having careers. Some of this cultural shift is probably due to the entry of massive numbers of women into the labor force as the American economy shifted from industry to services and the demand for secretaries and other service workers mushroomed. As women had fewer children and saw growing opportunities for themselves outside the home, they had new reason to question the terms on which they were living their lives and to seek alternatives. With so many women working outside the home, it was only a matter of time before cultural ideas about men and women began to adjust to this structural change (see Chapter 13).

We turn now to the ways in which the functional and conflict approaches explain social change in terms of the effects of culture and social structure on societies.

## The Functional Perspective

Durkheim developed the idea that a society is a complex network of interdependent parts—such as the family, government, religion, and economy—each of which either contributes to or interferes with the maintenance of the whole. Parsons (1937, 1951, 1966b, 1971) built on Durkheim's work by exploring what he regarded as the most important sociological problem: What causes groups and societies to stay together or to fall apart? How do culture and social structure affect the adaptability and maintenance of society?

Parsons believed that societies have built-in mechanisms that help them adapt and remain relatively stable. Shared cultural ideas and the relationships between their various parts help a society maintain equilibrium—or "balance"—among its different parts. When strain develops within the system or is introduced from the outside, it stimulates change that helps to reduce it. Social change, then, is a process through which societies "regain their balance" as they adjust to strain that arises through their normal functioning as complex systems.

Consider, for example, what happens in a large city when the police step up enforcement of the law. This produces a bumper crop of arrests, which then strains the ability of court system to conduct trials. More arrests and trials result in a larger number of convictions, and this, in turn, places greater demands on the prison system. The criminal justice system is functioning just as it is supposed to; but, clearly, "something has to give" if breakdown is to be avoided.

Several changes are possible. Crimes such as drug use, prostitution, public drunkenness, and vagrancy, might be reclassified as legal acts, thus reducing the number of arrests and prosecutions. More prisons might be built, diverting resources from other uses, such as the relief of poverty. Or, courts might dispense with some civil rights that "slow down" trials—such as the right of appeal. Each of these changes is a possible response to strain that develops through the normal operation of the interdependent parts that make up the whole of society.

Although Parsons' ideas had considerable influence in the 1940s and 1950s, they came under attack during the 1960s. Because he was interested primarily in the problem of how societies maintain themselves as systems of social relationships and cultural ideas, he paid relatively little attention to social conflict and social change. Like all investigators, he was selective in his choice of research problems; but his focus on social order during a period of intense unrest and awareness of injustice in existing social conditions led many sociologists

For many states, overcrowded prisons and jails have produced a crisis in the criminal justice system.

to misperceive Parsons and the entire functional perspective as inherently supportive of the status quo, including social inequality. As civil rights and antiwar protests challenged the status quo in the United States, any focus on the maintenance of social order as a theoretical problem became increasingly unpopular among sociologists.

In fact, however, leading functional theorists had recognized since the late 1940s that "strain, tension, contradiction, and discrepancy between the component parts of social structure" are inevitable in any society and that these often produce positive social change (Merton, 1948). Merton and others, such as Lewis Coser (1956, 1967), incorporated important elements of social conflict into the functional perspective and highlighted the fact that cultural ideas and social structures can be dysfunctional as well as functional.

## The Conflict Perspective

While Parsons' functional theory views change as an adaptive response to disturbances in an otherwise balanced society, the conflict perspective focuses on fundamentally different aspects of society and social change. Both perspectives view change as a normal social process, but they differ in their basic view of what holds societies together. To Parsons, for example, society is held together primarily by a shared consensus over major values. The conflict perspective, however, views society as held together by the ability of the powerful to coerce the weak, and the resulting conflict among different segments of a society is a continuing source of change.

Marx and Engels (1848/1932) believed that "All history is the history of class conflict"—which in capitalist societies means a struggle between those who own the means of production and those who do not. The exploitation of some groups by others inevitably leads to struggles to alter cultural ideas and social structures that produce and support exploitation and inequality. As Schaff (1970) summarized some of Marx's early ideas,

> To liberate the individual . . . it is necessary to effect a change in social relations and institutions, to overthrow them by overthrowing the prevalent pattern of class relations. (p. 31)

From a conflict perspective, oppressed groups cannot depend on and wait for their society to reach an equilibrium that includes social justice, for without conflict, social arrangements change slowly and tend to remain stable. Consequently, Marx believed that societies inevitably change, but not necessarily for the better; rather, they often perpetuate inequality and injustice in the name of stability and in the interests of powerful elites.

The conflict perspective identifies important aspects of social change, but, like Parsons' functional views, in its extreme form it oversimplifies societies and the process of change. As Dahrendorf (1958) pointed out, the functional and conflict perspectives focus on different aspects of social life and are complementary, not contradictory. All societies, at all times, represent an ongoing tension between social forces that would pull them apart and those that keep them together. Social structure is a source of both social cohesion and social conflict (Merton, 1968).

It is important to note as Simmel did in 1904 that conflict is often functional in societies, and serves the interests of cultural values. In the simplest sense, in order to fight with one another we must *interact*, both with our allies and with our enemies. Increased interaction, in turn, can both increase solidarity in groups and reveal important differences in points of view that must then be dealt with. Thus, conflict can improve relations both within and between groups.

Conflict is often functional in a larger sense, as well (Coser, 1956, 1967). Our legal system, for example, is based on "adversarial" relationships in which both sides in a dispute are represented by lawyers who openly conflict as they fight for their clients. American government is based on conflict among various political parties, an arrangement that we consider more desirable than rule by a single group. Thus, in many ways, conflict is deliberately used to ensure that our society functions as we want it to.

Social conflict arises because internal contradictions are inevitable in any complex society. Americans generally value equality and fairness and yet our society includes cultural ideas and social structures that discriminate against minorities

### PUZZLES:

## WHAT MADE ABORTION A PUBLIC ISSUE?

Prior to the 1970s abortion was never a seriously debated moral issue in the United States. Why did it suddenly emerge as a hotly contested passionate debate that involved primarily women?

The answer has much to do with the women's movement and the Supreme Court, as you will discover in this chapter.

such as nonwhites and women. We value both economic progress and a physical environment free of pollution; and we value the efficiency of rationally structured bureaucracies, and yet we also value the attention to individuals and their feelings that bureaucracies ignore.

The division of industrial societies into social classes that are based on unequal distributions of wealth, power, and prestige produces an inherent structural contradiction: each class often prospers at the expense of the other. Thus, the structure of industrial society produces conflict between social classes, and recurring conflict, in turn, produces pressures for new arrangements and accommodations.

**Social Movements** As we saw in Chapter 20, social movements are one of the most noticeable manifestations of social conflict and are a major source of social change. Social movements are structural in that they are organized and focus on changing some aspect of social relationships, particularly those that affect the distribution of wealth, power, and prestige.

It is important to remember that the appearance of social movements itself depends on both culture and social structure; that is, that social movements are as much an effect of social change as they are a cause. The importance of social conditions in the emergence of social movements, for example, is startlingly clear in the case of the abortion controversy in the United States. Luker (1984) has traced the history of abortion and found that before the 1850s there were no legal restrictions on abortion. Abortion was widespread and practiced primarily by nonphysicians such as midwives and herbalists, and the first attempts to restrict abortion were mounted by physicians primarily as part of their overall attempt to build a professional monopoly over medical care. To do this they attacked both the competence of nonphysicians and the relatively open availability of abortion to women. They were so successful in both areas that between 1850 and 1890 every state of the Union passed laws that allowed only physicians to perform abortions and then only when the pregnancy threatened the mother's life.

The effect of these laws was not to outlaw abortion, but to grant physicians a monopoly over the medical procedure and therefore to limit its availa-

bility somewhat. For the next half-century, abortion was not a public issue in the United States. It was regarded as a medical issue, not a moral one. In the early 1960s, some physicians became concerned over the fact that the law was ambiguous about the growing practice of performing abortions not only to save a mother's life, but to safeguard her mental health as well by, for example, terminating a pregnancy when the emotional strain of bearing a deformed child threatened to overwhelm the mother. This concern led 16 states to amend their statutes to explicitly include mental health as a valid consideration in abortion decisions. Once again the decision was prompted almost entirely by the medical community and did not involve a public moral debate.

In 1973, however, the Supreme Court's decision in *Roe* v. *Wade* overturned all laws designed to regulate abortion; by doing so, the Court returned to individual women control over the decision to have an abortion. The Court focused on the Fourteenth Amendment to the Constitution, which states that no State "shall deprive any person of life, liberty, or property without due process of law." A fetus, the Court ruled, is not a person subject to the protection of the Fourteenth Amendment.

Since that decision, abortion has been available on demand in the United States, and it was here, Luker argued, that the current struggle between the pro-life and pro-choice movements began. The pro-choice movement is led primarily by highly educated professional career women—such as doctors, lawyers, scholars—for whom the right to abortion is crucial to their ability to maintain their position in highly demanding, competitive, male-dominated careers. The pro-life movement, on the other hand, consists largely of less-educated housewives whose husbands are either skilled workers or small businessmen. For them, Luker argued, abortion on demand is nothing less than an attack on motherhood itself, and, therefore, on the role that provides their lives with much of their worth and meaning.

Both these social movements depended on a particular set of cultural and structural conditions in order to emerge as opposing forces. It is unlikely that the Supreme Court decision would have occurred without the activism of professional women

in a decade of intense feminist activity. It is also unlikely that the response of the pro-life movement would have been so extreme were it not for the threat to the roles of housewife and mother that many women experienced in the face of the women's movement and the continuing surge of mothers into the labor force.

## Some Problems with Functional and Conflict Theories

Functional theories explain cultural and structural change as adaptations to social and physical conditions. From this point of view, it is tempting to think of particular social arrangements as necessary. Some argue, for example, that divisions of labor based on gender allow societies to accomplish the essential tasks of production and reproduction more efficiently (Parsons and Bales, 1953). In some ways, such arguments are based on the commonsense notion that if something exists, there must be a good reason for it. After all, the complex relationships between men and women did not come about by accident, and so we may search for the cause that explains their origins as well as their continuing existence.

Goody (1976), for example, argued that in early hunter-gatherer societies, it was more efficient for men to hunt and women to care for children, since hunting requires days of extended travel and children require almost continuous attention. It would be relatively difficult, for example, for mothers to both tend to the breast-feeding of their children and participate in long, arduous hunting expeditions. Thus, physical and biological conditions provide an explanation for a gender-based division of labor in such societies. As revealing as such perspectives are, however, they can mislead us if we use them to explain or justify existing social arrangements by searching single-mindedly for their adaptive value to society. They must be used carefully, and for a variety of reasons.

First, if we think long and hard enough, we can always think of a reason for the existence of a cultural idea or social structure, and this may lead to the conclusion that all social arrangements are necessary simply because they exist. It is like the old story of a peasant who first shoots holes in the fence and then paints bull's-eyes around them (Geertz, 1973). As Merton (1948) pointed out some time ago, "whatever is, is right" is both a fallacy and a misapplication of the functional perspective.

Second, as we saw in Chapter 4, social structures are closely related to one another in webs of interdependence. Industrial societies, for example, are structured in such a way that most workers do not both live and work at home. Thus, in families with children it is difficult for both parents to work outside the home and still care for their children. Many argue from this that society suffers when mothers work and leave the care of their children to others, often relying on the justification that the identification of women with child care goes back thousands of years. This ignores the fact that the economy and the family are related to each other, and that if the economy were organized as it was before the Industrial Revolution, women would not experience this conflict. That is why some segments of the women's movement argue not for an end to the family, but for a restructuring of economic life and its relation to the family.

Third, as we have seen before, it is easy to argue that a social arrangement is necessary for the perpetuation of existing cultures and social structures, but this does not mean that existing aspects are desirable (Friedman, 1974; Harris, 1979). Existing social arrangements are often important to the functioning of societies; but as functional analysis has long indicated, they frequently benefit only some groups at the expense of others. The division of labor between men and women may have some adaptive value for society; but a male monopoly on the most culturally valued tasks—such as production, politics, and warfare—allows them to maintain a privileged position at the expense of women. State legislatures, for example, are controlled by men, and in 1984 the Equal Rights Amendment failed to win the support of the necessary two-thirds of the states.

Even when a social arrangement is in some way functional for society, it often not only harms members of some social categories, but also produces latent dysfunctions for society as a whole (Merton, 1968). Discrimination against women in the United States, for example, deprives American society of the skills and talents of more than half its adult population and has negative effects on the happiness and mental health of millions of women (Bernard, 1972). It is not enough to say, "we must

confine men and women to different roles in order to preserve our way of life," for we must raise a crucial additional question: Is our way of life worth preserving intact?

Finally, even if a social arrangement once had adaptive value, as conditions change, its usefulness to society may change as well. It is like the story of the man who watches his wife cut two inches from the end of a ham before she puts it in a large roasting pan. "Why do you do that?" he asks, "The pan is big enough for the whole ham."

"Because my mother always did," she replies.

He asks her mother, who answers, "Well, I guess because that's the way *my* mother always did it."

The grandmother's response is short and to the point: "We were poor, and my roasting pan was too short."

We do not feed ourselves by ranging far from home in search of wild game—economic production and military defense in industrial societies depend far more on brains than on brute physical strength. Some scholars estimate that some 29 percent of white American women born during the 1950s may remain childless (Bloom, 1982). In comparison with earlier generations, those women who do become mothers have fewer children and spend a far smaller portion of their lives caring for them. Infants no longer must depend on a mother's breast for nourishment, and children spend most of their waking hours in schools, with friends, and in front of television sets. Under such conditions, it is increasingly unclear that *any* role except the actual bearing of children must necessarily be performed exclusively by women or by men.

Just as single-minded attention to functional aspects of change can lead us astray, so can the attempt to explain all change in terms of social conflict. New technologies and their impact on social life, for example, often do not result from social conflict. Nor does conflict theory fully explain the complex ways in which changes in one area of social life, such as economic arrangements, affect others, such as the family.

A sensible approach to theories of change recognizes that each illuminates selected aspects of an enormously complex process. From a conflict perspective, the women's movement represents the organized dissatisfaction of millions of women with their social circumstances. From a functional point of view, denying women full equality is dysfunctional for many goals, including a healthy economy, the mental health of both women and men, and the achievement of social justice.

## Population, Ecology, and Social Change

Unlike functional and conflict theories, many theories focus on population and ecology as sources of change. These theories try to predict both patterns of change and the speed with which it occurs. Many early theories tended to be descriptive—which is to say they focused primarily on patterns of change; but some recent theories pay considerable attention to explanations as well. Before discussing and evaluating this set of theories, we begin by applying once again the ecological framework (represented by the acronym POET) that we introduced in Chapter 5. How do population, the physical environment, and technology stimulate change in the ways in which societies organize social life?

### Ecology and the Physical Environment

Because they represent interdependencies among living things in relation to physical environments, ecosystems constantly change, and the process through which they change is called **succession.** As one species thrives by consuming others, for example, its food sources decline as its population grows, and resulting starvation sends its population on a downward slide. Or, a change in the physical environment may benefit some forms of life at the expense of others: water pollution kills fish but supports bacteria and algae. Humans benefit from covering land with buildings, but most other forms of life do not (except, perhaps, for rats and cockroaches).

Human populations initiate succession by changing patterns of consumption (what and how much we consume); by altering the physical environment; and by changing population size or distribution. These sources of change depend heavily, in turn, on technology. Americans' preference for

eating beef, for example, leads them to use land inefficiently. Land that could be used to cultivate crops is, instead, used to grow food for cattle, and the nutritional value of their meat is less than that of the food they consume. Thus, it is more efficient to eat corn than it is to feed it to cattle that transform it into beef, therefore India's cultural taboo against eating beef is, in fact, a norm that supports the efficient use of both land and cows (Harris, 1974). The cow is more valuable as a source of labor than as a source of food.

Succession also takes place as humans alter their physical environments. Much of the early work of American sociologists such as Robert Park and Ernest Burgess focused on how urban areas develop as physical environments (Park, Burgess, and McKenzie, 1925). Over the last century, for example, New York City's Harlem changed from an area of pastures to an upper-class neighborhood, then a lower-middle-class neighborhood, and finally, today, a largely black ghetto (Osofsky, 1966). Succession is still commonplace in urban environments. "Urban renewal," for example, typically transforms run-down neighborhoods by restoring buildings and remodeling apartments. This, however, displaces residents who can no longer afford to live there, and what was, perhaps, a lower-class neighborhood becomes a middle-class neighborhood (see Chapter 9).

Such changes also result from the migration of new groups whose subculture differs from that of those already living there. One ethnic group moves in, and another moves out in search of a culturally homogeneous environment (Bressler, 1960).

### Population

Perhaps the most important source of ecological succession is the size and distribution of human population (see Chapter 5), for these factors directly affect how much people consume and how they use land (to build cities, for example). A growing population creates pressure that may lead to technological innovation—such as the invention of the plow—and this, in turn, both supports larger populations and alters their relationship with physical environments by, for example, making it possible to overcultivate the land and thereby exhaust the fertility of the soil and promote soil erosion (Harris, 1974).

The rapid growth of the world's population during the last two centuries has resulted primarily from increased production supported by new technology and increasingly complex divisions of labor, and from the dramatic lowering of death rates, particularly among infants and children. In many societies, however, rapidly expanding control over many causes of death has made populations grow faster than the production of goods needed to support them—a clear case of a latent dysfunction.

The technology for controlling infectious disease was first discovered in rapidly developing industrial societies in North America and Europe at a time when birth rates were falling steadily. As death rates declined in these countries, so did birth rates; and, while populations grew because death rates fell faster than birth rates, expanding industry allowed them to support more people. Once these medical technologies were discovered, however, they were easily and cheaply applied in societies whose birth rates remained at high levels and whose economies could barely support a rapidly expanding population. This ecological change has reached crisis proportions in much of the world in which population now grows much faster than production. While the world's population grew slowly prior to 1800—perhaps no more than 0.1 percent per year—it now grows by more than 1.7 percent. Thus, while it once took nearly 700 years for the world population to double, at current rates it will double in only 40 years (Dumond, 1975; Population Reference Bureau, 1984; Thompson and Lewis, 1965).

The resulting imbalance between population size and production contributes to extreme poverty in rural areas that make up most of developing countries, whose people migrate in droves to already crowded cities, seeking opportunities that simply do not exist. Such "overurbanization" plagues many developing countries, such as India, Egypt, and Mexico. In New Delhi, India, for example, thousands of urban "squatters" sleep in vacant lots, school playgrounds, and city streets (Ashish, 1973). As we saw in Chapter 5, Mexico City is rapidly becoming the largest city in the world—inhabited primarily by unemployed peasants—and demands for water will soon outrun the supply. It is ironic that what threatens to become a major ecological and social disaster was precipitated by an undeniably positive innovation—the elimination of many diseases as major causes of death.

When we realize that humans affect ecosystems in countless ways by initiating thousands of ecological changes, we can appreciate how difficult (if not impossible) it is to understand where the continuing process of ecological succession will lead. For societies, the danger of this is that our ecosystems may change in ways that no longer support human life. In ecosystems, one form of life is no more "valuable" than another: to us humans, a polluted lake may be an "awful sewer," but to bacteria and algae, it is a supportive, ideal physical environment. Although most cultures may value humanity as the most important form of life, in ecosystems, we enjoy no such privileged standing.

**Cohorts**  As we saw in Chapter 5, a birth cohort consists of all people born in the same year. The cohort is an important concept in the study of social change, for as each new generation is socialized, its members both continue existing traditions and modify them through their own fresh experience (Ryder, 1965). Each generation has a comparatively low level of commitment to a past it has not experienced, and so it brings with it an openness to new ideas and social relationships (Mannheim, 1952). The inevitable movement of new cohorts through the stages of the life course under historical circumstances that differ for each generation makes social change inevitable.

During the 1960s, for example, older generations of Americans had a hard time understanding or accepting the antiwar activities of many young people. Many older people identified the Vietnam War with their experience of World War II and the Korean War—it was simply another occasion for patriotism, self-sacrifice, and obedience to the government's call. Young people who were not even born when World War II ended were far less likely to identify Vietnam with previous wars and were thus able to be far more critical of the American government's policies. In turn, many of those who now read this book have no memory of the Vietnam War and the protest movements of the 1960s, and so might have difficulty understanding why young men would refuse to fight.

New generations are both a source of new ideas and a continuing threat to the perpetuation of cultural and structural aspects of social environ-

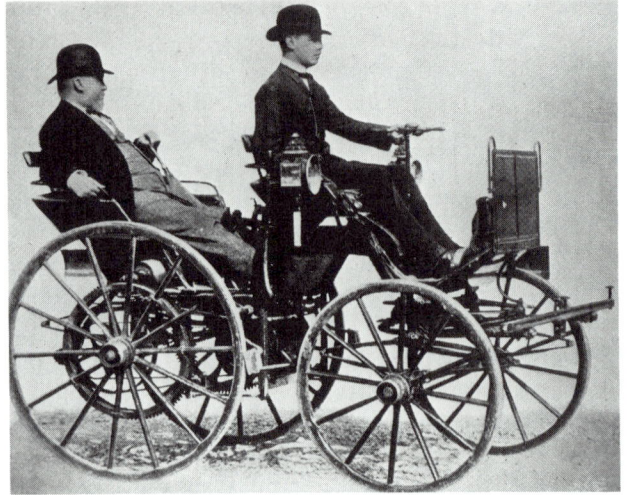

ments. In the Israeli Kibbutz, younger members often feel a strong pull toward the comforts of city life, for they did not share in the early years of excitement and challenge when the Kibbutz was first tried as a radical new form of community and family life (Bettelheim, 1969). Many Jews also worry because the number of people who actually experienced the Holocaust grows smaller each year. There are fewer "witnesses" who can speak of the horror, who can perpetuate the memory of it in order to ensure that it will never happen again.

## Technology

Technological change occurs in three basic ways. A **discovery** is an instance of finding out about something that already exists (such as gravity or the effects of marijuana on the human brain), whereas an **invention** is something new created from things that already exist (such as the plow, the computer chip, or the potato chip). Although discovery and invention obviously have been crucial sources of innovation in the world as a whole, the introduction of new technology in most societies has oc-

curred through the process of **diffusion,** which is the borrowing of knowledge from other societies (see Rogers, 1983). As far as we know, for example, printing was invented in the early sixth century by Chinese who used engraved wooden blocks. During the next 1,000 years printing technology spread from China through the Middle East and Europe, and a German printer named Johann Gutenberg is credited with inventing movable reusable type in the mid-fifteenth century. Printing technology is now used around the world, and yet it was not invented anew in each society.

A major part of the ecological perspective focuses on the ways in which societies apply discoveries and inventions to physical environments. As we have seen, technology affects the niches human societies occupy in ecosystems; but it also profoundly affects the cultural and structural characteristics of social environments. Money, for example, transformed economic activity by making it possible for people to engage in trade for profit, and without money, capitalism could never have developed (see Chapter 17). The invention of printing and movable type made books available to a wide population for the first time in human history. This greatly increased literacy, and the rapid dissemination of ideas stimulated the development of scientific, political, religious, and philosophical thought (see Eisenstein, 1980). In similar ways, the computer is now revolutionizing the ability of humans to store, retrieve, and communicate vast amounts of information with phenomenal speed and accuracy.

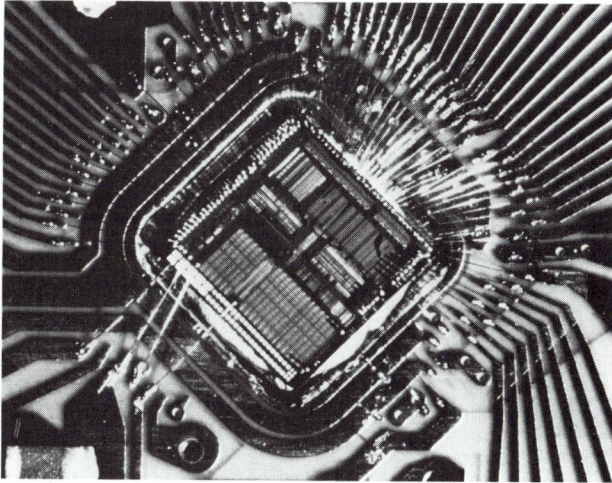

The invention of the cotton gin in the late 1700s made the production of cotton in the American South far more profitable, and this led to a dramatic increase in the slave population (Rasmussen, 1982). The Industrial Revolution rested on an astonishingly rapid series of innovations in the design of machinery and the development of nonhuman sources of energy (see Chapter 5). Industrialization, in turn, virtually transformed work and profoundly affected institutions such as the family and schools (see Chapters 15 and 16).

The mechanization of agriculture in the 1930s and 1940s helped to transform the United States from a nation of farmers into a nation of urban workers whose entire food supply is provided by less than 3 percent of the population (Rasmussen, 1982). The decline in the demand for manual farm labor also stimulated a mass migration of southern blacks from rural areas, first to southern cities, and then to the cities of the North. The urbanization of American blacks led to better education and job opportunities, and these, in turn, helped to lay the groundwork for the civil rights movement of the 1960s.

Technological innovation often has social effects that are not readily apparent. The automobile, for example, is more than a means of transportation: in the early 1900s it provided young people with a way to escape the watchful eyes of their parents. The mass migration of people from northern to southern states such as Texas in recent decades has been due in no small part to the development of air conditioning, which has made life in

## PUZZLES:

## WHAT IS CULTURE LAG?

In 1981 an Australian married couple discovered that the only way they could have children was through test tube fertilization. Several eggs were removed from the wife and fertilized with the husband's sperm. Two of the resulting embryos were frozen while the third was implanted in the wife. She miscarried 10 days later. In 1983 the couple was killed in a plane crash and left an estate valued at several million dollars.

Are the frozen embryos heirs to the estate? Does anyone own them? Can they be destroyed? If they are implanted in a woman who becomes their mother, can she claim part of the estate on their behalf?

These and other difficult questions that faced Australian legal authorities are examples of the kinds of problems that arise when technology allows us to do things faster than we create norms, beliefs, and values to deal with the consequences. William F. Ogburn called this "culture lag."

the southern climate far more bearable than it was.

Technology often creates dilemmas around deeply held values, in part because technological change moves at a faster pace than changes in cultural ideas that "lag" behind: we develop new technologies faster than we develop new cultural ideas that regulate how we use them (Ogburn, 1922). Medical technology, for example, enables doctors to prolong life by connecting people to machines that literally keep them alive. This, however, raises the problem of deciding when someone is actually dead. Is someone who functions only in relation to a machine actually alive? Is it murder or an act of mercy to "pull the plug"? These kinds of ethical questions never arose before, because until now it was impossible to keep people's hearts and lungs functioning through artificial means. Medical technology is also rapidly developing the ability to alter human genes. While this promises to eliminate birth defects and genetically carried diseases such as hemophilia and sickle cell anemia, it also

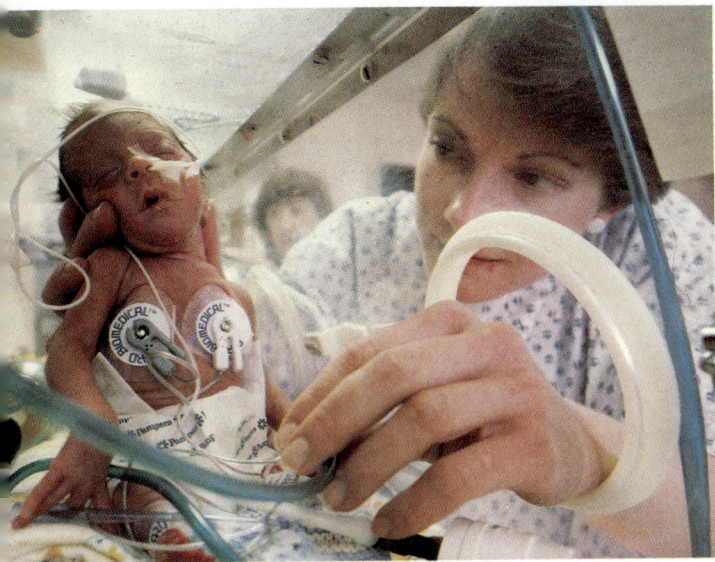

The increased ability of medical technology to sustain human life far beyond what would otherwise be possible raises profound moral questions.

Sarders © 1983 Milwaukee Journal.

raises the possibility of controlling human characteristics in ways that can only be imagined at this point. Our grasp of ethical issues involved in "human engineering"—for example, should we "tamper" with human genes at all?—lags far behind our technology.

Culture lag also involves norms, for the introduction of new technology often alters human behavior and interaction patterns faster than groups and societies are able to construct new norms to regulate them. Prior to the widespread use of computers, for example, most records in business, government, and other organizations were kept in written form, and this made it relatively easy to control who had access to them. As computers have taken over the job of filing and keeping track of vast quantities of information, however, entirely new security problems are introduced (Parker, 1983). In 1983, for example, operators of home computers—called "hackers"—began to figure out how to "break into" large computers by guessing passwords. When hospitals, banks, the military, and government agencies became alarmed at the prospect of unauthorized entry into and alteration of highly important information, they discovered that no laws existed which dealt with "breaking and entering" a computer through the use of a telephone.

The rapid growth of computer technology introduces other problems as well. For example, because most information held by governments in the past was in written form, it was relatively difficult to keep track of detailed information from diverse sources about millions of citizens. Computers, however, make it possible for government agencies to compile and access detailed records about citizens quickly and efficiently, and Marx and Reichman (1984) and others have argued that this gives the state an unprecedented ability to invade the privacy of individuals.

The rate at which new ideas and technologies are introduced depends on a variety of social and ecological factors (see Rogers, 1983). In the simplest sense, scientific and technological knowledge is largely cumulative: the more we know, the more we are able to know. Since inventions are new combinations of existing ideas and inventions, the more we start with, the more combinations we can invent. Large populations can be conducive to innovation because the more people there are, the more likely it is that someone will come up with something new (Ogburn, 1922). Population size, however, like any other factor, is not sufficient to guarantee innovation, as the examples of India and China during the last few centuries illustrate. A quarter of the world's population lives in China, and yet in terms of industrial technology China is an underdeveloped country.

## Voices: The Computer as Letterbox, Singles Bar, and Seminar

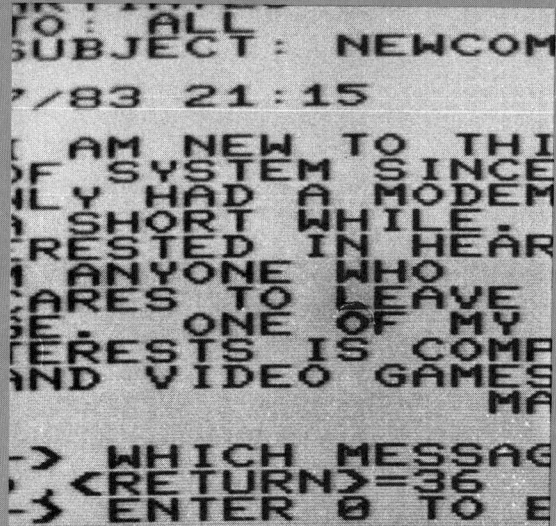

For thousands of Americans, the personal computer is becoming the ham radio of the 1980's, a forum for dialogues on politics, religion and other matters, matchmaking and courtship.

Protected by the anonymity of a computer screen and the length of a cross-country telephone line, strangers debate and harangue; shy people lose their shyness; and many people invent fantasy lives about themselves, fabricating identities and accomplishments, in the hope of impressing electronic pen pals they never meet.

"For many people, it's a lot easier to express themselves on the computer, when they're not face to face," observed [Karyn] Zoldan, who said that once-anonymous conversations on her computer had led to dates with several men. "It's turned my social life around," she said, "and it's safer than going to a bar." . . .

Hundreds of owners of small computers in the last year or so have organized electronic bulletin boards.

These are essentially switchboards in the owners' homes that other computer owners can get access to by dialing a special telephone number and where they can leave a message and obtain one left by another owner.

There are more than 200 bulletin boards in the Los Angeles area alone, ranging from one called Computers for Christ to at least a dozen restricted to the exchange of erotic messages.

There are more than a dozen bulletin boards in California devoted exclusively to heterosexual and homosexual matchmaking and at least one devoted to debate on nuclear disarmament.

In Nebraska, Iowa and other farm states, farmers have organized bulletin boards to exchange information about crops and to list equipment they want to sell.

In New York City, more than 1,000 people have dialed their computers into a matchmaking service called MMMMMM, or Marc the Martian's Mixed-Up Matching and Message Machine. Several marriages have resulted from the computer matching, operators of the system say.

"There are boards for everything, business boards, dating boards, gay boards," said Andrew M. Appel, a 19-year-old computer user in New Hyde Park, L.I. "Whatever people are interested in, there's a board for it."

Source: Lindsey, *New York Times*, December 2, 1984.

A third factor affecting the rate of innovation is the stability of social and physical environments. A society that must adapt to rapidly changing physical or social conditions will tend to produce more innovations than a society that exists in stable conditions. In the 1970s, for example, oil-producing nations in the Middle East refused to sell oil to the United States, and the ensuing shortages stimulated the development of solar energy technology. The nuclear arms race between the United States and the Soviet Union is another example of rapidly shifting environmental conditions that stimulate an equally rapid pace of technological development as each country struggles to "keep up" with the other.

Since most innovation occurs through diffusion, a fourth factor affecting the rate of innovation is the amount of contact between societies. Isolated societies simply have less opportunity to borrow from others than societies that are, for example, actively engaged in trade or other forms of exchange.

In some cases, societies try to isolate themselves from other societies in order to avoid the introduction of new ideas. This was true of Japan prior to the nineteenth century and in important ways is still true of the Soviet Union, whose government fears the diffusion of Western culture into Soviet society. The importation of magazines, films, and books from the West is tightly controlled and restricted by the government, and Soviet citizens are discouraged from interacting with visiting tourists from Western countries such as the United States.

Having examined the effects of population and ecology on societies, we look now at some specific theories that draw heavily on these factors in their attempts to predict and explain social change.

## Evolutionary and Unilinear Theory

Early thinkers tried to identify laws that govern change in all societies, and they often used the biological evolution of animal species as a model. The nineteenth-century English thinker Herbert Spencer, for example, drew heavily on Darwin's ideas about natural evolution to develop a theory of **social evolution** through which all societies naturally change toward superior forms (Spencer, 1891,

1896). From this point of view, social change is **unilinear,** which means that all societies pass through predictable stages: from primitive to civilized, simple to complex, "inferior" to "superior," and from militant and coercive to peaceful and industrial.

Like all ideas, Spencer's reflected to some extent the social environment in which he lived, for England was rapidly colonizing much of the world and encountering a vast array of peoples living in relatively simple societies at comparatively low levels of economic development. The theory of social evolution supported the Europeans' belief in their own superiority by focusing on economic development as the most important indicator of a superior society.

The American sociologist Thorstein Veblen also used evolutionary theory as a framework, but he focused more on the effect of technology on social change (see Lerner, 1948). Like later theorists, however, Veblen did not believe that evolutionary social change is unilinear, for he was aware of how easily technology can be transplanted from one society to another. China, for example, is still a largely agricultural society, and yet trade agreements signed with the United States in 1984 may soon bring computer and nuclear power technology to what is otherwise a relatively technology-poor society.

## Cyclical Theory

Early in this century, the German philosopher Spengler (1926) produced a variation on evolutionary theory by suggesting that societies change in predictable cycles, in the same way that individuals progress from birth toward maturity, old age, and death. Like Spencer's theory, Spengler's ideas about **cyclical change** reflected his environment, for the chaos and seemingly mindless destruction caused by World War I shook Europeans' belief that societies naturally progress toward better forms. Obviously, change did not necessarily imply an improvement in social life, for in the midst of the greatest spurt of economic progress known to humanity, millions of people were systematically slaughtering one another.

The Russo-American sociologist Pitirim Sorokin also believed that societies change in cycles. According to his principle of **immanent**

**change,** cultures have material and nonmaterial characteristics that cause societies to develop in certain directions. Eventually they are taken to their logical extreme, after which they go too far and "become less and less capable of serving as an instrument of adaptation, as an experience for real satisfaction of the needs of its bearers, and as foundation for their social and cultural life" (Sorokin, 1937–1941).

Sorokin argued, for example, that as a society develops the ability to produce goods, it will tend to go too far in that direction, and as people dwell on owning more and more possessions, life begins to lose its sense of meaning and they will turn away from the material aspects of their culture to nonmaterial aspects such as religious belief. During the two decades that followed World War II the United States enjoyed a period of great economic prosperity. In the 1960s there was a strong movement away from "materialism" and toward various forms of spiritualism, especially in the form of

Eastern religions such as Zen Buddhism. This movement was strongest among college students, many of whom came from relatively prosperous families. In the 1970s and into the 1980s there also has been a strong growth in fundamentalist religion and religious cults.

In spite of the insights that the earliest evolutionary and cyclical theories of change provide, they have a number of drawbacks that make them of relatively little interest to today's sociologists (Zeitlin, 1981). Their most obvious shortcoming is that they often do not fit the facts: as Veblen noted, societies often "skip" stages of development, especially when technology is introduced from the outside. It took the Industrial Revolution to ultimately produce the telephone, television, computer, nuclear reactor, and such deadly weapons as hydrogen bombs. These technologies, however, have spread rapidly to societies that have yet to industrialize. India, for example, has developed its own

ARRIVALS

| PESTILENCE | 4:02 |
|---|---|
| FAMINE | 4:15 |
| MARTIAL LAW | 4:21 |
| TRIPLE LOCKS | 5:00 |
| UNEMPLOYMENT | 5:20 |
| INFLATION | 5:32 |
| SHORTER SUMMERS | 5:43 |
| LONGER ZIP CODES | 5:46 |
| PLASTIC SILVERWARE | 6:01 |

DEPARTURES

| GOOD TASTE | 3:32 |
|---|---|
| SLEIGH RIDES | 3:49 |
| ALL-BEEF BURGERS | 4:25 |
| HAPPINESS | 5:11 |
| SECURITY | 5:15 |
| FRIENDLY LOAN COMPANIES | 5:58 |
| WARM BLANKETS | 6:10 |
| HARDWOOD FLOORS | 6:15 |
| HOMEMADE ICE CREAM | 6:31 |

Drawing by Ziegler; © 1979, The New Yorker Magazine, Inc.

nuclear weapons. These theories also do not appreciate the enormous complexity of social change and the phenomenal variation found among societies.

## Multilinear Theories

More recent evolutionary theories show greater appreciation for the complexity of social change. **Multilinear** theories in particular identify certain changes that appear to be universal—from small, simple, rural, and low technology to large, complex, urban, and high technology—and yet acknowledge that such changes take place in a variety of ways and do not necessarily result in "progress" and better lives for the members of a society (Smelser, 1973; Steward, 1955).

Perhaps the best-developed of the recent multilinear theories is Lenski's theory of social evolution (Lenski and Lenski, 1982). There are important similarities between the biological evolution of living species and the social evolution of human societies. Both, for example, depend on the transmission of information—via DNA molecules in genes in the case of biological evolution and via cultural symbol systems in social evolution. Both forms of evolution arise from the interaction of populations with their environments, and in each case the evolutionary trend involves an increase in amount and complexity of information. In comparison with the simplest virus, for example, human genes hold a million times more information (Curtis and Barnes, 1981). In similar ways, modern industrial societies are far more complex than the simple hunting and gather societies that existed thousands of years ago.

Biological and social evolution differ in important ways, however. The genetic information that controls biological evolution can be transmitted only through reproduction, and two different species cannot mate—that is, they cannot exchange genetic information. Since different species of life cannot share the same genetic information, biological evolution tends to produce greater diversity as each species develops in its own way.

Human societies, on the other hand, can exchange and share information quite easily with one another, and in this way they tend to become more similar. Less than a century ago, basic technologies such as electricity and telecommunications were found in only a few countries, but now exist in almost every society. Other aspects of culture, from MacDonald's restaurants and computers to designer jeans and rock music, have spread rapidly throughout many parts of the world.

Like some earlier theorists, Lenski regards information—technology in particular—as the key to social change. It was new technology that enabled human populations and societies to grow. The expanding human resources of larger societies spawned new cultural and structural developments: systems of written language, for example, new vocabularies, more complex divisions of labor, and greater production of material goods. According to modern evolutionary theory, in short, information is the engine of social change. Social change, in turn, creates pressures for new information and further change. One consequence of industrial technology, for example, has been damage to the physical environment (pollution, toxic waste) and, therefore, to the well-being of human populations. This, in turn, has created pressures both for new technology (such as pollution control devices and more fuel-efficient cars) and for change in political arrangements (such as greater government regulation of industry in capitalist societies).

## Modernization Theory

The concept of **modernization** refers to a process through which the cultural, structural, and ecological characteristics of societies change in fairly predictable ways (Parsons, 1951; Rostow, 1960). In its earliest form, which was most popular during the 1950s and 1960s, modernization theory was actually a form of evolutionary theory that tried to describe the development of nonindustrial societies into industrial societies. For two decades the idea of modernization dominated thinking about economic and social change in underdeveloped countries, and it held out the expectation that the economic prosperity and democratic political institutions found in the countries of North America and Western Europe would spread throughout the world.

According to modernization theory, modernization is not limited to the introduction of complex technology into the production process, for it involves a variety of structural and cultural changes. Cultures become more heterogeneous and subcultures flourish. People become more oriented to the future and open to change, and the rights of the individual increase in value. Social relationships shift from informal and primary to formal, bureaucratic, and secondary, and populations become more urban. Social inequality increases during the early stages of modernization as an elite profits from the easily exploitable labor of an unsophisticated, unskilled labor force; but as a society industrializes, social mobility increases and rigid stratification systems based on ascribed social statuses such as race and gender tend to break down. Traditional sources of authority—such as respect for the elderly—also tend to weaken as formal social institutions such as schools and the state take on increasing responsibility and power.

At the heart of modernization, of course, is technological innovation that makes industrialization possible, and scientific research and technological innovation are highly valued in modern societies. With industrialization comes an increasingly specialized division of labor, a more skilled and highly educated work force, and greater alienation in the workplace. Contact with modern working conditions, in turn, tends to make workers more modern in their values and beliefs, more supportive of democratic institutions, and more committed to the rights of individuals (Inkeles and Smith, 1974). As we saw in Chapter 17, some theo-

As this traditionally dressed Jordanian woman working at a computer terminal illustrates, the modernization process often produces sharp contrasts in traditional cultures with modern technologies.

rists believe that the most advanced stage of modernization is *postindustrial* society, in which sophisticated technology replaces much of human labor and most people work as service providers (such as nurses and computer programmers) rather than as producers of goods (Daniel Bell, 1973).

There is little doubt that most of the world's societies are committed to industrialization and economic development, for the lure of higher standards of living is a strong one. What is not clear, however, is how useful the theory of modernization is for predicting the patterns of change in today's underdeveloped societies. As we saw in Chapter 11, for example, there is considerable evidence that the gap between rich and poor nations has been growing, not shrinking. Is economic prosperity an attainable goal for all countries of the world as modernization theory seems to suggest? Supporters of world-system theory believe the answer is no.

## World-System Theory

**World-system** (or **dependency**) **theory** was developed in the 1970s as a direct challenge to modernization theory, most notably by Immanuel Wallerstein (1976, 1979, 1980). As we saw in Chapter 17, Wallerstein divides societies into three categories. Core societies such as Britain, the United States, and Japan occupy dominant positions in the world economy by controlling the development and flow of new technology as well as the wealth necessary for the creation of new capital. Countries in the periphery—such as most of Africa and much of Asia—are generally poor and underdeveloped and supply core industrial societies with raw materials, food, and other products that can be produced without sophisticated technology or an educated work force. Semiperiphery countries such as Brazil and South Korea stand between the core and the periphery and often provide cheap but well-trained industrial labor when labor costs in core countries go up. Many automobile spare parts, for example, are manufactured in Brazil, just as many American companies have their products made in Korea, Taiwan, or Mexico.

A world-system perspective has important implications for social change, for it is based on the view that development and change in a society depend not simply on its internal structure, culture, population, and ecology, but also on its position in the world economic system. It argues, for example, that even the leading socialist country in the world—the Soviet Union—cannot be completely socialist so long as it must deal with a largely capitalist world economy (Wallerstein, 1979). It also argues that "backward" conditions found in many peripheral societies arise not only from some internal dynamic in those societies, but also from their relationship with societies at the core or in the semiperiphery of the world-system. We cannot understand, for example, the phenomenal economic growth in Taiwan over the past 30 years without taking into account Taiwan's close relationship with the United States.

An important aspect of world-system theory focuses on the ways in which both core and peripheral societies change due to their positions in the system (see Chirot, 1977). For example, when Great Britain was an empire, it systematically destroyed the textile industry in India—one of its colonies—and forced Indians to purchase cloth made in Britain by not allowing them to produce any themselves. This both eliminated competition and provided a captive market for British goods. One result of this policy was increased revenues for Britain, which contributed to the industrial revolution that was the basis for modern core societies (Baran, 1957).

Thus, the economic problems of many countries are also tied to dependency relationships in the world system. Mexico, for example, is an urban, industrial, rich country compared to most underdeveloped nations, and yet in spite of its wealth of oil and natural resources it has widespread poverty and an enormous gap between rich and poor. Gonzalez Casanova (1980) argued that this is due in part to the relationship between Mexico and corporations in core countries, the United States in particular. So much of Mexico's industry is owned by foreigners, and so much of its foreign sales depend on a relative few customers, that Mexican leaders lack the flexibility they need to make the domestic investments that lead to improved living conditions. This kind of dependency is found in many countries, including Brazil and South Korea.

Like all theories, world-system theory has its shortcomings. Few social scientists would deny that a world-system exists or that there are strong dependent relations between core and other societies. What is unclear, however, are the reasons that some societies are at the core and others are in the periphery or semiperiphery. Brenner (1976), for example, showed that economic "backwardness" in eastern Europe arose less from economic dependence than on an absence of sophisticated technology that preceded the development of its dependent position in the world system (see also Chirot, 1980; Chirot and Hall, 1982; and Lenski, 1976b).

For all their flaws and shortcomings, theories of social change have come a long way from the relatively simplistic notions of unilinear evolution. Multilinear evolutionary theory and world-system and dependency theory show a development toward more comprehensive theories that appreciate the complexity of social change.

## Summary

1. Social change refers to the ways in which culture, social structure, and ecological arrangements change.

2. Cultural ideas often promote change. New beliefs, for example, alter ways of perceiving the world; shifting values affect the goals we pursue; and changing norms alter expectations in social relationships.

3. The structure of social relationships also causes change. Prejudice, for example, may be reduced by changing patterns of interaction between members of different groups. Social movements focus explicitly on change or resistance to change.

4. A functional perspective views social change as an adaptive response to the strains that arise through normal activity in a society. When mothers enter the labor force in increasing numbers, for example, subsequent changes in beliefs, values, attitudes, and norms that apply to working mothers are adaptations that affect social cohesion and order.

5. The conflict perspective focuses on social change as the result of antagonisms between groups. For example, this perspective would focus on social protest as a source of changing beliefs, values, attitudes, and norms that apply to working mothers.

6. Succession is the process through which ecosystems change, and it often causes social change. The shift from hunter-gather to horticultural and then agricultural societies, for example, laid a foundation for the emergence of social stratification and complex divisions of labor.

7. Rapid population growth and the changing characteristics of populations promote social change in a variety of ways. The pressure of an expanding population stimulates the development of new cultural technology; overpopulation contributes to poverty, urban congestion, and pollution; the inevitable movement of new cohorts through the life course under historical circumstances that differ for each generation makes change inevitable, for each generation matures in different circumstances and interprets society in its own way.

8. New technology acquired through discovery, invention, or diffusion is one of the most important sources of change. Culture lag occurs when technology changes faster than other aspects of culture, as when medical technology raises moral questions that have yet to be resolved.

9. The rate of innovation in a society depends on existing knowledge, population size, the stability of social and physical environments, and the extent of contact with other societies.

10. Early evolutionary theory drew on Darwin's theory of evolution and argued that societies progress toward superior forms. Some theorists believed that change is unilinear, always taking place in the same stages.

11. According to Spengler's cyclical theory, societies have periods that correspond to youth, middle- and old-age in humans. Sorokin believed that societies tend to overdevelop dominant cultural characteristics and then go into a period of decline.

12. More recent multilinear evolutionary theories show greater appreciation for the complexity of change. Lenski's theory suggests that social and biological evolution have much in common, especially their reliance on the accumulation and transmission of information.

13. Modernization theory attempts to describe a complex process through which all societies eventually change from traditional to modern, rural to urban, nonindustrial to industrial, simple to complex, and from primary, informal relationships to those that are predominantly secondary, formal and bureaucratic.

14. World-system theory argues that modernization is not a universal phenomenon but rather depends on the position a society occupies—core, semiperiphery, or periphery—in the world economic system. Dependent relationships between periphery and core societies, for example, often make it difficult if not impossible for periphery societies to modernize.

## Key Terms

## Recommended Readings

BERGESEN, A. (Ed.). (1983). *Crises in the world system.* Beverly Hills, CA: Sage. A collection of articles, all of which try to understand the cycles of recurring crisis believed by world-system theorists to characterize the world economy.

CHIROT, D. (1977). *Social change in the twentieth century.* New York: Harcourt Brace Jovanovich. An interesting look at social change in this century from a world-system perspective.

JENKINS, J. C. (1983). "Resource mobilization theory and the study of social movements." *Annual Review of Sociology 9,* 527–553. A comprehensive, up-to-date review of an important theoretical approach to social change.

LAUER, R. H. (Ed.). (1981). *Perspectives on social change* (3rd ed.). Boston: Allyn and Bacon. An introduction to social change that focuses on both theory and research.

MARSH, J. C., GEIST, A., and CAPLAN, N. (1982). *Rape and the limits of law reform.* Boston: Auburn House. A case study that examines the effect of a radical, much-heralded rewriting of Michigan's sexual assault laws on the ways in which subsequent cases were actually handled. Illustrates the difficulty of bringing about change through legal reform alone in an area of entrenched beliefs and values such as those that surround gender and violence.

MCADAM, D. (1982). *Political process and the development of black insurgency.* Chicago: University of Chicago Press. A clear, interesting analysis of the black civil rights movement that includes a well-reasoned critique of various theoretical approaches to social movements and social change.

PRICE, J. (1982). *The antinuclear movement.* Boston: Twayne. A richly drawn historical portrait of the antinuclear movement, starting with its beginnings in the 1950s.

ROBERTSON, C. C. (1984). *Sharing the same bowl: A socioeconomic history of women and class in Accra.* Bloomington: Indiana University Press. A book that adds an important piece to dependency and world-system theory by looking at the ways in which colonialism, capitalism, and peripheral status in the world system have changed the status of women in urban Africa.

# A Student Research Guide

At some point during your study of sociology, you may be required to write a research paper, and this appendix is intended to give you some help in going about it. You have probably never done original sociological research; and even if you are an old hand at using libraries, sociology has its own resources, of which you should be aware before you start.

## Deciding What You Want to Know

Whether you do your own research or sift through the results of someone else's in order to write a paper, you cannot get very far without a clear idea of what it is you want to know. Without a doubt, this is the most difficult part of research for most people, amateurs and professionals alike. Notice that saying, "I want to write a paper on the family" is not a statement of what you want to know; rather, it defines a general area within which lie hundreds of different topics.

One of the best ways to define a clear topic is to put it in the form of questions to which you can imagine clear answers. For example: How common is family violence in the United States? What kinds of families are the most prone to violence? How is the likelihood of violence affected by such things as the age of spouses and their children, the employment status and relative earnings of wives and husbands, whether or not both parents are living at home, whether or not parents themselves were victims of abuse as children? Is family violence more common in some societies than in others? Why? With each of these questions, you can have a clear idea of what you are looking for—an idea you cannot have with something like "I want to write a paper on the family."

So, you must be specific about what you want to know, and one good way to force yourself to do that is to make up clear questions. Once you have done that, you will probably still have to narrow your topic even further since you are working at a disadvantage that you do not share with most other researchers: College terms rarely last more than 12 or 13 weeks, and you may have less than a month to complete your work. Any one of the questions in the preceding paragraph, for example, could lead to a substantial term paper.

## Designing Your Research

Once you have decided what you want to know, the next thing to do is to plan how you are going to go after it. You may decide to use only published sources—in other words, to use information gathered by other people—or you may supplement this by gathering new information. You might, for example, be interested in finding out just how prevalent family violence is in the United States. As part of your research, you would use the library to review what is known about family violence in America. You might want to supplement this, however, by doing a survey of students in your college in order to find out how many of them come from families in which violence has taken place during the past year.

If you decide to supplement library research with your own fieldwork, I suggest that you assume that it will take you at least twice as long to do your fieldwork as you think it will. This is not meant to discourage you from gathering your own data—far from it. There are few things as exciting in academic work as doing your own research. It is meant to help you to be realistic about the time constraints you are probably working under. Writing questionnaires, for example, and having them typed, duplicated, distributed, returned, tabulated, and analyzed all takes a lot of time which you may not have. One excellent way to deal with this problem—if your professor allows it—is to work in teams so that you can divide the labor among several people.

## How to Use a Library

Many people go through their entire educational career without realizing what extraordinary resources libraries and their staffs are. To use a library well, however, you have to get to know your way around it, which is mostly a matter of time and attention.

The first thing you have to know is how a library is laid out. In writing this book, I have spent a great deal of time just wandering through the stacks of my library, getting a sense of what is located where. You will find that most sociology books are shelved in the same general area, and you can get an excellent feel for any discipline by spending an hour or so just browsing. You can benefit from this both in getting to know the field as a whole and in becoming familiar with specific areas within it, such as demography, the sociology of gender, stratification, urban studies, or the family. How do you find out what is where? Ask a librarian. Most librarians are justifiably proud of their libraries and are more than happy to show other people how to use them.

Some subjects will be catalogued in several different locations. You will find sources that discuss family violence, for example, under sociology as well as anthropology, psychology, and government studies that treat family violence as a problem in law enforcement.

Whether or not you decide to gather data of your own, at some point you should make yourself aware of what others have found and had to say about the topic you are investigating. Out of the millions of books and articles contained in many libraries, you need ways of locating just the ones that are most likely to help you understand the relatively narrow subject you have selected.

### General Sources

The most obvious place for you to begin is with the references in *Human Arrangements*, provided that this book discusses the topic you are interested in. For example, the section in Chapter 15 on family violence indicates several recent sources. Rather than spend hours finding them on your own, take advantage of the fact that I have already done some of your work for you—just as other authors did some of my work for me.

Another place to look is a general source such as an encyclopedia. In addition to widely known ones such as *Britannica*, there is the *International Encyclopedia of the Social Sciences*, which contains hundreds of articles written by specialists. Although it is a bit dated for some purposes (it was published in 1968), for general background discussions of major concepts and areas of social science it is an excellent resource for sociology students.

You might also look at recent issues of *Annual Review of Sociology*, a hardbound book containing reviews of entire areas of sociological inquiry. If you are lucky enough to find a recent review of your area of interest, the *Annual Review* can save you a great deal of time.

### Specific Sources in Sociology

Sociological articles appear in a large number of journals (see Table A-1), and you would do well to familiarize yourself with them if you plan to write a paper in sociology. An hour or so spent browsing through the tables of contents for the previous year can give you a good idea of the kinds of subjects found in each.

### Tracking Down Sources

If you want to find scholarly writings, there are several ways to go about it. Card catalogues usually consist of two sections. One lists books by author and title and the other lists them by subject. Doing a project on family violence, for example, you might look under "family," "violence," "domestic violence," or "child abuse." In general, it is best to go after the most recent titles, since they are likely to include summaries of previously published books and articles.

In addition to the card catalogue, there are books in the reference department that you can use to locate books and articles about a particular subject. The multivolume annual *Books in Print* lists all currently published books by subject, author, and title, and it can be a useful guide to books that your library does not own but which may be

**Table A-1**

Useful Journals in Sociological Research

**MAJOR SOCIOLOGICAL JOURNALS**

American Sociological Review
American Journal of Sociology
British Journal of Sociology
Social Forces

**MORE SPECIALIZED JOURNALS IN SOCIOLOGY**

Journal of Marriage and the Family
Journal of Health and Social Behavior
Public Opinion Quarterly

Social Problems
Sociology of Education
Demography
Population Problems

**JOURNALS IN SOCIAL PSYCHOLOGY**

Social Psychology Quarterly
Journal of Experimental Social Psychology
Journal of Applied Social Psychology
Journal of Abnormal and Social Psychology
Personality and Social Psychology

obtained through interlibrary loan systems. The *Social Science Index* and *Sociological Abstracts* are published each year and contain brief descriptions of every article and book of interest to sociologists. There are similar volumes for other areas, such as education, psychology, and crime. As before, begin with the most recent year and work backward. Most reference departments also have a variety of annotated bibliographies: books that describe articles and books that focus on a particular subject, such as blacks or women. These can be enormously useful.

For some topics, none of these sources will provide you with information, and this often happens when you are interested in a subject that focuses on recent events. If you cannot find what you need in scholarly sources, turn to the *Reader's Guide to Periodical Literature*, which is published each year and gives listings by subject of articles that appear in magazines such as *Newsweek*. In addition, newspapers of record, such as the *New York Times* and the London *Times*, publish annual indexes that list every person, event, or subject that has appeared in their newspapers. Be careful when using popular sources such as those found in the *Reader's Guide*, however, for they are not generally bound by the same rigorous scientific standards that sociologists try to follow.

## Finding Statistical Information

Perhaps the best source of statistical information about the United States is the U.S. government.

Some libraries are Government Document Depositories which contain almost every major document published by the federal government (and usually have a documents librarian to help you find them). The Census Bureau publishes not only the results of the census conducted every ten years but also the periodic *Current Population Reports*, whose highly scientific surveys cover such important areas as race, income and poverty, marital status and living arrangements, divorce and marriage, and migration.

The National Center for Health Statistics publishes detailed information on births, deaths, marriages, and divorces each year, often broken down by race, gender, and age. The Department of Labor publishes reports on work and earnings and the Justice Department reports on crime and law enforcement.

If you do not have access to a depository library, the best source is the annual *Statistical Abstract of the United States*, which presents the highlights of all federal statistics, with supplements from other sources as well. In addition, the federal government publishes other excellent statistical source books, including *Historical Statistics of the United States from Colonial Times to 1970* and *Social Indicators*, the latter being a series of volumes that periodically report on selected social conditions and trends in the United States, with some comparative data from other countries.

Many libraries also own annual volumes of the Gallup Opinion Poll Index (usually found in the reference section), which lists each question asked along with the responses, which are often broken down by characteristics such as age, gender, race, religion, education, or income.

For statistical information about countries in addition to the United States, the best source is the United Nations *Demographic Yearbook*, which contains the most complete and accurate information available on the social, political, and economic conditions of all states belonging to the United Nations. For more recent information on issues related to population, a good source is the Population Reference Bureau, whose current, inexpensive publications are available from them at Box 35012, Washington, DC 20013.

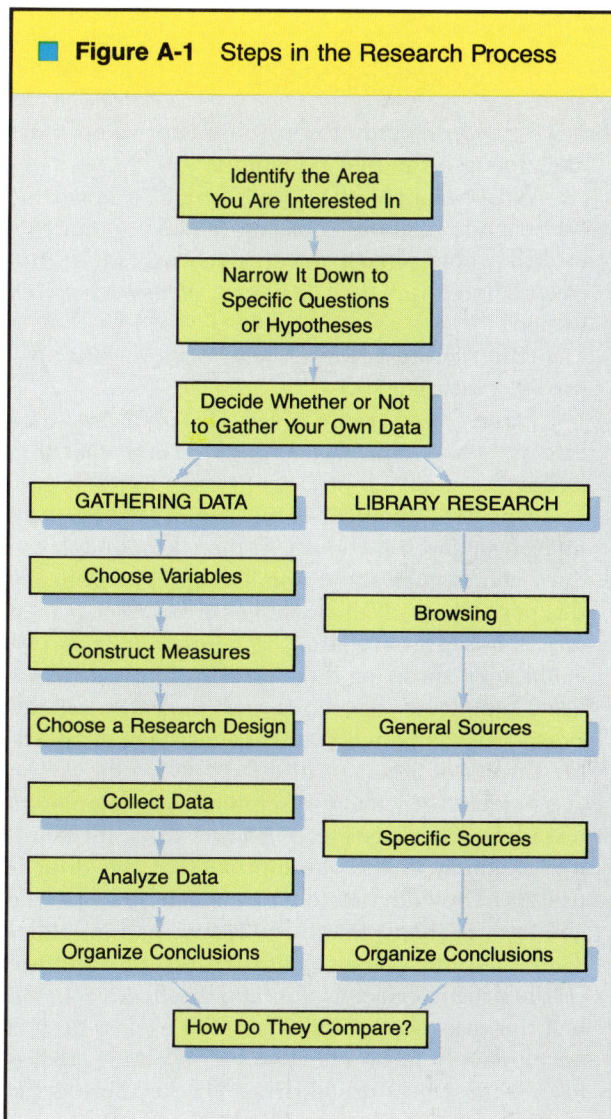

■ **Figure A-1**   Steps in the Research Process

Identify the Area You Are Interested In

Narrow It Down to Specific Questions or Hypotheses

Decide Whether or Not to Gather Your Own Data

GATHERING DATA

LIBRARY RESEARCH

Choose Variables

Browsing

Construct Measures

Choose a Research Design

General Sources

Collect Data

Specific Sources

Analyze Data

Organize Conclusions

Organize Conclusions

How Do They Compare?

# APPENDIX B

# Using Samples: A Primer on Statistical Inference

Researchers often try to describe very large populations, such as the adult population of the United States, with the results of surveys that involve only a relatively small sample, such as 1,300 to 1,500 people. If you have ever followed a national election, you know that such polls can predict results with astonishing accuracy. How is this possible? The procedure is called **statistical inference.** It involves some sophisticated mathematics that we will not go into here; but you can get some idea of the reasoning behind it by considering the following example.

Suppose you shoot dice with Fred (using his dice) and he rolls a total of "7" three times in a row. "Lucky throws," you think. Then he rolls three more 7s, for a total of six straight. *"Very* lucky," you think. "Maybe *too* lucky." As Fred keeps rolling 7s, you begin to doubt the "fairness" of the dice, and at some point you will conclude that something is fishy with the dice, and perhaps with Fred.

Without knowing it, you are performing some sophisticated statistical reasoning. You start with a **null hypothesis,** a testable assumption that both dice are "fair," which means that on each throw, all numbers have an equal chance to come up. You then watch the dice, and after a sample of three rolls, you note the result: "all 7s." At this point, there are two possibilities: (1) the dice are fair (the null hypothesis is correct) and Fred is lucky, or (2) a fair pair of dice would hardly ever give a total of "7" three times in a row, and the null hypothesis

is wrong. After only three rolls, you would most likely choose the first possibility.

With a sample of ten rolls of all 7s, however, the second possibility looks more likely: A fair pair of dice would almost never give you ten 7s in a row. Therefore, the dice are *almost certainly* loaded.

"But," protests Fred, "ten 7s in a row isn't *impossible* with fair dice."

"True," you reply, "but if I call the dice loaded, *the chances are mighty slim that I'm wrong.*"

This last statement is an example of statistical inference, and it is the key to the use of samples to draw conclusions about populations. Theoretically the population of all possible throws of a pair of dice is not just very large, it is *infinitely* large (we could keep throwing dice forever); but instead we use a sample of only ten throws to draw a conclusion about the population that consists of "all possible throws of a pair of dice."

Scientists in many disciplines use samples to test ideas. Physicians testing a new drug, for example, begin with the assumption that the drug is useless. They administer it to a sample of people and find, perhaps, that it is effective half the time. They then must choose between two possibilities: (1) the drug is in fact useless and its effectiveness in half the cases was a "fluke" or (2) a useless drug is very unlikely to be effective half the time; therefore, it must be a useful drug. The key here is the phrase "very unlikely" (and this is where the sophisticated mathematics come in): *if the sample is properly selected, it is possible to mathematically calculate the chances that a useless drug would be effective half the time simply by chance.*

This is essentially how pollsters predict election winners long before all the votes are in. If they draw a sample that shows candidate Mary Jones the winner, they start with the assumption that, at best, the election will end in a tie when all votes are counted. They then ask, "How likely is it that Jones would win in a sample we drew from a population in which she actually has no more votes than her opponent? (the same reasoning as "How likely are ten 7s with a pair of fair dice?"). If this possibility is very *un*likely, they reject the assumption that at best Jones will tie, and predict her victory.

There are four important points to be made here. First, when scientists draw conclusions from samples, there is always a possibility that they are wrong (just as ten 7s in a row is possible, however improbable it is). The mathematics of statistical inference, however, allows researchers to know just how likely such a mistake is. When election predictors say, "It's too close to call," they are in effect saying that if they predict a winner, the chances of being wrong are unacceptably high.

Second, they can make such statements only if they can *calculate* the chance of making an error, and this can only be done with samples selected so that every member of the population has an equal chance of being included. Thus, with "haphazard" samples there is no way to draw a conclusion and calculate the chances of making a mistake. They might be right; they might be wrong. More than that, they cannot say.

In the 1936 U.S. presidential election, for example, the *Literary Digest* selected a sample of adults from telephone directories and found overwhelming support for Republican Alfred Landon among its two million replies. The magazine predicted an easy victory over his Democratic opponent, Franklin Roosevelt. George Gallup, however, used a far smaller sample and correctly predicted Roosevelt's victory. What happened?

The *Literary Digest* violated the most important principle of scientific sampling when it used telephone directories to select its sample. During the Depression, only middle- and upper-class people could afford telephones, and such people tended to vote Republican. Less-affluent people,

on the other hand, heavily favored Roosevelt and were never considered for the *Digest* sample. By using scientific techniques to draw his sample, Gallup accurately predicted the outcome with a far smaller sample (Hennessy, 1971).

Third, note that the conclusion, "Jones will win the election" rests on the *rejection of other possible outcomes.* This illustrates a basic aspect of scientific research. We cannot explain something, for example, merely by finding an explanation that "fits the facts," because there may be many competing explanations that also might "fit the facts." The only way to prove a theory, then, is to systematically eliminate every alternative theory. To test the theory that employers discriminate against women by paying them less than men for doing the same work, for example, we must first eliminate alternative explanations—men are more competent, have more experience or higher educations. Only if we eliminate all possible alternative causes of pay differences, can we attribute any differences in earnings to discrimination.

Fourth, statistical inferences must be carefully interpreted. When a drug company tests its toothpaste against competing brands, it selects samples of children. One group uses "Brand A" and the other uses "Brand B," and after several years, the two groups are compared. The null hypothesis in this case is: "There is no difference between the two Brands." Suppose the Brand A group has fewer cavities than the Brand B group. Does this mean Brand A is better?

The problem is that it is possible to have two equally effective products produce differences *by chance* in a sample of users (just as it is possible to get six 7s in a row with a fair pair of dice). Researchers then use the mathematics of statistical inference to answer the question: "Could the difference between the two groups have occurred simply by chance?" Suppose they conclude the following: "It's *very* unlikely that two samples using equally effective toothpastes would differ this much simply by chance. Therefore, the two brands must *not* be equally effective: Brand A is better."

Such conclusions are frequently presented as "Children using Brand A had *significantly* fewer cavities." This is where caution is needed, for to most people, "significant," means "important" or "substantial"; but scientific "significance" has a much narrower meaning. To say that two groups are "significantly different" means *only* that we are very certain they are not exactly the same. By itself, it does *not* mean that the difference is either large or important.

Many studies show, for example, that when punishment is swift and certain, crime rates tend to fall. Thus, the swiftness and certainty of punishment have "significant effects" on crime rates. While this is an important finding, it is also important to ask, "How much of an effect?" The answer, disappointingly, is, "Not very much" (Andenaes, 1975; Tittle, 1975). Thus, whenever you read a scientific report that refers to "significant differences," be sure to search for statements that indicate the actual magnitude of the difference.

Used correctly, samples and statistical inference are very efficient research tools, for they enable us to study populations that would otherwise be too large to study at all.

# Glossary

**Aberrant behavior (aberrance)** Behavior that violates norms for personal gain. **283**

**Absolute deprivation** A lack of some basic necessity relative to a fixed standard such as the amount of food necessary for survival. **650**

**Abstract ideal** (See **Ethical religion.**)

**Academic subculture** The type of student subculture that encourages hard work and learning for its own sake. **505**

**Achieved status** A status entered after birth and due at least in part to individual behavior. **89**

**Acquired status** (See **Achieved status.**)

**Acting collective behavior** Behavior oriented to specific goals. **635**

**Affirmative action** A social policy of preferential treatment for minorities, the purpose of which is to erase disadvantages caused by a history of prejudice and discrimination. **385**

**Age group** One of the categories into which the life span is divided in a particular culture. **431**

**Ageism** Prejudice based on age. **433**

**Age structure** The relative number of people of each age in a population. **125, 450**

**Aggregate** A collection of people who happen to be in the same place at the same time. **94** (See also **Situational status.**)

**Agrarian society** A society in which agriculture is the primary means of subsistence. **133**

**Alienation** The psychological condition in which individuals feel detached from work, social relationships, and the results of their own behavior. **239, 349, 551**

**Aligning action** An action that signals an actor's acceptance of a new definition of the situation. **195**

**Amalgamation** The combination of several cultures in a society to produce a new culture. **359**

**Ancestor worship** The religious worship of ancestors based on the belief that they possess supernatural power. **607**

**Androgyny** The combining of masculine and feminine personality traits in a single individual. **422**

**Animism** A religion based on the belief that spirits and ghosts inhabit sacred objects such as trees and rocks. **607**

**Anomie** A social condition in which members of groups, organizations, communities, or societies no longer feel allegiance to norms. **298**

**Anthropology** The study of culture in small, preindustrial societies.

**Anticipatory socialization** The process of learning how to perform a role attached to a status we do not yet occupy. **164**

**Apartheid** South Africa's rigid policy of racial discrimination and segregation. **344**

**Ascribed status** A status assigned at birth. **89**

**Assimilation** The conformity of members of ethnic groups to the culture of the dominant group. **359**

**Attitudes** Positive or negative evaluations of people, objects, or situations, that often predispose people to feel and behave positively or negatively toward them. **15, 81**

**Audience segregation** In the dramaturgical approach, the effort by social actors to keep their "frontstage" and "backstage" selves separate. **193** (See also **Backstage; Frontstage.**)

**Authoritarian leadership structure** A leadership structure in which power is concentrated in the hands of a relative few. **101**

**Authoritarianism** In political sociology, the degree to which the state controls the lives of its citizens. **576**

**Authoritarian leader** A leader who dominates social interaction in a group. **215**

**Authority** Power assigned according to norms and accepted as legitimate by those over whom it is exercised. **101, 188, 567**

**Autocracy** A state that is ruled by a single person. **576**

**Automation** The replacement of human labor with machines. **541**

**Backstage** In the dramaturgical approach, the place where players are freed from the requirements of their role. **193** (See also **Frontstage.**)

**Balance theory** A theoretical perspective on social interaction that suggests that people organize their perceptions of people and objects into units and strive for some consistency in the positive and negative feelings among them. **200**

**Behavioral approach (to learning)** A theoretical approach to learning and behavior that focuses on the importance of reward and punishment and classical and operant conditioning. **148**

**Beliefs** Statements about what is real. **14, 72**

**Bias** The tendency of research results to be in error in one respect more than in any other. **40**

**Bilateral descent** Kinship arrangements in which descent is traced through both the mother's and father's blood relatives. **468**

**Bilocal society** A society in which married couples must live near or in the household of the wife's mother or the husband's father.

**Biological determinism** The belief that individual differences are biologically caused and, therefore, unchangeable. (See also "Nature versus nurture" debate; Social Darwinism.)

**Birth cohort** People who share the same year of birth. **126, 439**

**Birth order** A child's position in a family determined by his or her age relative to other children in a family. **166**

**Birth rate** The number of children born each year for every thousand members of a population. **115**

**Blue-collar** Referring to occupations that primarily involve manual work. **318**

**Boundary** The specification of who may occupy a particular status. **94** The **clarity** of boundaries describes how easily people can tell who occupies a status. **94** The **openness** of boundaries refers to how easy it is for individuals to occupy a particular status. **94**

**Bourgeoisie** (See **Capitalist**.)

**Bureaucracy** A complex set of formal, secondary relationships in which (1) entry into social statuses is controlled by rigid norms; (2) people specialize in narrowly-defined tasks; (3) roles are clearly and rigidly defined by rules and regulations; (4) power is distributed in a clear hierarchy; (5) managers specialize in making sure everything works according to the rules; and (6) decisions are based on rational considerations of the organization's best interests rather than on personal feelings and the welfare of individuals. **105, 220**

**Capital** Property such as machinery that can be used to produce goods or services. Also, wealth that can be used to produce more wealth. **535**

**Capitalism** An economic system in which the means of production are privately owned and controlled. **535**

**Capitalist** A person who owns means of production. **315, 535**

**Case study** A study that focuses on a single example rather than a representative sample in order to gather more detailed information. **41**

**Caste** A social class in which membership depends on ascribed statuses and cannot be changed after birth. **333**

**Casual collective behavior** Behavior that involves no common goal or purpose around which people interact or focus their attention. **635**

**Census** A gathering of information on all members of a population. **39**

**Charismatic authority** Authority that is based on people's belief that a particular individual possesses special abilities or characteristics. **567**

**Church** The second most powerful religious institution, with a broad membership that includes a majority of the members of a society, a formally trained and bureaucratic clergy, governed by legal-rational and traditional authority, focusing on highly abstract unemotional ritual, and often although not always allied with the ruling class. **613**

**Circular reaction** In Blumer's theory of collective behavior, the belief that people not only copy one another, but amplify one another's emotional state in the process. **643** (See also **Contagion**.)

**Civil disobedience** The deliberate and open violation of a norm for the purpose of changing it because it is perceived as being unjust. **574**

**Civil law** A norm that regulates social relationships in order to prevent or undo the negative effects of particular acts. **81**

**Civil religion** A set of cultural ideas, symbols, and practices oriented to the direct worship of a society by its members. **626**

**Clarity** (See **Boundary**.)

**Class consciousness** An awareness among members of a social class of the true extent and causes of inequality in a society. **349**

**Classical conditioning** A form of learning in which a biological reflex is conditioned to respond to a new stimulus. **148**

**Classical social movement theory** A theory (including several specific approaches) that is based on the following general model: some kind of strain or disturbance in the social environment (such as an economic depression) creates disruptive psychological states in individuals (such as anxiety) and individuals then channel their energy into social movements in order to relieve their emotional difficulties. **649**

**Closed (stratification) system** A stratification system in which class membership is based on ascribed statuses and movement from one class to another is difficult if not impossible. **333**

**Coalition** A subgroup whose members join forces in order to increase their control over group process. **191, 227, 586**

**Coercive power** Power that lacks the social legitimacy of authority and is based on fear and the use of force. **568**

**Cognitive development perspective (theory)** A theory of socialization that focuses on the growth of mental abilities to make increasingly complex judgments about ourselves as well as our physical and social environments. **150**

**Cohort** (See **Birth cohort**.)

**Cohort effect** Effects on people's lives that arise from the characteristics of the historical periods during which they experienced different stages of life such as childhood, adolescence, or middle age. **450**

**Collective behavior** The relatively unstructured behavior of people in crowds and masses. **635**

**"Collective conscience"** The term—used by proponents of the functional perspective—for the moral consensus that is violated by deviant acts. **280**

**Collectivity** A set of people who share a common culture and think of themselves as a unit, but do not interact with one another. **224**

**Collegiate subculture** The type of student subculture that values social activities above others. **505**

**Colonialism** The relationship between countries in which one dominates the other and exploits its natural and human resources. **345**

**Commodity** A good or service produced primarily for its exchange value, not for direct consumption by the producer. **532**

**Communal economy** An economy based on collective ownership of means of production, primary ties, and sharing.

**Communication structure** The frequency and duration of interaction among members of a group. **102**

**Communism** A utopian economic system in which the means of production are communally owned and there is no state. **558**

**Community** A collection of people who share a common territory and meet their basic physical and social needs through daily interaction with one another. **245**

**Compound family** A nuclear family in which children are directly related to only one of the parents. **473**

**Compound status** A status that consists of one or more statuses joined together as one—as "policewoman" joins occupation with gender. **91–92** (See also **Role strain; Status strain**.)

**Concentric-zone theory (model)** A theory of urban land use according to which cities develop in rings around a core of business activity; outer rings are higher in social class than inner rings. **265**

**Conflict perspective** A theoretical perspective that focuses on the struggle among different social groups over scarce rewards. **21**

**Conformity** Behavior or appearance consistent with norms. **277**

**Conglomerate** A collection of companies in different industries that are owned by a single corporation. **544**

**Conspicuous consumption** Consumption intended to affirm or enhance an individual's prestige. **218, 330**

**Constant** A behavior or characteristic that does not vary from one individual, group, or society to another. **35**

**Contagion** In Le Bon's theory of collective behavior, the belief that people uncritically copy one another's behavior, setting off a chain reaction. **641**

**Content analysis** Analysis of words and images contained in written, spoken, and visual media. **46**

**Control group** A group of people in an experiment who are not exposed to the experimental stimulus under study. **43**

**Control variable** A variable introduced into a statistical analysis to see if a statistical relationship holds among people who are alike on a particular characteristic. **52**

**Conventional collective behavior** Behavior that involves a specific purpose such as watching a parade. **635**

**Convergence theory** Le Bon's belief that crowds consist of like-minded people who assemble in one place. **641**

**Core society** In world-system theory, a society that is in an economically dominant position. **560**

**Correlation** A measure of association used in regression analysis. **55**

**Coup d'état** An attempt to illegally replace one government with another, often through the use of force. **594**

**Crime** The term for acts that violate laws. **285**

**Crime rate** The number of crimes per year per one thousand people in a population. **286**

**Criminal justice system** A set of institutions including police, courts, and prisons. **293**

**Criminal law** A norm that links specific acts with punishments. **81**

**Cross-cultural study** Research that tries to identify the origins of cultural ideas, social structures, or ecological arrangements by comparing different societies. **48**

**Crowd** A relatively temporary collection of people who happen to be in the same place at the same time in close enough proximity to one another so that they can interact with and be affected by one another. **635**

**Crude birth rate** (See **Birth rate**)

**Crude death rate** (See **Death rate.**)

**Cult** A relatively temporary religious group whose members are generally recruited among poor people in a state of emotional crisis, which has an informal, loosely organized structure governed by charismatic leadership, involves no formal rituals, relies on highly emotional displays during ceremonies, and actively rejects the major institutions of the surrounding society. **614**

**Cultural analysis** The analysis of (1) relationships among different cultural ideas; (2) the effects of culture on perceptions of reality; (3) the influence of culture on individuals' experience and behavior; (4) functions and dysfunctions of cultural ideas in relation to groups and societies; and (5) the ways in which cultural ideas contribute to social conflict. **65–83**

**Cultural determinism** The belief that individual differences are caused by the socialization process and are, therefore, changeable. (See also "**Nature versus nurture**" debate.)

**Cultural relativism** A concept that refers to the fact that the importance of a particular cultural idea varies from one society or subgroup to another. **74**

**Cultural universal** A cultural idea or practice found in all societies. **73**

**Culture** The entire set of beliefs, norms, values, and attitudes that govern social relationships in groups, communities, or societies. **14, 65** (See also **Material culture; Nonmaterial culture.**)

**Culture lag** An instance in which technological change occurs before cultural norms can be introduced to govern its use. **673, 674**

**Cyclical theory of social change** The theory that the development of societies occurs in cycles (rather than a straight line) that parallel the lives of individuals. Societies are "born," mature, age, and die. **676**

**Death rate** The number of people who die in a given year for every thousand people in a population. **117**

**Decision theory** A theoretical perspective that views collective behavior—and human behavior in general—as the result of rational attempts to solve problems. **644**

**De facto segregation** Segregation that is an unintended consequence of social or ecological arrangements. **373**

**Definition of the situation** The determination of which statuses and roles are relevant in a social situation. **91, 180**

**Degradation ceremony** An important part of the socialization process in total institutions, in which inmates are subjected to humiliation and labeled inferior human beings. **296**

**De jure segregation** Segregation that is required by law. **373**

**Democracy** A social structure in which power is evenly distributed. **574** (See also **Representative democracy.**)

**Democratic leader** A leader who exercises little authority and acts primarily as a moderator in group interactions. **101, 215**

**Democratic socialism** An economic system in which the state owns and controls only selected important means of production such as utilities and airlines. **557**

**Demographic transition theory** A theory describing the pattern of falling death and birth rates that has characterized the recent history of now industrialized countries of the world. **121**

**Demography** The study of the size, composition, growth, and distribution of human populations. **113**

**Denomination** The third most powerful type of religious institution, with a membership generally dominated by a single social class, a formal but not bureaucratic role structure, a trained clergy, traditional authority, abstract relatively unemotional ritual, and a condition of coexistence between it and dominant political and economic institutions. **613**

**Dependency theory** (See **World-system theory.**)

**Dependent variable** A variable affected by another variable. **51**

**Deviance** Any behavior or appearance that violates a norm. **277**

**Differential association (theory)** A theory of deviance that argues that in the socialization process people vary in the norms and values they feel allegiance to because they are not equally exposed to the same norms and values. **299**

**Diffusion** The process through which knowledge spreads from one society to another. **672**

**Discovery** An instance of finding out about something that already exists. **672**

**Discrimination** Positive or negative behavior directed toward the occupants of a social status based on stereotyped beliefs about them. **362**

**Division of labor** The allocation of different roles among the members of a group, organization, community, or society.

**Dramaturgy (dramaturgical approach)** The study of social interaction as theater in which actors play roles before audiences. **193**

**Dual economy** An economy that is part monopolistic and part competitive. **548**

**Dyad** A group with two members. **93, 190**

**Dysfunction** The interference of a cultural idea or social structure with the achievement of one or more valued goals. **22**

**Ecclesia** The most powerful of religious institutions, including most members of a society, dominated by a formal and bureaucratic clergy, governed by legal-rational and traditional authority, focusing on highly abstract ritual, and closely identified with dominant political and economic institutions. **612**

**Ecological analysis** The analysis of (1) how numbers of people and spatial arrangements affect individuals' perceptions and behavior; and (2) the effects of population size and distribution, physical environments, and technology on the development of cultural ideas and social structures. **113–137**

**Ecological succession** The process through which ecosystems change. **670**

**Ecology** The study of the relationship between populations and their physical environments, including the ability to use natural resources and technology. **17, 114**

**Economic institutions** Enduring arrangements of cultural ideas and socially structured relationships through which goods and services are produced and distributed in societies. **531**

**Ecosystem** All forms of life that live in relation to one another and a shared physical environment. **130**

**Education** The systematic formal transmission of skills, knowledge, beliefs, values, attitudes, and norms. **499**

**Egalitarian family (marriage)** A family in which authority is evenly divided between husbands and wives. **477**

**Ego** In Freudian theory, the rational part of the self that "manages" the desires of the id and the demands of the superego. **154**

**Emergent norm theory** A theory of collective behavior that tries to explain how patterns of expectation and interaction emerge in crowds that involve no prior planning. **643**

**Emigrant** Someone who moves out of a territory. **123** (See also **Immigrant.**)

**Endogamy** A marriage rule that requires people to marry someone belonging to their own social group or community. **471**

**Ethical religion** A religion that focuses more on sets of abstract ideals than on supernatural powers vested in gods, objects, or animals. **608**

**Ethnic group** A set of people who identify with a common cultural heritage. **353**

**Ethnicism** Prejudice based on ethnicity. **356**

**Ethnicity** A concept that refers to statuses based on a shared cultural heritage. **353**

**Ethnocentrism** The tendency of people to regard the ideas and practices of other cultures as incorrect, if not inferior. **74**

**Ethnomethodology** The study of the unspoken rules and meanings through which people interpret one another's behavior and form expectations of one another. **28**

**Evolutionary theories of social change** Theories that argue that all societies develop along predetermined paths that take them from inferior to superior forms, from simple to complex and from "primitive" to "civilized." **676** (See also **Social evolution.**)

**Exchange theory** An approach to social interaction that focuses on how people exchange one thing for another in social relationships. **197**

**Exchange value** The attribution of value to goods or services based upon how much can be gotten for them in exchange for other goods and services. **532**

**Exogamy** A marriage rule that requires people to marry someone outside their own social group or community. **471**

**Experiment** A research design in which similar groups of subjects are exposed to conditions that differ in only one respect (the independent variable) in order to establish cause-and-effect relationships. **43**

**Expressive collective behavior** Behavior that focuses on the expression of feelings toward some common object or event. **635**

**Expressive role** A role that focuses on maintaining harmony among members. **213** (See also **Task role.**)

**Expulsion** A form of social oppression in which minorities are forced to leave their communities or societies. **375**

**Extended family** A family that includes a nuclear family plus additional relatives such as grandparents, uncles, aunts, or cousins. **473**

**External causes** In social attribution, aspects of people's social situations that are used to explain their behavior. **182**

**Extrapolation** An estimate of future conditions based on the assumption that "current trends will continue."

**Extrinsic reward** A reward given to someone by someone else. **504** (See also **Intrinsic reward.**)

**Fad** A short-lived standard of appearance or behavior marked by great enthusiasm among its followers. **636**

**False consciousness** A state of unawareness of, or misperception of, social conditions and their causes, especially when applied to social stratification. **325**

**Family** A primary group organized around kinship ties and designed to regulate sexual behavior and reproduce, nurture, protect, and socialize the young. **463**

**Family disorganization** The result of unoccupied statuses or inadequately performed roles within a family. **484**

**Fashion** A relatively temporary standard of appearance or behavior that is considered to be socially acceptable or desirable. **635**

**Fatalism** The belief that humans can do nothing to control events. **618**

**Femininity** A set of beliefs describing the ideal female. **396**

**Feminism** An ideology that directly opposes sexism by supporting gender equality. **422**

**Feudalism** The social, economic, and political structure that characterized medieval Europe and other preindustrial societies. **533**

**Field experiment** An experiment conducted in real-world settings. **44**

**Folkways** The set of manners and customary acts that characterize everyday life in a society. **77**

**Formal organization (group)** A group that exists for a specific purpose and is dominated by social relationships governed by clearly stated, rigidly enforced norms. **220** (See also **Informal organization [group].**)

**Formal relationship** A relationship governed by specific rules that rigidly define and control interactions among status occupants. **103** (See also **Informal relationship.**)

**Formal sanction** A clearly defined sanction with specific people empowered to impose it. **80–81, 285** (See also **Informal sanction.**)

**Front** In the dramaturgical approach, a person's physical appearance, behavior, and definition of the situation. **193**

**Frontstage** In the dramaturgical approach, the place where roles are performed before an audience. **193** (See also **Backstage.**)

**Frustration-aggression theory** A theory that argues that collective behavior is a way of relieving feelings of frustration. **649**

**Function** A contribution of a cultural idea or social structure to the achievement of one or more valued goals.

**Functional perspective** A theoretical perspective that focuses on the ways in which cultural ideas and social structures contribute to or interfere with the attainment of valued goals. **22**

**Game theory** A theoretical perspective that views collective behavior—and human behavior in general—as an attempt by people to maximize their rewards while minimizing costs. **645**

**Gemeinschaft** A concept (attributed to Tönnies) that describes communities in which social cohesion is based on primary relationships, shared culture, and similarity of life experience. **235, 261** (Referred to by Durkheim as **Mechanical solidarity.**)

**Gender** Social statuses to which males and females are assigned in a society. **391**

**Gender role** A role that applies to people of different genders. **399**

**Generalized belief** In Smelser's theory of social movements, an irrational belief seized upon as a way of justifying collective behavior and reducing uncertainty and feelings of anxiety. **653**

**Generalized other** Our perceptions of the social environment including cultural ideas that regulate social interaction. **156**

**Genocide** The systematic attempt to kill all occupants of a particular status. **374**

**Gentrification** A process of community change through which housing in old neighborhoods is restored, resulting in higher rents and the displacement of previous tenants who can no longer afford to live there. **271**

**Gerontocracy** A society that is ruled by an elderly elite. **446**

**Gerrymandering** In politics, the practice of defining election districts in ways that maximize the political power of a particular group or social category. **587**

**Gesellschaft** A concept (attributed to Tönnies) that describes communities in which social cohesion is based on secondary relationships and interdependencies created by complex divisions of labor. **237, 261** (Referred to by Durkheim as **Organic solidarity.**)

**Gesture** An action that has symbolic meaning. **65**

**Government** The collection of people who happen to occupy positions of authority within the framework of social relationships that define the state. **570** (See also **State.**)

**Group** Two or more people who interact with each other in patterned ways and are identified as members by themselves and others. **93, 207**

**Group effectiveness** The extent to which a group accomplishes the goals it sets for itself. **229**

**Group process** What group members actually do, regardless of role expectations. **225**

**Groupthink** An example of group process in which a shared desire for consensus outweighs members' better judgment. **230**

**Hawthorne effect** A distortion of research results caused by the response of subjects to the special attention they receive from researchers. **43**

**Hidden curriculum** In schools, knowledge, values, attitudes, norms, and beliefs that people acquire because of the process that is used to learn something else. **506**

**Historical (analysis) research** The use of historical documents to analyze the development and change of culture, social structure, and ecology. **47**

**Horticultural society** A society in which subsistence needs are met primarily through cultivation of small gardens, but without the use of the plow. **132**

**Hospice** An organization designed to care for the terminally ill. **441**

**Hunter-gatherer society** A society in which subsistence needs are met primarily by hunting wild game and gathering existing vegetation. **132**

**Hypothesis** A statement that predicts a relationship between variables. **51**

**Hysteria** A state of rapidly spreading anxiety that affects people in crowds and masses. **639**

**I** George Herbert Mead's concept that refers to that part of us that directly experiences ourselves and others. **155** (See also **Me.**)

**Id** In Freudian theory, that part of the self that is the source of unregulated desires and impulses. **153**

**Ideal self** Our image of ourselves as we believe we ought to be. **162**

**Ideal type** A concept that describes a "pure" type that does not actually exist. **261**

**Ideology** A set of interrelated beliefs, values, attitudes, and norms that are used to explain and/or justify existing social relationships. **325, 358, 393**

**Immanent change** Sorokin's principle that cultures have material and nonmaterial characteristics that cause societies to develop in certain directions. **676**

**Immigrant** Someone who moves into a territory. **123** (See also **Emigrant.**)

**Incest taboo** A norm that forbids sexual intercourse between people who are culturally defined as kin. **463**

**Income** Money that people receive each year. **328**

**Independence** The condition in which one variable has no effect on another. **50**

**Independent primary (labor market) jobs** In the primary labor market, jobs that involve relatively high levels of creativity, autonomy, and power. **547**

**Independent variable** A variable considered to cause variation in a second variable. **51**

**In-depth interview** An interview or series of interviews designed to collect extensive information. **45**

**Infant mortality rate** The number of infants under the age of one who die in a given year for every 100,000 births that occur during that year. **116**

**Informal organization (group)** A group in which social relationships are governed by flexible, implicit norms. **220** (See also **Formal organization [group].**)

**Informal relationship** A relationship governed by flexible, implicit norms. **103**

**Informal sanction** A loosely defined sanction with no specific people authorized to impose it. **80, 285** (See also **Formal sanction.**)

**In-group** A group to which we belong and in which we share a sense of "we-ness" that often excludes and devalues members of other groups. **212**

**Innovation** A form of deviance in which a person accepts values but rejects the norms that define legitimate means for achieving them. **283**

**Institution** An enduring set of cultural ideas and social relationships that are designed to accomplish valued goals. **108, 461**

**Insulation** The practice of managing our role performances so that role partners cannot observe our behavior in two or more conflicting roles. **92**

**Integration** The degree to which members of different groups in a community are distributed according to their relative numbers. **387** (See also **Isolation.**)

**Interaction** (See **Social interaction.**)

**Interest group** An organization that attempts to affect political decisions by supporting candidates who are sympathetic to their interests and by influencing those who are already in positions of authority. **584**

**Intergenerational mobility** When the class position of children differs from that of their parents. **333**

**Internal causes** In social attribution, personal motives, abilities, and emotional states that are used to explain people's behavior. **182**

**Internal migration** Migration within a society.

**International migration** Migration between societies.

**International stratification** Stratification between societies. **341**

**Interview** A method of gathering data through which people are asked a series of questions by an interviewer. **41**

**Intrinsic reward** A reward that people give to themselves. **504**

**Invention** Something new created from things that already exist. **672**

**Iron rule of oligarchy** Michels' theory that all states inevitably become oligarchies.

**Isolation** The degree to which groups do not share the same communities. **387**

**J-curve theory** A theory of social movements that argues that movements are most likely to occur when a period of rising expectations is followed by sharp and rapidly worsening conditions for members of deprived groups. **651**

**Juvenile delinquency** Criminal acts committed by minors. **287**

**Kinship** Social relationships that are based on common ancestry, adoption, or marriage. **467**

**Kin** People who are bound together with kinship ties.

**Labor** The production of goods or services that can either be used directly or exchanged. **315, 536**

**Labor market segmentation** The division of job markets into distinct parts to which access is unequally distributed among workers. **548** (See also **Primary labor market** and **Secondary labor market.**)

**Labor power** The potential to produce goods—usually measured in terms of time—which workers sell to employers in return for wages. **316, 536**

**Laissez-faire leader** A leader who does not participate in group interaction unless asked to do so. **215**

**Language** A collection of symbols (words) and rules for their usage (syntax and grammar) that allows people to represent thought and experience. **67**

**Latent dysfunction** A negative unintended effect of a cultural idea or social structure on the achievement of one or more socially valued goals. **22**

**Latent function** A positive unintended effect of a cultural idea or social structure on the achievement of one or more socially valued goals. **22**

**Latent status** A status that is not included in the definition of a situation, but nonetheless affects the expectations of the participants. **92**

**Law** A norm whose sanctions are formal. **80** (See also **Criminal law** and **Civil law.**)

**Leadership** The exercise of authority that is supported by group norms and accepted by members. **101**

**Leadership structure** A structure that exhibits the distribution of authority in a group or organization. **101**

**Legal-rational authority** Power that is based on culturally defined rules that regulate social interaction. **567**

**Life course** The culturally defined "normal" set of passages from one age group to another. **431**

**Life expectancy** The average number of remaining years people can expect to live if current death rates remain unchanged throughout their lifetime. **117**

**Lifetime mobility** The degree to which individuals change class position within their own lifetimes. **333**

**Lobbyist** A representative of an interest group who meets with government officials and tries to influence decisions by providing information that tends to support the goals of the group. **585**

**Longitudinal (study) survey** A research design in which information is gathered from the same sample of people at specified intervals of time. **42**

**Looking-glass self** Our perception of how other people perceive and evaluate us. **160**

**Macrosociology (macrolevel)** A branch (level) of sociology that focuses on the cultural and social structural characteristics of groups and societies. **15–16**

**Manifest dysfunction** A negative intended effect of a cultural idea or social structure on the achievement of social goals. **22**

**Manifest function** An intended positive effect that a cultural idea or social structure has on the achievement of social goals. **22**

**Manifest status** A status that is explicitly included in the definition of a situation. **92**

**Market economy** An economy based primarily upon exchange of goods and services rather than sharing. **532**

**Marriage** A socially supported union between individuals in what is intended to be a stable, enduring relationship that involves sexual interaction as a key element. **463**

**Marriage rules** Norms that regulate whom people may marry, when, and under what circumstances. **470**

**Masculinity** A set of beliefs describing the ideal male. **396**

**Mass** A collection of people who pay attention to and react to the same thing without being in one another's presence. **635**

**Mass society theory** Kornhauser's theory that collective behavior is caused by a social condition in which people feel isolated from one another and from their communities. **652**

**Master status** A status that is treated as more important than any other status in a status set. **90, 304**

**Material culture** Objects made by people as they interact with one another and the physical world. **14**

**Matriarchy** A society formally dominated by females. **409, 477**

**Matrilineal descent** A kinship arrangement in which descent is traced through mothers and their blood relatives. **468**

**Matrilocal family (society)** A kinship arrangement in which married couples live in or near the household of the wife's mother. **471**

**Me** Mead's concept that refers to the part of the self that looks upon the self as an object. **155** (See also **I.**)

**Mean** A statistical measure used to describe the average score in a sample or population. It is computed by adding all the scores together and dividing by the number of people. **50**

**Means of production** The physical means through which goods and services are produced in a society. **531**

**Measurement instrument** A procedure that classifies individuals, groups, or societies according to a behavior or characteristic. **36**

**Measure of association** A number varying between +1.0 and −1.0 that indicates how accurately an independent variable can be used to predict a dependent variable. **56** (See also **Correlation.**)

**Mechanical solidarity 235, 252** (See **Gemeinschaft.**)

**Median** A statistical measure used to describe the typical score in a sample or population. It is equal to the score that divides a sample or population so that half the members are above the median and half are below. **50**

**Merchants** In a market economy, those who do not produce, but make a living by buying and selling what others produce. **534**

**Metropolitan area** A city with at least 50,000 inhabitants, *or* an urbanized area that is socially and economically integrated with surrounding communities that bring the total population to 100,000 or more. **247**

**Microecology** The study of how the number of people involved in a social situation and their physical arrangement in relation to one another affect social interaction. **190**

**Microsociology (microlevel)** A branch (level) of sociology that focuses on social relationships among individuals. **15**

**Migration** The movement of people from one place to another, either between societies or within them. **123**

**Military-industrial complex** A coalition consisting of the military and industrialists who make huge profits by manufacturing arms and selling them to the government. **586**

**Mind** The ability to use symbols in order to understand other people's thoughts, feelings, and expectations. **155**

**Minority (group)** A collection of people who, because of physical or cultural characteristics, are singled out from others for differential and unequal treatment. **354**

**Misanthropy** Hatred of all people. **394**

**Misogyny** Hatred of females. **394**

**Mob** An emotionally aroused, acting crowd that typically has a leader and focuses on a specific goal, the achievement of which usually involves some form of violence. **637**

**Mobilization** In Smelser's theory of collective behavior, the phase in which people gather into a crowd. **654**

**Mob psychology** A theoretical approach that tries to explain collective behavior solely on the basis of the psychological states of its members. **640**

**Mode** A statistical measure used to describe groups, equal to the most frequent score in a sample or population. **49**

**Model** A person whose behavior or appearance we use as an example of what to imitate or what to avoid. **149**

**Mode of production** The way in which a society goes about producing goods and services, consisting of the means of production and the relations of production. **531**

**Modern community** A community with a relatively complex division of labor, whose inhabitants tend to welcome change, use sophisticated technology, have well-developed mass media, and rely more on formal, secondary relationships than on primary or informal relationships. **248**

**Modernization** A concept describing a process through which societies are believed to change from less to more developed forms through the introduction of new technology and other social change. **679**

**Monogamy** Marriage to only one spouse at a time. **471**

**Monopoly** An arrangement in a market economy in which a partic-

ular good or service has only one provider who, therefore, controls the market. **544**

**Monotheism** Religious belief in a single supreme being. **607**

**Mores** The set of deeply held ideas about how people ought to behave. **79**

**Multilinear (change) theory** Theories of change that identify some change as universal, but also acknowledge that change takes place in ways that do not necessarily result in "progress." **678**

**Multinational corporation** A large business organization whose operations extend across international boundaries.

**Multiple-nuclei theory (model)** A theory of urban land use according to which cities have many different "cores" of activity. **265**

**Multistage sample** A sample selected in stages, beginning with the most unspecific level (such as regions of the country) and ending with the most specific (such as houses on selected city blocks). **41**

**"Nature versus nurture" debate** A debate arising from the question of whether nature (genetics) or nurture (environment) plays a greater role in human development. **146**

**Negative relationship** A statistical relationship in which high scores on one variable are related to low scores on another variable.

**Neighborhood** Collections of people who live close to one another within a community. **248**

**Neolocal society (family)** A kinship arrangement in which married couples start new households. **471**

**Niche** The position a species of life occupies in an ecosystem. **130**

**Nominal member** Someone who is considered to be a member of a group but who rarely if ever participates in group activities. **211**

**Nonconformist behavior (nonconformity)** Behavior that openly violates norms in order to bring about positive social change. **283**

**Nonconformist subculture** The type of student subculture that values rebellion against authority and open deviation from the academic, collegiate, and vocational subcultures. **505**

**Nonmaterial culture** The products of collective human activity that have no physical reality, including symbols, language, music, art, beliefs, values, norms, and attitudes. **14**

**Norm** A rule that attaches sanctions to the behavior of status occupants. **14, 77**

**"The Norm"** The common behaviors of a society. **277**

**Nuclear family** A family consisting of parents and their natural or adopted children. **473**

**Null hypothesis** A testable assumption about a population. (See Appendix B.)

**Oligarchy** A state that is ruled by a privileged elite. **575**

**Oligopoly** An economic arrangement in a market economy in which production of a good or service is controlled by a few organizations. **542**

**Openness** (See **Boundary.**)

**Open (stratification) system** A stratification system in which people are allowed to move from one class to another regardless of their ascribed statuses. **334**

**Operant conditioning** A form of learning in which punishment and reward are used to reinforce or discourage a behavior. **148**

**Opportunity structure** The distribution of opportunities to achieve culturally valued goals (among the occupants of different social statuses). **306**

**Organic solidarity 237, 252** (See **Gesellschaft.**)

**Organization** A situation in which two or more subgroups are related to each other through shared expectations and goals.

**Out-group** A group toward which hostile attitudes are directed by members of another group. **212** (See also **In-group.**)

**Overpopulation** An ecological condition in which a society is unable to support all its members with available technology and natural resources.

**Panic** A form of collective behavior in which people try to escape from a perceived danger in an uncooperative, often irrational way. **638**

**Participant observation** A research method in which researchers observe behavior in real-life settings in which they are participants. **44**

**Party** Weber's term for people who share similar levels of social power. **317**

**Party platform** A statement of a political party's position of important issues. **584**

**Patriarchy** A society or family system dominated by males. **409, 477**

**Patrilineal descent** A kinship arrangement in which descent is traced through fathers and their blood relatives. **468**

**Patrilocal family (society)** A kinship arrangement in which married couples live near or in the household of the husband's father. **471**

**Pattern of communication** (See **Communication structure.**)

**Peer group** People who share a level of social standing, especially in terms of age. **168**

**Percentage** The number of people in a sample or population who have a particular characteristic, divided by the size of the population or group, and multiplied by 100.

**Performative language** A meaningful utterance that alters people's positions in social relationships. **71**

**Peripheral member** A group member who meets with other members but rarely interacts with them. **211**

**Peripheral society** In world-system theory, a society that is in an economically subordinate position. **560**

**Personality** The complex patterns of thought, feeling, and behavior that make each individual unique.

**Personal power** Power that is based not on status occupancy, but on personal attributes such as physical strength or persuasiveness. **187**

**Pluralism (ethnic)** The coexistence of diverse ethnic groups in the same society. **359**

**Pluralism (political)** The distribution of power among several members of a group. **101, 216**

**Pluralistic leadership structure** A structure in which the right to make decisions is divided among different specialists. **101**

**Pluralist theory** The theory that holds that power in communities is distributed among a wide variety of groups and individuals. **260**

**Political economy** The sets of social arrangements through which political and economic institutions support and maintain each other. **592**

**Political institution** The relatively permanent cultural ideas and social structures through which power is distributed and exercised in societies. **567**

**Political party** An organization whose main goal is to acquire political power by placing members in positions of authority in political institutions. **582**

**Political process theory** An approach to social movements that concentrates both on what goes on within movements and on the relationship between movements and the institutions in the surrounding society. **657**

**Politics** The social process through which power and authority are distributed among and used by groups, communities, and societies. **567**

**Polyandry** Marriage between a woman and more than one man at a time. **471**

**Polygamy** Marriage to more than one spouse at a time. **471**

**Polygyny** Marriage between a man and more than one woman at a time. **471**

**Polytheism** In religion, the belief in more than one god. **607**

**Population** A collection of people who share a geographic territory. **17** (See also **Society.**) In research, a population is any precisely defined set of objects, people, groups, or societies. **39, 113**

**Population density** The number of people per unit of area (e.g., per square mile).

**Population distribution** A concept that refers to (1) the density of populations, (2) how people of different social statuses are distributed spatially, and (3) the physical arrangement of individuals as they interact with each other. **127**

**Population growth rate** The net result of births, deaths, in-migration, and out-migration in a population. **119–125**

**Positive relationship** A statistical relationship in which high scores on one variable are related to high scores on another variable.

**Postindustrial society** A society in which the production of goods is overshadowed by the provision of services, and in which relations between people and machines are gradually replaced by relationships between people. **550**

**Power** The possibility of imposing one's will upon the behavior of others in spite of their resistance. **100, 186**

**Power elite** A group of people who dominate decision making in all important areas of life in a community or society.

**Power-elite theory** The theory that argues that power in communities is concentrated in the hands of a relatively small group. **260** (See also **Power elite.**)

**Power structure** The distribution of power among members of groups, organizations, communities, or societies. **100**

**Precipitating incident** In Smelser's theory of collective behavior, an event that triggers a collective response. **654**

**Prejudice** A positive or negative attitude directed toward people who occupy a social status simply because they occupy that status. **356**

**Prestige** Respect accorded to people because of the social statuses they occupy. **101, 330**

**Primary deviance** Behavior that is not identified as deviant by the actor or by significant others. **303**

**Primary group** A group valued by its members for its own sake rather than for the achievement of specific goals, which endures through time and involves many aspects of its members' lives. **219**

**Primary labor market** The portion of the segmented labor market that includes jobs that require stable work habits, involve skills that are often learned on the job, are relatively high-paying, and have job ladders. **547** (See also **Subordinate primary jobs; Independent primary jobs.**)

**Primary relationship** A social relationship that exists for its own sake, endures through time, and involves people in many aspects of each other's lives. **103**

**Prisoner's dilemma** An experimental situation in which actors must choose between the risks of cooperation and competition.

**Profane** In religion, the designation of an object, experience, or person as being part of the natural human world. **602** (See also **Sacred.**)

**Profession** An occupation that is based on systematic, formal knowledge about a particular field (such as law) and involves high levels of autonomy and codes of conduct formulated and administered by other members of the occupation. **549**

**Professionalization** The social process through which an occupation acquires the cultural and structural characteristics of a profession. **550**

**Proletariat** In Marx's framework, the working class, which neither owns nor controls any means of production. **315**

**Pull factor** In migration, a positive social or ecological condition in one area that motivates people living in another area to move there. **123** (See also **Push factor.**)

**Push factor** In migration, a negative social or ecological condition in people's home areas that motivate them to leave. **123** (See also **Pull factor.**)

**Questionnaire** A method of gathering information in which respondents complete a written form. **41**

**Race (biological)** A collection of people with distinct physical characteristics that are passed on through reproduction. **353**

**Race (social)** A social status defined in terms of beliefs about biological race. **353**

**Racism** Prejudice that is based on perceived racial differences. **356**

**Random sample** A sample drawn so that all members of the population have an equal chance of being included. **41** (See also **Systematic sample** and **Multistage sample.**)

**Rate of natural increase** The difference between birth and death rates in a population. **119** (See also **Population growth rate.**)

**Realigning action** An action through which an actor tries to introduce a new definition of the situation. **196**

**Rebellion** A form of deviance in which a person challenges values and norms that define legitimate means for achieving them. **283** In politics, a **rebellion** challenges the policies of a government without trying to change the cultural or structural characteristics of the state. **593**

**Reference group** A group that someone uses as a standard of desirable or undesirable appearance or behavior. **163**

**Reference individual** An individual that someone uses as a standard of desirable or undesirable appearance or behavior. **163**

**Reform movement** A social movement that seeks to improve existing social environments. **647**

**Reincarnation** Rebirth in new bodies. **607**

**Relations of production** The social relationships through which goods or services are produced. **531**

**Relative deprivation** The perception that one's position in a stratification system is worse than the position of others with whom one compares oneself. **339, 650**

**Reliability** The degree to which a measurement instrument gives the same results with repeated measurements (assuming that whatever is being measured does not change). **37**

**Religion** A set of cultural ideas, symbols, and practices that focus on the meaning of life and the nature of the unknown. **601**

**Replication** The scientific practice of repeating research studies in order to confirm the original findings. **43**

**Representative democracy** A state in which citizens delegate authority to elected representatives. **574**

**Research design** The set of procedures that guide the gathering of research data. (See Appendix A.)

**Resistance movement** A social movement intended to stop social change. **649**

**Resocialization** The process of learning new roles that replace ones we once performed. **165**

**Resource mobilization theory** An approach to social movements that tries to explain their emergence, success, or failure in terms of access to resources such as time, money, people, and leadership and organizational skills. **655**

**Retreatism** A form of deviance in which a person withdraws from social life by rejecting values and norms without offering alternatives. **283**

**Revolution** A social movement seeking to change the fundamental character of one or more social institutions in a society. **595, 648**

**Riot** A leaderless, unorganized crowd whose members often focus on destruction and the expression of frustration and anger. **638**

**Rising expectations** The hope or expectation of a deprived group that social conditions will improve in the near future—thought by some sociologists to be a cause of social movements. **651**

**Rite of passage** A ceremony marking the transition of individuals from one social status to another. **165, 437**

**Ritual** A religious practice intended to maintain the relationship between believers and the supernatural and among one another. **608**

**Ritualism** Conformity to norms in the absence of a commitment to values. **307**

**Role** A set of beliefs, values, norms, and attitudes shared by status occupants in their relationships with the occupants of other statuses. **90**

**Role distance** The disassociation or "distancing" of people from a role they are performing in order to distract themselves and others from negative aspects of the role performance. **93**

**Role partner** The occupant of a particular status in relation to whom we perform roles as status occupants. **91** (See also **Role set.**)

**Role performance** The actual behavior of individuals who occupy a status. **90**

**Role segregation** The practice of avoiding occupying statuses for which specific individuals are role partners for more than one of our roles. **92**

**Role set** A set of roles attached to a single status. **91** (See also **Role partner.**)

**Role strain** The tension that results when we have difficulty performing a role or satisfying the conflicting demands of two or more roles in a role set. **92**

**Role structure** The set of roles performed by members of a group. **99, 450**

**Rumor** An unverified belief that arises from informal social interaction. **646**

**Rural community** A small, homogeneous, and sparsely settled community. **247**

**Sacred** In religion, the designation of an object, person, or experience as having meaning and value that inspire feelings of awe and place it outside of the natural human world. **602** (See also **Profane.**)

**Sanction** A social punishment or reward associated with obeying or violating a norm. **77** (See also **Formal sanction; Informal sanction.**)

**Scapegoat** A person blamed for the troubles of others. **379**

**School** A formal organization whose primary function is education. **499**

**Scientific method** A method of posing and answering questions that relies on clear, objective guidelines for gathering and interpreting observable evidence. **33**

**Secondary analysis** The use of information already gathered by others, such as government agencies, corporations, and universities. **46**

**Secondary deviance** Deviant acts performed in order to conform to people's expectations of those labeled "deviant." **303**

**Secondary group** A group valued by its members only insofar as it enables them to achieve specific and limited goals. **219**

**Secondary labor market** That segment of the labor market that includes jobs that do not require stable work habits, are relatively low-paying, have few chances for advancement, and have a high turnover. **547**

**Secondary relationship** A relationship that is limited to goals that, once achieved, usually end a person's involvement. **103**

**Sect** A religious group that draws most members by persuasion from the lower class, that has an informal structure and an untrained clergy, is governed with minimal authority, has few formal rituals, involves spontaneous displays of emotion, and generally opposes the dominant institutions of its society. **613**

**Sector theory (model)** A theory of urban land use according to which cities grow in "pie-shaped" segments going out of a central business core. **265**

**Secularization** The social change process through which religious beliefs and practices lose influence in a society. **623** (See also **Civil religion.**)

**Segregation** The practice of physically separating the occupants of some social statuses from the occupants of others. **372**

**Self-concept** The sum total of our thoughts and feelings about ourselves. **157**

**Self-esteem** The positive and negative feelings people feel toward themselves. **162**

**Self-fulfilling prophecy** A false belief that becomes true because we think and act as if it were. **180**

**Semiperipheral society** In world-system theory, a society that is in the process of industrializing. **560**

**Separatism** An ideology that holds that increased segregation is the only way to preserve minority cultures and end social oppression. **387**

**Serfs** In a feudal economy, those who give a share of what they produce to the nobility in exchange for protection and use of the noble's land. **533**

**Sex** Biological differences that define male and female. **391** (See also **Gender.**)

**Sexism** Prejudice based on gender. **399**

**Sex role** (See **Gender role.**)

**Significant other** A particular individual whose beliefs, evaluations, attitudes, and expectations are important to us. **155**

**Single-parent family** A nuclear family in which one parent is absent. **473**

**Situational status** A status occupied only in a particular social situation. **89**

**Social action** The behavior of people in relation to social environments. **23**

**Social attribution** The process through which we interpret and explain other people's behavior. **181**

**Social boundary** The protection from various kinds of social contact, offered by the roles attached to social statuses.

**Social category** Two or more people who have one or more social statuses in common, but who do not interact in patterned ways. **94**

**Social change** The ways in which cultural and structural characteristics of social environments change. **663**

**Social class (Marx)** A set of people who occupy a similar position in relation to the means through which goods and services are produced in a society. **315**

**Social class (Weber)** A set of people who have similar levels of wealth. **317**

**Social cohesion** The degree to which members of groups, organizations, communities, or societies feel committed to group beliefs, values, attitudes, and norms, as well as to the well-being of other members. **234**

**Social Darwinism** A late nineteenth-century theory (used to explain and justify social inequality) that held that the most capable people will and should gain more in the struggle for survival than the less capable. **20**

**Social environment** Culture and social structure.

**Social evolution** Spencer's theory (adapted from Darwin's ideas about natural evolution) that all societies naturally change toward superior forms. **676**

**Social identity** The sum total of who we think we are in relation to other people. **161**

**Social institution** (See **Institution.**)

**Social interaction** The process through which individuals act in relation to one another. **26, 177**

**Socialism** An economic arrangement in which the means of production are owned and controlled by the state, not by private individuals or groups. **556**

**Socialization** The process through which people learn to think, feel, evaluate, and behave as individuals in relation to social and physical environments. **143**

**Social labeling perspective** A perspective that holds that societies often reinforce their boundaries by labeling people as well as their acts as deviant. **303**

**Social learning theory (perspective)** A theory of socialization that focuses on learning through the imitation of models. **149**

**Social mobility** The process through which people move from one position in a stratification system to another. **332** (See also **Lifetime mobility; Intergenerational mobility.**)

**Social movement** A collective effort aimed at either changing or preserving some aspect of social environments or ecological arrangements. **647**

**Social oppression** The systematic, socially supported mistreatment and exploitation of one group or social category by another. **355**

**Social promotion** A practice in which students who have not mastered the skills of a particular grade or level are nevertheless sent on to the next higher grade. **512**

**Social psychology** The study of the effects of social environments on the psychological functioning and behavior of individuals. **26**

**Social script** In the dramaturgical approach to social interaction, the role we perform in relation to a particular audience. **193**

**Social status** A position in a social relationship, a characteristic that locates individuals in relation to other people and sets of role expectations. **88** (See also **Achieved status; Ascribed status; Temporary status; Situational status.**)

**Social stratification** The systematic, uneven distribution of valued products of social life such as wealth, power, and prestige among the occupants of different social statuses. **315**

**Social structure** The arrangement of people in relation to one another and the patterns of expectation attached to positions in social relationships. The concept also refers to patterns of expectation between groups, to the distribution of people among various social positions, and to the distribution of social rewards. **15, 88**

**Society** A population whose members share a cultural identity and way of life and interact in patterned ways. **17, 113**

**Socioeconomic status** A single, overall rank many sociologists use to describe people's positions in stratification systems. **318**

**Sociogram** A method of "mapping" patterns of loyalty and affection among group members. **100**

**Sociology** The systematic study of social environments and their effects on human experience and behavior. **7**

**Sociometry** The study of patterns of affection and loyalty that bind some group members more closely than others. **100**

**Special language** A language developed by a subgroup in order to set themselves apart from others. **69**

**Speech community** A set of people who share a common language. **69**

**Spurious relationship** When two variables that have no causal connection are, nonetheless, statistically related to each other. **54**

**State** The social institution that claims the monopoly of the use of force within a given territory. **569** (See also **Government.**)

**Statistical independence** A condition in which scores on one variable do *not* differ according to scores on another. **50**

**Statistical inference** A mathematical procedure used to test null hypotheses by comparing sample information with an assumption about a population. (See Appendix B.)

**Statistical relationship** A condition in which scores on one variable differ according to scores on another. **51**

**Statistics** A collection of numerical data; also, the branch of mathematics dealing with the collection and analysis of numerical data. **49** (See also Appendix B.)

**Status** Weber's term for the amount of prestige people receive. **317** (See also **Social status** for additional meaning.)

**Status inconsistency** The occupancy of statuses whose levels of prestige are inconsistent with each other. **318**

**Status segregation** (See **Role segregation.**)

**Status set** The entire collection of social statuses occupied by an individual. **90**

**Status strain** The tension that results from the inability to satisfy the requirements of roles attached to different statuses in a status set. **91**

**Stereotype** A rigid oversimplified belief that is applied to all members of a group or social category. **179, 382**

**Stigma** Personal characteristics that others treat as "not quite human" and therefore deviant. **282, 285**

**Structural analysis** The analysis of (1) how social statuses affect perceptions of reality and behavior; (2) how different statuses in individuals' status sets combine to limit their choices and produce conflict; (3) the functions and dysfunctions of structural arrangements; (4) how social structures contribute to social conflict; and (5) how the structures of different groups, organizations, and societies are related to one another.

**Structural strain** In Smelser's theory of collective behavior, the result when people perceive a contradiction between the reality of social life and what their values say it ought to be. **653**

**Structural unemployment** Unemployment caused by changes in the structure of occupational opportunities, such as when a steel factory closes and the number of steelworker jobs declines. **553**

**Student subculture** A subculture within the educational environment. **505**

**Subculture** A distinctive set of cultural ideas that sets a group of people apart from the culture of a surrounding community or society. **74**

**Subfamily** A family that shares a household with another family. **493**

**Subgroup** A group that is part of a larger group. **93**

**Subordinate primary (labor market) jobs** In the primary labor market, jobs that involve routine tasks and encourage workers to be obedient to authority. **547**

**Suburb** A community lying close to a city. **247**

**Succession** (See **Ecological succession.**)

**Superego** In Freudian theory, the conscience—the part of the self that is concerned with morality and living up to the expectations of adult society. **154**

**Surplus value** The value of goods and services that is kept by employers as profit after paying workers whatever is needed to sustain their labor power and reproduce themselves. **535**

**Survey** A method of gathering data through which people are asked a series of questions either by an interviewer or in questionnaire form. **41**

**Symbols** Objects, characteristics of objects, gestures, or words that represent more than themselves. **65**

**Symbolic interaction** The use of symbols by people to present themselves to others and interpret each other's behavior. **28**

**Syndicated crime** Highly bureaucratic crime, with rigid authority structures and complex divisions of labor. **291**

**Systematic sample** A sample drawn by selecting a random starting point in a list of a population and skipping through the list at regular intervals. **41**

**Task role** A role that focuses on achieving goals. **213** (See also **Expressive role.**)

**Technology** A society's accumulated knowledge of how to use the natural environment. **17, 114, 131**

**Temporary status** A status occupied for a limited time. **89** (See also **Situational status; Transitional status.**)

**Theory** A set of interrelated propositions designed to explain a phenomenon.

**Time structure** The ways in which social relationships are defined, conditioned, and regulated by time. **96**

**Token** People who have a social characteristic that is unusual in a particular social situation.

**Total institution** An organization such as a prison in which all aspects of people's daily lives are controlled by authorities. **296**

**Totalitarianism** The political condition in which the state attempts to control not only people's behavior, but virtually all aspects of their private lives as well. **577**

**Totem** In totemist religions, a sacred object believed to possess supernatural power. **605, 607**

**Totemism** A religion based on the belief that sacred objects (totems) possess supernatural power. **607**

**Tracking** An educational practice in which students are divided into groups on the basis of such factors as ability as measured by test scores. **522**

**Traditional authority** Authority that rests on the belief that the occupants of certain statuses are legitimately powerful because "that's the way it's always been." **568**

**Traditional community** A community with a relatively simple division of labor, whose inhabitants tend to resist change, use unsophisticated technology, have less-developed mass media, and rely more on informal relationships than on secondary, formal relationships. **248**

**Transitional status** A status occupied for a limited time as a "stepping stone" toward the occupancy of other statuses. **89**

**Triad** A group with three members. **190**

**Unilinear (change) theory** A theory of social change according to which all societies follow the same path of development. **676**

**Urban community** A large, heterogeneous, and densely settled community. **247**

**Urbanized area** A city and the densely settled territory around it that, together, contain 50,000 or more people. **247**

**Use value** The attribution of value to goods and services based upon their usefulness to those who consume them. **532**

**Validity** The degree to which a measurement instrument measures what it is intended to measure. **36**

**Value** An idea about what is desirable or undesirable, good or bad. **15, 75**

**Variable** In sociology, a behavior or characteristic that varies from one individual, group, or society to another. **35**

**Victimless crime** Criminal acts that violate legal norms but do not involve individuals as victims. **292**

**Vocational subculture** The type of student subculture that values hard work for its "pay off" in terms of a good job after graduation. **505**

**Wealth** Valued possessions not needed for immediate consumption. **328**

**White-collar** Referring to occupations that primarily involve mental work. **318**

**White-collar crime** Crimes that people are able to commit because of the power and opportunities afforded by social statuses—usually occupations—they occupy. **288**

**Worker** (See **Proletariat**.)

**World economy (system)** The economic arrangement among all nations, in which there is a division of labor and no nation is self-sufficient. **559** (See also **World-system theory**.)

**World-system (dependency) theory** A theory that divides nations into three groups (based on the worldwide distribution of wealth and power) and argues that the economic development of societies depends on their position in the world system. **559, 681** (See also **Core society; Peripheral society; Semiperipheral society**.)

**Xenophobia** The fear of strangers and outsiders. **254**

**Zero-sum game** A game in which the success of one player requires the failure of another. **503**

# References

Boldface numerals indicate pages on which references have been cited. References without page numbers, although not cited in the text, have been included because they may be of interest to the reader.

**AACJC (American Association of Community and Junior Colleges).** (1977, May). *Students in two-year colleges.* **508, 514**

**Abadinsky, H.** (1983). *The criminal elite: Professional and organized crime.* Westport, CT: Greenwood Press. **291**

**Aberle, D.** (1961). Matrilineal descent in cross-cultural perspective. In D. Schneider and K. Gough (Eds.), *Matrilineal kinship* (p. 677). Berkeley, CA: University of California Press. **468**

**Abrahamson, M.** (1980). *Urban sociology* (2nd ed.). Englewood Cliffs, NJ: Prentice-Hall. **258**

**Abrams, F.** (1983, September 25). The new effort to control information. *New York Times Magazine.*

**Abramson, L. Y., Seligman, M. E., and Teasdale, J. D.** (1978). *Learned helplessness in humans: Critique and reformulation. Journal of Abnormal Psychology,* 87, 49–74. **190**

**Abu-Lughod, J.** (1965). The emergence of differential fertility in urban Egypt. *Milbank Memorial Fund Quarterly,* 43(April), 235–253. **480**

**Acland, H.** (1972). *Streaming in British junior schools.* Cambridge, MA: Harvard University, Harvard Center for Educational Policy Research. **522**

**Adelman, I., and Morris, C.** (1973). *Economic growth and social inequality in developing countries.* Stanford, CA: Stanford University Press.

**Adorno, T. W., et al.** (1950). *The authoritarian personality.* New York: Harper & Row. **380**

**Alba, R. D., and Chamlin, M. B.** (1983). A preliminary examination of ethnic identification among whites. *American Sociological Review,* 48(April), 240–47.

**Albert, E.** (1971). The unmothered woman. In H. Garskof (Ed.), *Roles women play.* Belmont, CA. **417**

**Alexander, K. L., and Reilly, T. W.** (1981). Estimating the effects of marriage timing on educational attainment. *American Journal of Sociology,* 87, 143–156. **401**

**Alexander, N. C., and Wiley, M. G.** (1981). Situated activity and identity formation. In M. Rosenberg and R. Turner (Eds.), *Sociological perspectives on social psychology.* New York: Basic Books. **203**

**Allan, L. J.** (1978). Child abuse: A critical review of the research and the theory. In J. P. Martin (Ed.), *Violence and the family.* New York: Wiley. **448**

**Allen, I. L.** (1983). *The language of ethnic conflict.* New York: Columbia University Press. **69, 212**

**Allport, F. H.** (1920). The influence of the group upon association and thought. *Journal of Experimental Psychology,* 3, 159–82.

**Allport, G. W.** (1935). Attitudes. In C. Murchison (Ed.), *A handbook of social psychology.* Worcester, MA: Clark University Press. **15, 81**

**Allport, G. W.** (1954). *The nature of prejudice.* Garden City, NY: Doubleday/Anchor Books. (1958 refers to the paperback edition.) **356, 383, 664**

**Allport, G. W., and Postman, L.** (1947). *The psychology of rumor.* New York: Holt. **646**

**Altman, I., Taylor, D. A., and Wheeler, L.** (1971). Ecological aspects of group behavior in social isolation. *Journal of Applied Social Psychology,* 1, 76–100. **186**

**Ambron, S. R.** (1978). *Child development* (2nd ed.). New York: Holt, Rinehart & Winston. **157**

**American Society of Plastic and Reconstructive Surgeons.** (1985). In *Newsweek,* May 27, 1985, pp. 66–67. **397**

**Amin, S.** (1975). Toward a structural crisis of world capitalism. *Socialist Review,* 5(April), 9–44. **561, 563**

**Andenaes, J.** (1975). *Punishment and deterrence.* New York: Elsevier. **690**

**Anderson, A. G.** (1979). *The business of organized crime.* Stanford, CA: Hoover Institution Press. **291**

**Anderson, G. R.** (1983). Medicine versus religion: The case of Jehovah's Witnesses. *Health and Social Work,* 8(1, Winter), 31–38. **613**

**Anderson, R. T.** (1965). From Mafia to Cosa Nostra. *American Journal of Sociology,* 71(November), 302–310.

**Ann, J.** (1970). The secretarial proletariat. In R. Morgan (Ed.), *Sisterhood is powerful* (pp. 94–110). New York: Vintage. **411**

**Argyle, M., Lefebvre, L., and Cook, M.** (1974). The meaning of five patterns of gaze. *European Journal of Social Psychology,* 4, 125–136.

Argyris, C. (1957). The individual and organization: Some problems of mutual adjustment. *Administrative Science Quarterly, 1,* 1–24. **238**

Ariès, P. (1962). *Centuries of childhood: A social history of family life.* New York: Knopf. **435, 441**

Aronowitz, S. (1973). *False promises.* New York: McGraw-Hill. **521**

Aronson, S. H. (1971). The city: Illusion, nostalgia, and reality. In D. H. Wrong and H. L. Gracey (Eds.), *Readings in introductory sociology* (2nd ed.) (pp. 288–300). New York: Macmillan. **262**

Asch, S. E. (1952). *Social psychology.* Englewood Cliffs, NJ: Prentice-Hall. **209, 210**

Ash, D. (1967). *Automobile Almanac.* New York: Essandess/Simon & Schuster. **543**

Ash, T. G. (1984). *The Polish revolution: Solidarity.* New York: Charles Scribner's Sons. **594, 658**

Ashish, B. (1973). *Studies in India's urbanization: 1901–1971.* New York: McGraw-Hill. **671**

Atchley, R. C. (1982). Retirement as a social institution. *Annual Review of Sociology, 8,* 263–287. **453**

Auden, W. H. (1965). Prologue: The birth of architecture. In *About the house.* New York: Random House. **182**

Axelrad. S. (1952). Negro and white male institutionalized delinquents. *American Journal of Sociology,* (May), 569–574. **294**

Babst, D. V., et al. (1976). Assessing length of institutionalization in relation to parole outcome. *Criminology, 14*(May), 41–54. **295**

Bachman, J. G. (1970). *Youth in transition, vol. II: The impact of family background and intelligence on tenth-grade boys.* Ann Arbor, MI: Survey Research Center, Institute for Social Research.

Back, K. W. (1951). Influence through social communication. *Journal of Abnormal and Social Psychology, 46,* 9–23. **201**

Back, K. W. (1981). Small groups. In M. Rosenberg and R. H. Turner (Eds.), *Social psychology: Sociological perspectives* (pp. 320–43). New York: Basic Books. **211**

Balch, R. W., and Kelly, D. H. (1974). Reactions to deviance in a junior high school: Student views of the labeling process. *Journal of Instructional Psychology, 1*(1). **303**

Baldassare, M. (1983). Residential crowding and social behavior. In J. S. Pipkin, M. LaGory, and J. R. Blau (Eds.), *Remaking the city* (pp. 148–162). Albany, NY: State University of New York Press. **263**

Baldridge, J. V., and Deal, T. (1983). *The dynamics of organizational change in education.* Berkeley, CA: McCutchan. **512**

Bales, R. F. (1950). *Interaction process analysis: A method for the study of small groups.* Cambridge, MA: Addison-Wesley. **98, 213, 226**

Bales, R. F. (1954). Task roles and social roles in problem-solving groups. In E. E. Maccoby, T. M. Newcomb, and E. L. Hartley (Eds.), *Readings in social psychology* (3rd ed.). New York: Holt, Rinehart & Winston. **101**

Bales, R. F. (1968). Interaction process analysis. In D. L. Sills (Ed.), *The international encyclopedia of the social sciences* (Vol. 7). New York: The MacMillan Company/The Free Press. **227**

Bales, R. F., and Borgatta, E. F. (1955). A study of group size: Size of group as a factor in the interaction profile. In A. P. Hare, E. F. Borgatta, and R. F. Bales, *Small groups.* New York: Knopf. **232**

Bales, R. F., and Slater, P. E. (1955). Role differentiation in small decision-making groups. In T. Parsons, R. F. Bales, and P. E. Slater, *The family, socialization, and interaction process.* New York: The Free Press. **101**

Bales, R. F., and Strodtbeck, F. L. (1951). Phases in group problem-solving. *Journal of Abnormal and Social Psychology, 46,* 485–495. **226**

Ball, D. (1981, November 18). Reported in *The New York Times.*

Bamberger, J. (1974). The myth of matriarchy: Why men rule in primitive society. In M. Z. Rosaldo and L. Lamphere (Eds.), *Women, culture, and society* (pp. 263–280). Stanford, CA: Stanford University Press. **410, 477**

Bandura, A. (1977). *Social learning theory.* Englewood Cliffs, NJ: Prentice-Hall. **150**

Bandura, A., and Kupers, C. J. (1964). The transmission of patterns of self-reinforcement through modeling. *Journal of Abnormal and Social Psychology, 69,* 1–9.

Bandura, A., Ross, D., and Ross, S. (1963a). Imitation of film-mediated aggressive models. *Journal of Abnormal and Social Psychology, 66,* 3–11.

Bandura, A., Ross, D., and Ross, S. (1963b). Vicarious reinforcement and imitative learning. *Journal of Abnormal and Social Psychology, 67,* 601–607. **412**

Bane, M. J. (1976). *Here to stay: American families in the twentieth century.* New York: Basic Books. **480, 486, 487, 495**

Bane, M. J., and Jencks, C. (1972, September 16). The schools and equal opportunity. *Saturday Review of Education,* pp. 37–42. **337, 520, 524, 525**

Banfield, E. C. (1965). *Political influence.* New York: The Free Press. **260**

Banfield, E. C. (1967). *The moral basis of a backward society.* New York: The Free Press. **619**

Baran, P. A. (1957). *The political economy of growth.* New York: Monthly Review Press. **681**

Baran, P. A., and Sweezy, P. M. (1966). *Monopoly capital.* New York: Modern Reader Paperbacks. **544**

Barnet, R. J., and Muller, R. J. (1974). *Global reach.* New York: Simon & Schuster. **341, 343, 345**

Barnett, R. C., and Baruch, G. K. (1983). *Women's involvement in multiple roles, role strain, and psychological distress.* (Working Paper 107). Wellesley, MA: Wellesley College Center for Research on Women. **400**

Baron, H. M. (1976). The demand for black labor. In J. H. Skolnick and E. Currie (Eds.), *Crisis in American institutions* (3rd ed.). Boston: Little, Brown. **372**

Barsh, R. L., and Henderson, J. Y. (1980). *The road: Indian tribes and political liberty.* Berkeley and Los Angeles, CA: University of California Press. **360**

Bart, P. B. (1971). Depression in middle-aged women. In V. Gornick and B. K. Moran (Eds.), *Woman in sexist society* (pp. 163–186). New York: Signet. **419, 437**

Barth, H. (1976). *Truth and ideology.* Berkeley, CA: University of California Press.

Bartlett, F. C. (1932). *Remembering.* Cambridge, England: Cambridge University Press. **646**

Barton, E. M., Baltes, M. M., and Orzech, M. J. (1980). Etiology of dependence in older nursing home residents during morning care. *Journal of Personality and Social Psychology, 38,* 423–431. **447**

Basler, B. (1982, April 18). Auto thefts in city. *New York Times.* **308**

Bass, B. M. (1960). *Leadership, psychology, and organizational behavior.* New York: Harper & Row. **216**

Baumrind, D. (1964). Some thoughts on the ethics of research: After reading Milgram's 'Behavior study of obedience.' " *American Psychologist, 19,* 421–423. **302**

Baumrind, D. (1966). Effects of authoritative parental control on child behavior. *Child Development, 37,* 887–907.

Bavelas, A. (1950). Communication patterns in task-oriented groups. *Journal of the Acoustical Society of America, 22,* 725–730. **102**

Baxandall, R., Gordon, L., and Reverby, S. (1976). *America's working women.* New York: Vintage. **47, 404**

Beal, F. M. (1969). Double jeopardy: To be black and female. In R. Morgan (Ed.), *Sisterhood is powerful* (pp. 382–396). New York: Vintage.

Beale, C. L. (1976). A further look at nonmetropolitan growth since 1970. *American Journal of Agricultural Economics, 58,* 953–958.

Beale, H. K. (1975). The education of Negroes before the Civil War. In J. Barnard and D. Burner (Eds.), *The American experience in education* (pp. 88–90). New York: Watts. **515**

Beard, C. A., and Beard, M. R. (1944). *A basic history of the United States.* New York: The New Home Library. **578**

Beauvoir, S. de. (1952). An androgynous world. In B. Roszak and T. Roszak (Eds.), *Masculine/feminine* (pp. 148–157). New York: Harper & Row. **422**

Becker, G. (1981). *A treatise on the family.* Cambridge, MA: Harvard University Press. **121**

Becker, H. S. (1953). Becoming a marijuana user. *American Journal of Sociology, 59*(November), 235–242.

Becker, H. S. (Ed.). (1964). *The other side.* New York: The Free Press. **303**

Becker, H. S. (1973). *Outsiders: Studies in the sociology of deviance* (rev. ed.). New York: The Free Press. **303**

Becker, H. S., and Geer, B. (1958). The fate of idealism in medical school. *American Sociological Review, 23,* 50–56. **170**

Beeghley, L. (1983). *Living poorly in America.* New York: Praeger. **348**

Bell, D. (1973). *The coming of postindustrial society.* New York: Basic Books. **550, 680**

Bell, D. A., Jr. (1973). Racism in American courts. *California New Law Review, 61,* 165–203. **294**

Bell, W. (1969). Urban neighborhoods and individual behavior. In P. Meadows and E. H. Mizburchi (Eds.), *Urbanism, urbanization, and change.* Reading, MA: Addison-Wesley. **250**

Bellah, R. N. (1964). Religious evolution. *American Sociological Review, 29,* 358–374.

Bellah, R. N. (1970). *Beyond belief.* New York: Harper & Row.

Bellah, R. N. (1973). *The broken covenant.* New York: Seabury Press. **626, 627**

Bellah, R. N., and Hammond, P. E. (1980). *Varieties of civil religion.* New York: Harper & Row. **626**

Bem, S., and Bem, D. (1976). Training the woman to know her place: The power of nonconscious ideology. In S. Cox (Ed.), *Female psychology: The emerging self.* Chicago: St. Martin's Press. **153**

Bendix, R., and Lipset, S. M. (1966). Karl Marx's theory of social classes. In Bendix and Lipset (Eds.), *Class, status, and power.* New York: The Free Press.

Benedict, R. (1934). *Patterns of culture.* New York: New American Library. **11, 76, 87, 147**

Benedict, R. (1946). *The chrysanthemum and the sword.* Boston: Houghton Mifflin. **197**

Bennett, L., Jr. (1966). *Confrontation: Black and white.* Baltimore, MD: Penguin.

Benoliel, J. Q. (1973). *The nurse and the dying patient.* New York: Macmillan. **440**

Bensman, J., and Rosenberg, B. (1979). The peer group. In P. I. Rose (Ed.), *Socialization and the life cycle.* New York: St. Martin's Press.

Benston, M. (1969). The political economy of women's liberation. *Monthly Review, 21,* 13–27.

Ben-Yehuda, N. (1980). The European witch craze of the 14th and 17th centuries: A sociologist's perspective. *American Journal of Sociology, 86*(1), 1–31. **397**

Berger, B. M. (1960). *Working class suburb: A study of autoworkers in suburbia.* Berkeley, CA: University of California Press. **250**

Berger, P. L. (1963). *Invitation to sociology: A humanistic perspective.* Garden City, NY: Anchor Books. **19, 57**

Berger, P. L. (1967). *The sacred canopy.* New York: Doubleday. **623, 624**

Berger, P. L. (1970). *A rumor of angels.* Garden City, NY: Doubleday.

Berger, P. L., and Kellner, H. (1964). Marriage and the Construction of reality. *Diogenes, 45,* 1–25. (Reprinted in H. Robboy, S. L. Greenblatt, and D. Clark (Eds.). *Social interaction* (pp. 308–322). New York: St. Martin's Press.) **201, 476**

Berger, P. L. and Luckman, T. (1967). *The social construction of reality.* Garden City, NY: Anchor Books. **69**

Bergesen, A. (Ed.). (1980). *Studies of the modern world system.* New York: Academic Press. **559**

Berk, R. A. (1974a). A gaming approach to crowd behavior. *American Journal of Sociology, 79*(June), 355–373. **645**

Berk, R. A. (1974b). *Collective behavior.* Dubuque, IA: William C. Brown. **645**

Berk, R. A., and Berk, S. F. (1979). *Labor and leisure at home: Content and organization of the household day.* Beverly Hills, CA: Sage. **405**

Berk, R. A., and Berk, S. F. (1983). Supply-side sociology of the family. *Annual Review of Sociology, 9,* 375–395.

Berk, S. F., and Loseke, D. R. (1981). Handling family violence: Situational determinants of police arrest in domestic disturbances. *Law and Society Review, 15,* 315–346. **489**

Berkowitz, L. (1978). Decreased helpfulness with increased group size through lessening the effects of the needy individual's dependency. *Journal of Personality, 46,* 299–310. **178**

Berle, A. A., Jr., and Means, G. C. (1968). *The modern corporation and private property* (rev. ed.). New York: Harcourt Brace and World. (Original work published 1932). **545**

Bernard, J. (1971). The paradox of the happy marriage. In V. Gornick and B. K. Moran (Eds.), *Woman in sexist society* (pp. 145–162). New York: Signet.

Bernard, J. (1972). *The future of marriage.* New York: Bantam. **419, 669**

Berreman, G. D. (1973). *Caste in the modern world.* Morristown, NJ: General Learning Press. **343**

Berry, B. J. L., and Kasarda, J. D. (1977). The congruence of social and spatial structure: Neighborhood status and white resistance to residential integration as an example. In *Contemporary urban ecology* (Chapter 2). New York: Macmillan. **254, 257, 269, 270, 273**

Besser, J. D. (1979, January). Gentrifying the ghetto. *The Progressive,* pp. 30–32. **271**

Best, M. H., and Connolly, W. E. (1976). *The politicized economy.* Lexington, MA: D. C. Heath. **545**

Bettelheim, B. (1969). *Children of the dream.* New York: Macmillan. **270, 672**

Bettelheim, B., and Janowitz, M. (1950). *Dynamics of prejudice: A psychological and sociological study of veterans.* New York: Harper & Row. **380**

Bierstedt, R. (1978). Sociological thought in the eighteenth century. In T. Bottomore and R. Nisbet (Eds.), *A history of sociological analysis.* New York: Basic Books.

Biggar, J. C. (1979). The sunning of America: Migration to the Sunbelt. *Population Bulletin, 34.* **125**

Binder, F. M. (1974). *The age of the common school: 1830–1865.* New York: Wiley. **524**

Birren, J. E. (1968). Psychological aspects of aging and intellectual functioning. *The Gerontologist, 8*(1, Part II), 19. **432, 433**

Black, D. J. (1971). The social organization of arrest. *Stanford Law Review, 23*(6), 1104–1110. **293**

Blake, J. (1972). Coercive pronatalism and American population policy. In R. Parke, Jr., and C. F. Westoff (Eds.), *Aspects of population growth policy* (Vol. 6 of U.S. Commission on Population and the American Future Research Reports). Washington, DC: U.S. Government Printing Office. **117**

Blake, J. (1982). Demographic revolution and family evolution: Some implications for American women. In P. W. Berman and E. R. Ramey (Eds.), *Women: A developmental perspective* (pp. 299–312) (NIH Publication No. 82-2298). Washington, DC: U.S. Department of Health and Human Services. **469**

Blake, J. (1985). Number of siblings and educational mobility. *American Sociological Review, 50*(1), 84–93.

Blau, P. M. (1964). *Exchange and power in social life.* New York: Wiley. **197**

Blau, P. M. (1973). *The dynamics of bureaucracy* (2nd rev. ed.). Chicago: University of Chicago Press. **298**

Blau, P. M. (1974). Parameters of social structure. *American Sociological Review, 39,* 615–635.

Blau, P. M. (Ed.). (1975). *Approaches to the study of social structure.* New York: The Free Press.

Blau, P. M., Blum, T. C., and Schwartz, J. E. (1982). Heterogeneity and intermarriage. *American Sociological Review, 47*(1), 45–62. **472**

Blau, P. M., and Duncan, O. D. (1967). *The American occupational structure.* New York: Wiley. **334, 337, 340, 345, 371**

Blau, Z. S. (1982). *Old Age in a Changing Society* (2nd ed.). New York: Watts.

Blauner, R. (1964). *Alienation and freedom.* Chicago: University of Chicago Press. **552**

Blauner, R. (1972). Racism as the negation of culture. In *Racial oppression in America.* New York: Harper & Row. **359**

Bloch, M. (1961). *Feudal society.* Chicago: University of Chicago Press. **533**

Block, A. A., and Chambliss, W. J. (1981). *Organizing crime.* New York: Elsevier North Holland. **291**

Block, J. (1973). Conceptions of sex role: Some cross-cultural and longitudinal perspectives. *American Psychologist, 28,* 512–526. **299, 399**

Block, N. J., and Dworkin, G. (Eds.). (1976). *The IQ controversy.* New York: Pantheon.

Blood, R. O., Jr., and Wolfe, D. M. (1960). *Husbands and wives.* New York: The Free Press. **484**

Bloom, D. E. (1982). What's happening to the age at first birth in the United States? A study of recent cohorts. *Demography, 19*(3), (August), 351–370. **418, 669**

Bluestone, B., and Harrison, B. (1982). *The deindustrialization of America: Plant closings, community abandonment, and the dismantling of basic industry.* New York: Basic Books. **260**

Blumenthal, M. D., et al. (1972). *Justifying violence: Attitudes of American men.* Ann Arbor, MI: Institute for Social Research. **490**

Blumer, H. (1951). Collective Behavior. In A. M. Lee (Ed.), *New outline of the principles of sociology.* New York: Barnes and Noble. (Original work published 1939). **635, 636, 643**

Blumstein, A., and Nagin, D. S. (1974). *Analysis of arrest rates for trends in criminality.* Pittsburgh: Carnegie Mellon University School of Urban and Public Affairs. **307**

Bock, E. W. (1972, January). The significance of marital kinship and alternative relations. *The Family Co-ordinator,* pp. 71–78. **416**

Bogardus, E. S. (1928). *Immigration and race attitudes.* Boston: D. C. Heath. **368**

Bogardus, E. S. (1959). Race reactions by sexes. *Sociology and Social Research, 43,* 439–441. **368**

Bok, S. (1979). *Lying: Moral choice in public and private life.* New York: Vintage. **80**

Bollen, K. (1983). World system position, dependency, and democracy. *American Sociological Review, 48*(August), 468–479. **574**

Bose, N. K. (1965). Calcutta: A premature metropolis. *Scientific American, 113,* 91–102.

Bosrup, E. (1981). *Population and technological change.* Chicago: University of Chicago Press. **127, 137**

Boss, P. G. (1980). Normative family stress: Family boundary changes across the life span. *Family Relations, 29,* 445–450. **490**

Bottomore, T. (Ed.). (1963). *Karl Marx: Early writings.* London: Watts.

Bottomore, T. Structure and history. (1975). In P. M. Blau (Ed.), *Approaches to the study of social structure.* New York: The Free Press.

Bottomore, T., and Nisbet, R. (Eds.). (1978). *A history of sociological analysis.* New York: Basic Books.

Bottomore, T., and Rubel, M. (Eds.). (1965). *Karl Marx: Selected writings in sociology and social philosophy.* New York: McGraw-Hill. **306**

Bouvier, L. F., Shryock, H. S., and Henderson, H. W. (1977). International migration: Yesterday, today, and tomorrow. *Population Bulletin, 30,* 3–24. **124**

Bowles, S., and Gintis, H. (1976). *Schooling in capitalist America: Educational reform and the contradictions of economic life.* New York: Basic Books.

Bowles, S., and Nelson, V. (1974). The 'inheritance of IQ' and the intergenerational reproduction of economic inequality. *Review of Economics and Statistics, 56*(1, February). **338**

Bowser, B. P., and Hunt, R. G. (1981). *Impacts of racism on white Americans.* Beverly Hills, CA: Sage.

Bradbury, K., Downs, A., and Small, K. A. (1982). *Urban decline and the future of American cities.* Washington, DC: The Brookings Institution. **268**

Braithwaite, J. (1981). The myth of social class and criminology reconsidered. *American Sociological Review, 46*(February), 36–57. **289**

Braudel, F. (1977). *Afterthoughts on material civilization and capitalism.* Baltimore: Johns Hopkins University Press.

Braudel, F. (1983). *The wheels of commerce: Civilization and capi-*

*talism, 15th–18th century, volume two.* (S. Reynolds, Trans.). New York: Harper & Row. **559**

Braverman, H. (1974). *Labor and monopoly capital.* New York: Monthly Review Press. (1976 refers to the paperback edition.) **338, 535, 550, 551**

Brehm, J. W. (1966). *A theory of psychological reactance.* New York: Academic Press. **216**

Breland, H. M. (1973). Birth order effects: A reply to Schooler. *Psychological Bulletin, 80,* 210–212.

Brend, R. M. (1975). Male-female intonation patterns in American English. In B. Thorne and N. Henley (Eds.), *Language and sex: Difference and dominance.* Rowley, MA: Newbury Press. **395**

Brenner, R. (1976). Agrarian class structure and economic development in pre-industrial Europe. *Past and Present, 70,* 30–75. **681**

Bressler, M. (1960). The Myers' case: An instance of successful racial invasion. *Social Problems, 8,* 133. **670**

Brim, O. G., Jr. (1966). Socialization after childhood. In O. G. Brim, Jr., and S. Wheeler, *Socialization after childhood: Two essays.* New York: Wiley.

Brim, O. G., Jr. (1974, September). *The sense of personal control over one's life.* Address to the annual convention of the American Psychological Association. **449**

Brody, E. M. (1978). The aging of the family. *Annals of the American Academy of Political and Social Science, 438*(July), 18–21.

Brody, J. A. (1983). Life expectancy and the health of older people. *American Journal of Geriatric Sociology.* **440**

Bronfenbrenner, U. (1970). *Two worlds of childhood.* New York: Russel Sage Foundation.

Broverman, I. K., Broverman, D., Clarkson, F., Rosenkrantz, P., and Vogel, S. (1970). Sex-role stereotypes and clinical judgements of mental health. *Journal of Consulting and Clinical Psychology, 34,* 1–7. **396**

Broverman, I. K., Vogel, S., Broverman, D., Clarkson, F., and Rosenkrantz, P. (1972). Sex-role stereotypes: A current appraisal. *Journal of Social Issues, 28,* 59–79. **396**

Brown, D. L., and Wardwell, J. M. (Eds.). (1980). *New directions in urban-rural migration: The population turnaround in rural America.* New York: Academic Press. **124**

Brown, H. (1954). *The challenge of man's future.* New York: The Viking Press.

Brown, R. (1965). *Social psychology.* New York: The Free Press. **77, 155**

Brown, R. S., Moon, M., and Zoloth, B. S. (1980). Incorporating occupational attainment in studies of male-female earnings differentials. *Journal of Human Resources, 15,* 3–28. **406**

Brownmiller, S. (1975). *Against our will: Men, women, and rape.* New York: Simon & Schuster. **186, 292, 403, 469**

Burch, P. H., Jr. (1972). *The managerial revolution reassessed.* Lexington, MA: D. C. Heath. **545**

Bureau of National Affairs. (1984). *Pay equity and comparable worth* (Report 45 LDSR 28). Washington, DC: Bureau of National Affairs. **406**

Burke, K. (1935). *Permanence and change.* New York: Republic.

Burke, K. (1945). *A grammar of motives.* Englewood Cliffs, NJ: Prentice-Hall. **152**

Burke, P. J., and Reitzes, D. C. (1981). The link between identity and role performance. *Social Psychology Quarterly, 44,* 83–92. **203**

Burnette, R. (1971). *The tortured Americans.* Englewood Cliffs, NJ: Prentice-Hall. **365**

Burns, H. (1973). Black people and the tyranny of American law. *The Annals, 407*(May), 156–166. **280, 282, 579**

Burnside, I. M. (1975). Sexuality and the older adult: Implications for nursing. In I. M. Burnside (Ed.), *Sexuality and aging.* Los Angeles: Ethel Percy Andrus Gerontology Center. **433**

Bush, D. M., and Simmons, R. G. (1981). Socialization processes over the life course. In M. Rosenberg and R. H. Turner (Eds.), *Social psychology: Sociological perspectives* (pp. 133–164). New York: Basic Books. **143, 165**

*Business Week.* (1979, May 21). (p. 68). **307**

Buss, T. F., and Redburn, F. S. (1983). *Shutdown at Youngstown: Public policy for mass unemployment.* Albany, NY: State University of New York Press. **260, 553**

Butterfield, F. (1982). *China: Alive in the bitter sea.* New York: Times Books.

Cahalan, D., and Room, R. (1974). *Problem drinking among American men.* New Brunswick, NJ: Rutgers Center of Alcohol Studies.

Calhoun, J. B. (1962). Population density and social pathology. *The Scientific American, CCVI,* pp. 139–148. **263**

Callahan, R. E. (1962). *Education and the cult of efficiency.* Chicago: University of Chicago Press. **511**

Calvert, R. (1974). Criminal and civil liability in husband-wife assaults. In S. K. Steinmetz and M. A. Straus (Eds.), *Violence in the family* (pp. 88–90). New York: Harper & Row. **490**

Campbell, A. A. (1947). Factors associated with attitudes towards Jews. In T. Newcomb and E. Hartley (Eds.), *Readings in social psychology.* New York: Holt, Rinehart & Winston. **380**

Campbell, A. A. (1971) *White attitudes toward black people.* Ann Arbor, MI: Institute for Social Research, University of Michigan. **380**

Campbell, A. A., et al. (1976). *The quality of American life.* New York: Russel Sage Foundation.

Campbell, A. A., and Schuman, H. (1968). Racial attitudes in fifteen American cities. In *Supplementary studies for the National Advisory Commission on Civil Disorders* (see Kerner Commission). Washington, DC: U.S. Government Printing Office.

Camus, A. (1946). *The stranger* (S. Gilbert, Trans.) New York: Knopf.

Cantor, M. G., and Pingree, S. (1983). *The soap opera.* Beverly Hills, CA: Sage. **169**

Cantril, H. (1963). *The psychology of social movements.* New York: Wiley. **637**

Caplow, T. (1947). Rumors in war. *Social Forces, 25,* 298–302. **646**

Caplow, T. (1952). Urban structure in France. *American Sociological Review, XVII,* 544–549. **265**

Caplow, T. (1956). A theory of coalitions in the triad. *American Sociological Review, 21,* 489–493. **227**

Caplow, T. (1964). *The sociology of work.* New York: McGraw-Hill. **550**

Caplow, T. (1968). *Two against one: Coalitions in triads.* Englewood Cliffs, NJ: Prentice-Hall. **191, 227**

Caplow, T. (1982). Christmas gifts and kin networks. *American Sociological Review, 47*(June), 383–392. **197**

Caplow, T., and McGee, R. J. (1958). *The academic marketplace.* New York: Arno Press. **505**

Carnegie Council on Policy Studies in Higher Education. (1979, December 3). Giving youth a better chance: Options for education, work, and service. *The Chronicle of Higher Education,* pp. 11–13. **504, 512**

Carroll, B. (1980). Review essay: Political science, part II. International politics, comparative politics, and feminist radicals. *Signs, 5,* 449–458.

Carter, A. (1978). *The Sadeian woman and the ideology of pornography.* New York: Harper & Row. **397**

Castelli, J. (1983). *The bishops and the bomb: Waging peace in a nuclear age.* New York: Image. **623**

Castells, M. (1977). *The urban question: A Marxist approach.* (A. Sheridan, Trans.) Cambridge, MA: The MIT Press. **250**

Castells, M. (1980). *The economic crisis of American society.* Princeton, NJ: Princeton University Press. **563**

Cater, D., and Strickland, S. (1975). *TV violence and the child.* New York: Russell Sage Foundation.

Cath, S. H., Gurwitt, A. R., and Ross, J. M. (Eds.). (1982). *Father and child: Developmental and clinical perspectives.* Boston: Little, Brown. **426**

Caudill, W., and Weinstin, H. (1966). Maternal care and infant behavior in Japanese and American urban middle class families. In R. Konig and R. Hill (Eds.), *Yearbook of the international sociological association.*

Chafetz, J. *Masculine, feminine, or human?* (1978). Ithaca, IL: Peacock. **399**

Chalfant, H. P., Beckley, R. E., and Palmer, L. E. (1981). *Religion in contemporary society.* Palo Alto, CA: Mayfield. **613, 614, 623**

Chamberlin, E. H. (1962). *Theory of monopolistic competition.* Cambridge, MA: Harvard University Press. **542**

Chambliss, W. J. (1969). *Crime and legal process.* New York: McGraw-Hill. **294**

Chambliss, W. J. (1973). The Saints and the Roughnecks. *Society, 11,* 24–31. **281, 282, 293**

Chambliss, W. J. (1978). Toward a political economy of crime. In C. E. Reasons and R. M. Rich (Eds.). *The sociology of law: A conflict perspective.* Toronto: Butterworths. **306, 309**

Chapman, J. I. (1976). An economic model of crime and police: Some empirical results. *Journal of Research in Crime and Delinquency, 13*(January), 48–63. **295**

Cherlin, A. (1981). *Marriage, divorce, remarriage.* Cambridge, MA: Harvard University Press. **481**

Cherlin, A. (1983). Changing family and household: Contemporary lessons from historical research. *Annual Review of Sociology, 9,* 51–66. **404, 482**

Cherlin, A., and Furstenberg, F. F. (1983, June). The American family in the year 2000. *The Futurist,* pp. 7–14. **477**

Chernin, K. (1981). *The Obsession: Reflections on the tyranny of slenderness.* New York: Harper & Row. **396, 397, 435**

Childe, V. G. (1953). *Man makes himself.* New York: Mentor. **132**

Childe, V. G. (1964). *What happened in history.* Baltimore: Penguin. **132, 133**

Chilton, R., and Spielberger, A. (1971). Is delinquency increasing? Age structure and the crime rate. *Social Forces, 49*(3), 487–493. **126**

Chiricos, T. G., and Waldo, G. P. (1975). Socioeconomic status and criminal sentencing: An empirical assessment of the conflict proposition. *American Sociological Review, 40,* 753–772. **294**

Chirot, D. (1977). *Social change in the twentieth century.* New York: Harcourt Brace Jovanovich. **681**

Chirot, D. (1980). Changing fashions in the study of the social causes of economic and social change. In J. F. Short (Ed.), *The state of sociology* (pp. 259–282). Beverly Hills, CA: Sage. **681**

Chirot, D., and Hall, T. D. (1982). World-system theory. *Annual Review of Sociology, 8,* 81–106. **681**

Chomsky, N. (1957). *Syntactic structures.* The Hague: Mouton.

Chomsky, N. (1966). *Cartesian linguistics.* New York: Harper & Row. **146**

Christian Science Monitor. (1983, November 1). P. 1. **556**

Christian Science Monitor. (1983, December 5). **558**

Cicourel, A. V. (1974). *Cognitive sociology.* New York: The Free Press.

Clark, B. R. (1960). The cooling-out function in higher education. *American Journal of Sociology, 65*(May). **523**

Clark, B. R., and Trow, M. (1966). The organizational context. In B. R. Clark and M. Trow (Eds.), *College peer groups.* Chicago: Aldine. **505**

Clark, G. K. (1962). *The making of Victorian England.* Cambridge, MA: Harvard University Press. **20**

Clark, G. K., and Piggott, S. (1965). *Prehistoric societies.* New York: Knopf. **132**

Clark, K. B. (1965). *Dark ghetto.* New York: Harper & Row. **370**

Clausen, J. A. (1976). Drug use. In R. K. Merton and R. Nisbet (Eds.), *Contemporary social problems.* New York: Harcourt Brace Jovanovich. **280, 304**

Clinard, M., and Yeager, P. C. (1980). *Corporate crime.* New York: The Free Press. **281**

Cloward, R. A., and Ohlin, L. E. (1960). *Delinquency and opportunity: A theory of delinquent gangs.* New York: The Free Press. **306**

Clymer, A. (1981, August 28). Polls find black-white gaps on variety of issues. *New York Times.* **358**

Coale, A. J. (1964). How a population ages or grows younger. In R. Freedman (Ed.). *Population: The vital revolution.* New York: Anchor Books. **125**

Cobb, S., and Kasl, S. V. (1971). *Some medical aspects of unemployment.* (Report to Respondents). Ann Arbor, MI: University of Michigan Survey Research Center.

Cohen, A. K. (1955). *Delinquent boys: The culture of the gang.* New York: The Free Press.

Cohen, A. K., and Short, J. F., Jr. (1976). Crime and juvenile delinquency. In R. F. Merton and R. Nisbet (Eds.), *Contemporary social problems* (4th ed.). New York: Harcourt Brace Jovanovich. **287, 295**

Cohen, W. H., and Mause, P. J. (1968). The Indian: The forgotten American. *Harvard Law Review, 81*(8), 1818–1858. **360**

Cohen, Y. (1978). The disappearance of the incest taboo. *Human Nature, 1*(7), 72–78.

Cole, M., and Scribner, S. (1974). *Culture and thought: A psychological introduction.* New York: Wiley.

Cole, S. G., and Cole, M. W. (1954). *Minorities and the American promise.* New York: Harper & Row. **359**

Coleman, J. C. (1959). *Abnormal psychology and modern life.* New York: Scott-Foresman. **297**

Coleman, J. S. (1960). The adolescent subculture and academic achievement. *American Journal of Sociology, 65,* 337–347. **168, 505**

Coleman, J. S. (1961). *The adolescent society.* New York: The Free Press. **168, 169, 299, 505, 518**

Coleman, J. S., et al. (1966). *Equality of educational opportunity.* Washington, DC: U.S. Government Printing Office. **374, 515, 522**

Coleman, J. S., et al (1974). *Youth: Transition to adult.* Chicago: University of Chicago Press. **457**

Coleman, J. S., Kelly, S. D., and Moore, J. A. (1975). *Trends in school segregation: 1968–1973*. Washington, DC: The Urban Institute. **387**

Coleman, R. P., and Rainwater, L. (with McClelland, K. A.). (1978). *Social standing in America*. New York: Basic Books. **347**

Coles, R. (1968). *Children in crisis*. New York: Dell. **370**

Congressional Quarterly. (November 10, 1984). **368, 410**

Conklin, N. F., and Lourier, M. A. (1983). *A host of tongues: Language communities in the United States*. New York: Free Press. **359**.

Connor, W. P. (1979). *Socialism, politics, and equality*. New York: Columbia University Press. **343**

Conrad, R. E. (1983). *Children of God's fire: A documentary history of black slavery in Brazil*. Princeton, NJ: Princeton University Press. **362**

Conyers, J., Jr. (1979, January 3). Rampant crime in the boardroom. *The Los Angeles Times*, Part II, p. 5. **293, 309**

Cook, R. C. (1957). World migration: 1945–1955. *Population Bulletin, 13*, 77–94. **124**

Cooley, C. H. (1927). *Life and the student*. New York: Knopf. **157, 160, 368**

Cooley, C. H. (1962). *Social organization*. New York: Schocken Books. (Original work published 1909) **103, 219**

Cooley, C. H. (1964). *Human nature and the social order*. New York: Schocken. (Original work published 1902) **26, 152, 160, 161, 186**

Coombs, L. C. (1977). Preferences for sex of children among U.S. couples. *Family Planning Perspectives, 9*(6), 259–265. **396**

Coon, C. S. (1971). *The hunting peoples*. Boston: Little, Brown. **481**

Cooper, H. M., and Good, T. L. (1983). *Pygmalion grows up*. New York: Longman. **511**

Cordes, C. (1984, November). Easing toward perfection at Twin Oaks: Walden Two model now 17. *APA Monitor*, p. 1. Washington, DC: American Psychological Association. **248**

Coser, L. A. (1956). *The functions of social conflict*. Glencoe, IL: The Free Press. **89, 237, 489, 666**

Coser, L. A. (1967). *Continuities in the study of social conflict*. New York: The Free Press. **666**

Coser, L. A. (Ed). (1975a). *The idea of social structure*. New York: Harcourt Brace Jovanovich.

Coser, L. A. (1975b). Structure and conflict. In P. M. Blau (Ed.), *Approaches to the study of social structure*. New York: The Free Press.

Coser, L. A. (1977). *Masters of sociological thought* (2nd ed.). New York: Harcourt Brace Jovanovich. **26, 27**

Coser, R. L. (1966). Role distance, sociological ambivalence, and transitional status systems. *American Journal of Sociology, 77*(2), 173–187. **89**

Coulton, G. G. (1926). *The medieval village*. London: Cambridge University Press. **441**

Courtney, A. E., and Whipple, T. W. (1983). *Sex stereotyping in advertising*. Lexington, MA: Lexington Books. **169, 415**

Coverman, S. (1983). Gender, domestic labor time, and wage inequality. *American Sociological Review, 48*, 623–637. **426, 427**

Crain, R. L. (1975). School integration and occupational achievement of Negroes. In Pettigrew (1975), pp. 206–224. **374**

Cressey, D. R. (1969). *Theft of the nation: The structure of organized crime in America*. New York: Harper & Row. **291**

Cressey, P. F. (1938). Population succession in Chicago: 1889–1930. *American Journal of Sociology, 44*(1), 56–59.

Crowne, D. P., and Marlowe, D. (1964). *The approval motive*. New York: Wiley. **38**

Csikszentmihalyi, M. and Rochberg-Halton, E. (1981). *The meaning of things: Symbols in the development of the self*. Cambridge: Cambridge University Press. **161**

Curran, T. J. (1974). Xenophobia in America. In F. J. Coppa and P. C. Dolce (Eds.), *Cities in transition: From the ancient world to urban America*. Chicago: Nelson Hall. **255**

Curtin, P. D. (1969). *The Atlantic slave trade*. Madison, WI: University of Wisconsin Press. **124**

Curtis, H. (1968). *Biology*. New York: Worth. **68**

Curtis, H., and Barnes, N. S. (1981). *Invitation to biology* (3rd ed.). New York: Worth. **678**

Curtis, L. (1974). *Criminal violence: National patterns and behavior*. Lexington, MA: Lexington Books. **489**

Dadrian, W. N. (1971). Factors of anger and aggression in genocide. *Journal of Human Relations, 19*, 394–417. **374**

Dahl, R. A. (1961). *Who governs? Democracy and power in an American city*. New Haven: Yale University Press. **260**

Dahrendorf. R. (1958). Out of utopia: Toward a reorientation of sociological analysis. *American Journal of Sociology, 64*, 115–127. **28, 666**

Dahrendorf, R. (1959). *Class and class conflict in industrial society*. Stanford, CA: Stanford University Press.

Dahrendorf, R. (1973). Toward a theory of social conflict. In A. Etzioni and E. Etzioni-Halevy (Eds.), *Social change: Sources, patterns, and consequences*. New York: Basic Books. **28**

Daly, M. (1972, February). Abortion and sexual caste. *Commonweal*, pp. 415–419.

Daly, M. (1973). *Beyond God the Father*. Boston: Beacon Press. **611, 622**

Daner, F. J. (1976). *The American children of Krsna*. New York: Holt, Rinehart & Winston.

Dantin, H. M., and Carver, C. S. (1982). Induced competences and the bystander effect. *Journal of Applied Social Psychology, 12*(2), 100–111. **177**

Darwin, C. (1962). *On the origin of species*. New York: Macmillan. (Original work published 1859)

Davidowicz, L. S. (1975). *The war against the Jews: 1933–1945*. New York: Holt, Rinehart & Winston. **374, 379**

Davies, J. C. (1962). Toward a theory of revolution. *American Sociological Review, 27*, 5–18. **651**

Davies, J. C. (1969). The J-curve of rising and declining satisfactions as a cause of some great revolutions and a contained rebellion. In H. D. Graham and T. R. Gurr (Eds.), *Violence in America: Historical and comparative perspectives*. Washington, DC: U.S. Government Printing Office.

Davis, J. A. (1977). *General Social Surveys, 1972–1977: Cumulative Codebook*. Chicago: National Opinion Research Center. **490**

Davis, J. A. (1980). *General Social Surveys, 1972–1980: Cumulative codebook*. Chicago: National Opinion Research Center. **298, 358**

Davis, J. A. (1982). *General social surveys, 1972–1982: Cumulative codebook*. Chicago: National Opinion Research Center. **298, 318, 398, 400, 423, 501, 581, 587**

Davis, J. A. (1983). *General Social Surveys, 1972–1983: Cumulative codebook*. Chicago: National Opinion Research Center. **439, 490, 583**

Davis, J. A. (1984). *General social surveys, 1972–1984: Cumulative codebook*. Chicago: National Opinion Research Center. **36, 212, 280, 286, 295, 308, 309, 318, 325, 339, 374, 439, 469, 471, 485, 490, 492, 525, 552, 580, 581, 583, 584, 624, 627**

Davis, K. (1940). Extreme social isolation of a child. *American Journal of Sociology, 45,* 554–564. **147**

Davis, K. (1947). Final note on a case of extreme isolation. *American Journal of Sociology, 50,* 432–437. **147**

Davis, K. (1949). *Human society.* New York: Macmillan. **570**

Davis, K. (1953). Reply to Tumin. *American Sociological Review, 18*(August), 394–397. **348**

Davis, K. (1955). The origin and growth of urbanization in the world. *American Journal of Sociology, 60,* 429–437. **133**

Davis, K. (1963). The theory of change and response in modern demographic history. *Population Index, 29*(4), 345–366. **122**

Davis, K. (1967). Population: Will current programs succeed? *Science, 158,* p. 7.

Davis, K. (1974). The migrations of human populations. *Scientific American, 231,* 92–105. **124**

Davis, K. (1976). The world population crisis. In R. K. Merton and R. Nisbet (Eds.), *Contemporary social problems* (4th ed.). New York: Harcourt Brace Jovanovich. **137**

Davis, K., and Blake, J. (1956). Social structure and fertility: An analytic framework. *Economic Development and Cultural Change, 4,* 211–235. **115**

Davis, K., and Moore, W. E. (1945). Some principles of stratification. *American Sociological Review, 10,* 242–249. **348, 418**

Davis, M. H., and Stephan, W. G. (1980). Attributions for exam performance. *Journal of Applied Social Psychology, 10*(3), 235–248. **182**

Davis-Friedmann, D. (1983). *Long lives: Elderly and the Communist Revolution.* Cambridge: Harvard University Press. **435**

Deane, P., and Cole, W. A. (1962). *British economic growth 1688–1959: Trends and structure.* London: Cambridge University Press. **135**

Deaux, K. (1972). To err is humanizing. But sex makes a difference. *Representative Research in Social Psychology, 3,* 20–28. **182**

Deaux, K. (1976, December). Ahhh, she was just lucky. *Psychology Today 10*(7), p. 70ff. **401, 403**

Deci, E. L. (1975). *Intrinsic motivation.* New York: Plenum. **504**

Deci, E. L. (1980). *The psychology of self-determination.* Lexington, MA: Lexington Books. **190**

Demos, J. (1970). *A little commonwealth: Family life in Plymouth Colony.* New York: Oxford University Press. **404**

Deutsch, M. and Collins, M. (1951). *Interracial housing: A psychological evaluation of a social experiment.* Minneapolis: University of Minnesota Press. **383**

Deutsch, M., and Gerard, H. B. (1955). A study of normative and informational social influences upon individual judgement. *Journal of Abnormal and Social Psychology, 51,* 629–636. **210**

Devine, J. A. (1983). Class inequality and state policy. *American Sociological Review, 48*(October), 606–622. **324, 348**

Dewey, J., and Bentley, A. (1976). *Knowing and the known.* Westport, CT: Greenwood.

Diaz, B. (1974). *The conquest of New Spain* (J. M. Cohen, Trans.). London: The Folio Society. **608**

Disraeli, B. (1955). Address, House of Commons, May 1, 1866. Quoted in J. Bartlett (Ed.), *Familiar quotations* (13th ed., p. 512). Boston: Little, Brown.

Dobash, R. E., and Dobash, R. (1979). *Violence against wives.* New York: The Free Press. **489**

Dobb, M. (1947). *Studies in the development of capitalism.* New York: International Publishers. **534, 536**

Dobbs, J. (1972). *Sex, setting, and reactions to crowding on sidewalks.* Paper presented at the American Psychological Association meeting, Honolulu. **403**

Dobzhansky, T. (1962). *Mankind evolving.* New York: Bantam Books.

Dobzhansky, T. (1973). *Genetic diversity and human equality.* New York: Basic Books. **353**

Doering, C. H., Brodie, H. K. H., Kraemer, H., Becker, H., and Hamburg, D. A. (1974). Plasma testosterone levels and psychologic measures in men over a 2-month period. In R. C. Friedman (Ed.), *Sex differences in behavior* (pp. 413–431). **393**

Dohrenwend, B. P., and Dohrenwend, B. S. (1976). Sex differences in psychiatric disorders. *American Journal of Sociology, 81,* 1447–1454. **419**

Dollard, J., et al. (1939). *Frustration and aggression.* New Haven: Yale University Press. **649, 650**

Dollard, J., and Miller, N. E. (1950). *Personality and psychotherapy.* New York: McGraw-Hill.

Domhoff, G. W. (1967). *Who rules America?* Englewood Cliffs, NJ: Prentice-Hall. **330, 579**

Domhoff, G. W. (1971). *The higher circles.* New York: Random House. **330**

Domhoff, G. W. (1983). *Who rules America now?* Englewood Cliffs, NJ: Prentice-Hall. **330, 579, 593**

Domhoff, G. W., and Ballard, H. T. (Eds.). (1968). *C. Wright Mills and the power elite.* Boston: Beacon Press. **579**

Domhoff, G. W., and Zweigenhaft, R. L. (1983, April 24). Jews in the corporate establishment. *New York Times.* **367**

Douglas, J. D. (1968). Suicide: Social aspects. In D. L. Sills (Ed.), *The international encyclopedia of the social sciences, (Vol. 15).* New York: The Macmillan Company/The Free Press. **279**

Douglas, J. D., and Waksler, F. C. *The sociology of deviance: An introduction.* Boston: Little, Brown. **288**

Douvan, E., and Adelson, J. (1966). *The adolescent experience.* New York: Wiley. **299**

Dowd, D. F. (1974). *The twisted dream: Capitalist development in the United States since 1776.* Cambridge, MA: Winthrop. **536**

Draper, T. (1962). *Castro's revolution: Myths and realities.* New York: Praeger. **655**

Drew, E. (1983). *Politics and money.* New York: Macmillan. **585**

Dudley, J. R. (1983). *Living with stigma: The plight of people we label mentally retarded.* Springfield, IL: Charles C. Thomas. **285**

Dumond, D. (1975, February 28). The limitations of human population: A natural history. *Science, 187,* p. 714. **671**

Duncan, O. D. (1961). From social system to ecosystem. *Sociological Inquiry, 31,* 140–149. **113**

Duncan, O. D. (1969). Inheritance of poverty or inheritance of race? In D. P. Moynihan (Ed.), *On understanding poverty* (pp. 85–110). New York: Basic Books. **365, 371**

Duncan, O. D., and Duncan, B. (1955). Residential distribution and occupational stratification. *American Journal of Sociology, 60*(5), 493–503. **372**

Duncan, O. D., and Lieberson, S. (1959). Ethnic segregation and assimilation. *American Journal of Sociology, 64*(January), 364–74. **372**

Duncan, O. D., and Schnore, L. F. (1959). Cultural, behavioral, and ecological perspectives in the study of social organization. *American Journal of Sociology, 65.* **113**

Dunn, J., and Kendrick, C. (1982). *Siblings: Love, envy, and understanding.* Cambridge, MA: Harvard University Press. **167**

Durden-Smith, J., and DeSimone, D. (1983). *Sex and the brain.* New York: Arbor House. **392**

Durkheim, E. (1933). *The division of labor in society*. New York: The Free Press. (Original work published 1893) **81, 235, 237, 238, 252**

Durkheim, E. (1938). *The rules of the sociological method*. New York: The Free Press. (Original work published 1895) **13, 18, 21, 280, 285, 298**

Durkheim, E. (1951). *Suicide*. New York: The Free Press. (Original work published 1897) **33, 238, 298**

Durkheim, E. (1965). *The elementary forms of religious life*. New York: The Free Press. (Original work published 1912) **602, 605**

Durkheim, E. (1974). *Sociology and philosophy*. New York: The Free Press. (Original work published 1924) **77, 280**

Duverger, M. (1959). *Political parties* (B. North and R. North, Trans.). London: Methuen. **582, 627**

Dworkin, A. (1974). *Woman hating*. New York: E. P. Dutton. **397**

Easterlin, R. A. (1967). Effects of population growth on the economic development of developing countries. *Annals of the American Academy of Political and Social Science, 371*, 98–108. **126**

Easterlin, R. A. (1978). What will 1984 be like? Socioeconomic implications of recent twists in age structure. *Demography, 15*, 397–432. **121**

Edelman, M. W., and Howe, H., et al. (1985). *Barriers to excellence: Our children at risk*. Boston: National Coalition of Advocates for Students. **522**

Ehrlich, P. R., and Ehrlich, A. H. (1970). *Population, resources, environment*. San Francisco: W. H. Freeman.

Eisenstadt, S. N. (1956). *From generation to generation*. New York: The Free Press. **168, 431, 433, 449**

Eisenstein, E. (1980). *The printing press as an agent of change*. Cambridge, England: Cambridge University Press. **672**

Elder, G. H. (1974). *Children of the Great Depression*. Chicago: University of Chicago Press. **448**

Eldridge, H. T. (1968). Population policies. In D. L. Sills (Ed.), *The international encyclopedia of the social sciences (Vol. 12)*. New York: The Macmillan Company/The Free Press. **116**

Elkins, S. M. (1963). *Slavery: A problem in American institutional and intellectual life*. New York: Grosset and Dunlap. **367**

Elliott, D. S., and Ageton, S. S. (1980). Reconciling race and class differences in self-reported and official estimates of delinquency. *American Sociological Review, 45*(February), 95–110. **288**

Ellis, G. J., Lee, G. R., and Peterson, L. R. (1978). Supervision and conformity. *American Journal of Sociology, 84*, 386–403. **166**

Ellison, R. (1952). *The invisible man*. New York: Random House. **178**

Emerson, R. (1968). Colonialism: Political aspects. In D. L. Sills (Ed.), *The international encyclopedia of the social sciences (Vol. 3)*. New York: The Macmillan Company. **345**

Emerson, R. M. (1981). Social exchange theory. In M. Rosenberg and R. H. Turner (Eds.), *Social psychology: Sociological perspectives* (pp. 30–65). New York: Basic Books. **197**

Emerson, R. M. (1981). Observational field work. *Annual Review of Sociology, 7*, 351–378. **44**

Emmerich, W., et al. (1976). *Development of gender constancy in economically disadvantaged children*. Report of the Educational Testing Service, Princeton, New Jersey.

Engels, F. (1959). On authority. In L. S. Feuer (Ed.), *Marx and Engels, Basic writings in politics and philosophy*. Garden City, NY: Doubleday/Anchor.

Engels, F. (1962). *Conditions of the working class in England in 1844*. Moscow: Foreign Languages Publishing House. (Original work published 1845) **441**

Engels, F. (1972). The origin of the family, private property, and the state. New York: Pathfinder Press. (Original work published 1891) **404, 419, 478**

Entwistle, D. R., and Doering, S. G. (1981). *The first birth: A family turning point*. Baltimore: Johns Hopkins University Press. **426, 476**

Epstein, A. L. (1967). Urbanization and social change in Africa. *Current Anthropology, 8*, 275–295. **269**

Epstein, C. F. (1970). Encountering the male establishment. *American Journal of Sociology, 75*, 965–982. **41, 416**

Epstein, C. F. (1975). Tracking and careers: The case of women in American society. In E. L. Zuckerman (Ed.), *Women and men* (pp. 26–34). New York: The Radcliffe Club.

Epstein, C. F. (1983). *Women in law*. New York: Doubleday/Anchor. **408**

Epstein, C. F., and Coser, R. L. (Eds.). (1981). *Access to power: Cross-national studies of women and elites*. London: Allen Unwin. **410**

Erikson, E. H. (1963). *Childhood and society* (2nd ed.). New York: Norton.

Erikson, E. H. (1968). *Identity, youth, and crisis*. New York: Norton.

Erikson, K. T. (1966). *Wayward Puritans: A study in the sociology of deviance*. New York: Wiley. **280, 298**

Ernst, C., and Angst, J. (1983). *Birth order: Its influence on personality*. New York: Springer-Verlag. **166**

Espenshade, T. (1980). Raising a child can now cost $85,000. *Intercom, 8*, 1–2. **121**

Etienne, M., and Leacock, E. (Eds.). (1980). *Women and colonization: Anthropological perspectives*. New York: Praeger. **393, 399, 404**

Etzioni, A. (1969). *The semi-professions and their organization*. New York: The Free Press. **549**

Etzioni-Halévy, E. (1983). *Bureaucracy and democracy: A political dilemma*. Boston: Routledge and Kegan Paul. **575**

Eurich, N. P. (1981). *Systems of higher education in twelve countries*. New York: Praeger. **508**

Evans, P. B. (1981). Recent research on multinational corporations. *Annual Review of Sociology, 7*, 199–223. **346, 560, 561**

Evans, P. B., and Timberlake, M. (1980). Dependence, inequality, and the growth of the tertiary: A comparative analysis of less developed countries. *American Sociological Review, 45(4)*, 531–552. **346**

Farb, P. (1973). *Word play: What happens when people talk*. New York: Knopf. (1975 refers to the Bantam paperback edition.) **68, 69, 394**

Farley, R. (1980). The long road: Blacks and whites in America. *American Demographics, 2(2)*, 11–17. **384, 385**

Farley, R., Bianchi, S., and Colasanto, D. (1979). Barriers to the racial integration of neighborhoods: The Detroit case. *Annals of the American Academy of Political and Social Science, 441* (January), 97–113.

Farley, R., and Neidert, L. J. (1984). *How effective was the melting pot? An analysis of current ethnic differences in the United States* (Population Studies Center Research Report 84-68). Ann Arbor: University of Michigan. **366, 370**

Farley, R., Richards, T., and Wurdock, C. (1980). School desegregation and white flight: An investigation of competing models and their discrepant findings. *Sociology of Education, 53*(3), 123–139. **387**

Farley, R., Schuman, H., Bianchi, S., Colasanto, D., and Hatchett, S. (1978). 'Chocolate city, vanilla suburbs:' Will the trend toward racially separate communities continue? *Social Science Research, 7*(4), 319–344. **256, 372, 373**

Fatemi, N. S., Williams, G. W., and de Saint-Phalle, T. L. T. (1982). *Multinational corporations* (rev. 2nd ed.). New Jersey: A. S. Barnes. **561**

Federal Bureau of Investigation. (1976). *Uniform crime reports for the United States: Crime in the United States: 1976.* Washington, DC: U.S. Government Printing Office. **296**

Fein, R. (1966). An economic and social profile of the American Negro. In T. Parsons and K. B. Clark (Eds.), *The Negro American* (pp. 114–115). Boston: Beacon Press. **365**

Feldman, A. S., and Tilly, C. (1960). The interaction of social and physical space. *American Sociological Review, 25,* 877–884. **372**

Feldman-Summers, S., and Kiesler, J. (1974). Those who are number two try harder: The effects of sex on attributions of causality. *Journal of Personality and Social Psychology, 30,* 846–855. **182**

Ferdinand, T. N. (1970). Demographic shifts and criminality: An inquiry. *British Journal of Criminology,* (April), 169–175. **307**

Ferrarotti, F. (1970). Roma da capitale a pereferia. Rome: Laterza. **250**

Festinger, L. (1948). A study of rumor: Its origin and spread. *Human Relations, 1,* 464–485. **646**

Festinger, L. (1954). A theory of social comparison processes. *Human Relations, 7,* 117–140. **163**

Festinger, L., Pepitone, A., and Newcomb, T. M. (1952). Some consequences of de-individuation in a group. *Journal of Abnormal and Social Psychology, 47,* 382–389.

Festinger, L., Riecken, H. W., and Schacter, S. (1956). *When prophecy fails.* New York: Harper & Row. **44**

Fettner, A. G., and Check, W. A. (1984). *The truth about AIDS.* New York: Holt, Rinehart & Winston.

Feuer, L. (Ed.). (1959). *Marx and Engels: Basic writings on politics and philosophy.* Garden City, NY: Doubleday. **614**

Fidell, L. (1970). Empirical verification of sex discrimination in hiring practices in psychology. *American Psychologist, 25,* 1094–1097. **44**

Fiedler, F. E., Chemers, M. M., and Mahan, L. (1976). *Improving leadership effectiveness.* New York: Wiley. **234**

Field, M. H., and Field, H. F. (1973). Marital violence and the criminal process: Neither justice nor peace. *Social Service Review, 47*(2), 221–240. **490**

Fieldhouse, D. K. (1968). Colonialism: Economic aspects. In D. L. Sills (Ed.), *The international encyclopedia of the social sciences (Vol. 3).* New York: The Macmillan Company/The Free Press. **345**

Findley, L. J., and Redstone, P. M. (1982). Blood transfusions in adult Jehovah's Witnesses: A case study of one congregation. *Archives of Internal Medicine, 142*(3, March), 606. **613**

Finifter, A. W. (Ed.) (1972). *Alienation and the social system.* New York: Wiley.

Firey, W. (1945). Sentiment and symbolism as ecological variables. *American Sociological Review, 10*(April), 140–148. **258**

Firestone, S. (1970). *The dialectic of sex: The case for feminist revolution.* New York: William Morrow. **422**

Fischer, C. S. (1975). Toward a subcultural theory of urbanism. *American Journal of Sociology, 80* (May), 1319–1941. **250, 262**

Fischer, C. S. (1982). *To dwell among friends: Personal networks in town and city.* Chicago: University of Chicago Press. **250, 252, 262**

Fischer, C. S. (1984). *The urban experience* (2nd ed.). San Diego: Harcourt Brace Jovanovich. **250, 252, 262**

Fischer, H. W., and Lazerson, A. (1984). *Human development.* New York: W. H. Freeman. **143, 411**

Fishbein, M. (1966). A consideration of beliefs, attitudes, and their relationship. In I. D. Steiner and M. Fishbein (Eds.), *Current studies in social psychology.* New York: Holt, Rinehart, & Winston. **15**

Fisher, H. T., and Fisher, M. H. (Eds.). (1966). *Life in Mexico: The letters of Fanny Calderon de la Barca.* Garden City, NY: Doubleday. **113**

Fisher, J. D., Nadler, A., and DePaulo, B. M. (Eds.). (1983). *New directions in helping: Recipient reactions to aid,* (Vol. 1). New York: Academic Press. **79, 181**

Fishman, P. (1975). *Study of male-female conversations.* Paper Presented at the American Sociological Association Annual Meeting, San Francisco. **401**

Flacks, R. (1970, June). Young intelligentsia in revolt. *Transaction.* **525**

Flynn, J. (1977). Recent findings related to wife abuse. *Social Casework, 58,* 13–20. **293**

Foa, E. B., and Foa, U. G. (1974). *Societal structures of the mind.* Springfield, IL: Charles C. Thomas.

Foa, E. B., and Foa, U. G. (1980). Resource theory: Interpersonal behavior as exchange. In K. J. Gergen, M. S. Greenberg, and R. H. Willis (Eds.), *Social exchange: Advances in theory and research.* New York: Plenum.

Foote, C. (1965). The coming constitutional crisis in bail. *University of Pennsylvania Law Review, 113,* 959. **293**

*Footnotes.* (1980). Sociology in China: Its restoration and future role. Volume 8, No. 4 (October). **520**

Forer, L. G. (1984). *Money and justice.* New York: Norton. **293**

Fortes, M., Steel, R. W., and Ady, P. (1947). Ashanti survey, 1945–46: An experiment in social research. *Geographical Journal, 110,* 149–179. **472**

Fox, R. W. (1981). Mexico City shows global 2000 stresses. *Intercom, 9*(7), 1. Washington, DC: Population Reference Bureau. **124**

Fox, T., and Miller, S. M. (1965). Intra-country variations: Occupational stratification and mobility. *Studies in Comparative International Development, 1,* 3–10. **345**

Franklin, B. (1974). *Observations concerning the increase of mankind.* (Original work published 1751) **254**

Franks, L. (1981, November 22). The seeds of terror. *The New York Times Magazine,* p. 34.

Franks, V., and Rothblum, E. D. (Eds.). (1983). *The stereotyping of women: Its effects on mental health.* New York: Springer. **419**

Frederickson, G. M. (1981). *White supremacy: A comparative study in American and South African history.* New York: Oxford University Press. **333, 344, 360, 367**

Freedman, D. S., Freedman, R., and Whelpton, P. K. (1960). Size of family and preference for children of each sex. *American Journal of Sociology, 66,* 141–146. **115**

Freeman, D. (1983). *Margaret Mead and Samoa: The making and unmaking of an anthropological myth.* Cambridge, MA: Harvard University Press. **45**

**Freeman, J.** (1975). The women's liberation movement: Its origins, structures, impact, and ideas. In J. Freeman (Ed.), *Women: A feminist perspective* (pp. 448–460). Palo Alto, CA: Mayfield. **420**

**Freeman, R. B.** (1975, April). *Changes in job market discrimination and black economic well-being.* Paper delivered at Notre Dame Civil Rights Conference, South Bend, Indiana. **385**

**Freeman, R. B.** (1976). *The overeducated American.* New York: Academic Press. **347**

**Freire, P.** (1972). *Pedagogy of the oppressed.* New York: Herder and Herder. **510, 525**

**Freitag, P.** (1975). The Cabinet and big business: A study of interlocks. *Social Problems, 2* (December), 137–152. **579**

**Freud, S.** (1952). *Totem and taboo.* New York: Norton. (Original work published 1913) **154**

**Freud, S.** (1960). *Beyond the pleasure principle.* New York: Norton (Original work published 1920)

**Freud, S.** (1960). *The Ego and the Id.* New York: Norton. (Original work published 1923) **153**

**Freud, S.** (1961). *Civilization and its discontents.* New York: Norton. (Original work published 1930) **154**

**Freud, S., and Dann, S.** (1951). An experiment in group upbringing. *Psychoanalytic study of the child.* New York: International Universities Press. **147**

**Frey, W. H.** (1983). *Lifecourse migration of metropolitan whites and blacks and the structure of demographic change in large central cities* (Research Report No. 83-47). Ann Arbor, Michigan: University of Michigan Population Studies Center. **257, 267**

**Friedan, B.** (1963). *The feminine mystique.* New York: Dell. **422**

**Friedl, E.** (1962). *Vasilika: A village in modern Greece.* New York: Holt, Rinehart & Winston. **469**

**Friedl, E.** (1975). *Men and women: An anthropologist's view.* New York: Holt, Rinehart & Winston. **403**

**Friedman, H. S., Riggio, R. E., and Segall, D. O.** (1980). Personality and the enactment of emotion. *Journal of Nonverbal Behavior, 5,* 35–48. **401**

**Friedman, J.** (1974). Marxism, structuralism, and vulgar materialism, *Man, 9,* 444–469. **669**

**Friedrich, C. J., and Brzezinski, Z.** (1965). *Totalitarian dictatorship and autocracy* (Vol. 2). Cambridge, MA: Harvard University Press. **577**

**Froebel, F., Heinrichs, J., and Kreye, O.** (1980). *The new international division of labor.* New York: Cambridge University Press. **559**

**Froissart, Sir J.** (1961). *The chronicles of England, France, and Spain.* New York: Dutton. **324**

**Froman, C.** (1984). *The two American political systems: Society, economics, and politics.* Englewood Cliffs, NJ: Prentice-Hall. **593**

**Frost, R.** (1969). Mending wall. In E. C. Lathem (Ed.), *The poetry of Robert Frost.* New York: Holt, Rinehart & Winston. **183**

**Gagliani, G.** (1981). How many working classes? *American Journal of Sociology, 87*(2), 259–285. **317**

**Gallup Opinion Index.** (1978). *How Americans view the public schools.* (Report No. 151).

**Gamson, W. A.** (1961). An experimental test of a theory of coalition formation. *American Sociological Review, 26,* 565–573. **227**

**Gamson, W. A.** (1964). Experimental studies in coalition formation. In L. Berkowitz (Ed.), *Advances in experimental social psychology* (Vol. 1). New York: Academic Press. **227**

**Gamson, W. A.** (1968a). A theory of coalition formation. *American Sociological Review, 22,* 373–379. **191**

**Gamson, W. A.** (1968b). *Power and discontent.* Homewood, IL: Dorsey Press.

**Gamson, W. A.** (1974, July). Violence and political power: The meek don't make it. *Psychology Today, 8*(2), pp. 35–41. **386**

**Gamson, W. A.** (1975). *The strategy of social protest.* Homewood, IL: Dorsey Press. **386**

**Gans, H. J.** (1962). Urbanism and suburbanism as ways of life: A re-evaluation of definitions. In A. Rose (Ed.), *Human behavior and social processes.* Boston: Houghton Mifflin and Routledge & Kegan Paul. **250**

**Gans, H. J.** (1968). *People and plans.* New York: Basic Books. **272**

**Gans, H. J.** (1973). *More equality.* New York: Pantheon. **322**

**Gans, H. J.** (1980). *Deciding what's news.* New York: Vintage. **169**

**Gans, H. J.** (1982). *The urban villagers* (2nd ed.). New York: The Free Press. **248, 250, 256, 262, 272**

**Garfinkel, H.** (1956). Conditions of successful degradation ceremonies. *American Journal of Sociology, 61,* 420–424. **296**

**Garfinkel, H.** (1967). *Studies in ethnomethodology.* Englewood Cliffs, NJ: Prentice-Hall. **28, 162**

**Gartner, A., Greer, C., and Riessman, F. (Eds.).** (1973). *After deschooling, what?* New York: Harper & Row. **527**

**Gecas, V.** (1981). Contexts of socialization. In M. Rosenberg and R. Turner (Eds.), *Social psychology: Sociological perspectives.* New York: Basic Books. **165, 170, 203**

**Gecas, V.** (1982). The self-concept. *Annual Review of Sociology, 8,* 1–33. **157, 160**

**Geertz, C.** (1973). *The interpretation of cultures.* New York: Basic Books. **65, 602, 604, 668**

**Geller, D. M., Goodstein, L. S., M., and Sternberg, W. C.** (1974). On being ignored: The effects of violation of implicit rules of social interaction. *Sociometry, 37,* 541–556. **178**

**Gelles, R. J.** (1972). *The violent home: A study of physical aggression between husbands and wives.* Beverly Hills, CA: Sage. **220, 489, 490**

**Gelles, R. J.** (1978). Violence in the American family. In J. P. Martin (Ed.), *Violence and the family* (pp. 169–182). New York: Wiley.

**Gelles, R. J.** (1979). *Family violence.* Beverly Hills, CA: Sage.

**Genicut, L.** (1966). Crisis from the Middle Ages to modern times. In M. M. Postan (Ed.), *The agrarian life of the Middle Ages* (Vol. 1 of *The Cambridge economic history of Europe*). Cambridge: The University Press. **324**

**George, A. L.** (1971). Primary groups, organization, and military performance. In R. W. Little (Ed.), *Handbook of military institutions* (pp. 293–318). New York: Russel Sage Foundation. **211**

**Gergen, M. M.** (1980). The effects of age and type of residence on forms of social explanation. Unpublished doctoral dissertation, Temple University, Philadelphia. Cited in Gergen, K. J., and Gergen, M. M., (1981). *Social psychology,* p. 331. New York: Harcourt Brace Jovanovich, 1981. **417**

**Gerstel, N. R.** (1976). The feasibility of commuter marriage. In P. J. Stein, J. Richman, and N. Harmon (Eds.), *The family.* Reading, MA: Addison-Wesley. **487**

**Giddens, A.** (1973). *The class structures of advanced societies.* New York: Harper & Row.

**Gilbert, M.** (1970). Women in medicine. In R. Morgan (Ed.), *Sisterhood is powerful.* New York: Vintage. **402**

**Gillespie, D.** (1971). Who has the power? The marital struggle. *Journal of Marriage and the Family, 33,* 445–458. **404, 477**

Giniger, H. (1981, October 5). Quebec meets defiance in enforcing language law. *The New York Times*, p. 2. **70**

Glaser, B. G. (1966). Disclosure of terminal illness. *Journal of Health and Human Behavior, 7*, 83–91. **440**

Glaser, B. G., and Strauss, A. (1965). *Awareness of dying*. Chicago: Aldine. **440**

Glenn, N. D. (1976). The contribution of marriage to the psychological well-being of males and females. *Journal of Marriage and the Family*.

Glick, P. C. (1975). A demographer looks at American families. *Journal of Marriage and the Family, 37*, 15–26.

Glick, P. C., and Norton, A. J. (1979). Marrying, divorcing, and living together in the U.S. today. *Population Bulletin, 32*(5). Washington, DC: Population Reference Bureau. **479**

Glock, C. Y., and Stark, R. (1968). *American piety: The nature of religious commitment*. Berkeley: University of California Press. **609**

Glueck, S., and Glueck, E. (1950). *Unraveling juvenile delinquency*. New York: The Commonwealth Fund. **297**

Glueck, S., and Glueck, E. (1972). *Physique and crime: A biopsychosocial approach*. New York: Seminar Press. **297**

Goffman, E. (1951). Symbols of class status. *The British Journal of Sociology, 2*, 294–304.

Goffman, E. (1956–1957). Embarrassment and social organization. *Americal Journal of Sociology, 62*, 264–271. **195**

Goffman, E. (1959). *The presentation of self in everyday life*. New York: Doubleday and Company. **8, 28, 193**

Goffman, E. (1961a). *Asylums*. New York: Anchor Books. **41, 44, 296**

Goffman, E. (1961b). *Encounters*. Indianapolis, IN: Bobbs-Merrill. **92, 93, 195, 203**

Goffman, E. (1963a). *Behavior in public places*. New York: The Free Press. **195, 510**

Goffman, E. (1963b). *Stigma: Notes on the management of a spoiled identity*. New York: Prentice-Hall. **163, 282, 285, 370**

Goffman, E. (1967). *Interaction ritual*. New York: Anchor Books. **401, 402**

Goffman, E. (1976). *Gender advertisements*. New York: Harper Colophon. **169, 415**

Goffman, E. (1981), *Forms of talk*. Philadelphia: University of Pennsylvania Press. **28, 193**

Goldberg, P. (1968). Are women prejudiced against women? *Trans-action, 5*, 28–30. **43**

Goldberg, S. (1973). *The inevitability of patriarchy*. New York: William Morrow. Excerpted in J. Bensman and B. Rosenberg (Eds.), *Sociology* (pp. 136–140). New York: Praeger. **410**

Goldstein, S., and Mayer, K. B. (1965). The impact of migration on the socio-economic structure of cities and suburbs. *Sociology and Social Research, 50*(1), 5–23. **257**

Goldstein, S., and Sly, D. F. (1977). Recent and projected trends in world urbanization. In S. Goldstein and D. F. Sly (Eds.), *Patterns of urbanization: Comparative country studies*. Bolhain: Ordina Editions. **308**

Goldstone, J. A. (1982). The comparative and historical study of revolutions. *Annual Review of Sociology, 8*, 187–207. **596, 597, 648**

Gonzalez Casanova, P. (1980). The economic development of Mexico. *Scientific American, 243*, 192–204. **137, 681**

Goode, W. J. (1956). *The family*. Englewood Cliffs, NJ: Prentice-Hall.

Goode, W. J. (1959). The theoretical importance of love. *American Sociological Review, 24*, 38–47. **481**

Goode, W. J. (1962). Marital satisfaction and instability: A cross-cultural class analysis of divorce rates. *International Social Science Journal, 14*, 507–526. **484**

Goode, W. J. (1963). *World revolution and family patterns*. New York: The Free Press. **481**

Goode, W. J. (1976). Family disorganization. In R. K. Merton and R. Nisbet (Eds.), *Contemporary social problems* (4th ed., pp. 513–554). New York: Harcourt Brace Jovanovich. **484, 485, 486, 487**

Goodman, L. W. (1980). Horizons for research on international business in developing nations. *Latin American Research Review, 15*, 225–240. **561**

Goody, J. (1976). *Production and reproduction*. New York: Cambridge University Press. **404, 668**

Goolrich, W., and Tanner, O. (1980). *The battle of the bulge*. New York: Time-Life Books. **95**

Gora, J. G. (1982). *The new female criminal: Empirical reality or social myth?* New York: Praeger. **287**

Gordon, C. (1976). Development of evaluated role identities. *Annual Review of Sociology, 2*, 405–433. **161**

Gordon, D. M. (Ed.). (1977). *Problems in political economy: An urban perspective* (2nd ed.). Lexington, MA: D. C. Heath. **553**

Gordon, D. M., Edwards, R., and Reich, M. (1982). *Segmented work, divided labor*. Cambridge: Cambridge University Press. **339, 547**

Gordon, M. (1978). *Final payments*. New York: Ballantine. **436**

Gordon, S. L. (1981). The sociology of sentiments and emotion. In M. Rosenberg and R. H. Turner (Eds.), *Social psychology: Sociological perspectives*. New York: Basic Books. **82, 171**

Goring, C. (1913). *The English convict*. London: His Majesty's Stationery Office. **297**

Gornick, V. (1979). Introduction. In E. Goffman, *Gender advertisements*. New York: Harper Colophon. **416**

Gottfredson, M. R., and Hindelang, M. J. (1981). Sociological aspects of criminal victimization. *Annual Review of Sociology, 7*, 107–128. **286**

Gough, E. K. (1952). Changing kinship usages in the setting of political and economic change among the Nayars of Malabor. *The Journal of Royal Anthropological Institute of Great Britain and Ireland, 82*, 71–87. **463**

Gough, E. K. (1974). Nayar: Central Kerala. In D. Schneider and E. K. Gough (Eds.), *Matrilineal kinship*. Berkeley, CA: University of California Press. **468, 469, 472**

Gould, R. E. (1973, June). Measuring masculinity by the size of a paycheck. *Ms*. **416**

Gould, W. B. (1968). Discrimination and the unions. In J. Larner and I. Howe (Eds.), *Poverty: Views from the left* (pp. 168–183). New York: William Morrow. **377**

Gouldner, A. W. (1960). A norm of reciprocity: A preliminary statement. *American Sociological Review, 25*, 161–178. **79, 198**

Gouldner, A. W. (1970). *The coming crisis of western sociology*. New York: Avon. **28**

Gove, E., and Tudor, J. (1973). Adult sex roles and mental illness. *American Journal of Sociology, 78*, 812–835. **419**

Gove, W. R., and Carpenter, G. R. (1982). *The fundamental connection between nature and nurture*. Lexington, MA: Lexington Books. **392**

Grabill, W. H., Kiser, C. V., and Whelpton, P. K. (1959). *The fertility of American women*. New York: Wiley. **480**

Gracey, H. L. (1972a). Morality in the organized society. In D. H.

Wrong and H. L. Gracey (Eds.), *Readings in introductory sociology* (2nd ed.). New York: Macmillan. **240**

Gracey, H. L. (1972b). *The civil structure and ideology of an elementary school.* Chicago: University of Chicago Press. **506**

Grady, W. R. (1980). "Remarriages of women 15–44 years of age whose first marriage ended in divorce: United States, 1976. *Advancedata,* 58(February), 1–12. **470**

Graebner, I., and Britt, S. H. (Eds.). (1942). *Jews in a gentile world.* New York: Macmillan. **379**

Graebner, W. (1980). *A history of retirement: The meaning and function of an American institution, 1885–1978.* New Haven: Yale University Press. **442**

Graham, H. D., and Gurr, T. R. (Eds.). (1979). *The history of violence in America.* National Commission on the Causes and Prevention of Violence. New York: Bantam. **651**

Greeley, A. M. (1975). *Ethnicity, denomination, and inequality.* Unpublished paper. **370**

Greene, S. (1976). Attitudes toward working women have a long way to go. *The Gallup Opinion Index* (Report No. 128, March). **402**

Greenstein, F. I. (1968). Political socialization. In D. L. Sills (Ed.), *The international encyclopedia of the social sciences* (Vol. 14). New York: The Macmillan Company/The Free Press.

Greenwood, E. (1962). Attributes of a profession. In S. Nosow and W. H. Form (Eds.), *Man, work, and society.* New York: Basic Books. **549**

Greer, S. (1968). Neighborhood. In D. L. Sills (Ed.), *The International Encyclopedia of the Social Sciences, Vol. 11,* (pp. 121–125). New York: The MacMillan Company/The Free Press. **248**

Griffin, S. (1978). *Woman and nature.* New York: Harper & Row. **394**

Griffith, J. (1973). Social pressure on family size intentions. *Family Planning Perspectives,* 5(4), 237–242. **117**

Guest, A. M. (1976). Occupation and the journey to work. *Social Forces,* 55, 161–181. **265**

Gulliver, P. H. (1968). Age differentiation. In D. L. Sills (Ed.), *The international encyclopedia of the social sciences* (Vol. 1, pp. 157–162). New York: Macmillan. **437**

Gurr, T. R. (1970). *Why men rebel.* Princeton, NJ: Princeton University Press. **650, 651**

Guthfill, T., and Avery, N. (1977). Multiple overt incest as family defense against loss. *Family Process,* 16(1), 105–116.

Gutkind, P. C. W. (1966). African urban family life and the urban system. *Journal of Asian and African Studies,* 1, 35–42. **252**

Guzzardi, W. (1976, January). The uncertain passage from college to job. *Fortune Magazine.* **523**

Haber, C. (1983). *Beyond sixty-five.* Cambridge: Cambridge University Press. **442**

Hacker, H. (1951). Women as a minority group. *Social Forces,* 30, 60–69. **391, 410**

Hadden, J. K., and Swann, C. E. (1981). *Prime time preachers: The rising power of Telvangelism.* Reading, MA: Addison-Wesley. **626, 627**

Hagan, J., and Abonnetti, C. (1982). Race, class, and the perception of criminal injustice in America. *American Journal of Sociology,* 88(2), 329–355. **293, 384**

Hagan, J., and Bumiller, K. (1983). Making sense of sentencing: A review and critique of sentencing research. In A. Blumstein, J. Cohen, S. Martin, and M. Tonry (Eds.), *Research on sentencing: The search for reform* (Vol. 2, pp. 1–54). Washington, DC: National Academy Press. **294**

Hagen, R., and Kahn, A. (1975). Discrimination against competent women. *Applied Social Psychology,* 5, 362–376. **402**

Hakeem, M. (1958). A critique of the psychiatric approach to the prevention of juvenile delinquency. *Social Problems,* 5, 194–205. **297**

Halberstam, D. (1972). *The best and the brightest.* New York: Random House. **299**

Hale, M. (1847) A husband cannot be guilty. In *History of the pleas of the crown* (Vol. I, p. 628). Philadelphia: R. H. Small. **187**

Hall, B. (1981). The cost of raising a child—Update. *Consumer Close-Ups* #8. Ithaca, NY: Cornell University Cooperative Extension. **121**

Hall, E. T. (1959). *The silent language.* Greenwich, CT: Fawcett. **97, 183, 621**

Hall, E. T. (1969). *The hidden dimension.* Garden City, NY: Anchor. **77, 97, 183, 184, 191**

Hall, J., and Watson, W. H. (1970). The effects of normative intervention on group decision-making performance. *Human Relations,* 23, 299–317. **230**

Hall, J. A. (1978). Gender effects in decoding nonverbal cues. *Psychological Bulletin,* 85, 845–857. **401**

Hall, J. R. (1979, September/October). Apocalypse at Jonestown. *Society,* pp. 52–61. **616**

Hallman, H. W. (1984). *Neighborhoods: Their place in urban life.* Beverly Hills, CA: Sage. **248, 273**

Hamblin, R. L. (1958). Leadership and crisis. *Sociometry,* 21, 322–335. **216**

Hammel, L. (1974, July 2). Why do few women hold apprenticeships? *The New York Times,* p. 26. **41**

Haney, C., Banks, C., and Zimbardo, P. G. (1973). Interpersonal dynamics in a simulated prison. *International Journal of Criminology and Penology,* 1, 69–97. **188**

Hansberry, L. (1950). *A raisin in the sun.* New York: Random House. **5**

Hare, A. P. (1952). A study of interaction and consensus in different sized groups. *American Sociological Review,* 17, 261–267.

Hare, A. P. (1962). *Handbook of small group research.* New York: The Free Press. **98**

Hare, A. P. (1968). Group role structure. In D. L. Sills (Ed.), *The international encyclopedia of the social sciences* (Vol. 6). New York: The MacMillan Company/The Free Press. **98**

Hare, A. P., Borgatta, E. F., and Bales, R. F. (Eds.). *Small groups: Studies in social interaction* (2nd ed.). New York: Knopf.

Harkins, S. G. (1981). *Effects of task difficulty and task responsibility on social loafing.* Presentation to the First International Conference on Social Processes in Small Groups, Kill Devil Hills, NC. **229**

Harkins, S. G., Latané, B., and Williams, K. (1980). Social loafing: Allocating effort or taking it easy? *Journal of Experimental Social Psychology,* 16, 457–465. **229**

Harlow, H. F. (1958). The nature of love. *The American Psychologist,* 69 (December), 685. **417**

Harlow, H. F., and Harlow, M. K. (1965). The affectional system. In A. M. Scjroer, H. F. Harlow, and F. Stollnitz (Eds.), *Behavior of non-human primates* (Vol. 2). New York: Academic Press.

Harlow, H. F., and Harlow, M. K. (1969). Effects of various mother-infant relationships on rhesus monkey behaviors. In B. M. Foss (Ed.), *Determinants of infant behavior* (Vol. 4). London: Methuen. **417**

Harlow, H. F., and Zimmerman, R. Z. (1959). Affectional responses in the infant monkey. *Science, 130,* 421–432.

Harrington, M. (1963). *The other America: Poverty in the United States.* Baltimore: Penguin Books. **371**

Harris, C. D., and Ullman, E. L. (1945). The nature of cities. *The Annals of the American Academy of Political and Social Science, 242,* 7–17. **265**

Harris, L. (1977, September 12). Disagreement on discrimination. *The Harris Survey.* **358, 383**

Harris, M. (1974). *Cows, pigs, wars, and witches.* New York: Random House. **11, 12, 80, 330, 622, 670**

Harris, M. (1977). *Cannibals and kings: The origins of cultures.* New York: Random House. **218, 403**

Harris, M. (1979). *Cultural materialism.* New York: Random House. **131, 136, 218, 420, 669**

Harrison, B. G. (1978). *Visions of glory: A history and a memoir of Jehovah's Witnesses.* New York: Simon & Schuster.

Hart, C. W. M., and Pilling, A. R. (1960). *The Tiwi of North Australia.* New York: Holt, Rinehart & Winston. **469**

Hart, H. H. (1970). *Summerhill: For and against.* New York: Hart. **527**

Hart, R. J. (1978). Crime and punishment in the Army. *Journal of Personality and Social Psychology, 36,* 1456–1471.

Harter, C. L. (1977). *The 'good times' cohort of the 1930s* (PRB Report 3, April). Washington, DC: Population Reference Bureau. **126, 127**

Hartley, E. L. (1946). *Problems in prejudice.* New York: Columbia University Press/King's Crown Press. **356**

Haskell, T. L. (Ed.). (1984). *The authority of experts.* Bloomington, IN: Indiana University Press. **568**

Hastorf, A. H. (1965). The 'reinforcement' of individual actions in a group situation. In L. Krasner and L. P. Ullmann (Eds.), *Research in behavior modification: New developments and implications.* New York: Holt, Rinehart & Winston. **217**

Hastorf, A. H., and Cantril, H. (1968). They saw a game: A case study. In H. Toch and H. C. Smith (Eds.), *Social perception.* New York: D. Van Nostrand.

Hatt, P. K., and North, C. C. (1947, September). Jobs and occupations: A popular evaluation. *Opinion News, 9,* pp. 1–13.

Hauser, P. (1959). Cultural and personal obstacles to economic development in the less developed areas. *Human Organization, 18,* 82. **269**

Haviland, J. J., and Malatesta, C. Z. (1981). The development of sex differences in nonverbal signals: Fallacies, facts, and fantasies. In C. Mayo and N. M. Henley (Eds.), *Gender and nonverbal behavior* (pp. 184–208). New York: Springer-Verlag. **401**

Hawley, A. H. (1968). Human ecology. In D. L. Sills (Ed.), *The international encyclopedia of the social sciences* (Vol. 4, pp. 328–337). **129**

Hawley, A. H. (1981), *Urban society: An ecological approach.* New York: Wiley. **263, 268**

Hawley, A. H., and Zimmer, B. (1970). *The metropolitan community: Its people and government.* Beverly Hills, CA: Sage.

Hawthorne, N. (1979). *The scarlet letter.* New York: Dodd. **280, 303**

Hayes, C. D., and Kamerman, S. B. (1983). *Children of working parents: Experiences and outcomes.* Washington, DC: National Academy Press. **400**

Hazarika, S. (1983, February 21). 600 reported dead after Hindu raids on Indian villages. *New York Times,* p. 1. **375**

Heer, D. M. (1966). Economic development and fertility. *Demography, 3,* 423–444. **126**

Heer, D. M. (1979). What is the annual net flow of undocumented Mexican immigrants to the United States? *Demography, 16,* 417–423. **124**

Hegedus, R. (1976). Voucher plans. In S. E. Goodman (Ed.), *Handbook on contemporary education* (pp. 128–131). New York: Bowker. **527**

Heider, F. (1946). Attitudes and cognitive organization. *Journal of Personality, 21,* 107–112. **200**

Heider, F. (1958). *The psychology of interpersonal relations.* New York: Wiley. **181, 182**

Heider, K. G. (1970). *The Dugum Dani: A Papaun culture in the highlands of West New Guinea.* New York: Wenner-Gren Foundation. **68**

Heider, K. G. (1972). *The Dani of West Irian.* Andover, MD: Warner Modular. **463, 474**

Heilbroner, R. L. (1977). *The economic transformation of America.* New York: Harcourt Brace Jovanovich. **546**

Heiss, J. (1981). Social roles. In M. Rosenberg and R. H. Turner (Eds.), *Social psychology: Sociological perspectives* (pp. 94–129). New York: Basic Books. **90**

Heller, J. (1961). *Catch-22.* New York: Dell. (Original work published 1955) **178**

Hellman, L. (1979). *The children's hour.* In *Six plays by Lillian Hellman.* New York: Vintage. (Original work published 1934) **646**

Helsing, K. J., and Szklo, M. (1981). Mortality after bereavement. *American Journal of Epidemiology, 114,* 41–52. **172**

Henley, N. M. (1973). Status and sex: Some touching observations. *Bulletin of the Psychonomic Society, 2,* 91–93. **401, 402**

Henley, N. M. (1977). *Body politics: Power, sex, and nonverbal communication.* Englewood Cliffs, NJ: Prentice-Hall. **190, 402**

Hennessy, B. (1971). *Public opinion* (2nd ed.). North Scituate, MA: Duxbury. **689**

Henry, J. (1963). *Culture against man.* New York: Random House. **507**

Hentoff, N. (1977). Who's to blame? The politics of educational malpractice. *Learning, 6*(October), 40–49. **512**

Herman, E. S. (1975, January 3). The income 'counter-revolution'. *Commonweal.* Reprinted in J. H. Skolnick and E. Currie (Eds.). (1976). *Crisis in American institutions* (3rd ed.). Boston, MA: Little, Brown. **341, 346, 347**

Herman, E. S. (1981). *Corporate control, Corporate power.* New York: Cambridge University Press. **545**

Hersch, S. M. (1970). *My Lai 4: A report on the massacre and its aftermath.* New York: Vintage. **301**

Herzig, A. C., and Mali, J. L. (1980). *Oh boy! Babies!* Boston: Little, Brown. **417**

Herzog, A. R., Bachman, J. G., and Johnston, L. D. (1983). Paid work, child care, and housework: A national survey of high school seniors' preferences for sharing responsibility between husband and wife. *Sex Roles, 9*(1). **404**

Hess, R. D. (1970). Social class and ethnic influences upon socialization. In P. H. Mussen (Ed.), *Carmichael's manual of child psychology* (Vol. 2). New York: Wiley. **477**

Hess, R. D., and Shipman, V. C. (1965). Early experience and the socialization of cognitive modes in children. *Child Development, 34,* 869–886. **477**

Hetherington, E. M. (1967). The effects of familial variables on sex-typing on parent-child similarity, and on imitation in children. In J. P. Hill (Ed.) *Minnesota Symposium on Child Psychology* (Vol. 1). Minneapolis: University of Minnesota Press. **150**

HEW. (1974). *Alcohol and health: New knowledge.* DHEW Publication No. ADM 74–124, June. Washington, DC: U.S. Government Printing Office. **309**

Heyl, B. S. (1977). The madam as teacher: The training of house prostitutes. *Social Problems,* 24(5). **299**

Heyns, B. (1971). Curriculum assignment and tracking policies in forty-eight urban public high schools. PhD. Dissertation, University of Chicago, 1971. **522**

Hightower, J. (1980). Food monopoly. In M. Green and R. Massie (Eds.), *The big business reader* (pp. 9–18). New York: Pilgrim. **543**

Hill, C. (1961). *The century of revolution.* Edinburgh: Thomas Nelson and Sons. **536**

Hill, G. W. (1982). Group versus individual performance: Are n + 1 heads better than one? *Psychological Bulletin, 91,* 517–539. **229**

Hill, R. J. (1967). *Reformation to Industrial Revolution.* London: Weidenfeld and Nicolson. **539**

Hill, R. J. (1981). Attitudes and behavior. In M. Rosenberg and R. H. Turner (Eds.), *Social psychology: Sociological perspectives* (pp. 347–377). New York: Basic Books. **15, 81**

Hilton, I. (1967). Differences in the behavior of mothers toward first- and later-born children. *Journal of Personality and Social Psychology, 7,* 282–290.

Hindelang, M. J. (1978). Race and involvement in common law personal crimes. *American Sociological Review, 43,* 93–109. **287**

Hirschi, T. (1969). *Causes of delinquency.* Berkeley, CA: University of California Press. **298**

Hirschi, T. and Gottfredson, M. (1983). Age and the explanation of crime. *American Journal of Sociology,* 89(3, November), 552–584. **287**

Hitler, A. (1948). *Mein Kampf* (R. Mannheim, Trans.). Boston: Houghton Mifflin. (Original work published 1924) **590**

Hobsbawm, E. (1971). *Bandits.* New York: Dell. **324**

Hochschild, A. (1979). Emotion work, feeling rules, and social structure. *American Journal of Sociology, 85,* 551–575. **181**

Hodge, R. W., Siegel, P. M., and Rossi, P. H. (1964). Occupational prestige in the United States, 1925–1963. *American Journal of Sociology, 70,* 286–302. **162, 319, 320, 331**

Hodge, R. W., and Treiman, D. J. (1968). Class identification in the United States. *American Journal of Sociology, 73,* 535–547. **339**

Hodge, R. W., Treiman, D. J., and Rossi, P. H. (1966). A comparative study of occupational prestige. In R. Bendix and S. M. Lipset (Eds.), *Class, status, and power: Social stratification in comparative perspective* (2nd ed.). New York: The Free Press. **320, 332**

Hoebel, A. (1972). *Anthropology: The study of man* (4th ed.). New York: McGraw-Hill. (1966 refers to the third edition.) **68**

Hoffman, L. (1977). Changes in family roles, socialization, and sex differences. *American Psychologist, 32,* 644–657. **415**

Hoffman, M. L., and Saltzstein, H. D. (1967). Parents' discipline and the child's moral development. *Journal of Personality and Social Psychology, 5,* 45–57.

Hofstadter, R. (1955). *Social Darwinism in American thought.* Boston: Beacon. **26, 368, 374**

Hogan, D. P. (1980). The transition to adulthood as a career contingency. *American Sociological Review,* 45(April), 261–276. **431**

Hollander, E. P. (1960). Competence and conformity in the acceptance of influence. *Journal of Abnormal and Social Psychology, 51,* 365–369. **217**

Hollander, P. (1982). Research on Marxist societies: The relationship between theory and practice. *Annual Review of Sociology, 8,* 319–351. **343, 556, 557, 590**

Holmstrom, L. L., and Burgess, A. W. (1983). *The victim of rape.* New Brunswick, NJ: Transaction Books. **294, 403**

Holt, J. (1964). *How children fail.* New York: Dell. **506**

Holt, J. (1972, June). The little red prison. *Harper's, 244,* pp. 80–82. **506**

Homans, G. C. (1950). *The human group.* New York: Harcourt Brace Jovanovich. **93, 207, 211**

Homans, G. C. (1974). *Social behavior: Its elementary forms* (rev. ed.). New York: Harcourt Brace Jovanovich. **197**

Hood, J. C. (1983). *Becoming a two-job family.* New York: Praeger. **404, 477**

Horowitz, D. L. (1983). Racial violence in the United States. *Bulletin of the American Academy of Arts and Sciences,* 37(No. 3), 8–30.

Horowitz, I. L. (1965). *The rise and fall of Project Camelot.* Cambridge, MA: MIT Press. **58**

Hout, M. (1984). Occupational mobility of black men: 1962–1973. *American Sociological Review,* 49(June), 308–322. **365**

Howe, I. (Ed.). (1983). *1984 revisited: Totalitarianism in our century.* New York: Harper & Row. **577**

Hoyt, D. (1965). The relationship between college grades and adult achievement. *American Council on Testing Research Reports.* **522**

Hoyt, H. (1939). *The structure and growth of residential neighborhoods in American cities.* Washington, DC: Federal Housing Authority. **265**

Hoyt, M. F., and Raven, B. H. (1973). Birth order and the 1971 Los Angeles earthquake. *Journal of Personality and Social Psychology, 28,* 123–130. **167**

Huber, J. (1976). Sociology: Review essay. *Signs: Journal of Women in Culture and Society,* 1(3, Part 1), 605–697. **403**

Huber, J., and Spitze, G. (1981). Wife's employment, household behaviors, and sex-role attitudes. *Social Forces, 60,* 150–169. **426**

Huber, J., and Spitze, G. (1983). *Sex stratification: Children, housework, and jobs.* New York: Academic Press. **117, 121, 404, 405, 426**

Huber, R. M. (1971). *The American idea of success.* New York: McGraw-Hill. **500**

Hughes, E. C. (1963). Race relations and the sociological imagination. *American Sociological Review,* 28(December), 879–887. **386**

Humphreys, L. (1970). *Tearoom trade: Impersonal sex in public places.* Chicago: Aldine. **58**

Humphreys, L. (1975). *Tearoom trade: Impersonal sex in public places* (2nd ed.). Chicago: Aldine. **58**

Hunt, C. (1965). Female occupational roles and urban sex ratios in the United States, Japan, and the Philippines. *Social Forces, 43* (March), 407–417. **257**

Hunt, C., and Walker, L. (1974). *Ethnic diversity.* Homewood, IL: Dorsey Press. **358**

Hunt, M. (1974). *Sexual behavior in the 1970s.* New York: Dell.

Hunter, F. (1953). *Community power structure: A study of decision makers.* Chapel Hill, NC: University of North Carolina Press. **260, 579**

Hunter, F. (1980). *Community power succession.* Chapel Hill, NC: University of North Carolina Press. **260**

Huston, A. C. (1983). Sex typing. In P. H. Mussen (Ed.), *Handbook of child psychology* (4th ed.), Vol. 4: E. M. Hetherington (Ed.), *Socialization, personality, and social behavior.* New York: Wiley.

Hutchinson, E. P. (1965). *Immigrants and their children.* New York: Wiley. **366**

Hyman, H. H. (1942). The psychology of status. *Archives of Psychology, 269.* **163**

Hyman, H. H. (1960). Reflections on Reference Groups. *Public Opinion Quarterly, 24,* 383–396.

Hyman, H. H. (1968). Reference groups. In D. L. Sills (Ed.), *The international encyclopedia of the social sciences* (Vol. 13, pp. 353–361). New York: The Macmillan Company/The Free Press.

Hyman, H. H. (1972). *Secondary analysis of sample surveys.* New York: Wiley. **46**

Hyman, H. H. (1983). *Of time and widowhood.* Durham, NC: Duke University Press. **172**

Hyman, H. H., and Singer, E. (Eds.). (1968). *Readings in reference group theory and research.* New York: The Free Press. **163**

Ianni, F. A. J. (1972). *A family business: Kinship and social control in organized crime.* New York: Russell Sage Foundation. **291**

Illich, I. (1971). *Deschooling society.* New York: Harper & Row. **526**

Inkeles, A., and Smith, D. H. (1974). The fate of personal adjustment in the process of modernization. *International Journal of Comparative Sociology, 11*(June), 101–103. **248, 249, 266, 679**

Institute for Social Research. (1980, August) Faltering economy takes its toll on Americans' mental health. *Institute for Social Research Newsletter,* p. 3. **553, 561**

Irons, P. (1983). *Justice at war.* New York: Oxford University Press. **376**

Itard, J.-M.-G. (1962). *The wild boy of Aveyron* (G. and M. Humphrey, Trans.). Englewood Cliffs, NJ: Prentice-Hall. (Original work published 1801) **147**

Jackson, D. (1974, January 11). Justice for none. *New Times,* pp. 48–57. **294**

Jackson, E. F., and Crockett, H. J., Jr. (1964). Occupational mobility in the United States. *American Sociological Review, 24,* 5–15. **335**

Jackson, P. (1968). *Life in classrooms.* New York: Holt, Rinehart & Winston. **506**

Jacobs, D. (1981). Inequality and economic crime. *Sociology and Social Research, 66*(1), 12–28. **305**

Jacobs, J. (1961). *The death and life of great American cities.* New York: Vintage. **252**

Jacobson, P. H. (1959). *American marriage and divorce.* New York: Rinehart. **487**

Jaeger, M. L., Anthony, S., and Rosnow, R. L. (1979). Some determining factors in the transmission of a rumor. Unpublished study, London School of Economics, London, and Temple University, Philadelphia. Cited and discussed in K. J. Gergen and M. M. Gergen. (1981). *Social psychology* (p. 366). New York: Harcourt Brace Jovanovich. **647**

James, D., and Soref, M. (1981). Profit constraints on managerial autonomy: Managerial theory and the unmaking of the corporation president. *American Sociological Review, 46,* 1–18. **545**

James, J. (1951). A preliminary study of the size determinant in small group interaction. *American Sociological Review, 16,* 474–477. **231**

Janeway, E. (1971). *Man's world, woman's place.* New York: Dell. **400, 401, 410, 427**

Janis, I. L. (1951). *Air war and emotional stress: Psychological studies of bombing and civilian defense.* New York: McGraw-Hill. **237**

Janis, I. L. (1968). Group identification under conditions of extreme danger. In D. Cartwright and A. Zander (Eds.), *Group dynamics: Research and theory.* Harper & Row. **230**

Janis, I. L. (1982). *Victims of groupthink.* Boston: Houghton Mifflin. **230**

Jaret, C. (1983). Recent neo-Marxist urban analysis. *Annual Review of Sociology, 9,* 499–525. **250**

Jaynes, G. (1982, September 30). Suit on race recalls lines drawn under slavery. *The New York Times,* p. B16. **353**

Jencks, C. (1983a, March 3). Discrimination and Thomas Sowell. *New York Review of Books,* p. 33ff. **366**

Jencks, C. (1983b, March 17). Special treatment for blacks? *New York Review of Books,* p. 12ff. **385**

Jencks, C., and Reisman, D. (1968). *The academic revolution.* New York: Doubleday. **523**

Jencks, C., et al. (1972). *Inequality: A reassessment of the effect of family and schooling in America.* New York: Basic Books. **337, 371, 516**

Jencks, C., et al. (1979). *Who gets ahead? The determinants of economic success in America.* New York: Basic Books. **347**

Jenkins, J. C. (1981a). On the neofunctionalist theory of inequality. *American Journal of Sociology, 87*(1), 177–179. **322**

Jenkins, J. C. (1981b). Sociopolitical movements. In S. Long (Ed.), *Handbook of political science* (pp. 81–153). Plenum Press. **656, 657**

Jenkins, J. C. (1983). Resource mobilization theory and the study of social movements. *Annual Review of Sociology, 9,* 527–553. **655, 656**

Jenkins, J. C., and Perrow, C. (1977). Insurgency of the powerless: Farm workers movements (1946–72). *American Sociological Review, 42*(April), 249–268. **655, 656**

Jensen, A. R. (1969). How much can we boost IQ and scholastic achievement? *Harvard Educational Review, 39*(Winter), 1–123. **358**

Johnson, A. G. (1977a). Recent trends in sex mortality differentials in the United States. *Journal of Human Stress, 3*(1), 22–32.

Johnson, A. G. (1977b). Sex differentials in coronary heart disease: The explanatory role of primary risk factors. *Journal of Health and Social Behavior, 18*(1, March), 46–54.

Johnson, A. G. (1977c). *Social statistics without tears.* New York: McGraw-Hill.

Johnson, A. G. (1980). On the prevalence of rape in the United States. *Signs: Journal of Women in Culture and Society, 6*(1), 136–146. **403**

Johnson, B. (1975). *Functionalism in modern sociology: Understanding Talcott Parsons.* Morristown, NJ: General Learning Press.

Johnson, D. A., et al. (1971). Racial discrimination in apartment rentals. *Journal of Applied Social Psychology, 1,* 364–377. **362**

Johnson, K. A. (1983). *Women, the family, and peasant revolution in China.* Chicago: University of Chicago Press. **408**

Johnson, R. E. (1980). Social class and delinquent behavior: A new test. *Criminology, 18,* 86–93. **288**

**Joint Center for Political Studies.** (1975, June) Black elected officials triple since 1969. *Focus.* **368**

**Jones, E. E., and Nisbett, R. E.** (1971). *The actor and the observer: Divergent perceptions of the cause of behavior.* Morristown, NJ: Silver Burdett/General Learning Press. **182**

**Jones, G.** (1980). *Social Darwinism and English thought: The interaction of biological and social theory.* Atlantic Highlands, NJ: Humanities Press. **20**

**Jones, R.** (1977). *The other generation: The new power of older Americans.* Englewood Cliffs, NJ: Prentice-Hall. **433**

**Josephy, A. M., Jr.** (1973). Freedom for the American Indian. *The Critic.* Chicago: Thomas More Associates. Reprinted in J. Skolnick and E. Currie (Eds.). (1976). *Crisis in American institutions* (3rd ed.). Boston: Little, Brown. **360**

**Juster, F. T. (Ed.).** (1974). *Education, income, and human behavior.* New York: McGraw-Hill. **370**

**Kagan, J., and Havemann, E.** (1980). *Psychology: An introduction* (4th ed.). New York: Harcourt Brace Jovanovich. **149**

**Kahl, J. A.** (1961). *The American class structure* (2nd ed.). New York: Holt, Rinehart & Winston. **334**

**Kalish, R. A.** (1976). Death and dying in a social context. In R. H. Binstock and E. Shanas (Eds.), *Handbook of aging and the social sciences.* New York: Van Nostrand Reinhold. **440**

**Kalish, R. A.** (1981). *Death, grief, and caring relationships.* Monterey, CA: Brooks/Cole. **440**

**Kalleberg, A., and Griffin, L.** (1980). Class, occupation, and inequality in job rewards. *American Journal of Sociology, 85,* 731–768. **552**

**Kalton, G.** (1984). *Introduction to survey sampling.* Beverly Hills, CA: Sage. **41**

**Kalven, H., Jr., and Zeisel, H.** (1966). *The American jury.* Boston: Little, Brown. **294**

**Kamenetsky, C.** (1984). *Children's literature in Hitler's Germany.* Athens, OH: Ohio University Press. **520**

**Kamii, C. K., and Radin, N. L.** (1967). Class differences in the socialization practices of Negro mothers. *Journal of Marriage and the Family, 29,* 302–310. **477**

**Kanter, R. M.** (1972) *Commitment and community: Communes and utopias in sociological perspective.* Cambridge, MA: Harvard University Press. **248**

**Kanter, R. M.** (1976). Why bosses turn bitchy. *Psychology Today* 9(May), pp. 56–59. **402**

**Kanter, R. M.** (1977a). *Men and women of the corporation.* New York: Basic Books. **44, 46, 318**

**Kanter, R. M.** (1977b). Some effects of proportions on group life: Skewed sex ratios and responses to token women. *American Journal of Sociology, 82,* 965–990. **44, 211, 402**

**Kaplan, N.** (1955). *Reference group theory and voting behavior.* Unpublished doctoral dissertation, Columbia University. Quoted in R. K. Merton, (1957/1968). **95**

**Karlins, M., Coffman, T., and Walters, G.** (1969). On the fading of social stereotypes: Studies in three generations of college students. *Journal of Personality and Social Psychology, 13,* 1–16. **356**

**Karnow, S.** (1983). *Vietnam: A history.* New York: Viking Press. **623**

**Karp, D. A., and Yoels, W. C.** (1979). The college classroom: Some observations on the meanings of student participation. In Robboy, H., Greenblatt, S. L., and Clark, C. (Eds.), *Social interaction.* New York: St. Martin's Press. **195, 510**

**Kart, C. S., and Manard, B. B. (Eds.).** (1976). *Aging in America: Readings in social gerontology, Part III.* Alfred. **433**

**Kasarda, J. D., and Janowitz, M.** (1974). Community attachment in mass society. *American Sociological Review, 39,* 328–339. **262**

**Katz, D., and Braly, K. W.** (1933). Racial stereotypes of 100 college students. *Journal of Abnormal and Social Psychology, 28,* 280–290. **356**

**Keller, S.** (1975). The planning of communities: Anticipations and hindsights. In L. A. Coser (Ed.), *The idea of social structure.* New York: Harcourt Brace Jovanovich. **272**

**Kelley, H. H.** (1950). The warm-cold variable in first impressions of people. *Journal of Personality, 18,* 431–439. **179**

**Kelley, H. H.** (1952). Two functions of reference groups. In G. E. Swanson, T. M. Newcomb, and E. L. Hartley (Eds.), *Readings in social psychology* (rev. ed.). New York: Holt. **210**

**Kelley, H. H.** (1967). Attribution theory in social psychology. In D. Levine (Ed.), *The Nebraska symposium on motivation.* Omaha, NE: University of Nebraska Press.

**Kelley, H. H., and Michela, J. L.** (1980). Attribution theory and research. *Annual Review of Psychology, 31,* 457–501. **181**

**Kempis, T. A.** (1976). *The imitation of Christ.* New York: Doubleday. (Original work published 1420)

**Kendall, P. M.** (1962). *The Yorkist age.* Garden City, NY: Doubleday. **605**

**Kephart, W. M.** (1981). *The family, society, and the individual* (5th ed.). Boston: Houghton Mifflin. **487**

**Kephart, W. M.** (1982). *Extraordinary groups: the sociology of unconventional life-styles* (2nd ed.). New York: St. Martin's Press. (1976 refers to the first edition.) **248, 299, 617**

**Kerbo, H. R.** (1983). *Social stratification and inequality: Class conflict in the United States.* New York: McGraw-Hill. **58, 341, 380**

**Kerner Commission (National Advisory Commission on Civil Disorders).** (1968). *Report of the National Advisory Commission on Civil Disorders.* New York: Bantam.

**Kessler, R. C., and McRae, J. A., Jr.** (1981). Trends in the relationship between sex and psychological distress: 1957–1976. *American Sociological Review, 46*(August), 443–452. **419**

**Kessler, R. C., and McRae, J. A., Jr.** (1982). The effects of wives' employment on the mental health of married men and women. *American Sociological Review, 47*(April), 216–227. **427**

**Kessler, S.** (1975). Psychiatric genetics. In D. A. Hamburg and K. Brodie (Eds.), *American handbook of psychiatry* (Vol. VI). New York: Basic Books. **146**

**Kessler, S., and McKenna, W.** (1979). *Gender.* New York: Wiley. **162**

**Kessler-Harris, A.** (1982). *Out to work: A History of wage-earning women in the United States.* London: Oxford University Press. **427**

**Keyes, R.** (1980). *The height of Your life.* Boston: Little, Brown.

**Kiesler, S. B., Morgan, J. N., and Oppenheimer, V. K.** (1981). *Aging: Social change.* New York: Academic Press.

**Kinsey, A. C., et al.** (1948). *Sexual behavior in the human male.* Philadelphia: W. B. Saunders.

**Kipnis, D.** (1972). Does power corrupt? *Journal of Personality and Social Psychology, 24,* 33–41. **189, 397**

**Kipnis, D., Castell, P., Gergen, M. M., and Mauch, D.** (1976). Metamorphic effects of power. *Journal of Applied Psychology, 61,* 127–135. **397**

**Kirschenbaum, H., et al.** (1971). *Wad-ja-get?* New York: A & W. **501, 522, 526**

Klein, D. (1982). The dark side of marriage: Battered wives and the domination of women. In N. H. Rafter and E. A. Stanko (Eds.), *Judge, lawyer, victim, thief: Women, gender roles, and criminal justice.* Boston, MA: Northeastern University Press. **489**

Klockars, C. B. (1974). *The professional fence.* New York: The Free Press.

Kluckhohn, C. (1949). *Mirror for man.* New York: McGraw-Hill.

Kluegel, J. R., and Smith, E. R. (1982). Whites' beliefs about blacks' opportunity. *American Sociological Review, 47*(August), 518–532. **325, 384**

Knoke, D. (1981). Power structures. In S. Long (Ed.), *Handbook of political behavior.* New York: Plenum. **580**

Knox, R. E., and Safford, R. K. (1976). Group caution at the racetrack. *Journal of Experimental Social Psychology, 12,* 317–324. **230**

Kohlberg, L. (1963). The development of children's orientations toward a moral order: I. Sequence in the development of moral thought. Vita hum., Basel. **76**

Kohlberg, L. (1964). A cognitive-developmental analysis of children's sex-role concepts and attitudes. In E. E. Maccoby (Ed.), *The development of sex differences.* Stanford, CA: Stanford University Press.

Kohlberg, L., and Gilligan, C. (1971). The adolescent as philosopher: The discovery of the self in the post-conventional world. *Daedalus, 100*(Fall), 1051–1086.

Kohlberg, L., and Turiel, E. (1971). Moral development and moral education. In G. Lesser (Ed.), *Psychology and educational practice.* Chicago: Scott-Foresman.

Kohn, M. L. (1974). Social class and parent-child relationships: An interpretation. In R. F. Winch and L. W. Goldman (Eds.), *Selected studies in marriage and the family* (4th ed.). New York: Holt, Rinehart & Winston. **166**

Kohn, M. L. (1977). *Class and conformity.* Chicago: University of Chicago Press. **166**

Kohn, M. L., and Schooler, C. (1983). *Work and personality: An inquiry into the impact of social stratification.* Norwood, NJ: Ablex. **552**

Kolata, N. B. (1974, September 13). !Kung hunters-gatherers: Feminism, diet, and birth control. *Science, 185,* p. 932.

Kolb, W. (1954). The social structure and function of cities. *Economic Development and Cultural Change, III,* 30–46. **269**

Kollock, P., Blumstein, P., and Schwartz, P. (1985). Sex and power in interaction. *American Sociological Review, 50*(1), 34–46. **401**

Kolson, A. (1979, February 4). Sexual harrassment on the job. *Detroit Free Press,* p. 1C. **403**

Korbin, J. E. (Ed.). (1983). *Child abuse and neglect: Cross-cultural perspectives.* Berkeley, CA: University of California Press. **396**

Kornhauser, W. (1959). *The politics of mass society.* New York: The Free Press. **651**

Kornhauser, W. (1966). 'Power elite' or 'veto groups'? In R. Bendix and S. M. Lipset (Eds.), *Class, status, and power.* New York: The Free Press. **580**

Koslin, S., Amarel, M., and Ames, N. (1969). A distance measure of racial attitudes in primary grade children. *Psychology in the Schools, 6,* 382–385. **383**

Kramer, B. M. (1950). *Residential contact as a determinant of attitudes toward Negroes.* Unpublished doctoral dissertation, Harvard University, Cambridge, MA. **383**

Kramer, J. (1974, April 8). The Uganda Asians. *The New Yorker,* pp. 47–93. **375**

Kreuz, L. E., and Rose, R. M. (1972). Assessment of aggressive behavior and plasma testosterone in a young criminal population *Psychosomatic Medicine, 34,* 321–332. **393**

Kübler-Ross, E. (1969). *On death and dying.* New York: Macmillan. **172, 441**

Kübler-Ross, E. (1975). *Death, the final stage of growth.* Englewood Cliffs, NJ: Prentice-Hall. **172, 441**

Kuhn, M. H., and McPartland, T. (1954). An empirical investigation of self-attitudes. *American Sociological Review, 19,* 68–76. **161**

Kuper, H. (1963). *The Swazi: A South African kingdom.* New York: Holt, Rinehart & Winston. **469**

Kuper, L. (1977). *The pity of it all: Polarization of racial and ethnic relations.* Minneapolis: University of Minnesota Press. **374**

Kutner, B., et al. (1952). Verbal attitudes and overt behavior involving racial prejudice. *Journal of Abnormal and Social Psychology, 47*(July), 649–652. **362**

LaFree, G. D. (1980). The effect of sexual stratification by race on official reactions to rape. *American Sociological Review, 45*(October), 842–854. **294**

Lakoff, R. (1975). *Language and woman's place.* New York: Harper & Row. **394, 395**

Lamb, M. E., and Goldberg, W. A. (1982). The father-child relationship: A synthesis of biological, evolutionary, and social perspectives. In L. W. Hoffman, R. Gandelman, and H. R. Schiffman (Eds.), *Parenting: Its causes and consequences* (pp. 55–73). Hillsdale, NJ: Lawrence Erlbaum. **426, 476**

Landes, J. B. (1977–1978). Women, labor, and family life. *Science and Society, 41*(Winter), 386–409. **484**

Lane, D. (1982). *The end of social inequality? Class, status, and power under state socialism.* London: Allen Unwin. **556, 557**

Langer, S. K. (1962). The growing center of knowledge. In *Philosophical sketches.* Baltimore: Johns Hopkins Press. **427**

La Noue, G. R. (Ed.). (1972). *Educational vouchers: Concepts and controversies.* New York: Teachers College Press, Columbia University. **527**

Lao, R., Upchurch, W., Corwin, B., and Grossnickle, W. (1975). Biased attitudes toward females as indicated by ratings of intelligence and likeability. *Psychological Reports, 37,* 1315–1320. **396**

Lapidus, G. (1978). *Women in Soviet society.* Berkeley, CA: University of California Press. **408**

Lapiere, R. T. (1934). Attitudes versus actions. *Social Forces, 13* (December), 230–237. **362**

Larson, O. F. (1968). Rural society. In D. L. Sills (Ed.), *The international encyclopedia of the social sciences* (Vol. 13, pp. 580–588). New York: The Macmillan Company/The Free Press. **249, 267**

Lasch, C. (1977). *Haven in a heartless world: The family besieged.* New York: Basic Books. **167, 518**

Laska, S. B., Seaman, J. M., and McSeveney, D. R. (1982). Inner-city reinvestment: Neighborhood characteristics and spatial patterns over time. *Urban Studies, 19,* 155–165. **271**

Lasko, J. K. (1954). Parent behavior toward first- and second-born children. *Genetic Psychology Monograph, 49.*

Latané, B., and Darley, J. M. (1968) Group inhibition of bystander intervention in emergencies. *Journal of Personality and Social Psychology, 10,* 215–221.

Latané, B., and Darley, J. M. (1970). *The unresponsive bystander: Why doesn't he help?* New York: Appleton-Century-Crofts. **177, 510**

Latané, B., and Nida, S. (1981). Ten years of research on group size and helping. *Psychological Bulletin, 89,* 308–324. **177**

Lauer, R. H. (1981). *Temporal man: The meaning and uses of social time.* New York: Praeger. **97**

Laughlin, P. R. (1980). Social combination processes of cooperative problem-solving groups on verbal intellective tasks. In M. Fishbein (Ed.), *Progress in social psychology.* Hillsdale, NJ: Lawrence Erlbaum. **229**

Lazonick, W. (1974). Karl Marx and enclosures in England. *The Review of Radical Economics, 6*(2, Summer), 1–32. **536**

Leacock, E. (1969). *Teaching and learning in city schools.* New York: Basic Books. **522**

Leavitt, H. J. (1951). Some effects of certain communication patterns on group performance. *Journal of Abnormal and Social Psychology, 46,* 38–50. **102**

Leavitt, R. (1971). Women in other cultures. In V. Gornick and B. K. Moran (Eds.), *Woman in sexist society* (pp. 393–427). New York: Basic Books. **48, 404**

Le Bon, G. (1960). *The crowd: A study of the popular mind.* New York: Viking. (Original work published 1895). **641**

Lederer, L. (Ed.). (1980). *Take back the night: Women on pornography.* New York: William Morrow. **397**

Lee, E. S. (1966). A theory of migration. *Demography, 3,* 47–57.

Lee, M. T. (1968). The founders of the Chinese Communist Party. *Civilizations, 18.* **655**

Lefkowitz, M., Blake, R. R., and Mouton, J. S. (1955). Status factors and pedestrian violation of traffic signals. *Journal of Abnormal and Social Psychology, 51,* 704–706.

Leibert, R. M., Sprafkin, J. N., and Davidson, E. S. (1982). *The early window: Effects of television on children and youth* (2nd ed.). New York: Pergamon. **143**

LeMasters, E. E. (1975). *Blue-collar aristocrats.* Madison, WI: University of Wisconsin Press. **98, 476**

Lemert, E. M. (1951). *Human deviance, social problems, and social control.* New York: McGraw-Hill. **303**

Lenin, V. I. (1949). *The state and revolution.* Moscow: Progress Publishers. (Original work published 1917) **573**

Lenski, G. E. (1966). *Power and privilege.* New York: McGraw-Hill. **322, 457, 605**

Lenski, G. E. (1975). Social structure in evolutionary perspective. In P. M. Blau (Ed.), *Approaches to the study of social structure.* New York: The Free Press. **98**

Lenski, G. E. (1976a). History and social change. *American Journal of Sociology, 82*(3, November), 548–564.

Lenski, G. E. (1976b). Immanuel Wallerstein. The modern world system. *Social Forces, 54,* 701–702. **681**

Lenski, G. E., and Lenski, J. (1982). *Human societies* (4th ed.). New York: McGraw-Hill. **222, 485, 618, 619, 678**

Lepper, M. R., Greene, D., and Nisbett, R. E. (1973). Undermining children's intrinsic interest with extrinsic reward: A test of the 'overjustification' hypothesis. *Journal of Personality and Social Psychology, 28,* 129–137. **504**

Lerner, M. (Ed.). (1948). *The portable Veblen.* New York: Viking Press. **676**

Leslie, G. R. (1982). *The family in social context* (5th ed.). New York: Oxford University Press. **472**

Lesser-Blumberg, R. (1983). Kibbutz women: From the fields of revolution to the laundries of discontent. In M. Palgi, J. R. Blasi, M. Rosner, and M. Safir (Eds.), *Sexual equality: The Israeli kibbutz tests the theories* (pp. 130–150). Norwood, PA: Norwood Editions. **474**

Lester, D. (1983). *Why people kill themselves.* Springfield, IL: Charles C Thomas. **10**

Lever, H. (1981). Sociology of South Africa: Supplementary comments. *Annual Review of Sociology, 7,* 249–262. **344**

Levi, C. (1947). *Christ stopped at Eboli.* New York: Farrar, Straus. **619**

Lévi-Strauss, C. (1956). The family. In H. L. Shapiro (Ed.), *Man, culture, and society.* New York: Oxford University Press. **471**

Levy, H. (1966). *Chinese footbinding.* New York: Walton Rawls. **397**

Lewis, M., and Kreitzberg, V. S. (1979). Effects of birth order and spacing in mother-infant interactions. *Developmental Psychology, 15,* 617–625. **167**

Lewontin, R. (1970, March). Race and intelligence. *Bulletin of the Atomic Scientists,* pp. 23–25. **358**

Lewontin, R., Rose, S., and Kamin, L. J. (1984). *Not in our genes: Biology, ideology, and human nature.* New York: Pantheon.

Licht, H. (1932). *Sexual life in ancient Greece.* London: Routledge. **280**

Lieberman, S. (1956). The effects of changes in roles on the attitudes of role occupants. *Human Relations, 9,* 385–402. **202**

Lieberson, S. (1961). The impact of residential segregation on ethnic assimilation. *Social Forces, 40,* 52–57. **372**

Lieberson, S. (1971). An empirical study of military-industrial linkages. *American Journal of Sociology, 76* (January), 562–583. **579**

Lieberson, S. (1982). Stereotypes: Their consequences for race and ethnic interaction. In R. M. Hauser, D. Mechanic, A. O. Haller, and T. S. Hauser (Eds.), *Social structure and behavior* (pp. 47–68). New York: Academic Press. **357**

Liebert, R. M., and Baron, R. A. (1972). Some immediate effects of televised violence on children's behavior, *Developmental Psychology, 6,* 3.

Linton, R. (1936). *The study of man.* New York: Appleton-Century Crofts. **88, 90**

Lippitt, R., and White, R. K. (1947). An experimental study of leadership and group life. In T. M. Newcomb and E. L. Hartley (Eds.), *Readings in social psychology.* New York: Holt, Rinehart & Winston. **215**

Lipset, S. M. (1959). Democracy and working-class authoritarianism. *American Sociological Review, 24,* 482–501. **574, 583**

Lipset, S. M. (1963). *Political man.* New York: Anchor Books.

Lipset, S. M. (1975). Social structure and social change. In P. M. Blau (Ed.), *Approaches to the study of social structure.* New York: The Free Press.

Lipset, S. M. (1976). Equality and inequality. In R. K. Merton and R. Nisbet (Eds.), *Contemporary social problems* (4th ed.). New York: Harcourt Brace Jovanovich.

Lipset, S. M., and Bendix, R. (1959). *Social mobility in industrial society.* Berkeley, CA: University of California Press. **334, 335, 344, 378**

Lipset, S. M., Trow M., and Coleman, J. S. (1956). *Union democracy.* Glencoe, IL: The Free Press. **483, 552**

Lipton, D., Martinson, R., and Wilks, J. (1975). *The effectiveness of correctional treatment.* New York: Praeger. **296**

Lo, C. Y. H. (1982). Countermovements and conservative movements in the contemporary U.S. *Annual Review of Sociology, 8,* 107–134. **649**

Lofland, J. (1968). The youth ghetto. *Journal of Higher Education, 39* (March).

Lofland, J. (1977). *Doomsday cult* (enlarged ed.). New York: Irvington. **626**

**Lofland, J.** (1981). Collective behavior: Elementary forms and processes. In M. Rosenberg and R. Turner (Eds.), *Social psychology: Sociological perspectives*. New York: Basic Books. **635, 636**

**Lombroso, C.** (1911). *Crime: Its causes and remedies*. Boston: Little, Brown. **297**

**Long, J.** (1982, June 21). Serious crime by the elderly is on the rise. *Wall Street Journal.*

**Long, J. E.** (1981). Population deconcentration in the United States. (Special Demographic Analysis COS-81-5). Washington, DC: U.S. Government Printing Office. **250**

**Long, L. H., and Boertlein, C.** (1976). *The geographic mobility of Americans* (Current Population Reports, Series P-23, No. 64). Washington, DC: U.S. Government Printing Office. **308**

**Long, L. H., and De Are, D.** (1981, September). The suburbanization of blacks. *American Demographics*. **267**

**Long, L. H., and Hansen, K. A.** (1975). Trends in return migration to the South. *Demography, 12*, 601–614. **125**

**Lopata, H. Z.** (1971). *Occupation housewife*. New York: Oxford.

**Lopata, H. Z.** (1979). *Women as widows*. New York: Elsevier. **416**

**Lott, B.** (1981). A feminist critique of androgyny: Toward the elimination of gender attributions for learned behavior. In C. Mayo and N. M. Henley (Eds.), *Gender and nonverbal behavior* (pp. 171–180). New York: Springer-Verlag. **396, 422**

**Lowen, A.** (1969). *The betrayal of the body*. New York: Collier. **148**

**Luce, R. D., and Raiffa, H.** (1957). *Games and decisions*. New York: Wiley. **198, 644, 645**

**Luckmann, T.** (1967). *The invisible religion*. New York: Macmillan. **624, 627**

**Luker, K.** (1984). *Abortion and the politics of motherhood*. Berkeley, CA: University of California Press. **398, 426, 667**

**Lukes, S. and Scull, A. (Eds.).** (1983). *Durkheim and the law*. New York: St. Martin's Press. **252**

**Lynd, H.** (1958). *On shame and the search for identity*. New York: Harcourt Brace. **162**

**Lynd, R. S.** (1939). *Knowledge for what?* Princeton, NJ: Princeton University Press.

**Lynd, R. S., and Lynd, H. M.** (1929). *Middletown: A study in American culture*. New York: Harcourt Brace. **41, 260**

**Lynd, R. S., and Lynd, H. M.** (1937). *Middletown in transition: A study in cultural conflicts*. New York: Harcourt Brace. **260**

**Maccoby, E. E.** (1980). *Social development: Psychological growth and the parent-child relationship*. New York: Harcourt Brace Jovanovich.

**Maccoby, E. E., and Jacklin, C. N.** (1974). *The psychology of sex differences*. Stanford, CA: Stanford University Press. **392, 412, 414, 417**

**Maccoby, E. E., and Martin, J. A.** (1983). Socialization in the context of the family: Parent-child interaction. In P. H. Mussen (Ed.), *Handbook of child psychology* (4th ed.), Vol. 4: E. M. Hetherington (Ed.), *Socialization, personality, and social behavior*. New York: Wiley. **166**

**MacKenzie, M.** (1980). The politics of body size: Fear of fat. Los Angeles, CA: Pacifica Tape Library. **397**

**Macpherson, C. B.** (1973). *Democratic theory: Essays in retrieval*. Oxford: Clarendon Press. **539**

**Malandro, L. A., and Barker, L. L.** (1983). *Nonverbal communication*. Reading, MA: Addison-Wesley. **65**

**Malbix/Ricks Music, BMI.** (1976). Chocolate city. (Available on Casablanca Records, NBLP 7014). **372**

**Malinowski, B.** (1922). *Argonauts of the western Pacific*. New York: Dutton. **197, 532**

**Malinowski, B.** (1929). *The sexual life of savages*. New York: Harcourt Brace and World. **468, 469**

**Malinowski, B.** (1948). *Magic, science, and religion*. New York: The Free Press. **609**

**Malthus, T.** (1960). *Essay on the principle of population*. New York: Modern Library. (Original work published 1798) **137**

**Mamdani, M.** (1981). The ideology of population control. In K. L. Michaelson (Ed.), *And the poor get children* (pp. 39–49). New York: Monthly Review Press. **137**

**Mann, H.** (1842). *Fifth annual report to the secretary of the board*. Boston: Dutton and Wentworth, State Printers. **500**

**Mann, L.** (1970). The social psychology of waiting lines. *American Scientist, 58*(July), 390–398.

**Mann, T.** (1956). *The magic mountain*. New York: Knopf. **96**

**Mannheim, K.** (1952). *Essays on the sociology of knowledge*. London: Routledge and Kegan Paul. **671**

**Marak, G. E., Jr.** (1964). The evolution of leadership structure. *Sociometry, 27*, 174–182. **216**

**Marcus, G. E.** (1983, March 27). One man's Mead. *New York Times Book Review*, p. 3. **45**

**Marini, M. M.** (1980), Sex differences in the process of occupational attainment. *Social Science Research, 9*, 307–361. **406**

**Markham, J. M.** (1982, April 4). In barren Iceland, culture blossoms. *The New York Times*. **308**

**Markides, K. C., and Cohen, S. F.** (1982). External conflict/internal cohesion: A reevaluation of an old theory. *American Sociological Review, 47*(February) 88–98. **237**

**Markovsky, B., Smith, L. R. F., and Berger, J.** (1984). Do status interventions persist? *American Sociological Review, 49*(June), 373–382. **102, 217**

**Mars, G.** (1983). *Cheats at work: An anthropology of workplace crime*. Winchester, MA: Allen Unwin. **288**

**Marshall, L.** (1965). The !Kung Bushmen of the Kalahari Desert. In J. Gibbs (Ed.), *Peoples of Africa*. New York: Holt, Rinehart & Winston. **127, 322**

**Martinez, R. A.** (1974). The New York barrio: Cultures in conflict. In F. J. Coppa and P. C. Dolce (Eds.), *Cities in transition: From the ancient world to urban America*. Chicago: Nelson Hall.

**Martinson, R.** (1974). What works? Questions and answers about prison reform. *The Public Interest, 35*(Spring), 22–54. **296**

**Marx, G. T., and Reichman, N.** (1984). Routinizing the discovery of secrets: Computers as informants. *American Behavioral Scientist, 27*(4, March/April), 423–452. **674**

**Marx, K.** (1935). Theses on Feuerbach. In F. Engels, *Ludwig Feuerbach and the outcome of classical German philosophy* (pp. 73–75). New York: International Publishers. (Original work published 1845) **551**

**Marx, K.** (1961). *Economic and philosophical manuscripts of 1884*. (T. B. Bottomore, Trans.). **82, 349, 563**

**Marx, K.** (1967). Critiques of Hegel's Philosophy of Right. In L. D. Easton and K. Guddat (Trans. and Eds.), *Writings of the young Marx on philosophy and society*. New York: Doubleday. (Original work published 1843) **325**

**Marx, K.** (1970). *A contribution of the critique of political economy*. New York: International Publishers. (Original work published 1859)

**Marx, K.** (1975). *Capital: A critique of political economy*. New York: International Publishers. (Original work published 1867) **137, 306, 315, 535**

**Marx, K., and Engels, F.** (1932). *Manifesto of the Communist* *party.* New York: International Publishers. (Original work published 1848) **21, 324, 666**

Marx, K., and Engels, F. (1976). The German ideology. In *Collected works of Marx and Engels* (Vol. 5). New York: International. (Original work published 1846) **21, 306, 322, 348**

Mason, K. O. (1982). Norms relating to the desire for children. In R. A. Bulatao and R. D. Lee (Eds.), *Determinants of Fertility in developing countries: A summary of knowledge* (Panel on Fertility Determinants, Report No. 3). Washington, DC: National Academy Press. **480**

Mason, K. O. (1984a). Commentary: Strober's theory of occupational sex segregation. In B. F. Reskin (Ed.), *Sex segregation in the workplace: Trends, explanations, remedies* (pp. 157–170). Washington, DC: National Academy Press.

Mason, K. O. (1984b). *The status of women, fertility, and mortality: A review of interrelationships* (Population Studies Center Research Report 84-85). Ann Arbor: University of Michigan.

Massey, D. S. (1981a). Dimensions of the new immigration to the United States and prospects for assimilation. *Annual Review of Sociology, 7,* 57–85. **124**

Massey, D. S. (1981b). Hispanic residential segregation: A comparison of Mexicans, Cubans, and Puerto Ricans. *Sociology and Social Research, 65.* **372**

Massey, D. S., and Denton, N. A. (1985). Spatial assimilation as a socioeconomic outcome. *American Sociological Review, 50*(1), 94–105. **372**

Mathais, P. (1983). *The first industrial revolution: An economic history of Britain 1700–1914* (2nd ed.). London and New York: Methuen. **134**

Matsueda, R. L. (1982). Testing control theory and differential association. *American Sociological Review, 47*(August), 489–504. **299**

Matthiessen, P. (1984). *Indian country.* New York: Viking Press. **324**

Mayo, C., and Henley, N. M. (Eds.). (1981). *Gender and nonverbal behavior.* New York: Springer-Verlag. **402**

McAdam, D. (1982). *Political process and the development of black insurgency 1930–1970.* Chicago: University of Chicago Press. **649, 651, 654, 656, 657, 659**

McArthur, L. Z. (1982). Television and sex role stereotyping. *The Brandeis Quarterly, 2*(January), 12–13. **415**

McCall, G., and Simmons, J. (1978). *Identities and interactions* (rev. ed.). New York: The Free Press. **179**

McCarthy, J. D., and Zald, M. N. (1973). *The trend of social movements in America: Professionalization and resource mobilization.* Morristown, NJ: General Learning Press. **656, 657**

McClelland, D. C. (1973). Testing for competence rather than for 'intelligence'. *American Psychologist, 29*(January). **522**

McClosky, H., and Brill, A. (1983). *Dimensions of tolerance: What Americans believe about civil liberties.* New York: Russel Sage Foundation. **574**

McDougall, W. (1950). *An introduction to social psychology* (30th ed.). London: Methuen. (Original work published 1908) **146**

McGlen, N., and O'Connor, K. (1983). *Women's rights: The struggle for equality in the 19th and 20th centuries.* New York: Praeger. **587**

McGuire, W. J., McGuire, C. V., Child, P., and Fujioka, T. (1978). Salience of ethnicity in the spontaneous self-concept as a function of one's ethnic distinctiveness in the social environment. *Journal of Personality and Social Psychology, 36,* 511–520. **164**

McHugh, P. (1968). *Defining the situation: The organization of meaning in social interaction.* Indianapolis, IN: Bobbs-Merrill.

McPhail, C., and Miller, D. (1973). The assembling process: A theoretical and empirical examination. *American Sociological Review,* (December). **654**

McPhail, C., and Wohlstein, R. R. (1983). Individual and collective behaviors within gatherings, demonstrations, and riots. *Annual Review of Sociology, 9,* 579–600. **641**

Mead, G. H. (1934). *Mind, self, and society.* Chicago: University of Chicago Press. **27, 28, 154, 155, 156, 157, 160**

Mead, M. (1953). *Coming of age in Samoa.* New York: Modern Library. (Original work published 1928) **45, 48, 438, 469**

Mead, M. (1963). *Sex and temperament in three primitive societies.* New York: Morrow. (Original work published 1935) **398**

Mead, M. (1968). Incest. In D. L. Sills (Ed.), *The international encyclopedia of the social sciences* (Vol. 7, pp. 115–122). New York: MacMillan. **471, 482**

Mead, M., and Wolfenstein, M. (Eds.). (1955). *Childhood in contemporary cultures.* Chicago: Phoenix Books.

Medea, A., and Thompson, K. (1974). *Against rape.* New York: Farrar, Straus, and Giroux. **186, 294, 402, 403**

Mehrabian, A. (1972). *Nonverbal communication.* Chicago: Aldine-Atherton. **190**

Meier, R. F., and Short, J. F., Jr. (1982). The consequences of white-collar crime. In H. Edelhertz and T. D. Overcast (Eds.), *White-collar crime: An agenda for research* (pp. 23–50). Lexington, MA: Lexington Press. **309**

Melbin, M. (1978). Night as frontier. *American Sociological Review, 43*(February), 3–22. **257, 457**

Memmi, A. (1964). *Dominated man.* New York: Orion Press. **356, 358**

Merton, R. K. (1934). Durkheims's division of labor in society. *American Journal of Sociology, 40,* 319–328.

Merton, R. K. (1936). The unanticipated consequences of purposive social action. *American Sociological Review, 1,* 894–904.

Merton, R. K. (1938). Social structure and anomie. *American Sociological Review, 3,* 672–682. **305, 307**

Merton, R. K. (1940). Fact and factitiousness in ethnic opinionnaires. *American Sociological Review, 5,* 13–28. **42**

Merton, R. K. (1948). Discrimination and the American creed. In R. M. MacIver (Ed.), *Discrimination and national welfare* (pp. 99–126). New York: Harper and Brothers. **362, 374, 666, 669**

Merton, R. K. (1957). *Social theory and social structure.* New York: The Free Press. **330, 511**

Merton, R. K. (1968). *Social theory and social structure* (enlarged ed.). New York: The Free Press. **22, 88, 90, 91, 92, 171, 180, 211, 212, 218, 224, 233, 277, 283, 305, 307, 330, 511, 617, 666, 669**

Merton, R. K. (1971). Social problems and sociological theory. In R. K. Merton and R. A. Nisbet (Eds.), *Contemporary social problems* (3rd ed.). New York: Harcourt Brace Jovanovich.

Merton, R. K. (1972). Insiders and outsiders. *American Journal of Sociology, 78,* 9–47.

Merton, R. K. (1975). Structural analysis in sociology. In P. Blau (Ed.), *Approaches to the study of social structure* (pp. 21–52). New York: The Free Press.

Merton, R. K. (1976a). The sociology of social problems. In R. K. Merton and R. Nisbet (Eds.), *Contemporary social problems* (4th ed.). New York: Harcourt Brace Jovanovich. **283, 309**

**Merton, R. K.** (1976b). *Sociological ambivalence and other essays.* New York: The Free Press. **28**

**Merton, R. K., and Rossi, A. S.** (1968). Contributions to the theory of reference group behavior. In Merton (1968), pp. 279–334. **164**

**Meyer, J., and Sobieszek, B.** (1972). Effect of a child's sex on adult interpretations of its behavior. *Developmental Psychology, 6,* 42–48. **412**

**Michels, R.** (1911). *Political parties.* (1967). New York: The Free Press. **575**

**Mickish, G.** (1971). Can women function as successfully as men in the role of elementary principal? *Research Reports on Educational Administration, 2*(4) (ERIC Documentation Reproduction Service, ED 062 679). **415**

**Milavsky, J. R., Kessler, R. C., Stipp, H. H., and Rubens, W. S.** (1982). *Television and aggression: A panel study.* New York: Academic Press. **170**

**Milgram, S.** (1965). Some conditions of obedience and disobedience to authority. *Human Relations, 18,* 57–76. **301**

**Milgram, S.** (1974). *Obedience to authority.* New York: Harper & Row. **302**

**Milgram, S.** (1977). *The individual in a social world.* Reading, MA: Addison-Wesley. **646**

**Miliband, R.** (1969). *The state in capitalist society.* New York: Basic Books. **597**

**Miller, G.** (1978). *Odd jobs: The world of deviant work.* Englewood Cliffs, NJ: Prentice-Hall. **291**

**Miller, J., and Garrison, H. H.** (1982). Sex roles: The division of labor at home and in the workplace. *Annual Review of Sociology, 8,* 237–262. **404**

**Miller, N., and Brewer, M. B.** (Eds.). (1984). *Groups in contact: The psychology of desegregation.* New York: Academic Press.

**Miller, W. B.** (1958). Lower-class culture as a generating milieu of gang delinquency. *Journal of Sociological Issues, 14* (Summer), 5–19. **299**

**Millett, K.** (1971). *Sexual politics.* Garden City, NY: Doubleday.

**Mills, C. W.** (1951). *White collar.* New York: Oxford University Press. **327, 349, 540**

**Mills, C. W.** (1956). *The power elite.* New York: Oxford University Press. **329, 579**

**Mills, C. W.** (1959). *The sociological imagination.* New York: Oxford University Press. **18, 28**

**Miner, H. M.** (1968). Community-society continua. In D. L. Sills (Ed.), *The international encyclopedia of the social sciences* (Vol. 3, pp. 174–180). New York: The MacMillan Company/The Free Press. **261, 267**

**Mitchell, J.** (1966, November/December). The longest revolution. *New Left Review,* pp. 11–37. **420**

**Mitford, J.** (1973). *Kind and usual punishment.* New York: Knopf. **281, 293**

**Mitroff, I. I., Mason, R. O., and Barabba, V. P.** (1983). *The 1980 census: Policymaking amid turbulence.* Lexington, MA: Lexington Books. **39**

**Mixon, D.** (1972). Instead of deception. *Journal of the Theory of Social Behavior, 2,* 146–177. **302**

**Miyamato, S. F., and Dornbusch, S.** (1956). A test of the symbolic interactionist hypothesis of self-conception. *American Journal of Sociology, 61,* 399–403. **160**

**Moede, W.** (1927). Die Richtlinien der Leitungspsychologie. *Industrielle Psychotechnik, 4,* 193–209. Cited and discussed in Raven (1968). **229**

**Mol, H.** (1976). *Identity and the sacred: A sketch for a new social-scientific theory of religion.* Oxford: Blackwell. **604**

**Money, J., and Ehrhardt, A.** (1972). *Man and woman, boy and girl.* Baltimore, MD: Johns Hopkins University Press. **162**

**Monson, T. C., and Hesley, J. W.** (1982). Causal attributions for behaviors consistent or inconsistent with an actor's personality traits: Differences between those offered by actors and observers. *Journal of Experimental Social Psychology, 18*(5), 416–432. **182**

**Montagu, A. M. F.** (1971). *Touching: The human significance of the skin.* New York: Columbia University Press. **147, 469, 482**

**Montagu, A. M. F.** (1974). *Man's most dangerous myth: The fallacy of race.* New York: Oxford University Press.

**Moore, W. E.** (1962). *The conduct of the corporation.* New York: Random House. **239, 240**

**Moore, W. E.** (1969). Occupational socialization. In D. A. Goslin (Ed.), *Handbook of socialization theory and research* (pp. 861–884). Chicago: Rand McNally. **171**

**Moreno, J. L.** (1943). Sociometry and the cultural order. *Sociometry, 6,* 299–344. **100**

**Morgan, R.** (1970). *Sisterhood is powerful.* New York: Random House. **397, 427**

**Morgan, S. P., and Hirosima, K.** (1983). The persistence of extended family residence in Japan. *American Sociological Review, 48*(April), 269–281. **483**

**Morgenstern, O.** (1968). Game theory: Theoretical aspects. In D. L. Sills (Ed.), *The international encyclopedia of the social sciences* (Vol. 6). New York: The MacMillan Company/The Free Press. **503**

**Morison, S. E.** (1965). *The Oxford history of the American people.* New York: Oxford University Press. **123, 375, 539, 593**

**Morris, D.** (1967). *The naked ape.* New York: McGraw-Hill. **191**

**Morse, S. J., and Gergen, K. J.** (1970). Social comparison, self-consistency and the concept of self. *Journal of Personality and Social Psychology, 16,* 149–156.

**Mortimer, J. T., Finch, M. D., and Kumka, D.** (1981). Persistence and change in human development: The multidimensional self-concept. In P. B. Bates and O. G. Brim, Jr. (Eds.), *Life-span development and behavior* (Vol. 4). New York: Academic Press. **203**

**Moskos, C. C., Jr.** (1969). Why men fight: American combat soldiers in Vietnam. *Transaction, 7*(1). **211, 237**

**Moss, Z.** (1970). It hurts to be alive and obsolete: The ageing woman. In R. Morgan (Ed.), *Sisterhood is powerful* (pp. 188–194). New York: Vintage. **416**

**Mottaz, C. J.** (1981). Some determinants of work alienation. *The Sociological Quarterly, 22*(Autumn), 515–529. **552**

**Ms.** (1982, October). Name styles of the future, p. 11. **468**

**Mullen, B.** (1983). Operationalizing the effect of the group on the individual: A self-attention perspective. *Journal of Experimental Social Psychology, 19*(4), 295–322. **232**

**Muller, E. N.** (1985). Income inequality, regime repressiveness, and political violence. *American Sociological Review, 50*(1), 47–61.

**Mulligan, M. A.** (1977). An investigation of factors associated with violent modes of conflict resolution in the family. Unpublished master's thesis, University of Rhode Island. Cited in Gelles (1978), p. 173. **488**

**Mumford, L.** (1961). *The city in history.* New York: Harcourt Brace Jovanovich.

**Munley, A.** (1983). *The hospice alternative: A new context for* *death and dying.* New York: Basic Books. **441**

Munsinger, H. (1975). The adopted child's IQ: A critical review. *Psychological Bulletin, 82,* 623–659. **146**

Murdock, G. P. (1943). The common denominator of cultures. In R. Linton (Ed.), *The science of man in the world crisis.* New York: Columbia University Press. **73**

Murdock, G. P. (1949). *Social structure.* New York: MacMillan. **468, 469, 471, 472**

Murdock, G. P. (1967). *Ethnographic atlas.* Pittsburgh, PA: Pittsburgh University Press. **132, 222, 468, 532, 619**

Mussen, P. H., Conger, J. J., and Kagan, J. (1984). *Child development and personality* (6th ed.). New York: Harper & Row.

Myrdal, G. (1945). *An American dilemma.* New York: Harper & Row. **381**

NAEP (National Assessment of Educational Progress). (1977). Basic skills improve, but . . . *NAEP Newsletter, 10*(February), pp. 1–2. **512**

Nag, M. (1962). *Factors affecting human fertility in nonindustrial societies: A cross-cultural study.* New Haven, CT: Yale University Press. **480**

Nag, M. (1967). Family type and fertility. *Proceedings of the World Population Conference, Volume II,* pp. 160–163. New York: United Nations. **480**

Nasaw, D. (1979). *Schooled to order.* New York: Oxford University Press. **515, 519**

Nash, M. (1965). *The golden road to modernity: Village life in contemporary Burma.* New York: Wiley. **442**

National Commission on Excellence in Education. (1983). *A nation at risk: The imperative for educational reform.* Washington, DC: U.S. Government Printing Office. **105, 503, 512, 519, 526**

National Conference on Bail and Criminal Justice. (1964). *Bail in the United States.* Washington, DC. **293**

National Council on Aging. (1975). *The myth and reality of aging in America* (Mimeograph). Washington, DC. **433, 439**

National Education Association. (1968). *Ability grouping, research summary 1968-Se.* Washington, DC. **522**

National Institute of Mental Health. (1982). *Television and behavior: Ten years of scientific progress and implications for the eighties.* Washington, DC: U.S. Government Printing Office. **170**

National Law Review. (1984, May 21). **408**

National Office of Vital Statistics. (1956). *Death rates by age, race, and sex, United States, 1900–1953: Suicide* (Vital Statistics—Special Reports, 43, 30). Washington, DC: U.S. Government Printing Office. **11**

National Opinion Research Center. (1972, Spring). *National Data Program for the Social Sciences (General Social Survey).* National Opinion Research Center, University of Chicago. **372**

Neill, A. S. (1961). *Summerhill.* New York: Hart. **526**

Nelson, M. (1975). Why witches were women. In J. Freeman (Ed.), *Women: A feminist perspective* (pp. 335–350). Palo Alto, CA: Mayfield.

Neugarten, B. L., et al. (1965). Age norms, age constraints, and adult socialization. *American Journal of Sociology, 70,* 710–717. **441**

Newcomb, T. M. (1947). Autistic hostility and social reality. *Human Relations, 1,* 69–86. **382**

Newcomb, T. M. (1956). The prediction of interpersonal attraction. *American Psychologist* (Vol. 1, pp. 575–586). **201**

Newcomb, T. M. (1961). *The acquaintance process.* New York: Holt, Rinehart & Winston. **201**

Newfield, J. (1974). *Cruel and unusual justice.* New York: Holt, Rinehart & Winston. **294**

Newman, G. (1976). *Comparative deviance: Perception and law in six cultures.* New York: Elsevier. **299**

Newman, G., and Trilling, C. (1975). Public perceptions of criminal behavior. *Criminal Justice and Behavior, 2.* **299**

Newsweek. (1977, February 27).

Newsweek. (1982, October 18). Growth industries of the future, p. 83. **335**

Newsweek. (1982, October 25). Guns, grass—and money, p. 40. **280**

Newsweek. (1983, January 24). The Social Security crisis: Who will pay? **453**

Newsweek. (1983a, January 31). Getting off the tenure track, p. 50. **515**

Newsweek. (1983, February 14). The prisoners of conscience, p. 40ff. **307**

Newsweek. (1983b, May 9). Can the schools be saved?, p. 56. **519**

Newsweek. (1983, July 11). **545**

Newsweek. (1983, October 24). **623**

Newsweek. (1984, January 2). **271**

New York Times. (1982, January 10). 'Gypsy scholars' roam academic landscape. **515**

New York Times. (1982, June 3). Ford to test lifetime guaranteed jobs. **328**

New York Times. (1982, November 3). P. C1. **553**

New York Times. (1983, February 23). **375**

New York Times. (1983, March 22). **323**

New York Times. (1983, April 24). **567**

New York Times. (1983, June 12). **562**

New York Times. (1984, January 29). **288**

New York Times. (1984, March 4). **120**

New York Times Magazine. (1976, July 18). P. 39. **295**

Ngai, S. (1974). *Long-distance commuting as a solution to geographical limitation to career choices of two-career families.* Unpublished master's thesis, Cornell University. **487**

Niebuhr, R. (1929). *The social sources of denominationalism.* New York: Holt.

Nielson, J. (1978). *Sex in society: Perspectives on stratification.* Belmont, CA: Wadsworth. **403**

Noel, D. (1968). A theory of the origin of ethnic stratification. *Social Problems, 16*(Fall), 156–172. **377, 456**

North, C. C., and Hatt, P. K. (1947). Jobs and occupations: A popular evaluation. *Opinion News, 9,* 3–13. **332**

Oakley, A. (1974). *Woman's work: The housewife, past and present.* New York: Pantheon. **411**

Oberschall, A. (1973). *Social conflict and social movements.* Englewood Cliffs, NJ: Prentice-Hall. **654, 655, 656**

O'Callaghan, M. L. (1983, June 24). China finds it is not easy to enforce policy of one child per family. *Christian Science Monitor.* **116**

O'Connor, J. (1973). *The fiscal crisis of the state.* New York: St. Martin's Press. **454, 591, 593**

Ofshe, R. (1970). Cognitive consistency and language behavior. *Human Relations, 23,* 139–151. **201**

Ogburn, W. F. (1922). *Social change.* New York: Viking Press. **673, 674**

Ogburn, W. F. (1964). Cultural lag as theory. In W. F. Ogburn (Ed.), *On culture and social change* (pp. 86–95). Chicago: University of Chicago Press.

Oppenheimer, V. K. (1974). The life-cycle squeeze: The interaction of men's occupational and family life cycles. *Demography*, *11*(2), 227–244. **456**

Orum, A. M. (1972). *Black students in protest*. Washington, DC: The American Sociological Association. **651**

Orwell, G. (1946). *Animal farm*. New York: Harcourt Brace and Company.

Orwell, G. (1971). *Nineteen eighty-four*. New York: Signet. (Original work published 1949) **577**

Osborn, J. J., Jr. (1979). *The paper chase*. New York: Popular Library. **170**

Osgood, C. E., Suci, G. J., and Tannenbaum, P. H. (1957). *The measurement of meaning*. Urbana, IL: University of Illinois Press.

Osherow, N. (1981). Making sense of the nonsensical: An analysis of Jonestown. In E. Aronson (Ed.), *Readings about the social animal* (3rd ed.). San Francisco: W. H. Freeman.

Osofsky, G. (1966). *Harlem: The making of a ghetto*. Irvington. **670**

Page, B. I. (1983). *Who gets what from government*. Berkeley: University of California Press. **348**

Parenti, M. (in press). *Inventing reality*. New York: St. Martin's Press. **543**

Park, R. E. (1926). The urban community as a spatial pattern and moral order. In E. W. Burgess (Ed.), *The urban community*. Chicago: University of Chicago Press.

Park, R. E. (1950). The nature of race relations. In R. E. Park, *Race and culture* (pp. 81–116). Glencoe, IL: The Free Press. (Original work published 1939) **203**

Park, R. E., and Burgess, E. (Eds.). (1921). *An introduction to the science of sociology*. Chicago: University of Chicago Press. **129**

Park, R. E., Burgess, E., and McKenzie, R. D. (Eds.). (1925). *The city*. Chicago: University of Chicago Press. **265, 670**

Parker, D. P. (1983). *Fighting computer crime*. New York: Charles Scribner and Sons. **674**

Parkinson, C. N. (1957). *Parkinson's law*. Boston: Houghton Mifflin. **233**

Parnas, R. I. (1967). The police response to domestic disturbance. *Wisconsin Law Review*, *914*(Fall), 914–960. **489**

Parsons, H. M. (1982). More on the Hawthorne effect. *American Psychologist*, *37*(7, July), 856–857. **43**

Parsons, J. E. (Ed.). (1980). *The psychobiology of sex differences and sex roles*. Washington, DC: Hemisphere. **392**

Parsons, T. (1937). *The structure of social action*. New York: McGraw-Hill. **28, 664**

Parsons, T. (1951). *The social system*. Glencoe, IL: The Free Press. **28, 89, 664, 679**

Parsons, T. (1964). A revised approach to the theory of social stratification. In T. Parsons, *Essays in sociological theory* (pp. 386–439). New York: The Free Press. **318, 320, 330**

Parsons, T. (1966a). On the concept of political power. In R. Bendix and S. M. Lipset (Eds.), *Class, status, and power* (2nd ed.). New York: The Free Press.

Parsons, T. (1966b). *Societies: Evolutionary and comparative perspectives*. Englewood Cliffs, NJ: Prentice-Hall. **664**

Parsons, T. (1968). Social interaction. In D. L. Sills (Ed.), *The international encyclopedia of the social sciences* (Vol. 7, pp. 429–441). New York: The Macmillan Company/The Free Press.

Parsons, T. (1969). *Politics and social structure*. New York: The Free Press. **570**

Parsons, T. (1971). *The system of modern societies*. Englewood Cliffs, NJ: Prentice-Hall. **320, 664**

Parsons, T., and Bales, R. F. (1953). *Family, socialization, and interaction process*. Glencoe, IL: The Free Press. **417, 668**

Pascal, B. *Pensées*, Section XIV, No. 894. **620**

Pastner, C. (1974). Accommodations to Purdah: The female perspective. *Journal of Marriage and the Family*, *36*(May), 408–414. **469**

Patterson, M. L. (1983). *Nonverbal behavior*. New York: Springer-Verlag. **65**

Pavlov, I. P. (1960). *Conditioned reflexes*. New York: Dover. (Original work published 1927) **148**

Pear, R. (1982, December 19). How poor are the elderly? *New York Times*. **446**

Peattie, L., and Aldrete-Haas, J. A. (1981). 'Marginal' settlements in developing countries. *Annual Review of Sociology*, *7*, 157–175. **269**

Pechman, J. A. (1984). *Who paid the taxes?* Washington, DC: Brookings Institution. **325**

Pechman, J. A., and Okner, B. (1974). *Who bears the tax burden?* Washington, DC: Brookings Institution.

Pellegrin, R. J. (1953). The achievement of high status and leadership in the small group. *Social Forces*, *32*, 10–16. **102**

Perlmutter, H. V., and Montmollin, G. (1952). Group learning of nonsense syllables. *Journal of Abnormal and Social Psychology*, *47*, 762–769. **229**

Perlo, V. (1973). *The unstable economy*. New York: International Publishers.

Perls, F. S., Hefferline, R. F., and Goodman, P. (1965). *Gestalt therapy*. New York: Dell. **186**

Perrin, S., and Spencer, C. (1980). The Asch effect—A child of its time? *Bulletin of the British Psychology Society*, *32*, 405–406. **209**

Peter, L. J., and Hull, R. (1969). *The Peter Principle*. New York: William Morrow. **233**

Petersen, A. C. (1980). Biopsychosocial processes in the development of sex-related differences. In Parsons (1980), pp. 31–56. **392**

Peterson, R. E. (1976). California makes plans for lifelong learning. *ETS Findings*, *3*, 1–4. **527**

Peterson, W., and Gist, N. P. (1951). Rumor and public opinion. *American Journal of Sociology*, *57*, 159–167. **646**

Pettigrew, T. F. (1967). Social evaluation theory: Convergences and applications. In D. Levine (Ed.), *Nebraska Symposium on Motivation*. Lincoln, NE: University of Nebraska Press.

Pettigrew, T. F. (1968). Race relations: Social and psychological aspects. In D. L. Sills (Ed.), *The international encyclopedia of the social sciences* (Vol. 13, pp. 277–282). New York: The Macmillan Company. **356, 366, 379**

Pettigrew, T. F. (1971). *Racially separate or together?* New York: McGraw-Hill. **372**

Pettigrew, T. F. (1975). *Racial discrimination in the United States*. New York: Harper & Row. **372**

Pettigrew. T. F. (1976). Race and intergroup relations. In R. K. Merton and R. Nisbet (Eds.), *Contemporary social problems* (4th ed.). New York: Harcourt Brace Jovanovich. **371, 381**

Pfeffer, J. (1981). *Power in organizations*. Marshfield, MA: Pitman. **214**

Pfeiffer, E., Verwoedt, A., and Davis, G. (1972). Sexual behavior in middle life. *American Journal of Psychiatry*, *128*(10), 82. **433**

Piaget, J. (1965). *The moral judgement of the child*. Glencoe: IL: The Free Press.

Piaget, J., and Inhelder, B. (1969). *The psychology of the child*. New York: Basic Books. **150**

Piliavan, I., and Briar, S. (1964). Police encounters with juveniles. *American Journal of Sociology, 70,* 206–214. **293**

Piven, F. F., and Cloward, R. A. (1979). *Poor people's movements.* New York: Vintage. **657, 659**

Pleck, J. (1976). The male sex role: Definitions, problems, and sources of change. *Journal of Social Issues, 32,* 155–164.

Pleck, J. (1977). The work-family role system. *Social Problems, 24,* 417–427. **398, 483**

Polatnick, M. (1973). Why men don't rear children: A power analysis. *Berkeley Journal of Sociology, 18,* 45–86. Reprinted in J. W. Petras (Ed.). (1975). *Sex: Male; Gender:Masculine* (pp. 199–235). Port Washington, NY: Alfred Publishing Company. **411, 419, 427**

Pollock, L. A. (1984). *Forgotten children: Parent-child relations from 1500 to 1900.* Cambridge: Cambridge University Press. **435**

Polsby, N. W. (1968). Community: The study of community power. In D. L. Sills (Ed.), *The international encyclopedia of the social sciences* (Vol. 3, pp. 157–163). New York: The Macmillan Company/The Free Press. **259**

Pomerance, B. (1979). *The elephant man.* New York: Grove Press. **285**

Pomeroy, S. (1975). *Goddesses, whores, wives, and slaves.* New York: Schocken. **397**

Pope, L. (1942). *Millhands and preachers.* New Haven: Yale University Press. **622**

Population Reference Bureau. (1975). *World urbanization: 1800–2000.* Washington, DC: Population Reference Bureau. **267**

Population Reference Bureau. (1979). *World population data sheet: 1979.* Washington, DC: Population Reference Bureau.

Population Reference Bureau. (1980). *World's women data sheet.* Washington, DC: Population Reference Bureau. **479**

Population Reference Bureau. (1984). *World population data sheet: 1984.* Washington, DC: Population Reference Bureau. **115, 116, 118, 119, 120, 122, 127, 136, 143, 587, 671**

Porter, J. N. (Ed.). (1982). *Genocide and human rights: A global anthology.* Lanham, MD: University Press of America.

Powers, M. G. (Ed.). (1982). *Measures of socioeconomic status.* Boulder, CO: Westview Press. **318**

Pratt, J. W. (1935). The ideology of American expansion. In *Essays in honor of William E. Dodd* (p. 344). Chicago. **366**

President's Commission on Law Enforcement. (1967). *Final Report.* Washington, DC: U.S. Government Printing Office. **288**

Price, R. M., and Rosberg, C. G. (1980). *Apartheid regime: Political power and racial domination.* Berkeley, CA: University of California Institute of International Studies. **367**

Projector, D., and Weiss, G. (1966). *Survey of financial characteristics of consumers.* (Federal Reserve Technical Paper, p. 148). Washington, DC: U.S. Government Printing Office. **325**

Quadagno, J. S. (1976). Occupational sex-typing and internal labor market distributions: An assessment of medical specialties. *Social Problems, 23*(4), 442–453. **41**

Quinn, O. W. (1954). The transmission of racial attitudes among white Southerners. *Social Forces, 33*(1), 41–47. **150**

Quinney, R. (1970). *The social reality of crime.* Boston: Little, Brown.

Quinney, R. (1972). The ideology of law: Notes for a radical alternative to legal oppression. *Issues in Criminology, 7*(1), 1–35. **281**

Quinney, R. (1979). Capitalist society in the world system: Introduction. In R. Quinney (Ed.), *Capitalist society* (pp. 353–357). Homewood, IL: Dorsey Press.

Rabin, A. I. (1965). *Growing up in the kibbutz.* New York: Springer. **463**

Radcliffe-Brown, A. R. (1948). *The Andaman Islanders.* Glencoe, IL: The Free Press. **435**

Radecki, C., and Walstedt, J. J. (1980). Sex as a status position in work settings: Female and male reports of dominance behavior. *Journal of Applied Social Psychology, 10*(1), 71–85. **190**

Raiffa, H. (1970). *Decision analysis.* Reading, MA: Addison-Wesley. **644**

Raines, J. C. Berson, L. E., and Gracie, D. (1982). *Community and capital in conflict.* Philadelphia: Temple University Press. **260**

Rands, M., and Levinger, G. (1979). Implicit theories of relationship: An intergenerational study. *Journal of Personality and Social Psychology, 37,* 645–661. **403**

Ransford, H. E., and Miller, J. (1983). Race, sex and feminist outlooks. *American Sociological Review, 48*(February), 46–59.

Raper, A. (1933). *The tragedy of lynching.* Chapel Hill: University of North Carolina Press. **637**

Rappoport, D. C., and Alexander, Y. (Eds.). (1982). *The morality of terrorism: Religious and secular justifications.* New York: Pergamon Press. **284**

Raskin, A. H. (1982, September 5). Frustrated and wary, labor marks its day. *The New York Times Business Section,* p. 1. **328**

Rasmussen, W. D. (1982). The mechanization of agriculture. In *Scientific American. The mechanization of work* (pp. 15–30). San Francisco: W. H. Freeman. **554, 673**

Raven, B. H. (1968). Group performance. In D. L. Sills (Ed.), *The international encyclopedia of the social sciences* (Vol. 6). New York: The Macmillan Company/The Free Press.

Raven, B. H. (1974). The comparative analysis of power and power preference. In J. Tedeschi (Ed.), *Perspectives on social power.* Chicago: Aldine.

Ravitch, D. (1983). *The troubled crusade: American education, 1945–1980.* New York: Basic Books. **373, 502, 503, 508, 515, 520**

Reckless, W. C. (1973). *The crime problem.* Englewood Cliffs, NJ: Prentice-Hall. **288**

Redfield, R. (1947). The folk society. *American Journal of Sociology, 52,* 293–308. **262**

Reed, J. (1960). *Ten days that shook the world.* New York: Random House.

Reeder, G. D., and Spores, J. M. (1983). The attribution of morality. *Journal of Personality and Social Psychology, 44*(4), 736–745. **182**

Reich, M. (1981). *Racial inequality: A political-economic analysis.* Princeton, NJ: Princeton University Press. **378**

Reich, M., Gordon, D. M., and Edwards, R. C. (1973). A theory of labor market segmentation. *American Economic Review, LXIII*(2, May). **548**

Reinhold, R. (1982, September 26). Houston's great thirst is sucking city down into the ground. *The New York Times,* p. 28. **265**

Reiss, A. J. (1971). *The police and the public.* New Haven, CT: Yale University Press. **307**

Reiss, A. J., and Biderman, A. D. (1980). *Data sources on white-collar law-breaking.* Washington, DC: Bureau of Social Research. **288**

Reiss, I. L. (1980). *Family systems in America* (3rd ed.). New York: Holt, Rinehart & Winston.

Reynolds, P. D. (1971). Comment on 'The distribution of participation in group discussions' as related to group size. *American Sociological Review, 36,* 704–706. **216**

Reynolds, P. D. (1979). *Ethical dilemmas and social science research.* San Francisco: Jossey-Bass. **58**

Reynolds, P. D. (1982). *Ethics and social science research.* Englewood Cliffs, NJ: Prentice-Hall. **58**

Reynolds, V. (1980). *The biology of human action.* San Francisco: W. H. Freeman. **146**

Rich, A. (1976). *Of woman born: Motherhood as experience and institution.* New York: Norton. **410, 416**

Richardson, K., and Spears, D. (Eds.). (1972). *Race and intelligence.* Baltimore: Penguin Books. **353**

Richardson, L. W. (1977). *The dynamics of sex and gender.* Boston: Houghton Mifflin. **401**

Richardson, L. W. (1981). *The dynamics of sex and gender* (2nd ed.). Boston: Houghton Mifflin. **393**

Ridgeway, C. L. (1981). Nonconformity, competence, and influence in groups. *American Sociological Review, 46*(June), 333–347. **217**

Riding, A. (1983, May 15). Problems of Mexico City: Warning to the third world. *New York Times,* p. 1. **113**

Riesman, D. (1961). *The lonely crowd.* New Haven, CT: Yale University Press. **330, 579**

Riley, J. W., Jr. (1983). Dying and the meanings of death: Sociological inquiries. *Annual Review of Sociology, 9,* 191–216. **441**

Riley, M. W. (1974). The perspective of age stratification. *School Review, 82*(1). **457**

Riley, M. W. (1976). Age strata in social systems. In J. E. Birren (Ed.), *Handbook of aging and the social sciences.* New York: Van Nostrand Reinhold. **450**

Riley, M. W. (1983). The family in an aging society: A matrix of latent relationships. *Journal of Family Issues,* (September). **477**

Riley, M. W., et al. (1969). Socialization for the middle and later years. In D. A. Goslin (Ed.), *Handbook of socialization theory and research* (pp. 951–982). Chicago: Rand McNally. **172**

Riley, M. W., et al. (1970). *Aging and society* (Vol. 2). New York: Russell Sage Foundation. **433, 435**

Riley, M. W., and Foner, A. (1968). *Aging and society* (Vol. 1). New York: Russell Sage Foundation. **433, 435, 437, 452**

Riley, M. W., and Foner, A. (1972). *Aging and Society* (Vol. 3). New York: Russell Sage Foundation. **172, 450**

Riley, M. W., and Stoll, C. S. Content analysis. (1968). In D. L. Sills (Ed.), *The international encyclopedia of the social sciences* (Vol. 3, pp. 371–377). New York: Macmillan. **47, 442**

Riley, M. W., and Waring, J. (1976). Age and aging. In R. K. Merton and R. Nisbet (Eds.), *Contemporary social problems* (4th ed.). New York: Harcourt Brace Jovanovich. **420, 434, 456**

Rindfuss, R., Bumpass, L., and St. John, C. (1980). Education and fertility: Implications for the roles women occupy. *American Sociological Review, 45,* 431–447. **123**

Rist, K. (1979). Incest: Theoretical and clinical views. *American Journal of Orthopsychiatry, 49*(4, October), 680–691.

Roberts, R. E., and Lee, E. S. (1974). Minority group status and fertility revisited. *American Journal of Sociology, 80,* 503–523.

Robertson, D. (1982, February 15). The overprotected professors. *Newsweek,* p. 17. **515**

Robinson, J. C. (1984). Racial inequality and the problem of occupation-related injury and illness. *Milbank Memorial Fund Quarterly, 62*(4), 567–590. **365**

Robinson, J. G. (1980). Estimating the approximate size of the illegal alien population in the United States by the comparative trend analysis of age-specific death rates. *Demography, 17,* 159–176. **124**

Robinson, P. (1969). Poor black women. In B. Roszak and T. Roszak (Eds.), *Masculine/feminine* (pp. 208–213). New York: Harper & Row.

Robinson, R. V. (1984). Reproducing class relations in industrial capitalism. *American Sociological Review, 49*(June), 182–196. **166**

Robinson, W. P. (1972). *Language and social behavior.* Baltimore, MD: Penguin Books. **71**

Rodin, J., and Langer, E. (1977). Long-term effects of a control-relevant intervention with the institutionalized aged. *Journal of Personality and Social Psychology, 35,* 897–902. **190**

Roethlisberger, F. J., and Dickson, W. (1939). *Management and the worker.* Cambridge, MA: Harvard University Press. **43, 208**

Rogers, E. M. (1983). *Diffusion of innovations* (3rd ed.). New York: The Free Press. **672, 674**

Rogers, W. (1931, June 28). Syndicated newspaper column. In *Bartlett's quotations* (13th ed., p. 904). (1955). Boston: Little, Brown. **585**

Rokeach, M. (1968). The nature of attitudes. In D. L. Sills (Ed.), *The international encyclopedia of the social sciences* (Vol. 1). New York: The MacMillan Company/The Free Press.

Roos, P. A. (1985). *Gender and work: A comparative analysis of industrial societies.* Albany, NY: State University of New York Press.

Rose, P. I. (Ed.). (1979). *Socialization and the life cycle.* New York: St. Martin's Press.

Rose, P. I. (1981). *They and we: Racial and ethnic relations in the United States.* New York: Random House. **365**

Rosenberg, M. (1965). *Society and the adolescent self-image.* Princeton, NJ: Princeton University Press. **163**

Rosenberg, M. (1979). *Conceiving the self.* New York: Basic Books. **157, 160, 161, 162, 203**

Rosenberg, M. (1981). The self-concept: Social product and social force. In M. Rosenberg and R. H. Turner (Eds.), *Social psychology: Sociological perspectives* (pp. 593–624). New York: Basic Books. **157**

Rosenberg, M., and Kaplan, H. B. (Eds.). (1982). *Social psychology of the self-concept.* Arlington Heights, IL: Harlan Davidson. **157**

Rosenberg, M., and Simmons, R. B. (1971). *Black and white self-esteem: The urban school child.* Washington, DC: The American Sociological Association. **370**

Rosenhan, D. L. (1973, January 19). On being sane in insane places. *Science, 179* (No. 4070), pp. 1–9. **304, 305**

Rosenthal, K. M. and Keshet, H. F. (1978). Childcare responsibilities of part-time and single fathers. *Alternative Lifestyles, 1*(4, November), 465–491. **171**

Rosenthal, R. (1967). Covert communication in the psychological experiment. *Psychological Bulletin, 67,* 356–367. **57**

Rosenthal, R. (1982). *Experimenter effects in behavioral research.* New York: Irvington. **58**

Rosenthal, R., and Jacobson, L. (1968). *Pygmalion in the classroom: Teacher expectation and pupils' intellectual development.* New York: Holt, Rinehart & Winston. **511, 522**

Rosnow, R. L., and Fine, G. A. (1976). *Rumor and gossip.* New York: Elsevier. **646**

Rosow, I. (1974). *Socialization to old age.* University of California Press.

Ross, H. L. (1984). Social control through deterrence: Drinking-and-driving laws. *Annual Review of Sociology, 10,* 21–35. **295**

Rossi, A. S. (1969). Sex equality: The beginning of ideology. In B. Roszak and T. Roszak (Eds.), *Masculine/feminine* (pp. 173–186). New York: Harper & Row. **422**

Rossi, A. S. (1982). *Feminists in politics.* New York: Academic Press.

Rossi, A. S. (1984). Gender and parenthood. *American sociological review, 49*(February), 1–19. **393, 417, 426**

Rostow, W. W. (1960). *The stages of economic growth: A non-communist manifesto.* Cambridge: Cambridge University Press. **679**

Roszak, B., and Roszak, T. (Eds.). (1969). *Masculine/feminine.* New York: Harper & Row. **423**

Rothbart, M. K. (1971). Birth order and mother-child interaction in an achievement situation. *Journal of Personality and Social Psychology, 17,* 113–120. **167**

Rousseau, J.-J. (1950). New York: E. P. Dutton. (Original work published 1762) **591**

Rowbotham, S. (1973). *Woman's consciousness, Man's world.* New York: Penguin Books. **483**

Rubin, L. B. (1976). *Worlds of pain.* New York: Basic Books. **45, 484**

Rubin, N. (1982, January 10). Learning how children learn from the first moments of life. *The New York Times* (Education Supplement). **151**

Rubin, R., and Byerly, G. (1983). *Incest: The last taboo* (An annotated bibliography). New York: Garland. **470**

Rubin, Z. (1973). *Liking and loving.* New York: Holt, Rinehart & Winston. **403**

Russell, J. C. (1972). *Medieval regions and the cities.* Bloomington, IN: Indiana University Press. **263**

Ryder, N. B. (1965). The cohort as a concept in the study of social change. *American Sociological Review, 30,* 843–861. **127, 439, 450, 671**

Ryder, N. B., and Westoff, C. F. (1971). *Reproduction in the United States, 1965.* Princeton, NJ: Princeton University Press. **470**

Rytina, J. H., Form, W. H., and Pease, J. (1970). Income and stratification ideology: Beliefs about the American opportunity structure. *American Journal of Sociology, 75*(January), 703–716. **326**

Rytina, N. F. (1981). Occupational segregation and earnings differences by sex. *Monthly Labor Review, 104*(January), 49–53. **406**

Sabini, J., and Silver, M. (1982). *Moralities of everyday life.* New York: Oxford University Press. **240, 241**

Sacks, K. (1974). Engels revisited: Women, the organization of production, and private property. In M. Z. Rosaldo and L. Lamphere (Eds.), *Woman, culture, and society* (pp. 207–222). Stanford, CA: Stanford University Press. **404, 420, 426**

Safilios-Rothschild, C. (1974). *Women and social policy.* Englewood Cliffs, NJ: Prentice-Hall.

Sagatun, I. J., and Knudsen, J. H. (1982). Attributional self presentation for actors and observers in success and failure situations. *Scandinavian Journal of Psychology, 23,* 243–252. Cited in Annual Review of Sociology 9 (1983), p. 441. **193**

Sahlins, M. D. (1976). *The use and abuse of biology: An anthropological critique of sociobiology.* Ann Arbor, MI: University of Michigan Press. **67, 468**

Sahlins, M. D., and Service, E. R. (Eds.). (1960). *Evolution and culture.* Ann Arbor, MI: University of Michigan Press.

St. Peter, S. (1979). Jack went up the hill . . . but where was Jill?

*Psychology of Women Quarterly, 4,* 256–260. **47, 167, 415**

Sampson, A. (1983). *The changing anatomy of Britain.* New York: Random House. **500**

Sampson, E. A., and Hancock, F. T. (1967). An examination of the relationship between ordinal position, personality, and conformity. *Journal of Personality and Social Psychology, 5,* 398–407. **167**

Sanday, P. R. (1981). *Female power and male dominance.* Cambridge: Cambridge University Press. **399**

Satir, V. (1972). *Peoplemaking.* Palo Alto, CA: Science and Behavior Books.

Sauvigny, G. de B. de. (1966). *The Bourdon restoration.* Philadelphia: University of Pennsylvania Press. **20**

Sawyer, J. (1970, February 25). The case against grades. *Emphasis, Daily Northwestern Magazine, 44.* **522**

Schachter, S. (1959). *The psychology of affiliation.* Stanford, CA: Stanford University Press. **167**

Schachter, S., and Singer, J. L. (1962). Cognitive, social, and physiological determinants of emotional state. *Psychological Review, 65,* 121–128.

Schafer, S. (1974). *The political criminal.* New York: The Free Press. **285**

Schaff, A. (1970). *Marxism and the human individual.* New York: McGraw-Hill. **82, 83, 666**

Schaffer, K. F. (1981). *Sex roles and human behavior.* Cambridge, MA: Winthrop. **167, 415, 419, 426**

Scheff, T. J. (1968). Negotiating reality: Notes on power in the assessment of responsibility. *Social Problems, 16*(Summer), 3–17.

Scheff, T. J. (1975). *Labeling madness.* Englewood Cliffs, NJ: Prentice-Hall. **304**

Scheff, T. J. (1984). *Becoming mentally ill: A sociological theory* (2nd ed.). Chicago: Aldine. **304**

Scheider, J., and Hacker S. (1973). Sex role imagery in the use of the generic 'man.' in introductory texts: A case in the sociology of sociology. *American Sociologist, 8,* 12–18. **394**

Schein, E. J. (1957). Reaction patterns to severe chronic stress in American army prisoners of war of the Chinese. *Journal of Social Issues, 13,* 21–30. **225**

Schlesinger, A. (1983, September 25). Familiar barbarities [Review of Howe, 1983]. *New York Times Book Review,* p. 1. **578**

Schnore, L. F. (1973). Community: Theory and research on structure and change. In N. J. Smelser (Ed.), *Sociology: An introduction* (2nd ed.). New York: Wiley. **245**

Schroeder, R. C. (1974). Policies on population around the world. *Population Bulletin, 29.* Washington, DC: Population Reference Bureau. **116**

Schuessler, K. F., and Cressey, D. R. (1950). Personality characteristics of criminals. *American Journal of Sociology, 55,* 476–484. **297**

Schulz, R. (1976). Control, predictability, and the institutionalized aged. *Journal of Personality and Social Psychology, 33,* 563–573. **190, 447**

Schulz, R., and Hanusa, B. H. (1980). Experimental social gerontology: A social psychological perspective. *Journal of Social Issues, 36*(2), 30–46. **190**

Schuman, H., and Converse, J. M. (1971). The effects of black and white interviewers on black responses in 1968. *Public Opinion Quarterly, 35,* 44–68. **38**

Schuman, H., and Presser, S. (1981). *Questions and answers in attitude surveys.* New York: Academic Press. **37, 41**

Schur, E. M. (1965). *Crimes without victims.* Englewood Cliffs, NJ: Prentice-Hall. **292, 298**

Schur, E. M. (1971). *Labeling deviant behavior.* New York: Harper & Row. **277**

Schutz, A. (1962). *Collected papers, I: The problem of social reality.* The Hague: Martinus Nijhoff.

Schutz, A. (1970). In H. R. Wagner (Ed.), *Alfred Schutz on phenomenology and social relations: Selected writings.* Chicago: University of Chicago Press.

Schwartz, B. (1973). Waiting, exchange, and power: The distribution of time in social systems. *American Journal of Sociology, 79,* 841–870.

Schwartz, R. D., and Skolnick, J. H. (1962). Two studies of legal stigma. *Social Problems, 10*(2). **304**

*Scientific American.* (1982). The mechanization of work. San Francisco: W. H. Freeman.

Seeman, M. (1959). On the meaning of alienation. *American Sociological Review, 24,* 783–789. **552**

Seeman, M. (1981). Intergroup relations. In M. Rosenberg and R. H. Turner (Eds.), *Social psychology: Sociological perspectives* (pp. 378–410). New York: Basic Books. **356**

Seligman, M. E. P. (1975). *Helplessness.* San Francisco: W. H. Freeman. **189**

Selsam, H., and Martel, H. (1963). *Reader in Marxist philosophy.* New York: International Publishers.

Selznick, G. J., and Steinberg, S. (1969). *The tenacity of prejudice.* New York: Harper & Row. **380**

Sennett, R. (1981). *Authority.* New York: Vintage. **188**

Sennett, R., and Cobb, J. (1973). *The hidden injuries of class.* New York: Vintage.

Serbin, L., and O'Leary, K. (1975, December). How nursery schools teach girls to shut up. *Psychology Today, 9,* pp. 56–58. **167, 415**

Service, E. (1962). *Primitive social organization: An evolutionary perspective.* New York: Random House. **483**

Service, E. (1966). *The hunters.* Englewood Cliffs, NJ: Prentice-Hall. **481**

Service, E. (1975). *Origins of the state and civilization.* New York: Norton. **570**

Sewell, W. H., Hauser, R. M., and Wolf, W. C. (1980). Sex, schooling, and occupational status. *American Journal of Sociology, 8,* 551–583. **406**

Seymour, W. N. (1973). Social and ethical considerations in assessing white-collar crime. *American Criminal Law Review, 11,* 821–834. **294**

Shafer, W. E., et al. (1967). *Delinquency in schools* (The President's Commission on Law Enforcement and Administration of Justice, Task Force Report: Delinquency and Youth Crime). Washington, DC: U.S. Government Printing Office. **167, 522**

Shaw, G. B. (1904). *Plays pleasant and unpleasant* (Vol. II, Preface). Chicago, IL: H. S. Stone. (Original work published 1898) **69**

Shaw, M. E. (1954). Some effects of problem complexity upon problem solution efficiency in various communication nets. *Journal of Experimental Psychology, 48,* 211–217. **102, 234**

Sheehy, G. (1974). *Passages: The predictable crises of adult life.* New York: E. P. Dutton. **170, 171, 172, 431**

Sheldon, W. R. (1949). *Varieties of delinquent behavior.* New York: Harper. **297**

Sherif, M. (1935). A study of some social factors in perception. *Archives of Psychology, 27* (No. 187).

Sherif, M. (1936). Formation of social norms: The experimental paradigm. In M. Sherif, *The psychology of social norms.* New York: Harper & Row. Reprinted in H. Proshansky and B. Seidenberg (Eds.). (1966). *Basic studies in social psychology.* New York: Holt, Rinehart & Winston. **210**

Sherif, M., and Sherif, C. W. (1968). Group formation. In D. L. Sills (Ed.), *The international encyclopedia of the social sciences* (Vol. 6). New York: The MacMillan Company/The Free Press.

Sherman, L. W., and Berk, R. A. (1984). The specific deterrent effects of arrest for domestic assault. *American Sociological Review, 49*(June), 261–272. **489**

Shibutani, T. (1966). *Improvised news: A sociological study of rumor.* Indianapolis, IN: Bobbs Merrill. **647**

Shibutani, T. (1968). Rumor. In D. L. Sills (Ed.), *The international encyclopedia of the social sciences* (Vol. 13, pp. 576–580). New York: The Macmillan Company/The Free Press. **647**

Shiels, D. (1975). Toward a unified theory of ancestor worship. *Social Forces, 54*(December), appendix, part B. **468, 618**

Shils, E. A., and Janowitz, M. (1948). Cohesion and disintegration in the Wehrmacht in World War II. *Public Opinion Quarterly, 12*(Summer), 280–315. **235**

Shipler, D. K. (1983, October 16). Russia: A people without heroes. *New York Times Magazine,* p. 29. **575, 593, 620**

Shorter, E., and Tilly, C. (1974). *Strikes in France: 1830–1968.* London: Cambridge University Press. **651, 657, 658**

Shrauger, J. S., and Schoeneman, T. J. (1979). Symbolic interactionist view of self-concept: Through the looking glass darkly. *Psychological Bulletin, 86,* 549–573. **160**

Silberman, C. (1971). *Crisis in the classroom.* New York: Random House. **507, 509**

Silk, L. (1983, October 9). Andropov's economic dilemma. *New York Times Magazine.* **557, 593**

Silverman, M. (1976). Toward a theory of criminal deterrence. *American Sociological Review, 41,* 442–461. **295**

Silverstein, M. (1972). The history of a short, unsuccessful academic career. *Insurgent Sociologist*(Fall), 4–19. **416**

Simmel, G. (1950). *The sociology of Georg Simmel* (K. H. Wolff Ed. and Trans.). New York: The Free Press. (Original work published between 1902 and 1917) **26, 104, 211, 220, 224, 227, 230, 232, 263, 617, 666**

Simmel, G. (1965). The poor (C. Jacobson, Trans.). *Social Problems, 13,* 118–140. (Original work published 1908) **190, 191, 249**

Simpson, G. E., and Yinger, J. M. (1972). *Racial and cultural minorities: An analysis of prejudice and discrimination* (4th ed.). New York: Harper & Row.

Simon, W., Puntil, J. E., and Peluso, E. (1978). Continuities in delinquency research. In J. F. Short (Ed.), *Crime, delinquency, and society.* Chicago: University of Chicago Press.

Singer, C., Holmyard, E. J., and Hall, A. R. (1954). *A history of technology* (4 volumes). New York: Oxford University Press.

Singer, E. (1981). Reference groups and social evaluations. In M. Rosenberg and R. H. Turner (Eds.), *Social psychology: Sociological perspectives* (pp. 66–93). New York: Basic Books. **163**

Skinner, B. F. (1938). *The behavior of organisms.* New York: Appleton-Century-Crofts. **148**

Skinner, B. F. (1948). *Walden Two.* New York: Macmillan. **248**

Skinner, B. F. (1971). *Beyond freedom and dignity.* New York: Knopf.

Skinner, B. F. (1981). Selection by consequences. *Science, 213,* pp. 501–504. **148**

Skocpol, T. (1979). *States and social revolutions.* New York: Cambridge University Press. **595, 596, 648, 657**

Skolnick, A. (1975). The family revisited. *Journal of Interdisciplinary History, 5*(4), 715. **483**

Skolnick, J. H. (1975). *Justice without trial* (2nd ed.). New York: Wiley. **307**

Slambrouck, P. V. (1983, May 27). South Africa: The limits of dissent. *Christian Science Monitor,* p. 1. **386**

Slater, P. E. (1958). Contrasting correlates of group size. *Sociometry, 21,* 129–139. **231, 232**

Slater, P. E. (1970). *The pursuit of loneliness.* Boston: Beacon. (1971 refers to the paperback edition.) **75, 238**

Slomczynski, K. M., Miller, J., and Kohn, M. L. (1981). Stratification, work, and values. *American Sociological Review, 46,* 720–744. **166**

Smelser, N. J. (1959). *Social change in the Industrial Revolution.* Chicago: University of Chicago Press. **441**

Smelser, N. J. (1962). *Theory of collective behavior.* New York: The Free Press. **652**

Smelser, N. J. (1973). Toward a theory of modernization. In A. Etzioni and E. Etzioni-Halevy (Eds.), *Social change: Sources, patterns, and consequences.* New York: Basic Books. **678**

Smelser, N. J. (1976). *Comparative methods in the social sciences.* Englewood Cliffs, NJ: Prentice-Hall.

Smelser, N. J. (1981). *Sociology.* Englewood Cliffs, NJ: Prentice-Hall. **472**

Smith, A. (1982). *The wealth of nations.* New York: Penguin. **535**

Smith, D. A., and Visher, C. A. (1980). Sex and involvement in deviance/crime. *American Sociological Review, 45*(August), 691–701. **287**

Smith, H. (1976). *The Russians.* New York: Quadrangle Books.

Smith, J. (1981). *Social issues and the social order: The contradictions of capitalism.* Cambridge, MA: Winthrop. **168, 419, 454, 521, 540, 542, 553, 560, 561, 572**

Snow, D. A., Zurcher, L. A., and Eckland-Olson, S. (1980). Social networks and social movements. *American Sociological Review, 45,* 787–801. **655**

Sommer, R. (1969). *Personal space: The behavioral analysis of design.* Englewood Cliffs, NJ: Prentice-Hall. **185, 191, 225**

Sorensen, A., et al. (1974). *Indexes of racial residential segregation for 109 cities in the United States, 1940 to 1970* (Studies in Racial Desegregation, No. 1). Madison, WI: University of Wisconsin Institute for Research on Poverty. **372**

Sorokin, P. A. (1937–1941). *Social and cultural dynamics* (Vol. 4). New York: American Book Company. **677**

Sorokin, A., and Merton, R. K. (1937). Social time: A methodological and functional analysis. *American Journal of Sociology, 42,* 615–629. **97**

Speizer, J. J. (1981). Role models, mentors, and sponsors: The elusive concepts. *Signs: Journal of Women in Culture and Society, 6,* 692–712. **416**

Spencer, H. (1891). *The study of sociology.* New York: Appleton. **676**

Spencer, H. (1896). *The principles of sociology.* New York: Appleton. **676**

Spengler, O. (1926). *The decline of the West.* New York: Knopf. **676**

Spenner, K. I., Otto, L. B., and Call, V. R. A. (1982). *Career lines and careers.* Lexington, MA: Lexington Books. **53, 408**

Spinrad, W. (1965). Power in local communities. *Social Problems, V*(12, Winter), 335–356. **259**

Spiro, M. E. (1956). *Kibbutz: Venture in utopia.* Cambridge, MA: Harvard University Press. **270**

Spring, J. (1976). *The sorting machine.* New York: McKay. **520**

Stacey, J. (1975). When patriarchy kowtows: The significance of the Chinese family revolution for feminist theory. *Feminist Studies, 2,* 64–112.

Stacey, J. (1983). *Patriarchy and socialist revolution in China.* Berkeley: University of California Press. **408**

Stampp, K. (1956). *The peculiar institution.* New York: Knopf. **622**

Standard and Poor. (1978). *Standard and Poor's industrial survey.* New York: Standard and Poor Corporation. **542**

Standard and Poor. (1979). *Standard and Poor's industrial survey.* New York: Standard and Poor Corporation. **542**

Staples, R. (1976). *Introduction to black sociology.* New York: McGraw-Hill.

Staples, R. (1981). *The world of black singles.* Westport, CT: Greenwood Press. **171**

Stein, D. D., Hardyck, J. A., and Smith, M. B. (1965). Race and belief: An open and shut case. *Journal of Personality and Social Psychology, 1*(4), 281–289. **208**

Stein, D. (1978). Women to burn. *Signs, 4,* 253–268. **279**

Stein, P. J. (Ed.). (1981). *Single life.* New York: St. Martin's. **171**

Steinbeck, J. (1969). *The grapes of wrath.* New York: Bantam Books. (Original work published 1939) **124, 323**

Steinhart, P. (1981, October 25). The new green revolution. *The New York Times Magazine.* **135**

Steinzor, B. (1950). The spatial factor in face-to-face discussion groups. *Journal of Abnormal and Social Psychology, 45.* Reprinted in Hare et al., (1961), pp. 348–353. **225**

Stephan, G. E., and McMullin, D. R. (1982). Tolerance of sexual nonconformity: City size as a situational and early learning determinant. *American Sociological Review, 47*(June), 411–415. **249**

Stephens, W. N. (1963). *The family in cross-cultural perspective.* New York: Holt, Rinehart & Winston. **485, 486**

Sternglanz, S., and Serbin, L. (1974). Sex role stereotyping in children's television programs. *Developmental Psychology, 10,* 710–715. **47**

Stevens, G. (1985). Nativity, intermarriage, and mother-tongue shift. *American Sociological Review, 50*(1), 74–83. **359**

Steward, J. H. (1955). *Theory of culture change: The methodology of multilinear evolution.* Urbana, IL: University of Illinois Press. **678**

Steward, J. H. (1956). Cultural evolution. *Scientific American, 194,* 70–80.

Stimpson, C. (1971). 'Thy neighbor's wife, thy neighbor's servants': Women's liberation and black civil rights. In V. Gornick and B. Moran (Eds.), *Women in sexist society* (pp. 622–657). New York: New American Library. **427**

Stinchcombe, A. (1975). Merton's theory of social structure. In L. A. Coser (Ed.), *The idea of social structure.* New York: Harcourt Brace Jovanovich.

Stojanovic, S. (1981). *In search of democracy in socialism.* Buffalo, NY: Prometheus Books. **563, 589**

Stolnitz, G. J. (1964). The demographic transition. In R. Freedman (Ed.), *Population: The vital revolution.* New York: Anchor.

Stone, K. (1974). The origins of job structures in the steel industry. In R. C. Edwards, M. Reich, and D. M. Gordon (Eds.), *Labor market segmentation* (pp. 27–84). Lexington, MA: D.C. Heath Company. **339, 340, 548**

Stoner, J. A. F. (1961). A comparison of individuals and group decisions involving risk. Unpublished master's thesis, Massachusetts Institute of Technology, Cambridge, MA. **230**

Stouffer, S. A., et al. (1949). *The American Soldier.* Princeton, NJ: Princeton University Press. **236**

Straus, M. A., Gelles, R. J., and Steinmetz, S. K. (1980). *Behind closed doors.* New York: Anchor. **220, 488**

Straus, R. (1976). Alcoholism and problem drinking. In R. K. Merton and R. Nisbet (Eds.), *Contemporary social problems* (4th ed.). New York: Harcourt Brace Jovanovich.

Strauss, A. L. (1959). *Mirrors and masks.* New York: The Free Press.

Strodtbeck, F. L., and Hook, L. H. (1961). The social dimensions of a twelve-man jury table. *Sociometry, 24*(December), 397–415. **225**

Strodtbeck, F. L., James, R. M., and Hawkins, C. (1957). Social status in jury deliberations. *American Sociological Review, 22,* 713–719. **102, 217**

Strong, D. S. (1941). *Organized anti-Semitism in the United States.* American Council on Public Affairs. **380**

Stryker, S. (1981). Symbolic interactionism: Themes and variations. In M. Rosenberg and R. H. Turner (Eds.), *Social psychology: Sociological perspectives* (pp. 3–29). New York: Basic Books. **28, 161**

Sudnow, D. (1967). *Passing on: The social organization of dying.* Englewood Cliffs, NJ: Prentice-Hall. **440**

Suedfeld, P. (1969). Sensory deprivation stress. *Journal of Personality and Social Psychology, 11,* 70–74. **167**

Sullivan, E. V. (1977). A study of Kohlberg's structural theory of moral development: A critique of liberal social science ideology. *Human Development, 20,* 352–376.

Summers, G. F., and Hammonds, A. D. (1966). Effects of racial characteristics of investigator on self-enumerated responses to a negro prejudice scale. *Social Forces, 44,* 515–518. **38**

Sumner, W. G. (1883). *What social classes owe to each other.* New York: Harper. **26, 325**

Sumner, W. G. (1906). *Folkways.* Boston: Ginn & Company. **74, 77, 79, 212**

Sutherland, E. H. (1949). *White collar crime.* New York: Dryden. **288**

Sutherland, E. H. (1983). *White collar crime: The uncut version.* New Haven, CT: Yale University Press. **288**

Sutherland, E. H., and Cressey, D. R. (1978). *Criminology* (10th ed.). Philadelphia: Lippincott. **299**

Suttles, G. D. (1972). *The social construction of communities.* Chicago: University of Chicago Press. **253**

Sutton, J. R. (1983). Social structures, institutions, and the legal status of children. *American Journal of Sociology, 88*(5), 915–947. **287**

Suzuki, D. T., Griffiths, A. J. F., and Lewontin, R. C. (1981). *An introduction to genetic analysis* (2nd ed.). San Francisco: W. H. Freeman. **146**

Swanson, G. E. (1960). *The birth of the gods: The origin of primitive beliefs.* Ann Arbor: University of Michigan Press.

Sweezy, P. M. (1942). *The theory of capitalist development: Principles of Marxian political economy.* New York: Modern Reader Paperbacks. **555**

Sykes, G. (1958). *The society of captives: A study of a maximum security prison.* Princeton, NJ: Princeton University Press. **69, 98, 296**

Symonds, R., and Carder, M. (1973). *The United Nations and the population question.* New York: McGraw-Hill. **137**

Szymanski, A. (1977). Capital accumulation on a world scale and the necessity of imperialism. *The Insurgent Sociologist, 7*(2, Spring), 35–53.

Szymanski, A. (1978). *The capitalist state and the politics of class.* Cambridge, MA: Winthrop.

Taeuber, K. E. (1964). Negro residential segregation: Trends and measurement. *Social Problems, 12*(1), 42–50.

Taeuber, K. E. (1965). Residential segregation. *Scientific American, 213*(2), 12–19.

Talmon, Y. (1969). Pursuit of the millennium: The relation between religious and social change. In N. Birnbaum and G. Lenzer (Eds.), *Sociology and religion: A book of readings.* Englewood Cliffs, NJ: Prentice-Hall.

Tannenbaum, A. S. (1968). Leadership: Sociological aspects. In D. L. Sills (Ed.), *The international encyclopedia of the social sciences* (Vol. 9). New York: The MacMillan Company/The Free Press. **575**

Tannenbaum, F. (1947). *Slave and citizen: The negro in America.* New York: Knopf. **362**

Tavris, C., and Wade, C. (1984). *The longest war: Sex differences in perspective* (2nd ed.). New York: Harcourt Brace Jovanovich. **405**

Tawney, R. H. (1947). *Religion and the rise of capitalism.* New York: Mentor.

Taylor, F. W. (1911). *The principles of scientific management.* New York: Harper & Row. **540**

Tedeschi, J. T., and Riess, M. (1981). Identities, the phenomenal self, and laboratory research. In J. Tedeschi (Ed.), *Impression management theory and social psychological research* (pp. 3–22). New York: Academic Press. **193**

Terkel, S. (1974). *Working.* New York: Pantheon. **332**

Tetlock, P. E. (1981). The influence of self-presentation goals on attributional reports. *Social Psychology Quarterly, 44,* 300–311. **182**

Thomas, E. J., and Fink, C. F. (1963). Effects of group size. *Psychological Bulletin, 60,* 371–384.

Thomas, J., and Levin, H. M. (1983). *Public dollars for private schools: The case of tuition tax credits.* Philadelphia, PA: Temple University Press. **527**

Thomas, L. (1974). *Lives of a cell: Notes of a biology watcher.* New York: Viking Press. **129**

Thomas, R. K. (1966–1967). Powerless politics. *New University Thought, 4*(Winter). **371**

Thomas, W. I. (1931). *The unadjusted girl.* Boston: Little, Brown. **67**

Thomas, W. I., and Thomas, D. S. (1928). *The child in America.* New York: Knopf. **180**

Thompson, S. K. (1975). Gender labels and early sex-role development. *Child Development, 46,* 339–347. **157**

Thompson, S. K., and Bentler, P. M. (1971). The priority of cues in sex discrimination by children and adults. *Developmental Psychology, 5,* 181–185. **157**

Thompson, W. (1942). *Population problems* (3rd ed.). New York: McGraw-Hill. **121**

Thompson, W., and Lewis, D. (1965). *Population problems* (5th ed.). New York: McGraw-Hill. **671**

Thompson, W., and Whelpton, P. K. (1933). *Population trends in the United States.* New York: McGraw-Hill. **481**

Thornberry, T. P. (1973). Race, socioeconomic status, and sentencing in the juvenile justice system. *Journal of Criminal Law and Criminology, 64*, 90–98. **294**

Thornton, A., Alwin, D. F., and Camburn, D. (1983). Causes and consequences of sex-role attitudes and attitude change. *American Sociological Review, 48*(April), 211–227.

Thornton, A., and Freedman, D. (1982). Changing attitudes toward marriage and single life. *Family Planning Perspectives, 14*(6, November/December), 297–303. **492**

Thornton, A., and Freedman, D. (1983). The changing American family. *Population Bulletin, 38*(4). Washington, DC: Population Reference Bureau. **485, 494**

Thornton, A., and Rodgers, W. L. (1983, February). *Changing patterns of marriage and divorce in the United States* (Final Report Prepared for the National Institute for Child Health and Human Development, Ann Arbor, MI). **470**

Thurow, L. (1975). *Generating inequality*. New York: Basic Books. **322, 337, 347, 365**

Tilly, C. (1978a). *From mobilization to revolution*. Reading, MA: Addison-Wesley. **651, 654, 657, 658**

Tilly, C. (Ed.) (1978b). *Historical studies of changing fertility*. Princeton, NJ: Princeton University Press. **115**

Tilly, C., Tilly, L., and Tilly, R. (1975). *The rebellious century*. Cambridge, MA: Harvard University Press. **658**

Tilly, L. A., and Scott, J. W. (1978). *Women, work, and the family*. New York: Holt, Rinehart & Winston. **404**

Tilly, L. A., and Tilly, C. (Eds.). (1981). *Collective action and class conflict*. Beverly Hills, CA: Sage. **658**

*Time Magazine.* (1979, December 31). Was Robin just a hood? **525**

Tisdale, H. (1942). The process of urbanization. *Social Forces, 20*, 311–316. **133**

Tissue, T. (1979). Downward mobility in old age. In P. I. Rose (Ed.), *Socialization and the life cycle* (pp. 355–367). New York: St. Martin's Press. **446**

Tittle, C. R. (1975). Deterrence of labeling? *Social Forces, 53* (March), 399–419. **690**

Tittle, C. R., and Villemez, W. J. (1977). Social class and criminality. *Social Forces, 56*(2), 474–502. **288, 289**

Tittle, C. R., Villemez, W. J., and Smith, D. A. (1978). The myth of social class and criminality: An empirical assessment of empirical evidence. *American Sociological Review, 43*, 643–656. **288**

Toch, H. H., and Schulte, R. (1961). Readiness to perceive violence as a result of police training. *British Journal of Psychology, 52*, 389–393.

Tocqueville, A. de. (1954). *Democracy in America II*. New York: Random House. (Original work published 1835) **347, 578**

Tönnies, F. (1963). *Community and society*. New York: Harper. (Original work published 1887) **235, 237, 261**

Toynbee, A. (1956). *The Industrial Revolution*. Boston: Beacon Press.

Treiman, D. J. (1977). *Occupational prestige in comparative perspective*. New York: Academic Press. **332**

Treiman, D. J., and Hartmann, H. I. (Eds.). (1981). *Women, work and wages: equal pay for jobs of equal value*. Washington, DC: National Academy Press. **52, 406, 409**

Treiman, D. J., and Roos, P. A. (1983). Sex and earnings in industrial society. *American Journal of Sociology, 89*(3, November), 612–650. **418**

Trimberger, E. K. (1971). The ideological function of grading in American education. Paper Read at the Annual Meeting of the American Sociological Association. **523**

Troeltsch, E. (1931). *The social teaching of the Christian churches.*

New York: Macmillan. (Original work published 1912) **613**

Trow, M. (1961). The second transformation of American secondary education. *International Journal of Comparative Sociology, 2*, 144–165. **500**

Tuchman, B. W. (1978). *A distant mirror*. New York: Knopf. **121**

Tuddenham, R. D., and McBride, P. (1959). The yielding experiment from the subject's point of view. *Journal of Personality, 27*, 259–271. **210**

Tullock, G. (1974). Does punishment deter? *The Public Interest*, (Summer), 103–111. **295**

Tumin, M. M. (1953). Some principles of stratification: A critical analysis. *American Sociological Review, 18*, 378–394. **320**

Tumin, M. M. (1964). Business as a social system. *Behavioral Science 9*, 2(April), 120–130. **221**

Tumin, M. M. (1973). *Patterns of society*. Boston: Little, Brown. **358**

Turk, A. (1969). *Criminality and the legal order*. Chicago: Rand McNally. **280**

Turk, A. (1976). Law as a weapon in social conflict. *Social Problems, 23*(3), 276–291. **280**

Turnbull, C. (1961). *The forest people*. New York: Simon & Schuster. **618**

Turnbull, C. (1965). The Mbuti Pygmies of the Congo. In J. L. Gibbs, Jr. (Ed.), *People of Africa*. New York: Holt, Rinehart & Winston. **607**

Turner, R. H. (1941). *The great cultural traditions: The foundations of civilization*. New York: McGraw-Hill.

Turner, R. H. (1964). Collective behavior. In R. E. L. Faris (Ed.), *Handbook of modern sociology*. Chicago: Rand McNally. **641, 647**

Turner, R. H., and Killian, L. (1972). *Collective behavior* (2nd ed.). Englewood Cliffs, NJ: Prentice-Hall. **643**

Twain, M. (1922). *Pudd'nhead Wilson and those extraordinary twins*. New York: Harper.

Unger, A. (1983, May 10). TV is offering a fairer image, but mainly for certain groups. *Christian Science Monitor*, p. 12. **356**

Unger, R. K. (1979). *Female and male: Psychological perspectives*. New York: Harper & Row. **422**

United Nations. (1956). *The determinants and consequences of population trends* (Vol. 1). New York: Author. **433**

United Nations. (1973). The determinants and consequences of population trends: New summary of findings on interaction of demographic, economic, and social factors. I. *Population Studies, 50*. New York: United Nations Department of Economic and Social Affairs. **122, 137**

United Nations. (1974). *Demographic yearbook 1971: Table 1*. New York: Author.

United Nations. (1979). *Demographic yearbook 1976*. New York: Author.

United Press International. (1978, July 16). Crimes against business are frequently crimes by business. **293**

United Press International. (1983, December 11). **653**

U.S. Census Bureau. (1918). *Negro population: 1790–1915*. Washington, DC: Government Printing Office. **372**

U.S. Census Bureau. (1975a). *Historical statistics of the United States: Colonial times to 1970*. Washington, DC: U.S. Government Printing Office. **109, 442, 450, 455, 484, 485, 500, 501, 508, 511, 514**

U.S. Census Bureau. (1975b). *Statistical abstract of the United States: 1975*. Washington, DC: U.S. Government Printing Office.

**U.S. Census Bureau.** (1975c). *The social and economic status of the black population in the United States.* (Current Population Reports, Series P–23, No. 54). Washington, DC: U.S. Government Printing Office. **368**

**U.S. Census Bureau** (1976). *Statistical abstract of the United States: 1976.* Washington, DC: U.S. Government Printing Office.

**U.S. Census Bureau.** (1978a). *Geographical mobility: March 1975 to March 1978.* (Current Population Reports, Series P–20, No. 331). Washington, DC: U.S. Government Printing Office.

**U.S. Census Bureau.** (1978b). *Social and economic characteristics of the metropolitan population: 1977 and 1970* (Current Population Reports, Series P–23, No. 75). Washington, DC: U.S. Government Printing Office. **308**

**U.S. Census Bureau.** (1979a). *Estimates of the population of the United States, by age, sex, and race: 1976 to 1978* (Current Population Reports, Series P–25, No. 800). Washington, DC: U.S. Government Printing Office.

**U.S. Census Bureau.** (1979b). *Fertility of American women: June 1978* (Current Population Reports, Series P–20, No. 341). Washington, DC: U.S. Government Printing Office. **115**

**U.S. Census Bureau.** (1980a). *Households and families by type: March, 1980* (Advanced Report, Current Population Reports, Series P–20, No. 357). Washington, DC: U.S. Government Printing Office.

**U.S. Census Bureau.** (1980b). *Social indicators III.* Washington, DC: U.S. Government Printing Office. **262, 267, 286, 295, 324, 329, 334, 336, 341, 370, 385, 516, 580**

**U.S. Census Bureau.** (1981). *Statistical abstract of the United States: 1981.* Washington, DC: U.S. Government Printing Office. **339, 341, 384, 448, 452, 455, 480**

**U.S. Census Bureau.** (1982). *Statistical abstract of the United States, 1982.* Washington, DC: U.S. Government Printing Office. **257, 263, 267, 286, 290, 295, 348, 354, 363, 365, 368, 370, 418, 433, 443, 445, 453, 455, 470, 479, 509, 511, 514, 524, 547, 553, 581**

**U.S. Census Bureau.** (1983a). *Households, families, marital status, and living arrangements: March, 1983.* Washington, DC: U.S. Government Printing Office. **479**

**U.S. Census Bureau.** (1983b). *Money income and poverty status of families and persons in the United States, 1982* (Current Population Report, Series P–60, No. 140). Washington, DC: U.S. Government Printing Office. **49, 50, 53**

**U.S. Census Bureau.** (1983c). *Statistical Abstract of the United States: 1984.* Washington, DC: U.S. Government Printing Office. **91, 109, 125, 172, 224, 247, 248, 263, 267, 268, 286, 287, 289, 290, 298, 307, 308, 318, 327, 328, 329, 334, 337, 338, 339, 341, 345, 346, 348, 364, 385, 387, 406, 407, 408, 409, 410, 416, 418, 419, 426, 427, 442, 443, 446, 450, 454, 455, 457, 472, 474, 477, 478, 479, 480, 484, 488, 492, 493, 500, 508, 514, 515, 516, 519, 527, 540, 542, 544, 545, 547, 549, 581, 617**

**U.S. Census Bureau.** (1984a). *After-tax money income estimates of households: 1982* (Current Population Reports, Series P–23, No. 137). Washington, DC: U.S. Government Printing Office. **325**

**U.S. Census Bureau.** (1984b). *Money income of families and persons in the United States: 1982* (Current Population Reports, Series P–60, No. 142, Table 46). Washington, DC: U.S. Government Printing Office. **445**

**U.S. Census Bureau.** (1984c). *Money income of families and persons in the United States: 1982* (Current Population Reports, Series P–60, No. 142, Table 47). Washington, DC: U.S. Government Printing Office. **447**

**U.S. Commission on Civil Rights.** (1967). *Racial isolation in the public schools (Vol. 1).* Washington, DC: U.S. Government Printing Office. **374**

**U.S. Department of Health, Education, and Welfare.** (1961). *U.S. health examination survey: 1959–1961.* Washington, DC: U.S. Government Printing Office. **172**

**U.S. Department of Health, Education, and Welfare.** (1973). *Work in America.* Cambridge, MA: M.I.T. Press. **552**

**U.S. Department of Housing and Urban Development.** (1981). *Residential displacement: An update.* Washington, DC: U.S. Government Printing Office. **271**

**U.S. Department of Justice.** (1976). *Criminal victimization in the United States: A comparison of 1973 and 1974 findings.* Washington, DC: U.S. Government Printing Office.

**U.S. Department of Justice.** (1980a). *Criminal victimization in the United States: A comparison of 1977 and 1978 findings.* Washington, DC: U.S. Government Printing Office. **286**

**U.S. Department of Justice.** (1980b). *Intimate victims: A study of violence among friends and relatives.* Washington, DC: U.S. Government Printing Office. **292, 489**

**U.S. Department of Justice.** (1983). *Criminal victimization in the United States, 1981.* Washington, DC: U.S. Government Printing Office. **290, 291**

**U.S. Department of Labor.** (1979). *The earnings gap between women and men.* Washington, DC: U.S. Government Printing Office.

**U.S. Department of Labor.** (1981). *Employment and earnings: January, 1981.* Washington, DC: U.S. Government Printing Office. **409**

**U.S. Department of Labor.** (1982). *Analyzing 1981 earnings data from the current population survey* (Bulletin 2149). Washington, DC: U.S. Government Printing Office. **50, 51**

**U.S. Department of Labor.** (1983). *Educational attainment of workers, March 1981* (Bulletin 2159). Washington, DC: U.S. Government Printing Office. **52**

**Useem, M.** (1983). *The inner circle: Large corporations and the rise of business political activity in the U.S. and U.K.* New York: Oxford University Press. **330, 579**

**Uyeki, E. S.** (1964). Residential distribution and stratification. *American Journal of Sociology, 69*(5), 491–498. **372**

**Van Creveld, M.** (1982). *Fighting power: German and U.S. Army Performance, 1939–1945.* Westport, CT: Greenwood Press. **235**

**Vander Zanden, J. W.** (1972). *American minority relations: The sociology of race and ethnic groups* (3rd ed.). New York: Ronald Press. **377, 456**

**Vanek, J.** (1974). Time spent in housework. *Scientific American, 231* (November), 116–120.

**Van Gennep, A.** (1960). *The rites of passage.* Chicago: University of Chicago Press. (Original work published 1909) **165, 437**

**Van Til, J.** (1980). Citizen participation in neighborhood transformation: A social movements approach. *Urban Affairs Quarterly, 15,* 439–452. **273**

**Veblen, T.** (1934). *The theory of the leisure class.* New York: Modern Library. (Original work published 1928) **218, 330**

**Vinacke, S., and Arkoff, A.** (1957). Experimental study of coalitions in a triad. *American Sociological Review, 22,* 406–415. **227**

**Vockell, E. L., Felker, D. W., and Miley, C. H.** (1973). Birth order literature 1967–1971: Bibliography and index. *Journal of Individual Psychology, 29,* 39–53. **167**

**Von Neumann, J., and Morgenstern, O.** (1964). *Theory of games and economic behavior* (3rd ed.). New York: Wiley. **199, 503**

**Walker, K.** (1973). Effect of family characteristics on time contributed for household work by various members. Paper presented at the American Home Economics Association Meeting.

**Wallace, M., and Kalleberg, A. L.** (1982). Industrial transformation and the decline of craft: The decomposition of skill in the printing industry, 1931–1978. *American Sociological Review*, 47(June), 307–324. **541**

**Wallerstein, I.** (1976). *The modern world system.* New York: Academic Press. **559, 681**

**Wallerstein, I.** (1979). *The capitalist world-economy.* Cambridge: Cambridge University Press. **559, 681**

**Wallerstein, I.** (1980). *The modern world system II: Mercantilism and the consolidation of the European world economy, 1600–1750.* New York: Academic Press. **559, 681**

**Wallston, B., Foster, M., and Berger, M.** (1978). I will follow him: Myth, reality, or forced choice. Job seeking experiences of dual-career couples. *Psychology of Women Quarterly*, 3, 9–21. **426, 487**

**Walton, R. E.** (1972). How to counter alienation in the plant. *Harvard Business Review*, 50(6, November–December), 70–82. **542**

**Walum, L. R.** (1974). The changing door ceremony: Notes on the operation of sex roles. *Urban Life and Culture*, 2, 506–515. **77**

**Warner, C. D.** (1870). *My summer in a garden.* Quoted in Bartlett's, p. 645. **586**

**Warner, W. L.** (1961). *The family of God.* New Haven: Yale University Press. **605**

**Warnick, D. H., and Sanders, G.** (1980). The effects of group discussion on eyewitness accuracy. *Journal of Applied Social Psychology*, 10(3), 249–259. **229**

**Watson, G. B.** (1928). Do groups think more efficiently than individuals? *Journal of Abnormal and Social Psychology*, 23, 328–336. **231**

**Watson, J. B.** (1928). *Psychological care of infant and child.* New York: Norton. **146**

**Watson, J. B.** (1929). *Psychology from the standpoint of a behaviorist* (3rd ed., rev.). Philadelphia and London: Lippincott. (Original work published 1919)

**Watson, J. B., and Rayner, R..** (1920). Conditioned emotional reactions. *Journal of Experimental Psychology*, 3, 1–14. **148**

**Watson, T. J.** (1980). *Sociology, work, and industry.* London: Routledge and Kegan Paul.

**Watzlawick, P.** (1976). *How real is real? Confusion, disinformation, communication.* New York: Random House. **180**

**Weber, M.** (1946). *From Max Weber: Essays in sociology* (H. H. Gerth and C. W. Mills, Eds. and Trans.). New York: Oxford University Press. **238, 317, 500**

**Weber, M.** (1947). *The theory of social and economic organization.* New York: Oxford University Press. (Original work published 1925) **100, 188, 215, 567**

**Weber, M.** (1949). *The methodology of the social sciences.* New York: The Free Press. **38**

**Weber, M.** (1950). *General economic history.* New York: The Free Press. (Original work published 1923) **622**

**Weber, M.** (1922a/1954). In M. Rheinstein (Ed.), *Max Weber on law in economy and society.* Cambridge, MA: Harvard University Press. (Original work published 1922). **23, 105, 220, 238, 261**

**Weber, M.** (1922b/1958). Bureaucracy. In H. H. Gerth and C. W. Mills, (Eds. and Trans.), *From Max Weber: Essays in sociology.* New York: Oxford University Press (Original work published 1922) **105, 186, 220**

**Weber, M** (1958). Politics as a vocation. In H. H. Gerth and C. W. Mills (Eds. and Trans.), *From Max Weber.* New York: Oxford University Press. (Original work published 1921) **569**

**Weber, M.** (1958). *The Protestant ethic and the spirit of capitalism.* New York: Charles Scribner's and Sons. (Original work published 1904) **26, 535, 663**

**Weed, J.** (1982). Divorce: Americans' style. *American Demographics*, 4(3, March), 13–17. **485**

**Weede, E.** (1980). Beyond misspecification in sociological analysis of income inequality. *American Sociological Review*, 45, 497–501. **341**

**Weg, R. B.** (1975). Changing physiology of aging: Normal and pathological. In D. S. Woodruff and J. E. Birren (Eds.), *Aging: Scientific perspectives and social issues.* New York: Van Nostrand. **435, 442**

**Weiner, H.** (1958). Diagnosis and symptomatology. In L. Bellak (Ed.), *Schizophrenia.* New York: Logos Press. **148**

**Weinstein, J.** (1969). *The corporate ideal in the liberal state: 1900–1918.* Boston: Beacon Press. **546**

**Weinstein, J. A.** (1976). *Demographic transition and social change.* Morristown, NJ: General Learning Press. **121**

**Weintraub, B.** (1975, March 14). Uganda exiles—In Britain I miss . . . . *New York Times* p. 24. **375**

**Weisbord, R.** (1975). *Genocide? Birth control and the black American.* Westport, CT: Greenwood Press. **387**

**Weiss, C. S.** (1981). The development of professional role commitment among graduate students. *Human Relations*, 34, 13–31. **419**

**Weiss, L., and Lowenthal, M. F.** (1975). *Life course perspectives on friendship.* In M. F. Lowenthal, M. Thurner, and D. Chiriboga (Eds.), *Four stages of life.* San Francisco: Jossey-Bass. **403**

**Weiss, R. S.** (1979). The emotional impact of marital separation. In G. Levinger and O. C. Moles (Eds.), *Divorce and separation.* New York: Basic Books. **171**

**Weissberg, R.** (1981). *Understanding American government* (alternate ed.). New York: Holt, Rinehart & Winston. **260**

**Weitz, S.** (1977). *Sex roles.* New York: Oxford. **47, 394**

**Weitzman, L.** (1981). *The marriage contract.* New York: The Free Press. **187, 492**

**Weller, R. H.** (1977). Demographic correlates of women's participation in economic activities. *International Population Conference: Mexico 1977*, (pp. 497–516). Liege, Belgium: International Union for the Scientific Study of Population. **480**

**Weller, R. H.** (1979). The differential attainment of family size goals by race. *Population Studies*, 33, 157–164.

**Weller, R. H., and Bouvier, L. F.** (1981). *Population: Demography and policy.* New York: St. Martin's Press. **118, 125, 136, 480, 481**

**Weller, R. P., and Guggenheim, S. E. (Eds.).** (1982). *Power and protest in the countryside: Studies of rural unrest in Asia, Europe, and Latin America.* Durham, NC: Duke University Press. **269**

**Welsh, W. A. (Ed.).** (1981). *Survey research and public attitudes in Eastern Europe and the Soviet Union.* New York: Pergamon Press. **563**

**West, C.** (1982). Why can't a woman be more like a man? *Sociology of Work and Occupations*, 9, 5–29. **190**

**West, S. G., Gunn, S. P., and Chernicky, P.** (1975). Ubiquitous Watergate: An attributional analysis. *Journal of Personality and Social Psychology*, 32, 55–65. **182**

**Westing, A.** (1981). Cited in the *New York Times*, October 6, 1981. **136**

**Westoff, C. F.** (1978a). Some speculations on the future of marriage and fertility. *Family Planning Perspectives*, 10, 79–83. **120**

**Westoff, C. F.** (1978b). Marriage and fertility in the developed countries. *Scientific American*, 239(6), 51–57. **469**

**Westoff, C. F.** (1983). Fertility decline in the West: Causes and prospects. *Population and Development Review*, 9, 99–105. **120**

**Westoff, C. F., and Bumpass, L.** (1973). The revolution in birth control practices of U.S. Roman Catholics. *Science*, 179(5), pp. 41–44. **116**

**Westoff, C. F., and Jones, E. F.** (1979). The end of 'Catholic' fertility. *Demography*, 16(May), 209–217. **480**

**Wheeler, L., and Nezlek, T.** (1977). Sex differences in social participation. *Journal of Personality and Social Psychology*, 35, 742–754. **403**

**White, K. L., and Brinkerhoff, D. B.** (1981). The sexual division of labor: Evidence from childhood. *Social Forces*, 60, 170–181. **414**

**Whiting, B. (Ed.).** (1963). *Six cultures—Studies in child rearing.* New York: Wiley. **482**

**Whiting, J. W. M.** (1964). The effects of climate on certain cultural practices. In W. Goodenough (Ed.), *Explorations in cultural anthropology.* New York: McGraw-Hill.

**Whiting, J. W. M.** (1968). Socialization: Anthropological aspects. In D. L. Sills, (Ed.), *The international encyclopedia of the social sciences* (Vol. 14, pp. 545–551). New York: The Macmillan Company/The Free Press.

**Whorf, B. L.** (1956). *Language, thought and reality.* Cambridge, MA: MIT Press.

**Whyte, W. F.** (1950). The social structure of the restaurant. *American Journal of Sociology*, 54, 302–310. **222, 225**

**Whyte, W. F.** (1955). *Street corner Society* (2nd enlarged ed.). Chicago: University of Chicago Press.

**Whyte, W. F.** (1981). *Street corner society* (3rd ed.). Chicago: University of Chicago Press. **41, 44, 214**

**Whyte, W. H.** (1956). *The organization man.* New York: Simon & Schuster.

**Wiatrowski, M. D., Griswold, D. B., and Roberts, M. K.** (1981). Social control theory and delinquency. *American Sociological Review*, 46(October), 525–541. **298**

**Wice, P. B.** (1973). *Bail and its reform: A national survey.* Washington, DC: U.S. Government Printing Office. **368**

**Wilkinson, R.** (1964). *Gentlemanly power: British leadership and the public school tradition.* London: Oxford University Press. **500**

**Willett, R. S.** (1971). Working in 'a man's world': The woman executive. In V. Gornick and B. K. Moran (eds.), *Woman in sexist society: Studies in power and powerlessness* (pp. 511–532). New York: New American Library. **402**

**Williams, J. E., and Best, D. L.** (1982). *Measuring sex stereotypes: A thirty nation study.* Beverly Hills, CA: Sage.

**Williams, R. M., Jr.** (1975). Relative deprivation. In L. A. Coser (Ed.), *The idea of social structure* (pp. 355–378). New York: Harcourt Brace Jovanovich. **339**

**Williamson, J.** (1984). *The crucible of race.* New York: Oxford University Press.

**Williamson, N.** (1976). Sex preferences, sex control, and the status of women. *Signs: Journal of Women in Culture and Society*, 1, 847–862. **115, 396**

**Willick, D. H., Gehlker, G., and Watts, A. M.** (1975). Social class as a factor affecting judicial disposition. *Criminology*, 13, 57–77. **294**

**Willner, A. R.** (1984). *The spellbinders: Charismatic political leadership.* New Haven, CT: Yale University Press. **568**

**Wilner, D. M., et al.** (1955). *Human relations in interracial housing: A study of the contact hypothesis.* Minneapolis: University of Minnesota Press. **383**

**Wilson, B.** (1982). *Religion in sociological perspective.* New York: Oxford University Press. **604, 606, 609, 610, 613, 617, 621, 624**

**Wilson, E. O.** (1975). *Sociobiology.* Cambridge, MA: Belknap. **392**

**Wilson, E. O.** (1977). Biology and the social sciences. *Daedalus*, 106(Fall), 127–140. **392**

**Wilson, J.** (1978). *Religion in American society: The effective presence.* Englewood Cliffs, NJ: Prentice-Hall. **623, 624**

**Wilson, J. Q.** (1968). The police and the delinquent in two cities. In S. Wheeler (Ed.), *Controlling delinquents.* New York: Wiley. **294**

**Wilson, R. S., and Harpring, E. B.** (1972). Mental and motor development in infant twins. *Developmental psychology*, 7, 277–287. **146**

**Wilson, T. C.** (1985). Urbanism and tolerance. *American Sociological Review*, 50(1), 117–123. **249**

**Wilson, W. J.** (1973). *Power, racism, and privilege.* New York: Macmillan.

**Wilson, W. J.** (1978). *The declining significance of race.* Chicago: University of Chicago Press. **365, 379**

**Winsborough, H. H.** (1965). The social consequences of high population density. In T. R. Ford and G. F. DeJong (Eds.), *Social demography.* Englewood Cliffs, NJ: Prentice Hall. **263**

**Winter, D. G.** (1973). *The power motive.* New York: The Free Press. **167**

**Wirth, L.** (1938). Urbanism as a way of life. *American Journal of Sociology*, 44, 1–24. **247, 249, 261, 263, 268**

**Wirth, L.** (1945). The problem of minority groups. In R. Linton (Ed.), *The science of man in the world crisis.* New York: Columbia University Press. **354**

**Wise, D.** (1976). Cloak and dagger operations: An overview. In J. H. Skolnick and E. Currie (Eds.), *Crisis in American institutions* (3rd ed.). Boston, MA: Little, Brown.

**Wissler, C.** (1911). The social life of the Blackfoot Indians. *Anthropological Papers of the American Museum of Natural History*, 7(1). New York: American Museum of Natural History. **469**

**Withey, S. B., and Abeles, R. P. (Eds.).** (1980). *Television and social behavior.* Hillsdale, NJ: Erlbaum. **169, 356**

**Witkin, H. A., et al.** (1976). Criminality in XYY and XXY men. *Science*, 193(August), 547–555. **297**

**Wolfe, T.** (1979). *The right stuff.* New York: Farrar, Straus & Giroux. **395**

**Wolfgang, M. E., Figlio, R. M., and Sellin, T.** (1972). *Delinquency in a birth cohort.* Chicago: University of Chicago Press. **287**

**Wolfgang, M. E., and Reidel, M.** (1973). Race, judicial discretion, and the death penalty. *Annals of the American Academy of Political and Social Science*, 407, 119–133. **294**

**Women on Words and Images.** (1975a) *Dick and Jane as victims: Sex stereotyping in children's readers* (Enlarged Ed.). Princeton, NJ. **47, 167, 415**

**Women on Words and Images.** (1975b). *Channeling children: Sex stereotyping on prime TV.* Princeton, NJ. 47, 415

**Women's Research and Education Institute.** (1984). *Gender at work.* Washington, DC: Women's Research and Education Institute. 406

**Woodward, B., and Bernstein, C.** (1974). *All the President's men.* New York: Simon & Schuster.

**Woolf, V.** (1929). *A room of one's own.* New York: Harcourt, Brace and World. 410

**Woolley, Sir L.** (1963). *Prehistory* (Vol. 1, Pt. 2). New York: Harper & Row. 612

**World Bank.** (1983) *World Development Report 1983.* New York: Oxford University Press. 346

**World Heath Organization.** (1978). *World Health Statistics Annual* (Vol. 1). Geneva, Switzerland: World Health Organization. 118

**Woytinsky, W. S., and Woytinsky, E. S.** (1953). *World population and production: Trends and outlook.* New York: Twentieth Century Fund. 135

**Wren, C. S.** (1981, November 11). In China, millions use fuel produced from wastes. *New York Times,* p. C1. 135

**Wright, E. O., Hacken, D., Costello, C., and Sprague, J.** (1982). The American class structure. *American Sociological Review, 47*(December), 709–726. 317

**Wright, J. D., and Wright, S. R.** (1976). Social class and parental values for children: A partial replication and extension of the Kohn thesis. *American Sociological Review, 41*(June), 527–548. 166

**Wrong, D. H.** (1961). The oversocialized conception of man in modern sociology. *American Sociological Review, 26,* 183–193. 173

**Wrong, D. H.** (1980). *Power: Its forms, bases, and uses.* New York: Harper & Row. 100

**Wurdock, C.** (1979) Public school resegregation after desegregation: Some preliminary findings. *Sociological Focus, 12*(4), 263–274. 387

**Wurdock, C. and Farley, R.** (1979). School integration and enrollments in the nation's largest cities: An analysis of recent trends. *Proceedings of the American Statistical Association (Social Statistics Section),* 359–363. 373, 387, 515

**Yarrow, L. J., Rubenstein, J. L., and Pedersen, F. A.** (1975). *Infant and environment: Early cognitive and emotional development.* Washington, DC: Hemisphere Publishing Company (Distributed by Wiley). 147

**Young, M.** (1961). *The rise of the meritocracy.* Baltimore: Penguin. 456

**Zablocki, B.** (1980). *The joyful community.* Chicago: University of Chicago Press. 248, 299

**Zagare, F. C.** (1984). *Game theory: Concepts and applications.* Beverly Hills, CA: Sage. 199, 645

**Zald, M. N., and McCarthy, J. D.** (Eds.). (1979). *The dynamics of social movements.* Cambridge, MA: Winthrop.

**Zangwill, I.** (1933). *The melting pot.* New York: Macmillan. (Original work published 1909) 359

**Zborowski, M.** (1953). Cultural components in responses to pain. *Journal of Social Issues, 8,* 16–31.

**Zeitlin, I. M.** (1981). Karl Marx: Aspects of his social thought and their contemporary relevance. In B. Rhea (Ed.), *The future of the sociological classics* (pp. 1–15). London: Allen Unwin. 677

**Zelnick, M., and Kanter, J. F.** (1976). Sexual and contraceptive experience of young unmarried women in the United States, 1976 and 1971. *Family Planning Perspectives, 9*(March–April), 55–71. 480

**Zelnick, M., and Kanter, J. F.** (1978). First pregnancies to women aged 15–19: 1976 and 1971. *Family Planning Perspectives, 10*(January–February), 11–20. 480

**Zimbardo, P. G.** (1971). *The psychological power and pathology of imprisonment.* A statement prepared for the U.S. House of Representatives Committee on the Judiciary, Subcommittee No. 3; Hearings on Prison Reform, San Francisco, California, October 25. Cited and quoted in D. G. Myers. (1983). *Social psychology* (pp. 179–180). New York: McGraw-Hill. 188

**Zimmerman, D., and West, C.** (1975). Sex roles, interruptions and silences in conversation. In B. Thorne and N. Henley (Eds.), *Language and sex: Difference and dominance.* Rowley, MA: Newbury House. 401

**Zorbaugh, H. W.** (1929). *The Gold Coast and the slum: A sociological study of Chicago's Near North Side.* Chicago: University of Chicago Press.

**Zuboff, S.** (1982). New worlds of computer-mediated work. *Harvard Business Review,* (September/October). 551

**Zucker, L.** (1983). Organizations as institutions. In S. B. Bacharach (Ed.), *Research in the sociology of organizations* (Vol. 2). Greenwich, CT: JAI Press. 224

**Zwerdling, D.** (1980). *Workplace democracy.* New York: Harper & Row. 542

# ILLUSTRATION CREDITS

## Figures

**Figure 5–2:** Copyright © 1981 by the New York Times Company. Reprinted with permission. **Figure 8–1:** Solomon E. Asch, *Social Psychology* (Englewood Cliffs, NJ: Prentice–Hall, Inc., 1952). **Figure 8–3:** Reprinted from *The Business of Organized Crime: A Cosa Nostra Family* by Annelise Graebner Anderson with permission of the publisher Hoover Institution Press. © 1979 by the Board of Trustees of the Leland Stanford Jr. University. **Figure 9–2:** Chauncy D. Harris and Edward L. Ullman, "The Nature of Cities," *Annals of the American Academy of Political and Social Science* 242 (November 1945). **Figure 11–1:** Wright, Hacken, Costello, and Sprague, "The American Class Structure," *American Sociological Review* 47 (December 1982): 709–726. **Figure 14–1:** Kurt Fischer and Arlyne Lazerson, *Human Development* (New York: W. H. Freeman): 45. **Figures 20–1 and 20–2:** Doug McAdam, *Political Process and the Development of Black Insurgency: 1930–1970* (Chicago: The University of Chicago Press, 1982): 7, 9, 51.

## Pictures

PART OPENING PHOTOS **One:** © Ron Cooper/EKM–Nepenthe; **Two:** © Eve Arnold/Magnum Photos; **Three:** © Eve Arnold Magnum Photos; **Four:** © Ron Cooper/EKM–Nepenthe; **Five:** © Ulrike Welsh/Stock, Boston; **Six:** © Bruce Hoertel/*Newsweek*

**CHAPTER 1: Page 5:** Friedman–Abeles photo, courtesy Robert Nemiroff; **6:** © Elliot Erwitt/Magnum Photos; **7:** (left) © Jerry Schad; (right) © Kurt Thorson/EKM–Nepenthe; **11:** The Bettmann Archive, Inc.; **13:** Detail, *Hell*, from *Garden of Earthly Delights* by Hieronymus Bosch, c. 1505, Museo Nacional del Prado, Madrid; **15:** © Susan Holtz; **16:** © Ray Manley/Shostal Associates, Inc.; **17:** © J. P. Laffont/Sygma; **21:** Brown Brothers; **22:** The Bettmann Archive, Inc.; **23:** German Information Center; **24:** (top left) UPI/Bettmann Newsphotos; (top right) © Paul Conklin; (bottom) © Jim Harrison/Stock, Boston; **25:** (top) © Hilda Bijur/Monkmeyer Press; (bottom) ©

Charles Gupton/Southern Light; **27:** Courtesy of Chicago Historical Society

**CHAPTER 2: Page 37:** (left) © Harvey Stein 1979; (right) © Margaret Thomas/*The Washington Post*; **38:** © Richard Wood/The Picture Cube; **40:** AP/Wide World Photos; **45:** Institute for Intercultural Studies/Photo Reo Fortune; **48:** Pennsylvania Historical and Museum Commission; **49:** © Napoleon Chagnon/Anthro–Photo; **54:** © Gary Benson/Black Star; **59:** © E. C. P. Armees/*Newsweek*

**CHAPTER 3: Page 66:** (top left) © Paul Conklin; (top right) © Fabian/Sygma; (bottom left) © George Malave/Stock, Boston; (bottom right) © Elizabeth Crews; **71:** AP/Wide World Photos; **72:** © Donald Yeager for Camera M. D. Studios, Inc., 1973; **74:** (left) © Eric A. Roth/The Picture Cube; (right) © Owen Franken/Stock, Boston; **76:** Courtesy Chrysler Corporation; **80:** AP/Wide World Photos; **82:** The Bettmann Archive, Inc.; **83:** Courtesy Apple Corp.

**CHAPTER 4: Page 87:** Ringling Museum of the Circus, Sarasota, Florida; **88:** The Museum of Modern Art/Film Stills Archive; **89:** © Stanley Tretick/*Newsweek*; **93:** © Eve Arnold/Magnum Photos; **95:** © Sara Krulwich/NYT Pictures; **97:** (left) © Alan Carey/The Image Works; (right) Bob Daemmrich/TexaStock ©; **101:** UPI/Bettmann Newsphotos; **104:** Michael D. Sullivan/TexaStock ©; **106:** (top) © Erika Stone/Peter Arnold, Inc.; (bottom left) © Alan Carey/The Image Works; (bottom right) © Fred Ward/Black Star; **107:** HBJ Collection

**CHAPTER 5: Page 113** © Urraca/Sygma; **114:** (left) © Greg Plattka/Southern Light; (right) © Cary Wolinsky/Stock, Boston; **115:** © Hazel Hankin/Stock, Boston; **116:** © Richard J. Quataert/Taurus Photos; **119:** © Baldev/Sygma; **121:** The Bettmann Archive, Inc.; **123:** Culver Pictures; **124:** © Phil Huber/Black Star; **125:** © George W. Gardner; **128:** UN Photo 152, 113/Shelley Rother; **129:** © Alain Nogues/Sygma; **130:** Australian News and Information Bureau Photograph by J. Tanner; **133:** Courtesy of the Oriental Institute of the University of Chicago; **134:** The Bettmann Archive, Inc.

**CHAPTER 6: Page 143:** © Douglas Faulk-

ner/S. Faulkner Collection; **144:** (top left) Courtesy Gary Burke; (top right) Courtesy Mrs. Joe H. McNaul; (bottom left) Courtesy Howard W. Rollins; (bottom right) Courtesy Doris Holtz; **145:** (top left) Courtesy Candace C. Young; (top right) Courtesy Gary Burke; (bottom left) Courtesy Maryanne De Leo; (bottom right) Courtesy William McNaul; **149:** © David S. Strickler/Monkmeyer Press; **152:** © Owen Franken/Stock, Boston; **154:** © Charles Gatewood/The Image Works; **156:** (both) © Elizabeth Crews; **158:** (both) © Ira Kirschenbaum/Stock, Boston; **159:** (top) © James R. Holland/Stock, Boston; (bottom) Courtesy DuPont Co.; **163:** © Tannenbaum/Sygma; **164:** © Ellis Herwig/The Picture Cube; **165:** © Bill Gillette/Stock, Boston; **168:** © Catherine Ursillo/Photo Researchers; **173:** The Bettmann Archive, Inc.

**CHAPTER 7: Page 178:** (left) © Yan Lukas/Photo Researchers; (right) Jerry Cooke, *Life* Magazine © 1955 Time Inc.; **183:** © Allan L. Price/Photo Researchers; **185:** (top) © Aaron M. Levin/Taurus Photos; (bottom) © Robert Eckert/Stock, Boston; **189:** Courtesy of Professor Philip G. Zimbardo, Department of Psychology, Stanford University; **192:** © Owen Franken/Stock, Boston; **194:** (both) © Jerry Berndt/The Picture Cube; **196:** © Steve Stone/The Picture Cube; **199:** © Randy Taylor/Sygma

**CHAPTER 8: Page 209:** © Ken Robert Buck/The Picture Cube; **214:** © Lee Snider/Photo Images; **215:** (top) Bob Daemmrich/TexaStock ©; (bottom left) © Robert V. Eckert, Jr./EKM–Nepenthe; (bottom right) © Bohdan Hrynewych/Stock, Boston; **222:** NYT Pictures; **231:** Imperial War Museum, London; **234:** © Toshi Matsumoto/Sygma; **235:** Library of Congress; **236:** U.S. Signal Corps, Al Chang; **239:** Ralph Barrera/TexaStock ©; **241:** (top) © P. Vauthey/Sygma; (bottom) General Services Administration F. W. from Black Star

**CHAPTER 9: Page 245:** (top) USDA Photo; (bottom) © George W. Gardner; **247:** Photo © Joel Gordon 1978; **249:** © 1978 Dan Budnik/Woodfin Camp & Associates; **251:** © Patrick Ward/Stock, Boston; **254:** SEF/Art Resource, New York; **255:** Library of Congress; **258:** © G. B. Jones/Taurus Photos; **263:** © Toshi Matsumoto/Sygma;

# Index

Page references in **boldface** indicate tables, figures, and other illustrative material.

A
B
C
D
E
F
G
H
I
J